HANDBOOK OF NEUROPSYCHOLOGY

HANDBOOK OF NEUROPSYCHOLOGY

Series Editors

FRANÇOIS BOLLER

Unit 324 INSERM, Centre Paul Broca, Paris, France

and

JORDAN GRAFMAN

Medical Neurology Branch, NINCDS, Bethesda, MD, U.S.A.

ELSEVIER

Amsterdam – New York – Oxford

HANDBOOK OF NEUROPSYCHOLOGY

Section Editors

L. SQUIRE
G. GAINOTTI

VOLUME 3

1991

ELSEVIER

Amsterdam – New York – Oxford

ISBN Series: 0-444-90492-1

First published (hardbound edition) by Elsevier Science Publishers B.V. (Biomedical Division), 1989.
ISBN: 0-444-81090-0.

This edition (paperback) published by Elsevier Science Publishers B.V., 1991.
ISBN: 0-444-89168-4.

This book is printed on acid-free paper

Published by:
ELSEVIER SCIENCE PUBLISHERS B.V.
P.O. BOX 211

Library of Congress Cataloging-in-Publication Data
(Revised for vol. 3)

Handbook of neuropsychology.

Includes bibliographies and indexes.
1. Clinical neuropsychology. 2. Neuropsychology.
[DNLM: 1. Neuropsychology.] I. Boller, Francois.
II. Grafman, Jordan.
RC343.H225 1988   616.8   88-21312
ISBN 0-444-90492-1 (set)

Printed in The Netherlands

Preface

In the preface to the first volume of the Handbook of Neuropsychology, we stated that in recent years there has been an enormous increase in interest in disorders of higher cortical functions and brain-behavior relationships. This is certainly exemplified by the success met so far by the Handbook, the third volume of which we now present.

The Handbook of Neuropsychology has been planned as a reference source in order to provide for the first time comprehensive and current coverage of both experimental and clinical aspects of neuropsychology. To this end the chapter authors have produced in-depth reviews that go beyond a summary of their results and points of view. Each chapter is up-to-date, covering the latest developments in methodology and theory. Discussion of bedside evaluations, laboratory techniques and theoretical models are all to be found in the Handbook.

The first two volumes comprised an introductory section (edited by Boller and Grafman) and sections on attention (Rizzolatti), language, aphasia and related disorders (Goodglass) and disorders of visual behavior (Damasio).

The present volume comprises two sections. The first one (Section Five of the Handbook) has as Topic Editor Professor L. Squire and deals with memory and its disorders. Specific topics include the organization and neurological foundations of memory, the neuropsychological assessment of learning and memory, and a discussion of which structures and connections must be damaged to produce memory disorders. Specific syndromes are also discussed, including post-traumatic amnesia, transient global amnesia and functional amnesia. This section concludes with chapters on rehabilitation and pharmacological treatment of memory disorders.

The Topic Editor of the second section of this volume (Section Six) is Professor G. Gainotti. It deals with emotional behavior and its disorders. It includes a review of theories of emotion, of the anatomical and neurochemical bases of emotional behavior, lateralization and hemispheric specialization, as well as of specific disorders of emotion and emotional arousal, including anxiety and depression.

Volume Four will also consist of two sections. The first one (Topic Editor: Professor R. Nebes) will deal with the neurobehavioral sequelae of congenital and surgically induced lesions of the corpus callosum and hemispherectomy in animals and humans. The following section of Volume Four, Section Eight (Topic Editor: Professor S. Corkin), will deal with aging, age-related disorders and dementia. It will cover the neuropsychology of aging in animals and humans; clinical and pathological correlates of

v

dementia; and modern clinical and experimental techniques such as PET and NMR spectroscopy. Also included will be chapters on psychiatric symptoms in dementia, sleep studies of demented patients, statistical considerations, and issues related to pharmacological therapy of dementia. Due to the considerable size of this section, only the first part will be found in Volume Four. The rest will be included in Volume Five, in which there will also be Section Nine (edited by Grafman and Boller), dealing with cognitive models, neurolinguistic approaches to aphasia and a chapter on contemporary trends in neuropsychology. This will conclude the part of the Handbook dedicated to the neuropsychology of adulthood and aging. Two additional volumes are currently in preparation with Professor Isabelle Rapin and Professor Sidney Segalowitz as Topic Editors. These two volumes will deal with developmental neuropsychology. In this context, we wish to welcome and thank Professor Howard Gardner, who has also joined the Editorial Board.

The Handbook is expected to be an essential reference source for clinicians such as neurologists, psychiatrists and psychologists, as well as for all scientists engaged in research in the neurosciences.

Many people have contributed to the successful preparation of the Handbook. We again wish to emphasize our appreciation for the commitment of the Topic Editors, who have spent long hours both in the planning stage and in the actual compiling of the various sections. Dr. Marie-Cécile Masure has painstakingly prepared the index of this volume as well as that of the two preceding volumes and we are most grateful to her for her effort. Ms Annette Grechen in Pittsburgh and the editorial staff of Elsevier in Amsterdam continue to provide invaluable technical assistance.

François BOLLER
Jordan GRAFMAN

List of contributors

N. Butters Psychology Service (116B), V.A. Medical Center, 3350 La Jolla Village Drive, San Diego, CA 92161, U.S.A.

C. Caltagirone Clinica Neurologica, II Università di Roma 'Tor Vergata', Rome, Italy

A.R. Damasio Department of Neurology, University of Iowa Hospitals and Clinics, Iowa City, IA 52242, U.S.A.

H. Damasio Department of Neurology, University of Iowa Hospitals and Clinics, Iowa City, IA 52242, U.S.A.

R.J. Davidson University of Wisconsin, Department of Psychology, Psychophysiology Laboratory, 1202 West Johnson Street, Madison, WI 53706, U.S.A.

D.C. Delis Psychology Service (116B), V.A. Medical Center, 3350 La Jolla Village Drive, San Diego, CA 92161, U.S.A.

N.L. Etcoff Department of Brain and Cognitive Sciences, Massachusetts Institute of Technology, Cambridge, MA 02139, U.S.A.

P. Feyereisen Unité Nexa, UCL 5545, Avenue Hippocrate, B-1200 Brussels, Belgium

P. Flor-Henry Alberta Hospital Edmonton, Box 307, Edmonton, Alberta, Canada T5J 2J7

G. Gainotti Institute of Neurology, Policlinico Gemelli, Largo A. Gemelli, 8, 00168 Rome, Italy

List of contributors

E.L. Glisky   Amnesia and Cognition Unit, Department of Psychology, University of Arizona, Tucson, AZ 85721, U.S.A.

K.M. Heilman   Department Neurology – Box J236, J. Hills Miller Health Center, University of Florida, College of Medicine, Gainesville, FL 32610, U.S.A.

J.M. Hill   Section on Brain Biochemistry, Clinical Neuroscience Branch, National Institute of Mental Health, Building 10, Room 3N256, 9000 Rockville Pike, Bethesda, MD 20892, U.S.A.

J.F. Kihlstrom   Amnesia and Cognition Unit, Department of Psychology, University of Arizona, Tucson, AZ 85721, U.S.A.

M. Kritchevsky   V.A. Medical Center (127), 3350 La Jolla Village Drive, San Diego, CA 92161, U.S.A.

H.S. Levin   Division of Neurosurgery, The University of Texas Medical Branch, Galveston, TX 77550, U.S.A.

M. Liotti   University of Oregon, Psychology Clinic, Eugene, OR 97403, U.S.A.

G. Macchi   Institute of Neurology, Catholic University, Policlinico Gemelli, Largo A. Gemelli, 8, 00168 Rome, Italy

C.B. Pert   Section on Brain Biochemistry, Clinical Neuroscience Branch, National Institute of Mental Health, Building 10, Room 3N256, 9000 Rockville Pike, Bethesda, MD 20892, U.S.A.

M. Petrides   Department of Psychology, McGill University, 1205 Dr. Penfield Avenue, Montreal, Quebec H3A 1B1, Canada

L. Pizzamiglio   Dipartimento di Psicologia, Università degli Studi di Roma 'La Sapienza', Via degli Apuli, 00185 Rome, Italy

D.L. Schachter   Amnesia and Cognition Unit, Department of Psychology, University of Arizona, Tucson, AZ 85721, U.S.A.

A.P. Shimamura   V.A. Medical Center (V116), 3350 La Jolla Village Drive, San Diego, CA 92161, U.S.A.

M.L. Smith   Department of Psychology, Erindale College, University of Toronto, Mississauga, Ontario L5L 1C6, Canada

E. Strauss   Department of Psychology, University of Victoria, Victoria, British Colombia, Canada V8W 2Y2

D.T. Stuss   Rotman Research Institute of Baycrest Centre, 3560 Bathurst St., Toronto, Ontario M6A 2E1, and Departments of Psychology and Medicine, University of Toronto, Toronto, Ontario M5S 1A7, Canada

L.J. Thal   Neurology Service (127), V.A. Medical Center, 3350 La Jolla Village Drive, San Diego, CA 92161, U.S.A.

A.J. Tomarken   University of Wisconsin, Department of Psychology, Psychophysiology Laboratory, 1202 West Johnson Street, Madison, WI 53706, U.S.A.

D. Tranel   Department of Behavior Neurology and Cognitive Neuroscience, University of Iowa College of Medicine, Iowa City, IA 52242, U.S.A.

D.M. Tucker   University of Oregon, Psychology Clinic, Eugene, OR 97403, U.S.A.

R.T. Watson   Department Neurology – Box J236, J. Hills Miller Health Center, University of Florida, College of Medicine, Gainesville, FL 32610, U.S.A.

B. Zipser   Department of Physiology, Michigan State University, East Lansing, MI 48824-1101, U.S.A.

P. Zoccolotti   Dipartimento di Psicologia, Università degli Studi di Roma 'La Sapienza', Via degli Apuli, 00185 Rome, Italy

Acknowledgements

The editors and publisher gratefully acknowledge Sandoz Ltd, Basle, Switzerland, CIBA-Geigy, Summit, NJ, U.S.A., Fondation IPSEN, Paris, France, and Farmitalia Carlo Erba, Milan, Italy, for partially supporting the publication of this volume.

Contents

Contents

Section 6: Emotional Behavior and its Disorders (Gainotti)

Section 5

Memory and its Disorders

editor

L. Squire

© 1989 Elsevier Science Publishers B.V. (Biomedical Division)
Handbook of Neuropsychology, Vol. 3
F. Boller and J. Grafman (Eds)

CHAPTER 1

Neuropsychological assessment of learning and memory

Dean C. Delis

Veterans Administration Medical Center, San Diego, and University of California, San Diego, School of Medicine, CA 92161, U.S.A.

Human learning and memory depend on numerous cognitive processes mediated by diverse cerebral regions. As such, in the presence of brain injury or disease, these functions rarely escape compromise. The nature of a patient's memory impairment can vary greatly depending on the type and location of the pathology.

Clinical neuropsychologists and neurologists have tended to provide cursory examination of learning and memory abilities. Commonly used tests such as the original Wechsler Memory Scale (Wechsler, 1945) are limited in their standardized format, because they assess immediate recall *only*. A severely amnesic patient, who may have no recollection of even taking this test only a few minutes after its completion, may still be able to echo back a number of target items on immediate recall. Bedside mental-status testing is limited in that the patient is traditionally asked to remember only three words or hidden objects. The assessment of memory for only a few items often fails to detect mild to moderate memory deficits caused by insidious and debilitating neurologic disorders.

The role of memory assessment in complex clinical dilemmas: three cases

The importance of conducting a comprehensive memory assessment is illustrated in the following complex cases (details of the first case were presented to the author while he was serving as a consultant to a local hospital; the other two cases were evaluated by the author):

Case 1: A 63-year-old diabetic man, who was negligent in taking insulin and avoiding sweets, suffered a series of hypoglycemic comas. His physician referred him to a psychotherapist to enhance treatment compliance. The therapist, believing the patient was 'overly defended', attempted to confront his 'denial' of his illness so he would be more motivated to comply with medical treatment. The patient appeared to be making gains in therapy by discussing his feelings about his illness. He then suffered another diabetic coma, this time resulting in death. Autopsy revealed a highly atrophied brain. It is possible that the patient became caught in a deadly neuropathological cycle: metabolic encephalopathy secondary to diabetes caused memory problems, which in turn resulted in increased forgetfulness in complying with treatment, which gradually led to greater encephalopathy and eventual death. A comprehensive neuropsychological examination may have detected a memory disorder, and recommendations could have been made for daily supervision of the patient's medication compliance and diet.

Case 2: While at a stop sign, a 54-year-old woman with no prior psychiatric or neurological history was rear-ended by a car going 5 miles per hour. She complained of a sore back but did not seek medical attention, and she returned to work the next day. Over the next four months, she experienced increasing difficulty with her job as a grocery clerk; her family claimed that these difficulties were related to back problems. She took disability leave and fell into a severe depression, with suicidal ideation, psychomotor slowing, and weight loss. She underwent psychiatric hospitalization, first receiving antidepressant medication and then ECT. Her mood improved and she was discharged, but she remained confused and disoriented over the next six months. Her family initiated a civil law suit against the driver who caused the accident. They claimed that the patient had injured her back, which disrupted her ability to work and eventually precipitated the depressive episode. A forensic neuropsychological examination revealed a profile of spared and impaired cognitive functions commonly seen in patients with early-stage Alzheimer's disease. The results of memory testing were particularly telling: new learning was her most impaired function and was characterized by disruption in both encoding and retrieval processes, severely deficient delayed recall, exceptionally high intrusion rate, failure to show vulnerability to proactive interference, and a 'Yes' response bias on recognition testing. Follow-up testing one year later verified a progressive deterioration of most cognitive functions while her mood continued to improve. On the basis of the combined results from the neuropsychological and neurological examinations, the woman was diagnosed as having putative Alzheimer's disease with secondary depressive features in the early stages. The automobile accident was considered to be a coincidental event.

Case 3:   A renal-failure patient who was targeted for kidney transplant suffered a small, left subcortical stroke while on hemodialysis. Several months after the stroke, he continued to display severe memory impairment. The physicians on the Kidney Transplant Board were considering cancelling his scheduled surgery, because the demand for kidney organs far exceeds the supply and the patient was now thought to be at high risk for failing to comply with the complex medication regimen required after kidney transplant. The board was faced with a life-or-death decision: it was thought the patient would not survive long without a donor

kidney. Neuropsychological assessment was requested to evaluate the extent of the patient's memory disorder and to offer recommendations about his cognitive capacity to comply with treatment. Test results indicated that the patient's encoding processes were considerably more intact than his retrieval processes, and that he was able to remember much more information than he could express in the 'free recall' demands of his conversations with his renal treatment team. Therefore, the team was instructed to inquire about his memory using probes and recognition testing. Relatives provided signed statements saying that they would rotate supervision of his daily medication compliance. The Transplant Board voted unanimously to proceed with surgery. Follow-up neuropsychological evaluations were scheduled at six month intervals to monitor the patient's memory and cognitive functions over time.

These three cases demonstrate the importance of conducting a thorough evaluation of patients' spared and impaired memory processes in order to address clinical issues that literally can save patients' lives. As Squire (1987) poignantly wrote, "It is extraordinary how unremarkable amnesia can appear on first impression, yet how profound and devastating an effect it can nevertheless have" (p. 178). Unfortunately, most clinical tests of learning and memory in use today continue to provide insufficient assessment. We can understand this shortcoming by examining the model of test construction upon which these early tests were based.

Traditional clinical tests: the global achievement model

The scoring method employed in the vast majority of intellectual and neuropsychological tests yields *only* a single achievement score (i.e., the number of items passed or recalled). For example, performance on each subtest of the WAIS-R, WMS, Stanford-Binet, and Halstead-Reitan Neuropsychological Battery is measured in terms of a single achievement score. As a number of critics have argued, this scoring procedure provides insufficient and sometimes erroneous evaluation of cognitive functioning, because it fails to measure whether examinees use effective or ineffective strategies to reach particular achievement levels (Eysenck, 1983; Gardner, 1983; Sternberg, 1977; Werner, 1937). For example, two examinees may recall the same *number* of words on a list-learning task, but one may have used an active semantic clustering strategy resulting in more stable long-term storage, whereas the other may have passively echoed back the last words on the list, resulting in deficient encoding and greater vulnerability to retroactive interference. Furthermore, Kaplan (1983) demonstrated that brain-damaged patients with markedly different cognitive deficits may obtain the same overall score on intellectual and neuropsychological tests. She has stressed that global scores are insufficient for characterizing patients' spared and impaired cognitive functions. As Berger (1982) states, "The basis of intelligence measurement, the total test score, confounds a number of components and is thus unsuitable as the basic unit for the analysis of test performance" (p. 15).

Psychometric instruments were initially developed at a time when behaviorism was the dominant school of psychology and research on mental functions was eschewed. Developers of the early clinical tests did not have access to the wealth of knowledge about the structures and processes of cognition which has accrued in the last two decades in the field of cognitive psychology. Consequently, most clinical tests still in use today are unsophisticated in terms of measuring components of cognitive functions.

New clinical tests: the cognitive science model

An exciting new direction in clinical test construction involves the integration of principles of cognitive science with psychometric assessment techniques. In this approach, the goal of test construction is to 'maximize the number of categories into which test-taking behavior can be classified and ultimately scored' (Berger, 1982), and to derive these categories from constructs developed in cognitive psychology and neuroscience (Butters, 1984; Delis and Ober, 1986; Horn, 1979; Kaplan, 1983; Mayes 1986; Russell, 1981; Squire, 1986a, b; Sternberg, 1977). The clinical utility of each scoring category should be tested empirically. Factor analytic studies can reveal whether or not additional, meaningful component factors underlie test performance when results from the new scoring categories are analysed. Clinical investigations can evaluate whether or not particular scoring categories enhance the test's capacity to differentiate and characterize the cognitive profiles of different patient populations.

The three clinical cases discussed above illustrate the importance of a cognitive-science approach to memory assessment. Critical diagnostic information is gained by quantifying components of learning and memory, such as indices reflecting learning strategy, encoding and retrieval processes, error types, and types of learning interference. The advantages of this approach for all types of intellectual and cognitive assessment are that it (1) affords quantification and normative data for multiple variables reflecting *how* tasks are solved in addition to the overall level of achievement obtained; (2) provides measurement of the spared and impaired cognitive processes in brain-damaged patients; (3) allows neuroscientists to analyse more rigorously the correlations between brain imaging and other neurophysiological indices with patients' spared and impaired cognitive processes; (4) facilitates the development of vocational, residential and therapeutic programs tailored to each examinee's specific deficits and strengths; and (5) contributes to overcoming a major shortcoming in modern psychology by bridging the gap between experimental and clinical psychology.

Memory assessment in the context of a comprehensive neuropsychological examination

Learning and memory are higher-level functions that are dependent upon the integrity of numerous other cognitive abilities. For instance, verbal memory is dependent in part on attention, auditory or visual perception, and linguistic processing. A patient may have severe anterograde amnesia for verbal material with relative preservation of attention, perception and language functions; however, verbal memory will suffer if one of these other cognitive abilities is disrupted. The implication for clinical assessment is that diagnosis of memory impairment must include a comprehensive evaluation of the cognitive skills upon which learning and memory functions are dependent.

A comprehensive neuropsychological evaluation is also essential for greater diagnostic specificity in patients with similar amnesic disorders. As an example, the memory deficits in patients with alcoholic Korsakoff syndrome and Alzheimer's disease are often strikingly similar: impaired immediate recall, little or no recall after a delay interval, high intrusion rate, and poor recognition performance characterized by a strong 'Yes' response bias and high false positive rate (Butters, 1985; Butters and Cermak, 1980; Fuld et al., 1982; Moss et al., 1986; Wilson et al., 1983). Additional neuropsychological findings which facilitate differentiation between these two patient groups include: (1) Alzheimer but not Korsakoff patients are also prone to suffer from anomia, apraxia and acalculia; (2) Alzheimer patients tend to display greater visuospatial and problem-solving deficits than Korsakoff patients; and (3) Korsakoff but not Alzheimer patients have IQ scores that tend to remain within the normal range over time (Butters and Cermak, 1980; Squire, 1987). Thus, a patient's memory deficits should always be interpreted vis-à-vis other cognitive strengths and weaknesses. As in any neuropsychological evaluation, a patient's medical and psychiatric history, demographic background and current emotional and behavioral functioning must also always be considered in formulating interpretations (Lezak, 1983).

The clinical utility of proposed divisions in memory

Perhaps more than any other cognitive domain, memory has inspired researchers to hypothesize numerous conceptual dichotomies. Although lively debate surrounds the validity of these divisions and their interrelationships (e.g., Cermak, 1984; Warrington and Weiskrantz, 1973), clinicians can nevertheless enrich their assessment of memory disorders by understanding how these dissociations may be manifested in patients' test performance. Only the most well-known distinctions will be briefly discussed here; for more in-depth discussions, see Butters and Miliotis, 1985; Cermak, 1984; Squire, 1987; Warrington and Weiskrantz, 1973; Shimamura, Chapter 2 of this volume.

Short- versus long-term memory
The grandfather of all memory divisions is the distinction between short- and long-term memory (or primary and secondary memory; Atkinson and Schiffrin, 1971; James, 1980; Waugh and Norman, 1965). Short-term memory generally refers to recall of material *immediately* after it is presented or during uninterrupted rehearsal of the material; it is thought to be limited in its capacity (Miller, 1956). Long-term memory refers to recall of information after a delay interval in which the examinee's attention is focused away from the target items; it is thought to have an extraordinarily large capacity. The clinical significance of this distinction is exemplified in famous cases such as H.M. (Scoville and Milner, 1957; Milner et al., 1968) and N.A. (Squire and Moore, 1979; Teuber et al., 1968) as well as in patients with alcoholic Korsakoff syndrome (Butters and Cermak, 1980). These patients often perform within or close to the normal range on immediate recall of supra-span material presented once; however, they are neither able to increase their level of recall on subsequent

presentations of the same material nor to remember any information once a delay interval is interposed between presentation and recall.

There is considerable controversy in the experimental literature surrounding this dichotomy. For example, one researcher's temporal definition of short-term memory is another's criterion for long-term memory (Cermak, 1972; Klatzky, 1980). For this reason, I recommend that clinicians do not employ the terms short- and long-term memory in describing patients' performance; rather, it is less ambiguous to use task-descriptive phrases such as 'immediate recall', '2-minute delay recall', '20-minute delay recall'.

Many experimentalists believe that the short-term/long-term distinction is altogether spurious (see reviews by Crowder, 1982; Wickelgren, 1973). They propose that there are levels of successful encoding of information into memory which exist on a continuum (Craik and Lockhart, 1972). However, the fact that amnesic patients display such an abrupt drop in memory performance as soon as their attention is drawn away from the target material provides clinical justification for continuing to distinguish between immediate and delayed recall (see also Squire, 1987).

Learning versus memory

As Squire (1987) writes:

The concepts of learning and memory are closely related. Learning is the *process* of acquiring new information, while memory refers to the *persistence* of learning in a state that can be revealed at a later time. (p. 3)

Most existing clinical tests evaluate memory per se, that is, the *amount* of information retained on immediate or delayed recall. Tests involving multiple presentations of the same material (e.g., the Paired-Associate subtest of the Wechsler Memory Scale (Wechsler 1945, 1981); the selective reminding procedure (Buschke, 1973); the Rey Auditory Verbal Learning Test (Lezak, 1983)) afford an evaluation of whether learning increases on successive trials. Although these tests do not provide formal indices that quantify the rate of learning

across trials or the different strategies that reflect how examinees learn the material, such indices could potentially be incorporated into these tests (see Delis et al., 1988b). The California Verbal Learning Test (Delis et al., 1987) formally quantifies and provides normative data for numerous indices reflecting how examinees learn, or fail to learn, verbal material in addition to the amount of information retained.

Patients vary widely in their patterns of performance on repeated learning trials of supra-span material. For example, examinees who are highly anxious often perform poorly on the first trial but improve considerably on subsequent trials (Lezak, 1983). In contrast, patients with frontal lobe damage have been reported to perform normally on the first trial but quickly reach a learning plateau on subsequent trials (Luria, 1981). Thus, assessment of both learning and memory variables contributes valuable diagnostic information.

Encoding versus retrieval

Encoding refers to the process by which physical information is transformed into a stored, mental representation; retrieval, to the process of later bringing stored information into conscious awareness. Brain-damaged patients vary greatly in terms of whether the locus of their memory problem is at the encoding or the retrieval level. A common procedure for testing this distinction clinically is to compare examinees' memory for the same material using first free recall and then recognition testing. If information has been encoded but cannot be adequately retrieved, then performance, relative to normal controls, should be poor on free recall (which places maximal demands on retrieval) and disproportionately better on recognition testing (which maximally aids retrieval and allows testing of the limits of information encoded). Evidence for this pattern of memory performance has been reported in patients with Huntington's disease (Butters et al., 1985) and frontal lobe lesions (Janowsky et al., in press). In contrast, if deficits in encoding are present, then aiding retrieval through recognition testing will not enhance performance. Butters and Cermak (1980) reported this pattern of performance in patients with Korsakoff syndrome. There are, however, difficulties inherent in separating encoding and retrieval processes using behavioral techniques (e.g., recognition may be disproportionately better than free recall because the target material was only partially encoded); consult Squire (1980, 1982) and Albert et al. (1981a) for caveats regarding these distinctions.

Proactive versus retroactive interference
Two proposed mechanisms fundamental to memory difficulty in normal subjects are proactive interference (i.e., the decremental effect of prior learning on the retention of subsequently learned material) and retroactive interference (i.e., the decremental effect of subsequent learning on the retention of previously learned material; Postman, 1971; Underwood, 1948). Examples of clinical instruments that assess both types of interference are the Rey Auditory Verbal Learning Test (Lezak, 1983) and the California Verbal Learning Test (Delis et al., 1987). On these tests, examinees are presented with two word lists to learn. If learning List A significantly interferes with learning List B, then an unusually high degree of proactive interference may be occurring. Conversely, if learning List B significantly interferes with subsequent recall of List A, then an unusually high degree of retroactive interference may be occurring.

Evaluating both types of interference can play an important role in testing different diagnostic hypotheses. For example, patients with multiple sclerosis or early stage Parkinson's disease, whose overall recall levels are below average, nevertheless show normal sensitivity to proactive and retroactive interference (Delis et al., 1987). In contrast, patients with Alzheimer's disease have been found to show *less* vulnerability to proactive interference than normal control subjects, and considerably more sensitivity to retroactive interference (Kramer et al., 1985; Wilson et al., 1983). Further support for the clinical utility of this distinction derives from a factor analytic study of the California Verbal Learning Test, which found that indices

of proactive and retroactive interference load on independent factors (Delis et al., 1988b).

Retrograde versus anterograde amnesia
Acute insult to neural systems responsible for memory can disrupt recall of information acquired before the injury (retrograde amnesia) as well as information presented for learning after the insult (anterograde amnesia). Retrograde amnesia can be assessed by asking the patient to recall autobiographical information which the examiner has obtained from relatives and other sources (Barbizet, 1970). There are also standardized instruments which evaluate patients' memory for past public information such as famous celebrities or television shows from different years (Albert et al., 1979; Squire and Slater, 1975; see below). Anterograde amnesia is evaluated whenever a patient is asked to learn new material.

Patients vary greatly in terms of their relative levels of retrograde and anterograde amnesia (Buttes and Miliotis, 1985; Squire, 1987). Some patients show greater anterograde than retrograde amnesia (Corkin, 1984; Zola-Morgan et al., 1986), some show greater retrograde than anterograde amnesia (Goldberg et al., 1981), while others show equally severe anterograde and retrograde amnesia (Damasio et al., 1985). Given the heterogeneity in the patterns of anterograde and retrograde memory loss among neurological patients, it behoves the clinician to assess both aspects of memory.

Recent versus remote memory
This distinction usually applies to the temporal dimension of retrograde memory. Information learned just prior to a cerebral insult is considered to be in recent memory, whereas knowledge acquired years or decades before the injury is thought to be in remote memory. Retrograde amnesia often adheres to a temporal gradient in which memory for recent events is more impaired than memory for remote events. Temporal gradients in retrograde amnesia have been reported in patients with alcoholic Korsakoff syndrome (Albert et al., 1979; Squire et al., 1989) and with mild Alzheimer's disease (Beatty et al., 1987). In contrast, patients

with Huntington's disease (Albert et al., 1981a; Beatty et al., 1987) and with moderate to severe Alzheimer's disease (Wilson et al., 1981) have been found to display a 'flat' retrograde amnesia (i.e., they are equally impaired in recalling events from different past decades).

The recent/remote memory dichotomy is helpful clinically in characterizing the nature of a patient's retrograde amnesia. Similar to the short-term/long-term distinction, there is no consensus among researchers regarding the temporal demarcation between these constructs. Thus, clinicians are advised to state specifically the estimated time duration of a patient's retrograde amnesia. The recent/remote distinction has occasionally been used synonymously with short-term/long-term memory, which again illustrates the need to use highly descriptive phrases in reporting patients' memory performance.

Declarative versus procedural memory
One of the most unintuitive and therefore exciting distinctions to emerge from modern neuropsychological research is that between declarative and procedural knowledge (Cohen et al., 1981; Squire, 1982; Squire and Cohen, 1984). Declarative memory refers to the acquisition of facts, knowledge and events which are directly accessible to conscious awareness. Procedural memory refers to learning on perceptual-motor tasks (e.g., pursuit rotor or mirror reading), which is not accessible to awareness. Because there are other types of implicit memory tasks that are not perceptual-motor in nature (e.g., semantic priming, which refers to unconscious memory for recently presented information that can be cued by associated information; see Chapter 2 of this volume), more conservative terms such as 'declarative/nondeclarative' (Squire and Zola-Morgan, 1988) and 'explicit/implicit' (Graf and Schacter, 1985) have also been advanced to denote this division.

The clinical relevance of this distinction derives from the finding that patients with severe amnesic syndromes often show normal procedural learning in the face of almost complete disruption of declarative memory (Gardner et al., 1973; Graf et al., 1984; Jacoby and Witherspoon, 1982; for review, see Shimamura, 1986). In contrast, patients with Huntington's disease are more impaired relative to amnesic patients on procedural learning tasks (e.g., pursuit rotor; Heindel et al., 1988) and less impaired on recognition tasks of declarative memory (Martone et al., 1984). Interestingly, Huntington patients have been found to show normal semantic priming (Shimamura et al., 1987), suggesting dissociable components of nondeclarative memory (i.e., between perceptual-motor and cognitive skills).

Because the neuropsychological significance of this distinction has only recently been discovered, standardized procedures for testing procedural memory clinically have not been developed. Existing tests could, however, be modified to provide such assessment. The Hooper Visual Organization Test (Hooper, 1958), for example, requires the subject to arrange mentally the mixed-up pieces of pictured objects and then to identify the objects. Equivalent alternative forms of this task could be administered for several trials to assess whether an examinee becomes faster and more accurate in reporting responses (procedural learning), followed by a delayed recall condition in which the examinee is asked to remember the actual objects (declarative memory). Perceptual-motor tasks such as pursuit rotor could also be normed and standardized, although motor dysfunction per se (e.g., peripheral neuropathy) may preclude a valid assessment of procedural learning on such tasks. New clinical tests of procedural learning will undoubtedly be developed in the future (e.g., adaptation of Cohen and Squire's, 1980, mirror reading procedure).

Episodic versus semantic memory
Declarative knowledge can be further divided into episodic and semantic memory (Tulving, 1983). Episodic memory refers to information learned at a particular time and place in one's life. Asking an examinee to recall what he or she ate for breakfast that day, or to recall a list of words presented 20

minutes earlier, taps episodic memory. Semantic memory refers to general knowledge of the world which is not linked to a particular temporal-spatial context. Asking examinees to define 'Breakfast', name the capital of Italy, or report which states border Kansas assesses different aspects of semantic memory. The term 'semantic memory' can be confusing, because it overlaps with some constructs used to describe other cognitive domains. For example, while defining the meaning of words is clearly a language task, it can also be thought of as a verbal semantic memory task (i.e., *recalling* the meaning of words). It follows then that a globally aphasic patient by definition has impaired semantic memory for linguistic knowledge.

Some researchers have proposed that amnesia represents a selective disruption of episodic memory with relative sparing of semantic memory (Kinsbourne and Wood, 1975; Weingartner et al., 1983). Amnesic patients typically perform at floor levels on tasks of new learning, whereas they achieve average or above-average scores on tasks assessing linguistic and cultural knowledge. These findings, however, may be better explained by the retrograde/anterograde distinction than by the episodic/semantic dichotomy (Squire and Cohen, 1984; Squire, 1987). Most semantic knowledge is learned in the early decades of life and thus has undergone the 'crystallizing' effects of long-term consolidation. Episodic knowledge acquired early in life (i.e., early autobiographical events) is also often preserved in amnesics. The temporal gradient of retrograde amnesia parsimoniously accounts for the findings that amnesic patients perform well in recalling both semantic and episodic information acquired early in life, and poorly in recalling both types of knowledge learned in later decades. When presented with *new* episodic or semantic information, amnesic patients are impaired in acquiring both types equally (Cermak and O'Connor, 1983; Gabrieli et al., 1982; Ostergaard, 1987).

Cermak (1984) has attempted to reconcile this issue by positing an interaction between the episodic/semantic and retrograde/anterograde distinctions. All new declarative learning (events or facts) reflects episodic memory, because a neurologically intact individual is likely to remember the learning context. Over time, acquired episodic knowledge gradually crystallizes into semantic memory, as evidenced, for example, by one's forgetting of the precise context of many childhood events. In this revised formulation, both the episodic/semantic and retrograde/anterograde distinctions are consistent with the data from amnesic patients.

It remains to be seen whether CNS pathology can cause selective disruption of episodic memory as originally formulated by Tulving (1972, 1983). Patients with Huntington's disease may show such a dissociation. They display a flat retrograde amnesia on a visual confrontation naming test of remote events (Albert et al., 1981a), and thus they are impaired in recalling episodic information even from early decades. In contrast, their language functioning as assessed by a visual confrontation naming test of common and uncommon objects (Boston Naming Test; Kaplan et al., 1983) is often within or close to the normal range until the terminal stages of the disease (Butters et al., 1978); verbal semantic memory is thus relatively preserved. This episodic/semantic dissociation in Huntington patients is valid, however, only within certain constraints. For example, it occurs only for retrograde memory testing, as these patients show impaired anterograde memory for both episodic and semantic knowledge. In addition, some aspects of verbal semantic memory, such as controlled word association, are impaired in Huntington patients (Butters et al., 1986). These constraints call into question the explanatory and clinical utility of the episodic/semantic distinction.

Clinical tests of learning and memory

The last two decades have witnessed a proliferation of memory tests, particularly in the experimental literature. Because of space limitations, only a sampling of commonly used clinical memory tests, revised versions of these tests, and recently developed instruments are described and briefly appraised here. In order to gain familiarity with the gamut of tests available, the reader is referred to several excellent reviews by Butters (1985), Butters and Cermak (1980), Lezak (1983), Loring and Papanicolaou (1987), Mayes (1986), Poon (1987), Russell (1981), Squire (1986) and Squire and Butters (1984).

Verbal tests

Immediate recall span
The repetition of information immediately after its initial presentation requires attentional abilities and what many researchers would term 'short-term memory' capacity. Patients with classic amnesic syndrome may perform within, or close to, the normal range on immediate recall span tests. Individuals who have impaired attentional skills, such as patients with severe depression (Breslow et al., 1980; Stromgren, 1977) or dementia of the Alzheimer's type (Corkin, 1982; Kaszniak et al., 1979), often perform poorly on immediate recall span tests.

Digit span. The most commonly used span tests are those found on Wechsler's scales (Wechsler, 1945, 1955, 1981). The examiner presents increasingly long sequences of random digits, and the examinee is asked to repeat each sequence. A second set of random digits is then presented, and the examinee is asked to repeat them backwards. Repetition of digits provides a good measure of immediate recall span for verbal material in general, because digits can be thought of as verbal symbols which are relatively homogeneous with respect to frequency of occurrence in the English language, abstractness, meaningfulness and imageability.

Wechsler's Digit Span subtest has been criticized in terms of its scoring method (Lezak, 1983). Although repetition of digits forwards and backwards taps different cognitive processes (i.e., digits backwards places more demand on mental control and symbol transformation than digits forwards), both types of testing have been traditionally collapsed into one scaled score. This single score can

obscure the fact that amnesic patients can show normal digits forwards and impaired digits backwards. Thus, the level of an examinee's immediate recall span should not be estimated from this test's scaled score, but rather from the number of digits an examinee is able to repeat in the forward direction. This scoring problem has finally been rectified on the new Wechsler Memory Scale-Revised (WMS-R; Wechsler, 1987), which provides separate percentile scores for both digits forwards and backwards (see below).

It is also questionable whether repeating digits *forwards* represents the best measure of an examinee's immediate verbal recall span, because most verbal memory tests do not require that the target items be recalled in the exact order in which they were presented. For these memory tests, the best measure of immediate recall span may be simply the length of a digit sequence accurately repeated, regardless of the order of the digits. Kaplan et al. (in press) have developed a new scoring system for Wechsler's Digit Span subtest which yields indices for (a) digit span regardless of order, (b) digit span forward, (c) digit span backward, and (d) error types (i.e., transpositions, omissions, commissions).

Word and sentence span. Tests have been developed which require the examinee to repeat increasingly long sequences of words (Miller, 1973; Talland, 1965) or sentences (e.g., from "Take this home" to "The members of the committee have agreed to hold their meeting on the first Tuesday of each month"; Benton and Hamsher, 1976). As Lezak (1983) points out, it is important to consider several variables such as number of syllables per word, frequency, abstractness, imageability and meaningfulness in clinically interpreting results from these tests.

Memory for word lists
Paired-associate subtest, WMS. (Wechsler, 1945). This test involves the presentation of 10 word pairs. The examiner then reads the first word of each pair and the examinee is asked to provide the second word. Three learning trials are presented.

Four of the word pairs are 'hard' associates (e.g., 'School-Grocery') and six are 'easy' (e.g., 'Baby-Cries'). The advantages of this test are: (1) paired-associate learning, especially for the 'hard' items, is sensitive to memory dysfunction in general (Squire, 1986); (2) this subtest has been used extensively in clinical research, and thus a large body of comparative data is available from a variety of patient populations (Delaney et al., 1980; Gilleard, 1980; Perez et al., 1975); and (3) it assesses differential learning of high-frequency and low-frequency associations.

One problem with this subtest is that two of the 'easy' associates are too easy: for 'north-south' and 'up-down', amnesic patients can often guess the correct answer. In addition, this subtest does not provide formal assessment of delayed recall. Both of these problems, however, have been ameliorated on the WMS-R (Wechsler, 1987). In her revision of this subtest, Kaplan (see Milberg et al., 1986) includes an additional recall trial after the first three trials: the examiner reads the *second* word of a pair and the examinee must report the first word. Patients who encode word pairs on a more superficial, phonetic level, rather than a 'deeper' semantic level, will often perform worse on this trial compared to the third trial because the phonemic sequence of the word pairs is altered.

In addition to the Paired-Associate subtest of the WMS, a large number of different paired-associate learning tasks can be found in the experimental literature (Bowers, 1972; Jones, 1974; Paivio, 1965).

Selective reminding procedure. (Buschke, 1973; Buschke and Fuld, 1974). In this procedure, a word list is presented once, followed by immediate recall. On the next trial, only those words the examinee failed to recall on the preceding trial are presented, and the examinee attempts to recall the entire list. This procedure is repeated for several trials until the examinee recalls all the target words or a predetermined number of trials has been administered. A number of different versions of this procedure have been developed (Buschke and Fuld, 1974; Caine et al., 1977; Hannay and Levin,

1985; Ober et al., 1985; Randt and Brown, 1983).

The selective reminding procedure represents one of the first attempts to bridge the gap between clinical assessment and cognitive science. Several memory constructs are operationally defined and quantified by the procedure, including 'short-term retrieval' (i.e., the number of words recalled that were presented on a trial), 'long-term retrieval' (the number of words recalled on a trial that were not presented on that trial because they had been recalled on the previous trial), 'long-term storage' (the total number of words that were recalled on two consecutive trials at least once), and 'consistent long-term retrieval' (the subset of long-term retrieval items that are recalled on all successive trials following their initial recall). The validity of some of these constructs has, however, been called into question. Loring and Papanicolaou (1987) discussed problems related to the operational definition of retrieval:

Although the attempt to isolate different components of memory is admirable, the distinction between long-term storage and retrieval is arbitrary. According to Buschke's definition, a word has entered LTS if it has been successfully recalled on two consecutive trials. Therefore, by definition, and definition only, failure to recall is due to retrieval failure. Just as plausible and conceptually appealing, however, is that these 'memory traces' have been stored in a weak or degraded form . . . Therefore, operationally defined retrieval may have in fact little to do with retrieval itself. (p. 349)

Inferences about the relative integrity of encoding and retrieval processes are typically made by contrasting free-recall and recognition performance (Lezak, 1983). Because only free recall is usually assessed with the selective reminding procedure, its operational definition of retrieval may not be adequate.

The procedure's definition of 'long-term storage' may also be invalid for certain patient populations. For example, Ober et al. (1985) found that moderate-to-severe Alzheimer patients actually showed better 'long-term storage' than mild Alzheimer patients on a selective reminding test. One possible explanation for this unexpected finding was that the moderate-to-severe patients tended to perseverate one or two words across trials. Labeling these perseverations as responses from 'long-term storage' may be an incorrect characterization of pathological performance. More descriptive terms such as 'reminded recall' instead of 'short-term retrieval' and 'unreminded recall' instead of 'long-term storage' would overcome this labeling problem.

Rey Auditory Verbal Learning Test. (RAVLT; Lezak, 1983). On Rey's test, a list of 15 unrelated words is presented for five immediate-recall trials. A second, interference list of unrelated words is presented for one trial, followed by recall and then recognition testing of the first list. Many examiners test for recall of the first list again after a delay interval (Lezak, 1983). Preliminary normative data are provided for total number of words recalled on each of the recall trials of the first list (Lezak, 1983; Query and Berger, 1980). In addition, the examiner can make qualitative interpretations about various learning parameters, such as primacy-recency effects, learning rate across trials, and increased vulnerability to proactive and retroactive interference. A scoring system quantifying many of these parameters could easily be developed for the RAVLT (see Delis et al., 1988b).

The California Verbal Learning Test. (CVLT; Delis et al., 1987). The general format of the CVLT was modeled after Rey's test. One major difference between the two tests is that the CVLT lists contain four words from each of four semantic categories (e.g., 'fruits'; 'tools'). Words from the same category are never presented consecutively, which affords an assessment of the degree to which an examinee uses an active semantic clustering strategy in recalling the words. Another difference between the tests is that the CVLT's scoring system quantifies and provides normative data for numerous learning and memory variables in addition to total levels of recall and recognition. These variables include semantic and serial-order clustering strategies, primacy-recency effect, learning rate across trials, consistency of item recall across trials, degree of vulnerability to proactive and retroactive interference, retention of information after short and longer (20-minute) delays,

enhancement of recall performance by category cuing and recognition testing, indices of recognition performance derived from signal-detection theory (discriminability and response bias), and frequency of error types (intrusions, perseverations and false positives). Optional computerized scoring automatically computes the multiple learning and memory indices and converts raw scores into standardized scores based on the examinee's age and sex (Fridlund and Delis, 1987).

The advantage of the CVLT for clinical practice is that its scoring system quantifies the strategies, processes and errors an examinee displays in learning verbal material. As such, the test fully embraces a cognitive-science approach to neuropsychological assessment. Normative data from 273 normal subjects and 145 carefully diagnosed neurological patients are provided for 26 memory variables. An alternate form is available, and a children's version of the CVLT has also been developed (Delis et al., in press). For clinical research purposes, the CVLT allows an assessment of the extent to which multiple aspects of memory covary in one test. The disadvantage of the test for research is that it does not provide formal measures of specific memory processes in isolation.

Memory for stories
Logical Memory subtest, WMS. (Wechsler, 1945). The most commonly used story memory test is the Logical Memory subtest of the WMS. In its standardized format, two stories are each read once for immediate recall. The revision of this subtest to include delayed recall is critical for detecting subtle memory deficits and for highlighting the sometimes complete disruption of long-term recall in amnesic patients (Lezak, 1983; Milberg et al., 1986; Russell, 1975). The new WMS-R includes both immediate and delayed recall, and a better scoring system for quantifying units of story ideas recalled (for problems associated with scoring story recall, see Crosson et al., 1984; Lezak, 1983; Loring and Papanicolaou, 1987; Power et al., 1979; Russell, 1975).

Other clinical tests of story memory have been

developed by Babcock (1930), Kramer et al. (1988), Heaton et al. (1985), Lezak (1983), Randt and Brown (1983) and Talland (1965b). The Kramer et al. (1988) test includes immediate and 20-minute delayed free recall, cued recall, and recognition testing; the test's scoring system quantifies verbatim and paraphrased recall, gist recall, primacy/recency effect, and error types. On Heaton's test (Heaton et al., 1985), one paragraph is presented for up to five trials or until a criterion score is reached, which affords an assessment of story learning. Free recall of the story after a four-hour delay is also assessed. Normative data for over 200 normal subjects are forthcoming (Heaton, personal communication).

It is not uncommon for a patient to perform considerably better in recalling stories than word lists. These examinees often have difficulty adopting an active learning strategy such as semantic clustering in recalling word lists, but they are able to benefit from the thematic organization inherent in stories.

Visuospatial tests

Immediate recall span
Corsi Blocks. (De Renzi et al., 1977; Kaplan et al., in press; Lezak 1983; Milner, 1971). On this test, nine 1½ inch cubes are fastened randomly on a board. The examiner touches increasingly long sequences of blocks, and the examinee is asked to repeat each sequence in the same order. In the backwards condition, the examinee touches each sequence in the reverse order from the examiner. The Corsi Block test represents a spatial analogue of the Digit Span subtest, and assesses an examinee's attentional skills and span capacity for visuospatial stimuli. A similar test will be included as a supplemental subtest of the WAIS-R (Kaplan et al., in press). A pictorial version of this task is included in the WMS-R (Wechsler, 1987).

Memory for visual stimuli
Benton Visual Retention Test. (BVRT; Benton, 1974). The BVRT involves the presentation of ten

visual stimuli. The first two stimuli consist of one geometric shape each, and the remaining eight stimuli each consist of two large and one small geometric design (see Fig. 1). The examiner can choose between different administration conditions (e.g., 10-second exposure of each stimulus followed by immediate recall; 10-second exposure of each stimulus followed by 15-second delayed recall), and three alternative forms. The BVRT is one of the first clinical instruments to use a scoring system that quantifies and provides normative data for multiple variables (e.g., accuracy and error types are analysed).

The BVRT has been used extensively in neuropsychological investigations (Benton, 1962; Marsh and Hirsch, 1982; Nickols, 1972; Sterne, 1969). It has been found to be sensitive to hemispatial processing deficits in unilateral brain-damaged patients (Heilbrun, 1956). Most of the designs can be easily verbalized (e.g., large triangle), and, as with many visuospatial memory tasks, it is difficult to ascertain the degree to which an examinee uses a spatial and/or verbal learning strategy (Lezak, 1983).

If an examinee shows impaired performance on a visuospatial memory test which involves a constructional response (e.g., drawing), the locus of the deficit may be at the perceptual, constructional or memory level. Asking the examinee to copy the same designs he or she previously drew from memory will often elucidate the nature of the impairment (i.e., whether constructional or memory skills are more impaired; see Kaplan, 1983). If the patient's copied drawings are deficient, then a matching task in which the examinee selects the target design displayed with several similar designs will help determine whether the patient has a percep-

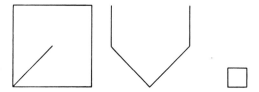

FIG. 1. Example of target stimulus from the Benton Visual Retention Test (Benton, 1974).

tual problem. Benton and his colleagues have developed tests of copying, visual discrimination, and visual recognition memory for greater diagnostic specificity (Benton, 1974; Benton et al., 1983).

Visual Reproduction subtest. (WMS; Wechsler, 1945). On this test, the examinee studies each of three stimulus cards for 10 seconds, and attempts to recall each one immediately after its presentation. The first two cards display one design each, and the last one displays two designs. The figures are relatively simple and can be easily verbalized. Most revisions of the subtest include a delayed recall condition of the test (Lezak, 1983; Milberg

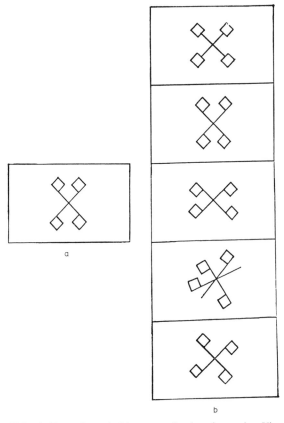

FIG. 2. Examples of (a) target stimulus from the Visual Reproduction subtest of the Wechsler Memory Scale (Wechsler, 1945); and (b) multiple-choice alternatives used in testing recognition memory for the Visual Reproduction designs. The distractor items were developed by Edith Kaplan (see Milberg et al., 1986) and represent prototypical errors made by patients with focal and diffuse brain damage in their free-recall drawings of the target designs.

et al., 1986; Russell, 1975), and the WMS-R has formally incorporated a 30-minute delayed recall condition. Kaplan (see Milberg et al., 1986) also developed recognition memory, matching and copying tasks for this subtest in order to assess the integrity of component functions it taps (i.e., perception, construction and memory; see Fig. 2).

An advantage of the Visual Reproduction subtest is that comparison data are available from numerous investigations with focal brain-damaged patients (Delaney et al., 1980), elderly subjects (Hulicka, 1966; Ivison, 1977), amnesics (Butters and Cermak, 1980), and patients with different types of dementia (Gilleard, 1980; Perez et al., 1975). A problem with the test is that considerable variance in performance occurs in the normal elderly. For example, normal subjects between 70 and 79 years old had a mean score of 4.95 out of 14 possible points and a standard deviation of 3.42 (Wechsler, 1945). An elderly individual could obtain a score of only 1.5, which would still fall within one standard deviation of the mean for his or her age group.

In Heaton et al.'s (1985) revision of this subtest, the designs are displayed for 10 seconds each, and the examinee attempts to draw them only after all three designs have been presented. This procedure is repeated for up to five trials or until the examinee reaches a criterion score. Four-hour delayed recall for the drawings is also assessed. Normative data for over 200 normal subjects are forthcoming.

Recognition Memory Test (Warrington, 1984). This test assesses recognition memory for 50 pictorial stimuli (i.e., photographs of unknown faces) and 50 visually presented verbal stimuli (i.e., printed words). Examinees make 'pleasantness' ratings for each item in a set, followed by a two-choice recognition test. Normative data are provided for 310 subjects. This test affords a rigorous assessment of modality-specific recognition memory. It has been found to be sensitive to unilateral brain damage (Warrington, 1984).

Rey-Osterrieth Complex Figure Test (Lezak, 1983). This is a favorite visuospatial memory test among many neuropsychologists. The examinee first copies the complex figure (see Fig. 3), and then draws it from memory both immediately and after a delay interval (Brooks, 1972; Milberg et al., 1986; Taylor, 1979; Waber and Holmes, 1986). Taylor (1979) developed a second complex figure that serves as an alternative form of the original test.

One advantage of this test is that the examiner can assess the relationship between the examinee's copying strategy and subsequent recall performance. Just as semantic clustering is the most effective strategy for recalling categorized word lists, so too *perceptual clustering* is the most effective strategy for recalling a complex visual stimulus such as the Rey-Osterrieth figure. By perceptual clustering, I mean perceiving and copying the complex figure in terms of perceptual wholes or similar features (e.g., large rectangle; side triangle; two diagonal lines; etc.), rather than drawing the figure in a disorganized, piecemeal manner (Paterson and Zangwill, 1944). Perceptual clustering organizes the numerous line segments of a complex figure into a smaller number of perceptual units for more efficient encoding and retrieval. Although perceptual clustering tends to correlate with memory accuracy, impulsive patients may copy the figure in a piecemeal manner but nevertheless draw it from memory in a perceptually organized manner. This

finding indicates that they are slow to adopt a perceptual clustering strategy but still capable of doing so during consolidation. In order to analyse the examinee's constructional strategy, Kaplan (see Milberg et al., 1986) recommends that the examiner record exactly what an examinee draws, numbering the lines to indicate the order in which they are generated and placing arrows on the lines to indicate directionality of construction.

Another advantage of the Rey-Osterrieth test is that the figure contains both larger configural features (e.g., the large rectangle) and smaller internal details (e.g., the dots and circle). This configural/detail stimulus parameter helps dissociate the differential processing strategies of unilateral brain-damaged patients. Left-hemisphere damaged patients often have difficulty remembering the internal details, whereas right-hemisphere damaged patients are impaired in remembering the general configuration (Binder, 1982; Goodglass and Kaplan, 1979; Lezak, 1983; see Fig. 4 for examples of patients' drawings).

A limitation of the Rey-Osterrieth figure is that it does not have clear demarcation between stimulus features perceived as larger wholes versus smaller parts. For instance, although the large base rectangle can be classified as a larger configural shape and the dots within the circle as internal details, other features that fall in between these two levels of structure (e.g., the diagonal lines within the rectangle) cannot be unambiguously classified as configural or detail (Robertson and Delis, 1986). Thus, the Rey-Osterrieth figure does not lend itself to rigorous quantification of performance differences in constructing configural versus detail features.

Different scoring systems for the Rey-Osterrieth test are available (Binder, 1982; Taylor, 1959; Waber and Holmes, 1986). Taylor's (1959) system yields a single achievement score that reflects final accuracy only. Both Binder (1982) and Waber and Holmes (1986) have developed scoring systems that quantify an examinee's constructional strategy in addition to overall level of achievement.

California Global-Local Learning Test (CGLT;

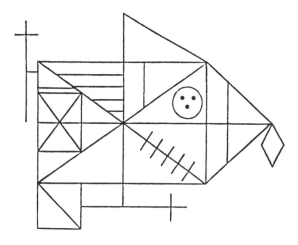

FIG. 3. The Rey-Osterrieth figure (Lezak, 1983).

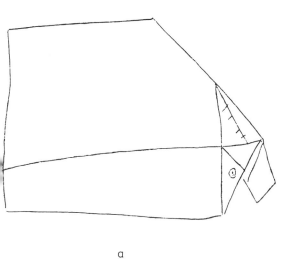

a

numerous smaller letters and shapes (see Fig. 5). These stimuli provide precise demarcation between features perceived as larger wholes (the global letter or shape) and smaller details (the local letter or shape). In order to control for the ease of verbalizing the stimuli, three types of stimuli are used: linguistic forms (letters), high-frequency nonlinguistic forms (e.g., trapezoid), and low-frequency nonlinguistic forms (shapes without established names). The hierarchical stimuli are presented in pairs, one stimulus in each hemispace, to assess hemispatial processing defects. Three pairs of visual hierarchical stimuli are presented for five seconds each, followed by recall drawing of each pair immediately after its presentation. The pairs are presented for three trials to assess learning of

b

FIG. 4. Examples of 20-minute delayed recall of the Rey-Osterrieth figure (Lezak, 1983) by (a) a left-hemisphere damaged patient illustrating better recall of the outer configuration than of details; and (b) a right-hemisphere damaged patient illustrating better recall of details than of the outer configuration.

Delis and Kaplan, 1988). Because unilateral brain pathology tends to disrupt analysis of wholes and parts selectively (Kaplan, 1983; Warrington et al., 1966), the CGLT was developed to quantify this parameter more rigorously. The test involves the presentation of visual hierarchical stimuli consisting of a larger letter or shape constructed from

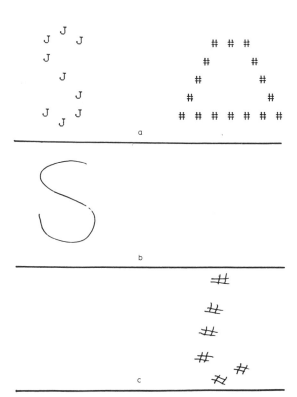

FIG. 5. Examples of (a) a pair of target hierarchical stimuli from the California Global-Local Learning Test (Delis and Kaplan, 1988); (b) immediate free-recall by a left-hemisphere damaged patient illustrating correct memory only for the global form presented in left hemispace; and (c) immediate free-recall by a right-hemisphere damaged patient illustrating correct memory only for the local forms presented in right hemispace.

17

visuospatial material. Multiple-trial presentation of the same stimuli also reduces the large performance variance that the elderly often show on visuospatial memory tests (see Visual Reproduction subtest above). Twenty-minute delayed free recall, recognition and copy are then tested.

The CGLT provides indices and normative data for learning rate and retention of forms that are global or local, linguistic or nonlinguistic, and presented in left or right hemispace. Previous studies have found that left-hemisphere damaged patients are selectively impaired in learning local forms, especially when they are presented in right hemispace, whereas right-hemisphere damaged patients are selectively impaired in learning global forms, especially when they are presented in left hemispace (Delis et al., 1986, 1988c; see Fig. 5 for examples of patients' drawings).

Tactile memory test
Tactual Performance Test (TPT; Halstead, 1947; Reitan and Davison, 1974). The examinee is blind-folded and asked to place cut-out shapes into a formboard, in turn using his or her preferred hand, nonpreferred hand, and both hands. On the memory part of the test, the blindfold is removed and test equipment hidden, and the examinee is asked to draw the shapes and their relative locations. The shapes are high-frequency geometric figures (e.g., square), which can elicit a verbal strategy. Although the original 'cut-off' scores for 'impaired' performance have been found to yield too high a false-positive rate in the elderly (Bak and Green, 1980; Blusewicz et al., 1977), Heaton et al. (1985) have gathered more extensive normative data for this population. Lezak (1983) recommends using the TPT in order to evaluate tactile learning with blind persons.

Memory scales

Wechsler Memory Scale (Wechsler, 1945). The WMS consists of seven subtests: Information, Orientation, Mental Control, Digit Span, Logical Memory, Visual Reproduction, Paired-Associate

Learning. Its wide use in clinical and research practice is matched by the criticism it has received in its original version (Erickson and Scott, 1977; Loring and Papanicolaou, 1987; Prigatano, 1978). The Memory Quotient has been particularly assailed, because it confounds numerous cognitive and memory functions and it reflects only immediate recall performance. The revisions offered by Russell (1975), Kaplan (see Milberg et al., 1986) and Heaton et al. (1985) have improved the scale considerably. The most important revisions include delayed recall for the three subtests of new learning (Logical Memory, Visual Reproduction, and Paired-Associate Learning), improved scoring for the Logical Memory stories (Russell, 1975), and recognition memory, copying and matching trials for the Visual Reproduction designs (Milberg et al., 1986).

Wechsler Memory Scale-Revised (WMS-R; Wechsler, 1987). The WMS-R represents a significant improvement over the original WMS, and clearly indicates that the revision authors have listened carefully to the criticisms of the older version. Both immediate and 30-minute delayed recall are systematically assessed on the Logical Memory, Visual Reproduction, Verbal Paired Associates, and Visual Paired Associates subtests. The subtests are well-balanced in terms of testing verbal and visuospatial memory. There are now 13 subtests: Information and Orientation, Mental Control, Figural Memory, Logical Memory I (immediate recall) and II (delayed recall), Visual Paired Associates I and II, Verbal Paired Associates I and II, Visual Reproduction I and II, Digit Span, and Visual Memory Span. A Memory Rating Form is also included which is filled out by the examinee or a significant other.

The scoring rules for the Logical Memory stories have been improved considerably, and examples of acceptable paraphrases are provided for each story unit. The stories have also been updated (e.g., Anna Thompson is now robbed of $56 instead of $15). A more elaborate scoring procedure is also provided for the Visual Reproduction subtest, with examples of drawings. The original verbal paired-associates are used, with the exception that the two associates that were too easy (i.e., up-down, north-south) have been eliminated. Another major improvement is that *separate* scores are derived for the forward and backward conditions of the Digit Span and Visual Memory Span subtests. Thus, the problem in past Wechsler scales of collapsing forward and backward span testing into a single score has been rectified.

New subtests include a recognition test for visual patterns that cannot be easily verbalized (Figural Memory), a color patch/design paired associate test, and a visuospatial span test similar to Corsi blocks (see Fig. 6 for example stimuli from these new subtests). In addition to assessing visuospatial

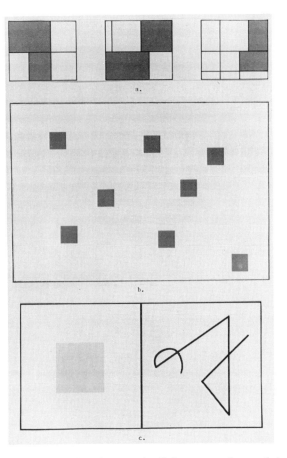

FIG. 6. Examples of target stimuli from new subtests of the Wechsler Memory Scale-Revised (Wechsler, 1987): (a) Figural Memory item; (b) Visual Memory Span stimulus; and (c) Visual Paired Associates item.

recognition memory, the Figural Memory subtest affords an analysis of hemispatial processing defects. One problem with the Visual Paired Associates subtest is that patients with hemi-inattention may be especially handicapped, because the color patch is always presented on the left side of the card and the design on the right side. This problem may be corrected by rotating the cards 90 degrees during presentation so that the color patch and design are vertically aligned (a study will be needed to determine whether or not this modification alters normal performance).

A normative study has been completed involving 316 normal subjects and 346 clinical patients. Based empirically on factor analytic results from this normative sample, five composite standardized scores are derived for each examinee: General Memory, Attention/Concentration, Verbal Memory, Visual Memory, and Delayed Recall. These indices are scaled to a mean of 100 and standard deviation of 15. Percentile scores are also computed for immediate and delayed recall of the Logical Memory passages and Visual Reproduction designs, and for the forward and backward conditions of the Digit Span and Visual Memory Span subtests. Recent investigations indicate that the WMS-R has considerable utility in characterizing the memory disorders of patients with Alzheimer's disease, Huntington's disease, multiple sclerosis, alcoholic Korsakoff syndrome, long-term alcoholism, closed head injury, exposure to neurotoxins, schizophrenia and depression (Butters et al., 1988; Borstein and Chelune, 1988; Chelune and Borstein, 1988; Fischer, 1988; Ryan and Lewis, 1988; see also Wechsler, 1987). In a study comparing the WMS-R and CVLT, numerous strong correlations were found (e.g., $r = .910$ between the WMS-R Verbal Memory Index and CVLT List A Trials $1-5$ Total Recall Index; Delis et al., 1988a). These findings suggest a high degree of convergence between the two instruments.

Randt Memory Test (Randt and Brown, 1983). Seven subtests comprise the Randt Memory Test: general information, a five-item list-learning task, digit span, paired-associate learning, a short story, picture recognition memory, and an incidental learning test of the names of the previous tasks. On some of the subtests, a Brown-Peterson distraction task is used in which the examinee must count backwards by threes between presentation and recall. Twenty-four-hour delayed recall is also solicited. A selective reminding procedure is employed on the five-item learning task. As the authors state, the test provides a 'global survey' of patients' memory complaints; it 'is *not* intended to assist in the localization of brain lesions or functions, nor is it intended for detailed research investigations into specific facets of normal human memory'. Optional computerized scoring of test scores is available.

An advantage of the test is that five alternative forms are available. Normative data are provided for 290 normal subjects. One limitation is that patients with moderate to severe memory disturbance may have difficulty understanding and remembering the complex instructions of some of the tasks (e.g., 'In a moment I will read a list of five unrelated words to you and ask you to recall these items, in any order, after a brief period of time, during which I will ask you to subtract some numbers'). The examiner is instructed in the manual to ask those examinees who may be too impaired to count backwards by threes to count backwards by twos or ones. This unsystematic variation in administration may lessen the test's psychometric rigor. Another problem is that examinees are told before tasks of new learning that they will have to remember the material 'again tomorrow'. This instruction may be confounding in that highly motivated examinees have the opportunity to write down target items after leaving the examiner. Finally, the stimuli on the Picture Recognition task are all high-frequency objects (e.g., telephone, clock), which probably elicits a verbal strategy for many examinees. Thus, visuospatial memory is not adequately assessed by this battery.

Memory scale, Luria-Nebraska Neuropsychological Battery. (Golden et al., 1983). The Luria-Nebraska battery contains 14 scales, one of which is a memory scale. This scale has drawn extensive criticism, because of low content validity, heterogeneity of items (e.g., confounding of memory and nonmemory questions and of verbal and visuospatial items), and failure to assess delayed recall (Adams, 1980; Russell, 1986; Spiers, 1981). As Spiers (1981) remarked:

> The composition of the Luria-Nebraska memory scale suggests that the authors were either unaware of [the] component aspects of memory functioning or chose to ignore them. Of the 13 items making up this scale, 1 item tests rhythm (228); 1 is confounded by representational praxis (229); 1 is a visual item that requires appreciation of color, shape, and sequence (226); and 1 is a sentence repetition task (223). This leaves 9 items supposedly related to memory, all of which are immediate recall tasks. (p. 336)

The Luria-Nebraska battery has been found to be useful in identifying 'brain damage' per se (Golden et al., 1983). The items within the memory scale, however, are so heterogeneous that an examinee's score may have little bearing on the integrity of his or her specific memory functioning.

Retrograde memory tests

The assessment of patients' memory for events that occurred prior to the onset of their brain dysfunction can be done informally by eliciting autobiographical recall. Because amnesic patients are prone to confabulate, verification with relatives or administration of this task a second time after a delay interval may be necessary to determine the validity of the patient's responses (Schacter et al., 1982). If the responses are valid, then a time-line can be constructed reflecting the presence, nature (i.e., flat versus temporal gradient) and extent of a patient's retrograde amnesia (Barbizet, 1970; Squire and Slater, 1983).

In experimental investigations, memory tests of public information have been developed in order to quantify patients' retrograde amnesia more rigorously. Because of large individual differences in exposure to public information, these tests are best suited for the assessment of retrograde amnesia in groups of subjects. They can, however,

e used by clinicians for making tentative inferences about a patient's recall of information
that he or she was likely to have learned during
particular past years or decades.

Boston Retrograde Amnesia Battery. (BRAB;
Albert et al., 1979). This test assesses memory for
public events and famous actors, politicians, celebrities and other individuals who were in the public
spotlight from the 1930s to the 1970s. There are
three components to the battery: a famous faces
test, a verbal recall questionnaire, and a multiple-
choice recognition questionnaire. An examinee's
performance level in remembering information
from each decade is graphed, which reveals
whether a patient's retrograde amnesia is equally
severe across all decades (flat retrograde amnesia)
or less severe for more remote decades (temporal
gradient). A creative feature of the test is that some
of the pictures of famous people were taken during
different decades (e.g., Jimmy Stewart during the
1930s and 1970s; see Fig. 7); patients whose retrograde amnesia adheres to a temporal gradient will
often recognize the earlier but not the later picture.

Comparison data from normal control subjects
are available. The BRAB has been used in numerous investigations which have documented the
nature of retrograde memory loss in various patient populations, including alcoholic Korsakoff
syndrome, Huntington's disease and Alzheimer's

disease (Albert et al., 1979, 1980, 1981a, b).

Television test (Squire and Fox, 1980; Squire and
Slater, 1975). A methodological problem inherent
in testing retrograde memory is possible differences in item difficulty across decades (Sanders
and Warrington, 1971). Many amnesics may show
better memory for remote than for recent events
because the earlier events are easier to recall due to
their longer period of exposure and fame. Squire
and Slater (1975), however, developed a retrograde
memory test that circumvents this problem. To
maximize equivalent public exposure across years,
they used as test items television programs broadcast for one season. Both recall and recognition
testing conditions are employed. The validity of
this test has been demonstrated in studies documenting the nature of retrograde amnesia in
depressed patients who have undergone ECT treatment (Squire et al., 1975), in amnesic patients
(Cohen and Squire, 1981), and in repeated administrations of an updated version of the test to
subjects over a seven-year period (Squire and Fox,
1980). Normative data are available for 250 normal subjects.

Information subtest, WAIS-R (Wechsler, 1981).
This subtest of the WAIS-R assesses recall of
famous people (e.g., Louis Armstrong), and cultural and scientific facts likely to have been learned
in school (e.g., 'On what continent is Brazil?'). As
with all WAIS-R subtests, Information has been
normed on 1,880 subjects who are representative
of the U.S. population on a number of demographic variables (e.g., sex, race). Kaplan et al. (in
press) have developed a recognition test for this
subtest in order to evaluate selective deficits in
retrieval of remote knowledge.

For middle-aged and older individuals, this
subtest can serve as a gross measure of memory for
remote information. However, because the items
of this subtest are neither selected systematically
from different decades nor equated for ease of
recall, important qualitative features of a patient's
retrograde amnesia cannot be evaluated. Patients
with retrograde amnesia that extends only a few
years or decades prior to their disease onset may

FIG. 7. Pictures of Jimmy Stewart from (a) the 1930s and
(b) the 1970s which are used as items on the Boston Retrograde
Amnesia Battery to assess temporal gradients in retrograde
memory (Albert et al., 1979).

still perform well on this test, since most of the items tap knowledge acquired during more remote school years. For patients who perform poorly on the test, it becomes important to differentiate between a naming deficit and remote memory loss.

Memory profiles of selected clinical populations

A brief overview of the memory profiles of selected patient populations reveals how different components of learning and memory can be selectively disrupted or spared.

Unilateral brain damage
For years it was thought that left-hemisphere damage (LHD) impairs memory for verbal material, whereas right-hemisphere damage (RHD) disrupts memory for visuospatial material (Gerner et al., 1972; Kimura, 1963; Milner, 1971). The search for elementary principles of hemispheric specialization was reopened, however, by subsequent findings indicating that RHD patients suffer subtle deficits in verbal memory, while LHD patients are impaired in remembering certain types of visual stimuli.

RHD patients were found to remember an equivalent *number* of idea units of thematically organized stories as normal controls, but they were more prone to lose the gist of a story (Wapner et al., 1981). Forgetting the gist of a story can functionally be as serious a memory problem as failing to remember the basic idea units themselves. Normal subjects are likely to paraphrase the words of stories that do not fit into their everyday vocabulary (e.g., saying 'felt sorry for her' rather than 'touched by the woman's story'). Paraphrasing is a more efficient way of remembering less familiar stimulus words (Bartlett, 1932). RHD patients, in contrast, often recall story segments using the exact words, and thus do not benefit from active paraphrasing (Wapner et al., 1981). These patients also tend to introject personal information into their recall, which can further obscure the original gist of the story (Gardner et al., 1983; Wapner et al., 1981).

For randomly presented, categorized word-lists RHD patients do not actively adopt a semantic clustering strategy relative to normal subjects (Villardita, 1987). Consequently, when a supraspan word list is presented for multiple trials, the number of words they recall is lower than that recalled by normal controls (Raymond et al., 1987; Villardita, 1987).

Regardless of whether or not they display aphasic deficits, LHD patients as a group show significantly more impairment than RHD patients and normal controls in recalling stories and word lists (Gerner et al., 1972; Milner, 1971; Wapner et al., 1981). For aphasic patients, the examiner must often conclude that the language impairment precludes a valid assessment of verbal memory function. Sometimes recognition testing, which bypasses verbal expression, will reveal greater verbal memory retention than recall testing conditions for aphasic patients.

Kaplan (1983) reported a dissociation in memory for visuospatial material following unilateral brain damage. She observed that LHD patients displayed more impairment in remembering the internal details relative to the outer configural features of complex stimuli such as the Rey-Osterrieth figure, whereas RHD patients showed the opposite pattern (see Figs. 4 and 5). As discussed above, Delis et al. (1988c) found that LHD patients were selectively deficient in remembering local forms of visual hierarchical stimuli, especially when they were presented in right hemispace. In contrast, RHD patients were selectively impaired in remembering global forms, especially when the stimuli were presented in left hemispace (see Fig. 6). These findings occurred regardless of whether or not the patients displayed visual field cuts, hemi-inattention, or aphasic deficits (Delis et al., 1986, 1988c; see also Robertson and Delis, 1986; Delis et al., 1988d).

One possible reason why earlier investigations found that memory for visuospatial material was impaired only in RHD patients is that these studies tended to employ visual stimuli which have minimal or no internal details (e.g., the outline of a eometric shape). Consequently, the LHD patients' deficit in remembering more local features of complex stimuli would not have been detected.

Alcoholic Korsakoff syndrome

Alcoholic Korsakoff syndrome is caused by damage to the dorsomedial nucleus of the thalamus, the mammillary bodies, and frontal and diffuse atrophy secondary to acute Wernicke's encephalopathy from thiamine deficiency (Victor et al., 1971). For these patients, immediate recall span ranges from the normal to low normal range, but the ability to encode new information into more permanent storage is often severely arrested (Butters and Cermak, 1980). This severe anterograde amnesia is restricted to declarative knowledge; procedural learning and semantic priming are preserved (Butters et al., 1987; Cohen and Squire, 1980; Shimamura et al., 1987). The patients' declarative amnesia encompasses all stimulus categories (e.g., verbal and visuospatial material) and stimulus features (e.g., global and local forms). On delayed recall tasks, these patients frequently have no recollection of previously being tested let alone remembering the target items.

The combination of severely impaired declarative memory in conjunction with intact linguistic skills may explain in part these patients' tendency to confabulate and make intrusion errors (Butters and Cermak, 1980; Zangwill, 1966). For example, when asked, 'Tell me all the shopping items I read to you earlier', these patients often respond as if they are free associating to 'shopping items'. In essence, they are overly relying on one of their cognitive strengths, language. Category cuing will similarly elicit high-frequency associates to the category names (Cermak and Stiassny, 1982); for this reason, prototypical members of categories should not be included on categorized word lists (Delis et al., 1987). Preserved ability to draw common objects may contribute to their tendency to confabulate on delayed recall testing of visuospatial material. One Korsakoff patient, for instance, drew a house on 15-minute delayed recall of the Rey-Osterrieth figure (see Fig. 8).

On yes/no recognition testing, these patients typically adopt a liberal response bias, endorsing both hits and false positives (Butters et al., 1985). Relative to normal subjects, their overall recognition discriminability is often as severely impaired as their free-recall performance.

Recall of past autobiographical events and public information reveals a retrograde amnesia characterized by a temporal gradient, with considerably better recall for remote than for recent events (Albert et al., 1979; Marsler-Wilson and Teuber, 1975; Seltzer and Benson, 1974; Squire and Cohen, 1982). Because of the gradual increase in memory problems secondary to long-term alcohol abuse (Albert et al., 1980; Cohen and

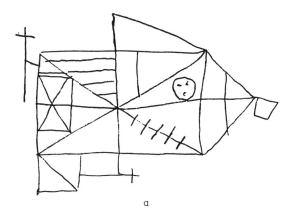

a

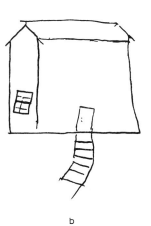

b

FIG. 8. Copy (a) and 15-minute delayed recall (b) of the Rey-Osterrieth figure (Lezak, 1983) by an alcoholic Korsakoff patient illustrating an intrusion error on visuospatial memory testing.

Squire, 1981), the mechanisms underlying failure to recall events from recent past years may represent some combination of anterograde amnesia secondary to chronic alcoholism and retrograde amnesia secondary to the acute Wernicke's encephalopathy (Butters and Miliotis, 1985; Squire, 1987).

Although alcoholic Korsakoff patients often achieve IQ scores that fall within the normal range, they usually suffer some decline in novel problem-solving and visuospatial skills (Glosser et al., 1977; Kapur and Butters, 1977; Squire, 1982). This decline may be related to frontal and diffuse atrophy associated with long-term alcohol abuse (Lishman, 1981).

Chronic alcoholism

Detoxified chronic alcoholics often display mild to moderate deficits on more challenging tests of new learning and memory (Bowden, 1988; Brandt et al., 1983; Cutting, 1978; Miglioli et al., 1979; Ryan and Butters, 1980). Memory for visuospatial stimuli is often worse than for verbal material (Miglioli et al., 1979), which parallels the findings that these patients tend to show greater dysfunction in visuospatial skills relative to verbal abilities (e.g., Goldstein and Shelly, 1971; Glosser et al., 1977; Kapur and Butters, 1977; Parsons and Farr, 1981; Ryan and Butters, 1983; Wilson et al., 1987). Some researchers have interpreted these findings in accordance with the traditional verbal/spatial theory of hemispheric specialization, concluding that the right hemisphere is more vulnerable than the left to the toxic effects of ethanol (Jones, 1971; Jones and Parsons, 1972; Miglioli et al., 1979). There are, however, a number of problems with this right-hemisphere vulnerability hypothesis of alcoholism. First, neuropathological changes have not been found to be greater in the right hemisphere compared with the left (Hudolin, 1980; Ron, 1983). Second, the finding that alcoholics show less memory impairment for verbal material than visuospatial stimuli has not always been supported (Nixon et al., 1987). Third, although chronic alcoholics were found to be impaired in remembering visual hierar-

chical stimuli, they did not display selective memory impairment for global or local forms (Kiefner and Delis, 1986). This result indicates that chronic alcoholics do not show the same type of visuospatial memory dysfunction as found in RHD patients. Rather, their impairment encompasses memory for both global and local forms.

In testing alcoholics, it is advisable to allow a period of 3 to 6 weeks of sobriety before conducting the evaluation, because acute intoxication or the detoxification process will exacerbate a patient's cognitive dysfunction (Grant et al., 1984). There is evidence that chronic alcoholics will continue to show improvement in cognitive functioning for at least five years of sobriety (Brandt et al., 1983). Relatively young alcoholics (in their thirties) may show little neuropsychological impairment (Grant et al., 1979; but see Bowden, 1988). Because alcoholics frequently incur head injuries from falls or driving accidents, focal and/or more extensive diffuse damage may be present. Thus the memory and cognitive deficits in this population can vary greatly.

Alzheimer's disease

Severe anterograde amnesia for declarative knowledge is often one of the first neuropsychological findings contributing to an early diagnosis of Alzheimer's disease (Albert and Moss, 1984; Katzman, 1981). Immediate recall span is often lower in Alzheimer patients than Korsakoff patients, because of additional deficits in attention, naming and visuospatial functioning (Corkin, 1982; Kaszniak et al., 1979; Morris and Baddeley, 1988). Like Korsakoff patients, Alzheimer patients fail to show learning on repeated, immediate recall trials of the same supra-span material (Moss et al., 1986; Ober et al., 1985; Wilson et al., 1983). They tend to recall items from the recency region of the list, which reflects a highly passive learning style (Delis et al., 1987; Miller, 1971; Wilson et al., 1983). They also report numerous intrusion errors (Fuld et al., 1982; Kramer et al., 1988), though their intrusions may not be as closely related semantically to target items or category cues as seen in Korsakoff patients because of naming deficits. On delayed recall, these patients recall few if any target items (Moss et al., 1986; Ober et al., 1985; Wilson et al., 1983). They adopt a liberal response bias on recognition testing, endorsing high numbers of both hits and false positives (Post, 1975; Kramer et al., 1988). Their deficient recognition discriminability suggests impaired encoding processes.

On tests of retrograde memory, patients with moderate to severe Alzheimer's disease are impaired in recalling past events from all periods of their lives equally (Albert et al., 1981; Wilson et al., 1981). A recent study, however, reports that the impaired retrograde amnesia of Alzheimer patients in earlier stages of the disease is characterized by a temporal gradient (Beatty et al., 1987).

Two studies have reported that Alzheimer patients show less vulnerability to proactive interference than normal control subjects (Kramer et al., 1985; Wilson et al., 1983). That is, they performed better on a second word list than on a first list. This may occur because (1) little or no information is being encoded from the first list that would later interfere with the learning of the second list; and (2) they may be better able to focus on the nature of the task on the second list than the first due to attentional deficits and set acquisition problems (Wilson et al., 1983).

Recent investigations have reported a dissociation in different aspects of nondeclarative learning in Alzheimer patients. Although they show normal acquisition on a perceptual-motor task (i.e., pursuit rotor; Eslinger and Damasio, 1986; Heindel et al., 1988), they are impaired in semantic priming (Shimamura et al., 1987).

As with any progressive disease, there is considerable variability in the spared and impaired cognitive functions among Alzheimer patients. One source of this variability is individual differences in emotional reaction to the disease. Some patients develop a reactive depression in the earlier stages, which exacerbates their memory and cognitive impairment (Miller, 1980). There is also variability in the cerebral regions most affected by the

neuropathological process. Positron emission tomography indicates that Alzheimer patients show significantly more lateral asymmetry of brain glucose metabolism than age-matched normal subjects (Friedland et al., 1985; Haxby et al., 1985). Patients with greater metabolic dysfunction in the left or right cerebral hemisphere tend to perform significantly worse on verbal or visuospatial tests, respectively (Foster et al., 1983; Koss et al., 1985; Martin et al., 1986).

Results from a pilot study we recently conducted suggest asymmetric visuospatial memory profiles in some Alzheimer patients. A modified version of the California Global-Local Learning Test (Delis and Kaplan, 1988) was administered to six Alzheimer patients who showed lateralized cognitive deficits on other clinical tests. Five patients displayed normal performance on the Boston Naming Test and impaired performance on the WAIS-R Block Design subtest, whereas the other patient showed the opposite pattern. The target hierarchical stimuli were presented individually for 10 seconds, followed by immediate free recall. The patients with normal naming recalled primarily local forms (93% accuracy for local forms and 32% accuracy for global forms), a performance similar to unilateral right CVA patients (Delis et al., 1988c). In contrast, the patient with normal block constructions recalled only global forms (66% accuracy for global forms and 0% accuracy for local forms), a performance similar to left CVA patients (see Fig. 9 for examples of patients' drawings). A third group of Alzheimer patients who were impaired in both naming and block constructions (but matched with the other patients in overall dementia severity; Mattis, 1976) showed less discrepancy in their recall of global and local forms (28% accuracy in recalling global forms and 41% accuracy in recalling local forms). These results suggest the presence of subgroups of Alzheimer patients who show different types of visuospatial memory impairment.

In the later stages of the disease, Alzheimer patients often develop such severe impairment in fundamental skills of attention, language and visuo-

FIG. 9. Examples of (a and b) target hierarchical stimuli presented individually for 10 seconds; (c and d) immediate recall by an Alzheimer's patient with normal naming and impaired block constructions, illustrating accurate memory for local but not global forms; and (e and f) immediate recall by an Alzheimer's patient with normal block constructions and impaired naming, illustrating accurate memory for global but not local forms.

spatial functioning that it precludes valid assessment of memory ability.

Huntington's disease

Huntington patients matched in overall cognitive severity with Alzheimer patients display equally impaired immediate free recall, but they show better retention of information over delay intervals (Butters et al., 1985). When presented with multiple trials of different verbal stimuli, they reveal normal sensitivity to proactive interference (Butters et al., 1976). Compared with Alzheimer patients and amnesics, they make significantly fewer intrusion and perseveration errors (Butters et al., 1987; Kramer et al., 1988).

Recognition performance, though impaired, tends to be disproportionately better in Hun-

tington patients than in Alzheimer or amnesic patients (Butters et al., 1985; Kramer et al., 1988). Butters et al. (1986) posit that one mechanism of their memory failure is deficient retrieval search. A recent study reported that Huntington patients in the most advanced stages are as impaired as Alzheimer patients in recognition discriminability (Kramer et al., 1988). This finding suggests that encoding processes are progressively more affected as the disease advances.

Huntington patients are impaired in retrograde memory recall, but their performance differs qualitatively from Korsakoff patients. They show a flat retrograde amnesia, with equally deficient recall of events from all decades (Albert et al., 1981; Beatty et al., 1987). The performance of recently diagnosed Huntington patients improves on recognition testing of remote events, which further implicates a retrieval search deficit in this group of patients (Albert et al., 1981).

Martone et al. (1984) reported a cross-over effect between declarative and procedural learning in Huntington and Korsakoff patients. Huntington patients showed better recognition memory for declarative knowledge than amnesics, whereas amnesics displayed superior procedural learning (mirror reading) than Huntington patients. Although oculomotor defects may have contributed to the Huntington patients' difficulty in mirror reading, other studies have reported that these patients are also impaired on perceptual-motor tasks which place fewer demands on eye movements (Butters et al., 1985; Heindel et al., 1988). Interestingly, Huntington patients have been found to show normal learning on a semantic priming task (Shimamura et al., 1987). Thus, the caudate nucleus and other basal ganglia, the locus of the pathology in Huntington's disease, may mediate processes important for nondeclarative learning on perceptual-motor but not semantic priming tasks (Heindel et al., 1988).

Affective disorder

Patients suffering from depression represent a heterogeneous group in terms of their cognitive profiles (Niederehe, 1986). Depressed patients whose vegetative symptoms are not too severe and who obsessively castigate themselves will show considerable variability in their performance on memory and other cognitive tasks. Their performance waxes and wanes with the intensity of their self-deprecation. Initial poor performance feeds upon itself, giving the depressed patient further ammunition to be self-critical and anxious.

Because their naturally limited attentional capacity is often involuntarily consumed with obsessive thinking, depressed patients frequently show impaired immediate recall span (Breslow et al., 1980) and immediate recall of supra-span material (Cronholm and Ottosson, 1961; Henry et al., 1973). They tend to be minimal responders, reporting not only few target items but also few errors (i.e., intrusions and perseverations). They are deficient in adopting an active semantic clustering strategy in recalling randomized, categorized word lists (Weingartner et al., 1981). The information they do report on immediate recall trials is typically retained to a normal degree after a delay interval, since brain systems which mediate memory processes are structurally intact (this applies, of course, to depressed patients without CNS damage; Henry et al., 1973). Their memory performance often improves on recognition testing, which probably compensates for retrieval difficulties that arise from being minimal responders (Caine, 1986). Depressed patients are more likely to make recognition errors of misses and incorrect rejections rather than false positives (Miller and Lewis, 1977; Niederehe and Camp, 1985; Post, 1975), because the negativism of their depression seems to invite a 'No' response bias. At least one study, however, reported a tendency for depressed patients to make both misses and false positive errors (Frith et al., 1983).

Patients with severe vegetative symptoms of psychomotor retardation, weight loss and insomnia will appear to be a more homogeneous group cognitively, simply because they often perform close to or at floor levels on neuropsychological tests. Floor effects are especially common on tests assessing higher-order functions such as memory and novel problem-solving. These patients represent one of the most difficult diagnostic dilemmas. Major depression can co-occur with CNS damage and mask the impaired and spared cognitive functions related to the structural damage. For example, Alzheimer patients in early stages can develop such a severe depression that their initial pattern of strengths and weaknesses may not be detected (Miller, 1980). A clinical rule of thumb is to treat the depression psychiatrically. Repeated assessment of memory and other cognitive functions then becomes diagnostically important for documenting possible improvement in mental functioning that corresponds with alleviation of mood disturbance, and/or possible decline that corresponds with progressive neuropathology.

A common referral question for clinical neuropsychologists is to determine whether the memory and cognitive dysfunction in a depressed patient is 'functional' versus 'organic', or reflects a 'pseudodementia' as opposed to some type of 'real' dementia. There is increasing evidence, however, that the cognitive abnormalities of depressed patients may occur secondary to genuine neuropathology (Caine, 1986). This pathology may be related largely to changes in neurotransmitter systems such as serotonin and norepinephrine. A more sophisticated clinical examination would thus inquire whether cognitive dysfunction in a depressed patient is consistent with reversible neurochemical changes associated with the psychiatric disorder, irreversible structural lesions, or some combination of the two. Sensitive scanning instruments such as magnetic resonance imaging (MRI) will increasingly play a role in this difficult differential diagnosis. In a preliminary study, for example, Dupont et al. (1987) found that 8 out of 14 bipolar patients showed focal areas of signal hyperintensity within the deep white matter and periventricular regions. Those patients with positive MRI findings had significantly greater memory dysfunction and higher numbers of psychiatric hospitalizations for mood disturbance than those with normal MRI scans. For subgroups of psychiatric patients with chronic affective disorders, small subcortical lesions and subsequent neurochemical changes may affect both cognitive and emotional functioning.

Conclusion

We are entering a particularly exciting era of clinical and research practice which integrates principles and techniques from neuropsychology, cognitive science, neurology and psychiatry. The complexity inherent in the structure of mind and brain necessitates this multidisciplinary approach. The advances that are being made in the understanding and clinical assessment of memory function and dysfunction attest to the rich fruition of this work.

Acknowledgement

The author is grateful to Larry Squire and Edith Kaplan for their valuable critiques of the manuscript, and to Amy Bihrle, Munro Cullum, Bill Heindel and Paula Shear for their helpful comments. The preparation of this manuscript was supported in part by a research grant from the Veterans Administration.

References

Adams KM: In search of Luria's battery: a false start. *J. Consult. Clin. Psychol.: 48*, 511 – 516, 1980.

Albert MS, Moss MB: The assessment of memory disorders in patients with Alzheimer's disease. In Squire LR, Butters N (Editors), *Neuropsychology of Memory*. New York: Guilford Press, 1984.

Albert MS, Butters N, Levin J: Temporal gradients in the retrograde amnesia of patients with alcoholic Korsakoff disease. *Arch. Neurol.: 36*, 211 – 216, 1979.

Albert MS, Butters N, Brandt J: Memory for remote events in alcoholics. *J. Stud. Alcohol.: 41*, 1071 – 1081, 1980.

Albert MS, Butters N, Brandt J: Development of remote memory loss in patients with Huntington's disease. *J. Clin. Neuropsychol.: 3*, 1 – 12, 1981a.

Albert MS, Butters N, Brandt J: Patterns of remote memory in amnesic and demented patients. *Arch. Neurol.: 38*, 495 – 500, 1981b.

Atkinson RC, Shiffrin RM: The control of short-term memory. *Sci. Am.: 224*, 82 – 90, 1971.

Babcock H: An experiment in the measurement of mental deterioration. *Arch. Psychol.: 117*, 105, 1930.

Bak JS, Greene RL: Changes in neuropsychological functioning in an aging population. *J. Consult. Clin. Psychol.: 48*, 395 – 399, 1980.

Barbizet J: *Human Memory and its Pathology*. San Francisco: Freedman and Company, 1970.

Bartlett FC: *Remembering*. Cambridge, England: Cambridge University Press, 1932.

Beatty WW, Salmon DP, Butters N, Heindel WC, Granholm EP: Retrograde amnesia in patients with Alzheimer's disease or Huntington's disease. *Neurobiol. Aging: 9*, 181 – 186, 1987.

Benton AL: The Visual Retention Test as a constructional praxis task. *Confin. Neurol.: 22*, 141 – 155, 1962.

Benton AL: *The Revised Visual Retention Test* (4th edn.). New York: The Psychological Corporation, 1974.

Benton AL, Hamsher K deS: Multilingual Aphasia Examination. Iowa City: University of Iowa, 1976.

Benton AL, Hamsher K deS, Varney NR, Spreen O: *Contributions to Neuropsychological Assessment*. New York: Oxford University Press, 1983.

Berger M: The 'scientific approach' to intelligence: an overview of its history with special reference to mental speed. In Eysenck HJ (Editor), *A Model for Intelligence*. New York: Springer-Verlag, pp. 13 – 43, 1982.

Binder LM: Constructional strategies on complex figure drawings after unilateral brain damage. *J. Clin. Neuropsychol.: 4*, 51 – 58, 1982.

Blusewicz MJ, Dustman RE, Schenkenberg T, Beck EC: Neuropsychological correlates of chronic alcoholism and aging. *J. Nerv. Mental Dis.: 165*, 348 – 355, 1977.

Bornstein RA, Chelune GA: Factor structure of the Wechsler Memory Scale-Revised. *Clin. Neuropsychol.: 2*, 107 – 115, 1988.

Bowers GH: Mental imagery and associative learning. In Gregg L (Editor), *Cognition in Learning and Memory*. New York: Wiley, 1972.

Brandt J, Butters N: The neuropsychology of Huntington's disease. *Trends Neurosci.: 9*, 118 – 120, 1986.

Brandt J, Butters N, Ryan C, Bayog R: Cognitive loss and recovery in long-term alcohol abusers. *Arch. Gen. Psychiatry: 40*, 435 – 442, 1983.

Breslow R, Kocsis J, Belkin B: Memory deficits in depression: evidence utilizing the Wechsler Memory Scale. *Percept. Motor Skills: 51*, 541 – 542, 1980.

Brooks DN: Memory and head injury. *J. Nerv. Mental Dis.: 155*, 350 – 355, 1972.

Buschke H: Selective reminding for analysis of memory and behavior. *J. Verbal Learn. Verbal Behav.: 12*, 543 – 550, 1973.

Buschke H, Fuld PA: Evaluating storage, retention, and retrieval in disordered memory and learning. *Neurology: 24*, 1019 – 1025, 1974.

Butters N: The clinical aspects of memory disorders: Contributions from experimental studies of amnesia and dementia. *J. Clin. Neuropsychol.: 6*, 17 – 36, 1984.

Butters N: Alcoholic Korsakoff syndrome. *J. Clin. Exp. Neuropsychol.: 7*, 181 – 210, 1985.

Butters N, Cermak LS: *Alcoholic Korsakoff's Syndrome*. New York: Academic Press, 1980.

Butters N, Miliotis P: Amnesic disorders. In Heilman KM, Valenstein E (Editors), *Clinical Neuropsychology*. New

York: Oxford University Press, pp. 403–452, 1985.

Butters N, Tarlow S, Cermak LS, Sax D: A comparison of the information processing deficits in patients with Huntington's chorea and Korsakoff's syndrome. *Cortex: 12,* 134–144, 1976.

Butters N, Sax D, Montgomery K, Tarlow S: Comparison of the neuropsychological deficits associated with early and advanced Huntington's disease. *Arch. Neurol.: 35,* 585–589, 1978.

Butters N, Wolfe J, Martone M, Granholm E, Cermak LS: Memory disorders associated with Huntington's disease: verbal recall, verbal recognition and procedural memory. *Neuropsychologia: 6,* 729–744, 1985.

Butters N, Wolfe J, Granholm E, Martone M: An assessment of verbal recall, recognition and fluency abilities in patients with Huntington's disease. *Cortex: 22,* 11–32, 1986.

Butters N, Martone M, White B, Granholm E, Wolfe J: Clinical Validators: Comparisons of demented and amnesic patients. In Poon LW (Editor), *Clinical Memory Assessment of Older Adults.* Washington, DC: American Psychological Association, 1987.

Butters N, Cairns P, Salmon DP, Cermak LS, Moss MB: Differentiation of amnesic and demented patients with the Wechsler Memory Scale-Revised. *Clin. Neuropsychol.: 2,* 133–148, 1988.

Caine ED: The neuropsychology of depression: the pseudodementia syndrome. In Grant I, Adams KM (Editors), *Neuropsychological Assessment of Neuropsychiatric Disorders.* New York: Oxford University Press, 1986.

Caine ED, Ebert MH, Weingartner H: An outline for the analysis of dementia: the memory disorder of Huntington's disease. *Neurology: 27,* 1087–1092, 1977.

Cermak LS: *Human Memory: Research and Theory.* New York: Ronald Press, 1972.

Cermak LS: The episodic-semantic distinction in amnesia. In Squire LR, Butters N (Editors), *Neuropsychology of Memory.* New York: Guilford Press, 1984.

Cermak LS, O'Connor M: The anterograde and retrograde retrieval ability of a patient with amnesia due to encephalitis. *Neuropsychologia: 21,* 213–234, 1983.

Cermak LS, Stiassny, D: Recall failure following successful generation and recognition of responses by alcoholic Korsakoff patients. *Brain Cognition: 1,* 165–176, 1982.

Chelune GJ, Bornstein RA: Wechsler Memory Scale-Revised patterns among patients with unilateral brain lesions. *Clin. Neuropsychol.: 2,* 121–132, 1988.

Cohen D, Eisdorfer C, Walford RL: Histocompatibility antigens (HLA) and patterns of cognitive loss in dementia of the Alzheimer type. *Neurobiol Aging: 2,* 277–280, 1981.

Cohen NJ, Squire LR: Preserved learning and retention of pattern analyzing skill in amnesia: dissociation of knowing how and knowing that. *Science: 210,* 207–209, 1980.

Corkin, S: Some relationships between global amnesias and the memory impairments in Alzheimer's disease. In Corkin S, Davis KL, Growdon JH, Usdin E, Wurtmen RL (Editors), *Aging, Vol. 19. Alzheimer's Disease: A Report of Progress.* New York: Raven, pp. 149–164, 1982.

Corkin S: Lasting consequences of bilateral medial temporal lobectomy: clinical course and experimental findings in H.M.

Semin. Neurol.: 4, 249–259, 1984.

Craik FIM, Lockhart RS: Levels of processing: a framework for memory research. *J. Verbal Learn. Verbal Behav.: 11,* 671–684, 1972.

Cronholm B, Ottosson J: Memory functions in endogenous depression. *Arch. Gen. Psychiatry: 5,* 193–197, 1961.

Crosson B, Hughes CW, Roth DL, Monkowski PG: Review of Russell's (1975) norms for the logical memory and visual reproduction subtests of the Wechsler Memory Scale. *J. Consult. Clin. Psychol.: 52,* 635–641, 1975.

Crowder, R.G: The demise of short-term memory. *Acta Psychol.: 50,* 291–323, 1982.

Cutting J: Specific psychological deficits in alcoholism. *Br. J. Psychiatry: 133,* 119–122, 1978.

Damasio AR, Eslinger PJ, Damasio H, Van Hoesen GW, Cornell S: Multimodal amnesic syndrome following bilateral temporal and basal forebrain damage. *Arch. Neurol.: 42,* 252–259, 1985.

Delaney RC, Rosen AJ, Mattson RH, Novelly RA: Memory function in focal epilepsy: a comparison of non-surgical, unilateral temporal lobe and frontal lobe samples. *Cortex: 16,* 103–117, 1980.

Delis DC, Kaplan E: The California Global-Local Learning Test. Submitted for publication, 1988.

Delis DC, Ober BA: Cognitive neuropsychology. In Knapp TJ, Robertson LC (Editors), *Approaches to Cognition: Contrasts and Controversies.* Hillsdale: Erlbaum, pp. 243–266, 1986.

Delis DC, Robertson LC, Efron R: Hemispheric specialization of memory for visual hierarchical stimuli. *Neuropsychologia: 24,* 205–214, 1986.

Delis DC, Kramer JH, Kaplan E, Ober BA: *The California Verbal Learning Test.* New York: The Psychological Corporation, 1987.

Delis DC, Cullum CM, Butters N, Cairns P: The Wechsler Memory Scale-Revised and California Verbal Learning Test: convergence and divergence. *Clin. Neuropsychol.: 2,* 188–196, 1988a.

Delis DC, Freeland J, Kramer JH, Kaplan E: Integrating clinical assessment with cognitive neuroscience: construct validation of the California Verbal Learning Test. *J. Consult. Clin. Psychol.: 56,* 123–130, 1988b.

Delis DC, Kiefner MG, Fridlund AJ. Visuospatial dysfunction following unilateral brain damage: dissociations in hierarchical and hemispatial analysis. *J. Clin. Exp. Neuropsychol.: 10,* 421–431, 1988c.

Delis DC, Kramer JH, Kiefner MG: Visuospatial functioning before and after commissurotomy: disconnection in hierarchical processing. *Arch. Neurol.: 45,* 462–465, 1988d.

Delis DC, Kramer JH, Kaplan E, Ober BA: *The California Verbal Learning Test – Children's Version.* New York: The Psychological Corporation; in press.

De Renzi E, Faglioni P, Previdi P: Spatial memory and hemispheric locus of lesion. *Cortex: 13,* 424–433, 1977.

Dupont RM, Jernigan TL, Gillin JC, Butters N, Delis DC, Hesselink JR: Presence of subcortical signal hyperintensities in bipolar patients detected by magnetic resonance imaging. *Psychiatric Res.: 21,* 357–358, 1987.

Erickson RC, Scott ML: Clinical memory testing: a review. *Psychol. Bull.: 84,* 1130–1149, 1977.

Eslinger PJ, Damasio AR: Preserved motor learning in Alzheimer's disease: implications for anatomy and behavior. *J. Neurosci.: 6,* 3006 – 3009, 1986.

Eysenck HJ (Editor): *A Model for Intelligence.* New York: Springer-Verlag, 1982.

Fischer JF: Using the Wechsler Memory Scale-Revised to detect and characterize memory deficits in multiple sclerosis. *Clin. Neuropsychol.: 2,* 149 – 172, 1988.

Foster NL, Chase TN, Fedio P, Patronas NJ, Brooks RA, Chiro GD: Alzheimer's disease: focal cortical changes shown by positron emission tomography. *Neurology: 33,* 961 – 965, 1983.

Fridlund AJ, Delis DC: *Computer-assisted Administration and Scoring Program for the California Verbal Learning Test.* New York: The Psychological Corporation, 1987.

Friedland RP, Budinger TF, Koss E, Ober BA: Alzheimer's disease: anterior-posterior and lateral hemispheric alterations in cortical glucose utilization. *Neurosci. Lett.: 53,* 235 – 240, 1985.

Frith CD, Stevens M, Johnstone EC et al. Effects of ECT and depression on various aspects of memory. *Br. J. Psychiatry: 142,* 610 – 617, 1983.

Fuld PA, Katzman R, Davies P, Terry RD: Intrusions as a sign of Alzheimer dementia: chemical and pathological verification. *Ann. Neurol.: 11,* 155 – 159, 1982.

Gabrieli JDE, Cohen NJ, Cohen S: The acquisition of lexical and semantic knowledge in amnesia. *Soc. Neurosci. Abstr.: 9,* 238, 1982.

Gardner H: *Frames of Mind.* New York: Basic Books, 1983.

Gardner H, Boller F, Moreines J, Butters N: Retrieving information from Korsakoff patients: effects of categorical cues and reference to the task. *Cortex: 9,* 165 – 175, 1973.

Gardner H, Brownell HH, Wapner W, Michelow D: Missing the point: the role of the right hemisphere in the processing of complex linguistic material. In Perceman E (Editor), *Cognitive Processes in the Right Hemisphere.* New York: Academic Press, pp. 169 – 191, 1983.

Gerner P, Ommaya A, Fedio P: A study of visual memory: verbal and nonverbal mechanisms in patients with unilateral lobectomy. *Int. J. Neurosci.: 4,* 231 – 238, 1972.

Gilleard CJ: Wechsler Memory Scale performance of elderly psychiatric patients. *J. Clin. Psychol.: 36,* 958 – 960, 1980.

Glosser G, Butters N, Kaplan E: Visuoperceptual processes in brain-damaged patients on the Digit-Symbol Substitution test. *Int. J. Neurosci.: 7,* 59 – 66, 1977.

Goldberg E, Antin SP, Bilder RM, Hughes JEO, Mattis S: Retrograde amnesia: possible role of mesencephalic reticular activation in long-term memory. *Science: 213,* 1392 – 1394, 1981.

Golden CJ, Hammeke TA, Purisch AD: *The Luria-Nebraska Neuropsychological Battery.* Los Angeles: Western Psychological Services, 1983.

Goldstein G, Shelly C: Field dependence and cognitive, perceptual, and motor skills in alcoholics: a factor analytic study. *Q. J. Stud. Alcohol: 32,* 29 – 40, 1971.

Goodglass H, Kaplan E: Assessment of cognitive deficit in the brain-injured patient. In Gazzaniga MS (Editor), *Handbook of Behavioral Neurobiology, Vol. 2.* New York: Plenum Press, 1979.

Goodglass H, Kaplan E: *Assessment of Aphasia and Related Disorders.* Philadelphia: Lea & Febiger, 1983.

Graf P, Schacter DL: Implicit and explicit memory for new associations in normal and amnesic subjects. *J. Exp. Psychol. Learn. Memory Cognition: 11,* 501 – 518, 1985.

Graf P, Squire LR, Mandler G: The information that amnesic patients do not forget. *J. Exp. Psychol. Learn. Memory Cognition: 10,* 164 – 178, 1984.

Grant I, Adams K, Reed R: Normal neuropsychological abilities of alcoholic men in their late thirties. *Am. J. Psychiatry: 136,* 1263 – 1269, 1979.

Grant I, Adams K, Reed R: Aging, abstinence, and medical risk factors in the prediction of neuropsychologic deficit among long-term alcoholics. *Arch. Gen. Psychiatry: 41,* 710 – 718, 1984.

Halstead WC: *Brain and Intelligence.* Chicago: University of Chicago Press, 1947.

Hannay HJ, Levin HS: Selective reminding test: An examination of the equivalence of four forms. *J. Clin. Exp. Neuropsychol.: 7,* 251 – 263, 1985.

Haxby JV, Duara R, Grady CL, Cutler NR, Rapoport SI: Relations between neuropsychological and cerebral metabolic asymmetries in early Alzheimer's disease. *J. Cereb. Blood Flow Metab.: 5,* 193 – 200, 1985.

Heaton RK, Nelson LM, Thompson DS, Burks JS, Franklin GM: Neuropsychological findings in relapsing-remitting and chronic-progressive multiple sclerosis. *J. Consult. Clin. Psychol.: 53,* 103 – 110, 1985.

Heilburn AB: Psychological test performance as a function of lateral localization of cerebral lesion. *J. Comp. Physiol. Psychol.: 49,* 10 – 14, 1956.

Heindel WC, Butters N, Salmon DP: Impaired learning of a motor skill in patients with Huntington's disease. *Behav. Neurosci.: 102,* 141 – 147, 1988.

Henry GM, Weingartner H, Murphy DL: Influence of affective states and psychoactive drugs on verbal learning and memory. *Am. J. Psychiatry: 130,* 966 – 971, 1973.

Hooper HE: *The Hooper Visual Organization Test.* Los Angeles: Western Psychological Services, 1958.

Horn JL: Trends in the measurement of intelligence. *Intelligence: 3,* 229 – 239, 1979.

Hudolin V: Impairments of the nervous system in alcoholics. In Richter D (Editor), *Addiction and Brain Damage.* Baltimore: University Park Press, pp. 168 – 200, 1980.

Hulicka IM: Age differences in Wechsler Memory Scale scores. *J. Genet. Psychol.: 109,* 135 – 145, 1966.

Ivison DJ: The Wechsler Memory Scale: preliminary findings toward an Australian standardization. *Austr. Psychol.: 12,* 303 – 312, 1977.

Jacoby LL, Witherspoon D: Remembering without awareness. *Can. J. Psychol.: 32,* 300 – 324, 1982.

James W: *Principles of Psychology.* New York: Holt, 1890.

Janowsky JS, Shimamura AP, Kritchevsky M, Squire LR: Cognitive impairment following frontal lobe damage and its relevance to human amnesia. *Behav. Neurosci.:* in press.

Jones BM: Verbal and spatial intelligence in short- and long-term alcoholics. *J. Nerv. Ment. Dis.: 153,* 292 – 297, 1971.

Jones BM, Parsons OA: Specific vs generalized deficits of abstracting ability in chronic alcoholics. *Arch. Gen. Psychiatry: 26,* 380 – 384, 1972.

Jones MK: Imagery as a mnemonic aid after left temporal

lobectomy: Contrasts between material-specific and generalized memory disorders. *Neuropsychologia: 12,* 21 – 30, 1974.

Kaplan E: Process and achievement revisited. In Wapner S, Kaplan B (Editors), *Toward a Holistic Developmental Psychology.* Hillsdale: Erlbaum, pp. 143 – 156, 1983.

Kaplan E, Goodglass H, Weintraub S: *The Boston Naming Test.* Philadelphia: Lea & Febiger, 1983.

Kaplan E, Fein D, Morris R, Delis DC: *Manual for the WAIS-R as a Neuropsychological Instrument.* New York: The Psychological Corporation; in press.

Kapur N, Butters N: An analysis of visuoperceptive deficits in alcoholic Korsakoffs and long-term alcoholics. *J. Stud. Alcohol: 38,* 2025 – 2035, 1977.

Kaszniak AW, Garron DC, Fox JH: Differential effects of age and cerebral atrophy upon span of immediate recall and paired-associate learning in older patients suspected of dementia. *Cortex: 15,* 285 – 295, 1979.

Katzman R: Early detection of senile dementia. *Hosp. Pract.: 12,* 61 – 76, 1981.

Kessler HR, Lauer K, Kausch DF: The performance of multiple sclerosis patients on the California Verbal Learning Test. Paper presented at the meeting of the International Neuropsychological Society, San Diego, CA, Feb. 1985.

Kiefner MG, Delis DC: Effects of chronic alcohol abuse on visual hierarchical processing. Paper presented at the meeting of the International Neuropsychological Society, Washington, DC, 1987.

Kimura D: Right temporal lobe damage: perception of unfamiliar stimuli after damage. *Arch. Neurol.: 8,* 264 – 271, 1963.

Kinsbourne M, Wood F: Short-term memory processes and the amnesic syndrome. In Deutsch D, Deutsch JA (Editors), *Short-term Memory.* New York: Academic Press, 1975.

Klatzky RL: *Human Memory: Structure and Processes.* San Francisco: Freeman, 1980.

Koss E, Friedland RP, Ober BA, Jagust WJ: Differences in lateral hemispheric asymmetries of glucose utilization between early- and late-onset Alzheimer-type dementia. *Am. J. Psychiatry: 142,* 638 – 640, 1985.

Kramer JH, Blusewicz MJ, Brandt J, Delis DC: The assessment of multiple memory processes in Alzheimer's disease patients. Paper presented at the meeting of the International Neuropsychological Society, San Diego, 1985.

Kramer JH, Delis DC, Blusewicz MJ, Brandt J, Ober BA, Strauss M: Verbal memory errors in Alzheimer's and Huntington's dementias. *Dev. Neuropsychol.: 4,* 1 – 5, 1988.

Kramer JH, Delis DC, Kaplan E: *The California Discourse Memory Test.* Submitted for publication, 1988.

Lezak MD: *Neuropsychological assessment.* New York: Oxford University Press, 1983.

Lishman WA: Cerebral disorder in alcoholism: syndromes of impairment. *Brain: 104,* 1 – 20, 1981.

Loring DW, Papanicolaou AC: Memory assessment in neuropsychology: Theoretical considerations and practical utility. *J. Clin. Exp. Neuropsychol.: 9,* 340 – 358, 1987.

Luria AR: *Higher Cortical Functions in Man.* New York: Basic Books, 1981.

Marsh GG, Hirsch SH: Effectiveness of two tests of visual retention. *J. Clin. Psychol.: 38,* 115 – 118, 1982.

Marslen-Wilson WD, Teuber HL: Memory for remote events in anterograde amnesia: recognition of public figures from news photographs. *Neuropsychologia: 13,* 347 – 352, 1975.

Martin A, Brouwers P, Lalonde F, Cox C, Teleska P, Fedio P, Foster NL, Chase TN: Towards a behavioral typology of Alzheimer's patients. *J. Clin. Exp. Neuropsychol.: 8,* 594 – 610, 1986.

Martone M, Butters N, Payne M, Becker JT, Sax DS: Dissociations between skill learning and verbal recognition in amnesia and dementia. *Arch. Neurol.: 41,* 965 – 970, 1984.

Mattis S: Mental status examination for organic mental syndrome in the elderly patient. In Bellack L, Karasu TB (Editors), *Geriatric Psychiatry.* New York: Grune and Stratton, 1976.

Mayes AR: Learning and memory disorders and their assessment. *Neuropsychologia: 24,* 25 – 39, 1986.

McKhann G, Drachman D, Folstein M, Katzman R, Price R, Stadlan EM: Clinical diagnosis of Alzheimer's disease: Report of the NINCDS-ADRDA Work Group under the auspices of Department of Health and Human Services Task Force on Alzheimer's disease. *Neurology: 34,* 939 – 944, 1984.

Miglioli M, Buchtel HA, Campanin T, DeRisio C: Cerebral hemispheric lateralization of cognitive deficits due to alcoholism. *J. Nerv. Ment. Dis.: 167,* 212 – 217, 1979.

Milberg WP, Hebben N, Kaplan E: The Boston process approach to neuropsychological assessment. In Grant I, Adams KM (Editors), *Neuropsychological Assessment of Neuropsychiatric Disorders.* New York: Oxford University Press, 1986.

Miller E: On the nature of the memory disorder in presenile dementia. *Neuropsychologia: 9,* 75 – 78, 1971.

Miller E: Short- and long-term memory in patients with presenile dementia. *Psychol. Med.: 3,* 221 – 224, 1973.

Miller E, Lewis P: Recognition memory in elderly patients with depression and dementia: a signal detection analysis. *J. Abnorm. Psychol.: 86,* 84 – 86, 1977.

Miller GA: The magical number seven, plus or minus two: some limits on our capacity for processing information. *Psychol. Rev.: 63,* 81 – 97, 1956.

Miller NE: The measurement of mood in senile brain disease: examiner ratings and self-ratings. In Cole J, Barret J (Editors), *Psychopathology in the Aged.* New York: Raven Press, pp. 97 – 118, 1980.

Milner B: Interhemispheric differences in the localization of psychological processes in man. *Br. Med. Bull.: 27,* 272 – 277, 1971.

Milner B, Corkin S, Teuber HL: Further analysis of the hippocampal amnesic syndrome: a 14-year follow-up study of H.M. *Neuropsychologia: 6,* 215 – 234, 1968.

Morris RG, Baddeley AD: Primary and working memory functioning in Alzheimer-type dementia. *J. Clin. Exp. Neuropsychol.: 10,* 279 – 296, 1988.

Moss MB, Albert MS, Butters N, Payne M: Differential patterns of memory loss among patients with Alzheimer's disease, Huntington's disease and alcoholic Korsakoff's syndrome. *Arch. Neurol.: 43,* 239 – 246, 1986.

Nickols J: Mental deficit, schizophrenia and the Benton Test. *J. Nerv. Ment. Dis.: 136,* 279 – 282, 1963.

Niederehe G: Depression and memory impairment in the aged.

In Poon LW (Editor), *Clinical Memory Assessment of Older Adults*. Washington, DC: American Psychological Association, 1987.

Niederehe G, Camp CJ: Signal detection analysis of recognition memory in depressed elderly. *Exp. Aging Res.: 11*, 207 – 213, 1985.

Ober BA, Koss E, Friedland RP, Delis DC: Processes of verbal memory failure in Alzheimer-type dementia. *Brain Cognition: 4*, 90 – 103, 1985.

Ostergaard AL: Episodic, semantic and procedural memory in a case of amnesia at an early age. *Neuropsychologia: 25*, 341 – 357, 1987.

Paivio A: Abstractness, imagery, and meaningfulness in paired-associate learning. *J. Verbal Learn. Verbal Behav.: 4*, 32 – 38, 1965.

Parsons OA, Farr SD: The neuropsychology of alcohol and drug use. In Filskov SB, Boll TJ (Editors), *Handbook of Clinical Neuropsychology*. New York: Wiley, pp. 320 – 365, 1981.

Paterson A, Zangwill OL: Disorders of visual space perception associated with lesions of the right cerebral hemisphere. *Brain: 67*, 331 – 358, 1944.

Perez FI, Rivera VM, Meyer JS, Gay JRA, Taylor RL, Mathew NT: Analysis of intellectual and cognitive performance in patients with multi-infarct dementia, vertebrobasilar insufficiency with dementia, and Alzheimer's disease. *J. Neurol. Neurosurg. Psychiatry: 38*, 533 – 540, 1975.

Poon LW (Editor) *Clinical Memory Assessment of Older Adults*. Washington, DC: American Psychological Association, 1987.

Post F: Dementia, depression, and pseudodementia. In Benson DF, Blumer B (Editors), *Psychiatric Aspects of Neurologic Disease*. New York: Grune & Stratton, 1975.

Postman L: Transfer, interference and forgetting. In Kling JW, Riggs LA (Editors), *Experimental Psychology*. New York: Holt, Rinehart and Winston, 1971.

Power DG, Logue PE, McCarthy SM, Rosenstiel AK, Ziesat HA: Inter-rater reliability of the Russell revision of the Wechsler Memory Scale: an attempt to clarify some ambiguities in scoring. *J. Clin. Neuropsychol.: 1*, 343 – 345, 1979.

Prigatano GP: Wechsler Memory Scale: a selective review of the literature. *J. Clin. Psychol.: 34*, 816 – 832, 1978.

Query WT, Berger RA: RAVLT memory scores as a function of age among general medicine, neurologic, and alcoholic patients. *J. Clin. Psychol.: 36*, 1009 – 1012, 1980.

Rao SM: Neuropsychology of multiple sclerosis: a critical review. *J. Clin. Exp. Neuropsychol.: 8*, 503 – 542, 1986.

Randt CT, Brown ER: *Randt Memory Test*. Bayport: Life Science Associates, 1983.

Raymond PM, Stern RA, Authelet AM, Penny D: A comparison of California Verbal Learning Test performance among patients with multiple sclerosis, right-hemisphere vascular lesions, and normal controls. Paper presented at the meeting of the International Neuropsychological Society, Washington, DC, 1987.

Reitan RM, Davison LA: *Clinical Neuropsychology: Current Status and Applications*. Washington, DC: Winston & Sons, 1974.

Robertson LC, Delis DC: 'Part-whole' processing in brain damaged patients: dysfunctions of hierarchical organization. *Neuropsychologia: 24*, 363 – 370, 1986.

Ron MA: The alcoholic brain: CT scan and psychological findings. *Psychol. Med.: 3*, 1 – 33, 1983.

Russell EW: A multiple scoring method for the assessment of complex memory functions. *J. Consult. Clin. Psychol.: 43*, 800 – 809, 1975.

Russell EW: The pathology and clinical examination of memory. In Filskov SB, Boll TJ (Editors), *Handbook of Clinical Neuropsychology*. New York: Wiley, 1981.

Russell EW: The psychometric foundation of clinical neuropsychology. In Filskov SB, Boll TJ (Editors), *Handbook of Clinical Neuropsychology, Vol. 2*. New York: Wiley & Sons, pp. 45 – 80, 1986.

Ryan C, Butters N: Learning and memory impairments in young and old alcoholics: evidence for the premature-aging hypothesis. *Alcoholism: 4*, 288 – 293, 1980.

Ryan C, Butters N: The neuropsychology of alcoholism. In Wedding D, Horton AM and Webster J (Editors), *The Neuropsychology Handbook: Behavioral and Clinical Perspectives*. New York: Springer, 1986.

Ryan JJ, Lewis CU: Comparison of normal controls and recently detoxified alcoholics on the Wechsler Memory Scale-Revised. *Clin. Neuropsychol.: 2*, 173 – 180, 1988.

Salmon DP, Lasker BR, Butters N, Beatty WW: Remote memory in a patient with circumscribed amnesia. *Brain Cognition: 7*, 201 – 211, 1988.

Sanders HI, Warrington EK: Memory for remote events in amnesic patients. *Brain: 94*, 661 – 668, 1971.

Schacter D, Wang PL, Tulving E, Freedman PC: Functional retrograde amnesia: a quantitative case study. *Neuropsychologia: 20*, 523 – 532, 1982.

Scoville WB, Milner B. Loss of recent memory after bilateral hippocampal lesions. *J. Neurol. Neurosurg. Psychiatry: 20*, 11 – 21, 1957.

Seltzer B, Benson DF: The temporal pattern of retrograde amnesia in Korsakoff's disease. *Neurology: 24*, 527 – 530, 1974.

Shimamura AP. Priming effects in amnesia: evidence for a dissociable memory function. *Q. J. Exp. Psychol.: 38*, 619 – 644, 1986.

Shimamura AP, Salmon DP, Squire LR, Butters N: Memory dysfunction and word priming in dementia and amnesia. *Behav. Neurosci.: 101*, 347 – 351, 1987.

Spiers P: Have they come to praise Luria or to bury him? The Luria-Nebraska Battery controversy. *J. Consul. Clin. Psychol.: 49*, 331 – 341, 1981.

Squire LR: The neuropsychology of human memory. *Ann. Rev. Neurosci.: 5*, 241 – 273, 1982.

Squire LR: Mechanisms of memory. *Science: 232*, 1612 – 1619, 1986a.

Squire LR: The neuropsychology of memory dysfunction and its assessment. In Grant I, Adams KM (Editors), *Neuropsychological Assessment of Neuropsychiatric Disorders*. New York: Oxford University Press, 1986b.

Squire LR: *Memory and Brain*. New York: Oxford University Press, 1987.

Squire LR, Butters N (Editors) *The Neuropsychology of Memory*. New York: Guilford Press, 1984.

Squire LR, Cohen NJ: Remote memory, retrograde amnesia,

and the neuropsychology of memory. In Cermak LS (Editor), *Human Memory and Amnesia*. Hillsdale: Erlbaum, 1982.

Squire LR, Cohen NJ: Human memory and amnesia. In Lynch G, McGaugh JL, Weinberger NM (Editors), *Neurobiology of Learning and Memory*. New York: Guilford Press, 1984.

Squire LR, Fox MM: Assessment of remote memory: validation of the television test by repeated testing during a seven-year period. *Behav. Res. Methods Instrum.: 12*, 583 – 586, 1980.

Squire LR, Moore RY: Dorsal thalamic lesions in a noted case of chronic memory dysfunction. *Ann. Neurol.: 6*, 503 – 506, 1979.

Squire LR, Slater PC: Forgetting in very long-term memory as assessed by an improved questionnaire technique. *J. Exp. Psychol. Hum. Learn. Memory: 104*, 50 – 54, 1975.

Squire LR, Slater PC: Electroconvulsive therapy and complaints of memory dysfunction: a prospective three-year follow-up study. *Br. J. Psychiatry: 142*, 1 – 8, 1983.

Squire LR, Zola-Morgan S: Memory: brain systems and behavior. *Trends Neurosci.:* (Special Issue) *11*, 170 – 175, 1988.

Squire LR, Slater PC, Chase PM: Retrograde amnesia: temporal gradient in very long-term memory following electroconvulsive therapy. *Science: 187*, 77 – 79, 1975.

Squire LR, Haist F, Shimamura AP: The neurology of memory: quantitative assessment of retrograde amnesia in two groups of amnesic patients. *J. Neurosci.: 9*, 828 – 839, 1989.

Sternberg RJ: *Intelligence, Information Processing, and Analogical Reasoning: The Componential Analysis of Human Abilities*. Hillsdale: Erlbaum, 1977.

Sterne DM: The Benton, Porteus and WAIS Digit Span Tests with normal and brain-injured subjects. *J. Clin. Psychol.: 25*, 173 – 175, 1969.

Stromgren LS: The influence of depression on memory. *Acta Psychiatr. Scand.: 56*, 109 – 128, 1977.

Talland GA: Three estimates of the word span and their stability over the adult years. *J. Exp. Psychol.: 17*, 301 – 307, 1965a.

Talland GA: *Deranged Memory*. New York: Academic Press, 1965b.

Taylor EM: *The Appraisal of Children with Cerebral Deficits*. Cambridge, MA: Harvard University Press, 1959.

Taylor LB: Psychological assessment of neurosurgical patients. In Rasmussen T, Marino R (Editors), *Functional Neurosurgery*. New York: Raven Press, 1979.

Teuber HL, Milner B, Baughan HG: Persistent anterograde amnesia after stab wound of the basal brain. *Neuropsychologia: 6*, 267 – 282, 1968.

Tulving E: Episodic and semantic memory. In Tulving E, Donaldson W (Editors), *Organization of Memory*. New York: Academic Press, 1972.

Tulving E: *Elements of Episodic Memory*. Oxford: Clarendon Press, 1983.

Underwood BJ: Retroactive and proactive inhibition after 5 and 48 hours. *J. Exp. Psychol.: 38*, 29 – 38, 1948.

Victor M, Adams RD, Collins GH: *The Wernicke-Korsakoff Syndrome*. Philadelphia: Davis, 1971.

Villardita C: Verbal memory and semantic clustering in right brain-damaged patients. *Neuropsychologia: 25*, 277 – 280, 1987.

Waber DP, Holmes JM: Assessing children's memory productions of the Rey-Osterrieth complex figure. *J. Clin. Exp. Neuropsychol.: 8*, 563 – 580, 1986.

Wapner W, Hamby S, Gardner H: The role of the right hemisphere in the apprehension of complex linguistic material. *Brain Lang.: 14*, 15 – 32, 1981.

Warrington EK: *Recognition Memory Test*. Windsor: Nfer-Nelson, 1984.

Warrington EK, James M, Kinsbourne M: Drawing disability in relation to laterality of cerebral lesion. *Brain: 89*, 53 – 82, 1966.

Warrington EK, Weiskrantz L: An analysis of short-term and long-term memory defects in man. In Deutsch JA (Editor), *The Physiological Basis of Memory*. New York: Academic Press, 1973.

Waugh NC, Norman DA: Primary memory. *Psychol. Rev.: 72*, 89 – 104, 1965.

Wechsler D: A standardized memory scale for clinical use. *J. Psychol.; 19*, 87 – 95, 1945.

Wechsler D: *Manual for the Wechsler Adult Intelligence Scale*. New York: The Psychological Corporation, 1955.

Wechsler D: *Manual for the Wechsler Adult Intelligence Scale-Revised*. New York: The Psychological Corporation, 1981.

Wechsler D: *Wechsler Memory Scale-Revised*. New York: The Psychological Corporation, 1987.

Weingartner H, Grafman J, Boutelle W, Kaye W, Martin P: Forms of memory failure. *Science: 221*, 380 – 382, 1983.

Werner H: Process and achievement: a basic problem of education and developmental psychology. *Harv. Educ. Rev.: 7*, 353 – 368, 1937.

Wickelgren WA: The long and the short of memory. *Psychol. Bull.: 80*, 425 – 438, 1973.

Wilson B, Kolb B, Odland L, Wishaw IQ: Alcohol, sex, age, and the hippocampus. *Psychobiology: 15*, 300 – 307, 1987.

Wilson RS, Kaszniak AW, Fox JH: Remote memory in senile dementia. *Cortex: 17*, 41 – 48, 1981.

Wilson RS, Bacan LD, Fox JH, Kaszniak AW: Primary memory and secondary memory in dementia of the Alzheimer type. *J. Clin. Neuropsychol.: 5*, 337 – 344, 1983.

Zangwill OL: The amnesic syndrome. In Whitty CWM, Zangwill OL (Editors), *Amnesia*. London: Butterworths, 1966.

Zola-Morgan S, Squire LR, Amaral DG: Human amnesia and the medial temporal region: enduring memory impairment following a bilateral lesion limited to field CA 1 of the hippocampus. *J. Neurosci.: 6*, 2950 – 2967, 1986.

© 1989 Elsevier Science Publishers B.V. (Biomedical Division)
Handbook of Neuropsychology, Vol. 3.
F. Boller and J. Grafman (Eds)

CHAPTER 2

Disorders of memory: the cognitive science perspective

Arthur P. Shimamura

Department of Psychology, University of California, Berkeley, CA, U.S.A.

Introduction

Cognitive science has generated useful tools and concepts for the study of memory disorders. Indeed, many theories of amnesia are derived from investigations of normal cognition. Cognitive science has its roots in the tradition of experimental psychology and artificial intelligence (see Gardner, 1985, for an interesting historical perspective). The approach can be traced to research conducted in the 1950s (e.g., Broadbent, 1958; Miller, 1956; Newell et al., 1958), but its inception as a discipline of its own was marked more recently by the establishment of the journal *Cognitive Science* in 1977 and the establishment of the Cognitive Science Society, which first met in 1979. The purpose of this new field was to study cognition from a broad interdisciplinary perspective, drawing on cognitive psychology, computer science, anthropology, linguistics, neuroscience and philosophy (see Collins, 1977; Norman, 1980). Of these various disciplines, cognitive psychology has produced an abundance of experimental data on human memory (see Anderson, 1982; Crowder, 1976; Glass and Holyoak, 1986).

The cognitive science perspective views behavior in terms of the operation of mental or 'cognitive' processes. Cognitive scientists develop theories to explain how such processes (e.g., perception, attention, memory) operate and interact with each other. One useful strategy has been to identify dissociations between cognitive processes. Thus, it

is generally believed that one can dissociate the operations of some cognitive processes from others — just as one can dissociate the operations of a carburetor from the operations of a battery in an automobile or the operations of an input device (e.g., keyboard) from the operations of a memory device (e.g., disk drive) in a computer. Some important theoretical dissociations of memory that have been investigated include the distinction between short-term and long-term memory (Atkinson and Shiffrin, 1968), verbal and nonverbal memory (Kosslyn, 1975; Paivio, 1971), episodic (autobiographical) and semantic (generic) memory (Tulving, 1972, 1983), and skill learning and fact memory (Anderson, 1983).

There are several parallels between the field of cognitive science and neuropsychology. First, the topics of interest are similar: both study aspects of human cognition or what is often termed in neuropsychology 'higher cortical function'. Of course, rather than investigating the composition of normal cognitive function, the neuropsychological researcher investigates the breakdown of cognitive function as a result of brain damage. Another parallel between the two fields is the strategy of locating dissociations between cognitive functions. In neuropsychology, it is often the case that focal brain damage produces a relatively selective cognitive deficit. That is, a circumscribed brain lesion may severely affect one function but not impinge on others. In fact, one of the main goals of experimental neuropsychology is to determine which neurological deficits can be dissociated from others (see Broadbent and Weiskrantz, 1982; Butters, 1985; Shallice, 1979; Shimamura, in press). Evidence of dissociable functions provides important clues about the organization of brain systems. It provides the starting point for basic neurobiological research concerning the neural substrate and architecture underlying these systems.

As a result of these parallels between cognitive science and neuropsychology, one might suppose that researchers have developed general and integrative theories which incorporate findings from both normal and brain-injured patients. In reality, it has been only during the last 8 – 10 years that the two fields have had considerable interaction. Indeed, during the 1970s only two neuropsychological studies of amnesic patients appeared in the volumes of the *Journal of Experimental Psychology* (Cermak and Reale, 1978; Oscar-Berman et al., 1976). Yet during the 1980s a total of 16 studies of amnesia have been published in the same journal volumes. Such an increase in the publication of amnesia research in psychological journals marks a new shift in the importance of neuropsychological findings to the study of normal memory functions. In recent years, memory researchers have tried to integrate both cognitive and neuropsychological research (see Cermak, 1982; Hirst, 1982; Schacter, 1987b; Squire, 1982b, 1987). This increased interest in neuropsychological research was forecast in 1982 by Schacter and Tulving:

" . . . there is reason to believe that we may be on the verge of a 'golden age' in which the interaction between the experimental psychology of normal memory and the investigation of amnesic deficits will be more thorough and meaningful than it has been in the past". (p. 2, Schacter and Tulving, 1982).

This chapter will describe some of the fruitful interactions between cognitive science and neuropsychology in the study of memory and amnesia.

Memory impairment and neurological disorders

The amnesic syndrome

Complaints about memory are ubiquitous among psychiatric and neurological patients (Strubb and Black, 1977). This symptomatology is probably related to the fact that memory pervades nearly all aspects of daily living, and thus any disorder of mood or cognition can affect learning and remembering. Moreover, in dementing illnesses, such as Alzheimer's disease or Huntington's disease, many cognitive processes, including memory, can be severely impaired, while some neurological disorders can produce a rather selective impairment of memory. In such cases, other cortical functions such as intelligence, language, affect and motor abilities are preserved. The term 'amnesic syndrome' has been used to characterize a rather selective memory disorder that can occur as a result of neurological disease or injury.

The amnesic syndrome is characterized by two general disorders − anterograde amnesia and retrograde amnesia. Anterograde amnesia is impairment of new learning ability and can be assessed by such measures as free recall, paired-associate learning and recognition memory. On free recall tests, subjects are shown a list of stimuli (e.g., words, pictures) and then asked to recollect as many of the stimuli as possible. This test can be quite difficult because no cues or hints are provided. On paired-associate learning tests, subjects are shown word pairs (e.g., TABLE-DOLLAR) and then asked to recollect the second word in the pair when given the first word as a cue (e.g., TABLE-?). On recognition tests, subjects are shown a list of stimuli and then given test trials in which they are asked to determine whether a test item was or was not in the study list (yes/no recognition test) or asked to choose a study item from a set of possible choices (forced-choice recognition test). Amnesic patients exhibit deficits on such tests, even when testing is conducted only minutes after learning. The Wechsler Memory Scale-Revised (Wechsler, 1987) is a useful memory battery for neuropsychological assessment of anterograde amnesia. A variety of other neuropsychological tests of anterograde amnesia are available (see Chapter 1 of this volume; Lezak, 1983; Mayes, 1986).

Retrograde amnesia is impairment of memory for events which occurred before the onset of

mnesia. It often accompanies anterograde amne-
ia. In general, the exact nature and severity of
etrograde amnesia is difficult to assess, partly
ecause testing is almost always conducted retro-
pectively. That is, the experimenter typically has
o prior knowledge of who will become amnesic
except for cases involving neurosurgery or elec-
roconvulsive therapy), and thus study material
annot be introduced prior to the onset of amne-
ia. Consequently, on tests of retrograde amnesia
here is little control over the degree and form of
earning (or whether any learning has occurred at
ll). Researchers must generally rely on tests that
ssess memory for public information. For exam-
le, tests of public information assess memory for
ublic events (Cohen and Squire, 1981; Warr-
ngton and Sanders, 1971), famous faces (Albert et
l., 1979; Cohen and Squire, 1981; Marslen-
Vilson and Teuber, 1975; Sanders and Warr-
ngton, 1971), past television programs (Cohen
nd Squire, 1981; Squire and Slater, 1978) and
amous voices (Meudell et al., 1980). One problem
vith such tests is that patients vary widely in terms
f their exposure to public information. Some investigators have attempted to assess retrograde
mnesia with autobiographical material (Baddeley
nd Wilson, 1986; Butters and Cermak, 1986;
Zola-Morgan et al., 1983). For example, patients
an be asked to recollect a specific
utobiographical incident or episode that involved
a particular object (e.g., bird, window) and then
sked to date the incident. One problem with tests
f autobiographical memory is that it is often difficult to verify the accuracy of responses.

The term 'amnesic syndrome' has been used to
characterize a rather selective impairment of
anterograde and retrograde amnesia. Recently,
however, the term has lost some impact as a result
of controversy over what symptoms are used to
define the 'syndrome'. Moreover, it is unclear
whether there is one or more 'amnesic syndrome'.
These issues are relevant to questions about the
nature of the memory impairment associated with
the syndrome (e.g., What specific memory process
or processes are part of the syndrome?) and to

questions about the neural substrate of amnesia
(e.g., What are the brain areas that when damaged
cause amnesia?). These issues will be discussed in
subsequent sections. In this chapter, the term is used descriptively as a way to distinguish between the
broad cognitive impairment seen in patients with
dementia and the relatively selective memory impairment seen in patients with more circumscribed
brain damage. The next two sections describe some
neurological disorders that have been associated
with the amnesic syndrome.

Patient H.M.

Perhaps the best known amnesic case is patient
H.M., who in 1953 underwent surgery for relief of
severe epilepsy (Scoville and Milner, 1957). The
surgery involved bilateral excision of the medial
temporal region, which reportedly included removal of the hippocampal gyrus, amygdala and the anterior two-thirds of the hippocampus. Following
surgery, H.M. exhibited a profound anterograde
amnesia – he was unable to remember information encountered since his operation (for review,
see Corkin, 1984; Iversen, 1977; Milner et al.,
1968). Despite his severe amnesic disorder, there
was no detectable impairment in intelligence or
language abilities. In fact, his IQ score two years
after his operation was increased by 8 points compared with his pre-operative IQ score (112 vs. 104).
There was some retrograde amnesia – H.M. could
not remember the layout of the hospital wards or
recognize members of the attending medical staff.
Moreover, he could not recall the death of a
favorite uncle who had died three years previously
(Iversen, 1977). Recent evidence suggests some
amnesia for even more remote events (Corkin,
1984). Nevertheless, H.M.'s retrograde amnesia
was not severe, as indicated by the fact that he was
as good as control subjects at recognizing faces
that became famous before 1950 (Marslen-Wilson
and Teuber, 1975).

H.M.'s anterograde amnesia affected information received from all sensory modalities and included impairment of both verbal and nonverbal
memory. He exhibited impairment on a variety of

memory tests, including tests of free recall memory, paired-associate learning, and recognition memory (see Corkin, 1984; Milner et al., 1968). He has also failed to learn new vocabulary words that have been added to the dictionary since his surgery (Gabrieli et al., 1983). In addition to these psychometric tests of memory, clinical observations indicate that memory for ongoing events is severely impaired. In fact, 30 minutes after eating lunch, H.M. could not recall what he had eaten or whether he had even had lunch at all. H.M. reflected upon his impairment as follows:

Right now, I'm wondering. Have I done or said anything amiss? You see, at this moment everything looks clear to me, but what happened just before? That's what worries me. It's like waking from a dream; I just don't remember. (p. 115, Milner, 1966)

The quote above suggests that H.M.'s short-term memory is intact; information could be stored momentarily if it were kept in mind. In fact, if H.M. was not distracted he could retain a short string of digits for as long as 15 minutes. Presumably, he could rehearse the information in short-term memory. As soon as his attention is diverted or as soon as the information exceeds his short-term memory capacity, the information is apparently forgotten. Thus, H.M.'s memory impairment appears to be in the domain of long-term memory retention: yet not all long-term memory abilities are impaired. He exhibits considerable skill-learning abilities (see later section).

Patient H.M. represents a landmark case in the study of amnesia. The selectivity and the severity of his amnesia is strong evidence for the modularity of memory functions. Furthermore, this case offers the strongest evidence for the crucial role of the medial temporal region in learning and memory. Indeed, studies of H.M. have provided the impetus for numerous animal studies on the psychobiology of memory – research which has come to fruition with recent primate models of medial temporal amnesia (see Mahut and Moss, 1984; Mishkin, 1982; Squire and Zola-Morgan, 1983).

Etiologies of amnesia

Various neurological disorders can produce an amnesic syndrome similar to that seen in H.M. Some of these disorders will be discussed briefly in this section. More extensive reviews can be found in other chapters in this volume (see also Corkin et al., 1985; Whitty and Zangwill, 1977).

Korsakoff's syndrome. Korsakoff's syndrome can develop after nutritional deficiency and many years of chronic alcohol abuse (see Butters, 1984, 1985; Butters and Cermak, 1980; Korsakoff 1887/1955; Talland, 1965). Patients typically undergo an acute phase (i.e., Wernicke's encephalopathy), in which motor, cognition and affect are all impaired. Following this acute phase, amnesia can persist as a chronic symptom. Neuropathological studies indicate that Korsakoff's syndrome involves bilateral lesions along the walls of the third and fourth ventricles, as well as cortical atrophy and cerebellar damage (Mair et al., 1979; Victor et al., 1971). A recent study using quantitative analyses of CT data from patients with Korsakoff's syndrome corroborated these neuropathological findings by identifying structural abnormalities in both diencephalic and cortical areas (Shimamura et al., 1988). In that study, abnormalities in both thalamic and frontal regions were correlated with impairment on neuropsychological tests.

Patients with Korsakoff's syndrome are the most available and best-studied neuropsychological cases of amnesia. They exhibit severe anterograde amnesia, despite relatively preserved intellectual abilities. Like H.M., patients with Korsakoff's syndrome exhibit a rather global impairment of new learning ability, which can be observed on a variety of verbal and nonverbal tests (see Butters and Cermak, 1980; Squire and Shimamura, 1986; Talland, 1965; Warrington and Weiskrantz, 1982). Unlike H.M., who exhibited relatively mild impairment of premorbid memories, tients with Korsakoff's syndrome can exhibit severe and extensive retrograde amnesia, which can span several decades (Albert et al., 1979; Cohen and Squire, 1981; Sanders and Warrington,

1971; Seltzer and Benson, 1974; Squire et al., 1988).

In patients with Korsakoff's syndrome, the extent and severity of retrograde amnesia is particularly difficult to assess, because the disease is associated with prolonged alcohol abuse. Thus, poor performance on tests of remote memories actually may be the result of lack of exposure to test information or to the result of new learning impairment due to alcohol intoxication. On tests of remote memory, impairment is often temporally graded, so that memory for more recent events is more affected than memory for very remote events (Albert et al., 1979; Cohen and Squire, 1981; Seltzer and Benson, 1974; but see Sanders and Warrington, 1971). Butters (1984; Butters and Cermak, 1986) describes an interesting case of retrograde amnesia in a patient with Korsakoff's syndrome (case P.Z.), who was an eminent scientist and had written an autobiography 3 years before the onset of Wernicke's encephalopathy. Like other Korsakoff patients, P.Z. exhibited severe and extensive remote memory impairment. Interestingly, he exhibited impairment for events published in his autobiography that had occurred during the past two decades. Consequently, P.Z. exhibited retrograde amnesia (i.e. true loss of premorbid memories), because he was severely amnesic for premorbid information which was available to him only 3 years before. This finding suggests that remote memory impairment in Korsakoff's syndrome cannot be attributed solely to poor learning habits.

In addition to anterograde and retrograde amnesia, patients with Korsakoff's syndrome vary greatly in terms of additional cognitive impairment. These patients are often emotionally flat, apathetic, and without insight about their deficit (Butters and Cermak, 1980; Squire and Zouzounis, 1988; Talland, 1965). Moreover, they exhibit cognitive deficits not seen in other amnesic patients. For example, patients with Korsakoff's syndrome exhibit deficits in encoding, short-term memory and metamemory (see Butters and Cermak, 1980; Shimamura and Squire, 1986b; Squire, 1982).

These deficits are not typically exhibited by other amnesic patients (see later section for details) and may be related to frontal lobe dysfunction (Moscovitch, 1982; Squire, 1982). As a result of the extent and severity of cognitive impairment, careful neuropsychological assessment must be performed on patients with Korsakoff's syndrome (see Butters, 1984; Jacobson and Lishman, 1987; Warrington and Weiskrantz, 1982; Squire, 1982; Squire and Shimamura, 1986; Talland, 1965). In fact, because they do form such a heterogeneous group − ranging from a rather selective amnesic disorder to amnesia with many other cognitive deficits (i.e., dementia) − only a subset of clinical patients with Korsakoff's syndrome can be truly described as having an amnesic syndrome.

Amnesia due to an ischemic or hypoxic episode. A persistent and relatively selective amnesic syndrome can occur following ischemic or hypoxic injury. Such injury can arise as a result of cardiac arrest, near-drowning, carbon monoxide poisoning, or loss of consciousness (Volpe and Hirst, 1983; Whitty et al., 1977; Zola-Morgan et al., 1986). Anterograde amnesia is typically the outstanding cognitive impairment, though loss of premorbid memory can also occur (Squire and Shimamura, 1986; Volpe and Hirst, 1983). General intellectual abilities and short-term memory (i.e., digit span) are often intact. Depending upon the duration of the ischemic or hypoxic episode, the involvement of other cortical areas could be present in the form of additional infarcts.

A recent case of amnesia following an ischemic episode (patient R.B.) has provided some important information concerning the role of the hippocampus in memory (Zola-Morgan et al., 1986). Patient R.B. was given extensive neuropsychological assessment during the four years following his injury. In 1983, R.B. suffered a fatal cardiac arrest, and, with the consent and encouragement of his family, a comprehensive histological examination of his brain was performed. This examination revealed a circumscribed bilateral lesion of the CA1 subfield of the hippocampus. Thus, R.B. represents the first extensively studied case of amnesia that occurred as a result of a lesion primarily restricted to the hippocampus. Along with case H.M., case R.B. exemplifies the crucial role of the medial temporal region in memory. It is important to note that although R.B.'s amnesia was clinically significant, it was not as severe as H.M.'s. Because H.M.'s lesion extended beyond the hippocampus and included bilateral removal of parahippocampal gyrus and amygdala, it is likely that the extent of the damage within the medial temporal region can determine the severity of amnesia.

Viral encephalitis. Herpes simplex encephalitis produces somewhat widespread neuropathology which includes bilateral damage to various cortical areas, such as medial temporal lobe (including hippocampus and amygdala), orbitofrontal cortex and cingulate areas, as well as bilateral damage to the basal forebrain (see patient D.R.B., Damasio et al., 1985b). Initial complications include episodes of confusion, seizure activity, fever and loss of consciousness. Following these acute symptoms, severe anterograde amnesia and extensive retrograde amnesia are prominent features of this disease (Cermak, 1976; Cermak and O'Connor, 1983; Damasio et al., 1985b; Rose and Symonds, 1960).

A comprehensive assessment of memory functions in one patient with amnesia due to herpes simplex encephalitis (case S.S.) has been performed by Cermak (1976; Cermak and O'Connor, 1983). S.S.'s premorbid intellectual capabilities were quite high – he had received a masters degree in physics and was president of an optical firm. Moreover, two years after S.S. had contracted encephalitis, he still exhibited a high IQ score of 133, and he showed no indication of language, short-term memory or perceptual-motor impairment. Nevertheless, his anterograde and retrograde amnesia was severe and comparable to that seen in patients with alcoholic Korsakoff's syndrome (Cermak and O'Connor, 1983). Attempts to encourage S.S. to use mnemonic techniques, such as providing cues during study and test,

did little to facilitate the acquisition of new information.

Transient amnesic disorders. Transient global amnesia (TGA) is a temporary condition of memory impairment that closely resembles the permanent amnesic syndrome seen in the etiologies described above (Fisher and Adams, 1964; Kritchevsky et al., 1988; Steinmetz and Vroom, 1972; Whitty, 1977). The onset of anterograde and retrograde amnesia is sudden, and the amnesia typically lasts for several hours. Patients can appear neurologically intact on examination on the day after the TGA attack (Kritchevsky et al., 1988). Both epileptic seizures and transient cerebrovascular disorder have been considered as causes of TGA, but vascular etiology is widely favored (see Fisher and Adams, 1964; Whitty, 1977). There is indication of EEG abnormalities in the region of the temporal lobes in some but not all TGA patients (Rowan and Protass, 1979; but see Cole et al., 1987).

Another transient form of amnesia can occur after electroconvulsive therapy (ECT). Following a postical confusional period of about 30 – 60 minutes, amnesia is present as a relatively circumscribed disorder. In fact, by 60 minutes after treatment patients can exhibit normal scores on tests of verbal intelligence. ECT causes both anterograde and retrograde amnesia (Squire, 1984; Williams, 1977). Anterograde amnesia can be quite severe, particularly in patients prescribed bilateral ECT. Retrograde amnesia is often temporally graded, affecting memory for recent events more than memory for very remote events (Squire et al., 1975, 1981). By several months after ECT treatment, there is extensive recovery of both new learning capacity (Squire and Chace, 1975) and memory for premorbid information (Squire et al., 1981).

Traumatic head injury can cause a transient and rather selective memory impairment (Russell and Nathan, 1946; Whitty and Zangwill, 1977). Following initial stages of unconsciousness and confusion, both anterograde and retrograde amnesia are present, and the severity of anterograde amnesia is often correlated with the temporal extent of retro-grade amnesia (Russell and Nathan, 1946). Amnesia following head trauma can last for minutes, days, or even weeks. In severe cases, both amnesia and other cognitive impairment can be chronic (Sunderland et al., 1983; Whitty and Zangwill, 1977).

Other etiologies of amnesia. Depending upon the brain areas damaged, brain tumors, head injury or vascular disorders can cause memory impairment to be the most prominent cognitive deficit. Typically, these etiologies produce extensive cognitive impairment in addition to amnesia. Brain tumors in diencephalic and medial temporal structures can cause a selective memory impairment (see McEntee et al., 1976; Whitty et al., 1977). For example, tumors in the area of the third ventricle can produce memory disorders characteristic of Korsakoff's syndrome (see Williams and Pennybacker, 1954). One head-injury case, patient N.A., has been studied extensively. In 1960, N.A. sustained a brain injury in an accident in which a miniature fencing foil entered his right nostril, took an oblique trajectory, and penetrated his left diencephalon (Teuber et al., 1968; Kaushall et al., 1981). Since then, N.A. has had a material-specific amnesia that mainly involves the ability to learn new verbal information (see Squire and Shimamura, 1986; Teuber et al., 1968). His ability to learn non-verbal information and his premorbid remote memory are relatively intact. Previous computed tomography scans showed a lucency in the region of the left dorsomedial thalamus (Squire and Moore, 1979), but recent evidence from magnetic resonance imaging scans of N.A. revealed more extensive midline damage that included other midline thalamic nuclei and mammillary nuclei (Squire et al., in press).

Several cases of amnesia resulting from vascular disorders have been reported. For example, amnesia can occur in patients with occlusion of the posterior cerebral arteries (see Whitty et al., 1977; Victor et al., 1961), in patients with thalamic infarcts (see Mori et al., 1986; von Cramon et al., 1985), and in patients with rupture and repair of anterior cerebral or anterior communicating artery aneurysms (Damasio et al., 1985a; Phillips et al., 1987; Talland et al., 1967; Vilkki, 1985; Volpe and Hirst, 1983). Amnesia following occlusion of the posterior cerebral arteries is presumably related to lesions in the medial temporal region which can accompany this vascular disorder (Victor et al., 1961). Amnesia from thalamic infarcts is consistent with findings from patients with Korsakoff's syndrome, who also exhibit thalamic damage. It should be noted, however, that patients with thalamic infarcts often exhibit more extensive cognitive decline, including perceptual and affective disorders (see Graff-Radford et al., 1985). Damage to the anterior cerebral or anterior communicating arteries produces pathology in the basal forebrain and in ventromedial areas of the frontal lobes (Damasio et al., 1985a; Phillips et al., 1987).

Summary. Neurobehavioral studies have implicated the medial temporal lobe and the diencephalic midline as critical areas for the establishment of new memories. Fig. 1 displays a schematic drawing of the medial surface of the brain which illustrates some of the structures that when damaged cause memory impairment (e.g., hippocampus,

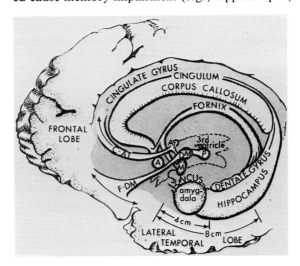

Fig. 1. Schematic drawing of the medial surface of the human brain showing structures in the medial temporal lobe (e.g., hippocampus, amygdala, dentate gyrus) and in the diencephalic midline (e.g., dorsomedial [DM] and anterior [AT] thalamic nuclei, mammillary nucleus [M]). Figure reprinted from Squire (1984).

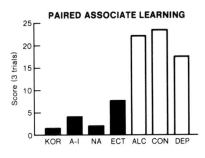

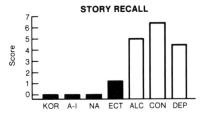

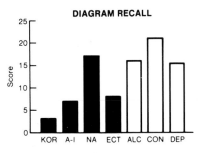

Fig. 2. Performance by amnesic patients and control subjects on three tests sensitive to anterograde amnesia (KOR = patients with Korsakoff's syndrome; A-I = patients with amnesia due to anoxia or ischemia; NA = patient N.A.; ECT = patients prescribed electroconvulsive therapy; ALC = alcoholic control subjects; CON = healthy control subjects; DEP = depressed patients tested before ECT). Note: N.A.'s good performance on the diagram recall test is indicative of his left unilateral diecephalic lesion. Figure reprinted from Squire and Shimamura (1986).

dorsomedial thalamic nuclei, mammillary nuclei). Fig. 2 displays performance by some amnesic patients and control subjects on three measures of anterograde amnesia. The rather selective memory disorder defined as the amnesic syndrome can be seen in patients with neurosurgical lesions of the medial temporal lobe (e.g., H.M.), patients with Korsakoff's syndrome, patients with lesions due to an anoxic or ischemic episode (e.g., R.B.), patients with damage due to viral encephalitis (e.g., D.R.B., S.S.), and patients with damage due to

rupture and repair of the anterior communicating artery. In addition, patients with circumscribed lesions from head injury, tumors or vascular disorders can also exhibit a selective memory impairment. Finally, transient amnesic syndromes can be observed in cases of traumatic head injury, transient global amnesia and ECT.

The status of memory functions in amnesia

As illustrated in the previous section, it is possible to identify patients who exhibit severe amnesia, in the presence of normal language, intellectual and social skills. Studies of patients with rather selective impairment can help to define the brain regions that contribute to memory functions. In fact, careful neuropsychological studies have shown that even some memory functions are preserved in amnesia. That is, amnesic patients can exhibit *entirely normal* performance on some memory tests. This fact suggests that some memory functions are completely dissociated from the memory functions impaired in amnesia. In other memory tests, amnesic patients exhibit considerable retention or 'relatively preserved' retention, though in these tests performance is still below normal. In contrast to examples of normal or near-normal memory functions, other functions appear to be disproportionately impaired in some amnesic patients. This section reviews the status of various memory functions in patients, including those functions that are preserved in amnesia and those functions that can be particularly impaired.

Preserved memory functions

Short-term memory. One of the first memory functions that was claimed to be unimpaired in amnesic patients is short-term memory. Short-term memory refers to the temporary memory store used to hold information that is currently in use or in mind (Atkinson and Shiffrin, 1968; Baddeley, 1986; Miller, 1956). Some investigators have used the term 'span of apprehension' or 'consciousness' to characterize short-term memory (see Miller,

1956). Others have used terms such as 'primary memory', 'immediate memory', or 'working memory' to describe a similar function (see Baddeley, 1986; James, 1890; Waugh and Norman, 1965). Short-term memory can be contrasted with permanent storage of information or 'long-term memory' (Atkinson and Shiffrin, 1968). Some of the first descriptions of amnesia suggested a sparing of a process that permits short-term memory. For example, Korsakoff (1889/1955) noted that patients with severe memory disorders can exhibit 'relatively good preservation of consciousness'.

Three psychological findings have been used to demonstrate preserved short-term memory in amnesia. The first finding is intact digit span. Amnesic patients can repeat a short list of digits immediately after presentation as well as control subjects (Baddeley and Warrington, 1970; Drachman and Arbit, 1966; Talland, 1965). The second finding is an intact 'recency effect' in list learning. The recency effect refers to a heightened level of recall performance for the last few items in a list. Typically the last items presented in a list are the first items recalled; and it has been suggested that the recency effect is due to recalling items from short-term memory (Atkinson and Shiffrin, 1968; Glazner and Cunitz, 1966; Murdock, 1962). Baddeley and Warrington (1970) showed that amnesic patients recall the last 2 items in a 10-word list as well as control subjects (see also Brooks and Baddeley, 1976).

The third – and most controversial – finding is the report of intact performance by amnesic patients on the Brown-Peterson task (Brown, 1958; Peterson and Peterson, 1959). In this task, subjects are presented with three words and then given a distraction task (e.g., counting backwards by threes) for a certain time period before they are asked to recall the words. The distraction task can last from 5 to 60 seconds. Baddeley and Warrington (1970) reported that both amnesic patients and control subjects exhibited similar levels of performance in this task. However, other investigators failed to replicate the finding of intact performance in amnesic patients (Butters and Grady,

1977; Cermak and Butters, 1972; Meudell et al., 1978). Differences in methodology between studies were partly responsible for the conflict in findings (see Butters and Cermak, 1974; Butters and Grady, 1978), yet these differences could not fully account for the impaired performance in this task by some amnesic patients. Thus, it appears that impairment in the Brown-Peterson task by amnesic patients can occur, particularly if the memory impairment is severe or if more widespread cognitive impairment is observed (Butters and Grady, 1978; Baddeley, 1982a; see also Cermak, 1982b; Warrington, 1982).

The equivocal findings from the Brown-Peterson task stem not only from differences in the severity or extent of impairment in patient groups but also from the problem of its use as a pure measure of short-term memory. The Brown-Peterson task taps memory after a distraction task; that is, after it has been removed from consciousness. Efficient encoding strategies and facile use of associations in long-term memory could help to boost memory performance in this task. Thus, the Brown-Peterson task may not be an appropriate measure of short-term memory store, because impaired performance may be the result of poor encoding or associative strategies in some patients.

The findings of intact digit span and intact recency effects are less subject to the criticisms about the findings from the Brown-Peterson task. In general, the findings from these two tasks suggest preserved short-term memory, but even these findings have been subjects of debate. For instance, intact digit span is not always observed in amnesic patients (see Parkinson, 1982), though it should be noted that H.M.'s digit span actually increased when it was assessed postoperatively (Milner, 1966). One problem with the digit span test is that it is a rather insensitive measure, as it is based on only a few (4 – 7) items and usually only tested on one occasion for a given patient. Although the recency effect has been demonstrated in amnesia, it only occurred for the last two items in a list (Baddeley and Warrington, 1970). Some have suggested that the recency effect should have included more than the last two items of a list (see Cermak, 1982b).

In summary, the normal or near-normal performance on tests of digit span and recency effects suggests a distinction between short-term and long-term memory. Even if mild or moderate deficits occur on some short-term memory tasks, the disproportionate deficit in long-term memory is certainly the central impairment. More importantly, double dissociations between short-term and long-term memory have been reported. That is, findings from other neuropsychological patients suggest that verbal short-term memory can be impaired, despite intact long-term memory (Vallar and Baddeley, 1984; Warrington and Shallice, 1969).

Skill learning. During the 1960s, several studies indicated that H.M. could show considerable retention of perceptual-motor skills. For example, he exhibited good performance on a mirror drawing task in which he was required to trace the outline of a star while viewing the star through a mirror (Milner, 1962). He also improved his performance across trials in a simple tactual maze task in which a stylus must be guided through a short route (Milner et al., 1968). Corkin (1968) found similar results from H.M. on two perceptual-motor tracking tasks: a pursuit rotor task and a bimanual tracking task. In both tracking tasks, the subject must keep a stylus on a moving target. In the maze-learning and tracking tasks, H.M. exhibited considerable improvement across trials, even when trials were separated by 24 h. His performance on these tasks, however, fell below that of control subjects.

Two factors could explain why H.M.'s skill-learning performance was not always normal. First, H.M. exhibits slow latencies on simple reaction time tests (Corkin, 1968), and thus subnormal skill learning on the perceptual-motor tasks may be a result of slowed motor responses. Second, some skill-learning tasks may benefit from verbal learning ability, which is severely impaired in H.M. For example, explicit verbal knowledge of successful strategies or knowledge of performance on prior sessions could facilitate skill learning in normal

subjects. H.M. had no verbal memory of his performance on previous sessions and was not aware of the extensive number of learning trials given to him. H.M., however, could recognize the test apparatus from session to session (Corkin, 1968).

Preserved skill learning has been observed in other cases of amnesia (for review, see Cohen, 1984; Parkin, 1982). Talland (1965) found some evidence for skill learning in patients with Korsakoff's syndrome using a task which required subjects to move beads from one bowl to another using a forceps. Cermak et al. (1973) found good learning and retention of the tactual maze and pursuit-rotor task in patients with Korsakoff's syndrome. The encephalitic patient, S.S., also exhibited good skill learning and retention on the tactual maze task (Cermak, 1976). As with H.M., maze-learning performance in patient S.S. and in patients with Korsakoff's syndrome was below that of control subjects.

Brooks and Baddeley (1976) found entirely normal pursuit-rotor skill learning and 1-wk retention in three patients with Korsakoff's syndrome and two patients with amnesia due to encephalitis. Also, in a jig-saw puzzle assembly task, these amnesic patients exhibited shorter completion times across six trials and good retention when the same puzzle was given 1 week later. Performance on the puzzle task by encephalic patients was comparable to performance by control subjects, yet performance by patients with Korsakoff's syndrome was initially poorer than the performance by control subjects, and this deficit was maintained across trials. Thus, amnesic patients performed well on these skill tasks, despite severe verbal memory impairment on tests of free recall and paired-associate learning.

Cohen and Squire (1980) observed entirely normal skill learning and retention by amnesic patients on a mirror reading task, which measured the time it takes subjects to read three words presented in mirror-reversed fashion. Patients with Korsakoff's syndrome, patients given ECT and patient N.A. exhibited normal learning and retention of the skill, even when retention was assessed one

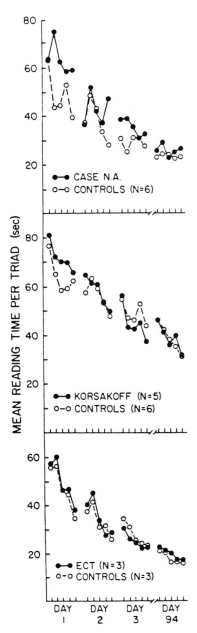

Fig. 3. Acquisition of a mirror-reading skill (e.g., *vagueness, nebulous sauerkraut*) during three daily sessions and retention of the skill 3 months later. The skill in reading non-repeated mirror-reversed words was acquired at a normal rate by case N.A., patients with Korsakoff's syndrome, and patients prescribed ECT. Figure reprinted from Cohen and Squire (1980).

month after learning (see Fig. 3). Recognition memory for the words used in the task was severely

impaired. Interestingly, this skill-learning ability was intact in ECT patients when training was administered before the onset of amnesia (i.e., before ECT treatment) and tested when these patients were amnesic (Squire et al., 1984). Intact performance by amnesic patients in this mirror reading task indicates that skill learning can be preserved, even when the skill requires basic cognitive functions, such as word identification and naming, in addition to perceptual-motor functions.

It is not clear whether amnesic patients exhibit preserved skill learning on complex tasks. Wood et al. (1982) briefly described an experiment in which patients with Korsakoff's syndrome were asked to learn the Fibonacci series rule in which the correct number in a series is the sum of the previous two numbers (e.g., 2, 3, 5, 8, 13, 21, etc.). The Fibonacci rule could be learned by amnesic patients, but performance was reported to be below that of control subjects. Unfortunately, scores of control subjects were not reported, and it is not known whether performance on this task was any better than performance on a verbal memory task such as recognition memory.

Another task that involves rather complex cognitive skill learning is the Tower of Hanoi puzzle. In this task, subjects must move five wooden blocks from one peg to another. Three rules must be followed: the blocks must be moved one at a time, the blocks must be placed on one of three pegs, and a larger block cannot be placed on a smaller one. The solution to the puzzle requires an iterative strategy which, if performed perfectly, consists of 31 moves. Cohen and Corkin (1981; see Cohen, 1984) reported normal acquisition and retention of this complex skill in patient H.M. Other laboratories, however, have been unable to replicate normal performance in the Tower of Hanoi puzzle in other amnesic patients (e.g., Butters et al., 1985). It may be that such tasks require extensive problem-solving abilities which may be impaired in patients with additional damage (e.g., patients with Korsakoff's syndrome). Also, the procedure used by Cohen and Corkin (1981) involved prompting and cuing when the subjects

45

were confronted with critical choice points during the task. Such prompts and cues may have been used more extensively with H.M. than with control subjects or with other amnesic patients. In fact, when the Tower of Hanoi puzzle was later given to H.M. without prompting, he failed to improve his performance across trials (Gabrieli et al., 1987). Thus, there is no conclusive evidence for intact skill learning on tasks that require complex cognitive operations.

Priming effects. Amnesic patients exhibit preserved priming effects; that is, their performance can be facilitated or biased by recently encountered information (for review, see Shimamura, 1986). The first evidence for preserved priming in amnesia came from cued recall studies by Warrington and Weiskrantz (1970a,b, 1968). In these studies, subjects were presented with fragmented words or pictures and were asked to identify each one. If the subject failed to identify a word or picture, then a succession of less fragmented versions of the stimulus was shown until the subject could identify it. In a retention test, this procedure was repeated, and subjects were asked to use the fragmented cues as aids to facilitate identification of previously presented stimuli. When testing occurred 1 min after presentation, amnesic patients and control subjects exhibited the same level of cued recall performance. That is, performance by both groups was facilitated by previous exposure to the fragments. Amnesic patients were impaired on tests of free recall and recognition memory (Warrington and Weiskrantz, 1970a). At longer intervals (e.g., 1 h or 24 h), amnesic patients exhibited savings in re-learning by performing better than they had done during the initial study phase, but they performed more poorly than control subjects (Warrington and Weiskrantz, 1968; 1970b).

From these findings, Warrington and Weiskrantz (1970a, 1974) initially suggested that amnesia causes a deficit in retrieval. That is, the impairment could be circumvented by supplying patients with efficient retrieval cues (e.g., fragmented words or pictures). One problem with this interpretation was that amnesic patients did not always

exhibit normal performance when retrieval cues were provided (Mayes et al., 1978; Mortensen, 1980; Squire et al., 1978; Warrington and Weiskrantz, 1968; 1970b). Other researchers offered a different interpretation, which viewed the good cued recall performance as evidence for a process of memory that was preserved in amnesia. Rozin (1976) likened this process to a 'hot tubes' effect. After a vacuum tube radio has been turned off, the tubes remain hot for a while. Mortensen (1980) suggested that amnesic patients can activate memory representations and that 'this activation may result in some kind of ′priming″ (p. 81).

The concept of 'priming' or 'activation' has been extensively studied in cognitive science (for review, see Collins and Loftus, 1975; Richardson-Klavehn and Bjork, 1988; Schacter, 1987a). An important property of priming effects is that they occur automatically; that is, without awareness or conscious recollection (Jacoby and Witherspoon, 1982; Neely, 1977). Both Gardner et al. (1973) and Graf et al. (1984) provided important evidence to suggest that unconscious recollection is a critical factor for the finding of normal priming effects in amnesia. In both studies, subjects were provided cues at test and instructed either (1) to use the cues as aids to recall previously presented words (explicit cued recall instructions) or (2) to say the first word that came to mind for each cue (implicit priming instructions). For example, Graf et al. (1984) used a word completion paradigm in which words (e.g., MOTEL) are presented for study and then cued by three-letter beginnings of the words (e.g., MOT). Amnesic patients exhibited entirely normal word-completion performance under implicit priming instructions but impaired performance under cued recall instructions. The dissociation of priming effects and explicit tests of memory (e.g., free recall, recognition memory) was confirmed in a study of ECT patients (Squire et al., 1985) in which intact word-completion priming was observed even when patients exhibited chance levels on a test of recognition memory.

These findings suggest that normal performance by amnesic patients depends on the way in which information is sought. If both control subjects and amnesic patients are asked simply to say the first word that comes to mind, then they perform similarly. Words appear to 'pop' into mind, and amnesic patients exhibit this automatic activation of previously presented stimuli. If subjects are asked to use the cues as aids to recollect a prior learning session, then control subjects exhibit better performance than amnesic patients. Preserved priming effects in amnesia have been observed under a variety of test paradigms. For example, amnesic patients (including H.M.) exhibit facilitation in a task in which previously presented words are represented briefly for word identification (Cermak et al., 1985; Nissen et al., 1981). In this task, amnesic patients can identify previously presented words at briefer exposure times than novel words. In another study (Jacoby and Witherspoon, 1982), patients with Korsakoff's syndrome exhibited priming in a test that first biased the meaning of a critical word which could be spelled in more than one way (e.g., Name a musical instrument that employs a *reed*). When patients were asked to spell the word, they tended to use the infrequent, but recently encountered, spelling (e.g., *reed* instead of *read*).

Several studies have attempted to define the boundary conditions under which normal priming effects are observed in amnesic patients. As shown above, the first boundary condition is that implicit priming instructions must be used at test. That is, the test should be presented as a puzzle or completion test rather than an explicit test of memory. Graf et al. (1985) extended the boundary of preserved priming effects by showing that normal priming is observed under cross-modality priming conditions. In that study, words were presented visually or aurally and then tested in a word-completion task with the cues presented visually. Amnesic patients exhibited normal priming when words were presented aurally but tested visually. This cross-modality priming effect was smaller than the within-modality priming, but the effect of modality was the same for normal subjects and amnesic patients. Another boundary condition for

entirely normal priming is the use of preexisting or unitized representations, such as words or pictures. Preexisting semantic associates can also be used to prime recently presented words. For example, Shimamura and Squire (1984) presented words (e.g., BABY) and later asked subjects to 'free associate' to related words (e.g., CHILD). At immediate testing, patients and control subjects exhibited a two-fold increase in their priming performance over their baseline tendency to use these words if they had not been presented. After a 2-h delay, priming performance declined to baseline levels for both amnesic patients and control subjects (see Fig. 4). Other semantic priming effects have been demonstrated with different paradigms (see Graf et al., 1985; Mayes et al., 1987; Schacter, 1985).

Priming can sometimes be shown by amnesic patients in the form of preference biases. In studies of normal subjects, stimuli which have been shown repeatedly are often preferred over novel stimuli (Zajonc, 1980). A similar preference bias was

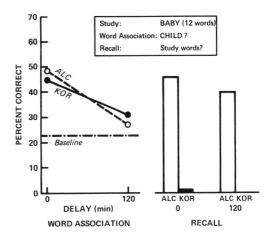

Fig. 4. Patients with Korsakoff's syndrome (KOR) exhibit intact semantic priming as measured by a word association test (left panel). After a 120-min delay, performance drops to baseline levels for both patients with Korsakoff's syndrome and alcoholic control subjects (ALC). Patients with Korsakoff's syndrome exhibit severely affected free recall performance at both immediate and 120 min delay conditions (right panel). Figure reprinted from Shimamura and Squire (1984).

found in patients with Korsakoff's syndrome using repeated melodies (Johnson et al., 1985), which suggests that biasing of this affective judgment can be preserved in amnesia. However, in another study (Redington et al., 1984) a mixed group of amnesic patients (e.g., amnesia following a hypoxic-ischemic event, stroke, or rupture-repair of anterior communicating artery) did not exhibit a normal preference bias for repeated photographs of faces. Thus, an intact preference bias is not a general phenomenon in amnesia. Preference biases may be sensitive to the type of task or stimuli that is used.

Another important feature of priming is that the effects are sometimes shorter-lasting in amnesic patients than in control subjects. Several studies have shown that word-completion priming and free-association priming disappear in both amnesic patients and control subjects after a 2-h retention interval (Graf et al., 1984; Mayes et al., 1987; Shimamura and Squire, 1984). In these studies, the decay rates in both groups are comparable; yet in other priming paradigms used with normal subjects, priming can last across retention intervals of days and even weeks (Tulving et al., 1982). When amnesic patients are tested in such priming paradigms, however, they still exhibit only short-lasting priming effects (Squire et al., 1987).

There are reports of long-lasting priming effects in amnesic patients, but in each case performance by amnesic patients was not entirely normal (Moscovitch et al., 1986; McAndrews et al., 1987; Warrington and Weiskrantz, 1970; 1978). In one provocative study (McAndrews et al., 1987), subjects were given ambiguous sentences (e.g., 'The haystack was important because the cloth ripped.'). Each sentence could be understood when a critical word (e.g., parachute) was presented. Amnesic patients were given critical words of ambiguous sentences at study, and after a 1-wk retention interval they were asked to explain the sentences without the critical words. Amnesic patients exhibited good retention of the meaning of such sentences, though performance was not normal. Thus, unlike the entirely normal (transient)

priming effects observed on tests of word completion or free association, priming performance by amnesic patients in this study was significantly poorer than that of control subjects. Further studies are needed to determine whether normal long-lasting priming effects can be observed in amnesic patients and whether such priming effects are qualitatively different from weak normal memory.

Some have also suggested that priming of newly established associations can be preserved in amnesia. For example, the finding of good comprehension of ambiguous sentences (McAndrews et al., 1987) suggests that some novel associations can be primed, though not at a normal level. Graf and Schacter (1985) tested priming of new associations by asking subjects to generate sentences using unrelated words pairs (e.g., WINDOW-REASON). At test, subjects were shown the first word and the three-letter beginning of the second word (WINDOW-REA) and were asked to say the first word that came to mind that could be used to complete the last word. This condition was compared to the priming effect obtained when the cue was paired with a different word (BREAD-REA). It was initially reported that amnesic patients exhibited a greater priming effect when cued with the same word used during study compared to the effect when a different word was used (Graf and Schacter, 1985). However, further assessment of the effect showed that none of the severely impaired amnesic patients exhibited this priming of new associations (Schacter and Graf, 1986). Recent studies have shown that amnesic study patients generally fail to exhibit priming of new associations in this paradigm (Cermak et al., 1988; Shimamura and Squire, in press). For example, on two testing occasions patients with Korsakoff's syndrome and patients with amnesia due to an anoxic or ischemic episode failed to show a reliable priming effect for new associations (Shimamura and Squire, in press), though these same patients exhibit entirely normal word-completion and free-association priming effects for preexisting words and word associates.

The phenomenon of priming is one of the most extensively studied topics in both neuropsychological and cognitive studies of learning and memory. There is general agreement that at least some aspects of this phenomenon reflect a preserved form of memory that can be successfully established in amnesic patients. Many questions about the nature of preserved priming in amnesia still remain to be answered. In particular, further studies are needed to address the issue of long-lasting priming effects and the issue of priming of newly learned information in amnesic patients. Interestingly, patients with mild to moderate dementia who were diagnosed as having Alzheimer's disease exhibited impaired priming in both the word-completion and free-association priming tests (Salmon et al., 1988; Shimamura et al., 1987). These findings suggest that priming effects may depend on neocortical areas that are damaged in Alzheimer's disease.

Other examples of preserved memory functions. One of the earliest anecdotes of unconscious preserved learning was presented by Claparede (1911/1951). While interviewing a patient with Korsakoff's syndrome, Claparede hid a pin between his fingers and surreptitiously pricked the patient on the hand. When he once again reached for the patient's hand, the patient quickly withdrew her hand, but she did not have any conscious memory of having her hand pricked before. The patient simply stated: 'Sometimes pins are hidden in people's hands'. This anecdote provides an example of stimulus-response learning without awareness of the learning episode itself. Another form of stimulus-response learning was demonstrated by Weiskrantz and Warrington (1979). In that study, simple classical conditioning of the eyeblink response was observed in two amnesic patients. These patients retained the effect for as long as 24 h, even though they failed to recognize the test apparatus. In that study, however, data from control subjects were not presented so it is not clear whether performance was normal in amnesic patients.

These are several reported observations of preserved perceptual aftereffects in amnesic patients. The first observation is the finding of visual persistence of the McCollough color aftereffect by amnesic patients (Warrington and Weiskrantz, unpublished observation, as cited by Weiskrantz, 1982). The second observation is the facilitation in perceiving random-dot stereograms after repeated exposures (Ramachandran, as cited by Weiskrantz, 1982). Recently, the finding of a facilitation effect for repeated random-dot stereograms has been replicated in a group of amnesic patients (Benzing and Squire, in press). Finally, Benzing and Squire (in press) report a biasing effect in a perceptual adaptation-level experiment. In that experiment, judgments about the weights of objects were influenced by previous experience of lifting a set of heavy objects or a set of light objects. Amnesic patients and control subjects exhibited comparable biasing effects in this adaptation-level experiment. These observations of preserved aftereffects suggest that the areas damaged in amnesia operate independently of the areas that can store some transient perceptual representations.

Summary. Amnesic patients can exhibit intact performance on a variety of memory tests. Short-term memory, as measured by digit span and recency effects, is intact in many amnesic patients. Also, patients can exhibit intact performance on tests of priming effects and perceptual aftereffects. These effects are relatively transient in both amnesic patients and intact subjects, but they can last longer than the span of short-term memory. Finally, long-term retention can be observed on tests of skill learning and classical conditioning.

Memory functions disproportionately impaired in some amnesic patients

As mentioned previously, the hallmark feature of amnesia is an impairment of new learning ability which can be observed on a variety of memory tests, including tests of recall, recognition and paired-associate learning. Findings from the previous section help to define better the status of memory functions by identifying functions that are apparently preserved in amnesia (e.g., short-term memory, skill learning, priming). This section outlines some memory functions that are disproportionately impaired in some but not all amnesic patients. In particular, many of these functions are disproportionately impaired in patients with Korsakoff's syndrome, which suggests that Korsakoff's syndrome involves a broader spectrum of memory impairment than is observed in other amnesic patients. One obvious possibility is that the extent of the memory impairment is related to the severity of amnesia. Behavioral methods have been established to test whether disproportionate findings are due simply to quantitative effects, and some of these methods are described in this section. Another possibility is that damage to other brain areas (that is, qualitatively different neuropathology) is needed to produce these additional deficits. One candidate structure is the frontal lobes, because it is known that patients with Korsakoff's syndrome have frontal lobe damage (Shimamura et al., 1988) and that some of these additional memory deficits are correlated with tests sensitive to frontal lobe dysfunction (see Janowsky et al., in press; Moscovitch, 1982; Squire, 1982). The memory functions discussed in this section are encoding, memory for spatial/temporal context, metamemory, and free recall versus recognition memory.

Encoding. Several lines of evidence suggest that some amnesic patients (particularly patients with Korsakoff's syndrome) can exhibit disproportionate deficits in encoding features of stimulus information (for review, see Cermak, 1979; 1986; Squire, 1982a). The first line of evidence comes from studies of impaired short-term memory in patients with Korsakoff's syndrome. As mentioned earlier, some investigators have found impaired performance on the Brown-Peterson task (Butters and Grady, 1977; Cermak and Butters, 1972; Meudell et al., 1978). Because the task requires multiple study/test trials, one explanation for the deficit is that patients with Korsakoff's syndrome are more sensitive to proactive interference; that is,

interference from previous learning trials causes an encoding deficit on subsequent trials (see Butters, 1985; Warrington and Weiskrantz, 1978; Winocur and Weiskrantz, 1976).

If amnesic patients exhibit increased interference from previous learning trials, then they should make more prior item intrusion errors on tasks with multiple study/test trials. In fact, patients with Korsakoff's syndrome do make more intrusion errors. For example, on the Brown-Peterson task, Meudell et al. (1978) found that patients with Korsakoff's syndrome made more prior item intrusion errors than control subjects or patients with Huntington's disease. Similar effects of increased proactive interference can also be shown in paired-associate learning tests in which information acquired on the first learning trial interferes with learning on subsequent trials. In these tests, associations learned in the first learning trial (e.g., SOLDIER-ARMY) interfered with performance on subsequent trials because new responses are paired with the same cue word (e.g., SOLDIER-BATTLE). In such paired-associate learning tasks (called A-B, A-C tasks), intrusion errors are more frequent in patients with Korsakoff's syndrome than in control subjects (Winocur and Weiskrantz, 1976; see also Warrington and Weiskrantz, 1978).

A related encoding deficit concerns the phenomenon of the 'release from proactive interference' (Wickens, 1970). Subjects are first given four study/test trials of the Brown-Peterson task using words from the same semantic category (e.g., all bird names). For each trial, three words are presented and followed by a 15–20-second distraction task. Across the four trials, normal subjects exhibit a decrement in recall performance (i.e., proactive interference), which is due to the similarity of the word stimuli. On the fifth trial, words from a different semantic category are presented for study, and on this trial normal subjects perform at the same level as they did on the first trial (Wickens, 1970). This 'release from proactive interference' indicates that subjects can improve their performance by noticing (encoding) the shift in the meaning of the word stimuli. Patients with

Korsakoff's syndrome, however, do not exhibit a release from proactive interference (Cermak et al., 1974; Squire, 1982a). Presumably, these patients do not adequately encode information in a semantic manner. Interestingly, normal release from proactive interference can be observed in other amnesic patients, such as patient N.A., patient S.S., patients with amnesia due to an anoxic or ischemic episode, and patients prescribed ECT (Cermak, 1976; Janowsky et al., in press; Squire, 1982a).

Deficits in semantic encoding by amnesic patients can also be demonstrated in the 'levels-of-processing' paradigm, which was originally investigated in cognitive studies of normal subjects (see Craik and Lockhart, 1972; Craik and Tulving, 1975; Hyde and Jenkins, 1969; Walsh and Jenkins, 1973). For example, in normal subjects, words which were encoded meaningfully (e.g., is this word an animal name?) were remembered better than words which were encoded phonetically (does this word rhyme with TRAIN?) (Craik and Tulving, 1975). In several studies of patients with Korsakoff's syndrome, it was demonstrated that semantic encoding did not improve memory performance (Cermak et al., 1973; Cermak and Reale, 1978; McDowell, 1979; Wetzel and Squire, 1980). Consequently, patients with Korsakoff's syndrome failed to encode information at a deep, semantic level of processing. Other amnesic patients, however, can exhibit normal 'levels-of-processing' effects (Cermak and O'Connor, 1982; Wetzel and Squire, 1980). In fact, this semantic encoding deficit is not even seen in all patients with Korsakoff's syndrome (Squire, 1982a), which suggests that this deficit may only be present in patients with Korsakoff's syndrome who exhibit extensive cognitive impairment.

Memory for spatial/temporal context and source amnesia. One useful description of memory is the distinction between memory for facts (i.e., what information is learned) and memory for spatial/temporal context (i.e., where and when the information is learned). This distinction has been cogently argued by Tulving (1972, 1983), who suggested a dissociation between semantic and episodic memory. Indeed, some investigators have applied this distinction to the analysis of amnesia. It has been suggested that amnesia produces a particular impairment in episodic memory or memory for spatial/temporal context (see Cermak, 1984; Kinsbourne and Wood, 1975; Hirst, 1982; Huppert and Piercy, 1976; Williams and Zangwill, 1950; for review, see Mayes et al., 1985; Schacter and Tulving, 1982b). Interestingly, even Korsakoff (1889/1955) acknowledged the possibility of this distinction: 'In some cases the facts themselves are remembered, but not the time when they occurred.'

Huppert and Piercy (1976, 1978) provided important evidence for the view that memory for temporal context is impaired in patients with Korsakoff's syndrome. In one study (Huppert and Piercy, 1976), subjects were presented 80 pictures on one day; and on the next day, they were presented another 80 pictures: 40 new pictures and 40 pictures from the previous day. Following a 10-min delay, subjects were given a recognition test in which they were asked to determine which pictures were presented only on that day ("Which of these two pictures did you see today?") [two-choice test] or "Did you seen this picture today?" [yes/no test]). Patients with Korsakoff's syndrome tended to make false positive errors for those pictures that were presented on the previous day (50.6%), whereas control subjects made few false positive errors (3.1%). That is, patients with Korsakoff's syndrome were poor at discriminating those pictures presented 24 h ago from those pictures presented 10 min ago. In another study (Huppert and Piercy, 1978), it was found that patients with Korsakoff's syndrome appeared to confuse memory strength with recency. In that study, pictures presented more frequently (3 times) were judged to have occurred more recently than pictures presented only once.

Findings of impaired temporal context memory in patients with Korsakoff's syndrome have been replicated in other studies (Meudell et al., 1985; Squire, 1982a). In an important extension of the findings, Meudell et al. (1985) found that patients exhibit a greater impairment in judging the recency of stimuli, even when item recognition memory performance by control subjects is matched to that of patients with Korsakoff's syndrome, by using longer retention intervals for the control subjects (i.e., 'delayed control subjects'). In a similar test of temporal order, Squire et al. (1981) showed that recency judgments were not disproportionately impaired in patient N.A. or in patients prescribed ECT, relative to delayed control subjects. Yet, in the same paradigm, temporal order judgments by patients with Korsakoff's syndrome were disproportionately impaired (Squire, 1982a).

Interestingly, the deficit in temporal order judgments in patients with Korsakoff's syndrome was correlated with impairment on tests sensitive to frontal lobe damage (Squire, 1982a). The possibility that damage to the frontal lobes may contribute to impaired temporal order judgments was supported by a study of recency judgments in patients with frontal lobe pathology (Corsi, as cited by Milner, 1971). In that study, subjects were shown a series of stimuli (words or pictures) and on certain trials they were asked to judge which of two stimuli was more recently presented. Patients with frontal lobe lesions exhibited poor recency memory, whereas patients with temporal lobe lesions were not particularly impaired on the recency memory but were impaired on item recognition memory (i.e., whether a stimulus had been previously presented or never presented).

In addition to impaired temporal order judgments of recently presented stimuli, amnesic patients also exhibit impaired temporal order judgments for past public events (Hirst and Volpe, 1982). For example, subjects were asked to determine which public event occurred more recently: (a) Reagan is inaugurated or (b) Sadat is assassinated. In this test, recency judgments were impaired, but recognition memory for public events was not different from control subjects. Although these findings suggest a particular deficit in temporal order judgments for public events, there were some anomalies in the report. First, a rather

mixed group of six amnesic patients was used (3 patients with amnesia following a hypoxic/ischemic event, 1 patient with rupture and repair of anterior communicating artery, 1 patient with temporal lobe damage due to a stroke, and 1 patient with a hematoma in the left parietooccipital area due to closed head trauma and coma). Second, recognition memory for the public events was not impaired, which is quite unexpected considering the fact that memory for public events is usually impaired in amnesic patients (Albert et al., 1979; Cohen and Squire, 1981). The failure to find a recognition deficit in amnesia may have been due to ceiling effects, insensitive tests, or other scaling problems. Finally, it is not certain whether the public events were premorbid events or whether they occurred after the onset of amnesia. Nevertheless, these findings do suggest that patients can exhibit impairment on temporal order judgments when public events are used as stimuli.

If amnesic patients fail to encode or retrieve contextual information, then it may be possible to improve their memory by making contextual information more distinctive. In a series of experiments, Winocur and Kinsbourne (1978) tested this notion by varying the distinctiveness of the experimental room. Patients with Korsakoff's syndrome and control subjects were given an A-B, A-C paired-associate learning task using related word pairs (e.g., ARMY-SOLDIER, ARMY-BATTLE). As mentioned above, learning the first pair produces proactive interference, so that learning the second pair is impaired. In the study by Winocur and Kinsbourne (1978), the first pair was tested in a distinctive context, a room which was lit by a red lamp and in which classical music was playing. After a 20–30-min delay, the second pair was presented and tested in a room with standard lighting and with no music. For patients with Korsakoff's syndrome, the shift in context improved paired-associate learning for the second list of word pairs compared to learning in standard (no-shift) conditions; yet performance did not reach normal levels. Winocur and Kinsbourne (1978) suggested that amnesic patients exhibit a deficit in

trieving contextual information and that by pro-
ding distinctive contextual cues one could
cilitate their performance. This view was sup-
orted by the fact that performance by patients
ith Korsakoff's syndrome was facilitated even
hen both study and test were conducted in the
istinctive room.

Further evidence for a selective impairment of
atial/temporal context memory comes from
udies of *source amnesia*. Often, one remembers
me fact (e.g., news item, research idea, name of
good restaurant) but forgets the source of the in-
rmation – who presented the information or
here or when it was learned. Claparede (1911/
951) noted an instance of source amnesia in a pa-
ent with Korsakoff's syndrome:

hen one told her a little story, read to her various items of a
wspaper, three minutes later she remembered nothing, not
en the fact that someone had read to her; but with certain
lestions one could elicit in a reflex fashion some of the details
f those items. (p 69, Claparede, 1911/1951)

chacter et al. (1984) tested source amnesia in
mnesic patients in a paradigm previously used in
:udies of post-hypnotic suggestion (e.g., Evans
nd Thorn, 1966). They presented made-up 'facts'
.g., Bob Hope's father was a fireman) to a group
f memory-impaired patients (e.g., patients with
lzheimer's disease, head injury, encephalitis) and
en gave a recall test for the fact. If a fact was
ecalled, patients were asked how they had ac-
uired the information. Frequently, patients ex-
ibited source amnesia: they recalled some facts
ut stated that the facts were learned before the ex-
erimental session. This deficit could not be at-
ributed simply to poor memory because delayed
ontrol subjects (tested 1 wk after learning) did not
xhibit source amnesia even though their fact
lemory performance was matched to that of
lemory-impaired patients. Interestingly, source
lemory impairment in the patients was correlated
ositively with impairment on neuropsychological
:sts of frontal lobe pathology.

In another study, Shimamura and Squire (1987)
ested source amnesia and fact memory in 6 pa-

tients with Korsakoff's syndrome, 3 patients with
amnesia due to an anoxic or ischemic episode, and
case N.A. In that study, patients and control subjects were presented obscure facts (e.g., Angel
Falls is located in Venezuela) and after a 2-h (Experiment 1) or 5-min (Experiment 2) delay were
given tests of fact memory (e.g., Where is Angels
Falls located?) and tests of source information
(e.g., How did you know that answer?). Severe
source amnesia was observed in four amnesic patients (3 Korsakoff patients and 1 anoxic patient).
These patients could recall some obscure facts
which had recently been presented, but they never
mentioned that a recalled fact had been presented
previously by the experimenter. These patients
often attributed a television show or a newspaper
article as the source of the recalled facts. Although
these four amnesic patients exhibited severe source
amnesia, the other amnesic patients exhibited no
source amnesia or only occasional source errors.
Interestingly, the level of fact memory performance did not appear to be related to the level of
source memory impairment. The four patients who
exhibited source amnesia exhibited the same level
of fact memory performance as those patients who
did not exhibit source amnesia. Consequently, a
disproportionate deficit in memory for spa-
tial/temporal memory was found in some but not
all amnesic patients. Moreover, this deficit did not
appear simply to be a consequence of poor fact
memory performance, because delayed control
subjects did not exhibit source amnesia.

In summary disproportionate deficits of spa-
tial/temporal context can be observed on tests of
recency judgments for presented information and
for public events, on tests of contextual cueing using standard versus distinctive room characteristics, and on tests of source amnesia. An important
feature of this deficit is that it does not appear
simply to be a consequence of weak memory. That
is, the spatial/temporal memory deficit seen in
some patients is greater than that seen in delayed
control subjects whose item memory matches that
of amnesic patients tested after shorter delays
(Meudell et al., 1985; Schacter et al., 1984;

Shimamura and Squire, 1987; Squire et al., 1981).
Metamemory. Knowledge about one's own memory capabilities and knowledge about strategies that can aid memory are termed *metamemory* (Flavell and Wellman; Gruneberg, 1983; Nelson and Narens, 1980). The 'tip-of-the-tongue' phenomenon is an everyday example of metamemory processes in operation. In that situation, some knowledge about what one is trying to remember is present (e.g., what the initial sound of the word is or how many syllables the word has), yet complete recall is not available. Such examples of the 'tip-of-the-tongue' of 'feeling of knowing' phenomenon have been investigated in normal subjects (Freedman and Landauer, 1966; Gruneberg and Monks, 1974; Hart, 1965; Nelson and Narens, 1980). Also, some have suggested (and it seems reasonable) that deficits in metamemory could contribute to or even cause amnesia (Crowder, 1985; Hirst, 1982). Hirst (1982) noted that patients with Korsakoff's syndrome appear to have limited knowledge about mnemonic strategies. Moreover, they seemed to take longer in applying the strategies they know. Hirst (1982) also reported that other amnesic patients (e.g., patients with temporal lobe lesions) have good knowledge about mnemonic strategies. Similarly, Squire and Zouzounis (1988) demonstrated that patients with Korsakoff's syndrome were unreliable and inaccurate in making self-rating judgments about their own memory abilities, though patients with amnesia due to an anoxic or ischemic event could make reliable self-ratings.

Shimamura and Squire (1986a) compared metamemory and memory in patients with Korsakoff's syndrome, patients prescribed ECT, patients with amnesia due to an anoxic or ischemic event, and patient N.A. Patients and control subjects were asked general information questions of varying degrees of difficulty (e.g., What is the name of the ship on which Charles Darwin made his famous voyage? [Beagle], or Who invented the wireless radio? [Marconi]). If the correct answer to a question could not be recalled, then subjects rated their feeling of knowing; that is, they rated on a four-point scale the probability that they would be able to recognize the answer if some choices were given. To verify feeling-of-knowing judgments, subjects were then given a recognition test for nonrecalled questions. Of all the amnesic patients tested, only patients with Korsakoff's syndrome exhibited deficits in feeling-of-knowing accuracy. These patients were poor at predicting whether they would know the answer to a question in a subsequent recognition test. Other amnesic patients were as accurate as control subjects in their ability to predict subsequent recognition memory performance.

Thus, metamemory impairment is not an obligatory feature of anterograde amnesia. That is, some amnesic patients can express knowledge about what they know and what they do not know, despite having severe impairment of new learning ability. Patients with Korsakoff's syndrome, however, exhibited impaired feeling of knowing and this impairment may contribute to their memory impairment. It has also been shown that patients with closed head injuries which resulted in loss of consciousness were poor at rating their memory abilities (Sunderland et al., 1984). One possibility is that poor planning and organizational strategies contribute to impaired metamemory. If so, then patients with frontal lobe damage might exhibit impaired metamemory. In fact, recent findings suggest that certain aspects of feeling-of-knowing judgments are poor in patients with circumscribed frontal lobe damage (Janowsky et al., 1989).

Free recall versus recognition memory. A distinction is often made between the processes underlying free recall performance and those underlying recognition memory performance (see Anderson and Bower, 1972; Crowder, 1976; Tulving, 1983). On tests of free recall, subjects are not given any cues to facilitate memory retrieval. On tests of recognition memory, however, subjects are given the answer, either singly on yes/no tests or together with incorrect alternatives on forced-choice tests. Thus, on tests of recognition memory subjects only have to make familiarity judgments (e.g., "Was this item presented before?"). On ossible difference between tests of free recall and recognition is that tests of free recall require more extensive use of retrieval or search processes. Hirst and colleagues (Hirst et al., 1986, 1988) provided evidence that amnesic patients exhibit a disproportionate deficit in free recall. In these studies, amnesic patients exhibited impairment on both tests of free recall and recognition memory; but they exhibited disproportionate free recall impairment when their performance was compared with control subjects whose recognition memory performance was matched to that of amnesic patients. Memory was matched by testing control subjects after a longer retention interval or by presenting stimuli to control subjects at a shorter exposure time.

The finding of disproportionate free recall impairment suggests that amnesic patients fail to initiate or plan appropriate search strategies. This impairment may be related to the deficit in contextual memory seen in some amnesic patients. That is, the failure to encode and retrieve contextual information may particularly affect free recall test performance, because such tests require search strategies which probably use contextual information to gain access to item memory. Deficits in initiation and planning have been associated with frontal lobe pathology. One possibility is that the particular impairment in free recall is due to frontal lobe dysfunction observed in some patients (e.g., patients with Korsakoff's syndrome, patients with basal forebrain damage). Interestingly, patients with circumscribed frontal lobe damage do exhibit a mild but significant free recall impairment, despite good recognition memory performance (Janowsky et al., in press). In addition, even patients with Korsakoff's syndrome were found to be more impaired on free recall tests compared with four patients with amnesia due to an anoxic or ischemic episode, despite the fact that recognition memory performance was similar in the two groups (Janowsky et al., in press).

A recent finding suggests that free recall performance may be particularly impaired, even compared with cued recall performance (Shimamura

and Squire, 1988; see also Glisky et al., 1986a). Amnesic patients can fail to make any correct responses on free recall tests, particularly if recency effects are reduced; yet on cued recall tests there is often above-chance residual memory. Shimamura and Squire (1988) presented a set of sentences (e.g., "The dog chased the cat into the barn") and tested memory for the last word in each sentence by cueing the subject with the rest of the sentence (e.g., "The dog chased the cat into the ____" [direct cued recall condition]). A recognition test for the missing word was also given. In addition, some sentences were cued less directly by providing a question (e.g., "Where did the dog go?"). This 'indirect cued recall' condition was used to make subjects initiate more search or retrieval strategies. Amnesic patients (patients with Korsakoff's syndrome, patients with amnesia due to an anoxic or ischemic episode) were tested after a 1 h delay, and control subjects were tested after a 2-wk delay, in order to match performance in the direct cued recall condition. Unlike performance on free recall tests, amnesic patients did not exhibit disproportionate impairment in the cued recall tests compared with recognition memory performance. Moreover, they did not exhibit disproportionate impairment on the indirect cued recall condition, compared with the direct cued recall condition. These findings suggest that even rather weak cues can facilitate recall performance. Free recall tests may be particularly difficult for amnesic patients, because on such tests they must initiate their own retrieval or contextual cues (see Glisky et al., 1986a).

Summary

Table 1 summarizes the status of various cognitive functions in amnesic patients and compares the neuropsychological profile of amnesic patients to the profiles of patients with frontal lobe lesions and patients with Alzheimer's disease. As shown in Table 1, the profile of impairment is quite similar for patient H.M., patients with amnesia due to an anoxic-ischemic episode, post-encephalitic patients, patients prescribed ECT, and patients with

Korsakoff's syndrome. All patients exhibit impairment of new learning ability and premorbid memory, in spite of relatively preserved I.Q., language, skill learning and priming. Of all etiologies of amnesia, Korsakoff's syndrome appears to cause the broadest spectrum of cognitive impairment. For example, aspects of encoding, short-term memory, contextual memory and metamemory all appear to be particularly impaired in patients with Korsakoff's syndrome.

Some of the additional cognitive deficits observed in patients with Korsakoff's syndrome appear to be related to frontal lobe dysfunction. Frontal lobe atrophy can be detected on CT scans of patients with Korskoff's syndrome (Carlen et al., 1981; Jacobson and Lishman, 1987; Shimamura et al., 1988), and the extent of frontal atrophy in patients with Korsakoff's syndrome is correlated with cognitive and memory test performance (Shimamura et al., 1988). As shown in Table 1, patients with frontal lobe lesions share some of the cognitive deficits seen in patients with Korsakoff's syndrome. For example, both frontal and Korsakoff patients exhibit deficits of short-term memory, encoding, contextual memory and metamemory (see Janowsky et al., 1989; in press;

Moscovitch, 1982; Schacter, 1987b). Yet patients with frontal lobe lesions typically perform in the normal range on standard tests of new learning ability, though they appear to have a mild impairment of free recall (Janowsky et al., in press).

Finally, the neuropsychological profile of amnesic patients can be compared with the rather global cognitive impairment observed in patients with mild to moderate dementia due to Alzheimer's disease. Patients with Alzheimer's disease exhibit anterograde and retrograde amnesia, but they also exhibit impairment on tests of intelligence, language, short-term memory and metamemory (see Butters, 1984; Corkin, 1982; Huppert and Tym, 1986; Martin and Fedio, 1983; Morris and Kopelman, 1986). Also, recent findings demonstrate that patients with mild to moderate Alzheimer's disease exhibit impairment on the same priming tests on which amnesic patients have been known to perform normally (Salmon et al., 1988; Shimamura et al., 1987). The status of skill learning in Alzheimer's disease is somewhat mixed. One report indicated preserved learning on the pursuit-rotor task (Eslinger and Damasio, 1986), whereas another report indicated impaired learning on the mirror reading task (Groeber, 1985).

TABLE 1

Neuropsychological profile of cognitive impairment in amnesic patients, patients with frontal lobe damage, and patients with Alzheimer's disease

Cognitive function	H.M.	Anoxia/ ischemia	Encephalitis	ECT	Korsakoff's syndrome	Frontal lobe damage	Alzheimer's disease
I.Q.	+	+	+	+	+	+ / −	−
Language	+	+	+	+	+	+ / −	−
New learning	−	−	−	−	−	+	−
Premorbid memory	−	−	−	−	−	?	−
Short-term memory	+	+	+	+	+ / −	+ / −	−
Perceptual/motor skills	+	+	+	+	+	?	+ / −
Priming	+	+	+	+	+	?	−
Encoding	+	+	+	+	−	−	−
Contextual memory	−	−	−	−	− *	−	?
Metamemory	?	+	?	+	− *	−	−

+, unimpaired; −, impaired; + / −, findings are mixed or some aspects impaired; − *, function disproportionately impaired compared with other patients; ?, status of function not known.

Comparisons between patients with Alzheimer's disease and patients with amnesia highlight the rather selective disorder of memory observed in patients with amnesia.

Theoretical descriptions of amnesia

In this section, various cognitive theories and models of amnesia are evaluated. None of the theoretical descriptions provides a full account of amnesia. Some descriptions focus on particular aspects of memory dysfunction, whereas others suggest different forms of memory impairment. Perhaps the best way to view theoretical descriptions is to follow Baddeley's position: "I regard models as tools, useful fictions that summarize what one already knows in ways that make it easier to ask sensible further questions" (Baddeley, 1982a, p. 306).

Consolidation theory

Consolidation theory views amnesia as a deficit in *storing* recently acquired information (see Milner, 1966; Muller and Pilzecker, 1900; Squire, 1987). It was the initial theoretical description used to explain the memory impairment of H.M. (Milner, 1966), and it was widely popular during the 1960s and 1970s as a way to provide a neurological basis for the distinction between short-term and long-term memory (see Atkinson and Shiffrin, 1968; Crowder, 1976; Klatzky, 1975). Evidence for the consolidation theory was based on the finding that H.M. could exhibit intact language skills and short-term memory, but could not learn and remember events, episodes or facts which had occurred since the onset of amnesia. Thus, it was suggested that H.M., as well as other amnesic patients, could not transfer or consolidate information from short-term to long-term memory. Consolidation theory has been popular in neurobiological descriptions of memory (see, Gerard, 1955; Hebb, 1949; McGaugh and Herz, 1972). It explains memory as a storage process that either creates new synaptic connections or restructures previously existing ones.

The consolidation theory, as it was initially described, cannot completely account for the findings from human amnesia. First, the theory views amnesia as a storage deficit, and thus it cannot easily account for retrograde amnesia, because premorbid memories are presumed to have been already stored or consolidated. Second, the theory does not account for examples of intact new learning, such as intact learning of perceptual-motor skills. Third, an impaired consolidation process suggests rapid forgetting in amnesia, but this is not always the case. It was originally reported that H.M. did exhibit rapid forgetting (Huppert and Piercy, 1979, Experiment 1), yet subsequent experiments did not replicate this finding (Freed et al., 1987). Patients undergoing ECT exhibit rapid rates of forgetting (Squire, 1981), yet patients with Korsakoff's syndrome do not (Huppert and Piercy, 1978; Squire, 1981). Finally, the theory does not account for the particular impairment of encoding processes and spatial/temporal context memory observed in some amnesic patients.

Squire et al. (1984) proposed a more specific consolidation theory that attempts to solve some of the problems associated with the earlier theory (see also Wickelgren, 1979). Squire et al. (1984) suggest that the time course of consolidation is much more gradual, lasting for months or even several years for some types of information. Consolidation involves the reactivation, elaboration or rehearsal of newly learned information so that the information can be established in a long-lasting way. The gradual nature of the consolidation process can account for temporally limited retrograde amnesia. For example, if the time of consolidation process is extensive, then some memories acquired during the months or several years before the onset of amnesia may not have been fully consolidated. From this viewpoint, retrograde amnesia could be explained by a deficit in consolidating premorbid memories.

Squire et al. (1984) also specify that the consolidation process depends on the interaction of the medial temporal region with neocortex. In addition, they suggest that the interaction between the medial temporal region and neocortex occurs only for certain kinds of knowledge. Because this consolidation theory is specific to amnesia caused by damage to the medial temporal region (e.g., H.M., R.B.), it is not relevant to the finding of extensive retrograde amnesia that is often seen in patients with Korsakoff's syndrome; nor is it relevant to impairments of encoding processes and spatial/temporal memory often seen in these patients. Finally, because the consolidation process only occurs for certain kinds of knowledge (i.e., *declarative* knowledge, see below), it is compatible with findings of preserved perceptual-motor skills.

The consolidation theory best explains the impairment observed in patients with selective loss of new learning ability (i.e., anterograde amnesia). The theory defines a process that depends on the medial temporal lobe and that is particularly involved in storing the products of cognitive processing (see Squire, 1987). The two amnesic patients with damage that is known to be restricted to the medial temporal region (patients H.M. and R.B.) provide the best evidence for the consolidation theory as an explanation of amnesia. Yet one practical limitation of the theory is the fact that neuropathological information from well-studied amnesic patients is rare and thus it is generally not known whether patients exhibit selective medial temporal damage. Perhaps the theory can be tested best by investigations of nonhuman primate models of amnesia and by neural system analyses of the medial temporal lobe (see Lynch, 1986; Mishkin, 1982; Squire and Zola-Morgan, 1983). That is, it is critical to determine whether the neural architecture and physiological properties of the medial temporal lobe can act as a storage mechanism. Recently, several investigators have postulated ways in which the medial temporal lobe could function as a storage mechanism (see McNaughton and Morris, 1987; Rolls, in press; Squire et al., in press; Teyler and DiSenna, 1986).

Encoding theory and other processing theories
Craik and Lockhart (1972) proposed a theoretical framework of memory which suggested that the level or depth of semantic processing during learning determined the degree of memory retention. This view shifted attention away from structural descriptions of memory (e.g., short-term vs. long-term memory) to descriptions about the way information is used or processed. As mentioned earlier, the general finding from normal subjects was that material encoded in a meaningful way was remembered better than material encoded only visually or phonetically. Based on this 'levels-of-processing' framework, it was suggested by Cermak (1979, 1986) that the memory deficit in patients with Korsakoff's syndrome was at least partly due to a deficit in encoding or processing information. As mentioned earlier, these patients often fail to benefit from semantic encoding strategies. An impairment of semantic encoding can also be used to explain other deficits exhibited by patients with Korsakoff's syndrome, such as deficits in short-term memory (e.g., Cermak and Butters, 1972) and the failure to release from proactive interference (Cermak et al., 1974; Squire, 1982a).

An impairment of encoding is certainly a feature of the neuropsychological profile of Korsakoff's syndrome. However, it is important to note that encoding deficits typically are not seen in amnesic patients with other etiologies (Cermak, 1976; Squire, 1982a). In fact, severe amnesia can occur without any detectable deficit in encoding (e.g., patient H.M.). Moreover, some encoding deficits (e.g., short-term memory impairment, levels of processing impairment) are not always seen in patients with Korsakoff's syndrome (Squire, 1982a). Thus, a deficit in encoding is not sufficient to account for the amnesic syndrome, nor is it sufficient to account for all the memory deficits seen in patients with Korsakoff's syndrome. For example, encoding deficits cannot easily explain why patients with Korsakoff's syndrome exhibit impairment on tests of remote memory, memory for spatial/temporal context, and metamemory.

Encoding theory, however, can be used to address several important issues about amnesia. First, to establish a deficit in *encoding,* as opposed to a deficit in *memory,* patients should exhibit impairment on tasks that tap information acquisition, not just memory. In other words, questions about the ability of amnesic patients to perform on tests of on-line cognitive processing (e.g., stimulus registration or stimulus manipulation) need to be addressed in order to distinguish an encoding deficit from a storage deficit. That is why findings of impaired immediate memory are critical for support of an encoding theory. The possibility of an encoding deficit in amnesia forces the researcher to investigate aspects of cognition other than memory — aspects such as selective attention, access to semantic memory and problem solving. Some of these aspects have already been studied (e.g., Oscar-Berman, 1980; Cermak et al., 1978; Janowsky et al., in press), but further investigations may help to elucidate more precisely the encoding deficit that is present in at least some amnesic patients.

Another important issue for an encoding theory of amnesia is to determine the extent to which encoding deficits contribute to anterograde amnesia. Is the severity of encoding deficits related directly to the severity of anterograde amnesia, or can these two deficits be dissociated from one another? Such questions may be addressed by correlating performance on tests of encoding with performance on tests of anterograde amnesia. Also, it may be possible to evaluate memory performance of patients with attention disorders. For example, patients with circumscribed frontal lobe lesions exhibit impairment on tests of attention and problem solving, and recent findings (Janowsky et al., 1989; in press) suggest that they share some of the deficits observed in patients with Korsakoff's syndrome (e.g., deficits in initiation, metamemory). Yet patients with frontal damage do not exhibit amnesia. Further studies of patients with frontal lobe damage and other patient groups with encoding deficits may help to determine the ways in which encoding deficits affect memory performance.

Other processing theories of amnesia suggest that the impairment includes a broader array of processing deficits than just encoding impairment. For example, Jacoby (Jacoby, 1983; Jacoby and Witherspoon, 1982) suggested that amnesia produces a deficit in 'deliberate remembering' or 'memory with awareness.' What is preserved in amnesia is a 'perceptual fluency' for recently acquired information; and what is impaired is the acquisition of nonperceptual (e.g., semantic) information. Another way to characterize this distinction is to contrast 'data-driven' processes from 'conceptually driven' ones (Jacoby, 1983; Roediger and Blaxton, 1987). Based on this view, amnesic patients can exhibit a normal perceptual enhancement from stimulus presentation. What is impaired is the ability to gain awareness about the acquired information. This description of amnesia incorporates some of the tenets of the 'levels-of-processing' encoding view of amnesia, but it broadens the deficit to include retrieval processes as well (i.e., deliberate remembering).

The explanation of amnesia as a sparing of data-driven processes and a deficit of conceptually driven ones captures many aspects of the cognitive impairment seen in amnesic patients. First, the description emphasizes an impairment of deliberate or conscious remembering as a critical part of the amnesic syndrome. Second, the findings of preserved perceptual fluency on tests of perceptual-motor skills and perceptual priming conform nicely with this view of amnesia. Some inconsistencies, however, are apparent. For example, some semantic (i.e., conceptually driven) modes of memory are entirely preserved in amnesia: amnesic patients exhibit normal priming of words when they are cued by semantically related words that were never presented during study (Graf et al., 1985, Experiment 2; Shimamura and Squire, 1984). Also, if amnesic patients exhibit spared perceptual fluency, but impaired semantic processing, then patients should exhibit modality-specific priming but little cross-modality priming. Yet amnesic patients can exhibit normal word comple-tion priming of words when the words are pre-sented in the auditory mode but tested in the visual mode (Graf et al., 1985, Experiment 1).

Another processing theory by Johnson (1983) distinguishes between three processing modes: sen-sory, perceptual and reflective modes. Similar to the view of Jacoby, Johnson (1983) suggests that sensory and perceptual processes are spared in amnesia, but reflective processes are impaired. Reflective processes refer to such processes as "planning, creating images, organizing, elabor-ating, and rehearsing" (p. 86, Johnson, 1983). Also, Johnson (1983, p. 86) states: "The reflection system helps us to find relationships between new information and old knowledge so that we can comprehend and draw inferences." Tests of free recall are supposed to depend heavily on reflective processes, tests of recognition memory are suppos-ed to tap both reflective and perceptual processes, and tests of perceptual-motor skill learning are thought to depend on sensory processes.

A deficit in reflective processes may be too broad a term to use as a theoretical description of amnesia. Amnesic patients can exhibit a wide array of preserved reflective processes: they can form plans and make inferences, they can create images, and they can organize their thoughts (see Janowsky et al., in press; Shimamura and Squire, 1986). All of these on-line reflective processes are intact. The problem is that amnesic patients fail to *store* the products of cognitive processing. A deficit in reflective processes may help to explain the additional cognitive deficits observed in pa-tients with Korsakoff's syndrome but not in other amnesic patients. For example, it could account for the poor performance by patients with Kor-sakoff's syndrome on tests of attention, encoding, free recall, metamemory and problem solving (see Butters and Cermak, 1980; Janowsky et al., 1989; in press; Oscar-Berman, 1980; Shimamura and Squire, 1986; Squire, 1982; Talland, 1965).

In summary, the argument for a processing theory – in contrast to a structural theory – is often a matter of emphasis or heuristics. In many cases, a processing theory does not necessarily preclude a structural one. For example, a struc-tural theory becomes a processing theory when it describes the *processes* by which information is stored or consolidated. A processing theory becomes a structural theory when it describes the way amnesia affects memory *storage*. Thus, in order to adhere strictly to a processing theory of amnesia, one must argue that the critical feature of amnesia is a deficit in on-line processing (e.g., en-coding processes or reflective processes). The most appropriate way to test such processing theories is to assess processing when memory, per se, is *not* required for performance. At present there is little evidence that any processing (*sans* memory) deficit generally occurs in amnesia.

Contextual memory theories

Contextual memory theories specify that the deficit in amnesia is a particular dysfunction of spatial/temporal memory (Huppert and Piercy, 1976; for review see Mayes et al., 1985). Amnesia is viewed as a specific deficit in contextual memory that also prevents efficient learning and remember-ing of other kinds of memory, including fact memory. That is, a general amnesic disorder is thought to be a consequence of impaired memory for spatial and/or temporal information. Findings of disproportionate impairment of recency judgments and source memory, as well as findings of preserved memory for some 'context-free' in-formation (e.g., skill learning), suggest a particular impairment of contextual memory in amnesia. In addition, findings from animal models of memory have led some researchers to suggest that the hip-pocampus may be related specifically to spatial memory (O'Keefe and Nadel, 1978) or to temporal memory (Rawlins, 1985).

As mentioned previously, another contextual memory theory suggests that amnesia causes a par-ticular deficit in episodic memory but leaves semantic memory intact (Cermak, 1984; Kins-bourne and Wood, 1975; for review see Schacter and Tulving, 1982b). The episodic – semantic distinction was originally developed by Tulving

(1972, 1983) as a way to characterize two general forms of human memory. Episodic memory is 'a system that receives and stores information about temporally dated episodes or events, and temporal-spatial relations among them' (p. 21, Tulving, 1983). Semantic memory is general knowledge that is important for language, comprehension, and fact memory: 'it is a mental thesaurus' (p. 21, Tulving, 1983). An important feature of episodic memory, and one that distinguishes it from semantic memory, is the autobiographical or personal quality of episodic memory. For episodic memories one can identify a personal time and place associated with a memory (e.g., 'I remember eating donuts this morning at the cafeteria'). It is the autobiographical or episodic nature of memory that some have suggested is impaired in amnesia. This aspect of the amnesic disorder is similar to that described by Claparede (1911/1951), who suggested that amnesic patients exhibit a deficit in feelings of familiarity or 'me-ness' (translated from *moiité*).

Some of the evidence that has been used to argue in favor of the semantic/episodic distinction is not well-founded. For example, some researchers have used the finding of preserved premorbid language and generic knowledge as evidence for preserved semantic memory in amnesia; yet these findings confound the semantic nature of the memory with the fact that such memories were acquired before the onset of amnesia and were also highly over-learned. Amnesic patients do exhibit retrograde amnesia on tests of public events (i.e., premorbid semantic memory) (Albert et al., 1979; Cohen and Squire, 1981), which is often comparable to their retrograde amnesia for autobiographical events (Butters, 1985; Zola-Morgan et al., 1983). Also, amnesic patients exhibit anterograde amnesia for some 'context-free' semantic information, such as learning new vocabulary words or new facts (Gabrieli et al., 1983; Ostergaard, 1987; Shimamura and Squire, 1987). Finally, evidence from priming studies has been used to argue for a preserved semantic memory system; yet it should be noted that the phenomenon of priming is broader and in-

cludes priming of perceptual memory in addition to semantic memory (see Graf et al., 1985).

Perhaps evidence from studies of disproportionate spatial/temporal memory impairment provides the strongest evidence for a distinction between episodic and semantic memory (or between context and fact memory). For example, some amnesic patients fail to remember where or when a fact was learned (i.e., source amnesia), though they can sometimes remember the fact itself (Schacter et al., 1984; Shimamura and Squire, 1987). Also, patients with Korsakoff's syndrome exhibit disproportionately impaired temporal order memory (Huppert and Piercy, 1976; Meudell et al., 1985; Squire, 1982). Yet is it important to note that not all amnesic patients exhibit source amnesia or disproportionate impairment of temporal order memory. Thus, it is difficult to explain all amnesia solely in terms of a deficit of episodic or contextual memory. Interestingly, spatial/temporal memory has been linked to frontal lobe dysfunction (Milner, 1971; Schacter et al., 1984; Squire, 1982). Finally, if amnesia is explained as a selective deficit in episodic memory, then one must argue that findings of impaired performance on tests of semantic memory are the result of episodic memory impairment (see Cermak, 1984). But if semantic memory always occurs as a consequence of episodic, then the distinction cannot be easily evaluated empirically (for discussion, see McKoon et al., 1986; Ostergaard, 1987; Shimamura and Squire, 1987).

Rather than viewing amnesia as a selective deficit in episodic or contextual memory, it may be more appropriate to consider the deficit as a contributing factor in at least some amnesic patients (Huppert and Piercy, 1976; Schacter et al., 1984; Shimamura and Squire, 1987). That is, some but not all amnesic patients exhibit a *disproportionate* deficit in episodic memory, and this deficit could contribute to impairment on many tests of memory. For example, failure to store contextual information during a learning session could affect subsequent performance on tests of new learning. Furthermore, failure to use contextual cues as a retrieval strategy could cause retrograde amnesia. Nevertheless, the amnesic deficit appears to include semantic memory itself, based on the finding of impaired retrograde and anterograde amnesia of semantic memory and on the finding that comparable deficits of semantic and episodic memory can be demonstrated in some amnesic patients. In other words, not all amnesic patients exhibit a disproportionate deficit of episodic or contextual memory. Consequently, there may be multiple forms of memory impairment.

Retrieval theories

Retrieval theories maintain that amnesia does *not* impair the encoding or storing of information but instead causes an impairment in the ability to recollect information. That is, it is presumed that amnesic patients can encode and consolidate information in a normal fashion but cannot initiate appropriate retrieval processes. General retrieval theories predict that the retrieval of premorbid memories should be just as impaired as the retrieval of memories learned since the onset of amnesia. Perhaps the strongest argument against such theories is the finding that severe anterograde amnesia can occur in the presence of relatively preserved premorbid memories. For example, H.M., who exhibits severe anterograde amnesia, did not exhibit severe impairment on tests of premorbid memories (Marslen-Wilson and Teuber, 1975). Also, amnesic patient R.B., who had bilateral lesions restricted to the hippocampus, did not exhibit any detectable impairment of premorbid memory (Zola-Morgan et al., 1986).

Other findings also suggest that a deficit in retrieval cannot completely account for the amnesic syndrome. First, the severity of retrograde amnesia is rather variable in patients and can be influenced by such factors as premorbid I.Q., the extent of brain injury, or the extent of intellectual decline. Second, the severity of retrograde amnesia is not always correlated with the severity of anterograde amnesia. For example, patients with Korsakoff's syndrome exhibit rather extensive remote memory impairment, but the severity of

anterograde amnesia was not correlated with the severity of amnesia for very remote memories, such as memory for information dating back 20 – 30 years before the onset of amnesia (Shimamura and Squire, 1986b). These findings suggest that impairment of retrieval processes may not be sufficient to account for the rather debilitating deficit of memory for information that occurred after the onset of amnesia. Although retrieval deficits may not completely account for the amnesic syndrome, they may contribute to the rather extensive retrograde amnesia observed in some amnesic patients (e.g., patients with Korsakoff's syndrome), as well as in patients with dementia (e.g., patients with Alzheimer's disease).

One particular retrieval view that has been studied rather rigorously is the 'disinhibition' hypothesis (Warrington and Weiskrantz, 1970, 1974, 1978). In this view, amnesia is caused by an inability to inhibit or suppress inappropriate responses. In other words, amnesic patients are particularly sensitive to proactive interference, which interferes with retrieval. Several findings by Warrington and Weiskrantz were used in support of the disinhibition hypothesis. First, amnesic patients appeared to be disproportionately benefitted by cued recall tests compared to recognition memory tests (Warrington and Weiskrantz, 1970). It was thought that cued recall tests better restrict the number of possible alternatives and thus reduce proactive interference. Second, amnesic patients tended to exhibit more interference from prior list learning than control subjects (Warrington and Weiskrantz, 1974). Third, amnesic patients tended to exhibit poor memory on cued recall tests in which the cues had a larger number of possible alternative responses (Warrington and Weiskrantz, 1974).

However, further studies failed to support the disinhibition hypothesis. As mentioned earlier, the disproportionate benefit of cued recall tests over recognition tests was not repeatable (Mayes et al., 1978; Mortensen, 1980; Squire et al., 1978; Warrington and Weiskrantz, 1968) or was primarily due to priming effects (Graf et al., 1984; for further discussion, see Shimamura, 1986). Warrington and Weiskrantz (1978) themselves rejected the disinhibition hypothesis on the grounds that amnesic patients were not particularly sensitive to manipulations of response competition. For example, cued recall performance by amnesic patients was not always predicted by the number of interfering response alternatives (Warrington and Weiskrantz, 1978). Also, cued recall performance by amnesic patients on multiple study/test learning trials was not impaired as much as expected (see Warrington and Weiskrantz, 1978).

Consequently, retrieval theories do not provide a complete explanation of the amnesic syndrome. Interestingly, heightened levels of proactive interference (i.e., disinhibition) have been used to explain *both* retrieval and encoding deficits. One possibility is that an inability to suppress competing responses impairs both learning and retrieval. Response competition could affect attentional and other encoding functions that contribute to new learning ability. From this viewpoint, anterograde memory should be particularly impaired because increased interference occurred at the time of study and at the time of retrieval. One way to test this viewpoint is to determine whether encoding deficits are correlated with retrieval failures. Perhaps this broader version of the disinhibition hypothesis can help account for the additional cognitive impairment observed in patients with Korsakoff's syndrome. Such patients exhibit greater attentional and encoding deficits as well as greater remote memory impairment than is seen in other amnesic patients. The finding of frontal lobe damage in patients with Korsakoff's syndrome (Shimamura et al., 1988) and the finding that some of the additional impairment is correlated with tests of frontal lobe dysfunction (Janowsky et al., in press; Squire, 1982a) suggest the possibility that disinhibition is caused by damage to frontal lobes.

Multiple forms of memory
Evidence of preserved memory functions (e.g., skill learning, priming, classical conditioning) in

amnesia has led to a growing consensus that some forms of long-term memory can be entirely dissociated from the forms of memory that are affected in amnesia. The term 'forms' is meant to characterize both the structures and the processes underlying memory functions. Various dichotomies have been used to distinguish the memory forms that are preserved in amnesia from those that are affected. In general, these characterizations share many aspects in common. In particular, it is thought that amnesic patients cannot explicitly or consciously recollect information learned since the onset of amnesia. The term 'conscious' recollection is often used to describe the form of memory that is impaired in amnesia (Baddeley, 1982b; Moscovitch, 1982; Squire, 1987). The impairment is often thought to affect the ability to store and also to retrieve newly learned information. Amnesic patients, however, can often perform in a normal fashion on certain 'indirect' tests of memory − tests not requiring conscious recollection of past learning sessions (see Richardson-Klavehn and Bjork, 1988; Schacter, 1987a; Shimamura, 1986). For example, skill learning and priming can be demonstrated without subjects even knowing that their memory is being tested. On indirect or implicit tests, subjects are simply asked to perform tasks, such as read mirror-reversed words, work at puzzles, complete word stems, identify degraded pictures, or make preference judgments. Target items appear simply to pop into mind.

One often cited description of memory that incorporates the conscious versus nonconscious distinction is the view that amnesia impairs *declarative* memory and spares *procedural* memory (Cohen, 1984; Cohen and Squire, 1980; Squire, 1982b, 1987). This distinction was first applied in memory models from cognitive science (see Anderson, 1976). The distinction is also similar to earlier views that distinguished between *knowing how* and *knowing that* (Ryle, 1949) or *memory without record* and *memory with record* (Bruner, 1969). Cohen and Squire (1980) applied the distinction to characterize amnesia. Declarative memory is available to conscious awareness and includes facts and episodes of everyday experiences. Procedural memory is implicit and is available only by engaging the specific operations in which the memory is embedded. The ability to acquire or consolidate new declarative memory depends on the integrity of the medial temporal and diencephalic brain areas. In particular, it is suggested that the circuitry of the hippocampus and its associated input and output connections are critical for the establishment of long-term, declarative memory (see Squire et al., 1984; in press). More recently, it has been acknowledged that various preserved forms of memory (e.g. priming) may not be the same as those that have been traditionally described as procedural or skill-like. Because little is known about the relationship between forms of memory that are preserved in amnesia, a more conservative distinction has been made between *declarative* and *nondeclarative* forms of memory (Squire and Zola-Morgan, 1988).

Other terms have been used to distinguish between forms of memory that are preserved in amnesia and those that are impaired. Some distinctions that relate to both human and nonhuman findings are those between *habit* and *memory* (Mishkin et al., 1984), *horizontal* and *vertical* associations (Wickelgren, 1979), and *dispositional* and *propositional* memory (Thomas, 1984). Like the procedural (nondeclarative)/declarative distinction, these descriptions suggest that the medial temporal region is critical for some forms of memory but not for others. In cognitive science, distinctions have been made between a form of memory described as *automatic, semantic, skill-like* and *integrative* on the one hand, and a form described as *conscious, mediational* and *elaborative* on the other.

Warrington and Weiskrantz (1982) developed a similar but slightly different distinction. Although they view amnesia as affecting only some forms of memory, they propose that amnesia may be best viewed as a disconnection syndrome that severs communication between the temporal and frontal lobes. The temporal lobes are thought to subserve semantic memory functions, such as verbal knowledge and object recognition. The frontal lobes are thought to engage in cognitive mediation, which includes processes such as elaboration, imagery and organization. Skills and priming are considered to be operations that can occur without the cognitive mediational (frontal lobe) system, whereas explicit recall and recognition are considered to require the interactions between the cognitive mediational and semantic systems. It is not clear if this approach makes any different predictions about the behavioral consequences of amnesia than the other descriptions mentioned above. The theory, however, does make specific predictions about the neuroanatomy of memory.

Graf and Schacter (1985; see also Schacter, 1987a) have used the term *implicit* and *explicit* memory. Implicit memory refers to memory without conscious recollection of the learning session in which the memory was established, whereas explicit memory requires conscious recollection. Implicit and explicit memory are terms that are meant to be strictly atheoretical or theoretically neutral. That is, they are meant to describe the state of the organism at the time of retrieval and are not meant to be related to any specific cognitive or neurobiological theory. These terms are useful for describing the quality of memory retrieval following various memory tasks. The characterization of implicit memory and how it differs from explicit memory is currently under extensive study in both cognitive and neuropsychological investigations (see Schacter, 1987a; Schacter and Graf, 1987; Shimamura and Squire, 1988).

An orientation towards multiple forms of memory (and of multiple forms of memory disorders) may help untangle the many facts and findings from studies of amnesia. For example, it may be possible to distinguish between forms of memory associated with diencephalic regions and those associated with medial temporal regions. Furthermore, there may be forms of memory that are particularly affected by frontal lobe dysfunction. Thus, the status of frontal lobe functions in amnesic patients will be important for theoretical descriptions about the organization of memory.

Moreover, findings from patients with circumscribed frontal lobe lesions may help identify processes and memory forms that depend specifically on the frontal lobes; for example, encoding and spatial/temporal processes or forms of memory that depend on cognitive mediation.

Computational models of memory and amnesia
It should be noted that all of the descriptions mentioned above are heuristic: that is, they are used to interpret a large body of experimental results and to provide a useful framework for generating further research. None of these descriptions provides enough detail to be able to predict in advance which memory tasks will show spared learning in amnesia and which tasks will show impairment. Although such verbal descriptions may provide a taxonomy of memory and may help guide research, they typically lack the precision necessary for a complete understanding of the brain systems and processes that are affected in amnesia. Recent advances in the development of computational models have marked a new interchange between brain and cognitive scientists. One reason for this recent cooperation is a convergence in a modeling style called *connectionism* or *parallel distributed processing* (see Anderson and Hinton, 1981; Ballard, 1986; Byrne and Berry, in press; Rumelhart and McClelland, 1986). Connectionistic models have adopted principles of neuronal behavior as basic building blocks. Thus, computations are based on the pattern of activation across a matrix of neuron-like units, with the level of activation in each unit dependent on the degree of excitation and inhibition received from input units. Key factors in this kind of modeling are that units are activated in parallel and that information flow and storage are distributed across a matrix of units.

Connectionistic models may provide a useful link between behavior and the neural systems that subserve behavior. Several models have been proposed that attempt to simulate plasticity in known neural architectures, such as olfactory cortex (Lynch and Granger, in press) and hippocampus

(see McNaughton and Morris, 1987; Rolls, in press). Other connectionistic models of memory have been proposed to simulate cognitive behavior, such as learning and recognition (see Anderson and Hinton, 1981; Rumelhart and McClelland, 1986). The advantage of such models is that assumptions about memory processes are made explicitly. Also, computational models can be tested to determine how well they conform to actual data and actual neural substrates.

In terms of neuropsychological issues, it may be possible to simulate memory disorders by disrupting various functions of a computational model. In fact, an attempt has been made to model findings from amnesia (McClelland and Rumelhart, 1986). In this model, a single hypothetical mechanism was employed as a way to account for anterograde amnesia, temporally limited retrograde amnesia, and the relative sparing of some forms of skill learning. The mechanism incorporated the basic characteristics of the consolidation theory proposed by Squire et al. (1984). That is, a mechanism was formalized that strengthened new memory traces gradually across time. The interesting characteristic of the model was that both anterograde amnesia and temporally limited retrograde amnesia were exhibited by introducing a 'deficit' in the hypothetical consolidation mechanism. No additional deficit in retrieval was required to explain retrograde amnesia. Although this model was not based on known neural circuitry nor on known biochemistry, it has stimulated interactions between cognitive scientists and neuroscientists. Further developments in this and other computational models of amnesia could improve our understanding of memory at the neural systems level as well as at the behavioral level.

Conclusions

As indicated by the research represented in this review, significant progress has been achieved by the interchange between cognitive science and neuropsychology. This progress is reflected in an increase in our understanding of amnesia as well as an increase in our understanding of the organization of normal memory functions. The two fields strengthen one another: clinical observations and intuitions provide clues about memory dysfunction, whereas cognitive studies of specific memory processes in both normal and impaired subjects help to corroborate clinical observations. It is also extremely important to characterize memory at the neural level. A complete understanding of memory functions cannot be achieved without basic neuroscience research, from studies of cellular mechanisms to systems analyses (see Amaral, 1987; Kandel and Schwartz, 1982; Lynch, 1986; Mishkin, 1982). Further developments in behavioral analyses of amnesia and in computational models are already apparent on the horizon. In fact, there is evidence of a still accelerating interest in the relationship between cognition and brain functions as indicated by the inception of such fields as *cognitive neuropsychology* and *cognitive neuroscience* (for review, see Churchland, 1987; Delis and Ober, 1986; Squire, 1987).

Many unanswered questions still remain about memory and amnesia, and several new directions may help resolve some of these issues. First, further research is needed to identify more clearly the boundary conditions of preserved memory in amnesia. What kinds of cognitive skills are preserved in amnesia? Can entirely preserved long-lasting priming effects be demonstrated in patients? Also, can entirely preserved priming of new associations occur in patients? Is there a relationship between skill learning and priming effects?

Another important issue is the identification of different subtypes of amnesia. As reviewed here, there is ample evidence to suggest that Korsakoff's syndrome produces a pattern of amnesia different from that seen in other patients with amnesia. Are there other subtypes of amnesia? One type of amnesia that has not been well studied is the memory disorder associated with basal forebrain damage (e.g., amnesia following rupture and repair of the anterior communicating artery). Issues of subtypes can be addressed only by careful empirical investigations of two or more etiological groups within the same experiment. One of the problems of previous investigations is that for practical reasons many studies tended to use only one etiological group (typically Korsakoff's syndrome) or tended to use a mixed group of patients (which would sometimes include patients with more widespread pathology, such as patients with Alzheimer's disease or head injury). A comparative approach to the study of patients with relatively circumscribed memory impairment may help to resolve some of the inconsistent or equivocal findings within the field (e.g., the status of spatial/temporal memory or encoding in patients).

The advent of newly developed in vivo imaging techniques, such as magnetic resonance imaging (MRI) and positron emission tomography (PET), will certainly increase our knowledge of the relationship between functional impairment and structural damage in brain-injured patients (see Andreason, 1988; Petersen et al., 1988). Although important findings have been established using computed tomography (see Jacobson and Lishman, 1987; Shimamura et al., 1988), the finer resolution of MRI may provide a clearer view of the brain areas damaged in amnesia. PET scans, as well as cortical blood flow measures, could help in detecting physiological defects in amnesia, such as hyperactivity in certain subcortical and cortical areas. The hope is that physiological and structural changes could be detected in amnesic patients and then correlated with memory impairment.

Finally, it is hoped that a better understanding of memory and amnesia will facilitate efforts of rehabilitation. As Wilson (1987) has indicated, it is important to assess the relationship between performance on laboratory tests of memory and performance on everyday memory applications and usages. Further studies are needed to assess practical aspects of memory in amnesia (for discussion, see Baddeley, 1986; Gruneberg et al., 1988; Wilson, 1987). As this review has indicated, there are aspects of memory that are preserved, even in severely amnesic patients. It may be possible to facilitate memory in patients by focusing on preserved functions (e.g., see Glisky et al., 1986a, b). Also, it may be possible to extend methods of memory rehabilitation to patients with dementia from Alzheimer's disease or Huntington's disease. Although it is acknowledged that rehabilitation of memory in severely impaired patients cannot be completely successful, it may be possible to provide the patient with some coping skills. Also, it may be possible to develop external (e.g., computerized) aids that could reduce the demand on one's own memory. The use and practicality of external mnemonic aids has not be well studied. Such aids may be most helpful for mild or moderate disorders of memory. With the increase in the mean age of the general population, such aids may be useful not only for neuropsychological patients but also for aging neuropsychological researchers and practitioners as well.

Acknowledgements

This work was supported by the Medical Research Service of the Veterans Administration, by National Institute of Mental Health Grant MH24600, and by the Office of Naval Research.

References

Albert MS, Butters N, Levin J: Temporal gradients in the retrograde amnesia of patients with alcoholic Korsakoff's disease. *Arch. Neurol.: 36,* 211–216, 1979.

Amaral DJ: Memory: the anatomical organization of cadidate brain regions. In Mountcastle V, Plum F (Editor), *Handbook of Physiology: Higher Functions of the Nervous System.* Bethesda, MD: American Physiological Society, 1987.

Anderson JA, Hinton GE (Editors): *Parallel Models of Associative Memory.* Hillsdale, NJ: Erlbaum, 1981.

Anderson JR: *Language, Memory and Thought.* Hillsdale, NJ: Erlbaum, 1976.

Anderson JR: *Cognitive Psychology and its Implications.* San Francisco, CA: Freeman, 1980.

Anderson JR, Bower GH: *Human Associative Memory,* Washington, DC: Winston, 1973.

Andreason NC: Brain imaging: applications in psychiatry. *Science: 239,* 1381–1388, 1988.

Atkinson RC, Shiffrin RM: Human memory: a proposed system and its control process. In Spence KW, Spence JT (Editors), *The Psychology of Learning and Motivation, Vol. 2.* New York: Academic Press, 1968.

Aubel PM, Franks JJ: Effort toward comprehension: elabora-tion or 'aha'? *Memory Cognition: 7,* 426–434, 1979.

Baddeley AD: Amnesia: a minimal model and an interpretation. In Cermak LS (Editor), *Human Memory and Amnesia.* Hillsdale, NJ: Erlbaum, pp. 305–336, 1982a.

Baddeley AD: Domains of recollection. *Psychol. Rev.: 89,* 708–729, 1982b.

Baddeley AD: *Working Memory.* Oxford: Oxford University Press, 1986.

Baddeley AD, Warrington EK: Amnesia and the distinction between long- and short-term memory. *J. Verbal Learn. Verbal Behav.: 9,* 176–189, 1970.

Baddeley AD, Wilson BA: Amnesia, autobiographical memory and confabulation. In Rubin DC (Editor), *Autobiographical Memory.* Cambridge, MA: Cambridge University Press, pp. 225–252, 1986.

Ballard DH: Cortical connections and parallel processing: structure and function. *Behav. Brain Sci.: 9,* 67–120, 1986.

Benzing WC, Squire LR: Preserved learning and memory in amnesia: intact adaption-level effects and learning of stereoscopic depth. *Behav. Neurosci.:* in press.

Broadbent DE: *Perception and Communication.* London: Pergamon Press, 1958.

Broadbent DE, Weiskrantz L (Editors): *The Neuropsychology of Cognitive Function.* London: The Royal Society, 1982.

Brooks DN, Baddeley AD: What can amnesic patients learn? *Neuropsychologia: 14,* 111–122, 1976.

Brown J: Some tests of decay theory of immediate memory. *Q. J. Exp. Psychol.: 10,* 12–21, 1958.

Bruner JS: Modalities of memory. In Talland GA, Waugh NC (Editors), *The Pathology of Memory.* New York: Academic Press, pp. 253–259, 1969.

Butters N: Alcoholic Korsakoff's syndrome: an update. *Semin. Neurol.: 4,* 226–244, 1984.

Butters N: Alcoholic Korsakoff's syndrome: some unresolved issues concerning etiology neuropathology and cognitive deficits. *J. Clin. Exp. Neuropsychol.: 7,* 181–210, 1985.

Butters N, Cermak L: Some comments on Warrington and Baddeley's report of normal short-term memory in amnesic patients. *Neuropsychologia: 12,* 283–285, 1974.

Butters N, Cermak LS: *Alcoholic Korsakoff's Syndrome: An Information Processing Approach.* New York: Academic Press, 1980.

Butters N, Cermak LS: A case study of the forgetting of autobiographical knowledge: implications for the study of retrograde amnesia. In Rubin DC (Editor), *Autobiographical Memory.* Cambridge, MA: Cambridge, University Press, pp. 253–289, 1986.

Butters N, Grady M: Effect of predistractor delays on the short-term memory performance of patients with Korsakoff's and Huntington's disease. *Neuropsychologia: 15,* 701–706, 1977.

Butters N, Wolfe J, Martone M, Granholm E, Cermak LS: Memory disorders associated with Huntington's disease: verbal recall verbal recognition and procedural memory. *Neuropsychologia: 23,* 729–743, 1985.

Byrne J, Berry W (Editors): *Neural Models of Plasticity.* New York: Academic Press, in press.

Carlen PL, Wilkinson DA, Wortzman G, Holgate R, Cordingley J, Lee MA, Huszar L, Moddel G, Singh R, Kiraly L, Rankin JG: Cerebral atrophy and functional deficits in

Ch. 2 A.P. Shimamura

alcoholics without clinically apparent liver disease. *Neurology: 31,* 377 – 385, 1981.

Cermak LS: The encoding capacity of a patient with amnesia due to encephalitis. *Neuropsychologia: 14,* 311 – 326, 1976.

Cermak LS: Amnesic patients' level of processing. In Cermak LS, Craik FIM (Editors), *Levels of Processing in Human Memory.* Hillsdale, NJ: Erlbaum, 1979.

Cermak LS (Editor): *Human Memory and Amnesia.* Hillsdale, NJ: Erlbaum, 1982a.

Cermak LS: The long and short of it in amnesia. In Cermak LS (Editor), *Human Memory and Amnesia.* Hillsdale, NJ: Erlbaum, pp. 43 – 59, 1982b.

Cermak LS: The episodic-semantic distinction in amnesia. In Squire LR, Butters N (Editors), *Neuropsychology of Memory.* New York: Guilford Press, pp. 55 – 62, 1984.

Cermak LS: Amnesia as a processing deficit. In Goldstein G, Tarter E (Editors), *Advances in Clinical Neuropsychology, Vol. 3.* New York: Plenum Press, pp. 265 – 290, 1986.

Cermak LS, Butters N: The role of interference and encoding in the short-term memory deficits of Korsakoff patients. *Neuropsychologia: 10,* 89 – 96, 1972.

Cermak LS, O'Connor M: The retrieval capacity of a patient with amnesia due to encephalitis. *Neuropsychologia: 21,* 213 – 234, 1983.

Cermak LS, Reale L: Depth of processing and retention of words by alcoholic Korsakoff patients. *J. Exp. Psychol. Hum. Learn. Mem.: 4,* 165 – 174, 1978.

Cermak LS, Butters N, Gerrein J: The extent of verbal encoding ability of Korsakoff patients. *Neuropsychologia: 11,* 85 – 94, 1973a.

Cermak LS, Lewis R, Butters N, Goodglass H: Role of verbal mediation in performance of motor tasks by Korsakoff patients. *Percept. Motor Skills: 37,* 259 – 262, 1973b.

Cermak LS, Butters N, Moreines J: Some analyses of the verbal encoding deficit of alcoholic Korsakoff patients. *Brain Lang.: 1,* 141 – 150, 1974.

Cermak LS, Reale L, Baker E: Alcoholic Korsakoff patients' retrieval from semantic memory. *Brain Lang.: 5,* 215 – 226, 1978.

Cermak LS, Talbot N, Chandler K, Wolbarst LR: The perceptual priming phenomenon in amnesia. *Neuropsychologia: 23,* 615 – 622, 1985.

Cermak LS, Bleich RP, Blackford SP: Deficits in the implicit retention of new associations by alcoholic Korsakoff patients. *Brain Cognition: 7,* 312 – 323, 1988.

Churchland PS: *Neurophilosophy: Toward a Unified Science of the Mind-Brain.* Cambridge: MIT Press, 1986.

Claparede E: Reconnaissance et moiité. *Archiv. Psychol.: 11,* 79 – 90, 1911 [Recognition and 'me-ness.' Translation in Rapaport D (Editor), *Organization and Pathology of Thought.* New York: Columbia University Press, 1951].

Cohen NJ: Preserved learning capacity in amnesia: evidence for multiple memory systems. In Squire L, Butters N (Editors), *The Neuropsychology of Memory.* New York: Guilford Press, pp. 83 – 103, 1984.

Cohen NJ, Corkin S: The amnesic patient H.M.: learning and retention of a cognitive skill. *Soc. Neurosci. Abstr.: 7,* 235, 1981.

Cohen NJ, Squire LR: Preserved learning and retention of pattern analyzing skill in amnesia: association of knowing how

and knowing that. *Science: 210,* 207 – 209, 1980.

Cohen NJ, Squire LR: Retrograde amnesia and remote memory impairment. *Neuropsychologia: 19,* 337 – 356, 1981.

Collins AM: Why cognitive science. *Cognitive Sci.: 1,* 1 – 2, 1977.

Collins AM, Loftus EF: A spreading-activation theory of semantic processing. *Psychol. Rev.: 82,* 407 – 428, 1975.

Corkin S: Acquisition of motor skill after bilateral medial temporal lobe excision. *Neuropsychologia: 6,* 225 – 265, 1968.

Corkin S: Some relationships between global amnesia and the memory impairment in Alzheimer's disease. In Corkin S, Davis K, Crowdon JH (Editors), *Alzheimer's Disease: A Report of Progress in Research.* New York: Raven Press, 1982.

Corkin S: Lasting consequences of bilateral medial temporal lobectomy: Clinical course and experimental findings in H.M. *Semin. Neurol.: 4,* 249 – 259, 1984.

Corkin S, Cohen NJ, Sullivan EV, Clegg RA, Rosen TJ, Ackerman RH: Analyses of global memory impairments of different etiologies. *Ann. N.Y. Acad. Sci.: 444,* 10 – 40, 1985.

Craik FIM, Lockhart RS: Levels of processing: a framework for memory research. *J. Verbal Learn. Verbal Behav.: 11,* 671 – 684, 1979.

Craik FIM, Tulving E: Depth of processing and retention of words in episodic memory. *J. Exp. Psychol. Gen.: 104,* 268 – 294, 1975.

Crowder RG: *Principles of Learning and Memory.* Hillsdale, NJ: Erlbaum Press, 1976.

Crowder RG: On access and the forms of memory. In Weinberger NM, McGaugh JL, Lynch G (Editors), *Memory Systems of the Brain.* New York: Guilford Press, pp. 433 – 441, 1985.

Damasio AR, Eslinger PJ, Damasio H, Van Hoesen GW, Cornell S: Multimodal amnesic syndrome following bilateral temporal and basal forebrain damage. *Arch. Neurol.: 42,* 252 – 259, 1985a.

Damasio AR, Graff-Radford NR, Eslinger PJ, Damasio H, Kassell N: Amnesia following basal forebrain lesions. *Arch. Neurol.: 42,* 263 – 271, 1985b.

Delis DC: Neuropsychological assessment of learning and memory. In Boller F, Grafman J (Editors), *Handbook of Neuropsychology, Vol. 3.* Amsterdam, The Netherlands: Elsevier, 1989 (Chapter 1 of this volume).

Delis DC, Ober BA: Cognitive neuropsychology. In Knapp TJ, Robertson LC (Editors), *Approaches to Cognition: Constrasts and Controversies.* Hillsdale, NJ: Erlbaum, pp. 243 – 266, 1986.

Diamond R, Rozin P: Activation of existing memories in the amnesic syndromes. *J. Abnorm. Psychol.: 93,* 98 – 105, 1984.

Drachman DA, Arbit J: Memory and the hippocampal complex. *Arch. Neurol.: 15,* 52 – 61, 1966.

Eslinger PJ, Damasio AR: Preserved motor learning in Alzheimer's disease: implications for anatomy and behavior. *J. Neurosci.: 6,* 3006 – 3009, 1986.

Evans FJ, Thorn WAF: Two types of posthypnotic amnesia: Recall amnesia and source amnesia. *Int. J. Clin. Exp. Hypn.: 14,* 162 – 179, 1966.

Flavell JH, Wellman HM: Metamemory. In Kail Jr RV, Hagen JW (Editors), *Perspectives on the Development of Memory and Cognition*. Hillsdale, NJ: Erlbaum, pp. 3 – 33, 1977.

eed DM, Corkin S, Cohen NJ: Forgetting in H.M.: a second look. *Neuropsychologia: 25,* 461 – 471, 1987.

eedman JL, Landauer TK: Retrieval of long-term memory: 'Tip-of-the-tongue' phenomenon. *Psychonomic Sci.: 4,* 309 – 310, 1966.

abrieli JDE, Cohen NJ, Corkin S: Acquisition of semantic and lexical knowledge in amnesia. *Soc. Neurosci. Abstr.: 9,* 28, 1983.

abrieli JDE, Keane MM, Corkin S: Acquisition of problem-solving skills in global amnesia. *Soc. Neurosci. Abstr.: 13,* 1455, 1987.

ardner H: *The Mind's New Science.* New York: Basic Books, 1985.

ardner H, Boller F, Moreines J, Butters N: Retrieving information from Korsakoff patients: effects of categorical cues and reference to the task. *Cortex: 9,* 165 – 175, 1973.

erard RW: Physiology and psychiatry. *Am. J. Psychiatry: 105,* 161 – 173, 1949.

lass AL, Butters N: The effects of associations and expectations on lexical decision making in normals alcoholics and alcoholic Korsakoff patients. *Brain Cognition: 4,* 465 – 476, 1985.

lass AL, Holyoak KJ: *Cognition.* New York: Addison-Wesley, 1986.

lazner M, Cunitz AR: Two storage mechanisms in free recall. *J. Verbal Learn. Verbal Behav.: 5,* 351 – 360, 1966.

lisky EL, Schacter DL, Tulving E: Learning and retention of computer-related vocabulary in memory-impaired patients: method of vanishing cues. *J. Clin. Exp. Neuropsychol.: 8,* 292 – 312, 1986a.

lisky EL, Schacter DL, Tulving E: Computer learning by memory-impaired patients: acquisition and retention of complex knowledge. *Neuropsychologia: 24,* 313 – 328, 1986b.

raf P, Schacter DL: Implicit and explicit memory for new associations in normal and amnesic subjects. *J. Exp. Psychol. Learn. Mem. Cognition: 11,* 501 – 518, 1985.

raf P, Schacter DL: Selective effects of interference on implicit and explicit memory for new associations. *J. Exp. Psychol. Learn. Mem. Cognition: 13,* 45 – 53, 1987.

raf P, Mandler G, Haden PE: Simulating amnesic symptoms in normals. *Science: 218,* 1243 – 1244, 1982.

raf P, Squire LR, Mandler G: The information that amnesic patients do not forget. *J. Exp. Psychol. Learn. Mem. Cognition: 10,* 164 – 178, 1984.

raf P, Shimamura AP, Squire LR: Priming across modalities and priming across category levels: extending the domain of preserved function in amnesia. *J. Exp. Psychol. Learn. Mem. Cognition: 11,* 386 – 396, 1985.

rober E: Encoding of item-specific information in Alzheimer's disease. *J. Clin. Exp. Neuropsychol.: 7,* 614, 1985.

iruneberg MM: Memory processes unique to humans. In Mayes A (Editor), *Memory in Animals and Man.* London: Van Nostrand, pp. 253 – 281, 1983.

iruneberg MM, Monks J: Feeling of knowing and cued recall. *Acta Psychol.: 41,* 257 – 265, 1974.

iruneberg MM, Morris PE, Sykes RN (Editors): *Practical Aspects of Memory: Current Research and Issues.* New York: Wiley, 1988.

Hart JT: Memory and the feeling-of-knowing experience. *J. Educ. Psychol.: 56,* 208 – 216, 1965.

Hebb DO: *The Organization of Behavior.* New York: Wiley, 1949.

Hirst W: The amnesic syndrome: descriptions and explanations. *Psychol. Bull.: 91,* 435 – 460, 1982.

Hirst W, Volpe BT: Temporal order judgments with amnesia. *Brain Cognition: 1,* 294 – 306, 1982.

Hirst W, Johnson MK, Kim JK, Phelps EA, Risse G, Volpe BT: Recognition and recall in amnesics. *J. Exp. Psychol. Learn. Mem. Cognition: 12,* 445 – 451, 1986.

Hirst W, Johnson MK, Phelps EA, Volpe BT: More on recognition and recall with amnesics. *J. Exp. Psychol. Learn. Mem. Cognition: 14,* 758 – 762, 1988.

Huppert FA, Piercy M: Recognition memory in amnesic patients: effect of temporal context and familiarity of material. *Cortex: 12,* 3 – 20, 1976.

Huppert FA, Piercy M: The role of trace strength in recency and frequency judgements by amnesic and control subjects. *Q. J. Exp. Psychol.: 30,* 346 – 354, 1978.

Huppert FA, Piercy M: Normal and abnormal forgetting in organic amnesia: Effect of locus of lesion. *Cortex: 15,* 385 – 390, 1979.

Huppert FA, Tym E: Clinical and neuropsychological assessment of dementia. *Br. Med. Bull.: 42,* 11 – 18, 1986.

Hyde TS, Jenkins JJ: Differential effects of incidental tasks on the organization of recall of a list of highly associated words. *J. Exp. Psychol.: 82,* 472 – 481, 1969.

Iversen SD: Temporal lobe amnesia. In Whitty CWM, Zangwill OL (Editors), *Amnesia.* London: Butterworths, 136 – 182, 1977.

Jacobson RR, Lishman WA: Selective memory loss and global intellectual deficits in alcoholic Korsakoff's syndrome. *Psychol. Med.: 17,* 649 – 655, 1987.

Jacoby LL: Perceptual enhancement: Persistent effects of an experience. *J. Exp. Psychol. Learn. Mem. Cognition: 9,* 21 – 38, 1983.

Jacoby LL, Witherspoon D: Remembering without awareness. *Can. J. Psychol.: 32,* 300 – 324, 1982.

James W: *Principles of Psychology.* New York: Holt, 1890.

Janowsky JS, Shimamura AP, Squire LR: Memory and metamemory: comparisons between patients with frontal lobe lesions and amnesic patients. *Psychobiology: 17,* 3 – 11, 1989.

Janowsky JS, Shimamura AP, Kritchevsky M, Squire LR: Cognitive impairment following frontal lobe damage and its relevance to human amnesia. *Behav. Neurosci.:* in press.

Johnson MK: A multiple-entry modular memory system. In Bower GH (Editor), *The Psychology of Learning and Motivation: Advances in Research Theory, Vol. 17.* New York: Academic Press, pp. 81 – 123, 1983.

Johnson MK, Kim JK, Risse G: Do alcoholic Korsakoff's syndrome patients acquire affective reactions? *J. Exp. Psychol. Learn. Mem. Cognition: 11,* 22 – 36, 1985.

Kandel ER, Schwartz JH: Molecular biology of learning: modification of transmitter release. *Science: 218,* 433 – 442, 1982.

Kaushall PI, Zetin M, Squire LR: A psychosocial study of chronic circumscribed amnesia. *J. Nerv. Ment. Dis.: 169,* 383 – 389, 1981.

Kinsbourne M, Wood F: Short-term memory processes and the amnesic syndrome. In Deutsch D, Deutsch JA (Editors), *Short-term Memory*. New York: Academic Press, pp. 258–291, 1975.

Kinsbourne M, Wood F: Theoretical considerations regarding the episodic-semantic memory distinction. In Cermak LS (Editor), *Human Memory and Amnesia*. Hillsdale, NJ: Erlbaum Press, pp. 194–217, 1982.

Klatzky RL: *Human Memory: Structures and Processes*. San Francisco: WH Freeman, 1975.

Korsakoff SS: Uber eine besondere Form psychischer Storung Kombiniert mit multiplen Neuritis. *Arch. Psychiatrie Nervenkrankh.: 21,* 669–704, 1889 [Translation in Victor M, Yakovlev: Psychic disorders in conjunction with multiple neuritis. *Neurology: 5,* 394–406, 1955].

Kosslyn SM: Information representation in visual images. *Cognitive Psychol.: 7,* 341–370, 1975.

Kritchevsky M, Squire LR, Zouzounis, JA: Transient global amnesia: characterization of anterograde and retrograde amnesia. *Neurology: 38,* 213–219.

Lishman WA: Cerebral disorder in alcoholism: syndromes of impairment. *Brain: 104,* 1–20, 1981.

Lezak MD: *Neuropsychological Assessment* (2nd Edn). New York: Oxford University Press, 1983.

Loftus E: Activation of semantic memory. *Am. J. Psychol.: 86,* 331–337, 1973.

Luria AR: *The Working Brain*. Basic Books: New York, 1973.

Lynch G: *Synapses, Circuits and the Beginnings of Memory*. Cambridge: MIT Press, 1986.

Lynch G, Granger RH: Plasticity in olfactory cortex. In Byrne J, Berry W (Editors), *Neural Models of Plasticity*. New York: Academic Press, in press.

Mair WGP, Warrington EK, Weiskrantz L: Memory disorder in Korsakoff's psychosis: a neuropathological and neuropsychological investigation of two cases. *Brain: 102,* 749–783, 1979.

Mahut H, Moss M: Consolidation of memory: the hippocampus revisited. In Squire LR, Butters N (Editors), *Neuropsychology of Memory*. New York: Guilford Press, 1984.

Mandler G: Recognizing: the judgment of previous occurrence. *Psychol. Rev.: 87,* 252–271, 1980.

Marslen-Wilson WD, Teuber H-L: Memory for remote events in anterograde amnesia: recognition of public figures from news photographs. *Neuropsychologia: 13,* 353–364, 1975.

Martin A, Fedio P: Word production and comprehension in Alzheimer's disease: the breakdown of semantic knowledge. *Brain Lang.: 19,* 124–141, 1983.

Mayes AR: Learning and memory disorders and their assessment. *Neuropsychologia: 24,* 25–39, 1986.

Mayes AR, Meudell PR: How similar is the effect of cueing in amnesics and normal subjects following forgetting? *Cortex: 17,* 113–124, 1981.

Mayes AR, Meudell PR, Neary D: Must amnesia be caused by either encoding or retrieval disorders? In Gruneberg MM, Morris PE, Sykes RN (Editors), *Practical Aspects of Memory*. London: Academic Press, pp. 712–719, 1978.

Mayes AR, Meudell PR, Pickering A: Is organic amnesia caused by a selective deficit in remembering contextual information? *Cortex: 21,* 167–202, 1985.

Mayes AR, Pickering A, Fairbairn A: Amnesic sensitivity to proactive interference: its relationship to priming and t causes of amnesia. *Neuropsychologia: 18,* 211–220, 198

McAndrews MP, Glisky EL, Schacter DL: When priming p sists: long-lasting implicit memory for a single episode amnesic patients. *Neuropsychologia: 25,* 497–506, 1987.

McDowall J: Effects of encoding instructions and retrieval c ing on recall in Korsakoff patients. *Mem. Cognition:* 232–239, 1979.

McGaugh JL, Herz MJ: Memory Consolidation. San Fra cisco: Albion, 1972.

McKoon G, Ratcliff R, Dell GS: A critical evaluation of t semantic-episodic distinction. *J. Exp. Psychol. Learn. Me Cognition: 12,* 295–306, 1986.

McNaughton BL, Morris RGM: Hippocampal synaptic e hancement and information storage within a distribut memory system. *Trends Neurosci.: 10,* 408–415, 1987.

Meudell PR, Butters N, Montgomery K: The role of rehears in the short-term memory performance of patients with Kc sakoff's and Huntington's disease. *Neuropsychologia: I* 507–510, 1978.

Meudell PR, Northern B, Snowden JS, Neary D: Long ter memory for famous voices in amnesics and normal subjec *Neuropsychologia: 18,* 133–139, 1980.

Miller GA: The magical number seven plus or minus two: sor limits on our capacity for processing information. *Psychc Rev.: 63,* 81–97, 1956.

Milner B: Les troubles de la memoire accompagnant des lesio hippocampiques bilaterales [Memory impairment accor panying bilateral hippocampal lesions]. In *Physiologie l'Hippocampe*. Paris: Centre National de la Recherche Scie tifique, 1962.

Milner B: Some effects of frontal lobectomy in man. In Warre JM, Akert K (Editors), *The Frontal Granular Cortex ar Behaviour*. New York: McGraw-Hill, 1964.

Milner B: Interhemispheric differences in the localization (psychological processes in man. *Br. Med. Bull.: 12* 272–277, 1971.

Milner B: Amnesia following operation on the temporal lobe In Whitty CWM, Zangwill OL (Editors), *Amnesia*. Londo Butterworths, pp. 109–133, 1966.

Milner B, Corkin S, Teuber H-L: Further analysis of the hi pocampal amnesic syndrome: 14-year follow-up study (H.M. *Neuropsychologia: 6,* 215–234, 1968.

Milner B, Petrides M: Behavioural effects of frontal-lobe l sions in man. *Trends Neurosci.: 7,* 403–407, 1984.

Mishkin M: A memory system in the monkey. In Broadbe DE, Weiskrantz L (Editors), *The Neuropsychology c Cognitive Function*. London: The Royal Society, pp. 85–9! 1982.

Mishkin M, Malamut B, Bachevalier J: Memories and Habit Two neural systems. In McGaugh JL, Lynch G, Weinberge N (Editors), *The Neurobiology of Learning and Memory* New York: Guilford Press, pp. 65–77, 1984.

Morris RG, Kopelman MD: The memory deficits in Alzheimer type dementia: a review. *Q. J. Exp. Psychol.: 38A* 575–602, 1986.

Mortensen EL: The effects of partial information in amnesi and normal subjects. *Scand. J. Psychol.: 21,* 75–82, 1980.

Moscovitch M: Multiple dissociations of function in amnesia In Cermak L (Editor), *Human Memory and Amnesia*

Hillsdale, NJ: Erlbaum, pp. 337–370, 1982.

Moscovitch M, Winocur G, McLachlan D: Memory as assessed by recognition and reading time in normal and memory impaired people with Alzheimer's disease and other neurological disorders. *J. Exp. Psychol. Gen.: 115*, 331–347, 1986.

Müller GE, Pilzecker A: Experimentelle Beitrage zur Lehre vom Gedachtniss [Experimental contributions to the theory of memory]. *Z. Psychol.: 1*, 1–288, 1900.

Murdock BB: The serial position effect of free recall. *J. Exp. Psychol.: 64*, 482–488, 1962.

Neely JH: Semantic priming and retrieval from lexical memory: the role of inhibitionless spreading activation and limited capacity attention. *J. Exp. Psychol. Gen.: 106*, 226–254, 1977.

Nelson TO, Narens L: A new technique for investigating the feeling of knowing. *Acta Psychol.: 46*, 69–80, 1980.

Newell A, Shaw JC, Simon HA: Elements of a theory of human problem solving. *Psychol. Rev.: 65*, 151–166, 1958.

Nissen MJ, Cohen NJ, Corkin S: The amnesic patient H.M.: learning and retention of perceptual skills. *Soc. Neurosci. Abstr.: 7*, 235, 1981.

Norman D: Twelve issues for cognitive science. *Cognitive Sci.: 4*, 1–32, 1980.

O'Keefe J, Nadel L: *The Hippocampus as a Cognitive Map*. London: Oxford University Press, 1978.

Oscar-Berman M: The neuropsychological consequences of long-term chronic alcoholism. *Am. Sci.: 68*, 410–419, 1980.

Oscar-Berman M, Sahakian BJ, Wikmark G: Spatial probability learning by alcoholic Korsakoff patients. *J. Exp. Psychol. Hum. Learn. Mem.: 2*, 215–222, 1976.

Ostergaard AL: Episodic semantic and procedural memory in a case of amnesia at an early age. *Neuropsychologia: 25*, 341–357, 1987.

Paivio A: *Imagery and Verbal Processes*. New York: Holt Rinehart and Winston, 1971.

Parkin AJ: Residual learning capability in organic amnesia. *Cortex: 18*, 417–440, 1982.

Parkinson SR: Performance deficits in short-term memory tasks: a comparison of amnesic Korsakoff patients and the aged. In Cermak LS (Editor), *Human Memory and Amnesia*. Hillsdale, NJ: Erlbaum, pp. 77–96, 1982.

Petersen SE, Fox PT, Posner MI, Mintun M, Raichle ME: Positron emission tomographic studies of the cortical anatomy of single-word processing. *Nature: 331*, 585–589, 1988.

Peterson LR, Peterson MJ: Short-term retention of individual verbal items. *J. Exp. Psychol.: 58*, 193–198, 1959.

Rawlins JNP: Associations across time: the hippocampus as a temporary memory store. *Behav. Brain Sci.: 8*, 479–496, 1985.

Richardson-Klavehn A, Bjork RA: Measures of memory. *Annu. Rev. Psychol.: 39*, 1988.

Redington K, Volpe BT, Gazzaniga MS: Failure of preference formation in amnesia. *Neurology: 34*, 536–538, 1984.

Roediger HL III, Blaxton TA: Retrieval modes produce dissociations in memory for surface information. In Gorfein DS, Hoffman RR (Editors), *Memory and Cognitive Processes: The Ebbinghaus Centennial Conference*. Hillsdale, NJ: Erlbaum, pp. 349–379, 1987.

Rolls ET: Functions of neuronal networks in the hippocampus and neocortex in memory. In Byrne J, Berry W (Editors), *Neural Models of Plasticity*. New York: Academic Press, in press.

Rose FC, Symonds CP: Persistent memory defect following encephalitis. *Brain: 83*, 195–212, 1960.

Rozin P: The psychobiological approach to human memory. In Rosenzweig MR, Bennett EL (Editors), *Neural Mechanisms of Learning and Memory*. Cambridge, MA: MIT Press, pp. 3–46, 1976.

Rumelhart DE, McClelland JL (Editors): *Parallel Distributed Processing*. Cambridge, MA: MIT Press, 1986.

Ryle G: *The Concept of Mind*. San Francisco: Hutchinson, 1949.

Salmon DP, Shimamura AP, Butters N, Smith S: Lexical and semantic priming deficits in patients with Alzheimer's disease. *J. Clin. Exp. Neuropsychol.: 4*, 477–494, 1988.

Sanders HI, Warrington EK: Memory for remote events in amnesic patients. *Brain: 94*, 661–668, 1971.

Schacter DL: Priming of old and new knowledge in amnesic patients and normal subjects. *Ann. N.Y. Acad. Sci.: 444*, 41–53, 1985.

Schacter DL: Implicit memory: history and current status. *J. Exp. Psychol. Learn. Mem. Cognition: 13*, 501–518, 1987a.

Schacter DL: Memory amnesia and frontal lobe dysfunction: a critique and interpretation. *Psychobiology: 15*, 21–36, 1987b.

Schacter DL, Graf P: Preserved learning in amnesic patients: perspectives from research on direct priming. *J. Clin. Exp. Neuropsychol.: 6*, 727–743, 1986.

Schacter DL, Tulving E: Amnesia and memory research. In Cermak LS (Editor), *Human Memory and Amnesia*. Hillsdale, NJ: Erlbaum, pp. 1–32, 1982a.

Schacter DL, Tulving E: Memory amnesia and the episodic/semantic distinction. In Isaacson RL, Spear NE (Editors), *The Expression of Knowledge*. New York: Plenum Press, pp. 33–65, 1982b.

Schacter DL, Harbluck J, McLaughlin D: Retrieval without recollection: an experimental analysis of source amnesia. *J. Verbal Learn. Verbal Behav.: 23*, 593–611, 1984.

Scoville WB, Milner B: Loss of recent memory after bilateral hippocampal lesions. *J. Neurol. Neurosurg. Psychiatry: 20*, 11–21, 1957.

Seltzer B, Benson DF: The temporal pattern of retrograde amnesia in Korsakoff's disease. *Neurology: 24*, 527–530, 1974.

Shallice T: Neuropsychological research and the fractionation of memory systems. In Nillson L-G (Editor), *Perspectives in Memory Research*. Hillsdale, NJ: Erlbaum, pp. 257–277, 1979.

Shimamura AP: Priming effects in amnesia: Evidence for a dissociable memory function. *Q. J. Exp. Psychol.: 38A*, 619–644, 1986.

Shimamura AP: Forms of memory: Issues and directions. In McGaugh JL, Weinberger NM, Lynch G (Editors), *Brain Organization and Memory: Cells Systems and Circuits*. New York: Oxford University Press, in press.

Shimamura AP, Squire LR: Paired-associate learning and priming effects in amnesia: a neuropsychological study. *J. Exp. Psychol. Gen.: 113*, 556–570, 1984.

Shimamura AP, Squire LR: Memory and metamemory: a study of the feeling-of-knowing phenomenon in amnesic patients. *J. Exp. Psychol. Learn. Mem. Cognition: 12,* 452–460, 1986a.

Shimamura AP, Squire LR: Korsakoff's syndrome: the relationship between anterograde amnesia and remote memory impairment. *Behav. Neurosci.: 100,* 65–100, 1986b.

Shimamura AP, Squire LR: A neuropsychological study of fact memory and source amnesia. *J. Exp. Psychol. Learn. Mem. Cognition: 13,* 464–473, 1987.

Shimamura AP, Squire LR: Long-term memory in amnesia: Cued recall recognition memory and confidence ratings. *J. Exp. Psychol. Learn. Mem. Cognition: 14,* 763–770, 1989.

Shimamura AP, Squire LR: Impaired priming of new associations in amnesia. *J. Exp. Psychol. Learn. Mem. Cognition:* in press.

Shimamura AP, Salmon DP, Squire LR, Butters N: Memory dysfunction and word priming in dementia and amnesia. *Behav. Neurosci.: 101,* 347–351, 1987.

Shimamura AP, Jernigan TL, Squire LR: Korsakoff's syndrome: radiological (CT) findings and neuropsychological correlates. *J. Neurosci.: 8,* 4400–4410, 1988.

Squire LR: Two forms of human amnesia: an analysis of forgetting. *J. Neurosci.: 1,* 635–640, 1981.

Squire LR: Comparison between forms of amnesia: Some deficits are unique to Korsakoff's syndrome. *J. Exp. Psychol. Learn. Mem. Cognition: 8,* 560–571, 1982a.

Squire LR: The neuropsychology of human memory. *Annu. Rev. Neurosci.: 5,* 241–273, 1982b.

Squire LR: ECT and memory dysfunction. In Lerer B, Weiner RD, Belmaker RH (Editors), *ECT: Basic Mechanisms.* London: John Libbey, pp. 156–163, 1984.

Squire LR: *Memory and Brain.* New York: Oxford University Press, 1987.

Squire LR, Chace P: Memory functions six to nine months after electroconvulsive therapy. *Arch. Gen. Psychiatry: 32,* 1557–1564, 1975.

Squire LR, Moore RY: Dorsal thalamic lesion in a noted case of human memory dysfunction. *Annu. Neurol.: 6,* 503–506, 1979.

Squire LR, Shimamura AP: Characterizing amnesic patients for neurobehavioral study. *Behav. Neurosci.: 100,* 866–877, 1986.

Squire LR, Slater P: Anterograde and retrograde memory impairment in chronic amnesia. *Neuropsychologia: 16,* 313–322, 1978.

Squire LR, Zola-Morgan S: The neurology of memory: the case for correspondence between the findings for human and nonhuman primates. In Deutsch JA (Editor), *The Physiological Basis of Memory* (2nd Edn), New York: Academic Press, 1983.

Squire LR, Zola-Morgan S: Memory: brain systems and behavior. *Trends Neurosci.: 22,* 170–175, 1988.

Squire LR, Zouzounis JA: Self-ratings of memory dysfunction: different findings in depression and amnesia. *J. Clin. Exp. Neuropsychol.: 10,* 727–738, 1988.

Squire LR, Slater P, Chace PM: Retrograde amnesia: temporal gradient in very long-term memory following electroconvulsive therapy. *Science: 187,* 77–79, 1975.

Squire LR, Wetzel CD, Slater PC: Anterograde amnesia following ECT: an analysis of the beneficial effect of parti information. *Neuropsychologia: 16,* 339–347, 1978.

Squire LR, Slater P, Miller PL: Retrograde amnesia followi ECT: long-term follow-up studies. *Arch. Gen. Psychiatr 38,* 89–95, 1981.

Squire LR, Cohen NJ, Zouzounis JA: Preserved memory retrograde amnesia: sparing of a recently acquired ski *Neuropsychologia: 22,* 145–152, 1984.

Squire LR, Shimamura AP, Graf P: Independence of recogn tion memory and priming effects: a neuropsychologic analsysis. *J. Exp. Psychol. Learn. Mem. Cognition: 1, 37*–44, 1985.

Squire LR, Amaral DG, Zola-Morgan S, Kritchevsky M, Pre G: Description of brain injury in the amnesic patient N.′ based on magnetic resonance imaging. *Exp. Neurol.:* press.

Squire LR, Shimamura AP, Graf P: Strength and duration c priming effects in normal subjects and amnesic patient *Neuropsychologia: 25,* 195–210, 1987.

Squire LR, Shimamura AP, Amaral D: Memory and the hi pocampus. In Byrne J, Berry W (Editors), *Neural Models c Plasticity.* New York: Academic Press, in press.

Squire LR, Haist F, Shimamura AP: The neurology o memory: quantitative assessment of retrograde amnesia i two groups of amnesic patients. *J. Neurosci.: 9,* 828–839 1989.

Strubb RL, Black FW: *The Mental Status Examination i Neurology.* Philadelphia: FA Davis, 1977.

Talland GA: *Deranged Memory.* Academic Press: New York 1965.

Teuber HL, Milner B, Vaughan HG: Persistent anterograd amnesia after stab wound of the basal brain. *Neuro psychologia: 6,* 267–282, 1968.

Teyler TJ, DiScenna P: The hippocampal memory indexin theory. *Behav. Neurosci.: 100,* 147–154, 1986.

Thomas GJ: Memory: Time binding in organisms. In Squir LR, Butters N, (Editors), *Neuropsychology of Memory.* Ne York: Guilford Press, pp. 374–384, 1984.

Tulving E: Episodic and semantic memory. In Tulving E Donaldson W (Editors), *Organization of Memory.* Ne York: Academic Press, pp. 381–403, 1972.

Tulving E: *Elements of Episodic Memory.* Oxford: Clarendo Press, 1983.

Tulving E, Schacter D, Stark HA: Priming effects in word fragment completion are independent of recognitio memory. *J. Exp. Psychol. Learn. Mem. Cognition: 8 352*–373, 1982.

Vallar G, Baddeley AD: Fractionation of working memory neuropsychological evidence for a phonological short-term store. *J. Verbal Learn. Verbal Behav.: 23,* 151–161, 1984.

Victor M, Adams RD, Collins GH: *The Wernicke-Korsakof Syndrome.* Philadelphia: Davis Company, 1971.

Walsh DA, Jenkins JJ: Effects of orienting tasks on free recal in incidental learning: 'difficulty' 'effort' and 'process' ex planations. *J. Verbal Learn. Verbal Behav.: 12,* 481–488 1973.

Warrington EK: Selective impairment of semantic memory. *Q J. Exp. Psychol.: 27,* 635–657, 1974.

Warrington EK: The double dissociation of short- and long-term memory deficits. In Cermak L (Editor), *Human*

Memory and Amnesia. Hillsdale, NJ: Erlbaum, pp. 61 – 76, 1982.

Warrington EK, Sanders HI: The fate of old memories. *Q. J. Exp. Psychol.: 23,* 432 – 422, 1971.

Warrington EK, Shallice T: The selective impairment of auditory verbal short-term memory. *Brain: 92,* 885 – 896, 1969.

Warrington EK, Weiskrantz L: New method of testing long-term retention with special reference to amnesic patients. *Nature: 217,* 972 – 974, 1968.

Warrington EK, Weiskrantz L: The amnesic syndrome: consolidation or retrieval? *Nature: 228,* 628 – 630, 1970a.

Warrington EK, Weiskrantz L: A study of forgetting in amnesic patients. *Neuropsychologia: 8,* 281 – 288, 1970b.

Warrington EK, Weiskrantz L: The effect of prior learning on subsequent retention in amnesic patients. *Neuropsychologia: 12,* 419 – 428, 1974.

Warrington EK, Weiskrantz L: Further analysis of the prior learning effect in amnesic patients. *Neuropsychologia: 16,* 169 – 177, 1978.

Warrington EK, Weiskrantz L: Amnesia: a disconnection syndrome? *Neuropsychologia: 20,* 233 – 248, 1982.

Wechsler D: *Wechsler Memory Scale-Revised.* San Antonio, Texas: Psychological Corporation (Harcourt, Brace, Jovanovich), 1987.

Weiskrantz L: Comparative aspects of studies of amnesia. In Broadbent DE, Weiskrantz L (Editors), *Neuropsychology of Cognitive Function.* London: The Royal Society, pp. 97 – 109, 1982.

Weiskrantz L, Warrington EK: Conditioning in amnesic patients. *Neuropsychologia: 17,* 187 – 194, 1979.

Wetzel CD, Squire LR: Encoding in anterograde amnesia. *Neuropsychologia: 18,* 177 – 184, 1980.

Whitty CWM, Zangwill OL (Editors): *Amnesia.* London: Butterworths, 1977.

Whitty CWM, Stores G, Lishman WA: Amnesia in cerebral disease. In Whitty CWM, Zangwill OL (Editors), *Amnesia.* London: Butterworths, 52 – 92, 1977.

Wickelgren WA: Chunking and consolidation: a theoretical synthesis of semantic networks configuring in conditioning S-R versus cognitive learning normal forgetting the amnesic syndrome and the hippocampal arousal system. *Psychol. Rev.: 86,* 44 – 60, 1979.

Wickens DD: Encoding strategies of words: an empirical approach to meaning. *Psychol. Rev.: 22,* 1 – 15, 1970.

Williams M: Memory disorders associated with ECT. In Whitty CWM, Zangwill OL (Editors), *Amnesia.* London: Butterworths, 183 – 198, 1977.

Williams M, Pennybacker J: Memory disturbances in third ventricle tumours. *J. Neurol. Neurosurg. Psychiatry: 17,* 115, 1954.

Williams M, Zangwill OL: Disorders of temporal judgment associated with amnesic states. *J. Ment. Sci.: 96,* 484 – 493, 1950.

Wilson BA: *Rehabilitation of Memory.* New York: Guilford Press, 1987.

Winocur G, Weiskrantz L: An investigation of paired-associate learning in amnesic patients. *Neuropsychologia: 14,* 97 – 110, 1976.

Wood F, Ebert V, Kinsbourne M: The episodic-semantic memory distinction in memory and amnesia: clinical and experimental observations. In Cermak LS (Editor), *Human Memory and Amnesia.* Hillsdale NJ: Erlbaum, pp. 167 – 194, 1982.

Woods RT, Piercy M: A similarity between amnesic memory and normal forgetting. *Neuropsychologia: 12,* 437 – 445, 1974.

Zajonc RB: Feeling and thinking: preferences need no inferences. *Am. Psychol.: 35,* 151 – 175, 1980.

Zola-Morgan S, Cohen NJ, Squire LR: Recall of remote episodic memory in amnesia. *Neuropsychologia: 21,* 487 – 500, 1983.

Zola-Morgan S, Squire LR, Amaral DG: Human amnesia and the medial temporal region: enduring memory impairment following a bilateral lesion limited to field CA1 of the hippocampus. *J. Neurosci.: 6,* 2950 – 2967, 1986.

© 1989 Elsevier Science Publishers B.V. (Biomedical Division)
Handbook of Neuropsychology, Vol. 3
F. Boller and J. Grafman (Eds)

CHAPTER 3

Frontal lobes and memory

Michael Petrides

*Department of Psychology, McGill University, 1205 Dr. Penfield Avenue, Montreal, Quebec, H3A 1B1, and the Montreal
Neurological Institute, McGill University, 3801 University Street, Montreal, Quebec, H3A 2B4 Canada*

Introduction

The frontal lobe occupies a very large area of the
primate cerebral cortex. Its posteriormost part,
which lies immediately in front of the central
sulcus, consists of motor cortex. The vast area that
lies further forward extends as far as the frontal
pole on the lateral surface of the cerebral
hemispheres, covers the orbital part of the frontal
bone ventrally, and occupies a large part of the
rostral half of the medial surface of the brain. A
great many functions have been ascribed to this
large expanse of cortex which reaches its maximum
development in the human brain. Early investigators have often referred to the frontal cortex
as the 'seat of intelligence', and its involvement in
the highest forms of mental activity has frequently
been asserted. Despite these claims, many studies
have repeatedly shown that even extensive damage
to this region of the brain need not impair performance on conventional intelligence tests (e.g.
Hebb, 1939; Mettler, 1949; Milner, 1964; Teuber,
1964; Black, 1976). Over the past twenty years,
however, a number of carefully conducted investigations have demonstrated various cognitive
impairments in patients with damage to the frontal
cortex, these impairments being most evident in
situations that require a certain degree of planning
and flexibility of response (see Milner and
Petrides, 1984; Stuss and Benson, 1986). The present article reviews evidence pertaining to the involvement of the human frontal cortex in memory

processes. This is a complex issue which requires
consideration of both the site and the extent of
damage within the frontal lobe, as well as the way
memory performance is assessed. Emphasis will be
given to evidence derived from the examination of
patients with damage to the frontal cortex, but
relevant information from anatomical studies and
from investigations of the behavioral effects of
selective ablations within the frontal cortex in
nonhuman primates will also be discussed.

Anatomical aspects of the frontal cortex

Any attempt to deal with the functions of the
primate frontal cortex must recognize the fact that
it comprises many cytoarchitectonic areas which
exhibit marked differences in their connections
with various cortical and subcortical regions of the
brain (Figs. 1 – 3). Major inputs to various regions
of the frontal cortex have been shown to originate
from the prestriate, temporal and posterior
parietal neocortex (e.g. Nauta, 1964; Pandya and
Kuypers, 1969; Jones and Powell, 1970; Barbas
and Mesulam, 1981, 1985; Petrides and Pandya,
1984, 1988; Schwartz and Goldman-Rakic, 1984).
Most of these connections are reciprocal in nature,
implying that the frontal cortex can modulate, as
well as receive input from, posterior cortical areas
that are involved in the processing and, probably,
long-term storage of visual, auditory and
somatosensory information.

In addition to its close relationship with

posterior neocortical areas, major association systems link the frontal cortex with the amygdalo-hippocampal region in the mesial part of the temporal lobe, a region of the brain that has been shown to play a significant role in memory processes (Milner, 1972; Weiskrantz, 1978; Mishkin, 1982; Squire and Zola-Morgan, 1983). The fibers that form one of these association systems originate in the dorsolateral and medial frontal cortex and travel as part of the cingulum bundle just above the corpus callosum. Some of these fibers terminate within the cingulate cortex along

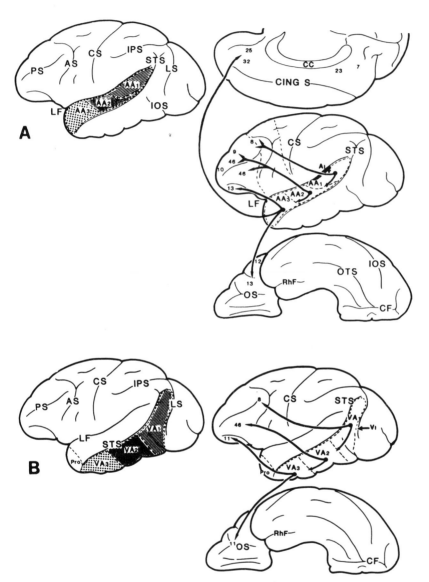

Fig. 1. Diagrams showing projections to the frontal cortex of the monkey. A, projections originating from different parts of the superior temporal gyrus (AA_1, AA_2, AA_3), and B, from visual regions in the prestriate and inferior temporal cortex (Va_1, VA_2, VA_3). Abbreviations: AS, arcuate sulcus; CC, corpus callosum; CF, calcarine fissure; CING S, cingulate sulcus: CS, central sulcus; IOS, inferior occipital sulcus; IPS, intraparietal sulcus; LF, lateral fissure, LS, lunate sulcus; OS, orbital sulcus; OTS, occipito-temporal sulcus; PS, sulcus principalis; RhF, rhinal sulcus; STS, superior temporal sulcus. The numbers within the frontal lobe indicate cytoarchitectonic areas. From Pandya and Barnes, 1987, with permission.

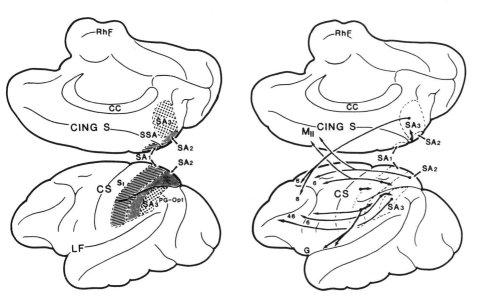

Fig. 2. Diagrams showing projections to the frontal cortex of the monkey originating from different parts of the posterior parietal cortex (SA$_1$, SA$_2$, SA$_3$). Abbreviations are the same as those used in Fig. 1. The numbers within the frontal lobe indicate cytoarchitectonic areas. From Pandya and Barnes, 1987, with permission.

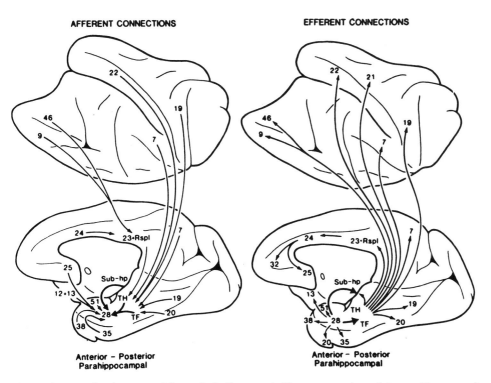

Fig. 3. Diagrams showing some of the cortical afferent and efferent connections of the parahippocampal gyrus. From Van Hoesen, 1982, with permission.

its whole antero-posterior extent, but a considerable number turn in a ventral direction at the level of the splenium of the corpus callosum to terminate within the presubiculum of the hippocampal complex (Adey and Meyer, 1952; Nauta, 1964; Goldman-Rakic et al., 1984). There is also an important projection from the dorsolateral frontal cortex to the caudomedial lobule that lies adjacent to the presubiculum at the most posterior part of the hippocampal formation (Goldman-Rakic et al., 1984). Another association system originates within the posterior orbitofrontal region and travels to the entorhinal cortex (area 28), as well as to transitional cortex along the rhinal sulcus, as part of the uncinate fasciculus (Van Hoesen et al., 1972, 1975). A smaller direct projection from the dorsolateral frontal region to cortex along the rhinal sulcus has also been identified (Goldman-Rakic et al., 1984). Thus, the frontal cortex can exert considerable influence over the hippocampal system, which in turn can modulate frontal neural activity via reciprocal connections originating in the subiculum and other areas of the hippocampal complex (Rosene and Van Hoesen, 1977; Goldman-Rakic et al., 1984; Vogt and Pandya, 1987).

The frontal lobe is also closely linked with the amygdaloid system. The orbital frontal cortex has both direct connections with the amygdala and indirect connections via the temporopolar cortex (Pandya and Kuypers, 1969; Jones and Powell, 1970; Aggleton et al., 1980; Van Hoesen, 1981; Moran et al., 1987). The amygdaloid nuclei, in turn, project back to the orbital and medial regions of the frontal lobe and, to a lesser extent, to the dorsolateral frontal cortex (Nauta, 1961; Jacobson and Trojanowski, 1975; Porrino et al., 1981; Amaral and Price, 1984).

The amygdalo-hippocampal region of the brain can also interact with the posterior orbital and medial frontal cortex via connections with the medial thalamus. Thus, the anterior nucleus of the thalamus, which receives input from the hippocampal complex directly and through connections with the mammillary bodies (Rosene and Van

Hoesen, 1977; Aggleton et al., 1986), projects to the anterior cingulate and subcallosal gyri (Baleydier and Mauguiere, 1980). In addition, the magnocellular part of the medial dorsal thalamic nucleus, which is linked with the amygdala (Nauta, 1961; Aggleton and Mishkin, 1984; Russchen et al., 1987), is connected with the orbital frontal region (Nauta, 1962; Tobias, 1975; Goldman-Rakic and Porrino, 1985; Russchen et al., 1987).

The brief review of the anatomical evidence provided above is intended to highlight some important connections of the frontal cortex for the discussion that follows. It must, however, be realized that the frontal cortex, like other cortical areas, has major projections directed toward the striatum, as well as various brainstem nuclei and that these connections will undoubtedly prove critical for some aspects of the learning of complex behavioral responses controlled by the frontal cortex.

Evidence from cases of tumor of the frontal lobe and ruptured aneurysms of the anterior communicating artery

The connections described above suggest the existence of a considerable degree of functional interaction between the frontal cortex and the mesial region of the temporal lobe, as well as the anterior and dorsomedial thalamic nuclei (see also Warrington and Weiskrantz, 1982). Extensive damage to the mesial temporal or thalamic regions of the brain gives rise to a severe memory disorder (cf. Milner, 1972; Weiskrantz, 1978; Mishkin, 1982; Squire and Zola-Morgan, 1983). Disturbances of memory have also been reported in patients with tumors affecting the frontal lobes (e.g. Kolodny, 1929; Strauss and Keschner, 1935; Rylander, 1939; Paillas et al., 1950; Hecaen, 1964; Avery, 1971; Luria, 1976). Any attempt, however, to draw conclusions concerning the functions of the frontal cortex from such cases is fraught with serious difficulties. Tumors of the frontal lobe, by compressing or infiltrating areas neighbouring on the frontal cortex (e.g. various basal forebrain areas) or by raising intracranial pressure, can give rise to a variety of symptoms that reflect pathological changes in widespread regions of the brain.

Similar problems of interpretation can be raised concerning the amnesic syndrome that has often been described in cases of ruptured aneurysms of the anterior communicating artery (e.g., Lindqvist et al., 1966; Talland et al., 1967; Luria, 1976; Gade, 1982; Volpe and Hirst, 1983; Damasio et al., 1985; Corkin et al., 1985; Phillips et al., 1987). Although damage to the posterior orbital and medial frontal cortex can often be demonstrated or presumed in these cases, the extent of damage is not restricted to the frontal cortex, but it also includes various basal forebrain structures such as the septal area, nucleus accumbens and parts of the nucleus basalis of Meynert. Many investigators have in fact suggested that damage to the latter neural structures may be responsible for the amnesia that has been observed in these cases (e.g. Gade, 1982; Alexander and Freedman, 1984; Eslinger and Damasio, 1985).

It is important, however, to note that the posterior parts of the orbital and medial frontal lobe (i.e. the anterior cingulate gyrus, the subcallosal gyrus, the posterior orbital cortex and adjoining areas) have cytoarchitectonic characteristics that indicate a close relationship with limbic structures in the mesial part of the temporal lobe

(Fig. 4). These regions of the frontal lobe are also the targets of outputs from the anterior and medial thalamic nuclei which, in turn, receive inputs from the hippocampal and amygdaloid systems respectively (cf. Baleydier and Mauguiere, 1980; Goldman-Rakic and Porrino, 1985; Russchen et al., 1987). Bachevalier and Mishkin (1986) have recently demonstrated that bilateral lesions of this region of the frontal lobe, but not of the dorsolateral frontal cortex (Fig. 5), give rise to an impairment in recognition memory. This observation and the earlier findings showing severe impairments in recognition memory in monkeys with bilateral mesial temporal-lobe lesions (Mishkin, 1982; Squire and Zola-Morgan, 1983) or lesions of the mesial diencephalon (Aggleton and Mishkin, 1983) suggest that the ventromedial frontal cortex may constitute a major component of a limbo-thalamic system underlying memory.

Evidence from psychosurgery

Since the end of World War II, the widespread use of frontal-lobe surgery for the symptomatic relief of psychiatric disorders has furnished the opportunity for a further examination of the effects of damage to the frontal cortex on cognitive functions. Unfortunately the observations made on these patients have often proved more confusing

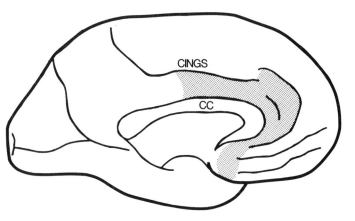

Fig. 4. Diagram of the medial surface of the left hemisphere of the human brain. The shaded area shows the proisocortical region of the medial frontal lobe. This region has cytoarchitectonic characteristics indicating a close relationship to limbic structures of the medial temporal lobe. Abbreviations: CC, corpus callosum; CINGS, cingulate sulcus.

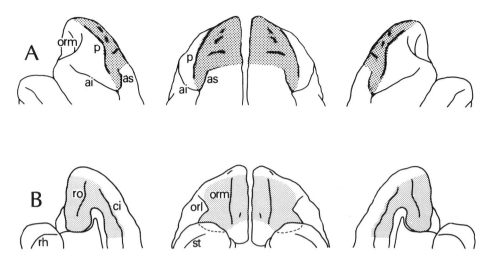

Fig. 5. Diagrams of the dorsolateral (A) and ventromedial (B) frontal cortical excisions studied by Bachevalier and Mishkin (1986). Abbreviations: ai, inferior arcuate sulcus; as, superior arcuate sulcus; ci, cingulate sulcus; orl, lateral orbital sulcus; orm, medial orbital sulcus; p, sulcus principalis; rh, rhinal sulcus; ro, rostral sulcus; st, superior temporal sulcus. Reproduced with permission.

than enlightening because of the difficulties in drawing conclusions from the study of patients with severe psychotic symptoms and because, in many cases, appropriate control groups were not examined. In addition, it must be stated that formal evaluation of memory function with appropriate tests can only rarely be found in the many publications on the effects of psychosurgical procedures.

One of the more ambitious investigations was carried out in the late 1940s (Mettler, 1949). In this study, 48 psychotic patients were examined. Twenty-four of these patients had bilateral excisions of different areas of the frontal cortex and the other 24 patients served as unoperated control subjects. The extensive psychological test battery administered to these patients included various learning and retention tasks, but no impairments could be demonstrated on any of these tasks. Smith et al. (1977) examined the effects of bilateral medial frontal operations on 34 patients who suffered from severe anxiety, depression or obsessional behavior. The Wechsler Adult Intelligence Scale (WAIS) and the Wechsler Memory Scale (WMS) were administered both before and six months after surgery. Postoperatively, a signifi-

cant improvement was noted on the WAIS and the WMS; the improved performance on the latter scale was evident both when the overall score was considered, and when performance on the subtests examining memory for short stories and verbal paired-associate learning was evaluated. This finding might be attributed to a reduction in the anxiety and depression levels of these patients.

Jus et al. (1973) studied 13 chronic schizophrenic patients who had undergone a 'prefrontal lobotomy' 10 to 22 years earlier, and 13 unoperated chronic schizophrenic patients matched with the operated group for age, sex, duration of illness, clinical symptomatology and type of pharmacological treatment. No significant differences in performance between the two groups could be demonstrated on a number of memory tasks requiring the repetition of digits, recall of objects, and the recall of two short stories.

More recently, Stuss et al. (1982) carried out an extensive evaluation of the memory of schizophrenic patients who had undergone 'prefrontal leucotomy' about 25 years earlier. In comparison with the performance of appropriate control groups, no impairments could be demonstrated on many standard verbal and nonverbal memory tasks both when recall was assessed after very short delays and when it was assessed after longer delays of 20 to 30 minutes. A significant decrease in the performance of the group that had undergone prefrontal leucotomy could only be shown on a test in which, on each trial, the subjects had to recall the particular three consonants that had been presented prior to a distracting task (counting backwards).

The reported absence of a major memory impairment in many investigations of the effects of psychosurgery must be interpreted with caution. A careful consideration of the operative procedures, in those studies in which sufficient information has been provided, raises the possibility that the absence of a severe and general memory loss may have been due to the fact that the lesions did not encroach *extensively* upon the posterior orbital and medial frontal lobe. Mishkin and Bachevalier (1986), for example, demonstrated that bilateral lesions *restricted* to either the orbital or the anterior cingulate cortex in the monkey resulted in only mild impairments in recognition memory; by contrast, a more severe memory loss was observed after lesions that invaded both of these areas. In this context it is interesting to note that significant impairments in memory were not observed in patients who had undergone bilateral anterior cingulotomy (see Corkin, 1980). Similarly Scoville, who introduced the psychosurgical procedure known as 'orbital undercutting' (i.e. sectioning of the white matter just above the orbital frontal cortex), reported no clinically evident memory loss in these patients, except for a few cases in which the operation extended too far posteriorly (Scoville and Bettis, 1977). It is possible that the posterior extension of the undercutting in these operations had brought about a more complete isolation of the orbitomedial frontal lobe from the rest of the brain than might have been the case in more limited psychosurgical procedures confined to either the orbitofrontal or the anterior cingulate regions.

Evidence from studies of the temporal organization of behavior

The generally negative findings from investigations in which the potential effects of psychosurgical operations on memory were examined are in agreement with the results of a few studies carried out with individuals who had suffered gunshot wounds to the frontal lobe (Ghent et al., 1962; Newcombe, 1969; Black, 1976). For instance, Ghent et al. (1962) tested patients with frontal-lobe injury, patients with brain lesions outside the frontal lobe, and a group of subjects without brain injury on various tasks of recent memory. No impairments could be demonstrated on any of these tasks in the group with frontal-lobe injury. Similar findings were reported in patients who had undergone unilateral excisions of frontal cortex for the relief of pharmacologically intractable epilepsy. It was shown that these patients could perform well on many tasks that had revealed significant memory loss in patients with unilateral anterior temporal lobectomies (Milner, 1967, 1968a; Smith and Milner, 1984). More recently, Janowsky et al. (1989) demonstrated that patients with lesions of the frontal cortex, caused by cerebrovascular accidents or surgical excision of an abscess, performed well on many memory tasks, in sharp contrast to patients with Korsakoff's syndrome.

Despite the absence of a general memory loss in patients with unilateral excisions of frontal cortex, performance on certain memory tasks requiring comparisons among a small set of recurring stimuli or judgements of the temporal order of recent events can be severely impaired (Milner, 1964, 1971). The requirements of the latter tasks are similar to those of delayed response and delayed alternation which were amongst the first tasks to reveal a significant behavioral impairment in monkeys with lesions of the frontal cortex (Jacobsen, 1935; Jacobsen and Nissen, 1937). In delayed response, the animal sees the experimenter bait one of two locations before an opaque screen is lowered to initiate a delay period of several seconds, whereas in delayed alternation the monkey must alternate its responses between the two locations following the delay. On every trial in both of these tasks, the animal must choose between the two locations on the basis of the most recent information, ignoring information from earlier trials that is no longer relevant. Impairments on these tasks have been reported only after bilateral frontal-lobe lesions in patients (see Freedman and Oscar-Berman, 1986).

Prisko (1963; reported in Milner, 1964) tested patients with unilateral frontal-lobe excisions on a task in which the subject had to decide whether the stimulus presented on a particular trial was the same as, or different from, the stimulus that had been presented 60 seconds earlier. Prisko's findings showed that when, over successive trials, a small set of stimuli were constantly recurring in different combinations, patients with frontal-lobe excisions performed very poorly.

On the basis of the above observations, Milner (1968b) suggested that excisions of the frontal cortex may affect the ability to discriminate the more recent stimuli from the ones appearing earlier in a sequence. Corsi and Milner (reported in Milner, 1971) went on to demonstrate that damage to the frontal cortex can impair memory for the order of occurrence of recent events. In this experiment, the subjects were shown a series of cards on which two different stimuli were presented (Fig. 6). Mixed with the stimulus-presentation cards were test cards which contained either two items that had already been presented or an earlier item paired with a novel one. The subjects had to indicate which of the two items they had seen more recently. There were three versions of the task which differed in the kind of stimulus material used: concrete words, representational drawings, and abstract designs. Patients with frontal-lobe damage had no problem in discriminating between the novel and the familiar items (i.e. in recognition memory), but were impaired when they were required to judge the relative recency of two familiar items. Patients with left frontal-lobe excisions were

Fig. 6. Recency-discrimination task in which representational drawings were used. Sample test card. The subject must point to the item seen more recently.

impaired on the verbal version of the task and patients with right frontal-lobe excisions on the tasks involving abstract designs and representational drawings.

More recently, Smith and Milner (1988) have shown that unilateral frontal-lobe lesions impair the recall of the frequency with which a series of abstract designs occurred. As was the case with recency discrimination, these patients had no difficulty in recognizing whether a particular design had appeared earlier in the sequence, indicating that the defect in the judgement of frequency was not secondary to a general memory impairment.

In another investigation, Petrides and Milner (1982) examined the role of the frontal cortex in the monitoring of self-generated responses. For this purpose, a task was developed in which the

ubjects were presented with a stack of cards, each
of which contained the same set of stimuli, but
with the position of these stimuli varying from
card to card (Fig. 7). The subjects had to go
through the stack of cards pointing to one stimulus
on each card, in any order they wished, but
without pointing to any one stimulus more than
once. There were four versions of this task which
differed only in terms of the stimulus material used: concrete words, abstract words, representational drawings, and abstract designs. In contrast
to the findings on the recency tests, patients with
left frontal-lobe excisions were severely impaired
on all four versions of the self-ordered pointing
task, whereas patients with right frontal-lobe
damage were mildly impaired on the two versions
that involved representational drawings and
abstract designs.

In the self-ordered pointing task, the subjects
have to plan their subsequent responses and at the
same time keep track of those responses that they
have already executed. In other words, in self-
ordered pointing, considerable demands are made
on executive functions within the context of a
working memory task. It is conceivable that an active working memory may depend more on the left
frontal cortex than on the right because the
strategy to be employed, as well as other executive
processes, may be aided by some degree of verbal
formulation.

In another study, patients with unilateral
frontal-lobe excisions were shown to be impaired
in the copying of sequences of arm and face
movements, making errors by omitting movements
and by reproducing them in the incorrect sequence
(Kolb and Milner, 1981). Deficits after frontal-
lobe excisions were also reported on a task requiring subjects to group pictures of common objects
into categories and to recall the names of these objects (Incisa della Rocchetta, 1986). Whereas poor

Fig. 7. Self-ordered pointing task: representational drawings. Two different test cards (A and B) are shown. Note that the relative positions of the drawings vary at random from card to card. The various test cards were presented to the subject in a stack. After having pointed to one of the drawings, the subject had to turn that card face downwards and point to another drawing on the next card.

categorization appeared to account for the impaired recall of patients with excisions from the right frontal lobe, an inadequate search strategy was thought to be a contributing factor in the performance of the left frontal group (Incisa della Rocchetta, 1986). Similar impairments in the recall of a list of words (Grafman et al., 1986; Jetter et al., 1986; Janowsky et al., 1989) or the names of objects (Smith and Milner, 1984) after frontal damage can be attributed to inefficient search strategies.

Functional heterogeneity of the frontal lobe

The anatomical evidence that has accumulated over the past thirty years has brought into focus the fact that the frontal lobe is not a homogeneous region of the brain but rather a large expanse of the cortical mantle encompassing many different cytoarchitectonic areas that have their own unique connections with other cortical and subcortical regions (Pandya and Barnes, 1987). The existence of a number of relatively distinct functional subsystems within the frontal cortex is also supported by investigations of the behavioral effects of ablations restricted to specific parts of the frontal lobe (see Fuster, 1980, and Goldman-Rakic, 1987, for a review). With regard to memory, the available evidence indicates that the posterior part of the orbital and medial frontal lobe and limbic structures in the mesial part of the temporal lobe may constitute important components of the same limbothalamic memory system (Bachevalier and Mishkin, 1986). The findings from the study of clinical cases, though not unambiguous, can be considered to be consistent with the above notion in so far as significant memory impairments have been observed in cases of basal frontal tumors (e.g. Avery, 1971; Luria, 1976).

Although damage to the lateral frontal cortex does not give rise to a general memory loss, significant impairments have been demonstrated after such damage on tasks requiring the recall of the temporal order of various stimuli (Milner, 1971) and the active planning and monitoring of se-

quences of responses (Petrides and Milner, 1982). Deficits on tasks that have similarities to the above have also been reported in monkeys with lesions restricted to the lateral frontal cortex (e.g. Jacobsen, 1935; Jacobsen and Nissen, 1937; Gross and Weiskrantz, 1964; Mishkin, 1964; Pinto-Hamuy and Linck, 1965; Goldman and Rosvold, 1970; Brody and Pribram, 1978; Mishkin and Manning, 1978; Passingham, 1985; Goldman-Rakic, 1987), and in rats with damage to a part of the anterior cortex considered to be equivalent to the primate frontal region (see Kolb, 1984, for review). The behavioral work with nonhuman primates has further shown that performance on spatial versions of delayed response and delayed alternation tasks can be severely disrupted after lesions restricted to the cortex within the sulcus principalis (e.g. Mishkin, 1957; Gross and Weiskrantz, 1964; Goldman and Rosvold, 1970). More recently, performance on an oculomotor version of the traditional delayed response task has also been shown to be impaired after such lesions (see Goldman-Rakic, 1987).

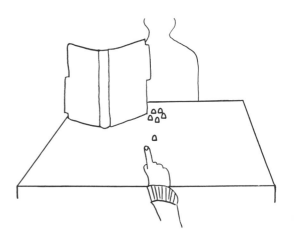

Fig. 8. Schematic diagram of the experimental arrangement in one of the conditional associative tasks. In this task, the subject first learns to make six different hand postures. Subsequently, six differently colored stimuli are placed on the table and, when one of these stimuli is placed in front of the others, the subject must respond by making the hand posture which is correct for that particular stimulus. If an incorrect response is made, the subject must perform the other hand postures until the correct response is produced (from Petrides, 1985).

Another indication of the existence of relatively distinct functional subsystems within the lateral frontal cortex emerged when patients with unilateral frontal lesions were tested on conditional tasks. In such tasks, the subject is faced with an experimental situation in which any one of a number of alternative responses will be correct provided that it is performed when the appropriate exteroceptive signal is given. Thus, to master such a task, the subject must learn to select the correct response for the particular stimulus that is present on a given trial (Fig. 8). Patients with excisions from the left or right frontal cortex were severely impaired in this kind of learning (Petrides, 1985). The work with patients suggested that the impairment observed in conditional learning could, to a certain extent, be dissociated from the impairment observed in self-ordered pointing (Petrides and Milner, 1982). This was strongly indicated by the performance of individual patients tested on both tasks and by the overall pattern of the results obtained in these two studies. In investigations with patients, however, the critical regions within the lateral frontal cortex for conditional learning and for the monitoring of self-generated responses are difficult to establish because the therapeutic excisions are rarely confined to anatomically distinct regions. This limitation can, of course, be overcome in work with nonhuman primates. Such work has now provided evidence for a striking dissociation between these two impairments by demonstrating that they result from damage to different parts of the lateral frontal cortex. Monkeys with excisions limited to the posterior part of the dorsolateral frontal lobe (i.e. rostral area 6 and area 8) were shown to be severely impaired in learning conditional tasks comparable to those used with patients (Petrides, 1982, 1987). Postoperative retention of a similar task has also been shown to be deficient after lesions to area 6 (Hals-

Fig. 9. Schematic diagram of the experimental arrangement in the self-ordered task used with nonhuman primates. In this task, the monkey is faced with three distinct boxes, all of which contain a reward. When the animal selects one of the three boxes by opening it to retrieve the reward, an opaque screen is lowered. The position of the three boxes is changed according to a random schedule and the screen is raised to allow the animal to choose another box. Daily testing continues in this manner until all three boxes have been opened.

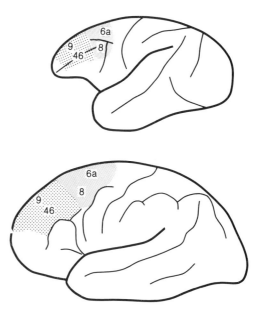

Fig. 10. Upper part: schematic diagram of the lateral surface of the brain of the monkey, showing the mid-lateral frontal cortex (areas 9 and 46) and the posterior part of the dorsolateral frontal region (area 8 and rostral part of area 6). Lower part: schematic diagram of the lateral surface of the human brain showing approximate location of regions comparable to the above.

band and Passingham, 1982). In a more recent investigation, the effect of selective lesions within the lateral frontal cortex on performance of a nonspatial self-ordered task, also modelled on the one administered to patients, was examined (Fig. 9). Monkeys with lesions confined to the mid-lateral frontal cortex (i.e. areas 46 and 9) were severely impaired, whereas monkeys with lesions to area 8 and rostral area 6 performed as well as the normal control animals (Fig. 10) (Petrides, 1988).

The specialized contributions of different regions of the lateral frontal cortex to learning and memory must not be viewed in isolation from its more general role in the organization of complex behavior. The capacity to monitor the performance of a series of actions or to recall the order of occurrence of a sequence of events is probably an essential component of a neural system which contributes significantly to the development of plans of action and to the execution of such plans. Similarly, the flexibility and adaptability of behavior must be considerably enhanced by conditional learning, i.e., the capacity to learn to perform different responses in a given situation according to the particular environmental signals that are present.

A number of recent anatomical investigations have reported that the various frontal areas are predominantly, though by no means exclusively, connected with other cortical areas exhibiting comparable cytoarchitectonic characteristics (e.g. Pandya and Barnes, 1987; Petrides and Pandya, 1988). Such observations suggest that different parts of the frontal lobe may have evolved in parallel with particular posterior cortical regions and it can be argued that the increase in perceptual and other cognitive processes resulting from the expansion of posterior neocortical regions was accompanied by a comparable increase in the complexity of control processes dependent on the frontal cortex.

Further evidence for the involvement of the lateral frontal cortex in some aspects of memory has been provided by investigations in which the activity of single neurons within this cortical region was recorded in monkeys performing various delayed response tasks. These investigations have demonstrated the existence within the lateral frontal cortex of a class of neurons that exhibit sustained increases in their rate of discharge during the delay period, some of these varying their rate of response depending on the particular cue presented before the initiation of the delay period (e.g. Fuster and Alexander, 1971; Kubota and Niki, 1971; Fuster, 1973; Niki, 1974a,b; Kojima and Goldman-Rakic, 1982). Such findings suggest that information provided just before the delay and which will be used to determine the next response is being actively maintained within the frontal cortex. Indeed, some degree of temporary storage of information may be a common phenomenon in many cortical areas and may be an inherent characteristic of particular aspects of the information being processed in these areas. For instance, in many studies in which the activity of individual neurons has been recorded in animals performing behavioral tasks, a certain proportion of cells is frequently observed to exhibit activation during delay periods and this activity has often been linked to the temporary storage of the processed information (e.g. Mikami and Kubota, 1980; Fuster and Jervey, 1982).

Concluding comments

The behavioral work reviewed above, particularly the work with nonhuman primates, has demonstrated the existence of marked functional differences between the various parts of the frontal lobe. The proisocortical regions on the orbital and medial surface of the frontal lobe appear to be an integral part of a basic limb-thalamic memory system. By contrast, the isocortical areas of the lateral and dorsomedial frontal cortex, which are closely interconnected with particular posterior neocortical areas, form important components of distributed cortical circuits. These isocortical frontal areas can be thought of as specialized functional modules subserving certain aspects of the organization of complex behavior and contributing to learning and memory in highly specific ays. For instance, it is now clear that certain aspects of memory, such as the capacity to maintain an ongoing record of self-generated responses, depend on the integrity of the mid-lateral frontal cortex, whereas the more posterior region of the frontal lobe plays a significant role in conditional learning.

Finally, it must be emphasized that the frontal cortex, in addition to its more direct involvement with certain aspects of memory, subserves a variety of executive functions concerned with the organization (planning) of sequences of responses, the selection and development of appropriate strategies in complex situations, the monitoring of the effectiveness of the organism's own behavior, the capacity to inhibit and change behavior in the face of changing circumstances, etc. (see Milner and Petrides, 1984). It is inevitable that these executive functions will find expression in memory as much as in any other aspect of an individual's cognitive and behavioral functioning. Overall memory performance is the outcome of complex interacting mechanisms. To the extent that efficient performance on any given memory task depends on some of the executive functions subserved by the frontal cortex, performance will be affected after damage to this region of the brain.

Acknowledgement

I would like to thank Dr. B. Milner for her helpful comments on this paper.

References

Adey WR, Meyer M: An experimental study of hippocampal afferent pathways from prefrontal and cingulate areas in the monkey. *J. Anat.: 86,* 58 – 75, 1952.

Aggleton JP, Mishkin M: Memory impairments following restricted medial thalamic lesions in monkeys. *Exp. Brain Res.: 52,* 199 – 209, 1983.

Aggleton JP, Mishkin M: Projections of the amygdala to the thalamus in the cynomolgus monkey. *J. Comp. Neurol.: 222,* 56 – 68, 1984.

Aggleton JP, Burton MJ, Passingham RE: Cortical and subcortical afferents to the amygdala of the rhesus monkey (*Macaca mulatta*). *Brain Res.: 190,* 347 – 368, 1980.

Aggleton JP, Desimone R, Mishkin M: The origin, course, and termination of the hippocampo-thalamic projections in the Macaque. *J. Comp. Neurol.: 243,* 409 – 421, 1986.

Alexander MP, Freedman M: Amnesia after anterior communicating artery aneurysm rupture. *Neurology: 34,* 752 – 757, 1984.

Amaral DG, Price JL: Amygdalo-cortical projections in the monkey (*Macaca fascicularis*). *J. Comp. Neurol.: 230,* 465 – 496, 1984.

Avery TL: Seven cases of frontal tumour with psychiatric presentation. *Br. J. Psychiatry: 119,* 19 – 23, 1971.

Bachevalier J, Mishkin M: Visual recognition impairment follows ventromedial but not dorsolateral prefrontal lesions in monkeys. *Behav. Brain Res.: 20,* 249 – 261, 1986.

Baleydier C, Mauguiere F: The duality of the cingulate gyrus in monkey. Neuroanatomical study and functional hypothesis. *Brain: 103,* 525 – 554, 1980.

Barbas H, Mesulam M-M: Organization of afferent input to subdivisions of area 8 in the rhesus monkey. *J. Comp. Neurol.: 200,* 407 – 431, 1981.

Barbas H, Mesulam M-M: Cortical afferent input to the principalis region of the rhesus monkey. *Neuroscience: 15,* 619 – 637, 1985.

Black FW: Cognitive deficits in patients with unilateral war-related frontal lobe lesions. *J. Clin. Psychol.: 32,* 366 – 372, 1976.

Brody BA, Pribram KH: The role of frontal and parietal cortex in cognitive processing. Tests of spatial and sequential functions. *Brain: 101,* 607 – 633, 1978.

Corkin S: A prospective study of cingulotomy. In Valenstein E (Editor), *The Psychosurgery Debate.* San Francisco: Freeman Press, Ch. 9, pp. 164 – 204, 1980.

Corkin S, Cohen NJ, Sullivan EV, Clegg RA, Rosen TJ, Ackerman RH: Analyses of global memory impairments of different etiologies. *Ann. N.Y. Acad. Sci.: 444,* 10 – 40, 1985.

Damasio AR, Graff-Radford NR, Eslinger PJ, Damasio H, Kassell N: Amnesia following basal forebrain lesions. *Arch. Neurol.: 42,* 263 – 271, 1985.

Eslinger PJ, Damasio AR: Severe disturbance of higher cognition after bilateral frontal lobe ablation: patient EVR. *Neurology: 35,* 1731 – 1741, 1985.

Freedman M, Oscar-Berman M: Bilateral frontal lobe disease and selective delayed response deficits in humans. *Behav. Neurol.: 100,* 337 – 342, 1986.

Fuster JM: Unit activity in prefrontal cortex during delayed-response performance: neuronal correlates of transient memory. *J. Neurophysiol.: 36,* 61 – 76, 1973.

Fuster JM: *The Prefrontal Cortex. Anatomy, Physiology, and Neuropsychology of the Frontal Lobe.* New York: Raven Press, 1980.

Fuster JM, Alexander GE: Neuron activity related to short-term memory. *Science: 173,* 652 – 654, 1971.

Fuster JM, Jervey JP: Neuronal firing in the inferotemporal cortex of the monkey in a visual memory task. *J. Neurosci.: 2,* 361 – 375, 1982.

Gade A: Amnesia after operations on aneurysms of the anterior communicating artery. *Surg. Neurol.: 18,* 46 – 49, 1982.

Ghent L, Mishkin M, Teuber H-L: Short-term memory after frontal-lobe injury in man. *J. Comp. Physiol. Psychol.: 55,* 705 – 709, 1962.

Goldman PS, Rosvold HE: Localization of function within the dorsolateral prefrontal cortex of the rhesus monkey. *Exp. Neurol.: 27,* 291 – 304, 1970.

Goldman-Rakic PS: Circuitry of primate prefrontal cortex and regulation of behavior by representational memory. In Plum F, Mountcastle V (Editors), *Handbook of Physiology – The Nervous System*. American Physiological Society, Vol. 5, pp. 373 – 417, 1987.

Goldman-Rakic PS, Porrino LJ: The primate mediodorsal (MD) nucleus and its projection to the frontal lobe. *J. Comp. Neurol.: 242,* 535 – 560, 1985.

Goldman-Rakic PS, Selemon LD, Schwartz ML: Dual pathways connecting the dorsolateral prefrontal cortex with the hippocampal formation and parahippocampal cortex in the rhesus monkey. *Neuroscience: 12,* 719 – 743, 1984.

Grafman J, Vance SC, Weingartner H, Salazar AM, Amin D: The effects of lateralized frontal lesions on mood regulation. *Brain: 109,* 1127 – 1148, 1986.

Gross CG, Weiskrantz L: Some changes in behaviour produced by lateral frontal lesions in the macaque. In Warren JM, Akert K (Editors), *The Frontal Granular Cortex and Behavior*. New York: McGraw-Hill Book Company, Ch. 5, pp. 74 – 101, 1964.

Halsband U, Passingham R: The role of premotor and parietal cortex in the direction of action. *Brain Res.: 240,* 368 – 372, 1982.

Hebb DO: Intelligence in man after large removals of cerebral tissue: report of four left frontal lobe cases. *J. Gen. Psychol.: 21,* 73 – 87, 1939.

Hecaen H: Mental symptoms associated with tumors of the frontal lobe. In Warren JM, Akert K (Editors), *The Frontal Granular Cortex and Behavior*. New York: McGraw-Hill Book Company, Ch. 16, pp. 335 – 352, 1964.

Incisa della Rocchetta A: Classification and recall of pictures after unilateral frontal or temporal lobectomy. *Cortex: 22,* 189 – 211, 1986.

Jacobsen CF: Functions of the frontal association area in primates. *Arch. Neurol. Psychiatry: 33,* 558 – 569, 1935.

Jacobsen CF, Nissen HW: Studies of cerebral function in primates: IV. The effects of frontal lobe lesions on the delayed alternation habit in monkeys. *J. Comp. Physiol. Psychol.: 23,* 101 – 112, 1937.

Jacobson S, Trojanowski JQ: Amygdaloid projections to prefrontal granular cortex in rhesus monkey demonstrated with horseradish peroxidase. *Brain Res.: 100,* 132 – 139, 1975.

Janowsky JS, Shimamura AP, Kritchevsky M, Squire LR: Cognitive impairment following frontal lobe damage and its relevance to human amnesia. *Behav. Neurosci.:* in press.

Jetter W, Poser U, Freeman RB Jr., Markowitsch HJ: A verbal long term memory deficit in frontal lobe damaged patients. *Cortex: 22,* 229 – 242, 1986.

Jones EG, Powell TPS: An anatomical study of converging sensory pathways within the cerebral cortex of the monkey. *Brain: 93,* 793 – 820, 1970.

Jus A, Jus K, Villeneuve A, Pires A, Lachance R, Fortier J, Villeneuve R: Studies on dream recall in chronic schizophrenic patients after prefrontal lobotomy. *Biol. Psychiatry: 6,* 275 – 293, 1973.

Kojima S, Goldman-Rakic PS: Delay-related activity of prefrontal neurons in rhesus monkeys performing delayed response. *Brain Res.: 248,* 43 – 49, 1982.

Kolb B: Functions of the frontal cortex of the rat: a comparative review. *Brain Res. Rev.: 8,* 65 – 98, 1984.

Kolb B, Milner B: Performance of complex arm and facial movements after focal brain lesions. *Neuropsychologia: 19,* 491 – 503, 1981.

Kolodny A: Symptomatology of tumor of the frontal lobe. *Arch. Neurol. Psychiatry: 21,* 1107 – 1127, 1929.

Kubota K, Niki H: Prefrontal cortical unit activity and delayed alternation performance in monkeys. *J. Neurophysiol.: 34,* 337 – 347, 1971.

Lindqvist G, Norlen G:. Korsakoff's syndrome after operation on ruptured aneurysm of the anterior communicating artery. *Acta Psychiatr. Scand.: 42,* 24 – 34, 1966.

Luria AR: *The Neuropsychology of Memory*. New York: John Wiley and Sons, 1976.

Mettler FA: *Selective Partial Ablation of the Frontal Cortex*. New York: Paul B. Hoeber Inc., 1949.

Mikami A, Kubota K: Inferotemporal neuron activities and color discrimination with delay. *Brain Res.: 182,* 65 – 78, 1980.

Milner B: Some effects of frontal lobectomy in man. In Warren JM, Akert K (Editors), *The Frontal Granular Cortex and Behavior*. New York: McGraw-Hill Book Company, Ch. 15, pp. 313 – 334, 1964.

Milner B: Brain mechanisms suggested by studies of temporal lobes. In Darley FL (Editor), *Brain Mechanisms Underlying Speech and Language*. New York: Grune & Straton, pp. 122 – 132, 1967.

Milner B: Visual recognition and recall after right temporal lobe excision in man. *Neuropsychologia: 6,* 191 – 209, 1968a.

Milner B: Memory. In Weiskrantz L (Editor), *Analysis of Behavioral Change*. New York: Harper and Row, pp. 328 – 375, 1968b.

Milner B: Interhemispheric differences in the localization of psychological processes in man. *Br. Med. Bull.: 27,* 272 – 277, 1971.

Milner B: Disorders of learning and memory after temporal lobe lesions in man. *Clin. Neurosurg.: 19,* 421 – 446, 1972.

Milner B, Petrides M: Behavioural effects of frontal-lobe lesions in man. *Trends Neurosci.: 7,* 403 – 407, 1984.

Mishkin M: Perseveration of central sets after frontal lesions in monkeys. In Warren JM, Akert K (Editors), *The Frontal Granular Cortex and Behavior*. New York: McGraw-Hill Book Company, Ch. 11, pp. 219 – 241, 1964.

Mishkin M: Effects of small frontal lesions on delayed alternation in monkeys. *J. Neurophysiol.: 20,* 615 – 622, 1957.

Mishkin M: A memory system in the monkey. *Phil. Trans. R. Soc. Lond. B: 298,* 85 – 95, 1982.

Mishkin M, Bachevalier J: Differential involvement of orbital and anterior cingulate cortices in object and spatial memory functions in monkeys. *Soc. Neurosci. Abstr.: 12,* 742, 1986.

Mishkin M, Manning FJ: Non-spatial memory after selective prefrontal lesions in monkeys. *Brain Res.: 143,* 313 – 323, 1978.

Moran MA, Mufson EJ, Mesulam MM: Neural inputs into the temporopolar cortex of the rhesus monkey. *J. Comp. Neurol.: 256,* 88 – 103, 1987.

Nauta WJH: Fibre degeneration following lesions of the amygdaloid complex in the monkey. *J. Anat.: 95,* 515 – 531,

1961.

auta WJH: Neural associations of the amygdaloid complex in the monkey. *Brain: 85,* 505–520, 1962.

auta WJH: Some efferent connections of the prefrontal cortex in the monkey. In Warren JM, Akert K (Editors), *The Frontal Granular Cortex and Behavior.* New York: McGraw-Hill Book Company, Ch. 19, pp. 397–409, 1964.

ewcombe F: *Missile Wounds of the Brain. A Study of Psychological Deficits.* New York: Oxford University Press, 1969.

iki H: Prefrontal unit activity during delayed alternation in the monkey. I. Relation to direction of response. *Brain Res.: 68,* 185–196, 1974a.

iki H: Prefrontal unit activity during delayed alternation in the monkey. II. Relation to absolute versus relative direction of response. *Brain Res.: 68,* 197–204, 1974b.

aillas JE, Bourdouresque J, Bonnal J, Provansal J: Tumeurs frontales. Considerations anatomo-cliniques a propos de 72 tumeurs operees. *Rev. Neurol.: 83,* 470–473, 1950.

andya DN, Barnes CL: Architecture and connections of the frontal lobe. In Perecman E (Editor), *The Frontal Lobes Revisited.* New York: The IRBN Press, Ch. 3, pp. 41–72, 1987.

andya DN, Kuypers HGJM: Cortico-cortical connections in the rhesus monkey. *Brain Res.: 13,* 13–36, 1969.

assingham RE: Memory of monkeys (Macaca mulatta) with lesions in prefrontal cortex. *Behav. Neurosci.: 99,* 3–21, 1985.

etrides M: Motor conditional associative-learning after selective prefrontal lesions in the monkey. *Behav. Brain Res.: 5,* 407–413, 1982.

etrides M: Deficits on conditional associative-learning tasks after frontal- and temporal-lobe lesions in man. *Neuropsychologia: 23,* 601–614, 1985.

etrides M: Conditional learning and the primate frontal cortex. In Perecman E (Editor), *The Frontal Lobes Revisited.* New York: The IRBN Press, Ch. 5, pp. 91–108, 1987.

etrides M: Performance on a nonspatial self-ordered task after selective lesions of the primate frontal cortex. *Soc. Neurosci. Abstr.: 14,* 2, 1988.

etrides M, Milner B: Deficits on subject-ordered tasks after frontal- and temporal-lobe lesions in man. *Neuropsychologia: 20,* 249–262, 1982.

etrides M, Pandya DN: Projections to the frontal cortex from the posterior parietal region in the rhesus monkey. *J. Comp. Neurol.: 228,* 105–116, 1984.

etrides M, Pandya DN: Association fiber pathways to the frontal cortex from the superior temporal region in the rhesus monkey. *J. Comp. Neurol.: 273,* 52–66, 1988.

hillips S, Sangalang V, Sterns G: Basal forebrain infarction. A clinico-pathologic correlation. *Arch. Neurol.: 44,* 1134–1138, 1987.

into-Hamuy T, Linck P: Effect of frontal lesions on performance of sequential tasks by monkeys. *Exp. Neurol.: 12,* 96–107, 1965.

orrino LJ, Crane AM, Goldman-Rakic PS: Direct and indirect pathways from the amygdala to the frontal lobe in rhesus monkeys. *J. Comp. Neurol.: 198,* 121–136, 1981.

risko L: Short-term memory to focal cerebral damage. Unpublished Ph.D. thesis: Montreal: McGill University, 1963.

Rosene DL, Van Hoesen GW: Hippocampal efferents reach widespread areas of cerebral cortex and amygdala in the rhesus monkey. *Science: 198,* 315–317, 1977.

Russchen FT, Amaral DG, Price JL: The afferent input to the magnocellular division of the mediodorsal thalamic nucleus in the monkey, *Macaca fascicularis. J. Comp. Neurol.: 256,* 175–210, 1987.

Rylander G: *Personality Changes after Operations on the Frontal Lobes.* London: Oxford University Press, 1939.

Schwartz ML, Goldman-Rakic PS: Callosal and intrahemispheric connectivity of the prefrontal association cortex in rhesus monkey: relation between intraparietal and principal sulcal cortex. *J. Comp. Neurol.: 226,* 403–420, 1984.

Scoville WB, Bettis DB: Results of orbital undercutting today: a personal series. In Sweet WH, Obrador S, Martin-Rodriguez JG (Editors), *Neurosurgical Treatment in Psychiatry, Pain, and Epilepsy.* Baltimore: University Park Press; 189–202, 1977.

Smith JS, Kiloh LG, Boots JA: Prospective evaluation of prefrontal leucotomy: results of 30 months' follow-up. In Sweet WH, Obrador S, Martin-Rodriguez JG (Editors), *Neurosurgical Treatment in Psychiatry, Pain, and Epilepsy.* Baltimore: University Park Press, pp. 217–224, 1977.

Smith ML, Milner B: Differential effects of frontal-lobe lesions on cognitive estimation and spatial memory. *Neuropsychologia: 22,* 697–705, 1984.

Smith ML, Milner B: Estimation of frequency of occurrence of abstract designs after frontal or temporal lobectomy. *Neuropsychologia: 26,* 297–306, 1988.

Squire LR, Zola-Morgan S: The neurology of memory: The case for correspondence between the findings for human and nonhuman primate. In Deutsch JA (Editor), *The Physiological Basis of Memory* (2nd Edn). New York: Academic Press, pp. 199–267, 1983.

Strauss I, Keschner M: Mental symptoms in cases of tumor of the frontal lobe. *Arch. Neurol. Psychiatry: 33,* 986–1007, 1935.

Stuss DT, Kaplan EF, Benson DF, Weir WS, Chiulli S, Sarazin FF: Evidence for the involvement of orbitofrontal cortex in memory functions: an interference effect. *J. Comp. Physiol. Psychol.: 96,* 913–925, 1982.

Stuss DT, Benson DF: *The Frontal Lobes.* New York: Raven Press, 1986.

Talland GA, Sweet WH, Ballantine HT: Amnesic syndrome with anterior communicating artery aneurysms. *J. Nerv. Ment. Dis.: 145,* 179–192, 1967.

Teuber H-L: The riddle of frontal lobe function in man. In Warren JM, Akert K (Editors), *The Frontal Granular Cortex and Behavior.* New York: McGraw-Hill Book Company, Ch. 20, pp. 410–444, 1964.

Tobias TJ: Afferents to prefrontal cortex from the thalamic mediodorsal nucleus in the rhesus monkey. *Brain Res.: 83,* 191–212, 1975.

Van Hoesen GW: The parahippocampal gyrus. *Trends Neurosci.: 5,* 345–350, 1982.

Van Hoesen GW: The differential distribution, diversity and sprouting of cortical projections to the amygdala in the rhesus monkey. In Ben-Ari Y (Editor), *The Amygdaloid Complex.* New York: Elsevier/North-Holland Biomedical

Press, 77 – 90, 1981.

Van Hoesen GW, Pandya DN, Butters N: Cortical afferents to the entorhinal cortex of the rhesus monkey. *Science: 175,* 1471 – 1473, 1972.

Van Hoesen GW, Pandya DN, Butters N: Some connections of the entorhinal (area 28) and perirhinal (area 35) cortices of the rhesus monkey. II. Frontal lobe afferents. *Brain Res.: 95,* 25 – 38, 1975.

Vogt BA, Pandya DN: Cingulate cortex of the rhesus monkey: II. Cortical afferents. *J. Comp. Neurol.: 262,* 271 – 289, 1987.

Volpe BT, Hirst W: Amnesia following the rupture and repair of an anterior communicating artery aneurysm. *J. Neurol. Neurosurg. Psychiatry: 46,* 704 – 709, 1983.

Warrington EK, Weiskrantz L: Amnesia: a disconnection syndrome? *Neuropsychologia: 20,* 233 – 248, 1982.

Weiskrantz, L: A comparison of hippocampal pathology in man and other animals. In Elliot K, Whelan J (Editors) *Functions of the Septo-hippocampal System.* Amsterdam: Elsevier, 1978.

CHAPTER 4

Memory disorders associated with temporal-lobe lesions

Mary Lou Smith

Department of Psychology, Erindale College, University of Toronto, Mississauga, Ontario, Canada L5L 1C6

Introduction

Historically, the first evidence that the temporal lobes have a specialized role in memory can be traced back to the beginning of this century, when Bekhterev (1900) reported a case of severe memory impairment. On autopsy, the brain of this patient was found to have bilateral abnormalities in the uncus, hippocampus and adjoining medial temporal cortex. Since that time, our knowledge of the memory disorders associated with temporal-lobe lesions has increased, largely through the study of patients who have undergone unilateral brain surgery for the relief of medically intractable epilepsy (see Ojemann, 1987, and Penfield and Baldwin, 1952, for discussion of the indications for and outcome of the surgical treatment of epilepsy).

This population is an ideal one for study because the patients tend to be young (with an average age ranging from the mid-20s to mid-30s) and the operation produces a discrete, well-defined removal. For the most part, the epileptogenic lesions are static and atrophic, dating from birth or early life, although temporal lobectomies are also performed on patients with tumours; in the cases where the tumour is indolent, it has been reported that the cognitive effects of the surgery are similar to those seen with static lesions (Cavazzuti et al., 1980).

The typical temporal lobectomy always includes the anterior temporal neocortex, and, in some neurosurgical centres, the amygdala and varying amounts of the hippocampus and parahippocampal gyrus are also removed. The extent of excision from the hippocampal region is often individually tailored, either because of the presence of documented abnormality (Crandall, 1987; Olivier, 1987), or because of the risk of memory disturbance (Jones-Gotman, 1987; Olivier, 1987). As we shall see later, the appearance or the severity of memory deficits on certain tasks is dependent upon the degree of encroachment of the removal upon the hippocampal region. In those studies reviewed here which examined this factor, the patients had been subdivided into groups according to whether they had had small or large hippocampal removals, the decision for such classification being based on the surgeon's drawings and report at the time of operation. The excision was considered small if the hippocampus had been spared entirely or the removal had not exceeded the pes; large hippocampal excisions were those which extended beyond the pes into the body of the hippocampus and/or the parahippocampal gyrus. Fig. 1 depicts examples of representative temporal lobectomies, and of small and large hippocampal removals. This figure also shows that the size of the excision along the medial temporal region is independent of the extent of the lateral cortical removal.

With respect to cognitive function, the effects of a unilateral temporal lobectomy are specific. There is no lasting generalized loss in intellectual functioning, at least as measured by standardized tests of intelligence, although there is a transient lowering in IQ ratings seen in the immediate postoperative period. This finding is illustrated in Fig.

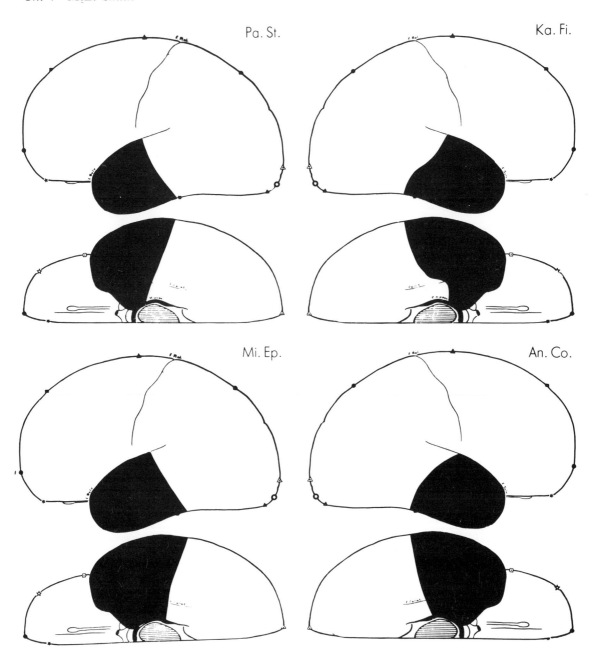

Fig. 1. Brain maps based on the surgeon's drawings at the time of operation, showing representative left and right temporal lobectomies. The lateral surface is shown above and the inferior surface below. The blackened area indicates the extent of cortical excision. Case Pa.St.: left temporal, small hippocampal removal; Case Mi.Ep.: left temporal, large hippocampal removal; Case Ka.Fi.: right temporal, small hippocampal removal; Case An.Co.: right temporal, large hippocampal removal. (From Milner B: Memory and the human brain. In Shafto M (Editor), *How We Know*. San Francisco: Harper & Row, Ch. 2, pp. 31 – 59, 1985. Reprinted with permission.)

2, which gives Full Scale IQ ratings for a group of 116 patients with temporal lobe lesions who were seen for neuropsychological assessments prior to surgery, 14 days postoperatively and again 2 or more years after the operation at the Montreal Neurological Institute (Smith and Milner, 1984). Data for 45 patients with lesions of either the frontal lobe, or with combined lesions of the frontal and temporal lobes, are included for the purpose of comparison. For all groups, the immediate postoperative effect is a significant decline in Full Scale IQ, but over time there is recovery to the preoperative level. It has been reported that at follow-up testing in some cases the overall level of intelligence is significantly improved relative to the baseline obtained preoperatively, an effect presumed to be due to the relief of the widespread, noxious effects of an epileptigenic focus (Blakemore et al., 1966; Milner, 1975; Novelly et al., 1984).

Against this background of normal intellectual functioning, the patient with a unilateral temporal-lobe lesion nonetheless experiences difficulty in the realm of learning and memory. These deficits are often apparent preoperatively, but are exacerbated by the surgery (Fedio and Mirsky, 1969; Meyer and Yates, 1955; Milner, 1958, 1967, 1975). For the

large part, the memory impairments are material-specific in nature as related to the hemisphere of the lesion; in patients with speech representation in the left hemisphere, a left temporal lobectomy results in impairments on tasks of verbal learning and verbal memory, whereas a right temporal lobectomy impairs performance on tasks in which the memoranda are difficult to verbalize. The few exceptions to the finding of material-specific memory disorders have generally been documented in studies in which the tasks contain memoranda that can be processed using either a verbal or a visual code (Eskenazi et al., 1986; Jones-Gotman, 1986b; Read, 1981; Zatorre, 1985).

Disorders of memory associated with left temporal-lobe lesions

One of the first demonstrations (Milner, 1958) of a deficit in verbal memory in patients with lesions of the left, or dominant, temporal lobe was for the recall of the information contained in the short prose passages of the Logical Memory Subtest of the Wechsler Memory Scale (Wechsler, 1945). In this task, recall is obtained immediately after the patient has heard each story and again one and a half hours later, the deficit being particularly marked after the delay. The patients forget many of the important details of the stories, recalling sparse and fragmented versions. A similar deficit is also seen on the verbal paired-associate learning task of the Wechsler Memory Scale (Meyer and Yates, 1955; Milner, 1967). Because of the similarity in the results from these two tests, Milner (1967) developed a composite score of delayed verbal memory, consisting of the mean number of items correctly recalled from the prose passages plus the number of word associates retained after a delay. Fig. 3 shows the composite recall scores for the same group of patients whose IQ ratings had been illustrated earlier. These data demonstrate that lesions in the left frontal or left temporal lobe produce a post-operative decline in ability to retain verbal information. When the lesion involves the frontal lobe alone, however, the impairment is

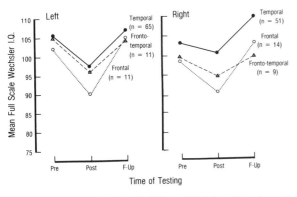

Fig. 2. Graphs showing the Full Scale Wechsler IQ ratings at three different times of testing. Results for patients with lesions of the left hemisphere are shown on the left, and for those with right hemisphere lesions on the right (Pre, pre-operative testing; Post, post-operative testing approximately two weeks after surgery; F-Up, follow-up assessment two or more years after surgery.)

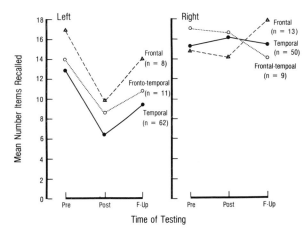

Fig. 3. Graphs showing the mean number of items recalled on a verbal memory test as related to time of assessment. Results for patients with lesions of the left hemisphere are shown on the left, and for those with right hemisphere lesions on the right. (Pre, pre-operative testing; Post, post-operative testing approximately two weeks after surgery; F-Up, follow-up assessment two or more years after surgery.)

transient, probably reflecting interference with function in adjacent cortical areas, and is not evident in follow-up testing. In this study, the recall scores at the time of follow-up testing of the small group of patients with left frontal-lobe lesions did not differ significantly from the scores they obtained pre-operatively.

Although the patients in whom the lesion invades the temporal lobe of the left hemisphere show some recovery of function over time, two or more years after surgery their verbal recall scores remain significantly depressed relative to their pre-operative scores. This evidence for a residual impairment in verbal recall represents a specific cognitive deficit, contrasting both with the recovery in general intelligence seen over the same time span, and with the normal verbal memory of patients with similar lesions in the right hemisphere, a finding also illustrated in Fig. 3.

The role of the left temporal lobe in verbal memory has been demonstrated in many centres and with a variety of learning and memory tasks. Not only is the deficit apparent with information presented in the auditory modality (Meyer and Yates, 1955; Milner, 1958, 1967) but it is also

elicited under conditions of visual presentation (Milner, 1967; Milner and Kimura, 1964). The finding of the impairment has been extended to other story-learning tasks (Frisk and Milner, 1985), to learning and recalling lists of unrelated words (Dennis et al., 1988), to the recall of the names of pictured objects (Incisa della Rochetta, 1986; Jaccarino, 1975, cited in Milner, 1978) or the names of toy models of objects (Smith and Milner, 1981), and to recognition as well as recall paradigms (Milner and Kimura, 1964; Dennis et al., 1988).

It is true that the deficit in verbal memory is not the only impairment exhibited by patients with lesions of the left temporal lobe. Mild impairments have also been noted on verbal perceptual tasks, such as identifying digits presented by dichotic listening techniques (Kimura, 1961), and on speeded reading comprehension tasks (Milner, 1967). Nonetheless, it has also been true that the difficulty in retaining verbal material is disproportionate to the deficits on these other types of tasks. For this reason, several investigations have been aimed at trying to uncover the mechanisms underlying the memory impairment.

Along this line, one approach has drawn on the work with normal subjects showing the interdependence of memory and other cognitive processes. For example, it has been demonstrated that the organization inherent in stimulus material influences the subsequent recall of that material (Bousfield, 1953; Marshall, 1967) and, furthermore, that when subjects impose their own organization on otherwise unorganized material, recall is also enhanced (Mandler, 1967, 1970; Tulving, 1962). Such findings have raised the question of whether the verbal memory impairment of patients with left temporal-lobe lesions is associated with a corresponding impairment in cognitive organization. Several studies bearing on this question have yielded mixed results. For example, a reduction in clustering during recall of taxonomically organized (Jaccarino-Hiatt, 1978; Moscovitch, 1976) or associatively organized words (Weingartner, 1968) has been found after left temporal lobectomy, In contrast, Incisa della Rocchetta (1986) demonstrated that left temporal lobectomy does not impair the ability to sort pictures of objects into appropriate taxonomic categories, although it does impair the ability to recall later the names of those pictures. Such patients also show the normal pattern of recalling more words from a taxonomically organized list than from a non-organized list (Jaccarino-Hiatt, 1978; Weingartner, 1968).

In those experiments mentioned above, the material to be remembered contained a preimposed organization. With a different kind of task, one which contained no inherent organization of the material but which made demands of the patients to impose subjective organization, Jaccarino-Hiatt (1978) found that lists of unrelated words were sorted into fewer categories than were designs by patients with left temporal-lobe lesions; the opposite pattern of results was seen in patients with right temporal-lobe lesions. No correlation was found, however, between the number of categories sorted and the number of items later recalled. Thus, the evidence relating the verbal memory impairment to deficits in cognitive organization is inconclusive, and any such cognitive impairments are mild in comparison to the impoverished verbal recall associated with left temporal lobectomy.

The previously described experiments emphasized learning and retention in the realm of episodic memory, or memory for unique, specific, personally experienced events (Tulving, 1972). Wilkins and Moscovitch (1978) investigated the possibility that semantic memory, the system involving memory for general principles, facts and associations (Tulving, 1972), is also impaired after anterior temporal lobectomy. Two classification tasks were used, one in which patients were asked to classify common objects (represented by drawings or words) as larger or smaller than a chair, and the other requiring a decision as to whether objects were living or man-made. Patients with right temporal-lobe lesions performed normally on both tasks, but those with left temporal-lobe lesions were impaired on the living/man-made classification. The authors suggested that left temporal lobectomy disrupts the semantic memory

systems that involve verbal or lexical representations. They also emphasized, however, that the observed semantic deficits appeared to be mild relative to the deficits in episodic memory seen in such patient groups.

Another aspect of cognitive functioning that has been investigated in relation to the verbal memory impairment is the type of emphasis given to the memoranda at the time of encoding. In normal subjects, orienting tasks involving semantic aspects of words result in better recall than do tasks that draw attention to phonemic or physical aspects (Craik and Lockhart, 1972). Rains (1987) hypothesized that if defective encoding formed the basis of the deficit in verbal memory, then the recall and recognition performance of patients with left temporal-lobe lesions should show a relationship to the depth of processing different from that seen in normal subjects. He used an incidental-learning task adapted from Craik and Tulving (1975), which varied the type of encoding performed on each word in a list and then tested the recall and recognition of the previously processed words.

During presentation, each word was preceded by a question that emphasized either the semantic aspects of the word, or the phonemic aspects, or the physical structure of the word. The results indicated that left temporal lobectomy produced the expected verbal memory impairment, reflected in an overall lower level of recall and recognition of the words, but that the patients nonetheless showed the normal pattern of deriving benefit from semantic encoding. This finding suggested to Rains, and corroborated the point made earlier by Wilkins and Moscovitch (1978), that impairment of the semantic memory system per se cannot account for the extent of the verbal memory impairment.

Despite showing a benefit of semantic encoding, the patients with left temporal-lobe lesions in Rains' study did not show an advantage in recall of phonemic over physical encoding. A similar deficit in the use of phonemic features to aid recall was obtained by Read (1981; see also Milner, 1985) on a variant of the Slamecka and Graf (1978) word-generation task, in which subjects had to generate words on the basis of either semantic (e.g., a synonym – BIG: LARGE) or phonetic cues (e.g., a rhyme – RICE: NICE). Immediately after generating a list of words, patients with left temporal-lobe lesions were impaired in recalling the rhymes, whereas an impairment for the recall of the synonyms appeared only in a delayed recall (24 hour) condition. Taken together, the results of Rains and Read provide evidence that the left temporal lobe is specialized for the encoding and/or utilization of phonemic information for subsequent recall of verbal material.

Recently, attention has once again been focused on the severe impairment in story recall evident in patients with left temporal-lobe dysfunction. Their recall tends to be sparse, containing only a few details, often not given in the order in which these facts had appeared in the original story. This poor quality of recall led Frisk and Milner (1985) to ask whether the underlying basis of the impairment was an inability to integrate information contained in the sentences comprising the text. For this reason, they varied the textual continuity inherent in prose passages by using stories presented either in the normal fashion or in a scrambled fashion, where the order of the sentences was randomized. Frisk and Milner hypothesized that if patients with left temporal-lobe lesions did have a deficit in integration, their recall would be less severely affected by the scrambling manipulation than would that of normal subjects. The results indicated, however, that recall of scrambled text was poor for all groups, but that there was no interaction between group and type of story. On this basis, poor integration had to be ruled out as a major source contributing to the impairment in recall. One other feature of this experiment emphasized the severity of the verbal memory deficit; Frisk and Milner found that cuing recall with specific questions about the content of the story did not compensate totally for the inability of the left temporal-lobe group to remember the details that they had heard.

Thus, attempts to delineate the factors underlying the impairment in verbal memory have yielded clues to the function of the left temporal lobe, but have left unanswered questions. The implications of a poor verbal memory for the person with left temporal-lobe dysfunction are important, for the deficit often proves to be troublesome in everyday living. Milner (1958) has described examples of difficulty experienced with a variety of activities, ranging from formal studies to handling the give-and-take of demanding conversation. Attempts to compensate for such impairments are often made with techniques such as keeping notes as reminders. Jones (1974) demonstrated that patients with left temporal-lobe lesions can use visual imagery to improve their performance on verbal paired-associate learning tasks, although not to normal levels.

Right temporal-lobe contributions to memory

The verbal learning and verbal memory tasks described above, in which performance is so sensitive to the effects of left temporal lobectomy, are accomplished normally by patients with comparable lesions in the right hemisphere. The right, non-dominant temporal lobe, like the left, is specialized in function for memory, but for memoranda that are not easily verbalized or coded into words. As was the case for the memory deficits characteristic of left temporal-lobe lesions, the nonverbal memory impairments associated with temporal lobectomy on the right are not modality-specific, and have been demonstrated for information presented via the auditory (Shankweiler, 1966), visual (Kimura, 1963; Milner, 1965, 1968) and tactile senses (Corkin, 1965; Rains, 1981).

Right temporal lobectomy impairs the recall of geometric designs as long as they do not lend themselves easily to the use of verbal mnemonics to aid recall (Jones-Gotman, 1986a, b; Taylor, 1969). These deficts are evident even though the patients are able to copy the designs accurately and do not show distortions or neglect in their drawings. Furthermore, the impairment in memory for designs is not restricted to free recall by drawing, but is also seen when the task requires the subject to learn to recognize abstract figures which recur throughout a long list (Kimura, 1963).

Abstract designs are not the only stimuli that can elicit the visual memory deficit associated with right temporal lobectomy. Faces also represent the kind of complex visual pattern resistant to accurate verbal coding. Milner (1968) demonstrated that when patients with right anterior temporal lobe lesions are asked to study a set of photographs of faces and after a short delay are required to choose these faces from among a larger array, they show a pronounced failure of recognition.

Thus far, it has been emphasized that the memory functions of the right temporal lobe are specific for material that is essentially nonverbal in nature. The contribution of this area to visual memory has been emphasized in a different context by Jaccarino (1975), in a study in which she presented line drawings of common objects, one at a time, in varying order over several trials. Immediately after the final trial, and again 24 hours later, the subjects were required to name from memory as many of the pictures as possible. In immediate recall, a mild impairment was evident for patients with left temporal-lobe lesions, whereas, as expected, patients with right temporal-lobe lesions performed as well as the normal control subjects. Twenty-four hours later, however, both groups of patients showed a marked deficit in recall. Jaccarino interpreted these results as emphasizing the duality of memory processing, the notion that in many circumstances both a verbal and an imaginal code are used to mediate recall (Paivio, 1971). In this instance she presumed that the verbal code was sufficient for the initial recall of the pictures, but that recall after a long delay also has an important visual component.

Further evidence of the role of the right temporal lobe in the recall of material that can be dually encoded is provided by the work of Jones-Gotman (1979) and Jones-Gotman and Milner (1978) on image-mediated verbal learning. Patients who have undergone right temporal lobectomy are indistinguishable from normal control subjects in learning lists of single words or word pairs when verbal mediational strategies are emphasized. In contrast, when visual imagery is used as a learning strategy, these same patients are impaired. They do not have any difficulty in generating appropriate images, and, in fact, in certain conditions showed normal recall immediately after learning the list, with the deficits emerging only after a delay (Jones-Gotman, 1979). These findings suggest that the images became less accessible over time so that the critical fault lay in the re-evocation of the images from memory.

There is convincing evidence to show that the structures of the right temporal lobe contribute to memory on tasks with a spatial component. Thus, impairments are seen in maze learning, whether it be in the visual (Milner, 1965) or tactual modality (Corkin, 1965), in the recall of simple position, again for information presented either visually (Corsi, 1972) or tactually (Rains, 1981), in spatial conditional associative learning (Petrides, 1985), and in the recall of the locations of small objects in a visually presented array (Smith and Milner, 1981, in press). An important feature of these tasks is that either the very presence of a deficit or the degree of severity of the deficit is related to the extent to which the lesion encroaches upon the hippocampal region. The spatial memory deficit associated with lesions of the right temporal lobe will be discussed in more depth in the section on the contribution of the hippocampal region to memory.

Hippocampal contributions to memory

In 1957, Scoville and Milner reported the now famous case of H.M., a young man who had undergone bilateral medial temporal-lobe removal for the relief of intractable seizures. The resection was said to have extended back 8 cm along the medial surface of both temporal lobes, destroying the amygdala, the uncus, and the anterior two-thirds of the hippocampus and the parahippocampal gyrus, but sparing the lateral neocortex. The surgery left H.M. with a severe, global anterograde amnesia, the characteristics of which have been extensively studied over the past 30 years (Corkin, 1984; Milner, 1959; Milner et al., 1968; Scoville and Milner, 1957).

The amnesia documented in H.M. focused attention on the contribution of the hippocampus to memory, and led to the question of whether the material-specific impairments observed after unilateral temporal lobectomy are contingent upon encroachment of the lesion into the hippocampal region. This possibility was first examined systematically by Corsi (1972, reported also in Milner, 1974, 1978), using formally similar verbal and nonverbal learning and memory tasks. One such set of tasks required the learning of supraspan sequences. The verbal version of these learning tasks was the Hebb (1961) recurring digits test, for which Corsi devised a nonverbal analogue, a block-tapping test, in which the subject must tap out a series of blocks, repeating exactly a sequence demonstrated by an examiner. In these tasks, each sequence exceeds by one digit or block, repectively, the subject's immediate memory span. Each task consists of 24 sequences in total, with the same sequence repeating every third trial (a feature of which the subject is not informed), whilst the intervening sequences occur only once. Under these conditions, normal subjects show learning of the recurrent sequence, while continuing to make errors on the non-recurrent sequences (Corsi, 1972; Hebb, 1961; Melton, 1963; Milner, 1978).

Although unilateral temporal lobectomy did not impair immediate memory span for either the digit or block sequences, Corsi demonstrated a double dissociation in the effects of left and right temporal-lobe lesions on the performance of these tasks, with deficits on the verbal version being seen only after left temporal lobectomy, and deficits on the nonverbal version seen only after right temporal lobectomy. More importantly, when he divided the patients into four groups based on the extent of hippocampal removal, he found that the degree of impairment was proportional to the size of the hippocampal lesion. Milner (1978) subsequently demonstrated that these sequence-learning tasks can also be used to detect hippocampal dys-

function in patients tested pre-operatively.

This relationship between the size of the hippocampal lesion and the severity of the memory deficit so clearly demonstrated by Corsi does not, however, hold true for all tests of memory. Performance on many of the tasks described earlier in the discussion of the memory disorders associated with left or right temporal lobectomy is not sensitive to the effects of hippocampal dysfunction. For certain tasks, a lesion of the lateral neocortex alone is sufficient to bring out the impairment, and that impairment is not exacerbated further by excision from the hippocampal region.

Examination of the tasks on which deficits are or are not contingent upon degree of medial temporal-lobe damage does not yield a simple explanation of the particular contribution of the hippocampus to memory. Lateral neocortical lesions in the left temporal lobe are sufficient to produce the impairment in recall of stories (Milner, 1967; Ojemann and Dodrill, 1985), in the recall of words generated as rhymes (Read, 1981, and cited in Milner, 1985), and in the recall of the names of pictured (Incisa della Rochetta, 1986) or real objects (Smith and Milner, 1981). Lateral right temporal-lobe lesions impair performance on the recall of complex geometric designs (Taylor, 1969), and on the recognition of faces (Milner, 1968), recurring nonsense figures (Kimura, 1963), and unfamiliar tonal melodies (Zatorre, 1985). The hippocampus appears to contribute when the tasks require sequence learning (Corsi, 1972) or when the material to be remembered lacks intrinsic structure (Milner, 1980), such as consonant trigrams (Corsi, 1972), or a complex geometric design presented in a piecemeal fashion so that its organization is not apparent (Jones-Gotman, 1986a). In addition, hippocampal lesions have been associated with reduced primacy effects, both for lists of words (Read, 1981) and for lists of designs (Jones-Gotman, 1986b). Table 1 indicates a variety of memory tasks on which deficits are or are not related to the extent of hippocampal excision included in the temporal lobectomy.

The diversity of tasks in which the hippocampus

is implicated emphasizes the interaction between the medial temporal-lobe structures and widespread areas of the ipsilateral neocortex (Pandya et al., 1981; Seltzer and Pandya, 1976; Seltzer and Van Hoesen, 1979; Van Hoesen, 1982; Van Hoesen and Pandya, 1975a, b; Van Hoesen et al., 1975). Thus, the hippocampal region may be part of a memory circuit involving a variety of cortical systems (Hirsh, 1974; Milner, 1959; Mishkin, 1982; O'Keefe and Nadel, 1978; Petrides and

TABLE 1

Material-specific memory deficits associated with unilateral temporal lobectomy: the contribution of the hippocampal region[a]

Side of temporal lobectomy	Tasks on which deficits are not related to extent of hippocampal lesion	Tasks on which deficits are related to extent of hippocampal lesion
Left	Recall of Wechsler Memory Scale prose passages and paired associates (Milner, 1967; Ojemann and Dodrill, 1985)	Learning of recurring supraspan digit sequences (Corsi, 1972; Milner, 1974)
	Recall of phonemically encoded words (Read, 1981; Rains, 1981)	Recall of consonant trigrams (Corsi, 1972)
	One-trial learning of supraspan digit sequences (Corsi, 1972)	Immediate recall of words generated as synonyms (Milner, 1985; Read, 1981)
	Delayed recall of semantically encoded words (Milner, 1985; Read, 1981)	Non-spatial conditional associative learning (Petrides, 1985)
	Recall of object names (Incisa della Rochetta, 1986; Jaccarino, 1975; Smith and Milner, 1981)	
Right	Recall of Rey-Osterrieth Complex Figure (Jones-Gotman, 1986a; Taylor, 1969)	Recall of spatial location (Corsi, 1972; Rains, 1981; Smith and Milner, 1981, in press)
	Recognition of unfamiliar faces (Milner, 1968[b]; Rains, 1981)	Maze learning (Corkin, 1965; Milner, 1965)
	Recognition of recurring designs (Kimura, 1963)	Learning of recurring supraspan block sequences (Corsi, 1972)
		Spatial conditional associative learning (Petrides, 1985)
		Self-ordered pointing to abstract designs and representational drawings (Petrides and Milner, 1982)
	Delayed recall of simple designs (Jones-Gotman, 1986a)	Recall of words learned with imagery mediation (Jones-Gotman, 1979; Jones-Gotman and Milner, 1978)
	Design-learning: trials to criterion (Jones-Gotman, 1986b)	Delayed recall of object names (Smith and Milner, 1981)
		Recall of complex design presented for copy in a piecemeal form (Jones-Gotman, 1986a)
		Design learning: accuracy scores in immediate recall (Jones-Gotman, 1986b)

[a] Adapted from Jones-Gotman, 1987.
[b] Although Milner (1968) reported an association between an impairment in face recognition and the extent of hippocampal damage, this association was found in only 1 of 3 test conditions; furthermore, in an expanded study with a much larger N, this finding for the hippocampal region was not replicated, although a deficit was still clearly demonstrated after right temporal lobectomy (Milner, personal communication).

Milner, 1982; Squire et al., 1984). According to this viewpoint, for tasks on which a temporal neocortical lesion is sufficient to impair performance, additional damage to hippocampal structures would not increase the severity of the impairment. If, however, successful performance on a task with a memory component requires a cortical area other than the temporal lobe, a deficit would be expected after damage to the hippocampal region because of the interruption of the critical memory circuit involving that part of the cortex.

One consistent finding with respect to the functions of the hippocampal region in the right hemisphere is that this area is implicated in spatial learning and spatial memory. This function was first noted in 1965, when Corkin and Milner published their papers on stylus maze-learning in the tactual and visual modalities, respectively. Patients with right temporal-lobe lesions were impaired in learning the correct path through the maze relative to patients with left temporal-lobe lesions or normal control subjects. When the right temporal-lobe group was subdivided into those with little or no involvement of the hippocampus in the removal, and those with radical excisions of this structure, the results indicated that the impairment was contingent upon the inclusion of a large part of the hippocampus in the excision. As described earlier, Corsi (1972) was able to demonstrate, using his recurring block-sequence task, an impairment in spatial learning that was dependent upon the extent of damage to the right hippocampal region. Performance on a spatial conditional associative learning task has also been demonstrated to be sensitive to extensive right hippocampal damage (Petrides, 1985).

In his series of experiments, Corsi (1972) also included a task requiring the memorization of the location of a dot positioned along an eight-inch line, and again found a deficit related to right hippocampal damage. Later, Rains (1981) demonstrated a similar impairment in memory for simple position, but for spatial information derived from touch, instead of by vision. The similarity in the findings, like that seen in the Corkin (1965) and

Milner (1965) studies on maze-learning, emphasizes that the important aspect of the task that is sensitive to the function of the right hippocampus is the spatial nature of the memoranda and not the modality of presentation.

Smith and Milner (1981, in press) examined the right hippocampal contribution to spatial memory using more complicated materials and with demands closer to those imposed in everyday life. Instead of requiring their subjects to remember the position of a single, meaningless stimulus like a dot on a line, they employed arrays of real objects, in which not only the absolute location but also the relative location of each object was important. The results from a series of experiments showed that patients with right temporal-lobe lesions which included radical hippocampal excisions showed normal ability to recall the locations of objects immediately after viewing the array, but were impaired when recall was tested after a delay as short as four minutes. This contrast in performance suggests that despite a normal ability to encode location, the patients with large right hippocampal lesions are susceptible to rapid forgetting of that information.

Although the above results do suggest a contribution by the right hippocampal region specifically to the learning and recall of spatial memoranda, there are other findings that do not fit the notion of such a complete specialization. Impairments in the retrieval of visual information to mediate verbal recall have been found to be related to the extent of right hippocampal damage (Jones-Gotman, 1979; Jones-Gotman and Milner, 1978; Smith and Milner, 1981). In addition, certain requirements of design learning and recall tasks have been demonstrated to elicit deficits in patients with radical right hippocampal lesions (Jones-Gotman, 1986a, b). For example, in a study examining both the learning of and memory for a list of abstract designs, Jones-Gotman (1986b) found that patients with either large or small hippocampal lesions were impaired in terms of the number of learning trials taken to reach criterion, but that the accuracy of the drawings reproduced across the arning trials was reduced only in the group with the large hippocampal excisions. Furthermore, ones-Gotman (1986a) demonstrated that presenting a complex drawing for copy in a piecemeal orm results in an impairment directly related to the extent of right hippocampal removal, whereas a similar design presented in an organized fashion ields a deficit that is not related to the size of the ippocampal lesion.

Attempting to assign a role specifically to the ippocampus is difficult because the lesions in the atients in whom these impairments have been emonstrated also include the amygdala, together ith varying amounts of the parahippocampal gy- us and the anterior temporal neocortex. Whether uch impairments would be found if the lesions ere to be restricted to the hippocampus remains > be seen. There is considerable evidence from ʹork in monkeys that the amygdala makes a signi- icant contribution to memory (Spiegler and Mish- in, 1981; Saunders et al., 1984), and that combin- d lesions of the amygdala and hippocampus are ecessary to produce severe impairments on cer- ain memory tasks (Mishkin, 1978). However, a ecently reported clinicopathological case study as demonstrated that amnesia can result from a esion confined to the hippocampus. Zola-Morgan t al. (1986) extensively examined a patient, R.B., ʹho developed an anterograde amnesia after an schemic episode. Five years after the onset of mnesia, R.B. died. Histological examination evealed a bilateral circumscribed lesion in the ʹA1 field of the hippocampus, with sparing of the ʹther medial temporal-lobe regions.

ʹarotid amytal studies of memory function

ʹodium Amytal was first used as a method of in- ʹestigating hemispheric function by Juhn Wada 1949, 1951) in his studies of the mechanisms ınderlying the spread of epileptic discharge be- ʹween the cerebral hemispheres in man. Intra- ʹarotid injection of sodium Amytal produces a ʹransient loss of function in the ipsilateral hemi- phere, a property that led to the appreciation of this method as a test for determining the lateraliza- tion of cerebral speech dominance. Injection of the dominant hemisphere results in a variety of apha- sic symptoms, including speech arrest, dysnomia, comprehension deficits and difficulty on verbal serial ordering tasks such as counting or reciting the days of the week, whereas injection of the non- dominant hemisphere does not cause interference with speech (Milner et al., 1964; Rasmussen and Milner, 1975; Wada and Rasmussen, 1960).

A few years after the adoption of the sodium Amytal procedure for assessing speech lateraliza- tion, it was realized that the procedure could also yield valuable information regarding memory function. The need for a pre-operative assessment of the risk of global memory deficit following unilateral temporal lobectomy became evident with the appearance of rare cases in which uni- lateral anterior temporal lobectomy (including the amygdala and hippocampus) produced a global and persistent amnesic syndrome. One such case, reported by Penfield and Milner in 1958, was the patient P.B., who underwent a two-stage removal from the left temporal region. During the first operation, the anterior 4 cm of the temporal lobe were excised, but the hippocampal region was left intact. The post-operative phase was marked by only a brief period of dysphasia. Five years later, because P.B. was still having seizures, a second operation was undertaken, in which the excision was extended to include the uncus, amygdala and hippocampus. This procedure was not followed by any aphasia, but there was a serious and generaliz- ed loss of recent memory, an anterograde amnesia that persisted for the remainder of P.B.'s life.

To explain the appearance of this amnesia, Pen- field and Milner hypothesized that there had been an additional and possibly more extensive lesion in the hippocampal region in the right hemisphere. Essentially, then, the removal of the epileptogenic but still partially functioning hippocampus on the side of operation deprived the patient of hip- pocampal function bilaterally. Several years later, P.B. died of a pulmonary embolism, and this hypothesis was confirmed by the findings on autopsy (Penfield and Mathieson, 1974). Examination of the brain indicated that approximately 22 mm of the left posterior hippocampus remained. On the right, the lateral neocortex and the amygdala appeared normal; in contrast, the right hippocampus was shrunken and histological studies revealed dense gliosis in the pyramidal cell layer and, to a lesser extent, in the dentate gyrus.

The findings in this and a few other such cases led Milner et al. (1962) to use the technique of intracarotid injection of sodium Amytal as a safeguard against the risk of severe memory loss after unilateral removal of the hippocampus. The rationale of the test is as follows: the procedure allows the assessment of memory in patients temporarily deprived of the functions of most of one hemisphere by the action of the drug. Inactivation of one temporal lobe should not in itself provoke a generalized amnesia, so that a global memory loss is not expected after unilateral injection unless there is a hippocampal lesion in the opposite hemisphere. If there is such a lesion, a transient generalized memory disorder characteristic of the amnesia seen in patients with bilateral medial temporal-lobe damage should be seen (Milner, 1975, 1978). It is important to stress that the transient amnesia is expected to be a generalized one, and not to be material-specific in nature. The critical test is one for anterograde amnesia, or failure to remember material presented while the functions of the hemisphere are inactivated by the Amytal, not material presented before the injection.

The assessment of memory using the intracarotid Amytal procedure is limited by the short-acting nature of the drug, which necessitates the use of simple tests. There is no standardized protocol in existence, and the actual procedure used varies widely from centre to centre (Blume et al., 1973; Fedio and Weinberg, 1971; Klove et al., 1969, 1970; Mateer and Dodrill, 1983; Milner, 1978; Rausch et al., 1984). At the Montreal Neurological Institute, where Amytal memory testing was pioneered, the patient is presented with five items while under the effect of the drug: two line-drawings of objects, a real object, a simple sentence and a concrete wor (see Jones-Gotman, 1987, and Milner, 1975, 1978 for complete details of the test procedure). Aft the drug has worn off, and speech functions hav returned to baseline levels (when the injection made into the dominant hemisphere), the patient first tested for recall of these items, and, if nee essary, for recognition using multiple-choice pro cedures. The time between the presentation of th stimuli and the memory test varies somewhat fro case to case, but averages approximately 1 minutes. The criterion for significant memory im pairment is taken as two or more errors of recogn tion.

In a recent retrospective study (Smith an Milner, 1985) of patients seen at the Montrea Neurological Hospital between 1979 and 1984, 11 cases with temporal-lobe lesions were identifie who had had sodium Amytal tests of both hemis pheres, and in whom the results of both tests wer unambiguous. Of these cases, 59 had a clear defined epileptic focus in the left temporal lobe, 3 had a right temporal-lobe focus, and 20 had epile tic activity occurring independently in both ten poral lobes. Table 2 shows the incidence c memory impairment as related to the nature of th epileptic focus (unilateral vs. bilateral). In patien with a clear, unilateral focus, injection of th hemisphere contralateral to the lesion is associate with a significantly higher failure rate than inje tion of the ipsilateral hemisphere.

This pattern of findings replicates the resul reported earlier by Milner (1975, 1978) with

TABLE 2

Incidence of anterograde amnesia after intracarotid injection sodium amytal

Temporal-lobe group	Side injected	
	Ipsilateral to planned operation	Contralateral to planned operation
Unilateral focus	14/96 (14.6%)	39/96 (40.6%)
Bilateral focus	10/20 (50%)	12/20 (60%)

milar group of patients, and using an earlier form
f the memory test containing only three items.
he data presented in Table 2 also demonstrate
at when there is dysfunction in both temporal
bes, the side of injection has no significant bear-
g on the incidence of memory impairment. Pa-
ents in whom there is evidence of bitemporal-lobe
ysfunction are especially at risk for memory loss
ter unilateral temporal lobectomy, and the
sults of the Amytal memory testing can be used
y the surgeon as an indication of whether to spare
e hippocampus and parahippocampal gyrus in
e temporal-lobe removal.

The incidence of failure on the memory test is
early related to the presence of a lesion con-
alateral to the side of injection. The early cases of
terograde amnesia resulting from unilateral tem-
oral lobectomy (Penfield and Milner, 1958) all
ad had excisions from the left, dominant hemi-
here, leading to the notion that removal from the
ominant hemisphere was instrumental in the am-
esia. Smith and Milner (1985) subdivided their
ses with unilateral foci according to side of leon and dominance for speech, and found no rela-
onship between memory impairment in the Amy-
l test and speech lateralization (see Table 3).

The results of the Amytal test for memory in pa-
ents with a unilateral epileptogenic focus has
ed light on normal memory processing. Several

studies have documented a striking failure of
recall, even for very simple test material seen when
only one hemisphere of the brain is active (Lesser
et al., 1986; Milner, 1978; Risse and Gazzaniga,
1978; Silfvenius et al., 1984). In a series of 48 patients with well-lateralized temporal-lobe lesions,
Milner (1978) contrasted recall and recognition
after injection of the hemisphere ipsilateral to the
lesion, so that the intact, normally functioning
hemisphere was responsible for memory. She
found that 60% could not recall either of two pictures presented to them just minutes earlier under
the effect of the sodium Amytal. That figure rose
to 72% for the recall of a sentence, a simple line
from a nursery rhyme which they had repeated correctly when it had been read to them. When
memory was tested by a multiple-choice recognition procedure, all correctly recognized the pictures, and 95% could identify the sentence from
among other familiar nursery rhymes. These findings, together with the evidence of memory
deficits in patients who have undergone cerebral
commissurotomy (Zaidel and Sperry, 1974), and
of the participation of both temporal lobes on
tasks leading to dual encoding (Jaccarino, 1975),
have led Milner (1978) to suggest that the successful re-evocation of a past experience depends
to some extent on the participation of both
hemispheres during the initial encoding.

Conclusions

In the eight decades since Bekhterev first suggested
that the temporal lobes are important for memory,
a vast amount of knowledge has been accumulated
to substantiate his hypothesis. In this chapter, the
material-specific deficits in learning and memory
associated with lateral and medial temporal-lobe
lesions were reviewed, along with corroborating
evidence from carotid Amytal studies of memory
function. The patterns of preserved and impaired
functions seen after temporal lobectomy and hippocampal lesions highlight the complexity both of
memory processing and of the interactions involved within the underlying neural systems.

ABLE 3

cidence of anterograde amnesia as related to locus of lesion
nd laterality of speech dominance

emisphere ominant or speech	Locus of lesion	Side injected	
		Ipsilateral to lesion	Contralateral to lesion
eft	Left temporal	8/45 (17.8%)	15/45 (33.3%)
	Right temporal	4/29 (13.8%)	12/29 (41.4%)
ight	Left temporal	0/14 (0%)	6/14 (43.9%)

Acknowledgements

The author wishes to thank the Natural Science and Engineering Research Council and the University of Toronto New Staff Fund for their support during the writing of this paper.

References

Bekhterev VM: Demonstration eines Gehirns mit Zerstorung der vorderen und inneren Theile der Hirnrinde beider Schlafenlappen. *Neurol. Zentralb.: 19,* 990 – 991, 1900.

Blakemore CB, Ettlinger G, Falconer MA: Cognitive abilities in relation to frequency of seizures and neuropathology of the temporal lobes in man. *J. Neurol. Neurosurg. Psychiatry: 29,* 268 – 272, 1966.

Blume WT, Grabow JD, Darley FL, Aronson AE: Intracarotid amobarbital test of language and memory before temporal lobectomy for seizure control. *Neurology: 23,* 812 – 819, 1973.

Bousfield WA: The occurrence of clustering in recall of randomly arranged associates. *J. Gen. Psychol.: 49,* 229 – 240, 1953.

Cavazzuti V, Winston K, Baker R, Welch K: Psychological changes following surgery for tumors in the temporal lobe. *J. Neurosurg.: 53,* 618 – 626, 1980.

Corkin S: Tactually-guided maze-learning in man: effects of unilateral cortical excisions and bilateral hippocampal lesions. *Neuropsychologia: 3,* 339 – 351, 1965.

Corkin S: Lasting consequences of bilateral medial temporal lobectomy: clinical course and experimental findings in H.M. *Semin. Neurol.: 4,* 249 – 259, 1984.

Corsi P: Human memory and the medial temporal region of the brain. Unpublished Ph.D. thesis, McGill University, Montreal, 1972.

Craik FIM, Lockhart RS: Levels of processing: a framework for memory research. *J. Verbal Learn. Verbal Behav., 11,* 671 – 684, 1972.

Craik FIM, Tulving E: Depth of processing and the retention of words in episodic memory. *J. Exp. Psychol. Gen.: 104,* 268 – 294, 1975.

Crandall PH: Cortical resections. In Engel Jr. J (Editor), *Surgical Treatment of the Epilepsies.* New York: Raven Press, pp. 377 – 404, 1987.

Dennis M, Farrell K, Hoffman HJ, Hendrick EB, Becker LE, Murphy EG: Recognition memory of item, associative, and serial-order information after temporal lobectomy for seizure disorder. *Neuropsychologia: 26,* 53 – 65, 1988.

Eskenazi B, Cain WS, Novelly RA, Mattson R: Odor perception in temporal lobe epilepsy patients with and without temporal lobectomy. *Neuropsychologia: 24,* 553 – 562, 1986.

Fedio P, Mirsky AF: Selective intellectual deficits in children with temporal-lobe or centrencephalic epilepsy. *Neuropsychologia: 7,* 276 – 300, 1969.

Fedio P, Weinberg LK: Dysnomia and impairment of verbal memory following intracarotid injection of sodium Amytal. *Brain Res.: 31,* 159 – 168, 1971.

Frisk V, Milner B: Retention of verbal information in scramble and unscrambled texts by patients with unilateral cerebral le sions. Paper presented at the annual meeting of the Canadia Psychological Association, Halifax, 1985.

Hebb DO: Distinctive features of learning in the higher anima. In Delafresnaye JF (Editor), *Brain Mechanisms and Learn ing.* London: Oxford University Press, pp. 37 – 51, 1961.

Hirsh R: The hippocampus and contextual retrieval of informa tion from memory: a theory. *Behav. Biol.: 12,* 421 – 444 1974.

Incisa della Rocchetta I: Classification and recall of picture after unilateral frontal or temporal lobectomy. *Cortex: 22* 189 – 211, 1986.

Jaccarino G: Dual encoding in memory: evidence fror temporal-lobe lesions in man. Unpublished M.A. thesis McGill University, Montreal, 1975.

Jaccarino-Hiatt G: Impairment of cognitive organization in pa tients with temporal-lobe lesions. Unpublished Ph.D. thesis McGill University, Montreal, 1978.

Jones MK: Imagery as a mnemonic acid after left tempora lobectomy: contrast between material-specific and generaliz ed memory disorders. *Neuropsychologia: 12,* 21 – 30, 1974.

Jones-Gotman M: Incidental learning of image-mediated o pronounced words after right temporal lobectomy. *Cortex 15,* 187 – 197, 1979.

Jones-Gotman M: Memory for designs: the hippocampal con tribution. *Neuropsychologia: 24,* 193 – 203, 1986a.

Jones-Gotman M: Right hippocampal excision impairs learnin and recall of a list of abstract designs. *Neuropsychologia: 24* 659 – 670, 1986b.

Jones-Gotman M: Psychological evaluation: testing hippocam pal function. In Engel J (Editor), *Surgical Treatment of th Epilepsies.* New York: Raven Press, pp. 203 – 211, 1987.

Jones-Gotman M, Milner B: Right temporal-lobe contributio to image-mediated verbal learning. *Neuropsychologia: 16* 61 – 71, 1978.

Kimura D: Some effects of temporal-lobe damage on auditor perception. *Can. J. Psychol.: 15,* 156 – 165, 1961.

Kimura D: Right temporal lobe damage. *Arch. Neurol.: 8* 264 – 271, 1963.

Klove H, Grabow JD, Trites RL: Evaluation of memory func tions with intracarotid Sodium Amytal. *Trans. Am. Neurol Assoc.: 94,* 76 – 80, 1969.

Klove H, Trites RL, Grabow JD: Intracarotid Sodium Amyta for evaluating memory function. *Electroencephalogr. Clin Neurophysiol.: 28,* 418 – 419, 1970.

Lesser RP, Dinner DS, Luders H, Morris HH: Memory for ob jects presented soon after intracarotid amobarbital sodiun injections in patients with medically intractable complex par tial seizures. *Neurology: 36,* 895 – 899, 1986.

Mandler G: Organization and memory. In Spence KW, Spenc JT (Editors), *The Psychology of Learning and Motivation Vol. 1.* New York: Academic Press, pp. 327 – 372, 1967.

Mandler G: Words, lists and categories: an experimental viev of organized memory. In Cowan JL (Editor), *Studies ii Thought and Language.* Tucson: University of Arizon. Press, pp. 99 – 131, 1970.

Marshall GR: Stimulus characteristics contributing to organiza tion in free recall. *J. Verbal Learn. Verbal Behav.: 6* 364 – 374, 1967.

Mateer CA, Dodrill CB: Neuropsychological and linguistic correlates of atypical language lateralization: evidence from sodium amytal studies. *Hum. Neurobiol.: 2*, 135 – 142, 1983.

Melton AW: Implications of short-term memory for a general theory of memory. *J. Verbal Learn. Verbal Behav.: 2*, 1 – 21, 1963.

Meyer V, Yates AJ: Intellectual changes following temporal lobectomy for psychomotor epilepsy. *J. Neurol. Neurosurg. Psychiatry: 18*, 44 – 52, 1955.

Milner B: Psychological defects produced by temporal lobe excision. *Res. Publ. Assoc. Nerv. Ment. Disord.: 36*, 244 – 257, 1958.

Milner B: The memory defect in bilateral hippocampal lesions. *Psychiatr. Res. Rep.: 11*, 43 – 58, 1959.

Milner B: Visually-guided maze-learning in man: effects of bilateral hippocampal, bilateral frontal, and unilateral cerebral lesions. *Neuropsychologia: 3*, 317 – 338, 1965.

Milner B: Brain mechanisms suggested by studies of the temporal lobes. In Darley FC (Editor), *Brain Mechanisms Underlying Speech and Language*. New York: Grune and Stratton, pp. 122 – 145, 1967.

Milner B: Visual recognition and recall after right temporal-lobe excision in man. *Neuropsychologia: 6*, 191 – 209, 1968.

Milner B: Hemispheric specialization: scope and limits. In Schmitt FO, Worden FG (Editors), *The Neurosciences: Third Study Program*. Boston: MIT Press, Ch. 8, pp 75 – 89, 1974.

Milner, B: Psychological aspects of focal epilepsy and its neurosurgical management. In Purpura DP, Penry JK, Walter RD (Editors), *Advances in Neurology, Vol. 8*. New York: Raven Press, Ch. 15, pp. 299 – 321, 1975.

Milner B: Clues to the cerebral organization of memory. In Buser P, Rougeul-Buser A (Editors), *Cerebral Correlates of Conscious Experience*. Amsterdam: Elsevier, pp. 139 – 153, 1978.

Milner B: Complementary functional specializations of the human cerebral hemispheres. In Levi-Montalcini R (Editor), *Nerve Cells, Transmitters and Behaviour*. Vatican City: Pontificia Academia Scientiarum, pp. 601 – 625, 1980.

Milner B: Memory and the human brain. In Shafto M (Editor), *How We Know*. San Francisco: Harper & Row, Ch. 2, pp. 31 – 59, 1985.

Milner B, Kimura D: Dissociable visual learning defects after unilateral temporal lobectomy in man. Paper presented at the annual meeting of the Eastern Psychological Association, Philadelphia, 1964.

Milner B, Branch C, Rasmussen T: Study of short-term memory after intracarotid injection of sodium amytal. *Trans. Am. Neurol. Assoc.: 87*, 224 – 226, 1962.

Milner B, Branch C, Rasmussen T: Observations on cerebral dominance. In DeReuck AVS, O'Connor M (Editors), *Ciba Foundation Symposium on Disorders of Language*. London: J and A Churchill, pp. 200 – 214, 1964.

Milner B, Corkin S, Teuber HL: Further analyses of the hippocampal amnesic syndrome: 14-year follow-up study of H.M. *Neuropsychologia: 6*, 215 – 234, 1968.

Mishkin M: Memory in monkeys severely impaired by combined but not by separate removal of amygdala and hippocampus. *Nature: 273*, 297 – 298, 1978.

Mishkin M: A memory system in the monkey. *Phil. Trans. R. Soc. Lond.: B298*, 85 – 95, 1982.

Moscovitch M: Verbal and spatial clustering in the free recall of drawings following left or right temporal lobectomy: evidence for dual encoding. Paper presented at the annual meeting of the Canadian Psychological Association, Toronto, 1976.

Novelly RA, Augustine, EA, Mattson RH, Glaser GH, Williamson PD, Spencer DD, Spencer SS: Selective memory improvement and impairment in temporal lobectomy for epilepsy. *Ann. Neurol.: 15*, 64 – 67, 1984.

Ojemann GA: Surgical therapy for medically intractable epilepsy. *J. Neurosurg.: 66*, 489 – 499, 1987.

Ojemann G, Dodrill C: Verbal memory deficits after left temporal lobectomy for epilepsy. *J. Neurosurg.: 62*, 101 – 107, 1985.

O'Keefe J, Nadel L: The hippocampus as a cognitive map. Oxford: Clarendon Press, 1978.

Olivier A. Commentary: cortical resections. In Engel Jr. J (Editor), *Surgical Treatment of the Epilepsies*. New York: Raven Press, pp. 405 – 418, 1987.

Paivio A: Imagery and verbal processes. New York: Holt, Rhinehart and Winston, 1971.

Pandya DN, Van Hoesen GW, Mesulam MM: Efferent connections of the cingulate gyrus in the rhesus monkey. *Exp. Brain Res.: 42*, 319 – 330, 1981.

Penfield W, Baldwin M: Temporal lobe seizures and the technique of subtotal temporal lobectomy. *Ann. Surg.: 136*, 625 – 634, 1952.

Penfield W, Mathieson G: An autopsy and a discussion of the role of the hippocampus in experiential recall. *Arch. Neurol.: 31*, 145 – 154, 1974.

Penfield W, Milner B: Memory deficit produced by bilateral lesions in the hippocampal zone. *Arch. Neurol. Psychiatry: 79*, 475 – 497, 1958.

Petrides M: Deficits on conditional associative-learning tasks after frontal- and temporal-lobe lesions in man. *Neuropsychologia: 23*, 601 – 614, 1985.

Petrides M, Milner B: Deficits on subject-ordered tasks after frontal- and temporal-lobe lesions in man. *Neuropsychologia: 20*, 249 – 262, 1982.

Rains GD: Aspects of memory in patients with temporal lobe lesions. Unpublished Ph.D. thesis, Cornell University, Ithaca, 1981.

Rains GD: Incidental verbal memory as a function of depth of encoding in patients with temporal-lobe lesions. *J. Clin. Exp. Neuropsychol.: 9*, 18, 1987.

Rasmussen T, Milner B: Clinical and surgical studies of the cerebral speech areas in man. In Zülch KJ, Creutzfeldt O, Galbraith GC (Editors), *Cerebral Localization*. Berlin: Springer-Verlag, pp. 238 – 257, 1975.

Rausch R, Fedio P, Ary CM, Engell J Jr, Crandall PH: Resumption of behavior following intracarotid sodium amobarbital injection. *Ann. Neurol.: 15*, 31 – 35, 1984.

Read DE: Effects of medial temporal-lobe lesions on intermediate memory in man. Unpublished Ph.D. thesis, McGill University, Montreal, 1981.

Risse GL, Gazzaniga MS: Well-kept secrets of the right hemisphere: a carotid amytal study of restricted memory transfer. *Neurology: 28*, 950 – 953, 1978.

Saunders RC, Murray EA, Mishkin M: Further evidence that

amygdala and hippocampus contribute equally to visual recognition. *Neuropsychologia: 22,* 785 – 796, 1984.

Scoville WB, Milner B: Loss of recent memory after bilateral hippocampal lesions. *J. Neurol. Neurosurg. Psychiatry: 20,* 11 – 21, 1957.

Seltzer B, Pandya N: Some cortical projections to the parahippocampal area in the rhesus monkey. *Exp. Neurol.: 50,* 146 – 160, 1976.

Seltzer B, Van Hoesen GW: A direct inferior parietal lobule projection to the presubiculum in the rhesus monkey. *Brain Res.: 179,* 157 – 161, 1979.

Shankweiler D: Defects in recognition and reproduction of familiar tunes after unilateral temporal lobectomy. Presented at the annual meeting of the Eastern Psychological Association, New York, 1966.

Silfvenius H, Blom S, Nilsson L-G, Christianson S-V: Observations on verbal, pictorial and stereognostic memory in epileptic patients during intracarotid Amytal testing. *Acta Neurol. Scand.:* 69 (Supplement 99), 57 – 75, 1984.

Slamecka NJ, Graf P: The generation effect: Delineation of a phenomenon. *J. Exp. Psychol. Hum. Learn. Mem.: 4,* 592 – 604, 1978.

Smith ML, Milner B: The role of the right hippocampus in the recall of spatial location. *Neuropsychologia: 19,* 781 – 793, 1981.

Smith ML, Milner B: Residual memory deficits after unilateral cerebral excision. Paper presented at the annual meeting of the International Neuropsychology Symposium, Beaune, 1984.

Smith ML, Milner B: Carotid Amytal studies of memory function. Paper presented at the annual meeting of the International Neuropsychology Society, San Diego, 1985.

Smith ML, Milner B: Right hippocampal impairment in the recall of location: encoding deficit or rapid forgetting? *Neuropsychologia: 27,* 71 – 82, 1989.

Spiegler BJ, Mishkin M: Evidence for the sequential participation of inferior temporal cortex and amygdala in the acquisition of stimulus-reward associations. *Behav. Brain Res.: 3,* 303 – 317, 1981.

Squire LR, Cohen NJ, Nadel L: The medial temporal region and memory consolidation: A new hypothesis. In Weingartner H, Parker E (Editors), *Memory Consolidation,* Hillsdale, NJ: Lawrence Erlbaum Associates, pp. 185 – 206, 1984.

Taylor, LB: Localization of cerebral lesions by psychological testing. *Clin. Neurosurg.: 16,* 269 – 287, 1969.

Tulving E: Subjective organization in free recall of 'unrelated' words. *Psychol. Rev.: 69,* 344 – 354, 1962.

Tulving E: Episodic and semantic memory. In Tulving E, Donaldson W (Editors), *Organization and Memory.* New York: Academic Press, pp. 381 – 403, 1972.

Van Hoesen GW: The parahippocampal gyrus: new observations regarding its cortical connections in the monkey. *Trends Neurosci.: 5,* 345 – 350, 1982.

Van Hoesen GW, Pandya DN: Some connections of the entorhinal (area 28) and perirhinal (area 35) cortices of the rhesus monkey. I. Temporal lobe afferents. *Brain Res.: 95,* 1 – 24, 1975a.

Van Hoesen GW, Pandya DN, Butters N: Some connections of the entorhinal (area 28) and perirhinal (area 35) cortices of the rhesus monkey. II. Frontal lobe afferents. *Brain Res.: 95,* 25 – 38, 1975.

Van Hoesen GW, Pandya DN: Some connections of the entorhinal (area 28) and perirhinal (area 35) cortices of the rhesus monkey. III. Efferent connections. *Brain Res.: 95,* 39 – 59, 1975b.

Wada J: A new method for the determination of the side of cerebral speech dominance. A preliminary report on the intracarotid injection of Sodium Amytal in man. *Igaku to Seibutsugaku (Medicine and Biology): 14,* 221 – 222, 1949 (Japanese).

Wada J: An experimental study on the neural mechanism of the spread of epileptic impulse. *Folia Psychiatr. Jap.: 4,* 289 – 301, 1951.

Wada J, Rasmussen T: Intracarotid injection of sodium Amytal for the lateralization of cerebral speech dominance: Experimental and clinical observations. *J. Neurosurg.: 17,* 266 – 282, 1960.

Wechsler D: A standardized memory scale for clinical use. *J. Psychol.: 19,* 87 – 95, 1945.

Weingartner H: Verbal learning in patients with temporal lobe lesions. *J. Verbal Learn. Verbal Behav.: 7,* 520 – 526, 1968.

Wilkins B, Moscovitch M: Selective impairment of semantic memory after temporal lobectomy. *Neuropsychologia: 16,* 73 – 79, 1978.

Zaidel D, Sperry RW: Memory impairment after commissurotomy in man. *Brain: 97,* 263 – 272, 1974.

Zatorre R: Discrimination and recognition of tonal melodies after unilateral cerebral excisions. *Neuropsychologia: 23,* 31 – 41, 1985.

Zola-Morgan S, Squire LR, Amaral DG: Human amnesia and the medial temporal region: Enduring memory impairment following a bilateral lesion limited to field CA1 of the hippocampus. *J. Neurosci.: 6,* 2950 – 2967, 1986.

© 1989 Elsevier Science Publishers B.V. (Biomedical Division)
Handbook of Neuropsychology, Vol. 3
F. Boller and J. Grafman (Eds)

CHAPTER 5

Diencephalic amnesia

Nelson Butters[1] and Donald T. Stuss[2]

[1] Psychology Service, San Diego Veterans Administration Medical Center and Psychiatry Department, University of California, San Diego, CA, U.S.A. and [2] Rotman Research Institute of Baycrest Centre and Departments of Psychology and Medicine, University of Toronto, Toronto, Canada

Introduction

Amnesia following damage to the medial portions of the diencephalon (e.g., mammillary bodies, dorsomedial nucleus of the thalamus) (Fig. 1) has been associated with a number of etiologies including vascular events, traumas, neoplasms and the combination of malnutrition (thiamine) and long-term alcoholism. In reviewing the literature of the past 25 years, five issues appear to have dominated investigators' interests. (1) What are the cognitive processes underlying the patients' anterograde amnesia? (2) What are the clinical features of their retrograde amnesia? (3) What aspects of memory are preserved in diencephalic amnesia? (4) In addition to memory, what other cognitive functions (e.g., attention, problem solving) are compromised, and how do they confound the diencephalic patients' amnesic symptoms? (5) What are the critical diencephalic structures involved in these severe memory deficits?

Because most of the published studies concerned with the first four issues have utilized alcoholics with Korsakoff's syndrome, our discussion of these alcoholic patients shall be separated for didactic reasons from those whose diencephalic amnesia emanates from other etiologies. In the first part of this chapter the neuropsychological impairments and anatomical features associated with vascular, traumatic and neoplastic etiologies will be considered. The second section will be reserved for a review of studies focusing upon alcoholic Korsakoff's syndrome.

Diencephalic amnesia associated with vascular, traumatic and neoplastic etiologies

Anterograde amnesia

Immediately following acute diencephalic damage, confusion and disorientation are the most obvious psychological changes (Graff-Radford et al., 1984; Spiegel et al., 1956). After several days or weeks, this confusional state remits, and the patient presents with a severe anterograde amnesia as his/her most evident and consistent neuropsychological impairment. Studies of patients with ischemic infarcts (Barbizet et al., 1981; Guberman and Stuss, 1983; Mills and Swanson, 1978), traumatic injury (Jarho, 1973; Squire and Moore, 1979; Teuber et al., 1968) and neoplastic growths (Butters, 1984a; McEntee et al., 1976; Sprofkin and Sciarri, 1952) are consistent in demonstrating that patients with bilateral mesial diencephalic lesions have extensive difficulty in learning and retaining new verbal and nonverbal information. Both animal and human studies have shown that this memory disorder, and at times disorientation, can persist for years, apparently representing a permanent disability (Castaigne et al., 1981; Michel et al., 1982; Stuss et al., 1988; Zola-Morgan and Squire, 1985).

Examinations of patients with unilateral thalamic pathology have indicated that hemispheric spe-

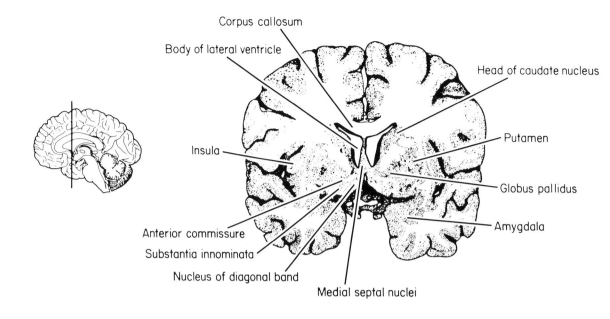

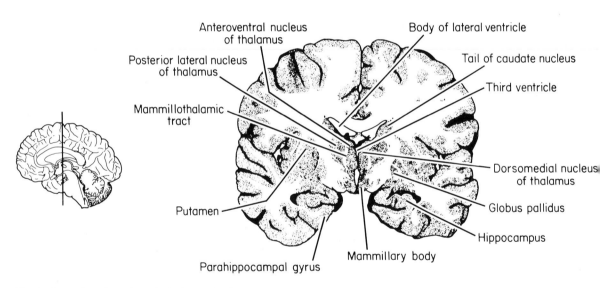

Fig. 1. Coronal sections through the human brain. The dorsomedial nucleus of the thalamus and the mammillary bodies (bottom section) are the diencephalic structures frequently associated with amnesic disorders. Damage to mesial temporal (hippocampus, amygdala) and basal forebrain (substantia innominata, nucleus of diagonal band, medial septal nuclei) structures (top section) have also been shown to result in amnesia.

cialization extends to diencephalic structures (Squire and Moore, 1979; Teuber et al., 1968). In general, right unilateral pathology results in non-verbal memory deficits, whereas left lesions are followed by primarily verbal memory impairments (Cappa and Vignolo, 1979; Michel et al., 1982; Mori et al., 1986; Reynolds et al., 1979; Speedie and Heilman, 1982, 1983; Squire, 1982; Squire and Moore, 1979; Squire and Slater, 1978; Vilkki, 1978). There has been controversy and a diversity of claims, with suggestions that right unilateral lesions produce minimal or no deficits, whereas damage limited to the left thalamus results in verbal memory impairment, disorientation and, suggested by some, possibly in dementia (Alexander and LoVerme, 1980; Choi et al., 1983; Graff-Radford et al., 1984; Graff-Radford et al., 1985; Squire, 1982; Squire and Slater, 1978).

Stuss et al. (1988) confirmed hemispheric asymmetries secondary to diencephalic pathology in patients tested 1 – 2 years following an acute onset of unilateral infarcts. However, the asymmetry was apparent only with relatively simple tasks (see Fig. 2). With more demanding memory tasks, the asymmetry was not evident, due either to the less specific nature of the more complex task, or to the obscuring of the asymmetry by impairments in focused attention.

In summary, diencephalic pathology from various etiologies results in a notable anterograde amnesia which is most severe if the damage is bilateral. Whether this is compounded by other behavioral disorders is less certain.

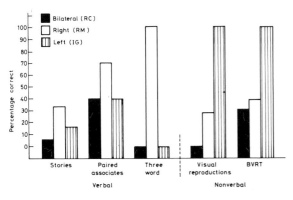

Fig. 2. Delayed recall of verbal and non-verbal measures of memory for all three patients with thalamic lesions (bilateral, primarily right and unilateral left) at least six months post-infarct. The visual reproductions, stories and paired associate tests were derived from the Wechsler Memory Scale. The multiple choice format was used for the Benton Visual Retention Test (BVRT). For the three word tests, the patient was asked to recall three words after a five minute delay. The figure clearly depicts the hemispheric asymmetry of recall of information, dependent upon lesion location. Reprinted with permission from Stuss et al., *Brain and Cognition, 1988.*

Neurologic structures underlying anterograde amnesia

There has been considerable controversy concerning the anatomical areas underlying diencephalic amnesia as well as the implications of such neurologic findings for the existence of multiple memory systems (Cramon et al., 1985; Mair et al., 1979; Weiskrantz, 1985). With few exceptions (e.g., Archer et al., 1981), diencephalic amnesia has been found to involve midline thalamic regions. Although the role of specific nuclei (e.g., dorsomedial nucleus of the thalamus, mammillary bodies) and fiber tracts (e.g., internal medullary lamina, mammillothalamic tract) has been debated (Weiskrantz, 1985), clarification has been slow due to a lack of patients with highly localized lesions and to technological limitations. For instance, most pathological studies have been based on relatively small sample sizes (e.g., Mair et al., 1979) and, in the case of in vivo documentation of pathology with modern radiological procedures, even high contrast CT scans and MRI often lack sufficient resolution to examine the millimeter differences needed to identify specific thalamic nuclei and white matter tracts.

The debate has focused primarily upon the dorsomedial (DM) nucleus, the mammillary bodies (MB) and the mammillothalamic tract (MTT) (Figs. 1 and 3). Perhaps influenced by trends in the study of alcoholic Korsakoff patients, the evidence from traumatic, ischemic and neoplastic etiologies may appear to favor the role of the DM nucleus. Tumors of the third ventricle in the area of the DM nucleus result in severe memory disorders (Cairns and Mosberg, 1951; Ignelzi and Squire, 1976). These deficits were present even in the absence of involvement of the MB, MTT and anterior thalamus (McEntee et al., 1976). Past studies using patients with different etiologies have suggested that damage to the dorsomedial thalamus may be sufficient to result in severe memory dysfunctions (Choi et al., 1983; Guberman and Stuss, 1983; Squire and Moore, 1979; Winocur et al., 1984). Whether pathology extending beyond the dorsomedial nucleus is necessary is uncertain.

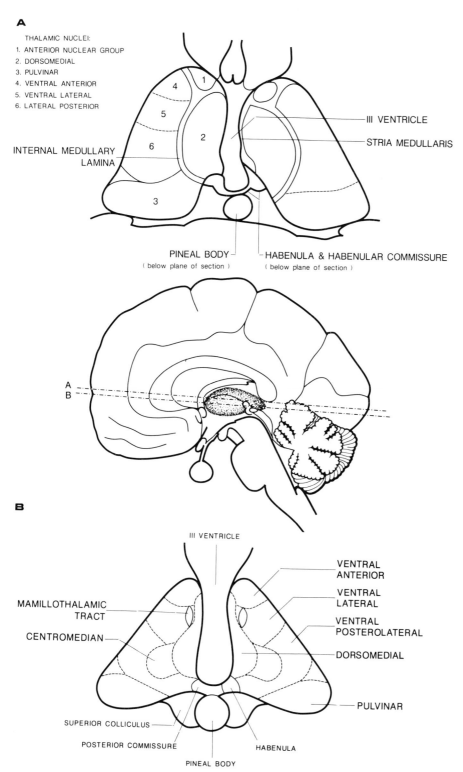

Fig. 3. A schematic representation of two horizontal cuts through the thalamus (DeArmond et al., 1976). Centre, level of the two planes; top and bottom, depiction of the paramedian thalamic region at each of the two levels.

Squire (1982, p. 264) has suggested that "the tradi-tional view that damage to the fornix/mammillary system causes amnesia seems less secure than it once was, while damage to the dorsal thalamus seems able to cause amnesia".

Despite this evidence, investigators remain cautious with regard to localization within the midline thalamic region. While the DM nucleus appears to be involved in memory, lesions have rarely been confined to this thalamic nucleus (Aggleton and Mishkin, 1983a, b; Markowitsch, 1982, 1984; Markowitsch and Pritzel, 1985; McEntee et al., 1976; Mills and Swanson, 1978; Schott et al., 1980; Smyth and Stern, 1938). Moreover, the involvement of the DM nucleus does not exclude a role for other proximate regions. This difficulty in determining precise anatomical localization can perhaps be best exemplified by Squire's series of investigations of patient N.A. who had endured a traumatic lesion to the diencephalon. Based upon CT scan analyses (Squire and Moore, 1979), patient N.A. initially appeared to have a lesion limited to the DM nucleus of the left hemisphere. However, a subsequent evaluation with magnetic resonance imaging (MRI) has shown the lesion to encompass several thalamic nuclei in the left hemisphere and the mammillary bodies bilaterally (Squire et al., in press).

The evidence for the involvement of the MB in memory is equally prominent (Castaigne et al., 1966; Castaigne et al., 1981; Pierrot-Deseilligny et al., 1982; Swanson and Schmidley, 1985). Some investigations have focused not only on the MB per se, but also on the MTT and its terminus, the anterior thalamic nucleus. Cramon et al. (1985) carefully examined the CT scans of patients with hemorrhagic diencephalic lesions, six of their own and five already published in the literature. Their analyses showed that the apparent critical structures for diencephalic amnesia were the MTT and the ventral portion of the internal medullary lamina (IML), but not the DM nucleus (Fig. 3). Cramon et al. concluded that the amnesic symptoms associated with diencephalic lesions may be due to a disconnection of the thalamus from mesial

temporal lobe structures. The MTT connects the medial diencephalon with the hippocampus via the subiculum and entorhinal cortex; the IML is comprised of fibers connecting the medial portions of the thalamus with the amygdala. If Cramon et al.'s data and conclusions are correct, Warrington and Weiskrantz's (1982) contention that all amnesias (i.e., both hippocampal and diencephalic) have a common neurological and psychological base appears well supported.

A compromise position, similar to that proposed for hippocampal amnesia (Mishkin, 1978, 1982) has also evolved. While a lesion in either the MB or the DM nucleus may be sufficient to cause mild amnesic symptoms, a lesion in both may be needed for severe memory dysfunction (Squire, 1982). Aggleton and Mishkin (1983a) have reported that medial thalamic lesions in monkeys result in an inability to retain new information. However, since their surgical procedures damaged the medial portions of the anterior nucleus of the thalamus as well as the DM nucleus, significant degeneration of MB was noted. In a second study in which lesions were limited to either the monkeys' DM or anterior thalamic nuclei, Aggleton and Mishkin (1983b) found that damage to either nucleus was followed by mild-to-moderate retention deficits, whereas severe anterograde amnesia required lesions in both diencephalic regions. While these findings appear consistent with those of Kritchevsky and colleagues (1987) who reported two patients with no memory deficits following infarcts damaging less than 15% of the DM nucleus, they conflict with an animal investigation by Zola-Morgan and Squire (1985). These investigators noted that damage limited to 32 – 44% of the posterior sector of the DM nucleus was followed by acquisition deficits similar in severity to those associated with combined anterior DM nucleus and MTT damage (Aggleton and Mishkin, 1983a, b). It is, however, difficult to compare the severity of DM lesions in the various studies because of differences in methodologies such as the presence or absence of pre-operative training.

The demonstrated difficulty in establishing the

neuroanatomical basis of diencephalic amnesia has its roots not only in the physical proximity of critical structures but also in the possible interconnectedness of these neurological entities. The DM nucleus is adjacent to the anterior nucleus, with the MTT tract traversing between the two (see Stuss et al., 1988). Given these considerations, selective damage to either the DM nucleus or to the MB and MTT is, and will likely continue to be, very rare in nature and animal lesion studies. Also, the possibility that still other unspecified structures adjacent to or interconnected with the DM nucleus and the MB play an important role in diencephalic amnesia cannot be discounted.

Retrograde amnesia

The assessment of remote memory loss in diencephalic amnesics with vascular, traumatic or neoplastic etiologies has been infrequent and when reported, evidence is frequently limited to clinical observations without quantitative documentation. This dearth of empirical data may reflect the fact that most neuropsychological studies of diencephalic amnesia, with the exception of those employing alcoholic Korsakoff patients, involve single case reports.

Patient N.A., who endured a tramatic lesion to the mesial diencephalon, was originally unable to recall any significant personal, national or international events for at least two years preceding the acute onset of his disorder (Teuber et al., 1968). His retrograde amnesia apparently diminished over time, leaving N.A. with a minimal if any remote memory loss (Cohen and Squire, 1981; Squire, 1982; Squire and Moore, 1979; Squire and Slater, 1978). Although the exact duration of his retrograde amnesia is difficult to determine (Squire and Cohen, 1982), there remains a striking dissociation between the severity of patient N.A.'s anterograde and retrograde amnesias. This disparity is most difficult to interpret given that N.A.'s lesion involves at least mesial thalamic nuclei in the left hemisphere and the mammillary bodies bilaterally (Squire et al., in press). It is conceivable that if N.A.'s lesion had involved both right and

left thalamus, a much extended RA might have been present.

Diencephalic patients whose anterograde amnesia has a vascular etiology often have relatively intact, or even normal, memory for remote events (Cramon and Eilbert, 1979; Michel et al., 1982; Schott et al., 1980; Winocur et al., 1984). This relative preservation has been reported with MB, MTT and medial thalamic lesions (Cramon and Eilert, 1979; Winocur et al., 1984). This predominance of anterograde over retrograde amnesia in diencephalic patients has prompted theoretical discussions concerning the nature of their memory deficiencies. Some investigators (e.g., Winocur et al., 1984) have interpreted the diencephalic patients' lack of retrograde amnesia as evidence of a storage rather than a retrieval deficit. That is, if the patients' overall memory problems stem from deficiencies in retrieving successfully stored information, they should exhibit difficulties in accessing information learned prior to as well as after their injury. A similar dissociation between anterograde and retrograde amnesia in the early reports of patient H.M. (Corkin, 1984; Milner, 1966, 1974) has also been frequently cited as evidence that amnesia represents a failure to consolidate (i.e., store) new information (Squire, 1987).

Other studies have challenged these observations concerning retrograde amnesia in diencephalic amnesia. Patients with tumors located within the diencephalon have been reported to have a severe, extended retrograde amnesia encompassing their entire lives (Butters, 1984a; McEntee et al., 1976; Ziegler et al., 1977). Several patients with bilateral, paramedian insults have been shown to have severe retrograde (as well as anterograde) amnesias for both personal and public events (Barbizet et al., 1981; Graff-Radford et al., 1984; Katz et al., 1987; Spiegel et al., 1956; Sprofkin and Sciarra, 1952; Stuss et al., 1988). It may be of some import to note that many of these extended retrograde amnesias were 'flat', i.e., there was no relative sparing of events from early childhood and adulthood.

Stuss et al. (1988) have described the retrograde amnesia of a well-educated patient (i.e., patient .C.) with an isolated bilateral paramedian thalamic infarct. In addition to his inability to learn and retain new information, patient R.C. could recall ttle about major public events that had occurred ver the past five decades. This severe impairment a remote memory was also evident when recognion measures were used, and appeared equivalent .e., no temporal gradient or sparing of very emote memories) for all periods of the patient's fe (Fig. 4). When patient R.C.'s memory for utobiographical events was evaluated, his severe hability to remember past episodes was again very pparent. Although this loss of personal memories eemed most severe for the years immediately prior o his infarct, there was at least a patchy loss for much of his life.

While the latter results certainly indicate that patents with paramedian thalamic damage can pre-sent with a severe retrograde amnesia, the neurological basis for this impairment remains obscure. Katz et al. (1987) have suggested that the severe retrograde amnesias noted in some thalamic patients are similar to those seen in patients with global dementias such as Alzheimer's disease. From this viewpoint, severe retrograde amnesia represents the superimposition of other cognitive deficiencies upon a focal anterograde memory loss. If this notion has validity then the presence of retrograde amnesia in diencephalic patients may be indicative of pathology beyond the DM nucleus, MB, MTT and IML. The possibilty that damage to frontal cortices may play some role in the amnesia of alcoholics with Korsakoff's syndrome will be considered later in this chapter.

In summary, our knowledge of the retrograde amnesia associated with vascular, traumatic and neoplastic lesions of the diencephalon is very limited. Most published case reports focus on the anterograde deficits and pay little, or no, attention to the patients' inability to recall remote events. When this lack of clinical evaluation is combined with the limitations imposed by neuroradiological techniques, it should not be surprising that few explanations exist for the great variability in the published reports of these patients' retrograde amnesias. Comparative studies of numerous patients with sophisticated neuropathological, neuro-radiological and neuropsychological techniques are needed before the roles of various diencephalic and surrounding structures in the recall of remote events can be appreciated.

Other cognitive and personality changes
Patients with diencephalic amnesia often have other cognitive impairments which, in some cases, may be so prominent that they significantly limit the assessment of their memory disorders. However, these ancillary cognitive deficiencies may not be apparent on standardized IQ tests where discrepancies of 1−3 standard deviations between general intelligence and memory functioning remain the psychometric hallmark of amnesia. In the acute stages, diencephalic lesions are followed by

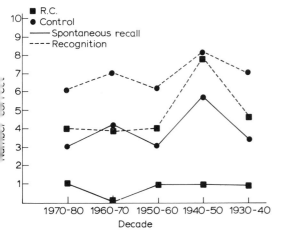

ig. 4. Spontaneous recall and recognition results of R.C., the atient with bilateral paramedian thalamic infarcts, is demon-rated for a remote memory test devised for a Canadian pop-lation. The 'control' data are the mean of three neurologically ormal individuals matched in age, education, cultural ackground and socioeconomic status to the patient. Reprinted ith permission from Stuss et al., *Brain and Cognition,* 1988.

impaired performances on IQ tests, but there is frequently recovery to average, or even premorbid levels, over a period of weeks or months (Graff-Radford et al., 1984; Mills and Swanson, 1978; Squire and Moore, 1979; Stuss et al., 1988; Teuber et al., 1968; Winocur et al., 1984). It is important to stress that recovery to normal limits should not be confused with a return to premorbid levels of overall intelligence (Stuss et al., 1988).

After acute thalamic insult patients may be initially comatose (Guberman and Stuss, 1983; Katz et al., 1987; Stuss et al., 1988). Although this comatose condition occurs most frequently with bilateral damage, some exceptions have been reported. Coma was reported in a patient with an apparent unilateral, non-dominant thalamic infarct (Friedman, 1985), and, conversely, a patient with bilateral thalamic lesions is said not to have lost consciousness (Karabelas et al., 1985).

In the early stages of recovery, unilateral and bilateral paramedian lesions are often accompanied by stupor, profound lethargy and hypersomnia (Castaigne et al., 1981; Mills and Swanson, 1978; Teuber et al., 1968). Even as the level of alertness improves, attention can be severely impaired, with notable fluctuations from moment to moment (Graff-Radford et al., 1984, 1985). Months later, when the patients have entered the chronic state of the disorder, they are usually fully alert but may still exhibit hypersomnia when left alone (Katz et al., 1987; Stuss et al., 1988). Despite the patients' now relatively normal arousal level, deficits involving many levels of attention are prominent (Castaigne et al., 1981; Katz et al., 1987; Mills and Swanson, 1978; Vilkki, 1978; Ziegler et al., 1977).

Although some authors have suggested that attentional impairments are not evident during the chronic stages (Archer et al., 1981; Graff-Radford et al., 1985; Schott et al., 1980), their observations may depend on how attention is defined and assessed. For example, patients with bilateral diencephalic lesions may recover their ability to perform digit span tasks (Stuss et al., 1988; Swanson and Schmidley, 1985; Winocur et al., 1984),

but still remain easily distractible and unable to sustain attention when placed in unstructured situations. These attentional problems likely contribute to the patients' deficiencies in problem solving, shifting of mental sets, conceptual regulation and to their slow cognitive processing (Katz et al., 1987; Speedie and Heilman, 1982, 1983; Stuss et al., 1988).

Pathological explanations of these altered states of arousal have focused upon biochemical and neuroanatomical deficiencies in the ascending activation of the cortex. Though the exact localization of the diencephalic lesions may vary, they all interrupt ascending neuroadrenergic pathways (Castaigne et al., 1981; Katz et al., 1987). Involvement of the reticular activating system through centrum medianum, the DM nucleus and/or proximal brainstem regions has been suggested (Graff-Radford et al., 1985; Katz et al., 1987; Mills and Swanson, 1978). Although all of these regions have been shown to be involved with cortical arousal (e.g., Magoun, 1958; Starzl and Whitlock, 1952), the DM nucleus may have a very specific role to play since it contributes to the production and regulation of different phases of sleep and wakefulness (Imeri et al., 1988; Lugaresi et al., 1986).

A neuropathological model to account for the selective attention deficits against a background of relatively normal alertness has also been proposed. Several investigators have postulated an impairment in the alerting function which facilitates or gates orientation and directed attention (Jurko and Andy, 1977; Luria, 1977; Mateer and Ojemann, 1983; Ojemann, 1977). The actual nuclei involved in such processes are less certain, although the centrum medianum and diffuse thalamic reticular nuclei have been suggested as having some special importance (Fuster and Alexander, 1973). Vilkki (1978), based on thalamotomy research, proposed that the destruction of the ventrolateral nucleus can lead to disruption of active conceptual regulation and control of memory.

The role of the DM nucleus in attentional processes has been prominent, particularly because of its massive reciprocal prefrontal connections. Schulman (1964), based on impaired delayed response performance in monkeys with bilateral DM nucleus lesions, postulated that these thalamic nuclei play an essential role in representing and retaining new information in short-term memory. This latter suggestion has been extended to include the afferent connections between the DM nucleus and the prefrontal association cortex (as well as the prefrontal cortex itself) as vital structures in the maintenance of sustained attention during a short delay period (Alexander and Fuster, 1973; Fuster and Alexander, 1973).

In addition to problems with selective attention, patients with medial diencephalic lesions manifest other behavioral deficits similar to those described after frontal lobe dysfunction (Luria, 1973; Milner, 1964; Stuss and Benson, 1984, 1986). Confabulation, reduplication and perseveration may occur even years after damage to the thalamus (Brion et al., 1983; Guberman and Stuss, 1983; Speedie and Heilman, 1983; Stuss et al., 1988; Swanson and Schmidley, 1985). Diencephalic patients may have difficulty chunking (i.e., organizing) information, be impaired in arranging data in logical sequences, fail to activate and attend rapidly to stimuli, be deficient in maintaining stable intentions and be highly susceptible to interference (Katz et al., 1987; Speedie and Heilman, 1982, 1983; Stuss et al., 1988).

Major personality and mood changes have also been observed in diencephalic patients. They are described as apathetic, akinetic, withdrawn, abulic, unconcerned, euphoric, slow, occasionally irritable and lacking spontaneity (Katz et al., 1987; Mills and Swanson, 1978; Schott et al., 1980; Speedie and Heilman, 1983; Stuss et al., 1988; Teuber et al., 1968). These emotional changes are not surprising in view of the multiple reciprocal connections between the thalamus and the limbic system. The type of behavioral change may vary with the location of the lesions (Graff-Radford et al., 1984). Interruption of dorsomedial-orbital frontal connections may be responsible for the patients' euphoric behavior and lack of insight,

whereas the withdrawn, akinetic personality features may be due to damage to the anterior thalamus-cingulate projections (Graff-Radford, et al., 1984). Despite these behavioral parallels between diencephalic and frontal insults, it is important to stress that the two patterns of symptoms may differ. For example, frontal patients were impaired in release from proactive interference (Moscovitch, 1982), while a patient with a primarily right paramedian thalamic astrocytoma had total release (Butters, 1984a). The vital question for our understanding of diencephalic amnesia is the influence such cognitive deficits have upon the patients' presentation of their anterograde and retrograde amnesias. This issue will be addressed in our review of the memory disorders of alcoholic Korsakoff patients.

Visuoperceptual and visuospatial deficits have also been reported in patients with diencephalic pathology, the impairments being more prominent in the acute than in the chronic stages (Jurko and Andy, 1973) of the disorder (Speedie and Heilman, 1982; Squire and Moore, 1979; Stuss et al., 1988; Teuber et al., 1968). Right and bilateral thalamic lesions are most likely to result in perceptual disturbances, although such dysfunctions have been reported after left thalamic lesions (Graff-Radford et al., 1984; Jurko and Andy, 1973; Stuss et al., 1988). Also, the greater the complexity of the task, the more likely a deficit is to be found (Graff-Radford et al., 1984, 1985; Henderson et al., 1982; Speedie and Heilman, 1982; Squire and Moore, 1979; Stuss et al., 1988, Teuber et al., 1968). Whether these are true visuoperceptual impairments dissociable from the diencephalic patients' other deficiencies in initiation, sustained attention and organizational abilities remains an unresolved issue (Graff-Radford et al., 1985; Henderson et al., 1982; Stuss et al., 1988).

In summary, diencephalic amnesia secondary to vascular, traumatic and neoplastic etiologies is associated with significant cognitive and personality change. Most prominent are disturbed motivation and mood, impaired selective attention and deficient planning and organization abilities.

Dementia as a feature of diencephalic amnesia

Are diencephalic amnesics demented? Based on the above descriptions, there appears to be little doubt that diencephalic patients, particularly those with bilateral pathology, meet the general criteria for dementia in that they have impaired abilities in more than one cognitive function (e.g., problem solving as well as memory deficits). There is also sufficient evidence to indicate that they do not have a dementia comparable to that of patients with Alzheimer's disease (Cummings and Benson, 1983). Their slowness in information processing; their absence of apraxia, agnosia or a true aphasia; their relatively intact IQ; their impairment in the use of acquired information and in the organization of new or complex facts; their inertia, unconcern, apathy and euphoria – all are characteristics more typical of so-called 'subcortical' dementia (Albert, 1978; Albert et al., 1974; Benson, 1983; Cummings and Benson, 1983; Katz et al., 1987; McHugh and Folstein, 1975). The reader should be cautioned, however, that the amnesic symptoms of diencephalic patients do not resemble, either qualitatively or quantitatively, the memory deficiencies of patients with basal ganglia (i.e., subcortical) dementias (Butters, 1984b; Butters et al., 1987b). Also, since many of the diencephalic patients' cognitive problems are similar to those ascribed to patients with focal frontal and/or anterior limbic pathology (Damasio, 1979; Poirier et al., 1983; Stuss and Benson, 1986), 'frontal-limbic' dementia may be a more appropriate term for describing the overall neuropsychological profile of patients with bilateral diencephalic damage.

Although the presence of some form of dementia is apparent in patients with bilateral damage, the picture is far more uncertain for patients with unilateral diencephalic damage. Graff-Radford et al. (1984) have suggested that left thalamic lesions do result in a dementia consistent with established neuropsychiatric criteria, (i.e., DSM-III), but other reports have stressed the transitory and mild nature of the unilateral patients' cognitive problems (Speedie and Heilman, 1982, 1983; Squire

and Moore, 1979; Stuss et al., 1988). When one considers that unilateral patients may return to relatively normal life, it would seem ecologically invalid to consider them 'demented'.

Alcoholic Korsakoff's syndrome

Alcoholic Korsakoff's syndrome represents the chronic state of the Wernicke-Korsakoff disorder (Victor et al., 1971). Although the etiology of the disorder has usually been associated with severe thiamine deficiencies (Victor et al., 1971), there is also considerable evidence that the neurotoxic effects resulting from long-term alcohol abuse may play a direct or indirect role in the development of the disorder (for review, see Butters, 1984a). In the acute Wernicke stage the patients present with a global confusional state, ophthalmoplegia, nystagmus, ataxia and polyneuropathy in the arms and legs. The confusional state is characterized by disorientation for time and place, inattention, an inability to recognize familiar people and failure to maintain a coherent conversation. If the patient with Wernicke's encephalopathy is not treated with large doses of thiamine, he is in danger of fatal midbrain hemorrhages. However, with the administration of appropriate vitamin therapy there is rapid improvement in the noted neurological dysfunctions. In most cases, the ocular palsies will disappear, the ataxia and peripheral neuropathies will improve and the confusional state will clear (Victor et al., 1971). At this point, the patient has passed the acute Wernicke stage and entered the chronic Korsakoff phase of the disorder. Relatively few patients with Wernicke's encephalopathy (about 25%) show evidence of a complete recovery to their premorbid intellectual levels (Victor et al., 1971).

General neuropsychological features

As will be detailed in following sections, the most obvious neuropsychological deficits of alcoholic Korsakoff patients are their severe anterograde and retrograde amnesias. Despite these memory deficiencies, their general intelligence as measured by the original or revised Wechsler Intelligence Scales (WAIS or WAIS-R) (Wechsler, 1955, 1981) remains remarkably intact (Butters and Cermak, 1980; Squire, 1987; Talland, 1965). In fact, it is this relative sparing of overall intelligence that differentiates the alcoholic Korsakoff patient from the patient with alcoholic dementia. Since the latter patient demonstrates a general and often severe intellectual decline associated with decades of alcohol abuse, his memory problems do not stand out as his most prominent cognitive deficiency (Cutting, 1978; Jacobson and Lishman, 1987; Lishman, 1981, 1987). When alcoholic Korsakoff patients and intact nonalcoholic control subjects are matched on relevant demographic variables (years of education, age, socioeconomic class), the performances of the two groups are often indistinguishable in terms of verbal, performance and full-scale WAIS IQs (Butters and Cermak, 1980). However, the Korsakoff patients have been found to be consistently impaired on the Digit-Symbol subtest of the WAIS (and WAIS-R), but this task should not be considered a special marker because detoxified long-term alcoholics without any clinical signs of amnesia are usually impaired on the same and similar substitution tests (Glosser et al., 1977; Kapur and Butters, 1977). Special note should be made of the alcoholic Korsakoff's normal performance on the Digit-Span subtest, a task that is often considered a measure of immediate memory and attention (Butters and Cermak, 1980; Talland, 1965).

Compared to his intelligence scores, the alcoholic Korsakoff patients' memory quotients (MQs) and indices are moderately-to-severely impaired depending upon the particular psychometric test that is administered. With the original Wechsler Memory Scale (WMS) (Wechsler, 1945) a 20 – 30 point scatter between IQ and MQ (e.g., IQ = 100, MQ = 75) has typically been observed (Butters and Cermak, 1980; Squire, 1987). Although this quantitative discrepancy seems substantial, it represents an underestimation of the differences between the patients' general intelligence and their ability to retain new information. Because two measures of attention (Digit Span, Mental Control) are included in the calculation of the MQ, the alcoholic Korsakoff patients' memory capacities are usually overestimated. Fortunately, the recently revised Wechsler Memory Scale (WMS-R) (Wechsler, 1987) provides separate indices for Attention/Concentration and for General (immediate) and Delayed Memory, thereby separating the measurement of attentional and memory processes. Butters and his collaborators (Butters et al., 1988) have reported that this revised scale provides more valid measures of the Korsakoff patients' memory disorders. They found that the mean General and Delayed Memory indices of 11 alcoholic Korsakoff patients were 65 and 57, respectively. The resulting 43 point scatter (almost three standard deviations) between a full-scale IQ of 100 and this Delayed Memory Index seems to be a more valid indicator of the severity of the Korsakoff patients' memory impairments.

Despite the alcoholic Korsakoff patients' normal IQ, their cognitive performance is not completely intact. A full neuropsychological evaluation usually reveals a number of secondary defects that may or may not contribute to the patients' severe memory problems. The most common deficits involve visuoperceptive, visuospatial and conceptual capacities. Alcoholic Korsakoff patients are dramatically impaired on symbol-digit as well as on digit-symbol substitution tasks (Glosser et al., 1977; Kapur and Butters, 1977), on hidden or embedded figures tests (Glosser et al., 1977; Kapur and Butters, 1977; Talland, 1965) and on various concept formation tests that require the learning and shifting of problem-solving strategies (Becker et al., 1986; Oscar-Berman, 1973; Squire, 1982; Talland, 1965). Such visuoconceptual and visuoperceptual deficits should not be surprising, since chronic alcoholics who are not clinically amnesic have been reported to have the same perceptual and problem-solving difficulties (for review, see Parsons and Farr, 1981; Ryan and Butters, 1986). Although there are some indications that these visuoperceptual and conceptual deficits, like the patients' memory disorders, may be due to damage to diencephalic structures surrounding the third ventricle (Jahro, 1973), other investigators have attributed these disorders to atrophy of cortical association areas (Mayes et al. 1988; Parsons, 1975; Squire, 1982, 1987).

In addition to their visuoperceptive and conceptual deficits, Jones and her collaborators (Jones et al., 1978; Jones et al., 1975) have reported that alcoholic Korsakoff patients are significantly impaired in their basic olfactory and gustatory senses. For both smell and taste stimuli, these investigators found that alcoholic Korsakoff patients have heightened intensity thresholds and noticeable difficulty in making qualitative discriminations. Mair and his colleagues (Mair et al., 1980) also found patients with Korsakoff's syndrome to be impaired in their ability to discriminate among similar odorants, but they concluded on the basis of a signal detection procedure that this deficit was not due to heightened intensity thresholds. Both groups of investigators agree that the patients' sensory problems can be traced to atrophy of several diencephalic structures anatomically associated with the olfactory and gustatory systems.

Another common clinical feature of alcoholics with Korsakoff's syndrome is their tendency to confabulate when faced with questions they cannot answer (Kopelman, 1987; Lishman, 1987; Victor et al., 1971). When asked to recall his activities of the previous day, an alcoholic Korsakoff patient may 'fill in' a gap in his memory with a story concerning a trip to his home or to a sporting event that may (or may not) actually have occurred many years ago. This tendency is not a constant or necessarily permanent feature of amnesic patients, and there are marked individual differences among amnesic populations. In general, confabulation is most apparent during the acute stages of the illness and becomes progressively less noticeable as the patient adjusts to his disorder. It is relatively easy to elicit confabulation from a patient in a Wernicke-Korsakoff confusional state, but such responses are less frequent in chronic Korsakoff patients who have had this disorder for five or more years.

Kopelman (1987) has categorized the confabulation of alcoholic Korsakoff patients into two types: spontaneous and provoked. The spontaneous form which is typically emitted without any probing or queries by the examiner may be due to some 'frontal lobe' disinhibition superimposed on the patients' organic amnesia. In contrast, provoked confabulations, which occur during examination of the patients' memory capacities, may represent an attempt to conceal or compensate for a severely deficient memory. As noted by both Kopelman (1987) and by Butters and his associates (1986, 1987), the Korsakoff patients' attempted recall of prose passages is often characterized by the intrusion of episodes, objects and individuals not included in the original story. Such extra-story intrusion errors may be confabulations provoked by the recall demands of the task and the patients' faulty memory.

Personality changes

Besides the general memory and cognitive changes, alcoholic Korsakoff patients demonstrate dramatic changes in personality. They often have premorbid histories of antisocial behavior characterized by impulsive aggressive acts and petty crimes designed to support their chronic alcoholism. Many were 'barroom brawlers' who also violently attacked members of their immediate families. With the onset of Korsakoff's syndrome, a dramatic change occurs in these motivational-affective characteristics. Impulsivity, aggression and severe alcohol abuse are replaced by apathy, passivity, a lack of initiative and a virtual disinterest in alcohol. The patient is also unable to formulate, organize and initiate a series of plans. Left to his own devices, the Korsakoff patient is likely to remain seated before a television set or even in bed for long periods of time. He makes few demands or inquiries of hospital staff and will obey all instructions in a passive indifferent manner. Since these personality changes are apparent as soon as the patient enters the chronic Korsakoff stage, they cannot be attributed to the consequence of institutionalization.

An issue that has received little attention is the relationship between the Korsakoff patients' personality change and their cognitive deficits. Talland (1965) proposed that the patients' difficulties in memory and perception are due to a faulty organization of cognitive strategies (a perseveration or rigidity of cognitive sets) resulting from a premature closure of activating mechanisms. That is, the patients' motivational and arousal deficits prevent a thorough coding of new information (anterograde amnesia) and the organization of suitable search strategies for scanning stored information (retrograde amnesia). Since it is commonly believed that arousal and attentional processes are dependent upon the reticular activating system (RAS), Talland assumed that the alcoholic Korsakoff's midline diencephalic lesions interrupted the facilitative influence of the RAS on cognitive (that is, cortical) functions. Although Oscar-Berman's (1980) report that positive reinforcement has more control of the operant responses of normal subjects than of Korsakoff patients lends some support to Talland's hypothesis, we shall later review evidence that the beneficial effects of increased arousal and attention may be restricted to perceptual functions and have little effect upon retention (Davidoff et al., 1984; Granholm et al., 1985).

Anterograde amnesia

Most of the studies of alcoholic Korsakoff patients' anterograde amnesia have focused on the processes (e.g., storage, retrieval, encoding) underlying their almost total inability to acquire new verbal and nonverbal information. Although there is still some controversy as to whether these patients are impaired on short-term memory tasks*

---

* Short-term memory tasks should not be confused with the Digit Span subtest of the WAIS or WAIS-R. The short-term tasks involve a delay (usually filled with distractor activity) of to 60 seconds between stimulus presentation and recall, whereas on the Digit Span subtest recall is attempted immediately after the stimulus is exposed.

(Baddeley and Warrington, 1970; Butters and Cermak, 1974; Butters and Cermak, 1980; Kinsbourne and Wood, 1975; Kopelman, 1985; Mair et al., 1979; Meudell et al., 1978; Piercy, 1977), all investigators agree that Korsakoff patients have inordinate difficulty in retaining information in long-term memory due to an increased sensitivity to proactive interference (PI) (Butters, 1985; Butters and Cermak, 1980; Squire, 1982, 1987; Warrington and Weiskrantz, 1973). Whether these patients are tested with paradigms employing list learning, paired-associates or prose passages, previously learned materials intrude into and seem to prevent the acquisition of new information. For example, Butters and his colleagues (Butters et al., 1986, 1987a) presented alcoholic Korsakoff patients and other brain-damaged and intact control subjects with a series of four short prose passages. Thirty seconds after the presentation of each story, the subjects were required to recall as much of the story as possible. Not surprisingly, the Korsakoff patients recalled little information about each passage, but what characterized their poor performance was the tendency to commit prior-story intrusion errors. If the phrase "Tim had a brown dog" was part of the first story and was recalled correctly, it would then often be included in the patient's subsequent attempts to recall the second, third and even fourth stories. Several investigations have noted that, while this sensitivity to PI is a prominent feature of the alcoholic Korsakoff patients' anterograde amnesia, it is far less apparent in the severely impaired recall of other amnesic and even demented patient populations (Butters et al., 1986, 1987; Cermak, 1976; Cermak and O'Connor, 1983; Squire, 1982).

Other evidence of the alcoholic Korsakoffs' sensitivity to PI are found in demonstrations of improved performance when the learning conditions are structured to reduce proactive interference. In a now classic series of studies Warrington and Weiskrantz (1968, 1970, 1974) showed that although amnesic patients are severely impaired when unaided recall and recognition tests are employed these patients do retrieve normally when partial information, such as the first two letters of the word, is provided. Warrington and Weiskrantz (1970, 1973) concluded that the superiority of the partial information method originated from the limitations it places on interference from previously learned information. If the first two letters of the word are 'ST', the number of words that can possibly interfere with the recall of the target word 'STAMP' is greatly limited. Apparently, free recall and recognition are not as successful as the partial information procedure in limiting the influence of PI. Later in this chapter we shall note that Warrington and Weiskrantz' reports of the positive effects of partial information was also the first demonstration of what is now recognized as amnesic patients' intact *implicit* memory system.

While acknowledging the importance of the Korsakoff patients' increased sensitivity to PI and their apparent deficiencies on some retrieval tasks, other investigators have viewed these phenomena as largely descriptive rather than explanatory and have offered more extensive hypotheses to account for the patients' severe anterograde amnesia. Cermak and Butters (1973, 1976) suggested that the alcoholic Korsakoff patients' verbal memory impairment is related to a failure to encode, at the time of storage, all of the attributes of the stimulus. The Korsakoff patients may fully categorize verbal information according to its phonemic and associative attributes, but they seem inadequate in their analyses of the semantic features of the materials (Cermak et al., 1976, 1980). Similarly, when confronted with photographs of unfamiliar faces, the alcoholic Korsakoff patient may analyse or focus upon some superficial piecemeal feature (such as hair style or color) rather than upon the configurational aspects (the relationship among the eyes, nose and mouth) of the faces (Biber et al., 1981; Dricker et al., 1978). Information that is not fully analysed (encoded) may be stored in a degraded fashion and thus be more sensitive to interference and more difficult to retrieve.

Some evidence supporting this conclusion stems from cueing studies in which phonemic (such as rhymes) and semantic (such as superordinate) cues were compared in terms of their ability to facilitate recall. In general, phonemic cues worked as well for alcoholic Korsakoff patients as for control subjects but semantic cues only aided the recall of the control subjects (Cermak and Butters, 1972; Cermak et al., 1973a).

In an attempt to demonstrate the relationship between sensitivity to PI and limited semantic encoding Cermak et al. (1974) adapted Wickens' (1970) release from PI technique for use with alcoholic Korsakoff patients. Wickens had discovered that the PI generated by several consecutive trials with material from a single class of information can be released by introducing materials from a new class of information. This finding was interpreted to mean that the extent of interference during recall is primarily dependent upon the subject's ability to differentiate words in memory by their semantic features (i.e., semantic encoding). In applying Wickens' notions to their amnesic patients, Cermak et al. (1974) reasoned that, if Korsakoff patients' increased sensitivity to PI is due to their lack of semantic encoding, then the amount of PI release shown by these patients should vary with the encoding requirements of the verbal materials. When the verbal materials involved only rudimentary categorizations (e.g., *letters* versus *numbers*) the Korsakoff patients would be expected to show normal release; when the stimulus materials involved more abstract semantic differences (e.g., taxonomic differences such as *animals* versus *vegetables*), the Korsakoff patients should evidence far less release from PI.

Cermak et al.'s (1974) findings were consistent with their predictions. Their alcoholic Korsakoff patients showed normal release from PI when shifting from letters to numbers or vice versa (i.e., alphanumeric shift), but virtually no release when shifting from names of animals to names of vegetables or vice versa (i.e., taxonomic shift). In interpreting these results, Cermak et al. (1974) concluded that the alcoholic Korsakoffs' failure to release with taxonomic materials was indicative of a deficiency in semantic encoding. If the Korsakoff patients did not encode the verbal materials along semantic dimensions then the PI accumulating during the test session was likely not specific to any one semantic category. Under such conditions, shifting categories would consequently have little effect on recall.

Other evidence suggesting that encoding deficiencies play some role in Korsakoff's patients' amnesia has emanated from 'orientation' studies that have attempted to induce alcoholic Korsakoff patients to thoroughly analyse stimuli that must be remembered at a later time. Cermak and Reale (1978), utilizing a technique developed by Craik and Tulving (1975), attempted to ameliorate the alcoholic Korsakoff patients' verbal learning deficits with orientation tasks that required their subjects to analyse and judge the semantic attributes of sequentially presented words. Their basic premise was that the higher the level of encoding their subjects performed on a word, the greater the probability that they would remember the word on a subsequent unannounced recognition test. For each word presented, a question was asked that required the subjects to process on one of the three levels: a shallow orthographic level ("Is [this word] printed in upper case letters?''); a phonemic level ("Does [this word] rhyme with fat?''); a semantic level ("Does [this word] fit into the following sentence?''). Following the presentation of the entire series of questions, the patients were administered a recognition test to determine how many of the exposed words could be correctly identified.

In one experiment in which a 60-word stimulus list and a 180-word recognition test were divided into a series of short encoding and recognition tasks, Cermak and Reale (1978) found evidence that was at least partially consistent with the semantic encoding hypothesis. Although the alcoholic Korsakoff patients were still impaired under all encoding conditions, they did benefit from the semantic orientation task. The Korsakoff patients' best recognition occurred for the semantic words, their poorest recognition for the words that had been associated with orthographic questions. Unfortunately, Cermak and Reale (1978) did not find that their semantic orientation task had a differentially greater effect upon alcoholic Korsakoff patients than upon their control subjects. Thus, while Korsakoff patients may be impaired in their encoding of new verbal information, it is unlikely that this deficiency is sufficient to explain their severe inability to store new information. The observation that Korsakoff patients, like intact controls, can learn semantically-related word pairs more easily than unrelated ones suggests that their appreciation of semantic relationships is not as impaired as originally suggested (Weiskrantz, 1985; Winocur and Weiskrantz, 1976).

Biber et al. (1981), using an orientation procedure in an attempt to improve face recognition, reported evidence that is consistent with the limited encoding hypothesis. Patients with alcoholic Korsakoff's syndrome, patients with a progressive dementia (Huntington's disease), patients with damage confined to the right hemisphere and normal control subjects were administered a face recognition task under three experimental conditions that presumably induced different levels of facial analysis. The recognition scores of the Korsakoff patients, but not those of the other two patient groups, improved significantly following a 'high level' orientation task requiring the subjects to judge the likability of the faces to be remembered. Under baseline conditions (no orientation task), normal control subjects appeared spontaneously to encode faces in a manner induced by the 'high-level' task, whereas Korsakoff patients employed strategies consistent with the 'low-level' orientation task (judgment of nose size).

Although the findings of Biber et al. (1981) seem to support the limited encoding hypothesis, their data can also be explained by motivational-arousal concepts. As noted previously, other investigators (Oscar-Berman, 1980; Talland, 1965) have remarked on the passivity and lack of initiative of alcoholic Korsakoff patients, and have suggested that reduced motivation may contribute to these patients' severe learning and memory problems. Adapting methods borrowed from animal learning studies, Oscar-Berman and her collaborators (Oscar-Berman et al., 1976) reported that alcoholic Korsakoff patients have reduced responsiveness to the effects of positive reinforcement. When confronted with a two-choice spatial probability learning test in which the two spatial alternatives were reinforced on a 70 − 30 or 30 − 70 ratio, normal control subjects altered their response tendencies to match the reinforcement contingencies. In marked contrast to the malleability of normal behavior, the alcoholics with Korsakoff's syndrome continued to respond to each spatial alternative 50% of the time and seemed totally unaffected by the prevailing reinforcement contingencies. In another experiment (Oscar-Berman et al., 1980), alcoholic Korsakoff patients and normal control subjects were placed on a complex concurrent variable schedule of reinforcement. As with the spatial probability learning test, the responses of the normal control subjects, but not that of the Korsakoff patients, matched the reinforcement contingencies present in the experimental situation.

In view of such demonstrations of motivational anomalies in alcoholic Korsakoff patients, Oscar-Berman (1980) has urged caution in explaining all of the Korsakoff patients' memory deficits strictly from a cognitive perspective. For example, in the study by Biber et al. (1981), the process of making a likability judgment (high-level orientation task) may have motivational as well as cognitive consequences, and the significant improvement in the memory of the alcoholic Korsakoff patients following these judgments may reflect some form of affective-motivational arousal.

Further evidence that motivational-arousal factors may play some role in the overall cognitive performance of alcoholic Korsakoff patients has been reported in three investigations of memory for prose passages (Davidoff et al., 1984; Granholm et al., 1985; Kovner et al., 1983). Kovner et al. (1983) used a training procedure which associated word-list items in a novel manner by embedding them in ridiculous-imaged stories (RIS). After eight weekly training sessions with RIS two

alcoholic Korsakoffs (and three other amnesics) could successfully recall an average of 14 of the 20 words on the list. In contrast, the same patients showed virtually no learning of a similar word list administered with a modifed selective reminding procedure. The investigators concluded that the novel, often bizarre, nature of the stories increased the patients' arousal and subsequently their retention of the key words. Kopelman's (1986) demonstration that Korsakoff patients are capable of considerable learning and retention of highly anomalous sentences also suggests that increased arousal can have some ameliorating effects on Korsakoff patients' dense anterograde amnesia.

Davidoff et al. (1984) read alcoholic Korsakoff patients and control subjects a series of nine short passages (stories) similar in length to those comprising the Logical Memory test of the Wechsler Memory Scale (Wechsler, 1945). Three of the nine stories contained a sexual phrase, three an aggressive phrase and three a neutral phrase in the middle of the passages. The findings showed that, although the Korsakoff patients' immediate recall of the entire story was facilitated by the introduction of a sexual phrase, the resulting beneficial effects were transient and did not improve the ultimate retention of the stories. That is, on delayed recall, the alcoholic Korsakoff patients, in comparison with the control subjects, demonstrated rapid forgetting of the details of all stories regardless of their affective-motivational value. Granholm et al. (1985) replicated the Korsakoffs' transient improvement with sexual stories and showed that similar changes did not occur in the recall of patients with Huntington's Disease. Both Davidoff et al. and Granholm et al. concluded that motivational factors may affect the amount of information the Korsakoff patients attend to and register at the time of presentation, but that such affective variables have little, if any, influence upon the ultimate storage and retention of this material.

Granted that motivational-arousal factors may be responsible for some aspects of the alcoholic Korsakoff patients' memory problems, it remains unlikely that most of the patients' severe amnesia can be explained by such concepts. Patients with bilateral frontal lesions, including those who have undergone frontal lobotomies, often present with the personality alterations and problem solving deficits similar to those seen in alcoholic Korsakoff patients, but they do not show the dramatic amnesic symptoms (Stuss and Benson, 1986). Thus, since marked alterations in activation can occur without equally impressive changes in storage functions, some skepticism must remain as to the causal role of the noted motivational changes in the Korsakoffs' memory and cognitive deficits.

Another influential theoretical approach to the Korsakoff patients' memory deficits has stressed their deficiencies in the encoding and use of temporal and spatial contextual cues to aid retrieval (Huppert and Piercy, 1976; Kinsbourne and Wood, 1975; Winocur and Kinsbourne, 1978; Winocur et al., 1981). It has been proposed that alcoholic Korsakoff patients may be able to analyse many of the specific physical or semantic attributes of a stimulus but fail to discriminate the temporal and spatial contexts in which the stimulus was encountered. Due to this deficit, the patients may later recognize, or even recall, some information but may still be unable to specify when or where they experienced the stimulus (i.e., source amnesia). This hypothesis is consistent with the often noted clinical observation that alcoholic Korsakoff patients can accurately select from a room full of people those individuals they have seen before, but they are unable to recall under what circumstances the interaction occurred. It is important to note that these context theories focus on retrieval rather than storage processes. Although the Korsakoff patients are viewed as having normal encoding processes, it is believed that they are severely impaired in generating efficient temporal and spatial retrieval strategies.

Kinsbourne and Wood (1975) tied their context-retrieval theory to Tulving's (1972, 1983) distinction between *episodic* and *semantic* memory and suggested that the amnesic syndrome represents a loss of episodic memory. The amnesic patients' ability to remember the meaning of words, the rules of syntax and basic arithmetical procedures is considered by Kinsbourne and Wood (1975) as evidence of an intact semantic memory. Weingartner and his associates (Weingartner et al., 1983) expanded this episodic-semantic distinction to encompass patients with progressive dementias as well as patients with relatively pure amnesic syndromes (such as alcoholic Korsakoff patients). According to these investigators, amnesia represents a loss of episodic memory, whereas dementia involves failure in both episodic and semantic memory systems. Although this proposal has proven very useful in explaining several features of Korsakoff patients' total amnesic syndrome (Cermak, 1984), there is some question as to whether semantic memory is totally intact in amnesia. As noted by Butters and Cermak (1986) and Beatty and his collaborators (Beatty et al., 1987), amnesic patients may fail to remember much of the highly specialized information pertaining to their professions. Also, several recent studies have stressed that sufferers of different forms of dementia (e.g., Alzheimer's and Huntington's diseases) may fail semantic memory tasks for quite distinct reasons (Butters et al., 1987).

Experimental evidence supporting context theories of the alcoholic Korsakoff's anterograde amnesia has been reported by Huppert and Piercy (1976). These investigators showed 80 pictures to alcoholic Korsakoff patients and normal controls on Day 1, and then 80 more on Day 2. Day 2 pictures consisted of 40 new pictures and 40 repeats from Day 1. Ten minutes after the exposure of the 80th picture on Day 2, the subjects were presented with 160 pictures and asked to respond to the questions, "Did you ever see this picture before?" and "Was it presented today?" Of the 160 pictures, 120 had been exposed previously (on Day 1 and Day 2) and 40 were 'fillers' that had not been used on either day. Of the 120 that had been exposed previously, 40 had been shown only on Day 1, 40 only on Day 2, and 40 on Days 1 and 2. The alcoholic Korsakoff patients had no difficulty determining whether they had or had not seen a given picture previously, but they did make many false positive responses in answering the second question. In other words, the patients frequently said they had seen pictures on Day 2 that had actually been presented only on Day 1. The patients were able to recognize that they had viewed a picture, but they could not place this experience in a particular temporal context.

Winocur and Kinsbourne (1978) reported additional data suggesting that contextual factors play some role in the alcoholic Korsakoff patients' memory deficits. Amnesic patients were required to learn lists of verbal paired associates under conditions that maximized the interference between successive lists (both lists contained the same stimulus but different response elements). Although this proactive interference made learning almost impossible for the alcoholic Korsakoff patients, their performance could be greatly improved by increasing the salience (for example, use of different colored inks or background music) of the contextual cues in the learning environment.

Winocur et al. (1981) suggested that the alcoholic Korsakoff patients' inability to discriminate contexts is responsible for their failure to release from PI (Cermak et al., 1974). Alcoholic Korsakoff patients and normal subjects were asked to recall successive lists of nine nouns drawn from the same taxonomic category (occupations, body parts, sports). In the no-shift (control) condition, the same category of nouns was used for five successive lists; in the shift (experimental) condition, a new taxonomic category (sports) was introduced on the fifth list after the same category (body parts) had been employed on the first four lists. Both the alcoholic Korsakoff patients and the control subjects demonstrated progressive decrements in performance over the five lists (i.e., due to the accumulation of PI) in the no-shift condition. When no effort was made to increase the contextual salience between the fourth and fifth lists in the shift condition, only the normal control subjects showed a significant improvement in performance on the fifth (shift) list (i.e., release from PI). However, if the subjects were provided with

an instructional set warning them of the impending taxonomic change or if the words comprising the fourth and fifth lists were printed in ink of different colors, the alcoholic Korsakoff patients also recalled more words on the fifth than on the fourth list (i.e., release from PI). On the basis of these findings, Winocur et al. (1981) concluded that the alcoholic Korsakoff patients' failure to release from proactive interference is not due to a deficit in semantic encoding (Cermak et al., 1974), but rather to an inability to discriminate contextually the words comprising the fourth and fifth lists. Winocur et al.'s (1987) demonstration that providing Korsakoff patients with contextual cues during recall improved performance also may be viewed as supporting the context theory of amnesia.

At this point, it is important to consider whether some of the features of the Korsakoff patients' memory disorders are possible indicators of 'frontal lobe' dysfunction rather than phenomena closely linked to amnesia resulting from diencephalic lesions (Moscovitch, 1982; Schacter, 1987a; Shimamura and Squire, 1986; Squire, 1982). Moscovitch (1982) reported that nonamnesic patients with damage to the prefrontal cortex, like alcoholic Korsakoff patients, failed to release from PI following taxonomic shifts. Squire (1982) found that although alcoholic Korsakoff patients failed to release from PI, other patients with chronic or transient amnesias did so. Furthermore, although the alcoholic Korsakoff patients and the other amnesic patients were equally impaired on a sentence recognition task, the Korsakoff patients were significantly more impaired than the others in making temporal recency judgments about the same verbal materials. Since impairments in recency judgments had been reported in nonamnesic frontal lobe patients (Milner, 1971), Squire suggested that alcoholic Korsakoff patients have a number of cognitive deficits attributable to some functional frontal lobe dysfunction. His findings of a 0.79 correlation between Korsakoff patients' performances on the release from PI and recency judgment tasks and tests with demonstrated sensitivity to 'frontal' dysfunction (e.g., Wisconsin Card Sorting Test, verbal fluency, embedded figures) were highly consistent with this conclusion. When these findings are combined with the demonstration by Winocur et al. (1981) that contextual factors are important in release from PI, it follows that impairments in the discrimination and retrieval of contextual cues may be more related to the Korsakoff patients' ancillary cognitive problems than to their anterograde amnesia.

In a study comparing alcoholic Korsakoff patients and amnesics of other etiologies, Shimamura and Squire (1986) reached a similar conclusion about metamemory (i.e., accuracy of feeling of knowing). Whereas both the alcoholic Korsakoffs and the other amnesics were impaired in the recall of answers to general information questions and of sentences, only the Korsakoff patients were impaired in their predictions of the likelihood they would accurately identify the correct answers (i.e., feeling-of-knowing predictions) in a recognition paradigm. Since failures in metamemory did not appear to be an obligatory feature of amnesia, Shimamura and Squire (1986) proposed that the alcoholic Korsakoffs' impairments on this type of task reflect their ancillary cognitive problems.

Other evidence suggesting that frontal dysfunction can contribute to the memory disorders of Korsakoff patients has been reported in a recent radiological (CT) study (Shimamura et al., 1988). When rank-order correlations between numerous CT scan and memory measures derived from seven alcoholic Korsakoff patients were calculated, only thalamic CT density and the amount of fluid in the region of the frontal sulci resulted in significant findings. Eighteen of the possible 24 correlations between thalamic density indices (each hemisphere treated separately) and memory tests were positive, with the median correlation being 0.34. Similarly, 18 of the 24 correlations between frontal fluid indices and memory scores were positive, with the median correlation being 0.43. Although there is some question whether increased sulcal fluid should be considered a sign of cortical atrophy, these findings do suggest that other structures

besides the diencephalon affect the memory performances of alcoholic Korsakoff patients.

In considering these possible effects of 'frontal dysfunction' on the Korsakoff patients' memory disorders one should note that the dorsomedial nucleus of the thalamus (i.e., the structure most frequently implicated in this disorder) is the primary thalamic source of afferent input to the prefrontal association cortices. Thus, bilateral damage to this midline diencephalic structure can lead to a disconnection between the frontal lobes and thalamus similar to that seen after frontal lobotomies (Stuss and Benson, 1986). If such a disconnection is responsible for the alcoholic Korsakoff patients' increased sensitivity to PI and failures on recency judgment and problem solving tasks, their 'frontal' signs should be considered as an inseparable part of diencephalic amnesia, and not as a set of ancillary (non-obligatory) deficits related to the neurotoxic effects of alcohol on the frontal lobes (Squire, 1982). Salmon and Butters' (1987) demonstration that the mild short-term disorders of chronic alcoholics (non-Korsakoff) are not characterized by an increased sensitivity to PI suggests that the Korsakoffs' problems with PI as well as their anterograde amnesia appear simultaneously following acute damage to diencephalic (or other subcortical) structures. Also, since alcoholics have repeatedly been shown to be impaired on various card sorting and other problem solving tasks (for review, see Ryan and Butters, 1986), there would appear to be no necessary association between performance on such 'frontal' tasks and sensitivity to PI.

This dissociation between frontal lobe damage and PI is clearly demonstrated in Freedman and Cermak's (1986) comparison of bilateral frontal patients with and without memory disorders. Sensitivity to PI and semantic encoding were assessed using Wickens' release from PI paradigm. The results showed that frontal patients with memory disorders, and alcoholic Korsakoff patients, failed to release from PI, whereas frontal patients without memory problems released in normal fashion. Freedman and Cermak (1986) concluded that dysfunction of the frontal lobes by itself is unlikely to be responsible for amnesics' semantic encoding deficiencies and increased sensitivity to PI.

In summary, the alcoholic Korsakoff patients' severe inability to learn new factual information and their increased sensitivity to PI is likely to reflect some combination of encoding, motivational and retrieval problems, especially as they pertain to the contextual features of the materials. These deficiencies in identifying and utilizing the temporal and source cues (i.e., context cues) associated with new materials signifies these patients' special problems with episodic memory. Unfortunately, it is still not clear which characteristics of their learning failures represent an integral part of their amnesia and which are due to ancillary cognitive problems (i.e., 'frontal lobe' dysfunction). There is evidence that some aspects of the Korsakoff patients' memory problems may represent 'frontal lobe' dysfunction, but it remains uncertain whether these features are due to direct structural damage to the frontal cortices or to the frontal deafferentation which invariably follows lesions of specific medial diencephalic nuclei (e.g., dorsomedial nucleus of the thalamus). If deafferentation is the critical factor, then these ancillary cognitive problems may prove to be inseparable from other features of the alcoholic Korsakoff patients' anterograde amnesia.

Retrograde amnesia
Retrograde amnesia is also a distinct and consistent clinical feature of alcoholic Korsakoff's syndrome (Butters and Cermak, 1980; Talland, 1965; Victor et al., 1971). The Korsakoff patient has severe difficulty retrieving information concerning major public and autobiographical events that occurred prior to the onset of the illness. In general, this difficulty in retrieving old memories is usually more pronounced for events just from the 20–30 year period immediately prior to the onset of the illness, whereas remote events from the patient's childhood and early adulthood are relatively well remembered. Most alcoholic Korsakoff patients

who served in World War II or Korea can describe their tours of duty in great detail and with apparent accuracy, but they are unable to recall any of the major public events (such as John Kennedy's assassination, the Watergate scandal, America's bombing of Libya) of the 1960s, 1970s and 1980s.

This temporal 'gradient' is not only evident during a mental status examination but has been demonstrated in numerous experimental studies. Seltzer and Benson (1974) used a multiple-choice public events questionnaire and found that their alcoholic Korsakoff patients could remember famous events from the 1930s and 1940s better than events from the 1960s and 1970s. Marslen-Wilson and Teuber (1975) presented alcoholic Korsakoff patients with photographs of famous people and found that the patients had much more difficulty identifying famous faces from the 1960s than faces from the 1930s and 1940s. Meudell et al. (1980) demonstrated this relative preservation of very remote memories with a test consisting of voices of famous people recorded in the last 50 years. Alcoholic Korsakoff patients showed a retrograde amnesia for famous voices extending over several decades, but did correctly identify more voices from the remote than from the recent past.

Zola-Morgan et al.'s (1983) investigation of remote episodic memory indicates that this temporal gradient is also apparent when alcoholic Korsakoff patients attempt to remember specific personal experiences. These investigators presented alcoholic Korsakoff patients and alcoholic control subjects with 10 stimulus words (e.g., *bird, flag*) and asked them to recall specific episodes from their past that involved the stimuli. If the patients did not initially recall an episode for a specific stimulus word, the examiner 'probed' (i.e., cued) the patients by providing an example. The results showed that although the Korsakoff patients and control subjects did not differ in their overall ability to retrieve episodic memories under cued conditions, they varied significantly in terms of the periods of their lives from which the memories emanated. Unlike the alcoholic control subjects, who remembered personal episodes from both the recent and the remote past, the Korsakoff patients recalled events almost exclusively from their childhood and early adulthood. Thus, with no temporal restrictions placed on their retrieval processes, the Korsakoff patients limited their recall to episodes that had occurred 30–40 years ago.

Despite the consistency with which investigators have noted the relative sparing of very remote memories, Sanders and Warrington (1971) have raised a serious issue concerning the validity of most test instruments used to assess temporal gradients in retrograde amnesia. They suggested that most tests demonstrating a sparing of remote memories may have reflected failures to control for the difficulty and overexposure of the faces and events associated with the decades under study. That is, events from the 1940s and 1950s may be easier to recall than those from the 1970s and 1980s because the former have been overlearned and are of more lasting fame due to overexposure in subsequent decades. For example, pictures of Franklin Roosevelt and Winston Churchill have been exposed to the public during every decade since the 1930s.

Since Sanders and Warrington's (1971) emphasis on the control of item difficulty and overlearning had face validity, it forced a reevaluation of retrograde amnesia with more carefully developed test instruments. Albert et al. (1979) constructed a remote memory battery that statistically controlled for item difficulty. Their test battery included a famous persons (i.e., faces) test (i.e., photographs of well-known, public individuals), a recall questionnaire focusing on major public events and a multiple-choice recognition questionnaire also concerned with highly publicized historical events. Each test consisted of items from the 1930s to the 1970s that had been standardized on a population of normal controls before their inclusion in the final test battery. Half of the items were 'easy' (e.g., picture of Franklin Roosevelt) as judged by the performance of the standardization group; the other half were difficult or 'hard' (e.g., picture of

Rosemary Clooney), judged by the same criterion. In addition, the famous persons test included photographs of some individuals both early and late in their careers. For example, photographs of Marlon Brando from both the 1950s and the 1970s were included in the test battery.

When this remote memory battery was administered to alcoholic Korsakoff patients and normal control subjects (Albert et al., 1979), little evidence supporting Sanders and Warrington's (1971) proposal was found. As shown in Fig. 5, the alcoholic Korsakoff patients still identified more faces from the 1930s and 1940s than from the 1960s, regardless of the fame of the individual pic-

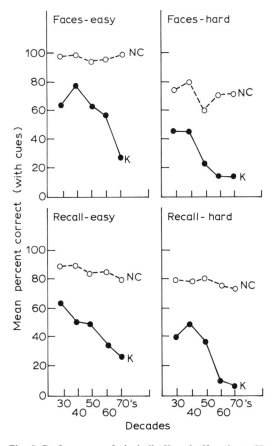

Fig. 5. Performance of alcoholic Korsakoff patients (K) and nonalcoholic control subject (NC) on Albert et al.'s (1979) Famous Persons (Faces) Test and Public Events Questionnaire. Results for easy and hard items are shown separately. (From Butters, 1984a.)

tured. Furthermore, although the normal controls were more accurate in identifying famous people later rather than earlier in their careers, the Korsakoff patients performed in the opposite manner. On the recall test of public events, the same pattern emerged. For both easy and hard items, the Korsakoff patients recalled more information from the 1930s and 1940s than from the 1960s. Similar gradients were reported for the recognition test of public events (Albert et al., 1979).

Squire and Cohen (1982) suggested that Albert et al.'s (1979) statistical approach to item difficulty may have actually confounded rather than solved the equivalence and overlearning issue. They questioned whether two public events (or pictures of famous people) from two separate decades (e.g., one from the 1930s and the other from the 1970s) can ever be considered intrinsically equal in difficulty, even if both are recalled by 80% of all controls. That one event occurred 40 years prior to the other and is still remembered as well suggests that the very remote event is more famous and overlearned than the recent one. The mere passage of 30 years since original acquisition should have weakened the memory trace more than a 5-year interval since original learning. From their viewpoint, statistical equality might simply be a mask for an intrinsic inequality manifested by the temporal gradients of amnesic patients.

Butters and Albert (1982) have offered some additional empirical evidence for their statistical approach. They reanalysed their original data on the famous persons test so that 'easy' items from the recent past could be compared with 'hard' items from the remote past. They found that normal controls, as expected, identified significantly fewer faces from the remote than from the recent past, but alcoholic Korsakoff patients evidenced the opposite trend. That is, the amnesic Korsakoff patients correctly identified more hard faces from the remote past (e.g., the 1930s and 1940s) than easy faces from the recent past (e.g., the 1970s). Butters and Albert (1982) noted that this relative preservation of very remote memories under conditions of planned statistical inequality offers strong support

that temporal gradients characterize the retrograde amnesia of alcoholic Korsakoff patients.

Like Albert et al. (1979), Squire and his colleagues have attempted to develop a remote memory test that circumvents the overlearning and overexposure problems noted by Sanders and Warrington (1971). To ensure limited but equivalent public exposure, Squire and Slater (1975) used the titles of television programs that had been aired for one season or less in the construction of their recall and recognition tests. The individual items on these tests were matched for public exposure on the basis of known viewing histories and, since each item had a brief exposure period, the time of learning could be specified.

In two extensive reports, Cohen and Squire (1981) and Squire and Cohen (1982) administered their television tests, several tests of public events and Albert et al.'s famous persons test to alcoholics with Korsakoff's syndrome, to long-term alcoholics with no clinical signs of amnesia, to depressed patients one hour following their fifth administration of bilateral ECT, and to the well-studied diencephalic patient N.A. The results of this testing showed a clear distinction between the remote memory losses of the Korsakoff patients and those of N.A. and the ECT patients. The alcoholic Korsakoff patients' loss of remote memories was severe, extended over several decades and was characterized by a temporal gradient in which very remote memories (from the 1940s) were relatively spared, whereas both patient N.A. and the ECT patients had only mild-to-moderate retrograde amnesias that were limited on some tests to the four-year period immediately preceding trauma or shock treatment. On the television recognition test and the famous persons test, the long-term (non-Korsakoff) alcoholics' retrieval of remote memories was mildly depressed, especially for events and people who were famous during the past 10 years.

It is important to stress that many systematic evaluations of the retrograde amnesias of patients other than alcoholic Korsakoff patients have reported temporally limited (e.g., $1-4$ years) forgetting of old memories. In addition to Squire's patient N.A. and patients receiving ECT, patient H.M. (Milner, 1966; Marslen-Wilson and Teuber, 1975; Corkin, 1984), many traumatic amnesics (Benson and Geschwind, 1967; Levin et al., 1982; Russell and Nathan, 1946) and patients whose amnesia is associated with anterior communicating artery aneurysms (Butters et al., 1984; Damasio et al., 1985) all have been reported to have deficiencies in remote memory limited to the 3 – 5 year period immediately preceding their illness or the beginning of shock treatment (ECT). While many patients with hippocampal damage due to hypoxia may, like alcoholic Korsakoffs, evidence an extended and temporally-graded retrograde amnesia (for review, see Squire et al., 1989), it is still evident that there is no necessary correlation between overall severity of anterograde and retrograde amnesia. These two symptoms probably depend upon distinct neurological and psychological processes.

Both Squire and Cohen (1982) and Butters and Albert (1982) have addressed the psychological factors underlying the Korsakoff patients' loss of remote memories. These investigators have suggested that the alcoholic Korsakoff patients' loss of remote memories may be secondary to a primary defect in establishing new memories during the 20 years of alcohol abuse that preceded the diagnosis of the amnesic syndrome. If chronic alcoholics acquire less information each year due to a progressive anterograde memory deficit, then at the time an alcoholic patient is diagnosed as having Korsakoff's syndrome one would expect to find a retrograde amnesia with a temporal gradient. From this viewpoint, the Korsakoff patients' loss of remote memories would be considered an artifact related to a primary defect in establishing new memories. A corollary of this hypothesis is that true retrograde amnesias, uncontaminated by deficiencies in original learning, are temporally limited and are far less severe and devastating than the amnesic patients' anterograde memory problems.

To evaluate this 'chronic' interpretation of the alcoholic Korsakoff patients' retrograde amnesia two investigations (Albert et al., 1980; Cohen and Squire, 1981) assessed the remote memories of detoxified, long-term alcoholics. If the learning deficit related to alcoholism was responsible for the Korsakoff patients' difficulties in recalling past events, two predictions could be made: (1) alcoholics should be impaired in their identification of famous persons and public events; and (2) since the detrimental effects of alcohol on the learning of new information are likely to be related to years of alcohol abuse, the alcoholics' deficits in recalling past events should be most apparent for the years immediately preceding testing. The results of both studies only partially confirmed these expectations. Long-term alcoholics demonstrated mild-to-moderate deficits only on the most difficult tests and items, although this impairment was most apparent for the 10-year period immediately prior to testing. For example, Albert et al. (1980) found that their alcoholics' impairments were limited to hard public events questions from the 1970s. On the famous persons test and on the easy items of the public events questionnaire there were no significant differences between their alcoholic and nonalcoholic subjects.

Although these noted deficits in the remote memory capacities of non-Korsakoff alcoholics are not of sufficient magnitude to allow the Korsakoff patients' retrograde amnesia to be reduced to an anterograde problem, they do suggest that two separate etiological factors may be involved. One is the impact of chronic alcohol abuse on anterograde memory processes. Since long-term alcoholics may retain somewhat less information each year due to a chronic learning deficit (for review, see Ryan and Butters, 1986), their store of remote memories for the recent past may be mildly or moderately deficient. The second may be a forgetting of or a loss of access to old memories that appears acutely during the Wernicke stage of the illness and results in a severe and equal loss for all time periods prior to the onset of the disease. When this acute loss of remote memories is superimposed on the patients' already deficient store, a severe retrograde amnesia with a temporal gradient would be expected. Patients should be impaired with respect to controls at all time periods, but memory for recent events should be most severely affected because less had been learned initially during this period.

The most convincing evidence for this two-factor model of the alcoholic Korsakoff patients' retrograde amnesia emanates from a single-case study of autobiographical memory (Butters and Cermak, 1986). This patient (with the fictitious initials P.Z.), an eminent scientist and university professor who developed alcoholic Korsakoff's syndrome at the age of 65, had written several hundred research papers and numerous books and book chapters, including an extensive autobiography three years prior to the acute onset of Wernicke's encephalopathy in 1981. Like all alcoholics with Korsakoff's syndrome, P.Z. had severe anterograde and retrograde amnesia as assessed by clinical and formal psychometric techniques. He was unable to learn verbal-verbal and symbol-digit paired associates, and evidenced no recall of day-to-day events 30 minutes after they occurred. On Albert et al.'s (1979) remote memory battery P.Z. was severely impaired in his recall of famous people and major historical events, but he did show some sparing of faces and episodes from the 1930s and 1940s.

To assess P.Z.'s amnesia for famous individuals in his scientific specialty, a famous scientists test was constructed. This task consisted of the names of 75 famous investigators and scholars, all of whom should have been well known to P.Z. The vast majority of these names were mentioned prominently in one or more of P.Z.'s books or major scholarly papers. Other names were chosen because of their documented professional interactions with P.Z. (such as editors of major journals in P.Z.'s area of expertise). Twenty-eight of these scholars had reached the pinnacle of their prominence prior to 1965, 24 of the scientists had made major contributions both before and after 1965, and 23 had attained a high level of fame and visibility since 1965. At the time of testing, P.Z.

was presented with each name and asked to describe the scholar's major area of interest and specific contributions to this area. P.Z.'s answers were tape-recorded and later scored on a three-point (0, 1, 2) ordinal scale in terms of their adequacy. For example, if P.Z. could identify the scientist's area of expertise but could not recall a specific major contribution, the response was rated as a '1.' If, however, P.Z. identified accurately both the scientist's area of research and a specific scholarly contribution to this area, his response was assigned a score of '2'. Only a total failure to recognize the scientist and to identify the scientist's major area of interest accurately resulted in a score of '0.' In order to evaluate P.Z.'s memory for famous scientists, another 65-year-old, highly prominent scholar in P.Z.'s area of specialty was administered the same famous scientists test.

The results for the famous scientists test are shown in Fig. 6. It is obvious from even a casual inspection of these data that P.Z. has a severe retrograde amnesia for individuals who were once well known to him. Although this deficit is apparent for all three temporal categories, it is most evident for those scientists who attained prominence since 1965. The percentage of '0' scores increases dramatically from the 'before 1965' to the 'after 1965' category, whereas the percentage of '1' rankings shows the opposite trend (highest percentage was for scientists prominent prior to 1965). Thus, P.Z. appears to have developed a temporally graded loss of professional knowledge which, by all accounts and documentation, was familiar to him prior to the acute onset of the Wernicke's stage of his disorder.

To determine whether P.Z. had also lost access to autobiographical material that was very familiar to him before his illness, a retrograde amnesia test based upon his autobiography was developed. The test consisted of questions about relatives, colleagues, collaborators, conferences, research assistants, research reports and books mentioned prominently in his autobiography.

Patient P.Z.'s recall of these autobiographical facts is shown in Fig. 7. As with the results from the famous scientists test, two points are evident. First, P.Z. has a very severe retrograde amnesia for autobiographical events, with considerable sparing of information from the very remote past. Second, P.Z.'s retrograde amnesia for autobiographical material cannot be secondary to a deficiency in original learning. Since all the questions were drawn from his own autobiography, the possibility that he had never acquired the information can be eliminated. Just three years prior to the onset of his Wernicke-Korsakoff's syndrome, patient P.Z. could retrieve this information, which he considered most important in his professional and personal life. Clearly, P.Z.'s illness marked the acute onset of his inability to access information that was once readily available to him.

The most severe impairment in retrieval of information acquired during the most recent two decades suggests that this autobiographical infor-

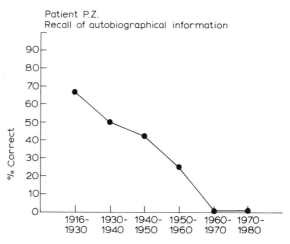

Fig. 7. Patient P.Z.'s retrograde amnesia for information from his published autobiography. (From Butters, 1984a.)

mation might not have achieved as stable a level as information acquired earlier in patient P.Z.'s lifetime. There are a number of plausible interpretations. One possibility is that this instability represents a progressive loss of P.Z.'s ability to acquire new information during his 35-year history of alcoholism (Albert et al., 1980; Cohen and Squire, 1981). Thus, due to the increasingly deleterious (i.e., neurotoxic) effects of alcohol, P.Z.'s memory for episodes and facts from the past 20 years may have been based upon partial or 'degraded' engrams. The more degraded or partial the memories, the more vulnerable they may have been to the acute brain damage that occurred in 1981.

A second plausible explanation for the temporal gradients that characterized P.Z.'s retrograde amnesia involves the notion that information acquired decades previously might be retrieved from a more general knowledge system than is the case for recently acquired information. Cermak (1984) has suggested that newly acquired knowledge may be *episodic* in nature but that with time and continued rehearsal the memories become independent of specific temporal and spatial contexts (i.e., *semantic* memory). From this viewpoint, the gradients evidenced by P.Z. (and other alcoholic Korsakoff patients) are due to the greater vulnerability

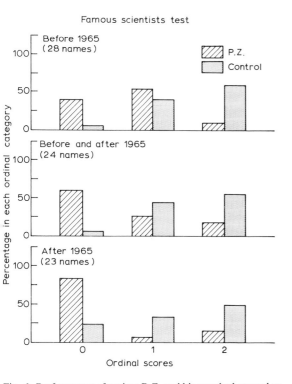

Fig. 6. Performance of patient P.Z. and his matched control on the identification of famous scientists. Scores 0, 1 and 2 represent an ordinal scaling of the adequacy of the two subjects' responses. (From Butters, 1984a.)

of episodic than of semantic memory to extensive damage to diencephalic or mesial temporal lobe structures. Knowledge of public events and personal experiences from the 1930s and 1940s may be part of semantic memory, whereas public and personal happenings from the past decade may still be associated with specific spatial and temporal contexts. This hypothesis stressing the loss of episodic memory is unique among theories of amnesia because it attempts to account for both the patients' anterograde and their retrograde amnesias.

Shimamura and Squire's (1986) findings concerning the degree of correlation between alcoholic Korsakoff patients' anterograde and retrograde amnesias lend support to Cermak's proposed dichotomization of remote memories. They administered nine tests of new learning (i.e., tests of episodic memory) and three tests of remote memory to alcoholic Korsakoff patients. Although there were no significant correlations between the new learning tests and overall severity of retrograde amnesia (1940s – 1970s), a different picture emerged when the very remote (1940s – 1950s) and recent remote (1960s – 1970s) memories were considered separately. Significant correlations between tests of new learning and recent remote (1960s – 1970s) memories were found, whereas no relationship between these anterograde tasks and very remote (1940s – 1950s) memories were noted. This significant relationship between the episodic tests of new learning and the recent remote memories suggests that they both may be involved in the same *episodic* memory system and that the very remote memories from the 1940s and 1950s may, as suggested by Cermak (1984), belong to a different memory system (e.g., *semantic* memory).

Given the previously noted evidence of 'frontal' dysfunction in Korsakoff patients, the possibility that these patients' retrograde amnesias may be a reflection of their impaired problem solving and planning should be considered. Such deficits in executive and sequencing functions could lead to a general inability to initiate systematic retrieval of old memories about public and autobiographical events.

Although some retrograde amnesias may be a consequence of cortically mediated cognitive deficits beyond the domain of the amnesic syndrome, there is evidence from single-case reports that signs of frontal (or other) cortical damage are not necessary for the existence of extended losses of remote memories. Cermak's postencephalitic patient S.S. (Cermak, 1976; Cermak and O'Connor 1983) has almost a total loss of all memories for personal and public events that occurred prior to the onset of his illness, without any significant impairments on complex problem solving or other 'frontal lobe' tests. Similarly, Stuss et al.'s (1988) patient R.C., who suffered a vascular infarct limited to the paramedian thalamic region, was severely impaired on public events and famous persons tests for all decades of his life (see Fig. 4). Squire et al.'s (1989) comparison of the retrograde amnesias of alcoholic Korsakoff patients and of patients with circumscribed lesions of mesial temporal lobe structures provides strong evidence that neither frontal dysfunction nor retrieval failures are sufficient to account for extended retrograde amnesias. Despite intact performance on cognitive tasks sensitive to frontal damage, patients with mesial temporal damage had retrograde amnesias similar in extent and form (i.e., temporally graded) to those of alcoholic Korsakoff patients. When the patients and normal controls were readministered the remote memory tests on several occasions, their performances for individual items remained highly consistent from one administration to another. In other words, since neither amnesic group showed unusual variability in their recall and recognition of individual items, there was no evidence that their performances represented a failure in retrieval processes (Squire et al., 1989).

In summary, the extended, temporally-graded retrograde amnesias of alcoholic Korsakoff patients are a highly consistent, yet poorly understood, feature of the disorder. The failure to reduce retrograde amnesia to deficient learning prior to the onset of amnesic symptomatology emphasizes its acute onset during the Wernicke stage of the syndrome. At the present time, the relative paring of remote events seems best explained by Cermak's (1984) proposed shift of information from a fragile episodic to a stable semantic memory store. Although it is possible that some features of the Korsakoff patients' retrograde amnesia may be attributable to ancillary frontal lobe dysfunctions, there is substantial evidence that extended losses of remote memory can occur without any functional or structural evidence of damage to anterior association cortices.

Preserved memory capacities

In recent years there has been increasing interest in exploring those memory capacities and systems that remain intact despite the alcoholic Korsakoff patients' dense anterograde and retrograde amnesias. One series of studies has focused upon the patients' rate of forgetting newly acquired materials. Huppert and Piercy (1977, 1978) reported that when alcoholic Korsakoff patients, Scoville and Milner's (1957) patient H.M. (who developed a severe amnesia following extensive, bilateral removal of the mesial region of his temporal lobes), and intact controls attained the same level of initial learning, important differences were apparent in their rates of forgetting of pictorial materials over a seven-day period. So that all subjects would attain approximately the same level of learning (i.e., recognition) after a 10-minute delay period, exposure time during the initial presentation of the pictures was manipulated (i.e., increased for the amnesics) to ensure a performance level of at least 75% correct. The results of these studies showed that, although H.M., normal subjects and alcoholic Korsakoff patients all performed more poorly on recognition tasks with increasing retention intervals (one day, seven days), patient H.M.'s performance evidenced a much steeper rate of forgetting than that of the two subject groups. Indeed, the rates of forgetting of the alcoholic Korsakoff patients and the normal control subjects were indistinguishable. Based on these data, Huppert and Piercy (1977, 1978) suggested that the anterograde amnesias of H.M. and of the alcoholic

Korsakoff patients involve different deficits in information processing. The alcoholic Korsakoff patients' learning difficulties appear to emanate from a decrement in stimulus analysis, whereas patient H.M.'s rapid forgetting of newly acquired materials may be an indicator of a problem with consolidation and storage.

While other investigations using Huppert and Piercy's technique (Martone et al., 1986; Kopelman, 1985; Squire, 1981) have also reported normal forgetting rates for Korsakoff patients, recent studies of patient H.M. and of other patients with bilateral mesial temporal damage (e.g., patients with Alzheimer's disease) have resulted in contradictory findings. Freed et al. (1987) attempted to replicate Huppert and Piercy's data with patient H.M. but found little difference between him and intact controls in the forgetting of pictorial materials. Kopelman (1985) compared alcoholic Korsakoff and Alzheimer patients' rate of forgetting of pictorial material and found that only the Alzheimer patients demonstrated rapid forgetting. Squire (1981) evaluated alcoholic Korsakoff patients and depressed patients receiving bilateral electroconvulsive therapy (ECT) on pictorial and verbal forgetting tasks. He found that the Korsakoff patients forgot at normal rates over a 32-hour period, whereas the patients receiving ECT had an accelerated decay of both types of materials during the same period. Squire (1981) proposed that ECT affects memory by disrupting hippocampal mechanisms concerned with the consolidation process and concluded, like Huppert and Piercy, that amnesic symptoms associated with diencephalic and hippocampal dysfunction are dissociable in terms of the stage of information processing adversely affected.

Martone and her collaborators (Martone et al., 1986) replicated and extended the previous findings. In the first of three experiments, alcoholic Korsakoff patients and patients with Huntington's disease demonstrated normal rates of forgetting of pictorial materials over a one-week period when overexposure of stimulus materials was used to equate initial recognition. The second experiment explored whether the Korsakoff and Huntington patients learned as much about the features of the pictorial stimuli as did intact individuals. After the subjects viewed a series of pictorial stimuli, recognition was assessed 10 minutes later using the whole pictures, isolated main features of the pictures, or isolated peripheral features of the pictures. The results showed that with prolonged exposure times the two patient groups did not differ from a normal control group in terms of the features of the stimuli they analysed and remembered.

The third experiment in Martone et al.'s (1986) study assessed the validity of Huppert and Piercy's technique, i.e., whether overexposure of stimuli to achieve equivalent immediate recognition necessarily results in identical levels of learning and storage. Young and old normal controls were shown a series of pictorial stimuli for half a second and one second each, respectively. Although the two age groups did not differ in recognition performance 10 minutes after presentation, the young subjects who viewed each picture for half a second showed more rapid forgetting over a one-week period than did the old subjects. Since there is no apparent explanation for young individuals to be more prone to rapid forgetting, Martone et al. concluded that under some exposure conditions similar recognition scores (10 minutes after presentation) do not necessarily imply equivalent amounts of learning. The young subjects may have acquired limited knowledge of each picture, but this deficiency was not apparent until some forgetting had occurred over a seven-day period.

When these data with normal subjects are extrapolated to comparisons of patient groups, the lessons to be gleaned are evident. The Huppert and Piercy (1977, 1978) procedure for equating patients' and controls' initial recognition levels does not assure that the amount of information acquired is equivalent (for review, see Weiskrantz, 1985). If alcoholic Korsakoff patients are provided extensive overexposure of stimulus materials, they may actually learn more about the materials than do intact and/or other brain-damaged patient

groups. If such is the case, the superior storage o the Korsakoff patients may mask a very rapid rat of forgetting. As noted previously, Butters et al.' (1988) validation study with the WMS-R reportec that alcoholic Korsakoff patients showed mor rapid forgetting on the Logical Memory and Visua Reproduction tests than did patients with Hun tington's disease, even though the two patien groups showed almost identical levels of impaired immediate recall. However, on tasks (i.e., Verba and Visual Paired Associate) where the Korsakof patients had twice as many learning trials as did th intact controls, differences in forgetting rate ove a 30-minute period were small (Butters et al. 1988).

In stark contrast to their inability to learn anc retain most factual material, alcoholic Korsakof patients, like all amnesics and even patients with Alzheimer's disease, show normal acquisition o motor and visuoperceptual skills. Cermak et al. (1973b) compared alcoholic Korsakoff patients alcoholics (non-Korsakoff) and intact control sub jects in the acquisition of a pursuit-rotor task anc of four and six choice-point mazes. The pursuit rotor task required the patients to learn to maintain contact between a stylus and a small metallic disk on a rotating turntable. For the two finger mazes the subjects were instructed to discover with their index finger the correct pathway from the bottom to the top of the maze which remained hidden from view. The Korsakoff patients proved to be severely impaired in learning the sequence o right-left choices needed to master the two mazes, but they showed normal acquisition and retention of the pursuit-rotor motor skill over a five-day period. Brooks and Baddeley (1976) replicated Cermak et al.'s findings with the pursuit-rotor task and showed that the Korsakoff patients' intact skill learning extended to the assembly of jig-saw puzzles and the Porteus Maze.

Cohen and Squire (1980) reported that alcoholic Korsakoff patients can learn and retain over a 94-day period the general visuomotor and visuoperceptual skills needed to read mirror-reflected words. The alcoholic Korsakoff patients acquired his mirror-reading skill despite a severe amnesia for the previous training sessions and for the specific words they had read. The investigators proposed that alcoholic Korsakoff patients, like all patients with amnesic conditions, are severely impaired in learning specific *declarative (data-based) knowledge* (e.g., the actual words employed), but they are capable of normal acquisition and retention *procedural (skill-based) knowledge* (e.g., the reading of mirror-reflected words).

These findings for skill-based and data-based knowledge have been replicated and extended by Martone and her collaborators (Martone et al., 1984). These investigators found a double dissociation between procedural and declarative memory for alcoholic Korsakoff patients and for patients with Huntington's disease. As Cohen and Squire (1980) had reported, Korsakoff patients demonstrated normal rates of skill learning (mirror reading) coupled with impaired recognition of the actual verbal materials used on the task; in contrast, patients with Huntington's disease were impaired in the acquisition of the skill but could identify with great accuracy the words presented during the experiment. Based upon their data, Martone et al. (1984) proposed that the limbic-diencephalic structures and the basal ganglia mediate the acquisition and retention of data-based and skill-based knowledge, respectively. Heindel et al.'s (1988) demonstration of a double dissociation between amnesic and Huntington patients on verbal recall and pursuit-rotor tasks is consistent with Martone et al.'s (1984) conclusions.

Whether the Korsakoff patients' intact procedural memory extends to cognitive skills is still unclear. Cohen (1984), in a brief report, claimed that amnesics (none of whom were alcoholic Korsakoffs) were capable of acquiring the complex rules underlying the solution of the Tower of Hanoi puzzle. This Tower task requires the shifting of five blocks arranged according to size from a start to a goal (i.e., end) peg while maintaining the established order by size. Subjects are permitted to move only one block at a time and can never place a larger block on top of a smaller one. Cohen

reported that his amnesics (including Scoville and Milner's patient H.M.) showed the same rate of improvement (as measured by the number of moves to achieve solution) as did intact controls over two days of testing.

When Butters et al. (1985) used the Tower of Hanoi with alcoholic Korsakoff patients, they found little evidence of learning over 16 test trials. One possible explanation for the Korsakoffs' failure is that solution of the Tower puzzle relies heavily upon problem-solving abilities in addition to the capacity to acquire skill-based procedural knowledge. Like many other problem solving tasks, the Tower puzzle requires the identification, sequencing and retention of moves (i.e., strategies) to ensure an efficient solution. On such tasks, subjects can rarely confine themselves to the specific move or choice immediately confronting them; rather, the current move must be considered in the context of the immediately succeeding situation. Because alcoholic Korsakoff patients are impaired in the initiation and ordering of problem solving strategies (Becker et al., 1986; Oscar-Berman, 1973; Talland, 1965), the failure of Butters et al.'s patients to show significant improvement on the Tower of Hanoi puzzle may not be indicative of a deficit in acquiring skill-based information. Saint-Cyr et al.'s (1988) report that some demented as well as amnesic patients can learn a similar, but simpler, cognitive skill (i.e., Tower of Toronto) when they are first trained on the problem solving features of the task is supportive of this explanation.

The Korsakoff patients' ability to acquire and retain skill-based information is just one example of their generally intact *implicit* memory. Whereas *explicit* memory refers to conscious and intentional attempts to recall or recognize specific episodes or facts, *implicit* memory is apparent when previous experiences unconsciously facilitate performance (Schacter, 1987b, c; Schacter et al., 1988; Graf and Schacter, 1985). In normal individuals both types of memory are unimpaired and easily demonstrable, but in amnesics explicit memory is severely impaired while implicit memory remains intact

(Schacter, 1987b; Shimamura, 1986). Lexical, semantic and perceptual priming, classical conditioning and skill learning have all been cited as examplars of implicit memory. It is commonly assumed that implicit memory represents the unconscious activation of memory traces, often in semantic memory, that later affect an individual's performance on stem-completion, reaction time, free association, perceptual and even judgment tasks.

The first demonstration of intact implicit memory in alcoholic Korsakoff patients was provided by Warrington and Weiskrantz (1968, 1970, 1974). They showed that amnesics (including alcoholic Korsakoff patients) could exhibit almost normal performance when fragmented words and pictures and two-letter words stems were used to cue recall. That is, amnesics who were severely impaired in their attempted (i.e., intentional) recall and recognition of common words evidenced rapid, accurate identification when shown highly fragmented visual representations of the words or the first two letters of the word. Weiskrantz and Warrington (1970) reported that learning accomplished with these degraded (i.e., fragmented) stimuli was surprisingly well retained 24 and 72 hours later, even by alcoholic Korsakoff patients. As noted previously, Warrington and Weiskrantz (1973) initially interpreted these findings as evidence for their retrieval theory of memory, but have more recently proposed that such cuing is an example of implicit memory (i.e., automatic facilitatory effect) (Warrington and Weiskrantz, 1982).

The second formal demonstration of intact implicit memory in alcoholic Korsakoff patients was provided by Gardner and his collaborators (Gardner et al., 1973). After subjects were presented with a list of common words (e.g., tennis, lettuce), belonging to one of six general categories (e.g., sports, vegetables), their recall was assessed under three different conditions. In one condition the subjects were simply asked to recall the words that had been read to them (i.e., free recall); in another, their attempted (i.e., conscious and intentional) recall was cued by category (e.g., "A few moments ago I asked you to remember some words. One of them was a *sport*. What was it?''); in the third condition, the subjects were simply given a category name (e.g., vegetables) and asked to produce the first example of this category that came to mind. The results showed that although the Korsakoff patients were significantly impaired in comparison to intact subjects on the first two recall conditions, they did not differ from controls on the third (i.e., free association) condition. Both the alcoholic Korsakoff patients and intact controls tended to produce previously presented words (e.g., tennis) when asked to 'free associate' to the category names (e.g., sports). Thus, the Korsakoff patients were very impaired when recall was under conscious control (i.e., explicit memory), but did not differ from normal controls when there was no conscious intention to recall the previously presented words (i.e., implicit memory). This finding that the activation underlying implicit memory in Korsakoff patients spreads along semantic hierarchies (i.e., from category exemplars to category labels) has been replicated by Graf et al. (1985).

During the past eight years numerous studies demonstrating the existence and limits of implicit memory in other experimental paradigms have been published (for review, see Schacter, 1987b,c; Shimamura, 1986). Jacoby and Witherspoon (1982) demonstrated the roles of implicit activation of semantic memory on a spelling bias task. They asked normal control subjects and alcoholic Korsakoff patients a series of questions such as, "Name a musical instrument that employs a *reed*.'' Later all subjects were asked to spell homophonic words such as *reed/read*. Like the control subjects, the Korsakoff patients evidenced a strong spelling bias for the words previously presented in the questions. However, despite this spelling bias, the Korsakoff patients were severely impaired when they attempted to recognize the words used in the questions. These findings, like those of Gardner et al. (1973), indicated that implicit memory can involve the activation of associative networks in semantic memory, and is not limited to the facilitation of specific words (as in the stem-completion and degraded stimuli paradigms). Although Cermak et al. (1986) have replicated this semantically biased spelling preference in alcoholic Korsakoff patients, they have shown that it is easily disrupted by the passage of time and the presentation of new verbal materials.

Johnson et al. (1985) have also reported preference biasing in alcoholic Korsakoff patients. They presented melodies from Korean songs and asked Korsakoff patients and normal subjects to rate each melody as to how Chinese or American they sounded. After a brief delay, the subjects listened to a series of melodies comprised of the previously presented and new ones and rated each melody in terms of how much they liked it. Although Korsakoff patients showed very poor recognition of the previously presented melodies, they and normal control subjects exhibited the same preference bias for the repeated melodies.

Graf et al. (1984) extended the findings of Warrington and Weiskrantz (1968, 1970) with the stem-completion priming paradigm. While Warrington and Weiskrantz had tested only with explicit memory instructions, Graf et al. (1984) compared stem-completion priming in Korsakoff patients and intact controls using both explicit and implicit memory procedures. Under the explicit condition, the subjects were told to utilize three-letter word stems to facilitate recall of the previously presented words; with implicit instructions, the subjects were simply asked to complete the stems with the first words that came to mind. The results showed that with explicit instructions (as well as with free recall and recognition procedures) alcoholic Korsakoff patients produced significantly fewer of the to-be-remembered words than did intact control subjects. However, when free association instructions (i.e., implicit) were operative, the two subject groups were equivalent in their tendency to generate words from the presentation list. As part of a study concerned with implicit memory in dementia, Shimamura et al. (1987) have replicated the free-association, stem-completion effects for alcoholic Korsakoff patients.

This interaction between subject groups and instructions (Graf et al., 1984) was primarily due to changes in the performances of the control subjects who were significantly less likely to produce a list word with implicit than with explicit memory instructions. In contrast, the alcoholic Korsakoff patients' tendency to produce list words did not change as a function of the test instructions. This shift in performance by intact controls with explicit and implicit instructions was also noted by Gardner et al. (1973) who attributed the change to their normal subjects' interpretation of the demands of their free association task. Since normal individuals have intact explicit memories, they may interpret the implicit free association condition as a challenge to generate words other than those on the presentation list. Schacter (1987b) has reviewed the likelihood and implications of such instructional biases for the stem-completion model.

Shimamura and Squire (1984) have shown that the implicit activation of traces is also apparent when alcoholic Korsakoff patients attempt to learn semantically related paired-associates (e.g., table-chair). When given explicit memory instructions, Korsakoff patients proved to be superior at learning semantically related than unrelated word pairs (see also, Winocur and Weiskrantz, 1976), although they were significantly impaired for both types of stimuli. However, when the Korsakoff patients were tested with implicit memory instructions requiring the subjects to free associate to the first member of the stimulus pair (e.g., table), they were as good as their control subjects in acquiring the list. Shimamura and Squire (1984) suggest that the alcoholic Korsakoff patients rely upon their intact implicit memory processes regardless of the explicit or implicit demands of the learning task. In contrast, normal individuals can superimpose the intact encoding processes of explicit memory upon the unconscious implicit traces and thereby facilitate the transfer of new information into a permanent store.

Graf et al. (1985) have reported that priming effects can cross sensory modalities. After either oral or visual presentation of a list of words, alcoholic Korsakoff patients and control subjects were asked to recall the words and then administered a visual stem-completion (word-completion) task. Thus, the presentation words were exposed either in the same (visual) or different (auditory) sensory modality as the stem cues. The results indicated that although both amnesic and control groups exhibited better stem-completion priming when the words had been presented visually, the Korsakoff patients performed as well as their controls on both the visual-visual and auditory-visual conditions. On the free recall test, the alcoholic Korsakoff patients were severely impaired regardless of the sensory modality used for presentation. These findings suggest that implicit memory engages semantic memory and is not bound by the physical attributes of the stimuli.

Further evidence that implicit memory in amnesics relies heavily upon the activation of semantic knowledge has been provided by Cermak et al. (1985). In the first of two experiments, they presented alcoholic Korsakoff patients and alcoholic control subjects with lists of real words and then assessed the subjects' recognition and perceptual identification (i.e., temporal thresholds) for these and for distractor words. With one minute delays between presentation and testing, the Korsakoff patients were impaired on recognition memory, yet demonstrated normal levels of facilitation on the perceptual identification task. That is, although the Korsakoff patients were severely impaired in differentiating target from distractor words on the recognition task, they identified the target words more rapidly (i.e., with briefer exposure times) than the distractor stimuli. In the second experiment, the same procedures were followed with pseudowords serving as the stimuli. Under these conditions the Korsakoff patients failed to show any facilitation on the perceptual identification task. As Cermak et al. (1985) conclude, this dissociation between real and pseudowords indicates that for amnesics' priming must activate previously acquired information in semantic memory.

In summary, despite their severe anterograde and retrograde amnesias, alcoholic Korsakoff patients, like most amnesics, appear to have a remarkably intact implicit memory system. Besides their ability to acquire and retain motor, visuo-perceptual and perhaps cognitive skills, the Korsakoff patients' semantic memory can be unconsciously activated in a manner that can facilitate their performance on word-completion, paired-associate, perceptual identification and judgment tasks. This activation of semantic memory does not seem bound by the sensory modality engaged, although priming effects may be temporally more limited and fragile for Korsakoff patients than for intact subjects. Also, the frequently cited evidence of alcoholic Korsakoff patients' normal forgetting rates may be exaggerated. Since Huppert and Piercy's elegant procedure may inadvertently result in overlearning, demonstrations of normal forgetting may be a reflection of an initial inequality in acquisition.

Neurological bases of the Wernicke-Korsakoff syndrome

Since several reviews of the neurological basis of the Wernicke-Korsakoff syndrome have already appeared (Brierly, 1977; Mair et al., 1979; Markowitsch, 1982; Markowitsch and Pritzel, 1985; Victor et al., 1971), we shall cite only their major findings and then discuss in some detail the results of some recent investigations related to this topic. As Brierly (1977) notes, most of the literature supports the conclusion that the neurological symptoms of Wernicke's encephalopathy are related to lesions of the brainstem and cerebellum, whereas the amnesic symptoms of the chronic Korsakoff state involve damage to several thalamic and hypothalamic structures surrounding the third ventricle of the brain. The dorsomedial nucleus of the thalamus and the mammillary bodies of the hypothalamus are the specific structures most often associated with the alcoholic Korsakoff patients' amnesic symptoms (Fig. 1).

Adams et al. (1962) combined neuropathological findings with careful clinical and psychometric examinations of 300 Wernicke-Korsakoff patients. They found that the onset of the Wernicke stage was acute and subsided rapidly with the administration of large doses of thiamine. As the confusion, ataxia, nystagmus and ocular palsies cleared, the patients' major remaining symptoms were severe anterograde and retrograde amnesia. Of the 300 cases, 54 brains were eventually studied. The investigators attributed the symptoms of Wernicke's encephalopathy to lesions in the brainstem (for example, oculomotor nucleus) and cerebellum. The severe memory disorder of the Korsakoff stage of the illness was correlated with the presence of lesions in the mammillary bodies and several thalamic nuclei (dorsomedial, anteroventral and pulvinar).

Victor et al. (1971) carefully examined the dorsomedial nucleus of the thalamus in the brains of 43 Wernicke-Korsakoff patients. Their results showed that the dorsomedial nucleus and the mammillary bodies were extensively atrophied in 38 cases and that the mammillary bodies alone were affected in five cases. Since there had been no reports of chronic memory disorders in the five cases with isolated mammillary body damage, Victor et al. (1971) concluded that the dorsomedial nucleus, and not the mammillary bodies, is the critical structure for the amnesic syndrome.

Two recent neuropathological studies (Harper, 1979, 1983) suggest that the atrophic and vascular diencephalic changes associated with the Wernicke-Korsakoff syndrome may also be common among non-amnesic, long-term alcoholics. In one investigation of 51 cases of Wernicke's encephalopathy diagnosed at necropsy, only seven had been diagnosed clinically during life (Harper, 1979). In a second and more extensive study, Harper (1983) found that 83% of 131 brains of alcoholics evidenced significant medial diencephalic changes (including atrophy of the mammillary bodies, hemorrhagic lesions of the thalamus, dilatation of the third ventricle) even though only 20% of the cases had been reported to have signs

of Wernicke's encephalopathy prior to death. Although Harper's conclusions (Harper and Finlay-Jones, 1986) stress the underdiagnosis of the Wernicke-Korsakoff syndrome among alcoholics, his findings also demonstrate the presence of significant medial diencephalic lesions in alcoholic patients with apparently mild neurological and neuropsychological deficits.

One explanation of Harper's findings rests upon quantitative differences in neurological damage between alcoholics with and without the clinical signs of the Wernicke-Korsakoff syndrome. That is, non-Korsakoff alcoholics may simply have less atrophy and fewer hemorrhagic lesions than do alcoholics with Korsakoff's syndrome. For an alcoholic to progress to the Wernicke's state the amount of diencephalic damage may have to exceed a critical threshold necessary for the maintenance of neurological and neuropsychological functioning. As Harper (1983) has suggested, alcoholics whose malnutrition is chronically mild-to-moderate in severity may have numerous subclinical Wernicke episodes before their sensory, motor and mental status changes are noted. The observation that 20 – 25% of all Korsakoff patients (and probably all alcoholics with general dementia) have chronic progressive rather than acute onsets (Victor et al., 1971) is consistent with Harper's (1983) notions.

A second explanation of Harper's findings concerns the involvement of other brain structures besides the medial diencephalon in the Wernicke-Korsakoff syndrome. Arendt et al.'s (1983) neuropathological findings have suggested that the basal forebrain, the major source of cholinergic input to the cerebral cortex and hippocampus, may play a vital role in Korsakoff's syndrome. They reported that three cases of alcoholic Korsakoff's syndrome showed a 47% reduction in the number of neurons in the basal forebrain in comparison to 14 control cases and five cases of chronic alcoholism without dementia. Although Arendt et al.'s observations must be considered preliminary due to the small number of cases and lack of detailed clinical descriptions, they certainly raise the possibility that the acute onset of Wernicke's encephalopathy in alcoholics may be associated with more than a sudden increment in medial diencephalic damage. Lishman's (1986) suggestion that damage to the basal forebrain may be more common in alcoholic dementia than in Korsakoff's syndrome also emphasizes the need for more studies of these structures in alcoholics with different degrees and patterns of neuropsychological impairments.

Although much of the neuropathological interest in the Wernicke-Korsakoff syndrome has focused upon subcortical structures, such as the mammillary bodies and the dorsomedial nucleus of the thalamus, the use of CT scans with living alcoholics (with and without Korsakoff's syndrome) had caused investigators to question whether the damage associated with long-term abuse is limited to a small number of subcortical structures and whether all of the symptoms associated with Korsakoff's syndrome should be attributed to atrophy of structures surrounding the third ventricle (Moscovitch, 1982; Schacter, 1987a; Squire, 1982, 1987). All recent reviews of the CT literature concerned with alcoholics conclude that the vast majority of those who have been abusing alcohol for more than 10 years demonstrate significant cortical as well as subcortical abnormalities (Jacobson and Lishman, 1987; Lishman, 1981, 1987; Wilkinson, 1987; Bergman, 1987; Ron, 1987). The changes are usually characterized as symmetric shrinkage of the cortex of the cerebral hemispheres in addition to dilation of the lateral and third ventricles. Shrinkage of the vermis of the cerebellum and cerebellar hemispheres is also present in all advanced stages. Despite the diffuseness of this atrophy, the frontal lobes show the most marked shrinkage, as indicated by a widening of the interhemispheric fissure and frontal horns of the lateral ventricles.

In a recent study employing computer-generated measures derived from CT scans, Shimamura et al. (1988) examined seven alcoholic Korsakoff patients, seven detoxified alcoholics and seven intact (nonalcoholic) control subjects. The Korsakoff patients were found to have lower density values in the region of the thalamus and greater fluid volumes in the third ventricle than did the alcoholic and intact subjects. Signs of anterior cortical atrophy (e.g., increased sulcal size) were noted in both groups of alcoholics. As noted previously, for the Korsakoff patients several cognitive measures, including indices of memory functioning, correlated significantly with density measures of the thalamus and fluid volumes in the region of the frontal lobes. The authors conclude that dysfunction of both midline thalamic and anterior cortical structures contribute to the Korsakoff patients' memory and other cognitive problems.

While most studies of the neurological basis of Korsakoff's syndrome have focused upon structural correlates, a few have emphasized the role of specific neurotransmitter systems (McEntee and Mair, 1978, 1980; Mair and McEntee, 1986). McEntee and Mair (1978) reported that the cerebrospinal fluid of nine Korsakoff patients contained significantly deficient levels of MHPG, the primary monoamine metabolite of norepinephrine. They also reported a significant correlation between the severity of the patients' memory impairment and the levels of MHPG in their cerebrospinal fluid.

Further evidence linking damage to norepinephrine-containing neurons in subcortical centers with patients' memory disorders was provided in a second study (McEntee and Mair, 1980). In this investigation, several drugs that facilitate central norepinephrine activity were administered to eight patients with Korsakoff's disease. Each patient was examined on a neuropsychological test battery, which included measures of memory, perceptual and conceptual functions, before and after two weeks of drug administration. The results indicated that the administration of one drug, clonidine, was associated with significant improvements on several measures of anterograde memory functions, including short-term memory tests and specific subtests of the WMS. Mair and McEntee (1986) replicated their previous findings with clonidine and found that this drug's effects were limited to measures of the Korsakoff patients' anterograde amnesia. Clonidine did not ameliorate the patients' severe retrograde amnesia or their deficits on a digit-symbol substitution task. It should be noted that the small improvements found on some retention tests may have actually resulted from clonidine's beneficial effects on cognitive processes (e.g., attention, problem-solving) other than memory.

These neurochemical studies of McEntee and Mair have received some support from a recent neuropathological investigation. Mayes et al. (1988) reported psychometric and neuropathological findings for two alcoholic Korsakoff patients. Although both patients had extensive atrophy of the mammilary bodies and a band of gliosis in the medial thalamus, only the patient with the more severe anterograde amnesia had significant neuronal loss in locus coeruleus, a major source of noradrenalin for both limbic and cortical structures. Mayes et al. suggest that the etiology of Korsakoff's syndrome may involve a 'proclivity towards destroying neurons that release or receive noradrenalin.'

In summary, studies of the neurological basis of Korsakoff's syndrome have tended to implicate most frequently the dorsomedial nucleus of the thalamus and the mammillary bodies of the hypothalamus as the critical structures involved in the patients' amnesia. However, given the presence of these medial diencephalic lesions in non-Korsakoff alcoholics, the influence of other neurological entities (e.g., basal forebrain) must be considered. Also, since damage to the medial diencephalon frequently involves pathways connecting the thalamus and mesial temporal lobe structures (Cramon et al., 1985; Mayes et al., 1988; Mair et al., 1979), there is a distinct likelihood that Korsakoff's syndrome represents, at least in part, a disconnection syndrome. Finally, McEntee and Mair's studies of MHPG and clonidine suggest that further evaluations of the roles of specific neurotransmitter substances in this amnesic syndrome are warranted.

Conclusions

With regard to five issues discussed at the beginning of this review, the following conclusions can be noted.

(1) The *anterograde amnesia* associated with diencephalic damage is often severe and reflects some combination of deficiencies in storage, encoding, the use of temporal and spatial contextual cues for retrieval, motivation and arousal and an increased sensitivity to proactive interference. While there is evidence that all these factors are of some import, it is unlikely that any one deficit can account for the anterograde amnesia by itself.

(2) Despite a few clinical reports of relatively brief *retrograde amnesias,* most systematic investigations have indicated that diencephalic amnesia is characterized by an extended loss of both remote public and personal events. Although this deficit in remote memory may be flat in some patients with acute vascular etiologies, it is usually characterized by a temporal gradient in which public and personal episodes from the very remote past are relatively spared. At present, the most plausible explanation for this temporal gradient involves the transfer of remote memories from a fragile *episodic* to a stable *semantic* store. This transfer (i.e., consolidation) seems to occur years following the initial storage of the experience in episodic memory.

(3) Like patients whose memory disorders originate from mesial temporal lobe damage, diencephalic amnesics have *intact procedural* and *implicit memory* capacities. Alcoholic Korsakoff patients can acquire and retain motor, visuoperceptual, and perhaps cognitive skills and also manifest normal implicit memory on various word-completion, free association, perceptual identification, preference and judgment tasks.

(4) Diencephalic amnesics often have *problem solving, visuoperceptual, attentional* and *motivational changes* similar to those reported for patients with damage to the prefrontal association cortices. Although there is ample evidence that these 'frontal' dysfunctions may account for some of the features of diencephalic amnesics' memory disorders, the neurological bases for these seemingly ancillary impairments are not clear. Some amnesics, such as alcoholics with Korsakoff's syndrome, have demonstrable structural changes within the frontal lobes, but others, especially those with vascular etiologies, usually show no neuroradiological evidence of damage to association cortices. Furthermore, since lesions of medial diencephalic structures are likely to lead to extensive deafferentation of the frontal lobes, the likelihood that these so-called frontal features can ever be disentangled from the diencephalic patients' amnesia is very problematical.

(5) Although the dorsomedial nucleus of the thalamus and the mammillary bodies of the hypothalamus are often considered the *critical neurologic entities* involved in diencephalic amnesia, there is now increasing evidence that this amnesic syndrome may also involve other subcortical structures (e.g., basal forebrain) and/or fiber tracts (e.g., mammillothalamic tract and internal medullary lamina) connecting the diencephalon with mesial temporal lobe structures. If the latter proves to be the case, diencephalic amnesia may ultimately be viewed as a disconnection syndrome which is inseparable from amnesias following lesions of the hippocampus and adjacent structures.

Acknowledgements

The preparation of this chapter was supported in part by funds from the Medical Research Service of the Veterans Administration, grants AG05131 and AG08204 to the University of California, grant AA00187 to Boston University and by funds from the Medical Research Council of Canada and the Ontario Mental Health Foundation. The authors wish to express their gratitude to P. Grillo, M. Lecompte and L. Stethem for their help in preparing the manuscript. Part of this chapter represents an updated version of Dr. Butters' article 'Alcoholic Korsakoff's syndrome: an update' (*Seminars in Neurology: 4*, 226 – 244, 1984).

References

Adams RD, Collins GH, Victor M: Troubles de la memoire et de l'apprentissage chez l'homme; leurs relations avec des lesions des lobes temporaux et du diencephale. In *Physiologie de l'Hippocampe*. Paris: Centre National de la Recherche Scientifique, 1962.

Aggleton JP, Mishkin M: Memory imparments following restricted medial thalamic lesions. *Exp. Brain Res.: 52*, 199 – 209, 1983a.

Aggleton JP, Mishkin M: Visual recognition impairment following medial thalamic lesions in monkeys. *Neuropsychologia: 21*, 189 – 197, 1983b.

Albert ML: Subcortical dementia. In Katzman R, Terry RD, Bick KL (Editors), *Alzheimer's Disease: Senile Dementia and Related Disorders*. New York: Raven Press, pp. 173 – 180, 1978.

Albert ML, Feldman RG, Willis AL: The 'subcortical dementia' of progressive supranuclear palsy. *J. Neurol. Neurosurg. Psychiatry: 37*, 121 – 130, 1974.

Albert MS, Butters N, Brandt J: Memory for remote events in alcoholics. *J. Stud. Alcohol: 41*, 1071 – 1081, 1980.

Albert MS, Butters N, Levin J: Temporal gradients in the retrograde amnesia of patients with alcoholic Korsakoff's disease. *Arch. Neurol.: 36*, 211 – 216, 1979.

Alexander GE, Fuster JM: Effects of cooling prefrontal cortex on cell firing in the nucleus medialis dorsalis. *Brain Res.: 61*, 93 – 105, 1973.

Alexander MP, Lo Verme SR: Aphasia after left hemispheric intracerebral hemorrhage. *Neurology: 30*, 1193 – 1202, 1980.

Archer CR, Ilinsky IA, Goldfader PR, Smith Jr KR: Aphasia in thalamic stroke: CT stereotactic localization. *J. Comput. Assist. Tomography: 5*, 427 – 432, 1981.

Arendt T, Bigl V, Arendt A, Tennstedt A: Loss of neurons in the nucleus basalis of Meynert in Alzheimer's disease, paralysis agitans and Korsakoff's disease. *Acta Neuropathol.: 61*, 101 – 108, 1983.

Baddeley AD, Warrington EK: Amnesia and the distinction between long- and short-term memory. *J. Verbal Learn. Verbal Behav.: 9*, 176 – 189, 1970.

Barbizet J, Degos JD, Louarn F, Nguyen JP, Mas JL: Amnesia from bilateral ischemic lesions of the thalamus. *Rev. Neurol.: 137*, 415 – 424, 1981.

Beatty W, Salmon D, Bernstein N, Butters N: Remote memory in a patient with amnesia due to hypoxia. *Psychol. Med.: 17*, 657 – 665, 1987.

Becker J, Butters N, Rivoira P, Miliotis P: Asking the right questions: problem solving in male alcoholics and male alcoholics with Korsakoff's syndrome. *Alcohol. Clin. Exp. Res.: 10*, 641 – 646, 1986.

Benson DF: Subcortical dementia: a clinical approach. *Adv. Neurol.: 38*, 185 – 194, 1983.

Benson DF, Geschwind N: Shrinking retrograde amnesia. *J. Neurol. Neurosurg. Psychiatry: 30*, 539 – 544, 1967.

Bergman H: Brain dysfunction related to alcoholism: some results from the KARTAD project. In Parsons O, Butters N, Nathan P (Editors) *Neuropsychology of Alcoholism: Implications for Diagnosis and Treatment*. New York: Guilford Press, pp. 21 – 44, 1987.

Biber C, Butters N, Rosen J, Gerstmann L, Mattis S: Encoding strategies and recognition of faces by alcoholic Korsakoff and other brain-damaged patients. *J. Clin. Neuropsychol.: 3,* 315 – 330, 1981.

Brierly JB: Neuropathology of amnesic states. In Whitty CWM, Zangwill OL (Editors), *Amnesia,* 2nd ed. Boston: Butterworths, 1977.

Brion S, Mikol J, Plas J: Memoire et specialisation fonctionelle hemispherique. Rapport anatomo-clinique. *Rev. Neurol.: 139,* 39 – 43, 1983.

Brooks DN, Baddeley AD: What can amnesic patients learn? *Neuropsychologia: 14,* 111 – 122, 1976.

Butters N: Alcoholic Korsakoff's syndrome: an update. *Semin. Neurol.: 4,* 226 – 244, 1984a.

Butters N: The clinical aspects of memory disorders: contributions from experimental studies of amnesia and dementia. *J. Clin. Neuropsychol.: 6,* 17 – 36, 1984b.

Butters N: Alcoholic Korsakoff's syndrome: some unresolved issues concerning etiology, neuropathology, and cognitive deficits. *J. Clin. Exp. Neuropsychol.: 7,* 181 – 210, 1985.

Butters N, Albert MS: Processes underlying failures to recall remote events. In L.S. Cermak (Editor), *Human Memory and Amnesia.* New Jersey: L. Erlbaum Associates, pp. 257 – 274, 1982.

Butters N, Cermak LS: *Alcoholic Korsakoff's syndrome: An Information-Processing Approach to Amnesia.* New York: Academic Press, 1980.

Butters N, Cermak LS: A case study of the forgetting of autobiographical knowledge: implications for the study of retrograde amnesia. In Rubin D (Editor), *Autobiographical Memory.* New York: Cambridge University Press, pp. 253 – 272, 1986.

Butters N, Tarlow S, Cermak LS, Sax D: A comparison of the information processing deficits of patients with Huntington's chorea and Korsakoff's syndrome. *Cortex: 12,* 134 – 144, 1976.

Butters N, Miliotis P, Albert MS, Sax DS: Memory assessment: Evidence of the heterogeneity of amnesic symptoms. In Goldstein G (Editor), *Advances in Clinical Neuropsychology, Vol. 1.* New York: Plenum Press, pp. 127 – 159, 1984.

Butters N, Wolfe J, Martone M, Granholm E, Cermak L: Memory disorders associated with Huntington's disease: verbal recall, verbal recognition and procedural memory. *Neuropsychologia: 23,* 729 – 743, 1985.

Butters N, Wolfe J, Granholm E, Martone M: An assessment of verbal recall, recognition and fluency abilities in patients with Huntington's disease. *Cortex: 22,* 11 – 32, 1986.

Butters N, Granholm E, Salmon D, Grant I, Wolfe J: Episodic and semantic memory: a comparison of amnesic and demented patients. *J. Clin. Exp. Neuropsychol.: 9,* 479 – 497, 1987a.

Butters N, Salmon D, Granholm E, Heindel W, Lyon L: Neuropsychological differentiation of amnesic and dementing states. In Stahl S, Iversen S, Goodman EC (Editors), *Cognitive Neurochemistry.* London: Oxford University Press, pp. 3 – 20, 1987b.

Butters N, Salmon D, Cullum CM, Cairns P, Troster A, Jacobs D, Moss M, Cermak L: Differentiation of amnesic and demented patients with the Wechsler Memory Scale - Revised. *Clin. Neuropsychol.: 2,* 133 – 148, 1988.

Cairns H, Mosberg WH: Colloid cyst of the third ventricle. *Surg. Gynecol. Obstet.: 92,* 545 – 570, 1951.

Cappa SF, Vignolo LA: 'Transcortical' features of aphasia following left thalamic hemorrhage. *Cortex: 15,* 121 – 130, 1979.

Castaigne P, Buge A, Cambier J, Escourolle R, Brunet P, Degos JD: Demence thalamique d'origine vasculaire par ramollissement bilateral, limite au territoire du pedicule retro-mamillaire. A propos de deux observations anatomo-cliniques. *Rev. Neurol.: 114,* 89 – 107, 1966.

Castaigne P, Lhermitte F, Buge A, Escourolle R, Hauw JJ, Lyon-Caen O: Paramedian thalamic and midbrain infarcts: clinical and neuropathological study. *Ann. Neurol.: 10,* 127 – 148, 1981.

Cermak LS: The episodic-semantic distinction in amnesia. In Squire L, Butters N (Editors), *Neuropsychology of Memory.* New York: Guilford Press, pp. 55 – 62, 1984.

Cermak LS, Butters N: The role of interference and encoding in the short-term memory deficits of Korsakoff patients. *Neuropsychologia: 10,* 89 – 96, 1972.

Cermak LS, Butters N: Information processing deficits of alcoholic Korsakoff patients. *Q. J. Stud. Alcohol.: 34,* 1110 – 1132, 1973.

Cermak LS, Butters N: The role of language in the memory disorders of brain-damaged patients. *Ann. N.Y. Acad. Sci.: 280,* 857 – 867, 1976.

Cermak LS, O'Connor M: The anterograde and retrograde retrieval ability of a patient with amnesia due to encephalitis. *Neuropsychologia: 21,* 213 – 234, 1983.

Cermak LS, Reale L: Depth of processing and retention of words by alcoholic Korsakoff patients. *J. Exp. Psychol. Hum. Learn. Mem.: 4,* 165 – 174, 1978.

Cermak LS, Butters N, Gerrein J: The extent of the verbal encoding ability of Korsakoff patients. *Neuropsychologia: 11,* 85 – 94, 1973a.

Cermak LS, Lewis R, Butters N, Goodglass H: Role of verbal mediation in performance of motor tasks by Korsakoff patients. *Percept. Motor Skills: 37,* 259 – 262, 1973b.

Cermak LS, Butters N, Moreines J: Some analyses of the verbal encoding deficit of alcoholic Korsakoff patients. *Brain Lang.: 1,* 141 – 150, 1974.

Cermak LS, Naus M, Reale L: Rehearsal and organizational strategies of alcoholic Korsakoff patients. *Brain Lang.: 3,* 375 – 385, 1976.

Cermak LS, Uhly B, Reale L: Encoding specificity in the alcoholic Korsakoff patient. *Brain Lang.: 11,* 119 – 127, 1980.

Cermak LS, Talbot N, Chandler K, Wolbarst LR: The perceptual priming phenomenon in amnesia. *Neuropsychologia: 23,* 615 – 622, 1985.

Cermak LS, O'Connor M, Talbot N: Biasing of alcoholic Korsakoff patients' semantic memory. *J. Clin. Exp. Neuropsychol.: 8,* 543 – 555, 1986.

Choi D, Sudarsky L, Schacter S, Biber M, Burke P: Medial thalamic hemorrhage with amnesia. *Arch. Neurol.: 40,* 611 – 613, 1983.

Cohen N: Preserved learning capacity in amnesia: evidence of multiple memory systems. In Squire L, Butters N (Editors), *Neuropsychology of Memory.* New York: Guilford Press, pp. 83 – 103, 1984.

Cohen N, Squire LR: Preserved learning and retention of pattern analyzing skills in amnesia: dissociation of knowing how and knowing that. *Science: 210,* 207–210, 1980.

Cohen NJ, Squire LR: Retrograde amnesia and remote memory impairment. *Neuropsychologia: 19,* 337–356, 1981.

Corkin S: Lastin consequences of bilateral medial temporal lobectomy: clinical course and experimental findings in H.M. *Semin. Neurol.: 6,* 249–259, 1984.

Craik FIM, Tulving E: Depth of processing and retention of words in episodic memory. *J. Exp. Psychol. Gen.: 104,* 268–294, 1975.

Cramon D v, Eilert P: Ein beitrag zum amnestischen syndrom des menschen. *Nervenarzt: 50,* 643–648, 1979.

Cramon D v, Hebel N, Schuri U: A contribution to the anatomical basis of thalamic amnesia. *Brain: 108,* 993–1008, 1985.

Cummings JL, Benson DF: *Dementia: A Clinical Approach.* Boston: Butterworth, 1983.

Cutting J: Relationship between Korsakoff's syndrome and alcoholic dementia. *Br. J. Psychiatry: 132,* 240–251, 1978.

Damasio A: The frontal lobes. In Heilman KM, Valenstein E (Editors), *Clinical Neuropsychology,* Second edition. New York/London: Oxford University Press, pp. 339–402, 1985.

Damasio AR, Graff-Radford NR, Eslinger PJ, Damasio H, Kassell N: Amnesia following basal forebrain lesions. *Arch. Neurol.: 42,* 263–271, 1985.

Davidoff D, Butters N, Gerstman L, Zurif E, Paul I, Mattis S: Affective-motivational factors in the recall of prose passages by alcoholic Korsakoff patients. *Alcohol: 1,* 63–69, 1984.

De Armond SJ, Fusco MM, Dewey MM: *Structure of the Human Brain. A Photographic Atlas,* Second edition. New York: Oxford University Press, 1976.

Degirolami U, Haas ML, Richardson EP Jr: Subacute diencephalic angioencephalopathy. A clinicopathological case study. *J. Neurol. Sci.: 22,* 197–210, 1974.

Dricker J, Butters N, Berman G, Samuels I, Carey S: Recognition and encoding of faces by alcoholic Korsakoff and right hemisphere patients. *Neuropsychologia: 16,* 683–695, 1978.

Freed D, Corkin S, Cohen N: Forgetting in H.M.: a second look. *Neuropsychologia: 25,* 461–471, 1987.

Freedman M, Cermak LS: Semantic encoding deficits in frontal lobe disease and amnesia. *Brain Cognition: 5,* 108–114, 1986.

Friedman JH: Syndrome of diffuse encephalopathy due to non-dominant thalamic infarction. *Neurology: 35,* 1524–1526, 1985.

Fuster JM, Alexander GE: Firing changes in cells of the nucleus medialis dorsalis associated with delayed response behavior. *Brain Res.: 61,* 79–91, 1973.

Gamper E: Zur frage der polioencephalitis haemorrhagic der chronischen alcoholiker. Anatomische befunde beim alkolischen Korsakov undihre Beziehungen zum klinischen bild. *Dtsch. Z. Nervenheilk.: 102,* 122–129, 1928.

Gardner H, Boller F, Moreines J, Butters N: Retrieving information from Korsakoff patients; effects of categorical cues and reference to the task. *Cortex: 9,* 165–175, 1973.

Glosser G, Butters N, Kaplan E: Visuoperceptual processes in brain-damaged patients on the digit-symbol substitution test. *Int. J. Neurosci.: 7,* 59–66, 1977.

Graf P, Squire LR, Mandler G: The information that amnesic patients do not forget. *J. Exp. Psychol. Mem. Learn. Cognition: 10,* 164–178, 1984.

Graf P, Shimamura AP, Squire LR: Priming across modalities and priming across category levels: extending the domain of preserved function in amnesia. *J. Exp. Psychol. Mem. Learn. Cognition: 11,* 386–396, 1985.

Graff-Radford NR, Damasio H, Yamada T, Eslinger PJ, Damasio AR: Nonhaemorrhagic thalamic infarction. Clinical, neuropsychological and electrophysiological findings in four anatomical groups defined by computerized tomography. *Brain: 108,* 485–516, 1985.

Graff-Radford NR, Eslinger PJ, Damasio AR, Yamada T: Nonhaemorrhagic infarction of the thalamus: behavioral, anatomic, and physiologic correlates. *Neurology: 34,* 14–23, 1984.

Granholm E, Wolfe J, Butters N: Affective-arousal factors in the recall of thematic stories by amnesic and demented patients. *Dev. Neuropsychol.: 4,* 317–333, 1985.

Guberman A, Stuss D. The syndrome of bilateral paramedian thalamic infarction. *Neurology: 33,* 540–546, 1983.

Harper C: Wernicke's encephalopathy: a more common disease than realized. *J. Neurol. Neurosurg. Psychiatry: 42,* 226–231, 1979.

Harper C: The incidence of Wernicke's encephalopathy in Australia – a neuropathological study of 131 cases. *J. Neurol. Neurosurg. Psychiatry: 46,* 593–598, 1983.

Harper C, Finlay-Jones R: Clinical signs in the Wernicke-Korsakoff complex: a retrospective analysis of 131 cases diagnosed at necropsy. *J. Neurol. Neurosurg. Psychiatry: 49,* 341–345, 1986.

Heindel W, Butters N, Salmon D: Impaired learning of a motor skill in patients with Huntington's disease. *Behav. Neurosci.: 102,* 141–147, 1988.

Henderson VW, Alexander MP, Naeser MA: Right thalamic injury, impaired visuospatial perception, and alexia. *Neurology: 32,* 235–240, 1982.

Huppert FA, Piercy M: Recognition memory in amnesic patients: effect of temporal context and familiarity of material. *Cortex: 12,* 3–20, 1976.

Huppert FA, Piercy M: Recognition memory in amnesic patients: a defect of acquisition? *Neuropsychologia: 15,* 643–652, 1977.

Huppert FA, Piercy M: Dissociation between learning and remembering in organic amnesia. *Nature: 275,* 317–318, 1978.

Ignelzi RJ, Squire LR: Recovery from anterograde and retrograde amnesia following percutaneous drainage of a cystic craniopharyngioma. *J. Neurol. Neurosurg. Psychiatry: 39,* 1231–1236, 1976.

Imeri L, Moneta ME, Mancia M: Changes in spontaneous activity of medialis dorsalis thalamic neurones during sleep and wakefulness. *Electroencephalogr. Clin. Neurophysiol.: 69,* 82–84, 1988.

Jacobson R, Lishman WA: Selective memory loss and global intellectual deficits in alcoholic Korsakoff's syndrome. *Psychol. Med.: 17,* 649–655, 1987.

Jacoby LL: Incidental vs intentional retrieval: remembering and awareness as separate issues. In Squire L, Butters N (Editors), *The Neuropsychology of Memory.* New York: Guilford Press, pp. 145–156, 1984.

Jacoby LL, Witherspoon D: Remembering without awareness. *Can. J. Psychol.: 36,* 300 – 324, 1982.

Jahro L: Korsakoff-like amnesic syndrome in penetrating brain injury. A study of English war veterans. *Acta Neurol. Scand.: 49,* Suppl. 54, pp. 1 – 156, 1973.

Johnson MK, Kim JK, Risse G: Do alcoholic Korsakoff's syndrome patients acquire affective reactions? *J. Exp. Psychol. Mem. Learn. Cognition: 11,* 22 – 36, 1985.

Jones BP, Butters N, Moskowitz HR, Montgomery K: Olfactory and gustatory capacities of alcoholic Korsakoff patients. *Neuropsychologia: 16,* 323 – 337, 1978.

Jones BP, Moskowitz HR, Butters N: Olfactory discrimination in alcoholic Korsakoff patients. *Neuropsychologia: 13,* 173 – 179, 1975.

Jurko MF, Andy OJ: Psychological changes correlated with thalamotomy site. *J. Neurol. Neurosurg. Psychiatry: 36,* 846 – 852, 1973.

Jurko MF, Andy OJ: Verbal learning dysfunction with combined centre median and amygdala lesions. *J. Neurol. Neurosurg. Psychiatry: 40,* 695 – 698, 1977.

Kapur N, Butters N: Visuoperceptive deficits in long-term alcoholics with Korsakoff's psychosis. *J. Stud. Alcohol: 38,* 2025 – 2035, 1977.

Karabelas G, Kalfakis N, Kasvikis I, Vassilopoulos D: Unusual features in a case of bilateral paramedian thalamic infarction. *J. Neurol. Neurosurg. Psychiatry: 48,* 186, 1985.

Katz DI, Alexander MP, Mandell AM: Dementia following strokes in the mesencephalon and diencephalon. *Arch. Neurol.: 44,* 1127 – 1133, 1987.

Kinsbourne M, Wood F: Short-term memory processes and the amnesic syndrome. In Deutsch D, Deutsch JA (Editors), *Short-Term Memory.* New York: Academic Press, 1975.

Kopelman M: Rates of forgetting in Alzheimer-type dementia and Korsakoff's syndrome. *Neuropsychologia: 23,* 623 – 638, 1985.

Kopelman M: Recall of anomalous sentences in dementia and amnesia. *Brain lang.: 29,* 154 – 170, 1986.

Kopelman M: Two types of confabulation. *J. Neurol. Neurosurg. Psychiatry: 50,* 1482 – 1487, 1987.

Kovner R, Mattis S, Goldmeier E: A technique for promoting robust free recall in chronic organic amnesia. *J. Clin. Exp. Psychol.: 5,* 65 – 71, 1983.

Kritchevsky M, Graff-Radford NR, Damasio AR: Normal memory after damage to medial thalamus. *Arch. Neurol.: 44,* 959 – 962, 1987.

Levin HS, Benton AL, Grossman RG: *Neurobehavioral Consequences of Closed Head Injury.* New York: Oxford Press, 1982.

Lishman WA: Cerebral disorder in alcoholism: syndromes of impairment. *Brain: 104,* 1 – 20, 1981.

Lishman WA: Alcoholic dementia: a hypothesis. *Lancet:* 1184 – 1186, 1986.

Lishman WA: *Organic Psychiatry,* 2nd edition. Blackwell Scientific Publications: London, 1987.

Lugaresi E, Medori R, Montagna R, Baruzzi A, Cortelli P, Lugaresi A, Tinuper P, Zucconi M, Gambetti P: Fatal familial insomnia and dysautonomia with selective degeneration of thalamic nuclei. *N. Engl. J. Med.: 315,* 997 – 1003, 1986.

Luria AR: *The Working Brain.* New York: Basic, 1973.

Luria AR: On quasi-aphasic speech disturbances in lesions of the deep structures of the brain. *Brain Lang.: 4,* 432 – 459, 1977.

Luria AR: *Higher Cortical Functions in Man.* New York: Basic, 1980.

Magoun HW: *The Waking Brain,* 2nd edn. Springfield, Il: Charles C. Thomas, 1958.

Mair RG, McEntee WL: Cognitive enhancement in Korsakoff's psychosis by clonidine: a comparison with L-dopa and ephedrine. *Psychopharmacology: 88,* 374 – 380, 1986.

Mair WG, Warrington EK, Weiskrantz L: Memory disorder in Korsakoff's psychosis: a neuropathological and neuropsychological investigation of two cases. *Brain: 102,* 749 – 783, 1979.

Mair RG, Capra C, McEntee WL, Engen T: Odor discrimination and memory in Korsakoff's psychosis. *J. Exp. Psychol. Hum. Percept. Performance: 6,* 445 – 448, 1980.

Markowitsch HJ: Thalamic mediodorsal nucleus and memory. A critical evaluation of studies in animals and man. *Neurosci. Biobehav. Rev.: 6,* 351 – 380, 1982.

Markowitsch HJ: Can amnesia be caused by damage of a single brain structure? *Cortex: 20,* 27 – 45, 1984.

Markowitsch HJ, Pritzel M: The neuropathology of amnesia. *Prog. Neurobiol.: 25,* 189 – 287, 1985.

Marslen-Wilson WD, Teuber HL: Memory for remote events in anterograde amnesia: recognition of public figures from news photographs. *Neuropsychologia: 13,* 347 – 352, 1975.

Martone M, Butters N, Payne M, Becker J, Sax DS: Dissociations between skill learning and verbal recognition in amnesia and dementia. *Arch. Neurol.: 41,* 965 – 970, 1984.

Martone M, Butters N, Trauner D: Some analyses of forgetting of pictorial material in amnesic and demented patients. *J. Clin. Exp. Neurpsychol.: 8,* 161 – 178, 1986.

Mateer CA, Ojemann GA: Thalamic mechanisms in language and memory. In Segalowitz SJ (Editor), *Language Functions and Brain Organization.* New York: Academic Press, pp. 171 – 191, 1983.

Mayes A, Meudell P, Mann D, Pickering A: Location of lesions in Korsakoff's syndrome: neuropsychological and neuropathological data on two patients. *Cortex: 24,* 367 – 388, 1988.

McDowall J: Effects of encoding instructions and retrieval cueing on recall in Korsakoff patients. *Mem. Cognition: 7,* 232 – 239, 1979.

McEntee WJ, Biber MP, Perl DP, Benson DF: Diencephalic amnesia: a reappraisal. *J. Neurol. Neurosurg. Psychiatry: 39,* 436 – 441, 1976.

McEntee WJ, Mair RG: Memory impairments in Korsakoff's psychosis: a correlation with brain noradrenergic activity. *Science: 202,* 905 – 907, 1978.

McEntee WJ, Mair RG: Memory enhancement in Korsakoff's psychosis by clonidine: further evidence for a noradrenergic deficit. *Ann. Neurol.: 7,* 466 – 470, 1980.

McHugh PR, Folstein MF: Psychiatric syndromes of Huntington's chorea: a clinical and phenomenological study. In Benson DF, Blumer D (Editors), *Psychiatric Aspects of Neurologic Disease.* New York: Grune & Stratton, pp. 267 – 286, 1975.

Meibach RC, Siegal A: Efferent connections of the septal area in the rat: an analysis utilizing retrograde and anterograde transport methods. *Brain Res.: 119,* 1–20, 1977.

Meudell PR, Butters N, Montgomery K: Role of rehearsal in the short-term memory performance of patients with Korsakoff's and Huntington's Disease. *Neuropsychologia: 16,* 507–510, 1978.

Meudell PR, Northern B, Snowden JS, Neary D: Long-term memory for famous voices in amnesic and normal subjects. *Neuropsychologia: 18,* 133–139, 1980.

Michel D, Laurent B, Foyatier N, Blanc A, Portafaix M: Infarctus thalamique paramedian gauche (etude de la memoire et du langage). *Rev. Neurol.: 138,* 533–550, 1982.

Mills RP, Swanson PD: Vertical oculomotor apraxia and memory loss. *Ann. Neurol.: 4,* 149–153, 1978.

Milner B: Some effects of frontal lobectomy in man. In Warren JM, Akert K (Editors), *The Frontal Granular Cortex and Behavior.* New York: McGraw-Hill, pp. 313–334, 1964.

Milner B: Amnesia following operation on the temporal lobes. In Whitty, CWM, Zangwill OL (Editors), *Amnesia.* London: Butterworths, pp. 109–133, 1966.

Milner B: Interhemispheric differences and psychological processes. *Br. Med. Bull.: 27,* 272–277, 1971.

Milner B: Hemispheric specialization: scope and limits. In Schmitt OF, Worden FG (Editors), *The Neurosciences: Third Study Program.* Massachusetts: MIT Press, pp. 75–89, 1974.

Mishkin M: Memory in monkeys severely impaired by combined but not by separate removal of amygdala and hippocampus. *Nature: 273,* 297–298, 1978.

Mishkin M: A memory system in the monkey. In Broadbent DE, Weiskrantz L (Editors), *The Neuropsychology of Cognitive Function.* London: The Royal Society, pp. 85–95, 1982.

Mori E, Yamadori A, Mitani Y: Left thalamic infarction and disturbance of verbal memory: A clinicoanatomical study with a new method of computed tomographic stereotaxic lesion localization. *Ann. Neurol.: 20,* 671–676, 1986.

Moscovitch M: Multiple dissociations of function in amnesia. In Cermak LS (Editor), *Human Memory and Amnesia.* New Jersey: Lawrence Erlbaum Associates, Inc., pp. 337–370, 1982.

Ojemann GA: Asymmetric function of the thalamus in man. *Ann. N.Y. Acad. Sci.: 299,* 380–396, 1977.

Oscar-Berman M: Hypothesis testing and focusing behavior during concept formation by amnesic Korsakoff patients. *Neuropsychologia: 11,* 191–198, 1973.

Oscar-Berman M: Neuropsychological consequences of long-term chronic alcoholism. *Am. Sci.: 68,* 410–419, 1980.

Oscar-Berman M, Sahakian BJ, Wikmark G: Spatial probability learning by alcoholic Korsakoff patients. *J. Exp. Psychol. Mem. Learn. Cognition: 2,* 215–222, 1976.

Oscar-Berman M, Heyman GM, Bonner RT, Ryder J: Human Neuropsychology: some differences between Korsakoff and normal operant performance. *Psychol. Res.: 41,* 235–247, 1980.

Parsons OA: Brain damage in alcoholics: Altered states of unconsciousness. In M. Gross (Editor), *Alcohol Intoxication and Withdrawal II.* New York: Plenum Press, pp. 564–584, 1975.

Parsons OA, Farr SP: The neuropsychology of alcohol and drug abuse. In Filskov SB, Boll TJ (Editors), *Handbook of Clinical Neuropsychology.* New York: Wiley, pp. 320–365, 1981.

Piercy MF: Experimental studies of the organic amnesic syndrome. In Whitty CWM, Zangwill OL (Editors), *Amnesia,* 2nd edn. London: Butterworths, pp. 1–51, 1977.

Pierrot-Deseilligny C, Chain F, Lhermitte F: A pontine reticular formation syndrome providing further data about the failure of the voluntary eye movements (Fren). *Rev. Neurol.: 138,* 517–532, 1982.

Poirier J, Barbizet J, Gaston A, Meyrignac C: Demence thalamique lacunes expansives du territoire thalamo-mesencephalique paramedian hydrocephalie par stenose de l'aqueduc de sylvius. *Rev. Neurol.: 139,* 349–358, 1983.

Reynolds AF, Turner PT, Harris AB, Ojemann GA, Davis LE: Left thalamic hemorrhage with dysphasia: a report of five cases. *Brain Lang.: 7,* 62–73, 1979.

Riggs H, Boles HS: Wernicke's disease: A clinical and pathological study of 42 cases. *Q. J. Stud. Alcohol: 5,* 361–370, 1944.

Ron M: The brain of alcoholics: An overview. In Parsons O, Butters N, Nathan P (Editors), *Neuropsychology of Alcoholism: Implications for Diagnosis and Treatment.* New York: Guilford Press, pp. 11–20, 1987.

Russell WR, Nathan PW: Traumatic amnesia. *Brain 69,* 280–300, 1946.

Ryan C, Butters N: The neuropsychology of alcoholism. In Wedding D, Horton A, Webster J (Editors), *The Neuropsychology Handbook.* New York: Springer Publishing Co. pp. 376–409, 1986.

Saint-Cyr JA, Taylor A, Lang A: Procedural learning and neostriatal dysfunction in man. *Brain: 111,* 941–959, 1988.

Salmon D, Butters N: The etiology and neuropathology of alcoholic Korsakoff's syndrome: some evidence for the role of the basal forebrain. In Galanter M (Editor), *Recent Developments in Alcoholism 5.* New York: Plenum Press, pp. 27–58, 1987.

Sanders HI, Warrington EK: Memory for remote events in amnesic patients. *Brain: 94,* 661–668, 1971.

Schacter DL: Memory, amnesia, and frontal lobe dysfunction. *Psychobiology: 15,* 21–36, 1987a.

Schacter DL: Implicit memory: history and current status. *J. Exp. Psychol. Mem. Learn. Cognition: 13,* 501–518, 1987b.

Schacter DL: Implicit expressions of memory in organic amnesia: learning of new facts and associations. *Hum. Neurobiol.: 6,* 107–118, 1987c.

Schacter DL, McAndrews MP, Moscovitch M: Access to consciousness: dissociations between implicit and explicit knowledge in neuropsychological syndromes. In Weiskrantz L (Editor), *Thought Without Language.* New York: Oxford University Press, pp. 242–277, 1988.

Schott B, Mauguiere F, Laurent B, Serclerat O, Fischer C: L'amnesie thalamique. *Rev. Neurol.: 136,* 117–130, 1980.

Schulman S: Bilateral symmetrical degeneration of the thalamus. *J. Neuropathol. Exp. Neurol.: 16,* 446–470, 1957.

Schulman S: Impaired delayed response from thalamic lesions (studies in monkeys). *Arch. Neurol.: 11,* 477–499, 1964.

Scoville WB, Milner B: Loss of recent memory after bilateral hippocampal lesions. *Neuropsychologia: 20,* 11–21, 1957.

Seltzer B, Benson DF: The temporal pattern of retrograde

amnesia in Korsakoff's disease. *Neurology: 24,* 527 – 530, 1974.

Shimamura A: Priming effects in amnesia: evidence for a dissociable memory function. *Q. J. Exp. Psychol.: 38A,* 619 – 644, 1986.

Shimamura A, Squire LR: Paired-associate learning and priming effects in amnesia: a neuropsychological study. *J. Exp. Psychol. Gen.: 113,* 556 – 570, 1984.

Shimamura A, Squire LR: Korsakoff's syndrome: a study of the relationship between anterograde and remote memory impairment. *Behav. Neurosci.: 100,* 165 – 170, 1986a.

Shimamura A, Squire LR: Memory and metamemory: a study of the feeling-of-knowing phenomenon in amnesic patients. *J. Exp. Psychol. Learn. Mem. Cognition: 12,* 452 – 460, 1986b.

Shimamura A, Salmon D, Squire L, Butters N: Memory dysfunction and word priming in dementia and amnesia. *Behav. Neurosci.: 101,* 347 – 351, 1987.

Shimamura A, Jernigan T, Squire L: Korsakoff's syndrome: radiological (CT) findings and neuropsychological correlates. *J. Neurosci.: 8,* 4400 – 4410, 1988.

Smyth GE, Stern K: Tumours of the thalamus – a clinico-pathological study. *Brain: 61,* 339 – 374, 1938.

Speedie LJ, Heilman KM: Amnestic disturbance following infarction of the left dorsomedial nucleus of the thalamus. *Neuropsychologia: 20,* 597 – 604, 1982.

Speedie LJ, Heilman KM: Anterograde memory deficits for visuospatial material after infarction of the right thalamus. *Arch. Neurol.: 40,* 183 – 186, 1983.

Spiegel EA, Wycis HT, Orchinik O, Freed H: Thalamic chronotaraxis. *Am. J. Psychiatry: 113,* 97 – 105, 1956.

Sprofkin BE, Sciarra D: Korsakoff's psychosis associated with cerebral tumours. *Neurology: 2,* 427 – 434, 1952.

Squire LR: Two forms of human amnesia: An analysis of forgetting. *J. Neurosci.: 1,* 635 – 640, 1981.

Squire LR: The neuropsychology of human memory. *Annu. Rev. Neurosci.: 5,* 241 – 273, 1982.

Squire LR: *Memory and the Brain.* New York: Oxford University Press, 1987.

Squire LR: Comparisons between forms of amnesia: some deficits are unique to Korsakoff's syndrome. *J. Exp. Psychol. Mem. Learn. Cognition: 8,* 560 – 571, 1982.

Squire LR, Cohen NJ: Remote memory, retrograde amnesia, and the neuropsychology of memory. In Cermak LS (Editor), *Human Memory and Amnesia.* New Jersey: L. Erlbaum Associates, pp. 275 – 303, 1982.

Squire LR, Moore RY: Dorsal thalamic lesion in a noted case of human memory dysfunction. *Ann. Neurol.: 6,* 503 – 506, 1979.

Squire LR, Slater PC: Forgetting in very long-term memory as assessed by an improved questionnaire technique. *J. Exp. Psychol. Hum. Learn. Mem.: 104,* 50 – 54, 1975.

Squire LR, Slater PC: Anterograde and retrograde memory impairment in chronic amnesia. *Neuropsychologia: 16,* 313 – 322, 1978.

Squire LR, Haist F, Shimamura AP: The neurology of memory: quantitative assessment of retrograde amnesia in two groups of amnesic patients. *J. Neurosci.: 9,* 828 – 839, 1989.

Squire LR, Amaral D, Zola-Morgan S, Krichevsky M, Press G:

Description of brain injury in the amnesic patient N.A. based on magnetic resonance imaging. *Ann. Neurol:* in press.

Starzl TE, Whitlock DG: Diffuse thalamic projection system in monkey. *J. Neurophysiol.: 15,* 449 – 468, 1952.

Stuss DT, Benson DF: Neuropsychological studies of the frontal lobes. *Psychol. Bull.: 95,* 3 – 28, 1984.

Stuss DT, Benson DF: *The Frontal Lobes.* New York: Raven Press, 1986.

Stuss DT, Guberman A, Nelson R, Larochelle S: The neuropsychology of paramedian thalamic infarction. *Brain Cognition: 8,* 348 – 378, 1988.

Swanson RA, Schmidley JW: Amnestic syndrome and vertical gaze palsy: early detection of bilateral thalamic infarction by CT and NMR. *Stroke: 16,* 823 – 827, 1985.

Talland GA: *Deranged Memory.* New York: Academic Press, 1965.

Teuber HL, Milner B, Vaughan HG: Persistent anterograde amnesia after stab wound of the basal brain. *Neuropsychologia: 6,* 267 – 282, 1968.

Tulving E: Episodic and semantic memory. In Tulving E, Donaldson W (Editors), *Organization of Memory.* New York: Academic Press, 1972.

Tulving E: *Elements of Episodic Memory.* New York: Oxford University Press, 1983.

Valenstein ES, Nauta WJ: A comparison of the distribution of the fornix system in the rat, guinea pig, cat and monkey. *J. Comp. Neurol.: 113,* 337 – 362, 1959.

Victor M, Adams RD, Collins GH: *The Wernicke-Korsakoff Syndrome.* Philadelphia: F.A. Davis, 1971.

Vilkki J: Effects of thalamic lesions on complex perception and memory. *Neuropsychologia: 16,* 427 – 437, 1978.

Warrington EK, Weiskrantz L: New method of testing long-term retention with special reference to amnesic patients. *Nature: 217,* 972 – 974, 1968.

Warrington EK, Weiskrantz L: Amnesic syndrome: consolidation or retrieval? *Nature: 228,* 628 – 630, 1970.

Warrington EK, Weiskrantz L: An analysis of short-term and long-term memory defects in man. In Deutsch JA (Editor), *The Physiological Basis of Memory.* New York: Academic Press, pp. 365 – 395, 1973.

Warrington EK, Weiskrantz L: The effect of prior learning on subsequent retention in amnesic patients. *Neuropsychologia: 12,* 419 – 428, 1974.

Warrington EK, Weiskrantz L: Amnesia: a disconnection syndrome? *Neuropsychologia: 20,* 233 – 248, 1982.

Wechsler D: A standardized memory scale for clinical use. *J. Psychol.: 19,* 87 – 95, 1945.

Wechsler D: *Wechsler Adult Intelligence Scale Manual.* New York: Psychological Corporation, 1955.

Wechsler D: *WAIS-R manual.* New York: Psychological Corporation, 1981.

Wechsler D: *Wechsler Memory Scale – Revised.* New York: Psychological Corporation, 1987.

Weingartner H, Grafman J, Boutelle W, Kaye W, Martin PR: Forms of memory failure. *Science: 221,* 380 – 382, 1983.

Weiskrantz L: On issues and theories of the human amnesic syndrome. In Weinberger N, McGaugh JL, Lynch G (Editors), *Memory Systems of the Brain.* New York: Guilford Press, pp. 380 – 415, 1985.

Weiskrantz L, Warrington EK: A study of forgetting in amnesic patients. *Neuropsychologia: 8,* 281 – 288, 1970.

Wilkinson DA: CT scan and neuropsychological assessments of alcoholism. In Parsons O, Butters N, Nathan P (Editors), *Neuropsychology of Alcoholism: Implications for Diagnosis and Treatment.* New York: Guilford Press, pp. 76 – 102, 1987.

Winocur G, Kinsbourne M: Contextual cueing as an aid to Korsakoff amnesics. *Neuropsychologia: 16,* 671 – 682, 1978.

Winocur G, Weiskrantz L: An investigation of paired-associate learning in amnesic patients. *Neuropsychologia: 14,* 97 – 110, 1976.

Winocur G, Kinsbourne M, Moscovitch M: The effect of cueing on release from proactive interference in Korsakoff amnesic patients. *J. Exp. Psychol. Hum. Learn. Mem.: 7,* 56 – 65, 1981.

Winocur G, Oxbury S, Roberts R, Agnetti V, Davis C: Amnesia in a patient with bilateral lesions to the thalamus. *Neuropsychologia: 22,* 123 – 143, 1984.

Winocur G, Moscovitch M, Witherspoon D: Contextual cuing and memory performance in brain-damaged amnesics and old people. *Brain Cognition: 6,* 129 – 141, 1987.

Ziegler K, Kaufman A, Marshall HE: Abrupt memory loss associated with thalamic tumor. *Arch. Neurol.: 34,* 545 – 548, 1977.

Zola-Morgan S, Cohen NJ, Squire LR: Recall of remote episodic memory in amnesia. *Neuropsychologia: 21,* 487 – 500, 1983.

Zola-Morgan S, Squire LR: Amnesia in monkeys after lesions of the mediodorsal nucleus of the thalamus. *Ann. Neurol.: 17,* 558 – 564, 1985.

1989 Elsevier Science Publishers B.V. (Biomedical Division)
andbook of Neuropsychology, Vol. 3
Boller and J. Grafman (Eds)

CHAPTER 6

Amnesia caused by herpes simplex encephalitis, infarctions in basal forebrain, Alzheimer's disease and anoxia/ischemia

A.R. Damasio, D. Tranel and H. Damasio

Department of Neurology, Division of Behavioral Neurology and Cognitive Neuroscience, University of Iowa College of Medicine, IA, U.S.A.

Introduction

Over the past decade, the systematic study of patients with amnesia caused by different neuropathological processes has revealed an extensive roster of brain regions implicated in memory, in both the cerebral cortex and in a variety of subcortical territories. As the data discussed in this chapter will indicate, it is now possible to propose an organization for those different brain loci, at the level of systems, and thus enlarge on the physiological picture derived from the study of previously identified regions such as the hippocampus and the thalamus. An important development in this regard has been the addition of Alzheimer's disease and cerebral anoxia to the traditional studies based on cerebrovascular disease, surgical ablations and herpes simplex encephalitis. While the latter pathological processes cause macroscopic lesions in cortex or subcortical nuclei, by means of massive brain tissue destruction, Alzheimer's disease and cerebral anoxia produce selective neuronal damage and a disruption of neural circuitry. The features of such damage can be identified under the microscope, with appropriate histological stains, and interpreted in terms of the rich new knowledge of connectional neuroanatomy accumulated over the past two decades from experimental studies in nonhuman

primates. This development means that the lesion method has been extended from the level of the macroscopic lesion, to the cellular level.

In the three sections below, we discuss the typical clinical presentation, the neuropsychological profile and the neuroanatomical findings that characterize the amnesias caused by herpes simplex encephalitis, infarctions in the basal forebrain, Alzheimer's disease and anoxic encephalopathy. The discussion concludes with an interpretation of the neuropsychological and neuroanatomical findings, in neural computational terms, using as a base a new model for the neural substrates of memory at systems level.

Amnesia caused by herpes simplex encephalitis

Introduction

Herpes encephalitis causes a severe necrotic process in cortical structures associated with the limbic system, some neocortical structures in the vicinity of the latter, and several subcortical limbic structures. Among the first, there are the parahippocampal gyrus, in particular its anterior region (area 28 or the entorhinal cortex), the polar limbic cortex (area 38), the cingulate gyrus (area 24), and the posterior orbital cortices of areas 11 and 12. All of these are masocortices located in the medial rim of the temporal and frontal regions. The nearby neocortices of the anterolateral and anteroinferior temporal lobe, however, which are neocortices rather than limbic cortices, may also be destroyed by the encephalitis (areas, 20, 21, anterior portion of 22, and parts of 37 and 36). The hippocampus proper, the amygdala and the basal forebrain nuclei are frequent targets of the encephalitis (Damasio and Van Hoesen, 1985).

Herpes encephalitis is usually a bilateral process, although in some cases it can be exclusively or predominantly unilateral. All the structures enumerated above can be destroyed in a single case, on both sides, the best recorded example being that of our patient Boswell discussed below. However, in some instances, the disease may spare some of the territories on one side or the other or even on both sides. Most commonly spared are the cingulate gyri or the orbital cortices, and the extent of damage to neocortices is often small. This variability is attributable to numerous factors, including the age of the patient, the type and speed of therapeutic intervention, and possibly genetic and infectivity factors which have not yet been identified. Whatever the cause, the availability of instances with different amnesia profiles related to different neuroanatomical profiles provides a unique opportunity to specify precise anatomical correlations for cognitive disturbances. In short, herpes encephalitis provides a relatively selective ablation of limbic telencephalic structures. The facts that most herpes lesions have sharply defined borders, that the process is self-limited and that the patients recover to a chronic state which permits extensive neuropsychological testing and experimentation make herpes encephalitis cases uniquely valuable for research in amnesia.

Clinical presentation

One of the best-studied cases of herpes encephalitis is that of patient Boswell, who has been investigated in our laboratories since 1975 (Damasio et al., 1985a, 1987). He illustrates the full extent of damage caused by herpes encephalitis.

Patient Boswell is a 60-year-old, fully right-handed (+100 on the Geschwind-Oldfield ques-

tionnaire) man who, at the age of 48, develope herpes simplex encephalitis. Before his illness, h had worked for nearly three decades as newspaper advertising and printing salesperson He had 13 years of schooling, and was successf in his profession and in his personal and famil life. He was, by all accounts, a normal, wel adjusted person, before the onset of his condition

The clinical presentation of Boswell's herpe encephalitis was fairly typical, with episodes o confusion, partial complex seizures and, late tonic-clonic seizures and fever. After a profoun three-day coma, his level of consciousness gradua ly improved, and in many respects he made remarkable recovery. One month after the onset o his condition, a neurological examination showe normal strength, normal motor coordination an normal perception except for complete bilatera anosmia. The major sequela was a profoun amnesic syndrome.

Neuropsychological profile

Boswell has been administered the Wechsler Adul Intelligence Scale (both the original form (1955 and the revised version (1981)) on several occa sions. His scores are generally low average, wit Verbal and Performance IQs in the 80 – 90 range In absolute terms these are below expectations bas ed on his background, but the primary reasons fo the low scores are his amnesia and distractibility It is important to note that his scores have bee stable over the entire 13 years of our contact wit him, and he shows no evidence of intellectua decline over this period. Nor is the extent of in tellectual compromise sufficient to account for th multitude of defects he demonstrates in memor paradigms.

Boswell's speech and language are normal i every respect, as documented by a variety of stan dardized and specialized probes, including th Multilingual Aphasia Examination (Benton, 1976 and the Boston Diagnostic Aphasia Examinatio (Goodglass and Kaplan, 1983). He is fluent an nonparaphasic, with normal articulation and pro sody, and he has normal use and comprehension o mantics, syntax and morphology.

There are no defects in visual perception, suospatial abilities or visual constructional func- ons. He performs normally on tasks such as the acial Discrimination Test, Judgment of Line rientation, three-dimensional block construc- on, right-left discrimination (Benton et al., 1983), awing to dictation, and the copy administration the Complex Figure Test (Lezak, 1983, p. 395).

Against this background of generally intact europsychological function, Boswell's amnesic ndrome is particularly striking. His performances standardized neuropsychological memory pro- s are uniformly abysmal. On the Wechsler emory Scale (Wechsler, 1945), his performances the Mental Control and Digit Span subtests are ormal, but on the paragraph recall and paired ssociate learning tests he performs at the zero ercentile. On the Rey Auditory-Verbal Learning est (Lezak, 1983, p. 422) his scores are also near e zero level, with no indication of improved per- ormance as a function of multiple exposures to e stimulus material. Performances on tests of isual memory, such as the Benton Visual Reten- on Test (Administration A) (Lezak, 1983, p. 447) nd the 3-minute delayed recall administration of e Complex Figure Test (Lezak, 1983, p. 444), are milarly severely impaired.

Boswell's orientation has been assessed on umerous occasions with the standardized pro- edures of Benton et al. (1983). In every instance, is scores have been severely defective. With egard to time, he can only produce a random uess as to the month, date, day of week, and year. Ie has never been accurately oriented to place dur- ig the 13 years of his amnesic condition. When sked the name of the city he is in, he provides a tandard list of alternatives, none of which is nything more than a sheer guess. Regarding rientation to personal information, there are four tandard items on the Benton et al. (1983) ques- ionnaire, including home town, address, date of irth, and age. Boswell nearly always gives the cor- ect answer to the home town item, and he gives his late of birth correctly on about half of the occa-

sions. He cannot provide his address, and he typically answers with some fictitious address from his home town. He consistently misstates his age as the 'late 40s' (he is now 60 years old). It is in- teresting to note that Boswell's response is actually at a point that corresponds to his age at the time of onset of his brain lesions (age = 48).

To assess Boswell's recognition of familiar faces learned before his amnesia, we administered the Boston Remote Famous Faces test (using 48 stimuli) (Albert et al., 1979), and two other customized sets of stimuli designed specifically for Boswell. One of the customized sets (PERSONAL) comprised 20 pictures of individuals with whom Boswell had been personally acquainted. The other set (FAMOUS) was made up of 10 pictures of per- sons with a high level of public exposure, such as politicians and actors. Each set of stimuli, in- cluding the Boston Famous Faces Test, was shown twice.

Boswell's scores on the two administrations of the Boston Famous Faces Test were 0/48 and 1/48 (he correctly named the picture of Betty Grable on the second exposure). For the PERSONAL set, he obtained scores of 2/20 and 2/20 on the two ad- ministrations. Both correct items on each trial were pictures of Boswell's parents, and on both occa- sions, the correct identifications occurred in the context of several similar or equal (but incorrect) responses to other faces in the set; e.g., Boswell responded 'that's my father' to pictures of his father, a close friend, and himself. His scores in the FAMOUS set were 0/10 and 0/10.

Two sets of tailor-made stimuli were used to assess Boswell's ability to learn new faces, i.e., faces that he has encountered since the onset of his condition, but not before. In one set (PROFES- SIONALS), the faces were of various professionals that Boswell has worked with extensively at our facility over the past decade. The second set (CARETAKERS) comprised faces of persons whom Boswell encounters regularly in the care facility in which he lives. Boswell's score was at the zero level for both sets.

Boswell's acquisition of new memory remains

confined to covert, nondeclarable forms of learning. Some of the tasks he masters conform to the concept of perceptuo-motor skills or priming. Examples are:

(1) *Rotor pursuit*. In a standard rotor persuit task (Corkin, 1968; Eslinger and Damasio, 1986), in which the subject attempts to maintain contact between a stylus and a small target on a rotating platter, Boswell showed a normal learning curve over five trials, a normal level of retention after a 20-min delay, and normal retention after a 2-year delay. He has never obtained declarative knowledge of the task.

(2) *Mirror tracing*. Boswell was tested with a standard mirror tracing task (Milner, 1962), on which he produced a normal learning curve across three consecutive trials, and normal 48-hour retention. Again, he had no declarative knowledge about the task.

(3) *Mirror reading*. This is another standard procedure that provides a contrast between declarable and nondeclarable learning (Squire et al., 1984). On the nondeclarable portion, i.e., the skill-learning part reflected by the subject's latencies in reading words in mirror image, Boswell performed at a level comparable to that of controls. In contrast, his acquisition of declarable information, i.e., knowledge about the actual words that served as stimuli, was at the zero level.

(4) *Word completion priming*. Boswell was given the standard procedure (Graf et al., 1984), using a 10-word list administered and tested under several different conditions. On the Free Recall test, Boswell was at the zero level. His Recognition score in forced choice, however, was above chance (80%), and he showed a small but significant 'priming' effect, achieving a higher word-completion rate for words with prior exposure, as compared to the base guessing rate.

Another interesting example of non-declarable learning was uncovered with the specially designed experiment described below.

'Good guy – bad guy' experiment. This experiment was designed to define the extent of Boswell's anterograde learning of people and faces. We exposed him to three different persons, manipulating

the affective valence and extent of exposure time of each person. One person (No. 1) assumed a very positive affective posture towards Boswell (e.g. granting requests for special treats) but was given minimal exposure time. Another person (No. 2) assumed a neutral affective valence but was given maximal exposure time. The third individual (No. 3) acted in a 'negative' manner towards Boswell (e.g., denying requests for treats), and was given the same exposure (high) as No. 2. Thus, there were three combinations of affective valence and exposure time: No. 1 = Positive-Low; No. 2 = Neutral-High; No. 3 = Negative-High.

Boswell's learning of these individuals was tested in a 2-alternative forced-choice paradigm. Slides depicting each of the three target faces (Nos 1, 2 and 3) were paired with slides of faces Boswell had never seen before, and for each pair Boswell was required to 'choose the person you like the best, who you would go to for rewards, treats and favors.' Each target face was tested 18 times.

At no point during or after this experiment did Boswell give any indication that he had learned anything about the three target individuals, despite, in the cases of Nos. 2 and 3, a very high degree of exposure time. Boswell never gave an indication that the persons were familiar, or that he recognized them as people he had been working with, or that he had any inkling as to their names or other identifying information. Against this complete absence of overt learning, the results of this experiment are intriguing. In the forced choice test, Boswell produced the following performance: target face No. 1 was chosen on 15 or 18 opportunities (83%); No. 2 was chosen 10/18 times (56%); and No. 3 was chosen on 4 of the 18 chances (22%). In other words, Boswell's tendency to choose No. 1 was significantly higher than chance (chance is 50%), and his tendency to choose No. 3 was much lower than chance. It can be concluded that Boswell did learn something about these individuals, although that learning was restricted to the affective valence of the person and thus was not enough to permit their specific identification.

Neuroanatomical findings

Boswell's lesions (see Fig. 1) have been studied with CT in both acute and chronic epochs (Damasio et al., 1985a) and most recently with MR (Damasio et al., 1987).

The critical anatomical points are as follows:

(a) *both* medial temporal regions are destroyed in their entirety, i.e., entorhinal cortex, hippocampus proper and amygdala;

(b) *both* temporal poles (area 38), and non-medial, anterior, high-order association cortices, are also entirely destroyed, i.e., areas 20, 21, anterior sector of 22;

(c) *both* insular cortices are destroyed;

(d) *both* posterior orbital cortices and basal forebrain regions are destroyed;

(e) *both* motor and premotor cortices, basal ganglia, internal capsules and cerebellum are intact;

(f) *all* primary and most early sensory association cortices are intact in occipital, temporal and parietal cortices; most association cortices in the prefrontal region are intact bilaterally.

Neural mechanisms

The bilateral medial temporal lobe damage in Boswell and in most patients with herpes encephalitis explains the severe learning defect that covers all aspects of declarable memory. In nature and magnitude, the defect is no different from that found in patient HM (Corkin, 1984). The loci of damage that correlate with the defect are the ones presumably also compromised in HM: entorhinal cortex, hippocampus proper and amygdala. Where Boswell appears to differ markedly from HM is in the presence of a major defect in retrograde memory, which entirely prohibits the retrieval of information at episodic level from any point of his

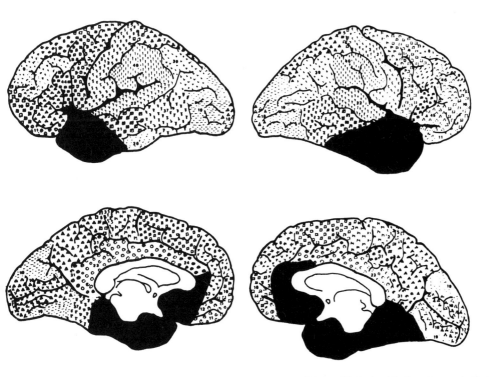

Fig. 1. Lateral and mesial views of the left and right hemispheres of Boswell's brain. Blackened areas indicate the damaged regions in both temporal and frontal cortices as described in the text. Plotting is based on both T_1 and T_2 weighted images obtained with an advanced magnetic resonance Picker Sinerview scanner.

life history, regardless of how remote. Earlier in the study of this patient we attributed this defect to the extensive involvement of the non-medial anterior temporal cortices and the insula. Our reasoning then was that such high-order association cortices constituted a virtual 'catalogue', cognitively and neurally separate from both (1) the hippocampal system, and (2) the 'early' sensory association cortices where fragmentary records would be laid down. This tripartite organization — hippocampal system, 'early' association cortices, 'catalogues' – was supposed to function in concert. Fragments of sensory activity in multiple sensory cortices would be stabilized 'in place', partly as a result of the influence of the hippocampal system. At the same time, the hippocampal system would also promote the establishment of an independent index of the combination of fragments that constituted a given perceptual set, on the basis of whose activation the set might be reconstituted later. Such an arrangement could account for learning impairment in patient HM (while permitting him to retrieve information from the retrograde compartment) and could also account for the combined anterograde and retrograde defect in Boswell (while permitting him to retrieve fragments of information unbound by the temporal and spatial arrangements in which they had occurred in his experience). The past decade of studies in Boswell, in other encephalitic patients and in patients with Alzheimer's disease (as discussed later in this chapter) and cerebral anoxia (see Zola-Morgan et al., 1986) have supported this account and have contributed to the development of a new model for the neural substrates of cognition (Damasio et al., 1989; Damasio, 1989a,b). The critical aspects of the model and the interpretation of Boswell's case according to its premises are summarized below.

The model is governed by two fundamental sets of constraints. The first, termed *neurobiological constraints,* corresponds to the basic structural design of the nervous system and to the neuroanatomically embodied values of the organism, prior to interactions with the environment. The other set

of constraints, termed *reality constraints,* corresponds (a) to the characteristics of physical structure, operation, frequency of occurrence of entities and events external to the perceiver's entire organism (environmental), and of entities and events external to the perceiver's brain but internal to the body, i.e., somatic; and (b) to the fact that entities and events necessarily occur in unique combinatorial sets defined by their *contextual complexity.* During perceptual interactions between the perceiver's brain and reality, the two sets of constraints lead to:

(1) *domain formation:* a process of categorization of entities based on their physical structure, operation, frequency of occurrence and value to perceiver, performed according to their *similarity;*

(2) the creation of records of *contextual complexity,* which code for the contextual complexity of entities and events (different degrees of contextual complexity can be designated by different taxonomic levels);

(3) *functional regionalization:* a process of assignment of fragmented, multimodal records of perceptuo-motor interactions, as well as of the codes binding their coincidence in time and space, to different regions of brain structure, according to domain and taxonomic level of entities and events.

The fundamental cognitive structures of the model are: (a) records of fragments of perceptual and motor events that preserve topographic/topological relationships; and (b) records of the codes binding the occurrence of the above representations in temporal and spatial terms (*convergence zones*). The representations embodied in those structures are interrelated according to combinatorial semantics and syntax.

The neuroanatomical substrates for the above cognitive structures are:

(1) primary and early association cortices, both sensory and motor, which constitute the substrate for topographic/topological records;

(2) association cortices of different orders, both sensory and motor, some limbic structures (entorhinal cortex, hippocampus, amygdala, cingulate

ortices), the neostriatum and the cerebellum, which constitute the substrate for binding code records;

(3) feed-forward and feedback connectivity interrelating (1) and (2);

(4) servosystem structures in thalamus, basal forebrain, hypothalamus and brain stem nuclei.

The cognitive/neural architecture outlined above can perform: (1) perceptuo-motor interactions with the brain's surround; (2) learning of these interactions; (3) problem-solving, decision-making, planning and creativity; and (4) communication with the environment. All these functions are predicated on a key operation: the attempted reconstitution of learned perceptuo-motor interactions on internal recall and motor performance. Attempted perceptuo-motor reconstitution is achieved by *retroactivation* of fragmentary records, in *multiple cortical regions,* as a result of feedback activity from convergence zones.

By reference to this model, the amnesia of patient Boswell and comparable patients can be interpreted as (1) the result of destruction of existing convergence zones in anterotemporal and insular cortices, and (2) the impossibility of creating new convergence zones (or new linkages to existing convergence zones) in the cortices which have been destroyed by the encephalitis. Had the lesions spared the hippocampus and amygdala, the amnesia might have been precisely the same. Boswell would have been unable to gain access to convergence zones in the damaged area and would have been equally unable to form new convergence zones or create new linkages to existing ones. Existing convergence zones in undamaged cortices, e.g., early association cortices of all modalities, dorsolateral association cortices in the frontal lobe and association cortices in the parietal lobe, which are all intact, can support recognition and recall at generic level in the absence of the anterotemporal and insular cortices necessary only for retrieval at contextually more complex (episodic) levels of operation. Based on this model, damage to the mesial temporal sector alone, which can on occasion occur as a result of encephalitis and which is

the anatomical highlight of patient HM, produces a different amnesic profile. Learning of new material, at any episodic level, and for any domain except that of perceptuomotor activities, is not possible because new convergence zones anywhere in the telencephalon cannot be formed, nor can new linkages be established with existing and intact convergence zones.

The preservation of cortical and subcortical structures of the motor system explains, in Boswell as well as in HM, the intact learning of 'procedural' type, perceptuo-motor tasks. It also indicates clearly that the learning of such tasks requires neither the hippocampal system nor the set of higher-order sensory association cortices of the anterior temporal lobe and insula.

Amnesia caused by infarctions in the basal forebrain

Introduction

In addition to causing major subarachnoid hemorrhages, the rupture of aneurysms located either in the anterior communicating artery or in the anterior cerebral artery almost invariably causes an infarction in one or two critical cerebral territories: (1) the region of the basal forebrain, a set of bilateral paramidline gray nuclei that includes the septal nuclei, the diagonal band of Broca and the substantia innominata; and (2) the posterior orbital cortices, a paralimbic region that includes part of cytoarchitectonic areas 11 and 12, in the gyrus rectus. The basal forebrain region is supplied directly from small arterioles arising directly from the anterior communicating artery, and in part from twigs out of the recurrent artery of Heubner, itself a branch of the anterior cerebral artery. Whether because of loss of blood flow during or following rupture, or the mechanical action of the hemorrhage, the basal forebrain may be more or less destroyed, unilaterally of bilaterally (the paramidline position of the region makes it prone to bilateral damage, although entirely unilateral damage is possible). It is important to note that because the vascular supply of this region is entirely independent from the vascular supply of the temporal lobe (which arises out of posterior cerebral artery and anterior choroidal artery) and from the vascular supply of the basal ganglia (which is provided by lenticular arteries arising out of the middle cerebral artery), basal forebrain infarctions are highly circumscribed and are unlikely to overlap with critical territories for cognitive function located nearby. Basal forebrain infarction is thus an ideal human condition for neuropsychological research.

Depending on the extent of damage, infarctions in this territory may disrupt (a) the bidirectional connectivity with the hippocampus and amygdala, (b) the cortical innervation for acetylcholine which largely arises out of the basal forebrain nuclei, and (c) the neurotransmitter projection systems for monoamines which traverse the area en route to cerebral cortex.

The damaged components in orbital cortex are usually unilateral and contribute to the overall clinical picture of these patients by involving yet another neural system.

Clinical presentation

Amnesia following basal forebrain lesions is an important and not infrequent condition (Damasio et al., 1985b). The typical presentation of a basal forebrain amnesic is captured in the case described below.

A 32-year-old right-handed man with a college education, who worked as a farmer and then as a mail carrier, developed a severe headache and shortly thereafter became comatose. On arrival at the hospital, no focal neurological abnormalities were evident. A CT showed hematomas in the left gyrus rectus and the midline septal nuclei. An angiogram showed an aneurysm at the junction of the A_1 and A_2 segments of the left anterior cerebral artery. A left frontal craniotomy was performed immediately to isolate and clip the aneurysm. During the procedure, the position of the hematomas seen in the CT was confirmed.

Postoperatively, the patient was disoriented to time and variably oriented to place and personal

information. Initially, his level of alertness and ability to concentrate fluctuated. During lucid periods, a significant impairment of memory was evident. He could not remember recent events or provide biographical details. However, the benefit of cuing was evident in his recall and recognition. For instance, at one point, the patient described himself as a college senior, but when told he had completed college eight years earlier, he was able to describe his current circumstances accurately. A similar effect occurred when the patient was questioned about his wife and family. He initially denied he was ever married, but, helped by successive cues, he gradually described his wife, her name, his children, their ages and their names.

Perhaps the central aspect of this patient's amnesia was the mismatch between auditory-verbal and visual memories and the lack of temporal tagging of either. We were able to document this phenomenon in the anterograde compartment of his memory. The patient learned the names of several physicians and the psychologist who handled his case, their faces and even some of their distinguishing features. However, he could not match those separate tokens of knowledge. He had no notion of when a specific encounter with these persons had taken place. In short, he appeared not to have been able to compute to co-occurrence of separate stimuli, although he was able to store each of them individually. Furthermore, there was no evidence that he could accomplish the temporal tagging of those individual tokens. This disturbance improved gradually but only partially.

During the acute phase, the patient exhibited bizarre and unusual fabrications. He would interweave current public events with imagined personal experiences. For instance, he believed he was a spaceship commander at the time of the Columbia space shuttle mission. Only occasionally did the patient seem to realize that his recalled experiences were not real. During the month following surgery there was substantial improvement in temporal orientation and evaluation of reality.

The following is a transcript from a videotaped interview with the patient, conducted by one of us

(A.R.D.) five weeks after onset. It brings to light some of the distinctive characteristics of basal forebrain amnesia.

Examiner: What important event took place in October?

Patient: Could we be having elections now?

Examiner: That is quite correct. What kind of election?

Patient: Local.

Examiner: That's correct. What about world events, nationally and internationally?

Patient: I think something happened in Iran. Did the Shah die?

Examiner: He did die, but not in October.

Patient: Oh, he died a while back. He was assassinated.

Examiner: No, he died of natural causes.

Patient: I suppose for that he can be thankful.

Examiner: There was another political leader assassinated in October.

Patient: I'm not aware of it. Who?

Examiner: He's from the general area you mentioned. It's not Iran.

Patient: Not Soviet?

Examiner: What about Egypt?

Patient: Oh, Anwar Sadat!

Examiner: What happened to him?

Patient: He was shot, wasn't he?

Examiner: Yes, he was. When?

Patient: In the past several months. When you mention that, it comes forth. It happens to me a lot of times when people talk about something. It just comes out.

Examiner: Tell me, what do you see when you picture the event?

Patient: An assassination. Was he killed near a wall with a lot of people running? I thought that as a loss for the West.

Examiner: Why was he assassinated?

Patient: I would imagine because he was anticommunist. Is that right?

Examiner: That's one way of putting it.

Patient: It's my guess.

Examiner: What happened after that?

Patient: I dont' know. I had a headache, I left the room.

Examiner: But what happened?

Patient: They elected a new president, No. 2 or 3 in the government.

Examiner: Yes. What was his name?

Patient: Does his name begin with an 'M'?

Examiner: Yes. Mubarak. What happened afterwards? Was there a funeral?

Patient: Yes, obviously there was. A state funeral. I didn't see it on television, but I suppose world leaders converged on Egypt.

Examiner: Who went to the funeral from this country?

Patient: Did two people go?

Examiner: More than two. Try to think who.

Patient: Was one of them Richard Nixon?

Examiner: One of them was Richard Nixon.

Patient: Richard Nixon went on his own.

Examiner: No. Let's work on that some more. Do you remember (President) Reagan going?

Patient: I don't remember Reagan going. Didn't he send somebody? I don't remember anybody else.

Examiner: You do remember Nixon. Was there anybody else?

Patient: Al Haig (correct).

Examiner: Anybody else? For instance, Kissinger?

Patient: Yes, Kissinger (correct).

Examiner: Ford:

Patient: Yes (correct). Now why didn't I recall that. This is the problem with the surgery. Somebody mentions something and it comes flying out of your head. It's like flashes of knowledge that unleash from the dark side of your head.

Examiner: Who is your immediate family?

Patient: My mother and father. Of course, I'm married now.

Examiner: When did you get married?

157

Patient: Aren't I married?

Examiner: I really don't know. (The patient is married and has two children.)

Patient: Maybe I'm not, maybe that's just a fantasy now.

Examiner: I really don't know if you're married.

Patient: No, I don't think I am.

Examiner: Yes, you are.

Patient: Then I must be (embarrassed laughter).

Examiner: If you're married, then who's your wife?

Patient: Karen (correct). I don't know, but I think I have memory of two children (correct).

Examiner: All right.

Patient: If this isn't right, it's going to look bad.

Examiner: Don't worry, we understand the problem.

Patient: I have a son, Steven . . . one daughter (correct). I'm not clear what her name is. (She was born shortly before this operation.)

Examiner: How long have you been married?

Patient: Several years . . . four, it may be going five. We have a house in the country (correctly names town in which he lives).

Examiner: How old is Steven?

Patient: He's about 3 years old (correct).

Examiner: When did you see them last?

Patient: Believe it or not, that's unclear.

Examiner: You had some peculiar ideas during your admission here. Can you tell us about some?

Patient: I was a pirate and I commanded a spaceship (embarrassed laughter). Now I realize it's not true. I *didn't dream* that; it was a total part of consciousness. To me, it was reality at that time. It's embarrassing now. At times, even reality is a dream. It was continuous throughout the day. I did believe it!

The patient was re-examined 20 weeks after onset. His wife noted a personality change characterized by sexual and verbal disinhibition and some instability of mood. The patient was usually cheerful and relaxed but prone to occasional sudden anger. His neuropsychological scores continued to improve, although verbal learning and visual memory impairments remained evident. He was able to return to work as a mail carrier and continued to manage his job satisfactorily.

Neuropsychological profile

Although the magnitude of basal forebrain amnesia can vary considerably from case to case, the neuropsychological characteristics of the defect are quite consistent and can be summarized as follows:

The patients are able to learn separate modal stimuli, such as the name and face of a person, as well as other associated features, e.g., speech accent, physical traits, or characteristics of an occupation. However, they are not able to integrate properly those differently learned components. Although they know a person's name and face, they cannot bring the two together. This is remarkably different from what occurs in patients HM and Boswell, in whom the failure to learn is at the level of the separate stimulus. Basal forebrain patients either fail to register the temporal relationship of stimuli, or appear not to use such a register, if it exists normally, to produce a proper evocation.

Basal forebrain patients have some resemblance to patients with Korsakoff's syndrome, although a modal memory mismatching defect exactly as noted above has not been described. The patients are also different from those with Korsakoff's syndrome in the nature and extent of their fabrications. Talland (1965) pointed out that the fabrication of patients with Korsakoff's syndrome draws on the previous life experience of the subjects and stays close to it.

Basal forebrain patients confabulate freely and wildly. The dreamlike fabrications are spontaneous. They occur before patients are engaged in questions they cannot answer properly, i.e., the fabrications are not prompted by a need to confabulate to fill in gaps of information. The internal experience of the patients in the wakeful 'resting state' includes fantasies that are *not* recognized as such. The disordered memory mechanism behind this phenomenon is probably the same that causes the mismatched recall previously described. The fabricated episodes are composed of unrelated memories, some of which record real experience and some of which are acquired through conversations, reading, the media and even dreaming. The patients use sensible and realistic items of knowledge to compose the unreal experiences. Their stories do not have a paranoid flavor and do not involve distorted perception.

The fabrications often include some salient element of current news. The combination of the elements is legitimate. i.e., it respects logic and is within the boundaries of the fictionally possible. It is the combinatorial arrangement that violates reality. The fabricated fantasies are partly incorporated in memory.

An apt description for these fabrications would probably be a dream in the waking state. Unlike what happens in a daydream, however, the patients are not actively directing the process of fabrication and are not aware, at least automatically, that the experience is not reality. Even after this is pointed out to them, they only gradually realize the oneiric nature of the experience. Later in the course of the illness, the patients become more aware of the fabrications, and are more cautious in reporting them to the examiners. Ultimately they become frankly embarrassed by the content of their untrue tales.

The first description of a comparable manifestation of which we are aware was given by Whitty and Levin (1957), in patients who underwent cingulectomy. The confabulations of those patients were often based on real experiences, but they had difficulty distinguishing between 'thoughts' and 'external events'. Their phenomenon lasted only a couple of days, compared with weeks or even months in our patients.

Cuing markedly improves recall and recognition in both the anterograde and retrograde compartments of memory. Improved performance for recently learned material could be related either to the manner of encoding and recording or to the manner of retrieval. Improved performance for retrograde memories, however, cannot be related to encoding-consolidation mechanisms because the allegedly defective memories were recorded before the onset of amnesia. Support for a predominant retrieval deficit comes not only from clinical observation, but also from performance on standard neuropsychological tests in which basal forebrain patients show an impaired learning curve during free recall trials but often improve to normal or near normal on a recognition trial. Impaired retrieval appears to be an important factor in basal forebrain amnesia.

Neuroanatomical findings
The common anatomic denominator in basal forebrain amnesics is the involvement of the septal nuclei, diagonal band nuclei and medial parts of the substantia innominata. Damage to the septal nuclei deprives the hippocampus of cholinergic innervation, but because lesions in this area also compromise a part of the nucleus basalis of Meynert the cerebral cortex is also deprived of cholinergic innervation. Projection pathways such as the precommissural fornix, medial forebrain bundle, diagonal band of Broca and ventroamygdalofugal tract may be damaged too. This means that critical bidirectional connections with the hippocampal region are likely to be interrupted, and that, in addition, cortically bound projections of such neurotransmitters as dopamine, norepinephrine and serotonin may be interrupted as well, with ensuing cortical deprivation of those substances.

In all basal forebrain patients who have been studied so far, the orbitofrontal damage component is always unilateral, left or right, and always in the posterior sector of the ventromedial part of these frontal cortices. The medial temporal region, the dorsomedial, anterior and nonspecific midline

159

nuclei of the thalamus and the dorsolateral frontal cortices are structurally intact.

An example of a typical basal forebrain lesion as depicted in coronal sections of X-ray computerized tomography is illustrated in Fig. 2.

Neural mechanisms

The neural condition of basal forebrain amnesics is remarkably different from that of patients with herpes encephalitis. Both limbic and neocortical temporal structures are intact and only subcortical nuclei are involved. Such damage, however, compromises the delivery of critical neurotransmitters, in generalized fashion, over large regions of cortex and of the hippocampal system. Because of the widespread contribution that such subcortical neurotransmitter nuclei make to telencephalic neural tissue, this defect alone means that virtually no modular unit of cortex or hippocampal system could possibly operate normally during processes

of learning or retrieval. It is possible, however, that the disruption of their directional circuitry which occurs with lesions in the basal forebrain adds another cause of dysfunction, unrelated to neurotransmitter physiology.

The mechanisms behind the learning and retrieval defects of patients with basal forebrain damage can be interpreted in the context of our model for the neural basis of cognition, discussed above in the section on herpes encephalitis. As noted, the key for storing and retrieving representations is a device known as the *convergence zone*. For memories encompassed under the broad class of 'declarative' memory, numerous convergence zones are located throughout higher-order association cortices. Convergence zones receive information by feed-forward projections, from other cortices, and also receive feedback projections from the cortical and subcortical limbic system, the basal forebrain and neurotransmitter nuclei in the

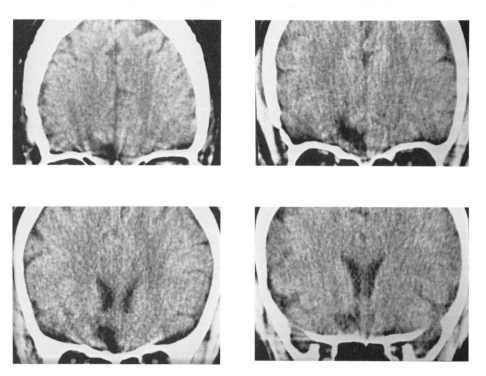

Fig. 2. Four consecutive coronal sections from a computerized X-ray tomography scan (CT) of patient RF, a basal forebrain amnesic. The sections cut through the posterior frontal lobe and basal forebrain region.

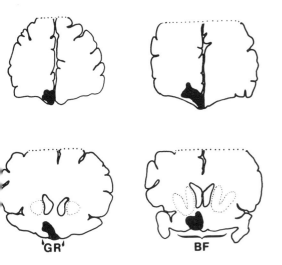

Fig. 3. Diagram of the lesion in patient RF as seen in the CT sections of Fig. 2. GR = gyrus rectus; BF = basal forebrain. As noted in the text, the lesion involves the left gyrus rectus and the left basal forebrain region.

brainstem. It is critical for the process of development of convergence zones, as well as for the processes of learning connected to a convergence zone, that activity from the multiple feed-forward and feedback projections be concurrent. The construct of convergence zone predicts that defective concurrence of activity at the convergence zone site, brought about by inadequate timing or by sheer absence of one of the projection components, ought to lead to defects in learning and retrieval. Damage to basal forebrain clearly implies a substraction of important subcortical projections to a large array of association cortices and the lack of a critical feedback component in numerous convergence zones. This means that, throughout the hemisphere, the process of forming new convergence zones, the attachment of new linkages to existing convergence zones and the normal activation of existing convergence zones during recall or recognition will be disturbed.

Amnesia caused by Alzheimer's disease and cerebral anoxia

Alzheimer's disease

Clinical presentation

In the advanced stages of Alzheimer's disease (AD) virtually all cognitive systems are disrupted. However, as the disease progresses in its earlier stages it is possible to detect selective impairments of some cognitive processes against a background of otherwise normal cognition. Furthermore, in some cases of AD, the selectivity is such that only one or very few systems are involved, for a long period of the evolution (see Van Hoesen and Damasio, 1987, for review).

In spite of considerable individual variability, the prevalent cognitive profile of AD always includes (1) an impairment of learning and retrieval in verbal and nonverbal domains, (2) an eventual impairment in problem-solving, decision-making and planning, and (3) an eventual impairment of emotion and affect.

The defect in the learning of information at episodic level appears early and is always present, i.e., learning of entities and events that have a unique temporal and spatial placement in the individual's autobiography is always defective. Equally marked is the inability to solve day-to-day problems and to plan activities correctly, which may be entirely secondary to this episodic learning defect. A defect in retrieval of episodic information, especially of information acquired recently rather than in the distant past, is also consistently present and proportional to the degree of episodic learning impairment. The 'autobiographical' update needed for the appropriate acquisition of new episodic information is gradually disrupted in AD to the point that only a few landmarks of personal history, e.g., the patient's name, the name of the spouse, and the like, remain accessible.

AD also disrupts memory processing at non-episodic level, i.e., the forms of memory generally referred to as semantic or generic. The breakdown of generic memory generally occurs later than that of episodic memory and encompasses both acquisition of new items and retrieval of items previously acquired. This is in keeping with the notion that acquisition of generic memory is not possible when there is a primary defect in acquisition of episodic memory. The meaning of numerous stimuli from diverse domains gradually eludes patients with AD. The defect for this particular type of memory is greater than that seen with amnesic syndromes caused by cerebrovascular disease, or herpes encephalitis. Furthermore, the defective retrieval of memory at generic level has special characteristics in AD. The responses are more erratic than with other etiologies of amnesia, less stable, and more likely to appear as a 'derailment' across an otherwise well-targeted semantic field. It is as if the activation of records pertinent to a given stimulus would occur only fleetingly and the patient would be unable to experience enough of such brief and dislocated activations to generate sufficient remembrances to yield the meaning of a given object.

A salient feature of the episodic retrieval defect is the inability to recognize locales, and to recognize the relationships of objects and persons to those topographic locations. This phenomenon explains the often noted bewilderment of patients with early AD when they have to negotiate rapidly changing scenes and locations.

All patients with AD have an impairment of language, which in our view is a special form of memory defect. The impairment does not compromise processing of syntax, or the use of phonemic information, nor does it cause incorrect phonetic implementation. The defect is squarely at the lexical level and is best described as an inability to retrieve lexical entries that tag specific nonverbal entities or events. For long periods into the evolution of the disease, patients might, in fact, be classified as anomic or amnestic aphasics. In some cases, this defect has progressed in virtual isolation, with little or no accompanying decline of other cognitive operations (Mesulam, 1982).

Patients with AD remain capable of learning new perceptuo-motor skills (Eslinger and Dama-

sio, 1986; Mickel et al., 1986). However, they have no conscious appreciation of that knowledge and have 'source amnesia', i.e., they are unable to recall the circumstances in which learning took place. The dissociation between the complete inability to learn the identity of new faces, or new names, and the preserved ability to perform as controls do in mirror tracing or rotor pursuit tasks, is most striking, and it is usually not until the very late stages of the disease that skill learning is compromised.

The neuropathology of Alzheimer's disease

The neuropathology of Alzheimer's disease is characterized by two signature phenomena: the neurofibrillary tangle and the neuritic plaque. The neurofibrillary tangle is the transformation of a once viable neuron whose cell body loses normal organelle architecture. Stained neurofibrillary tangles should be viewed as a useful way of marking the pathological process that leads to neuronal death. The development of neurofibrillary tangles leads to neuronal loss and to disruption of the cellular architecture of cortical layers (laminae) or subcortical nuclei. As neurons die and axons perish, normal connectivity is also disrupted. The cause of neuritic plaques and their role in the disruption of normal anatomy are not clear. They may signal the degeneration of axon terminals or be due to some other cause. They are not necessarily a factor in modifying normal connectivity. In short, Alzheimer's disease is the disruption of the intricate cortical architecture on which cognitive processes depend.

The accrual of neuropathological defects in Alzheimer's disease is gradual, over a long period of years, but the disease affects neural structures selectively, in terms of (a) brain regions, (b) laminae within the regions, and (c) cell types within the laminae. Using the neurofibrillary tangle, as stained by Congo red or thioflavin S, as the signature marker of the disease, the principal neuroanatomical features of the condition are as follows:

Damage to limbic system. The key feature is that the entorhinal cortex, the pivotal way station for input to and from hippocampus, is disrupted by neurofibrillary tangles in layers II and IV. The normal layer II of entorhinal cortex contains clusters of neurons that give rise to the perforant pathway, the main route for entry into the hippocampal formation. In Alzheimer's disease, layer II neurons are gradually substituted by neurofibrillary tangles in massive manner (Hyman et al., 1984; Ball et al., 1985; Pearson et al., 1985) and the perforant pathway is thus demyelinated (Hyman et al., 1986). In some of our cases, studied in collaboration with Robert Terry at the University of California, San Diego, more than 90% of such neurons are transformed into neurofibrillary tangles. The neurotransmitter used by this pathway, glutamate, is drastically reduced in the terminal zone of the projection within the dentate gyrus of the hippocampus (Hyman et al., 1987). As more and more neurons in the layer II clusters of the entorhinal cortex become inoperative, lesser and lesser signaling of cortical activity is available to the hippocampal formation, in a virtual deafferentation of the hippocampus from cortical inputs.

The disease also breaks the efferent linkage of the hippocampus back to cerebral cortex, by damage at two sites: (1) the subiculum, the hippocampal structure from which both efferents from hippocampus to cerebral cortex and efferents from hippocampus to subcortical structures take their origin; and (2) layer IV of the entorhinal cortex, a critical pivot in the projections from hippocampus to cerebral cortex.

Equally involved is the amygdala, a key component of the subcortical limbic system. Most of its nuclei are heavily disrupted by neurofibrillary tangles (Hyman et al., 1987).

Neuropathological involvement in basal forebrain nuclei has also been noted. The nucleus basalis of Meynert is compromised (Whitehouse et al., 1981) and other cholinergic nuclei of the region are too (Van Hoesen and Damasio, 1987). As noted in the basal forebrain section, those neurons are the providers of acetylcholine to the cerebral cortex and hippocampal structures. This is of some import, since most brains with Alzheimer's disease show a marked reduction of enzymatic indicators of acetylcholine (Davies and Maloney, 1976). It should be clear, however, that several dementias, of the degenerative type and not, show no deficiency whatsoever in acetylcholine, indicating that acetylcholine deficiency is not the critical element in the mechanisms leading to cognitive impairment.

Damage in cerebral cortices. From the point of view of neurofibrillary tangles, damage in cerebral cortices is most marked in higher-order association cortices (Van Hoesen and Damasio, 1987). The disruption is less marked in cortices progressively closer to the primary sensory regions, e.g., the higher-order visual cortices in areas 20 and 21 are more heavily invested with neurofibrillary tangles than cortices in areas 18 and 19; area 17 is free of neurofibrillary tangles although it can contain neuritic plaques. The so-called multimodal cortices in areas 37 and 39 are heavily involved and so are frontal association cortices. The most significant characteristics of this aspect of Alzheimer's neuropathology is that the laminar distribution is different from that found in entorhinal cortex, i.e., it is layers III and V and not II and IV that are the primary recipients of the damage (Van Hoesen and Damasio, 1987). Because these are pivotal layers for corticocortical projections, damage here disrupts the feed-forward and feedback projections that interconnect different cortical areas.

Motor system. Virtually all motor structures, areas 4 and 6, areas 3, 1, 2, as well as the basal ganglia and cerebellum, are less involved by neurofibrillary tangles than other parts of the telencephalon (Terry and Katzman, 1983; Van Hoesen and Damasio, 1987). This neuropathological finding is consistent with the cognitive counterpart; i.e., the intact learning and performance of motor-related skills in AD patients described above.

Neural mechanisms

The defective acquisition of memory at episodic level is attributable to impairments in a bilateral network that includes the amygdala, the hippocampal formation, their input and output staging areas in the entorhinal cortex, and their projections to higher-order association cortices, e.g., the polar, anterolateral and anteroinferior temporal cortices and the insular cortices. Damage in basal forebrain nuclei and in paramidline, non-specific nuclei of the thalamus probably contributes to the episodic learning defect. In our view, the defect in retrieval at episodic level is largely attributable to dysfunction in higher-order association cortices.

On the basis of current knowledge of the anatomical basis of the agnosias in humans and animals (Damasio, 1985; Mishkin et al., 1982), and from the contrast between patient HM and patient Boswell, the impairment of generic memory should be related to a network which includes the modal sensory cortices and some higher-order association cortices located in (a) posterior occipitotemporal and occipitoparietal regions (areas 18, 19, part of 37, 36, 35 and 39), (b) part of the anterior temporal cortices (areas 20, 21, 22, 38) and insular cortices. This network is more caudally located than the one hypothesized for retrieval of memory at episodic level, but partly overlaps with it. In both of these overlapping networks the disruption of feedforward and feedback circuitry might well explain the defects and probably explains the peculiar nature of the recognition responses in Alzheimer's patients.

The lack of impairments in phonemic programming and reception, as well as the normal phonetic implementation and syntactic processing, indicates that the classic language areas of the frontal operculum (areas 44 and 45), the posterior region of superior temporal gyrus (area 22) and the supramarginal gyrus (area 40) are not compromised in AD. On the other hand, a new set of neuropsychological and neuroanatomical findings in our laboratory indicates that the severe defect in naming is caused by dysfunction in the *dominant* temporal cortices of areas 20, 21 and 38, and in the ad-

joining dominant hippocampal system (Tranel and Damasio, 1988).

On the basis of current knowledge of cognitive disturbances caused by dysfunction in frontal cortices (Damasio, 1985; Eslinger and Damasio, 1985; Goldman-Rakic, 1984), the network related to defects in executive control (monitoring, higher-level problem-solving, goal development, planning, judgment) includes areas in prefrontal cortex working in concert with parietal and temporal cortical regions.

Cerebral anoxia/ischemia

Cerebral anoxia in the setting of cardiorespiratory arrest often leads to the selective destruction of cellular groups within the hippocampal formation. The extent of damage is linked to the number of minutes of the arrest. Brief periods of anoxia/ischemia may cause limited, albeit bilateral damage. Survival is possible with amnesia as the sole consequence. Judging from the best studies available in the literature, the characteristics of the amnesia resemble those found in patient HM: marked anterograde learning defect and minimal retrograde memory impairment. The recent histological analysis of the anoxic amnesic RB (Zola-Morgan et al., 1986) reveals that the damage was circumscribed to one of the ammonic fields, CA1. All other areas of the hippocampus, as well as the amygdala and entorhinal cortex, were intact. The fact that no significant retrograde memory impairment was noted in RB supports the hypothesis suggested by data on patient HM, according to which the hippocampus would not be involved in the permanent storage of past records. It also supports the hypothesis raised in connection with the data from patient Boswell, according to which it is damage in higher-order association neocortices of the anterior temporal lobe and insula that is related to a severe retrograde memory defect. It is possible, of course, that experiments aimed at the detailed study of retrograde memory within specific domains and highly subordinate taxonomic levels may eventually indicate that the hip-

campus is, in fact, more heavily involved in
retrieval of records from the retrograde compartment than the current data lead one to believe.
It is interesting to note that the type of cellular
damage described in Zola-Morgan et al.'s patient
disrupts the input-output circuitry of the hippocampal system, in much the same way as the
cellular damage in Alzheimer's disease, although
different points. The two sets of data converge
indicate the critical role of the hippocampal for-
ation in the acquisition of new records of experiences of the so-called declarative type.

Concluding remarks

Data derived from the study of amnesics with the
four neuropathological substrates described above
have both enlarged and made more precise our list
of the key cortical functional regions and subcortical structures involved in learning and memory.
At cortical level, the list includes the several
primary and early association cortices, the higher-
order association cortices of the temporal, frontal
and insular regions, the paralimbic cortices of the
temporal lobe (entorhinal cortex, area 38 and
posterior parahippocampal gyrus) and of the frontal lobe (posterior orbital cortices and cingulate
gyrus). At subcortical level, the list includes the
hippocampus, the amygdala, the basal forebrain
nuclei, the thalamus and hypothalamus, and
neurotransmitter nuclei in the brainstem. On the
basis of detailed neuropsychological investigations
of patients with lesions in these territories, it has
been possible to characterize in greater detail the
profiles associated with various subsidiary patterns
of neuroanatomical damage. In turn, this has
made way for a new theoretical account in which
the contents and processes of memory are related
to specific neural systems.

Acknowledgement

Supported by NINCDS Grant PO1 NS19632.

References

Ball MJ, Fisman M, Hachinski V, Blume W, Fox A, Kral VA, Kirshen AJ, Fox H, Merskey H: A new definition of Alzheimer's disease: a hippocampal dementia. *Lancet: 1;* 14–16, 1985.

Albert MS, Butters N, Levin J: Temporal gradients in the retrograde amnesia of patients with alcoholic Korsakoff's disease. *Arch. Neurol.: 36;* 211–216, 1979.

Benton AL: *Multilingual Aphasia Examination,* Department of Neurology: Iowa City: University of Iowa, 1976.

Benton AL, Hamsher K, Varney AR, Spreen O: *Contributions to Neuropsychological Assessment,* New York: Oxford University Press, 1983.

Corkin S: Acquisition of motor skill after bilateral medial temporal excision. *Neuropsychologia: 6;* 255–265, 1968.

Corkin S: Lasting consequences of bilateral medial temporal lobectomy: clinical course and experimental findings in HM. *Semin. Neurol.: 4;* 249–259, 1984.

Damasio A: Disorders of complex visual processing. In Mesulam M-M (Editor), *Principles of Behavioral Neurology, Contemporary Neurology Series.* Philadelphia: F.A. Davis, pp. 259–288, 1985.

Damasio AR: The brain binds entities and events by multiregional activation from convergence zones. *Neural Comput.: 1,* 123–132, 1989a.

Damasio A: Multiregional retroactivation: a systems level model of neural substrates of cognition. *Cognition:* 1989b; in press.

Damasio AR, Van Hoesen GW: The limbic system and the localization of herpes simplex encephalities. *J. Neurol. Neurosurg. Psychiatry: 48;* 297–301, 1985.

Damasio AR, Damasio H, Tranel D, Welsh K, Brandt J: Additional neural and cognitive evidence in patient DRB. *Soc. Neurosci.: 13;* 1452, 1987.

Damasio A, Eslinger P, Damasio H, Van Hoesen GW, Cornell S: Multimodal amnesic syndrome following bilateral temporal and basal forebrain damage. *Arch. Neurol.: 42;* 263–271, 1985a.

Damasio AR, Graff-Gradford NR, Eslinger PJ, Damasio H, Kassell, N: Amnesia following basal forebrain lesions. *Arch. Neurol.: 42;* 263–271, 1985b.

Damasio A, Damasio H, Tranel D: Impairments of visual recognition as clues to the processes of memory. In: Edelman G, Gall E, Cowan M (Editors), *Signal and Sense: Local and Global Order in Perceptual Maps;* Neuroscience Institute Monograph. New York: Wiley & Sons, 1989.

Davies P, Maloney AJF: Selective loss of central cholinergic neurons in Alzheimer's disease (letter) *Lancet: 2* (pt. 2), 1403, 1976.

Eslinger PJ, Damasio AR: Severe disturbance of higher cognition after bilateral frontal lobe ablation: patient EVR. *Neurology: 35;* 1731–1741, 1985.

Eslinger PJ, Damasio AR: Preserved motor learning in Alzheimer's disease. *J. Neurosci.: 6;* 3006–3009, 1986.

Goldman-Rakic PS: The frontal lobes: uncharted provinces of the brain. *Trends Neurosci.: 7;* 425–429, 1984.

Goodglass H, Kaplan E: *The Assessment of Aphasia and*

Related Disorders. Philadelphia: Lea & Febiger, 1972 (2nd edition 1983).

Graf P, Squire LR, Mandler G: The information that amnesic patients do not forget. *J. Exp. Psychol. Learn. Mem. Cognition: 10;* 164 – 178, 1984.

Hyman BT, Van Hoesen GW, Damasio A, Barnes CL: Cell specific pathology isolates the hippocampal formation in Alzheimer's disease. *Science: 225;* 1168 – 1170, 1984.

Hyman BT, Van Hoesen GW, Kromer LJ, Damasio A: Perforant pathway changes and the memory impairment of Alzheimer's disease. *Ann. Neurol.: 20;* 472 – 481, 1986.

Hyman BT, Van Hoesen GW, Damasio A: Alzheimer's disease: glutamate depletion in the hippocampal perforant pathway zone. *Ann. Neurol.: 22;* 37 – 40, 1987.

Lezak, MD: *Neuropsychological Assessment, Vol. 2*. New York: Oxford University Press, 1983.

Mesulam M-M: Slowly progressive aphasia without generalized dementia. *Ann. Neurol.: 11;* 592 – 598, 1982.

Mickel SF, Gabrieli JDE, Rosen TJ, Corkin S, Growdon JH: Mirror tracing: preserved learning in patients with global amnesia and some patients with Alzheimer's disease. *Soc. Neurosci. Abstr.: 12,* 20, 1986.

Milner B: Les troubles de la memoire accompagnant des lesions hippocampiques bilaterales. In *Physiologie de l'Hippocampe*. Paris: Centre National de la Recherche Scientifique, pp. 257 – 272, 1962.

Mishkin M, Spiegler BJ, Saunders RC, Malamut BJ: An animal model of global amnesia. In Corkin S, Davis KL, Growdon JH, Usdin E, Wurtman RJ (Editors), *Toward a Treatment of Alzheimer's Disease*. New York: Raven Press, 1982.

Pearson RCA, Esiri MM, Hiorns RW, Wilcox GK, Powell TPS: Anatomical correlates of the distribution of the pathological changes in the neocortex in Alzheimer disease.

Proc. Natl. Acad. Sci. USA: 82; 4531 – 4534, 1985.

Squire LR, Cohen NJ, Zouzounis JA: Preserved memory retrograde amnesia: sparing of a recently acquired skil. *Neuropsychologia: 22;* 145 – 152, 1984.

Talland GA: *Deranged Memory*. New York: Academic Pres 1965.

Terry RD, Katzman R: Senile dementia of the Alzheimer typ *Ann. Neurol.: 14;* 497, 1983.

Tranel D, Damasio AR: Dissociated verbal and nonverb retrieval and learning, following left anterior tempor damage. *J. Clin. Exp. Neuropsychol.: 10;* 17, 1988.

Van Hoesen GW, Damasio A: Neural correlates of cogniti impairment in Alzheimer's disease. In Mountcastle V, Plu F (Editors), *Handbook of Physiology; Higher Functions the Nervous System*. Bethesda, MD: American Physiologic Society, pp. 871 – 898, 1987.

Wechsler DA: A standardized memory scale for clinical use. *Psychol.: 19;* 87 – 95, 1945.

Wechsler DA: *Manual for the Wechsler Adult Intelligen Scale*. New York: The Psychological Corp., 1955.

Wechsler DA: *The Wechsler Adult Intelligence Scale-Revise* New York: The Psychological Corporation, 1981.

Whitehouse PJ, Price DL, Clark AW, Coyle JT, Delong Mł Alzheimer disease: evidence for selective loss of cholinerg neurons in the nucleus basalis. *Ann. Neurol.: 10;* 122 – 12 1981.

Whitty CWM, Levin W: Vivid day-dreaming, an unusual for of confusion following anterior cingulectomy. *Brain: 8* 72 – 76, 1957.

Zola-Morgan S, Squire LR, Amaral DG: Human amnesia ar the medial temporal region: enduring memory impairmer following a bilateral lesion limited to the CA1 field of tł hippocampus. *J. Neurosci.: 6;* 2950 – 2967, 1986.

1989 Elsevier Science Publishers B.V. (Biomedical Division)
ndbook of Neuropsychology, Vol. 3
Boller and J. Grafman (Eds)

CHAPTER 7

Transient global amnesia

Mark Kritchevsky

Neurology Service, Veterans Administration Medical Center, San Diego, and Department of Neurosciences, University of California, San Diego, U.S.A.

Introduction

ransient global amnesia (TGA) is a short-lasting eurological condition in which memory impairment is the prominent deficit. It was described independently by Bender (1956), Guyotat and Courjon (1956) and Fisher and Adams (1958). The ame transient global amnesia was introduced by isher and Adams (1958), who later published 17 xtensive case descriptions of patients with TGA nd discussed the nature of the memory disorder Fisher and Adams, 1964). Subsequent reports furner defined the clinical picture and natural history f TGA, debated the etiology of the syndrome, nd explored the neuropsychological profile of the 'GA patient during and after the episode. Table 1 ummarizes the characteristics of TGA.

Clinical picture of the patient with TGA

The episode

he episode of TGA is stereotyped (Fisher and Adams, 1964; Kritchevsky 1987). It usually begins uddenly, lasts for at least several hours, and esolves gradually over several hours to a day. The nean duration of the episode is 6 to 7 hours, with wo-thirds lasting 2 to 12 hours (Caplan, 1985; Miller et al., 1987a). Careful examination during 'GA shows that the patient has a relatively solated amnesic syndrome (Patten, 1971; Shuttleworth and Wise, 1973; Gordon and Marin, 1979; Donaldson, 1985). The general neurological ex-

amination is normal – the visual, motor, and somatosensory systems are intact. Evaluation of the mental status shows normal immediate memory for a list of numbers or words. In contrast, the TGA patient can recall little of any verbal or nonverbal material that was presented minutes before. He often repeats the same question many times because he cannot remember the answer that was just given. Frequently repeated questions include, 'Is there something the matter with me?,' and 'What's wrong, have I had a stroke?' During TGA the patient also has a patchy loss of recall for events dating from several hours to many years before the attack. Older memories are spared, and the patient does not lose personal identity. The TGA patient is often unusually passive during the attack; occasionally he is agitated. The mental status examination is otherwise normal. All other cognitive and behavioral abnormalities found at the bedside can be explained by the amnesic syndrome. The patient is often mistakenly reported to be 'confused', but the level of consciousness and the level of attention are normal. About 15% of TGA patients complain of a steady or throbbing headache, sometimes with associated nausea or vomiting, during or immediately after the episode (Miller et al., 1987a). TGA patients examined carefully after the episode are normal except for an inability to recall the episode.

Risk and precipitating factors

TGA generally occurs in persons over age 50, and

TABLE 1

Characteristics of TGA

The episode	A relatively isolated amnesic syndrome (passivity or headache may be present)
Time course	Relatively sudden onset, gradual recovery, 7 ± 4 hours duration
Age of patients	60 ± 10 years
Sex of patients	Slight male preponderance
Incidence in persons older than 50 years	23.5/100,000/year
Precipitating factors	Physical or psychological stress in 30%
Recurrence rate	3 – 5%/year
Incidence of subsequent TIA, stroke, permanent memory or intellectual problems	Not increased
Laboratory tests	Generally normal
Neuropsychological exam during TGA	Severe anterograde amnesia for verbal and nonverbal material, patchy retrograde amnesia for events that occurred several hours to many years before TGA, mild difficulty copying a complex diagram
Neuropsychological exam after TGA	Complete recovery

See text for discussion and references.

75% of patients are 50 to 69 years old (Fisher, 1982a; Caplan, 1985; Miller et al., 1987a). Men and women are affected with nearly equal frequency, although most reports include a slight preponderance of males (Caplan, 1985). The estimated incidence in Rochester, MN, was 5.2 per 100,000 per year for persons of all ages and 23.5 per 100,000 per year for persons older than 50 years (Miller et al., 1987a).

A third of TGA attacks are precipitated by physical or psychological stress including strenuous exertion, sexual intercourse, intense emotion, pain, exposure to intense heat or cold, and minor or major medical procedures (Fisher, 1982a; Miller et al., 1987a). The majority of episodes have no clear precipitating factor, and about 5% are present on awakening.

On rare occasions TGA occurs in members of the same family (Corston and Godwin-Austen, 1982; Munro and Loizou, 1982; Stracciari and Rebucci, 1986; Dupuis et al., 1987). The reason for this may be an increased awareness of the condition, or a higher incidence of a risk or precipitating factor.

On one occasion TGA has occurred in a woman who had separate strokes, focal seizures and episodes of temporary amnesia which occurred in association with transient, then permanent, skin lesions of livedo reticularis (Rumpl and Rumpl, 1979). The historical evidence suggested that each episode of amnesia was, indeed, an episode of TGA.

Several other potential risk factors should be discussed. Migraine does not appear to be a risk factor for TGA. About 15% of TGA patients have a history of common or classical migraine headaches (Miller et al., 1987a), and some patients complain of a typical migraine headache during or after the episode of amnesia (Frank, 1976; Caplan et al., 1981; Crowell et al., 1984; Miller et al., 1987a). Nonetheless, the incidence of migraine in TGA patients appears to be the same as that in an age-matched control group (Kushner and Hauser, 1985).

There is also no good evidence to suggest that cerebrovascular disease (that is, TIA or stroke) causes TGA. One study found that cerebrovascular disease occurred before or after TGA in 11% of patients, which was the expected incidence of stroke for a group of that age (Miller et al., 1987a). Prior reports of an association between TGA and cerebrovascular disease probably misdiagnosed patients with amnesic transient ischemic attack (TIA) as having had TGA (Mathew and Meyer, 1974; Jensen and Olivarius, 1980; Kushner and Hauser, 1985).

Brain tumor does not cause TGA. Although two patients with episodes of isolated amnesia similar to TGA had a temporal lobe tumor, they subsequently developed permanent memory or other neurological dysfunction (Hartley et al., 1974; Findler et al., 1983). In another patient, the association of TGA and brain tumor was probably a coincidence, as the tumor was a right anterior parietal meningioma which did not appear to be associated with seizures or significant mass effect (Collins and Freeman, 1986). Other reported cases of brain tumor and episodic memory loss (Boudin et al., 1975; Lisak and Zimmerman, 1977; Shuping et al., 1980b; Meador et al., 1985; Matias-Guiu et al., 1986) did not meet criteria for TGA (see discussion in Caplan, 1985).

No drug appears to cause TGA. The drug clioquinol can cause an episode of temporary memory impairment, sometimes labeled TGA (Mumenthaler et al., 1979; Kaeser, 1984), but the episode is often associated with abnormalities of consciousness, attention or thought (Kaeser, 1984). The drug triazolam, when taken with alcohol, can cause a period of normal behavior that is later not recalled (Morris and Estes, 1987). Such episodes have also been mistakenly called TGA.

Finally, it is unlikely that hydrocephalus, subdural hematoma, arachnoid cyst or subarachnoid hemorrhage causes TGA. Two patients with transient amnesia had otherwise asymptomatic hydrocephalus (Giroud et al., 1987). The first patient probably did not have TGA; he was 20 years old and had anterograde amnesia lasting about 20 minutes following a fall 'on his back.' The second patient was a 47-year-old man who had five episodes of anterograde amnesia over 15 years. Only one of the episodes may have met current criteria for TGA. Cases of probable TGA were also associated with minimally symptomatic bilateral subdural hematomas (Chatham and Brillman, 1985) and with an asymptomatic right anterior temporal arachnoid cyst (Stracciari et al., 1987a). These associations were most likely coincidental. A case reported to have TGA associated with subarachnoid hemorrhage (Sandyk, 1984) did not meet criteria for TGA.

Course and prognosis

Most TGA patients have only a single attack. Because TGA has a recurrence rate of 3 – 5% per year for at least 5 years after the initial episode, some patients will have two or more attacks (Nausieda and Sherman, 1979; Shuping et al., 1980a; Hinge et al., 1986; Miller et al., 1987a). Neither atherosclerotic risk factors nor migraine increase the recurrence rate, although a trend toward a higher incidence of recurrence was noted for migraine patients (Hinge et al., 1986). One report noted that 46% of TGA patients with mitral valve prolapse had recurrent episodes but did not state the duration of follow-up (Jackson et al., 1985).

The patient with TGA does not appear to have an increased risk of developing permanent memory deficit or other cognitive dysfunction (see discussion below). Moreover, TGA patients have an incidence of subsequent stroke equal to the incidence of a comparable population (Hinge et al., 1986; Miller et al., 1987a).

Laboratory investigation

Blood, urine and spinal fluid. Routine tests of blood, urine and spinal fluid are generally normal (Fisher and Adams, 1964; Kushner and Hauser, 1985). One investigator found that a group of TGA patients had a significantly higher hematocrit (the percent of whole blood volume taken up by red cells) than a group of control subjects (Matias-Guiu et al., 1985d). The difference was small, however, and was not confirmed by a difference in absolute red blood cell count. A mild elevation of total cholesterol in TGA patients has been reported (Matias-Guiu et al., 1984), but not confirmed (Crowell et al., 1984). Normal prolactin levels were found in three TGA patients during and after the episode (Matias-Guiu et al., 1985c). In contrast, 43% of patients with a partial complex seizure disorder, a proposed etiology of TGA, had elevated prolactin after a seizure (Wyllie et al., 1984).

Cardiological evaluation. Cardiac abnormalities generally reflect the age of TGA patients. Chest roentgenogram is usually normal but may show cardiomegaly (Fisher and Adams, 1964; Fogelholm et al., 1975; Shuping et al., 1980a; Crowell et al., 1984). Electrocardiogram (EKG) is also usually normal; when abnormal it generally reveals left ventricular hypertrophy or sinus bradycardia (Fogelholm et al., 1975; Shuping et al., 1980a; Crowell et al., 1984; Kushner and Hauser, 1985). Twenty-four-hour ambulatory electrocardiogram has shown sinus bradycardia or minor cardiac arrhythmias in several patients (Shuping et al., 1980a; Crowell et al., 1984).

Two reports suggest that mitral valve prolapse (MVP) may be unusually common in TGA patients. The first found echocardiographic evidence of MVP in two of six patients studied (Crowell et al., 1984). The second noted a 24.5% incidence of MVP in 53 TGA patients compared with a 7.5% incidence of MVP in 53 age- and sex-matched controls (Jackson et al., 1985). This report did not state diagnostic criteria for TGA, however, so patients with amnesic TIA may have been included in the TGA group.

Electroencephalography and event-related potentials. During TGA the electroencephalogram (EEG) is usually normal (Jaffe and Bender, 1966, Miller et al., 1987b). The incidence of nonspecific, nonepileptiform abnormalities, which remain unchanged on follow-up recordings, is appropriate for persons of this age group (Miller et al., 1987b).

The EEG after TGA also shows no significant abnormalities (Miller et al., 1987b). Nonspecific, nonepileptic abnormalities occur with the same frequency as in other patients of the same age. Previous reports of epileptic abnormalities in the EEG of TGA patients were either due to the patients actually having seizures that caused amnesia (Deisenhammer, 1981; Meador et al., 1985) or due to the misinterpretation of benign EEG variants as epileptiform (Greene and Bennett, 1974; Gilbert, 1978; Rowan and Protass, 1979).

The P300 response, a long latency event-related potential that has been linked to cognitive processing, was studied in a single TGA patient (Meador et al., 1988). The response was normal during TGA when compared with the responses one month and two years after TGA, and when compared with the responses of normal subjects.

Neuroimaging. Skull roentgenograms (Fogel-

holm et al., 1975; Shuping et al., 1980a), radionuclide brain scan (Fogelholm et al., 1975; Crowell et al., 1984) and cerebral angiography (Fogelholm et al., 1975; Shuping et al., 1980a; Crowell et al., 1984; Miller et al., 1987a) suggested the presence of atherosclerotic changes in the cerebral vessels of some TGA patients. Nonetheless, noninvasive carotid artery testing showed that atherosclerotic disease occurred less often in 56 consecutive TGA patients than in a group of TIA patients (Feuer and Weinberger, 1987).

Regional cerebral blood flow measured after Xenon 133 inhalation showed abnormal flow in five of seven patients studied 1 to 14 days after TGA (Crowell et al., 1984). The pattern of abnormalities was reported to be similar to changes seen in migraine patients and unlike the pattern of TIA patients. Abnormal flow was seen in different brain regions in different patients, however, and the significance of these data is uncertain.

A single patient was studied during TGA with positron emission tomography (PET) (Volpe et al., 1983). The PET study showed a global decrease in regional cerebral blood flow and oxygen metabolism compared to normal subjects. Moreover, in the medial temporal lobes there was a decrease in oxygen metabolism in excess of the decrease in cerebral blood flow, which suggested focal dysfunction of medial temporal structures during TGA. The PET study was normal one day after the patient's recovery.

The CT head scan after TGA is essentially normal. One report found that 77 of 102 scans obtained after the episode of amnesia were normal and 16 showed only atrophy (Miller et al., 1987a). Five scans revealed stroke, a reasonable number for this age group, and four showed other, incidental lesions. Prior reports of a high incidence of abnormal CT scans in TGA patients included some patients who had amnesia together with associated neurological deficits, presumably due to amnesic TIA or stroke, or to tumor (Shuping et al., 1980a; Ladurner et al., 1982; Crowell et al., 1984; Kushner and Hauser, 1985; Matias-Guiu et al., 1986).

Postmortem examination. One postmortem examination has been reported in a patient who had an episode of TGA 14 years before her death (Miller et al., 1987a). A small, old left parietal infarct and diffuse atherosclerotic vascular changes, particularly in vertebrobasilar vessels, were noted. No pathological findings could be directly related to the TGA.

Differential diagnosis

An episode of temporary isolated amnesia is almost always due to TGA. Nonetheless, other conditions may also produce an episode of transient amnesia.

Concussive head trauma can produce an amnesia identical to that of TGA, but the history or physical examination invariably reveals the true cause of memory impairment (Russell, 1971). Minor head trauma has also been reported to cause an episode of temporary isolated amnesia in a group of patients aged 11 to 28 years (Haas and Ross, 1986). Two of the three cases described in detail had scalp lacerations but one case had no signs of the witnessed head trauma. TGA is uncommon in young patients, and unwitnessed head injury should be suspected in young patients who appear to have TGA.

Whiplash injury of the neck without apparent head trauma or loss of consciousness can produce a syndrome similar to TGA (Fisher, 1982b; Matias-Guiu et al., 1985a; Hofstad and Gjerde, 1985). Two of the reported patients complained of neck pain, and all three had dizziness.

A *TIA* can produce temporary amnesia if brain structures important for memory are affected. Almost always, however, associated neurological findings such as aphasia, visual field defects, eye-movement abnormalities or hemiparesis suggest that a TIA is causing the amnesia. Permanent anterograde amnesia suggests the diagnosis of amnesic stroke (Benson et al., 1974; von Cramon et al., 1985).

A small left *temporal lobe hemorrhage* caused a transient, isolated amnesic syndrome identical to TGA in one patient (Landi et al., 1982). The lesion was located posteriorly and involved either the hippocampus or hippocampal connections.

A *brain tumor* that involves either temporal lobe can very rarely produce an episode of temporary amnesia similar to TGA (Hartley et al., 1974; Findler et al., 1983). Nonetheless, the subsequent development of permanent memory or other neurological deficits differentiates these episodes from TGA.

Epilepsy can occasionally produce episodes of isolated amnesia. In such cases the amnesia generally lasts less than 30 minutes and occurs several times over two or three days (Deisenhammer, 1981; Meador et al., 1985; Miller, 1987b).

A syndrome identical to TGA can occur as a complication of *cerebral angiography,* particularly during study of the vertebrobasilar circulation (Hauge, 1954; Wales and Nov, 1981; Cochran et al., 1982; Pexman and Coates, 1983). It is unlikely that this is an example of physical or psychological stress causing TGA because the amnesia generally develops during, or immediately after, the brief injection of contrast into blood vessels known to supply brain structures important for memory. The relation of this syndrome to TGA is uncertain.

Etiology

None of the proposed etiologies for TGA is entirely satisfactory. Several reports suggested that *epileptic seizures* involving structures important for memory were the likely cause of TGA (Fisher and Adams, 1958; Cantor, 1971; Gilbert, 1978; Fisher, 1982a). Epileptic amnesia is, however, clinically distinct from TGA, and there is no electroencephalographic evidence to support the connection of TGA and epilepsy (Miller et al., 1987b).

It was also hypothesized that TGA could be explained by the experimental phenomenon known as *Leao's spreading depression* (Oleson and Jørgensen, 1986). By this hypothesis, emotional stress causes a release of the neurotransmitter glutamate within the hippocampus that would in turn produce a spreading depolarization of hippocampal cortical neurons. Transient dysfunction of the hippocampus would then result in temporary amnesia. There is no direct support for this hypothesis in the TGA literature.

It is commonly accepted that TGA is caused by a general circulatory disturbance of the brain (Bender, 1956), although different types of disturbance have been considered. For example, *occlusive cerebrovascular disease* (TIA and stroke due to thrombotic or embolic blockage of one or more blood vessels of the brain) was said to be associated with TGA (Kushner and Hauser, 1985) or to cause TGA (Heathfield et al., 1973; Fogelholm et al., 1975; Shuping et al., 1980a). The benign course of TGA, however, makes TIA or stroke an unlikely cause.

Transient *migrainous vasospasm* of posterior circulation vessels was also proposed as a cause of TGA (Caplan et al., 1981; Crowell et al., 1984; Haas and Ross, 1986). This phenomenon could produce benign temporary ischemia of brain structures important for memory but is an unlikely cause of TGA because most TGA patients have neither a history of migraine nor migrainous manifestations during the episode.

Finally, it was hypothesized that TGA was due to *acute arterial dyscontrol* manifested as a transient period of altered vascular tone in the arteries of the vertebrobasilar territory (Caplan, 1985). Because these vessels supply brain structures important for memory, a temporary amnesic syndrome might result. The phenomenon may be similar to migraine, which would explain the occurrence of migrainous manifestations in some TGA patients. At present, this seems to be the most satisfactory explanation for the transient amnesia of TGA.

Evaluation and treatment of the patient

TGA is a benign condition and generally requires no medical treatment (Palmer, 1986; Kritchevsky, 1987). The diagnosis of TGA is made if the patient has a temporary isolated amnesic syndrome as described. If the patient has returned to normal or near normal, he can be reassured and sent home. The patient who is still amnesic at the time of evaluation should be observed in the hospital until he has recovered. Every TGA patient should probably have an elective CT or MRI head scan because of the rare brain tumor or stroke that may cause or be associated with an episode of amnesia. An EEG should be obtained if there is any question that the patient has had an amnesic seizure. An echocardiogram should be obtained if there is evidence of mitral valve prolapse on physical examination.

The patient with a single episode of TGA is generally treated with reassurance only, although some neurologists recommend antiplatelet therapy with aspirin (325 mg/day). Because recovery may not be complete until several days or perhaps weeks after the episode, the patient should be cautioned about engaging in complex business or professional activities for up to 1 month after the episode (Palmer, 1986). The patient with recurrent episodes is often treated with aspirin. If recurrent episodes are associated with headache, a trial of antimigraine prophylaxis is warranted. On the other hand, if recurrent attacks last less than 1 hour, or are associated with paroxysmal EEG abnormalities, then a trial of anticonvulsant therapy is indicated.

Diagnostic criteria for TGA

It seems likely that the majority of patients with a temporary, isolated amnesic syndrome have a single, well-defined, disorder with a specific pathogenesis, clinical picture and prognosis. The following diagnostic criteria attempt to define this disorder, for which the name transient global amnesia should be reserved. In general, the criteria are consistent with those of other authors (Logan and Sherman, 1983; Caplan, 1985). Absence of associated neurological deficits is an important criterion which was either not included (for example, Shuping et al., 1980a; Matias-Guiu et al., 1984; Kushner and Hauser, 1985; Miller et al., 1987a) or not followed (Crowell et al., 1984; Matias-Guiu et al., 1986) by some previous studies.

(1) *The patient with TGA should have an*

amnesic syndrome characterized by normal immediate memory with inability to learn new material. An experienced, knowledgeable observer must see the patient during the attack, or interview an eyewitness of the episode to be certain that this criterion is met. The patient almost always makes repetitive queries, and generally has a variable period of retrograde amnesia extending back several days to many years before the onset of TGA. Very old memories, including personal identity, are preserved.

(2) *The amnesic syndrome should be relatively isolated; there must be no other significant neurological symptoms or signs.* This must be ascertained by an experienced, knowledgeable observer who sees the patient during the attack or interviews an eyewitness of the episode. Essentially all abnormal behavior is accounted for by the amnesia. The patient has a normal level of consciousness and normal responsiveness. During the episode, the patient may be unusually passive, and he may have a headache during or after the attack. Formal neuropsychological examination may reveal other subtle deficits such as inability to copy accurately a complex diagram.

(3) *The onset of the attack should be relatively sudden; there must be no evidence of head trauma, neck trauma, seizure or loss of consciousness; there should be no evidence of transient vertebrobasilar hypoperfusion caused by cardiac arrhythmia, coronary angiography or, perhaps, cerebral angiography.* Ideally, the onset of the attack should be observed by a reliable eyewitness, or the eyewitness should have been nearby in order to rule out otherwise undetected head trauma or loss of consciousness at onset. In practice, the diagnosis is often made without an eyewitness of the onset if careful examination shows no evidence of head or neck trauma and the clinical picture is otherwise consistent with TGA. TGA may occur in relation to some physical or emotional stress such as sexual intercourse, swimming in the cold ocean, or a medical or surgical procedure.

(4) *The episode of amnesia should be transient; patient, family, and physician should agree that there has been complete recovery except for persistent inability to recall events that occurred during TGA and just prior to TGA.* The diagnosis of TGA is suspect in any episode of amnesia lasting less than 1 hour or greater than 24 hours. It is uncertain whether formal neuropsychological testing may demonstrate persistent minor cognitive deficits after recovery from TGA (see below).

(5) *CT or MRI brain scan, if performed, should show no evidence of a lesion which would account for the episode of amnesia.* The rare patient who develops a medial temporal or medial diencephalic lesion with an episode of temporary amnesia should not be diagnosed as TGA.

TABLE 2

TGA cases studied with formal memory tests during and after the episode

Report	No. of subjects	Anterograde tests		Retrograde tests	Studied course of recovery
		Verbal	Nonverbal		
Wilson et al. (1980)	1	+	−	+	−
Regard and Landis (1984)	2	+	+	−	+
Gallassi et al. (1986)	1	+	+	−	+
Stracciari et al. (1987b)	1	+	+	−	+
Kritchevsky et al. (1988)	5	+	+	+	−
Meador et al. (1988)	1	+	+	−	−
Kritchevsky and Squire (1989)	6	+	+	+	−
Hodges and Ward (in press)	5	+	+	+	+

Neuropsychological findings of TGA patients

During TGA

Twenty-two patients have been examined with formal neuropsychological tests during TGA (Table 2). All patients met criteria for TGA, although two were atypical. The first patient may have had amnesia due to whiplash injury (Regard and Landis, 1984, Case 1). He was 40 years old, developed amnesia during gymnastics, and complained shortly after the onset of amnesia that the back of his head was bruised. No injury was witnessed, however, and no signs of trauma were noted on examination. The second patient (Gallassi et al., 1986) may have had a small medial thalamic stroke. Her episode was not completely described, but it was unusually long, appeared to be associated with impairment of attention at the initial neuropsychological testing, and was associated with incomplete recovery. Nonetheless, neurological examination during the episode and CT brain scan during and one month after the episode were normal.

We have tested 11 patients during an episode of TGA (Kritchevsky et al., 1988; Kritchevsky and Squire, 1989). All patients were tested between 2 and 11 hours after the onset of TGA. All patients were amnesic at this time, although in four cases family members stated that the memory problems had begun to improve by the time of testing. Three other patients had some recovery during the testing session.

To establish a baseline against which to judge the extent of recovery, we also tested 10 normal subjects on the tests of anterograde amnesia. These subjects averaged 68.8 years of age (65.4 for the TGA patients) and 12.0 years of education (12.8 for the TGA patients).

Tests of anterograde amnesia.
We assessed anterograde amnesia with three tests: story recall, paired associate learning and diagram recall. Two forms of each of these tests were employed − one during TGA and the other after TGA. We administered the two forms in one order to six of the patients and in the opposite order to the other five patients.

In the *story recall* test, subjects were read a short prose passage (Gilbert et al., 1968) with the instruction, 'When I am finished I want you to tell me as much of it as you can remember.' Immediately thereafter, and again after a delay of 10−20 minutes, subjects attempted to recall the passage. The score was the number of story segments corrected recalled (maximum score = 19 or 21 segments).

In the *paired-associate learning* test, we presented 10 unrelated noun-noun pairs (for example army-table) on index cards at the rate of 6 seconds per pair, on each of three study trials (Jones, 1974). Following each study trial, we asked subjects to recall the second word of each pair upon seeing the first. For each trial the word pairs were presented in a different order. The maximum score for each trial was 10.

In the *diagram recall* test, subjects were asked to copy either the Rey-Osterrieth (Osterrieth, 1944) or Taylor (Milner and Teuber, 1968) diagram. After a 10−20 minute delay, without forewarning, we asked them to draw the diagram from memory. The maximum score was 36 points.

All 11 patients had anterograde amnesia for verbal material. Fig. 1 shows that delayed recall of verbal material on the story recall test was im-

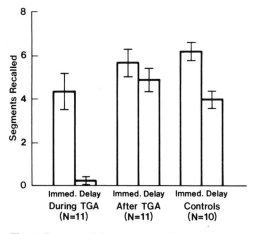

Fig. 1. Story recall by patients during and after TGA and by control subjects. Recall was tested immediately after presentation of the story (immed.) and again after a delay of 10−20 minutes (delay). Brackets show standard errors of the mean. (Data from Kritchevsky et al., 1988, and Kritchevsky and Squire, 1989.)

paired during TGA, both in comparison with performance after TGA ($t(10) = 8.9$, $p < 0.01$) and also in comparison with the performance of control subjects ($t(19) = 9.6$, $p < 0.01$). Similarly, Fig. 2 shows impairment of the ability to learn new verbal material on the paired-associate learning test. A two-way analysis of variance (during or after TGA × three learning trials) showed that learning was impaired during TGA ($F(1,10) = 31.9$, $p < 0.01$). The effect of trials was also significant ($F(2,20) = 38.3$, $p < 0.01$), as was the interaction of TGA × trials ($F(2,20) = 12.2$, $p < 0.01$). The trials effect indicates that learning did occur across trials; the interaction signifies that more learning occurred when memory was tested after recovery from TGA than when memory was tested during the episode. A comparison of the patients tested during TGA with the control subjects also showed that performance was impaired during TGA ($F(1,19) = 26.5$, $p < 0.01$).

All 11 patients also had anterograde amnesia for nonverbal material. Fig. 3 shows that the ability to draw a diagram from memory was markedly impaired during TGA, both in comparison with performance after TGA ($t(10) = 7.0$, $p < 0.01$) and

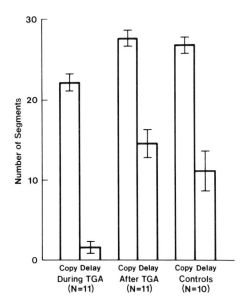

Fig. 3. Copy and recall of a complex figure by patients during and after TGA and by control subjects. Reconstruction of the figure was attempted 10 – 20 minutes after copying it. Brackets show standard errors of the mean. (Data from Kritchevsky et al., 1988, and Kritchevsky and Squire, 1989.)

in comparison with the performance of control subjects ($t(19) = 4.0$, $p < 0.01$).

Four other points concern the anterograde amnesia of TGA patients. First, during TGA the anterograde amnesia of all 11 patients was severe. The test scores of the TGA patients were similar to scores previously obtained by a group of well-studied patients with chronic amnesia (Squire and Shimamura, 1986). Those patients required supervisory care because of the severity of their memory impairment. Second, there appeared to be a correlation of severity of anterograde amnesia with time since onset of TGA. More severe anterograde amnesia may have been present in patients who were tested within 6 hours of the onset of TGA (Kritchevsky and Squire, 1989). Third, there was no evidence for material-specific, or partial, amnesia. None of the patients had a significant disparity between the degree of anterograde amnesia for verbal and nonverbal material. Finally, 11 other patients examined during TGA with various neuropsychological tests of new learning

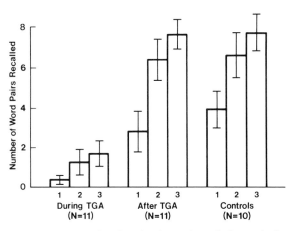

Fig. 2. Paired-associate learning by patients during and after TGA and by control subjects. Ten word pairs were presented on each of three study trials. After each study trial, the first word of each pair was presented, and subjects attempted to recall the second word of the pair. Brackets show standard errors of the mean. (Data from Kritchevsky et al., 1988, and Kritchevsky and Squire, 1989.)

ability were also found to have anterograde amnesia for verbal and, when tested, nonverbal material (Wilson et al., 1980; Regard and Landis, 1984; Gallassi et al., 1986; Stracciari et al., 1987b; Meador et al., 1988; Hodges and Ward, in press). *Tests of retrograde amnesia.* Of the 11 patients we have tested during TGA, 6 were given tests of *recall and recognition of public events* that had occurred from 1950 to 1985 (Kritchevsky and Squire, 1989). These patients were all tested between July 1, 1987, and December 31, 1987. We presented the recall test orally. We then gave the recognition test in a four-alternative, multiple-choice format to be completed by the subject.

Fig. 4 shows that the six patients exhibited a temporally graded retrograde amnesia covering at least 20 years prior to TGA onset. The left panel shows that recall during TGA was impaired compared with recall after TGA for the time periods 1980 – 1985 ($t(5) = 3.9$, $p < 0.05$), 1970 – 1979 ($t(5) = 4.3$, $p < 0.01$) and 1960 – 1969 ($t(5) = 4.6$, $p < 0.01$). Recall for events of the time period 1950 – 1959 was similar during and after TGA ($p > 0.1$). The right panel shows that recognition during TGA was impaired compared with after TGA for the time period 1980 – 1985 ($t(5) = 2.5$,

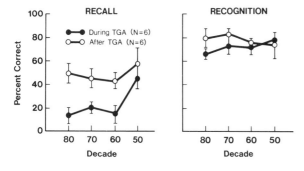

Fig. 4. Performance during and after TGA on public events recall and recognition tests. Patients were asked questions about public events that had occurred from 1950 to 1985 (left panel). They then attempted to recognize the correct answers to the same questions on a four-alternative, multiple-choice test (right panel). Patients were tested in 1987. Brackets show standard errors of the mean. (From Kritchevsky and Squire, *Neurology,* 1989; reprinted with permission.)

$p = 0.05$), but not for the other time periods ($p > 0.1$).

The performance of TGA patients on the public events tests was similar to the performance of other patients with chronic amnesia due to anoxia or ischemia, bilateral thalamic infarctions or Korsakoff's syndrome (Squire et al., 1989). By contrast, the amnesic patient R.B. had no detectable retrograde amnesia as measured by these tests (Zola-Morgan et al., 1986). R.B. had an ischemic brain injury which resulted in a bilateral lesion limited to field CA1 of the hippocampus.

Three of the patients who were given the public events tests were also given a *personalized test of past memory* (Kritchevsky and Squire, 1989). The examiner asked questions concerning specific public or personal events that could be dated either to a recent day or month or to a more remote time period. Patients were asked an average of 81 questions, selected on the basis of their interests and experiences. Only those questions answered correctly after TGA (mean = 67 questions) were considered in the analysis of memory function during TGA. Seventy-nine percent of the questions concerned public events. (These questions were different from those used in the public events recall and recognition tests.) The other 21% of the questions concerned personal events. Questions that could not be answered after TGA were considered to be outside the patient's fund of knowledge.

Table 3 shows that the personalized test of past memory also demonstrated a temporally graded retrograde amnesia. Thus, for the time period 1986 – 1987, only 30% of the 63 memories available after TGA could be recalled during TGA. (Ninety percent of the questions from this time interval concerned events that had occurred from 4 weeks to 1½ years before the onset of TGA.) For the time period 1930 – 1959, 92% of the memories available after TGA could be recalled during TGA. Recall from the intermediate time periods was 52% for 1980 – 1985, 57% for 1970 – 1979, and 79% for 1960 – 1969.

Table 3 also shows that the retrograde amnesia was patchy, inasmuch as all patients were able to recall some events that had occurred within the time interval affected by retrograde amnesia. Indeed, during TGA some memories were recalled, albeit incompletely, which were less than one to two months old. Additionally, Table 3 demonstrates that there was a similar temporally graded retrograde amnesia for both public and personal events.

Hodges and Ward (in press) also found a temporally graded retrograde amnesia in five TGA patients studied between 1984 and 1986 with a famous-faces recall test. Although two patients scored within the normal range during TGA, the other three patients had abnormal recall for faces dating from 1950 to the present. Additionally, when recall for all five patients was compared during and after TGA, memory was most impaired for faces of the 1970s, less impaired for faces of the 1950s and 1960s, and minimally impaired for faces of the 1930s and 1940s. Although these patients performed well during TGA on a recognition test of famous events, retrograde amnesia with a temporal gradient was found when patients attempted to date the events they recognized.

Several additional points concern the retrograde amnesia of TGA patients. First, two patients were reported in whom TGA apparently disrupted childhood memories (Kritchevsky et al., 1988). Second, some examples of incomplete, misdated and missequenced memories were noted (Kritchevsky

et al., 1988). These types of errors were also apparent in clinical interviews of other reported patients with TGA (Regard and Landis, 1984; Gallassi et al., 1986; Stracciari et al., 1987b). Finally, during TGA five patients had a reduced ability to recollect full and detailed autobiographical memories, which was largely attenuated when the examiner probed and questioned the subject (Kritschevsky et al., 1988). This finding may have been related to the unusually passive, quiet personalities exhibited by many of the subjects during the episode.

Tests of other cognitive abilities. The 11 TGA patients we have tested during the episode had a decreased ability to copy a diagram (Fig. 3) (Kritchevsky et al., 1988; Kritchevsky and Squire, 1989). The copy scores were lower during TGA than after recovery from TGA ($t(10) = 4.2$, $p < 0.01$) and they were also lower than the scores obtained by the control group ($t(19) = 3.1$, $p < 0.01$). This decreased ability to copy a diagram provides evidence for cognitive impairment during the episode of TGA separate from, and in addition to, the amnesic syndrome. Nine other patients have been asked to copy a complex diagram during TGA (Regard and Landis, 1984; Stracciari et al., 1987b; Meador et al., 1988; Hodges and Ward, in press). When we scored the two diagrams that were published (Regard and Landis, 1984), we obtained impaired scores similar

TABLE 3

Results of the personalized test of past memory

	1986 – 87	1980 – 85	1970 – 79	1960 – 69	1940 – 59	1930 – 39
Case 1	14% (22)	28% (21)	50% (14)	80% (10)	100% (3)	83% (6)
Case 2	36% (22)	63% (27)	64% (11)	67% (6)	100% (4)	50% (2)
Case 3	42% (19)	61% (18)	60% (5)	100% (3)	100% (2)	100% (7)
Public events	27% (48)	48% (54)	57% (30)	86% (14)	100% (7)	86% (7)
Personal events	40% (15)	67% (12)	– (0)	60% (5)	100% (2)	88% (8)

The percent scores show the proportion of memories that could be recalled from each time period during TGA. The numbers in parentheses indicate the total number of memories queried in each time period that could be recalled after TGA. The row labeled public events sums the data for all questions about public events asked during TGA. The row labeled personal events sums the data for all questions about autobiographical material asked during TGA. Patients were tested in 1987. (From Kritchevsky and Squire, *Neurology*, 1989; reprinted with permission.)

to those of our patients (Kritchevsky et al., 1988).

We asked six patients to name objects depicted in the series of 60 sketches of the Boston Naming Test (Kaplan et al., 1983). The score on the test was the number correct. The same test was given during and after TGA. During TGA, each patient correctly named a normal number of items (mean = 53.0 items). After TGA, each patient scored about one item better (mean = 54.5 items). Three other patients administered the same test of naming also had normal scores during TGA (Hodges and Ward, in press).

With the exception of one atypical patient (Gallassi et al., 1986), all TGA patients have performed normally on all other formal neuropsychological tests. One patient had normal forward digit span, normal immediate recall for a word list and normal verbal fluency (Wilson et al., 1980). Two other patients had normal performance on tests of forward digit span, reverse digit span, verbal fluency, nonverbal fluency and immediate recall of a word list (Regard and Landis, 1984). They also performed normally on the Stroop Color Word Test. Another patient had normal performance on tests of visual attention, forward digit span, spatial span, immediate recall of a word list and immediate recall of visual material (Stracciari et al., 1987b). Reverse digit span was 3 during and 4 after TGA. Three patients performed normally on tests of problem solving and language, four patients had normal verbal fluency, and five had normal forward digit and block-tapping spans (Hodges and Ward, in press). One atypical patient was reported to have impaired performance on a test of attention during TGA and had a reverse digit span of 2 (Gallassi et al., 1986).

During recovery from TGA

Serial neuropsychological testing of nine patients during recovery from TGA demonstrated that (1) deficits were still present when patients first felt completely recovered, (2) patients could be fully recovered as early as 36 hours after the episode, and (3) full recovery might not occur until 72 hours to more than 4 weeks after the onset of TGA. One patient had continued impairment on tasks of spatial supraspan and delayed recall of a diagram 12 hours after TGA although the patient had felt fully recovered for at least several hours (Stracciari et al., 1987b). Thirty-six hours after TGA her neuropsychological performance was normal, and no further change was observed 1 month and 9 months after TGA. Another patient had impaired learning of a list of words 24 and 48 hours after TGA (Gallassi et al., 1986). Her performance on this task was normal 72 hours and 1 month after TGA. Her delayed recall for the list of words improved gradually and was within the normal range 1 month after TGA. The performance of two other patients was significantly improved 24 hours after the onset of TGA, although some impairment of memory continued through the test session 72 hours after the episode (Regard and Landis, 1984). Only when the patients were next tested, 1 month after TGA, did they appear to be fully recovered (Fig. 5). The final five patients still had mild anterograde amnesia 24 hours after TGA onset, although all felt fully recovered (Hodges and Ward, in press). Four of the patients appeared to be recovered 4 weeks after TGA (see Table 2 of Hodges and Ward, in press). The final patient was still mildy impaired 4 weeks after TGA, but appeared recovered when next tested, 6 months after TGA.

After TGA

One month after TGA, permanent retrograde amnesia is often present for events that occurred immediately prior to TGA (Kritchevsky and Squire, 1989). Permanent retrograde amnesia may also be present for some events that occurred as long as three days prior to TGA.

Except for inability to recall events that occurred during the TGA episode or just prior to TGA, patients appear to perform normally on neuropsychological tests after TGA. The 11 patients we studied during TGA had normal ability to learn new verbal and nonverbal material when tested 2 to 35 days after the episode (Figs. 1, 2 and 3) (Kritchevsky et al., 1988; Kritchevsky and Squire,

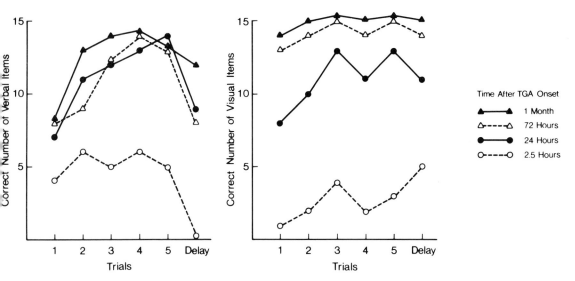

Fig. 5. Verbal and visual recall by a single patient during the course of recovery from TGA. Fifteen words or figures were presented on each of five trials. The subject was asked to recall as many of the words or figures as he could after each trial and after a 40-minute delay. (Adapted from Regard and Landis, 1984.)

1989). Their ability to copy a diagram was also normal after TGA (Fig. 3). Ten additional patients studied during and after TGA also had normal memory when tested 36 hours to 6 months after TGA (Wilson et al., 1980; Regard and Landis, 1984; Stracciari et al., 1987b; Meador et al. 1988; Hodges and Ward, in press). One other TGA patient was examined neuropsychologically 1 year before TGA as part of a study of normal older persons (Stracciari and Morreale, 1987). When tested again 15 months after TGA, his performance on tests of anterograde amnesia was normal and unchanged from the previous testing. Finally, the Wechsler Bellevue verbal and performance IQ of 29 patients studied after TGA was normal compared with the IQ of a control group (Matias-Guiu et al., 1985b; also reported in Matias-Guiu and Codina, 1985).

Other reports of memory impairment after TGA (Mazzuchi et al., 1980; Gallassi et al., 1986) were compromised by methodological problems. Persistent deficits of verbal IQ and verbal long-term memory were reported in 16 subjects studied after TGA (Mazzucchi et al., 1980). Yet the Wechsler Bellevue verbal IQ of these patients, although lower than their performance IQ, was not significantly different from the verbal IQ of the control group. Additionally, several of the TGA patients did not meet current diagnostic criteria for TGA, and two patients were tested within 1 week of the episode. One other patient was reported who could reverse only two digits, made frequent incorrect intrusive responses when learning a list of words, and was said to have an abnormal performance on a serial position curve free recall test when tested 1 month after TGA (Gallassi et al., 1986). Normative data were not presented for the latter test, however, and her decreased recall from the primacy region on that test was not consistent with her normal recall from this region when she was asked to learn a list of words.

Neuroanatomical substrate of TGA

It is likely that TGA is caused by temporary dysfunction of either (1) bilateral medial temporal structures including field CA1 of the hippocampus and adjacent, anatomically related structures, or (2) bilateral medial diencephalic structures including the dorsomedial nucleus of the thalamus, mammillothalamic tract and mammillary bodies. First, the normal memory test scores obtained by TGA patients after the episode indicate that the patients did not have significant preexisting damage to any brain structure important for memory. The fact that TGA patients have normal CT and MRI brain scans supports the lack of preexisting brain damage. Second, the impairment in learning both verbal and nonverbal material during the episode suggests that TGA causes bilateral dysfunction of brain structures important for memory. Third, bilateral lesions of medial temporal (Duyckaerts et al., 1985; Zola-Morgan et al., 1986) or medial diencephalic (Winocur et al., 1984; case 6 of Gentilini et al., 1987) structures may produce a relatively isolated amnesic syndrome similar to the amnesia of TGA. Fourth, because the patient R.B. (Zola-Morgan et al., 1986) had damage limited to field CA1 of the hippocampus but did not exhibit extensive retrograde amnesia, the area of dysfunction in TGA, if medial temporal, must involve more than just the CA1 region of the hippocampus. Additionally, the impairment in copying a complex figure, which appears to be a typical finding in TGA, raises the possibility that TGA is associated with dysfunction of brain regions beyond those responsible for the amnesia.

It has been suggested that some cases of apparent TGA are instead cases of material-specific ('partial') amnesia due to unilateral brain dysfunction (Damasio et al., 1983). Seven patients with transient amnesia have been said to have anterograde amnesia for verbal but not nonverbal material, or to have anterograde amnesia predominantly for verbal material (Damasio et al., 1983; Matias-Guiu and Codina, 1986; Okada et al., 1987). These patients were not tested neuropsychologically during the attack, however, and preservation of nonverbal memory was inferred from the patients' normal recognition of places or faces. Because the 21 patients who were tested neuropsychologically during TGA had anterograde amnesia for both verbal and nonverbal material (Regard and Landis, 1984; Gallassi et al., 1986; Stracciari et al., 1987b; Kritchevsky et al., 1988; Meador et al.,

1988; Kritchevsky and Squire, 1989; Hodges and Ward, in press), the existence of transient, material-specific amnesia remains unproven.

Conclusion

TGA is a benign neurological condition in which the prominent deficit is a temporary amnesic syndrome. Probably caused by transient dysfunction of bilateral medial temporal or medial diencephalic structures important for memory, it is a not uncommon condition that may serve as one more clinical probe of the nature of memory and amnesia.

Acknowledgement

I thank Barbara Reader for assistance in the preparation of the manuscript.

References

Bender MB: Syndrome of isolated episode of confusion with amnesia. *J. Hillside Hosp.: 5*, 212 – 215, 1956.

Benson DF, Marsden CD, Meadows JC: The amnesic syndrome of posterior cerebral artery occlusion. *Acta Neurol. Scand.: 50*, 133 – 145, 1974.

Boudin G, Pépin B, Mikol J, Haguenau M, Vernant JC: Gliome du système limbique postérieur, révélé par une amnésie globale transitoire: observation anatomo-clinique d'un cas. *Rev. Neurol. (Paris): 131*, 157 – 163, 1975.

Cantor FK: Transient global amnesia and temporal lobe seizures (abstract). *Neurology: 21*, 430 – 431, 1971.

Caplan LB: Transient global amnesia. In Frederiks JAM (Editor), *Handbook of Clinical Neurology, Vol. 1(45)*. Amsterdam: Elsevier Science Publishers, Ch. 15, pp. 205 – 218, 1985.

Caplan L, Chedru F, Lhermitte F, Mayman C: Transient global amnesia and migraine. *Neurology: 31*, 1167 – 1170, 1981.

Chatham PE, Brillman J: Transient global amnesia associated with bilateral subdural hematomas. *Neurosurgery: 17*, 971 – 973, 1985.

Cochran JW, Morrell F, Huckman MS, Cochran EJ: Transient global amnesia after cerebral angiography: report of seven cases. *Arch. Neurol.: 39*, 593 – 594, 1982.

Collins MP, Freeman JW: Meningioma and transient global amnesia: another report (letter). *Neurology: 36*, 594, 1986.

Corston RN, Godwin-Austen RB: Transient global amnesia in four brothers. *J. Neurol. Neurosurg. Psychiatry: 45*, 375 – 377, 1982.

Cramon DY von, Hebel N, Schuri U: A contribution to the anatomical basis of thalamic amnesia. *Brain: 108*, 993 – 1008, 1985.

owell GF, Stump DA, Biller J, McHenry Jr LC, Toole JF: The transient global amnesia-migraine connection. *Arch. Neurol.: 41,* 75 – 79, 1984.

amasio AR, Graff-Radford NR, Damasio H: Transient partial amnesia. *Arch. Neurol.: 40,* 656 – 657, 1983.

eisenhammer E: Transient global amnesia as an epileptic manifestation. *J. Neurol.: 225,* 289 – 292, 1981.

onaldson IM: 'Psychometric' assessment during transient global amnesia. *Cortex: 21,* 149 – 152, 1985.

upuis MJM, Pierre PH, Gonsette RE: Transient global amnesia and migraine in twin sisters (letter). *J. Neurol. Neurosurg. Psychiatry: 50,* 816 – 817, 1987.

uyckaerts C, Derouesne C, Signoret JL, Gray F, Escourolle R, Castaigne P: Bilateral and limited amygdalohippocampal lesions causing a pure amnesic syndrome. *Ann. Neurol.: 18,* 314 – 319, 1985.

euer D, Weinberger J: Extracranial carotid artery in patients with transient global amnesia: evaluation by real-time B-mode ultrasonography with duplex doppler flow. *Stroke: 18,* 951 – 953, 1987.

ndler G, Feinsod M, Lijovetzky G, Hadani M: Transient global amnesia associated with a single metastasis in the non-dominant hemisphere: case report. *J. Neurosurg.: 58,* 303 – 305, 1983.

sher, CM: Transient global amnesia: precipitating activities and other observations. *Arch. Neurol.: 39,* 605 – 608, 1982a.

isher, CM: Whiplash amnesia. *Neurology: 32,* 667 – 668, 1982b.

sher CM, Adams RD: Transient global amnesia. *Acta Neurol. Scand.: 40 (Suppl. 9),* 1 – 83, 1964.

isher CM, Adams RD: Transient global amnesia. *Trans. Am. Neurol. Assoc.: 83,* 143 – 145, 1958.

ogelholm R, Kivalo E, Bergström L: The transient global amnesia syndrome: an analysis of 35 cases. *Eur. Neurol.: 13,* 72 – 84, 1975.

rank G: Amnestische Episoden bei Migräne – Ein Beitrag zur Differentialdiagnose der transienten globalen Amnesie (Ictus amnésique). *Schweiz. Arch. Neurol. Neurochir. Psychiatrie: 118,* 253 – 274, 1976.

allassi R, Lorusso S, Stracciari A: Neuropsychological findings during a transient global amnesia attack and its follow-up. *Ital. J. Neurol. Sci.: 7,* 45 – 49, 1986.

entilini M, De Renzi E, Crisi G: Bilateral paramedian thalamic artery infarcts: report of eight cases. *J. Neurol. Neurosurg. Psychiatry: 50,* 900 – 909, 1987.

ilbert GJ: Transient global amnesia: manifestation of medial temporal lobe epilepsy. *Clin. Electroencephalogr.: 9,* 147 – 152, 1978.

ilbert JG, Levee RF, Catalano FL: A preliminary report on a new memory scale. *Percept. Motor Skills: 27,* 277 – 278, 1968.

iroud M, Guard O, Dumas R: Transient global amnesia associated with hydrocephalus: report of two cases. *J. Neurol.: 235,* 118 – 119, 1987.

ordon B, Marin OSM: Transient global amnesia: an extensive case report. *J. Neurol. Neurosurg. Psychiatry: 42,* 572 – 575, 1979.

reene HH, Bennett DR: Transient gloal amnesia with a previously unreported EEG abnormality. *Electroencephalogr. Clin. Neurophysiol.: 36,* 409 – 413, 1974.

Guyotat J, Courjon J: Les ictus amnésiques. *J. Méd. Lyon: 37,* 697 – 701, 1956.

Haas DC, Ross GS: Transient global amnesia triggered by mild head trauma. *Brain: 109,* 251 – 257, 1986.

Hartley TC, Heilman KM, Garcia-Bengochea F: A case of a transient global amnesia due to a pituitary tumor. *Neurology: 24,* 998 – 1000, 1974.

Hauge T: Catheter vertebral angiography. *Acta Radiol. (Suppl.): 109,* 1 – 219, 1954.

Heathfield KWG, Croft PB, Swash M: The syndrome of transient global amnesia. *Brain: 96,* 729 – 736, 1973.

Hinge HH, Jensen TS, Kjaer M, Marquardsen J, Olivarius B: The prognosis of transient global amnesia: results of a multicenter study. *Arch. Neurol.: 43,* 673 – 676, 1986.

Hodges JR, Ward CD: Observations during transient global amnesia: a behavioural and neuropsychological study of five cases. *Brain:* in press.

Hofstad H, Gjerde IO: Transient global amnesia after whiplash trauma (letter). *J. Neurol. Neurosurg. Psychiatry: 48,* 956 – 957, 1985.

Jackson AC, Boughner DR, Bolton CF, Hopkins M, Barnett HJM: Transient global amnesia associated with mitral valve prolapse (abstract). *Neurology: 35 (Suppl. 1),* 215, 1985.

Jaffe R, Bender MB: E.E.G. studies in the syndrome of isolated episodes of confusion with amnesia 'transient global amnesia'. *J. Neurol. Neurosurg. Psychiatry: 29,* 472 – 474, 1966.

Jensen TS, Olivarius B: Transient global amnesia as a manifestation of transient cerebral ischemia. *Acta Neurol. Scand.: 61,* 115 – 124, 1980.

Jones MK: Imagery as a mnemonic aid after left temporal lobectomy: contrast between material-specific and generalized memory disorders. *Neuropsychologia: 12,* 21 – 30, 1974.

Kaeser HE: Transient global amnesia due to clioquinol. *Acta Neurol. Scand.: 70 (Suppl. 100),* 175 – 179, 1984.

Kaplan E, Goodglass H, Weintraub S: *Boston Naming Test.* Philadelphia: Lea & Febiger, 1983.

Kritchevsky M: Transient global amnesia: when memory temporarily disappears. *Postgrad. Med.: 82,* 95 – 100, 1987.

Kritchevsky M, Squire LR: Transient global amnesia: evidence for extensive, temporally graded retrograde amnesia. *Neurology: 39,* 213 – 218, 1989.

Kritchevsky M, Squire LR, Zouzounis JA: Transient global amnesia: characterization of anterograde and retrograde amnesia. *Neurology: 38,* 213 – 219, 1988.

Kushner MJ, Hauser WA: Transient global amnesia: a case-control study. *Ann. Neurol.: 18,* 684 – 691, 1985.

Ladurner G, Skvarc A, Sager WD. Computer tomography in transient global amnesia. *Eur. Neurol.: 21,* 34 – 40, 1982.

Landi G, Giusti MC, Guidotti M: Transient global amnesia due to left temporal haemorrhage. *J. Neurol. Neurosurg. Psychiatry: 45,* 1062 – 1063, 1982.

Lisak RP, Zimmerman RA: Transient global amnesia due to a dominant hemisphere tumor. *Arch. Neurol.: 34,* 317 – 318, 1977.

Logan W, Sherman DG: Transient global amnesia. *Stroke: 14,* 1005 – 1007, 1983.

Mathew NT, Meyer JS: Pathogenesis and natural history of transient global amnesia. *Stroke: 5,* 303 – 311, 1974.

Matias-Guiu J, Codina A: Neuropsychological functions in the follow-up of transient global amnesia (letter). *J. Neurol. Neurosurg. Psychiatry: 48,* 713, 1985.

Matias-Guiu J, Codina A: Transient global amnesia: criteria and classification (letter). *Neurology: 36,* 441 – 442, 1986.

Matias-Guiu J, Davalos A, Antem M, Codina A: High density lipoprotein cholesterol in transient global amnesia (letter). *J. Neurol. Neurosurg. Psychiatry: 47,* 1139 – 1140, 1984.

Matias-Guiu J, Buenaventura I, Cervera C, Codina A: Whiplash amnesia (letter). *Neurology: 35,* 1259, 1985a.

Matias-Guiu J, Davalos A, Codina A: Transient global ischemia (letter). *Stroke: 16,* 132 – 133, 1985b.

Matias-Guiu J, Garcia C, Galdos L, Codina A: Prolactin concentrations in serum unchanged in transient global amnesia (letter). *Clin. Chem.: 31,* 1764, 1985c.

Matias-Guiu J, Masagué I, Codina A: Transient global amnesia and high haematocrit levels (letter). *J. Neurol.: 232,* 383 – 384, 1985d.

Matias-Guiu J, Colomer R, Segura A, Codina A: Cranial CT scan in transient global amnesia. *Acta Neruol. Scand.: 73,* 298 – 301, 1986.

Mazzucchi A, Moretti G, Caffarra P, Parma M: Neuropsychological functions in the follow-up of transient global amnesia. *Brain: 103,* 161 – 178, 1980.

Meador KJ, Adams RJ, Flanigin HF: Transient global amnesia and meningioma. *Neurology: 35,* 769 – 771, 1985.

Meador KJ, Loring DW, King DW, Nichols FT: The P3 evoked potential and transient global amnesia. *Arch. Neurol.: 45,* 465 – 467, 1988.

Miller JW, Petersen RC, Metter EJ, Millikan CH, Yanagihara T: Transient global amnesia: clinical characteristics and prognosis. *Neurology: 37,* 733 – 737, 1987a.

Miller JW, Yanagihara T, Petersen RC, Klass DW: Transient global amnesia and epilepsy: electroencephalographic distinction. *Arch. Neurol.: 44,* 629 – 633, 1987b.

Milner B, Teuber H-L: Alteration of perception and memory in man: reflections on methods. In Weiskrantz L (Editor), *Analysis of Behavioral Change.* New York: Harper & Row, pp. 268 – 375, 1968.

Morris HH, Estes ML: Traveler's amnesia: transient global amnesia secondary to triazolam. *J. Am. Med. Assoc.: 258,* 945 – 946, 1987.

Mumenthaler M, Kaeser HE, Meyer A, Hess T: Transient global amnesia after clioquinol: five personal observations from outside Japan. *J. Neurol. Neurosurg. Psychiatry: 42,* 1084 – 1090, 1979.

Munro JM, Loizou LA: Transient global amnesia – familial incidence (letter). *J. Neurol. Neurosurg. Psychiatry: 45,* 1070, 1982.

Nausieda PA, Sherman IC: Long-term prognosis in transient global amnesia. *J. Am. Med. Assoc.: 241,* 392 – 393, 1979.

Okada F, Ito N, Tsukamoto R: Two cases of transient partial amnesia in the course of transient global amnesia. *J. Clin. Psychiatry: 48,* 449 – 450, 1987.

Olesen J, Jørgensen MB: Leao's spreading depression in the hippocampus explains transient global amnesia: a hypothesis. *Acta Neurol. Scand.: 73,* 219 – 220, 1986.

Osterrieth PA: Le test de copie d'une figure complexe. *Arch. Psychol.: 30,* 206 – 356, 1944.

Palmer EP: Transient global amnesia and the amnestic syndrome. *Med. Clin. N. Am.: 70,* 1361 – 1374, 1986.

Patten BM: Transient global amnesia syndrome. *J. Am. Med. Assoc.: 217,* 690 – 691, 1971.

Pexman JHW, Coates RK: Amnesia after femorocereb angiography. *Am. J. Neuroradiol.: 4,* 979 – 983, 1983.

Regard M, Landis T: Transient global amnesia: neuropsyc ological dysfunction during attack and recovery in two 'pu cases. *J. Neurol. Neurosurg. Psychiatry: 47,* 668 – 672, 198

Rowan AJ, Protass LM: Transient global amnesia: clinical a electroencephalographic findings in 10 cases. *Neurology:* 869 – 872, 1979.

Rumpl E, Rumpl H: Recurrent transient global amnesia in case with cerebrovascular lesions and livedo reticularis (Sne don syndrome). *J. Neurol.: 221,* 127 – 131, 1979.

Russell WR: *The Traumatic Amnesias.* London: Oxfo Univeristy Press, 1971.

Sandyk R: Transient global amnesia: a presentation subarachnoid hemorrhage (letter). *J. Neurol.: 23* 283 – 284, 1984.

Shuping JR, Rollinson RD, Toole JF: Transient glob amnesia. *Ann. Neurol.: 7,* 281 – 285, 1980a.

Shuping JR, Toole JF, Alexander Jr E: Transient glob amnesia due to glioma in the dominant hemisphe *Neurology: 30,* 88 – 90, 1980b.

Shuttleworth EC, Wise GR: Transient global amnesia due arterial embolism. *Arch. Neurol.: 29,* 340 – 342, 1973.

Squire LR, Haist F, Shimamura AP: The neurology memory: quantitative assessment of retrograde amnesia two groups of amnesic patients. *J. Neurosci.: 9,* 828 – 83 1989.

Squire LR, Shimamura AP. Characterizing amnesic patien for neurobehavioral study. *Behav. Neurosci.: 100,* 866 – 87 1986.

Stracciari A, Morreale A: Memory performance before ar after transient global amnesia (letter). *Stroke: 18,* 813 – 81 1987.

Stracciari A, Rebucci GG: Transient global amnesia ar migraine: familial incidence (letter). *J. Neurol. Neurosur Psychiatry: 49,* 716, 1986.

Stracciari A, Ciucci G, Bissi G: Transient global amnes associated with a large arachnoid cyst of the middle crani fossa of the non dominant hemisphere. *Ital. J. Neurol. Sci 8,* 609 – 611, 1987a.

Stracciari A, Rebucci GG, Gallassi R: Transient glob amnesia: neuropsychological study of a 'pure' case. *Neurol.: 234,* 126 – 127, 1987b.

Volpe BT, Herscovitch P, Raichle ME, Hirst W, Gazzanig MS: Cerebral blood flow and metabolism in human amnesi *J. Cereb. Blood Flow Metab.: 3, (Suppl. 1),* S5 – S6, 1983

Wales LR, Nov AA: Transient global amnesia: complication cerebral angiography. *Am. J. Neuroradiol.: 2,* 275 – 27 1981.

Wilson RS, Koller W, Kelly MP: The amnesia of transie global amnesia. *J. Clin. Neuropsychol.: 2,* 259 – 266, 1980

Winocur G, Oxbury S, Roberts R, Agnetti V, Davis C: Amnes in a patient with bilateral lesions to the thalamus. *Neur psychologia: 22,* 123 – 143, 1984.

Wyllie E, Lüders H, MacMillan JP, Gupta M: Serum prolacti levels after epileptic seizures. *Neurology: 34,* 1601 – 160 1984.

Zola-Morgan S, Squire LR, Amaral DG: Human amnesia an the medial temporal region: enduring memory impairmer following a bilateral lesion limited to field CA1 of the hip pocampus. *J. Neurosci.: 6,* 2950 – 2967, 1986.

1989 Elsevier Science Publishers B.V. (Biomedical Division)
ndbook of Neuropsychology, Vol. 3
Boller and J. Grafman (Eds)

CHAPTER 8

Memory deficit after closed head injury

Harvey S. Levin

Division of Neurosurgery, The University of Texas Medical Branch, Galveston, TX 77550, U.S.A.

athophysiology of head injury: implications for emory deficit

osttraumatic amnesia (PTA) and residual disturnce of memory are characteristic features of osed head injury (CHI) which vary in degree and uration according to the severity of trauma. In ontrast to etiologies of memory disorders such as coholic Korsakoff's syndrome and ruptured inacranial aneurysms, CHI primarily affects dolescents and young adults, with an annual indence of about 180 hospital admissions per 00,000 population (Kraus et al., 1984). Males redominate among admissions for head injury ncidence of 247/100,000 versus 111/100,000 for omen), a disparity which reflects their high risk or injury in vehicular accidents and assaults. A te rise in incidence occurs after age 70 due to alls.

Pertinent to clinical assessment of memory eficit after CHI, it is generally agreed that antecent cerebral insults such as previous head injury, lcohol and drug abuse are overrepresented in this roup of patients as compared with the general opulation (Levin et al., 1982). Predisposing ehavioral patterns characterized by disinhibition, npulsivity and sensation-seeking have also been ıggested as contributing factors in at least a ıbgroup of CHI patients. Although investigators ave not analysed the influence of these predisposıg factors, collection of historical information rom consecutive admissions suggests that preexiting problems of sufficient severity to potentially

compromise memory function are present in about 10% to 15% of the cases depending on the population served by the hospital.

Despite recent advances in experimental models of head injury and neuropathological studies, our understanding of the mechanisms of CHI which contribute to impairment of memory is incomplete. Both diffuse cerebral insult and focal intracranial lesions have been implicated in memory problems after CHI (Jennett, 1969). The Glasgow Coma Scale (GCS) of Teasdale and Jennett (1974), which is a widely accepted measure of impaired consciousness, will be referred to as an indicator of severity of injury in the following discussion.

Diffuse brain injury

The frequent occurrence of memory disturbance in CHI patients rendered comatose on impact without evidence of intracranial mass lesion implies that diffuse cerebral insult is contributory (Levin et al., 1982a). Features of diffuse cerebral insult include axonal injury which is produced by the shearing forces on impact and results in degeneration of the white matter (Adams et al., 1982). Following previous neuropathological studies demonstrating ventricular enlargement after severe diffuse injury (Strich, 1956), Levin et al. (1981) measured the ventricle/brain ratio (VBR) for the lateral ventricles from computed tomographic (CT) scans in young adults who had sustained a moderate or severe CHI at least one month earlier. Consistent with the postulation of periventricular white matter degeneration, the investigators found that three-fourths of the head-injured patients had a VBR which exceeded the upper limit of the distribution of ventricular size in a comparison group of age-matched, neurologically intact patients. Moreover, the degree of ventricular enlargement in the head-injured patients was positively related to the presence of a memory deficit.

A second common mechanism of diffuse cerebral insult in CHI is ischemic necrosis, a consequence of reduced cerebral perfusion which is related to increased intracranial pressure arising from cerebral swelling or an expanding mass lesion (Adams et al., 1980). Of relevance to post-traumatic memory disorder, necropsy studies have shown that the hippocampus is a frequent site of ischemic necrosis (Adams et al., 1980). However, the extent to which the hippocampus is damaged in survivors of CHI is unknown. Hypoxia, a complication of head injury frequently related to airway obstruction, may also be a factor in producing hippocampal damage.

Recent investigations using magnetic resonance imaging (MRI) in chronic survivors of severe CHI have raised the question of multifocal lesions primarily involving the parasagittal frontal lobes, the subcortical white matter including the temporal lobes, the corpus callosum and upper brainstem in cases diagnosed as diffuse brain injury (Jenkins et al., 1986; Levin et al., 1985a). Fig. 1 reveals the presence of increased signal intensity in the right temporal lobe of a young woman who had sustained a severe, presumably diffuse brain injury in an automobile accident five years earlier. Consistent with the presumption of diffuse brain injury (Adams et al., 1982), she was rendered comatose (GCS score = 6) immediately on impact and remained in that condition for about a month. Initial and follow-up CT provided no evidence of a focal intracranial mass lesion. Neuropsychological assessment at the time of the MRI scan revealed marked difficulty in recognition memory of recurring, random designs (Kimura, 1963) despite adequate performance on a recognition procedure using line drawings of familiar living things (Hannay

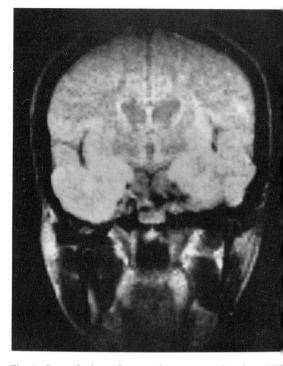

Fig. 1. Coronal view of magnetic resonance imaging (MR) scan shows increased signal intensity in the right temporal lobe of a 24-year-old woman who sustained a severe closed head injury five years previously. The area of increased intensity in the right temporal lobe was also present in the transaxial slice of the MRI scan. Serial CT scans revealed no evidence of a temporal lobe lesion in this patient with a presumably diffuse brain injury. Reproduced from Levin et al. (1985a), with permission from the authors and publisher.

et al., 1979). Although analysis of focal brain lesions by MRI is at an early stage, these preliminary findings raise the possibility that the neuroanatomic localization may be related to memory disturbance. Studies implicating areas of hypometabolism using positron emission tomography might also provide clinicopathological correlation for memory deficit after CHI (Langfitt et al., 1986).

Focal intracranial lesions

Intracranial hematomas and contusions after CHI are most frequently situated in the orbitofrontal and anterior temporal regions (Adams et al., 1980). Temporal lobe lesions have been related to PTA (Jennett, 1969) and residual impairment of memory which differentially affects verbal and nonverbal processing depending on the lateralization of lesion (Alexandre et al., 1979; Levin et al., 1982a). Preliminary findings also raise the possibility that a parenchymal lesion has a more adverse effect on memory function than extradural hematomas (Alexandre et al., 1979). Although the size of focal temporal lobe lesions and contralateral shift of midline structures may also influence the effects on memory, the data bearing on these features of brain injury are preliminary (Levin et al., 1987a). In a series of patients with mild to moderate head injuries who underwent MRI within two weeks of the trauma, we found that the estimated size of temporal lobe lesions was directly related to the degree of memory impairment (Levin et al., 1987a). However, confirmation of a relationship between size of focal lesion and memory disturbance after CHI awaits further investigation.

The relationship between the presence of temporal lobe lesions and both the specificity and persistence of memory disturbance (as distinguished from global cognitive impairment) also depends on the severity of diffuse cerebral insult. Recovery of verbal learning and memory in patients with evacuated left temporal intracerebral hematomas has been documented in patients whose duration of impaired consciousness was confined to periods of less than one week, whereas impairment persisted on similar tests in patients who survived prolonged periods of coma (Levin et al., 1982a).

Effects of severity of closed head injury on long-term memory

In studies of long-term memory assessed after a relatively uniform postinjury interval, a moderate relationship between duration of impaired consciousness and degree of impairment has emerged (Brooks, 1972, 1974a,b, 1975, 1976: Levin et al., 1979a; Lezak, 1979; Parker and Serrats, 1976; Schacter and Crovitz, 1977). Table 1 summarizes the results of studies which have analysed various indices of brain injury. The GCS score (typically recorded after resuscitation or the lowest score) has been employed in some studies primarily to select the patients according to the initial impairment of consciousness. As indicated in Table 1, durations of coma (not necessarily measured by the Glasgow Scale) and PTA have been used by other investigators to evaluate severity of injury. Duration of impaired consciousness has emerged as the most consistently reported correlate of impaired memory, with correlation coefficients typically accounting for approximately one-third of the variance in test performance. However, the procedure for assessing duration of impaired consciousness in most of the studies listed in Table 1 is unclear. Although Levin and co-workers (1979) specified use of the GCS to select cases of severe head injury and they defined duration of impaired consciousness according to the resumption of obeying commands, most investigations listed in Table 1 did not mention the Glasgow Scale and failed to specify the method for evaluating coma. Retrospective estimates of PTA duration in these studies typically reflected both the duration of coma and period of marked anterograde amnesia without differentiating these components (Brooks, 1972, 1974a,b, 1975, 1976). In view of these differences across studies in the methods for evaluating severity of injury, variability in the relationship of these indices to long-term memory is to be expected (Table 1).

Potential bias has been introduced by the selection of patients capable of undergoing memory assessment and severity has been frequently confounded with chronicity of injury (e.g., longer intervals between trauma and testing necessitated by more severe injuries) in some studies. Failure to exclude (or at least identify and analyse separately) patients with antecedent cerebral insult (e.g., previous head injury, alcohol or drug abuse) might also account for variability in the relationship between neurological indices of CHI and memory function across the studies summarized in Table 1. Relatively small sample sizes comprising heterogeneous injuries (i.e., diffuse, focal injuries) have also conspired to attenuate the effects of indices of severity such as duration of PTA. In conclusion, the studies summarized in Table 1 are

TABLE 1

Summary of studies analysing effects of neurological indices of closed head injury on long-term memory

Study	Measure of memory	n	Mean injury interval	GCS score	Duration of coma	Duration of PTA	CT/ MRI	Neuro deficit	Findings concerning severity of injury
Brooks (1972)	Prose recall, paired associates, Rey figure, continuous recognition	27	7 months			+			Significant correlation of PTA with all memory scores in patients older than 30 years, but not in younger cases (age effect)
Brooks (1974a, b)	Visual recognition memory	34	12.0 months			+		+	PTA duration related to deficient recognition memory using total correct or d'
Brooks (1975)	Free recall digit span	30	15 months			+		+	No relation to severity
Brooks (1976)	Wechsler Memory Scale	82	13.1 months			+		+	PTA durations up to one month were related to poor performance on all subtests except digit span forward and errors on Mental Control of Wechsler Memory Scale
Gronwall and Wrightson (1979)	Wechsler Memory Scale, selective reminding	71	4 days for mild cases, 26 days for more severe injuries			+			PTA duration > 24 hours related to lower Memory Quotient. Effects were most evident for prose recall and paired-associate learning, but minimal for digit span. PTA duration was related to storage, but not retrieval measure of selective reminding
Hannay et al. (1979)		47	1.8 months		+		+	+	Duration of coma was positively related to impaired visual recognition memory

ABLE 1 *(continued)*

tudy	Measure of memory	n	Mean injury interval	GCS score	Duration of coma	Duration of PTA	CT/ MRI	Neuro deficit	Findings concerning severity of injury
evin et al. 1987a)	Selective reminding	20	8.8 days	used to select mild and moderate injuries			+		Size of temporal lobe lesion estimated by MRI was negatively correlated with long-term memory
evin et al. 1976)	Short-term visual recognition	24	Post-PTA		+			+	Duration of coma and oculovestibular deficit were related to defective recognition of random designs
evin et al. 1979a)	Selective reminding	27	12.6 months	used to select patients in coma on admission	+			+	Impaired verbal learning and memory related to duration of coma, oculovestibular deficit and hemiparesis
ezak (1979)	Rey's Auditory-Verbal Learning Test	24	0 – 6, 7 – 12 13 – 24 and 25 – 36 months		+				Percentage of patients with abnormal verbal learning/memory was greater for group who were unconsciousness longer than two weeks vs. patients with briefer periods of impaired consciousness
Parker and errats (1976)	Free recall of 10 lists of words	108	1 – 24 months		+				Percentage of patients with abnormal verbal recall was directly related to the duration of PTA. The percentage of patients with abnormal verbal memory improved up to 12 months with only slight change up to 24 months

CT = computed tomography; CGS = Glasgow Coma Scale; MRI = magnetic resonance imaging; PTA = posttraumatic amnesia.

generally in agreement that residual memory deficit is unusual for CHI patients who are briefly unconscious (e.g., one or two hours), while memory disturbance is far more likely to persist in patients with long periods of impaired consciousness (e.g., one month). Prospective, serial assessment of impaired consciousness using the Glasgow Scale is likely to impart greater reliability among examiners in evaluating severity of injury and presumably more robust prediction of memory deficit. At the same time, preliminary findings using new techniques for neuroimaging indicate that intracranial mass lesions situated in the temporal lobes may be related to memory problems (which persist for at least three months) in patients with moderate head injury (Levin et al., 1987a). Future research using the GCS together with prospective measurement of PTA and other neurological findings (e.g., integrity of eye movements and pupillary reactivity) could better elucidate the relationship between indices of brain injury and recovery of memory function.

Posttraumatic and retrograde amnesia

Posttraumatic amnesia
In 1932 Ritchie Russell initially characterized the postinjury interval preceding restoration of memory for ongoing events as the 'loss of full consciousness' which included the duration of coma. This formulation of PTA evolved from a condition of disturbed consciousness (Russell and Nathan, 1946) to emphasize anterograde amnesia, i.e., a period during which 'current events have not been stored' (Russell and Smith, 1961). In addition to the marked anterograde amnesia during the initial stage of recovery after resolution of coma, PTA also involves a variable constellation of behavioral disturbances including defective attention, agitation, lethargy, inappropriate and disinhibited behavior, confusion and incoherent speech.

Russell and his colleagues assessed PTA by questioning 1000 patients who had been evacuated to the Military Hospital for Head Injury in Oxford. These investigators estimated the duration of PTA

based on an interview in which the patient indicated the point when continuous memory for ongoing events was first restored. Although this technique has yielded prognostically useful information concerning resumption of daily activities (Russell and Smith, 1961), it is frequently difficult to distinguish between actual memory for events during the initial hospitalization and information subsequently provided by the nursing staff or families . 'Islands' (i.e., fragments) of relatively preserved memory for events during the period of presumed PTA further complicate efforts to collect reliable data on a retrospective basis. In fact, Gronwall and Wrightson (1980) reported that retrospective estimates of PTA duration were frequently discrepant from reports given by the patient during early stages of recovery.

Given that disorientation is characteristic of PTA, Russell (1971) recommended use of the 'return of orientation' to define the end of this initial stage of recovery. To evaluate the concurrence between anterograde amnesia and disorientation, Gronwall and Wrightson (1980) serially interviewed a consecutive series of patients with mild head injury whom they initially studied in the emergency room (an average interval of less than two hours postinjury). The investigators found an overall relationship between return of continuous memory (i.e., accurate recall of ongoing events related to medical treatment) and recovery of orientation, but there was a sufficient number of dissociations (e.g., impaired recall of ongoing events despite normal orientation) to question the functional equivalence of disorientation and PTA. Although it is unclear whether a similar dissociation occurs after severely injured patients have emerged from coma, clinical experience suggests that marked disorientation and impaired memory are closely linked during the early stages of recovery following coma. In any case, the sequence of cognitive changes during PTA warrants further study.

In view of the aforementioned problems in the retrospective estimate of PTA, investigators have developed quantitative techniques to evaluate PTA beginning when the patient is able to obey com-

TABLE 2

Questions comprising the Galveston Orientation and Amnesia Test

GALVESTON ORIENTATION AND AMNESIA TEST (GOAT)	Error points

1. What is yout name? (2) _____   _____

   Where were you born? (4) _____   _____

   Where do you live? (4) _____   _____

2. Where are you now? (5) city _____   _____

   (5) hospital _____   _____

   (unnecessary to state name of hospital)

3. On what date were you admitted to this hospital? (5) _____   _____

   How did you get here? (5) _____   _____

4. What is the first event you can remember after the injury? (5) _____   _____

   Can you describe in detail (e.g., date, time, companions) the first event you can recall after injury?

   (5) _____   _____

5. Can you describe the last event you recall before the accident? (5) _____   _____

   Can you describe in detail (e.g., date, time, companions) the first event you can recall before the in-

   jury? (5) _____   _____

6. What time is it now? _____ (1 for each ½ hour removed from correct   _____

   time to maximum of 5)

7. What day of the week is it? _____ (1 for each day removed from cor-   _____

   rect one)

8. What day of the month is it? _____ (1 for each day removed from   _____

   correct date to maximum of 5)

9. What is the month? _____ (5 for each month removed from correct   _____

   one to maximum of 15)

10. What is the year? _____ (10 for each year removed from correct one   _____

   to maximum of 30)

Adapted from Levin et al. (1979b) with permission from authors and publisher.

mands (Fortuny et al., 1980; Levin et al., 1979b). These brief bedside examinations assess orientation to time, place and person and recall of information pertaining to the circumstances of injury and hospital admission. A limitation of these techniques for serial monitoring of PTA is that inattentiveness, distractibility and other behavioral manifestations are not specifically tested.

The Galveston Orientation and Amnesia Test (GOAT) of Levin et al. (1979b) was derived from a previously developed questionnaire of temporal orientation (Benton et al., 1964) which was expanded to include items pertaining to orientation to person, place and circumstances and a detailed description of the first postinjury memory and the last event before the injury (Table 2). Although these latter items are difficult to verify, they provide traditional measures of PTA and retrograde amnesia. Error points for each question (shown in parenthesis) are summed and the total is deducted from 100 to yield a total GOAT score. Based on the distribution of scores in young adults who had recovered from mild head injury, various levels of performance on the GOAT were defined (e.g., the normal range corresponded to a GOAT score of 75 – 100).

A recovery curve depicting resolution of PTA is derived from serial scores obtained through daily administration of the GOAT (Fig. 2). Levin et al. (1979b) operationally defined duration of PTA as the interval during which the GOAT score is below 75 (corresponding to the eighth percentile of the standardization group). Accordingly, they employed a chi-square analysis to show that severity of initial CHI as reflected by the GCS score was strongly related to the duration of PTA measured by the GOAT. In a series of 50 severely injured patients studied serially with the GCS and GOAT during the pilot phase of the National Institute of Neurologic Diseases and Stroke's Coma Data Bank, Levin and Eisenberg (1986) obtained a Spearman rank order correlation of 0.44 ($p < 0.001$) between the duration of coma and duration of PTA. A similar technique for measuring PTA was developed by Fortuny et al. (1980)

which includes a brief picture-recall test and recall of the examiner's name. These investigators defined the termination of PTA as the point when the patient had had three consecutive days of correct recall.

By utilizing the GOAT to assess 31 neurosurgery inpatients recovering from head injury, Levin et al. (1987c) recently compared the rate of forgetting in relation to PTA. Initial learning was controlled on a visual recognition memory test by presenting colored slides for longer durations to patients in PTA as compared to the exposure durations used for patients who had GOAT scores above 75 (out of PTA) and normal subjects. Despite disorientation and confusion, this technique permitted most patients tested during PTA to reach a criterion of initial acquisition on a recognition memory test administered 10 minutes after the presentation series. However, retesting at 2 hours and 32 hours following the presentation series revealed more rapid forgetting in patients studied during PTA as com-

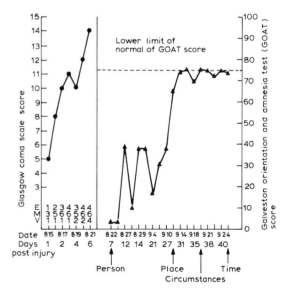

Fig. 2. Serial scores on the Galveston Orientation and Amnesia Test depicting gradual resolution of posttraumatic amnesia after a severe head injury complicated by bifrontal contusions. Note the stages of reorientation to biographic information place, time and circumstances of injury. The marked anterograde amnesia was accompanied by confabulation concerning the reasons for hospitalization and disinhibited behavior which eventually improved.

pared to head-injured cases tested after resolution of PTA and normal controls. These results are consistent with findings obtained using a similar technique which also showed rapid forgetting following a course of electroconvulsive therapy (Squire, 1981). Other parallels between PTA and the amnesia produced by electroconvulsive therapy have been described (Crovitz, 1987).

Retrograde amnesia

Retrograde amnesia (RA) refers to the abolition of memory for events before the injury. In contrast to PTA, which frequently extends for periods exceeding several hours (if not days) in moderate to severe CHI, Russell and Nathan (1946) found that the retrograde effects of amnesia rarely exceeded 30 minutes except in cases of quite severe injury. However, persistent RA extending over a period of 20 years before a severe CHI was recently documented in a case study of a patient who sustained right hemisphere and mesencephalic lesions (Goldberg et al., 1981). The phenomenon of shrinking RA, which refers to a progressive reduction in the preinjury interval for which the patient is amnesic, was first reported in 1932 by Russell. He described a head-injured patient during PTA who initially exhibited an RA that extended nine years into the past. Over a period of 10 weeks, the patient gradually recollected events in the remote past, beginning with the earliest memories until his recall of past events had recovered to within a few minutes of the accident. Similar parallels between the sequential recovery of remote memory and the resolution of PTA have been confirmed (Benson and Geschwind, 1967; Russell and Nathan, 1946). These clinical reports provide support for the law of regression as formulated by Ribot (1882), which holds that the susceptibility of memory to disruption is inversely proportional to its age.

To evaluate the possibility of relative sparing of the oldest memories of CHI patients during PTA, Levin et al. (1985b) revised a recognition memory test (Squire and Slater, 1975) for titles of former television programs. This technique maintained the level of item difficulty across time periods. To

modify this test for use with young head-injured patients, the investigators deleted the oldest television programs. The revised questionnaire was administered orally while presenting each item on an index card to CHI patients who were in PTA (i.e., GOAT score < 75) and a second head-injured group whose PTA had resolved as reflected by sustained increments of their GOAT scores above 75. To mitigate the effects of attentional deficit, only 10 of the 30 questionnaire items were administered in each session. Fig. 3 depicts the percentage of correct recognition of the names of television programs plotted against the time period during which they were broadcast. Head-injured patients consistently recognized fewer programs than the control group irrespective of the time period. As shown in Fig. 3, there was no consistent temporal gradient compatible with sparing of the oldest memories in the CHI patients, as their performance paralleled the pattern obtained in the control group.

Admittedly, assessment of memory for titles of previous television programs might have questionable relevance to long-term retention of more

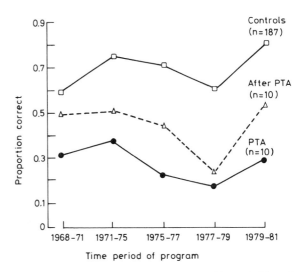

Fig. 3. Mean proportion of correct recognition of titles of television programs plotted across the time period of broadcast for patients tested after resolution of PTA as compared to head-injured patients assessed during PTA and control subjects. Reproduced from Levin et al. (1985b), with permissioin from the authors and publisher.

personally salient information. In the same investigation, Levin et al. (1985) assessed recall of autobiographical events (e.g., names of previous teachers) sampled from various periods of the patient's life and verified by interviewing a relative. In contrast to the television questionnaire, it was not feasible to control for variation in item difficulty across the time periods encompassed by the autobiographical memory interview. As depicted in Fig. 4, recall of autobiographical events was characterized by a temporal gradient, with selective sparing of the earliest memories. The investigators interpreted the dissociation between these two measures of remote memory as support for the relative invulnerability of older memories which become integrated into a semantic framework.

The results for remote memory using the television program technique are at variance with

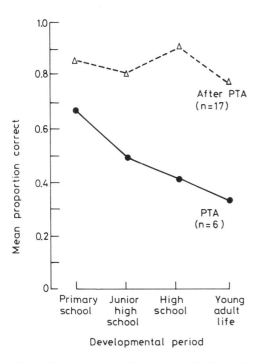

Fig. 4. Mean proportion of correct recall of autobiographical events plotted against developmental periods for head-injured patients assessed or studied during PTA versus after PTA. Reproduced from Levin et al. (1985b), with permission from the authors and publisher.

previous findings of relative sparing of the oldest memories in patients with alcoholic Korsakoff's syndrome (Albert et al., 1979). It is conceivable that Korsakoff patients have a progressive disruption of learning new material which results in a temporal gradient characterized by a disproportionate impairment of memory for relatively recent events. In contrast, CHI produces an immediate onset of RA which affects previously learned material and is relatively uniform across time periods (Levin et al., 1985). By confining studies to young survivors of CHI without previous neuropsychiatric disorder, it is plausible to assume that their preinjury learning and retention capabilities were normal (Levin et al., 1985). At the same time, it must be acknowledged that general cognitive impairment might tend to disrupt retention of remote information equivalently across time periods and thereby attenuate a temporal gradient in RA. However, the lack of evidence for sparing of the oldest memories in CHI patients given the television test is at variance with the finding of a temporally graded RA in depressed patients given a similar test following a course of electroconvulsive therapy (Squire and Cohen, 1979; Squire et al., 1975). Squire and colleagues found that information about television programs acquired one to three years previously was disrupted by the electroconvulsive treatment, whereas retention of material pertaining to programs broadcast earlier was unaffected. Application of other techniques to evaluate remote memory could further elucidate the type of material for which a temporal gradient is present after CHI.

Mechanisms of posttraumatic and retrograde amnesia

It is plausible to postulate that encoding and storage of information are compromised during PTA, but failure at these stages of long-term memory (i.e., a relatively stable, potentially permanent memory with a high capacity for retention of information) can hardly account for RA. Impaired memory for events which occurred shortly before injury could conceivably be attributed to isruption of ongoing memory storage. Inability to ecall or recognize material which was acquired ong before the head injury implies difficulty in etrieval because of the ample time for consolida- ion. In this context consolidation refers to the process by which memory gradually becomes resis- ant to disruption by an amnesic agent (Squire, 987). Further research is necessary to elucidate he mechanisms of PTA and RA, including onverbal measures and assessment of the con- ribution of attentional problems. Given the precisely defined onset of PTA following CHI, this venue of investigation offers an opportunity to est hypotheses concerning the formation and lissolution of memory.

Residual disorder of memory after head injury

Resolution of PTA is characterized by clearing of onfusion, reorientation and improved memory or ongoing events such as ongoing therapy ses- ions and other aspects of the hospital environ- ment. Although head-injured patients may exhibit no obvious memory deficit during an interview fter resolution of PTA, quantitative evaluation requently demonstrates a residual deficit in long- erm memory. Whether memory is dispropor- ionately impaired relative to other cognitive apacities or secondarily affected by attentional problems remains unclear (Schacter and Crovitz, 977).

The degree and persistence of memory deficit end to be related to the severity of acute head in- ury (Russell, 1971). Based on examination of ,766 servicemen who had sustained CHI during World War II (including 266 consecutive admis- ions within three days of injury and 239 relatively nselected cases admitted within three weeks of CHI), Russell (1971) found that 23% had a esidual memory deficit. This figure was increased o about 55% in a subgroup who had initial dura- ions of PTA which exceeded a week. However, confirmation of this estimate (which was presumably based on a neurological examination nd presenting complaints) requires administration of tests of long-term memory to consecutive CHI cases for whom prospective clinical data on neurological indices of injury are available. Con- secutive admissions of head-injured patients (with exclusion of cases at risk for memory deficit because of preinjury neuropsychiatric disorder) provide data more representative of the CHI population than patients who are referred for neuropsychological evaluation or rehabilitation because of persistent complaints or disability. Data obtained on the selective reminding and paired- associate tests about one month after predomin- antly moderate head injuries (e.g., PTA duration < 1 month) indicate that about one-fourth of the patients exhibit a residual memory deficit (Gron- wall and Wrightson, 1981).

Short-term memory

Short-term (or immediate) memory has been studied primarily by assessment of forward digit span. Backward digit span, which necessitates that the patient hold the numbers in memory before repeating them, engages long-term memory. Con- sequently, this section is confined to studies which evaluated forward digit span (apart from backward digit span) by determining the longest string of digits which the patients could recall in correct sequence.

Ruesch (1944) serially studied forward digit span in 53 patients during their initial hospitalization for CHI. Although measures of coma or PTA were not employed, the clinical description provided by the authors suggests that these samples were of predominantly mild to moderate head injuries. The term mild CHI as used here is denoted by brief (< 20 minutes) or no loss of consciousness, an ad- mission GCS score which ranges from 13 (i.e., con- fused, disoriented) to 15 (oriented in all spheres) without deterioration in level of consciousness, in- tracranial lesions detected by computed tomography (CT), neurological deficits or com- plications (e.g., shock, hypoxia). In contrast, moderate CHI is characterized by impaired con- sciousness (e.g., eyes open, but unable to obey commands) corresponding to a GCS score of

9 – 12 on admission without deterioration to a comatose level (i.e., GCS score < 8). Ruesch compared the mean forward span of 5.8 within 24 hours of injury to results obtained four to 12 weeks later (mean = 6.2) and found only slight improvement. Consequently, the authors inferred that forward span was relatively unaffected by the injury. Early recovery of forward digit span has since been confirmed, primarily in patients studied relatively early after mild head injury. Cronholm and Jonsson (1957) found that forward digit span was comparable in mildly head-injured patients (mean = 5.2 digits) to the results obtained in a control group of hospitalized patients matched on age and education (mean = 5.0 digits). Brooks (1972, 1975) compared the forward digit span of patients who sustained CHI of varying severity and were tested at different intervals following injury. In contrast to the generally impaired long-term memory exhibited by these patients as compared to control subjects, forward digit span was relatively well preserved (e.g. 6.5 digits vs. 6.7 in a control group reported in the 1975 paper). An exception to the general recovery of short-term auditory recall following CHI is the finding by Thomsen (1977) that auditory digit span was still reduced more than two years after severe injury in patients with residual aphasia. However, nonaphasic CHI cases assessed in the same study had a normal digit span.

In summary, short-term (or immediate) memory, as measured by forward digit span, is comparatively resistant to the effects of CHI. Patients sustaining mild injury may exhibit no evidence of reduced forward digit span even when tested early after hospital admission. Although digit span is disturbed during initial stages of recovery from more severe injury, persistent deficit is primarily confined to backward span and short-term visual memory.

Residual impairment of long-term memory
Verbal learning and memory. The distinction between short- and long-term memory was investigated by Brooks (1975) in CHI patients and control subjects whom he tested on a free recall

task (i.e., recall of a list of words in any order immediately after presentation). As depicted in Fig 5, normal subjects characteristically exhibit a 'recency effect' in which the probability of recall i highest for the items at the end of the list and decreased for words occupying positions in the middle of the list. Recall from the terminal portion of the word list is presumed to depend on short term memory, whereas long-term memory mediates recall from the midportion of the list because of the longer retention interval and the in terference from both earlier and later words Recall of words from the initial portion of the list which is free of proactive interference, tends to be better than for words in the middle of the list.

Evidence for a dissociation between short-term and long-term memory on this task was provided in a study of amnesic patients (primarily Korsakof cases) by Baddeley and Warrington (1970). These investigators found that the magnitude of memory impairment was greatest for words at the beginning of the list (long-term memory), whereas retention was relatively normal for words presented las (short-term memory). To analyse short-term and

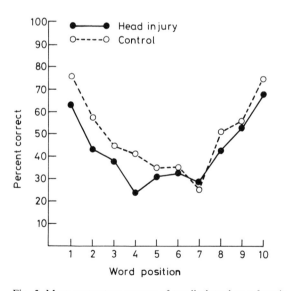

Fig. 5. Mean percentage correct of recall plotted as a function of word position for closed head injured and control patients Reproduced from Brooks (1975), with permission from the author and publisher.

long-term memory components in the free recall of CHI patients, Brooks (1975) employed the method of Tulving and Colotla (1970), which classifies a word according to the number of intervening presentations by the examiner and other words recalled by the subject (retention interval) on each trial. Accordingly, retention of a word which followed a total of seven or fewer intervening words (either presented or recalled) was defined as short-term memory, whereas long-term memory corresponded to an interval of eight or more words. Under this classification, Brooks found that short-term recall for the CHI patients did not differ from the performance of the control group. In contrast, Fig. 5 shows that there was an unequivocal long-term memory deficit in the head-injured cases.

Utilizing the Selective Reminding Test (Buschke and Fuld, 1974), Levin et al. (1979a) reported that the degree of long-term memory impairment one year after severe head injury corresponds to the overall level of disability in survivors. Patients who had attained a good recovery (i.e., resumption of work and normal social functioning) consistently recalled words without further reminding (which is interpreted by Buschke and Fuld as evidence for retrieval from long-term memory) at a level comparable to that of normal adults. In contrast, consistent recall was grossly impaired in patients who were moderately or severely disabled at the time of the study. The investigators interpreted the inconsistency in recall of words over trials by the disabled groups as evidence for impaired organization of memory and inefficient search process associated with retrieval. Investigation of this feature of verbal learning and memory after CHI is discussed in a later section of this chapter.

Verbal learning and memory have also been studied following mild CHI as defined by GCS score ranging from 13 on admission to the hospital (i.e., a confused, disoriented state) to 15 (intact orientation). In a three-center investigation of patients admitted for mild CHI uncomplicated by multiple trauma requiring surgery or previous neuropsychiatric disorder, Levin et al. (1987b) ad-

ministered a modified version of the Selective Reminding Test (Mattis and Kovner, 1978) at baseline (following resolution of PTA), one month and three months after injury. This eight-trial selective reminding procedure consisted of 20 names of animals with probe recognition trials presented after recall trials four and eight. As depicted in Fig. 6, consistent long-term retrieval (i.e., consistent recall of words) summed across trials was initially impaired in each of the mild head-injury groups as compared to a control group of normal subjects matched on demographic features. In contrast to the residual difficulty in long-term memory frequently present in severely injured patients, Fig. 6 shows considerable improvement by one month after mild CHI. Verbal learning and memory, which closely approximated the level of normal controls by one month after mild head injury, improved only slightly between one and three months in a subgroup of patients tested a third time. Although it is conceivable that practice effects contributed to the observed improvement in the patients by one month after mild CHI, this explanation by itself appears insufficient given the persistent impairment of long-term memory in repeatedly tested patients sustaining more severe CHI.

Notwithstanding the finding of impressive recovery of long-term memory within the first one to three months after a mild head injury, a recent report has documented that mild head injury producing no loss of consciousness is sufficient to immediately precipitate an episode of transient global amnesia for periods of up to 24 hours (Haas and Ross, 1986). These amnesic episodes were accompanied by temporal disorientation and repeated queries by the patient concerning the present circumstances despite apparently preserved alertness and language. While atypical for mild head injury producing minimal or no loss of consciousness, the nine cases described by Haas and Ross developed extensive RA for periods of one day to a month before injury. Although the authors suggested that posttraumatic transient global amnesia may be related to distinctive pathophysiological features (e.g., migrainous phenomena) of head trauma in young persons (all nine patients were in the pediatric or young adult age range), the incidence of CHI peaks during this period of life. Whether predisposing conditions in these patients interacted with the mild trauma to produce their lengthy amnesia is unclear.

Organization of verbal memory
Semantic features. In contrast to the aforementioned studies reporting impaired long-term verbal memory in head-injured patients, there are relatively sparse data concerning qualitative features which characterize their amnesic disorder. In a case study of a patient who sustained a severe head injury 19 years earlier, Zatorre and McEntee

(1983) found that he had deficient semantic encoding despite an average level of verbal intelligence. This patient, who had CT evidence of lesions in the frontal and temporal lobes, failed to exhibit the usual release from proactive inhibition when the semantic category was shifted for triads of words presented on each trial. Consistent with this finding, he showed no facilitation of recognition memory under a condition in which he was asked questions about the semantic category of the word as compared to questions concerning the rhyme or physical appearance of the word (i.e. upper vs. lower case letters).

Levin and Goldstein (1986) studied the organization of memory after CHI by using a method developed by Weingartner et al. (1983) to

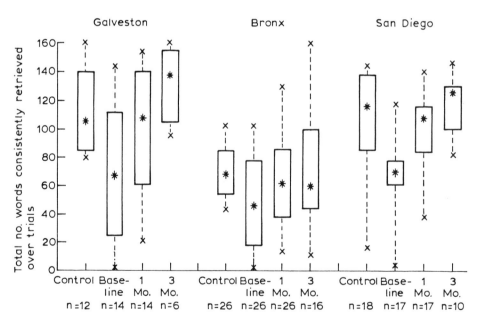

Fig. 6. Box plots showing the distribution of consistent retrieval of words from long-term memory for the control and mild head-injury groups studied at three university hospitals. Each asterisk signifies the median, while the upper and lower horizontal lines of each bar indicate the 75th and 25th percentile scores, respectively. The maximum and minimal scores are depicted by the letter 'x'. Distributions of scores are given for the head-injured groups at baseline (one week postinjury), at one month and three months after injury. Reproduced from Levin et al. (1987b), with permission from authors and publisher.

aracterize various forms of memory failure.
eingartner et al. (1981, 1983) found that patients
th degenerative dementia exhibited no enhance-
ent of memory under a condition which pro-
oted semantic organization in normal subjects.
vin and Goldstein (1986) applied similar techni-
es to chronic survivors of severe CHI who were
rolled in a residential rehabilitation program.
though both the patients and a control group of
mparable age and education exhibited improved
all of word lists consisting of semantically
ated words (i.e. exemplars of categories such as
rts of a house) presented in a clustered format
e. parts of a house, fruits, animals), there was a
sparity between the performance of the two
oups under a condition in which nouns drawn
om the same categories were presented in a ran-
mized order (i.e., unclustered, related lists).

In response to this unclustered, but related word
t, control subjects tended to spontaneously
ganize their recall by grouping the words. As
picted in Fig. 7, the head-injured patients less
equently utilized a clustering strategy, as

reflected by the lower proportion of clustered
words in their recall. When a subgroup of eight
head-injured patients were asked to sort index
cards showing the test words into groups which
made sense to them, only five individuals sorted
the words into the three categories. Levin and
Goldstein (1986) interpreted the results as evidence
for disruption of an active learning strategy. Consistent with previous studies of verbal learning
following CHI (Brooks, 1975; Levin et al., 1979a),
the patients had a greater number of intrusions
than control subjects. Taken in combination with
the reduced level of spontaneous clustering, these
findings suggest that severely head-injured patients
have difficulty in differentiating separate memory
stores. The finding that the recall by severe CHI
patients was enhanced under the clustered related
word condition indicates that they were able to
benefit from the organization inherent in a list at
presentation. In contrast, Weingartner and coworkers found that patients with degenerative
dementia were unable to improve their verbal
recall on word lists which promoted semantic
memory in control subjects.

Visual imagery in verbal learning. Alteration of
learning strategies has also been found in relatively
mild CHI. In a series of experiments performed
after resolution of PTA in cases of mild to
moderate injury, Richardson and colleagues
(1979a,b, 1984a,b, 1985) found that free recall was
disproportionately impaired for concrete, but not
abstract, words. This finding was consistent with
earlier work showing that head-injured patients
had difficulty using mental imagery. Richardson
and associates showed that the deficient recall of
concrete words primarily affected initial learning
trials rather than later recall of several word lists.
There was no evidence of an impairment in visual
perception or of more rapid forgetting of visual
material to account for the difficulty in recalling
concrete words. Consequently, the investigators
inferred that the head-injured patients had a
specific problem in encoding words into an imaginary format. However, the head-injured patients
adequately compensated for this deficiency when

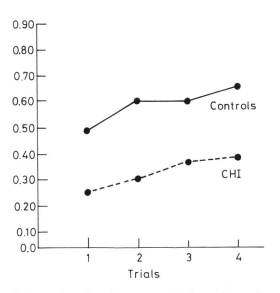

g. 7. Proportion of words spontaneously clustered according
category in the recall by closed head-injured patients as com-
red to the recall by control subjects under a condition of
ated-unclustered word lists. Reproduced from Levin and
oldstein (1986), with permission from authors and publisher.

they were instructed to use an imaginary strategy.

In general, it appears that head injury can disrupt use of active strategies such as semantic organization or visual imagery during encoding. The underutilization of active encoding strategies is particularly evident in spontaneous memory performance, whereas the patients can respond to specific instructions or enhance their recall under conditions which organize the material to be remembered.

Memory for nonverbal visual material

Studies of patients undergoing cortical excisions for treatment of intractable epilepsy have implicated the role of the right mesial temporal region in retention of relatively nonverbal, visual material such as nonsense designs (Kimura, 1963) or faces (Milner, 1978). A parsimonious interpretation of these findings implicates specialization of both the nondominant hemisphere for processing visuospatial information and the temporal lobes for long-term memory. This role of the temporal lobes is in accord with the hierarchical model of visual information processing and visual memory which Mishkin and Appenzeller (1987) have proposed on the basis of experimental ablation studies in monkeys.

Residual impairment of memory for relatively nonverbal material has been demonstrated in CHI patients using both recall (e.g., reproduction of designs) and recognition techniques. Brooks (1972, 1974a) found that CHI patients examined after resolution of PTA performed below the level of patients with orthopedic injuries on reproduction of geometric designs (which were presented for 10 seconds), reproduction of the Rey Complex Figure and on Kimura's recurring figure recognition memory test consisting of both nonsense and geometric designs. Although severity of CHI (as reflected by duration of PTA) was positively related to impaired memory on these visual tasks, this relationship was especially robust for the number of false-positive errors and the total corrected score (number correct responses minus false-positive errors) on the recognition memory task.

Recognition memory for relatively nonverbal, randomly generated designs was investigated by Levin et al. (1976) in groups of patients who differed with respect to severity of CHI. Patients who had sustained a mild head injury (i.e., brief or no loss of consciousness) were tested within two weeks of injury, whereas severely injured cases were studied from one month to more than a year following the traumatic insult. Each design was presented for 10 seconds followed by a 10 second delay and presentation of the four-choice display from which the patient selected the correct design. Impaired recognition memory, which was defined as a score falling below the range of performance in a control group, was confined to severely injured patients. In contrast, the recognition performance of mildly injured patients did not differ from that of the control group.

The signal detection theory by Green and Swets (1966) has been used to analyse recognition memory. Brooks (1974b) reanalysed his recognition memory data and found a lower d' (memory sensitivity) in CHI patients, which he interpreted as evidence for reduced efficiency of memory. Brooks also found a higher response criterion (β) from which he inferred that the head-injured patients were more cautious than control subjects in identifying a stimulus as having been presented previously. Duration of PTA was related to d' but not to β, suggesting that memory efficiency decreases with severity of diffuse brain injury, whereas a shift in response criterion may be a nonspecific effect.

This application of β has since been questioned because of the underlying assumptions of signal detection theory. As pointed out by Hannay et al. (1979), β is an index of whether the subject is behaving optimally, i.e., setting a response criterion to maximize the number of correct responses. This interpretation of β assumes that the subject (1) remembers the values of sensory input produced by the stimulus events, (2) has received feedback concerning the correctness of responses, and (3) thereby uses the feedback to select an optimal response criterion. Contrary to these assumptions, the continuous recognition

emory procedures employed in studies of head-
jured patients provide no feedback to the pa-
ent. Moreover, the capacity of the patients to re-
in information across trials is disputable.

An alternative to β is the response criterion *(c),*
hich depends entirely on the false alarm rate and
as fewer underlying assumptions. As a response
·iterion, c is a level of sensory input above which
ie subject always indicates that a signal is present
nd below which he responds that the signal is ab-
:nt. Thus, c equals $-Z[P(S/n)]$, where $P(S/n)$ is
ie probability of false alarms and Z corresponds
) its standard score transformation. In contrast, β
dependent on both the rate of hits and the rate
f false alarms. Consequently, β will be different
a two subjects who choose the same level of sen-
)ry input as their response criterion, but differ in
:nsitivity (i.e., β will be smaller in the subject with
ie larger d'). In a reanalysis of the recognition
iemory data reported by Brooks (1974a,b),
ichardson (1979b) found that head-injured pa-
ents had a markedly lower memory sensitivity
l'), but did not differ from controls with respect
) response criterion (c).

To further investigate visual recognition mem-
·y in patients with CHI, Hannay and colleagues
979) administered a test using line drawings of
amiliar plants and animals to patients with CHI
f varying severity. In this sample Grade I denoted
mild head injury characterized by brief or no loss
f consciousness, Grade II corresponded to im-
aired consciousness for periods as long as 24
ours and Grade III referred to severe injury
haracterized by impaired consciousness for inter-
als exceeding 24 hours. The authors found that
iemory sensitivity (d') decreased as a function of
uration of impaired consciousness, whereas
:sponse criterion (c) was inconsistently related to
:verity of injury. Determination of the percent of
:HI patients obtained scores which were worse
han the entire distribution of neurologically intact
ontrol patients revealed that 60% of the head-
ijured group had abnormal d' values as com-
ared to 46.7% with abnormal (c). Although d'
·as useful from a theoretical point of view, the

total correct responses (hits plus correct 'new' or
'no' responses to new stimuli) showed a comparable rate of impairment in the CHI patients
(66.7%).

As depicted in Fig. 8, group differences in total
correct responses and d' primarily reflect an increased false alarm rate in Grade II (i.e., generally
moderate) injuries and a higher rate of false alarms
combined with fewer hits in the Grade III (severe)
cases. In contrast, the recognition memory scores
of the Grade I (mild) injuries did not differ in any
respect from that of the control group. Although
the interval between injury and the study was
longer in the more severely injured patients, all
cases were tested after resolution of PTA. Hannay
et al. concluded that CHI of sufficient severity to
produce impaired consciousness persisting beyond
the time of admission results in impaired recognition memory in approximately two-thirds of the
cases, whereas alteration of response criterion is a

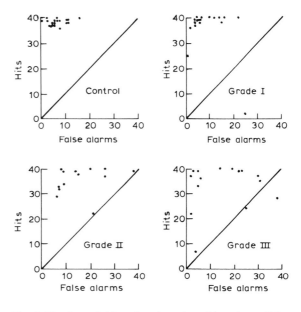

Fig. 8. Number of hits plotted against false alarm (false-
positive) errors for control subjects and each grade of head injury. It is seen that the number of false alarms increases with
severity of injury, whereas the number of correct detections
(hits) decreases, primarily in the most severely injured cases.
Reproduced from Hannay et al. (1979), with permission from
authors and publisher.

less consistent sequel. In regard to clinical utility, the findings reported by Hannay and associates indicate that the number of correct responses and the signal detection measures of sensitivity and response criterion provide improved discrimination of patients from controls as compared to the rates of hits and false alarms.

Analysis of recognition memory in relation to the neuroanatomic localization of mass lesions has been scarce in CHI patients. The only study to report these findings in detail was that of Alexandre et al. (1979), whose sample included 25 patients tested after undergoing intracranial surgery for repair of a depressed skull fracture or evacuation of a hematoma. Patients with temporal lobe lesions tended to perform at a lower level on the Kimura recognition memory test than patients with operated lesions situated in the frontal region. Analysis of the false negative errors (i.e. responding 'new' to a recurring picture) revealed that these mistakes occurred primarily on the nonverbal nonsense figures in patients with right temporal lobe lesions. In contrast, patients with left temporal lesions tended to incur negative errors on the relatively verbal geometric figures. While preliminary, the results reported by Alexandre and colleagues encourage the view that lateralization and localization of mass lesion influence the pattern of memory deficit after head injury.

Everyday memory after closed head injury
Investigators have recently inquired about memory problems in adaptive daily activities by administering structured interviews and checklists to head-injured patients and their relatives (Baddeley et al., 1987; Sunderland et al., 1983, 1984). Questionnaire items such as 'forgetting that you were told something yesterday or a few days ago, and maybe having to be reminded about it' have been frequently reported by both relatives and patients, whereas other items are infrequently endorsed (e.g., 'doing some routine thing twice by mistake . . .'). These studies have disclosed that self-report data obtained in structured interviews and questionnaires often disagree with the results of memory tests. Specifically, prose recall and paired-associate learning have a moderate relationship with subjective measures of everyday memory, whereas performance on tests such as continuous recognition memory and facial recognition have been unrelated to questionnaire and/or checklist data (Baddeley et al., 1987). However, the investigators have emphasized that these latter memory tests were still sensitive to the effects of traumatic brain injury despite their low correlation with subjective reports of everyday memory.

Interview and questionnaire data obtained from relatives have produced higher correlations with objective memory test scores than the self-report by head-injured patients. Sunderland and his colleagues have attributed this dissociation to diminished insight by severely injured patients. Although severely injured patients tended to underestimate their everyday memory problems as compared to reports by their relatives, mildly injured patients had complaints of memory disturbance which exceeded the degree of concern expressed by their relatives (Sunderland et al., 1984). While nonrepresentativeness of the mild head injured patients studied and differences in chronicity of injury between the mild and severe injury groups must be considered, these results are consistent with the impression that the degree of subjective complaints presented by patients is not commensurate with the severity of their head injury. It is plausible to attribute the impaired metamemory of severe CHI patients to frontal lobe involvement. However, evidence in support of this contention awaits further study of patients with focal lesions.

A promising development in clinical assessment and research concerning everyday memory is the Rivermead Behavioral Memory Test of Wilson et al. (1985). Designed to evaluate everyday memory problems in patients undergoing rehabilitation, the Rivermead Battery consists of 12 subtests such as remembering the name of someone and learning a new route (see Table 3) which simulate 'real-life' tasks and reflect the memory complaints of head

TABLE 3

Items in the Rivermead Behavioral Memory Test

Each item is scored pass (1 point) or fail (0 points) as follows:

Items 1 and 2	Name Score recall of first name and second name separately. In order to pass items 1 and 2 the subject needs to recall both names when asked, and without help.	Item 7	Face recognition The same rules apply here as in picture recognition. 1 point equals 100% success. Otherwise score 0 points.
Item 3	Belonging If the subject requests his/her belonging spontaneously and remembers where it was hidden, score 1 point. Otherwise score 0 points.	Item 8a	Route immediate If all 5 parts of the route are reproduced in the correct order, score 1 point. Otherwise score 0 points.
Item 4	Appointment If the subject asks the appropriate question when the alarm sounds, and without a reminder, score 1 point. Otherwise score 0 points.	Item 8b	Route delayed Score as for route immediate.
		Item 9	Delivering a message If the envelope is spontaneously picked up and left in the correct place in both the immediate and delayed routes, score 1 point. Otherwise score 0 points.
Item 5	Picture recognition In order to score 1 point the subject must select all ten pictures correctly, with no false positives. Otherwise score 0 points.	Item 10	Orientation Score 1 point if the subject is correct on all of the following questions: year, month, day of week, place and city of location, age, year born, present Prime Minister and present President. Otherwise score 0 points.
Item 6	Story recall In order to pass, the subject must score at least 6 on immediate recall and at least 4 on delayed recall. Otherwise score 0 points.	Item 11	Date Score 1 point if the subject gives the correct date. Otherwise score 0 points.

Adapted from Wilson B, Cockburn J, Baddeley A: *The Rivermead Behavioural Memory Test Manual.* Reading, England: Thames Valley Test Company, 1985.
The maximum number of points = 12. The cut-off point is 3 or more failures. Thus, subjects scoring 9 or less on the RBMT screening score are in the impaired range.

injured patients (Sunderland et al., 1983). Although this behavioral memory battery is still under investigation, preliminary findings indicate that it has a substantial correlation with the number of memory lapses reported by occupational therapists working with the patient (Baddeley et al., 1987). Assessment of memory by using practical tasks relevant to everyday activities holds considerable promise as an outcome measure in clinical trials of rehabilitation or other interventions.

Clinical assessment of memory deficit after closed head injury

Guidelines for clinical assessment of memory deficit following CHI must recognize the effects of heterogeneity in type of injury (e.g., diffuse versus mass lesion, presence of complications such as hypoxia) and chronicity of injury which influence the appropriate range of item difficulty (e.g., to mitigate 'floor' and 'ceiling' effects) and the presence of concomitant neurobehavioral impairments which can disrupt performance. Attentional problems during the initial hospitalization might be difficult to differentiate from memory deficit, whereas frontal lobe lesions might disrupt performance because of diminished motivation or difficulty in utilizing active strategies to encode information presented by the examiner and to organize recall. Word-finding disturbance and reduced speech intelligibility secondary to dysarthria are likely to adversely affect verbal recall, whereas primary visual disturbance and visuospatial impairment may compromise retention of relatively nonverbal material on tests utilizing the visual modality (e.g., random designs). Administration of memory tests requiring the drawing of designs may be inappropriate in patients with motor deficit.

Notwithstanding these caveats, serial administration of brief tests of orientation and memory for recent events is recommended during the phase of resolving PTA. As PTA recedes during the initial hospitalization and questions arise concerning disposition planning, clinical assessment of memory is essential for evaluating the patient's capacity for resumption of activities and indications for rehabilitation. To this end, procedures which stress long-term memory are particularly useful. Multitrial recall tests which present a number of items exceeding the immediate (forward) span are useful at this stage of recovery. Comparison of long-term memory for verbal material and relatively nonverbal information (e.g., novel designs) might reveal selective deficits which are related to the lateralization of intracranial mass lesion. Continuous recognition memory tests are also highly sensitive to the effects of CHI while offering the advantage of minimal demands on motor or oral response. In contrast to discrete trial recall procedures, continuous recognition memory tasks probably impose greater demand on sustained attention.

Assessment of the patient's capacity to gain access to previously acquired knowledge and utilize this information in organizing recall is pertinent to planning for remediation and providing the patient

and family with suggestions for mnemonic strategies. Can the patient utilize cuing such as the initial letter of a word? Does the patient utilize semantic information to organize memory? Interpretation of performance on memory tests is enhanced by placing these findings in perspective with other abilities such as problem-solving. Moreover, extrapolation of findings obtained on memory tests should consider observations of the patient in everyday activities which demand retention. Caution is advised in extrapolating from memory test data collected in a quiet environment by an individual examiner to long-term memory in everyday activities. It is essential to consider the specific mnemonic demands placed on the individual patient and the availability of resources (e.g., secretarial assistance) which might mitigate the effects of memory disturbance. Finally, prognostic statements can be imbued with greater confidence when they are based on the results of serial testing administered during the first several months after moderate or severe head injury as compared with a single assessment relatively early in the clinical course.

Memory remediation in head-injured patients

During the past decade numerous papers have been published concerning techniques to remedy the memory deficit in CHI patients (Crosson and Buenning, 1984; Crovitz et al., 1979; Glisky et al., 1986; Glasgow et al., 1977; Wilson and Moffat, 1984). The treatment methods, which have included techniques such as rote practice, semantic elaboration and visual imagery, have received preliminary support in selected case studies (Glasgow et al., 1977; Harris and Sunderland, 1981; Kovner et al., 1983). Although these reports suggest that young, mildly impaired patients might benefit from techniques which purport to generally improve memory, evidence from controlled clinical trials is limited to a single study which evaluated the efficacy of a total program rather than a specific technique (Prigatano et al., 1984). Moreover, no controlled investigations of rehabiliation of memory have adequately dealt with the methodological issues raised by Newcombe (1982) in her lucid review of this area.

Failure to comply with special instructions such as bizarre imagery, lack of generalization across situations and impersistence of gains after termination of training have been reported (Crosson and Buenning, 1984; Crovitz et al., 1979). More fundamentally, the feasibility of 'retraining' memory through rote exercise or specific techniques has been brought into question, as repeatedly tested amnesics such as patient H.M. have shown no improvement despite exhaustive drill and training in various mnemonic techniques (Milner et al., 1968). Slight gains in scores on memory tests after

cognitive rehabilitation do not necessarily imply enhanced retention in adaptive activities (Schacter and Glisky, 1986).

In view of recent evidence that even severely amnesic patients retain certain types of learning such as pattern-analysing skills (Cohen, 1984) and enhanced recall of previously presented words (Shimamura and Squire, 1984), the possibility of utilizing these spared abilities to assist patients in acquiring adaptive skills has been explored (Glisky et al., 1986). This strategy is aimed at the alleviation of specific problems associated with memory deficit by teaching patients the necessary knowledge or skills rather than attempting to globally restore mnemonic function. Utilizing the method

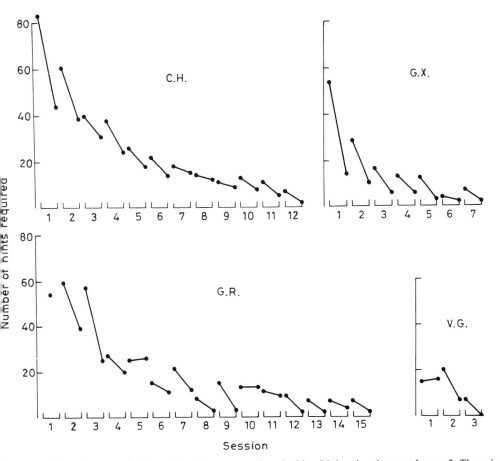

Fig. 9. Number of cues required by each of four memory-impaired head-injured patients on Lesson 2. The points represent performance on the first and last trials of each session. Sessions were conducted twice. Reproduced from Glisky et al. (1986), with permission from authors and publisher.

of vanishing cues (i.e., prompting with partial letter cues), Glisky et al. (1986) demonstrated that four CHI patients were capable of learning to interact with a microcomputer and perform simple programming despite their residual amnesic disorder. The remediation program began with computer operations, progressed to teaching the concept of programming and culminated in writing simple programs.

As depicted in Fig. 9, all four patients exhibited learning across sessions in the unit which dealt with an introduction to programming. It is seen that within-session learning was typically followed by between-session forgetting despite an overall decline in errors per session. Glisky et al. reported that a severely amnesic CHI patient who failed to recall his experiences with a computer nevertheless learned to write and edit simple programs and to perform disk storage and retrieval operations. At the same time, the authors acknowledged that many repetitions were required before the CHI patients attained error-free performance. Moreover, the generalization and persistence of this learning remain to be demonstrated. Nevertheless, the acquisition of computer operations is somewhat reminiscent of the skill acquisition that appears to be spared in patients with amnesic disorder of other etiologies (Cohen, 1984).

In conclusion, the exploitation of preserved learning capacities to assist head-injured patients acquire specific adaptive skills appears promising, whereas current evidence dictates that restoration of a general capacity for learning and memory is an unattainable goal. The repertoire of skilled acts could include performance of everyday activities (e.g., meal preparation) and operation of equipment necessary for specific jobs. Further investigation is necessary to evaluate the maintenance of gains and the degree to which these acquired skills generalize across situations. The influence of factors such as the patient's associated cognitive capacities and motivation and the highly supportive environment provided in experimental studies must also be considered in assessing the efficacy of memory remediation.

Directions for future research

Closer integration of research on outcome of head injury with cognitive neuroscience should produce new findings concerning PTA and residual disturbance of memory. Although research on memory deficit in head-injured patients has expanded remarkably during the past decade, relatively few studies have elucidated this disorder from a theoretical perspective similar to studies of the amnesia in patients with alcoholic Korsakoff's syndrome. The involvement of long-term memory following moderate to severe CHI has been convincingly demonstrated, but its manifestation as a relatively specific impairment is unclear. The appropriateness of describing a subgroup of severe CHI patients as amnesic awaits concurrent study of the recovery of memory and intellectual functioning. To the extent that memory deficit may persist as a relatively isolated deficit raises questions concerning the contributions of frontal versus temporal lobe lesions. Advances in neuroimaging could elucidate the relationship between the presence and type of residual memory disorder and focal areas of morphological and/or metabolic cerebral abnormalities.

The high incidence of CHI provides ample opportunity to investigate PTA, including features of memory which are preserved such as learning skilled acts and transfer of this information to the post-PTA period. In contrast to alcoholic Korsakoff's syndrome, PTA has a precisely defined onset and can be studied prospectively in young, previously healthy persons. Studies of remote memory after CHI have raised questions such as the relationship between the type of material (e.g., public events versus autobiographic memory) and the presence of a temporal gradient which invite further research.

Recent investigations comparing features of the memory disorder in Korsakoff's syndrome and dementia of various etiologies suggest that this line of research may be fruitful to pursue in head injury. For example, the memory deficits resulting from temporal lobe intracerebral hematoma versus temporal lobectomy have not been directly compared. Similarities between the memory deficit resulting from diffuse axonal injury and diseases which primarily involve the cerebral white matter such as multiple sclerosis have not yet been considered.

Finally, the recent resurgence of interest in preserved learning and retention of skilled acts in patients with memory disorder holds considerable promise for rehabilitation of head-injured patients. Application of experimental techniques to clinical trials of training skills could have far-reaching implications for rehabilitation, including a more theoretical approach bolstered by empirical validation. Other relatively preserved or 'latent' learning capacities of head-injured patients could be exploited in future studies.

Acknowledgements

The author is indebted to the co-investigators of the Galveston studies reviewed here and to Liz Zindler for manuscript preparation. Preparation of this manuscript was supported in part by the Javits Neuroscience Investigator Award, NS-21889, and Moody Foundation grant No. 82-241.

References

Adams JH, Graham DI, Murray LS, Scott G: Diffuse axonal injury due to nonmissile head injury in humans: an analysis of 45 cases. *Ann. Neurol.: 12,* 557 – 563, 1982.

Adams JH, Graham D, Scott G, Parker LS, Doyle D: Brain damage in fatal non-missile head injury. *J. Clin. Pathol.: 33,* 1132 – 1145, 1980.

Albert MS, Butters N, Levin J: Temporal gradients in the retrograde amnesia of patients with alcoholic Korsakoff's disease. *Arch. Neurol.: 36,* 211 – 216, 1979.

Alexandre A, Nertempi P, Farinello C, Rubini L: Recognition memory alterations after severe head injury. *J. Neurosurg. Sci.: 23,* 201 – 206, 1979.

Baddeley A, Sunderland A, Watts KP, Wilson BA: Closed head injury and memory. In Levin HS, Grafman J, Eisenberg HM (Editors), *Neurobehavioral Recovery from Head Injury.* New York: Oxford University Press, 1987.

Baddeley AD, Warrington EK: Amnesia and the distinction between long- and short-term memory. *J. Verbal Learn. Verbal Behav.: 9,* 176, 1970.

Benson DF, Geschwind N: Shrinking retrograde amnesia. *J. Neurol. Neurosurg. Psychiatry: 30,* 539 – 544, 1967.

Benton AL, Van Allen MW, Fogel ML: Temporal orientation in cerebral disease. *J. Nerv. Ment. Dis.: 139,* 110 – 119, 1964.

Brooks DN: Memory and head injury. *J. Nerv. Ment. Dis.: 155,* 350 – 355, 1972.

Brooks DN: Recognition memory, and head injury. *J. Neurol. Neurosurg. Psychiatry: 37,* 794 – 801, 1974a.

Brooks DN: Recognition memory after head injury: a signal detection analysis. *Cortex: 10,* 224 – 230, 1974b.

Brooks DN: Long and short term memory in head injured patients. *Cortex: 11,* 329 – 340, 1975.

Brooks DN: Wechsler Memory Scale performance and its relationship to brain damage after severe closed head injury. *J. Neurol. Neurosurg. Psychiatry: 39,* 593 – 601, 1976.

Buschke H, Fuld PA: Evaluating storage, retention, and retrieval in disordered memory and learning. *Neurology: 24,* 1019 – 1025, 1974.

Cohen NJ: Preserved learning capacity in amnesia. In Squire LR, Butters N (Editors), *Neuropsychology of Memory.* New York: Guilford Press, 1984.

Craik FIM, Lockhart RS: Levels of processing: a framework for memory research. *J. Verbal Learn. Verbal Behav.: 11,* 671 – 684, 1972.

Cronholm B, Jonsson I: Memory functions after cerebral concussion. *Acta Chir. Scand.: 113,* 263 – 271, 1957.

Crosson B, Buenning W: An individualized memory retraining program after closed-head injury: a single-case study. *J. Clin. Neuropsychol.: 6,* 287 – 301, 1984.

Crovitz HF: Techniques to investigate posttraumatic and retrograde amnesia after head injury. In Levin HS, Grafman J, Eisenberg HM (Editors), *Neurobehavioral Recovery from Head Injury.* New York: Oxford University Press, 1987.

Crovitz HF, Harvey MT, Horn RW: Problems in the acquisition of imagery mnemonics: three brain-damaged cases. *Cortex: 15,* 225 – 234, 1979.

Fortuny LAI, Briggs M, Newcombe F, Ratcliff G, Thomas C: Measuring the duration of posttraumatic amnesia. *J. Neurol. Neurosurg. Psychiatry: 43,* 377 – 379, 1980.

Glasgow RE, Zeiss RA, Barrera M Jr, Lewinsohn PM: Case studies on remediating memory deficits in brain-damaged individuals. *J. Clin. Psychol.: 33,* 1049 – 1054, 1977.

Glisky EL, Schacter DL, Tulving E: Computer learning by memory-impaired patients: acquisition and retention of complex knowledge. *Neuropsychologia: 24,* 313 – 328, 1986.

Goldberg E, Antin SP, Bilder RM Jr, Gerstman LJ, Hughes JEO, Mattis S: Retrograde amnesia: possible role of mesencephalic reticular activation in long-term memory. *Science: 213,* 1392 – 1394, 1981.

Green DM, Swets JA: *Signal Detection Theory and Psychophysics.* New York: Wiley, 1966.

Gronwall D, Wrightson P: Duration of post-traumatic amnesia after mild head injury. *J. Clin. Neuropsychol.: 2,* 51 – 60, 1980.

Gronwall D, Wrightson P: Memory and information processing capacity after closed head injury. *J. Neurol. Neurosurg. Psychiatry: 44,* 889 – 895, 1981.

Haas DC, Ross GS: Transient global amnesia triggered by mild head trauma. *Brain: 109,* 251 – 257, 1986.

Hannay HJ, Levin HS, Grossman RG: Impaired recognition memory after head injury. Cortex: 15, 269 – 283, 1979.

Harris JE, Sunderland A: A brief survey of the management of memory disorders in rehabilitation units in Britain. *Int. J. Rehabil. Med.: 3,* 206 – 209, 1981.

Jenkins A, Teasdale G, Hadley MDM, Macpherson P, Rowan JO: Brain lesions detected by magnetic resonance imaging in mild and severe head injuries. *Lancet: ii,* 445 – 446, 1986.

Jennett WB: Head injuries and the temporal lobe. In Herrington RN (Editor), *Current Problems in Neuropsychiatry,* British Journal of Psychiatry, special publication No. 4. Ashford, Kent, United Kingdom: Headley Brothers Ltd., 1969.

Kimura D: Right temporal-lobe damage. *Arch. Neurol.: 8,* 264 – 271, 1963.

Kovner R, Mattis S, Goldmeier E: A technique for promoting robust free recall in chronic organic amnesia. *J. Clin. Neuropsychol.: 5,* 65 – 71, 1983.

Kraus JF, Black MA, Hessol N, Ley P, Rokaw W, Sullivan C, Bowers S, Knowlton S, Marshall L: The incidence of acute brain injury and serious impairment in a defined population. *Am. J. Epidemiol.: 119,* 186 – 201, 1984.

Langfitt TW, Obrist WD, Alavi A, Grossman RI, Zimmerman R, Jaggi J, Uzzell B, Reivich M, Patton DR: Computerized tomography, magnetic resonance imaging, and positron emission tomography in the study of brain trauma. *J. Neurosurg.: 64,* 760 – 767, 1986.

Levin HS, Goldstein FC: Organization of verbal memory after severe closed-head injury. *J. Clin. Exp. Neuropsychol.: 8,* 643 – 656, 1986.

Levin HS, Grossman RG, Kelly PJ: Short-term recognition memory in relation to severity of head injury. *Cortex: 12,* 175 – 182, 1976.

Levin HS, Grossman RG, Rose JE, Teasdale G: Long-term neuropsychological outcome of closed head injury. *J. Neurosurg.: 50,* 412 – 422, 1979a.

Levin HS, O'Donnell VM, Grossman RG: The Galveston orientation and amnesia test: a practical scale to assess cognition after head injury. *J. Nerv. Ment. Dis.: 167,* 675 – 684, 1979b.

Levin HS, Meyers CA, Grossman RG, Sarwar M: Ventricular enlargement after closed head injury. *Arch. Neurol.: 38,* 623 – 629, 1981.

Levin HS, Benton AL, Grossman RG: *Neurobehavioral Consequences of Closed Head Injury.* New York: Oxford University Press, 1982a.

Levin HS, Eisenberg HM, Wigg NR, Kobayashi K: Memory and intellectual ability after head injury in children and adolescents. *Neurosurgery: 11,* 668 – 673, 1982b.

Levin HS, Handel SF, Goldman AM, Eisenberg HM, Guinto FC Jr: Magnetic resonance imaging after 'diffuse' nonmissile head injury. A neurobehavioral study. *Arch. Neurol.: 42,* 963 – 968, 1985a.

Levin HS, High WM, Meyers CA, Von Laufen A, Hayden ME, Eisenberg HM: Impairment of remote memory after closed head injury. *J. Neurol. Neurosurg. Psychiatry: 48,* 556 – 563, 1985b.

Levin HS, Amparo E, Eisenberg HM, Williams DH, High WM Jr, McArdle GB, Weiner RL: Magnetic resonance imaging and computerized tomography in relation to the neurobehavioral sequelae of mild and moderate head injuries. *J. Neurosurg.: 66,* 706 – 713, 1987a.

Levin HS, Mattis S, Ruff RM, Eisenberg HM, Marshall LF, Tabaddor K, High WM Jr, Frankowski RF: Neurobehav-

ioral outcome following minor head injury: a three center study. *J. Neurosurg.: 66,* 234 – 243, 1987b.

Levin HS, High WM Jr, Eisenberg HM: Learning and forgetting during posttraumatic amnesia in head injured patients. *J. Neurol. Neurosurg. Psychiatry:* 1987c.

Lezak MD: Recovery of memory and learning functions following traumatic brain injury. *Cortex: 15,* 63 – 72, 1979.

Mattis S, Kovner R: Different patterns of mnemonic deficits in two organic amnesic syndromes. *Brain Lang.: 6,* 179 – 191, 1978.

Milner B: Clues to the cerebral organization of memory. In Buser PA, Rougeul-Buser A (Editors), *Cerebral Correlates of Conscious Experience:* INSERM symposium No. 6. New York: Elsevier, pp. 139 – 153, 1978.

Milner B, Corkin S, Teuber ML: Further analysis of the hippocampal amnesic syndrome: 14 year follow-up study of H.M. *Neuropsychologia: 6,* 215 – 234, 1968.

Mishkin M, Appelzeller T: The anatomy of memory. *Sci. Am.: 256,* 80 – 89, 1987.

Newcombe F: The psychological consequences of closed head injury: assessment and rehabilitation. *Injury: 14,* 111 – 136, 1982.

Parker SA, Serrats AF: Memory recovery after traumatic coma. *Acta Neurochir.: 34,* 71 – 77, 1976.

Prigatano GP, Fordyce DJ, Zeiner HK, Roueche JR, Pepping M, Wood BC: Neuropsychological rehabilitation after closed head injury in young adults. *J. Neurol. Neurosurg. Psychiatry: 47,* 505 – 513, 1984.

Ribot T: *Diseases of Memory: An Essay in the Positive Psychology.* New York: Appleton, 1882.

Richardson JTE: Mental imagery, human memory, and the effects of closed head injury. *Br. J. Soc. Clin. Psychol.: 18,* 319 – 327, 1979a.

Richardson JTE: Signal detection theory and the effects of severe head injury upon recognition memory. *Cortex: 15,* 145 – 148, 1979b.

Richardson JTE: The effects of closed head injury upon intrusions and confusions in free recall. *Cortex: 20,* 413 – 420, 1984a.

Richardson JTE, Barry C: The effects of minor closed head injury upon human memory: further evidence on the role of mental imagery. *Cognitive Neuropsychol.: 2,* 149 – 168, 1985.

Richardson JTE, Snape W: The effects of closed head injury upon human memory: an experimental analysis. *Cognitive Neuropsychol.: 1,* 217 – 231, 1984b.

Ruesch J: Intellectual impairment in head injuries. *Am. J. Psychiatry: 100,* 480 – 496, 1944.

Russell WR: Cerebral involvement in head injury. *Brain: 55,* 549 – 603, 1932.

Russell WR: *The Traumatic Amnesias.* New York: Oxford University Press, 1971.

Russell WR, Nathan PW: Traumatic amnesia. *Brain: 69,* 183 – 187, 1946.

Russell WR, Smith A: Post-traumatic amnesia in closed head injury. *Arch. Neurol.: 5,* 4 – 17, 1961.

Schacter DL, Crovitz HF: Memory function after closed head injury: a review of the quantitative research. *Cortex: 8,* 150 – 176, 1977.

Schacter DL, Glisky EL: Memory remediation: restoration,

alleviation, and the acquisition of domain-specific knowledge. In Uzzell B, Gross Y (Editors), *Clinical Neuropsychology of Intervention*. Boston: Martinus Nijhoff, 1986.

Shimamura AP, Squire LR: Paired-associate learning and priming effects in amnesia: a neuropsychological study. *J. Exp. Psychol. Gen.: 113,* 556 – 570, 1984.

Squire LR: Two forms of human amnesia: an analysis of forgetting. *J. Neurosci.: 1,* 635 – 640, 1981.

Squire LR: *Memory and Brain*. New York: Oxford University Press, 1987.

Squire LR, Cohen N: Memory and amnesia: resistance to disruption develops for years after learning. *Behav. Neural Biol.: 25,* 115 – 125, 1979.

Squire LR, Slater PC: Forgetting in very long-term memory as assessed by an improved questionnaire technique. *J. Exp. Psychol. Hum. Learn. Mem.: 1,* 50 – 54, 1975.

Squire LR, Slater PC, Chace PM: Retrograde amnesia: temporal gradient in very long-term memory following electroconvulsive therapy. *Science: 187,* 77 – 79, 1975.

Strich SJ: Diffuse degeneration of the cerebral white matter in severe dementia following head injury. *J. Neurol. Neurosurg. Psychiatry: 19,* 163 – 185, 1956.

Sunderland A, Harris JE, Baddeley AD: Do laboratory tests predict everyday memory? A neuropsychological study. *J. Verbal Learn. Verbal Behav.: 22,* 341 – 357, 1983.

Sunderland A, Harris JE, Gleave J: Memory failures in everyday life following severe head injury. *J. Clin. Neuropsychol.: 6,* 127 – 142, 1984.

Teasdale G, Jennett B: Assessment of coma and impaired consciousness: a practical scale. *Lancet: ii,* 81 – 84, 1974.

Thomsen IV: Verbal learning in aphasic and non-aphasic patients with severe head injuries. *Scand. J. Rehabil. Med.: 9,* 73 – 77, 1977.

Tulving E, Colotla VA: Free recall of trilingual lists. *Cognitive Psychol.: 1,* 86 – 98, 1970.

Weingartner H. Kaye W, Smallberg S, Ebert MH, Gillin JC, Sitram N: Memory failures in progressive idiopathic dementia. *J. Abnorm. Psychol.: 90,* 187 – 196, 1981.

Weingartner H, Grafman J, Boutelle W, Kaye W, Martin PR: Forms of memory failure. *Science: 221,* 380 – 382, 1983.

Wilson BA, Cockburn J, Baddeley AD: *The Rivermead Behavioural Memory Test, Reading*. England: Thames Valley Test Company, 1985.

Wilson BA, Moffat N: *Clinical Management of Memory Problems*. Rockville, MD: Aspen Systems Corporation, 1984.

Zatorre RJ, McEntee WJ: Semantic encoding deficits in a case of traumatic amnesia. *Brain Cognition: 2,* 331 – 345, 1983.

1989 Elsevier Science Publishers B.V. (Biomedical Division)
Handbook of Neuropsychology, Vol. 3
F. Boller and J. Grafman (Eds)

CHAPTER 9

Functional amnesia

Daniel L. Schacter and John F. Kihlstrom

Amnesia and Cognition Unit, Department of Psychology, University of Arizona, AZ, U.S.A.

Introduction

Neuropsychological analyses of memory have traditionally relied on studies of patients with organic amnesias that are produced by lesions to specific brain structures. The general goals of this research have been to decompose memory into component processes and systems by documenting selective patterns of deficit across different kinds of memory tests, and to make inferences about the neural organization of memory on the basis of such observations. Research concerning organic amnesias has yielded a rich harvest of empirical findings and has led to important new insights about the nature and composition of memory (for review, see Cermak, 1982; Hirst, 1982; Smith, Ch. 8 of this volume; Schacter, in press; Squire, 1987).

Not all amnesias, however, result from brain damage. Amnesia may be produced by severe emotional trauma, psychological illness, hypnotic suggestion, or naturally occurring changes in state or arousal. These kinds of memory impairments are referred to collectively as *functional amnesias*. This chapter is concerned with functional amnesias, and has two main purposes: (1) to review data and ideas concerning the various functional amnesias that have been studied, and (2) to argue that functional amnesias can provide important insights into memory which are complementary to, and no less revealing than, insights gained from study of organic amnesias.

Before proceeding further, we should clarify some of the terminology that is used frequently in the chapter. *Functional amnesia* will be defined as memory loss that is attributable to an instigating event or process that does not result in damage or injury to the brain, and produces more forgetting than would normally occur in the absence of the instigating event or process. Of course, we recognize that functional amnesias are no doubt accompanied by correlated changes in brain state, and also recognize that it is not always a straightforward matter to determine what constitutes 'normal forgetting' in a particular situation. The purpose of the foregoing definition is to distinguish functional amnesia from organic amnesia on the one hand, and from 'ordinary' forgetting on the other.

We also find it useful to distinguish further between *pathological* and *non-pathological* functional amnesias. The former refers to cases in which amnesia is either a diagnostic symptom of psychopathology, or occurs within the context of a diagnosable psychological disorder. We will discuss two main kinds of pathological functional amnesias, which will be referred to as *functional retrograde amnesia* and *multiple personality amnesia*. Non-pathological amnesias, in contrast, either occur in the course of everyday living or are induced by psychological procedures (i.e., hypnotic suggestion) in people who are free of any diagnosable psychopathology. Under this general rubric we will consider *childhood amnesia, sleep and dream amnesia,* and *hypnotic amnesia.*

One further terminological distinction that will be used frequently merits brief introduction: the distinction between explicit and implicit forms of memory (Graf and Schacter, 1985; Schacter, 1987). Explicit memory refers to conscious recollection of previous experiences and is typically assessed by standard tests of recall and recognition, which require intentional retrieval of a prior experience. Implicit memory, on the other hand, refers to unintentional retrieval of previous experiences in the performance of tests that do not make explicit reference to those experiences. Implicit expressions of memory need not involve any conscious awareness of remembering on the part of the subject. It is now well established that patients with organic amnesia can show robust implicit memory for recent experiences despite severely impaired explicit memory (for review and discussion, see Schacter, 1987; Shimamura, 1986; Squire, 1987; Weiskrantz, 1987). One of the main points of the present chapter is that the dissociation between explicit and implicit memory can also be observed and profitably studied in cases of functional amnesia.

Pathological functional amnesias

Functional retrograde amnesia

Perhaps the most dramatic and frequently popularized form of memory loss, functional retrograde amnesia entails loss of personal identity and large sectors of one's personal past. The amnesia is usually precipitated by a severe emotional or psychological trauma (Abeles and Schilder, 1935; Thom and Fenton, 1920), and consists of several stages. Following the traumatic episode, patients enter a fugue state during which they may wander for variable periods of time, ranging from minutes to months (Abeles and Schilder, 1935; Abse, 1987; Fisher, 1945; Nemiah, 1979), and are unaware of any memory loss. The fugue, but not the amnesia, typically ends when patients are asked questions about their identity or past which they cannot answer (Stengel, 1941). Since the fugue is defined as that period during which patients are unaware of memory loss, it almost never comes to the atten-

tion of appropriate professionals until awareness i[s] achieved, and is therefore virtually impossible t[o] study while it is occurring. Information abou[t] fugue states is thus necessarily based on retrospec[-] tive accounts. Because patients generally remai[n] amnesic for the events of the fugue even after i[ts] termination, in most cases such retrospective ac[-] counts can only be obtained through hypnosis o[r] administration of appropriate barbiturates (Abse[,] 1987; Fisher, 1945). The reader is referred to th[e] reports of Fisher (Fisher, 1945; Fisher and Joseph[,] 1949), Geleerd et al. (1956), Luparello (1970) an[d] Stengel (1941) for careful retrospective analyses o[f] fugue states. More recent discussions of issues con[-] cerning diagnosis of fugue states are provided b[y] Akhtar and Brenner (1979), Freedman and Kapla[n] (1975) and Keller and Shaywitz (1986).

Some patients emerge directly from the fugue in[-] to a state of full recovery (Pratt, 1977), wherea[s] others proceed from the fugue to a second stag[e] that is characterized by awareness of loss of per[-] sonal identity and large sectors of the past. (Wha[t] we refer to as the first and second stages of func[-] tional retrograde amnesia can be viewed as distinc[t] clinical entities − fugue and psychogenic amnesi[a] − as they are in DSM-III. We do not take excep[-] tion to this characterization, and wish only to em[-] phasize the continuity between the two that exist[s] in many cases.) The second stage typically lasts fo[r] several days, although durations of weeks an[d] months have been recorded (Abeles and Schilder[,] 1935; Akhtar et al., 1981; Christianson an[d] Nilsson, in press; Kanzer, 1939; Lyon, 198[5] Suarez and Pittluck, 1975). In some cases, th[e] amnesia clears in response to the appearance of [a] relative or to a cue that is related to the emotiona[l] trauma that precipated the amnesia (Abeles an[d] Schilder, 1935; Christianson and Nilsson, in press[;] Jones, 1909; Schacter et al., 1982), whereas i[n] others hypnotic procedures or sodium amyta[l] treatment help to alleviate amnesia (e.g., Eise[n] 1989; Fisher, 1945; Kaszniak et al., 1988; Kenned[y] and Neville, 1957; Sargant and Slater, 194[1] Suarez and Pittluck, 1975). In many case[s] however, recovery of memory and identity i[s] 'spontaneous' in the sense that no salient external cues are present when patients suddenly recover memory function (Abeles and Schilder, 1935; Gillespie, 1937; Gudjonsson and Taylor, 1985; Kanzer, 1939). In the third stage, after patients have recovered their identity and personal past, the events of the second stage are accessible to conscious recall whereas the events of the first stage (fugue) are not (Fisher, 1945; Nemiah, 1979; Pratt, 1977).

Features of functional retrograde amnesia. What can be said about the characteristics of memory loss during stage two of functional retrograde amnesia and the nature of recovery in stage three? As pointed out by Schacter and Tulving (1982), surprisingly few studies have analysed the nature of memory processes during functional retrograde amnesia. Instead, many investigators have focussed on issues of psychiatric and clinical concern including the psychodynamic functions of amnesia and its relation to different forms of psychopathology (Berrington et al., 1956; Eisen, 1987; Geleerd et al., 1945; Keller and Shaywitz, 1986; Kennedy and Neville, 1957; Stengel, 1941; Wilson et al., 1950), the time course of recovery and the most effective treatment methods (Abeles and Schilder, 1935; Kennedy and Neville, 1957; Lyon, 1981; Sargant and Slater, 1941; Wilson et al., 1950), and the nature of the traumatic events that produce amnesia (Abeles and Schilder, 1935; Kanzer, 1939; Thom and Fenton, 1920). These clinical issues will not be considered here, and the reader is referred to discussions by Akhtar et al. (1981), Nemiah (1979) and Pratt (1977).

Despite the psychiatric orientation of much of the literature, several issues directly concerned with the nature of memory loss during functional retrograde amnesia have been addressed. Consider first the extent of patients' amnesia for their personal past. Clinical reports suggest that most patients present with amnesia for their entire personal past, although some show 'spotty' recollection of particular incidents or autobiographical facts (Abeles and Schilder, 1935; Jones, 1909; Wilson et al., 1950). Thus, for example, Jones

(1909) studied a patient who could recall nothing of his personal past except that he had recently been aboard a steamboat named 'Corona', and that he had spent a lot of time at sea; Keller and Shaywitz (1986) described an adolescent male who knew his age but nothing else about himself; and Akhtar et al. (1981) reported a case in which the only item of personal information the patient could supply was her name. Unfortunately, most clinical reports — which constitute the bulk of the literature on functional retrograde amnesia — provide virtually no information concerning the procedures used to probe memory, so they are of limited value when attempting to assess the extent of amnesia.

Quantitative information on this point has been provided in a study by Schacter et al. (1982) which used controlled cueing procedures for exploring autobiographical memory in a case of dense functional retrograde amnesia. The patient (P.N.) was a 21-yr-old man who was admitted to hospital complaining of excruciating back pains. When questioned about his identity, P.N. became aware that he did not remember his name or anything else about his personal past. The only piece of information that he could recall on his own was that he had once been given the nickname 'Lumberjack'. The amnesia had apparently been precipitated by the death and funeral of P.N.'s grandfather, to whom he had been extraordinarily close. To investigate autobiographical recall systematically, Schacter et al. used a cueing procedure that involved presenting the patient with a word and asking him to retrieve a specific personal experience related to it (Crovitz and Schiffman, 1974). P.N. was able to come up with episodic memories in response to 22 of the 24 cues presented, but 86% of them derived from the four days which intervened between the onset of amnesia and the test session; these memories concerned events that had transpired in the hospital where he was staying during this period. By contrast, when P.N. was given a similar cueing task several weeks later, after the amnesia had cleared, 92% of the retrieved memories predated the onset of the amnesia. Schacter et al.

included a second cueing condition in which P.N. was instructed to try to retrieve only memories that predated the onset of the amnesia. Under these conditions, the patient was able to come up with autobiographical episodes in response to 17 of the 24 cues. Several of these memories concerned isolated childhood experiences, but the majority of them derived from an extremely happy period of his life, one year prior to the amnesia, when he worked for a courier service. This preserved 'island' of autobiographical memories was accessible at a time when P.N. did not know his name, where he came from, or almost anything else about his personal past. Significantly, however, the nickname 'Lumberjack' – which was accessible from the time that P.N. entered the hospital – had been given to him when he worked for the courier service. These observations indicate that cueing procedures can be useful in uncovering preserved islands of autobiographical memories, and also suggest that the accessibility of such memories may depend on the availability of some sort of identity information (i.e., a nickname).

A second issue that has received some systematic investigation concerns whether functional retrograde amnesia is restricted to personal, autobiographical information or whether it also entails impaired access to general knowledge or semantic information on the one hand, and well-learned skills on the other. Some clinical observers have noted that general knowledge is preserved in patients with dense amnesia for personal information (Akhtar et al., 1981; Jones, 1909; Suarez and Pittluck, 1975; Wilson et al., 1950), but others have reported that it is impaired (e.g., Coriat, 1907; Kanzer, 1939). Abeles and Schilder (1935) noted that some of their patients ". . . retained an adequate fund of general information" (p. 595) whereas others ". . . professed no knowledge at all" (p. 595). One again, however, methodological inadequacies limit the usefulness of such statements because the empirical basis for them is unclear.

Several studies are somewhat more informative with respect to this issue. In the aforementioned

case study by Schacter et al., P.N. was given a test in which pictures of famous people from the past several decades are presented and the patient is required to identify them (Albert et al, 1979). On this test, P.N. performed about as well during the amnesia as he did after it cleared, and performed similarly to a matched control subject during both test sessions. In addition, P.N.'s vocabulary, as assessed by the Wechsler Adult Intelligence Scale (WAIS), was identical during and after the amnesic episode. These data suggest that general or semantic knowledge was preserved in this case. Similar observations were reported in the case of a male patient (M.R.) who became amnesic after homosexual rape (Kaszniak et al., 1988). M.R. exhibited an impressive spontaneous vocabulary while experiencing dense amnesia for all personal information, and performed similarly on the WAIS-R vocabulary subscale during the amnesia and after it cleared. Consistent with these findings, Gudjonsson and Taylor (1985) reported that the WAIS vocabulary performance of a man who developed a 20-yr retrograde amnesia for personal information following a series of stressful events showed little change during and after the amnesia. Note, however, that each of the foregoing studies sampled only a limited range of tests that probe semantic knowledge. Accordingly, caution must be exercised when interpreting the apparent preservation of semantic or general knowledge observed in these studies, especially in the light of clinical reports that some functional retrograde amnesia patients exhibit severe deficits in gaining access to semantic knowledge (Abeles and Schilder,, 1935; Kanzer, 1939). These observations suggest that functional retrograde amnesia may be a non-unitary syndrome characterized by a variable pattern of performance across patients.

Most clinical observers concur that previously acquired skills are preserved during episodes of functional retrograde amnesia (e.g., Abeles and Schilder, 1935; Gillespie, 1937; Kanzer, 1939; Nemiah, 1979). Yet despite this generally accepted view – or perhaps because of it – we know of no systematic empirical studies of skill retention or utilization in patients with functional retrograde amnesia. It seems clear that careful testing of patients' ability to execute acquired skills is needed to provide an empirical foundation for evaluating this issue.

A related issue that also requires more systematic investigation concerns whether functional retrograde amnesia is accompanied by generalized impairments of cognitive function. Clinical reports suggest that cognitive deficits may be observed in some patients and not others (Abeles and Schilder, 1935; Akhtar et al., 1981; Kanzer, 1939; Kennedy and Neville, 1957; Wilson et al., 1950). Studies that provide pertinent quantitative information have yielded varying results. Schacter et al. (1982) reported that their patient showed unchanged WAIS verbal IQ during (99) and after (98) his amnesic episode, whereas performance IQ was substantially lower during the amnesia (107) than after it (120). Since only three weeks separated the two test sessions, this latter improvement was attributed partly to practice effects, which are known to influence WAIS performance tests (e.g. Lezak, 1983). However, Kaszniak et al. (1988) found that their patient showed improvements on both WAIS-R verbal IQ (88 during amnesia, 95 after) and performance IQ (89 during amnesia, 110 after) with a 15-month separation between the two tests. Similarly, Gudjonsson and Taylor (1985) reported a 27-point improvement in full-scale WAIS IQ in a patient who was tested during an amnesic episode and again eight months later. These findings suggest some deterioration of intellectual function during the amnesic episode. More extensive investigation of cognitive function during functional retrograde amnesia is clearly required.

An issue of longstanding concern in the literature is whether patients with functional retrograde amnesia also exhibit some degree of anterograde amnesia. Several clinical observers have contended that little or no anterograde amnesia is observed: patients appear to remember reasonably well day-to-day events that occur while they are suffering from retrograde amnesia (e.g.,

Abeles and Schilder, 1935; Akhtar et al., 1981; Fisher and Joseph, 1949). By contrast, formal testing of anterograde function has revealed the existence of mild-to-moderate deficits on the Wechsler Memory Scale and laboratory tests of recall and recognition of recently presented materials (Gudjonsson and Haward, 1982; Gudjonsson and Taylor, 1985; Schacter et al., 1982). Yet even in these instances, it is not entirely clear how to interpret the observed anterograde deficits. For example, the patient studied by Schacter et al., P.N., showed significant impairment on the logical memory and paired-associated subtests of the Wechsler Memory Scale during amnesia relative to his performance several weeks later in a normal state. However, this patient showed excellent recall of day-to-day events while he was amnesic, as documented by his previously discussed performance on the Crovitz autobiographical cueing task. Thus, it would be inappropriate to assert that this patient suffered from clinically significant anterograde amnesia, even though Wechsler Memory Scale performance was low. It is possible that subtle anterograde impairments observed during functional retrograde amnesia may be secondary to cognitive deficits or to depressed mood.

The striking deficit in gaining access to autobiographical information that is the hallmark of functional retrograde amnesia is observed when patients are queried *explicitly* about their personal past. An important question concerns whether these patients can show *implicit* memory for autobiographical information that is inaccessible explicitly. Although this issue has received scant attention, several intriguing observations have been made. For example, Coriat (1907) used a procedure in which patients focussed attention on a monotonous stimulus and reported whatever came to mind; no explicit reference was made to the patient's personal past. He found that under these conditions, a patient with apparently complete functional retrograde amnesia produced bits and pieces of information about her past, but was entirely unaware of their autobiographical nature. As Coriat related, "These memory automatisms

. . . are not looked upon as memories, but as strange, unfamiliar and isolated phenomena, which Susan N. [the patient] well expressed by the term 'wonderments' . ." (1907, pp. 106 – 107). Similarly, Jones (1909) observed that a densely amnesic patient who could not explicitly remember either his wife or daughter produced their names correctly – without any conscious experience of familiarity – when asked to guess what names might fit them.

More recent observations are consistent with this early evidence of implicit memory in functional retrograde amnesia. Gudjonsson and Haward (1982) found that a young woman who had threatened to commit suicide before the onset of amnesia showed a preoccupation with death-related themes on a Rorschach test, even though she did not explicitly remember her suicide threat or the circumstances that produced it (see Gudjonsson and Taylor, 1985, for similar observations). In an earlier report concerning this patient, Gudjonsson (1979) reported that she showed heightened electrodermal responses to some, but not all, items of personal relevance at a time when she was amnesic for them. In their study of functional amnesia following male rape, Kaszniak et al. (1988) found that patient M.R. experienced severe distress when shown a TAT card which depicted one person attacking another from behind. He then left the testing session to go to his room, and attempted unsuccessfully to commit suicide – yet was unable at the time to remember explicitly the rape incident. In addition, M.R. produced under hypnosis images that he later confirmed were from his personal past, but were not experienced as memories when they were retrieved. Christianson and Nilsson (in press), in a study of a woman who developed amnesia after an assault and rape, observed that she became extremely upset when taken back to the scene of the assault, even though she did not explicitly remember what had happened or where. Lyon (1985) described a case in which a patient's implicit memory proved therapeutically useful. This patient was utterly unable to retrieve explicitly any autobiographical information. But

when asked to randomly dial numbers on the telephone, she unknowingly dialed the number of her mother, who then identified the patient.

The foregoing observations were made under clinical testing conditions that necessarily lack experimental rigor, and thus can be viewed as no more than suggestive. Nevertheless, they clearly support the idea that explicitly inaccessible autobiographical information can be expressed implicitly, and thereby encourage serious investigation of the phenomenon.

One further issue that merits brief mention concerns the role played by organic factors in the genesis of functional retrograde amnesia. By definition, organic brain damage is not the *immediate* cause of this form of amnesia. However several investigators have reported a prior history of head injury or other kinds of brain damage in functional retrograde amnesia patients (e.g., Abeles and Schilder, 1935; Kanzer, 1939; Schacter et al., 1982). These observations suggest that in some cases, subtle pre-existing neurological dysfunction may interact with emotional trauma to produce functional retrograde amnesia.

Theories of functional retrograde amnesia. In view of the fact that there have been relatively few controlled empirical attempts to delineate the characteristics of memory loss during functional retrograde amnesia, it is perhaps not surprising that there is a corresponding lack of well developed theories concerning the nature of the phenomenon. Nonetheless, because functional retrograde amnesia is a *reversible* disorder, all theoretical attempts begin with the assumption that it represents a temporary loss of access to stored information. An early account was put forward by Janet (1904), who argued that amnesia is produced by a process of *dissociation,* whereby traumatic mental contents are split off from the ego into a separate subconscious mental domain, and are thus rendered inaccessible to awareness. In Janet's view, dissociation is an automatic, pathological process of genetic origin that occurs in individuals without sufficient ego energy to accommodate the stress of emotional trauma. An important implication of

anet's view is that consciously inaccessible information is still expressed in the patient's behavior,
ia pathological symptoms, hallucinations and the
ke — subconscious 'fixed ideas' which, in the terminology adopted here, constitute implicit
memories of the amnesic patient's past. Prince
(916) put forward a similar view, except that he
id not view dissociation as an exclusively
athological process. Modern developments of
nese ideas, referred to as *neodissociationist*
neories, have been put forward by Hilgard (1977)
nd Kihlstrom (1984, 1987).

Freud and Breuer (1966), in contrast, argued
nat functional amnesia is attributable to an active
rocess of *repression* in which the ego works to in-
ibit the conscious expression of emotionally
nreatening traumata. This view has been widely
ccepted among psychiatric investigators of func-
onal amnesias, although the concept of repres-
ion remains controversial (e.g., Erdelyi and
joldberg, 1979). A somewhat different approach
vas taken by Schacter et al. (1982), who argued
nat functional amnesia represents a selective
ailure of an episodic memory system together with
paring of semantic memory. They suggested furner that the 'control elements' of episodic
nemory — higher order units of information such
s one's name — can be inhibited as a result of
sychological trauma and prevent conscious access
o the lower levels of autobiographical information
ested under them. Unfortunately, however, there
re no strong empirical grounds for distinguishing
etween these alternative accounts of functional
etrograde amnesia. A critical challenge for future
esearch is to construct and implement empirical
ests to discriminate between the different theories.
Limited amnesia. Not all cases of functional
etrograde amnesias entail loss of personal identity
nd large sectors of the personal past. In some in-
tances, amnesia is restricted to a single traumatic
vent or episode. This kind of memory loss, refer-
ed to elsewhere as *limited amnesia* (Schacter,
986a), is frequently observed in conjunction with
he commission of violent crimes (e.g., Hopwood
nd Snell, 1933; Taylor and Kopelman, 1984; see

Schacter, 1986a, for discussion). Little scientific
information exists concerning the properties of
limited amnesia. For example, it is not known how
often people remain permanently amnesic for
traumatic episodes and how often they recover
them. Some evidence suggests that amnesia for
emotionally traumatic episodes is state dependent,
inasmuch as the forgotten episode may become accessible when an amnesic individual re-experiences
the emotional state that prevailed during the
trauma (e.g., Bower, 1981; Watkins, 1949). In addition, early clinical observations provide some
evidence of implicit memory for consciously inaccessible episodes. Janet (1904), for example,
reported cases in which the contents of the
traumatic episode were experienced as involuntary
and unfamiliar 'hallucinations' by the patient. Accordingly, there is some reason to believe that
limited amnesia, like full-blown functional
retrograde amnesia, represents a reversible access
failure. Further investigations will be required to
provide a firmer basis for understanding limited
amnesia.

Multiple personality amnesia
Psychologists and psychiatrists have recently
displayed growing interest in multiple personality
disorders, in part because the syndrome is not as
rare as was once believed (e.g., Bliss, 1986; Boor,
1980; Putnam et al., 1986). Yet ever since the
earliest case reports of the phenomenon, amnesia
between personalities has been recognized as one
of the most striking features of these patients (Coriat, 1916; Janet, 1907; Mitchell, 1816; Prince,
1910; Sidis and Goodhart, 1898; Taylor and Martin, 1944). Most contemporary investigators, too,
view between-personality amnesia as a cardinal
symptom of multiple personality disorder (Abse,
1987; Coons, 1980; Greaves, 1980; Ludwig et al.,
1972; Silberman et al., 1985; Sutcliffe and Jones,
1962), and there is solid evidence to support this
notion: Putnam et al. (1986) found evidence for
amnesia in 98% of a sample of 100 cases. In fact,
the occurrence of unexplainable memory lapses in
everyday life is a frequent presenting symptom of

patients who are subsequently given a diagnosis of multiple personality. Such lapses can produce confusion and even bewilderment in both patients and others. For instance, Osgood et al. (1976) described a case in which the main personality earned a substantial income, yet was continually surprised to find that she had no money in her bank account at the end of each month. The money had been withdrawn and used by another personality, yet the main personality lacked any conscious recollection of the withdrawal or spending of the money. In a case reported by Bliss (1986), the patient had a personality named 'Willow' who worked as a prostitute. This personality's experiences, however, were inaccessible to the main personality, who was understandably perplexed when she encountered former customers: "People approach me and say they know me but I don't know them. Men say 'Hi, Willow, when are you going back to work?' They sometimes say shocking or insulting things which I don't want to repeat. I don't like forgetting things" (p. 140).

Features of multiple personality amnesia. Despite a general agreement that between-personality amnesia constitutes an integral aspect of multiple personality disorder, there has been remarkably little investigation of memory function in these patients (Schacter et al., in press). Clinical observations, however, point toward two possibly important features of between-personality memory impairment. First, the amnesia appears to be *asymmetrical:* although at least one personality shows dense amnesia for the experiences of the others, one or more typically has relatively unimpaired access to the experiences of some or all other personalities (e.g., Bliss, 1986; Coriat, 1916; Prince, 1910; Thigpen and Cleckley, 1957). Second, even when a particular personality lacks explicit memory for what has happened to others, some implicit memory can be observed. For instance, in his classic description of the case of Miss Beauchamp, Prince (1910) reported that personality 'B IV' had involuntary 'visions' that depicted the experiences of personality 'B I', but ". . . the visions were pure automatisms, excrescences in her

mind, without conscious association with the other experiences of the life which they pictured. When seeing a vision she [B IV] did not recognize the pictorial experiences as her own, even though it was of B I's life; there was no sense of memory connected with it" (p. 265). Similarly, B IV experienced strong emotional reactions to people and places that had affective significance for B I; B IV however, had no conscious recollection of the people or places that elicited the emotion and could not understand why she felt it. Similar observations of implicit memory across personalities were made by other early clinical observers (Coriat, 1916; Janet, 1907; Sidis and Goodhart, 1898).

More recently, a few experimental investigations of multiple personality amnesia have been reported; they confirm and extend the foregoing observations. In the first quantitative study of memory function in multiple personality, Ludwig et al. (1972) described a case in which there was a core personality, Jonah, and three other personalities, Sammy, Usoffa Abdulla and King Young. Jonah was completely amnesic for the other three personalities, who in turn had varying degrees of memory for Jonah and each other. Ludwig et al. examined whether information acquired by one personality could influence the performance of another on various learning and conditioning tasks, despite the existence of cross-personality amnesia for each other's experiences. For example, using the paired-associate learning tests from the two alternative forms of the Wechsler Memory Scale, they found that having either Jonah or Usoffa Abdulla study a particular list facilitated learning of that same list by each of the other personalities. Similarly, exposing either Jonah or Usoffa Abdulla to one of the WMS stories facilitated subsequent memory for that story in the other personalities. Evidence for transfer of classical conditioning (pairing of shock with a light or tone) from each of the personalities to some of the others was also obtained, as was evidence of cross-personality facilitation of performance on the WAIS block design test. In two additional paradigms, however, transfer was observed only from Jonah to other personalities, and not vice versa. One of these involved study of paired-associates and subsequent free association performance; the other involved GSR responses to words that had emotional significance for each of the personalities.

Based on these observations, Ludwig et al. suggested that affectively charged material transferred only from Jonah to other personalities, whereas affectively neutral material transferred among all personalities. This explanation is not entirely satisfying, however, because there are no strong reasons why the paired associate task showing asymmetrical transfer should be considered emotional while the one yielding symmetrical transfer should be viewed as neutral. Nor it is clear why a shock-conditioning procedure – which produced symmetrical transfer between all personalities – ought to be considered non-emotional. Whatever the explanation of the asymmetrical transfer, these instances of transfer can all be interpreted as implicit memory phenomena: a particular personality's performance is facilitated by the experiences of another personality under conditions in which conscious recollection of those experiences is not required and is in all likelihood precluded. Note, however, that Ludwig et al. did not distinguish between implicit and explicit memory and thus did not actually test whether any of the personalities could consciously remember what another had studied.

Similar considerations apply to a more recent study by Dick-Barnes et al. (1987). They tested three different personalities out of a total of 16 that had been identified in a 28-yr-old female patient. Like Ludwig et al., they found that having one of the personalities study a paired-associate list facilitated learning of that same list by any of the other personalities. Moreover, the amount of between-personality facilitation was roughly comparable to the amount of within-personality facilitation. A similar pattern of results was observed with a perceptual-motor learning task: acquisition of skill at the task by one personality facilitated skill acquisition by the others. Although

these observations can be viewed as implicit memory phenomena, Dick-Barnes et al., like Ludwig et al., did not make an implicit/explicit distinction and provided no data on whether the various personalities could explicitly remember the information studied by the others. Evidence on this point is provided in a study of cross-personality interference by Silberman et al. (1985) that included nine multiple-personality patients. They selected two personalities in each patient who were mutually amnesic, and examined performance in two different conditions: (1) similar categorized lists were studied successively by two different personalities, and (2) the lists were studied successively by the same personality. If information acquired by one personality does not interfere with performance in another, recall of individual list items should be higher in the first condition than in the second. However, Silberman et al. reported evidence of retroactive and proactive interference across personalities: recall was lower in the first than the second condition. Nevertheless, Silberman et al. found that "Subjectively, all MPD patients reported that all the words they remembered had been heard in the same personality state" (p. 257). Thus, it seems reasonable to interpret the observed interference effects as implicit expressions of memory by one personality for the experiences of another.

A study that specifically contrasted implicit and explicit memory across personalities has been reported recently by Nissen et al. (1988). They studied a 45-yr-old woman with a rather remarkable 22 diagnosed personalities. One personality has extensive awareness of and explicit memory for the experiences of the others, three receive 'advice' from some of the others, and the remaining 18 are densely amnesic for all experiences except their own. Nissen et al. focussed on eight mutually amnesic personalities that could each be elicited in response to an appropriate request by the experimenter. Target materials were studied by one personality (which was elicited by the patient's psychiatrist) and after retention intervals of approximately 5 – 10 minutes, another personality was elicited for memory testing. Little or no evidence of between-personality explicit memory was observed on a variety of tests. Thus, when the personality named Alice studied a list of words, and Bonnie was subsequently given a Yes/No recognition test and asked to pick out the words shown previously to Alice, she circled none of them. By contrast, evidence of cross-personality implicit memory was observed on several tests. For example, on a word fragment completion test in which personalities were required to try to complete graphemic fragments with a single correct solution (e.g., A___A___L_ for ASSASSIN; Tulving et al., 1982), Bonnie's performance was facilitated or primed by prior exposure of a word to Alice. Similar cross-personality implicit memory effects were observed on tasks that required identification of briefly exposed words (Jacoby and Dallas, 1981), and learning to respond to a sequential pattern of lights (Nissen and Bullemer, 1987). Significantly, however, no evidence of cross-personality transfer was observed on several other implicit memory tasks, including solution of semantically ambiguous sentence puzzles (McAndrews et al., 1987) and pictures (Bransford and Johnson, 1972), and free association to word stems with more than 10 possible completions (Graf et al., 1984). Moreover, repeated administration of the WMS logical memory passages did not yield any evidence of cross-personality facilitation of learning, as had been observed in the Ludwig et al. (1972) study. These data indicate that testing memory implicitly was a necessary but not sufficient condition for observing cross-personality transfer in this patient. Nissen et al. argued that the implicit tasks in which transfer was not observed required extensive semantic interpretation of stimulus material (e.g., solving ambiguous sentence puzzles, comprehending a story). Such interpretive activities may have drawn on prior knowledge idiosyncratic to each personality. Since this personality-specific knowledge would have been available only when the same personality performed at both study and test, cross-personality implicit memory may be observed only with tasks

and materials that do not tap personality specific knowledge.

Theories of multiple personality amnesia. Several ideas have been proposed to account for multiple personality amnesia. Janet (1904) and Prince (1910) applied their dissociation theories to the phenomenon, arguing that alternative personalities represent complex systems of subconscious ideas that are split off from, and function independently of, the central ego. This basic proposal has been developed and modified by Hilgard (1977) and Kihlstrom (1984). Bliss (1986) suggested that multiple personalities are hypnotic virtuosos who are victims of spontaneous self-hypnosis and suffer from a form of hypnotic amnesia. Bower (1981) portrayed multiple personality amnesia as an extreme manifestation of the phenomenon of state-dependent retrieval, whereby information acquired in one emotional state is inaccessible in another. Adopting a social psychological perspective, Kenny (1986), Sarbin and Coe (1979) and Spanos (1986) depicted multiple personality disorder as a kind of role-playing activity in which amnesia constitutes part of the role to be played.

As was the case in previous sections, there is little empirical evidence on which to base an assessment of alternative theoretical accounts of multiple personality amnesia. Accordingly, we can do no better at the present time than to register a plea for more systematic studies of the amnesic phenomena observed in multiple personality disorders.

Non-pathological functional amnesias

Infantile and childhood amnesia

Parents often remark that their offspring remember surprisingly little of the events of their early years – even events that would seem highly memorable. In *The Psychopathology of Everyday Life* (1901), Freud drew popular attention to the paucity of adult memories for the events of early childhood. He asserted that an infantile and childhood amnesia covered the first five to eight years of life, with only a few isolated fragments of experience – referred to as screen memories – remaining accessible to adult recall (see also Freud, 1899).

This developmental phenomenon was also appreciated by members of the first generation of experimental psychologists (Hall, 1899; Henri and Henri, 1895; Titchener, 1900), as well as by a number of literary figures (see De Mare, 1935; Salaman, 1972). Nevertheless, infantile/childhood amnesia has been virtually ignored by cognitive and developmental psychologists – perhaps because convincing empirical documentation has been so difficult to obtain. Consider, for example, the methodological problems attendant on demonstrating that 20-year-olds forget more events occurring from birth to age 5 than 50-year-olds do of events occurring from ages 30 to 35 – while controlling for adequacy of encoding, the number of events during the intervening retention interval, and the like.

Features of infantile and childhood amnesia. Prima facie evidence for infantile and childhood amnesia comes in two forms: surveys of subjects' earliest recollections (for a review, see Kihlstrom and Harackiewicz, 1982); and more extensive samplings of autobiographical memory (for a review, see Kihlstrom, 1981; Wetzler and Sweeney, 1986a; Rubin et al., 1986). For example, Kihlstrom and Harackiewicz (1982) found that high-school and college students' earliest personal recollections tended to be of events occurring between the third and fourth birthday – a figure that concurs with the findings on earlier generations of subjects (e.g., Dudycha and Dudycha, 1941). As another example, Waldfogel (1948) asked college students to freely recall *all* of their recollections up until their 8th birthday: relatively few memories were recovered before the 4th or 5th birthday, and almost nothing from the first three years of life (see also Crovitz and Harvey, 1979).

Evidence of a different kind comes from studies employing the cued recall procedure developed by Crovitz, which was discussed earlier in the chapter with respect to functional retrograde amnesia (1970; see also Crovitz et al., 1980; Crovitz and

Quina-Holland, 1976; Crovitz and Schiffman, 1974; Robinson, 1976). Wetzler and Sweeney (1986a), reanalysing data collected by Rubin (1982), concluded that subjects produce fewer memories from before age 5 than would be expected given the power function that describes the distribution of autobiographical memories across the lifespan. In that sense, then, the relative poverty of memory for events occurring before age 5 would seem to qualify as a true amnesia. Furthermore, it may be heuristically useful to distinguish between *infantile* amnesia, covering the first two years of life (i.e., before linguistic representations of memory are possible), and *childhood amnesia* covering the remaining period.

Theories of infantile and childhood amnesia. A remarkable feature of the literature on childhood amnesia is the vast proliferation of theories to account for the phenomenon before it had ever been convincingly established (see Wetzler and Sweeney, 1986b). For example, Freud (1901) argued that childhood amnesia resulted from the repression of conflict-laden sexual and aggressive ideas and impulses, occurring at the resolution of the Oedipal crisis at about age 5. This approach would be classified as a relatively pure retrieval theory, inasmuch as the repressed contents remain available in the memory store, if not accessible to conscious recall. More recently, White and Pillemer (1979) offered an encoding theory of the phenomenon, arguing that young children do not possess the information-processing capacity to encode memories well enough to make them accessible later on. Their viewpoint is congruent with psychobiological studies of nonhuman animals (e.g, Campbell and Coulter, 1976; Campbell and Spear, 1972; Coulter, 1979; Nadel and Zola-Morgan, 1984; Spear, 1979) and human neonates and infants (Nadel and Zola-Morgan, 1984; Schacter and Moscovitch, 1984) that relate infantile amnesia to the myelinization of neural tissue, development of hippocampus and other medial-temporal structures, or maturation of the cortex in general.

Other approaches may be classified as 'encoding

specificity' theories, in that they emphasize the relations between encoding and retrieval processes. An early example is Schactel (1947), whose theory represented an eclectic combination of Freud and Bartlett. He proposed that memories encoded in terms of pre-oedipal, primary process schemata were incompatible with the retrieval schemes characteristic of post-oedipal, secondary process thought. In a similar vein, Neisser (1962, 1967) combined Bartlett with Piaget and suggested that memories encoded by means of sensorimotor and preoperational schemata characteristic of early childhood were incompatible with the modes of retrieval characteristic of concrete or formal operations. In either case, the incompatibility between encoding and retrieval operations renders memories of early childhood that are available in memory storage inaccessible to adult recall — much in the manner of the state-dependent memory deficits produced by psychoactive drugs (Eich. 1980, 1989b).

At the same time, it is possible that infantile and childhood amnesias have less to do with the biological maturation and cognitive development of children than they do with the environments in which children live. Neisser (1962) has pointed out that the same period (ages 5 to 7) associated with such internal events as the development of the hippocampus, resolution of the oedipal crisis, shift from preoperational thought to concrete operations, and the acquisition of sophisticated strategies for memory processing is also marked by a major event in the external environment: the child goes to school. The onset of formal schooling provides the child, for the first time, with the temporal and spatial structures (weekdays vs. weekends; home vs. school) that permit one episode to be reliably distinguished from another. In the final analysis, the source of infantile and childhood amnesia is likely to be found in the interaction between the information-processing capacities of young children, and the information that their environment gives them to process.

At the same time as we consider theoretical explanations of infantile and childhood amnesia, we must remember that even neonates are capable of learning, and that a great deal of information acquired during childhood is retained by adults. Procedural and semantic knowledge, whose use does not require recollection of the specific circumstances under which it was acquired, is apparently unaffected by the amnesic process(es) that impair infants' remembering of specific events (Nadel and Zola-Morgan, 1986; Schacter and Moscovitch, 1984). Even within the domain of episodic memory, it may prove to be the case that infantile and childhood amnesia affects only explicit memory — the conscious recollection of past events — and spares the implicit effects of past experience on ongoing experience, thought, and action.

Posthypnotic amnesia

Posthypnotic amnesia occurs when subjects are unable to remember, after hypnosis has been terminated, the events and experiences that transpired while they were hypnotized (for reviews, see Kihlstrom, 1983, 1985; Kihlstrom and Evans, 1979). After the hypnotist administers a prearranged cue to cancel the suggestion, the amnesic subject will typically recover these memories — although some degree of residual amnesia may persist for a short period of time. This disruption in memory rarely occurs unless it has been suggested to the subject. And even with an explicit suggestion, the extent of amnesia is highly correlated with measured hypnotizability: insusceptible subjects show little if any response to the suggestion, while the very densest amnesias tend to be confined to the most highly hypnotizable subjects (sometimes called 'hypnotic virtuosos').

Features of posthypnotic amnesia. Like the other functional amnesias, posthypnotic amnesia is a phenomenon of episodic memory (Tulving, 1983). That is, amnesic subjects fail to remember specific events and experiences that occurred while they were hypnotized (suggested amnesia can also occur without termination of hypnosis; see Spanos, 1986). When amnesic subjects forget a wordlist that has been memorized during hypnosis, the vocabulary items themselves remain available for use in conversation, as word associations and category instances, and the like (Williamsen et al., 1965; Kihlstrom, 1980). It should be noted that appropriately worded suggestions can produce aphasias and agnosias as well as amnesia (Kihlstrom, 1985). Thus, subjects given the suggestion that they will be unable to pronounce the word *house* may be unable to understand a semantically related word such as *home* (Hilgard, 1977). In this chapter, however, we are concerned only with the apparent inability of hypnotized subjects to remember specific experiences that occurred while they were hypnotized (nothing systematic is known about the effectiveness of suggestions of amnesia for events occurring outside hypnosis).

Several studies from Hull's (1933) research program illustrate the selectivity of posthypnotic amnesia. For example, Patten (1932; cited in Hull, 1933) gave subjects practice in complex mental addition for 18 days; on Days 7–12, the practice took place in hypnosis. After termination of hypnosis the subjects were unable to remember the practice sessions which occurred in hypnosis; nevertheless, the learning curve for these sessions was continuous with that derived from the preceding and following nonhypnotic sessions. Similar findings were obtained by Coors (1928; cited in Hull, 1933) with subjects learning a stylus maze; and by Life (1929; cited in Hull, 1933) with subjects learning paired associates. Apparently, subjects retained procedural knowledge acquired in hypnosis, in the form of certain cognitive and motor skills; however, they were unable to remember the experiences through which they acquired that knowledge. The dissociation between procedural knowledge and episodic memory – the former spared, the latter disrupted – is characteristic of posthypnotic amnesia.

Another dissociation has been observed in posthypnotic source amnesia (Evans, 1979a; Evans and Thorn, 1966). In source amnesia experiments, hypnotized subjects are incidentally taught some items of obscure factual knowledge while they are hypnotized, and subsequently receive a suggestion to forget what happened during hypnosis. When tested posthypnotically, many subjects appear ignorant of this new factual information, just as they are unaware of the learning experience and other events of hypnosis. However, a substantial minority of subjects will forget the various hypnotic experiences, but nonetheless will correctly answer the questions whose answers they learned while hypnotized. When queried, these subjects seem unaware that they learned these facts while they were hypnotized, and may even attribute their knowledge to some nonhypnotic context – a tendency which gives the phenomenon its name. The factual information itself may be considered part of the subject's fund of semantic knowledge, the use of which is not impaired by the amnesia suggestion. Although Evans' experiments have been criticized on the grounds of demand characteristics (Spanos et al., 1985), it may be noted that a similar dissociation has been observed in cases of the amnesic syndrome due to brain damage (e.g., Schacter et al., 1984; Shimamura and Squire, 1987).

A further dissociative feature of posthypnotic amnesia is also illustrated by experiments in which subjects are asked to memorize lists of familiar words (Kihlstrom, 1980; Williamsen et al., 1965). If the acquisition phase is followed by suggestions of amnesia for the learning experience, hypnotizable subjects typically will be unable to remember the contents of the lists they have recently memorized. Nevertheless, they remain able to use the constituent items as word associations and category instances. Giving word associations and category exemplars are prototypical semantic memory tasks. These functions are unimpaired by suggestions for amnesia, although they may be affected by suggestions of other types (Bertrand and Spanos, 1987; Spanos et al., 1982a).

Theories of posthypnotic amnesia. The fact that amnesia does not occur spontaneously with the termination of hypnosis, and can be reversed without the reinduction of hypnosis, distinguishes posthypnotic amnesia from instances of state-dependent memory (e.g., Eich, 1980, 1989b). And the fact that it can be reversed at all distinguishes it from other forms of instructed forgetting (Kihlstrom, 1983). Moreover, reversibility clearly marks posthypnotic amnesia as a failure of memory retrieval: the critical memories are adequately encoded, and remain available in storage, but amnesic subjects seem to have trouble gaining conscious access to them. Nevertheless, the precise nature of this retrieval disruption has been subject to some controversy. Viewed from a psychoanalytic perspective, for example, posthypnotic amnesia may be attributed to the motivated repression of unwanted memories (for reviews, see Kihlstrom and Hoyt, 1988). From a social-psychological perspective, on the other hand, amnesia has been construed as a product of self-distraction and strategic self-presentation (e.g., Coe, 1978; Sarbin and Coe, 1979; Spanos, 1986; but see Kihlstrom, 1985). This chapter adopts the perspective of contemporary information-processing views of memory, which characterizes posthypnotic amnesia as a disruption in memory retrieval (for a more detailed account, see Kihlstrom, 1985).

On the basis of studies such as those described above, Kihlstrom (1980, 1984, 1985) has suggested that posthypnotic amnesia is characterized by dissociations between episodic memory and both procedural and semantic knowledge. However, the available literature is not completely organized by these distinctions. McKoon and her colleagues (McKoon et al., 1986) have pointed out that retroactive inhibition, in which memory for one wordlist impairs retrieval of another wordlist learned previously, is not affected by posthypnotic amnesia. For example, Graham and Patton (1968) asked subjects to learn two lists of adjectives; for some, the second list was learned in hypnosis. Those who received a suggestion to forget the second list were able to recall very little of it; nevertheless, they showed a level of retroactive interference on the first list equivalent to that displayed by subjects who remembered the interpolated list perfectly. Dillon and Spanos (1983) made similar observations in an experiment on proactive interference. The problem posed by

studies of interference in posthypnotic amnesia is that the interfering memory is episodic in nature, reflecting the residual trace of the subject's particular encounter with the interfering wordlist. Thus, the amnesia cannot be adequately characterized as reflecting a dissociation between episodic and semantic memory (Kihlstrom, 1985).

A finding with similar implications was obtained by Kihlstrom (1980) in two experiments originally intended to illustrate the dissociation between episodic and semantic memory. In the first experiment, subjects memorized a list of unrelated words, and then received a suggestion that they would not be able to remember the words they had learned. On an initial test of recall, the subgroup of 'virtuoso' hypnotic subjects remembered virtually none of the words they had previously memorized. At this point, the subjects were asked to give word associations to various probes. The critical probes had a high a priori probability of eliciting the items of the previously memorized wordlist; the neutral probes targeted carefully matched items that had not been learned. As noted earlier, the suggestion did not disrupt the word-association performance of the amnesic subjects: the items from the memorized wordlist remained available for use as vocabulary items. More important, there was a semantic priming effect observed in the word-association performance, such that the subjects were more likely to give the targeted response to critical as opposed to neutral probes. Most important, there was no difference in priming between amnesic and nonamnesic subjects. These findings were confirmed in a conceptual replication in which amnesic subjects memorized a categorized wordlist and were subsequently asked to provide instances of critical and neutral taxonomic categories (see also Spanos et al., 1982a).

Like retroactive and proactive interference, semantic priming is an effect of episodic memory; but, unlike free recall, it is not disrupted by suggestions for posthypnotic amnesia. However, while free recall is an expression of explicit memory, interference and priming are manifestations of implicit memory for a prior episode. That is, neither phenomenon requires that the subject be aware of the prior experience that is the source of the inhibitory and facilitative effects that are observed. In the final analysis, findings such as these suggest that the fundamental dissociation observed in posthypnotic amnesia is between explicit and implicit forms of episodic memory – the latter spared, the former impaired (Kihlstrom, 1987). In some respects, the explicit-implicit distinction subsumes the dissociations between episodic memory and procedural knowledge, and between episodic memory and semantic knowledge, described above. Most procedural and semantic knowledge is acquired through experience. But it is not necessary to remember the circumstances under which this knowledge was acquired in order to employ it in various tasks; nor do we, ordinarily; nor, when we do, does it help us in any way. Thus, the use of procedural and semantic knowledge can be an occasion for the subject to display implicit memory for some previous experience.

Sleep-induced amnesia

A great deal of activity transpires while we are asleep. Some of this activity is external to the sleeper: traffic passes in the street outside the house, the house cat knocks over a lamp in the living room, the couple next door has a marital spat. Other activity is internal: mental activity, including dreams and nightmares, occur in all the stages of sleep (Foulkes, 1985), and some of us sleepwalk or sleeptalk (Arkin et al., 1978). Yet virtually none of it is remembered upon awakening in the morning. This amnesia induced by (or at least associated with) sleep appears to be universally experienced.
Features of sleep-induced amnesia. Except in the twin cases of memory for dreams (Cohen, 1979; Koulack and Goodenough, 1976), and sleep learning (Aarons, 1976; Eich, 1989a), sleep-induced amnesia has not been the subject of much systematic inquiry (Arkin et al., 1978). Yet the anecdotal evidence from the laboratory provides ample evidence to supplement personal experience. Thus, although the typical night's eight hours of sleep encompass four or five full sleep cycles, most

people rarely remember any dreams at all save (perhaps) the one that occurred in the REM cycle out of which they awakened, and little or nothing of the mental activity that transpires during intervening NREM periods (for reviews, see Cohen, 1979; Goodenough, 1978; Koulack and Goodenough, 1976). Attempts at sleep learning are almost uniformly unsuccessful at yielding memory traces that are retrievable after awakening, regardless of the sleep stage during which the material is presented (Aarons, 1976; Eich, 1989a).

Still more evidence concerning post-sleep amnesia, if any were needed, comes from observations of sleepwalking and sleeptalking under both natural and laboratory conditions. Sleeptalkers may engage in fairly complex speech acts, including interchanges with real or imagined conversational partners (for reviews, see Arkin, 1978, 1981). These individuals rarely reveal secrets in their speeches, and this censorship itself would also seem to require extensive analysis of their content. Nevertheless, sleeptalkers typically remember little or nothing of what they have said the next morning. Similarly, sleepwalkers engage in relatively complex and coordinated behavioral activities as they navigate their environments (Gastaut and Broughton, 1964; Kales et al., 1966a; Sours et al., 1963), but display little memory for their sojourns upon awakening.

Additional evidence on memory for sleep episodes may be found in a remarkable series of studies on *sleep suggestion* performed by Evans and his associates (Evans et al., 1969, 1970; Perry et al., 1978; for a review, see Evans, 1979b). In these studies, subjects were administered hypnotic-like suggestions for simple motor responses during REM sleep. The cues were tested under three conditions: in the same REM period as that in which the suggestion had been administered; in a subsequent REM period, without repetition of the suggestion; and on a subsequent night. Although the subjects showed no signs of arousal (as indicated by EEG alpha activity), they responded appropriately to the cues approximately 20% of the time. After awakening, they did not remember the suggestions or the cues. Nevertheless, upon returning to the laboratory for a subsequent night's sleep, the subjects continued to respond to a significant number of cues even though the suggestions were not readministered. The findings are clearly reminiscent of the state-dependent memory phenomena induced by psychoactive drugs or moods (Eich, 1977, 1980, 1989b).

Theories of sleep-induced amnesia. One explanation of this universally experienced memory deficit is that the higher cortical centers which engage in complex information processing shut down during sleep, with the result that most events occurring while the person is asleep are not noticed and not processed; therefore accessible traces of these events fail to be encoded in memory. Thus, the most commonly accepted explanation of post-sleep amnesia is in terms of 'consolidation failure' (McGaugh, 1966), or, perhaps more properly, poor encoding (Cermak and Craik, 1979). For example, Koulack and Goodenough (1976; see also Goodenough, 1978) have proposed that the low level of cortical arousal characteristic of sleep effectively prevents the sleeper from performing the cognitive operations necessary to encode memory traces of dreams that are accessible in the subsequent waking state (Eysenck, 1976). In this view, dreams are remembered when the sleeper awakens during the dream, permitting retrieval from short-term memory. Alternatively, if the sleeper awakens shortly after a dream has occurred, residual information retrieved from short-term memory may serve as a cue to the retrieval of a highly degraded long-term memory trace of the dream. If retrieval is delayed until all trace of the dream has decayed or been displaced, the long-term memory trace of the dream will be virtually inaccessible.

This arousal-retrieval model of amnesia for dreams is based on classic multistore models of memory (Atkinson and Shifrin, 1968; Waugh and Norman, 1965), and has been adopted by Arkin (1981) as an explanation of amnesia for episodes of sleeptalking. Goodenough (1978) has also employed the model as an explanation of the general failure of research to find evidence for learning during sleep (Aarons, 1976; Eich, 1987). Thus, sleepers generally fail to remember information presented during sleep, unless the information was accompanied by evidence of physiological arousal (Simon and Emmons, 1955; Koukkou and Lehman, 1968; Lehman and Koukkou, 1973). It seems that the arousal-retrieval model provides an economical account of a wide variety of memory failures observed in the sleep context. (In passing, it may be noted that a similar explanation has been offered for the amnesia displayed by surgical patients given general anesthesia (Kihlstrom and Schacter, 1989; Trustman et al., 1977). However, more recent experiments, while not definitive, seem to indicate that this amnesia may affect only explicit memory for surgical events, and that under some circumstances adequately anesthetized patients may display memory (without awareness) of events that transpired during their surgery (Bennett, 1987, 1988; Goldmann, 1987; but see Eich et al., 1985).)

Although the hypothesis of encoding failure has the twin appeals of generality and parsimony, the strong view of cortical inactivity during sleep is contradicted by a variety of evidence. Certainly some degree of information-processing occurs during sleep. Anecdotally, it appears that sleepers may awaken readily to novel sounds, or to those that are unexpected or have special meaning (as when parents awaken to their child's cry), even though they remain unresponsive to other sounds of even greater stimulus intensity. Moreover, experimental evidence indicates that low-intensity environmental stimuli reliably evoke cortical, autonomic and behavioral responses in subjects who nevertheless remain asleep (Williams et al., 1964, 1966; for a review, see Williams, 1973), although these responses may not be entirely normal in terms of latency and amplitude. Further, environmental events can be incorporated into the contents of ongoing dreams (Dement and Wolpert, 1958; for a review, see Arkin and Antrobus, 1978). Although it may be the case that more complex information processing is possible in Stage REM than in NREM, these sorts of results indicate that sleepers remain capable of performing at least some (presumably automatized) information-processing functions.

This possibility raises the question of alternative explanations for the various phenomena of post-sleep amnesia, especially those affecting memory for dreams, that do not involve encoding failure. For example, Freud (1900) argued that memory for dreams was impaired by repression, which may be construed as a motivated failure to retrieve an available memory. However, while some early experimental tests seemed to support the repression theory (Goodenough, 1967), later work has not been persuasive (Goodenough, 1978; Goodenough et al., 1975). A more contemporary approach is represented by Cohen (1974, 1976, 1979), who has interpreted amnesia for dreams in terms of interference theory. While the interference hypothesis is supported by a considerable body of experimental research, most of the empirical data supporting interference are also compatible with the arousal-retrieval model (Cohen, 1979; Goodenough, 1978).

Finally, it has been suggested that the events of sleep may be encoded in long-term memory, but accessible only during the sleep state (Arkin, 1981; Cohen, 1979; Goodenough, 1978; Overton, 1973). Obviously, this hypnothesis of sleep-state-dependent memory is difficult to test. However, some supportive evidence is provided by Evans's (1979b) studies of sleep suggestion, described earlier. The sleep suggestion studies indicate that environmental events can be encoded in long-term memory, although access to this information may be dependent on the subject's being asleep at the time. This obviously bodes ill for those entrepreneurs who make strong claims for the effectiveness of sleep learning. From the point of view of accessibility, sleep-state dependency is effectively indistinguishable from consolidation failure or degraded encoding. However, it should be noted that observations of post-sleep amnesia are based mostly on measurements of explicit memory — that is, the subjects' ability to consciously remember episodes that occurred while they were asleep. It is possible that, if afforded the opportunity to do so, subjects who fail to show explicit memory for such episodes may nevertheless display implicit memory for them — that is, changes in task performance that are attributable to a preserved memory of some prior experience.

Some provocative hints of implicit memory for sleep experiences are provided in accounts of experiments on sleep learning conducted in the Soviet Union and Eastern Europe (for reviews, see Hoskovec, 1966; Hoskovec and Cooper, 1967; Rubin, 1968, 1971). For example, Svyadosch (1962; republished in Rubin, 1968) noted that in some cases the stimulus material was incorporated into dreams reported upon awakening; or it was experienced as entering consciousness unbidden, from an unknown source.

Unfortunately, these experiments generally fail to employ EEG indices of arousal from sleep, so their positive results are equivocal. Nevertheless, they hold open the possibility that material presented during sleep is successfully encoded and available in memory storage, but accessible to retrieval only in circumstances that do not require subjects to consciously remember a particular episode. Demonstration of sleep learning with measures of implicit rather than explicit memory would strengthen the argument that sleep events which do not awaken the subject, the contents of sleepspeeches, sleepwalks and dreams, are encoded and available in storage as well.

Interpretation of functional amnesias and the problem of simulation

The material covered in the preceding sections reveals that a rich variety of memory phenomena can be grouped under the general rubric of functional amnesia. It seems clear, however, that our current knowledge of each of the various functional amnesias is rather modest, and that our understanding of the relation between them is even more limited. We do not know, for example, whether fundamentally different mechanisms are involved in pathological and non-pathological functional amnesias, or for that matter, whether any of the individual amnesias discussed here share common mechanisms with any of the others. One feature that may provide important clues concerning these relationships is the extent to which a particular amnesia is reversible. Functional retrograde amnesia and hypnotic amnesia are both clearly reversible, and the evidence on multiple personality amnesia suggests that it, too, is reversed when personalities are integrated therapeutically (Bliss, 1986). In contrast, there is no compelling evidence that either infantile and childhood amnesias or sleep and dream amnesias are reversible. It is thus possible that different explanatory constructs need to be applied to reversible and non-reversible functional amnesias.

The reversibility/non-reversibility of functional amnesias may also be helpful in understanding their relation to the organic amnesias. For example, the classical amnesic syndromes associated with damage to the temporal lobes or Korsakoff's syndrome are typically stable, chronic disorders (e.g., Cermak, 1982; Squire, 1982). In contrast, some aspects of amnesia observed after closed head injury (Russell and Nathan, 1946; Schacter and Crovitz, 1977), transient ischemias (Fischer and Adams, 1958) and electroconvulsive therapy are reversible, although even these amnesias usually contain a non-reversible component. It is tempting to speculate that some of the mechanisms involved in reversible and non-reversible amnesias, respectively, are similar in functional and organic cases. This speculation must be tempered, however, by acknowledgement of known differences between functional and organic amnesia. For example, although some of the memory loss associated with both functional retrograde amnesia and organic retrograde amnesias produced by head injury and electroconvulsive therapy is reversible, the latter type of amnesia is frequently temporally graded (Squire, 1987) whereas the former is not (Schacter et al., 1982). In addition, there appears to be more variability in the nature of memory loss observed across cases in pathological functional amnesias than in organic amnesias.

A further issue that must be considered when discussing the relationship between functional and organic amnesias is the occurrence of simulated memory loss. Patients who present with pathological functional amnesias may be attempting to escape from an unpleasant or intolerable situation, such as military service, financial difficulties, or punishment for a crime, and therefore may benefit from similating amnesia (for a discussion, see Schacter, 1986a, c). The issue of simulation has also arisen with respect to hypnotic amnesias (e.g., Spanos et al., 1982b); Wagstaff 1982). Although simulation is not unknown following organic brain damage (Wiggins and Brandt, in press; Schacter, 1986c), it is not a serious concern when amnesia is produced by a verifiable lesion of a brain region known to be involved in memory. At the present time, no firm criteria exist for unequivocally distinguishing between genuine and simulated amnesias (Schacter 1986b, c). Nevertheless, investigators can minimize the possibility of confusing the two by carefully considering the circumstances surrounding each case and determining whether grounds for suspecting simulation exist. As far as we can determine, no such grounds exist in the cases discussed in this chapter. It would also be helpful if investigators examine and report the performance of non-amnesic subjects who are instructed to simulate amnesia, so as to determine whether features of an alleged instance of amnesia are intuitively obvious to naive individuals (e.g., Schacter, 1986b).

Although the interpretive difficulties that can arise when studying functional amnesias must be acknowledged, we think that further investigation of them as memory phenomena will provide new and useful insights into the nature of remembering and forgetting. Study of functional amnesias may be particularly informative with respect to the distinction between implicit and explicit forms of memory. Despite the striking failure of explicit remembering which defines the various functional amnesias we have considered, at least some evidence for implicit memory was observed with each type. Moreover, since reversible functional amnesias necessarily involve failures of explicit access to available memory representations, these amnesias should provide extremely fertile grounds for investigating implicit memory. More generally, functional amnesias may belong to an emerging class of dissociations, observed in both intact and brain-damaged populations, in which various types of knowledge that are not consciously accessible can be expressed implicitly (Kihlstrom, 1987; Schacter et al., 1988). Viewed within this context, further study of functional amnesias could provide important insights into the nature of both memory and consciousness.

Acknowledgements

Preparation of this paper, and the point of view represented therein, was supported in part by a Biomedical Research Support Grant from the University of Arizona to D.L.S. and a National Institute of Mental Health Grant MH-35856 to J.F.K. We thank Michael R. Berren, Irene P. Hoyt, Susan M. McGlynn, Douglas J. Tataryn, Betsy A. Tobias and James Wood for comments and discussion.

References

Aarons L: Sleep-assisted instruction. *Psychol. Bull.: 83,* 1 – 40, 1976.

Abeles M, Schilder P: Psychogenic loss of personal identity. *Arch. Neurol. Psychiatry: 34,* 587 – 604, 1935.

Abse DW: *Hysteria and Related Mental Disorders.* Bristol: IOP Publishing, 1987.

Akhtar S, Brenner I: Differential diagnosis of fugue-like states. *J. Clin. Psychiatry: 40* 381 – 385, 1979.

Akhtar S, Lindsey B, Kahn, FL: Sudden amnesia for personal identity. *Pa Med.: 84,* 46 – 48, 1981.

Albert MS, Butters N, Levin J: Temporal gradients in the retrograde amnesia of patients with alcoholic Kirsakoff's disease. *Arch. Neurol.: 36,* 311 – 216, 1979.

Arkin AM: Sleeptalking, In Arkin AM, Antrobus JS, Ellman SJ (Editors), *The Mind in Sleep.* Hillsdale, NJ: Erlbaum Ch. 15, pp. 513 – 532, 1978.

Arkin AM: *Sleep Talking: Psychology and Psychophysiology.* Hillsdale, NJ: Erlbaum, 1981.

Arkin AM, Antrobus JS: The effects of external stimuli applied prior to and during sleep on sleep experience. In Arkin AM, Antrobus JS, Ellman SJ, (Editors), *The Mind in Sleep.* Hillsdale, NJ: Erlbaum, Ch. 10, pp. 351 – 392, 1978.

Arkin AM, Antrobus JS, Ellman SJ (Editors): *The Mind in Sleep.* Hillsdale, NJ: Erlbaum, 1978.

Atkinson RC, Shiffrin RM: Human memory: a proposed system and its control processes. In Spence KW, Spence JT (Editors), *The Psychology of Learning and Motivation, Vol. 2.* New York: Academic Press, pp. 89 – 195, 1978.

Bennett HL: Learning and memory in anaesthesia. In Rosen M, Lunn JN (Editors), *Consciousness, Awareness, and Pain in General Anesthesia.* London: Butterworths, 132 – 139. 1987.

Bennett, HL: Perception and memory for events during adequate general anesthesia for surgical operations. In Pettinati H (Editor), *Hypnosis and Memory,* in press, 1988.

Berrington WP, Liddell DW, Foulds GA: A re-evaluation of the fugue. *J. Ment. Sci.: 102* 280 – 286, 1956.

Bertrand LD, Spanos NP: Contextual effects on priming during hypnotic amnesia. Unpublished manuscript, Carleton University, 1987.

Bliss EL: *Multiple Personality, Allied Disorders and Hypnosis.* New York: Oxford University Press, 1986.

Bower GH: Mood and memory. *Am. Psychol.: 36,* 129 – 148, 1981.

Brandt J, Rubinsky E, Lassen G: Uncovering malingered amnesia. *Ann. N. Y. Acad. Sci.: 444,* 502 – 503, 1985.

Bransford JD, Johnson MK: Consideration of some problems of comprehension. In Chase WG (Editor), *Visual Information processing.* New York: Academic Press, 1973.

Campbell BA, Coulter X: The ontogenesis of learning and memory. In Rosenzweig S, Bennett E (Editors), *Neurobiology of Learning and Memory.* Cambridge: MIT Press, Ch. 13, pp. 209 – 225, 1976.

Campbell BA, Spear NE: Ontogeny of memory. *Psychol. Rev.: 79,* 215 – 236, 1972.

Cermak LS (Editor): *Human Memory and Amnesia.* Hillsdale NJ: Lawrence Erlbaum Associates, 1982.

Cermak LS, Craik FIM (Editors): *Levels of Processing in Human Memory.* Hillsdale, NJ: Erlbaum, 1979.

Christianson SA, Nilsson LG: Hysterical amnesia: a case of aversively motivated isolation of memory. In Archer T, Nilsson LG (Editors), *Aversion, Avoidance, and Anxiety.* Hillsdale, NJ: Erlbaum Associates, in press.

Coe WC: The credibility of posthypnotic amnesia: a contextualist's view. *Int. J. Clin. Exp. Hypn.: 26,* 218 – 245, 1978.

Cohen DB: Toward a theory of dream recall. *Psychol. Bull.: 81,* 138 – 154, 1974.

Cohen DB: Dreaming: Experimental investigation of representational and adaptive properties. In Schwartz GE, Shapiro D (Editors), *Consciousness and Self-regulation: Advances in Research. Vol. 1.* New York: Plenum, Ch. 8, pp. 313 – 360, 1976.

Cohen DB: Remembering and forgetting dreaming. In Kihlstrom JF, Evans FJ (Editors), *Functional Disorders of Memory.* Hillsdale, NJ: Erlbaum, Ch. 8, pp. 239 – 274, 1979.

Coons PM: Multiple personality: diagnostic considerations. *J. Clin. Psychiatry: 41,* 330 – 336, 1980.

Coriat IH: *Abnormal Psychology.* New York: Moffat, Yard, and Co., 1916.

Coriat IH: The Lowell case of amnesia. *J. Abnorm. Psychol.: 2,* 93 – 111, 1907.

Coulter X: Determinants of infantile amnesia. In Spear NE,

Campbell BA (Editors), *The Ontogeny of Learning and Memory*. Hillsdale, NJ: Erlbaum, Ch. 10, pp. 245 – 270, 1979.

Crovitz HF: Galton's walk: *Methods for the Analysis of Thinking, Intelligence, and Creativity*. New York: Harper & Row, 1970.

Crovitz HF, Harvey MT: Early childhood amnesia: A quantitative study with implications for the study of retrograde amnesia after brain injury. *Cortex: 15,* 331 – 335, 1979.

Crovitz HF, Quina-Holland K: Proportion of episodic memories from early childhood by years of age. *Bull. Psychonomic Soc.: 7,* 61 – 62, 1976.

Crovitz HF, Schiffman H: Frequency of episodic memories as a function of their age. *Bull. Psychonomic Soc.: 4,* 517 – 518, 1974.

Crovitz HF, Harvey MT, McKee DC: Selecting retrieval cues for early childhood amnesia: implications for the study of shrinking retrograde amnesia. *Cortex: 16,* 305 – 310, 1980.

De La Mare W: *Early One Morning in the Spring: Chapters on children and on childhood as it is revealed in particular in early memories and in early writings*. New York: Macmillan, 1935.

Dement WC, Wolpert E: The relation of eye movements, body motility, and external stimuli to dream content. *J. Exp. Psychol.: 55,* 543 – 553, 1958.

Dick-Barnes M, Nelson RO, Aine U: Behavioral measures of multiple personality: The case of Margaret. *J. Behav. Ther. Exp. Psychiatry: 18,* 229 – 239, 1987.

Dillon RF, Spanos NP: Proactive inhibition and the functional ablation hypothesis: More disconfirmatory data. *Int. J. Clin. Exp. Hypn.: 31,* 47 – 56, 1983.

Dudycha GJ, Ducycha MM: Childhood memories: a review of the literature. *Psychol. Bull.: 38,* 668 – 682, 1941.

Eich JE: State-dependent retrieval of information in human episodic memory. In Birnbaum IM, Parker ED (Editors), *Alcohol and Human Memory*. Hillsdale, NJ: Erlbaum, Ch. 10, pp. 141 – 158, 1978.

Eich JE: The cue-dependent nature of state-dependent retrieval. *Mem. Cognition: 8,* 157 – 173, 1980.

Eich JE: Learning during sleep. In Bootzin RR, Kihlstrom JF, Schacter DL (Editors), *Cognition and Sleep*. Washington, DC: American Psychological Association, in press, 1989a.

Eich JE: Theoretical issues in state dependent memory. In Roediger HL, Craik FIM (Editors), *Varieties of Memory and Consciousness: Papers in Honor of Endel Tulving*. Hillsdale, NJ: Erlbaum, Ch. 17, pp. 331 – 354, 1989b.

Eich JE, Reeves JL, Katz RL: Anesthesia, amnesia and the memory/awareness distinction. *Anesth. Analg.: 64,* 1143 – 1148, 1985.

Eisen MR: Return of the repressed: hypnoanalysis of a case of total amnesia. *Int. J. Clin. Exp. Hypno.: 37,* 107 – 119, 1989.

Erdelyi MH, Goldberg B: Let's not sweep repression under the rug: toward a cognitive psychology of repression. In Kihlstrom JF, Evans FJ (Editors), *Functional Disorders of Memory*. Hillsdale NJ: Erlbaum Associates, Ch. 12, pp. 355 – 402, 1979.

Evans FJ: Contextual forgetting: posthypnotic source amnesia. *J. Abnorm. Psychol.: 88,* 556 – 563, 1979a.

Evans FJ: Hypnosis and sleep: techniques for exploring cognitive activity during sleep. In Fromm E, Shor RE (Editors), *Hypnosis: Developments in Research and New Perspectives*. New York: Aldine, Ch. 6, pp. 139 – 184, 1979b.

Evans FJ, Thorn WAF: Two types of posthypnotic amnesia recall amnesia and source amnesia. *Int. J. Clin. Exp. Hypn. 14,* 333 – 343, 1966.

Evans FJ, Gustafson LA, O'Connell DN, Orne MT, Shor RE Sleep-induced behavioral response. *J. Nerv. Ment. Dis.: 148* 467 – 476, 1969.

Evans FJ, Gustafson LA, O'Connell DN, Orne MT, Shor RE Verbally induced bahavior responses during sleep. *J. Nerv Ment. Dis.: 150,* 171 – 187, 1970.

Eysenck MW: Arousal, learning, and memory. *Psychol. Bull. 83,* 389 – 404, 1976.

Fisher C: Amnesic states in war neuroses: the psychogenesis o fugues. *Psychoanal. Q.: 14,* 437 – 468, 1945.

Fisher C, Adams RD: Transient global amnesia. *Trans. Am Neurol. Assoc.: 83,* 143 – 145, 1958.

Fisher C, Joseph E: Fugue with loss of personal identity *Psychoanal. Q.: 18,* 480 – 493, 1949.

Foulkes D: *Dreaming: A Cognitive-Psychological Analysis* Hillsdale, NJ: Erlbaum, 1985.

Freud S: Screen memories. In Strachey J (Editor), *The Standard Edition of the Complete Psychological works of Sigmund Freud. Vol. 3*. London: Hogarth, pp. 301 – 322, 1899.

Freud S: The interpretation of dreams. In Strachey J (Editor) *The Standard Edition of the Complete Psychological Work of Sigmund Freud. Vols. 4 – 5*. London: Hogarth, 1900.

Freud S: The psychopathology of everyday life. In Strachey (Editor), *The Standard Edition of the Complete Psychological Works of Sigmund Freud. Vol. 6*. London Hogarth, 1901.

Freud S, Brever J: *Studies on Hysteria*. New York: Avon Books, 1966.

Gastaut H, Broughton R: A clinical and polygraphic study o episodic phenomena during sleep. In Wortis J (Editor), *Recent Advances in Biological Psychiatry. Vol. 7*. New York Plenum, 1965.

Geleerd ER, Hacker FJ, Rapaport D: Contribution to the study of amnesia and allied conditions. *Psychoanal. Q.: 14* 199 – 220, 1956.

Gillespie RD: Amnesia. *Arch. Neurol. Psychiatry: 37* 748 – 764, 1937.

Goldmann L: Further evidence for cognitive processing unde general anesthesia. In Rosen M, Lunn JN (Editor), *Consciousness, Awareness, and Pain in General Anesthesia*. London: Butterworths, pp. 140 – 144, 1987.

Goodenough DR: Some recent studies of dream recall. In Witkin HA, Lewis HB (Editors), *Experimental Studies o Dreaming*. New York: Random House, 1967.

Goodenough DR: Dream recall: History and current status o the field. In Arkin AM, Antrobus JS, Ellman SJ (Editors) *The Mind in Sleep*. Hillsdale, NJ: Erlbaum, Ch. 5, pp 113 – 142, 1978.

Goodenough DR, Witkin HA, Lewis, HB, Koulack, D, Coher H: Repression, interference, and field dependence as factor in dream forgetting. *J. Abnorm. Psychol.: 83,* 32 – 44, 1974.

Graf P, Schacter DL: Implicit and explicit memory for new associations in normal and amnesic subjects. *J. Exp. Psychol. Learn. Mem. Cognition: 11,* 501 – 518, 1985.

Graf P, Squire LR, Mandler G: The information that amnesic patients do not forget. *J. Exp. Psychol. Learn. Mem. Cognition: 10*, 164–178, 1984.

Greaves GB: Multiple personality 165 years after Mary Reynolds. *J. Nerv. Ment. Dis.: 168*, 577–596, 1980.

Gudjonsson GH: The use of electrodermal responses in a case of amnesia (A case report). *Med. Sci. Law: 19*, 138–140, 1979.

Gudjonsson GH, Haward LRC: Case report – Hysterical amnesia as an alternative to suicide. *Med. Sci. Law: 22*, 68–72, 1982.

Gudjonsson GH, Taylor PJ: Cognitive deficit in a case of retrograde amnesia. *Br. J. Psychiatry: 147*, 715–718, 1985.

Hall GS: Note on early memories. *Pedagog. Semin.: 6*, 485–512, 1899.

Henri V, Henri C: On our earliest recollections of childhood. *Psychol. Rev.: 2*, 215–216, 1895.

Hilgard ER: *Divided Consciousness*. New York: John Wiley and Sons, 1977.

Hirst W: The amnesic syndrome: descriptions and explanations. *Psychol. Bull.: 91*, 435–460, 1982.

Hopwood JS, Snell HK: Amnesia in relation to crime. *J. Ment. Sci.: 79*, 27–41, 1933.

Hoskovec J: Hypnopedia in the Soviet Unon: a critical review of recent major experiments. *Int. J. Clin. Exp. Hypn.: 14*, 308–315, 1966.

Hoskovec J, Cooper LM: Comparison of recent experimental trends concerning sleep learning in the U.S.A. and the Soviet Union. *Act. Nerv. Super.: 9*, 93–96, 1967.

Hull CL: *Hypnosis and Suggestibility: An Experimental Approach*. New York: Appleton-Century-Crofts, 1933.

Jacoby LL, Dallas M: On the relationship between autobiographical memory and perceptual leaching. *J. Exp. Psychol. Gen.: 110*, 306–340, 1981.

Janet P: L'amesié et al dissociation des souvenirs par l'émotion. *J. Psychol. Norm. Pathol.: 1*, 417–453, 1904.

Janet P: *The Major Symptoms of Hysteria*. New York: Macmillan, 1907.

Jones E: Remarks on a case of complete autopsychic amnesia. *J. Abnorm. Psychol.: 4*, 218–235, 1909.

Kales A, Jacobson A, Paulson MJ, Kales JD, Walter RD: Somnambulism: psychophysiological correlates. I. All-night EEG studies. *Arch. Gen. Psychiatry: 14*, 586–594, 1966a.

Kales A, Paulson MJ, Jacobson A, Kales JD: Somnambulism: psychophysiological correlates. II. Psychiatric interviews, psychological testing, and discussion. *Arch. Gen. Psychiatry: 14*, 595–604, 1966b.

Kanzer M: Amnesia: a statistical study. *Am. J. Psychiatry: 96*, 711–716, 1739.

Kaszniak AW, Nussbaum PD, Berren MR, Santiago J: Amnesia as a consequence of male rape: a case report. *J. Abnorm. Psychology: 97*, 100–104, 1988.

Keller R, Shaywitz BA: Amnesia or fugue state: a diagnostic dilemma. *J. Dev. Behav. Pediatrics: 7*, 131–132, 1986.

Kennedy A, Neville J: Sudden loss of memory. *Br. Med. J.: 2*, 428–433, 1957.

Kenny MG: *The Passion of Ansel Bourne*. Washington DC: Smithsonian Institution Press, 1986.

Kihlstrom JF: Posthypnotic amnesia for recently learned material: interactions with 'episodic' and 'semantic'

memory. *Cognitive Psychol.: 12*, 227–251, 1980.

Kihlstrom JF: On personality and memory. In Cantor N, Kihlstrom JF (Editors), *Personality, Cognition, and Social Interaction*. Hillsdale, NJ: Erlbaum, Ch. 5, pp. 123–152, 1981.

Kihlstrom JF: Instructed forgetting: Hypnotic and nonhypnotic. *J. Exp. Psychol. Gen.: 112*, 73–79, 1983.

Kihlstrom JF: Conscious, subconscious, unconscious: a cognitive view. In Bowers KS, Meichenbaum D (Editors), *The Unconscious Reconsidered*. New York: Wiley-Interscience, Ch. 4, pp. 149–211, 1984.

Kihlstrom JF: Posthypnotic amnesia and the dissociation of memory. In Bower GH (Editor), *The Psychology of Learning and Motivation. Vol. 19*. San Diego: Academic Press, pp. 131–178, 1985.

Kihlstrom JF: The cognitive unconscious. *Science: 237*, 1445–1452, 1987.

Kihlstrom JF, Evans FJ (Editors): Memory retrieval processes during posthypnotic amnesia. In *Functional Disorders of Memory*. Hillsdale, NJ: Erlbaum, Ch. 6, pp. 179–218, 1979.

Kihlstrom JF, Harackiewicz JM: The earliest recollection: a new survey. *J. Pers.: 50*, 134–148, 1982.

Kihlstrom JF, Hoyt IP: Repression, dissociation, and hypnosis. In Singer JE (Editor), *Repression: Defense Mechanism and Personality Style*. Chicago: University of Chicago Press, in press 1988.

Kihlstrom JF, Schacter DL: Anaesthesia, amnesia, and the cognitive unconscious. In Bonke B, Fitch W, Millar K (Editors), *Awareness and Memory in Anaesthesia*. Amsterdam: Swets, in press, 1989.

Koukkou M, Lehman D: EEG and memory storage in sleep experiments with humans. *EEG Clin. Neurophysiol.: 25*, 455–462, 1968.

Koulack D, Goodenough DR: Dream recall and dream-recall failure: An arousal-retrieval model. *Psychol. Bull.: 83*, 975–984, 1976.

Lehman D, Koukkou M: Learning and EEG during sleep in humans. In Koella WP, Levin P (Editors), *Sleep: Physiology, Biochemistry, Psychology, Pharmacology, Clinical Implications*. Basel: Karger, pp. 43–47, 1973.

Lezak MD: *Neuropsychological Assessment* (2nd edition). New York: Oxford University Press, 1983.

Ludwig AM, Brandsma JM, Wilbur CB, Bendfeldt F, Jameson DH: The objective study of a multiple personality. *Arch. Gen. Psychiatry: 26*, 298–310, 1972.

Luparello TJ: Features of fugue. *J. Am. Psychoanal. Assoc.: 18*, 379–398, 1970.

Lyon LS: Facilitating telephone number recall in a case of psychogenic amnesia. *J. Behav. Ther. Exp. Psychiatry: 16*, 147–149, 1985.

McAndrews MP, Glisky EL, Schacter DL: When priming persists: long-lasting implicit memory for a single episode in amnesic patients. *Neuropsychologia: 25*, 497–506, 1987.

McGaugh JL: Time-dependent processes in memory storage. *Science: 153*, 1351–1358, 1966.

McKoon G, Ratcliff R, Dell G: A critical evaluation of the semantic-episodic distinction. *J. Exp. Psychol. Learn. Mem. Cognition: 12*, 295–306, 1986.

Mitchell SL: A double consciousness, or a duality of person in the same individual. *Med. Repos.: 3,* 185 – 186, 1816.

Nadel L: Down's syndrome in neurobiological perspective. Unpublished manuscript, University of Arizona, 1986.

Nadel L, Zola-Morgan S: Infantile amnesia: a neurobiological perspective. In Moscovitch M (Editor), *Infant Memory.* New York: Plenum, Ch. 7, pp. 145 – 172, 1984.

Neisser U: Cultural and cognitive discontinuity. In Gladwin TE, Sturtevant W (Editors), *Anthropology and Human Behavior.* Washington, DC: Anthropological Society of Washington, 1962.

Neisser U: *Cognitive Psychology.* New York: Appleton-Century-Crofts, 1967.

Nemiah J: Dissociative amnesia: a clinical and theoretical recantioration. In Kihlstrom JF, Evans FJ (Editors), *Functional Disorders of Memory.* Hillsdale, NJ: Erlbaum Associates, Ch. 10, pp. 303 – 324, 1979.

Nissen MJ, Bullemer P: Attentional requirements of learning: evidence from performance measures. *Cognitive Psychol.: 19,* 1 – 32, 1987.

Nissen MJ, Ross JL, Willingham DB, MacKenzie TB, Schacter DL: Memory and awareness in a patient with multiple personality disorder. *Brain Cognition: 8,* 21 – 38, 1988.

Osgood CE, Luria Z, Jeans RF, Smith SW: The three faces of Evelyn: a case report. *J. Abnorm. Psychol.: 85,* 247 – 286, 1976.

Overton DA: State-dependent retention of learned responses produced by drugs: Its relevance to sleep learning and recall. In Koella WP, Levin P (Editors), *Sleep: Physiology, Biochemistry, Psychology, Pharmacology, Clinical Implications.* Basel: Karger, pp. 48 – 52, 1973.

Perry C, Evans FJ, O'Connell DN, Orne EC, Orne MT: Behavioral response to verbal stimuli administred and tested during REM sleep: a further investigations. *Waking Sleeping: 2,* 35 – 42, 1978.

Pratt, TRC: Psychogenic loss of memory. In Whitty CWM, Zangwill OL (Editors), *Amnesia.* London: Butterworths, Ch. 9, 224 – 232.

Prince M: *The Dissociation of a Personality.* New York: Longmans, Green, 1910.

Putnam FW, Guroff JJ, Silberman EK, Barban L, Post RM: The clinical phenomenology of multiple personality disorder: 100 recent cases. *J. Clin. Psychiatry: 47,* 285 – 293, 1986.

Robinson JA: Sampling autobiographical memory. *Cognitive Psychol.: 8,* 578 – 595, 1976.

Rubin DC: On the retention function for autobiographical memory. *J. Verbal Learn. Verbal. Behav.: 21,* 21 – 38, 1982.

Rubin DC, Wetzler SE, Nebes RD: Autobiographical memory across the lifespan. In Rubin DC (Editor), *Autobiographical Memory.* Cambridge: Cambridge University Press, Ch. 12, pp. 202 – 224, 1986.

Rubin F: *Current Research in Hypnopaedia.* New York: American Elsevier, 1968.

Rubin F: *Learning and Sleep.* Bristol: John-Wright, 1971.

Russell WR, Nathan PW: Traumatic amnesia. *Brain: 69,* 280 – 300, 1946.

Salaman E: *A Collection of Moments: A Study of Involuntary Memory.* New York: St. Martin's Press, 1972.

Sarbin TR, Coe WC: Hypnosis and psychopathology: replacing old myths with fresh metaphors. *J. Abnorm. Psychol.: 88,* 506 – 526, 1979.

Sargant W, Slater E. Amnesic syndromes in war. *Proc. R. So Med.: 34,* 754 – 764, 1941.

Schachtel EG: On memory and childhood amnesia. *Psychiatr) 10,* 1 – 26, 1947.

Schacter DL: Amnesia and crime: how much do we real know? *Am. Psychol.: 41,* 286 – 295, 1986a.

Schacter DL: Feeling-of-knowing ratings distinguish betwee genuine and simulated forgetting. *J. Exp. Psychol. Learn Mem. Cognition: 12,* 30 – 41, 1986b.

Schacter DL: On the relation between genuine and simulate amnesia. *Behav. Sci. Law: 4,* 47 – 64, 1986c.

Schacter DL: Implicit memory: history and current status. *Exp. Psychol. Learn. Mem. Cognition: 13,* 501 – 518.

Schacter DL: Memory. In Posner MI (Editor), *Foundations c Cognitive Science.* Cambridge, MA: Bradford Books, i press.

Schacter DL, Crovitz HF: Memory function after closed hea injury: a review of the quantitative research. *Cortex: 1. 150 – 176, 1977.*

Schacter DL, Moscovitch M: Infants, amnesics, and dissociabl memory systems. In Moscovitch M (Editor), *Infant Memory New York: Plenum, Ch. 8, 173 – 216, 1984.*

Schacter DL, Tulving E: Memory, amnesia, and the episo dic/semantic distinction. In Isdacson RL, Spear N (Editors), *The Expression of Knowledge.* New York: Plenur Press, Ch. 2, pp. 33 – 65, 1982.

Schacter DL, Wang PL, Tulving E, Freedman M: Functiona retrograde amnesia: A quantitative case study. *Neuropsycho logia: 20,* 523 – 532, 1982.

Schacter DL, Harbluk JL, McLachlan DR: Retrieval withou recollection: an experimental analysis of source amnesia. *. Verb. Learning Verb. Behav.: 23,* 593 – 611, 1984.

Schacter DL, McAndrews MP, Moscovitch M: Access to con sciousness: dissociations between implicit and explici knowledge in neuropsychological syndromes. In Weiskrant L (Editor), *Thought Without Language.* Oxford: Oxfor University Press, pp. 242 – 278, 1988.

Schacter DL, Kihlstrom JF, Kihlstrom LC, Berren MB Autobiographical memory in a case of multiple personalit disorder. *J. Abnorm. Psychol.:* in press, 1989.

Shimamura AP: Priming effects in amnesia: evidence for dissociable memory function. *Q. J. Exp. Psychol.: 38A 619 – 644, 1986.*

Shimamura AP, Squire LR: A neuropsychological study of fac learning and source amnesia. *J. Exp. Psychol. Learn. Mem Cognition,* in press.

Sidis B, Goodhart SP: *Multiple personality.* New York: D. Ap pleton, 1898.

Silberman EK, Putnam FW, Weingartner H, Braun BG, Pos RM: Dissociative states in multiple personality disorder: quantitative study. *Psychiatry Res.: 15,* 253 – 260, 1985.

Simon CW, Emmons WH: Learning during sleep? *Psycho Bull.: 52,* 328 – 342, 1955.

Sours JA, Frumkin P, Indermill RR: Somnambulism: it clinical significance and dynamic meaning in late adolescenc and adulthood. *Arch. Gen. Psychiatry: 9,* 400 – 413, 1963.

Spanos NO: Hypnotic behavior: a social-psychological inter pretation of amnesia, analgesia, and 'trance logic'. *Behav Brain Sci.: 9,* 449 – 502, 1986.

Spanos N: Hypnosis, nonvolitional responding, and multipl

personality: a social-psychological perspective. In Maher BA (Editor), *Progress in Experimental Personality Research, Vol. 14.* New York: Academic Press, pp. 1 – 62, 1986.

panos NP, Radtke HL, Dubreuil DL: Episodic and semantic memory in posthypnotic amnesia: a reevaluation. *J. Pers. Soc. Psychol: 43,* 565 – 573, 1982a.

panos NP, Radtke HL, Bertrand LD, Addie DL, Drummond J: Disorganized reall, hypnotic amnesia and subjects' faking: more disconformatory evidence. *Psychol. Rep.: 50,* 383 – 389, 1982b.

panos NP, Della Malva L, Gwynn MI, Bertrand LD: Contextual demands and posthypnotic source amnesia. Unpublished manuscript, Carleton University, 1985.

pear NE: Experimental analysis of infantile amnesia. In Kihlstrom JF, Evans FJ (Editors), *Functional Disorders of Memory.* Hillsdale, NJ: Erlbaum, Ch. 3, pp. 75 – 102, 1979.

quire LR: The neuropsychology of human memory. *Annu. Rev. Neurosci.: 5,* 241 – 273, 1982.

quire LR: *Memory and Brain.* New York: Oxford University Press, 1987.

tengel E: On the aetiology of the fugue states. *J. Ment. Sci. 87,* 572 – 599, 1941.

uarez JM, Pittluck AT: Global amnesia: organic and functional considerations. *Bull. Am. Acad. Psychiatry Law: 3,* 17 – 24, 1975.

utcliffe JP, Jones J: personal identity, multiple personality, and hypnosis. *Int. J. Clin. Exp. Hypn.: 10,* 231 – 269, 1962.

aylor PJ, Kopelman MD: Amnesia for criminal offences. *Psychol. Med.: 14,* 581 – 588, 1984.

aylor WS, Martin MF: Multiple personality. *J. Abnorm. Soc. Psychol.: 29,* 281 – 300, 1944.

higpen C, Cleckley H: *The three faces of Eve.* New York: Popular Library, 1957.

hom DA, Fenton W: Amnesia in war cases. *Am. J. Psychiatry: 76,* 437 – 448, 1920.

itchener EB: Early memories. *Am. J. Psychol.: 11,* 435 – 436, 1900.

rustman R, Dubovsky S, Titley R: Auditory perception during general anesthesia: myth or fact? *Int. J. Clin. Exp. Hypn.: 25,* 88 – 105.

Tulving E: Elements of episodic memory. Oxford: Oxford University Press, 1983.

Tulving E, Schacter DL, Stark HA: Priming effects in word-fragment completion are independent of recognition memory. *J. Exp. Psychol. Learn. Mem. Cognition: 8,* 336 – 342, 1982.

Wagstaff GF: Disorganized recall, suggested amnesia, and compliance. *Psychol. Rep.: 51,* 1255 – 1258, 1982.

Waldfogel S: The frequency and affective character of childhood memories. *Psychol. Monogr.: 62* (Whole No. 291), 1948.

Watkins J: *Hypnotherapy of War Neuroses.* New York: Ronald Press, 1949.

Waugh NC, Norman DA, Primary memory. *Psychol. Rev.: 72,* 89 – 104, 1965.

Weiskrantz L: Neuroanatomy of memory and amnesia: a case of multiple memory systems. *Hum. Neurobiol.: 6,* 93 – 106, 1987.

Wetzler SE, Sweeney JA: Childhood amnesia: an empirical demonstration. In Rubin DC (Editor), *Autobiographical Memory.* Cambridge: Cambridge University Press, Ch. 11, pp. 191 – 201, 1986a.

Wetzler SE, Sweeney JA: Childhood amnesia: a conceptualization in cognitive-psychological terms. *J. Am. Psychoanal. Assoc.: 34,* 663 – 685, 1986b.

White SB, Pillemer DB: Childhood amnesia and the development of a socially accessible memory system. In JF Kihlstrom, Evans FJ (Editors), *Functional Disorders of Memory.* Hillsdale, NJ: Erlbaum, Ch. 2, pp. 29 – 74, 1979.

Wiggins ES, Brandt J: The detection of simulated amnesia. *Law Behav.:* in press.

Williams HL: Information processing during sleep. In Koella WP, Levin P (Editors), *Sleep: Physiology, Biochemistry, Psychology, Pharmacology, Clinical Implications.* Basel: Karger, pp. 36 – 42, 1973.

Williams HL, Hammack JT, Daly RL, Dement WC, Lubin A: Responses to auditory stimulation, sleep loss, and the EEG stages of sleep. EEG and Clinical *Neurophysiology: 16,* 269 – 279, 1964.

Williams HL, Morlock HC, Morlock JV: Instrumental behavior during sleep. *Psychophysiology: 2,* 208 – 216, 1966.

Wilson G, Rupp C, Wilson WW: Amnesia. *Am. J. Psychiatry: 106,* 481 – 485, 1950.

1989 Elsevier Science Publishers B.V. (Biomedical Division)
andbook of Neuropsychology, Vol. 3
Boller and J. Grafman (Eds)

CHAPTER 10

Models and methods of memory rehabilitation

Elizabeth L. Glisky and Daniel L. Schacter

Amnesia and Cognition Unit, Department of Psychology, University of Arizona, Tucson AZ 85721, U.S.A.

Introduction

Rehabilitation of memory disorders presents a major challenge to clinical and experimental neuropsychology. Memory impairment is one of the most debilitating consequences of brain injury and disease as well as among the most troublesome obstacles to successful rehabilitation (Auerbach, 1983; Glisky and Schacter, 1986; Grimm and Bleiberg, 1986; Levin et al., 1982; Miller, 1984; Schacter et al., 1989; Wilson, 1987). In the past few years several developments have fostered a surge of interest in the problems of cognitive/memory rehabilitation.

First, because of advances in medical research and technology, increased numbers of people are surviving brain trauma (Levin et al., 1982), and the demand for rehabilitation services is increasing correspondingly. Second, at the same time as the need for rehabilitation services has grown, the neuropsychology of memory disorders has advanced to a point where it can consider seriously its role as a rehabilitation science. Having accumulated an impressive body of knowledge describing the characteristics of memory dysfunction associated with various neurological conditions (for review, see Parkin, 1987; Squire and Butters, 1984), some researchers have turned to the task of trying to solve some of the problems that plague the memory-impaired survivors of brain injury and disease.

Third, cognitive psychologists, who until the past decade have eschewed serious interest in memory-impaired populations (Schacter and Tulving, 1982), have discovered that clinical populations can provide information about cognitive processes that is not easily obtainable from college students, and have begun to make experimental and theoretical contributions to neuropsychological research (e.g., Squire and Butters, 1984). This marriage of the two disciplines, clinical neuropsychology and cognitive/experimental psychology, has yielded new insights for both partners. Theoretical and empirical discoveries concerning memory processes are suggesting novel ways to structure remediation programs, while at the same time patient response to these interventions is contributing to a greater understanding of the underlying memory mechanisms (cf., Newcombe, 1985).

These recent trends suggest strongly that research on memory rehabilitation will occupy an increasingly prominent place in clinical and cognitive neuropsychology during the coming years. In the present chapter, we (a) outline the theoretical approaches that have guided much of the clinical research and practice in the past, (b) review the rehabilitation methods that have developed from these views, (c) discuss contemporary developments that are more closely tied to recent advances in experimental neuropsychology and cognitive psychology, and (d) conclude by delineating some directions that future research might profitably take.

Models of memory rehabilitation

In order to evaluate the various methods of remediation for memory disorders, it is necessary to consider the meaning of the term 'rehabilitation'. What exactly is implied by the word, and what expectations does its use engender in the minds of patients, therapists and researchers? A number of possible interpretations can be found in the literature. *Dorlands Pocket Medical Dictionary* (1982) defines rehabilitation as 'restoration to useful activity'. Grimm and Bleiberg (1986), in their chapter on rehabilitation following traumatic brain injury, state that 'rehabilitation generally refers to a set of therapeutic services designed to restore an individual to maximal level of functioning' (p. 506) and Gianutsos (1980) speaks of a 'service designed to remediate [cognitive] disorders' (p. 37) and 'restore lost function' (p. 38). These definitions seem to imply not only that a return to normal or near-normal functioning is an attainable goal but that a set of procedures to achieve that goal is available.

In the review of the literature that follows, there is little or no evidence that *restoration* of general mnemonic function in patients with organic memory disorders is possible. Nor is there any evidence of the existence of a set of sure-fire techniques that are invariably effective in enhancing the memory abilities of memory-impaired patients. Rather, the literature contains examples of methods that have sometimes been effective under some conditions, for some patients, with some kinds of materials, and to some limited degree.

Because evidence for general improvement in memory function has not been forthcoming, several investigators have adopted an alternative approach to the problems of memory rehabilitation (e.g., Harris, 1984; Mayer et al., 1986; Miller, 1978; Schacter and Glisky, 1986; Wilson and Moffat, 1984b). This approach is concerned with the *alleviation* of specific problems associated with memory disorders and is reflected in definitions of rehabilitation which specify somewhat more modest goals. For example, Whyte (1986) has proposed that a reasonable goal for clinicians working in the field of head trauma rehabilitation is the improvement of the 'quality of life in the natural environment' (p. ix) and Miller (1980) suggests that rehabilitation should be aimed at 'reducing the impact of the deficit on the individual's life' (p. 528). Similarly, Mayer et al. (1986) state that the goal of their functional approach to memory remediation is 'to produce an individual who will be adaptive . . . in his home and community environment' (p. 207) and Schacter and Glisky (1986) have focussed on 'the acquisition of domain-specific knowledge: knowledge pertaining to a particular task, subject, or function that is important to a patient in his or her everyday life' (p. 265). These latter definitions do not imply that damaged functions can be restored in any general sense. Rather they suggest that rehabilitation efforts should be directed towards finding solutions to problems of daily living that result from memory impairment. This, we will argue, is a much more realistic goal than the restoration of lost function.

From each of these approaches to memory rehabilitation there have emerged several different techniques for the management of memory problems. In the next section of this chapter, we describe the major methods of remediation, review the relevant experimental and clinical literature associated with each of them, and critically evaluate their effectiveness.

Methods of memory rehabilitation

Four main methods of memory rehabilitation have been investigated in the past decade: (a) use of repetitive exercises and drills, (b) teaching of mnemonic strategies, (c) use of external aids, and (d) teaching of domain-specific knowledge.

A. Exercises and drills

One of the oldest notions in cognitive psychology is that repeated practice facilitates memory (e.g., Newell and Rosenbloom, 1981). This idea is so pervasive that it can easily be misinterpreted. What is sometimes forgotten is that the effects of repeated practice accrue only to the material that is repeated; there is no evidence that repetitive practice improves memory in any general sense. William James (1890) distinguished between memory in general and memory for specific material, a distinction that he described as a difference between 'general physiological retentiveness' and 'the retention of particular things' (p. 565). The former, James claimed, was a physiological given that could never be changed, whereas the latter could be improved by changing one's study methods. Research has tended to confirm James's views that repeated practice with one kind of material can improve memory for that material but has no effect on memory for anything else. For example, Chase and Ericsson (1981) demonstrated that a college student (S.F.), who initially had an average digit span of approximately seven, was able after practising an hour a day for several months to increase that span to over 80 digits. However, his ability to remember letters of the alphabet (i.e., material with which he did not practice) did not change over the same interval; it remained at about seven items.

Although most psychologists today no longer believe that memory is like a muscle which needs to be exercised to maintain its potency, the notion that a damaged memory can be restored or improved in some general sense through repetitive exercises or drills continues to persist among many rehabilitation workers. In a survey of British rehabilitation services, Harris and Sunderland (1981) found that use of exercise regimens to strengthen memory was widespread. However, available empirical evidence indicates that, for memory-impaired patients as for normal individuals, repetitive practice in itself yields no general improvements in memory function.

Two clinical studies illustrate this claim. Godfrey and Knight (1985) found no difference in overall memory function between amnesic patients who were given 32 hours of memory skill training and those who engaged in the same amount of non-specific social activity. Even more dramatic were the findings of Prigatano and his colleagues (1984), who showed that after 625 hours of an intensive 'neuropsychological rehabilitation program', head-injured patients improved their performance on the Wechsler Memory Scale by an average of only one item on the subtests most sensitive to memory dysfunction. As noted previously (Schacter and Glisky, 1986), an improvement of 1/625 of an item per hour of memory training is hardly impressive.

A recent development which has had some impact on memory rehabilitation practices has been the increasing availability of inexpensive microcomputers and the corresponding proliferation of software for 'cognitive retraining' that has appeared on the market (Lynch, 1986). With their ease of administration and time-saving features, such software packages have considerable appeal for the often over-worked professionals in the field of rehabilitation. However, to the extent that such programs involve repeated presentation of relatively meaningless materials such as letters, digits, words and shapes, as many of them do, they have no therapeutic value (cf., O'Connor and Cermak, 1987). Simply presenting materials by computer does not alter the fact that benefits for memory in a general sense cannot be attained merely through exercise or practice.

The point made by James, that memory for particulars can be facilitated by practice but 'general retentiveness' cannot, applies well to research in memory rehabilitation. If the purpose of drilling is restoration of function, it will in all likelihood be unsuccessful. In contrast, if the purpose of repetitive practice is to help patients acquire specific information, then, as we shall see later, extensive practice is probably a necessary condition.

B. Mnemonic strategies
Visual imagery. The most thoroughly researched and most commonly used mnemonic technique is the ancient art of visual imagery (Yates, 1966). It has long been known that among normal subjects the formation of distinctive visual images renders information more memorable than would otherwise be the case (e.g., Bower, 1970; Paivio, 1969).

Because of the well-documented benefits for normal subjects, imagery has also been the most popular strategy for use with memory-impaired patients both in the clinic and in the laboratory. Attempts to produce general improvements in the memory abilities of organically impaired subjects by instructing them in the use of imagery mnemonics, however, have not been successful.

Early experiments concerning the benefits of visual imagery for brain-injured populations were performed with patients who had unilateral brain damage. Patten (1972) found that patients with verbal memory deficits associated with left hemisphere lesions could improve their recall performance substantially through the use of a 'pegword' technique. In this method, subjects form images of to-be-remembered items in association with previously learned number/word rhyming pairs (e.g., 'One is a bun, two is a shoe'). To later retrieve items, subjects simply run through the ordered pegwords (bun, shoe, etc.) and retrieve the items that had been imaged with them. Although Patten reported that this technique worked well for four patients with dominant hemisphere lesions, it was not successful for patients with midline lesions. In a later study, using interactive imaging techniques to teach memory-impaired patients lists of unrelated paired associates, Jones (1974) obtained results consistent with Patten's findings. She showed that patients who had undergone left temporal lobectomies benefitted from imagery instructions whereas patients with bilateral lesions did not. Similarly, Gasparrini and Satz (1979) demonstrated improved recall of paired associates when imagery was used by patients with left hemisphere damage.

Many studies of visual imagery have used groups of patients whose memory disorders varied in both etiology and severity. Results from these studies are confusing and inconclusive. Baddeley and Warrington (1973) studied a mixed group of amnesic patients, and failed to find benefits of visual imagery on a recall task. However, Cermak's (1975) study of Korsakoff patients did show advantages of imagery compared to simple rote

learning. Malec and Questad (1983) also reported positive effects of imagery training for word-list recall with a mildly impaired CHI patient. Lewinsohn et al. (1977), with a heterogeneous group of patients, found that imagery improved performance on a paired-associate task when recall was tested immediately, and that the advantage disappeared after a one-week delay. Some evidence that differing outcomes might be attributable to differences in severity of deficit was provided by Wilson (1987). She found that subjects with severe memory impairments did not benefit from visual imagery if they were required to construct mental images on their own, whereas moderately impaired patients did. When the experimenter drew pictures for them to image, however, both groups improved their recall performance.

This review of the literature on imagery mnemonics makes two points. First, the effects with memory-impaired patients are variable and no firm conclusions about the efficacy of imagery can be made. It may be that patients with mild-to-moderate memory disorders or with specific verbal memory deficits can benefit from imagery techniques whereas those with more severe disorders cannot (e.g., Wilson and Moffat, 1984b). Second, the bulk of this research has employed paired associates or unrelated lists of words as the material to be learned. Because learning this material has no value for patients in their everyday lives, we assume that the purpose of teaching patients these imaging techniques is to provide them with procedures which they could apply in everyday life. Unfortunately, evidence that such methods can be used beneficially in the real world is non-existent. In fact, it has been shown that even in the laboratory patients fail to spontaneously generate images unless specifically instructed to do so (Cermak, 1975; Crovitz, 1979).

Two reasons have been suggested for the failure of imagery mnemonics to generalize to everyday situations (Glisky and Schacter, 1986; Schacter and Glisky, 1986). First, many everyday problems do not lend themselves to the use of imagery and are more readily amenable to other solutions. This may be the reason why Harris (1978) has found that even normal adults seldom use these techniques in everyday life. A mnemonic such as the pegword technique may be useful for remembering things such as shopping lists, but as Parkin (1987) points out, a written list would probably be easier. Second, effective use of imagery strategies requires much effortful and elaborate processing, placing excessive demands on the already limited capacities of brain-damaged patients (Baddeley, 1982; Cermak, 1980; Schacter et al., 1985).

Despite these limitations, attempts to find real-life applications for imagery techniques have persisted. One kind of everyday problem that has been investigated is the problem of face-name association. Most memory-impaired patients report difficulty in remembering the names of new people whom they meet in daily life. Laboratory demonstrations of face-name learning through the use of imagery mnemonics, however, have not been impressive (Lewinsohn et al., 1977). Glasgow et al. (1977) suggested that traditional mnemonic procedures (Lorayne and Lucas, 1974), which require subjects to transform a name into an imageable noun and link it interactively with a prominent facial feature, are too difficult for brain-damaged patients to master, particularly when names are complex. They used a much simpler imagery-rehearsal technique that proved effective for a mildly impaired head-injured student in his everyday life. The subject wrote down names of people that he had trouble remembering. Then, at three scheduled times during his regular day, he read the names and visualized the corresponding faces. Glasgow et al. reported that the patient learned over 30 names, using this method.

Wilson (1982, 1987) also found that a simple imaging technique was effective for a variety of patients in learning the names of people with whom they had regular contact in their daily lives. Despite their ability to acquire several new names, however, patients in Wilson's studies never spontaneously used the methods to remember the names of new people that they encountered. That is, they were unable to maintain the strategy on their own or to generalize its use to other situations. Such an outcome would probably be interpreted as a failure if the goal of the intervention were to improve the learning abilities of the patients or to 'restore' lost function. Wilson's approach to rehabilitation, however, emphasizes amelioration of problems caused by memory deficits. In this context, her intervention was successful; patients learned the names of people in their environment that they had been unable to remember previously.

Summarizing the findings with respect to visual imagery mnemonics, we conclude that the benefits demonstrated to date have been rather limited. Although some patients seem able to profit from the techniques under some conditions, others, particularly those with severe deficits, do not. To the extent that new information can be learned through the use of these techniques, they have merit, although their usefulness in everyday life seems limited. As yet, no evidence exists that imagery strategies are used spontaneously by patients or that they generalize beyond the context of their acquisition. Nor do they improve, in any general sense, the memory or learning abilities of memory-impaired patients.

Verbal organization and semantic elaboration. Another class of strategies that has been used with memory-impaired patients entails verbal organization or semantic elaboration of to-be-learned material. These strategies, which rely on verbal rather than visual means for improving memory performance, have proven particularly useful for patients with right hemisphere damage. For example, Wilson (1982) found that a right-hemisphere CVA patient was able to learn rapidly a 10-item shopping list using a first-letter cuing technique. This strategy involved learning the first letters of list items by putting them in a coherent sentence. For example, the initial letters of the shopping items spelled the phrase 'GO SHOPPING'. Once this phrase was learned, the patient was able to use its letters as cues for the items on the shopping list (i.e., G = Grapes, O = Oranges, etc). He also learned a first-letter mnemonic to remind him to take his *g*lasses, *w*atch, *n*otebook, *m*emory aid and *p*en when he left his training session (i.e., Go With No Memory Problems). However, though he could use the verbal strategy when instructed to do so, he never spontaneously used it on his own.

A type of verbal cuing technique that has been used effectively with mildly impaired patients is the PQRST method (Robinson, 1970). PQRST, which stands for Preview, Question, Read, State and Test, is a procedure designed to facilitate learning of text such as newspaper articles or educational readings. Subjects *preview* material to be learned and formulate *questions* to guide their *reading* of the text; *stating* the answers to the questions is followed by a *test* of recall in which the questions act as cues. The benefits of this technique are thought to derive from the provision of an organizational framework during encoding and the furnishing of cues for retrieval. Glasgow et al. (1977) reported successful use of the procedure with a college student who had a mild memory complaint following concussion, and Wilson (1982) reported that her right-sided patient (WAIS IQ = 133) 'became very proficient at the PQRST strategy' (p. 587). Because of the complexity of this learning strategy, however, it has not been extensively investigated with amnesic patients and is probably of benefit primarily for patients with above-average intelligence and/or relatively mild memory deficits.

Other types of verbal cuing techniques that have been studied include the use of verbal mediators in paired-associate tasks (Cermak, 1975) and the provision of category labels to facilitate recall of categorized word lists (Jaffe and Katz, 1975). These studies have shown that cues can improve recall performance if they are provided to patients both at time of study and at time of test. Patients with memory disorders appear to have considerable difficulty in spontaneously generating their own cues, particularly at retrieval.

Similar kinds of findings have been obtained with semantic elaboration techniques such as story mnemonics or chain-linking procedures. Gianutsos and Gianutsos (1979; also Gianutsos, 1981) found

that elaborating a story about to-be-learned words increased the probability of recalling those words, and Crovitz (1979; also Crovitz et al., 1979) demonstrated that embedding words in a story chain which encouraged elaborate semantic encoding (and interactive imaging) improved retrieval. Once again, however, in these studies, amnesic patients were strongly dependent on the re-presentation of retrieval cues for successful recall.

Surprisingly good free recall by memory-impaired patients of mixed etiologies was reported by Mattis and Kovner (1984; Kovner et al., 1985). Using a training technique which initially included extensive cuing and repetition of words linked together in a story format, patients learned as many as 80 words, which they were able to freely recall even after several weeks. A recent attempt (Heinrichs, 1989) to replicate these findings with a severely amnesic Korsakoff patient, however, was not successful. Differences in severity of deficits may account for the differing outcomes in these two studies. It is also worth noting that even though Mattis and Kovner's patients demonstrated somewhat spectacular recall performance they still did not spontaneously apply the strategy that they had been taught either in the laboratory when concurrent control lists were presented or in the real world to improve memory of everyday events.

The findings with respect to verbal elaboration strategies can be summarized in much the same way as the imagery mnemonic studies. The strategies appear to be most useful for patients with mild memory disorders or right hemisphere damage, but even with these patients evidence of spontaneous use or generalization of techniques is lacking.

Rehearsal techniques. Because most mnemonic strategies require considerable cognitive effort, they may be beyond the capabilities of many brain-injured patients. For this reason, Schacter et al. (1985) suggested the use of a relatively simple rehearsal strategy known as spaced retrieval (Landauer and Bjork, 1978). This technique requires subjects to rehearse items at ever-increasing delays following initial presentation. In the Schacter et al. (1985) study, two patients with mild memory deficits and two severely impaired patients attempted to learn to associate personal characteristics of individuals (i.e., name, origin, occupation, hobby) with pictures of their faces. After an initial pairing of a face and a characteristic, the face was presented as a cue for rehearsal of the characteristic after a very short delay (5 seconds) and then at increasingly longer intervals thereafter. All four patients improved their recall performance relative to a no-training baseline but only two of the patients were able to maintain the strategy in the laboratory without prompting. No evidence of continued use outside the laboratory was reported. Although this rehearsal strategy thus has the advantage of being effective even for severely impaired patients, it suffers from the same shortcoming as do other mnemonic strategies: they do not appear to generalize to the real world. Practical benefits in everyday life are therefore likely to be limited.

C. External aids

The lack of evidence for long-term efficacy of mnemonic strategies, together with failures to 'restore' lost memory function, have recently prompted some researchers to focus on more ecologically relevant rehabilitation methods. These have most often involved the provision of external memory aids to help patients to bypass some of the problems created by their memory dysfunction (Harris, 1984; Wilson and Moffat, 1984b). At their simplest, external aids consist of environmental restructurings that decrease patients' reliance on their own memory functions. Such things as labels on cupboards, simple operating instructions on appliances, name tags on persons in the immediate environment, and signs or chalk lines on the floor to indicate locations or directions can substantially enhance patients' ability to function in everyday life as well as reduce some of the frustration that plagues their daily existence (Wilson and Moffat, 1984a).

Other external aids require some active par-

ticipation by patients. For example, if notebooks, lists and diaries are to serve as useful reminders or prompts for future actions, they must be meaningfully constructed, updated and consulted on a regular basis. It has often been observed, however, that many patients rarely consult the notebooks they carry, and when they do they are frequently unable to make sense out of the non-specific and incomplete notations that appear (e.g., Glisky and Schacter, 1986; Harris, 1978; 1984; Mateer et al., 1987; Milton, 1985; Wilson and Moffat, 1984b). Even mildly-impaired patients who use notebooks routinely have difficulty using the information because they fail to keep their notes current and tend to record the same messages repeatedly. Other external aids which serve cuing functions such as bell timers and alarm watches (e.g., Gouvier, 1982; Kurlychek, 1983) do not require that patients remember to consult them but they suffer from a lack of specificity. That is, although patients are prompted by a bell to perform some function, they may be unable to remember what function to perform. Some combination of notebook and signalling device may ultimately be necessary if an external aid is to serve as an effective remedial instrument (cf. Parkin, 1987).

These observations suggest that the use of even apparently simple external aids such as notebooks and alarm watches may require specific training. In the only study we know that has addressed this issue, Sohlberg and Mateer (in press) reported that memory-impaired patients required lengthy practice and extensive situational role playing before they were able to use a notebook effectively. In the case of a moderately impaired head-injury victim, these investigators provided approximately four months of intensive training in the use of a 'memory book' before the patient was able to use it adequately in daily living activities. Further research is needed to explore more efficient training procedures and to assess to what extent such training impacts on the everyday lives of patients with memory disorders. The capacity for greater independence in daily living that proficient application of these methods could provide would seem to make this a worthwhile research enterprise.

The external aid that may present the greatest potential for rehabilitation of the brain-injured is the microcomputer (e.g., Ager, 1985; Furst, 1984; Glisky et al., 1986a; Harris, 1984; Jones and Adam, 1979; Kirsch et al., 1987; Skilbeck, 1984). With its capacity to store large amounts of information, a computer has the capability to serve as a prosthetic or substitute memory for persons whose own memory is damaged. As is the case with all prostheses, however, beneficial use depends on successful acquisition of operating procedures. Until recently, the task of learning to operate a computer was considered to be well beyond the capabilities of amnesic patients. Attempts to teach patients to use even a simple computing device had been largely unsuccessful because patients were simply unable to remember how to input, access and update information (Wilson and Moffat, 1984b). Recent research, however, has demonstrated that, with appropriate training techniques, patients with severe memory deficits are capable of learning some of the basic functions associated with the operation of a microcomputer (Glisky et al., 1986a). In addition, Kirsch et al. (1987) have reported that a severely amnesic encephalitic patient was trained in the laboratory to use a specially adapted microcomputer to prompt her in the successive steps of cookie baking, a task she was unable to accomplish correctly on her own. These findings are encouraging in that they provide suggestive evidence that memory-impaired patients may eventually be able to benefit from a microcomputer in their daily lives.

In summary, preliminary results and anecdotal reports suggest that use of external aids may have ecologically important consequences for memory-impaired patients, but the research necessary to demonstrate this possibility conclusively remains to be done.

D. Domain-specific knowledge

Another approach that attempts to alleviate problems created by memory disorders focusses on the

acquisition of information relevant to the everyday functioning of the disabled individual – what Schacter and Glisky (1986) referred to as the *acquisition of domain-specific knowledge* (see also Mayer et al., 1986; Wilson, 1987). Although inability to learn new facts and knowledge has long been considered to be the hallmark of the amnesic syndrome, a number of studies have reported instances in which memory-impaired patients are able to acquire new facts concerning particular aspects of their environment. For example, Wilson (1982), using a variety of mnemonic techniques, taught a severely amnesic patient his daily timetable and the names of hospital personnel. Dolan and Norton (1977) reported that a contingent reinforcement technique was successful in teaching a group of brain-damaged patients the names of hospital staff members and appropriate ward behaviors, and Seidel and Hodgkinson (1979) used behavioral methods to alter the maladaptive smoking behavior of a Korsakoff patient. Wilson (1987), by means of the PQRST method, taught an aneurysm patient details concerning his illness and prognosis, and Cermak (1976) found that a severely amnesic encephalitic patient was able to learn considerable information about daily living activities through the use of visual and verbal strategies. Jaffe and Katz (1975) reported that they were successful in teaching a Korsakoff patient the location of his locker and the names of two hospital staff members by means of a first-letter cuing and fading technique.

These studies demonstrate that memory-impaired patients are capable of acquiring specific facts relevant to their everyday lives, and that a variety of mnemonic techniques can be used to facilitate their learning. However, in most of the studies just described, the knowledge acquired by patients was relatively simple, consisting of just a few pieces of information such as the names of one or two people in the environment. More critically, although patients learned information that was pertinent to particular aspects of everyday living, they were often unable to make use of what they had learned. For example, Dolan and Norton

(1977) found that, although patients learned to answer correctly a number of questions about their hospital surroundings, their behavior in the ward did not reflect this knowledge. Similarly, Cermak (1976) reported that his patient S.S. could recite many instructions that he had been taught concerning activities of his daily life but he never actually carried them out.

Such failures to benefit from newly acquired knowledge represent a serious problem for remedial techniques which focus on the acquisition of domain-specific knowledge. If patients are unable to make use of their new learning to increase their ability to function in the real world, then the raison d'être for this method of memory rehabilitation is in some doubt. Again, the problem seems to be one of inadequate generalization; that is, patients fail to apply knowledge acquired in one situation to another situation that is similar. Although it is certainly possible to teach information in the exact context in which it is to be applied, lack of generalization might seriously limit the benefits that could be derived from this technique. Research in this area, however, is just beginning. In the next section of the chapter, we will describe some extensions of the domain-specific approach that have emerged from basic research in cognitive psychology and neuropsychology.

New developments

Recent research has suggested that memory-impaired patients may well have the ability to learn much more information than was heretofore thought possible. For example, studies have shown that amnesic patients can acquire, in normal or near-normal fashion, motor skills such as rotor pursuit (Corkin, 1968; Milner et al., 1968), perceptual and cognitive skills such as mirror-reading (Cohen and Squire, 1980; Moscovitch, 1984) and puzzle-solving (Brooks and Baddeley, 1976), and even relatively complex skills such as mathematical rule learning (Kinsbourne and Wood, 1975; Milberg et al., 1988). Amnesic patients have also been shown to exhibit normal repetition priming

effects; that is, they are as likely as normals to produce previously experienced stimuli (e.g., CHAIR) in the presence of partial cues (e.g., CHA ——) (Cermak et al., 1985; Diamond and Rozin, 1984; Graf and Schacter, 1985; Graf et al., 1984; Schacter and Graf, 1986; Warrington and Weiskrantz, 1968, 1974). Of particular interest in both the skill learning and the priming studies are the findings that patients perform normally even though, in most cases, they do not remember any prior experience with the tasks or materials.

The foregoing findings have important implications for the remediation of memory disorders, insofar as they suggest that it may be possible for memory-impaired patients to acquire complex knowledge that could enhance their everyday functioning – even though they may not remember learning the information (cf. Salmon and Butters, 1987). Glisky and Schacter and their colleagues have developed and explored this idea in a series of recent articles (Glisky and Schacter, 1988a,b; Glisky et al., 1986a,b; Schacter and Glisky, 1986; Schacter et al., 1989).

Glisky et al. (1986b) investigated whether four memory-impaired patients (three closed-head injury, one encephalitic) with varying degrees of memory loss could acquire and retain the vocabulary associated with the use of an Apple IIe microcomputer. The teaching method that they used, referred to as *the method of vanishing cues,* was designed to make use of patients' preserved abilities to produce previously studied material in the presence of fragment cues. Definitions were presented on trial 1 (e.g., *to transfer a program from storage to computer*), and were followed by an ever-increasing fragment of the target word (e.g., L___, LO___, LOA__) until the subject responded correctly with the vocabulary item 'LOAD'. Across subsequent trials, letters in the target word were withdrawn one by one until eventually no letters were provided. If on any trial the patient was unable to produce the correct response, letters were again added to the fragment until the correct answer was generated. Across eight sessions (eight trials/session), all patients were able to acquire 20 – 30 items of new computer vocabulary, which they generated in the absence of letter cues. They also retained the vocabulary across a six-week interval.

In a follow-up experiment, Glisky et al. (1986a) explored whether patients could learn some of the basic operations associated with a microcomputer. Using the method of vanishing cues, four head-injured patients with memory disorders of varying severity learned to perform a variety of computer functions. By the end of training, they could display information on the computer screen, clear the display, perform a number of disk storage and retrieval operations, and write and edit simple computer programs. Even the most densely amnesic of the patients, who claimed that he had never worked on a computer despite over 100 hours of practice time, was able to complete correctly all of the assigned computer learning tasks. Furthermore, the learning appeared to be very durable. In a later study (Glisky and Schacter 1988b), which also included patients with memory disorders of etiologies other than head injury, little loss of the acquired computer knowledge was observed even after retention intervals of 7 – 9 months.

Learning achieved by patients in these studies, however, was not normal. They needed many more trials to acquire the information than did control subjects and their acquired knowledge seemed to be 'hyperspecific' (Glisky et al., 1986a; Schacter, 1985) in the sense that it was only accessible when original stimulus conditions were re-instated. This inflexibility once again suggests that transfer of learning to novel situations may be problematic. Although knowledge of computer operations is a potentially valuable skill, patients must be able to use that knowledge in the real world if they are to benefit significantly from the laboratory training.

A recent study provides some evidence that knowledge and skills acquired in the laboratory can be applied in at least one important domain of everyday life – the workplace. In a single-case study, Glisky and Schacter (1987) reported that they were able to train an amnesic post-encephalitic woman for a complex computer data-entry job in a big corporation. Using the method of vanishing cues and a laboratory simulation of the job, the patient, H.D., learned to extract information from company documents and enter it into coded columns of a computer display. To perform this task correctly, H.D. was required to learn the general terminology associated with the job, the meanings of the display codes, the location of appropriate information on the documents, the relationship between the documents and the computer display, and special procedures such as error-handling routines. She also had to perform the task quickly and without error. Although she initially needed 55 minutes to complete one trial of the training procedure, H.D. gradually acquired both the knowledge and skills associated with the job so that she was able to enter information from one card into the computer in as little as 13 seconds. More importantly, transfer of learning to the actual job situation was extremely smooth. After approximately three hours of supervised performance on the job, H.D. performed the task as accurately and efficiently as she had in the laboratory (see Glisky and Schacter, 1988a, for another vocational training study).

Reasons for the success of the vocational training studies are still uncertain, but Glisky and Schacter (1987, 1988a) suggest a few factors that are likely to be important. First, the jobs that appear to be most suitable for patients with memory disorders are those which require a set of relatively invariant procedures which can be taught explicitly and directly. Although memory-impaired patients may be able to learn complex tasks, they have considerable difficulty handling novel situations (e.g., Glisky et al., 1986a). To the extent that all possible variations of basic procedures can be specifically taught, problems of transfer should be minimized. Second, it may also be important to break complex tasks down into component steps and to teach each component directly. Such a task analysis approach has been used successfully in vocational training of the mentally retarded (e.g., Mithaug, 1979; Wacker & Hoffman, 1984; Wehman & Hill, 1981).

Finally, because the knowledge that amnesic patients acquire seems to be 'hyperspecific' and tightly bound to the stimulus situation, it is important that the learning context simulates the real-world environment as closely as possible.

More research within the domain-specific framework is needed before carefully considered long-term evaluations of the procedure can be made. As yet, real-world applications have been demonstrated with just a single patient. Almost certainly, patient characteristics will be an important determinant of response to interventions. The patient described above (H.D.), for example, retains excellent attentional capabilities despite her severe memory deficit. It remains to be demonstrated whether patients who have other cognitive deficits in conjunction with their memory disorders will be able to benefit similarly.

Future directions

Research concerning memory remediation is a relatively recent development, so it is not surprising that few firm conclusions concerning the efficacy of remedial interventions can be drawn. Nevertheless, existing evidence suggests that the most promising approaches are those concerned with alleviation of problems in everyday life, rather than with restoration of mnemonic function. Although research in these areas is still in its infancy, new techniques and developments have yielded some positive outcomes which suggest that the everyday lives of memory-impaired patients can be improved by an appropriate intervention.

Two recent advances should continue to have significant impact on future research. First, the ready availability of inexpensive microcomputers with their capacity to serve as powerful memory aids for impaired patients will probably continue to attract both practitioners and researchers in the field of memory rehabilitation. It is important that research should provide information and guidelines concerning the ways in which computers can and cannot be used productively to benefit disabled patients. Two beneficial uses of microcomput-

ers have been described in this chapter: (1) the provision of information and prompts for everyday activities (Kirsch et al., 1987), and (2) the teaching of domain-specific knowledge that can be used in daily life (Glisky and Schacter, 1987). In addition, it has also been demonstrated that patients with a variety of memory and cognitive disorders can operate a microcomputer, at least on a simple level (Glisky et al., 1986a, 1988b). Ways of exploiting this ability in order to enhance patients' capacities for independent living remain to be explored.

The second development that should influence the direction of future rehabilitation research is the finding that even patients with very serious memory disorders retain the ability for some learning. Based on this observation, studies of the acquisition of domain-specific knowledge have shown that even complex kinds of knowledge and skills can be acquired by memory-impaired patients (Glisky and Schacter, 1987, 1988a; Glisky et al., 1986a,b). Because no limits have yet been observed to the amount of knowledge that can be acquired, continued investigation along this line is likely to be profitable. In addition, only a few knowledge domains have been explored in the laboratory and even fewer real-world applications have been attempted. Many more possibilities for significant interventions – vocational, educational, social, domestic – have yet to be investigated.

Future research will also have to consider seriously problems of transfer of training and generalization. The domain-specific knowledge approach has attempted to minimize the problem by teaching all aspects of a task exactly as they would be required in everyday life. Although this method is effective, it is time-consuming and places limitations on the kinds of tasks that are suitable for memory-impaired patients. Greater efficiency of training might be achieved if it could be determined that the acquisition of some kinds of general knowledge and skills could provide benefits for the later learning of specific tasks. Experiments to determine what aspects of training are most likely to transfer and what kinds of knowledge tend to be most situation-specific will almost certainly form important segments of future research programs concerned with memory rehabilitation.

References

Ager A: Recent developments in the use of microcomputers in the field of mental handicap: implications for psychological practice. *Bull. Br. Psychol. Soc.: 38,* 142 – 145, 1985.

Auerbach SH: Cognitive rehabilitation in the head injured: a neurobehavioral approach. *Semin. Neurol.: 3,* 152 – 163, 1973.

Baddeley AD: Amnesia: a minimal model and interpretation. In Cermak LS (Editor), *Human Memory and Amnesia.* Hillsdale, NJ: Erlbaum, pp. 305 – 336, 1982.

Baddeley AD, Warrington EK: Memory coding and amnesia. *Neuropsychologia: 11,* 159 – 165, 1973.

Bower GH: Analysis of a mnemonic device. *Am. Sci.: 58,* 496 – 510, 1970.

Brooks DN, Baddeley AD: What can amnesic patients learn? *Neuropsychologia: 14,* 111 – 122, 1976.

Cermak LS: Imagery as an aid to retrieval for Korsakoff patients. *Cortex: 11,* 163 – 169, 1975.

Cermak LS: The encoding capacity of a patient with amnesia due to encephalitis. *Neuropsychologia: 14,* 311 – 322, 1976.

Cermak LS: Imagery and mnemonic training. In Poon LW, Fozard JL, Cermak LS, Arenberg KL, Thompson LW (Editors), *New Directions in Memory and Aging.* Hillsdale, NJ: Erblaum, pp. 507 – 510, 1980.

Cermak LS, Talbot N, Chandler K, Wolbarst LR: The perceptual priming phenomenon in amnesia. *Neuropsychologia: 23,* 615 – 622, 1985.

Chase WG, Ericcson KA: Skilled memory. In Anderson JR (Editor), *Cognitive Skills and Their Acquisition.* Hillsdale, NJ: Erlbaum, pp. 141 – 190, 1981.

Cohen NJ, Squire LR: Preserved learning and retention of pattern-analyzing skill in amnesia: dissociation of 'knowing how' and 'knowing that'. *Science: 210,* 207 – 209, 1980.

Corkin S: Acquisition of motor skill after bilateral medial temporal-lobe excision. *Neuropsychologia: 6,* 255 – 265, 1968.

Crovitz HF: Memory retraining in brain-damaged patients: the airplane list. *Cortex: 15,* 131 – 134, 1979.

Crovitz HF, Harvey MT, Horn RW: Problems in the acquisition of imagery mnemonics: three brain-damaged cases. *Cortex: 15,* 225 – 234, 1979.

Diamond R, Rozin P: Activation of existing memories in the amnesic syndrome. *J. Abnorm. Psychol.: 93,* 98 – 105, 1984.

Dolan MP, Norton JC: A programmed training technique that uses reinforcement to facilitate acquisition and retention in brain damaged patients. *J. Clin. Psychol.: 33,* 495 – 501, 1977.

Dorland's pocket medical dictionary. Philadelphia: Saunders, 1982.

Furst CJ: Utility of a computer prosthesis for impaired intention memory. Paper presented to the American Psychological Association, Toronto, Canada, 1984.

Gasparrini B, Satz P: A treatment for memory problems in left hemisphere CVA patients. *J. Clin. Neuropsychol.:* 137 – 150, 1979.

Gianutsos R: What is cognitive rehabilitation? *J. Rehabil.: 4,* 36 – 40, 1980.

Gianutsos R: Training the short- and long-term verbal recall of a post-encephalitic amnesic. *J. Clin. Neuropsychol.:* 143 – 153, 1981.

Gianutos R, Gianutsos J: Rehabilitating the verbal recall of brain-damaged patients by mnemonic training: an experimental demonstration using single-case methodology. *Clin. Neuropsychol.: 1,* 117 – 135, 1979.

Glasgow RE, Zeiss RA, Barrera M, Lewinsohn PM: Case studies on remediating memory deficits in brain-damaged individuals. *J. Clin. Psychol.: 33,* 1049 – 1054, 1977.

Glisky EL, Schacter DL: Remediation of organic memory disorders: Current status and future prospects. *J. Head Trauma Rehabil.: 1,* 54 – 63, 1986.

Glisky EL, Schacter DL: Acquisition of domain-specific knowledge in organic amnesia: training for computer-related work. *Neuropsychologia: 25,* 893 – 906, 1987.

Glisky EL, Schacter DL: Acquisition of domain-specific knowledge in patients with organic memory disorders. *J. Learn. Disabil.: 21,* 333 – 339, 1988a.

Glisky EL, Schacter DL: Long-term retention of computer learning by patients with memory disorders. *Neuropsychologia: 26,* 173 – 178, 1988b.

Glisky EL, Schacter DL, Tulving E: Computer learning by memory-impaired patients: acquisition and retention of complex knowledge. *Neuropsychologia: 24,* 313 – 328, 1986a.

Glisky EL, Schacter DL, Tulving E: Learning and retention of computer-related vocabulary in amnesic patients: method of vanishing cues. *J. Clin. Exp. Neuropsychol.: 8,* 292 – 312, 1986b.

Godfrey HPD, Knight RG: Cognitive rehabilitation of memory functioning in amnesiac alcoholics. *J. Consult. Clin. Psychol.: 53,* 555 – 557, 1985.

Gouvier W: Using the digital alarm chronograph in memory retraining. *Behav. Eng.: 7,* 134, 1982.

Graf P, Schacter DL: Implicit and explicit memory for new associations in normal and amnesic subjects. *J. Exp. Psychol. Learn. Mem. Cognition: 11,* 501 – 518, 1985.

Graf P, Squire LS, Mandler G: The information that amnesic patients do not forget. *J. Exp. Psychol. Learn. Mem. Cognition: 10,* 164 – 178, 1984.

Grimm BH, Bleiberg J: Psychological rehabilitation in traumatic brain injury. In Filskov SB, Boll TJ (Editors), *Handbook of Clinical Neuropsychology, Vol. 2.* New York: John Wiley & Sons, Ch. 17, pp. 495 – 560, 1986.

Harris JE: External memory aids. In Gruneberg MM, Morris PE, Sykes RN (Editors), *Practical Aspects of Memory.* London: Academic Press, pp. 172 – 179, 1978.

Harris JE: Methods of improving memory. In Wilson B, Moffat N (Editors), *Clinical Management of Memory Problems.* London: Aspen, pp. 46 – 62, 1984.

Harris JE, Sunderland A: A brief survey of the management of memory disorders in rehabilitation units in Britain. *Int. Rehabil. Med.: 3,* 206 – 209, 1981.

Heinrichs RW: Attempted clinical application of a technique for promoting robust free recall to a case of alcoholic Korsakoff's syndrome. *Brain Cognition: 9,* 151 – 157, 1989.

affe, PG, Katz AN: Attenuating anterograde amnesia in Korsakoff's psychosis. *J. Abnorm. Psychol.: 34,* 559–562, 1975.

ames W: *The Principles of Psychology, Vol. 1.* New York: Dover Publications Inc., 1890.

ones GH, Adam JH: Towards a prosthetic memory. *Bull. Br. Psychol. Soc.: 32,* 165–167, 1979.

ones MK: Imagery as a mnemonic aid after left temporal lobectomy: contrast between material-specific and generalized memory disorders. *Neuropsychologia: 12,* 21–30, 1974.

insbourne M, Wood F: Short term memory and the amnesic syndrome. In Deutsch DD, Deutsch JA (Editors), *Short-term Memory.* New York: Academic Press, pp. 258–291, 1975.

irsch NL, Levine SP, Fallon-Kreuger M, Jaros LA: The microcomputer as an orthotic device for patients with cognitive deficits. *J. Head Trauma Rehabil.: 2,* 77–86, 1987.

ovner R, Mattis S, Pass R: Some amnesic patients can freely recall large amounts of information in new contexts. *J. Clin. Exp. Neuropsychol.: 7,* 395–411, 1985.

urlychek RT: Use of a digital alarm chronograph as a memory aid in early dementia. *Clin. Gerontol.: 1,* 93–94, 1983.

andauer TK, Bjork RA: Optimum rehearsal patterns and name learning. In Gruneberg MM, Morris PE, Sykes RN (Editors), *Practical Aspects of Memory.* London: Academic Press, pp. 625–632, 1978.

evin HS, Benton AL, Grossman RG: *Neurobehavioral Consequences of Closed Head Injury.* New York: Oxford University Press, 1982.

ewinsohn PM, Danaher BG, Kikel S: Visual imagery as a mnemonic aid for brain-injured persons. *J. Consult. Clin. Psychol.: 45,* 717–723, 1977.

orayne H, Lucas J: *The Memory Book.* New York: Stein & Day, 1974.

ynch W: Technology. *J. Head Trauma Rehabil.: 1,* 78–80, 1986.

Malec J, Questad K: Rehabilitation of memory after craniocerebral trauma: case report. *Arch. Phys. Med. Rehabil.: 64,* 436–438, 1983.

Mateer CA, Sohlberg MM, Crinean J: Focus on clinical research: perceptions of memory function in individuals with closed-head injury. *J. Head Trauma Rehabil.: 2,* 74–84, 1987.

Mattis S, Kovner R: Amnesia is as amnesia does: toward another definition of the anterograde amnesias. In Squire LR, Butters N (Editors), *Neuropsychology of Memory.* New York: Guilford Press, pp. 115–121, 1984.

Mayer NJ, Keating DJ, Rapp D: Skills, routines, and activity patterns of daily living: a functional nested approach. In Uzzell B, Gross Y (Editors), *Clinical Neuropsychology of Intervention.* Boston, MA: Martinus Nijhoff, pp. 205–222, 1986.

Milberg W, Alexander MP, Charness N, McGlinchey-Berroth R, Barrett A: Learning of a complex arithmetic skill in amnesia: evidence for a disocciation between compilation and production. *Brain Cognition: 8,* 91–104, 1988.

Miller E: Is amnesia remediable? In Gruneberg MM, Morris PE, Sykes RN (Editors), *Practical Aspects of Memory.* London: Academic Press, pp. 705–711, 1978.

Miller E: Psychological intervention in the management and rehabilitation of neuropsychological impairments. *Behav. Res. Ther.: 18,* 527–535, 1980.

Miller E: *Recovery and Management of Neuropsychological Impairments.* New York: John Wiley & Sons, 1984.

Milner B, Corkin S, Teuber HL: Further analysis of the hippocampal amnesic syndrome: 14 year follow-up study of H.M. *Neuropsychologia: 6,* 215–234, 1968.

Milton SB: Compensatory memory strategy training: A practical approach for managing persisting memory problems. *Cognitive Rehabil.: 3,* 8–16, 1985.

Mithaug D: The relation between programmed instruction and task analysis in the prevocational training of severely and profoundly handicapped persons. *Am. Assoc. Educ. Severely/Profoundly Handicap. Rev.: 4,* 162–178, 1979.

Moscovitch M: The sufficient conditions for demonstrating preserved memory in amnesia: a task analysis. In Squire LR, Butters N (Editors), *Neuropsychology of Memory.* New York: Guilford Press, pp. 104–114, 1984.

Newcombe F: Rehabilitation in clinical neurology: Neuropsychological aspects. In Frederiks JAM (Editor), *Handbook of Clinical Neurology, Vol 2: Neurobehavioral Disorders.* Amsterdam: Elsevier Science Publishers, pp. 609–642, 1985.

Newell A, Rosenbloom PS: Mechanisms of skill acquisition and the law of practice. In Anderson JR (Editor), *Cognitive Skills and Their Acquisition.* Hillsdale, NJ, Erlbaum, pp. 1–56, 1981.

O'Connor M, Cermak LS: Rehabilitation of organic memory disorders. In Meier MJ, Benton AL, Diller L (Editors), *Neuropsychological Rehabilitation.* New York: Guilford, pp. 260–279, 1987.

Paivio A: Mental imagery in associative learning and memory. *Psychol. Rev.: 76,* 241–263, 1969.

Parkin AJ: *Memory and Amnesia.* London: Basil Blackwell, 1987.

Patten BM: The ancient art of memory. *Arch. Neurol.: 26,* 25–31, 1972.

Prigatano GP, Fordyce DJ, Zeiner HK, Roueche JR, Pepping M, Wood BC: Neuropsychological rehabilitation after closed head injury in young adults. *J. Neurol. Neurosurg. Psychiatry: 47,* 505–513, 1984.

Robinson FB: *Effective study.* New York: Harper & Row, 1970.

Salmon DP, Butters N: Recent developments in learning and memory: implications for the rehabilitation of the amnesic patient. In Meier MJ, Benton AL, Diller L (Editors), *Neuropsychological Rehabilitation.* New York: Guilford, pp. 280–293, 1987.

Schacter DL: Multiple forms of memory in humans and animals. In Weinberger N, McGaugh J, Lynch G (Editors), *Memory Systems of the Brain: Animal and Human Cognitive Processes.* New York: Guilford Press, pp. 351–379, 1985.

Schacter DL, Glisky EL: Memory remediation: restoration, alleviation, and the acquisition of domain-specific knowledge. In Uzzell B, Gross Y (Editors), *Clinical Neuropsychology of Intervention.* Boston: Martinus Nijhoff, pp. 257–282, 1986.

Schacter DL, Graf P: Preserved learning in amnesic patients: perspectives from research on direct priming. *J. Clin. Exp. Neuropsychol.: 8,* 727–743, 1986.

Schacter DL, Tulving E: Amnesia and memory research. In Cermak LS (Editor), *Human Memory and Amnesia*. Hillsdale, NJ: Erlbaum, pp. 1 – 32, 1982.

Schacter DL, Rich SA, Stampp MS: Remediation of memory disorders: experimental evaluation of the spaced-retrieval technique. *J. Clin. Exp. Neuropsychol.: 7,* 79 – 96, 1985.

Schacter DL, Glisky EL, McGlynn SM: Impact of memory disorder on everyday life: awareness of deficits and return to work. In Tupper D, Cicerone K (Editors), *The Neuropsychology of Everyday life*. Boston: Martinus Nijhoff, 1989.

Seidel H, Hodgkinson PE: Behavior modification and long-term learning in Korsakoff's psychosis. *Nurs. Times: 75,* 1855 – 1857, 1979.

Skilbeck, C: Computer assistance in the management of memory and cognitive impairment. In Wilson B, Moffat N (Editors), *Clinical Management of Memory Problems*. Rockville, MD: Aspen, pp. 112 – 133, 1984.

Sohlberg MM, Mateer CA: Training use of memory books: a three stage behavioral program. *J. Clin. Exp. Neuropsychol.:* in press.

Squire LR, Butters N (Editors): *Neuropsychology of Memory*. New York: Guilford Press, 1984.

Wacker DP, Hoffman RC: Vocational rehabilitation of severely handicapped persons. In Golden CJ (Editor), *Current Topics in Rehabilitation Psychology*. Orlando, FA: Grune & Stratton, pp. 139 – 171, 1984.

Warrington EK, Weiskrantz L: New method of testing long term retention with special reference to amnesic patients. *Nature: 217,* 972 – 974, 1968.

Warrington EK, Weiskrantz L: The effect of prior learning on subsequent retention in amnesic patients. *Neuropsychologia 12,* 419 – 428, 1974.

Wehman P, Hill JW: Competitive employment for moderately and severely handicapped individuals. *Except. Child.: 47* 338 – 345, 1981.

Whyte J: Preface. *J. Head Trauma Rehabil.: 1,* ix, 1986.

Wilson B: Success and failure in memory training following a cerebral vascular accident. *Cortex: 18,* 581 – 594, 1982.

Wilson B: *Rehabilitation of Memory*. New York: Guilford 1987.

Wilson B, Moffat N (Editors): *Clinical Management of Memory Problems*. London: Aspen, 1984a.

Wilson B, Moffat N: Rehabilitation of memory for everyday life. In Harris JE, Morris PE (Editors) *Everyday Memory Actions and Absentmindedness*. London: Academic Press pp. 207 – 233, 1984b.

Yates F: *The Art of Memory*. Chicago: University of Chicago Press, 1966.

1989 Elsevier Science Publishers B.V. (Biomedical Division)
andbook of Neuropsychology, Vol. 3
Boller and J. Grafman (Eds)

CHAPTER 11

Pharmacological treatment of memory disorders

Leon J. Thal

Neurology Service, Veterans Administration Medical Center, San Diego, CA, and Department of Neurosciences, University of California, San Diego, La Jolla, CA, U.S.A.

Introduction

The search for a treatment for memory disorders has been going on for many years. Senility was recognized in the bible and by Ponce de Leon during his quest for the fountain of youth. For the older aged population, few diseases are feared as much as the development of senility or loss of cognitive functioning. Until recently, the development of senility was viewed as a natural consequence of aging. Today, however, we know that a specific disease process is responsible for virtually all causes of memory loss. The most common disease responsible for memory loss is Alzheimer's disease (AD), which accounts for between 50 and 70% of all cases of memory disorders. Other diseases which account for significant numbers of cases of memory disorders include cerebrovascular disease, depression and Parkinson's disease (PD). Rarer causes include closed head trauma, electroconvulsive therapy, the Wernicke Korsakoff syndrome, and a wide variety of other medical, neurological and psychiatric disorders (Marsden and Harrison, 1972; Freeman 1976; Smith, 1981; Larson et al., 1986). With the 'graying of America' and the expected rise in the over age 65 population, the number of individuals with dementia in America will increase dramatically by the turn of the century.

Rationale for treatment

Dementing disorders
Alzheimer's disease. Until the late 1960s and early 1970s, the etiology of senile dementia was poorly understood. Most clinicians believed that dementia was due to cerebrovascular disease and brain ischemia. It was therefore logical to presuppose that treatment with vasodilators might ameliorate symptoms of 'senility'. Early drug trials employed compounds originally developed as peripheral vasodilators. That a state of chronic ischemia rarely occurred was not appreciated. There was little understanding of the difficulty of inducing persistent sustained dilatation of cerebral blood vessels. Finally, and most importantly, the underlying assumptions regarding the etiology of dementia in the majority of the population were incorrect. The vast majority of individuals with dementia are now known to suffer from AD rather than acquiring their dementia as a consequence of diminished blood flow or chronic ischemia.

It was only in the 1970s that the first biochemical pathology of AD was obtained. Significant losses of choline acetyltransferase (CAT), the synthetic enzyme for acetylcholine, were detected in the neocortex of individuals with AD (Davies and Malony, 1976; Perry et al., 1977; White et al., 1977) secondary to degeneration of cholinergic neurons in the nucleus basalis (Whitehouse, 1981). Subsequently, other investigators demonstrated changes of a lesser magnitude in the noradrenergic (Perry et al., 1981; Bondareff et al., 1982) and somatostatinergic systems (Davies et al., 1980; Rossor et al., 1980). Smaller changes in serotonin have been reported (Arai et al., 1984; Frances et al., 1985), while changes in dopamine concentration remain controversial (Adolfsson et al., 1978; Yates et al., 1979). Thus, AD is clearly not a disorder of the cholinergic system alone. Of all the neurotransmitter changes reported, however, decreases in CAT activity are the most consistent and are the only neurotransmitter changes that have been strongly correlated with changes in memory (Perry et al., 1978; Katzman et al., 1986). The cholinergic deficit in AD appears to be largely presynaptic, with most authors reporting either normal levels of muscarinic receptors (White et al., 1977; Davies and Verth, 1978) or small decreases (Rinne et al., 1985). The small decrease in receptor number may be secondary to a selective loss of presynaptic muscarinic receptors (Mash et al., 1985), further strengthening the concept of presynaptic cholinergic dysfunction.

The major pathological changes in AD consist of neuronal loss, and the presence of a characteristic distribution of neuronal plaques and neurofibrillary tangles (see Katzman, 1986, for review). Large numbers of plaques are characteristically seen in the hippocampus, entorhinal cortex and amygdala. Additionally, the pattern of cellular loss in the hippocampus is such that the hippocampal formation may be largely isolated from its many connections, thereby contributing to a memory disorder (Hyman et al., 1984).

The simplest rational pharmacological approach to this disorder has concentrated on a neurotransmitter replacement strategy. Attempts at altering the underlying pathology or restoring lost neuronal function have not yet been tried.

Vascular dementia. Vascular disease is reponsible for the second largest grouping of individuals with memory impairment after AD, accounting for approximately 25 to 30% of all patients who present with dementia (Marsden and Harrison, 1972 Freemon, 1976; Mölsä et al., 1985). Multiple forms of vascular dementia occur, including multi infarct dementia secondary to involvement of large- and medium-size vessels, the lacunar state characterized by arteriolar hyalinosis, Binswanger's disease characterized by the presence of small vessel disease in the subcortical white matter, a well as a small number of unusual vascular dementias, including microangiopathy and collagen vascular disease. The hallmark of the disorder is the appearance of cognitive deficits occurring in a step-wise manner, manifested by a patchy distribution of involvement, the presence of focal neurological signs and symptoms, and the presence of significant vascular disease (Am. Psychiatr Assoc., 1980).

The rationale for the treatment of vascular dementia is the assumption that this disorder is secondary to vessel narrowing due to cerebral atherosclerosis resulting in decreased blood flow and the production of a state of chronic ischemia If this assumption is correct, then vascular dementia could logically be treated by compounds that increase cerebral blood flow. While cerebral blood flow declines with aging (Ketty, 1956) and in most forms of dementia (Hachinsky et al., 1975) cerebral blood flow is quite resistant to change and there is only weak evidence that cerebral vasodilators can appreciably enhance blood flow More importantly, in normal subjects blood flow remains remarkably constant over a wide range of induced blood pressure. Less is known about blood flow in pathological states. However, except in very unusual conditions, a state of chronic ischemia rarely exists, because in most instances of vascular dementia frank infarction of tissue occurs secondary to vascular occlusion. It therefore seems unlikely that an increase in blood flow would enhance cerebral function. A more logical mechanism of improving memory in such individuals would be the use of agents designed to improve functioning of remaining brain tissue. Indeed, if cerebral vasodilators are effective in reducing symptoms associated with cerebrovascular ementia, their mechanism of action is likely to be an effect on something other than blood flow.

Parkinsonian dementia. The incidence of dementia in PD is generally thought to be about 30% (Mayeux and Stern, 1983), although the incidence clearly increases, reaching perhaps 70% in advanced states of disease (Martilla and Rinne, 1976). The dementia of PD is clinically characterized by memory loss and slowness without aphasia or apraxia.

The motor dysfunction of PD is linked to a decrease in dopamine (Barbeau, 1962). But what causes the cognitive dysfunction? Decreases of cortical CAT (Perry et al., 1983) and loss of cholinergic neurons in the nucleus basalis of Meynert have been reported in PD (Whitehouse et al., 1983). These changes occur in PD, both with and without dementia, but to a greater degree in demented subjects. Noradrenaline and serotonin are equally reduced in demented and nondemented PD patients (Scatton et al., 1983). Dopamine is decreased in both demented and nondemented patients (Price et al., 1978). Thus, the cause of the memory loss in PD is unknown but may involve changes in the cholinergic system.

Strategies for treatment based on neurotransmitter replacement therapy clearly involve restoration of brain dopamine, which should improve overall speed of performance. Attempts to correct cholinergic deficiencies with cholinomimetic agents may be limited by worsened motor symptoms in the face of cognitive improvement.

Amnesic disorders

Most compounds used for the treatment of amnesia were tried on empirical grounds alone. Some, such as the neuropeptides, were tried in humans based upon the demonstration of memory enhancement in animals. Hardly any are based on known alterations of neurochemistry in humans with amnesic disorders. The only exception has been the attempt to treat Wernicke Korsakoff patients with alpha agonists following the demonstration of a decreased norepinephrine metabolite in cerebrospinal fluid (CSF) (McEntee and Mair, 1978; McEntee et al., 1984).

Treatment of dementing disorders

Alzheimer's disease: non-cholinergic therapy

Vasodilators, metabolic enhancers

Early clinical trials of dementia concentrated on the use of vasodilators because of the mistaken notion that senile dementia was most frequently a consequence of cerebral atherosclerosis and chronic ischemia. Many methodological problems exist in interpreting these early studies. Most patient populations consisted of elderly patients with symptoms of senility. Attempts to separate etiologies such as vascular dementia and AD were generally not carried out. In many instances, only subjective impressions or subjective rating scales were utilized. In instances where objective psychometric testing was carried out, an extremely wide array of tests were used, making it very difficult to compare the numerous small studies. Nevertheless, it is clear that some of the agents tested produced small changes in either cognition or mood.

Papaverine (Pavabid). Papaverine is an alkaloid derived from opium but devoid of narcotic properties. It is a potent nonspecific smooth muscle relaxant that causes arteriolar dilatation. Acute intravenous administration increases cerebral blood flow (Meyer et al., 1965; McHenry et al., 1970), whereas oral therapy decreases cerebral blood flow in healthy volunteers (Wang and Obrist, 1976). A number of uncontrolled studies (LaBrecque, 1966; Dunlop, 1968) reported subjective improvement in memory, coordination, vertigo and headache in patients with chronic dementia. Several double-blind studies (Stern, 1970; Ritter et al., 1971; McQuillan et al., 1974) noted improvement in anxiety, depression, mental functioning and clinical global rating on papaverine. However, more than an equal number of studies failed to substantiate these findings (Lu et al., 1971; Bazo, 1973; Rosen, 1975). All of the studies reported have major methodological problems and most positive studies utilized subjective rating scales or failed to control for the increased attention being paid to the patient during the study.

Isoxsuprine (Vasodilan). Isoxsuprine is a derivative of epinephrine that induces cerebral and peripheral vasodilatation. Two double-blind controlled studies demonstrated a decrease in headaches without any change in mental functioning (Dhrymiotis and Whittier, 1962) and an increase on the similarities subtest of the Wechsler Adult Intelligence Scale (WAIS) (Affleck et al., 1961). Significant functional improvement was not reported in either study.

Cyclandelate (Cyclospasmol). Cyclandelate has structural similarities to papaverine. It is a direct-acting smooth muscle relaxant. Several early double-blind parallel studies demonstrated improvement on general questioning, orientation and picture interpretation, but not in self-care (Ball and Taylor, 1967; Fine et al., 1970). Later studies, however, were either equivocal (Aderman et al., 1972) or negative. In a careful study of 24 patients with a mixed population of both AD and vascular dementia, no improvement was seen on the Wechsler Memory Scale, WAIS or other tests administered (Westreich and Alter, 1975). Practical benefit from this compound appears to be lacking.

Ergoloid mesylates (Hydergine). Ergoloid mesylates are a mixture of three ergot alkaloids. These compounds have weak dopaminergic activity and some alpha-adrenoreceptor blocking activity. They therefore have properties of both vasodilators and agents that can alter multiple neurotransmitters. Ergoloid mesylates are undoubtedly the most extensively tested metabolic enhancing agents. They are also the most frequently prescribed drug for the treatment of cognitive impairment. Numerous double-blind, parallel, controlled studies of these compounds have been carried out and a careful review of most of these papers suggests that the majority of the individuals included in these studies had AD, while a minority had dementia secondary to cerebrovascular disease. Virtually all studies reviewed revealed improvement in such items as attention, mood, self-care, attitude, behavior, mental alertness, confusion and hostility (Hollister, 1955; Triboletti and Ferri, 1969; Ditch et al., 1971; Banen, 1972; Jennings, 1972; Rao and Norris, 1972; Roubicek et al., 1972; Arrigo et al. 1973; Bazo, 1973; Nelson, 1975; Rosen, 1975 Soni, 1975; Einspruch, 1976; Gaitz et al., 1977) Improvement has been demonstrated on a wide variety of different subjective rating scales, including the Brief Psychiatric Rating Scale (BPRS) The Nurses Observational Scale of Inpatient Evaluation (NOSIE), Sandoz Clinical Assessment Geriatric (SCAG), and Activity of Daily Living Scale, and other scales of behavior and mental functioning. Methodological procedures for completing the clinical behavioral scales were not specified by the majority of the investigators. Although over 1,500 patients have been included in these many trials, only a small number of investigators used objective testing such as subscales of the WAIS, or a verbal memory task such as the Buschke Selective Reminding Task, and these studies have generally failed to document changes in objective memory testing (Forster et al., 1955; Banen, 1972; Thienhaus et al., 1987). Overall symptom improvement has been found mainly in the area of subjective cognitive dysfunction, mood, depression and composite scores.

Almost all studies used doses of either 3 or 4.5 mg/day. Recently, two studies have been carried out comparing 6 mg to 3 mg (Yesavage et al., 1979) or 6 mg to placebo (Thienhaus et al., 1987). While both studies demonstrated limited improvement on subjective measures of short-term memory, a greater degree of efficacy was not demonstrated comparing the 6 mg dose to the 3 mg dose. Several excellent reviews of the many studies and current utilization of this preparation exist (McDonald, 1979; Hollister and Yesavage, 1984). Although virtually all controlled studies have demonstrated some degree of behavioral or psychological improvement in patients treated with ergoloid mesylates, improvement seems to be too small to be of clinical significance for the majority of patients. It seems likely that the ergoloid mesylates exert their influence on cognition by acting as mild antidepressants, probably by affecting multiple neurotransmitter systems. Ergoloid mesylates remain the only compound currently marketed in the

United States for the treatment of signs and symptoms of decline in mental capacity in the elderly. Almost every clinician has observed an individual patient with a striking response to this preparation. This factor probably accounts for its continued use for more than three decades.

Anticoagulants and hyperbaric oxygen. The rationale for the use of both anticoagulants and hyperbaric oxygen was again based on the erroneous assumption that most cases of dementia were secondary to vascular disease. An initial study of patients with dementia of various causes treated with the anticoagulant Coumadin apparently showed improvement on activities of daily living (Walsh, 1969), but the study could not be replicated (Ratner et al., 1972). A single study reported improvement on the Wechsler Memory Scale using hyperbaric oxygen (Jacobs et al., 1969) but two other studies failed to confirm these improvements on the Wechsler Memory Scale or other psychological tests (Goldfarb et al., 1972; Thompson et al., 1976). There is no justification for the use of either of these forms of therapy in the treatment of AD.

Nootropics

The word nootropic means 'acting upon the mind'. These compounds are a class of drugs that appear to alter mental functioning by unknown means. Additionally, they are virtually devoid of side-effects. In animal studies, these compounds facilitate learning and memory in a wide variety of tasks. The prototypic nootropic agent is piracetam, a cyclic relative of γ-aminobutyric acid (GABA). In a double-blind placebo-controlled study of 196 geriatric patients with dementia, piracetam was found to produce improvement in vertigo, physical fatigue and mental asthenia (Steginik, 1972). Two other studies, however, were entirely negative with respect to improvement in mental functioning (Abuzzahab et al., 1978; Gustafson et al., 1978). Additionally, piracetam plus lecithin failed to improve cognition in 18 patients tested with an extensive neuropsychological battery (Growdon et al., 1986). Multiple analogues

of piracetam have also been tested, including pramiracetam (Branconnier et al., 1983), oxiracetam (Saletu et al., 1985; Hjorther et al., 1987) and aniracetam (Sourander et al., 1987) with negative results. Naftidrofuryl (Praxilene) was reported to improve intelligence and memory in two preliminary double-blind trials (Judge and Urquhart, 1972; Bouvier et al., 1974) but these findings have not been subsequently confirmed. Unfortunately, although many of the preliminary open single-blind or small double-blind studies of nootropic agents seem to indicate improvement in AD, the large-scale American clinical trials of nootropics, including pramiracetam and rolziracetam (CI 911) (Gamzu, personal communication, 1987) have failed to demonstrate cognitive improvement in AD patients.

Neuropeptides

Vasopressin and analogues. The justification for the use of vasopressin and its analogues in the treatment of memory disorders emanates from animal data. Animals treated with vasopressin demonstrate improvement on a wide variety of experimental tasks, including active and passive avoidance, maze learning and ECT-induced amnesia (Bohus, 1977; de Wied, 1977; Hostetter et al., 1977). Additionally, loss of vasopressin by hypophysectomy or hereditarily, as in the Brattleboro rat, which is deficient in the production of vasopressin, impairs performance and learning (de Wied et al., 1975; de Wied, 1969). In AD, there are small decreases in hippocampal vasopressin, whereas cortical vasopressin levels are normal (Mazurek et al., 1986). A number of studies have now been carried out with vasopressin and its many analogues. Using lysine vasopressin, one open study reported improvement in verbal memory (Delwaide et al., 1980), but a more carefully controlled double-blind study reported only an increase in reaction time without improvement in list learning, verbal memory on a selective reminding task, paired associate learning, or memory passages (Durso et al., 1982). Using desamino-D-arginine-vasopressin (DDAVP), a vasopressin analogue without vasopressor activity, but which retains antidiuretic activity and has a longer duration of action, one study reported a small increase in category recall (Weingartner et al., 1981), while two other studies reported no improvement on a wide variety of tasks, including paired-associative learning and a Buschke Selective Reminding Task (Tinkelenberg et al., 1981; Peabody et al., 1986). Using desglycinamide-arginine-vasopressin (DGAVP), an analogue devoid of antidiuretic activity, three double-blind crossover studies reported essentially negative results on a wide variety of tasks, including list learning, selective reminding and nonverbal learning (Tinklenberg et al., 1982; Jennekens-Schinkel et al., 1985; Peabody et al., 1985). The effects of vasopressin appear to be on vigilance and attention as demonstrated by a faster reaction time. Overall, the therapeutic effects of vasopressin in AD are disappointing. Although some patients have more energy and less depression, cognitive improvement is lacking. The results suggest that vasopressin cannot exert a beneficial effect in individuals with extensive neuronal degeneration.

Adrenocorticotrophic hormone (ACTH). ACTH is a 39 amino acid peptide derived from a precursor protein. Amino acids 4 to 10 ($ACTH_{4-10}$) are responsible for most of the behavioral activity of the parent molecule (Bohus and de Wied, 1981). In animals, ACTH and its fragments increase resistance to extinction and restore acquisition of shock avoidance after hypophysectomy (de Wied, 1969; de Wied and Gispen, 1977). Corticotropin-releasing factor (CRF) promotes the release of ACTH. Recent studies have demonstrated decreases in CRF in brain (Bissette et al., 1985; Desouza et al., 1986) and CSF (May et al., 1987) as well as decreases in CSF ACTH (Facchinetti et al., 1984; May et al., 1987). Clinical trials with $ACTH_{4-10}$ have demonstrated mild elevation of mood but not a clear-cut improvement in cognition (Ferris et al., 1976; Branconnier et al., 1979; Will et al., 1978). An orally administered ACTH analogue, $ACTH_{4-9}$ (ORG2766), produced a small improvement on the SCAG in one study

(Kragh-Sorensen et al., 1986) but not in others (Martin et al., 1983; Soininen et al., 1985). Overall, there has been no convincing demonstration that ACTH or its fragments can improve memory in Alzheimer patients.

Opioids. A number of animal studies suggest that naloxone, an opiate antagonist, has a facilitory effect on memory performance whereas opiates have an inhibitory effect (see Kapp and Gallagher (1979) and Koob and Bloom (1983) for reviews). Therefore it was speculated that naloxone might be a useful compound for the treatment of memory loss in AD (Roberts, 1981). Initial results from a small double-blind placebo-controlled trial of five AD patients given 1, 5 and 10 mg of intravenous naloxone revealed an increase in the speed of performance and improvement on psychological testing, including category retrieval, digit span and digit symbol substitution (Reisberg et al., 1983). However, attempts to replicate this initial finding have been negative (Blass et al., 1983; Panella and Blass, 1984; Tariot et al., 1986). Since naloxone has an extremely short half-life, others have utilized orally active opiate antagonists with half-lives of up to 24 h such as naltrexone and nalmefene. Results have been conflicting, with most investigators reporting negative data on extensive neuropsychological batteries (Hyman et al., 1985; Serby et al., 1986; Weiss, 1987). One small double-blind, placebo-controlled crossover trial of nine patients reported improvement on the Mini-Mental State and Blessed Dementia Scale (Tennant, 1987) using 50 mg of naltrexone daily. A second uncontrolled trial reported improvement on the Rey Auditory Verbal Learning Task but not on other psychometric tests using naltrexone 150 and 300 mg/day (Knopman and Hartman, 1986). These studies do not suggest significant cognitive improvement in AD using opiate antagonists. However, large numbers of patients need to be studied and the question of an appropriate dose needs to be resolved before a final conclusion can be reached.

Somatostatin. Numerous studies have demonstrated a decrease in brain somatostatin concentrations in patients with AD (Davies et al., 1980; Rossor et al., 1980; Beal et al., 1986). Although a recent study has shown that somatostatin content from temporal cortex correlates with the WAIS full-scale IQ, the dementia rating does not demonstrate a similar correlation (Francis et al., 1987). Only a single attempt at somatostatin replacement has been carried out using a somatostatin analogue (L363,586). Ten AD patients were treated with this compound without benefit. However, CSF levels of this compound could not be detected (Cutler et al., 1985b). The lack of efficacy of this compound may be due to its failure to reach the central nervous system (CNS) or to the fact that somatostatin may not play a role in the memory disorder of AD as assessed by serial or paired-associate learning.

General conclusions regarding neuropeptide treatment of Alzheimer's disease. Improvements in memory and cognition following the use of neuropeptides in AD are less than striking. Many problems exist with this form of therapy. In many instances it is not known whether peptides act centrally or peripherally with a feedback loop to the CNS. Most peripherally administered peptides do not reach the brain directly, although very small quantities may cross the blood-brain barrier and produce behavioral changes. Peptides are rapidly degraded in blood and metabolic fragments are undoubtedly produced which may or may not exert behavioral effects. Peptides have short half-lives and in clinical studies brief treatment periods or suboptimal dosing may well occur. Finally, behavioral effects derived from studies using animals which are either normal or which have limited disease of the CNS are being extrapolated to patients with widespread and moderately advanced CNS disease. Future studies must address the questions of dose, duration of treatment, and entry into the brain before meaningful conclusions regarding the efficacy of these compounds can be reached.

Others

Compared to other neurotransmitters, little is known about the role of serotonin in memory disorders. Patients with AD have a moderate decrease in brain serotonin. Whether or not this diminution is related to a change in memory or cognition is not known. A trial of tryptophan in 28 demented, and in many cases depressed, patients failed to improve behavior on two geriatric rating scales; memory was not adequately measured (Smith et al., 1984). Similarly, zimelidine, a serotonin reuptake inhibitor, failed to improve memory on objective psychometric testing in four mildly demented AD patients (Cutler et al., 1985a).

Some AD patients may also have decreased norepinephrine (Bondareff et al., 1987) or dopamine levels (Yates et al., 1983). Brain monoamine oxidase-B activity has been reported to be increased in AD (Adolfsson et al., 1980). A recent trial of L-deprenyl in AD at 10 mg/day resulted in a small increase in both total and consistent recall on the Buschke selective reminding task (Tariot et al., 1987a) as well as decreased anxiety and depression (Tariot et al., 1987b). Changes in cognition and behavior following L-deprenyl therapy were small and may be mediated by an increase in attention or arousal. Confirmatory trials by other investigators are needed for replication of these results.

Alzheimer's disease: cholinergic agents

Cholinergic manipulation is the first logical and rational pharmacological treatment of AD. Using the experience derived from the treatment of PD, three approaches have been utilized. These include the use of precursor therapy designed to increase the production of acetylcholine, the use of cholinesterase inhibitors to augment the quantity of acetylcholine in the synapse, and the use of direct-acting agonists designed to directly stimulate postsynaptic muscarinic receptors.

Precursors

Following laboratory evidence demonstrating that administration of choline to rats increased rat brain acetylcholine levels (Cohen and Wurtman, 1975, 1976), numerous clinical studies attempted to ameliorate impairment of memory in AD with oral choline or lecithin. Studies using choline have been uniformly disappointing, with virtually all investigators reporting either minimal improvement on such items as a word-recognition task (Fovall et al., 1980) or negative results on objective measures including verbal learning, recall, constructions, verbal fluency and the Purdue pegboard (Boyd et al., 1977; Etienne et al., 1978; Signoret et al., 1978; Smith et al., 1978; Renvoize and Jerram, 1979; Thal et al., 1981). Studies using lecithin similarly failed to demonstrate memory improvement on a wide variety of tasks including learning, memory, constructions and self-care (Etienne et al. 1981; Brinkman et al., 1982; Dysken et al., 1982; Weintraub et al., 1983; Little et al., 1985). Failure to improve cognition with choline and lecithin is probably not caused by lack of absorption or failure to cross the blood-brain barrier because oral choline increases plasma and CSF levels of choline (Christie et al., 1979). It is more likely that in AD inadequate CAT is available to convert choline precursor into acetylcholine, or, more probably, that choline availability is not the rate-limiting step for the production of acetylcholine.

Cholinesterase inhibitors

Most studies with cholinesterase inhibition have attempted to use physostigmine because of its ready availability and safety. In double-blind studies using i.v. physostigmine, five of seven investigators reported improvement in 50 to 80% of subjects on cognitive tasks, including verbal memory (Peters and Levin, 1979; Schwartz and Kohlstaedt, 1980), recognition memory (Christie et al., 1981; Davis and Mohs, 1982) and a construction task (Muramoto et al., 1984). The two negative studies (Ashford et al., 1981; Franceschi et al., 1982) used patients with moderately severe dementia and employed only a single relatively low dose of physostigmine without any attempt at dose titration. These negative results in single-dose studies are not surprising, as multiple investigators (Peters and Levin, 1977; Berger et al., 1979) have reported improvement only when a moderate dose of

parenteral physostigmine was administered. Impairment occurred when high and low doses were given. Using oral physostigmine five double-blind studies have now been reported; three showed that physostigmine produced significant beneficial effects. Two studies demonstrated improvement on various aspects of the Buschke Selective Reminding Task (Thal et al., 1983; Beller et al., 1985), whereas the third demonstrated improvement on an Alzheimer Disease Assessment Scale (Mohs et al., 1985). The fourth study was negative in a group of patients too demented to complete a selective reminding task (Wettstein, 1983), while the fifth demonstrated a small improvement on digit symbol substitution and a shape cancellation task, but not on a selective reminding task (Stern et al., 1987). A marked limitation of this latter study was treatment of patients with the best dose for only three days. There have also been a number of open studies, some reporting positive results on a selective reminding task (Peters and Levin, 1982) whereas others reported negative results on other psychometric measures (Caltagirone et al., 1982, 1983; Jotkowitz, 1983).

Response to oral physostigmine is clearly not a uniform phenomenon. Patients with mild to moderate dementia appear to respond better than those with severe dementia. Dose is also important, since in many of the positive studies total daily doses of physostigmine were 15 – 16 mg for most patients, whereas the negative double-blind studies employed doses of 10 – 12 mg/day. That patients receiving the highest doses generally respond best strongly suggests that either the failure to induce adequate cholinesterase inhibition (probably secondary to poor drug absorption) or the advanced state of disease is responsible for many failures reported in the literature. Only two investigators attempted to monitor entry of drug into the CNS (Thal et al., 1983; Mohs et al., 1985).

In addition to physostigmine, three studies have used tetrahydroaminoacridine (THA), a longer-acting cholinesterase inhibitor. One study using low oral doses reported improvement in verbal memory only in less impaired patients treated with both THA and lecithin (Kaye et al., 1982), whereas intravenous THA alone resulted in global improvement in patients with early and moderate AD (Summers et al., 1981). Recently, striking improvement in global assessment and on psychometric testing was reported in 16 of 17 AD patients (Summers et al., 1986). Clearly, additional work using cholinesterase inhibitors with concomitant monitoring of drug absorption and entry of drug into the CNS is warranted. Several such trials are currently under way in the United States, Canada and Europe. At the present time the use of cholinesterase inhibitors appears to be the most promising simple pharmacological approach to the treatment of memory loss in AD.

Cholinergic agonists

Relatively few cholinergic agonists are available for testing in AD. Arecoline produced improvement at 2 and 4 mg in a small number of AD patients on a picture-recognition task (Christie et al., 1981). Oxotremorine induced significant depression, precluding evaluation of cognitive effects (Davis et al., 1987). Using RS 86, a direct-acting cholinergic agonist, negative results have been reported on a wide variety of tasks (Wettstein and Spiegel, 1984; Bruno et al., 1986; Hollander et al., 1987). A single study of pilocarpine in two patients was likewise negative (Caine, 1980). One investigator reported subjective improvement in a single blind study of four AD patients using intraventricular bethanechol (Harbaugh et al., 1984) but others have failed to replicate these findings (Penn et al., 1988). The results of trials with cholinergic agonists are not encouraging. Numerous peripheral side-effects including salivation, depression and changes in blood pressure and pulse limit these studies. It is clear that other safe muscarinic agonists are needed. An ideal compound would act as a postsynaptic agonist and a presynaptic antagonist, thereby simultaneously stimulating receptors as well as enhancing the release of endogenous acetylcholine. Such a compound is currently unavailable for clinical testing.

Vascular dementia

The multiple etiologies for vascular dementia as well as the patchy nature of the neuropsychological deficit result in the availability of a heterogeneous group of patients for clinical drug trials. The studies described below include patient populations in whom one can reasonably infer that vascular disease was the cause of the cognitive impairment.

Early studies designed to treat vascular dementia are difficult to interpret, since most used mixed patient populations containing individuals with both AD and multi-infarct dementia. Additionally, none of the studies reviewed attempted to ascertain the specific type of vascular dementia. The studies reviewed in this section include only patient populations in whom one can reasonably infer that vascular dementia was the cause of cognitive impairment.

Vasodilators

Papaverine. Clinical trials of papaverine are all flawed either by failure to use adequate controls or, more importantly, by use of patient populations who would be diagnosed as AD or mixed dementia by today's standards (LaBrecque, 1966; McQuillan et al., 1974; Stern, 1970).

Isoxsuprine (Vasodilin). A single study examined the effects of isoxsuprine in a mixed group of patients with dementia secondary to both vascular disease and AD. Only historical evidence of symptoms and signs suggesting cerebrovascular disease was inventoried. A decrease in headaches and dizziness without any change in mental status was noted (Dhrymiotis and Whittier, 1962).

Cyclandelate (Cyclospasmol). Two double-blind crossover studies examined the efficacy of cyclandelate in reasonably pure populations of vascular dementia (Fine et al., 1970; Hall, 1976). One study demonstrated an improvement in orientation, communication and socialization on a behavioral rating scale (Fine et al., 1970) and the second study demonstrated a small improvement in memory, constructional apraxia and ability to abstract

(Hall, 1976). Both studies used small numbers of patients and functional improvement was not striking.

Pentoxifylline. In a single very small study, 10 poststroke patients were demonstrated to show gradual improvement on a modified WAIS and Wechsler Memory Scale when treated with pentoxifylline in an uncontrolled study (Janaki, 1980), while 97 stroke patients treated in a controlled study showed improvement in subjective, but not objective, testing (Araki and Otomo, 1976).

Vinpocetine (Cavinton). Vincamine and apovincamine are alkaloids derived from the plant *Vinca minor*. These compounds have been extensively used in Europe as metabolic enhancers and cerebral vasodilators. They have numerous complex metabolic actions and alter levels of both phosphodiesterase and biogenic amines in animals. Increases in cerebral blood flow have been demonstrated after parenteral but not oral administration (Capon et al., 1977; Heiss and Podreka, 1978). Preliminary data available from an open study of 207 patients with both cerebral infarction and transient ischemic attacks demonstrated significant improvement on a Clinical Global Improvement of Change (CGIC) scale when vinpocetine was compared to the vasodilator ifenprobil and to an ergot preparation (Otomo et al., 1985). However, objective measurements of cognition were not carried out. In a small study of 10 patients with multi-infarct dementia, treated in a double-blind crossover design, both an increase in regional cerebral blood flow and an improvement in performance for verbal and sequence memory were demonstrated with bromvincamine. However, there were no significant changes of overall clinical state (Hagstadius et al., 1984). Three identically designed double-blind placebo-controlled trials of vinpocetine in patients with multi-infarct dementia were recently carried out in a total of 166 patients (Manconi et al., 1986; Peruzza and DeJacobis, 1986; Balestreri et al., 1987). All three studies demonstrated an improvement on the CGIC as well as improvement on several SCAG subfactors, including cognitive dysfunction. Additionally, a combined minimental state/cognitive capacity screening exam score improved with drug treatment as did speech and language dysfunction. Functional improvement was not commented upon. Two large-scale multicenter trials of vinpocetine in multi-infarct dementia were recently completed in the United States; results have not yet been reported or published.

Ergoloid mesylates (Hydergine). The majority of studies of ergoloid mesylates utilized patients with both AD and vascular dementia without distinguishing the etiology. An absence of improvement was reported in five patients with vascular dementia based on objective mental status testing in a double-blind crossover study (Forster et al., 1955) and a second study reported subjective improvement on mental, emotional, social and physical parameters in 32 vascular dementia patients treated with 4.5 mg of ergoloid mesylates for 9 months (Soni and Soni, 1975). During the convalescent phase following stroke, ergoloid mesylates failed to improve 11 drug-treated patients compared to 10 placebo-treated patients on tests of orientation, concentration and object recognition (Bochner et al., 1973). In contrast, in a large multicenter trial, comparing 3 mg of ergoloid mesylates in 270 patients to 6 mg in 280 poststroke patients, a higher percentage of patients treated with the 6 mg dose had subjective improvement of psychiatric and neurological symptoms (Yoshikawa et al., 1983). However, the time between stroke and initiation of therapy, which may influence spontaneous recovery, was not commented upon or controlled, and objective memory testing was not performed. At present, evidence for the efficacy of ergoloid mesylates poststroke seems equivocal.

Hyperbaric oxygen. Two small studies including six and eight patients, respectively, with vascular dementia were treated with hyperbaric oxygen without demonstration of significant improvement on objective memory testing (Goldfarb et al., 1972; Thompson et al., 1976).

Treatment of Parkinson's disease

A relatively small number of studies have examined the effect of pharmacological manipulation on cognitive dysfunction and memory in PD. Most studies were carried out in the early to mid 1970s shortly after the introduction of L-dopa. In an early open study of L-dopa, subjective improvement in thinking was reported by 12 of 29 PD patients and memory improvement was reported by 7 of 29 (Marsh et al., 1971a). On a follow-up study, the same authors reported an improvement on paired-associative learning in 20 PD patients on 3 g of L-dopa (Marsh et al., 1971b). Three studies revealed an overall improvement on full-scale IQ with maximum improvement on a variety of subtests, including similarities (Beardsley and Puletti, 1971), perceptual organization (Loranger et al., 1972) and performance subtests (Donnelly and Chase, 1973). On average, patients improved by 6 to 9 points of full-scale IQ in these three studies. Finally, it was demonstrated that even after 5 years of L-dopa therapy patients continued to demonstrate intellectual improvement compared to a group of patients treated with nondopaminergic therapies for PD (Riklan et al., 1976). Unfortunately, most of these studies were open so that the degree of placebo effect could not be ascertained. Additionally, detailed measurements of memory were not always performed and some of the improvement seen is probably secondary to both improved alertness and memory performance. Nevertheless, it seems probable that L-dopa improves many aspects of cognition and perhaps improves memory as well.

Treatment of amnesic disorders

Head trauma

A large number of small uncontrolled studies have been carried out with vasopressin and related neuropeptides in patients with closed head trauma. Two patients were reported to demonstrate improvement in memory and mood following intranasal vasopressin treatment (Oliveros et al.,

1978). In a larger double-blind study, 5 of 7 patients demonstrated improvement in attention and short-term visual retention following administration of lysine vasopressin (Timsit-Berthier et al., 1980). However, four other studies utilizing a variety of doses of lysine vasopressin, DDAVP and DGAVP administered to approximately 23 patients failed to note improvement on a wide battery of neuropsychological tests including both immediate and delay verbal and visual memory tests (Jenkins et al., 1979, 1981; Koch-Henriksen and Nielsen, 1981; Fewtrell et al., 1982). The reasons for the discrepancies reported are not immediately apparent but may relate to the attention-improving effect of vasopressin noted by others. Additionally, the location and degree of brain damage varies enormously following closed head injury.

Only a small number of additional studies of drug treatment following closed head injury have been reported. Fifty-one patients completed a double-blind, parallel, placebo-controlled trial of piracetam following concussion. Although multiple symptoms were reported to improve, including vertigo, headache and tiredness, there was no improvement in memory, even of a subjective nature (Hakkarainen and Hakamies, 1978). Finally, in a single well-studied case of severe open head trauma, oral physostigmine plus lecithin produced an improvement on the Wechsler Memory Scale from 102 to 115, as well as improvement on the Buschke Selective Reminding Task (Goldberg et al., 1982). The clinical drug trials carried out in patients with closed head trauma are too preliminary and fragmented to draw useful conclusions. Studies of the most extensively tested compound, vasopressin and its analogues, have produced conflicting results. Vasopressin appears to improve attention but not memory. At present there are no convincing studies demonstrating unequivocal improvement in memory with drug therapy following head trauma.

Electroconvulsive therapy

Few drug trials have been carried out in patients

with memory impairment secondary to electroconvulsive therapy (ECT). A single study of pemoline and magnesium hydroxide (Cylert) was carried out in 10 patients receiving drug and in 10 controls. Drug was administered daily during the course of bilateral ECT. Although memory loss occurred in both subjects and controls, there was less memory loss measured on the Wechsler Memory Scale in the pemoline and magnesium hydroxide-treated group at the end of treatment and 3 months following treatment (Small et al., 1968). Follow-up studies have not been carried out. Piracetam administered for 3 days following ECT was examined in 18 patients using a double-blind, placebo-controlled, crossover design following administration of bilateral ECT. Treatment with 4.8 g per day resulted in no difference in recognition memory, paired-associate learning or a verbal memory task (Mindus et al., 1975). Three studies have been carried out examining the ability of 15 or 30 mg of $ACTH_{4-10}$ to improve retrieval or consolidation at various times following ECT treatment. All three studies are negative using both verbal and nonverbal tests of both consolidation and retrieval (Small et al., 1977; d'Elia and Frederiksen, 1980a,b). After the report that vasopression partially reversed the retrograde amnesia following ECT in two depressed patients (Weingartner et al., 1981a), a double-blind crossover study of nine patients receiving 25 μg of vasopressin was carried out using the Wechsler Memory Scale. Drug was administered 2 – 3 h after the fourth or fifth ECT with memory testing 1 h later. No significant improvement was reported (Lerer et al., 1983). It should be noted that immediate rather than delayed recall was tested so that final conclusions regarding vasopressin following ECT cannot be drawn from this study. A single study using naloxone 0.1 mg intravenously administered 3 days after the final ECT with testing at 30 min and 24 h after administration failed to demonstrate improvement on tests of visual retention, digit sequence learning, word association, digit span and digit symbol in nine subjects (Nasrallah et al., 1985). In a double-blind study of 17 ECT patients

physostigmine was reported to decrease impairment in orientation and improve story recall, memory and category retrieval (Levin et al., 1987). Overall, the studies reporting treatment of memory impairment following ECT are either negative or have not been replicated. Issues of doses and time interval after drug administration have not been adequately addressed. In the positive studies, the issue of reduction of efficacy of ECT caused by anticonvulsant effects of the drugs has not been addressed. Finally, in some studies, inappropriate psychometric testing was utilized.

Wernicke Korsakoff syndrome

Only a small number of clinical trials have been carried out in individuals with the Wernicke Korsakoff syndrome. One double-blind trial of four Wernicke Korsakoff patients treated with a variety of doses of pemoline and magnesium hydroxide failed to demonstrate improvement on objective tests of learning, memory or performance (Talland et al., 1967). Vasopressin therapy has been reported to improve memory functioning in individual case reports by some (LeBoeuf et al., 1978; Oliveros et al., 1978; Drago et al., 1981) but not by others (Blake et al., 1978). Lack of improvement was noted in two double-blind studies of 8 and 6 subjects, respectively, on a battery of psychological tests designed to measure short- and long-term memory (Laczi et al., 1983; Franceschi et al., 1982).

Several studies have now been carried out using the alpha agonist clonidine in patients with Wernicke Korsakoff syndrome. The logic behind this form of therapy has been the demonstration that lumbar CSF methoxyhydroxyphenylglycol (MHPG), the major metabolite of norepinephrine, is significantly diminished in patients with Wernicke Korsakoff syndrome (McEntee and Mair, 1978; McEntee et al., 1984), and that the decrease correlates with deficits on psychometric testing (Mair et al., 1985), a finding not documented by others (Martin et al., 1984). Two double-blind crossover studies utilizing 8 and 7 individuals with well-characterized Wernicke Korsakoff syndrome have demonstrated that 0.3 mg of clonidine daily is able to induce memory improvement on several tasks of anterograde amnesia, including memory passages and visual reproduction; paired-associate learning, however, did not improve. In contrast, administration of L-dopa, ephedrine or amphetamine did not improve memory (McEntee and Mair, 1980; Mair and McEntee, 1986). The degree of functional improvement was not commented upon. Additional replications by separate investigational groups will be necessary to confirm these results.

Methodological issues

There are a number of methodological issues that involve virtually all of the studies reviewed. These methodological issues present more of a problem for studies of drugs designed to improve memory than in many other areas of psychopharmacology. The reasons for this are twofold. First, memory is not a unitary entity. There are numerous sites in the brain anatomically involved in the processing of memory that may be differentially involved in different disease states or even within the same disease state. Thus, the limbic system, including the hippocampus and association cortex, are particularly affected in AD (Brun, 1985), whereas the medial thalamic nuclei and the mamillary bodies are preferentially affected in the Wernicke Korsakoff syndrome (Victor and Adams, 1985). Second, there are many different types of memory. Memory has been dichotomized into short- and long-term memory, working and reference memory, procedural and declarative memory (see Squire, 1986, and Shimamura, Ch. 2 of this volume, for review). As a consequence, there are numerous methodologies for the testing of memory, making comparisons between studies difficult. The second major problem is the absence of a gold standard against which one can measure the efficacy of a new agent. At the present time, there are no compounds available that unequivocally enhance cognition. Thus, the merits of any

therapeutic agent must be demonstrated on one or more cognitive tests but without reference to a standard compound.

There are numerous problems related to choice of patient samples. In most early studies of senile dementia there was no differentiation made between individuals with AD and those with vascular dementia. A specific therapeutic agent developed for one disorder is not likely to improve memory for another disorder. Individuals with memory loss secondary to different etiologies will thus dilute the probability of demonstrating a positive effect in a drug study. In addition, even in populations of relatively pure AD, misdiagnosis is not infrequent (Sulkava et al., 1983; Mölsä et al., 1985; Wade et al., 1987).

The use of pharmacological agents to improve cognition presents a set of complex issues. In virtually every study reviewed, issues of dose-response curves, the optimum drug administration-test interval or drug entry into the CNS were not considered. Future drug studies must consider these variables, especially the existence of inverted U-shaped dose-response curves for psychopharmacological agents and the issue of drug delivery to the CNS. Many drugs are poorly absorbed. Others have only brief periods of action and require frequent administration. Others do not cross the blood-brain barrier and therefore do not reach their intended site of action.

A number of strategies will be utilized in the future to deal with each of these problems. In some instances, it will be possible to change the chemical nature of a molecule to make it resistant to breakdown by stomach acids without destroying drug activity. Alternative routes of administration must be tried, including the use of buccal preparations, transdermal absorption and controlled-release formulations to develop sustained blood levels for compounds with short half-lives. Drugs that do not cross the blood-brain barrier may be altered to make them more lipophilic or less charged. Finally, some drugs may require direct administration into the CNS. This approach has already been tried in AD patients using bethanechol (Harbaugh et al., 1984) and will un-doubtedly be tried again using nerve growth factor (NGF).

Testing methodologies need to be carefully ex-amined. Some of the tests used in the papers reviewed were sensitive to change in attention, memory and mood. Objective rather than subjec-tive tests are necessary to adequately evaluate memory. Equivalent forms are needed because repeated testing is required. In addition to reliabili-ty, face validity of testing must be demonstrated. Two approaches are needed. To meet research needs, objective memory tests designed to measure specific aspects of memory, such as verbal memory as assessed by the Buschke Selective Reminding Task or Rey Auditory Verbal Learning Task, are helpful (see Delis, Ch. 1 of this volume, for review). Equally important, however, is the need to demonstrate the overall clinical efficacy of a drug on a task that correlates with clinical im-provement. Few scales have been designed to meet these requirements. For dementia drug trials, the cognitive subscale of the Alzheimer Disease Assessment Scale (Rosen et al., 1984) may prove to be such an instrument as it combines objective measures of verbal memory, language function, orientation, constructions and praxis into a single scale that has a high test-retest reliability and demonstrates sufficient sensitivity to parallel clinical change in a dementia population. Similar instruments need to be validated for the study of other forms of memory dysfunction.

Future prospects and conclusion

At present, there are no agents that unequivocally improve memory. Nevertheless, it appears almost certain that pharmacological agents will be developed which will enhance memory. The greatest strides are likely to be made in the area of AD because the public health importance of this disorder has resulted in a marked increase in fund-ed research during the past 10 years. In addition to simple pharmacological interventions, several uni-que treatment modalities are likely to be tried in

AD patients within the next few years.

NGF, a protein with a molecular weight of ap proximately 13,000, has been shown to be essentia for the development of cholinergic neurons. Injec tion of NGF into the brains of newborn rat elevates septal choline acetyltransferase (Gnahn e al., 1983), stimulates growth of cholinergic neu rons in tissue culture (Gähwiler et al., 1987), an can prevent the death of adult medial septa cholinergic neurons following fimbria fornix le sioning (Williams et al., 1986). Additionally, ad ministration of NGF to aged behaviorally impaire rats partially reverses cholinergic neuronal atroph and improves retention of spatial memory on th Morris Water Maze Task (Fischer et al., 1987) This agent will certainly be tried in AD patients most probably by direct administration into th cerebrospinal fluid in a manner similar to the infu sion of bethanechol or chemotherapeutic agents.

Treatment of cholinergic deficiency by the use o brain grafting is almost certain to be tried in AD Already nearly 85 patients with PD have receive autologous adrenal medullary gland grafts to th caudate nucleus after an initial report of improve ment in two subjects (Madroza et al., 1987) However, it is still too early to determine whethe this form of therapy will prove useful in PD. I rats with septohippocampal lesions, transplanta tion of fetal embryonic cholinergic tissue to th hippocampus has resulted in improvement on a maze forced alternation task (Dunnett et al. 1982), while retention of passive avoidance ha been improved with cortical grafts followin unilateral lesions of the nucleus basalis (Fine et al. 1985). This technology requires a great deal o refinement before it will be ready for huma clinical trials.

During the previous 10 years, tremendous stride have been made in the diagnosing and understand ing of memory disorders. Modern biochemical an psychological techniques have taught us a grea deal about the deficits present in a variety o memory disorders. As a consequence, a whole hos of new therapeutic approaches have been explored During the next decade, the advances made i ellular neurobiology will also be applied to the study of disease. Although adequate treatments or ures for these disorders do not yet exist, there are many hopeful avenues currently being explored. Research is certain to continue along two lines. The first line will be the more immediate one designed to develop a treatment for individuals already afflicted with various disorders. It is clear that in modern medicine one is often able to treat diseases without fully understanding their cause. Thus, one can treat PD with L-dopa and diabetes with insulin without knowing the cause of either disease. At the same time the search must continue for the determination and biological understanding of the cause of each disease because it is by understanding the biochemical steps involved in the disease that effective therapies for prevention can be developed.

Acknowledgements

Supported by research grants from the Veterans Administration Research Service and NIH grant Ago 5386. I thank Barbara Reader for secretarial support.

References

Abuzzahab FS, Merwin GE, Zimmermann RL, Sherman MC. A double-blind investigation of piracetam (Nootropil) versus placebo in the memory of geriatric inpatients. *Psychopharmacol. Bull.: 14,* 23 – 25, 1978.

Aderman M, Giordina WJ, Koreniowski S: Effect of cyclandelate on perception, memory and cognition in a group of geriatric subjects. *J. Am. Geriatr. Soc.: 20,* 268 – 270, 1972.

Adolfsson R, Gottfries CG, Roos BE, Winblad B: Changes in the brain catecholamines in patients with dementia of Alzheimer type. *Br. J. Psychiatry: 135,* 216 – 223, 1979.

Adolfsson R, Gottfries, CG, Oreland L, Roos BE, Winblad B: Reduced levels of catecholamines in the brain and increased activity of monoamine oxidase in platelets in Alzheimer's disease: Therapeutic implications. In Katzman R, Terry RD, Bick KL (Editors), *Aging, Vol. 7: Alzheimer's Disease: Senile Dementia and Related Disorders.* New York: Raven Press, pp. 441 – 451, 1985.

Affleck DC, Treptow KR, Herrick HD: The effects of isoxsuprine hydrochloride (Vasodilan) on chronic cerebral arteriosclerosis. *J. Nerv. Ment. Dis.: 132,* 335 – 336, 1961.

American Psychiatric Association: *Diagnostic and Statistical Manual of Mental Disorders,* Edition 3. Washington, DC, 1980.

Arai H, Kosaka K, Iizuka R: Changes of biogenic amines and their metabolites in postmortem brains from patients with Alzheimer-type dementia. *J. Neurochem.: 43,* 388 – 393, 1984.

Araki G, Otomo E: Clinical efficacy of pentoxifylline (BL 191) and pyrithioxide hydrochloride (PTX) in treatment of cerebrovascular disorders. *Clin. Eval.: 4,* 213 – 215, 1976.

Arrigo A, Braun P, Kauchtschischwili GM, Moglia A, Tartara A: Influence of treatment of symptomatology and correlated electroencephalographic (EEG) changes in the aged. *Curr. Ther. Res.: 15,* 417 – 426, 1973.

Ashford JW, Soldinger S, Schaeffer J, Cochran L, Jarvik L: Physostigmine and its effect on six patients with dementia. *Am. J. Psychiatry: 138,* 829 – 830, 1981.

Balestreri R, Fontana L, Astengo F: A double-blind placebo controlled evaluation of the safety and efficacy of vinpocetine in the treatment of patients with chronic vascular senile cerebral dysfunction. *J. Am. Geriatr. Soc.: 35,* 425 – 430, 1987.

Ball JA, Taylor AR: Effect of cyclandelate on mental function and cerebral blood flow in elderly patients. *Br. Med. J. 3,* 525 – 528, 1967.

Banen DM: An ergot preparation (Hydergine) for relief of symptoms of cerebrovascular insufficiency. *J. Am. Geriatr. Soc.: 20,* 22 – 24, 1972.

Barbeau A: The pathogenesis of Parkinson's disease: a new hypothesis. *Can. Med. Assoc. J.: 87,* 802 – 807, 1962.

Bazo AJ: An ergot alkaloid preparation (Hydergine) versus papaverine in treating common complaints of the aged: double-blind study. *J. Am. Geriatr. Soc.: 21,* 63 – 71, 1973.

Beal MF, Benoit R, Mazurek MF, Bird ED, Martin J: Somatostatin-28 (1-12)-like immunoreactivity is reduced in Alzheimer's disease cerebral cortex. *Brain Res.: 368,* 380 – 383, 1986.

Beardsley JV, Puletti F: Personality (MMPI) and cognitive (WAIS) changes after levodopa therapy. *Arch. Neurol.: 25,* 145 – 150, 1971.

Beller SA, Overall JE, Swann AC: Efficacy of oral physostigmine in primary degenerative dementia. *Psychopharmacology: 87,* 147 – 151, 1985.

Berger PA, Davis KL, Hollister LE: Cholinomimetics in mania, schizophrenia and memory disorders. In Barbeau A, Growdon JH, Wurtman RJ (Editors), *Nutrition and the Brain, Vol 5.* New York: Raven Press, pp. 425 – 441, 1979.

Bissette G, Reynolds GP, Kilts CD, Widerlov E, Nemeroff CB: Corticotropin-releasing factor-like immunoreactivity in senile dementia of the Alzheimer types. *J. Am. Med. Assoc.: 254,* 3067 – 3069, 1985.

Blake DR, Dodd MJ, Groimley Evans J: Vasopressin in amnesia. *Lancet: i,* 608, 1978.

Blass JP, Reding MJ, Drachman D, Mitchell A, Glosser G, Katzman R, Thal LJ, Grenell S, Spar JE, Larue A, Liston E: Cholinesterase inhibitors and opiate antagonists in patients with Alzheimer's disease. *N. Engl. J. Med.: 309,* 556, 1983.

Bochner F, Eadie MJ, Tyrer JH: Use of an ergot preparation (Hydergine) in the convalescent phase of stroke. *J. Am. Geriatr. Soc.: 221,* 10 – 17, 1973.

Bohus B: Effects of desglycinamine-lysine vasopressin (DG-

LVP) on sexually motivated T-maze behavior of the male rat. *Horm. Behav.: 8,* 52–61, 1977.

Bohus B, de Wied D: Actions of ACTH- and MSH-like peptides on learning, performance, and retention. In Martinez J Jr, Jensen RA, Messing RB, Rigter H, McGaugh JJ (Editors), *Endogenous Peptides and Learning and Memory Process.* New York: Academic Press, pp. 39–74, 1981.

Bondareff W, Mountjoy CQ, Roth M: Loss of neurons of origin of the adrenergic projection to cerebral cortex (nucleus locus ceruleus) in senile dementia. *Neurology: 32,* 164–168, 1982.

Bondareff W, Mountjoy CQ, Roth M, Rossor MN, Iversen LL, Reynolds GP: Age and histopathologic heterogeneity in Alzheimer's disease. *Arch. Gen. Psychiatry: 44,* 412–417, 1987.

Bouvier JB, Passeron O, Chupin MP: Psychometric study of Praxilene. *J. Int. Med. Res.: 2,* 59–65, 1974.

Boyd WD, Graham-White J, Blackwood G, Glen I, McQueen J: Clinical effects of choline in Alzheimer senile dementia. *Lancet: ii,* 711, 1977.

Branconnier RJ, Cole JO, Gardos G: $ACTH_{4-10}$ in the amelioration of neuropsychological symptomatology associated with senile organic brain syndrome. *Psychopharmacology: 61,* 161–165, 1979.

Branconnier RJ, Cole JO, Dessain EC, Spera KF, Ghazvinian S, DeVitt D: The therapeutic efficacy of pramiracetam in Alzheimer's disease: preliminary observations. *Psychopharmacol. Bull.: 19,* 726–730, 1983.

Brinkman SD, Smith RC, Meyer JS, Vroulis G, Shaw T, Gordon JR, Allen RH: Lecithin and memory training in suspected Alzheimer's disease. *J. Gerontol.: 37,* 4–9, 1982.

Brun A: The structural development of Alzheimer's disease. *Dan. Med. Bull.: 32 (Suppl. 1):* 25–27, 1985.

Bruno G, Mohr E, Gillespie M, Fedio P, Chase TN: Muscarinic agonist therapy of Alzheimer's disease. *Arch. Neurol.: 43,* 659–661, 1986.

Caine ED: Cholinomimetic treatment fails to improve memory disorders. *N. Engl. J. Med.: 303,* 585–586, 1980.

Caltagirone C, Gainotti G, Masullo C: Oral administration of chronic physostigmine does not improve cognitive or mnesic performances in Alzheimer's presenile dementia. *Int. J. Neurosci.: 16,* 247–249, 1982.

Caltagirone C, Albanese A, Gainotti G, Masullo C: Acute administration of individual optimal dose of physostigmine fails to improve mnesic performances in Alzheimer's presenile dementia. *Int. J. Neurosci.: 18,* 143–148, 1983.

Capon A, de Rood M, Verbist A, Fruhling J: Action of vasodilators on regional cerebral blood flow in subacute or chronic ischemia. *Stroke: 8,* 25–29, 1977.

Christie JE, Blackburn IM, Glen AIM, Zeisel S, Sherry A, Yates CM: Effects of choline and lecithin on CSF choline levels and on cognitive function in patients with presenile dementia of the Alzheimer types. In Barbeau A, Growden JH, Wurtman RJ (Editors). *Nutrition and the Brain, Vol. 5.* New York: Raven Press, pp. 377–387, 1979.

Christie JE, Shering A, Ferguson J, Glen AIM: Physostigmine and arecoline: effects of intravenous infusions in Alzheimer presenile dementia. *Br. J. Psychiatry: 138,* 46–50, 1981.

Cohen EL, Wurtman RJ: Brain acetylcholine: increase after systemic choline administration. *Life Sci.: 16,* 1095–1102, 1975.

Cohen EL, Wurtman RJ: Brain acetylcholine: control by dietary choline. *Science: 191,* 561–562, 1976.

Cutler NR, Haxby J, Kay AD, Narang PK, Lesko LJ, Costa JL, Ninos M, Linnoila M, Potter WZ, Renfrew JW, Moore AM: Evaluation of zimelidine in Alzheimer's disease. *Arch. Neurol.: 42,* 744–746, 1985a.

Cutler NR, Haxby JU, Narung PK, May C, Burg C: Evaluation of an analogue of somatostatin (L363,586) in Alzheimer disease. *N. Engl. J. Med.: 312,* 725, 1985b.

Davis P, Malony AJF: Selective loss of central cholinergic neurons in Alzheimer's disease. *Lancet: ii,* 1403, 1976.

Davies P, Verth AH: Regional distribution of muscarinic acetylcholine receptor in normal and Alzheimer's-type dementia brains. *Brain Res.: 138,* 385–392, 1978.

Davies P, Katzman R, Terry RD: Reduced somatostatin-like immunoreactivity in cerebral cortex from cases of Alzheimer disease and Alzheimer senile dementia. *Nature: 288,* 279–280, 1980.

Davis KL, Mohs R: Enhancement of memory processes in Alzheimer's disease with multiple-dose intravenous physostigmine. *Am. J. Psychiatry: 139,* 1421–1424, 1982.

Davis KL, Hollander E, Davidson M, Davis BM, Mohs RC, Horvath TB: Induction of depression with oxotremorine in patients with Alzheimer's disease. *Am. J. Psychiatry: 144,* 468–471, 1987.

d'Elia G, Frederiksen S-O: $ACTH_{4-10}$ and memory in ECT treated and untreated patients. *Acta Psychiatr. Scand.: 62,* 418–428, 1980a.

d'Elia G, Frederiksen S-O: $ACTH_{4-10}$ and memory in ECT treated patients and untreated controls. *Acta Psychiatr. Scand.: 62,* 429–435, 1980b.

Delwaide PJ, DeVoitille, Ylieff M: Acute effect of drugs upon memory of patients with senile dementia. *Acta Psychiatr. Belg.: 80,* 748–754, 1980.

Desouza EG, Whitehouse PJ, Kuhar MJ, Price DL, Vale WW: Reciprocal changes in corticotropin-releasing factor (CRF)-like immunoreactivity and CRF receptors in cerebral cortex of Alzheimer's disease. *Nature: 319,* 593–595, 1986.

de Wied D: Effects of peptide hormones on behavior. In Ganong WF, Martini L (Editors), *Frontiers in Neuroendocrinology.* New York: Oxford Press, pp. 97–140, 1969.

de Wied D, Bohus B, van Wimersma Greidanus TJB: Memory deficits in rats with hereditary diabetes insipidus. *Brain Res.: 85,* 152–156, 1975.

de Wied D: Peptides and behavior. *Life Sci.: 20,* 195–204, 1977.

de Wied D, Gispen WH: Behavioral effects of peptides. In Gaines H (Editor), *Peptides in Neurobiology.* New York: Plenum Press, pp. 397–448, 1977.

Dhrymiotis AD, Whittier JR: Effect of a vasodilator, isoxsuprine, on cerebral ischemic episodes. *Curr. Ther. Res.: 4,* 124–129, 1962.

Ditch M, Kelly FJ, Resnick O: An ergot preparation (Hydergine) in the treatment of cerebrovascular disorders in the geriatric patient: double-blind study. *J. Am. Ger. Soc.: 19,* 208–217, 1971.

Donnelly EF, Chase TN: Intellectual and memory function in Parkinsonian and non-parkinsonian patients treated with L-dopa. *Dis. Nerv. Syst.: 34,* 119–123, 1973.

rago F, Rapisarda V, Calandra A, Filetti S, Scapagnini U: A clinical evaluation of vasopressin effects on memory disorders. *Acta Ther.: 7*, 345 – 352, 1981.

unlap E: Chronic cerebrovascular insufficiency treated with papaverine. *J. Am. Ger. Soc.: 16*, 343 – 349, 1968.

unnett SB, Low WC, Iversen SP, Stenevi U, Björklund A: Septal transplants restore maze learning in rats with fornix-fimbria lesions. *Brain Res.: 251*, 335 – 348, 1982.

urso R, Fedio P, Brouwers P, Cox C, Martin AJ, Ruggieri SA, Tamminga CA, Chase TN: Lysine vasopressin in Alzheimer disease. *Neurology: 32*, 674 – 677, 1982.

ysken MW, Foval P, Harris CM, Davis JM. Noronha A: Lecthin administration in Alzheimer dementia. *Neurology: 32*, 1203 – 1204, 1982.

inspruch BC: Helping to make the final years meaningful for the elderly residents of nursing homes. *Dis. Nerv. Syst.: 37*, 439 – 442, 1976.

tienne P, Gauthier S, Johnson G, Collier B, Mendis T, Dastoor D, Cole M, Muller HF: Clinical effects of choline in Alzheimer's disease. *Lancet: i*, 508 – 509, 1978.

tienne P, Dastoor D, Gauthier S, Ludwick R, Collier B: Alzheimer disease: Lack of effect of lecithin treatment for 3 months. *Neurology: 31*, 1552 – 1554, 1981.

acchinetti F, Nappin G, Petraglia F, Martignoni EJ, Sinforiani E, Genozzani AR: Central ACTH deficit in degenerative and vascular dementia. *Life Sci.: 35*, 1691 – 1697, 1984.

erris SH, Sathananthan G, Gershon S, Clark C, Moshinsky J: Cognitive effects of ACTH 4 – 10 in the elderly. *Neuropeptides: 5*, 73 – 78, 1976.

ewtrell WD, House AO, Jamie PF, Oates MR, Cooper JE: Effects of vasopressin on memory and new learning in a brain-injured population. *Psychol. Med.: 12*, 423 – 425, 1982.

ine EW, Lewis D, Villa-Landa I, Blakemore CB: The effect of cyclandelate on mental function in patients with arteriosclerotic brain disease. *Br. J. Psychiatry: 17*, 157 – 161, 1970.

ine A, Dunnett SB, Björklund A, Iversen SD: Cholinergic ventral forebrain grafts into neocortex improve passive avoidance memory in a rat model of Alzheimer's disease. *Proc. Nat. Acad. Sci. USA: 82*, 5227 – 5230, 1985.

ischer W, Wixtorin K, Björklund A, Williams LR, Varon S, Gage FH: Amelioration of cholinergic neuron atrophy and spatial memory impairment in aged rats by nerve growth factor. *Nature: 329*, 65 – 68, 1987.

orster W, Schults S, Henderson AL: Combined hydrogenated alkaloids of ergot in senile and arteriosclerotic psychoses. *Geriatrics: 10*, 26 – 30, 1955.

ovall P, Dysken MW, Lazarus LW, Davis JM, Kahn RL, Jope R, Finkel S, Rattan P: Choline bitartrate treatment of Alzheimer-type dementias. *Commun. Psychopharmacol.: 4*, 141 – 145, 1980.

ranceschi M, Tancredi O, Savio G, Smirne S: Vasopressin and physostigmine in the treatment of amnesia. *Eur. Neurol.: 21*, 388 – 391, 1982.

rancis PT, Palmer AM, Sims NR, Bowen DM, Davison AN, Esiri MM, Neary D, Snowden JS, Wilcock GK: Neurochemical studies of early-onset Alzheimer's disease. *N. Engl. J. Med.: 313*, 7 – 11, 1985.

rancis PT, Bowen DM, Lowe SL, Neary D, Mann DMA, Snowden JS: Somatostatin content and release measured in cerebral biopsies from demented patients. *J. Neurol. Sci.: 78*, 1 – 16, 1987.

Freeman FR: Evaluation of patients with progressive intellectual decline. *Arch. Neurol.: 33*, 658 – 659, 1976.

Gähwiler BH, Enz A, Hefti F: Nerve growth factor promotes development of the rat septo-hippocampal cholinergic projection in vitro. *Neurosci. Lett.: 75*, 6 – 10, 1987.

Gaitz CM, Varner RV, Overall JE: Pharmacotherapy for organic brain syndrome in late life. *Arch. Gen. Psychiatry: 34*, 839 – 845, 1977.

Gamzu E: Personal communication, 1987.

Goldberg E, Gerstman LJ, Mattis S, Hughes JEO, Sirio CA, Bilder RM Jr: Selective effects of cholinergic treatment on verbal memory in posttraumatic amnesia. *J. Clin. Neuropsychol.: 4*, 219 – 234, 1982.

Goldfarb AI, Hochstadt NJ, Jacobson JH, Weinstein EA: Hyperbaric oxygen treatment of organic mental syndrome in aged persons. *J. Gerontol.: 27*, 212 – 217, 1972.

Gnahn H, Hefti F, Heumann R, Schwab ME, Thoenes H: NGF-mediated increase of choline acetyltransferase (CHAT) in the neonatal rat forebrain: evidence for a physiological role of NGF in the brain? *Dev. Brain Res.: 9*, 45 – 52, 1983.

Growdon JH, Corkin S, Huff FJ, Rosen TJ: Piracetam combined with lecithin in the treatment of Alzheimer's disease. *Neurobiol. Aging: 7*, 269 – 276, 1986.

Gustafson L, Risberg J, Johanson M, Fransson M, Maximilian VA: Effects of piracetam on regional cerebral blood flow and mental functions in patients with organic dementia. *Psychopharmacology: 56*, 115 – 117, 1978.

Hachinski VC, Iliff LD, Zilhka E, DeBoulay GH, McAllister VL, Marshall J, Russell RWR, Symon L: Cerebral blood flow in dementia. *Arch. Neurol.: 32*, 632 – 637, 1975.

Hagstadius S, Gustafson L, Risberg J: The effects of bromvincamine and vincamine on regional cerebral blood flow and mental functions in patients with multi-infarct dementia. *Psychopharmacology: 83*, 321 – 326, 1984.

Hakkarainen H, Hakamies L: Piracetam in the treatment of post-concussional syndrome. A double-blind study. *Eur. Neurol.: 17*, 50 – 55, 1978.

Hall P: Cyclandelate in the treatment of cerebral arteriosclerosis. *J. Am. Geriatr. Soc.: 24*, 41 – 45, 1976.

Harbaugh RE, Roberts DW, Coombs DW, Saunders RL, Reeder TM: Preliminary report: intracranial cholinergic drug infusion in patients with Alzheimer's disease. *Neurosurgery: 15*, 514 – 518, 1984.

Heiss W-D, Podreka I: Assessment of pharmacological agents on cerebral blood flow. *Eur. Neurol.: 17 (Suppl. 1):* 135 – 143, 1978.

Hemmings WA: Vasopressin in amnesia. *The Lancet I:* 608 1978.

Hjorther A, Browne E, Jakobsen K, Viskum P, Gyntelberg F: Organic brain syndrome treated with oxiracetam. *Acta Neurol. Scand.: 75*, 271 – 276, 1987.

Hollander E, Davidson M, Mohs RC, Horvath TB, Davis BM, Zemishlany Z, Davis KL: RS 86 in the treatment of Alzheimer's disease: cognitive and biological effects. *Biol. Psychiatry: 22*, 1067 – 1078, 1987.

Hollister LE: Combined hydrogenated alkaloids of ergot in mental and nervous disorders associated with old age. *Dis. Nerv. Syst.: 16*, 259 – 262, 1955.

Hollister LE, Yesavage J: Ergoloid mesylates for senile dementias: unanswered questions. *Ann. Intern. Med.: 100,* 894 – 898, 1984.

Hostetter G, Jubb SL, Kolowski GP: Vasopressin affects the behavior of rats in a positively rewarded discrimination task. *Life Sci.: 21,* 1323 – 1328, 1977.

Hyman BT, Van Hoesen GW, Damasio AR, Barnes CL: Alzheimer's disease: cell specific pathology isolates the hippocampal formation. *Science: 225,* 1168 – 1170, 1984.

Hyman BT, Eslinger PJ, Damasio A: Effect of naltrexone on senile dementia of the Alzheimer type. *J. Neurol. Neurosurg. Psychiatry: 48,* 1169 – 1171, 1985.

Jacobs EA, Winter PM, Alvis HJ, Small SM: Hyperoxygenation effect on cognitive functioning in the aged. *N. Engl. J. Med.: 281,* 753 – 757 1969.

Janaki S: Pentoxifylline in strokes: a clinical study. *J. Int. Med. Res.: 8,* 56 – 62, 1980.

Jenkins JS, Mather HM, Coughlan AK, Jenkins DG: Desmopressin in post-traumatic amnesia. *Lancet: ii,* 1245 – 1246, 1979.

Jenkins JS, Mather HM, Coughlan AK, Jenkins DG: Desmopressin and desglycinamide vasopressin in post-traumatic amnesia. *Lancet: i,* 39, 1981.

Jennekens-Schinkel A, Wintzen AR, Lanser JBK: A clinical trial with desglycinamide arginine vasopressin for the treatment of memory disorders in man. *Prog. Neuro-Psychopharmacol. Biol. Psychiatry: 9,* 273 – 284, 1985.

Jennings WG: An ergot alkaloid preparation (Hydergine) versus placebo for treatment of symptoms of cerebrovascular insufficiency: double-blind study. *J. Am. Geriatr. Soc.: 20,* 407 – 412, 1972.

Jotkowitz S: Lack of the clinical efficacy of chronic oral physostigmine in Alzheimer's disease. *Ann. Neurol.: 14,* 690 – 691, 1983.

Judy TG, Urquhart A: Naftidrofuryl- a double-blind crossover study in the elderly. *Curr. Med. Res. Opin.: 1,* 166 – 172, 1972.

Kapp BS, Gallagher M: Opiates and memory. *Trends Neurosci.: 2,* 177 – 180, 1979.

Katzman R: Alzheimer's disease. *N. Engl. J. Med.: 314,* 964 – 973, 1986.

Katzman R, Brown T, Fuld P, Thal L, Davies P, Terry R: Significance of neurotransmitter abnormalities in Alzheimer's disease. In Martin JB, Barchas JD (Editors), *Neuropeptides in Neurologic and Psychiatric disease.* New York: Raven Press, pp. 279 – 286, 1986.

Kaye WH, Sitaram N, Weingartner H, Ebert MH, Smallberg S, Gillin JC: Modest facilitation of memory in dementia with combined lecithin and anticholinesterase treatment. *Biol. Psychiatry: 17,* 275 – 280, 1982.

Ketty SS: Human cerebral blood flow and oxygen consumption as related to aging. *J. Chron. Dis.: 3,* 478 – 486, 1956.

Knopman D, Hartman M: Cognitive effects of high-dose naltrexone in patients with probable Alzheimer's disease. *J. Neurol. Neurosurg. Psychiatry: 49,* 1321 – 1326, 1986.

Koch-Henriksen N, Nielson H: Vasopressin in post-traumatic amnesia. *Lancet: i,* 38 – 39, 1981.

Koob GF, Bloom FE: Behavioral effects of opiod peptides. *Br. Med. Bull.: 39,* 89 – 94, 1983.

Kragh-Sorensen P, Olsen RG, Lund S, Van Riezen H, Stef-fensen K: Neuropeptides: ACTH-peptides in dementia. *Prog. Neuro-Psychopharmacol. Biol. Psychiatry: 10,* 479 – 492, 1986.

LaBrecque DC: Papaverine hydrochloride as therapy for mentally confused geriatric patients. *Curr. Ther. Res.: 8,* 106 – 109, 1966.

Laczi F, Van Ree JM, Balogh L, Szasz A, Jardanhanzy T, Wagner A, Gaspar L, Valkusz Z, Dobranovics I, Szilard J, Laszlo FA, De Wied D: Lack of effect of desglycinamide-arginine-vasopressin (DGAVP) on memory in patients with Korsakoff's syndrome. *Acta Endocrinol.: 104,* 177 – 182, 1983.

Larson EB, Reifler BV, Sumi SM, Canfield CG, Chinn NM: Diagnostic tests in the evaluation of dementia. A prospective study of 200 elderly outpatients. *Arch. Int. Med.: 146,* 1917 – 1922, 1986.

LeBoeuf A, Lodge J, Eames PG: Vasopressin and memory in Korsakoff syndrome. *Lancet: ii,* 1370, 1978.

Lerer B, Zabow T, Egnal N, Belmaker RH: Effect of vasopressin on memory following electroconvulsive therapy. *Biol. Psychiatry: 18,* 821 – 824, 1983.

Levin Y, Elizur A, Korczyn AD: Physostigmine improves ECT-induced memory disturbances. *Neurology: 37,* 871 – 875, 1987.

Little A, Levy R, Chuaqui-Kidd P, Hand D: A double-blind, placebo-controlled trial of high-dose lecithin in Alzheimer's disease. *J. Neurol. Neurosurg. Psychiatry: 48,* 736 – 742, 1985.

Loranger AW, Goodell H, Lee JE, McDowell F: Levodopa treatment of Parkinson's syndrome. *Arch. Gen. Psychiatry: 26,* 163 – 168, 1972.

Lu L, Stotsky BA, Cole JO: A controlled study of drugs in long-term geriatric psychiatric patients. *Arch. Gen. Psychiatry: 25,* 284 – 288, 1971.

Madroza I, Drucker-Colin R, Giaz V, Martainez-Mata J, Torres C, Becerril JJ: Open microsurgical autograft of adrenal-medulla to the right caudate nucleus in two patients with intractable Parkinson's disease. *N. Engl. J. Med.: 316,* 831 – 834, 1987.

Mair RG, McEntee W: Cognitive enhancement in Korsakoff's psychosis by clonidine: a comparison with L-dopa and ephedrine. *Psychopharmacology: 88,* 374 – 380, 1986.

Mair RG, McEntee WJ, Zatorre RJ: Monoamine activity correlates with psychometric deficits in Korsakoff's disease. *Behav. Brain Res.: 15,* 247 – 254, 1985.

Manconi E, Binaghi B, Pitzus F: A double-blind clinical trial of vinpocetine in the treatment of cerebral insufficiency of vascular and degenerative origin. *Curr. Ther. Res.: 40,* 702 – 709, 1986.

Marsden CD, Harrison MJG: Outcome of investigation of patients with presenile dementia. *Br. Med. J.: 2,* 249 – 252 1972.

Marsh GG, Markham CM, Treciokas L: Parkinsonian patients' self-reports of levodopa effects on cognitive and memory changes. *Psychosomatics: 12,* 114 – 116, 1971a.

Marsh CG, Markham CM, Ansel R: Levodopa's awakening effect on patients with Parkinsonism. *J. Neurol. Neurosurg Psychiatry: 34,* 209 – 218, 1971b.

Martin JC, Ballinger BR, Cockram LL, McPherson FM Pigache RM, Tregaskis D: Effect of a synthetic peptide

ORG 2766, on inpatients with severe senile dementia. *Acta Psychiatr. Belg.: 67,* 205 – 207, 1983.

Martin PR, Weingartner H, Gordon EK, Burns S, Linnoila M, Kopin IJ, Ebert MH: Central nervous system catecholamine metabolism in Korsakoff's psychosis. *Ann. Neurol.: 15,* 184 – 187, 1984.

Marttila RJ, Rinne UK: Dementia in Parkinson's disease. *Acta Neurol. Scand.: 54,* 431 – 441, 1976.

Mash DC, Flynn DD, Potter LT: Loss of M2 muscarine receptors in the cerebral cortex in Alzheimer's disease and experimental cholinergic denervation. *Science: 228,* 1115 – 1117, 1985.

May C, Rapoport SI, Tomai TP, Chrousos GP, Gold PW: Cerebrospinal fluid concentrations of corticotropin-releasing hormone (CRH) and corticotropin (ACTH) are reduced in patients with Alzheimer's disease. *Neurology: 37,* 535 – 538, 1987.

Mayeux R, Stern Y: Intellectual dysfunction and dementia in Parkinson's disease. In Mayeux R, Rosen WG (Editors), *The Dementias.* New York: Raven Press, pp. 211 – 227, 1983.

Mazurek MF, Beal F, Bird ED, Martin JB: Vasopressin in Alzheimer's disease: a study of postmortem brain concentrations. *Ann. Neurol.: 20,* 665 – 670, 1986.

McDonald RJ: Hydergine: a review of 26 clinical studies. *Pharmakopsychiatr. Neuropsychopharmakol.: 12,* 407 – 422, 1979.

McEntee WJ, Mair RG: Memory impairment in Korsakoff's psychosis: a correlation with brain noradrenergic activity. *Neurology: 202,* 905 – 907, 1978.

McEntee WJ, Mair RG. Memory enhancement in Korsakoff's psychosis by clonidine: further evidence for a noradrenergic deficit. *Ann. Neurol.: 7,* 466 – 470, 1980.

McEntee WF, Mair RG, Langlais PJ: Neurochemical pathology in Korsakoff's psychosis: implications for other cognitive disorders. *Neurology: 34,* 648 – 652, 1984.

McHenry LC Jr, Jaffe ME, Kawamura J, Goldberg HI: Effect of papaverine on regional blood flow in focal vascular disease of the brain. *N. Engl. J. Med.: 252,* 1167 – 1170, 1970.

McQuillan LM, Lopec CA, Vibal JR: Evaluation of EEG and clinical changes associated with Pavabid therapy in chronic brain syndrome. *Curr. Ther. Res.: 16,* 49 – 58, 1974.

Meyer JS, Gotoh F, Gilroy F, Nara N: Improvement in brain oxygenation and clinical improvement in patients with strokes treated with papaverine hydrochloride. *J. Am. Med. Assoc.: 194,* 957 – 961, 1965.

Mindus P, Cronholm B, Levander SE: Does piracetam counteract the ECT-induced memory dysfunctions in depressed patients? *Acta Psychiatr. Scand.: 51,* 319 – 326, 1975.

Mohs RC, Davis BM, Johns CA, Mathe AA, Greenwald BS, Horvath TB, Davis KL: Oral physostigmine treatment of patients with Alzheimer's disease. *Am. J. Psychiatry: 142,* 28 – 33, 1985.

Mölsä PK, Paljärvi L, Rinne Jo, Rinne UK, Säkö E: Validity of clinical diagnosis in dementia: a prospective clinicopathological study. *J. Neurol. Neurosurg. Psychiatry: 48,* 1085 – 1090, 1985.

Muramoto O, Sugishita M, Ando K: Cholinergic system and constructional praxis: a further study of physostigmine in

Alzheimer's disease. *J. Neurol. Neurosurg. Psychiatry: 47,* 485 – 491, 1984.

Nasrallah HA, Varney N, Coffman JA, Bayless J, Chapman S: Effects of naloxone on cognitive deficits. *Psychopharmacol. Bull.: 21,* 89 – 90, 1985.

Nelson JJ: Relieving select symptoms of the elderly. *Geriatrics: 30,* 133 – 142, 1975.

Oliveros JC, Jandali MK, Timsit-Berthier M, Remy R, Benghezal A, Audibert A, Moeglen JM: Vasopressin in amnesia. *Lancet: i:* 42, 1978.

Otomo E, Atarashi J, Araki G, Ito E, Omae T, Kuzuya F, Nukada T, Ebi O: Comparison of vinpocetine with ifenprodil tartrate and dihydroergotoxine mesylate treatment and results of long-term treatment with vinpocetine. *Curr. Ther. Res.: 37,* 811 – 821, 1985.

Panella JJ, Blass JP: Lack of clinical benefit from naloxone in a dementia day hospital. *Ann. Neurol.: 15,* 308, 1984.

Peabody CA, Thiemann S, Pigache R, Miller TP, Berger PA, Yesavage J, Tinklenberg JR: Desglycinamide-9-arginine-8-vasopressin (DGAVP, Organon 5667) in patients with dementia. *Neurobiol. aging: 6,* 95 – 100, 1985.

Peabody CA, Davies H, Berger PA, Tinklenberg JR: Desamino-D-arginine-vasopressin (DDAVP) in Alzheimer's disease. *Neurobiol. Aging: 7,* 301 – 303, 1986.

Penn RD, Martin EM, Wilson RS, Fox JH, Savoy SM: Intraventricular bethanechol infusion for Alzheimer's disease: results of double-blind and escalating-dose trials. *Neurology: 38,* 219 – 222, 1988.

Perry EK, Perry RH, Blessed G, Tomlinson BE: Necropsy evidence of central cholinergic deficits in senile dementia. *Lancet: i,* 189, 1977.

Perry EK, Tomlinson BE, Blessed G, Bergmann K, Gibson PH, Perry RH: Correlation of cholinergic abnormalities with senile plaques and mental test scores in senile dementia. *Br. Med. J.: 2,* 1457 – 1459, 1978.

Perry EK, Tomlinson BE, Blessed G, Perry RH, Cross AJ, Crow TJ: Neuropathological and biochemical observations on the noradrenergic system in Alzheimer's disease. *J. Neurol. Sci.: 51,* 279 – 287, 1981.

Perry RH, Curtis M, Candy JM, Tomlinson BE, Candy JM, Blessed G, Foster JF, Bloxham CA, Perry ER: Cortical cholinergic deficit in mentally impaired Parkinsonian patients *Lancet: ii,* 788 – 789, 1983.

Peruzza M, DeJacobis M: A double-blind placebo controlled evaluation of the efficacy and safety of vinpocetine in the treatment of patients with chronic vascular or degenerative senile cerebral dysfunction. *Adv. Ther.: 3,* 201 – 209, 1986.

Peters BH, Levin HS: Memory enhancement after physostigmine treatment in the amnesic syndrome. *Arch. Neurol.: 34,* 215 – 219, 1977.

Peters B, Levin HS: Effects of physostigmine and lecithin on memory in Alzheimer's disease. *Ann. Neurol.: 6,* 219 – 221, 1979.

Peters BH, Levin HS: Chronic oral physostigmine and lecithin administration in memory disorders of aging. In Corkin S, Davis KL, Growdon J, Usdin E, Wurtman RJ (Editors), *Aging, Vol. 19.* New York: Raven Press, pp. 421 – 426, 1982.

Price KS, Farley IJ, Hornykiewicz O: Neurochemistry of Parkinson's disease: relationship between striatal and limbic dopamine. In Roberts PJ, Woodruff GN (Editors), *Ad-*

vances in Biochemical Psychopharmacology, Vol. 19. New York: Raven Press, pp. 293–300, 1978.

Rao DB, Norris JR: A double-blind investigation of Hydergine in the treatment of cerebrovascular insufficiency in the elderly. *Hopkins Med. J.: 130,* 317–324, 1972.

Ratner J, Rosenberg G, Kral VA, Engelsmann F: Anticoagulant therapy for senile dementia. *J. Am. Geriatr. Soc.: 20,* 556–559, 1972.

Reisberg B, Ferris SH, Anand R, Mir P, Geibel V, De Leon MJ, Roberts E: Effects on naloxone in senile dementia: a double-blind trial. *N. Engl. J. Med.: 308,* 721–722, 1983.

Renvoize EB, Jerram T: Choline in Alzheimer's disease. *N. Engl. J. Med.: 301,* 330, 1979.

Riklan M, Whelihan W, Cullinan T: Levodopa and psychometric test performance in parkinsonism--5 years later. *Neurology: 26,* 173–179, 1976.

Rinne JO, Laakso K, Lönnberg, P, Mölsä P, Paljärvi L, Rinne JK, Säkö E, Rinne YK: Brain muscarinic receptors in senile dementia. *Brain Res.: 336,* 19–25, 1985.

Ritter RM, Nail HR, Tatum P, Blazer M: The effect of papaverine on patients with cerebral atherosclerosis. *Clin. Med.: 78,* 18–22, 1971.

Roberts E: A speculative consideration on the neurobiology and treatment of senile dementia. In Crook T, Gershen S (Editors), *Strategies for the Development of an Effective Treatment for Senile Dementia.* New Canaan (CT): Mark Powley Associates, Inc., pp. 247–320, 1981.

Rosen HJ: Mental decline in the elderly: pharmacotherapy (ergot alkaloids versus papaverine). *J. Am. Geriatr. Soc.: 32,* 169–174, 1975.

Rosen WG, Mohs RC, Davis KL: A new rating scale for Alzheimer's disease. *Am. J. Psychiatry: 141,* 1356–1364, 1984.

Rossor MN, Emson PC, Mountjoy CQ, Roth M, Iversen LL: Reduced amounts of immunoreactive somatostatin in the temporal cortex in senile dementia of Alzheimer type. *Neurosci. Lett.: 20,* 373–377, 1980.

Roubicek J, Geiger CH, Abt K: An ergot alkaloid preparation (Hydergine) in geriatric therapy. *J. Am. Geriatr. Soc.: 20,* 222–229, 1972.

Saletu B, Linzmayer L, Grünberger J, Pietschmann H. Double-blind, placebo-controlled, clinical, psychometric and neurophysiological investigations with oxiracetam in the organic brain syndrome of late life. *Neuropsychobiology: 13,* 44–52, 1985.

Scatton B, Javoy-Agid F, Rouquier L, Dubois B, Agid Y: Reduction of cortical dopamine, noradrenaline, serotonin and their metabolites in Parkinson's disease. *Brain Res.: 275,* 321–328, 1983.

Schwartz AS, Kohlstaedt EV: Physostigmine effects in Alzheimer's disease: relationship to dementia severity. *Life Sci.: 38,* 1021–1028, 1986.

Serby M, Resnick R, Jordan B, Adler J, Corwin J, Rotrosen JP: Naltrexone and Alzheimer's disease. *Progr. Neuro-Psychopharmacol. Biol. Psychiatry: 10,* 587–590, 1986.

Signoret JL, Whiteley A, Lhermitte F: Influence of choline on amnesia in early Alzheimer's disease. *Lancet, ii,* 837, 1978.

Small IF, Sharpley P, Small JG: Influences of Cylert upon memory changes with ECT. *Am. J. Psychiatry: 125,* 837–840, 1968.

Small JG, Small IF, Milstein V, Dian DA: Effects of $ACTH_{4-10}$ on ECT-induced memory dysfunctions. *Acta Psychiatr. Scand.: 55,* 241–250, 1977.

Smith CM, Swase M, Exton-Smith AN, Phillips MJ, Overstall PW, Piper ME Bailey MR: Choline therapy in Alzheimer' disease. *Lancet: ii,* 318, 1978.

Smith DF, Strömnen E, Petersen HN, Williams DG, Sheldon W: Lack of effect of tryptophan treatment in demented geropsychiatric patients. *Acta Psychiatr. Scand.: 70,* 470–477, 1984.

Smith JS: The investigation of dementia: results in 200 consecutive admissions. *Lancet: ii,* 824–827, 1981.

Soininen H, Koskinen T, Helkala E-L, Pigache R, Riekkinen PJ: Treatment of Alzheimer's disease with a synthetic $ACTH_{4-9}$ analog. *Neurology: 35,* 1348–1351, 1985.

Soni SD, Soni SS: Dihydrogenated alkaloids of ergotoxine in nonhospitalised elderly patients. *Curr. Med. Res. Opin.: 3,* 464–468, 1975.

Sourander LB, Portin R, Mölsä P, Lahdes A, Rinne UK: Senile dementia of the Alzheimer type treated with aniracetam: a new nootropic agent. *Psychopharmacology: 91,* 90–95, 1987.

Squire L: Mechanisms of memory. *Science: 323,* 1612–1619, 1986.

Steginck AJ: The clinical use of piracetam, a new nootropic drug. *Arzneimittelforschung-Forschung: 22,* 975–977, 1972.

Stern FH: Management of chronic brain syndrome secondary to cerebral arteriosclerosis, with special reference to papaverine hydrochloride. *J. Am. Geriatr. Soc.: 18,* 507–512, 1970.

Stern Y, Sano M, Mayeux R: Effects of oral physostigmine in Alzheimer's disease. *Ann. Neurol.: 22,* 306–310, 1987.

Sulkava R, Haltia M, Paetau A, Wikström J, Palo J: Accuracy of clinical diagnosis in primary degenerative dementia: correlation with neuropathological findings. *J. Neurol. Neurosurg. Psychiatry: 46,* 9–13, 1983.

Summers WK, Viesselman JO, Marsh GM, Candelora K: Use of THA in treatment of Alzheimer-like dementia: pilot study in twelve patients. *Biol. Psychiatry: 16,* 145–153, 1981.

Summers WK, Majovski LV, Marsh GM, Tachiki K, Kling A: Oral tetrahydroaminoacridine in long-term treatment of senile dementia, Alzheimer type. *N. Engl. J. Med.: 315,* 1241–1245, 1986.

Talland GA, Hagen DQ, James M: Performance tests of amnesic patients with Cylert. *J. Nerv. Ment. Dis.: 144,* 421–429, 1967.

Tariot PN, Sunderland T, Weingarter H, Murphy DL, Cohen MR, Cohen RM: Naloxone and Alzheimer's disease. *Arch. Gen. Psychiatry: 43,* 727–732, 1986.

Tariot PN, Sunderland T, Weingartner H, Murphy DL, Welkowitz JA, Thompson K, Cohen RM: Cognitive effects of L-deprenyl in Alzheimer's disease. *Psychopharmacology: 91,* 489–495, 1987a.

Tariot PN, Cohen RM, Sunderland T, Newhouse PA, Yount D, Mellow AM, Weingartner H, Mueller EA, Murphy DL: L-Deprenyl in Alzheimer's disease. *Arch. Gen. Psychiatry: 44,* 427–433, 1987b.

Tennant FS: Preliminary observations on naltrexone for treatment of Alzheimer's type dementia. *J. Am. Geriatr. Soc.: 35,* 369–370, 1987.

Thal LJ, Rosen W, Sharpless S, Crystal H: Choline chloride fails to improve cognition in Alzheimer's disease. *Neurobiol. Aging: 2,* 205 – 208, 1981.

Thal LJ, Fuld PA, Masur DM, Sharpless NS: Oral physostigmine and lecithin improve memory in Alzheimer disease. *Ann. Neurol.: 13,* 491 – 496, 1983.

Thienhaus OJ, Wheeler BG, Simon S, Zemlan FP, Hartford JT: A controlled double-blind study of high dose dihydro-ergotoxine mesylate (Hydergine®) in mild dementia. *J. Am. Geriatr. Soc.: 35,* 219 – 223, 1987.

Thompson LW, Davis GC, Obrist WD, Heyman A. Effects of hyperbaric oxygen on behavioral and physiological measures in elderly demented patients. *J. Gerontol.: 31,* 23 – 28, 1976.

Timsit-Berthier M, Mantanus H, Jacques MC, Legros JJ: Utilite de la lysine-vasopressine dans le traitement de l'amnesie post-traumatique. *Acta Psychiatr. Belg.: 80,* 728 – 747, 1980.

Tinklenberg JR, Pfefferbaum A, Berger PA: 1-desamino-D-arginine vasopressin (DDAVP) in cognitively impaired patients. *Psychopharmacol. Bull.: 17,* 206 – 207, 1981.

Tinklenberg JR, Pigache R, Berger PA, Kopell BS: Desglycin-amide-9-arginine-8-vasopressin (DGAVP, Organon 5667) in cognitively impaired patients. *Psychopharmacol. Bull.: 18,* 202 – 204, 1982.

Triboletti F, Ferri H: Hydergine for treatment of symptoms of cerebrovascular insufficiency. *Curr. Ther. Res.: 11,* 609 – 620, 1969.

Victor M, Adams RD: The alcoholic dementias. In Frederiks JAM (Editor), *Handbook of Clinical Neurology, Vol. 46, Neurobehavioral Disorders.* Amsterdam: Elsevier Science Publishers, pp. 335 – 352, 1985.

Wade JP, Mirsen TR, Hachinski VC, Fisman M, Lau C, Merskey H: The clinical diagnosis of Alzheimer's disease. *Arch. Neurol.: 44,* 24 – 29, 1987.

Walsh AC. Prevention of senile and presenile dementia by bishydroxycoumarin (Dicumarol) therapy. *J. Am. Geriatr. Soc.: 17,* 477 – 487, 1969.

Wang HS, Obrist WD: Effect of oral papaverine on cerebral blood flow in normals: evaluation by the xenon-133 inhalation method. *Biol. Psychiatry: 11,* 217 – 225, 1976.

Weingartner H, Gold P, Ballenger JC, Smallberg SA, Summers R, Rubinow DR, Post RM, Goodwin FK: Effect of vasopressin on human memory function. *Science: 211,* 601 – 603, 1981a.

Weingartner H, Kaye W, Gold P, Smallberg S, Peterson R, Gillin JC, Ebert M: Vasopressin treatment of cognitive dysfunction in progressive dementia. *Life Sci.: 29,* 2721 – 2726, 1981b.

Weintraub S, Mesulam M-M, Auty R, Baratz R, Cholakos BN,

Kapust L, Ransil B, Tellers JG, Albert Ms, LoCastro S, Moss M: Lecithin in the treatment of Alzheimer's disease. *Arch. Neurol.: 40,* 527 – 528, 1983.

Weiss BL: Failure of nalmefene and estrogen to improve memory in Alzheimer's disease. *Am. J. Psychiatry: 144,* 386 – 387, 1987.

Westreich G, Alter M, Lundgren S: Effect of cyclandelate on dementia. *Stroke: 6,* 535 – 538, 1975.

Wettstein A: No effect from double-blind trial of physostigmine and lecithin in Alzheimer disease. *Ann. Neurol.: 13,* 210 – 212, 1983.

Wettstein A, Spiegel R: Clinical trials with the cholinergic drug RS 86 in Alzheimer's disease (AD) and senile dementia of the Alzheimer type (SDAT). *Psychopharmacology: 84,* 572 – 573, 1984.

White P, Goodhardt MJ, Keet JK, Hiley CR, Carrasio LH, Williams IEI: Neocortical cholinergic neurons in elderly people. *Lancet: i,* 668 – 671, 1977.

Whitehouse PJ, Price DL, Clark AW, Coyle JT, DeLong MR: Alzheimer's disease: evidence for selective loss of cholinergic neurons in the nucleus basalis. *Ann. Neurol.: 10,* 122 – 126, 1981.

Whitehouse PJ, Hedreen JC, White CL, Price DL: Basal forebrain neurons in the dementia of Parkinson's disease. *Ann. Neurol.: 13,* 243 – 248, 1983.

Will JC, Abuzzahab FS, Zimmerman RL: The effects of $ACTH_{4-10}$ versus placebo in the memory of symptomatic geriatric volunteers. *Psychopharmacol. Bull.: 14,* 25 – 27, 1978.

Williams LR, Varon S, Peterson GM, Wictorin K, Fischer W, Bjorklund A, Gage FH: Continuous infusion of nerve growth factor prevents basal forebrain neuronal death after fimbria fornix transection. *Proc. Natl. Acad. Sci. USA: 83,* 9231 – 9235, 1986.

Yates CM, Allisin Y, Sampon J, Maloney AJF, Gordon A: Dopamine in Alzheimer's disease and senile dementia. *Lancet: ii,* 851 – 852, 1979.

Yates CM, Simpson J, Gordon A, Maloney AFJ, Allison Y, Ritchie IM, Urquhart A: Catecholamines and cholinergic enzymes in pre-senile and senile Alzheimer-type dementia and Down's syndrome. *Brain Res.: 280,* 119 – 126, 1983.

Yesavage JA, Hollister LE, Burian E: Dihydroergotoxine: 6-Mg versus 3-Mg dosage in the treatment of senile dementia. Preliminary report. *J. Am. Geriatr. Soc.: 27,* 80 – 82, 1979.

Yoshikawa M, Hirai S, Aizawa T, Kuroiwa Y, Goto F, Sofue I, Toyokura Y, Yamamura H, Iwasaki Y: A dose-response study with dihydroergotoxine mesylate in cerebrovascular disturbances. *J. Am. Geriatr. Soc.: 31,* 1 – 7, 1983.

Section 6

Emotional Behavior and its Disorders

editor

G. Gainotti

© 1989 Elsevier Science Publishers B.V. (Biomedical Division)
Handbook of Neuropsychology, Vol. 3
F. Boller and J. Grafman (Eds)

CHAPTER 12

Theories of emotions and neuropsychological research

Pierre Feyereisen

Unité Nexa, UCL 5545, Avenue Hippocrate, B-1200 Brussels, Belgium

Introduction

Since the beginnings of modern psychology, the nature and the generation of the emotional states have been controversial issues and perhaps a larger number of papers have been devoted to the discussion of the respective theoretical positions than in other fields of psychology (see, for examples, the discussion of the James-Lange theory by Cannon in 1927, the criticism of 'emotion as disorganized response' by Lepper in 1948 with Young's, 1949, reply, and, more recently, the debate between Zajonc and Lazarus in 1984). And more often than in other fields of psychology, the discussions rely on the neurophysiological substrate of emotions. Accordingly, data from neuropsychology are of double interest as they provide arguments in theoretical discussions and means of testing specific hypotheses on the neural organization of emotional behavior.

The growing interest of comtemporary psychology in emotions and the development of experimental investigations in this area is testified by the launching of new journals like *Motivation and Emotion* or *Cognition and Emotion*. Numerous papers proposing theories of emotion have also been published. It is not certain, however, that all these 'theories' concern the same phenomena, and some discussions may be terminated by the simple statement that different things require different explanations. Emotions refer to a great diversity of behavioural processes, and the mechanisms underlying the different aspects of emotions probably differ from each other. Thus, theories of emotions have the problem of defining their object and specifying their domain of relevance so that the models they generate can be compared.

What are emotions?

People hold beliefs with which they explain behavior and the word emotion stems from such a folk psychology. One way to approach emotion is to describe the mental representations captured in ordinary language. For the layman, the set of mental states that can be said to be emotional have imprecise borders. Some common behaviours like laughing, being frightened or distress crying exemplify the concept of emotion, whereas other physical and mental states like sexual desire, fatigue, doubt or envy do not. Besides these clear examples, feelings like boredom, gratitude or pride are considered emotional by some people but not by others (Shields, 1984). Thus, the category of emotion may formally be described as fuzzy. Like other natural categories, the concept of emotion can be organized in such a way that some prototypes and some more peripheral exemplars can be identified. The structure of the mental representations of emotions can be evidenced in experimental tasks requiring subjects to list instances of emotion, to rate their typicality, to accept them as plausible substitutes for the word 'emotion' in sentences, etc. (Fehr and Russell, 1984; Ortony et al., 1987; Clore et al., 1987; Shaver et al., 1987).

It is not surprising that the concept of emotion, like other social cognitions, develops during childhood from the early discrimination of emotional cues to the late building of implicit theories of affect (for a general review, see Campos et al., 1983; for some recent representative studies see Nelson, 1987; Bretherton et al., 1986; Harris et al., 1987; Masters and Carlson, 1984; Strayer, 1986).

The psychology of emotions does not provide a much more precise picture of what an emotion is. Numerous definitions have been proposed, each stressing different aspects of emotions (for reviews, see Arnold, 1968; Kleinginna and Kleinginna, 1981; Plutchik, 1980; Strongman, 1973; Whissell, 1984). A comprehensive definition including all these dimensions fails to solve the definition problems, the first being the distinction between emotions and other mental states like moods or the ubiquitous affective consequences of non-emotional behaviour leading to pleasure or distress. Thus, the first aim of a theory of emotion is to show the specificity of the processes under study. In that task, neuropsychology offers one of the most helpful ways of showing that emotions constitute a separate domain (Feyereisen, in press). Under the assumption that emotions rely on specialized neural structures, selective impairments of affective processing may be expected in some cases of brain damage (LeDoux, 1984, 1986).

The second problem in the definition of emotion is raised by the diversity of the emotional states. Emotion refers to experiences like joy, anger, disgust, etc., which hardly constitute a homogeneous set of phenomena. For a 'theory of emotion', it is assumed that the different emotions one may experience are comparable and can be explained in similar ways. The specific emotions would be particular instances of a general mode of processing information emotionally. Emotional indifference in the Klüver and Bucy syndrome or hyper-emotionality in temporal lobe epilepsy (Bear, 1979, 1983) would affect in opposite ways this process in the diverse forms emotions may present. If, however, emotion refers to distinct specialized processes, dissociation of the various

emotional states could occur after brain lesions. For example, there may be pathological outbursts of anger without other emotional impairments (Moyer, 1976).

Third, emotions are built of different components. Inputs of different forms, actual or recollected events, may trigger emotional responses of different kinds: physiological arousal, motor activity or subjective feelings. A one-to-one correspondence between physiological states and subjective experiences is commonly assumed, which Schachter (1970) has called the assumption of identity. Theories of emotion propose different forms of integration between arousal, motor activity and subjective feeling. Conflicts between rival conceptions result from differences in the hypothesized sequence of events constituting emotions and thus in the identification of the main element of the emotional behaviour. Neuropsychology may also be useful in the description of the relationships between the different parts of an emotion. According to models of emotional processes, selective impairments of one component after a brain lesion are expected to have different effects on other processes. The study of these cases could also show the extent to which emotions can be fragmented into separable components.

Theories of emotion

How has the definition problem in the psychology of emotions been dealth with? Two families of conceptions may be distinguished schematically. For some theories, emotions are mainly bodily states: physiological arousal or motor activity. The affective system controlling these emotional responses is independent of and parallel to the cognitive system, two separate modes of information processing being suggested (Zajonc and Markus, 1984). Input of different kinds may activate either hard representations in the form of conditioned bodily response, for example, or soft representations like reminders of associated material (Bower and Cohen, 1982; Blaney, 1986). For the other class of theories, emotion can only result from some appraisal of the situation and thus a cognitive process takes place before the bodily response.

Emotions as bodily responses

Differential emotions theory
The primary affects. An influential conception in the study of emotions assumes the existence of a small number of basic affects (Ekman, 1982; Izard, 1977, 1984; Tomkins, 1962, 1980, 1984). Five to nine primary emotions are identified. Most often cited are joy, anger, fear, distress and disgust, and some authors add interest, surprise, shame or comtempt. Complex emotions arise from the simultaneous activation of several primary affects. For example, depression would result from a combination of distress with anger, disgust and contempt toward oneself and others. Emotional expressions are universal, innate and automatically triggered. However, they are also influenced by culture through learned 'display rules', which let one inhibit, exaggerate or disguise the primary spontaneous activity.

The facial feedback hypothesis. According to Tomkins and his followers, affects are primarily facial responses, so emotional experience depends on sensory feedback from the face. Patterns of facial activity, either overt behaviour or invisible electromyographic activity (Cacioppo et al., 1986; Schwartz et al., 1980), may differentiate affective states. Facial responses are diverse and rapid enough to be plausible candidates as a source of emotional experience. Several observations support the hypothesis that induced facial behaviour influences subjective feelings at least along the pleasant – unpleasant dimension (e.g., Rutledge and Hupka, 1985; Winton, 1986; for reviews, see Laird, 1984; Leventhal and Tomarken, 1986). For example, subjects requested to contract the zygomatic muscle while looking at slides are biased toward more positive ratings than control subjects (Laird, 1974). Posing for emotional expressions also influences physiological responses like heart rate and finger temperature (Ekman et al., 1983).

However, the effects of facial behaviour on emotional experience vary considerably with individual and situational characteristics (Buck, 1980; Tourangeau and Ellsworth, 1979). Hence, the interpretation of experimental data is still disputed.

The perceptual-motor theory
Leventhal (1980, 1984) also assumes automatic activation of a specific emotional system, but for him this system competes with a propositional one. Information is processed on three hierarchically organized levels. The first level controls the physiological activity that produces emotional arousal. On the second level, these visceral reactions are integrated into perceptual-motor schemata built during ontogeny from emotional experiences, and reactions to particular situations are coded in specific scripts. The input is also processed on the third, conceptual level where eliciting conditions and expected reactions are represented in a propositional code. The schematic and the conceptual processing constitute alternative ways of reacting to a situation: both the schematic and the conceptual processing may result in facial expressions and subjective feelings. The reactions under the control of the schematic processing are experienced as emotional. The facial expressions and the thoughts controlled on the conceptual level give access to consciousness in the form of a voluntary activity. Thus, emotional reactions to situations like painful stimulation or humorous movies may be inhibited by instructions switching from an emotional to a propositional mode of processing.

The prime theory
A similar concept suggesting parallel processing of information in emotional and propositional codes was developed by Buck (1985), who holds that emotion cannot be separated from motivation. It results from the functioning of several systems, or 'primes', that serve the adaptation of the organism. Emotional reactions constitute readout devices giving information about the state of the motivational systems. Four levels of organization are distinguished. The most primitive systems in-

volve maintenance of homeostasis via physiological responses. On the second level, expressive movements serve social functions by regulating the relationships between individuals. The third type of representation codes the state of the organism under the form of global subjective experiences. Thus, the functioning of the motivational systems gives rise to three kinds of feedback – visceral, proprioceptive and cognitive – all of them constituting in variable proportions the emotional experience. Apart from these emotional manifestations, analytic propositions, like those underlying verbal reports, constitute the fourth way of conceptually representing motivational states. From such a perspective, emotion does not occur as a discrete event but, outside or inside awareness, it constantly monitors ongoing behaviour.

Conclusions

Apart from their major differences, the diverse conceptions here reviewed converge in identifying emotions with automatically released bodily responses. Emotional processes parallel the cognitive processes and rely on separate neural bases. However, no precise criteria enable emotional behavior to be identified as different from other bodily responses. The reaction of being startled and facial expressions of pain may be considered either true emotional signals or reflexes aimed at protecting sense organs (Ekman et al., 1985; Craig and Patrick, 1985; LeResche and Dworkin, 1984).

Another obscure part of the assumed emotional processing is the way in which bodily responses are triggered by the situation. Facial expression of emotions is often compared to the elicitation of communicative displays in animal behaviour. However, ethology nowadays proposes more complex models of causation than the formerly described 'innate releasing mechanisms'. First, in most cases no key stimulus corresponds to vocal and facial signals of mammals. The same configuration may elicit threat, attack or avoidance, and the observed behaviour may result from conflicting tendencies. Accordingly, animal contests

may be described as 'negotiations' involving computation instead of automatic reactions (Hinde, 1985a, b). It is also suggested that some reactions depend on a comparison between expected and actual conditions (Andrew, 1972; Toates and Archer, 1978). Second, emotional terms are found inadequate to describe the diversity of responses to similar situations. For example, a general concept of fear cannot explain the differences between cases where freezing, flight or social displays are observed nor could it describe the production by some primates of different alarm calls depending on the nature of the predator (Seyfarth and Cheney, 1984). Finally, the idea that signals have evolved for a communicative purpose is disputed (Caryl, 1979; Hinde, 1981; see Wiley, 1983, for a review). Hiding intentions often offers more benefit than revealing them, so the primary function of emotional responses would not be the management of social relationships.

In general, somatic theories give no precise description of the conditions eliciting emotions. Anger, for example, would result from 'being either physically or psychologically restrained from doing what one intensely desires to do' (Izard, 1977, p. 329). Similarly, joy is considered the consequence of a 'reduction of tension'. Its origins, however, may be extremely diverse, from being tickled to a joke. The ontogenesis of smile and laughter and their pathology in some mentally handicapped children show their relationship to cognitive development (Sroufe, 1984; Ciccheti and Schneider-Rosen, 1984). The apparently simple reaction of disgust also depends on elaborate representations (Rozin and Fallon, 1987). Thus, affective reactions differ from reflex-like inescapable activity. Cognitive theories are aimed at describing the process by which some situations give rise to emotional responses.

Cognitive theories

The cognition-arousal theory

Development of cognitive theories of emotion was deeply influenced by the suggestion of Schachter and Singer (1962) that emotional experience depends on two factors, physiological arousal and attribution of arousal to an emotional source. Subjects who received an injection of epinephrine and who were informed of the arousing effects of the drug did not experience emotion because another explanation for the bodily state was available. The theory also predicts that no emotion can occur without arousal. Numerous experimental studies have attempted to analyse the influence of these two factors, cognition and arousal, on emotional experience, but they have failed to provide support for the model (for reviews, see Cotton, 1981; Leventhal and Tomarken, 1986; Manstead and Wagner, 1981; Reisenzein, 1983). Difficulties arise in the control of physiological states and cognitions. Some control subjects may truly be aroused by the injection of a placebo and by the laboratory situation. In the other control group of uninformed subjects receiving epinephrine, some of them may correctly guess the cause of the arousal. Furthermore, some data indicate that arousal is not neutral with respect to emotional attributions: high levels of arousal are rated negatively, and different emotions might be distinguished on the basis of physiological patterns.

Other conceptions derived from the Schachter's theory minimize the role of either arousal or cognition in emotional experience. The use of false autonomic feedback suggests that the true physiological responses play a reduced role in the generation of subjective feelings. Subjects led to believe that the sound of a recorded heartbeat corresponds to their own reactions are influenced in rating the pleasantness of the simultaneously presented slides (Valins, 1966). It remains to be determined, however, whether the false feedback influences physiological responses directly or by interacting with the bodily responses to the emotional stimuli (Hirschman and Clark, 1983; Parkinson, 1985). Other experimental data show a more robust effect. It was demonstrated that excitation may transfer from a previous condition to a subsequent one (Zillman, 1983). For example, subjects aroused by physical exercise react more aggressively to

provocation by the experimenter than control subjects. However, it seems that subjects are unaware of the manipulation and thus the observed effect is unlikely to be mediated by conscious interpretation of the physiological state.

The appraisal of situations

Schachter's theory does not explain how some conditions elicit physiological arousal. Other 'cognitive' theories describe the processes giving rise to an emotional response. For example, Scherer (1984) suggests a sequence of five 'stimulus evaluation checks'. Events are first judged for expectedness, then for pleasantness, goal relevance and coping potential, and finally for norm compatibility. Other similar models also consider the diverse emotions as different outcomes of successive tests called 'emotional interpretation rules' by Bower and Cohen (1982) and 'appraisals' by others (Frijda, 1984; Smith and Ellsworth, 1985). The main empirical data supporting such a perspective are produced in introspective reports of recollected emotional episodes (e.g. Scherer and Tannenbaum, 1986) or in simulation of human functioning by computers (Frijda and Swagerman, 1987). It is assumed, indeed, that true emotions cannot be experimentally induced in the laboratory.

The evaluations may occur on different levels and are not necessarily represented in consciousness (Leventhal and Scherer, 1987). Event novelty, for example, would be rapidly checked within a comparator that one could identify as the behavioural inhibition system described by Gray (1982). More subtle feelings of surprise may depend on expectations within the conceptual system. The locus at which pleasantness judgments occur in information processing has elicited controversy even since Zajonc (1980) formulated the thesis that 'preferences need no inferences'. For Zajonc, feelings do not depend on knowing, and stimuli are characterized by distinctive features or *discriminanda* that permit recognition and by affective features or *preferenda* that are used in liking judgments. The model of independent and parallel processes for familiarity and pleasantness ratings would fit the data concerning mere exposure effects (Moreland and Zajonc, 1979). Another experiment showed that stimuli previously shown at a subliminal threshold are not recognized below chance level but are nevertheless preferred to newly presented stimuli (Kunst-Wilson and Zajonc, 1980).

The thesis of the independence of affective and cognitive judgments has elicited several criticisms. First, mere exposure effects also fit an alternative model in which both recognition and liking depend on subjective familiarity (Birnbaum and Mellers, 1979). The terminological decision to call cognitive only conscious identification has also been disputed (Lazarus, 1982; Russell and Woudzia, 1986). Other examples of semantic activation without conscious identification are known from visual masking experiments (see review in Holender, 1986) and from the 'feeling of knowing' experience where some features of an unavailable word are retrieved (Brown and McNeill, 1966; Eysenck, 1979). Finally, Mandler (1982) considers that affective judgments do not depend on objective and isolated properties of an object but on its relations to the expectations and schemata of the subject. Accordingly, evaluation needs some computation and is not instantaneous. An experiment comparing recognition times and 'like-dislike' decision times for paintings of different styles showed that affective judgments are slower than non-affective ones (Mandler and Shebo, 1983).

The emotional control of cognitive processes
The last type of cognitive theory considers emotions as a way to interrupt ongoing activity and to solve conflicts between competing programs. Renewed interest is being paid to this old idea by people working from artificial intelligence perspectives (Simon, 1967, Mandler, 1980, 1984; Oatley and Johnson-Laird, 1987). It is assumed that organisms living in partially unpredictable environments and pursuing several objectives need some mechanism to flexibly re-orient their behaviour according to changing priorities. Oatley and Johnson-Laird (1987) assume two modes of control: a propositional mode relying on explicit representations of the system (people use a model of the self to guide conduct and interpret human action) and a simpler emotional mode allowing rapid transitions between concurrent plans. Sadness occurs when a major plan fails, anxiety when survival is threatened, anger follows frustration, etc. Complex adult emotions like remorse or jealousy result from a propositional evaluation of basic emotional states. Another kind of emotional influence on cognitive processing is described by Bower and Cohen (1982; see also Blaney, 1986). Results of appraisals are stored in an associative network under affective labels. These nodes may be reactivated by sensory input or by signals from connected units. Memory records may be primed in mood state-dependent retrievals similar to the way they are by episodic contextual cues (Davies, 1986; Guenther, 1988).

Conclusions
Cognitive theories have evolved from conceptions assuming causal attribution for physiological arousal to analyses of processes allowing for behavioural decisions when no obligatory reaction is programmed. Two kinds of procedure have been hypothesized: multi-dimensional appraisals of eliciting conditions or interruption mechanisms controlling ongoing activity. These models are intended to describe the conditions under which emotional bodily responses occur. Thus, they are not incompatible with somatic theories but only bear on different issues. However, empirical support is still lacking and it remains unclear whether or not the somatic and cognitive theories of emotion can solve the definition problems of specificity, diversity and identity raised in the first section of this chapter. Can neuropsychological data shed some light on these questions?

The use of neuropsychological data in building theories of emotions

The assumption of specific neural processes

The theories of emotions as bodily responses rely heavily on the assumption of specific processes expressing the functioning of specialized neural structures. For example, the differential emotions theory considers that emotions are built-in facial programs stored in specific neural structures. Some neuropsychological data support such an assumption. Spontaneous occurrences of facial reactions may be observed at the onset of epileptic seizures (Strauss et al., 1983). Brain damage may also result in pathological manifestations of anger, crying or laughter (Poeck, 1969). Similarly, the separation of propositional and emotional modes of processing as described in Leventhal's perceptual-motor theory or in Buck's prime theory is supported by the dissociation of spontaneous and voluntary facial behaviour (Rinn, 1984). In this context, the numerous studies on hemispheric specialization reviewed by Tucker (1981) are also referred to. However, these neuropsychological data are not sufficient to show the specificity of emotional processes. Emotion might only be a particular case of dissociation between automatic and controlled processes. Brain lesions sparing spontaneous expressions of emotion also leave non-emotional movements like swallowing or yawning unimpaired.

The specificity of processes generating emotions according to the cognitive theories also remains unquestioned. A right-hemisphere advantage in various tasks involving affective processing may reveal specialized processing units or derive from more general asymmetries in perceptual and motor activity. If, following Lindsley (1951/1966), arousal plays a central role in emotion generation, non-specific mechanisms underlying activation from sensory input or action readiness may be involved (Pribram and McGuiness, 1975; Kinsbourne and Bemporad, 1984; Tucker and Willamson, 1984). Attentional deficits such as

hemineglect would necessarily involve reduced arousal (Heilman et al., 1978). Emotional processing might also relate to other cognitive abilities. For example, the inability of right-brain-damaged patients to understand humour might depend on deficits in drawing inferences to establish text coherence (Brownell et al., 1983). The extent to which emotional impairments in the Klüver and Bucy syndrome or after frontal lesions relate to intellectual deficits is still unknown (Damasio and Van Hoesen, 1983; Lilly et al., 1983). Controls comparing emotional and nonemotional processing of similar stimuli have only rarely been presented (Campbell, 1982; Gainotti, 1984). In this regard, the most thorough analysis concerns the comprehension of facial expressions of emotions that dissociates from the perception of facial identity (Bowers et al., 1985; Etcoff, 1984). Such a dissociation between emotional and non-emotional processes was not observed in a study of the comprehension of prosody (Heilman et al., 1984).

The diversity of emotional states

The issue of homogeneity of the diverse emotions has only been indirectly addressed in neuropsychological research. The hypothesis of different hemispheric specialization for positive and negative emotions (Sackeim et al., 1982) or for approach and avoidance behaviour (Davidson, 1984) could suggest that several emotional processes have to be distinguished. Similarly, the description of distinct neuro-anatomical circuits for anger, fear, distress and expectancy (Panksepp, 1982, 1986) indicates that emotion refers to different kinds of processes which could be selectively impaired.

The dissociation of components of emotion

The main point of divergence between the different theories of emotion is the way the components relate to each other. The facial feedback hypothesis gives priority to the motor component. The neuropsychological evidence does not favour a strong version of the hypothesis according to which facial expression would constitute a necessary condition for subjective feeling. The motor and subjective components of emotions may dissociate in cases of pathological laughter or crying when the expression does not accompany changes in feelings (Poeck, 1969). Cases of emotional inexpressivity in spite of deep sorrow or anger have also been reported (Ross and Mesulam, 1979). These cases have yet to be analysed from the perspective of a weak version of the facial feedback hypothesis predicting that facial behaviour influences subjective experience to some extent or under some circumstances. Neurological impairments of facial motility (see Feyereisen, 1986, for a review) offer good opportunities for testing that hypothesis against the alternatives proposed by Leventhal (1984) and Buck (1985).

The influence that the perception of other bodily states exerts in the generation of emotional experience may also be studied, for example, in patients suffering from hypoarousal after spinal cord lesions (Bermond et al., 1985) or after right hemisphere damage (Heilman et al., 1978).

Cognitive theories suggest the possibility of emotional appraisal outside any motor manifestation if pathology dissociates input from output processes. Some data indicate that impairments in production and in comprehension of emotional cues may have a different basis (e.g., Borod et al., 1986; Zoccolotti et al., 1982). Emotional processes may also dissociate in the verbal and nonverbal modalities (Borod et al., 1985). Thus, neuropsychology opens the way to a finer analysis of emotional processes than can be offered by the crude dichotomies opposing right and left hemispheres or affect and cognition.

References

Andrew RJ: The information potentially available in mammal display. In Hinde RA (Editor) *Nonverbal Communication.* Cambridge: Cambridge University Press, pp. 179–206, 1972.

Arnold MB (Editor): *The Nature of Emotion.* Harmondsworth: Penguin, 1968.

Bear DM: Temporal lobe epilepsy: a syndrome of sensory limbic hyperconnection. *Cortex: 15,* 357–384, 1979.

Bear DM: Hemispheric specialization and the neurology of emotion. *Arch. Neurol.: 40,* 195–402, 1983.

Bermond B, Schuerman J, Niewenhuyse B, Fassotti L, Elshou J: Spinal cord lesions: effects upon mood states. Toulouse Communication at the 19th Ethological Conference, 1985.

Birnbaum MH, Mellers BA: Stimulus recognition may mediate exposure effects. *J. Pers. Soc. Psychol.: 37,* 391–394, 1979.

Blaney PH: Affect and memory: a review. *Psychol. Bull.: 99,* 229–246, 1986.

Borod JC, Koff E, Perlman M, Nicholas M: Channels of emotional expression in patients with unilateral brain damage. *Arch. Neurol.: 42,* 345–348, 1985.

Borod JC, Koff E, Perlman-Lorch M, Nicholas M: The expression and perception of facial emotion in brain-damaged patients. *Neuropsychologia: 24,* 169–180, 1986.

Bower GH, Cohen PR: Emotional influences in memory and thinking: data and theory. In Clark MS, Fiske ST (Editors) *Affect and cognition.* Hillsdale, NJ: Lawrence Erlbaum, pp. 291–331, 1982.

Bowers D, Bauer RM, Coslett HB, Heilman KM: Processing of faces by patients with unilateral hemisphere lesions. I. Dissociation between judgments of facial affect and facial identity. *Brain Cognition: 4,* 258–272, 1985.

Bretherton I, Fritz J, Zahn-Waxler C, Ridgeway D: Learning to talk about emotions: a functionalist perspective. *Child Dev. 57,* 529–448, 1986.

Brown R, McNeill D: The 'tip-of-the-tongue' phenomenon. *J. Verbal Learn. Verbal Behav.: 5,* 325–337, 1966.

Brownell HH, Michel D, Powelson J, Gardner H: Surprise but not coherence: sensitivity to verbal humor in right hemisphere patients. *Brain Lang.: 18,* 20–27, 1983.

Buck R: Nonverbal behavior and the theory of emotion: the facial feedback hypothesis. *J. Pers. Soc. Psychol.: 38,* 811–824, 1980.

Buck R: Prime theory: an integrated view of motivation and emotion. *Psychol. Rev.: 92,* 349–413, 1985.

Cacioppo JT, Petty RE, Losch ME, Kim HS: Electromyographic activity over facial muscle regions can differentiate the valence and intensity of affective reactions. *J. Pers. Soc. Psychol.: 50,* 260–268, 1986.

Campbell R: The lateralization of emotion: a critical review. *Int. J. Psychol.: 17,* 211–229, 1982.

Campos JJ, Barrett KC, Lamb ME, Goldsmith HH, Stenberg RC: Socioemotional development. In Mussen PH (Editor) *Handbook of Child Psychology II: Infancy and Developmental Psychobiology.* New York: Wiley, pp. 783–915, 1983.

Cannon WB: The James-Lange theory of emotions: a critical examination and an alternative theory. *Am. J. Psychol.: 39,* 106–124, 1927. Reprinted in Pribram KH (Editor), *Brain and Behaviour 4: Adaptation.* Harmondsworth: Penguin 1969.

Caryl PG: Communication by agonistic displays: what can game theory contribute to ethology? *Behaviour: 68,* 136–169, 1979.

Cicchetti D, Schneider-Rosen K: Theoretical and empirical considerations in the investigation of the relationship between affect and cognition in atypical populations of infants. In Izard CE, Kagan J, Zajonc RB (Editors), *Emotion, Cogni-*

tion, and Behavior. Cambridge: Cambridge University Press, pp. 366 – 405, 1984.

ore GL, Ortony A, Foss MA: The psychological foundations of the affective lexicon. *J. Pers. Soc. Psychol.:* 53, 751 – 766, 1987.

otton JL: A review of research on Schachter's theory of emotion and the misattribution of arousal. *Eur. J. Soc. Psychol.: 11,* 365 – 397, 1981.

raig KD, Patrick CJ: Facial expression during induced pain. *J. Pers. Soc. Psychol.: 48,* 1080 – 1091, 1985.

amasio AR, Van Hoesen GW: Emotional disturbances associated with focal lesions of the limbic frontal lobe. In Heilman KM, Satz P (Editors), *Neuropsychology of Human Emotion.* New York/London: Guilford Press, pp. 85 – 110, 1983.

avidson RJ: Affect, cognition, and hemispheric specialization. In Izard CE, Kagan J, Zajonc RB (Editors), *Emotion, Cognition, and Behavior.* Cambridge: Cambridge University Press, pp. 320 – 365, 1984.

avies G. Context effects in episodic memory: a review. *Cah. Psychol. Cogn.:* 6, 157 – 174, 1986.

kman P (Editor): *Emotion in the Human Face.* Cambridge: Cambridge University Press, 1982.

kman P, Levenson RW, Friesen WV: Autonomous Nervous System activity distinguishes among emotions. *Science: 221,* 1208 – 1210, 1983.

kman P, Friesen WV, Simons RC: Is the startle reaction an emotion? *J. Pers. Soc. Psychol.: 49,* 1416 – 1426, 1985.

tcoff NL: Selective attention to facial identity and facial emotion. *Neuropsychologia: 22,* 281 – 295, 1984.

ysenck MW: The feeling of knowing a word's meaning. *Br. J. Psychol.: 70,* 243 – 251, 1979.

ehr B, Russell JA: Concept of emotion viewed from a prototype perspective. *J. Exp. Psychol. Gen.: 113,* 464 – 486, 1984.

eyereisen P: Production and comprehension of emotional facial expressions in brain-damaged subjects. In Bruyer R (Editor), *The Neuropsychology of Face Perception and Facial Expression.* Hillsdale, NJ: Lawrence Erlbaum, pp. 221 – 245, 1986.

eyereisen P: What can be learned from lateral differences in emotional processing? In Gainotti G, Caltagirone C (Editor), *Emotions and the Dual Brain.* Berlin: Springer, in press.

rijda NH: Toward a model of emotion. In Spielberger CD, Sarason IG, Defares P (Editors), *Stress and Anxiety, Vol. 9.* Washington: Hemisphere, pp. 3 – 16, 1984.

rijda NH, Swagerman J: Can computers feel? Theory and design of an emotional system. *Cogn. Emot.:* 1, 235 – 257, 1987.

ainotti G: Some methodological problems in the study of the relationships between emotion and cerebral dominance. *J. Clin. Neuropsychol.: 6,* 111 – 121, 1984.

ray JA: Précis of the neuropsychology of anxiety: an inquiry into the functions of the septo-hippocampal system. *Behav. Brain Sci.: 5,* 469 – 534, 1982.

uenther K: Mood and memory. In Davies GM, Thomson DM (Editors), *Memory in Context, Context in Memory.* Chichester, New York: Wiley, pp. 55 – 80, 1988.

arris PL, Olthof T, Tervogt MM, Hardman CE: Children's knowledge of the situations that provoke emotion. *Int. J.*

Behav. Dev.: 10, 319 – 343, 1987.

Heilman KM, Bowers D, Speedie L, Coslett HB: Comprehension of affective and non-affective prosody. *Neurology: 34,* 917 – 921, 1984.

Heilman KM, Schwartz HD, Watson RT: Hypoarousal in patients with neglect syndrome and emotional indifference. *Neurology: 28,* 229 – 232, 1978.

Hinde RA: Animal signals: Ethological and games-theory approaches are not incompatible. *Anim. Behav.: 29,* 535 – 542, 1981.

Hinde RA: Was 'The expression of the emotions' a misleading phrase? *Anim. Behav.: 33,* 985 – 992, 1985a.

Hinde RA: Expression and negotiation. In Zivin G (Editor) *The Development of Expressive Behavior: Biology-environment Interactions.* Orlando, FL: Academic Press, pp. 103 – 116, 1985b.

Hirschman R, Clark M: Bogus physiological feedback. In Cacioppo JT, Petty RE (Editors), *Social Psychophysiology: A Sourcebook.* New York/London: Guilford, pp. 177 – 214, 1983.

Holender D: Semantic activation without conscious identification in dichotic listening, parafoveal vision, and visual masking: a survey and appraisal. *Behav. Brain Sci.: 9,* 1 – 66, 1986.

Izard CE: *Human Emotions,* New York/London: Plenum Press, 1977.

Izard CE: Emotion-cognition relationships and human development. In Izard CE, Kagan J, Zajonc RB (Editors), *Emotion, Cognition, and Behavior.* Cambridge: Cambridge University Press, pp. 17 – 37, 1984.

Kinsbourne M, Bemporad B: Lateralization of emotion: A model and the evidence. In Fox NA, Davidson RJ (Editors), *The Psychobiology of Affective Development.* Hillsdale, NJ: Lawrence Erlbaum, pp. 259 – 291, 1984.

Kleinginna PR, Kleinginna AM: A categorized list of emotion definitions, with suggestions for a consensual definition. *Motiv. Emotion: 5,* 345 – 379, 1981.

Kunst-Wilson WR, Zajonc RB: Affective discrimination of stimuli that cannot be recognized. *Science: 207,* 557 – 558, 1980.

Laird JD: Self attribution of emotion: The effects of expressive behavior on the quality of emotional experience. *J. Pers. Soc. Psychol.: 29,* 475 – 486, 1974.

Laird JD: The real role of facial response in the experience of emotion: A reply to Tourangeau and Ellsworth, and others. *J. Pers. Soc. Psychol.: 47,* 909 – 917, 1984.

Lazarus RS: Thoughts on the relations between emotion and cognition. *Am. Psychol.: 37,* 1019 – 1024, 1982.

Lazarus RS: On the primacy of cognition. *Am. Psychol.: 39,* 124 – 129, 1984.

LeDoux JE: Cognition and emotion: processing functions and brain systems. In Gazzaniga MS (Editor), *Handbook of Cognitive Neuroscience.* New York: Plenum Press, pp. 357 – 368, 1984.

LeDoux JE: The neurobiology of emotion. In LeDoux JE, Hirst W (Editors), *Mind and Brain: Dialogues in Cognitive Neuroscience.* Cambridge: Cambridge University Press, pp. 301 – 354, 1986.

Lepper RW: A motivational theory of emotion to replace 'emotion as disorganized response'. *Psychol. Rev.: 55,* 5 – 21,

1948. Reprinted in Pribram KH (Editor), *Brain and Behaviour 4: Adaptation.* Harmondsworth: Penguin, 1969.

LeResche L, Dworkin SF: Facial expression accompanying pain. *Soc. Sci. Med.: 19,* 1325 – 1330, 1984.

Leventhal H: Toward a comprehensive theory of emotion. In Berkowitz L (Editor), *Advances in Experimental Social Psychology, Vol. 13.* New York/London: Academic Press, pp. 139 – 207, 1980.

Leventhal H: A perceptual-motor theory of emotion. In Berkowitz L (Editor), *Advances in Experimental Social Psychology, Vol. 17.* New York/London: Academic Press, pp. 117 – 182, 1984.

Leventhal H, Scherer K: The relationship of emotion to cognition: a functional approach to a semantic controversy. *Cognition Emotion: 1,* 3 – 28, 1987.

Leventhal H, Tomarken AJ: Emotion: today's problems. *Annu. Rev. Psychol.:* 565 – 610, 1986.

Lilly R, Cummings JL, Benson DF, Frankel M: The human Klüver-Bucy syndrome. *Neurology: 33,* 1141 – 1145, 1983.

Lindsey DB: Emotions. In Stevens SS (Editor) *Handbook of Experimental Psychology.* New York/London: Wiley, pp. 473 – 516, 1966 (first edition, 1951).

Mandler G: The generation of emotion: a psychological theory. In Plutchik R, Kellerman H (Editors), *Emotion: Theory, Research, Experience. Vol. 1: Theories of Emotion.* New York/London: Academic Press, pp. 219 – 243, 1980.

Mandler G: The structure of value: accounting for taste. In Clark MS, Fiske ST (Editors), *Affect and Cognition.* Hillsdale, NJ: Lawrence Erlbaum, pp. 3 – 36, 1982.

Mandler G: *Mind and Body: Psychology of Emotion and Stress.* New York: Norton, 1984.

Mandler G, Shebo BJ: Knowing and liking. *Motivation Emotion: 7,* 125 – 144, 1983.

Manstead ASR, Wagner HL: Arousal, cognition and emotion: an appraisal of two-factor theory. *Curr. Psychol. Rev.: 1,* 35 – 54, 1981.

Masters JC, Carlson CR: Children's and adult's understanding of the causes and consequences of emotional states. In Izard CE, Kagan J, Zajonc RB (Eds), *Emotion, Cognition, and Behavior.* Cambridge: Cambridge University Press, pp. 438 – 463, 1984.

Moreland RL, Zajonc RB: Exposure effects may not depend on stimulus recognition. *J. Pers. Soc. Psychol.: 37,* 1085 – 1089, 1979.

Moyer KE: *The Psychobiology of Aggression.* New York/London: Harper and Row, 1976.

Nelson CA: The recognition of facial expressions in the first two years of life: mechanisms of development. *Child Dev.: 58,* 889 – 909, 1987.

Oatley K, Johnson-Laird PN: Towards a cognitive theory of emotions. *Cognition Emotion: 1,* 29 – 50, 1987.

Ortony A, Clore GL, Foss MA: The referential structure of affective lexicon. *Cogn. Sci.:* 11, 341 – 364, 1987.

Panksepp J: Toward a general psychobiological theory of emotions. *Behav. Brain Sci.: 5,* 407 – 467, 1982.

Panksepp J: The anatomy of emotions. In Plutchik R, Kellerman H (Editors), *Emotion: Theory, Research, Experience. Vol. 3: Biological Foundations of Emotion.* Orlando, FL: Academic Press, pp. 91 – 124, 1986.

Parkinson B: Emotional effects of false autonomic feedback.

Psychol. Bull.: 98, 471 – 494, 1985.

Plutchik R: *Emotion: A Psychoevolutionary Synthesis.* New York: Harper and Row, 1980.

Poeck K: Pathophysiology of emotional disorders associated with brain damage. In Vincken PJ, Bruyn GN (Eds), *Handbook of Clinical Neurology. Vol. 3: Disorders of Higher Nervous Activity.* Amsterdam: Elsevier, pp. 343 – 367, 1969.

Pribram KH, McGuiness D: Arousal, activation, and effort in the control of attention. *Psychol. Rev.: 82,* 116 – 149, 1975.

Reisenzein R: The Schachter theory of emotion: two decades later. *Psychol. Bull.: 94,* 239 – 264, 1983.

Rinn WE: The neuropsychology of facial expression: a review of the neurological and psychological mechanisms for producing facial expressions. *Psychol. Bull.: 95,* 52 – 77, 1984.

Ross ED, Mesulam MM: Dominant language functions in the right hemisphere? *Arch. Neurol.: 36,* 144 – 148, 1979.

Rozin P, Fallon AP: A perspective on disgust. *Psychol. Rev. 94,* 23 – 41, 1987.

Russell JA, Woudzia L: Affective judgments, common sense and Zajonc's thesis of independence. *Motivation Emotion 10,* 169 – 183, 1986.

Rutledge LL, Hupka RB: The facial feedback hypothesis: Methodological concerns and new supporting evidence. *Motivation Emotion: 9,* 219 – 240, 1985.

Sackeim HA, Greenberg MS, Weiman AL, Gur RC, Hungerbuhler JP, Geschwind N: Hemispheric asymmetry in the expression of positive and negative emotions. *Arch. Neurol. 39,* 210 – 218, 1982.

Schachter S: The assumption of identity and peripheralist-centralist controversies in motivation and emotion. In Arnold M (Editor), *Feelings and Emotions.* New York/London: Academic Press, pp. 111 – 121, 1970.

Schachter S, Singer J: Cognitive, social, and physiological determinants of emotional state. *Psychol. Rev.: 69,* 379 – 399, 1962.

Scherer KR: On the nature and function of emotion: a component process approach. In Scherer KR, Ekman P (Editors), *Approaches to Emotion.* Hillsdale, NJ: Lawrence Erlbaum, pp. 293 – 317, 1984.

Scherer KR, Tannenbaum PH: Emotional experiences in everyday life: a survey approach. *Motivation Emotion: 10,* 295 – 314, 1986.

Schwartz GE, Brown SL, Ahern GL: Facial muscle patterning and subjective experience during affective imagery: sex differences. *Psychophysiology: 17,* 75 – 82, 1980.

Seyfarth RM, Cheney DL: The natural vocalizations of non-human primates. *Trends Neurosci.: 7,* 66 – 73, 1984.

Shaver P, Schwartz J, Kirson D, O'Connor C: Emotion knowledge: further exploration of a prototype approach. *J. Pers. Soc. Psychol.: 52,* 1061 – 1086, 1987.

Shields SA: Distinguishing between emotion and non emotion. Judgments about experience. *Motivation Emotion: 8,* 355 – 369, 1984.

Simon HA: Motivational and emotional controls of cognition. *Psychol. Rev.: 74,* 29 – 39, 1967.

Smith CA, Ellsworth PC: Patterns of cognitive appraisal in emotion. *J. Pers. Soc. Psychol.: 48,* 813 – 838, 1985.

Sroufe A: The organization of emotional development. In Scherer KR, Ekman P (Editors), *Approaches to Emotion.* Hillsdale, NJ: Lawrence Erlbaum, pp. 109 – 128, 1984.

Strauss E, Wada J, Kosaka B: Spontaneous facial expressions occurring at the onset of focal seizure activity. *Arch. Neurol.: 40,* 545 – 547, 1983.

Strayer J: Children's attributions regarding the situational determinants of emotion in self and others. *Dev. Psychol.: 22,* 649 – 654, 1986.

Strongman KT: *The Psychology of Emotion.* New York: Wiley, 1973.

Toates FM, Archer J: A comparative review of motivational systems using classical control theory. *Anim. Behav.:* 26, 368 – 380, 1978.

Tomkins SS: *Affect, Imagery, and Consciousness. Vol. 1: The Positive Affects. Vol. 2: The Negative Affects.* New York/London: Tavistock/Springer, 1962.

Tomkins SS: Affect as amplification: some modifications in theory. In Plutchik R, Kellerman H (Editors), *Emotion: Theory, Research, Experience. Vol. 1. Theories of Emotion.* New York/London: Academic Press, pp. 141 – 164, 1980.

Tomkins SS: Affect theory. In Scherer KR, Ekman P (Editors), *Approaches to Emotion.* Hillsdale, NJ: Lawrence Erlbaum, pp. 163 – 195, 1984.

Tourangeau R, Ellsworth PC: The role of facial response in the experience of emotion. *J. Pers. Soc. Psychol.: 37,* 1519 – 1531, 1979.

Tucker DM: Lateral brain function, emotion and conceptualization. *Psychol. Bull.: 89,* 19 – 46, 1981.

Tucker DM, Williamson PA: Asymmetric neural control systems in human self-regulation. *Psychol. Rev.: 91,* 185 – 215, 1984.

Valins S: Cognitive effects of false heart-rate feedback. *J. Pers. Soc. Psychol.: 4,* 400 – 408, 1966.

Whissell CM: Emotion: A classification of current literature. *Percept. Motor Skills: 54,* 589 – 599, 1984.

Wiley RH: The evolution of communication: information and manipulation. In Halliday TR, Slater PJB (Editors), *Animal Behaviour, Vol. 2: Communication.* Oxford: Blackwell Scientific Publications, pp. 156 – 189, 1983.

Winton WM: The role of facial response in self reports of emotion: a critique of Laird. *J. Pers. Soc. Psychol.: 50,* 808 – 812, 1986.

Young PT: Emotion as disorganized response: a reply to professor Lepper. *Psychol. Rev.: 56,* 184 – 191, 1949.

Zajonc RB: Feeling and thinking: Preferences need no inferences. *Am. Psychol.: 35,* 151 – 175, 1980.

Zajonc RB: On the primacy of affect. *Am. Psychol.: 39,* 117 – 123, 1984.

Zajonc RB, Markus H: Affect and cognition: The hard interface. In Izard CE, Kagan J, Zajonc RB (Editors), *Emotion, Cognition, and Behavior.* Cambridge: Cambridge University Press, pp. 73 – 102, 1984.

Zillman D: Transfer of excitation in emotional behavior. In Cacioppo JT, Petty RE (Editors), *Social Psychophysiology: A Sourcebook.* New York/London: Guilford, pp. 215 – 240, 1983.

Zoccolotti P, Scabini D, Violani C: Electrodermal responses in patients with unilateral brain damage. *J. Clin. Neuropsychol.: 4,* 143 – 150, 1982.

© 1989 Elsevier Science Publishers B.V. (Biomedical Division)
Handbook of Neuropsychology, Vol. 3
F. Boller and J. Grafman (Eds)

CHAPTER 13

Anatomical substrate of emotional reactions

Giorgio Macchi

Institute of Neurology, Catholic University, Policlinico Gemelli, Largo A. Gemelli, 8, 00168 Rome, Italy

Phylogenetic considerations

The phylogenetic origins of what in mammals may be considered as the anatomical substrate of emotional reactions, i.e. the so-called 'limbic system', can be found in the telencephalic structures (rhinencephalon*) of submammals, which are closely related to the olfactory afferents and to the hypothalamic structures. In the reptile telencephalon, for instance (Crosby 1917), we find a dorsal-lateral pallial structure dominated by the olfactory afferents (palaeopallium), a dorso-medial structure (archipallium), also involved with the olfactory afferents but also closely connected with the hypothalamus and, lastly, subpallial structures (n. accumbens, anterior olfactory nucleus) linked to the olfactory and hypothalamic formations. A rudimentary outline of neocortex (general cortex, Crosby, 1917) rises between the dorso-medial cortex (archipallium or hippocampus) and the dorso-lateral cortex (paleopallium or olfactory cortex) (Fig. 1A). Its lateralmost portion receives thalamic afferents and thus represents a primitive system of thalamo-cortical relay (Butler, 1976), foreshadowing the mammal neocortex (general cortex), while its more medial portion is connected to the archipallial and palaeopallial cortex and the septo-hypothalamic region: it thus apparently belongs to the rhinencephalon. In mammals the insertion of the cingular and parahippocampal cortex, corresponding to the limbic lobe of Broca** (1878) (Figs. 1B,C and 2) is anatomo-functionally located between the hypothalamus and the rhinencephalon, on the one hand, and the neocortex, on the other (Beccari, 1943), thus forming one further level of limbic organization.

This level, found all the way up the mammal phylogenetic scale, is devoted to the integration of the rhinencephalic activities as they become increasingly independent of the olfactory afferents during the transition from macrosmatic mammals to microsmatic mammals (primates and man) and more and more closely related to the hypothalamic and brain stem activities as well as with more strict-

---

* In its original meaning the term 'rhinencephalon' (olfactory brain) includes the structures of the base of the encephalon connected with the olfactory sensory pathways, i.e. the areas of primary projection of the olfactory radiations originating in the olfactory bulb (Table 1). Taking the comparative anatomic (Beccari, 1943) and ontogenetic (Macchi, 1951) evidence into account, the rhinencephalic formations which, in non-mammal vertebrates, are reached by the olfactory radiations include not only the anterior olfactory n., the olfactory tubercle, the olfactory cortex (palaeocortex) and amygdala but in addition the septal region and the rostral hippocampus (archicortex). Therefore, if we follow a phylogenetic criterion, the rhinencephalic structures of mammals also include the ammonic formation and the septum even though they are not directly reached by the olfactory tracts.

** Historically, this term was coined by Broca (1878) and was used to refer to the portion of cortex dorsally enveloping the corpus callosum and which ventrally closes the hemispheric ilum in the form of a semi-circle and extends into the gyrus hyppocampi. These formations, sometimes referred to as paralimbic at the present time, are instead the actual structures previously attributed to the limbic lobe and which therefore retain the right to represent a fundamental part of the limbic system.

ly neocortical activities. Therefore, in mammals the '*limbic system*', which, according to Nauta (1986), 'is a collective and functionally neutral term denoting a heterogeneous group of neural structures arranged along the medial edge of the cerebral hemisphere (limbus) and having at its core the allocortex hippocampus and the largely subcortical amygdala', has three main levels of anatomical organization.

Level one is centered on the hypothalamus and its rostral and caudal connections; level two is

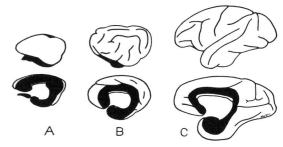

Fig. 2. Development of the limbic lobe in three animal species on the medial surface of the hemisphere in the phylogenetic evolution of the mammals's brain. The drawings are illustrative of Broca's observations that the limbic lobe is a common denominator of the brains of all mammals. A, rabbit; B, cat; C, monkey. From MacLean, 1954.

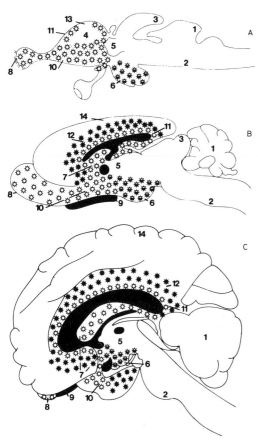

Fig. 1. Diagrammatic representation of the phylogenetic development of the limbic system in reptiles (A), mammals (rabbit, B) and man (C). (1) cerebellum, (2) brain stem, (3) mesencephalon, (4) basal ganglia, (5) thalamus, (6) hypothalamus, (7) septum, (8) olfactory bulb, (9) olfactory tract, (10) palaeopallium, (11) archipallium, (12) limbic lobe, (13) primordium neocortex (general pallium), (14) neopallium. Half stars, hypothalamus; white stars, rhinencephalon, black stars, limbic lobe.

represented mainly by the rhinencephalon, which is made up of the olfactory brain consisting of the olfactory bulb and its projections onto the olfactory cortex (prepyriform cortex, olfactory tubercle), the hippocampal formation (subiculum, Ammon's Horn and the fascia dentata), the amygdaloid complex, the septo-diagonal area; level three consists of the limbic lobe (gyrus cinguli and gyrus parahippocampi) and its connections with the hypothalamus and the rhinencephalon, on the one hand, and the neocortex, on the other. We shall now examine several important '*associated structures*' (see Mesulam, 1985) which have special relations with the limbic system and may therefore be included in an *enlarged limbic system*'. These consist of the ventral striopallidum (including the n. accumbens), the orbito-frontal-insular and polar temporal paralimbic areas, the anterior, dorso-lateral, medial portion of the dorso-medial and midline nuclei of the thalamus, the habenular complex and the brain stem nuclei, several of which have specific neurotransmitters (serotoninergic, noradrenergic, dopaminergic) (Table 1; Figs. 1, 3 and 4).

The phylogenetic development of the limbic system and associated structures is based on a general principle of nervous system organization in which, at each stage of development, the integration between the old and the new substratum is expressed through a reciprocal morpho-functional control. This implies that the 'command systems' of emotional reactions can change their behavioural expression as a function of the rostral extension of the neoencephalic structures, the more highly qualified substratum of which is located in the thalamo-cortical organization. Consequently, emotional reactions corresponding to the terms of *expectancy, fear, anger* and *panic* described by Panksepp (1982) as the four fundamental emotions (Fig. 5) share a common substratum in the basic organization of the three levels described above. However, emotional processing can differ in the rat, the cat, the monkey and in man in close relation to the development of the centres triggering the emotional reaction (e.g. perceptive centres) and centres affecting its behavioural expression at the motor, symbolic and psychic levels. In this sense, the terms of *expectan-*

TABLE I

Limbic system

Hypothalamus

Rhinencephalon
- Archicortex (hippocampus)
- Area olfactoria
  - Olfactory bulb
  - Anterior olfactory N.
  - Prepiriform cortex
  - Olfactory tubercle
- Amygdala
- Septo-diagonal area

Limbic lobe
- Cingular gyrus
- Parahippocampal gyrus

Associated structures

Ventral strio-pallidum

Paralimbic cortical areas
- Orbito-frontal cortex
- Insula
- Rostral temporal cortex

Limbic thalamic nuclei
- Medial part of medio-dorsal N.
- Midline NN.
- Anterior NN.
- Latero-dorsal N.

Habenular complex

Brain stem nuclei
- Serotoninergic neurons
- Noradrenergic neurons
- Dopaminergic neurons
- Periaqueductal gray
- Ventral and dorsal tegmental N.N.
- Interpeduncular N.
- Reticular tegmental pontine N.
- Parabrachial NN.
- Dorsal motor n. of the vagus
- N. of the solitary tract

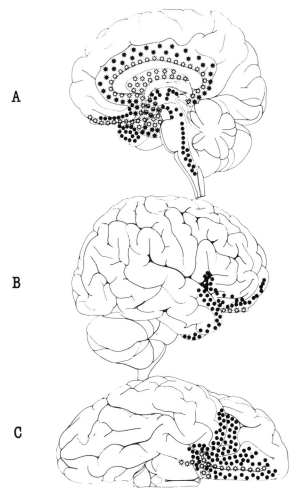

Fig. 3. Diagrammatic representation of the limbic system and associated structures on the medial-lateral and ventral surface of the cerebral hemisphere and the brain stem of man. Half stars, hypothalamus; white stars, rhinencephalon; black stars, limbic lobe; black circles, associated structures.

cy, fear, anger and *panic,* used either separately or in combination, cover a wide range of emotional behaviour observed also in man.

As Panksepp (1982) claims, the term expectancy could be replaced by that of desire or quest, which presupposes an appetite or consummatory action in its various forms (food, sex, knowledge), the performance of which leads to pleasure, joy and satisfaction, while failure to carry it out leads to unhappiness, pain, etc. Such expressions include a wide range of typically human emotional reactions.

Likewise, according to Panksepp, the panic reaction is indicative of distress verging on pain,

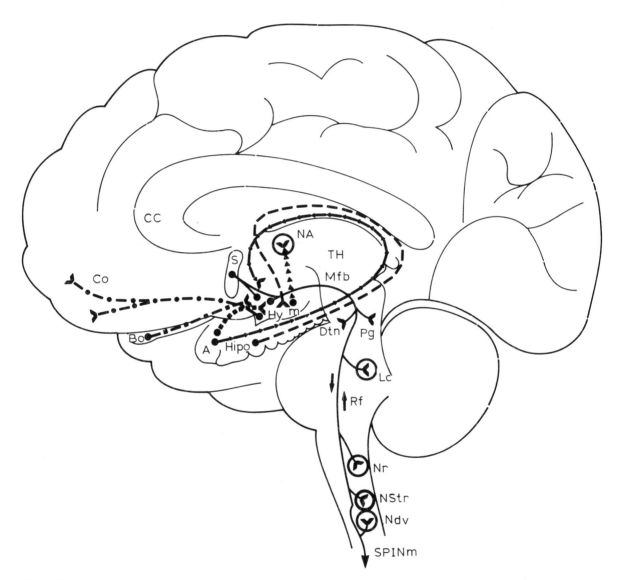

Fig. 4. Diagrammatic representation of the essential connections of the hypothalamus. Abbreviations: A, amygdaloid complex; B, olfactory bulb; CC, corpus callosum; Co, cerebral cortex; DTn, tegmental nuclei of the mesencephalon; Hipo, Hippocampus; Hy, Hypothalamus; Lc, Locus coeruleus; m, mammillary bodies; Mfb, medial forebrain bundle; NA, anterior nucleus of the thalamus; Ndv, dorsal nucleus of the vagus nerve; Nr, raphe nuclei; NStr, nucleus of the solitary tract; Pg, periaqueductal gray; Rf, reticular formation; SPINm, spinal cord; S, septum; TH, thalamus.

sadness and affliction. There are also other more complex (polyvalent) emotions involving more than one basic emotion, e.g. jealousy, which is made up of various components such as desire (expectancy), anger, fear, panic or shame, which is a mixture of fear and lack of self-esteem (panic reaction).

Levels of morphological organization of the limbic system

The first level of organization of the limbic system is the hypothalamus (see references in Nieuwenhuys et al., 1980; Brodal, 1981; Holstege, 1987). Cytoarchitecturally, it consists of three separate zones: periventricular and infundibular, medial (anterior, intermediate, and posterior or mammillary) and lateral (lateral hypothalamic region) and a rostral extension, the preoptic region.

The main connecting pathways are as follows (Fig. 4):

(1) the medial forebrain bundle (m.f.b.) joining the lateral preoptic-hypothalamic area rostrally to the rhinencephalon (olfactory brain and septo-diagonal area) and caudally to the associated mesencephalic limbic structures, thus forming a functionally homogeneous 'meso-limbic' circuit (Nauta, 1958);

(2) the dorsal longitudinal bundle, running from the posterior hypothalamus to the medulla

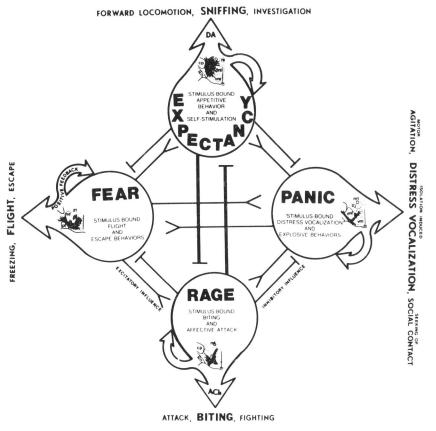

Fig. 5. Diagrammatic representation of the four basic emotions described by Panksepp and location of their hypothalamic command circuits in the brain of the rat. Abbreviations: cp, cerebral peduncle; dm, dorso-medial nucleus, mf, medial forebrain bundle; mt, mammillo-thalamic tract; ot, optic tract; re, n. reuniens; vm, ventro-medial nucleus; x, fornix; zi, zona incerta (reproduced from Panksepp, 1982, with kind permission of the author).

oblongata in a periventricular position (Nauta, 1958);

(3) the postcommissural fornix connecting the ventro-medial (mammillary) hypothalamic area with the hippocampal formation (especially the subiculum and Cal) (Swanson and Cowan, 1977);

(4) the stria terminalis and the ventral amygdalofugal projection bundles, which represent the main pathways between the lateral preoptic-hypothalamic zone and the ventro-medial and premammillary hypothalamus and the amygdaloid complex (Krettek and Price, 1978; Sarter and Markowitsch, 1985);

(5) the pathways between the mammillary hypothalamus and the anterior thalamus (mammillo-thalamic bundle) and the mesencephalic tegmental nuclei (mammillo-tegmental bundle);

(6) pathways between the habenular complex and the ponto-bulbar nuclei of the brain stem (see refs. in Brodal, 1981).

The second level of organization of the limbic system, the rhinencephalon, consists of four strategic centres composed of:

(A) *olfactory brain* (olfactory bulb, prepyriform cortex, anterior olfactory nucleus, olfactory tubercle),

(B) *septo-diagonal area,*

(C) amygdaloid complex and the *'bed nucleus of the stria terminalis'* (Holstege et al., 1985),

(D) the *hippocampal formation*. Simplified diagrams of the main connections of the amygdaloid complex, septo-diagonal area, and hippocampal formation are shown in Figs. 6, 7 and 8.

The area of olfactory projection reached by the olfactory tracts from the olfactory bulb and from the anterior olfactory nucleus is composed of the prepyriform 'allocortex' (paleocortex in the phylogenetic meaning of the term). The latter has a cytoarchitectural structure consisting of only two layers of cortex, an outer one made up of small triangular cells, and a deeper one occupied by pyramidal cells and granular clusters (Calleja's

islets) in the region of the olfactory tubercle.

The septo-diagonal area groups together several nuclear masses: the medial, lateral and dorsal septal nuclei, and the nucleus of the diagonal band, which continues ventrally and superficially into the diagonal area with rudimentary cortical structure

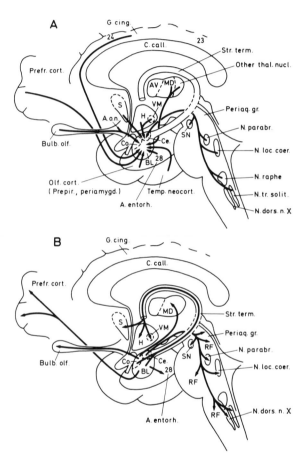

Fig. 6. Diagrammatic representation of the main afferents (A) and efferent (B) connections of the amygdaloid complex. See text for particulars. Abbreviations: AV, anteroventral thalamic n.; MD, dorso-medial thalamic n., H, hypothalamus; VM, ventromedial hypothalamic n.; BL, basolateral amygdaloid n.; Ce, central amygdaloid n.; Co, cortical amygdaloid n.; SN, substantia nigra; Prefr, prefrontal cortex; Bulb olf, olfactory bulb; olf cort, olfactory cortex; A entorh, area entorhinalis; temp. neocort, temporal neocortex; Str term, stria terminalis; Periaq gr., periacqueductal gray; N parabr., nucleus parabrachialis; N. loc. coer., nucleus locus coeruleus; G cing, cingular gyrus; N. Tr. solit, nucleus tract solitarii; RF, reticular formation; S, septum. (Reproduced with permission from Dr. A. Brodal.)

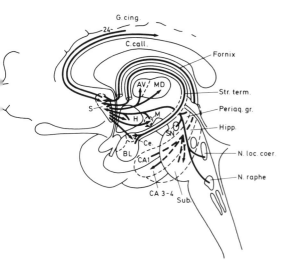

Fig. 7. Diagrammatic representation of the main afferent and efferent connections of the septal nuclei. Abbreviations: M, mammillary body; for the other abbreviations see legend to Fig. 6. CA1-CA-3-4, laminae of the Ammon's horn; sub, subiculum.

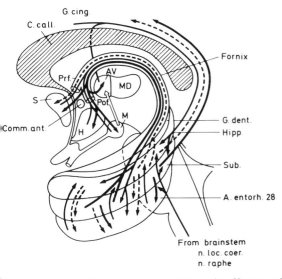

Fig. 8. Diagrammatic representation of the main afferent and efferent connections of the hippocampus. In the fornix the efferent fibers from the hippocampus proper (broken lines) supply the septal nuclei passing through the precommissural fornix. Efferent fibers from the subiculum (thick lines) follow the postcommissural fornix until the end stations. For abbreviations see legends to Figs. 6 and 7. See text for details. (Reproduced with permission from Brodal, 1981.)

and deeply into the Meynert's magnocellular nucleus.

The amygdaloid complex is also subdivided into several nuclear divisions (central, medial, lateral, medial and lateral basal, cortical, anterior amygdaloid area and nucleus of the lateral-olfactory tract).

Lastly, the *hippocampal formation* (archicortex) is an allocortical structure coiled up in the cavity of the temporal horn of the lateral ventricles. It includes three main elements: fascia dentata (deeper lying), Ammon's Horn (which stands out in the cavity of the ventricular horn) and the subiculum, which acts as an area of transition with the gyrus parahippocampi (Fig. 9). Ammon's horn consists of an efferent layer of pyramidal cells arranged in

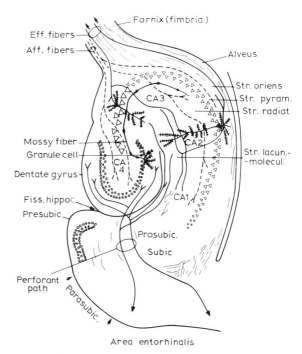

Fig. 9. Schematic drawing illustrating some main features in the organization of the hippocampal formation. The transverse section (medial to the left) shows the sequential arrangement of the following structures: dentate gyrus, areas CA4, CA3, CA2 and CA1 of the hippocampus proper, subiculum (with prosubiculum, presubiculum and parasubiculum) and entorhinal areas. The main cellular elements and layers in the dentatus gyrus and the hippocampus are shown. (Reproduced with some modifications from Brodal, 1981.)

topographically differentiated sheets (Cal-Ca2-Ca3-Ca4), whose axons extend outside the hippocampus through the alveus and the fimbria, while the apical dendrites are reached by the muscoid fibres, i.e. by the neurites originating in the fascia dentata (see refs. in Brodal, 1981). At the anatomical level, the four strategic rhinencephalic centres are characterized (1) by close connections between the various sectors examined, and (2) by extrinsic connections with the other limbic levels (hypothalamus, limbic lobe) and the various associated structures.

The *intrinsic* pathways (to the rhinencephalon) include:

(1) The pathways between the olfactory brain and the amygdala (nuclei of the lateral olfactory tract, medial n., central n.) and the parahippocampal gyrus (entorhinal cortex) (Lohman and Lammers, 1963; Room and Groenewegen, 1986).

(2) The cholinergic pathways between the hippocampus and the septodiagonal area (precommissural fornix) (see refs. in Brodal, 1981).

(3) The connections of the amygdala with the septo-diagonal area and the hippocampal subiculum (Krettek and Price, 1977a,b).

The most important *extrinsic* preferential pathways with the other limbic structures and associated structures are:

(1) Those between the olfactory brain and the hypothalamus (Scott and Leonard, 1971) and the dorso-medial n. of the thalamus (Heimer, 1972).

(2) Those between the amygdaloid complex and the hypothalamus (stria terminalis, ventral amygdalo-fugal projection bundle (Krettek and Price, 1978), the limbic lobe (entorhino-amygdaloid and cingulo-amygdaloid pathways (Krettek and Price, 1977a) and various associated structures: n. accumbens, pallidum ventralis (Nauta, 1986), dorso-medial n. of the thalamus (Krettek and Price, 1977a; Aggleton and Mishkin, 1984), nuclei of the brainstem, paralimbic and extralimbic cortices (neo-

cortex) (Krettek and Price, 1977a,b, 1978, Llamas et al., 1977; Macchi et al., 1978). See Fig. 6 for a survey of these connections.

(3) The pathways between the septo-diagonal area and the hypothalamus (medial forebrain bundle), the habenular complex, the medial thalamus, the limbic lobe (cingulate cortex), the brain stem (see refs. in Brodal 1981) and the Meynert n. (Aggleton et al., 1987). These connections are represented in Fig. 7.

(4) The connections of the hippocampus and the septum with the hypothalamus (see above) and the limbic lobe, in particular the *entorhinal area* through the perforating bundles directed towards the apical dendrites of the granular cells of the fascia dentata and the efferent fibers to the entorhinal cortex coming from Ca, and subiculum (see refs. in Van Groen et al., 1986; Witter et al., 1986). The most important pathways to the associated structures include the hippocampal-thalamic (n. reuniens, Yamagihara et al., 1985; Aggleton and Mishkin, 1986) and the hippocampal-mesencephalic bundles (Nauta, 1958). Some of these connections are shown in Fig. 8.

Level three of the limbic organization, the limbic lobe, comprises the gyrus cingularis, which surrounds the corpus callosum, and *the gyrus parahippocampi,* which is in close anatomic relation with the hippocampus. Architecturally, it is characterized by the cingulate cortex (mesocortex, Rose, 1926; or periarchicortex, Stephan, 1964), which approaches, but does not correspond to, the lamination observed in neocortex (prevalence of pyramidal layers), and by a parahippocampal (entorhinal and presubicular) cortex, with a structure intermediate between the paleocortex and the neocortex. This cortex is characterized by an external sheet of triangular and stellate cells and a main internal layer of pyramidal, fusiform and polymorphous cells. Between the two layers lies a plexiform layer rich in fibres and with only a few cells (lamina dissecans; Rose, 1926). The stratification of the posterior portion of the parahippocampal gyrus (proisocortex) in the primates resembles that of the cingulate cortex (mesocortex). The cingulate area is connected mainly with the thalamic afferents (thalamo-cingular pathways) coming from the anterior nuclei, n. reuniens and n. lateralis dorsalis. It also sends fibers to the precommissural fornix, and is connected with the septo-diagonal area and the ventral striato-pallidum, the hypothalamus and the brain stem nuclei (Fig. 10).

The parahippocampal cortex is connected not only to the cingulate cortex (Witter and Groenewegen, 1986a) but also to the rhinencephalon (hippocampus, amygdala, septo-diagonal regions) and to some associated structures of the thalamus and brain stem (Witter and Groenewegen, 1986b; Insausti et al., 1987).

Both sectors (cingular and parahippocampal) of the limbic lobe are also well connected with the Meynert n. (Mesulam, 1985), the paralimbic (orbito-fronto-temporo-insular) cortical areas and the uni- and multimodal prefrontal and parasensory associative areas (Van Hoesen, 1982; Pandya and Seltzer, 1982; Pandya and Yeterian, 1984) (Fig. 10). The great extension of these pathways during the transition from the lower mammals to the primates emphasizes an ever-increasing interdependence between the emotional structures and the highest levels of information-processing

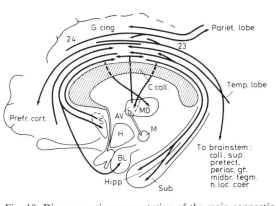

Fig. 10. Diagrammatic representation of the main connections of the cingular gyrus. M, mammillary body. The mammillo-thalamic bundle is indicated by the white arrow. For abbreviations see legends to Figs. 6–8. (Reproduced with permission from Brodal, 1981.)

and of decision-making, mediated by the neocortical centers.

Summing up the above anatomical evidence it could be concluded that an overall organization plan exists which enables the *three sectors* of the limbic system (as such) to be extensively interconnected and to have special links with the associated structures.

For example, at the level of *intralimbic pathways,* the olfactory brain is monosynaptically connected with the amygdala and the entorhinal cortex but not with the hippocampus. On the other hand, the amygdala is directly connected both to the olfactory brain and to the septo-diagonal area, and only with the subiculum of the hippocampus. The limbic lobe is connected with *all* the rhinencephalic sectors by means of well-defined preferential channels: (1) from the gyrus cinguli to the septo-diagonal area; (2) from the parahippocampal area to the amygdaloid complex, the septo-diagonal region and the hippocampus. Lastly, *all* the sectors of the rhinencephalon and of the limbic lobe are connected to either the same or to different sectors of the hypothalamus.

With regard to the *'associated' structures* there exist *diffuse* pathways between all the levels of the limbic system and the brain stem structures but also differentiated pathways, e.g. between the hypothalamus, the hippocampus, the septo-diagonal area, the amygdala and the limbic lobe and various thalamic structures; or between the limbic lobe, the amygdala and the hypothalamus and the paralimbic cortical areas, the n. accumbens and the ventral strio-pallidum (limbic strio-pallidal complex). Lastly, the limbic lobe and the amygdala, unlike other sectors of the limbic system, are linked by special pathways with the prefrontal and temporo-parietal-occipital cortical areas. Besides, it should be noted that: (1) specific neurotransmitter pathways mostly coming from the brain stem (ventral a. of Tsai (Albanese and Minciacchi, 1983), locus coerulus, raphe nuclei), are extensively afferent to the limbic system; (2) several intralimbic links are served by specific neurotransmitters (septo-hippocampal and septoamygdaloid cholinergic systems); (3) certain structures such as the amygdala and the hypothalamus are particularly rich in acetylcholine, gaba and various kinds of peptides, which are distributed differently in the various cytoarchitectonic subdivisions considered (Sarter and Markowitch, 1985).

Experimental stimulation and lesions

The relationship between the three-tier morphological organization of the limbic system and the neuropsychological responses that may be obtained with stimulation and demolition experiments carried out in various mammal species may be summed up as follows:

Stimulation experiments

(a) Behavioural responses corresponding 'mainly' to the four types of instinctive-emotional reaction described by Panksepp, i.e. 'expectancy', 'anger', 'fear', 'panic'. They appear in the form of extensive modifications of behaviour which may express only alertness and surprise, or else be transformed into attitudes of anger, aggressiveness, fear, flight or, on the other hand, pleasure.

These reactions can obviously be observed in unanaesthetized animals or, better still, ones which have implanted electrodes and are thus free to move. In the 'attention and surprise' response (heightened vigilance) a moving animal will stop still, or else take an attitude of particular alertness if already motionless, looking around as if something new had entered its perceptual field. This behaviour is usually accompanied by changes in breathing (inhibition followed by acceleration) and in pupillary reaction (midriasis). Sometimes the animal looks around, usually turning to the side ipsilateral to the direction of the stimulus, as though to seek something by means of oriented movements (Ursin and Kaada, 1960).

In the fear and aggressiveness response, the animal (e.g. the cat) takes up a defensive or aggressive attitude, grinding its teeth and trying to

bite even when not provoked; it makes typical 'grognements' and 'felissements', arching its back and lashing out with open claws; the pupils are midriatic and fur is bristling.

(b) Feeding habits. This refers to the modifications induced in behaviour leading to food intake and to the conditioned response of feeding or inhibition of feeding.

(c) Oral automatisms. These are typical responses reproducing the attitudes adopted by the animal when it is engaged in normal food-seeking and intake activities. This category includes the act of sniffing and nuzzling objects encountered by the animal, licking and chewing and swallowing movements.

(d) Somatomotor responses. These consist of true kinetic effects involving a small number of related muscles (facial contractions, eye and eyebrow movements) or a wider range of muscles (limb movements). Otherwise they consist of more complex acts such as tonic contralateral head and trunk rotation or the activation of synergic muscle groups involved in phonation (vocalization) or breathing (inhibition or acceleration of breathing rate).

(e) Vegetative and endocrine phenomena. These include the neurovegetative effects on the visceral motor functions (pupil diameter, gastrointestinal peristalsis, uterine motility, hair erection, urination and defecation), circulatory functions (increased or reduced pressure, pulse quickening or slackening) and secretory functions (salivation).

Furthermore, a number of endocrine modifications have also been reported (ovulation, release of ACTH and increase in the 17-ketosteroid content, modification of the hypothalamic secretion, hyperglycaemia).

(1) As far as the behavioural responses of greatest emotional significance are concerned, all the types of response which can be obtained by stimulation of the first level of limbic organization (*hypothalamus*) are characterized by taking on a different aspect depending on the point of stimulation, without excluding the possible overlapping of similar responses for different stimulated points.

non-specific component). This emerges clearly from Panksepp's (1982) description in which the stimulation of the lateral and dorsolateral hypothalamus, the rostral and caudal pathway of which is represented above all by the m.f.b., is considered to be closely linked to the manifestation of expectancy and exploratory activity on the one hand, and of anger on the other, with considerable overlap. On the other hand, stimulation of the antero-ventral and antero-basal hypothalamus, which is related essentially to the amygdaloid complex (stria terminalis, ventral amygdalofugal projection), is associated respectively with Panksepp's

flight and panic reactions (Figs. 5 and 11).

(2) In the case of stimulation of the second level of limbic organization (*rhinencephalon*), different responses are observed according to the point of stimulation. These responses are mainly superimposable on the emotional responses observed after hypothalamic stimulation although the effect varies with the intensity of the stimulus, the animal species considered and the environment (see refs. in Macchi, 1968) (Fig. 11).

In stimulating the *amygdalo-pyriform region* and its links with the septo-diagonal, limbic strio-pallidal complex, preoptic-hypothalamic and

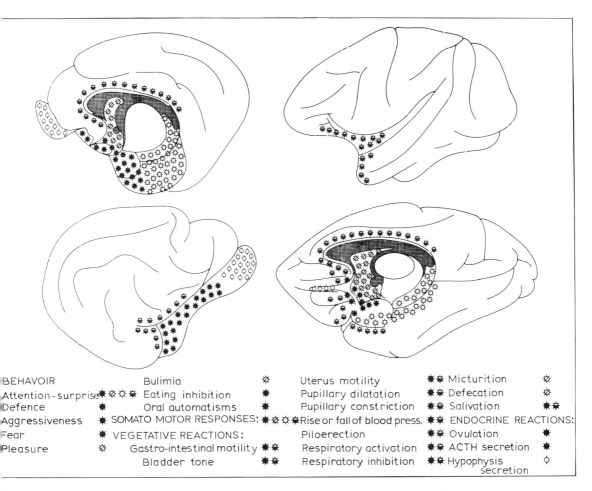

Fig. 11. Diagrammatic representation of the effect produced by stimulation of rhinencephalic and limbic lobe structures in the cat (left) and monkey (right). The different symbols indicate the telencephalic areas from which the various responses have been evoked. (Reproduced from Macchi, 1968.)

brain-stem regions (see Fig. 11), for instance, different responses are observed according to whether the baso-lateral, centro-medial or prepyriform-periamygdaloid regions are being stimulated, while by increasing the intensity of the stimulation an 'expectancy' response can be turned into an anger or a fear response.

In the 'expectancy' and 'surprise' response, different behavioural effects such as, for instance, the favouring or inhibiting of food, handling and the appearance of oral automatisms, can be induced by stimulating different nuclear subdivisions (basolateral n., central n., anterior amygdaloid area), while a different representation is used for the fear response (lateral n. and periamygdaloid area) and the anger response (baso-lateral and central n.) (Ursin and Kaada, 1960). Defence is believed to be dependent on the amygdalo-hypothalamic connections through the ventral amygdalofugal bundle (Zbrozyna, 1963) (see refs. in Macchi, 1968; Kaada, 1972; Brodal, 1981). On the other hand, according to Fonberg and Delgado (1961) emotional reactions are induced by stimulation of the whole dorso-medial region of the amygdala (central, medial, basal-parvocellular nuclei) and extend along the stria terminalis as far as the preoptic area and the rostral hypothalamus. This does not happen in the case of stimulation of the basal-magnocellular and lateral nuclei.

Fear and anger reactions and changes in sexual behaviour through amygdaloid stimulation have also been observed in man (Ferro-Milone et al., 1961; Gloor, 1986).

By stimulation of the *septo-diagonal area,* on the other hand, a pleasurable response is obtained which is the opposite of the fear or anger reaction obtained through amygdaloid stimulation and is associated with an inhibition of food-handling activity (Delgado, 1960).

Emotional responses are highly reduced by stimulation of the *hippocampal formation,* as they are limited to an 'alertness and surprise' reaction as long as the electrical activity (after discharge) due to stimulation of the hippocampus is restricted to the hippocampus itself (Carreras et al., 1958,

cat; Angeleri et al., 1961, man). Fear and anger reactions can be observed when the after-discharge spreads to other (hypothalamus, amygdala) structures (Kaada et al., 1961; Kaada, 1972; Brodal 1981).

Also somato-motor reactions such as facial contraction due to amygdaloid stimulation and coarse uni- or bilateral movements due to stimulation of the hippocampus and the septo-diagonal area can be observed via the connections with the associated pallido-striated limbic areas (Heimer et al., 1982) while endocrine and vegetative reactions are mainly caused by stimulation of the amygdalo-pyriform region (see refs. in Macchi, 1968; Poletti, 1986).

(3) Stimuli applied to level three of limbic organization (*limbic lobe*) can cause emotional responses, as in the case of hypothalamic and amygdaloid stimulation, but only when the stimulation is particularly intense and without any special relationship between the topography of the stimulated zone and the consequent effect. On the other hand, somatomotor and vegetative reactions are the ones most frequently observed after stimulation of the limbic lobe and the paralimbic structures (see refs. in Macchi, 1968; Brodal, 1981; Damasio and van Hoesen, 1983).

Effects of experimental lesions

As regards the effects of lesions of the three levels in question, no differences in emotional reactions were observed vis-à-vis the substrate under examination. The experimental material used consisted of marsupials, rats, cats, dogs and monkeys and the modifications induced by operations on the limbic system can be grouped as follows: (Fig. 12).

(1) Behaviour vis-à-vis the observer. The following were observed: (a) increased threshold of reaction to nociceptive stimuli, (b) reduced or non-existent fear and anger reaction, (c) aggressiveness, (d) docility and exaggerated affective reactions (cats typically purr, mew, rub themselves against the person and bite without intending to hurt).

(2) Behaviour vis-à-vis other animals of the same

pecies and of different species. The following
were observed: (a) increased contact reactions; (b)
hypersexuality: in such cases, hypersexual
behaviour takes the form of heterosexual and even
homosexual attitudes; (c) aggressiveness.

(3) Modification of appetite for food. The follow-
ing were observed: (a) hyperphagia or hypophagia,
(b) greedy search for food, (c) changed feeding
habits.

(4) Oral reactions. These include the whole range
of symptoms based on an exaggerated 'oral sinne',
and are characterized by: (a) continual concern
with sniffing at all the objects encountered by the
animal, (b) erroneous introduction into the oral
cavity of harmful objects, (c) exaggeration of oral
automatisms (licking oneself, sniffing, chewing,
swallowing).

(5) Visual reactions. (a) Manipulation of all the objects coming into the field of visual perception
(hypermetamorphosis), (b) visual agnosia (psychic

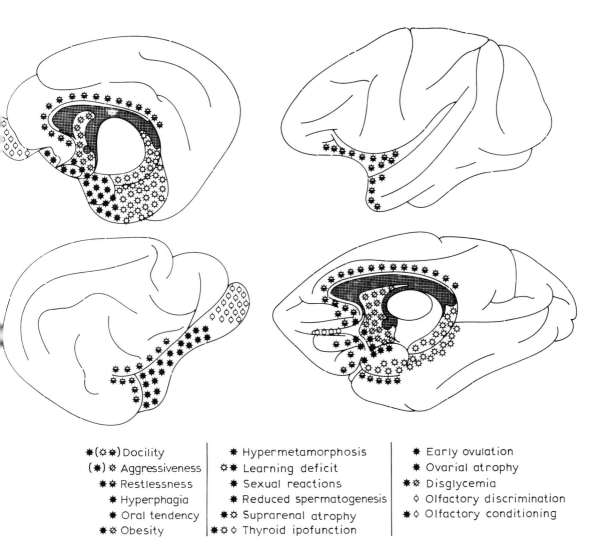

✸(✿✸) Docility	✸ Hypermetamorphosis	✸ Early ovulation
(✸) ✿ Aggressiveness	✿✸ Learning deficit	✸ Ovarial atrophy
✸✿ Restlessness	✸ Sexual reactions	✸✿ Disglycemia
✸ Hyperphagia	✸ Reduced spermatogenesis	◊ Olfactory discrimination
✸ Oral tendency	✸✿ Suprarenal atrophy	✸◊ Olfactory conditioning
✸✿ Obesity	✸✿◊ Thyroid ipofunction	

Fig. 12. Diagrammatic representation of the effects produced by rhinencephalic and limbic lobe ablations in the cat (left) and monkey (right). The symbols are as in Fig. 11. (Reproduced from Macchi, 1968.)

blindness).

(6) Postural modifications. These are generally manifested through a catatonoid and cataleptic attitude.

(7) Changes in motor behaviour. These consist above all of motor hypo- or hyperactivity.

(8) Modification of 'learning' and memory deficits.

(9) Modification of the vegetative and endocrino-metabolic functions. One group of symptoms includes changes both in nutrition and trophism (loss of weight and cachexia) or an abnormal accumulation of fat (obesity). A second group of symptoms is related to alterations observed in functional tests of endocrine and vegetative activity (glycaemic tolerance, reactions of the hypophysis-suprarenal axis, hormonal activation tests, testosterone administration, hypothermia) or of the function of the endocrine glands themselves.

Generally speaking, the *phenomena related to feeding, sexual and oral behaviour* are visible in the lesions caused above all at the level of the hypothalamus and the amygdalo-pyriform area (McLean, 1986) while docility and emotional indifference and, less frequently, aggressiveness, i.e. a *modification of the threshold of behaviour vis-à-vis man or individuals of the same species,* represent an emotional reaction that can be observed after lesions or ablations made at all three levels of limbic organization considered, or for lesions of several of the associated structures (e.g. paralimbic cortex). However, also in this case, effects are predominantly seen with level one and the amygdalo-pyriform region of level two (see refs. in Macchi, 1968; Magnus and Naquet, 1961; Passouant and Cadhilac, 1961; Brodal, 1981). Also worth mentioning are the contradictory reports often appearing in the literature which are due to the use of different species and different experimental methods.

In the *syndrome of Kluver and Bucy* (1937), achieved by means of a bilateral operation in the temporo-rhinencephalic region of primates, the symptoms related to instinctive-emotional behaviour (docility and increased emotional threshold, increased oral activity, hyperphagia and obesity, hypersexuality), which have also been confirmed in the subprimates (Macchi et al., 1963; see refs. in Macchi, 1968; Brodal, 1981) and in man (Terzian and Dalle Ore, 1955), appear after ablations performed at levels 2 and 3 of the limbic organization (rhinencephalic areas and gyrus parahippocampi), while visual agnosia (psychic blindness) has been broken down into two components (Cordeau, 1962): one of these consists of a deficit in visual discrimination and is caused by damage to the lateral temporal neocortex, while the other consists of a disturbance of memorization and is due to damage of the hippocampal-parahippocampal area (Fig. 13).

According to McLean (1961–1986), the fronto-temporal sector of the limbic system (which essentially comprises the amygdalo-pyriform zone and several associated structures) is a site of behaviour aimed at protecting the individual, while the septo-hippocampo-thalamo-cingular sector is the site of behaviour aimed at protecting the species.

A more radical view of the role played by basal temporo-diencephalic structures is that expressed by Poletti (1986). He views the ventral connections of the anterior hippocampus with the parahippocampal-amygdaloid structures, the hypothalamus and the brain stem as alternatives to the dorsal connections of the hippocampus via the fornix, the most suitable substrate for instinctive reactions linked to the preservation of the individual and the species and for memorization processes.

In experimental animals, as we shall see in the case of man, it is not often possible, except in small animals (Kaada et al., 1961), to make a separate evaluation of the parahippocampal and hippocampal component of the *memory deficit* (Scoville and Milner, 1957; Milner, 1965). This is doubtless one of the points to solve at the experimental level given the different phylogenetic position of one formation with respect to the other. However a recent anatomico-clinical contribution by Squire and Zola-Morgan (1988) would correlate the memory defect with a complete bilateral depletion of neurons in the CAI field of hippocampus.

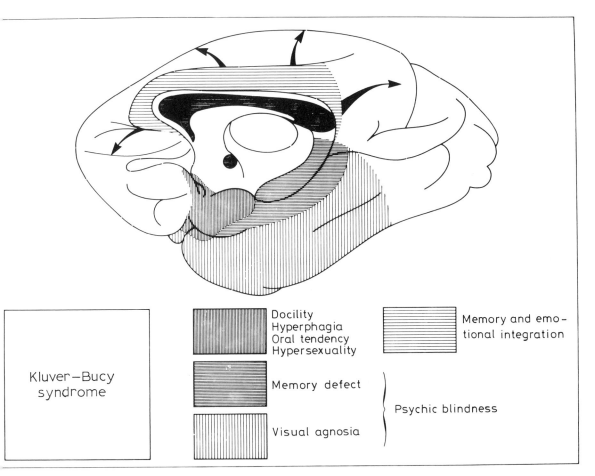

Fig. 13. Kluver and Bucy's syndrome. List of the symptoms related to the corresponding areas of the limbic system marked by the different symbols.

Likewise, a reappraisal will have to be made of the contribution of the amygdaloid complex and of the cingulate cortex and of their connections with the anterior and dorso-medial thalamus in memory processes (Mishkin, 1978; Markowitsch, 1982).

According to more recent literature, several components of the limbic system and associated structures are involved in memorization. For example, the persistence of mnemonic content is believed to be dependent on the hippocampo-parahippocampal structures (Zola-Morgan and Squire, 1986) and on the medial mammillo-thalamic structures (Aggleton and Mishkin, 1983a,b). On the other hand, the recording and recall of the signal to be memorized is thought to

depend on the action of other limbic system and associated structures. Therefore, the amygdala, which is connected to the parahippocampal cortex, the thalamus and the hippocampus, is believed to give the stimulus a special emotional significance, while the cingulate cortex would give the stimulus particular attention concerning its spatial location, performed in the hippocampal-parahippocampal structures (Pandya and Yeterian, 1984) (Fig. 12). The amygdalo-pyriform structures are known to be important in instinctive-emotional reactions and therefore in filtering the signals to be memorized more directly related to the individual's survival. On the other hand, cingular lesions can cause disorders of attention that can even attain

297

the level of akinetic mutism (Pandya and Yeterian, 1984).

On the basis of the above evidence a short comment can be made on Papez's (1937) concept of the 'anatomic bases of the emotions'. Since the 'emotional experience' can in no way be separated from the memory processes and since isolated lesions in the cingulate area do not cause the serious memory alterations found in the case of hippocampal-parahippocampal, mammillary and medial thalamic lesions (Aggleton and Mishkin, 1983a,b, 1985) but rather a reduction in emotional expression and a loss of interest in environmental stimuli (Messimy, 1965; see refs. in Brodal, 1981), it is likely that the cingulate areas are actually an area of convergence and integration of instinctive-emotional circuits connected to the anterior (olfacto-amygdaloid) rhinencephalon and hypothalamus, as well as of memory circuits connected to the parahippocampal-hippocampal-mammillo-thalamic areas (Fig. 10). This is confirmed by the abundant representation of the vegetative, endocrine and somatic functions (supplementary motor areas) and by the connections with the multimodal parasensory and prefrontal areas of the neocortex (Pandya and Yeterian, 1984) (Fig. 10). These functions are believed to affect the characterization of the mnemonic content and of the personality through special connections with level 3 of the limbic system (limbic lobe).

This interpretation also seems to be supported by the phylogenetic data, since the hippocampal and cingulate structures (limbic lobe) are known to have appeared at two different stages; the former are found in all the vertebrates, while the latter represent a structural level which appeared during the development of the neocortex and should therefore be considered the substrate most suitable for integrating the rhinencephalic functions with the neocortical ones.

In conclusion, at the experimental level, the anatomic substrate of the emotional circuits and related behavioural responses is located mainly in level one of the limbic system, in the amygdalo-pyriform-septal sector of level two and in the structures associated with them. On the other hand, mnemonic and learning activities depend mainly on the hippocampal-parahippocampal circuits connected to the amygdala, the hypothalamus and the anterior and medial thalamus, which are extensively represented in Papez's circuits.

The emotional and mnemonic learning activities are themselves integrated at the level of the limbic lobe (gyrus cinguli) through which they can influence the final behaviour by means of a special connection with the temporo-parieto-occipital and prefrontal centres of perception and operation (see Figs. 10 and 13).

We will, finally, recall that the anatomic substrate of the emotional reactions makes use of neurotransmitters which act specifically on some of the emotional content. For instance, the hyperactivity of the mesolimbic dopaminergic neurones connected to the fronto-orbitary cortex is known to cause anxiety, while a lesion of the dopaminergic pathways entering the cingulate cortex is believed to lead to a state of 'akinetic mutism' (Ross and Stewart, 1981). Likewise, the fear and anxiety threshold is lowered by the stimulation, or raised by the destruction, of the locus coeruleus (Kuhar, 1986). The septo-hippocampal cholinergic system, which is responsible for 'behavioural inhibition', is itself subject to modulation by the monoaminergic systems ascending from the brain stem (Kuhar, 1986). Lastly, it is worth mentioning the significant concentration of benzodiazepine receptors in the limbic system (particularly in the amygdala, the ventro-medial and mammillary hypothalamus and the anterior thalamus) and the changes in metabolism occurring in the prefronto-orbitary cortex and in the limbic system during anxiety and panic reactions (Kuhar, 1986).

Limbic pathology

Much of the experimental evidence outlined above concerning the substrate of emotional reactions has been confirmed by observations made in human pathology. The material of use for this pur-ose consists of lesions located in different areas of he limbic system, of paroxystic (epileptic) phenomena occurring at the level of epileptogenic foci situated inside the limbic system, and lastly of neurosurgical stimulation or demolition in several sectors of the limbic system (Table 2).

Since the critical phenomena ensuing from epileptic fits and stimulation performed on various limbic structures are dealt with by E. Strauss in Ch. 15 of the present volume, we shall discuss here only the consequences of localized lesions.

Lesions of the limbic system. These may have several causes of degenerative, vascular, traumatic, inflammatory or tumoral nature and may involve specific sectors of the limbic system (including also the associated structures). Otherwise they may involve numerous sectors of the limbic system and even be associated with diffuse lesions extending also into extralimbic areas. Let us consider the lesions occurring in four strategic points of the 'enlarged limbic system': (A) cingular; (B) fronto-orbitary; (C) temporo-medial; (D) inferomedial diencephalic; (E) hypothalamic.

Cingular lesions. According to a recent review by Damasio and Van Hoesen (1983) a bilateral lesion of the gyrus cinguli causes an affective disorder which precludes emotional expression and experience and all attempts to communicate them are impaired. In fact, spontaneous lesions, which are usually of a vascular nature owing to the involvement of the circulation of the anterior cerebral artery (Laplane et al., 1981), give rise to affective indifference and verbal aspontaneity even leading to 'akinetic mutism', in the absence of any true aphasic disorders. Unilateral lesions cause the same symptoms which, however, subsequently undergo total or partial remission.

Confirmation of the underlying function of the cingular circuits is found in surgical cingulectomy performed for psychiatric purposes as a result of its sedative effects on anxiety and psychomotor agitation (Le Beau and Parker, 1950) as well as in the cingular stimulations performed on epileptic subjects (Talairach et al., 1973). The latter result in increased alertness of the patient and induce an 'attention' reaction sometimes accompanied by an attitude of anxiety, sadness and fear. The close links with the supplementary motor area of the medial hemispheric surface can explain the special drive associated with stimulation of the cingular area and, on the other hand, the withdrawal from action in the case of lesions of the cingular area itself.

Lesions of the orbito-frontal paralimbic cortical areas. As in experiments involving primates (Butter et al., 1970), the effects previously reported by Kleist (1934) and subsequently observed in lesions of traumatic (apallic syndromes) or encephalitic origin (herpetic encephalitis) involving the fronto-orbitary regions have been confirmed also in man. They consist of a complex of symptoms which are opposite to those known to occur in cases of cingular lesion and which are characterized by the onset of punning, euphoria, irritability, intolerance and serious alterations of social behaviour (sexual disinhibition, boastfulness, etc.) (see refs. in Damasio and Van Hoesen, 1983).

Deep temporo-medial lesions. Deep temporo-medial lesions, which are normally associated with traumatic, vascular, tumoral or inflammatory pathology (temporo-limbic necrotizing encephalitis), with degenerative pathology (in this case associated with the involvement of other structures, for instance in Pick's disease), or else with neurosurgical demolition in epileptic subjects, are reminiscent of a symptomatology in many respects

TABLE 2

Pathology of the limbic system

Impairment of memory and learning
Alteration of emotional responses
Personality alterations
Akinetic mutism
Changes of autonomic responses

Paroxysmal disorders { Vegetative reactions
Emotional responses
Psychic disturbances
Amnesia
Motor disturbances

---

similar to that observed by Kluver and Bucy (1937) in an experimental model of primates (Fig. 13).

An essential component of this pathology is memory disturbance in the more posterior lesions, which may be observed in a transitory form in the so-called *'global transient amnesia'*, and in a definitive form in bilateral softening in the hippocampal-parahippocampal region (Grunthal, 1959; Van Buren and Borke, 1972; see refs. in Signoret, 1985). However, in the lesions involving the anteriormost sector together with the amygdala and associated structures, disturbances of instinctive behaviour arise. In man the most typical of them are 'oral tendencies', i.e. the tendency to grasp and bring to the mouth all objects which come to view, whether or not they are suitable for oral intake (see refs. in Poeck, 1969).

Other symptoms similar to those observed in Kluver and Bucy's syndromes in primates are found also in man, although with varying frequency and severity. They are also represented by 'tameness', as a result of which the subject becomes emotionally indifferent, by an alteration of the sex drive at both the verbal and the behavioural level, and by an exaggerated tendency to manipulate all objects falling within the visual field (hypermetamorphosis).

These phenomena, which according to Geschwind (1965) are determined by a 'limbic disconnection', are found in a more complex form and often with opposite characteristics in the 'limbic hyperconnections' syndrome observable in a paroxystic form during the crisis and which often persists during the interictal period in deep temporal focal epilepsy. According to Gloor (1986), the epileptogenic focus situated in the 'temporal lobe limbic system' and the stimulation of the temporal limbic structures in epileptic patients lead to the appearance of three fundamental syndrome complexes; perceptual, mnemonic and affective. The first complex comprises mainly hallucinatory phenomena (which are therefore considered to be extraneous by the subjects) and are of a visual, auditory, taste and olfactory nature. The second group is made up of re-emerging previous experiences which have the quality of an affective response. The third are characterized be the initial onset of highly emotionally charged phenomena such as fear (accompanied by related vegetative phenomena), anger, various kinds of erotic experience or a feeling of guilt or disgust.

According to Gloor, therefore, the emotions and their anatomic substrate, particularly the limbic structures of the temporal lobe, play an important role in determining which sensory data and which mnemonic contents exceed the threshold of consciousness at any given stage.

Infero-medial diencephalic region. Recorded anatomo-clinical cases of human pathology confirm the evidence previously reported by Aggleton and Mishkin (1983a,b, 1985) in medial diencephalic lesions in monkey. These authors have stressed the importance of these structures in memory processes; essentially, global anterograde diencephalic amnesia calls for an involvement which also includes the medial part of the dorsomedial n. and the median line thalamic nuclei, while the exclusive involvement of the mammillary body is not responsible for the major memory deficit (Victor et al., 1961; Gubermann and Stuss, 1983).

The importance of the thalamic dorso-medial and median location of the lesions and consequently the interruption of the connections with various limbic and paralimbic structures, including the amygdala, the hippocampal region and the fronto-orbitary region, in global diencephalic amnesia, apparently diminishes the importance of the hippocampo-mammillo-thalamo-cingular circuit in memory learning in man. This is confirmed by the absence of memory disturbances in subjects who have undergone bilateral sectioning of the fornix (Woolsey and Nelson, 1975; Zola-Morgan and Squire, 1986), although present-day CAT scanning in some cases (Barbizet et al., 1981) shows how bilateral lesions located in the Vic d'Azir bundle and in the polar thalamic region (Rousseaux et al., 1986) can result in prolonged disturbance of the persistence of memory traces. The experimental data and the human pathology evidence nevertheless confirm that the diencephalic circuits are essential to memorization while their importance as an emotional substrate, which is confirmed by the emotional reactions obtained by stimulation of the anterior thalamus (Ferro Milone et al., 1961), is probably linked to their connections with the limbic structures of level 1 and 2 (hypothalamorhinencephalic).

Hypothalamic lesions. In patients with hypothalamic lesions emotional disorders are usually obscured by more basic disturbances concerning the sleep mechanisms (as in the Kleine-Levin syndrome), thermoregulation, or other metabolic, nutritional, endocrine or vegetative functions (Boshes, 1969). Nevertheless, various kinds of emotional disturbances have been described in patients with hypothalamic lesions. Thus, emotional instability and disorders in visceral activity have been observed following tumors of the third ventricle as well as with infections of the hypothalamic structures. Increased motor activity has been described in lesions involving the rostral hypothalamus, whereas indifference and drowsiness, agitation and akinetic mutism, usually associated with Korsakoff's syndrome, have been noted in lesions involving the posterior hypothalamus, the mammillary region and the rostral mesencephalic transition. Finally, manifestations of severe rage have sometimes been observed in patients with lesions involving the basal hypothalamus (Plum and Uitert, 1978) and episodes of ictal laughter have often been recorded in patients with hypothalamic hamartomas (Berkovic et al., 1988).

References

Aggleton JP, Friedman DP, Mishkin M: A comparison between the connections of the amygdala and hippocampus with the basal forebrain in the macaque. *Exp. Brain Res.: 67,* 556 – 568, 1987.

Aggleton UP, Mishkin M: Visual recognition impairment following medial thalamic lesions in monkeys. *Neuropsychologia: 21,* 189 – 197, 1983a.

Aggleton JP, Mishkin M: Memory impairments following restricted medial thalamic lesions in monkeys. *Exp. Brain Res.: 52,* 109 – 209, 1983b.

Aggleton JP, Mishkin M: Projections of the amygdala to the thalamus in the cynomologus monkey. *J. Comp. Neurol.: 222,* 56 – 68, 1984.

Aggleton JP, Mishkin M: Mammillary body lesions and visual recognition in monkeys. *Exp. Brain Res.: 58,* 190 – 197, 1985.

Aggleton JP, Mishkin M, Desimone R: The origin, course, and termination of the hippocampothalamic projections in the macaque. *J. Comp. Neurol.: 243,* 409 – 421, 1986.

Albanese A., Minciacchi D: Organization of the ascending projection from the ventral tegmental area: a multiple fluorescent retrograde tracer study in the rat. *J. Comp. Neurol.: 216,* 406 – 420, 1983.

Angeleri F, Ferro-Milone F, Parigi S: Contributi delle registrazioni profonde simultanee dal cervello umano al problema della elettroencefalografia dell'epilessia con particolare riguardo per quella del lobo temporale. *Riv. Neurobiol.: 7,* suppl. 4: 901 – 943, 1961.

Barbizet J, Degos JD, Louarn F, Nguyen JP, Mas JL: Amnésie par lésion ischémique bi-thalamique. *Rev. Neurol. (Paris): 137,* 6 – 7, 415 – 424, 1981.

Beccari M: *Neurologia Comparata.* Firenze, Sansoni ed. med. scientifica, 1943.

Berkovic SF, Andermann F, Melanson D, Eithier RE, Feindel W, Gloor P: Hypothalamic hamartomas and ictal laughter. *Ann. Neurol.: 23,* 429 – 439, 1988.

Boshes B: Syndromes of the diencephalon. The hypothalamus and the hypophysis. In: Vinken PJ, Bruyn GW (Editors), *Handbook of Clinical Neurology, Vol. 3.* Amsterdam: Elsevier 343 – 367, 1969.

Broca P: Anatomie comparée des circonvolutions cérébrales. Le grand lobe limbique et la scissure limbique dans la série des mammifères. *Rev. Anthorap.: 1,* 385 – 498, 1878.

Brodal A: *Neurological Anatomy in Relation to Clinical Medicine.* New York, Oxford: Oxford University Press, pp. 1053, 1981.

Butler AB: Telencephalon of the Lizard Gekko gecko (Linnaeus) Some connections of the cortex and dorsal ventricular ridge. *Brain Behav. Evol.: 13,* 396 – 417, 1976.

Butter CM, Snyder DR, McDonald JA: Effects of orbital frontal lesions on aversive and aggressive behaviors in rhesus monkeys. *J. Comp. Physiol. Psychol.: 72,* 132 – 144, 1970.

Carreras M, Macchi G, Angeleri F: Ricerche sperimentali sulle fisiopatologie della formazione annonica. *Riv. Neurobiol.: 4,* 131 – 175, 473 – 498, 1958.

Crosby EC: The forebrain of alligator *Mississippiensis. J. Comp. Neurol.: 27,* 325 – 402, 1917.

Damasio AR, Van Hoesen GW: Emotional disturbances associated with focal lesions of the limbic frontal lobe. In Heilman K, Sotz P (Editors). *Neuropsychology of Human Emotion.* New York/London: The Guilford Press, pp. 85 – 110, 1983.

Delgado JMR: Emotional behavior in animals and humans. *Psych. Res, Rep.: 12,* 259 – 266, 1960.

Ferro-Milone F, Angeleri F, Parigi S: Effeti psichici per stimolazioni o lesioni talamiche e rinencefaliche: considerazioni introduttive alla psicochirurgia stereotassica. In: Contributi di fisiopatologia cerebrale a mezzo di esplorazioni e demolizioni stereotassiche nell'uomo (M. Benvenuti ed.) *Riv. Neurobiol.: 7,* suppl. 4: 1074 – 1094, 1961.

Fonberg E, Delgado JMR: Avoidance and alimentary reactions during amygdala stimulation. *J. Neurophysiol.: 24,* 651 – 664, 1961.

Geschwind N: Disconnexion syndromes in animals and man. *Part I. Brain: 88,* 237 – 294, 1965.

Gloor P: Role of the human limbic system in perception, memory and affect: lessons from temporal lobe epilepsy. In Doane BK, Livingston KE (Editors), *The Limbic System: Functional Organization and Clinical Disorders.* New York: Raven Press, pp. 159 – 169, 1986.

Grunthal E: Uber den derzeitigen Stand der Frage nach den klinischen Erscheinungen bei ausfall des Ammonshorns. *Psychiat. Neurol. (Basel): 138,* 145 – 159, 1959.

Güberman A, Stuss D: The syndrome of bilateral paramedian thalamic infarction. *Neurology: 33,* 540 – 545, 1983.

Heimer L: The olfactory connections of the diencephalon in the rat. An experimental light and electromicroscopy study with special emphasis on the problem of terminal degeneration. *Brain Behav.: 6,* 485 – 523, 1972.

Heimer L, Switzer RD, Van Hoesen GW: Ventral striatum and ventral pallidum. Components of the motor system? *Trends NeuroSci.: 5,* 83 – 87, 1982.

Holstege G: Some anatomical observations on the projections from the hypothalamus to brainstem and spinal cord: an HRP and autoradiographic tracing study in the cat. *J. Comp. Neurol.: 260,* 98 – 126, 1987.

Holstege G, Miners L, Ton K: Projections of the bed nucleus of the stria terminalis to the mesencephalon, pons and medulla oblongata in the cat. *Exp. Brain Res.: 58,* 379 – 391, 1985.

Insausti R, Amaral DG, Cowan WM: The entorhinal cortex of the monkey: III. Subcortical afferents. *J. Comp. Neurol.: 264,* 396 – 408, 1987.

Kaada BR, Wulff Rasmussen E, Kvlim O: Effects of hippocampal lesions on maze learning and retention in rats. *Exp. Neurol.: 3,* 333 – 355, 1961.

Kaada BR: Stimulation and regional ablation of the amygdaloid complex with reference to functional representation. In Eleftherion BE (Editor), *The Neurobiology of the Amygdala, Vol. 2.* New York: Plenum Press, pp. 205 – 281, 1972.

Kleist K: *Gehirnpathologie.* Leipzig: Barth 1935.

Kluver H, Bucy PC: Psychic blindness and other symptoms following bilateral temporal lobectomy in rhesus monkeys. *Am. J. Physiol.: 119,* 352 – 353, 1937.

Krettek JE, Price SL: Projections from the amygdaloid complex to the cerebral cortex and thalamus in the rat and cat. *J. Comp. Neurol.: 172,* 687 – 722, 1977a.

Krettek JE, Price JL: Projections from the amygdaloid complex and adjacent olfactory structures to the entorhinal cortex and to the subiculum in the rat and in the cat. *J. Comp. Neurol.: 172,* 723 – 752, 1977b.

Krettek JE, Price JL: Amygdaloid projections to subcortical structures within the basal forebrain and brainstem in the rat and cat. *J. Comp. Neurol.: 178,* 225 – 254, 1978.

Kuhar MJ: Neuroanatomical substrates of anxiety: a brief survey. *Trends NeuroSci.: 9,* 307 – 311, 1986.

Laplane D, Degos JD, Degos JD, Baulac M, Gray F: Bilateral infarction of the anterior cingulate gyri and of the fornices. *J. Neurol. Sci.: 51,* 289 – 300, 1981.

Le Beau J, Parker J: Etude de certaines formes d'agitation psychomotrice en cours de l'épilepsie et de l'arriération mentale, traités par la topecomie péricalleuse antérieuse bilateral. *Sem. Hôp. Paris: 26,* 1, 1950.

Leonard CM, Scott JW: Origin and distribution of the amygdalofugal pathways in the rat: an experimental neuroanatomical study. *J. Comp. Neurol.: 141,* 313 – 330, 1971.

Llamas A, Avendano C, Reinoso-Suarez F: Amygdaloid projections to prefrontal and motor cortex. *Science: 195,* 194 – 196, 1977.

Lohman AHM, Lammers HJ: On the connections of the olfactory bulb and the anterior olfactory nucleus in some mammals. In *Progress in Brain Research Vol. 3.* Amsterdam: Elsevier, pp. 149 – 162, 1963.

Macchi G: The ontogenetic development of the olfactory telencephalon in man. *J. Comp. Neurol.: 95,* 245 – 306, 1951.

Macchi G: Aspetti della organizzazione anatomo-funzionale delle strutture rinencefaliche. *Acta Neurol.: 23,* 964 – 1021, 1968.

Macchi G, Carreras M, Azzali G, Della Rosa V, Lechi A: Rinencefalo e comportamento istintivo: effetti provocati da lesioni operate sul lobo piriforme (Studio sperimentale nel gatto). *Boll. Soc. It. Biol. Sper.: 34,* 1: 37 – 41, 1963.

Macchi G, Bentivoglio M, Rossini P, Tempesta E: The basolateral amygdaloid projections to the neocortex in the cat. *Neurosci. Lett.: 9,* 347 – 351, 1978.

Magnus O, Naquet R: Physiologie normale et pathologique de l'amygdale. In *Physiologie et Pathologie du Rhinencéphale. Vol. II,* Paris: Masson pp. 191 – 221, 1961.

MacLean PD: Studies on limbic system ('Visceral brain') and their bearing on psychosomatic problems. In Meghorns R, Wittkower (Editors), *Recent Developments of Psychosomatic Medicine* London: Pitman and Sons Ltd, 495 pp., 1954.

MacLean PD: Le système limbique du point de vue de la self-protection et de la conservation de l'espèce. In Alajouanine T (Editor) *Physiologie et Pathologie du Rhinencéphale.* Paris: Masson & Cie, pp. 111 – 126, 1961.

MacLean PD: Culminating developments in the evolution of the limbic system: the thalamocingulate division. In Doane BK, Livingston KE (Editors), *The Limbic System: Functional Organization and Clinical Disorders.* New York: Raven Press, pp. 1 – 28, 1986.

Markowitsch HJ: Thalamic mediodorsal nucleus and memory: a critical evaluation of studies in animals and man. *Neur. Biobehav. Rev.: 6,* 351 – 380, 1982.

Messimy R: Physiopathologie des lobes cingulés. *Pathologie-Biologie: 13,* 676 – 688, 1965.

Mesulam NM: Patterns in behavioral neuroanatomy: association areas and limbic system and hemispheric specialization. In Mesulam MM (Editor), *Principles of Behavioural Neurology.* Philadelphia: FA Davis Co., p. 405, 1985.

Milner B: Visually-guided maze learning in man: effects of bilateral hippocampal, bilateral frontal, and unilateral cerebral lesions. *Neuropsychologia: 3,* 317 – 338, 1965.

Mishkin M: Memory in monkeys severely impaired by combined but not by separate removals of amygdala and hippocampus. *Nature: 273,* 297 – 298, 1978.

Nauta WJH: Hippocampal projections and related neural

pathways to the midbrain in the cat. *Brain: 81,* 319 – 340, 1958.

Nauta WJH: Circuitous connections linking cerebral cortex, limbic system and corpus striatum. In Doane B, Livingston K (Editors), *The Limbic System: Functional Organization and Clinical Disorders.* New York: Raven Press, pp. 43 – 54, 1986.

Nieuwenhuys R, Voogd J, Huijzen C: *Sistema Nervoso Centrale* (Nussdorfer G, Editor). Padova: Piccin Editore, pp. 249, 1980.

Pandya DN, Seltzer B: Association areas of the cerebral cortex. *Trends NeuroSci.: 5,* 386 – 390, 1982.

Pandya DN, Yeterian EH: Proposed neural circuitry for spatial memory in the primate brain. *Neuropsychologia: 22,* 109 – 122, 1984.

Panksepp J: Toward a general psychobiological theory of emotions. *Behav. Brain Sci.: 5,* 407 – 467, 1982.

Papez JW: A proposed mechanism of emotion. *Arch. Neurol. Psych. (Chicago): 38,* 725 – 743, 1937.

Passouant P, Cadilhac J: Physiologie normale et pathologique de l'hippocampe. In *Physiologie et Pathologie du Rhinencéphale, Vol. II.* Paris: Masson, pp. 343 – 367, 1961.

Poeck K: Pathophysiology of emotional disorders associated with brain damage. In Vinken PJ, Bruyn GW (Editors), *Handbook of Clinical Neurology, Vol. 3.* Amsterdam: Elsevier, pp. 343 – 367, 1969.

Poletti CE: Is the limbic system a limbic system? Studies of hippocampal efferents: their functional and clinical implications. In Doane BK, Livingston KE (Editors), *The Limbic System: Functional Organization and Clinical Disorders.* New York: Raven Press, pp. 79 – 94, 1986.

Plum F, Van Uitert R: Neuroendocrine diseases and disorders of the hypothalamus. *Res. Publ. Assoc. Res. Nerv. Ment. Dis.: 56,* 415 – 473, 1978.

Room P, Groenewegen HJ: Connections of the parahippocampal cortex. I. Cortical afferents. *J. Comp. Neurol., 251:* 415 – 450, 1986.

Rose M: Der Allocortex bei Tier und Mensch. *Int. J. Psychol. Neurol. (Lpz): 34,* 1 – 111, 1926.

Ross ED, Stewart N: Akinetic mutism from hypothalamic damage: successful treatment with dopamine agonists. *Neurology: 31,* 1435 – 1439, 1981.

Rousseaux M, Cabaret M, Lesoin F, Devos Ph, Dubois F, Petit G: L'amnésie des infarctus thalamiques restreints – 6 cas. *Cortex: 22,* 213 – 228, 1986.

Sarter M, Markowitsch HJ: Involvement of the amygdala in learning and memory: a critical review, with emphasis on anatomical relations. *Behav. Neurosci.: 99,* 342 – 380, 1985.

Scott JW, Leonard CM: The olfactory connections of the lateral hypothalamus in the rat, mouse and hamster. *J. Comp. Neurol.: 141,* 331 – 344, 1971.

Scoville WB, Milner B: Loss of recent memory after bilateral hippocampal lesions. *J. Neurol. Neurosurg. Psych.: 20,* 11 – 21, 1957.

Signoret JL: Memory and amnesias. In Mesulam MM (Editor), *Principles of Behavioural Neurology.* Philadephia: FA Davis, pp. 259 – 288, 1985.

Squire RL, Zola-Morgan S: Memory: brain systems and behavior. *Trends NeuroSci.: 11,* 170 – 175, 1988.

Stephan H: Die Kortikalen Anteile des Limbischen Systems (Morphologie und Entwicklung). *Nervenarzt: 35,* 396 – 401, 1964.

Swanson LW, Cowan WM: An autoradiographic study of the organization of the efferent connexions of the hippocampal formation in the rat. *J. Comp. Neurol.: 172,* 49 – 84, 1977.

Talairach J, Bancaud J, Geier S, Bordas-Ferrer M, Bonis A, Szikla G, Rusu M: The cingulate gyrus and human behaviour. *Electroencephalogr. Clin. Neurophysiol.: 34,* 45 – 52, 1973.

Terzian H, Dalle Ore GD: Syndrome of Kluver-Bucy reproduced in man by bilateral removal of the temporal lobes. *Neurology: 5,* 373 – 380, 1955.

Ursin H, Kaada BR: Functional localization within the amygdaloid complex in the cats. *Electroencephalogr. Clin. Neurophysiol.: 12,* 1 – 20, 1960.

Van Buren JM, Borke RC: The medial temporal substratum of memory. Anatomical studies in three individuals. *Brain: 95,* 599 – 632, 1972.

Van Groen T, Van Haren FJ, Witter MP, Groenewegen HJ: The organization of the reciprocal connection between the subiculum and the entorhinal cortex in the cat. I. A neuroanatomical tracing study. *J. Comp. Neurol.: 250,* 485 – 497, 1986.

Van Hoesen GW: The parahippocampal gyrus. New observations regarding its cortical connections in the monkey. *Trends Neurosci.: 5,* 345 – 350, 1982.

Victor M, Angevine JB Jr, Mancall EL, Fisher CM: Memory loss with lesions of the hippocampal formation. *Arch. Neurol. (Chicago): 5,* 244 – 263, 1961.

Witter MP, Groenewegen HJ: Connections of the parahippocampal cortex in the cat. III. Cortical and thalamic efferents. *J. Comp. Neurol.: 252,* 1 – 31, 1986a.

Witter MP, Groenewegen HJ: Connections of the parahippocampal cortex in the cat. IV. Subcortical efferents. *J. Comp. Neurol.: 251,* 51 – 77, 1986b.

Witter MP, Room P, Groenewegen HJ, Lohman AHM: Connections of the parahippocampal cortex in the cat. V. Intrinsic connections: comments on input/output connections with the hippocampus. *J. Comp. Neurol.: 252,* 78 – 94, 1986.

Woolsey EM, Nelson JS: Asymptomatic destruction of the fornix in man. *Arch. Neurol.: 32,* 566 – 568, 1975.

Yamagihara M, Ono K, Niimi K: Thalamic projections to the hippocampal formation in the cat. *Neurosci. Lett.: 61,* 31 – 35, 1985.

Zbrozyna AW: The anatomical basis of the patterns of autonomic and behavioural response effected via the amygdala. In: *Progress in Brain Research Vol. 3.* Amsterdam: Elsevier, pp. 50 – 70, 1963.

Zola-Morgan S, Squire LS: Memory impairment in monkeys following lesions limited to the hippocampus. *Behav. Neurosci.: 100,* 155 – 160, 1986.

CHAPTER 14

Neurochemical basis of emotional behavior

Candace B. Pert[1], Joanna M. Hill[1] and Birgit Zipser[2]

[1]*Section on Brain Biochemistry, Clinical Neuroscience Branch, National Institute of Mental Health, ADAMHA, Bethesda, MD 20892, and [2]Department of Physiology, Michigan State University, East Lansing, MI 48824-1101, U.S.A.*

Introduction

Neuropeptides are the largest and most diverse class of chemical messages in the brain. In addition to classical synaptic communication it has recently been suggested that peptidergic neurons can communicate with noncontiguous neurons parasynaptically through the diffusion of their secretions in the extracellular fluid of the brain.

This chapter will discuss recent evidence which has shown that both neuropeptides and their receptors are enriched in the limbic regions of the brain. The presence of numerous neuropeptides and their receptors in the emotion-mediating regions of the brain, through which cells can communicate both synaptically and parasynaptically, suggests that these molecules are the biochemicals of emotion. These findings also suggest that peptide-receptor-rich regions form nodes in an emotion-mediating system of the brain and body.

Neuropeptides

In addition to the classical neurotransmitters, recent evidence has shown that intercellular communication in the brain is also accomplished by numerous other informational substances (Schmitt, 1984), most of which are peptides. It has long been recognized that peptide hormones are effective in information transduction throughout the body. Forty years ago it was discovered that the peptide hormones oxytocin and vasopressin were secreted by neurons in the hypothalamus (Scharrer and Scharrer, 1940).

This discovery was closely followed by the realization that several additional hypothalamic hormones, released into the capillary bed of the hypophyseal stalk, were transported to the anterior pituitary where they regulated anterior pituitary function. However, the recent discoveries that peptidergic neurons ramify throughout the brain in extrahypothalmic sites (Morley, 1979; Vale et al., 1975), that the neuroactive compounds neurotensin and substance P are peptides (Carraway and Leeman, 1973; Brazeau et al., 1973), and that opiate peptides (Hughes et al., 1975) and their receptors (Pert and Snyder, 1973) are present in brain have resulted in the recognition that peptides act as neurotransmitters or neuromodulators and widely influence central nervous system function and behavior.

At this writing about 50 peptides have been found in brain (Table 1); however, this number represents only about one-quarter of the total number predicted (Snyder, 1980; Sternberger, 1980).

Peptides have many characteristics which make them well suited for information transfer in the brain (Schmitt, 1984). They are biologically active at extremely low concentrations, can be transported in extracellular fluids some distance before being degraded, one or more peptides can be synthesized by a larger precursor molecule, they often coexist with classical neurotransmitters, and can act as intercellular signals by diffusing in the extracellular fluid to receptors on noncontiguous cells, i.e., parasynaptic information transfer.

Parasynaptic intercellular communication, recently proposed by Schmitt (1984), is thought to exist in addition to the classical synaptic communication between contiguous neurons. Informational substances, including transmitters, modulators, peptides, etc., released from cells, diffuse through the extracellular fluid to act upon non-synaptic receptors, which can be several millimeters from the site of release. Nieuwenhuys (1985) has postulated a similar non-synaptic paracrine interneuronal communication in brain. He proposes that in thin, unmyelinated pathways in the core of the brain, peptides are able to influence neurons along their length as well as at their ultimate destination. An 'action at a distance' of transmitters at receptors on noncontiguous cells

serves to explain the well-documented mismatch between sites of transmitter release in the brain and the sites of their receptors (Herkenham and McLean, 1986; Herkenham, 1987).

Receptors in neuropeptide function

Because information transfer in the brain is conducted through the use of molecules synthesized and sometimes secreted at brain sites different from those regions where they are active, the specificity of function of a peptide is controlled by the peptide's receptor. To know the localization of a peptide receptor then is to know the site where that peptide is most active. Receptors, or recognition sites, are proteins localized in surface membranes of neurons and/or glial cells and typically recognize only a particular neuroactive substance and its close analogues. Recognition of an infor-

TABLE 1

Neuropeptides

Adrenocorticotropic hormone	Melanocyte-stimulating hormone-releasing hormone
Angiotensin I	Melatonin
Angiotensin II	(Met)enkephalin
Angiotensin III	Motilin
Bombesin	Nerve growth factor
Bradykinin	Neurohypophysial hormone
Calcitonin	Neuropeptide Y
Calcitonin gene-related peptide	Neurophysin
Carnosine	Neurotensin
Cholecystokinin	Oxytocin
Corticotropic-releasing factor	Pancreatic polypeptides
Ependymin (β and γ)	Physalaemin
β-Endorphin	Pituitary peptides
Gastrin	Proctolin
Gastrointestinal polypeptide	Prolactin
Glucagon	Secretin
Gonadotropin-releasing hormone	Somatostatin
Growth hormone	Substance K
Hypothalamic-releasing hormone	Substance P
Insulin	Thyroid hormone
Insulin-like growth factor I	Thyroid-stimulating hormone
Insulin-like growth factor II	Thyrotropin-releasing hormone
Interleukin I	Transferrin
(Leu)enkephalin	Arginine vasopressin
Luteinizing hormone	Lysine vasopressin
Luteinizing hormone-releasing factor	Vasoactive intestinal polypeptide
Melanocyte-stimulating hormone (α and β)	Vasotocin

national substance at the neuronal membranes initiates transduction of a message through the membrane to the internal workings of the cell.

Methods used in the study of peptide receptor distribution

The development of autoradiographic techniques in the mid-1970s led to the determination of the distribution patterns of receptors for peptides and other neuroactive compounds throughout the mammalian brain. Receptor autoradiography has been described fully elsewhere (Herkenham and Pert, 1982); therefore only a brief outline will be given here. After a preincubation step designed to remove endogenous peptides from their receptors, fresh frozen brain slices are incubated with a radiolabeled peptide. The specifically bound peptides are attached to the receptor and are not displaced in subsequent rinses which wash off excess and non-specifically bound peptides from the tissue. After drying, the slices are exposed to X-ray film, and after a few days (for iodinated compounds) or a few weeks (for tritiated compounds) the film is developed. On the film, the brain regions having receptors appear in shades of grey or black depending on the density of the receptors in that region. A characteristic pattern of distribution and relative density of receptors can be found for each peptide. The binding sites on brain are considered receptors, however, if among other things the specific binding can be displaced by excess non-radioactive peptide. In addition, often the pattern of displacement of the peptide by analogues serves to further characterize the receptor. If an antibody to the receptor is available, radioimmunocytochemistry can also serve as supportive evidence that the receptor recognition is specific (Hill et al., 1985, 1987). The radioimmunocytochemical method incorporates many steps from autoradiographic techniques. Fresh frozen brain sections are preincubated to remove endogenous peptide and then incubated with an anti-receptor antibody. After rinsing off excess antibody, the sections are then incubated in a labeled antibody, e.g., ^{125}I-immunoglobulin, which will bind to the primary antibody. The sections are then rinsed, dried, and exposed to film as described above.

Brain regions enriched with peptide receptors

While each type of neuropeptide receptor has a characteristic pattern of distribution we have found certain brain regions to be enriched. In a study of the distribution patterns of 22 different peptide receptors we found 23 brain regions which had receptors for 55% or more of the peptides studied (Table 2).

Fig. 1a,b illustrates seven different receptor distribution patterns on five different brain sections ranging from rostral forebrain to medulla or spinal cord. The receptor patterns for classical neuropeptides (opiates, substance P and neurotensin), hormones (insulin, somatostatin and cholecystokinin) and a growth factor (transferrin) are illustrated.

The amygdala has receptors for all the peptides examined except nerve growth factor (95%). Some types of receptor are distributed relatively evenly across the entire amygdala (e.g., insulin, Fig. 1a, and transferrin, Fig. 1b); others are contained in particular subnuclei (e.g., substance P, Fig. 1b). The dentate gyrus of the hippocampal formation has receptors for all the peptides but calcitonin and oxytocin (91%). However, considerable variation occurs in localization of receptors within the lamina and subregions of this structure (Fig. 1a,b). This is also true of the hippocampus proper (Ammon's horn, Fig. 1a,b), which has receptors for 86% of the peptides studied. The cerebral cortex has receptors for 19 of the 22 neuropeptides surveyed. Within the frontal, parietal and striatal cortex individual receptor types show little regional variation in receptor distribution pattern. The caudate putamen has receptors for 19 of the 23 (82%) peptides. These receptors usually occur at low densities, but occasionally at high densities (e.g., naloxone, Fig. 1a). Their distribution can either be homogeneous or occur in distinct patches (e.g., opiate receptors, Fig. 1a) or in an anterior-posterior gradient (e.g., insulin receptors, Fig. 1a).

The olfactory bulb, central grey and septum have receptors for 17 of the 22 (77%) peptides surveyed. In the olfactory bulb, receptor densities are typically high. However, different peptide receptors are abundant in different layers. For example, insulin (Fig. 1a), neurotensin (Fig. 1a) and substance P (Fig. 1b) have their highest binding in

the external plexiform layer of the olfactory bulb. On the other hand, the receptors for VIP (Fig. 1b), CCK (Fig. 1a), IL-1 and IGF-II (data not shown) are most abundant in the mitral cell layer and the glomerular layer in the olfactory bulb. In the septum, the dorsal lateral subnuclei frequently have denser receptor binding than the ventral and medial regions.

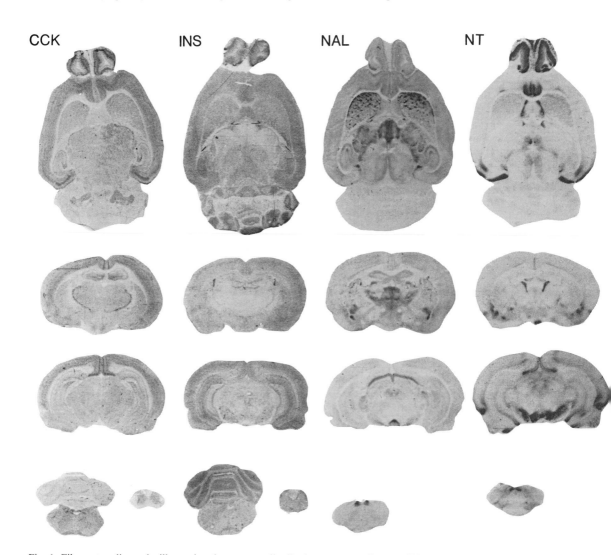

Fig. 1. Film autoradiographs illustrating the receptor distribution patterns of seven different neuropeptides in the horizontal plane and coronal view at the level of the thalamus and amygdala, at the level of the superior colliculus and hippocampus, at the level of the cerebellum and medulla, and at the level of the spinal cord. Abbreviations: Amy, amygdala; CCK, cholecystokinin; CCmol, cerebellar cortex, molecular layers; CG, central grey; CiC, cingulate cortex; CPu, caudate putamen; Ctx, cortex; DG, dentate gyrus; H, hippocampus; INS, insulin; M. Hab, medial habenula; NAL, naloxone; NT, neurotensin; OB, olfactory bulb; PaN, paraventricular nucleus; S, septum; SC, superior colliculus; SG, substantia gelatinosa; Sol, nucleus solilarius; SP, substance P; SU

Sixteen of 22 (73%) receptor types are present in the paraventricular nucleus. Fifteen out of 22 (68%) receptor types are present in the nucleus accumbens, bed nucleus of the stria terminalis, subiculum, superior colliculus superficial grey, interpeduncular nucleus, substantia gelatinosa and nucleus of the solitary tract. Fourteen of 22 (64%) receptor types are found in the entorhinal cortex and nucleus of the solitary tract. Thirteen of 22 (59%) receptor types are present in the olfactory tubercle, cingulate cortex and the molecular layer of the cerebellar cortex. Twelve of the 22 (55%) receptor types are found in the preoptic area, medial habenula and locus coeruleus.

It is quite likely that the incidence of receptors in the olfactory bulb and brain stem regions such as

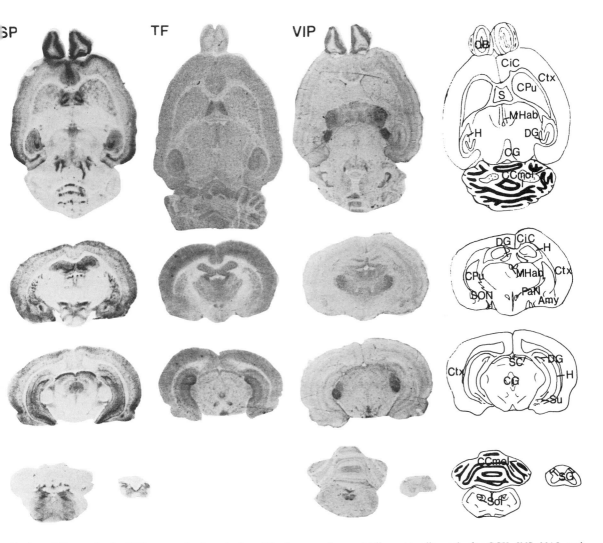

subiculum; TF, transferrin; VIP, vasoactive intestinal peptide. (a, opposite page) Film autoradiographs for CCK, INS, NAL and NT. (b, above) Film autoradiographs for SP, TF, VIP and line drawings with brain regions labeled. Tissue was prepared as described and serial brain sections radiolabeled according to the following procedures (Herkenham and Pert, 1982). CCK, (Gaudreau et al., 1983), INS (Hill et al., 1986), NAL (Herkenham and Pert, 1982), NT (Quirion et al., 1982), SP (Quirion et al., 1983), TF (Hill et al., 1985), VIP (Wiedermann et al., 1987).

TABLE 2

Peptide-receptor-rich regions of the brain

	AII	AVP	BN	CT	CGRP	CCK	CRF	INS	IGF-I	IGF-II	IL-I	NGF	NPY	NT	OP	OT	SS	SK	SP	TRH	TF	VIP	%
1. Amygdala	+	+	+	+	+	+	+	+	+	+	+	0	+	+	+	+	+	+	+	+	+	+	95
2. Dentate gyrus	+	+	+	0	+	+	+	+	+	+	+	+	+	+	+	0	+	+	+	+	+	+	91
3. Hippocampus proper	+	+	+	0	0	+	+	+	+	+	+	0	+	+	+	0	+	+	+	+	+	+	85
4. Cerebral cortex	+	+	+	0	+	+	+	+	+	+	+	+	+	+	+	0	+	+	+	+	+	+	86
5. Caudate putamen	0	+	+	+	+	+	+	+	+	.	+	0	+	+	+	0	+	+	+	0	+	+	82
6. Olfactory bulb	+	+	+	?	?	+	+	+	+	0	+	?	?	+	+	?	+	+	+	+	+	0	77
7. Septum	+	+	0	0	0	+	+	+	0	0	+	0	+	+	+	+	+	+	+	+	+	0	77
8. Central grey	+	0	+	+	+	+	+	+	0	0	+	0	+	0	0	0	+	0	+	+	+	+	77
9. Paraventricular nucleus	+	+	+	+	0	0	+	+	+	+	0	0	+	0	0	+	+	0	+	+	+	+	73
10. Nucleus accumbens	0	+	+	+	+	+	+	+	+	0	+	0	0	+	+	0	0	0	+	+	+	+	68
11. Nuclei of stria terminalis/stria terminalis	0	+	+	+	0	+	+	+	+	0	0	0	+	+	+	+	+	0	0	+	+	+	68
12. Subiculum	+	+	+	0	0	+	+	+	0	+	+	0	0	+	+	+	0	0	+	+	+	+	68
13. Superior colliculus, superficial grey	+	0	+	0	+	+	+	+	+	0	0	0	0	+	+	0	+	0	+	+	+	+	68
14. Interpeduncular nucleus	+	0	+	+	+	+	+	+	+	0	0	+	0	0	+	0	+	+	+	+	+	+	68
15. Substantia gelatinosa	+	0	+	0	?	?	+	+	+	0	?	+	+	+	+	0	+	+	+	+	?	+	68
16. Entorhinal cortex	0	+	0	0	+	+	+	+	+	+	+	0	0	0	+	0	+	0	+	+	+	+	64
17. Nucleus of the solitary tract																							
18. Olfactory tubercle	0	0	+	0	+	+	+	0	0	0	0	0	0	+	0	0	+	+	+	+	0	+	64
19. Cingulate cortex	0	0	+	0	+	+	+	+	0	0	+	0	+	+	+	+	+	0	+	+	+	+	59
20. Cerebellar cortex, molecular layer	+	+	0	0	0	0	+	+	+	0	+	0	+	+	0	0	0	0	0	+	+	+	59
21. Medial preoptic area	+	0	0	+	+	+	0	+	0	0	+	0	+	+	0	0	0	0	0	+	+	+	59
22. Medial habenula	+	0	0	0	0	+	+	0	0	+	+	0	0	+	0	0	+	0	+	+	+	+	55
23. Locus coeruleus	+	0	+	+	+	+	0	0	0	+	0	0	0	+	+	0	+	0	+	0	+	+	55

+, receptor present; 0, few or no receptors; ?, unreported; AII, angiotensen II; AVP, arginine-vasopressin; BN, bombesin; CT, calcitonin; CGRP, calcitonin gene-related peptide; CCK, cholecystokinin; CRF, corticotropin-releasing factor; INS, insulin; IGF-I, insulin-like growth factor I, IGF-II, insulin-like growth factor II; IL-I, interleukin-I; NGF, nerve growth factor; NPY, neuropeptide Y; NT, neurotensin; OP, opiates; OT, oxytocin; SS, somatostatin; SK, substance K; SP, substance P; TRH, thyrotropin-releasing hormone; TF, transferrin; VIP, vasoactive intestinal peptide.

the substantia gelantinosa, nucleus of the solitary tract and the locus coeruleus is higher than reported here because these anterior and posterior parts of the brain are frequently neglected in regional distribution studies.

Relationship of peptide-receptor-enriched regions to the limbic system

The receptor-rich regions of the brain were found to be widespread and to encompass diverse brain structures; they are involved in diverse functions, and all, in one context or another, have been considered limbic structures.

The concept of the limbic system evolved from a description by Papez (1937) of a brain circuit found on the border or limbus of the cortex, which functions in the modulation and expression of emotion. The components of the limbic system have never been clearly demarcated; however, the classical limbic regions (Fig. 2) usually include the structures of Papez circuit (the hypothalamus,

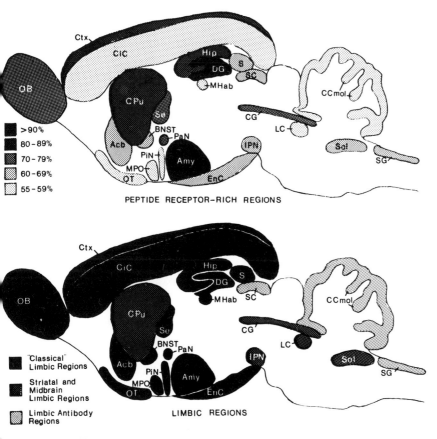

Fig. 2. Line drawings illustrating the peptide-receptor-rich regions of the brain (upper drawing) and the limbic regions of the brain (lower drawing) in which peptide receptors are enriched. Shades of grey in upper drawing correspond to the percentage of the 22 different peptide receptors found in each brain region (see Table 2). Shades of grey in lower drawing show which peptide-receptor-rich brain regions are considered classical limbic regions (Papez, 1937; MacLean, 1952), striatal (Gerfen, 1984; Kelley et al., 1982) and midbrain limbic regions (Nauta and Domesick, 1982) and limbic antibody regions (Levitt, 1984). See text for further discussion. Abbreviations: Acb, nucleus accumbens; Amy, amygdala; BNST, bed nucleus of the stria terminals; CCmol, cerebellar cortex, molecular layer; CG, central grey; CiC, cingulate cortex; CPu, caudate putamen; Ctx, cortex; DG, dentate gyrus; EnC, entorhinal cortex; Hip, hippocampus; IPN, interpeduncular nucleus; LC, locus coeruleus; M Hab, medial habenula; MPD, medial preoptic area; OB, olfactory bulb; OT, olfactory tubercle; PaN, paraventricular nucleus; PiN, periventricular nucleus; S, subiculum; Sc, superior colliculus; SE, septum; Sg, substantia gelatinosa; Sol, nucleus solitarius.

anterior thalamic nucleus, cingulate gyrus and hippocampus), and those regions added by MacLean (1952), the amygdala and many cortical and subcortical regions having reciprocal connections with the hypothalamus. The receptor-rich regions of the brain overlapping with these classical limbic areas and others, such as the striatum, parts of which have recently been found to have reciprocal hypothalamic connections (Gerfen, 1984; Kelly et al., 1982), appear in black in Fig. 2. (The cortex appearing in Fig. 2 represents the limbic cortex, i.e., the basal fronto-temporal region having reciprocal connections with the amygdala and/or hypothalamus). Recently Nauta and Domesick (1982) have expanded the concept of the limbic system by including a number of strongly interconnected mesencephalic structures. Together with the forebrain limbic structures these form a functional system, the 'limbic system – midbrain circuit.' The receptor-rich regions of the brain included in Nauta's circuit appear in dark grey in Fig. 2. The limbic system is further characterized by the identification of a limbic-system-specific antigen, a surface marker, recently isolated through monoclonal antibodies and postulated to play a role in the system's assembly (Levitt, 1984). This antigen is expressed by most of the limbic and associated regions appearing in black and dark grey in Fig. 2, and three other brain regions, the substantia gelantinosa, the superficial layer of the superior colliculus, and the molecular layer of the cerebellar cortex (Fig. 2, pale grey) previously not considered to be limbic-associated areas. In a recent paper, however, Haines and Dietrichs (1987) have reported reciprocal connections between the cerebellum and the hypothalamus, and the superior colliculus has been shown to receive synaptic input from the cingulate cortex (Domesick, 1969; Siegel et al., 1973).

Thus, the group of 23 regions that are distinguished through a high incidence of receptor localization overlap with the limbic and associated regions of the brain (Fig. 2).

Nieuwenhuys (1985), in an extensive review of the chemoarchitecture of the brain, has shown that the set of brain regions enriched with informational substances, primarily neuropeptides, also overlaps extensively with the limbic system. The limbic regions of the brain are, therefore, characterized by being enriched with both neuropeptide and neuropeptide receptors.

Relationship of receptor-rich regions to emotion

The limbic system has traditionally been viewed as the neuroanatomical substrate for emotion. Our demonstration that neuropeptide-receptor-enriched regions of the brain overlap with the limbic and associated regions supports the concept of neuropeptides as the biochemicals of emotion. In addition, it suggests that neuropeptide-receptor rich regions of the brain form nodes in an emotion mediating network of the brain.

The concept of the limbic system originally based on the connectivity of regions through synaptic connections expanded with modern tract-tracing methods. As a consequence, much of the brain was included in the 'limbic system'. At the same time these methods demonstrated that the interconnections among the components of the original Papez circuit of emotions were not the major connections of these structures. This resulted in the opinion, held by some, that the term 'limbic system' should be abolished, that Papez's circuit was of historical interest only (Brodal, 1981), and that the concept of the limbic system had perhaps outlived its usefulness (Heimer, 1983).

These criticisms, however valid, do not solve the problem of understanding the relationship of emotion to brain structures. Certain brain regions are involved in the subjective feeling and expression of emotions, and these regions have been considered a part of the limbic system by most authors. The hypothalamus, through its connections with the brain stem, regulates the expression of emotion. Therefore, brain regions with reciprocal hypothalamic connections are in a position to modify emotional expression. Ablation and stimulation experiments have identified other brain regions, for example, the amygdala cingulate gyrus, frontal cortex, septum/hippocampus and locus coeruleus, all considered limbic regions, which are involved somehow in the emotionality of the organism. Therefore, these regions and those to which they are connected can modulate emotion.

Levitt's (1984) discovery of a limbic-system-specific antigen provides a molecular basis for linking the limbic regions. Similarly, Nieuwenhuys's (1985) finding that the 'neuromediator-rich regions of the brain constitute a readily recognizable entity' which coincides largely with the limbic system, including the midbrain structures outlined by Nauta and Domesick (1982), suggests that limbic regions share both molecular and biochemical characteristics which bring them together as an entity. Our study of the peptide-receptor-rich regions of the brain both complements and extends the concept that the regions share molecular and biochemical features. The neuropeptide-receptor-rich regions of the brain form a recognizable entity which encompasses regions brought together originally on an anatomical basis and later on by molecular/biochemical similarities.

Although there is a mismatch between the sites of neurotransmitter release and the localization of its receptor (Herkenham and McLean, 1986; Herkenham, 1987), as discussed above, both the receptors, as we have shown, and the peptides, as shown by Nieuwenhuys (1985), are enriched in the limbic regions of the brain.

The neuropeptide-rich limbic regions of the brain can communicate with the neuropeptide-receptor-rich limbic regions of the brain not only through a multitude of reciprocal synaptic pathways but also through the extensive and versatile parasynaptic system. There are potentially 200 neuropeptides and their receptors in the limbic structures of the brain, peptides that are potent at extremely low concentrations and can diffuse for considerable time and distance before being degraded.

Therefore, what the 'limbic system' lacks in synaptic communication through strong anatomical connections between its various components perhaps is made up for by a potentially extensive parasynaptic communication.

This collection of brain regions may not function as a system in the same way as a neuronal circuit as originally envisaged by Papez (1937) or the documented circuits of the brain which today are referred to as systems. However, a function as complex as the modulation of emotion, requiring the integration and coordination of the perceptions of both the internal and external milieu, perhaps requires much of the brain and body and includes regions which overlap with many other systems.

Neuropeptide- and neuropeptide-receptor-enriched regions of the body and their relation to emotion

Most of the peptides and their receptors listed in Table 1 were originally discovered in other parts of the body and only later found to be present in the brain. The opposite is also true. Neuropeptides and neuropeptide receptors, such as the opiates, originally found in the brain have been found widely distributed throughout the body. The discovery that the brain and body utilize a common set of peptides and their receptors has important implications in understanding the relationship between emotion and health. Shared peptides and peptide receptors may form a molecular/biochemical framework for a bidirectional communication network between brain and body (Pert et al., 1985).

Peptides synthesized throughout the body and entering the brain through the circumventricular organs, crossing the blood-brain barrier, or being brought in by migrating macrophages (Ruff and Pert, 1986) can gain access to brain receptors. Thus, informational substances in the extracellular fluid reaching limbic receptors from any part of the brain or body can potentially modify emotions. Further, if the neuropeptide-receptor-rich regions of the brain form nodes in an emotion-mediating network of the brain, perhaps the neuropeptide-receptor-rich regions of the body can also be considered nodes in this communication network.

Acknowledgements

We gratefully acknowledge the expert technical assistance of Ms. Nicole Jelesoff and Ms. Sabine Jean-Paul. We also thank Ms. Yolanda Edwards for her careful preparation of this manuscript.

References

Brazeau P, Vale W, Burgus R, Ling N, Butcher M, Rivier J, Guillemin R: Hypothalamic polypeptide that inhibits the secretion of immunoreactive pituitary growth hormone. *Science: 179,* 77 – 79, 1973.

Brodal A: *Neurological Anatomy in Relation to Clinical Medicine.* 3rd Edn. New York: Oxford University Press, 1981.

Carraway R, Leeman SE: The isolation of a new hypothalamic peptide, neurotensin, from the bovine hypothalami. *J. Biol. Chem.: 248,* 6854 – 6861, 1973.

Domesick VB: Projections from the cingulate cortex in the rat. *Brain Res.: 12,* 296 – 320, 1969.

Gaudreau P, Quirion R, St-Pierre S, Pert CB: Characterization and visialization of cholecystokinin receptors in rat brain using (^{3}H) pentagastrin. *Peptides: 4,* 755 – 762, 1983.

Gerfen CR: The neostriatal mosaic: compartmentalization of corticostriatal input and striatonigral output systems. *Nature: 311,* 461 – 464, 1984.

Haines PE, Dietrichs: On the organization of interconnections between the cerebellum and hypothalamus. In King JS (Editor), *New Concepts in Cerebellar Neurobiology,* New York: Allan R. Liss, Inc. pp. 113 – 149, 1987.

Heimer L: *The Human Brain and Spinal Cord. The Functional Neuroanatomy and Dissection Guide.* New York: Springer-Verlag, 1983.

Herkenham M: Mismatches between neurotransmitter and receptor localizations in brain. Observations and implications. *Neuroscience:* in press, 1987.

Herkenham M, McLean S: Mismatches between receptor and transmitter localizations in the brain, observations and implications. In: Boast C, Snowhill EW, Altar CA (Editors), *Quantitative Receptor Autoradiography.* New York: Alan Liss, pp. 137 – 171, 1986.

Herkenham M, Pert CB: Light microscopic localization of brain opiate receptors: a general autoradiographic method which preserves tissue quality. *J. Neurosci.: 2,* 1129 – 1149, 1982.

Hill JM, Ruff MR, Weber RJ, Pert CB: Transferrin receptors in rat brain. Neuropeptide-like pattern and relationship to iron distribution. *Proc. Nat. Acad. Sci., USA: 82,* 4553 – 4557, 1985.

Hill JM, Lesniak MA, Pert CB, Roth J: Autobiographic localization of insulin receptors in rat brain: prominence in olfactory and limbic areas. *Neuroscience: 17,* 1127 – 1138, 1986.

Hill JM, Lesniak MA, Kiess W, Nissley SP: Radioimmunohistochemical localization of type II 1GF receptors in rat brain. *Peptides:* in press, 1987.

Hughes J, Smith TW, Koslerlitz HW, Fathergill LA, Morga BA, Morris HR: Identification of two related pentapeptide from brain with potent agonist activity. *Nature: 258* 577 – 580, 1975.

Kelly AE, Domesick VB, Nauta WJH: The amygdalostriata projections in the rat. An anatomical study by anterograd and retrograde tracing methods. *Neuroscience 1,* 615 – 630 1983.

Levitt P: A monoclonal antibody to limbic system neurons *Science: 223,* 299 – 301, 1984.

MacLean PD: Some psychiatric implications of physiologica studies on frontotemporal portion of limbic system (viscera brain). *Electroencephalogr. and Clin. Neurophysiol. J.: 4* 407 – 418, 1952.

Morley JE: Extrahypothalamic thyrotropin-releasing hormon (TRH): its distribution and its functions. *Life Sci.: 25* 1539 – 1550, 1979.

Nauta WJH, Domesick VB: Neural association of the limbi system. In Beckman AL (Editor), *The Neurological Basis o Behavior.* New York: Spectrum Publications, Inc., pp 175 – 206, 1982.

Nieuwenhuys R: *Chemoarchitecture of the Brain.* New York Springer Verlag, 1985.

Papez JW: A proposed mechanism of emotion. *Arch. Neurol. 38,* 725 – 743, 1937.

Pert CB, Ruff MR, Weber RJ, Herkenham M: Neuropeptide and their receptors: a psychosomatic network. *J. Immunol. 135,* 820s – 826s, 1985.

Pert CB, Snyder SH: Opiate receptor: demonstration in ner vous tissue. *Science: 179,* 1011 – 1014, 1973.

Quirion R, Gaudreau P, St-Pierre S, Rioux F, Pert CB Autoradiographic distribution of (^{3}H)neurotensin receptor in rat brain: visualization by tritium sensitive film. *Peptides 3,* 757 – 763, 1982.

Quirion R, Shults CWM, Moody TW, Pert CB, Chase TN O'Donohue TL: Autoradiographic distribution of substanc P receptors in rat central nervous system. *Nature: 303* 714 – 716, 1983.

Ruff MR, Pert CB: In Plotnikoff NP (Editor), *Enkephalins an Endorphins Stress and The Immune System.* New York Plenum, pp. 387 – 398, 1986.

Scharrer E, Scharrer B: Secretory cells within th hypothalamus. In *The Hypothalamus.* New York: Hafner 1940.

Schmitt FO: Molecular regulators of brain function: a nev view. *Neuroscience: 13,* 991 – 1001, 1984.

Siegel A, Troiano R, Royce A: Differential projections of th anterior and posterior cingulate gyrus to the thalamus in the cat. *Exp. Neurol.: 38,* 192 – 201, 1973.

Snyder SH: Brain peptides as neurotransmitters. *Science: 209,* 976 – 983, 1980.

Sternberger LA: What is brain? An immunocytochemica neuroendocrine approach. *Acta Histochem. Cytochem.: 13,* 66 – 70, 1980.

Vale W, Brazeau P, River C, Brown M, Bass B, Rivier J, Burgus R, Ling N, Guillemin R: Somatostatin. *Rec. Prog. Horm. Res.: 34,* 365 – 397, 1975.

Wiedermann CJ, Sertl K, Zipser B, Hill JM, Pert CB: Vasoac tive intestinal peptide receptors in rat spleen and brain: a shared communication network. *Peptides: 9* (Suppl. 1), 21 – 28, 1987.

© 1989 Elsevier Science Publishers B.V. (Biomedical Division)
Handbook of Neuropsychology, Vol. 3
F. Boller and J. Grafman (Eds)

CHAPTER 15

Ictal and interictal manifestations of emotions in epilepsy

Esther Strauss

Department of Psychology, University of Victoria, Victoria, British Columbia, Canada V8W 2Y2

Introduction

After more than a century of research, controversy still exists regarding the nature of the relationship between emotional disturbances and epilepsy. In part, the evaluation of this issue has been hampered by the weaknesses of vague constructs, the crudity of localizing techniques and the lack of methodological rigor in research (Hermann and Whitman, 1984; Kligman and Goldberg, 1975; Tizard, 1962). Yet because epilepsy is one of the most common neurological problems (affecting about 1% of the American population; National Commission of the Control of Epilepsy and Its Consequences, 1978), and because epileptics, as a group, have more psychological problems than normal people (Dodrill and Batzel, 1986; Hermann and Stevens, 1980), it would seem, from a practical standpoint, that the issue merits further investigation. Moreover, from a theoretical perspective, the study of emotional manifestations in epilepsy may provide a valuable tool in clarifying the neural mechanisms that underlie emotions, since it allows for direct correlation between specific aspects of affective behavior and localized dysfunction (Bear et al., 1984; Geschwind, 1975).

The purpose of this chapter is to review evidence bearing on the relationship between emotional disturbance and epilepsy. We consider first, ictal (that is, during seizure) manifestations of emotion; namely, fear, pleasure, laughter, depression, cry-

ing, aggressive and sexual behavior. By means of this review, we attempt to specify the nature, prevalence and neural structures associated with each of these behaviors. Since standard tests, especially surface electroencephalographic (EEG) recordings, can be very inaccurate in localizing the site of epileptogenic lesion (Mendius and Engel, 1985; Wieser, 1980), this section also examines the correlations between ictal emotions and electrical findings obtained via cerebral depth recording and stimulation.

Major portions of the limbic system are either contained within the temporal lobe or are in direct anatomic relation with structures within the temporal lobe (Gloor, 1975; Mirsky and Harmon, 1977). Since the limbic system is intimately concerned with aspects of emotional behavior (e.g. Gloor et al., 1982; Kluver and Bucy, 1939; MacLean, 1949, 1954; Papez, 1937), one might expect dysfunction in the temporal-limbic system to lead to disturbances of emotional behavior. The second section of this chapter examines interictal (that is, between seizure) manifestations of emotional disturbance in temporal-lobe epilepsy. Because considerable debate has centered on personality traits, aggression and sexual dysfunction in temporal-lobe epileptics, these topics are reviewed here. Psychotic illness, a clinical concern in some epileptic patients, will not form part of this chapter (for reviews of this topic see Flor-Henry, Ch. 22 of this volume; Hermann and Whitman,

1984; Toone, 1981; Trimble, 1984.

The final section provides some concluding remarks.

Ictal emotions

Fear

Hughlings Jackson (1879) was the first to describe fear as a sympton of an epileptic attack. He stated explicitly that he was not talking about the fear of a fit but of undirected fear, of 'fear which comes by itself — the sympton of fear'. Its intensity can vary from slight anxiety to stark terror and its duration can vary from several seconds to minutes (Daly, 1958; MacRae, 1954; Williams, 1956). Ictal fear is usually associated with other symptoms, particularly visceral ones, but can occur as an isolated syndrome (Bingley, 1958; MacRae, 1954; Williams, 1956).

Based on detailed clinical analysis of seizure patterns, investigators have noted that about 5% of epileptic patients experience an emotion as part of their seizure (Daly, 1958; Williams, 1956) and that fear is the ictal affect most commonly described (Bingley, 1958; Daly, 1958; Dalby, 1971; Gloor et al., 1982; King and Ajmone-Marsan, 1977; Preston and Atack, 1964; Schmid and Wieser, personal communication, 1987; Strauss et al., 1982; Williams, 1956). Williams (1956) reviewed over 2000 cases of epilepsy and reported that approximately 3% had ictal fear.

Ictal fear has typically been regarded as a symptom of temportal-lobe seizures (Daly, 1958; King and Ajmone-Marsan, 1977; MacRae, 1954; Williams, 1956). Estimates vary, but if we average incidence rates across studies (Bingley, 1958; Dalby, 1971; Gloor et al., 1982; King and Ajmone-Marsan, 1977; Strauss et al., 1982), then ictal fear is reported by about 20% of patients with temporal-lobe epilepsy. Both Williams (1956) and Strauss et al. (1982) concluded that ictal fear has no lateralizing value. This conclusion, however, must be tempered by the observation that in Williams's series (1956), ictal fear was twice as

common in patients with left-sided ($n = 30$) as compared to right-sided ($n = 16$) epileptic foci.

More precise information on the neuroanatomical correlates of fear has been obtained from electrical stimulation studies. During neurosurgical operations for the relief of intractable epilepsy, Penfield and his colleagues (Penfield and Jasper, 1954; Mullan and Penfield, 1959; Feindel and Penfield, 1954) noted that the most effective sites for producing fear were located in the mesial aspect of the temporal lobe (Gloor and Feindel, 1963). More recently, studies using chronic in-dwelling electrodes in patients with medically intractable seizures have shown that activation within the limbic system, especially the amygdala, is associated with an emotion of fear (Gloor, 1972; Gloor et al., 1981, 1982; Wieser, 1980). The results of the limbic stimulation, however, depend somewhat on the personality of the subject, his ongoing concerns and his environment (Gloor et al., 1982; Halgren et al., 1978; Halgren, 1982). In Halgren's series (1978), stimulation was most likely to result in the experience of fear or anxiety in those epileptic patients who scored higher on the 'psychaesthenia' (pt) scale of the Minnesota Multiphasic Personality Inventory (MMPI). This scale measures anxiety and tenseness.

There is additional evidence that stimulation of limbic structures, particularly the amygdala, is likely to be linked with a sensation of fear. Several investigators (Henriksen, 1973; McLachlan and Blume, 1980) have described epileptic patients whose attacks of fear stopped after temporal lobectomy which included removal of portions of the amygdala.

To summarize these observations on fear occurring with temporal-lobe seizures and stimulations, we can conclude that the emotion differs from the normal state in that it arises suddenly, out of context, and is undirected. Fear is the most common ictal emotion experienced during spontaneous seizures and upon experimental electrical stimulation. It is thought to be related to spread of the discharge to limbic structures, notably the amygdala.

Pleasure

Pleasurable emotions such as feelings of euphoria, completeness or gladness can also occur as ictal events. The most famous case is probably that of Dostoyevski (Ajouanine, 1963; Geschwind, 1984). Both Williams (1956) and Daly (1958) claimed that pleasure is typically accompanied by visceral sensations. The affect, however, may be inappropriate with regard to circumstances. Daly (1958) described a patient in whom nausea was associated with a pleasurable feeling.

Clinical observations indicate that ictal pleasure is an extremely rare event (Bingley, 1958; Dalby, 1971; Gloor et al., 1982; Strauss et al., 1982; Williams, 1956), occurring in probably less than 0.5% of epileptics. Most cases reported in the literature are suspected of showing a focus within the temporal lobe (Daly, 1958; Williams, 1956).

Given the fact that the occurrence of pleasurable experiences during a seizure is rare, it is not surprising that there are very few reports of electrical stimulation evoking this emotion. Penfield and Jasper (1954) reported that electrical stimulation at operation did not, in their experience, produce any emotional response such as joy or pleasure. Penfield wrote, "One is tempted to believe that there are no specific cortical mechanisms associated with these emotions, but absence of evidence proves nothing". Studies of epileptic patients implanted with electrodes have noted similar results (Gloor et al., 1981, 1982; Halgren et al., 1978). Among the few positive observations reported is that of Stevens et al. (1969). They described a case in which bipolar stimulation of the most medial points in the amygdalar complex on either side regularly gave a tremendous feeling of 'relaxation and relief' to the patient which persisted for minutes to hours after stimulation had stopped. Others (Heath et al., 1968, 1972; Obrador et al., 1973) have reported that septal stimulation may result in pleasurable feelings, although Gol (1967) was unable to confirm this finding.

In summary, pleasurable emotions as part of the ictal event are relatively rare occurrences. Most cases in the literature show evidence of a temporal-lobe focus and there are isolated reports that limbic stimulation can elicit this affect. However, localizing evidence is far less clear-cut than it had been for the ictal symptom of fear, this being due to the rarity of this category of emotion.

Laughter

Laughter has received relatively little attention as a manifestation of ictal emotion (Sackeim et al., 1982). The phenomenon was first described by Trousseau in 1873 and subsequently Daly and Mulder (1957) proposed the term 'gelastic' epilepsy. These attacks can be characterized by their stereotyped recurrence, absence of external precipitants, concomitance of other epileptic manifestations, presence of epileptiform discharges and the absence of diffuse neurological disorders such as bilateral corticobulbar or frontal-lobe disease (Gascon and Lombroso, 1971). The clinical features of epileptic laughter are variable (Loiseau et al., 1971; Lehtinen and Kivalo, 1965). In some cases the laughter sounds normal, while in other cases it is a caricature of a laugh. The duration of the laughter can vary. It is usually brief, a few seconds to 1 or 2 minutes, but longer attacks, up to half an hour, have been reported. The time in the attack when the outburst occurs is also variable, as is the memory for the attack. The laughter may or may not be accompanied by mood changes (e.g. Lehtinen and Kivalo, 1965; Loiseau et al., 1971; Money and Hosta, 1967; Rey-Pias, 1972; Yamada and Yoshida, 1977). It is worth noting, however, that the experience accompanying the laughter need not be a pleasant one. Roger and his colleagues (1967) described a patient with temporal-lobe epilepsy in whom the laughter was experienced as a disagreeable, incongruous happening which the patient tried to cover up.

Ictal laughter is a rare phenomenon. Since the time of Trousseau (1873), fewer than 200 cases have been reported in the literature. Chen and Forster (1973) reviewed a series of 5000 consecutive cases of epilepsy and found that 10 or 0.2% of the cases had gelastic epilepsy. These investigators pointed out that this incidence is probably higher than that which occurs in the total population of epileptics, since the majority of the cases studied in their center had temporal-lobe seizures.

There is no single anatomic lesion that can be held responsible for the occurrence of gelastic epilepsy (Black, 1982; Chen and Forster, 1973; Gascon and Lombroso, 1971; Loiseau et al., 1971). It may arise from lesions of the frontal and temporal cortex or in the hypothalamic-diencephalic structures. Some have proposed that epileptic foci in the temporal lobe will produce a gelastic seizure with an affective component, whereas seizures caused by diencephalic lesions are thought not to have an affective component (Gascon and Lombroso, 1971; Loiseau et al., 1971; Money and Hosta, 1967).

Just as there is no single neuroanatomic lesion responsible for the occurrence of gelastic epilepsy, so too the electroencephalographic studies have not revealed a characteristic pattern of electrical activity (Chen and Forster, 1973; Loiseau et al., 1971). Although many investigators report temporal-lobe abnormality, there are numerous exceptions. The conclusion that the EEG findings are extremely variable requires some qualification. Recently, Sackeim and his colleagues (1982) evaluated the laterality of epileptic foci in a large sample of published cases of gelastic epilepsy. They found that foci were twice as likely to be predominantly left- as opposed to right-sided. This asymmetry was more pronounced for men than for women.

Experimental electrical stimulation of brain structures rarely elicits laughter (Gloor et al., 1982; Halgren et al., 1978; Schmid and Wieser, personal communication, 1987). One of the few published observations is that by Delgado (1960). He reported a case in whom electrical stimulation of the temporal lobe induced 'expressions of pleasure, giggling, laughing, humorous comments', and a remark by the patient that she very much enjoyed the 'pleasant tingling sensation of the body'.

The findings with regard to ictal laughter in-

dicate it is a very rare phenomenon. There is no focal neuroanatomic 'center' for laughter. Rather, it is a complex neurophysiological event with recording changes most pronounced on the left side of the brain, in temporal, frontal and diencephalic structures.

Depression

Ictal depression has been described by several investigators (Bingley, 1958; Daly, 1958; Weil, 1955, 1956; Williams, 1956). The affect occurs suddenly, out of context and in all degrees. Patients may describe feelings of sadness, lonesomeness, futility, or a sinking hollow feeling. Like other ictal emotions, the depression appears unmotivated to the patient. The emotion may occur as an aura of the seizure, during the seizure or as a sequel to the seizure. The duration of depression is also variable. It may be brief, lasting for several minutes, but unlike other ictal emotions the mood may also persist for days or weeks after the attack (Weil, 1955, 1956; Williams, 1956). Persistence of depression is the more characteristic pattern. Weil (1955, 1956) proposed that the prolonged depressive episodes may be due to subclinical epileptiform activity in the hippocampal-amygdaloid-temporal lobe complex and/or due to after-discharges following activation of these same structures. Williams (1956) offered a different explanation for the relative persistence of ictal depression. He suggested that depression as an ictal mood has the same qualities as a naturally occurring mood and that 'moods are inevitably prolonged'.

Ictal depression is fairly uncommon, being described by about 1% of epileptic patients (Williams, 1956). Most cases show evidence of a temporal lobe focus (Daly, 1958; Weil, 1955, 1956; Williams, 1956), although even among this group of patients depression is a rare event. Less than 10% of patients with temporal-lobe epilepsy describe depression as part of their seizure.

Feelings of sadness, depression, can on occasion be elicited by electrical stimulation (Penfield and Jasper, 1954; Mullan and Penfield, 1959; Gloor et al., 1982). Gloor and his colleagues (1981, 1982) reported that among 35 patients in whom intracerebral depth electrodes were stereotaxically implanted, three described feelings of emotional distress in the form of depression, guilt or a less definable unpleasant emotional state. In all three patients, the emotional phenomenon did not occur unless the stimulation or seizure discharge involved the limbic system.

We can summarize these findings by noting that ictal depression is relatively rare. Unlike other emotions, ictal depression typically lasts for days after the attack. Finally, there is usually evidence of temporal-limbic discharge.

Crying

Crying as an epileptic phenomenon has received little attention in the literature. It has been referred to as 'dacrystic' epilepsy by Offen et al. (1976) and 'quiritarian' epilepsy by Sethi and Rao (1976).

The data on this condition are sparse, since to date fewer than 10 cases have been reported in the literature. The rarity of ictal crying is somewhat surprising in view of the fact that most emotions occurring as part of epileptic attacks are unpleasant (Sethi and Rao, 1976).

No focal area has been associated with ictal crying. Sackeim and his colleagues (1982) examined the lateralization of foci in cases of dacrystic epilepsy. An extensive literature search uncovered 6 cases. Only one case was rated as left-sided, four were rated as right-sided and the lateralization of one case was indeterminate. Based on these results, Sackeim et al. suspected a right-sided asymmetry for ictal crying, but they emphasized that too few cases have been reported in the literature to examine this issue adequately. Finally, we are not aware of any case in which experimental stimulation of brain structures has evoked crying behavior.

Aggression

Aggression, as an ictal manifestation, has been the subject of intense study and debate. At the turn of the century, there was widespread belief that

directed aggression could occur as part of an epileptic seizure (see for review Trieman, 1986). This view is still espoused in some modern textbooks of neurology and psychiatry (e.g. Kolb and Brodie, 1982). The weight of evidence, however, suggests that ictal aggression is an extremely rare phenomenon.

One of the first studies was conducted by Williams (1956). He reviewed a series of over 2000 cases of epilepsy and found that 17 or 0.9% of the cases showed ictal aggression. All were suspected of having a temporal lobe focus. He also noted that anger as a purely affective state, in the absence of aggression, occurred in only one case. Rodin (1982) has commented that, over a timespan of 21 years, he has observed more than 10,000 epileptic seizures with automatic components. Moderate ictal violence to a person was seen in only 3 cases (0.03%). Bingley (1958) reported that in his sample of 90 patients with temporal-lobe epilepsy, 17% showed anger and/or an expression of aggressivity. This incidence seems quite high in the light of other reports. Gloor (1967), speaking on the extensive experience of the Montreal Neurological Institute with patients having temporal lobe seizures, made the statement that "rage, with or without aggressive behavior, is an extremely rare phenomenon . . . I myself have never seen an instance of true ictal rage . . . Furthermore, I would suspect that some, perhaps even the reported cases of ictal rage, would not withstand a critical assessment of the evidence. Frequently, aggressive behavior associated with a fit is not at all ictal, but rather a postictal phenomenon, elicited in the postictal confusional state. This often occurs because the patient is restrained by well-meaning people in an attempt to protect him".

Other studies confirm Gloor's experience. In 1973, Rodin reported on 150 epileptic patients, including 42 with psychomotor automatisms, seen in the Lafayette clinic. All had seizures induced by drug for diagnostic purposes and were photographed during this time. There was no instance of ictal or postictal aggression. When there was danger of aggressive behavior, it could promptly be averted by abandoning restraint efforts. Studies by King and Ajmone-Marsan (1977) and Delgado-Escueta and his colleagues (1977, 1981) provide additional evidence. King and Ajmone-Marsan (1977) reported that of 199 patients with temporal-lobe foci whose seizures were observed by trained personnel (e.g. physicians, EEG technicians, nurses), 9 had perictal behavior that could be defined as violent. Of these 9 patients, 7 were combative (that is, pushing, struggling, flailing) while being restrained in the immediate postictal period. One, in whom there was doubt whether the attacks were genuinely epileptic, had episodes of beating her chest, and another picked up objects and threw them. Delgado-Escueta and his colleagues (1977, 1982) recorded on closed-circuit television (CCTV) and EEG 691 complex partial seizures in 79 patients. Seven exhibited resistive violence while fighting restraints and 3 had stereotyped automatic motions like thrashing and flailing of arms. Six walked or ran away during the early part of the seizures and knocked down objects or tried to break open a door as part of the ambulatory automatism. None exhibited directed aggression.

The most comprehensive study to date regarding ictal aggression has been reported by Delgado and his colleagues in 1981. Officials from 16 epilepsy programs in the United States, Canada, Germany and Japan selected from a group of 5400 epileptics the 19 patients (0.4%) who were believed to exhibit ictal aggression. A total of 33 attacks in these 19 patients were identified as possibly showing violent behavior. A panel of 18 epileptologists then convened in a workshop to review the case histories and the CCTV-EEG recordings of this group of patients. The clinical diagnosis of epilepsy was incontestable in 13 of these 19 patients.

The panel agreed on the definition of violence as the directed exertion of extreme and aggressive physical force, which if unrestrained would result in injury, destruction or abuse. In analysing aggressive behavior, the panel used the following rating scale. A rating of 0 represented no violence or aggressive behavior, 1 represented no directed aggressive behavior, 2 represented violence to pro-

perty, 3 denoted threatening violence to a person, 4 denoted mild actual violence to a person, 5 represented moderate violence to a person, and a rating of 6 indicated severe violence to a person such as the use of physical force which resulted in serious injury or death. On the basis of this rating scale, the panel agreed that 6 patients had no or minimal aggression. The remaining 7 patients exhibited aggression that was rated 2 to 4. In most cases, spontaneous, nondirected stereotyped aggressive movements, violence to property, shouting or spitting at persons, and mild to moderate violence to another person were observed during the height of epileptiform paroxysms. Nondirected aggression was seen at the end of a complex partial seizure in one case and after a tonic-clonic seizure in two patients. In the latter two patients, aggression appeared to be in relation to being restrained. All forms of aggressive behavior that rated 2 to 4 occurred during complex partial seizures. Amnesia for aggressive acts was present in every case. All aggressive acts appeared suddenly, without evidence of planning and lasted an average of 29 seconds, whereas complete complex partial seizures lasted an average of 145 seconds in this series. Aggressive acts were stereotyped, simple, unsustained and never supported by a consecutive series of purposive movements. In this group of patients, acts of aggression were never carried out with a lethal weapon.

In short, independent studies from diverse institutions reveal that ictal or even postictal aggression is rare. Admittedly, in these investigations, patients from a population with known aggressive or violent behavior were not included. This is an important distinction, since more harmful acts of aggression could characterize the seizures of more violence-prone epileptics. One way to correct for this potential bias is to select epileptic patients who are alleged to be aggressive and to evaluate their seizures. Ramani and Gumnit (1981) subjected 19 epileptic patients with significant histories of episodic aggressive behavior to intensive video-EEG monitoring. Ictal episodes were recorded successfully in 15 patients. None showed directed aggression, but one patient exhibited nondirected, aggressive behavior postictally while trying to free himself from restraints.

Another approach is to consider in detail each case reported in the literature in which an act of violence is alleged to have been due to an epileptic attack. Trieman and Delgado-Escueta (1983) reviewed 29 cases reported in the medical literature from 1872 to 1981 in which violent events were reported to be due to a seizure. In only 3 of the cases was the evidence strongly suggestive of a relationship between ictal epileptic attacks and violent automatisms. Trieman (1986) evaluated 75 cases of violence where epilepsy had been used as a defence in the courts in the United States. In none of the 75 cases, except for 4 cases of vehicular manslaughter, was there sufficient evidence to establish the ictal nature of the violent episode.

The conclusion that it is extremely unusual for epileptic patients to show any ictal aggression, especially if unrestrained, is not surprising, in view of the evidence advanced by Penfield (Penfield and Jasper, 1954; Mullan and Penfield, 1959), Gloor (1978, 1981, 1982) and others (Wieser, 1980; Halgren et al., 1978; Chapman, 1958; St- Hilaire et al., 1980) that limbic stimulation rarely evokes anger or aggression. Nevertheless, a few reports of ictal aggression have appeared in the literature (e.g. Heath et al., 1955; Stevens et al., 1969; St-Hilaire et al., 1980; Sweet et al., 1968; Wieser, 1983). One of the most famous cases is that of Julia P. described by Mark, Ervin and Sweet (Mark and Ervin, 1970; Sweet et al., 1968; Mark et al., 1972). Julia was a 22-year-old girl who had encephalitis at the age of 2. When she was 10 years old, she began having complex partial and generalized tonic-clonic seizures. Her behavior between seizures was marked by severe temper tantrums. On 12 occasions, Julia assaulted other people without provocation. By far the most serious attack occurred when she was 18. She was at a movie with her parents when she felt a wave of terror pass over her body. She told her father that she was going to have one of her 'racing spells' and agreed to wait for her parents in the ladies' lounge.

As she went to it, she took a small knife from her handbag. In the lounge, she looked in the mirror and perceived the left side of her face and trunk as 'shriveled, disfigured, and evil'. At the same time, she noticed a drawing sensation in her face and hands. Another girl entered the lounge and inadvertently bumped against Julia's left arm and hand. Julia, in a panic, stabbed the girl in the heart and then screamed loudly. Whether this assault represented an ictal epileptic attack is controversial (e.g. Trieman and Delgado-Escueta, 1983). Nonetheless, electrical stimulation of limbic structures in this patient did evoke aggressive behavior. During a sequence of electrical stimulations of the right amygdala, Mark and his colleagues produced an EEG discharge reminiscent of her habitual seizures. This ictal EEG event occurred just before an abnormal behavioral event in which she made a series of angry grimaces and sprang towards the wall.

St-Hilaire and his colleagues (1980) have also documented, by means of depth electrode and audio-visual records, two rare but definite cases of ictal aggression. Both patients had complex partial seizures. One patient shouted insults at people. The other patient shouted and tried to scratch the faces of people. In neither case was restraint a provocative element. In both cases, hippocampal discharge was associated with the aggressive behavior. It is noteworthy that in both cases, immediate environmental factors played a role in these aggressive outbursts. The target seemed to be chosen according to the patient's interpretation of his current situation. In short, both the site of stimulation and the patient's current context interacted to determine the quality of the response.

Although this review is not exhaustive, it seems sufficiently comprehensive to indicate that ictal anger or aggression, whether associated with temporal-lobe discharge or electrical stimulation, is an exceedingly rare phenomenon. Most of the recorded cases have shown aggression while being restrained at the end of a seizure rather than directed aggression. Aggressive acts are typically stereotyped, simple, unsustained, unplanned, never a part of a consecutive series of complex acts. They do not occur in response to preictal provocation, nor are they premeditated (Trieman, 1986). Finally, there is no focal centre for aggression. In the few well-documented cases, changes correlated with aspects of aggressive behavior invariably involved electrical abnormality in the limbic structures, particularly the hippocampus and amygdala.

Sexual behavior

Ictal sexual behavior can take three different forms (Remillard et al., 1983; Spencer et al., 1983). One type consists of somatosensory sensations in the genitalia that may be unpleasant or emotionally neutral. These sensations probably indicate discharges from the superior portion of the postcentral gyrus, in the interhemispheric fissure or the perisylvian region. A second form consists of sexual automatisms. These are defined as clinical mannerisms that encompass exhibitionism, masturbatory activity, or other sexual activity for which the patient is amnesic. Such automatisms have been related to frontal seizure origin. These manifestations must be distinguished from erotic feelings, with or without genital feelings or sensations of orgasm. This last form is reviewed here.

Patients may describe the ictal sensations as erotic, sexual or orgasmic (Remillard et al., 1983). One famous case, described by Mitchell (1954), is that of a patient with epilepsy accompanied by a fetish for safety pins. Seizures were specifically triggered whenever he looked at a bright shiny pin. The seizure was accompanied by a pleasurable sensation described as 'thought satisfaction' and as 'better than intercourse'. This patient had a left anterior temporal epileptic focus, the epilepsy and the fetish both being cured by left anterior temporal lobectomy. It is worth noting that the sexual feelings are typically, though not necessarily, pleasurable. Bente and Klug (1953) described a case (cited in Gloor and Feindel, 1963) of a female patient with libidinous feelings that were not felt to be pleasant. She experienced nymphomanic attacks leading to compulsory masturbation and

orgasm. Nonetheless, she was at the same time depressed and cried. However, this may have been a reactive emotion, explicable on the basis that, to this patient, the episodes were highly embarrassing and shameful. Finally, ictal sexual feelings are often associated with other symptoms, particularly genital visceral ones, and usually occur at the beginning of the seizure (Remillard et al., 1983).

Case reports of ictal erotic sensations have appeared in the literature (Bente and Klug, 1953; Blumer, 1970; Currier et al., 1971; Erickson, 1945; Hooshmand and Brawley, 1969; Jacome et al., 1980; Remillard et al., 1983; Van Reeth, 1958; Warnecke, 1976). The incidence of these ictal manifestations is unknown although the impression of this reviewer is that they are rather rare events. It is, however, possible that patients do not disclose these episodes and that their frequency may be higher than one would otherwise conclude from the available evidence. These phenomena are reported more frequently by women than by men, suggesting that the neural organization of psychosexual behavior may be different in men and women (Remillard et al., 1983). Alternatively, in view of the nature of these experiences, men may be more reluctant than women to relate them.

Ictal erotic feelings have typically been regarded as a symptom of temporal-lobe seizures (e.g. Currier, 1971; Freemon and Nevis, 1969; Jacome et al., 1980; Remillard et al., 1983; Warnecke, 1976). Lateralization of the epileptogenic foci is predominantly, though not invariably, right-sided (Flor-Henry, 1976; Remillard et al., 1983).

Not surprisingly, reports of electrical brain stimulation evoking erotic sensations are very rare (Penfield and Jasper, 1954). Remillard and his colleagues (1983) described two patients with temporal-lobe epilepsy who reported ictal sexual arousal. The feelings were reproduced by stimulation of deep temporal regions, indicating involvement of limbic structures. Quesney (cited in Gloor, 1986) produced a feeling of sexual arousal by right amygdaloid stimulation in a 40-year-old woman. She had an abdominal feeling like nausea, but in addition she experienced a pleasant feeling in her vulva and on the inner surface of her thighs, as if she were having sexual intercourse. She volunteered that she had the same sexual experience at the onset of her spontaneous seizures. Orgasmic feelings have also been observed with stimulation of the septal region (Heath, 1972) and the ventrolateral thalamic region (Bechterewa, 1973).

We can summarize these findings by noting that erotic ictal manifestations are rare, although their exact prevalence is unknown. These sensations are more often reported by women than by men. Characteristically, they indicate involvement of deep temporal-limbic structures, more often on the right than on the left side of the brain.

Summary

The literature reviewed in this section indicates that a wide variety of emotional responses can be produced by ictal discharge or electrical stimulation. Fear is the most common ictal emotion and is experienced by about 3% of epileptic patients. Ictal feelings of depression are somewhat less common, being reported by about 1% of epileptics. Experiences of pleasure, laughter, crying and aggression all appear to be rather rare ictal manifestations, each occurring in less than 1% of the epileptic population. Ictal sexual sensations are probably infrequent although their prevalence is unknown. The evidence tends to suggest that the most crucial structures for aspects of these emotional behaviors are those belonging to the limbic system. There is also evidence that certain limbic structures may be more involved than others in the mediation of some emotional behaviors. There is even the suggestion that some emotional responses are related to the laterality of the discharge or stimulation. However, it would be erroneous to conceive of a fine topographical differentiation, with discrete centers subserving separate emotional behaviors. The evidence available at present does not support this kind of interpretation (Gloor et al., 1982; Halgren et al., 1978; St-Hilaire, 1980). Moreover, responses occurring with temporal-limbic discharge or stimulation differ in one important respect from those evoked from primary motor or sensory areas of cortex. They are not 'hard-wired' but, as Halgren et al. (1978) and others (Gloor et al., 1982; St-Hilaire et al., 1980) have emphasized, the experiences are individualized. They depend somewhat on the subject's personality, his ongoing concerns and his environment. In short, these experiential phenomena reflect an interaction of both the site of seizure discharge or stimulation and the individual's personality and current concerns.

Interictal manifestations

There is an extensive literature on the relationship between interictal manifestions of emotional disturbance and epilepsy (for reviews see Guerrant et al., 1962; Trimble, 1983, 1984). Briefly, at the turn of the century, investigators considered that all epileptic people underwent intellectual and personality deterioration because of their fits. This view was subsequently challenged by a number of authors, most notably Lennox (1960). He argued that most epileptics were normal in intellect and personality, although some suffered psychological defects as a result of structural brain damage or the deleterious effects of chronic anticonvulsant therapy. The 'period of normalcy' continues to the present for epilepsy in general. The modern era, termed the 'period of psychomotor peculiarity' by Guerrant et al. (1962), began with more extensive use of the EEG, and with the reports of investigators such as Gibbs, Gibbs and their colleagues (1948, 1953, 1964) of a high incidence of emotional disorders in persons with psychomotor epilepsy. Although they acknowledged that psychological factors are important in creating the patient's emotional problems, these authors held that the location of the epileptogenic focus was critical. Gibbs and Stamps (1953) asserted that 'the patient's emotional reactions to his seizures, to his family and to his social situation are less important determinants of psychiatric disorder than the site and type of epileptic discharge'. This proposal, that people with epilepsy originating in the temporal lobe are at special risk for emotional disturbance, is still very controversial.

We examine here the interictal manifestations of emotional disturbance in epilepsy, especially with reference to temporal-lobe epilepsy, and we focus on three problem areas; namely personality traits, aggression, and sexual function. More specifically, the following questions are considered:

1. Do people with temporal-lobe epilepsy have different behavioral traits relative to other populations?

2. Is there a particular constellation of personality traits that is characteristic of persons with temporal-lobe epilepsy?

3. Is aggression more common among people with temporal-lobe epilepsy relative to other populations?

4. In comparison with other groups, do people with temporal-lobe epilepsy demonstrate more sexual problems?

Before turning to the literature review, it is important to note that the assessment of interictal disorders presents considerable methodological problems (for other detailed reviews, see Dodrill, 1986; Hermann and Whitman, 1984; Kligman and Goldberg, 1975). The first troublesome point concerns the use of the term temporal-lobe epilepsy. Individual investigators have used different definitions of temporal-lobe epilepsy and this may be one source of the divergent results in the literature. Researchers have used the terms 'psychomotor', 'temporal-lobe' or 'complex partial' seizures as if they were equivalent entities. However, many patients with a focus in the temporal lobe may never have the clinical manifestations of a 'psychomotor' seizure and patients with 'psychomotor' or 'complex partial' attacks may not have a temporal-lobe EEG focus. With the introduction of the International Classification of Seizure Disorders (Gastaut, 1970), investigators have recognized that old terms such as 'psychomotor' epilepsy are inadequate. According to this scheme, a distinction is made between seizures without focal onset (generalized seizures) and those with focal onset (partial seizures). Generalized seizures involve discharge through many brain structures. Grand

mal epilepsy falls in this category. Partial seizures are of two types. Those with elementary symptomatology have no impairment of consciousness, whereas those with complex partial seizures may be accompanied with such alterations. The term complex partial seizure is being used with increasing frequency. One should note, however, that here the EEG focus may arise from the temporal lobe but it may also originate from other cerebral regions. In this chapter, we refer to the attacks as temporal-lobe epilepsy to emphasize their anatomical correlates (see also Hermann and Whitman, 1984). In Tables 1–3, the specific terminology used by the individual investigators is given.

The variation in nomenclature is not the only source of confusion. A related problem concerns variation in the diagnostic criteria. Thus, some have diagnosed their patients primarily on the basis of clinical seizure patterns, whereas others have relied solely on EEG findings. Still others have used both clinical and EEG (interictal or ictal) criteria, and their selection criteria therefore can be considered more rigorous. To the extent that investigators employ divergent diagnostic criteria, they may not be studying the same disorders.

In addition, the adequacy of the EEG techniques has varied among studies. Most investigators made their diagnosis on the basis of interictal scalp EEG abnormalities. This is a very imprecise procedure. Only in the last 5–10 years have researchers recognized the importance of ictal EEG localization at the time of the habitual clinical seizure. Few studies, however, have relied on this technique. Furthermore, the scalp EEG can provide a reasonable overview of surface activity but may not detect abnormal activity arising from subcortical structures. Special extracranial electrode placements (nasopharyngeal, sphenoidal, suborbital, ethmoidal) or intracranial techniques (depth recording in combination with stimulation) increase the probability of detecting abnormalities in deep temporal-limbic structures, but few studies have used these special procedures. This failure may increase the likelihood of not detecting a temporal-obe focus in some patients, particularly those with generalized epilepsy. As a result, real behavioral differences may be obscured when making comparisons between epileptic subgroups.

Another important problem is that the majority of studies that contrasted temporal-lobe epilepsy with other convulsive disorders have used patients with generalized epilepsy as control subjects. Generalized epilepsy, however, involves abnormal firing through many brain structures, including deep temporal-limbic ones, thereby confounding the contrast. A more appropriate comparison would be with partial epilepsy, originating from other cerebral regions, but few studies have used this approach since such epilepsies are rare.

Finally, in discussing the behavior of a group of temporal-lobe epileptics, it is important to keep in mind (Hermann and Whitman, 1984; Kligman and Goldberg, 1975; Tizard, 1962) that temporal-lobe epilepsy is itself a complex phenomenon that does not represent a well-defined homogeneous entity. Rather there is no uniformity of etiology, pathology or clinical symptomatology. In fact, Symonds (1962) suggested substituting the term 'temporal-lobe epilepsies' to emphasize the diversity of forms. Grouping these diverse disorders together may complicate the interpretation of those behavioral trends that are observed and may mask others which are characteristic of only one subtype (Kligman and Goldberg, 1975).

It is clear that such methodological difficulties hinder the accurate assessment of behavior disturbance in temporal-lobe epilepsy. Consequently, any conclusions that one might draw in this area must be regarded as highly tentative.

Personality traits

According to the view of Gibbs and others, one would expect people with temporal-lobe epilepsy to show an increased incidence of atypical personality traits or behavioral characteristics. There are very few careful epidemiological surveys bearing on this issue. A number of studies of hospital patients have been conducted and these show a high incidence of emotional disturbance in in-

dividuals with temporal-lobe epilepsy (e.g. Currie et al., 1971; Dalby, 1971; James, 1960; Jensen and Larsen, 1979; Kogeorgos et al., 1982; Stevens, 1966; Slater and Beard, 1963; Taylor and Falconer, 1968). The value of these reports, however, is somewhat limited, since people attending hospitals manifest more disturbances than nonattenders (Pond and Bidwell, 1959, Pond, 1981). Two studies with nonselected adult epileptic populations have been reported, however, and both are consistent with Gibbs's proposal. Pond and Bidwell (1959), in a general practice survey, noted that 29% of their epileptic population showed psychological difficulties and 7% had been in a mental hospital before or during the survey year. About 5% had abnormal personalities. The patients with temporal-lobe epilepsy fared worse. More than 50% had serious psychological difficulties and nearly 20% had been in a mental hospital. About 30% showed abnormal personality traits. Gudmundsson's (1966) survey of the population of Iceland revealed that 50% of the epileptics had some type of abnormal personality. The frequency of psychological difficulties was higher in patients with temporal-lobe epilepsy (50%) than in non-temporal-lobe epileptics (24%).

In addition to these epidemiological surveys, a number of investigators have used objective tests and rating scales to compare persons with temporal-lobe epilepsy to other groups. Table 1 summarizes studies that have measured behavioral characteristics with a variety of objective procedures (either a test or rating form). Each study included in the table had to have at least one group with temporal-lobe epilepsy and one contrast group.

Let us consider first whether differences exist between people with temporal-lobe epilepsy and normal healthy individuals. There are 11 studies that have made such a comparison (Bear and Fedio, 1977; Bear et al., 1981; Bellur et al., 1985; Brandt et al., 1985; McIntyre et al., 1976; Mungas, 1982; Perini and Mendius, 1984; Rodin and Schmaltz, 1984; Stores, 1978; Strauss et al., 1982; Whitman et al., 1984). The conclusion from these studies,

TABLE I

Personality traits

Authors and subject groups	Evaluation procedure	Differences between TLE and:			Left vs. right
		Normals	Chronic	Other epil.	
Bear and Fedio, 1977; 15 RTLE, 12 LTLE, 12 normals, 9 pts with neuromuscular disease	– Pers. Inv. – Pers. Behav. Survey	TLE got higher scores	TLE got higher scores	–	RTLE underreported some qualities and LTLE gave more self-reports
Bear et al., 1981; 5 TLE, 7 normals	Verbal ratings and GSR to slides	Skin conduct. responses larger in TLE	–	–	–
Bear et al., 1982; 10 TLE, 10 other epil., 10 schizophr., 10 primary affective dis., 10 aggressive character dis.	Ratings of 14 traits derived from structured interview	–	TLE got higher scores	TLE higher on some traits	–
Bellur et al., 1985; 23 TLE, 7 non-TLE, 16 normals	Heart rate and electrodermal responses to stressful film	No diff.	–	No diff.	–
Brandt et al., 1985; 28 LTLE, 19 RTLE, 10 generalized epilepsy, 14 normals	Pers. Inv.	TLE and normals differed in overall profiles	–	TLE lower than GE on dependence circumstantiality	LTLE characterized by humorlessness; RTLE no different from controls
Cairns, 1974; 26 psychomotor, 12 non-psychomotor	16 PF	–	–	Psychomotor group less dependent, sensitive and conscientious	–
Dikmen et al., 1983; 34 CPS, 34 CPS with sec. generaliz., 48 generalized epilepsy	MMPI	–	–	CPS with sec. gen. scored higher on depression scale than CPS gp. No diff. between the two PCS gps.	–
Guerrant et al., 1962; 32 psychomotor, 26 grand mal, 26 chronic illness	Ratings derived from psychiatric interview and psychol. tests incl. MMPI	–	Chronic illness gp worse	TLE higher on phobias, obsessions, chronic fatigue. Grand mal higher on ideas of reference, excess alcohol and negativism. More clinical interpretations of psychotic profiles on MMPI in TLE	–

Study	Test				
47 TLE, 28 generalized epilepsy	—	—	—	of adolescent onset scored higher in psychol. dysfunction	—
Hermann and Riel, 1981; 14 TLE, 14 generalized epilepsy	Pers. Inv.	—	—	TLE scored higher on 4 of 18 trait scales	—
Hermann et al., 1982; 11 TLE with ictal fear, 14 TLE with olfactory or gustatory auras, 14 generalized epilepsy	MMPI	—	—	Subgroup of TLE with ictal fear showed more psychopathology	—
Hermann et al., 1983; 80 TLE, 31 non-TLE, 13 TLE + GE	Response to letters	—	—	TLE showed greater response rate	—
Kogeorgos et al., 1982; 66 epileptics	– General Health Quest. – Crown-Crisp Experiential Index	—	Epil, esp males, showed more anxiety, depression and hysteria	On Crown-Crisp, GE scored higher on hysteria scale	—
Lachar et al., 1979; 37 TLE, 28 non-TLE	MMPI	—	—	No diff.	—
Mathews and Klove, 1968; 52 major motor, 44 psychomotor, 38 mixed, 51 non-neurol. controls, 48 neurol. controls	MMPI	—	No diff.	No diff.	—
McIntyre et al., 1976; 11 LTLE, 11 RTLE, 12 normals	– Kagan Matching Familiar Figures Test – Davis Mattis Metaphor Test	LTLE more reflective and made more unusual responses	—	—	LTLE more reflective, RTLE more impulsive; LTLE made more unusual responses on DMMT
Mignone et al., 1970; 98 psychomotor, 53 non-psychomotor	MMPI	—	—	No diff.	No diff. but % deviant responses of LTLE higher than in those with RTLE
Mungas, 1982; *Study 1:* 14 TLE, 14 neurobehavior disorder, 14 psychiatric disorder	– Pers. Inv. – Pers. Behav. Survey	—	No diff.	—	—
Study 2: 12 neurobehavior disorder, 12 psychiatric disorder, 12 neurol. movement dis., 12 normals	Pers. Inv.	No diff.	No diff.	—	—

327

TABLE I (continued)

Authors and subject groups	Evaluation procedure	Differences between TLE and:			
		Normals	Chronic	Other epil.	Left vs. right
Perini and Mendius, 1984; 9 LTLE, 8 RTLE, 3 bilat., 19 normals	– State-Trait Anxiety Inv. – Beck Depression Inventory – Columbia Mania and Depression Scale	Depression and anxiety more common in TLE	–	–	LTLE more depressed and anxious; RTLE no diff from normals
Rodin et al., 1976; 78 TLE, 78 non-TLE	Pts rated on 887 vars. covering neurol., psychiatric psychol., social and EEG data	–	–	TLE, esp. those with multiple sz types, had more impaired peer relations, more personality disturbances, more psychotic tendencies, higher MMPI elevations on scales D and PA	–
Rodin and Schmaltz, 1984; 148 epil, 18 pain pts, 15 psychiatric, 40 normals, 89 family members of epileptics	– Pers. Inv. – Pers. Behav. Suvery	TLE scored higher on all traits	TLE scored higher on most traits	No diff. when sex and IQ effects taken into account	No diff.
Sachdev and Waxman, 1981; 9 TLE, 8 non-TLE	Response to letters	–	–	TLE responded more and wrote more extensively	–
Small et al., 1962; 25 TLE, 25 non-TLE	MMPI	–	–	no diff.	–
Standage and Fenton, 1975; 19 TLE, 15 generalized epilepsy, 3 non-temp. focal epil., 27 neuromuscular controls	– Wing Present State Exam – Eysenck Personality Inventory	–	No diff.	No diff.	–
Stevens et al., 1972; 29 psychomotor, 14 generalized epilepsy, 6 frontal	MMPI	–	–	No diff.	–
Stevens, 1975; 21 psychomotor, 18 generalized epilepsy	MMPI	–	–	No diff.	–

Study	Instrument				
Stores, 1978; 17 gen. epil. irreg. spike and wave, 17 gen. epil. reg. 3/sec spike and wave, 16 RTLE, 20 LTLE, 103 normal children	– Connors Teaching Rating Scale – Self-administered dependency quest.	Epil boys diff. from non-epil. boys	–	LTLE more dependent than children with generalized epilepsy	LTLE boys had conduct problems, anxiety, inattentiveness, overactivity and social isolation; LTLE more dependent than RTLE
Strauss et al., 1982; 30 LTLE, 31 LTLE, 53 generalized epilepsy, 35 carpal tunnel syndrome, 113 normals	Fear Inventory	LTLE reported more social and sexual fears	LTLE reported more social fears	No diff.	LTLE reported more social and sexual fears
Tucker et al., 1987; 51 LTLE, 25 RTLE, 31 primary gen. seizures, 27 with pseudoseizures	Wiggins Religiosity Scale of MMPI	–	No diff.	No diff.	No diff.
Whitman et al., 1984; 409 TLE, 258 generalized epilepsy, 142 other, 870 neurol. pts, 1107 chronic illness pts	MMPI	Epileptics at higher risk for psychopathology	No diff.	No diff.	–
Wieser, 1986; 10 temp.-limb., 6 temp.-neocort., 23 temp.-limb. + neocort., 16 frontal, 5 centroparietal, 3 occipital	Pers. Inv.	–	–	Humorlessness increased in frontals. In temp.-limbic pts, increase in circumstantiality and hypermoralism	Trend: Rt. showed increase in hypermoralism, humorlessness; L: increase in relig., hypergraph., altered sexual content
Willmore et al., 1980; 10 RTLE, 10 LTLE, 14 generalized epilepsy	Quest. on religiosity	–	–	Gen. epil. more religious	No diff.

summarized in Table 1, is that temporal-lobe epileptics, or subgroups of this larger category, have more behavioral problems than do normal people. All but 2 of the 11 studies (Bellur et al., 1985; Mungas, 1982) showed some type of difference between groups.

Another question is whether people with temporal-lobe epilepsy demonstrate more problems than do individuals with other chronic illnesses. The answer may depend on whether the control group's disease is associated with brain damage or dysfunction (Dodrill and Batzel, 1986). Eight studies included a control group with non-brain-related medical disorders (Bear and Fedio, 1977; Bear et al., 1982; Guerrant et al., 1962; Mungas, 1982; Rodin and Schmaltz, 1984; Standage and Fenton, 1975; Strauss et al., 1982; Whitman et al., 1984). Half of these studies (Bear and Fedio, 1977; Bear et al., 1982; Rodin and Schmaltz, 1984; Strauss et al., 1982) found that people with medical disorders had fewer problems than individuals with temporal-lobe epilepsy. Only 4 studies have compared temporal-lobe epileptics to people with cerebral disorders other than epilepsy (Kogeorgos et al., 1982; Mathews and Klove, 1968; Mungas, 1982; Whitman et al., 1984). All but one study (Kogeorgos et al., 1982) showed that individuals with brain-related neurological diseases had behavioral disorders as frequently as persons with temporal-lobe epilepsy. (Note: The study by Tucker et al. (1987) is not included for consideration, since it is not clear whether their contrast group, patients with pseudoseizures, had a neurologically based disorder).

We turn now to studies comparing patients with temporal-lobe epilepsy to those with other types of seizures. Many investigators have used the MMPI. There are a total of 12 such studies. The majority (Dikmen et al., 1983; Lachar et al., 1979; Mathews and Klove, 1968; Mignone et al., 1970; Small et al., 1962; Stevens et al., 1972; Stevens, 1975; Whitman et al., 1984) reported no differences between seizure groups. By contrast, Guerrant et al. (1962) reported more clinical interpretations of psychosis in the MMPI profiles of temporal-lobe epileptics.

Rodin et al. (1976) and Hermann et al. (1980, 1982) also noted some differences between epileptic groups, but these were attributed to subgroups of people with temporal-lobe epilepsy; namely, those with multiple seizure types (Rodin et al., 1976), temporal-lobe epilepsy of adolescent onset (Hermann et al., 1980) and ictal fear (Hermann et al., 1982).

Studies which use different rating scales and tests appear more likely to show differences between epileptic groups. There are 14 studies that fall in this category and all but 4 found significant differences between seizure groups (Rodin and Schmaltz, 1984; Standage and Fenton, 1975; Strauss et al., 1982; Tucker et al., 1987). Of the 10 studies that did find differences, 4 (Bear et al., 1982; Cairns, 1974; Guerrant et al., 1962; Hermann and Riel, 1981) reported that people with temporal-lobe epilepsy were more likely than individuals in other seizure groups to experience some type of behavioral problem. Three studies noted an increased incidence of behavioral difficulties in selected subgroups of patients with temporal-lobe epilepsy; namely, those with multiple seizure types (Rodin et al., 1976), a left-sided epileptogenic focus (Stores, 1978) and those with a temporal-limbic focus (Wieser, 1986). In three studies (Brandt et al., 1985; Kogeorgos et al., 1982; Willmore et al., 1980), patients with generalized epilepsy showed increased disturbance relative to those with temporal-lobe epilepsy.

Thus far, relatively little has been said about the particular behavioral characteristics thought to be associated with temporal-lobe epilepsy. Several investigators, most notably Geschwind (1979; Waxman and Geschwind, 1975) and Bear (1979; Bear and Fedio, 1977) have argued strongly for the existence of a specific interictal syndrome in temporal-lobe epilepsy, characterized by as many as 18 – 20 symptoms. These can be grouped (Benson, 1986) into three main divisions: (1) overinclusiveness in verbal output (circumstantiality), action (stickiness), and writing (hypergraphia), (2) alteration of sexuality (typically hyposexuality) and (3) intensification of mental activities (philosophic, religious) and emotional behavior (depression, paranoia, irritability).

Bear and Fedio (1977) developed their own rating scales to measure these traits. The Personal Inventory was a self-report form, while the Personal Behavior Survey assessed personality traits in the patient as reported by a close friend or relative. Bear and Fedio gave these forms to patients with unilateral temporal epileptic foci, and contrasted their profiles with those of people with neuromuscular disease and healthy individuals. A distinctive profile emerged for the temporal-lobe epilepsy group characterized by humorless sobriety, dependence, obsessionalism and religious and philosophic concerns. Furthermore, there were laterality differences. Patients with right temporal foci emphasized emotional traits (e.g. sexual alteration, sadness, emotionality), whereas left temporal epileptics displayed ideational traits (e.g. sense of personal destiny, paranoia, helplessness).

Bear (1979) attempted to explain this syndrome by proposing that repeated discharge in the temporal lobes results in increased functional connectivity between temporal neocortex and limbic structures. This 'sensory-limbic hyperconnection', he suggested, leads to increased limbic excitation during daily experience which produces deepened associations to overtly neutral events.

Table 1 summarizes the five studies that have used the Bear and Fedio (1977) questionnaires (Brandt et al., 1985; Hermann and Riel, 1981; Mungas, 1982; Rodin and Schmaltz, 1984; Wieser, 1986). Some reported a behavioral pattern specific to temporal-lobe epilepsy, or to a subgroup of temporal-lobe epileptics, but a consistent trait profile has not emerged. Hermann and Riel (1981) found only 4 of the 18 traits scores (personal destiny, dependence, paranoia, philosophical interest) significantly elevated in temporal-lobe epileptics relative to a matched group with generalized seizures. On the other hand, Brandt et al. (1985) reported that left and right temporal-lobe epileptics differed from persons with generalized epilepsy only on dependence and circumstantiality, with the temporal-lobe epileptics

obtaining the lower scores. Furthermore, contrary to the findings of Bear and Fedio (1977), left and right temporal-lobe epileptics differed from each other only on the trait of humorlessness. Other researchers (Mungas, 1982; Rodin and Schmaltz, 1984; Wieser, 1986) have noted that people with temporal-lobe epilepsy score higher on some traits than individuals with other types of cerebral disorder. Nevertheless, they claimed that the inventory does not assess a specific personality syndrome, nor can it distinguish those with right or left temporal-lobe foci. Rather, it is a measure of overall maladjustment. Interpretation of the individual scales is also not settled. For example, Mayeux and his colleagues (1980) found a significant negative correlation between the trait of circumstantiality and naming performance, suggesting that an overly detailed pedantic language pattern might be a form of compensatory circumlocution for anomia rather than a personality trait per se.

There have been additional attempts to evaluate whether specific traits are associated with temporal-lobe epilepsy. Waxman and Geschwind (1975) initially suggested a link between temporal-lobe epilepsy and hypergraphia. Subsequently, Sachdev and Waxman (1981) examined written responses of epileptics to letters. Patients with temporal-lobe epilepsy tended to reply more frequently, and wrote more extensively than others. Hermann et al. (1983), using a similar procedure to Sachdev and Waxman (1981), have also provided some support for the proposed relationship between hypergraphia and temporal-lobe epilepsy. Patients with temporal-lobe epilepsy demonstrated a higher response rate relative to patients with other convulsive disorders. In addition, the two longest letters were both written by people with temporal-lobe epilepsy. Based on a review of both personal and published cases, Roberts and his colleagues (1982) suggested that hypergraphia occurs more frequently in patients with right-sided as opposed to left-sided temporal-lobe epileptic foci.

Another behavioral characteristic that deserves attention is hyperreligiosity. Case reports and anecdotal observations have associated deepened religious concerns with temporal-lobe epilepsy (e.g. Dewhurst and Beard, 1970). Both Willmore et al. (1980) and Tucker et al. (1987) evaluated religiosity, comparing temporal-lobe epileptics to other groups. Willmore et al. (1980) used a specially designed questionnaire, while in the study by Tucker et al. (1987) the Wiggins Religiosity Scale of the MMPI was scored for each subject. Both studies failed to support the hypothesis that hyper-religiosity is a consistent interictal behavioral characteristic of individuals with temporal-lobe epilepsy.

Finally, mention should be made of two studies that have attempted to verify the mechanism – enhanced affective responsivity – presumed to underly the personality change. The results, however, do not agree well with one another. Bear et al. (1981) measured skin conductance responses to photographic slides depicting either emotionally neutral, pleasant or unpleasant stimuli. The patients with temporal-lobe epilepsy showed significantly greater amplitudes of electrodermal response to the slides than healthy controls. In contrast, however, Bellur et al. (1985) evaluated patients with temporal-lobe epilepsy, patients with other types of seizure and healthy controls as to their autonomic nervous system responsiveness to an emotionally stressing film. No differences were found between the groups. It is conceivable that specific subgroups of the temporal-lobe epileptic population manifest the phenomenon proposed by Bear, but that its existence is washed out in any evaluation of unselected patients with temporal-lobe epilepsy.

In the light of the methodological problems noted earlier, no strong conclusions can be made. Four points emerge from the existing literature. First, people with temporal-lobe epilepsy demonstrate significantly more behavioral difficulties than normal controls. Second, whether temporal-lobe epileptics also show more disturbances than people with chronic illnesses is uncertain. There is a hint in the data that temporal-lobe epileptics experience more behavioral difficulties than individuals with chronic non-neurological diseases but that they have behavioral problems as frequently as persons with other brain-related nonepileptic disorders. However, this proposal requires additional investigation. Third, whether differences exist between seizure groups seems to depend, at least in part, upon the particular evaluation procedure employed. Our review suggests that the MMPI is not a very useful test for detecting personality differences among groups with different seizure disorders (Bear and Fedio, 1977; Dodrill and Batzel, 1986; Trimble, 1983). When other measures are used, differences between seizure types are more likely to be uncovered. Finally, the question as to whether there is a specific set of characteristics associated with temporal-lobe epilepsy is still not settled. It may be that there is a characteristic constellation of traits but they may be difficult to measure with current procedures. It is also clear that not all patients with temporal-lobe epilepsy are prone to behavior disturbance. A number of risk factors can be identified (see also Hermann and Whitman, 1984), including the age of seizure onset (Hermann et al., 1980), the presence of multiple seizure types (Hermann et al., 1982; Rodin et al., 1976) and the laterality of the focus (Bear and Fedio, 1977; Brandt et al., 1985; McIntyre et al., 1976; Mendez et al., 1986; Nielsen and Kristensen, 1981; Perini and Mendius, 1984; Roberts et al., 1982; Stores, 1978; Strauss et al., 1982). Finally, studies by Nielsen and Kristensen (1981), Wieser (1986) and Hermann et al. (1982) indicate that people with dysfunction involving the limbic system may be more apt to display abnormal personality traits. Nielsen and Kristensen (1981) found that patients with medio-basal temporal foci were more likely to exhibit atypical behavioral characteristics than patients with a lateral focus. Wieser (1986) evaluated patients whose routine work-up included depth-electrode studies. Patients with a temporal-limbic focus appeared more likely than those with a temporal-neocortical focus to show increases on various trait scores of the Bear and Fedio Personal Inventory. Finally, Hermann et al. (1982), comparing patients with temporal-lobe epilepsy and generalized epilepsy, reported that temporal-lobe epileptics with an aura of fear were more apt to display pathological elevations on several MMPI scales, especially the scale for Schizophrenia. Recall from our earlier discussion (Ictal emotions) that ictal fear is thought to be related to spread of the discharge to limbic structures, particularly the amygdala (Gloor, 1972; Gloor et al., 1981, 1982; Wieser, 1980).

Aggression

There are two ways to address the question of aggression and temporal-lobe epilepsy. One approach is to look at the incidence of temporal-lobe epilepsy among people identified as aggressive. The other method is to evaluate the prevalence of aggression among individuals with temporal-lobe epilepsy.

Let us consider first whether the incidence of temporal-lobe epilepsy is increased among aggressive people. A number of EEG studies of aggressive individuals have been published (e.g. Hill and Pond, 1952; Williams, 1969), but these suffer from methodological problems such as the inclusion of variant EEG patterns that have no specific diagnostic implications (Trieman, 1986). The best study to date is by Riley and Neidermeyer (1978). They studied 229 records of 212 patients referred to the EEG laboratory because of acts of violence, recurrent aggressive behavior, destructive behavior or outbursts of anger, with or without provocation, serious enough to necessitate psychiatric or neurological evaluation. Only 14 of the patients showed EEG abnormalities. These were mild rather than marked and none was epileptiform. The percentage of abnormal records (6.6%) did not differ significantly from that found in healthy populations. In short, there was no evidence of an epileptic component in the episodic aggressive behavior of these individuals.

The study by Riley and Neidermeyer (1978) focussed on non-incarcerated individuals. Perhaps surveys of imprisoned people might reveal an increased incidence of temporal-lobe epilepsy. Gunn and his colleagues (1977) have conducted a series of studies of epilepsy in the British prison system. In one survey, they examined the receptions to all prisons and borstals in England and Wales during the month of November 1966. The second was a survey of all epileptic residents at the same institutions on the night of Dec 13/14 1966. They found an increased prevalence of epilepsy in custodial settings relative to that in the general English population. However, comparison of the offences of the prisoners with temporal-lobe epilepsy to those having other convulsive disorders failed to reveal more violent crimes among the temporal-lobe epileptics. Similar findings have been reported by Hermann and his colleagues (Hermann and Whitman, 1984).

We turn now to an examination of the prevalence of aggression in people with temporal-lobe epilepsy. A number of studies of neurosurgical candidates have been conducted (James, 1960; Serafetidines, 1965; Taylor, 1969a) and these show an increased incidence of aggressive behavior in temporal-lobe epileptics (about 33%). These data, however, were derived from a highly select population; namely, intractable temporal-lobe epileptics with severe psychiatric symptoms who were being considered for surgical intervention. Surveys of less select populations of temporal-lobe epileptics show a considerably lower incidence of aggression (less than 10%; Currie, 1971; King and Ajmone-Marsan, 1977; Rodin, 1973).

There are only a few controlled investigations in this area and these are summarized in Table 2. Two studies have compared temporal-lobe epileptics with normal populations. Nuffield (1961) reported that children with a temporal-lobe focus obtained higher behavior ratings of aggression (e.g. irritability, fighting). Similarly, Cairns (1974) found that a combined group of adult epileptics (psychomotor and non-psychomotor) scored higher on a measure of aggression relative to college students.

Two studies have contrasted patients with temporal-lobe epilepsy and individuals with (non-neurological) chronic illnesses. Guerrant et al. (1962) reported more anger and aggression among a combined convulsive group (psychomotor, grand

TABLE 2

Aggression

Authors and subject groups	Evaluation procedure	Differences between TLE and:			Left vs. right
		Normals	Chronic	Other epil.	
Cairns, 1974; 18 psychomotor, 14 non-psychomotor, 169 psychiatric, 86 students	Hostility and Direction of Hostility Quest.	Combined epil. scored higher than normals	TLE scored higher but signif. not reported	No diff.	–
Guerrant et al., 1962; 32 psychomotor, 26 grand mal, 26 non-neurol. chronic illness	Interview-based rating scale of Ss' anger and aggression	–	Epil. higher with main contribution from grand mal group	–	–
Hermann et al., 1980; 153 TLE, 79 generalized epilepsy	MMPI measure of agression	–	–	No diff.	–
Juul-Jensen, 1963; 1020 epileptics	Incidence of criminality, i.e. punishment worse than fines	–	–	No diff.	–
Mignone et al., 1970; 98 psychomotor, 53 non-psychomotor	Psychiatric assessment	–	–	No diff.	–
Nuffield, 1961; 30 temp. focus, 30 extra-temp., 28 3/sec spike and wave, 44 irreg. spike and wave, 32 diffuse spikes, 33 non-specific abnormal, 29 normals	Behavioral ratings based on psychiatric interview	TLE more aggressive	–	TLE more aggressive	–
Rodin, 1973; 34 aggressive epil., 34 non-aggressive epil.	History of destructive assaultive behavior	–	–	No diff.	–
Small et al., 1962; 25 TLE, 25 non-TLE	Interview-based rating scale assessing frequency and nature of aggression	–	–	No diff.	–

Small et al., 1966; *Medical:* 25 TLE, 25 Non-TLE *Psychiatric:* 25 TLE, 25 non-TLE	See Small et al., 1962	—	—	No diff.	—
Standage and Fenton, 1975; 19 TLE, 15 generalized epilepsy, 3 focal non-temporals, 27 chronic non-neurol.	Irritability defined by Present State Exam	—	No diff.	No diff.	—
Whitman et al., 1982; 35 TLE, 48 generalized epilepsy	Child Behavior Check-list	—	—	No diff.	—

mal), but noted that the main contribution came from the grand mal group. Standage and Fenton (1975) found no difference in irritability between the epileptic and control groups.

Finally, 10 studies have compared temporal-lobe epileptics with other seizure groups (Cairns, 1974; Hermann et al., 1980; Juul-Jensen, 1963; Mignone et al., 1970; Nuffield, 1961; Rodin, 1973; Small et al., 1962, 1966; Standage and Fenton, 1975; Whitman et al., 1982). All but one (Nuffield, 1961) showed that the incidence of aggression did not vary as a function of seizure type.

Again, due to methodological weaknesses in the existing literature, it is hazardous to make firm conclusions in this area. The available data suggest that temporal-lobe epilepsy has no special relationship to aggressive behavior. There is no increased prevalence of temporal-lobe epilepsy among aggressive individuals. Furthermore, rates of aggression are relatively low in non-neurosurgical, as compared to surgical, groups of temporal-lobe epileptics. The prevalence of aggression is somewhat higher in people with temporal-lobe epilepsy compared to that found in the normal population. However, the evidence to date does not point to an increased incidence of aggression in temporal-lobe epileptics relative to those with other chronic illnesses or other seizure types. Finally, some investigators have identified variables associated with an increased risk of aggressive behavior (see also Hermann and Whitman, 1982; Kligman and Goldberg, 1975). These include an early onset of seizures (James, 1960; Serafetinides, 1965), male sex (Rodin, 1973; Taylor, 1969a; Whitman et al., 1982), poor early environment (Serafetinides, 1965; Taylor, 1969a), low IQ (James, 1960; Rodin, 1973; Taylor, 1969a), a left-sided epileptic focus (Serafetinides, 1965; Taylor, 1969a) and multiple seizure types (Hermann et al., 1982). Some of these same variables (e.g. sex, early environment) are known to be related to aggression in the larger population (Hermann and Whitman, 1984).

Sexual behavior

Abnormal sexual behavior has also been linked with temporal-lobe epilepsy. The disorder can take three separate forms: hyposexuality, hypersexuality or perversity.

Gastaut and Collomb (1954) were the first to document that hyposexuality was a common symptom in temporal-lobe epilepsy. This abnormality occurred in 26 of 36 (72%) patients who were studied systematically and it post-dated the onset of the seizures. Gastaut and Collomb emphasized that the sexual alteration was specific to dysfunction in the temporal-limbic system although precise data for this assertion were not provided. Moreover, they indicated that the sexual disturbance was not a simple impotence or frigidity but, rather, a profound disinterest in all the usual libidinous aspects of life. Thus, there was a decrease or absence of sexual curiosity and coquetry, erotic fantasies and dreams, as well as a lack of desire for physical intercourse (Blumer and Walker, 1967).

A number of surveys of neurosurgical candidates have been reported. In line with the work of Gastaut and Collomb (1954), these show a high incidence (about 60%) of sexual dysfunction, particularly hyposexuality, in temporal-lobe epileptics. Blumer and Walker (1967) reported that of 21 epileptics who underwent temporal lobectomy, 11 (52%) were grossly hyposexual prior to surgery. Subsequently, Blumer (1970) reported on 50 temporal-lobe epileptics from the same neurosurgical unit. Twenty-nine of the 50 patients (58%) showed a marked lack of libidinal and genital arousal. Seven patients has distinct episodes of hypersexuality. However, these occurred on the cessation of seizures following either temporal lobectomy or drug treatment. Taylor (1969b) surveyed the sexual behavior of 100 epileptics selected for temporal lobectomy. Only a third showed adequate sexual function. The most common abnormality was low sexual drive and not failure of erection or ejaculation. Perversity, in the form of sadomasochism, bizarre fantasy and ex-

TABLE 3

Sexual behavior

Authors and subject groups	Evaluation procedure	Differences between TLE and:			
		Normals	Chronic	Other epil.	Left vs. right
Guerrant et al., 1962; 32 psychomotor, 26 grand mal, 26 non-neurol. illness	– Self-report impotence/ frigidity – psychiatric evaluation of pt's sexual adjustment	–	TLE more sexual problems	TLE more impotence/ frigidity	–
Kolarsky et al., 1967; 49 TLE, 31 non-TLE, 6 unknown	Clinical interview	–	–	TLE more sexual problems	–
Saunders and Rawson, 1970; 33 TLE, 65 idio-pathic, 2 cortical seizures	Clinical interview	–	–	TLE more sexual disturbances	–
Shukla et al., 1979; 70 TLE, 70 generalized epilepsy	Clinical interview	–	–	TLE were hyposexual	–

hibitionism, was somewhat less common and occurred in 15% of the patients. Hypersexuality was exceedingly rare. Only one patient had an excessive heterosexual appetite.

In non-neurosurgical samples, the prevalence of sexual disturbance is somewhat reduced, although it is still high (about 40%). Again, hyposexuality is observed most frequently, whereas hypersexuality and perversity are rare occurrences. Pritchard (1980) noted that of 33 men with complex partial seizures, 48% were hyposexual. In this series, however, the disorder was characterized by erectile dysfunction with preserved libido. Lindsay et al. (1979) found that of 41 men with temporal-lobe epilepsy, 14 (34%) showed no sexual interest. Saunders and Rawson (1970) reported that 12 of 33 (36%) men with temporal-lobe epilepsy showed some disturbance of sexual behavior. Hyposexuality was the most common sympton. Seven of the 12 men were impotent but libido was preserved, whereas only 2 men were globally hyposexual. There was one case of exhibitionism. No patient was hypersexual. Shukla et al. (1979) evaluated 79 patients with temporal-lobe epilepsy. More than 60% of both the men and the women demonstrated a global loss of performance and interest in sex. Only one patient was hypersexual. There were no cases of sexual deviation.

There are few controlled investigations in this area. As Table 3 shows, no study has contrasted temporal-lobe epileptics with healthy normal people. Only one report, by Guerrant et al. (1962), has compared people with temporal-lobe epilepsy to individuals suffering from chronic medical disorders. There were more instances of impotence and frigidity in the temporal-lobe epilepsy group. Four studies have contrasted temporal-lobe epileptics and individuals with other seizure disorders (Guerrant et al., 1962; Kolarsky et al., 1967; Saunders and Rawson, 1970; Shukla et al., 1979). All found that the temporal-lobe epileptics showed more sexual dysfunction.

It is clear that few studies have been carried out on the relationship between sexual disturbance and temporal-lobe epilepsy, and at present few firm conclusions can be drawn. What is certain is that a substantial proportion of patients with temporal-lobe epilepsy suffer from some kind of sexual dysfunction. Hypersexuality and sexual deviation appear to be quite rare, although isolated cases have been reported in the literature (Blumer, 1970; Ellison, 1982; Epstein, 1961; Hierons and Saunders, 1966; Hoenig and Kenna, 1979; Kolarsky et al., 1967; Saunders and Rawson, 1970; Shukla et al., 1979; Taylor, 1969). Hyposexuality is the more common abnormality in temporal-lobe epilepsy and appears to be uniquely associated with that seizure disorder. Some authors have described a global loss of performance and interest in sex (e.g. Blumer and Walker, 1967; Blumer, 1970; Lindsay et al., 1979; Shukla et al., 1979; Taylor, 1969), whereas others (Pritchard, 1980; Saunders and Rawson, 1970) have noted impotence/frigidity with intact libido. The difference may reflect, in part, the severity of the patient's seizure disorder and the age of seizure onset (Kolarsky et al., 1967; Lindsay et al., 1979; Saunders and Rawson, 1970; Taylor, 1969). Temporal-lobe epilepsy in childhood and adolescence may arrest psychosexual development, whereas later onset may induce impotence/frigidity while leaving libido relatively unaffected depending upon the severity of the seizure disorder (Hermann and Whitman, 1984).

A number of other factors may also influence sexual behavior. One important consideration is the patient's overall level of psychiatric adjustment (Mignone et al., 1970). A patient who is anxious or depressed may have no interest in sex. Another factor concerns the range of opportunities for sexual relationships (Taylor, 1969). Patients may manifest inadequate sexual behavior because they are institutionalized or socially isolated. The chronic effects of anticonvulsant medication (e.g. Toone, 1981) may also play an important role by altering sex hormone levels. Finally, sexual behavior appears also to be related to the functional integrity of the limbic system (Blumer, 1970; Gastaut and Collumb, 1954). Recently, Pritchard (1980) reported that hyposexual patients with complex partial seizures were more likely to have medio-basal than temporal-lobe convexity spike foci.

Concluding remarks

The papers reviewed in this chapter emphasize that, in recent years, a substantial amount of work has been carried out on the relationship between emotion and epilepsy. It is clear that many issues remain to be resolved and that at present there are few firm conclusions. In closing, we emphasize three points that have emerged in this review.

First, a number of methodological problems exist in the literature which must be overcome in order to provide accurate assessments of this area. From the point of view presented here, the most serious drawbacks of this work include problems in the definition and diagnosis of temporal-lobe epilepsy, in sample selection effects and in the choice of appropriate control groups. As a result, it is rarely clear who or what is being evaluated (for more detailed reviews see Halgren, 1982; Hermann and Whitman, 1984; Kligman and Goldberg, 1975; Mendius and Engel, 1985).

Second, the literature suggests that a variety of emotional responses can occur with electrical discharge or stimulation of temporal-limbic structures. However, this epileptic or experimental stimulation does not produce a pure emotional response. Rather, the response reflects an interaction between the functional role of the stimulated area, the individual's prior experience, and his current cues. Studies of this complex interaction, rather than of electrical stimulation or seizure discharge alone, may provide a more realistic understanding of emotional behavior (Gloor et al., 1982; Halgren et al., 1978; Kligman and Goldberg, 1975).

Finally, the 'period of psychomotor peculiarity' appears to be on the wane. There is a growing realization that behavioral abnormalities are not universal in temporal-lobe epilepsy. The emphasis has shifted from attempts to correlate behavioral disturbances and temporal-lobe epilepsy, to a detailed study of the critical variables, both psychosocial and biological, that promote or inhibit the development of the interictal behaviors. An important point here is that limbic system dysfunction is a critical variable predisposing epileptic patients to emotional-ideational disorders. However, these disorders may not take the same form or severity in each patient, but may depend on an interaction with other factors, including the individual's past experience and his current psychosocial situation (Hermann et al., 1982; Rodin and Schmaltz, 1984; Stevens and Hermann, 1981; Wieser, 1986). In this way, the work in this area has paralleled that on ictal emotions. These important research directions should bring additional order to an area where there has been much controversy.

Acknowledgements

I thank Drs. Don Read and Juhn Wada, who provided thoughtful and generous comments on this review. This chapter was written while the author was supported by grants from the Medical Research Council of Canada, the Natural Sciences and Engineering Research Council of Canada and the Vancouver Foundation.

References

Ajouanine T: Dostoieski's epilepsy. *Brain: 86*, 209–218, 1963.
Bear DM: Temporal lobe epilepsy: a syndrome of sensorylimbic hyperconnection. *Cortex: 15*, 357–384, 1979.
Bear DM, Fedio P: Quantitative analysis of interictal behavior in temporal lobe epilepsy. *Arch. Neurol., 34*, 454–467, 1977.
Bear D, Schenk L, Benson H: Increased autonomic responses to neutral and emotional stimuli in patients with temporal lobe epilepsy. *Am. J. Psychiatry: 138*, 843–845, 1981.
Bear D, Levin K, Blumer D, Chetham D, Ryder J: Interictal behavior in hospitalized temporal lobe epileptics: relationship to idiopathic psychiatric syndromes. *J. Neurol. Neurosurg. Psychiatry: 45*, 481–488, 1982.
Bear DM, Freeman R, Greenberg M: Behavioral alterations in patients with temporal lobe epilepsy. In Blumer D (Editor), *Psychiatric Asepects of Epilepsy*. Washington: American Psychiatric Press, Inc., pp. 97–227, 1984.
Bechterewa NP: Human response to brain stimulation. In Valenstein ES (Editor), *Brain Control*. New York: Wiley In-

terscience, pp. 105, 1973.

Bellur S, Camacho A, Hermann B, Kempthorne WJ, McCanne T: Autonomic responsiveness to affective visual stimulation in temporal lobe epilepsy. *Biol. Psychiatry: 20*, 73 – 78, 1985.

Benson DF: Interictal behavior disorders in epilepsy. *Psychiatr. Clin. N. Am.: 9*, 283 – 292, 1986.

Bente D, Klug E: Sexuelle Reizzustände im Rahmen des Uncinatus-syndroms. *Arch. Psychiatry: 190*, 357 – 376, 1953.

Bingley T: Mental symptoms in temporal lobe epilepsy and temporal lobe gliomas. *Acta Psychiatr. Neurol. Scand.: Suppl. 120, 33*, 1 – 151, 1958.

Black D: Pathological laughter. *J. Nerv. Ment. Dis.: 170*, 67 – 71, 1982.

Blumer D: Hypersexual episodes in temporal lobe epilepsy. *Am. J. Psychiatry: 126*, 1099 – 1106, 1970.

Blumer D, Walker AE: Sexual behavior in temporal lobe epilepsy. *Arch. Neurol.: 16*, 37 – 43, 1967.

Brandt J, Seidman LJ, Kohl D: Personality characteristics of epileptic patients: a controlled study of generalized and temporal lobe cases. *J. Clin. Exp. Neuropsychol.: 7*, 25 – 38, 1985.

Cairns VM: Epilepsy, personality and behavior. In Harris P, Maudsley C (Editors), *Epilepsy: Proceedings of the Hans Berger Centenary Symposium.* Edinburgh: Churchill-Livingstone, pp. 256 – 268, 1974.

Chapman WP: Studies of the periamygdaloid area in relation to human behavior. In Solomon HC, Penfield W (Editors), *The Brain and Human Behavior. Res. Publ. Res. Nerv. Ment. Dis.: 36*, 258 – 270.

Chen R-C, Forster FM: Cursive epilepsy and gelastic epilepsy. *Neurology: 23*, 1019 – 1029, 1973.

Currie S, Heathfield KWG, Henson RA, Scott DF: Clinical course and prognosis of temporal lobe epilepsy: a summary of 666 patients. *Brain: 94*, 173 – 190, 1971.

Currier RD, Little SC, Suess JF, Andy OJ: Sexual seizures. *Arch. Neurol.: 25*, 260 – 264, 1971.

Dalby MA: Antiepileptic and psychotropic effects of carbamazepine (Tegretol) in the treatment of psychomotor epilepsy. *Epilepsia: 12*, 325 – 334, 1971.

Daly D: Ictal affect. *Am. J. Psychiatry: 115*, 97 – 108, 1958.

Daly DD, Mulder DW: Gelastic epilepsy. *Neurology: 7*, 189 – 192, 1957.

Delgado JMR: Emotional behavior in animals and humans. *Psychiatr. Res. Rep.: 12*, 259 – 266, 1960.

Delgado-Escueta AV, Bascal FE, Treiman DM: Complex partial seizures on closed-circuit television and EEG: a study of 691 attacks in 79 patients. *Ann. Neurol.: 11*, 292 – 300, 1982.

Delgado-Escueta AV, Kunze U, Waddell G, Boxley J, Nadel A: Lapse of consciousness and automatisms in temporal lobe epilepsy: a video-tape analysis. *Neurology: 27*, 144 – 155, 1977.

Delgado-Escueta AV, Mattson RH, King L, Goldensohn ES, Spiegel H, Madsen J, Crandall P, Dreifus F, Porter RJ: The nature of aggression during epileptic seizures. *N. Engl. J. Med.: 305*, 711 – 716, 1981.

Dewhurst K, Beard AW: Sudden religious conversions in temporal lobe epilepsy. *Br. J. Psychiatry: 117*, 497 – 507, 1970.

Dikmen S, Hermann BP, Wilensky A, Rainwater G: The validity of the MMPI in psychopathology in epilepsy. *J. Nerv.*

Ment. Dis.: 171, 114 – 122, 1983.

Dodrill DB: Neuropsychology of epilepsy. In Filskov SB, Boll TJ (Editors), *Handbook of Clinical Neuropsychology, Vol. 2*, New York: Wiley, pp. 366 – 395, 1986.

Dodrill CB, Batzel LW: Interictal behavioral features of patients with epilepsy. *Epilepsia.: 27* (Suppl. 2), S64 – S76, 1986.

Ellison SM: Alterations of sexual behavior in temporal lobe epilepsy. *Psychosomatics: 23*, 499 – 509, 1982.

Epstein AW: Relationship of fetishism and transvestism to brain and particularly to temporal lobe dysfunction. *J. Nerv. Ment. Dis.: 133*, 247 – 252, 1961.

Erickson TC: Erotomania as an expression of cortical epileptiform discharge. *Arch. Neurol. Psychiatry: 53*, 226, 1945.

Feindel W, Penfield W: Localization of discharge in temporal lobe automatism. *Arch. Neurol. Psychiatry: 72*, 605 – 630, 1954.

Flor-Henry P: Temporal lobe epilepsy and sexual deviation. In Granville-Grossman K (Editor), *Recent Advances in Clinical Psychiatry 2.* London: Churchill-Livingstone, pp. 284 – 287, 1976.

Freemon FR, Nevis AH: Temporal lobe sexual seizures. *Neurology: 19*, 87 – 90, 1969.

Gascon GG, Lombroso CT: Epileptic (gelastic) laughter. *Epilepsia: 12*, 63 – 76, 1971.

Gastaut H: Clinical and electroencephalographic classification of epileptic seizures. *Epilepsia: 11*, 102 – 103, 1970.

Gastaut H, Collumb H: Etude du comportement sexuel chez les épileptiques psychomoteurs. *Ann. Med.-Psychol.: 112*, 657 – 696, 1954.

Geschwind N: The clinical setting of aggression in temporal lobe epilepsy. In Field WS, Sweet WH (Editors), *Neural Bases of Violence and Aggression* St. Louis, MO: Warren H. Green, pp. 273 – 284, 1975.

Geschwind N: Behavioral changes in temporal lobe epilepsy. *Psychol. Med.: 9*, 217 – 219, 1979.

Geschwind N: Dostoievsky's epilepsy. In Blumer D (Editor), *Psychiatric Aspects of Epilepsy.* Washington: American Psychiatric Press, pp. 325 – 334, 1984.

Gibbs FA, Gibbs EL: *Atlas of Electrocencephalography, Vol. 3.* Reading, MA: Addison Wesley, 1964.

Gibbs FA, Stamps FW: *Epilepsy Handbook.* Springfield, Il: Charles C. Thomas, 1953.

Gibbs FA, Gibbs EL, Fuster B: Psychomotor epilepsy. *Arch. Neurol. Psychiatry: 60*, 331 – 339, 1948.

Gloor P: Discussion. In Clemente CD, Lindsley DB (Editors), *Aggression and Defense – Brain Function, Vol. V.* Los Angeles: University of California Press, pp. 116 – 124, 1967.

Gloor P: Temporal lobe epilepsy: its possible contribution to the understanding of the functional significance of the amygdala and of its interaction with neocortical-temporal mechanisms. In Eleftheriou BE (Editor), *The Neurophysiology of the Amygdala* New York: Plenum Press, pp. 423 – 457, 1972.

Gloor P: Physiology of the limbic system. In Penry JK, Daly DD (Editors), *Advances in Neurology, Vol. 11.* New York: Raven Press, pp. 27 – 55, 1975.

Gloor P: Inputs and outputs of the amygdala: what the amygdala is trying to tell the rest of the brain. In Livingston KS, Hornykiewicz O (Editors), *Brain Mechanisms. The Con-*

tinuing Evolution of the Limbic System Concept. New York: Plenum Press, pp. 189 – 209, 1978.

oor P: Role of the human limbic system in perception, memory and affect: lessons from temporal lobe epilepsy. In Doane BK, Livingston KE (Editors), *The Limbic System: Functional Organization and Clinical Disorders.* New York: Raven Press, pp. 159 – 169, 1986.

oor P, Feindel W: Temporal lobe and affective behavior. In Monnier M (Editor), *Physiologie des Vegetativen Nervensystems, Vol. II.* Stuttgart: Hippokrates Verlag, pp. 685 – 716, 1963.

oor P, Olivier O, Quesney LF: The role of the amygdala in the expression of psychic phenomena in temporal lobe seizures. In Ben-Azi Y (Editor), *The Amygdaloid Complex* Amsterdam: Elsevier, pp. 489 – 498, 1981.

oor P, Olivier O, Quesney LF, Andermann F, Horowitz S: The role of the limbic system in experiential phenomena of temporal lobe epilepsy. *Ann. Neurol.: 12,* 129 – 144, 1982.

ol A: Relief of pain by electrical stimulation of the septal area. *J. Neurol. Sci.: 5,* 115 – 120, 1967.

.dmundsson G: Epilepsy in Iceland. *Acta Neurol. Scand.: 43, Suppl. 25,* 1 – 124.

.errant J, Anderson WW, Fischer A, Weinstein MR, Jaros JM, Deskins A: *Personality in Epilepsy.* Springfield, Il: Charles C Thomas, 1962.

.nn J: *Epileptics in Prison.* London: Academic Press, 1977.

.algren E: Mental phenomena induced by stimulation in the limbic system. *Hum. Neurobiol.: 1,* 251 – 260, 1982.

.algren E, Walter RD, Cherlow DG, Crandall PH: Mental phenomena evoked by electrical stimulation of the hippocampal formation and amygdala. *Brain: 101,* 83 – 117, 1978.

.eath RG: Pleasure and brain activity in man. *J. Nerv. Ment. Dis.: 154,* 3 – 18, 1972.

.eath RG, John SB, Fontana CJ: The pleasure response: studies by stereotaxic techniques in patients. In Kline N, Laska E (Editors), *Computers and Electronic Devices in Psychiatry.* New York: Grune & Stratton, pp. 178 – 179, 1968.

.eath RG, Monroe RR, Mickle W: Stimulation of the amygdaloid nucleus in a schizophrenic patient. *Am. J. Psychiatry: 111,* 862 – 863, 1955.

.enriksen GF: Status epilepticus partialis with fear as clinical expression. *Epilepsia: 14,* 39 – 46, 1973.

.ermann BP, Riel P: Interictal personality and behavioral traits in temporal lobe and generalized epilepsy. *Cortex: 17,* 125 – 128, 1981.

.ermann BP, Stevens JR: Interictal behavioral correlates of the epilepsies. In Hermann BP (Editor), *A Multidisciplinary Handbook of Epilepsy.* Springfield, Il: Charles C Thomas, pp. 272 – 307, 1980.

.ermann BP, Whitman S: Behavioral and personality correlates of epilepsy: a review, methodological critique, and conceptual model. *Psychol. Bull.: 95,* 451 – 497, 1984.

.ermann BP, Schwartz MS, Karnes WE, Vahdat P. Psychopathology in epilepsy: relationship of seizure type to age of onset. *Epilepsia: 21,* 15 – 23, 1980.

.ermann, BP, Dikmen S, Schwartz MS, Karnes WE: Psychopathology in TLE patients with ictal fear: A quantitative investigation. *Neurology: 32,* 7 – 11, 1982.

Hermann BP, Dikmen S, Wilensky A: Increased psychopathology associated with multiple seizure types: fact or artifact? *Epilepsia: 23,* 587 – 596, 1982.

Hermann BP, Whitman S, Arnston P: Hypergraphia in epilepsy: is there a specificity to temporal lobe epilepsy? *J. Neurol. Neurosurg. Psychiatry: 46,* 848 – 853, 1983.

Hierons R, Saunders M: Impotence in patients with temporal lobe lesions. *Lancet: ii,* 761 – 764, 1966.

Hill D, Pond DA: Reflections on 100 capital cases submitted to EEG. *J. Ment. Sci.: 98,* 23 – 43, 1952.

Hoenig J, Kenna JC: EEG abnormalities and transsexualism. *Br. J. Psychiatry: 134,* 293 – 300, 1979.

Hooshmand H, Brawley BW: Temporal lobe seizures and exhibitionism. *Neurology: 19,* 1119 – 1124, 1969.

Jackson JH: Lectures on the diagnosis of epilepsy. *Medical Times and Gazette,* 1, 29, 85, 141, 223. Reprinted in Taylor J (Editor), *Selected Writings of John Hughlings Jackson, Vol. 1, On Epilepsy and Epileptiform Convulsions.* London: Hodder and Stoughton pp. 276 – 307, 1931.

Jacome DE, McLain Jr W, FitzGerald R: Postural reflex gelastic seizures. *Arch. Neurol.: 37,* 249 – 251, 1980.

James IP: Temporal lobectomy for psychomotor epilepsy. *J. Ment. Sci.: 106,* 543 – 557, 1960.

Jensen I, Larsen JK: Psychoses in drug-resistant temporal lobe epilepsy. *J. Neurol. Neurosurg. Psychiatry: 42,* 948 – 954, 1979.

Juul-Jensen P: Epilepsy: a clinical and social analysis of 1020 adult patients with epileptic seizures. *Acta Neurol. Scand.: 5 (Suppl.),* S1 – S136, 1963.

King DW, Ajmone-Marsan C: Clinical features and ictal patterns in epileptic patients with EEG temporal lobe foci. *Ann. Neurol.: 2,* 138 – 147, 1977.

Kligman D, Goldberg DA: Temporal lobe epilepsy and aggression: Problems in clinical research. *J. Nerv. Ment. Dis.: 160,* 324 – 341, 1975.

Kluver H, Bucy PC: Preliminary analysis of function of the temporal lobes in man. *Arch. Neurol. Psychiatry: 42,* 979 – 1000, 1939.

Kogeorgos J, Fonagy P, Scott DF: Psychiatric symptom profies of chronic epileptics attending a neurologic clinic: a controlled investigation. *Br. J. Psychiatry: 140,* 236 – 243, 1982.

Kolarsky A, Freund K, Machek J, Polak O: Male sexual deviation: association with early temporal lobe damage. *Arch. Gen. Psychiatry: 17,* 735 – 743, 1967.

Kolb LC, Brodie HKM: *Modern Clinical Psychiatry.* 10th Edn. Philadelphia: Saunders, 1982.

Lachar D, Lewis R, Kupke T: MMPI in differentiation of temporal lobe and nontemporal lobe epilepsy: investigation of three levels of test performance. *J. Consult. Clin. Psychol.: 47,* 186 – 188, 1979.

Lehtinen L, Kivalo A: Laughter epilepsy. *Acta Neurol. Scand.: 41,* 255 – 261, 1965.

Lennox WG, Lennox MA: *Epilepsy and Related Disorders.* London: J. and A. Churchill, 1960.

Lindsay J, Ounsted C, Richards P: Long-term outcome in children with temporal lobe seizures: II. Marriage, parenthood, and sexual indifference. *Dev. Med. Child Neurol.: 21,* 433 – 440, 1979.

Loiseau P, Cohadon F, Cohadon S: Gelastic epilepsy. *Epilepsia: 12,* 313 – 323, 1971.

MacLean P: Psychosomatic disease and the 'visceral brain': recent developments bearing on the Papez theory of emotion. *Psychosom. Med.: 4*, 338 – 353, 1949.

MacLean P: The limbic system and its hippocampal function. *J. Neurosurg.: 11*, 29 – 44, 1954.

MacRae D: Isolated fear: a temporal lobe aura. *J. Nerv. Ment. Dis.: 120*, 385 – 393, 1954.

Mark VH, Ervin FR: Relief of pain by stereotactic surgery. In White JC, Sweet WH (Editors), *Pain and the Neurosurgeon: A Forty Year Experience* Springfield, II: Charles C Thomas, pp. 834 – 887, 1969.

Mark VH, Ervin FR: *Violence and the Brain*. New York: Harper and Row, 1970.

Mark VH, Ervin FR, Sweet WH: Deep temporal lobe stimulation in man. In Basil E (Editor), *Advances in Behavioral Biology, Vol. 2*. New York: Eleftheriou, pp. 485 – 507, 1972.

Mathews CG, Klove H: MMPI performance in major motor, psychomotor and mixed seizure classifications of known and unknown etiology. *Epilepsia: 9*, 43 – 53, 1968.

Mayeux R, Brandt J, Rosen J, Benson DF: Interictal memory and language impairment in temporal lobe epilepsy. *Neurology: 30*, 120 – 125, 1980.

McIntyre M, Pritchard PB, Lombroso C: Left and right temporal lobe epileptics: a controlled investigation of some psychological differences. *Epilepsia: 17*, 377 – 386, 1976.

McLachlan RS, Blume WT: Isolated fear in complex partial status epilepticus. *Ann. Neurol.: 8*, 639 – 641, 1980.

Mendez MF, Cummings JL, Benson DF: Depression in epilepsy: significance and phenomenology. *Arch. Neurol.: 43*, 766 – 770, 1986.

Mendius JR, Engel Jr J: Studies of hemispheric lateralization in patients with partial epilepsy. In Benson DF, Zaidel E (Editors), *The Dual Brain*. New York: Guilford Press, pp. 263 – 276, 1985.

Mignone RJ, Donnelly EF, Sadowsky D: Psychological and neurological comparisons of psychomotor and non-psychomotor epileptic patients. *Epilepsia: 11*, 345 – 359, 1970.

Mirsky AF, Harmon N: On aggressive behavior and brain disease – some questions and possible relationships derived from the study of men and monkeys. In Whalen RE (Editor), *Advances in Behavioral Biology. The Neuropsychology of Aggression, Vol. 12*. New York: Plenum Press, pp. 185 – 210, 1977.

Mitchell W, Falconer MA, Hill D: Epilepsy with fetishism relieved by temporal lobectomy. *Lancet: ii*, 626 – 630, 1954.

Money J, Hosta G: Laughing seizures with sexual precocity: report of two cases. *Johns Hopkins Med. J.: 120*, 326 – 336, 1967.

Mullan S, Penfield W: Illusions of comparative interpretation and emotion: production by epileptic discharge and electrical stimulation of the temporal cortex. *Arch. Neurol. Psychiatry: 81*, 269 – 284, 1959.

Mungas D: Interictal behavior abnormality in temporal lobe epilepsy: a specific syndrome or nonspecific psychopathology? *Arch. Gen. Psychiatry: 39*, 108 – 111, 1982.

National Commission of the Control of Epilepsy and Its Consequences. *Plan for Nationwide Action on Epilepsy*. Washington, DC: DHEW Publication No NIH 78 – 276, 1978.

Nielsen H, Kristensen O: Personality correlates of sphenoid EEG foci in temporal lobe epilepsy. *Acta Neurol. Scand.: 6* 289 – 300, 1981.

Nuffield EJA: Neurophysiology and behavior disorders epileptic children. *J. Ment. Sci.: 107*, 438 – 458, 1961.

Obrador S, Delgado JMR, Martin-Rodriguez JG: Emotic areas of the human brain and their therapeutic stimulatio In Zuelch KJ (Editor), *Cerebral Localization*. Berlir Springer, pp. 171 – 183, 1973.

Offen ML, Davidoff RA, Troost BT, Richey ET: Dacryst epilepsy. *J. Neurol. Neurosurg. Psychiatry: 39*, 829 – 83 1976.

Papez JW: A proposed mechanism of emotion. *Arch. Neuro Psychiatry: 38*, 725 – 743, 1937.

Penfield W, Jasper H: *Epilepsy and the Functional Anatomy the Human Brain*. Boston: Little, Brown, 1954.

Perini G, Mendius R: Depression and anxiety in complex parti seizures. *J. Nerv. Ment. Dis.: 174*, 287 – 290, 1984.

Pond DA, Bidwell BH: A survey of epilepsy in fourteen genera practices: II. Social and psychological aspects. *Epilepsia:* 285 – 299, 1959.

Preston DN, Atack EA: Temporal lobe epilepsy: A clinic study of 47 cases. *Can. Med. Assoc. J.: 91*, 1256 – 125 1964.

Pritchard PB: Hyposexuality: a complication of complex pa tial epilepsy. *Trans. Am. Neurol. Assoc.: 105*, 193 – 19ξ 1980.

Ramani V, Gumnit RJ: Intensive monitoring of epileptic pa tients with a history of episodic aggression. *Arch. Neurol 38*, 570 – 571, 1981.

Remillard GM, Andermann F, Testa GF, Gloor P, Aube N Martin JB, Feindel W, Guberman A, Simpson C: Sexual ict manifestations predominate in women with temporal lob epilepsy: a finding suggesting sexual dimorphism in th human brain. *Neurology: 33*, 323 – 330, 1983.

Rey-Pias JM: Gelastic epilepsy. *Arch. Suisses Neurc Neurochirur. Psychiatrie: 111*, 29 – 35, 1972.

Riley T, Niedermeyer E: Rage attacks and episodic violer behavior: electroencephalographic findings and general cor sideration. *Clin Encephalogr.: 9*, 131 – 139, 1978.

Roberts J, Robertson MM, Trimble MR: The lateralizir significance of hypergraphia in temporal lobe epilepsy. Neurol. Neurosurg. Psychiatry: 45*, 131 – 138, 1982.

Rodin EA: Psychomotor epilepsy and aggressive behavio *Arch. Gen. Psychiatry: 28*, 210 – 213, 1973.

Rodin EA: Aggression and epilepsy. In Riley TL, Roy (Editors), *Pseudoseizures*. Baltimore, MD: Wilkins Wilkins, pp. 185 – 212, 1982.

Rodin E, Schmaltz S: The Bear-Fedio personality inventory ar temporal lobe epilepsy. *Neurology: 34*, 591 – 596, 1984.

Rodin E, Katz M, Lennox K. Differences between patients wit temporal lobe seizures and those with other forms of epiler tic attacks. *Epilepsia: 17*, 313 – 320, 1976.

Roger J, Lob H, Waltregny A, Gastaut H: Attacks of epilept laughter; on 5 cases. *Electroencephalogr. Clin. Neurc physiol.: 22*, 278 – 282, 1967.

Sachdev HS, Waxman SG: Frequency of hypergraphia in ten poral lobe epilepsy: an index of interictal behavior syndrom *J. Neurol. Neurosurg. Psychiatry: 44*, 358 – 360, 1981.

Sackeim HA, Greenberg MS, Weiman AL, Gur RC, Humge

buhler JP, Geschwind N: Hemispheric asymmetry in the expression of positive and negative emotions: neurologic evidence. *Arch. Neurol.: 39*, 210–218, 1982.

⎾unders M, Rawson MR: Sexuality in male epileptics. *J. Neurol. Sci.: 10*, 577–583, 1970.

⎾rafetinides EA: Aggressiveness in temporal lobe epileptics and its relation to cerebral dysfunction and environmental factors. *Epilepsia: 6*, 33–42, 1965.

⎾thi PK, Rao TS: Gelastic, quiritarian, and cursive epilepsy: a clinicopathological appraisal. *J. Neurol. Neurosurg. Psychiatry: 39*, 823–828, 1976.

⎾ukla GD, Srivastava ON, Katiyar BC: Sexual disturbances in temporal lobe epilepsy: a controlled study. *Br. J. Psychiatry: 134*, 288–292, 1979.

⎾ater E, & Beard AW: The schizophrenic psychoses of epilepsy. *Br. J. Psychiatry: 109*, 95–150, 1963.

⎾mall JG, Milstein V, Stevens JR: Are psychomotor epileptics different? A controlled study. *Arch. Neurol.: 7*, 187–198, 1962.

⎾mall J, Small I, Hayden M: Further psychiatric investigations of patients with temporal and non-temporal lobe epilepsy. *Am J. Psychiatry: 123*, 303–310, 1966.

⎾pencer SS, Spencer DD, Williamson PD, Mattson RH: Sexual automatisms in complex partial seizures. *Neurology: 33*, 527–533, 1983.

⎾tandage KF, Fenton GW: Psychiatric symptom profiles of patients with epilepsy: a controlled investigation. *Psychol. Med.: 5*, 152–160, 1975.

⎾tevens JR: Psychiatric implications of psychomotor epilepsy. *Arch. Gen. Psychiatry: 14*, 461–471, 1966.

⎾tevens JR: Interictal clinical manifestations of complex partial seizures. In Penry JK, Daly DD (Editors), *Advances in neurology, Vol. 11*, New York: Raven Press, pp. 85–112, 1975.

⎾tevens JR, Hermann BP: Temporal lobe epilepsy, psychopathology, and violence: the state of the evidence. *Neurology: 31*, 1127–1132, 1981.

⎾tevens JR, Mark VH, Ervin F, Pacheco P, Suematsu K: Deep temporal stimulation in man. *Arch. Neurol.: 21*, 157–169, 1969.

⎾tevens JR, Milstein V, Goldstein S: Psychometric test performance in relation to the psychopathology of epilepsy. *Arch. Gen. Psychiatry: 26*, 532–538, 1972.

⎾t-Hilaire JM, Gilbert M, Bouvier G, Barbeau A: Epilepsy and aggression. Two cases with depth electrode studies. In Robb P (Editor), *Epilepsy Up-dated: Causes and Treatment*. Chicago: Year Book Medical Publ., pp. 145–176, 1980.

⎾tores G: School-children with epilepsy at risk for learning and behavior problems. *Dev. Med. Child Neurol.: 20*, 502–508, 1978.

⎾trauss E, Risser A, Jones MW: Fear responses in patients with epilepsy. *Arch. Neurol.: 39*, 626–630.

⎾weet WH, Ervin F, Mark VH: The relationship of violent behavior to focal cerebral disease. In Garattini S, Sigg EB (Editors), *Aggressive Behaviors*. Amsterdam: Exerpta Medica, pp. 336–352, 1968.

⎾ymonds C: Discussion. *Proc. R. Soc. Med.: 55*, 314–315, 1962.

⎾aylor DC: Aggression and epilepsy. *J. Psychosom. Res.: 13*, 229–236, 1969a.

Taylor DC: Sexual behavior and temporal lobe epilepsy. *Arch. Neurol.: 21*, 510–516, 1969b.

Taylor DC, Falconer MA: Clinical, socioeconomic and psychological changes after temporal lobectomy for epilepsy. *Br. J. Psychiatry: 114*, 1247–1261, 1968.

Tizard B: The personality of epileptics: A discussion of the evidence. *Psychol. Bull.: 59*, 196–210, 1962.

Toone BK: Psychoses of epilepsy. In Reynolds EH, Trimble MR (Editors), *Epilepsy and Psychiatry*. Edinburgh: Churchill-Livingstone, pp. 113–137, 1981.

Trieman DM: Epilepsy and violence: medical and legal issues. *Epilepsia: 27 (Suppl. 2)*, S77–S104, 1986.

Trieman DM, Delgado-Escueta AV: Violence and epilepsy: A critical review. In Pedley TA, Meldrum BS (Editors), *Recent Advances in Epilepsy, Vol. 1*. London: Churchill-Livingstone, pp. 179–209, 1983.

Trimble MR: Personality disturbance in epilepsy. *Neurology: 33*, 1332–1334, 1983.

Trimble MR: Psychiatric and psychological aspects of epilepsy. In Porter R, Marselli PL (Editors), *BIMR Neurology. Epilepsies. Vol. 5*. London: Butterworths, pp. 322–355, 1984.

Trosseau A: *Clinique medicale de l'Hotel Dieu de Paris*. 4th edn. Paris: Bailliere, p. 409, 1873.

Tucker DM, Novelly RA, Walker PJ: Hyperreligiosity in temporal lobe epilepsy: redefining the relationship. *J. Nerv. Ment. Dis.: 175*, 181–184, 1987.

Van Reeth PE: L'hypersexualité dans l'epilepsie et les tumeurs du lobe temporal. *Acta Neurol. Psychiatr. Belg.: 58*, 194–218, 1958.

Warnecke LB: A case of temporal lobe epilepsy with an orgasmic component. *Can. Psychiatr. Assoc. J.: 21*, 319–324, 1976.

Waxman SG, Geschwind N: The interictal behavior syndrome of temporal lobe epilepsy. *Arch. Psychiatry: 32*, 1580–1588, 1975.

Weil AA: Depressive reactions associated with temporal lobe-uncinate seizures. *J. Nerv. Ment. Dis.: 121*, 505–510, 1955.

Weil AA: Ictal depression and anxiety in temporal lobe disorders. *Am. J. Psychiatry: 113*, 149–157, 1956.

Whitman S, Hermann BP, Black RB, Chhabria S: Psychopathology and seizure type in children with epilepsy. *Psychol. Med.: 121*, 843–853, 1982.

Whitman S, Hermann BP, Gordon A: Psychopathology in epilepsy: How great is the risk? *Biol. Psychiatry: 19*, 213–236, 1984.

Wieser HG: Temporal lobe or psychomotor status epilepticus. A case report. *Electroencephalogr. Clin. Neurophysiol.: 48*, 558–572, 1980.

Wieser HG: Depth recorded limbic seizures and psychopathology. *Neurosci. Behav. Rev.: 7*, 427–440, 1983.

Wieser HG: Selective amygdalohippocampectomy: indications, investigative technique and results. In *Adv. Techn. Stand. Neurosurg., Vol. 13*, Vienna: Springer, pp. 39–133, 1986.

Williams D: The structure of emotions reflected in epileptic experiences. *Brain: 79*, 29–67, 1956.

Williams D: Neural factors related to habitual aggression: consideration of differences between those habitual aggressives and others who have committed crimes of violence. *Brain:* *92*, 503 – 520, 1969.

Willmore LJ, Heilman KM, Fennell E: Effects of chronic seizures on religiosity. *Trans. Am. Neurol. Assoc.: 105*,

85 – 87, 1980.

Yamada H, Yoshida H: Laughing attack: a review and report of nine cases. *Folia Psychiatr. Neurol. Jap.: 31*, 129 – 137 1977.

© 1989 Elsevier Science Publishers B.V. (Biomedical Division)
Handbook of Neuropsychology, Vol. 3
F. Boller and J. Grafman (Eds)

CHAPTER 16

Disorders of emotions and affect in patients with unilateral brain damage

Guido Gainotti

Institute of Neurology of the 2nd Faculty of Medicine of the University of Naples, Naples, Italy

Introduction

The classical views about the neural substrates of emotional behavior (summarized in Ch. 13 of this volume by Macchi) have held that emotions are subtended by a highly integrated anatomical system, extending from the hypothalamus and from the amygdala to the 'older' (i.e., less highly differentiated) cortical areas lying on the medial wall of the cerebral hemispheres. According to Panksepp (1982, 1985, 1986) the hypothalamus should be considered as the hard core of this system, containing the basic 'command circuits' for emotions, but a substantial body of evidence also points to a crucial role of the amygdala in various basic aspects of emotional behavior (LeDoux, 1987; Doty, 1989). On the other hand, Van Hoesen (1982) and Damasio and Van Hoesen (1983) consider the limbic areas lying on the medial edge of the cortical mantle as an interface between these hard-wired emotional circuits and the information coming from the outside world, since a strong connection exists at this level between the limbic system and modality-specific or multi-modal association areas. These views, being based on strong anatomical, experimental and clinical evidence, certainly account for most of the abnormal emotional phenomena observed in the fields of behavioral neurology and biological psychiatry. There are, however, some emotionally relevant phenomena, observed in brain-damaged patients or discovered in normal subjects under precise experimental conditions, which suggest that, in addition to the distinction between sub-cortical and cortical structures and the opposition between medial wall and lateral convexity of the cortical mantle, hemispheric specialization also plays a role in the regulation of emotions.

One big problem with this new variable is that we completely ignore the biological substrates of the hemispheric lateralization of the emotional functions. Our knowledge of this topic is, in fact, based only upon clinical, experimental and psychophysiological evidence. The aim of the present chapter will consist in reviewing the part of this evidence which stems from observation of the different emotional behavior shown by right and left brain-damaged patients and in discussing its meaning. Thus, our chapter will be organized according to the following guidelines:

We will first briefly review some important pioneering observations on the relationships between emotions and cerebral dominance;

We will then pass on to a fairly detailed account of the clinical studies which have described differing emotional behavior in right and left brain-damaged patients and of investigations which have assessed mood changes following unilateral brain damage by means of standardized psychiatric instruments or biological markers of depression.

Our next step will consist in discussing the three main interpretations advanced to explain these different emotional changes, namely: (a) the specialization of the right and left hemisphere for opposite aspects of mood; (b) the relative dominance of the right hemisphere for various aspects of emotions; (c) the critical role of the right hemisphere in non-verbal (emotional) communication.

Finally, the possible interactions between side and intra-hemispheric locus of lesion will be taken into account.

First observations on the hemispheric lateralization of functions related to emotion

The first observations on the possible lateralization of functions related to emotion are probably those of Jackson, who more than a century ago noticed that emotional language is often preserved in aphasic patients, and attributed to the right hemisphere the source of these affective utterances (Jackson, 1878).

The same author also observed that when an emotional experience, such as a 'dreamy state' or an emotion of fear 'occurs at the onset of a paroxysm . . . the first spasm is usually on the left side of the body' (Jackson, 1880).

Some decades later, Babinski (1914), after having observed that some patients affected by organic hemiplegia are seemingly unaware of their disability (anosognosia) or manifest an amazing indifference toward their paralysis (anosodiaphoria), raised the question of the relationship between these patterns of behavior and localization of damage to the right hemisphere.

Subsequent clinical and anatomo-clinical reports confirmed the relationship between anosognosia and right hemisphere lesions, but did not thoroughly discuss its nature. To be sure, Hirschl and Potzl (quoted by Schilder, 1935) advanced the hypothesis of a right hemisphere dominance for vegetative functions, but this idea was not taken up by other authors, probably because it was not in line with the prevailing concepts about cerebral dominance. The same holds for Critchley's (1955, 1957) suggestion that right brain-damaged patients might present a prevalence not only of anosognosia and anosodiaphoria, but also of other abnormal attitudes toward the disability, such as the personification of the paralysed limbs or an almost 'insane hatred of the paralysed extremity couched in exaggerated language' (misoplegia). Thus, until the beginning of the sixties the right and left hemisphere were considered as equally involved in the regulation of emotions and related behavior. For example, Hécaen (1962), reviewing the clinical work on the various facets of cerebral dominance, explicitly claimed: 'when there is a disturbance of the activities of synthesis (such as personality disturbances derived from cerebral lesions) no difference can be found between left and right lesions'.

Almost at the same time, however, Terzian and Cecotto (1959), Alemà and Donini (1960) and Perria et al. (1961) observed differing emotional behavior in patients submitted to pharmacological inactivation of the right and left cerebral hemispheres. Injection of sodium amytal into the left carotid artery produced a 'depressive catastrophic' reaction, whereas injection of the same drug into the right carotid artery was followed by an opposite 'euphoric' reaction. Although these observations have not been confirmed by all the authors who have used the same procedure (negative results have been reported, for example, by Milner, 1967; Tsunoda and Oka, 1976; and, more recently, by Kolb and Milner, 1981), the problem of the relationships between emotions and hemispheric specialization had been, in any case, definitely raised.

Emotional reactions associated with unilateral brain lesions

Clinical investigations

Interesting but sporadic observations of the emotional behavior of patients affected by lesions of the dominant and of the minor hemisphere seemed consistent with the finding of a different emotional change after injection of sodium amytal into the right as compared to the left carotid artery.

Goldstein (1939) had noticed, for example, that

catastrophic reactions usually prevail in aphasic left brain-damaged patients, whereas Hécaen et al. (1951) and Denny-Brown et al. (1952) had described an abnormal indifference to failure in subjects affected by right brain damage. Since no systematic study of this phenomenon had previously been carried out in patients with unilateral brain injury, I undertook toward the end of the sixties (Gainotti, 1969) a systematic investigation of the emotional reaction associated with lesion of the right and the left cerebral hemisphere. Results of this study were apparently in good agreement with the observations made during pharmacological inactivation of either hemisphere, since left brain-damaged patients presented, in addition to their communication disabilities, a prevalence of catastrophic reactions, with anxiety and bursts of tears, whereas right-sided patients more frequently showed an abnormal indifference toward their disability and other frustrations met during the test.

However, neither the subjective impression drawn from the observation of these emotional reactions nor the analysis of the clinical context in which they appeared was consistent with the interpretation given by the authors who had observed differing emotional behavior after pharmacological inactivation of the right and left hemispheres. These authors had assumed the existence at the level of the right and the left hemisphere of neurological structures subsuming respectively negative and positive aspects of the mood.

According to this model, normal mood would result from a balance between these opposite mechanisms, whereas depressive-catastrophic reactions of left brain-damaged patients would derive from a prevalence of the right-sided center for negative emotions, and euphoric-manic reactions of right brain-damaged patients would be due to the predominance of the left-sided center for positive emotions. The clinical impression we obtained from the analysis of our patients suggested, on the contrary, that the catastrophic reactions of left brain-damaged patients should be considered

as a dramatic but psychologically appropriate form of reaction to the devastating effect of the lesion on speech and motor abilities.

Much more difficult to explain was the abnormal indifference reaction of right brain-damaged patients. The qualitative features of this emotional change, consisting of a mixture of apathetic indifference and an inappropriate tendency to joke, were, in any case, very different from those observed in the euphoric excited behavior of manic patients. We tried, therefore, to clarify the meaning of this surprising form of emotional reaction by undertaking a more analytical study of the patterns of emotional behavior shown by right and left brain-damaged patients (Gainotti, 1972). In this research we tried to distinguish, within the 'Catastrophic Reactions', two separable groups of behaviors:

(i) those directly linked (such as anxiety reactions, bursts of tears, swearing, aggressive behavior, sharp refusal or desolate renunciation of the test) to the *violent emotional storm of the catastrophic reaction* considered, according to Goldstein (1939), as the anxious, desperate reaction of an organism faced with a task that it cannot solve;

(ii) those considered as suggestive of *a more stable depressive orientation of the mood* (expression of discouragement, anticipations and declarations of incapacity, excuses and extolling of past abilities).

A third group of patterns (anosognosia and minimization of the disability, indifference toward failures and tendency to joke) pointed, in contrast, to *indifference toward the disability*.

Finally, the last group of patterns (including confabulations of denial, delusions about parts of the body and expressions of hatred toward the paralysed limbs) was considered as indicative of *a strong need to deny illness and disabilities*.

Results of this second study showed that only patterns of behavior directly linked to the emotional storm of the catastrophic reaction were significantly more frequent in left brain-damaged patients, whereas patterns pointing to a more stable depressive orientation of the mood showed only a non-significant trend in the same direction.

As for the patterns of emotional behavior significantly associated with right hemisphere injury, they consisted on the one hand of anosognosia, indifference and tendency to joke and, on the other hand, of exaggerated expressions of hatred toward the paralysed limbs. This result is consistent with Critchley's suggestion that not only anosognosia and anosodiaphoria but also misoplegia usually prevails in right brain-damaged patients (Critchley, 1955, 1957).

Among the left brain-damaged patients, catastrophic reactions were highly associated with aphasia and were particularly sharp and violent in Broca's aphasic patients. Less dramatic but frequent anxiety reactions were also observed in patients with anomic aphasia, whereas Wernicke's aphasic patients were often unaware of their aphasic disturbances and showed less obvious catastrophic reactions. These subjects looked, however, sometimes aggressive and excited, showing a very high incidence of swearing, cursing or other affective utterances.

Among the right brain-damaged patients, all types of indifference or anosognosic reactions and expressions of hatred toward the paralysed limbs were significantly related to the presence of neglect phenomena. In conclusion, the general picture drawn from these studies can be summarized as follows:

Catastrophic reactions of left brain-damaged patients represent a dramatic but psychologically appropriate form of emotional reaction to a seriously disabling brain lesion and in particular to severe difficulty in verbal expression.

Indifference reactions of right hemisphere-damaged patients, on the other hand, are much more difficult to explain, consisting both of indifference and of exaggerated expressions of hatred toward the disability. In any case, since they are obviously emotionally inappropriate, we suggested that they could be due to disruption of a structure (the right hemisphere) critically involved in the regulation of emotions and affects.

Research on emotions and related behavior conducted in patients with unilateral brain injury after the first clinical studies

The attempt to clarify the meaning of the different emotional reactions observed in right and left brain-damaged patients has been further pursued following two main lines of research:
(a) an improved assessment of presence and severity of mood changes following unilateral brain injury by means of depression rating scales or biological markers of depression, such as the dexamethasone suppression test;
(b) the investigation of the ability of patients with unilateral brain damage to comprehend and express emotions.

The first of these lines of research will be reviewed and discussed here in some detail, since it specifically pertains to the content of this chapter, whereas the second one will only be briefly summarized, since this subject is reviewed in Chapters 17 and 18 of this volume.

(A) Investigations which have assessed mood changes following unilateral brain damage by means of depression rating scales or biological markers of depression

The first group of studies have tried to check under more controlled conditions the results of the previous clinical investigations, studying unselected groups of right and left brain-damaged patients by means of depression rating scales or other standardized psychiatric instruments. In the first period the most frequently used research tool was the Minnesota Multiphasic Personality Inventory (MMPI), a well-known structured questionnaire, giving separate scores for 10 different areas of psychopathology.

Then, many other subjective or objective rating scales (such as the Hamilton Depression Scale, the Beck Hopelessness Scale, the Zung Self-Rating Depression Scale, the Present State Examination and so on) have been used by various authors.

Finally, biological markers of depression, such as the dexamethasone suppression test, giving hints about the type and severity of depression, were taken into account. The basic assumptions underlying most of this research were, on one hand, the greater objectivity and sensitivity of the MMPI and the depression rating scales with respect to simple clinical observation and, on the other hand, the equivalence between depression and catastrophic reactions.

For simplicity's sake, the most significant data relative to investigations which have assessed mood changes by means of the MMPI or Depression Rating Scales are reported in Table 1.

These data show that only some authors have found a prevalence of depression in left brain-damaged patients, but that most have failed to demonstrate significant relationships between incidence of depression and laterality of brain injury. These results must be evaluated keeping in mind the following considerations. The first concerns the relevance of these findings to the prevalence of catastrophic reactions in left brain-damaged patients shown in previous studies. In our opinion depression and catastrophic reaction do not belong to the same order of phenomena, as is sometimes wrongly assumed, since catastrophic reaction is a dramatic form of reaction to a catastrophic event, and not a biologically determined and long-lasting mood deflection. Therefore, no discrepancy exists between data reported in Table I and results of previous clinical investigations. Second, it is quite possible that a sampling bias (namely the exclusion from most studies of severely aphasic patients, probably affected by depression, but unable to perform the MMPI or other self-rating depression rating scales) could explain why a trend toward a prevalence of depression in left brain-damaged patients often exists but seldom reaches the level of statistical significance.

However, there are at least two reasons that recommend caution in accepting the above-mentioned trend. The first is that results pointing in the opposite direction are sometimes reported in the neuropsychological literature. Right brain-damaged patients scored, for example, higher than left hemisphere patients on one of the measures of depression used by Sinyor et al. (1986), and a similar prevalence of depression in patients with right-sided lesion has been reported by Kulesha et al. (1981) and Lim and Ebrahim (1983) in two studies not listed in Table I, because they did not fit the criteria for inclusion in this table.

The second reason, recently stressed by Ross and Rush (1981), is that the detection of depression in right brain-damaged patients can be made difficult by the inability of these patients to overtly express affects and by their tendency to deny depression and related behavioral and vegetative disorders. So, we can conclude that psychometric studies of mood change in unilateral brain-damaged patients do not support the view that the emotional reac-

TABLE I

Investigations which have assessed mood changes by means of standardized depression measures

Those showing a prevalence of depression in left B.D. patients	Those showing no clear prevalence
Black (1975) (MMPI)	Dikmen and Reitan (1974) (MMPI)
Gasparrini et al. (1978) (MMPI)	Dikmen and Reitan (1977) (MMPI)
Pasoli et al. (1982) (MMPI)	Folstein et al. (1977) (Hamilton, PSE)
Finklestein et al. (1982) (Hamilton, PSE)	Black and Black (1982) (MMPI)
Robinson and Price (1982) (Hamilton, PSE)	Ruckdeschel-Hibbard (1984) (Hamilton, Beck)
Robinson et al. (1984) (Hamilton, Zung, PSE)	De Agostini et al. (1983) (Nurse's Scale)
	De Bonis et al. (1985)
	Reding et al. (1985) (Hamilton, Zung)
	Sinyor et al. (1986) (Zung, Beck, HSC)

MMPI = Minnesota Multiphasic Personality Inventory
Hamilton = Hamilton Depression Rating Scale
Beck = Beck Hopelessness Scale
Zung = Zung Depression (self-rating) Scale
HSC = Hopkins Symptom Checklist (depression)
PSE = Present Status Examination

tion of left brain-damaged patients is a sort of endogenous depression.

Further support for this claim comes from results of research using the dexamethasone suppression test as a biological marker of depression in stroke patients. Finklestein et al. (1982), Bauer et al. (1984), Reding et al. (1985) and Lipsey et al. (1985) have, indeed, consistently shown that the number of pathological responses to this test is very similar in patients with right and left hemispheric lesions.

A final observation concerning investigations reported in Table I refers to the incidence of indifference reactions in the few studies which have attempted a more rigorous analysis of previous clinical research, either considering indifference reactions as a single entity, or analysing in more detail the patterns of emotional reaction shown by right- and left-sided patients. Results obtained in these studies are in good agreement with those of previous clinical investigations. Finklestein et al. (1982) and Robinson et al. (1984) have noticed, in fact, that indifference reactions (globally considered) are observed almost only in right brain-damaged patients, with an incidence very close to that (30%) reported in my first study (Gainotti, 1969). Analogously, Pasoli et al. (1982) have confirmed, in their analytical report of the patterns of emotional behavior shown by right and left brain-damaged patients, that anxiety reactions and bursts of tears prevail in subjects with left-sided lesions, whereas indifference reactions, anosognosia and tendency to joke are in the foreground in patients with right-sided injury. The prevalence of indifference reactions in right brain-damaged patients is also confirmed by other studies (e.g. Cutting, 1978; Denes et al., 1982; Etcoff, 1989), which are not reported in Table I, since they were not devised to specifically assess the incidence of depression in right and left brain-damaged patients.

In conclusion, results of investigations which have assessed mood changes after unilateral brain damage have confirmed: (a) that a different emotional reaction follows damage to the right as compared to the left hemisphere; (b) that catastrophic reactions cannot be considered as a sort of endogenous depression; (c) that the emotional reaction of right brain-damaged patients typically consists of an abnormal tendency to deny the disability or to treat it with amazing indifference.

(B) Investigations which have studied comprehension and expression of emotions in patients with unilateral brain injury

Several authors (e.g. Heilman et al., 1975, 1984; Tucker et al., 1977; Ross, 1981, 1984; Ruckdeschel-Hibbard et al., 1984) have shown that right brain-damaged patients can easily understand the meaning of a sentence, but are unable to recognize the emotion expressed by the tone of voice of the speaker. Other authors (e.g. DeKosky et al., 1980; Cicone et al., 1980; Goldblum, 1981; Benowitz et al., 1983) have shown that patients with right hemisphere injury are also seriously impaired in recognizing facial emotional expressions (see Etcoff, Ch. 17 of this volume). Similar results have been obtained studying the capacity of right and left brain-damaged patients to express emotions through the tone of voice (Tucker et al., 1977; Ross and Mesulam, 1979; Ross, 1981, 1984; Hughes et al., 1983; Borod et al., 1985) and through facial expression (Buck and Duffy, 1980; Borod et al., 1986) (see Pizzamiglio et al., Ch. 18 of this volume).

All these data have suggested the hypothesis of a right hemisphere superiority for non-verbal communication, similar to the left hemisphere dominance for language functions. The authors who have advanced this hypothesis (Ross, 1981, 1984; Ruckdeschel-Hibbard et al., 1984) more precisely assume a strong correspondence between organization of various aspects of 'propositional' language at the level of the left hemisphere and organization of 'emotional' language at the level of the right hemisphere.

This general hypothesis has important implications for the interpretation of indifference reactions typically observed in right brain-damaged patients. Ross (1984) has maintained, indeed, that inner feelings are intact in right hemisphere patients and that the main defect of these subjects concerns the communicative aspects of emotions. According to this interpretation, indifference reactions should not be considered as an inappropriate form of reaction to the disability, but rather as the consequence of an inability to correctly express a normally experienced emotional reaction. As previously mentioned, Ross and Rush (1981) claim that right brain-damaged patients are as depressed as left hemisphere patients, but, being unable to adequately express their emotions, give the examiner a superficial impression of indifference.

Discussion of the main theories advanced to explain the emotional behavior of right and left brain-damaged patients

We can now summarize the three main theories advanced to explain the different emotional behavior of right and left brain-damaged patients.

(A) Right and left hemisphere are specialized for opposite aspects of the mood, with a left hemisphere dominance for 'positive' emotions, and a right hemisphere prevalence for 'negative' emotions

In the normal brain the balance between these mono-hemispheric structures would be maintained through reciprocal trans-callosal inhibition, whereas in patients with unilateral brain damage the overt emotional behavior would reflect the prevalent activation of the polar aspect of the mood represented in the intact hemisphere.

This interpretation was first advanced by the authors who observed a 'depressive-catastrophic' reaction after pharmacological inactivation of the left hemisphere and a 'euphoric-maniacal' reaction after injection of sodium amytal into the right carotid artery (Terzian, 1964; Rossi and Rosadini, 1967) and was subsequently supported by data obtained both in normal subjects and in brain-damaged patients.

Two main lines of evidence for a different specialization of the right and left hemisphere

respectively for negative and positive emotions have been reported in normal subjects. In the first, physiological measures of hemispheric activation were monitored during positive and negative mood states, whereas in the second the processing of positive and negative emotional stimuli was investigated during lateralized tachistoscopic presentation to the right and left half fields. Different indices of hemispheric activation were used by various authors in the first line of research. Schwartz et al. (1979) studied asymmetries in facial electromyographic activity; Ahern and Schwartz (1979) analysed the direction of lateral eye movements (LEM) and Davidson and coworkers (Davidson et al., 1979; Davidson and Fox, 1982) examined asymmetries in EEG desynchronization. All these studies consistently showed a greater activation of the right hemisphere during induction of negative emotions and a greater activation of the left hemisphere during induction of positive affects.

The weight of these results must, however, be considered with caution owing to the difficulties usually met in interpreting physiological indicators of cerebral activation (Ehrlichman and Weinberger, 1978; Silberman and Weingartner, 1986). Less clear-cut are results obtained from studying recognition of positive and negative emotions by the right and left hemisphere. The hypothesis that positive and negative emotions may be differently recognized by the two hemispheres is, indeed, supported by results obtained by Reuter-Lorenz and Davidson (1981), Reuter-Lorenz et al. (1983) and Natale et al. (1983), but is at variance with the results of Suberi and McKeever (1977), Campbell (1978), Buchtel et al. (1978), Ladavas et al. (1980), Strauss and Kaplan (1980), Strauss and Moscovitch (1981) Hirschman and Safer (1983), Duda and Brown (1984) and Gage and Safer (1985), who have shown that in normal subjects the left visual field is superior to the right in processing both negative and positive emotions.

Thus, the most substantial support for the hypothesis of a different hemispheric specialization for emotions comes from the retrospective study of uncontrollable outbursts of laughing and crying, conducted by Sackeim et al. (1982). These authors reviewed the literature on pathological laughing and crying and found that in cases of destructive brain pathology outbursts of laughter were associated with predominantly right-sided lesions, and outbursts of crying with predominantly left-sided damage. The opposite trend was observed in patients with irritative brain lesions, since ictal outbursts of laughing (gelastic epilepsy) were predominantly found in patients with left-sided foci. According to Sackeim et al. (1982) these data would show that 'the experience of positive mood and outbursts of uncontrollable laughing are most often due to excitation of regions in the left side of the brain . . ., whereas the reverse holds for negative emotions'. It must be acknowledged, however, that although interesting, Sackeim et al.'s data suffer the methodological weakness common to all retrospective studies and that inferences drawn from the lateralization of emotional outbursts to an analogous lateralization of the affective feelings are somewhat arbitrary. It is well known, in fact, that pathological laughing and crying of a lesional or epileptic nature may well be dissociated from the corresponding subjective mood, since patients who present these symptoms often claim that their concurrent mood is unrelated to the displayed emotion (Poeck, 1969; Lieberman and Benson, 1977). More relevant to the problem at issue could be results of investigations which have examined the localization of epileptic foci producing properly emotional ictal experiences, but these results are not consistent with Sackeim et al.'s theory. Thus, Williams (1956), who recorded the laterality of foci causing fear, depression, pleasure or displeasure as ictal manifestations, found no relationship between laterality of focus and type of positive or negative emotional experience. Analogously, Pazzaglia and D'Alessandro (1980) found a slight prevalence of right over left-sided foci in patients presenting an ictal manifestation of pleasure, a finding which is clearly at variance with Sackeim et al.'s suggestion. Finally, Strauss et al. (1983) have failed to confirm

Sackeim et al.'s data in a study in which they directly observed emotional facial expressions occurring at the onset of lateralized focal seizures.

Even less consistent with the implications of this theory are results of investigations which have assessed mood changes following unilateral brain damage, since a theory considering the emotional behavior of right and left brain-damaged patients as determined by an imbalance between a left-sided center for positive emotions and a right-sided center for negative affects should predict (a) a prevalence of depression in left brain-damaged patients and (b) a prevalence of euphoria in subjects with right-sided lesions. Now, if data reported in Table 1 are not inconsistent with the first part of this prediction, they are certainly at variance with the second part. A trend toward a prevalence of depression in left brain-damaged patients could, in fact, be observed in some studies reported in Table 1, but right brain-damaged patients, instead of being euphoric, were often as depressed as subjects with left-sided lesions. It is true that right brain-damaged patients were often unduly indifferent, but the equivalence between the indifference reaction and the euphoric state is even more inappropriate than that between catastrophic reactions and biological depression.

In conclusion, we think that, although stimulating and capable of accounting for many clinical and experimental data, the hypothesis of a different hemispheric specialization for positive and negative emotions meets serious empirical (and perhaps also theoretical) objections.

(B)   The   difference   between   right   and   left hemisphere in the regulation of emotions and affects is quantitative, rather than qualitative
Instead of assuming a different specialization of the right and left hemisphere for opposite aspects of mood, this theory maintains that *both hemispheres are involved in the regulation of each type of emotion, but the right hemisphere is dominant for this function.*

This hypothesis was prompted by the suggestion (Gainotti, 1972) that the difference between the emotional reactions of left and right brain-damaged patients could be better explained by considering the former as 'dramatic but emotionally appropriate' and the latter as clearly 'inappropriate' than by considering the former as 'depressive' and the latter as 'euphoric'.

Consequently, the emotional reaction of left brain-damaged patients would be appropriate because of the integrity of the hemisphere dominant for emotions (the right one) whereas the emotional reaction of right brain-damaged patients would be inadequate because of the disorganization of the emotionally dominant hemisphere.

Data supporting the hypothesis of an emotional inappropriateness of patients with right-sided lesions were subsequently obtained by different authors with different clinical and experimental methodologies. Finlayson and Rourke (1975) showed, for example, that right brain-damaged patients achieve particularly poor results on a test of social judgement. Gardner et al. (1975) noticed that these patients, although perfectly able to explain verbally the meaning of humorous cartoons, often react to them with an inappropriate emotional reaction. Finally, several authors (e.g. Marquarsden, 1969; Hurwitz and Adams, 1972; Held et al., 1975; Denes et al., 1982) have shown that the inappropriate emotional reaction of right brain-damaged patients has important implications for the outcome of recovery from hemiplegia. Left hemiplegics show, in fact, a lesser degree of spontaneous recovery (Hurwitz and Adams, 1972) and less social adjustment (Marquarsden, 1969) than patients with right hemiplegia. Furthermore, Held et al. (1975) and Denes et al. (1982) have shown that motor rehabilitation takes longer and is more difficult in left than in right hemiplegics, owing to the deleterious influence of the inappropriate social and emotional reaction of these patients. Another important body of data relevant to the issue has been obtained by studying hemispheric asymmetries in comprehension and expression of emotions. Several studies, conducted both in normal subjects and in brain-damaged patients with different experimental paradigms, have in fact

generally shown an advantage of the right hemisphere for various aspects of emotional communication (see Chs. 17 and 18 of this volume for exhaustive critical surveys of studies dealing respectively with comprehension and expression of emotions).

A third important group of data strongly supporting the hypothesis of a right hemisphere dominance for emotions and affects comes from studies of autonomic arousal in patients with unilateral brain lesions. These studies, which will also be discussed by Heilman and Watson (Ch. 19 of this volume), might perhaps cast some light on the basic mechanisms underlying the relative dominance of the right hemisphere for emotions and related behavior. A short discussion of this issue will, therefore, be found in the last part of this chapter.

(C) The strange indifference reaction of patients with right-side lesions results from the disorganization of a system critically involved in functions of non-verbal (emotional) communication and predominantly subserved by the right hemisphere
Both theoretical empirical reasons have prompted this hypothesis. A primary theoretical reason, stressed by Darwin (1872) more than a century ago, emphasizes the adaptive value for a social species of communication of emotions. This suggests that both sophisticated peripheral organs (such as the human facial musculature) and specialized cortical nervous structures may have evolved to improve expression and comprehension of emotions. Obviously, this theoretical reasoning suggests the existence of cortical structures critically involved in functions of emotional communication but gives no hints as to the possible lateralization of these structures. The second theoretical consideration suggests that if some components of the emotional functions are asymmetrically represented in the human brain, they should concern more the cognitive and communicative than the basic experiential aspects of emotions, which would be more likely to be represented in the sub-

cortically located hard core of the emotional system. The third, empirical reason is represented by results of clinical and experimental studies (discussed by Etcoff in this volume) which have documented the existence of a right hemisphere advantage for functions of emotional communication.

These theoretical and empirical reasons led Ross (1981, 1984) and Ruckdeschel-Hibbard et al. (1984) to hypothesize that right hemisphere injury primarily results in a defect of emotional communication. As a consequence, both the examiner and family members could draw an impression of emotional indifference or inappropriateness, not corresponding to the unexpressed, but otherwise intact, emotional experience of these patients. If this hypothesis is correct, then autonomic arousal should be normal in these patients, since a strong link exists between autonomic arousal and intensity of emotional experience (Duffy, 1962; Hohmann, 1966; Schachter, 1975; Reisenzein, 1983).

An important body of data, however, suggests that right brain-damaged patients show a defect of autonomic arousal during various kinds of emotionally loaded tasks. Heilman et al. (1978), Morrow et al. (1981) and Zoccolotti et al. (1982) have indeed observed a poor autonomic response both to painful stimuli and to emotionally loaded visual stimuli in right brain-damaged patients (see Ch. 19 of this volume). Even more recently, we have confirmed these findings, at the same time analysing in right and left brain-damaged patients (a) the emotional reaction shown during the neuropsychological test situation, (b) the comprehension of emotionally laden stimuli, (c) the spontaneous expression of emotions and (d) the autonomic response to emotional stimuli.

Both spontaneous expression of emotions and emotional arousal were elicited by showing the patients through a rear projector short movies, constructed to provoke positive, neutral and negative emotional states. Emotional facial expressions were videotaped and analysed by means of the FACS procedure (Ekman and Friesen, 1975). Galvanic skin responses and heart rate deceleration

were recorded and considered respectively as indices of sympathetic and parasympathetic arousal (Sandman, 1975; Lacey, 1967).

Results suggested that experience of emotion and autonomic correlates of inner experience are more selectively disrupted by right hemisphere injury than the ability to express emotions (Gainotti, 1987). No significant difference was, in fact, observed between right and left brain-damaged patients when we considered the ability to produce facial expressions congruent with the elicited emotion (Mammucari et al., 1988), but an interesting difference was observed between right-sided patients and normal controls or left-sided patients during the projection of the negative emotional movie. In this situation, normal subjects and left brain-damaged patients showed a tendency to move the eyes away from the most unpleasant scene (a bloody presentation of a surgical toilette), whereas similar avoidance eye movements were not observed in right brain-damaged patients. Results obtained studying the autonomic response to the same stimuli confirmed that the lack of avoidance eye movements was due to a sort of emotional indifference to stressing situations. Both normal subjects and left brain-damaged patients showed, in fact, the highest level of galvanic skin response and the greatest heart rate deceleration while viewing the unpleasant emotional film, whereas right brain-damaged patients showed a very weak sympathetic and parasympathetic reaction when faced with the same stimuli (Zoccolotti et al., 1986). These data indicate that the term 'indifference' is not misleading, but correctly describes the emotional reaction of right brain-damaged patients. These subjects, in fact, are not simply unable to express an otherwise intact emotional experience, but show a defective emotional arousal and a correlated diminished capacity to feel affects.

Emotional reaction, time course of the disease and intra-hemispheric locus of lesion in right and left brain-damaged patients

The patterns of emotional reaction considered

typical of right and left brain-damaged patients are certainly not observed in all (or even in the great majority) of the subjects presenting with signs of unilateral brain injury. The percentages of emotional reactions reported in our 1969 study (in which catastrophic reactions were observed in about 40% left and indifference reactions in 30% right brain-damaged patients) are representative of the prevalence of these two types of emotional reaction in unselected samples of unilateral brain-damaged patients. The prevalence of these two types of emotional behavior is, however, influenced both by the developmental stage of the disease and by the intra-hemispheric localization of damage. As for the first variable, Robinson and Price (1982) showed that depression was present in about 35% of their subjects with left hemisphere infarct during the acute stroke period, but this percentage rose to more than 75% from 6 months to 2 years after the stroke. Analogously, important developmental factors can be found when the patterns of emotional behavior usually observed in right brain-damaged patients are taken into account. In a longitudinal study conducted many years ago in patients affected by extensive lesions of the right hemisphere (Gainotti, 1968) we have shown, in fact, that anosognosia and delusions about parts of the body are usually observed only in the acute post-ictal periods. Then gradually anosognosic patients begin to admit the presence of hemiplegia, but minimize its importance or become fatuous, indifferent and, sometimes, frankly euphoric. Finally, in the chronic stage, some patients become much more aware or their disability and show a depressed mood, whereas others show a mixture of apathetic indifference, expressions of hatred toward the paralysed limbs and poorly expressed depression. This last picture corresponds to the cases reported by Ross and Rush (1981) showing a dissociation between internal mood states and external expressed affects. Our findings have been recently confirmed by Hier et al. (1983), studying the recovery of behavioral abnormalities in a group of stroke patients showing evidence of anosognosia during the acute post-stroke period.

The influence of the intra-hemispheric locus of lesion on the emotional behavior of right and left brain-damaged patients is particularly clear in subjects with left-sided lesions. It is well known, in fact, from the early anatomo-clinical studies of aphasia, that a very different emotional reaction is usually observed in Broca's and in Wernicke's aphasic patients, with the former presenting the most prototypical forms of catastrophic reactions, and the latter being described as unaware of their language disturbances, indifferent and sometimes inappropriately euphoric. Results of our 1972 study confirmed these clinical impressions, with the distinction that Wernicke's aphasic patients seemed agitated and irascible, rather than euphoric (a viewpoint shared by other authors, such as De Renzi and Vignolo, 1962, and Fisher, 1970). The meaning of these different forms of emotional reaction remains, however, controversial. The traditional interpretation, as summarized by Benson (1973) for example, considered the different emotional behavior of Broca's and Wernicke's aphasic patients in psychological terms, as conditioned by the presence of a speech defect and as resulting from a different degree of awareness of language disturbance. Broca's aphasics, having an effortful non-fluent speech, are acutely aware of being unable to express in words thoughts and feelings, whereas Wernicke's aphasics, showing a fluent (or even a hyper-fluent) paraphasic speech, associated with a severe comprehension disorder, do not realize that their own output is incomprehensible. They are, therefore, unaware of their disability and can be aggressive with the examiner, who fails to respond to their statements or questions.

More recent interpretations, however, assume that neurobiological rather than psychological explanations might account for these differences. In particular, Robinson and coworkers (Robinson and Benson, 1981; Robinson and Price, 1982; Robinson et al., 1984) maintain that it is the anatomical frontal location of lesions, rather than psychological factors, which accounts for the presence of severe depression in stroke patients with left hemisphere injury. Robinson et al. relate the prevalence of depression in patients with left anterior lesions to the disruption of catecholamine pathways, which would be depleted by left more than by right and by frontal more than by parietal lesions. They also provide data suggesting that the emotional disturbances usually described under the heading of 'frontal lobe syndrome' may have different features according to the side of the lesion. Specifically, they suggest that an abnormal emotional reaction is usually provoked by anterior rather than by posterior brain damage, but that left frontal lesions specifically produce depressive disturbances, whereas right frontal injury usually provokes indifference and inappropriate cheerfulness. The meaning of the emotional behavior of patients with left frontal lesions and the hypothesis of an interaction between laterality of frontal damage and type of emotional change will be discussed separately.

(1) The hypothesis that depressive-catastrophic reactions of patients with left frontal lesions may be considerd as a form of 'endogenous depression', resulting from an 'asymmetrical depletion in the cortical biogenic amine pathways' (Robinson et al., 1984), seems unconvincing for two reasons. The first is that the 'endogenous' nature of this depression is not confirmed by studies which have taken into account lesion localization, using the dexamethasone suppression test as a biological marker of depression (Finklestein et al., 1982; Lipsey et al., 1985). Neither of these studies has, in fact, found a greater incidence of pathological responses on this test in patients with left frontal damage. The second is that no independent evidence supports the assumption of an asymmetrical representation of noradrenergic pathways in the human cortex.

(2) The hypothesis that left frontal lesions provoke depressive-catastrophic disturbances, whereas right frontal damage produces inappropriate cheerfulness, revives the old views considering the frontal lobe as crucially involved in emotional behavior (see Macchi, Ch. 13 of this volume) but meets with both theoretical and empirical objec-

tions. The theoretical objection consists in the fact that the portions of the frontal lobes usually damaged in stroke patients do not coincide with those more deeply involved in emotional functions and more tightly linked with the limbic system. The former are located in the frontal convexity and supplied by the upper branches of the middle cerebral artery (Gacs et al., 1982; Kertesz and Black, 1985), whereas the latter are located on the medial surface and in the orbital portion of the frontal lobe and are supplied by the anterior cerebral artery. Now, emotional and personality disorders are frequently observed after vascular lesions in the latter territory, but they do not differ qualitatively in right-sided and left-sided lesions. Alexander and Freedman (1984) have recently reported the detailed clinical observation of seven patients presenting an infarct in the territory of the anterior cerebral artery after rupture of aneurisms of the anterior communicating artery. Severe personality disorders were observed in all these patients, but the essential features of these changes were the same, irrespective of the laterality of the lesion, consisting of apathy, jocularity and irritability. The only difference concerned the severity of the emotional disorder, which was greater in patients with right-sided than in those with left-sided infarcts. This finding supports the hypothesis of a greater involvement of the right frontal limbic cortex in the modulation of emotions and affects, rather than that of a differential involvement of the right and left frontal limbic systems in the regulation of different sorts of emotions. Data consistent with the first hypothesis have also been recently obtained by Grafman et al. (1986). These authors have found that patients with penetrating brain wounds located in the right orbitofrontal cortex present a higher incidence of psychiatric treatment, persistent feelings of anxiety and 'edginess' and altered sexual behavior than those with either left orbitofrontal injury or right nonfrontal lesions.

The empirical objection to the Robinson theory is that inconsistent results have been reported by the authors who have tabulated the incidence of indifference reactions in right brain-damaged patients with anterior and posterior brain lesions. Robinson et al. (1984) reported that an anterior lesion was present in 5 of the 6 right brain-damaged patients presenting an inappropriate cheerfulness, but Finklestein et al. (1982) found a parietal lesion in all the four right brain-damaged patients with an indifference reaction observed in their study. Furhermore, Finset (1982), in a study of 50 right brain-damaged patients with lesion localization based on CT and/or EEG data, found that patients with marked indifference reactions tended to have combined posterior and frontal lesions, suggesting a closer link with the extent of the right hemisphere damage than with its intrahemispheric localization. Finally, Starkstein et al. (1987) in a further study aiming to compare the influence of cortical and subcortical lesions in the production of post-stroke mood disorders have found that the incidence of indifference reactions was higher in right brain-damaged patients with posterior (43%) than in those with anterior (33%) lesions.

Taken together, these data do not support the hypothesis of a possible interaction between emotional behavior, laterality and intra-hemispheric focus of lesion.

Concluding remarks

Although the exact nature of the relationships between emotions and hemispheric specialization is still difficult to define, we think that the hypothesis of a right hemisphere dominance for emotions and related behavior remains the most convincing one. This hypothesis seems, in fact, not unreasonable from the evolutionary point of view and poses fewer difficulties than the competing theories assuming (a) a different specialization of the right and left hemisphere for opposite aspects of mood, (b) a simple specialization of the right hemisphere for non-verbal (emotional) communication.

Much more difficult is to specify the basic mechanisms which could underlie this right hemisphere superiority for emotional behavior. One could think of elementary factors, such as a greater autonomic reactivity or a stronger emotional arousal, or of higher-level cognitive factors, such as a better capacity to process non-verbal information and to control the motor expressive apparatus. Theoretical reasons could favor the latter hypothesis, but empirical data seem to support more the former than the latter interpretation. As a matter of fact, it would seem likely, from the theoretical point of view, that hemispheric asymmetries emerge at the interface between innate emotional circuits, located in subcortical structures and cortical hemispheric structures underlying the analysis of perceptual information designed to activate these internal circuits. However, differences observed between right and left brain-damaged patients on tasks of emotional comprehension and expression are generally not very impressive.

Some authors have even failed to observe significant differences between patients with right-sided and left-sided lesions both on tests of comprehension of emotional stimuli (Schlanger et al., 1976) and in the production of facial emotional expressions (see Ch. 18 of this volume for a discussion of this issue). In contrast, effects obtained studying the autonomic responses of right and left brain-damaged patients to emotional stimuli are, in general, much more robust.

This finding could suggest that the relationship between right hemisphere damage and disorders of emotional behavior lies more at the level of autonomic arousal, intimately linked with the experience of emotions, than at the interface between emotional experience and cognitive or communicative aspects of emotions (Gainotti, 1987).

Two points should, however, be stressed at the end of this discussion. The first is that the search for a basic mechanism underlying an interhemispheric difference may be intellectually rewarding but not entirely correct, since the superiority of one hemisphere over the other is not necessarily due to the influence of one leading factor, but could also be due to the co-occurrence of several (more or less related) factors. Thus, it is possible that both a greater level of emotional arousal and better equipment for processing emotional information may account for the right hemisphere superiority in emotional functions.

The second is that, since our knowledge of the whole problem is still uncertain, the above-mentioned interpretations should be considered more as attempts at systematization, aiming to orient future investigations, than as firmly established, internally consistent theories.

Acknowledgements

The author is very grateful to Professor E. De Renzi for his advice and assistance in the preparation of this paper, and to Mrs. M. Bonfante, who carefully typed the manuscript.

References

Ahern GL, Schwartz GE: Differential lateralization for positive versus negative emotion. *Neuropsychologia: 17*, 693 – 698, 1979.

Alemà G, Donini G: Sulle modificazioni cliniche ed elet-troencefalografiche da introduzione intracarotidea di iso-amil-etil-barbiturato di sodio nell'uomo. *Boll. Soc. Ital. Biol. Sper.: 36*, 900 – 904, 1960.

Alexander MP, Freedman M: Amnesia after anterior com-municating artery aneurysm rupture. *Neurology: 34*, 752 – 757, 1984.

Babinski J: Contribution à l'étude des troubles mentaux dans l'hémiplégie organique cérébrale (Anosognosie). *Rev. Neurol.: 27*, 845 – 848, 1914.

Bauer M, Gans J, Harley J: Dexamethasone suppression test and depression in a rehabilitation setting. *Arch. Phys. Med. Rehabil.: 64*, 421 – 422, 1983.

Benowitz LI, Bear DM, Mesulam MM, Rosenthal R, Zaidel EE, Sperry RW: Nonverbal sensitivity following lateralized cerebral injury. *Cortex: 19*, 5 – 12, 1983.

Benson DF: Psychiatric aspects of aphasia. *Br. J. Psychiatry: 123*, 555 – 566, 1973.

Black FW: Unilateral brain lesions and MMPI performance: A preliminary study. *Percept. Motor Skills: 40*, 87 – 93, 1975.

Black FW, Black IL: Anterior-posterior locus of lesion and per-sonality: Support for the caudality hypothesis. *J. Clin. Psychol.: 38*, 3, 468 – 477, 1982.

Borod JC, Koff E, Perlman M, Nicolas M: Channels of emo-tional expression in patients with unilateral brain damage. *Arch. Neurol.: 42*, 345 – 348, 1985.

Buchtel HA, Campari F, De Risio C, Rota R: Hemispheric dif-ferences in discriminative reaction time to facial expression. *Ital. J. Psychol.: 5*, 159 – 169, 1978.

Buck R, Duffy RJ: Nonverbal communication of affect in brain-damaged patients. *Cortex: 16*, 351 – 362, 1980.

Campbell R: Asymmetries in interpreting and expressing a po[s]-ed facial expression. *Cortex: 14*, 327 – 342, 1978.

Cicone M, Wapner W, Gardner H: Sensitivity to emotional e[x]-pressions and situations in organic patients. *Cortex: 1[6]* 145 – 158, 1980.

Critchley M: Personification of paralysed limbs in hemiplegic[s]. *Br. Med. J.: 30*, 284 – 286, 1955.

Critchley M: Observations on anosodiaphoria. *Encephale: 4[6]* 540 – 546, 1957.

Cutting J: Study of anosognosia. *J. Neurol. Neurosur[g] Psychiatry: 41*, 548 – 555, 1978.

Damasio AR, Van Hoesen GW: Emotional disturbance[s] associated with focal lesions of the limbic frontal lobe. I[n] Heilman K, Satz P (Editors), *Neuropsychology of Huma[n] Emotion*. New York: The Guilford Press, Ch. 4, p[p] 85 – 110, 1983.

Darwin C: *The Expression of Emotion in Man and Animal[s]* London: John Murray, 1872. (Current edition, Chicag[o] University of Chicago Press, 1986).

Davidson RJ, Fox NA: Asymmetrical brain activit[y] discriminates between positive versus negative stimuli in te[n] month old human infants. *Science: 218*, 1235 – 1237, 1982.

Davidson RJ, Schwartz GE, Saron C, Bennett J, Goleman D[J] Frontal versus parietal EEG asymmetry during positive an[d] negative affect. *Psychophysiology: 16*, 202 – 203, 1979.

De Agostini I, Blanc-Garin J, De Bonis M: Evaluation du com[-] portment émotionnel chez les malades avec lésion[s] cérébrales. Premiers résultats. In *C.R. Congr. Psychiatr[.] Neurol. Lang. Franç.: 81*, pp. 321 – 328, 1983.

De Bonis M, Dellatolas G, Rondot P: Mood disorders in lef[t] and right brain-damaged patients: comparison betwee[n] ratings and self ratings on the same adjective mood scale[.] *Psychopathology: 18*, 286 – 292, 1985.

DeKosky ST, Heilman KM, Bowers D, Valenstein E: Recogni[-] tion and discrimination of emotional faces and pictures[.] *Brain Lang.: 9*, 206 – 214, 1980.

Denes GF, Semenza C, Stoppa E, Lis A: Unilateral spatia[l] neglect and recovery from hemiplegia. A follow-up study[.] *Brain: 105*, 543 – 552, 1982.

Denny-Brown D, Meyer JS, Horenstein S: The significance o[f] perceptual rivalry resulting from parietal lesions. *Brain: 75* 433 – 471, 1952.

De Renzi E, Vignolo LA: Fattori verbali ed extraverbali dell[a] comprensione negli afasici. In Atti del XIV° Congresso Na[-] zionale della Società Italiana di Neurologia, pp. 443 – 46[8] 1962.

Dikmen S, Reitan R: MMPI correlates of localized cerebral le[-] sions. *Percept. Motor Skills: 39*, 831 – 840, 1974.

Dikmen S, Reitan R: MMPI correlates of adaptive abilit[y] deficits in patients with brain lesions. *J. Nerv. Ment. Dis.: 165*: 247 – 254, 1977.

Doty RW: Some anatomical substrates of emotions and thei[r] bihemispheric coordination. In Gainotti G, Caltagirone C[:] (Editors), *Emotions and the Dual Brain*. New York: Springe[r] Verlag, 1989.

Duda PD, Brown J: Lateral asymmetry of positive and negativ[e] emotions. *Cortex: 20*, 253 – 261, 1984.

Duffy E: *Activation and Behavior*. New York: Wiley, 1962.

Ehrlichman H, Weinberger A: Lateral eye movements an[d] hemispheric asymmetry: A critical review. *Psychol. Bull.: 85*

1080 – 1101, 1978.

kman P, Friesen WV: *Unmasking the Face.* Englewood Cliff, NJ: Prentice Hall, 1975.

tcoff N: Recognition and expression of emotion. In Gainotti G, Caltagirone C (Editors), *Emotions and the Dual Brain.* New York: Springer Verlag, 1989.

inklestein S, Benowitz LI, Baldessarini RJ, Arana GW, Levine D, Woo E, Bear D, Moya K, Stoll AL: Mood, vegetative disturbance, and dexamethasone suppression test after stroke. *Ann. Neurol.: 12,* 463 – 468, 1982.

inlayson MAJ, Rourke BP: Personality correlates of lateralized cerebral vascular disease. Paper presented at the American Psychological Association Convention, 1975.

inset A: Depressive behavior, outburst of crying and emotional indifference in left hemiplegics. Paper presented at the Second Symposium of Cognitive Rehabilitation. Indianapolis, 1982.

isher CM: Anger associated with dysphasia. *Trans. Am. Neurol. Assoc.: 95,* 240 – 242, 1970.

olstein MF, Maiberger R, McHugh PR: Mood disorder as a specific complication of stroke. *J. Neurol. Neurosurg. Psychiatry: 40,* 1018 – 1020, 1977.

iacs G, Merei FT, Bodosi M: Ballon catheter as a model of cerebral emboli in humans. *Stroke: 13,* 39 – 42, 1982.

iage DF, Safer MA: Hemisphere differences in the mood state-dependent effect for recognition of emotional faces. *J. Exp. Psychol. Learn. Mem. Cognition: 11,* 752 – 763, 1985.

iainotti G: Aspetti qualitativi ed evolutivi della sintomatologia conseguente a lesioni dell'emisfero destro. *Ann. Neurol. Psichiatria: 62,* 1 – 29, 1968.

iainotti G: Réactions 'catastrophiques' et manifestations d'indifférence au cours des atteintes cérébrales. *Neuropsychologia: 7,* 195 – 204, 1969.

iainotti G: Emotional behavior and hemispheric side of the lesion. *Cortex: 8,* 41 – 55, 1972.

iainotti G: Disorders of emotional behavior and of autonomic arousal resulting from unilateral brain damage. In Ottoson D (Editor), *The Dual Brain.* London: Macmillan. 1987.

iardner H, King PD, Flamm L, Silverman J: Comprehension and appreciation of humorous material following brain damage. *Brain: 98,* 399 – 412, 1975.

iasparrini WG, Satz P, Heilman KM, Goolidge FL: Hemispheric asymmetries of affective processing as determined by the Minnesota Multiphasic Personality Inventory. *J. Neurol. Neurosurg. Psychiatry: 41,* 470 – 473, 1978.

ioldstein K: *The Organism: A Holistic Approach to Biology, Derived from Pathological Data in Man.* New York: American Books, 1939.

irafman J, Vance S, Weingartner H, Salazar AM, Amin D: The effects of lateralized frontal lesions on mood regulation. *Brain: 109,* 1127 – 1148, 1986.

lécaen H: Clinical symptomatology in right and left hemisphere lesion. In Mountcastle VB (Editor), *Interhemispheric Relations and Cerebral Dominance.* Baltimore: Johns Hopkins, 1962.

lécaen H, Ajuriaguerra J de, Massonet J: Les troubles visuo-contructifs par lésion pariéto-occipitale droite. *Encéphale: 40,* 122 – 179, 1951.

leilman KM, Bowers D, Speedie L, Coslett HB: Comprehension of affective and nonaffective prosody. *Neurology: 34,*

917 – 921, 1984.

Heilman KM, Scholes R, Watson RT: Auditory affective agnosia: Disturbed comprehension of affective speech. *J. Neurol. Neurosurg. Psychiatry: 38,* 69 – 72, 1975.

Heilman KM, Schwartz HD, Watson RT: Hypoarousal in patients with neglect and emotional indifference. *Neurology: 28,* 229 – 232, 1978.

Held JP, Pierrot-Deseilligny E, Bussel B, Perrigot M, Malier M: Devenir des hémiplégies vasculaires par atteinte sylvienne en fonction de côté de la lesion. *Ann. Méd. Phys.: 4,* 592 – 604, 1975.

Hier DB, Mandlock J, Caplan LR: Recovery of behavioral abnormalities after right hemisphere stroke. *Neurology: 33,* 345 – 350, 1983.

Hirschman RS, Safer MA: Hemisphere differences in perceiving positive and negative emotions. *Cortex: 18,* 569 – 580, 1982.

Hohmann G: Some effects of spinal cord lesions on experimental emotional feelings. *Psychophysiology: 3,* 143 – 156, 1966.

Hughes CP, Chan JL, Su MS: Aprosodia in Chinese patients with right cerebral hemisphere lesions. *Arch. Neurol.: 50,* 732 – 736, 1983.

Hurwitz LJ, Adams GF: Rehabilitation of hemiplegia: indices of assessment and prognosis. *Br. Med. J.: 1,* 94 – 98, 1972.

Jackson JH: On the affections of speech from disease of the brain. *Brain: 1,* 304 – 330, 1878.

Jackson JH: On right- or left-sided spasm at the onset of epileptic paroxysms and on crude sensation warnings and elaborate mental states. *Brain: 3,* 192 – 206, 1880.

Kertesz A, Black SE: Cerebrovascular disease and aphasia. In *Speech and Language Evaluation in Neurology.* New York: Grune & Stratton, Ch. 4, pp. 83 – 122, 1985.

Kolb B, Milner B: Observations on spontaneous facial expression after focal cerebral excision and after intracarotid injection of sodium amytal. *Neuropsychologia: 19,* 505 – 514, 1981.

Kulesha D, Moldofsky H, Urowitz M, Zeman R: Brain scan lateralization and psychiatric symptoms in systemic lupus erythematosus. *Biol. Psychiatry: 16,* 407 – 411, 1981.

Lacey JI: Somatic response patterning and stress: Some revisions of activation theory. In Appley MH, Trumbull R (Editors), *Psychological Stress: Issues in Research.* New York: Appleton-Century-Crofts, pp. 14 – 42, 1967.

Ladavas E, Umiltà C, Ricci-Bitti PE: Evidence for sex differences in right-hemisphere dominance for emotions. *Neuropsychologia: 18,* 361 – 366, 1980.

LeDoux JE: Emotion. In Mountcastle VB, Plum R, Geiger SR (Editors), *Handbook of Physiology, Sect. I: The Nervous System, Vol. V, Higher Functions of the Brain.* Bethesda: American Physiological Soc., pp. 419 – 459, 1987.

Lieberman A, Benson DF: Control of emotional expression in pseudobulbar palsy. *Arch. Neurol.: 34,* 717 – 719, 1977.

Lim ML, Ebrahim SBJ: Depression after stroke: a hospital treatment survey. *Postgrad. Med.: 59,* 489 – 491, 1983.

Lipsey JR, Robinson RG, Pearlson GD, Rao K, Price TR: The dexamethasone suppression test and mood following stroke. *Am. J. Psychiatry: 141,* 317 – 323, 1985.

Mammucari A, Caltagirone C, Ekman P, Friesen W, Gainotti G, Pizzamiglio L, Zoccolotti P: Spontaneous facial expression of emotions in brain-damaged patients. *Cortex: 24,*

521 – 533, 1988.

Marquardsen J: The natural history of acute cerebrovascular disease: a retrospective study of 769 patients. *Acta Neurol. Scand. Suppl.: 38*, 1 – 192, 1969.

Milner B: Brain mechanisms suggested by studies of the temporal lobes. In Millikan CH, Darley FL (Eds), *Brain Mechanisms Underlying Speech and Language.* New York: Grune & Stratton, 1967.

Morrow L, Vrtunski B, Kim Y, Boller F: Arousal response to emotional stimuli and laterality of lesion. *Neuropsychologia: 19*, 65 – 71, 1981.

Natale M, Gur RE, Gur RC: Hemispheric asymmetries in processing emotional expressions. *Neuropsychologia: 21*, 55 – 565, 1983.

Panksepp J: Toward a general psychobiological theory of emotions. *Behav. Brain Sci.: 5*, 407 – 468, 1982.

Panksepp J: Mood changes. In Vinken PJ, Bruyn GW, Klawans HL (Editors), *Handbook of Clinical Neurology, Revised Series Vol. 1(45).* Amsterdam: Elsevier, pp. 272 – 285, 1985.

Panksepp J: The anatomy of emotions. In Plutchik R, Kellerman H (Editors), *Emotions: Theory, Research and Experience, Vol. 3, Biological Foundations of Emotions*, New York: Academic Press, pp. 91 – 124, 1986.

Pasoli EA, Trabucco G, Pasoli CA: Asimmetrie emotive e lesioni cerebrali lateralizzate. *Giornale Ital. Psicol.: 9*, 309 – 322, 1982.

Pazzaglia P, D'Alessandro R: Il sentimento di felicità come fenomeno critico: studio di 7 malati con epilessia parziale complessa. In Canger R, Avanzini G, Tassinari CA (Editors), *Progressi in Epilettologia.* Milan: Lega Italiana contro l'Epilessia, 1980.

Perria L, Rosadini G, Rossi GF: Determination of side of cerebral dominance with Amobarbital. *Arch. Neurol.: 4*, 173 – 181, 1961.

Poeck K: Pathophysiology of emotional disorders associated with brain damage. In Vincken PJ, Bruyn GN (Editors), *Handbook of Clinical Neurology, Vol. 3: Disorders of Higher Nervous Activity.* Amsterdam & New York: North-Holland & Wiley, pp. 343 – 367, 1969.

Reding M, Orto L, Willensky P, Fortuna I: The Dexamethasone suppression test. An indicator of depression in stroke but not a predictor of rehabilitation outcome. *Arch. Neurol.: 42*, 209 – 212, 1985.

Reisenzein R: The Schachter theory of emotion: two decades later. *Psychol. Bull.: 94*, 239 – 264, 1983.

Reuter-Lorentz P, Davidson RJ: Differential contribution of the two cerebral hemispheres to the perception of happy and sad faces. *Neuropsychologia: 19*, 609 – 613, 1981.

Reuter-Lorenz P, Givis R, Moscovitch M: Hemispheric specialization and the perception of emotion: evidence from right-handers and from inverted and non-inverted left handers. *Neuropsychologia: 21*, 687 – 692, 1983.

Robinson RG, Benson DF: Depression in aphasic patients: frequency, severity and clinical-pathological correlations. *Brain Lang.: 14*, 282 – 291, 1981.

Robinson RG, Kubos KL, Starr LB, Rao K, Price TR: Mood disorders in stroke patients: importance of lesion location. *Brain: 107*, 81 – 93, 1984.

Robinson RG, Price TR: Post-stroke depressive disorders: a

follow-up study of 103 outpatients. *Stroke: 13*, 635 – 641 1982.

Ross ED: The aprosodias. *Arch. Neurol.: 38*, 561 – 569, 1981.

Ross ED: Right hemisphere's role in language, affective behaviour and emotion. *Trends Neurosci.: 7*, 342 – 346 1984.

Ross ED, Mesulam M: Dominant language functions in the right hemisphere? *Arch. Neurol.: 36*, 144 – 148, 1979.

Ross ED, Rush AJ: Diagnosis and neuroanatomical correlates of depression in brain-damaged patients. *Arch. Gen Psychiatry: 38*, 1344 – 1354, 1981.

Rossi GF, Rosadini G: Experimental analysis of cerebra dominance in man. In Millikan CH, Darley FL (Editors) *Brain Mechanisms Underlying Speech and Language.* New York: Grune & Stratton Inc., pp. 167 – 174, 1967.

Ruckdeschel-Hibbard M, Gordon WA, Diller L: Affective disturbances associated with brain damage. In Filskov S, Boll T (Editors), *Handbook of Neuropsychology, Vol. 2.* New York: John Wiley & Sons, Inc., 1984.

Sackeim A, Greenberg MS, Weiman L, Gur RC, Hungerbuhler JP, Geschwind N: Hemispheric asymmetry in the expression of positive and negative emotions. *Arch. Neurol.: 39*, 210 – 218, 1982.

Sandman C: Physiological responses during escape and non escape from stress in field independent and field dependent subjects. *Biol. Psychol.: 2*, 205 – 216.

Schachter S: Cognition and peripheralist-centralist controversies in motivation and emotion. In Gazzaniga MS, Blakemore C (Editors), *Handbook of Psychobiology.* New York & London: Academic Press, pp. 529 – 564, 1975.

Schilder P: *The Image and Appearance of the Human Body.* London: K. Paul, 1935.

Schlanger BB, Schlanger P, Gerstman LJ: The perception of emotionally toned sentences by right hemisphere-damaged and aphasic subjects. *Brain Lang.: 3*, 396 – 403, 1976.

Schwartz GE, Ahern GL, Brown SL: Lateralized facial muscle response to positive and negative emotional stimuli. *Psychophysiology: 16*, 561 – 571, 1979.

Silberman EK, Weingartner H: Hemispheric lateralization of functions related to emotion. *Brain Cognition: 5*, 322 – 353, 1986.

Sinyor D, Jacques P, Kaloupek DG, Becker R, Goldenberg M, Coopersmith H: Poststroke depression and lesion location. *Brain: 109*, 537 – 546, 1986.

Starkstein SE, Robinson RG, Price TR: Comparison of cortical and subcortical lesions in the production of post-stroke mood disorders. *Brain: 110*, 1045 – 1059, 1987.

Strauss E, Kaplan E: Lateralized asymmetries in self-perception. *Cortex: 6*, 283 – 293, 1980.

Strauss E, Moscovitch M: Perception of facial expressions. *Brain Lang.: 13*, 308 – 332, 1981.

Strauss E, Wada J, Losaka B: Spontaneous facial expressions occurring at the onset of focal seizure activity. *Arch. Neurol.: 40*, 545 – 547, 1983.

Suberi M, McKeever WF: Differential right hemispheric memory storage of emotional and non-emotional faces. *Neuropsychologia: 15*, 757 – 768, 1979.

Terzian H: Behavioural and EEG effects of intracarotid sodium amytal injection. *Acta Neurochir.: 12*, 230 – 239, 1964.

Terzian H, Ceccotto C: Su un nuovo metodo per la determinazione e lo studio della dominanza emisferica. *Giornale Psichiatr. Neuropatol.: 87*, 889 – 924, 1959.

Tsunoda T, Oka M: Lateralization for emotion in the human brain and auditory cerebral dominance. *Proc. Jap. Acad.: 52*, 528 – 531, 1976.

Tucker DM, Watson RT, Heilman KM: Discrimination and evocation of facial recognition in patients with unilateral cerebral lesions. *Cortex: 3*, 317 – 326, 1977.

Van Hoesen GW: The parahippocampal gyrus. New observations regarding its cortical connections in the monkey. *Trends NeuroSci.: 5*, 345 – 350, 1982.

Williams D: The structure of emotions reflected in epileptic experience. *Brain: 79*, 29 – 67, 1956.

Zoccolotti P, Caltagirone C, Benedetti N, Gainotti G: Perturbation des réponses végétatives aux stimuli émotionnels au cours des lésions hémisphériques unilatérales. *Encéphale: 12*, 263 – 268, 1986.

Zoccolotti P, Scabini D, Violani V: Electrodermal responses in patients with unilateral brain damage. *J. Clin. Neuropsychol.: 4*, 143 – 150, 1982.

© 1989 Elsevier Science Publishers B.V. (Biomedical Division)
Handbook of Neurospsychology, Vol. 3
F. Boller and J. Grafman (Eds)

CHAPTER 17

Asymmetries in recognition of emotion

Nancy L. Etcoff

Department of Brain and Cognition Sciences, Massachusetts Institute of Technology, Cambridge, MA 02139, U.S.A.

Introduction

Any succcessful living being must have the means to monitor the changing states of the important objects in its environment. For humans, this means monitoring other humans, whose changes are often changes in emotion. No social being could prosper and survive (to say nothing of reproducing) if it could not tell whether others were angry or pleased. The ability to monitor the emotional states of others, then, is one of the most important human perceptual abilities.

To be good at recognizing emotions we must be sensitive to the diverse acts through which people communicate them. Our most precise communicative act, the spoken word, may not be the most informative when it comes to emotion. Even the man who put the greatest faith in our ability to talk about emotion, Sigmund Freud, acknowledged the difficulties he encountered in his attempts to talk to his patients about their emotional ills: they 'resisted'. Yet this did not mean that his patients did not communicate: 'when lips are silent, he chatters with his fingertips; betrayal oozes out of him at every pore' (Freud, 1905).

Communication about emotion, then, is often nonverbal, and much of the research literature has concentrated on the various kinds of nonverbal acts. By far the most studied vehicle is facial expressions. But recently a growing body of literature has investigated tone of voice or prosody. In this chapter, these vehicles of communication will be referred to as *channels* and the chapter will be organized around what is known about the recognition of emotion in each of them. The speech channel contains both tone and content (i.e., what is said), so the treatment of emotional tone of voice will also contain a treatment of emotional content, and attention will be paid to the relation between the two.

Once one isolates the individual channels of communication of emotion, one is led to the question of *how* each channel communicates its message. That is, what sort of information does the face or the voice provide that allows us to distinguish, for example, happiness from sadness? For each emotion, there must be a mapping between the physical form of the signals (for example, upturned versus downturned corners of the mouth, or lowered versus raised pitch) and the internal state. Before discussing the neuropsychology of emotion recognition, then, there will be a brief presentation of what is known about the perceptual cues or 'psychophysics of communication' in each channel.

Although it is logically possible that there is one perceptual analyser in the human brain for each sensory modality (e.g. a single analyser for all visual processing, and one for all auditory processing), there is increasing evidence that different brain areas are specialized for processing information about emotion. Indeed, it is findings such as this that make it possible to talk about a neuropsychology of emotion at all, as distinct from a neuropsychology of vision or audition or any higher general cognitive function. Much of this literature highlights the role of the right cerebral hemisphere, and it has been suggested that the circuits underlying recognition of emotion via each of these channels may have distinct representations within this hemisphere. This claim will be examined.

The overall plan of the chapter, then, is to review the neuropsychological literature on the recognition of emotion, considering each channel of communication independently. Within each section, the initial part will be devoted to a summary of the perceptual cues to emotion specific to that channel. Next, the literature from brain-damaged subjects, normal adults and split-brain subjects will be reviewed in the light of two major questions. The first concerns the neural substrates of the ability to recognize emotions: is recognition of emotion lateralized for all channels, and is it localized to a particular region within a hemisphere? The second concerns the specificity of brain circuits underlying recognition: are skills in recognizing emotion dissociable from more general perceptual skills? Are they dissociable from other aspects of emotion processing, such as the ability to respond emotionally or the ability to recognize emotion in other channels? Answers to questions such as these have important implications for the study of emotion, and may help clarify such issues as the role of general knowledge in processing emotion and the extent to which different components of emotion are functionally related.

Facial expression

When we emote, we tend to move. Herbert Spencer noted this as a general law: 'Feeling passing a certain pitch, habitually vents itself in bodily action' (1863). These movements are not random, nor uniform across emotions: a face displaying a lowered brow and tightened lips conveys not just an emotion, but the specific emotion of anger. We do not confuse it with surprise or happiness.

The particular forms of our facial expressions are non-arbitrarily related to the emotions they convey because of their evolutionary history: facial muscles originally used in noncommunicative acts of self-preservation such as biting, protecting the eyes, expelling food, and so on, took on value as signals, first as indicators of an intended action of which the facial movement was a part or a precursor, and more recently in evolutionary history as indicators of the internal emotional state associated with the facial movement (Darwin, 1872; see also Andrew, 1963; Chevalier-Skolnikoff, 1973). The adaptive value of such displays is evident – being able to display an intention to attack by biting is safer than actually biting at every provocation – but only if the organism at whom the display is directed is capable of understanding the signal. One must assume that selection forces were at work in the evolution not only of our ability to produce facial expressions of emotion but also of our ability to recognize them, and that both of these abilities are part of the biological inheritance of humanity.

There is a great deal of evidence that all humans are able to recognize the basic emotions of happiness, surprise, fear, anger, disgust and sadness from their facial appearances (see Ekman et al., 1982, for a review). A recent study suggests that contempt also has a unique facial display than can be recognized by widely divergent cultures (Ekman and Friesen, 1986). These displays usually involve the movement of several independent facial muscles, with some movements used in more than one emotional expression (for example, we lift our brows in both fear and surprise). The perceptual device capable of recognizing facial expressions of emotion must be able to discriminate complex visual displays in which any single, isolated visual feature may provide misleading or nondiscriminative information.

Data on errors in recognition of facial expressions suggest that, as in all other realms, the simpler and more distinctive a display, the easier it is to recognize. Happiness is probably the only emotional expression which can be produced in recognizable form by the movement of only one facial muscle (although more actions are involved in genuine smiles; see Ekman and Friesen, 1982).

Not surprisingly, it can be recognized at presentation times too brief and at distances too far to support the recognition of other expressions (O'Sullivan et al., in preparation; Hager and Ekman, 1979). The expressions of fear and surprise share many of the same facial actions and are visually similar. They are also one of the two emotion pairs (anger and disgust being the other) which are most likely to be confused with one another.

Interestingly, the expressions of anger and disgust are not visually similar. Their ready confusion seems due to a *conceptual* difficulty in distinguishing the two emotion categories (that is, people's idiosyncratic boundaries which define anger versus disgust), and suggests another component to the ability to recognize facial expressions: the ability to link each visual display with an underlying concept of the emotion it conveys.

No two individuals have the same facial appearance. Expressions will look slightly different on each individual depending on the shape and size of their features, their facial wrinkles, subcutaneous fat, and so on. In order to recognize an emotional expression we must be able to abstract out what is constant and informative in that facial expression (the movement of the muscles) from what is not (the individual's exact way of rendering those movements given his or her face). Finally, in order to recognize facial expressions of emotion we must be capable of recognizing a signal that is transient and only briefly available for analysis: research indicates that facial expressions of emotion typically appear on the face for one-half to four seconds (Ekman and Friesen, 1982).

All of these abilities must be present in any organism capable of recognizing facial displays: they are unlikely to be skills unique to people. Nonetheless, the human capacity to recognize facial expressions surely involves additional skills. First, humans speak, and their facial muscles are used not only to produce words but also to illustrate or emphasize those words and to regulate their flow among people (Ekman, 1978). This means that speech competes with emotion not just for the use of the muscles around the mouth, but

for the use of the muscles that raise and lower the brows (one of the chief facial illustrators of speech) and other facial areas. The visual signal for emotion is necessarily noisy – delivered not from an otherwise still background but from one which is moving and conveying other information.

Second, human facial expressions are enormously variable. We are capable of producing tens of thousands of expressions. Of the ones relevant to emotion, some reflect not just pure emotions such as happiness or anger but complex blends (this is not surprising given that our internal emotions are seldom pure states). We are also capable of some control over our facial muscles: we can augment or dampen an expression, suppress it entirely, or camouflage it with a simulated emotion (reviewed in Ekman, 1984).

All in all, the recognition of human facial expressions is a far from simple task and is likely to involve a sophistication in disentangling different sorts of information which was not needed when the skill originally evolved. In the next section, I will examine evidence concerning the neural substrate of this skill, and its relationship to a host of related skills: recognition of faces, recognition of linguistic information from facial movement, and recognition of and response to other emotional information.

Lateralization

An early and enduring focus of the neuropsychological literature on the recognition of facial expressions of emotion has been whether the skill is lateralized to one cerebral hemisphere. Converging evidence from studies of normal adults and from adults with many kinds of cerebral damage points to a right hemisphere superiority. In divided visual field studies with normal adults, the right cerebral hemisphere has been repeatedly demonstrated to be faster and/or more accurate at discriminating facial expressions than is the left cerebral hemisphere (e.g. Landis et al., 1979; Ladavas et al., 1980; Ley and Bryden, 1979; Natale et al., 1983; Pizzamiglio et al., 1983; Strauss and Moscovitch, 1981). In studies where 'chimeric' faces are presented to normal subjects in which the two halves of the face present conflicting information about emotional state (e.g. one half of the face is neutral while one half is smiling), the half-face presented to the left visual field (right cerebral hemisphere) has the most impact on judgement of emotion (e.g. Campbell, 1978; Heller and Levy, 1981). Patients who have suffered unilateral right cerebral damage (RH) show far greater impairment than do left hemisphere damaged patients (LH) in recognizing facial expressions (e.g. Benowitz et al., 1983, 1984; Bowers et al., 1985; Cicone et al., 1980; DeKosky et al., 1980; Etcoff, 1984a,b; Kolb and Taylor, 1981; Zoccolotti et al., 1982).

Although the number of patients tested is small, evidence to date from split-brain subjects and from a hemispherectomy patient also suggests that it is *only* the isolated right hemisphere that can recognize facial expressions adequately. Benowitz et al. (1983, 1984) showed filmed facial expressions from the standardized Profile of Nonverbal Sensitivity (PONS) test to each hemisphere of a split-brain patient who had been fitted with a contact lens restricting visual input to a single hemisphere. Right hemisphere responses were signaled by hand movements, left by verbal responses. The isolated right hemisphere performed in the normal range for recognizing facial expressions; the isolated left hemisphere was grossly impaired. Three additional split-brain subjects viewed the films in free vision and made verbal responses, presumably reflecting the choice of the left hemisphere (the right is believed to be largely mute). All three performed poorly (see also Gazzaniga et al., 1975). Finally, there is evidence that removal of the right hemisphere in childhood can all but eliminate skills in the recognition of facial expression: using the PONS test, Benowitz et al. (1983, 1984) reported that recognition of facial expressions was only at chance levels in a 20-year-old patient who had undergone a radical right hemispherectomy at age eight.

A common thread in the diverse studies on right hemisphere involvement in recognizing emotion is that the cerebral asymmetry is most apparent when subjects are required to assign an expression to a category − either to recognize it on different faces or to match it with a name. For example, in Strauss and Moscovitch's (1981) studies, the RH advantage was strongest when subjects were required to abstract a common facial expression from the faces of different individuals (rather than from a single individual), or were asked to compare expressions with a target held in memory. In addition, RH patients show significantly greater difficulties than do LH patients in tasks where they must demonstrate knowledge about the emotion conveyed (such as naming the emotion conveyed by a face, or pointing to a named emotional expression in an array) and where they must abstract a common emotion from different faces (e.g. Bowers et al., 1985; Cicone et al., 1980; DeKosky et al., 1980; Etcoff, 1984a,b). All of the above suggests that RH skill in recognizing facial expression involves an ability to form an abstract representation of the expression and to link that representation to an emotion label*.

Relation to other visuospatial skills
The finding of a right hemisphere superiority for recognizing facial expressions of emotion is not entirely unexpected, since right hemisphere advantages have been found for the recognition of spatial configurations (see Milner, 1974, for a review) and for faces in particular (e.g. De Renzi and Spinnler, 1966; Rizzolatti et al., 1971). If the right hemisphere's superiority in recognizing facial expressions is simply a reflection of its superiority in perceiving complex visuospatial patterns or in perceiving faces in particular, then this would tell us little about right hemisphere processing of facial *emotion*. Thus it is of great interest that an increasing body of research suggests that the recognition

---

* Safer (1981) argued that labeling an emotional expression would call on left hemisphere mechanisms and reported RH advantages when subjects were told to empathize with an emotional expression but not when subjects were told to label the expression. However, this result was not replicable (Safer, 1984).

of faces and the recognition of facial expressions of emotion are separate processes.

Relationship of the recognition of facial expression to face recognition. Evidence on this dissociation comes from many sources. First, there are case studies of prosopagnosics, patients with bilateral lesions involving the visual system (temporal-occipital lesions), whose cardinal symptom is a severe impairment in their ability to recognize familiar faces. Some of these patients, nonetheless, retain the ability to recognize facial expressions of emotion (e.g. Bruyer et al., 1983; Shuttleworth et al., 1982; Tranel and Damasio, 1987). In line with this, a study with normal adults has shown that knowledge about facial identity (familiar versus unfamiliar faces) does not improve one's ability to recognize and match facial expressions (Young et al., 1986). Although RH damaged patients as a group show deficits in the recognition of both emotion and identity in unfamiliar faces (e.g. Bowers et al., 1985; Cicone et al., 1980; DeKosky et al., 1980; Etcoff, 1984a), their patterns of performance on tests of face recognition and facial emotion recognition differ (e.g. Etcoff, 1984a), and individual patients are found whose deficits are confined to either the recognition of emotional expression or the recognition of identity (see Etcoff, 1986, for a review). Finally, studies with normal adults that have statistically partialled out performance on face identity tasks and facial emotion tasks have found the two effects to be dissociable (e.g. Pizzamiglio et al., 1983; Strauss and Moscovitch, 1981).

A final source of evidence comes from electrical stimulation mapping in humans and neurophysiological studies in monkeys. (These studies will come up again in the section entitled 'Localization'.) When discrete cortical sites are stimulated in patients undergoing right-sided intracranial operations for the treatment of epilepsy (Fried et al., 1982), a disruption of the ability to perceive or remember facial identity is caused by stimulation at sites different from those causing disruption of the ability to recognize facial expressions. Interestingly, although there is some variability among subjects in the exact localization of these functions, none shows an overlap between the areas where stimulation disrupts recognition of identity and where it disrupts recognition of emotion. Investigations of the activity of neurons in the temporal cortex of monkeys paint a similar picture: small populations of neurons sensitive to faces have been found, but these neurons are not sensitive to changes in facial expression. Neurons sensitive to static facial expressions are even rarer, but these also tend to be specialized, giving similar outputs across different faces (e.g. Rolls, 1984; Perrett et al., 1984).

In all, the evidence is overwhelmingly in support of the idea that the recognition of facial emotion is a process separable from the recognition of another complex visuospatial object (human faces) and that the dissociation of the two reflects different neural substrates.

Relationship of the recognition of facial expression to the recognition of facial speech. The movements of facial muscles do not just provide perceptual cues about emotion. They also provide cues about language: facial muscles move when we speak. The power of facial cues to influence speech perception has been illustrated by McGurk and MacDonald (1976). They found that when subjects saw a person uttering one sound and simultaneously heard that person uttering a different sound, they perceived an entirely new, blended sound, intermediate in terms of place of articulation between the heard and 'seen' sound. Another form of facial speech is important for deaf individuals who use American Sign Language (ASL): they use facial expressions to convey specific linguistic information, such as relative clauses and adverbs (e.g. Baker-Shenk, 1983; Liddell, 1980).

Movements of facial muscles provide a complex visual cue. When this cue is decoded for emotion, a right hemisphere advantage emerges. What happens when linguistic information is extracted from facial movement? A complex set of findings from hearing adults, deaf signers and patients with unilateral cortical lesions can best be summarized as follows: when the task involves minimal knowledge about language, such as deciding that two unfamiliar ASL linguistic expressions are the same or trying to read a limited set of vowels or consonants from the face, hearing adults may preferentially use their right hemisphere. However, when more sophisticated language judgements need to be made, the left hemisphere is equally or perhaps preferentially involved. Given the important role of the LH in language processing, known for over a century, this is not completely surprising, though it is interesting that the localization is strongly tied to the abstract nature of the task (language versus emotion) and not strongly tied to the sensory modality involved.

For example, Campbell (1986) found that hearing adults were better at matching photographs of a speaking person to a small set of spoken speech sounds when the photograph was presented to the right hemisphere. Corina (1987) found that hearing adults were more accurate at recognizing both facial expressions of emotion and unfamiliar facial expressions used in ASL (quantifiers and adverbs) when these expressions were presented to the right hemisphere. Crucially, these subjects did not understand the meaning of the ASL signs; they simply had to find the same expression in an array. In contrast, in normal deaf signers, the left hemisphere was as proficient as the right in matching linguistic facial expressions. (The case of normal deaf signers is complicated by the fact that they have learned complex ways of analysing facial movements for linguistic purposes. Although deaf signers show an RH advantage for recognizing facial expressions of emotion when these expressions are presented first, if *linguistic* facial expressions are shown first then a trend toward a *left* hemisphere advantage emerges. This is presumably because they fall into the 'set' of analysing expressions linguistically, which for this group might be a rich enough analysis to allow discrimination of emotions as well.)

Similarly, Campbell et al. (1986) found that LH but not RH damage disrupts lip-reading of phonemes, whereas the reverse is true for recognizing facial expressions of emotion. In line with earlier findings, Campbell et al.'s LH patient was able to perform facial speech tasks only when they were simple (e.g., when the number of choice alternatives was limited). Interestingly, the right but not the left hemisphere damaged patient showed the McGurk and MacDonald blend illusion, suggesting that the left hemisphere is crucially involved in the integration of visual and auditory linguistic signals.

An important point of all this research is that hemispheric specialization depends on the computation performed, such as the extraction of linguistic versus emotional information, and not on the complexity of the signal or its transmission through a particular channel. We will return to this point in our discussion of emotional prosody.

Relation to other aspects of emotional functioning

The right hemisphere seems to be crucially involved in the control of many other aspects of emotion, including the ability to show appropriate emotional concern (e.g. Gainotti, 1972), to regulate autonomic response to emotional stimuli (e.g. Zoccolotti et al., 1982), to recognize emotion through tone of voice (e.g. Ross, 1981) and to produce facial expressions of emotion and emotional tone of voice (e.g. Borod and Caron, 1980; Ross, 1981). Studies of the breakdown or preservation of each of these functions in individual right hemisphere patients could provide very valuable evidence as to whether the different aspects of emotion are indivisible or are organized as autonomous modules. Few neuropsychological studies have looked at the relationship between the recognition of facial expressions of emotion and other emotion functions. The ones that have strongly suggest that it operates in a modular, autonomous fashion.

Denial of illness. Patients with RH damage can manifest a peculiar lack of emotional concern about their illness and disability; they may joke about it or deny it altogether. Such 'denial' and 'indifference' is rarely found after left hemisphere damage: indeed the reactions of these patients are at times 'catastrophic', characterized by tears, swearing and expressions of fear and anger (e.g. Gainotti, 1972). Several authors have suggested that there may be a relationship between deficits in perception of emotion in patients with right hemisphere lesions and their emotional indifference. For example, both deficits could reflect a global disturbance in affect which could accompany right hemisphere damage. Others have suggested a causal link: if RH patients are reading the wrong emotion from the faces of the people they interact with, then their reactions may seem inappropriate. At the very least, this hypothesis requires that difficulty in perceiving emotion in faces and indifferent emotional behavior occur in the *same* right hemisphere damaged patients. The one study which explicitly tested this prediction (Etcoff, 1983), however, did not find evidence for it. In that study, some but not all RH patients were impaired at recognizing facial expressions and were indifferent (as rated by hospital staff). However, there was no correlation between degree of impairment in perceiving emotions and degree of indifference. This suggests that concern for the self and the recognition of facial expressions do not reflect a single global emotional skill. It is also unlikely that difficulty perceiving facial emotions causes emotional indifference (although it may exacerbate the problem).

Hypoarousal. RH patients have also been described as 'hypoaroused' (Heilman et al., 1978), that is, as showing dampened autonomic responsivity, particularly to emotionally charged stimuli (Morrow et al., 1981). When neutral slides (e.g. buildings and landscapes) and emotionally provocative slides (e.g. a cut hand or a woman in a bikini) are presented to LH patients or intact adults, they show greater autonomic responsivity (as measured by skin conductance) to the emotional slides. RH patients do not. However, Zoccolotti et al. (1982) found that the two deficits (hypoarousal and difficulty in recognizing expres-

sions) were dissociable: the difference between RH and LH patients' autonomic responsivity to visually arousing stimuli was not altered when the performance on a facial expression recognition task was partialled out.

This study and that of Etcoff (1983, 1986) provide evidence contrary to the idea that right hemisphere decoding of emotional stimuli is necessarily mediated by actual emotional changes in response to them (e.g. Safer, 1981; Silberman and Weingartner, 1986). The converse possibility – that emotional reactions are aberrant because of perceptual difficulties – is also not supported by these studies.

Production of facial expressions. It has been reported that normal adults express many emotions more intensely or more extensively on the left side of their face (e.g. Borod and Caron, 1980), and that adults with RH damage are less facially expressive than are those with left hemisphere damage (Buck and Duffy, 1980; Borod et al., 1985). Evidence such as this has been used to suggest that the right hemisphere may control the production of facial expression of emotion.

Only one study has reported evidence on the recognition and production of facial expressions in the same RH and LH patients. Borod and her collaborators (Borod et al., 1986) found that RH patients were more impaired than were LH patients or controls at both perceiving and expressing emotions (they assessed the ability to express emotion by having judges rate patients while they watched evocative slides and while they imitated facial expressions or produced them to command). But they found that the two deficits were not correlated, even within the same emotion category such as sadness. This finding is consistent with social psychologists' reports that skills in encoding and decoding emotions are largely independent, particularly evident when skills within a single emotion category are tested (e.g. Lanzetta and Kleck, 1970). It is also consistent with case studies which suggest that production of emotional behaviors involves neural substrates more anterior to those which govern the recognition of emotion (e.g. Ross, 1985). It is worth noting, however, that recent studies of intact and brain-damaged adults which have used actual measurements of facial movement rather than raters' judgements (Hager and Ekman, 1985; Pizzamiglio, 1986) have challenged the whole notion of right hemisphere control over the production of facial expressions of emotion (see also Kolb and Milner, 1981).

Recognition of tone of voice and of body movement. Finally, there is evidence that RH patients have trouble recognizing emotional expressions through channels other than facial expression, most notably through tone of voice or prosody (e.g. Ross and Mesulam, 1979; Ross, 1981). Case reports of individual patients suggest that although roughly similar lesions may impair the recognition of emotion through the two channels, each may have a separate neural representation. For example, Benowitz et al. (1984) found selective impairments within individual RH patients for recognizing emotion through facial expression or tone of voice using the PONS test. Etcoff (in preparation) reports on a patient with a selective impairment in recognizing emotion through tone of voice but not through facial expression. Ross (1981) found that in a patient who originally had both deficits, recognition of facial expressions recovered while the recognition of emotion prosody remained impaired.

Benowitz et al. (1984) also found that RH and LH patients did not differ in their ability to recognize emotion conveyed through body movements, and that the split-brain patient whose individual hemispheres could be tested showed a *left* hemisphere superiority in recognizing emotion through body movement. These results suggest that recognizing emotion per se is not the exclusive domain of the right hemisphere. Right hemisphere advantages for recognizing emotion are likely to emerge only for particular channels.

Finally, Benowitz et al. noted a striking phenomenon in one patient who was severely impaired in recognizing facial expressions: when only a voice or

only body movements were presented to him, his performance was intact, but when a voice or a set of body movements were presented together with a face, he was impaired. In other words, he kept on attending to the (for him) entirely uninformative face. This finding suggests that patients may appear globally impaired at recognizing emotion even if their deficit is confined to only one channel (such as faces) and that it may be useful in rehabilitation to direct their attention to preserved channels, something which they may not do spontaneously.

Emotional valence. I have been examining the different emotional *functions;* there are also differences among *emotions* themselves. Emotions have been studied either as a set of distinct, basic categories (such as happiness, disgust, and so on), or as points along continuous dimensions such as positive-to-negative. In the neuropsychological literature, the dimensions of emotion have received far more attention than the categories, and there have been suggestions that continua such as positive-negative or approach-avoidance are neuroanatomically significant dimensions whose poles can be localized to different hemispheres of the brain. Specifically, there have been suggestions that the left hemisphere mediates positive emotions and the right mediates negative emotions (Reuter-Lorenz and Davidson, 1981), or that the left mediates 'approach' emotions and the right 'avoidance' emotions (Davidson and Fox, in press; Kinsbourne and Bemporad, 1984).

If the 'positive-negative' dimension differentiates the hemispheres' role in the recognition of facial expressions, then consistent RH advantages should be found only for negative emotions (disgust, sadness, fear, anger) whereas LH advantages would be found for positive emotions (happiness and surprise). If it is the approach-avoidance dimension that captures the difference between the hemispheres, one would find RH advantages for avoidance emotions (disgust, sadness, fear and surprise) and LH advantages for approach emotions (anger and happiness). The overwhelming majority of studies on the recognition of facial expressions of emotion do not find evidence for either pattern (for reviews, see Etcoff, 1986; Ley and Strauss, 1986).

Because of the attention given to emotion dimensions, emotion categories are often not analysed separately. However, when they are, fear and, to a lesser extent, disgust emerge as the emotion categories showing strongest right hemisphere lateralization (e.g. Etcoff, 1984b; Hirschman and Safer, 1982; Ladavas et al., 1980; Pizzamiglio et al., 1983). Anger shows less consistent RH superiority: it is sometimes well recognized by RH patients, who as a group have difficulty recognizing facial expressions (Etcoff, 1984b; in press), and in one study with intact adults showed an LH advantage (Pizzamiglio et al., 1983). As Pizzamiglio et al. noted, this pattern of results cannot be explained simply by the visual complexity of these displays: the angry face used in his study involved more independent muscle movements than did the face displaying disgust. This again highlights the fact that RH advantages do not simply reflect the right hemisphere's ability to recognize complex visual displays.

Finally, authors have suggested two other ways in which valence may bear on the recognition of facial expressions. First, although the right hemisphere may show a general advantage in the recognition of most or all emotions, each hemisphere may impart a characteristic affective 'coloring' to perception. Previous studies have suggested that the RH may tend to cast a slightly negative light on visual input; for example, rating films as more 'horrific' or 'unpleasant' (Dimond et al., 1976). Natale et al. (1983) report that the RH of normal adults rates facial emotions (except happiness) as being more intensely negative than does the left (but see Davidson et al., 1985; Hirschman and Safer, 1982; for failures to replicate this difference). Second, some authors have suggested that positive or 'approach' facial expressions lead to a predominance of left frontal EEG activity whereas negative or 'avoidance' expressions are accompanied by enhanced right frontal activity. The authors suggest that this EEG activity does *not*

reflect the operation of perceptual analysers, but rather reflects emotional evaluation or reaction to the analysed input. Thus, they claim that perception of facial expressions and the emotional response to them may be separable, with valence an important dimension only when emotional response comes into play (see Davidson and Fox, in press, for a review).

Localization

The preceding review suggests that the recognition of facial expressions of emotion is a lateralized and modular skill, and one may then ask whether it has a distinct neural locus *within* the right hemisphere. Unfortunately, there are very few data with which to address this question from current studies of unilaterally brain-damaged patients. However, combining what evidence there is with that from electrical stimulation mapping in humans and neurophysiological studies with monkeys suggests that the most likely site is the right temporal region. Let us briefly review the evidence.

Studies with unilaterally brain-damaged patients as a whole have provided little evidence for intrahemispheric localization: some have even suggested that a lesion virtually anywhere in the right hemisphere can disrupt the recognition of facial expression. However, this body of research is mostly unsuitable for drawing conclusions about this issue one way or the other. First, many studies report composite data for 'anterior', 'posterior' or combined 'anterior-posterior' groups. Because this practice discards information, it may obscure underlying commonalities in lesion sites that produce deficits. For example, in Borod et al.'s (1986) study, RH patients were grouped together as either 'anterior and posterior' or 'posterior'. Looking closely at the composition of these groups one can see that they differ in a potentially important way: the majority of the patients in this study's 'anterior/posterior' group had damage to the temporal lobe, while the majority of the patients in this study's 'posterior' group did not. The fact that 'anterior/posterior' patients fared worse than did the 'posterior' group is thus hard to interpret: it could suggest the importance of anterior structures, the damaging effects of a larger lesion, or the importance of the temporal region. The second problem is that control tasks for more general visual deficits are not always included. For example, Kolb and Taylor (1981) found that lesions anywhere in the RH led to deficits in the recognition of facial expressions. However, their task was a complex one involving the matching of seven facial expressions to each of 24 magazine photographs of faces. No other visual task was included for comparison.

There are a few case reports of selective deficits in the recognition of facial expressions in patients whose lesion sites are reasonably specified. Three studies (Benowitz et al., 1984; Cicone et al., 1980; Etcoff, 1986) all report specific deficits in recognizing facial emotion in patients with right temporal involvement (temporal or frontotemporal or temporoparietal lesions), and two suggest that damage to the parietal lobe alone leaves the ability relatively intact (Benowitz et al., 1984; Cicone et al., 1980). Etcoff (1986), however, also reported a patient with a selective deficit in recognizing facial expression whose lesion was confined to frontoparietal regions. Clearly, future studies on the recognition of facial expression will need to be done to determine whether or not this skill has a distinct and localizable substrate. Studies which attempt to construct a composite picture (in terms of maximal lesion overlap) of only those patients who show a selective deficit in the recognition of facial expressions would provide the crucial evidence. Interestingly, Bisiach et al. (1986), using just such an approach in the study of denial of illness, have found evidence both for localization (to the infero-posterior right hemisphere) and for its dissociation from neglect and from more elementary neurological disorders.

Even when better anatomical and task-specific evidence is available from the literature on unilateral lesions, one problem will always remain; naturally occurring diseases and accidents tend to produce damage that is extensive and, even if the damage is circumscribed, it may cross functional boundaries. Yet another problem is that functionally distinct circuits may not lie in macroscopic regions with spatially crisp boundaries. The problem is no more clearly illustrated than in the literature on temporal lobe neurons in monkeys which are responsive to faces: such neurons are distributed in the superior temporal sulcus and inferior temporal areas intermixed with neurons that are not specifically face-sensitive (e.g. Rolls, 1984; Perrett et al., 1984). The neurophysiological studies of monkey temporal cortex and electrical stimulation mapping studies with humans thus may provide important data about the possible localization of specific skills that cannot be uncovered from studies of patients with naturally occurring lesions.

As mentioned earlier, electrical stimulation mapping with humans (Fried et al., 1982) suggests that the recognition of facial expressions of emotion is disrupted by stimulation of sites different from those which disrupt recognition of faces: specifically, stimulation of the middle temporal gyrus of the right hemisphere disrupts the recognition of facial expressions, while stimulation of other regions (in the superior temporal gyrus, inferior frontal gyrus and parieto-occipital junction) disrupts the ability to match and to remember faces. Interestingly, the disruption in the recognition of facial expression is manifested by difficulties in *labelling* the emotion, but not in any change in emotional state. This finding coincides well with the pattern of findings in patients with cortical lesions, where perception can be dissociated from emotional responses.

Finally, there are neurons in monkey's inferior temporal cortex and, more extensively, in their superior temporal cortex, that are selectively sensitive to faces but not to facial expressions (e.g. Perrett et al., 1984; Rolls, 1984). Neurons sensitive to expressions of static faces are rare in these areas, and their relevance to emotion uncertain (for example, these cells showed greater response to a yawning face than to a threat or a fear face). It is interesting, however, that small populations of neurons sensitive to faces have been uncovered in he amygdala, including a small number which esponded differentially to threat faces. This part f the amygdala receives inputs from relatively nterior temporal cortex but probably not directly rom the cortex in the superior temporal sulcus vhere the face-selective neurons are found (e.g. Rolls, 1984). These results not only point once gain to dissociations between neurons responsive o faces versus facial expressions, but they also uggest the importance of temporal-limbic amygdala) connections in the recognition of facial xpressions. Bear (1983) has also speculated on the mportance of specific temporal sites within what e calls the ventral visual-limbic circuit for the ecognition of facial expressions of emotion, a cir- uit involving the temporal cortex, the amygdala nd hippocampus and the orbital frontal cortex.

Prosody

Emotions are expressed nonverbally not only by he face but also by the voice, through speech *pro- sody:* the variations in pitch, timing and amplitude vhose perceptual correlates are intonation, length and stress. Just as facial expressions of emotion have been shown to be universal, affective fluctua- ions in pitch are also believed to exist in all languages (e.g. Lehiste, 1970; Bolinger, 1964). Vocal indicators of emotion are also likely to be phylogenetically continuous: the social functions they serve and the physiological mechanisms that produce them are highly similar in man and in nonhuman primates, and are related to their func- tions. Shrieks of fear, whether uttered by a man or an ape, will be high in amplitude because they need to be heard and rouse others to action, and high in pitch because they are produced by muscles which are tensed for flight or fight (see Cosmides, 1983; Scherer, 1981, 1986).

Although judgement studies have found a high level of agreement in categorizing emotion from prosodic cues (Scherer, 1981), psychacousticians have not yet specified the acoustic parameters which differentiate emotion categories. We do not know how many emotions are served by distinct acoustic signals nor whether the same pattern of acoustic cues will be associated with the same emo- tion in all cultures. Studies indicate some con- sistency, for example, in the association of sadness with low pitch, slow tempo and low amplitude, and of anger with high pitch, fast tempo and high amplitude (see Williams and Stevens, 1972; Scherer, 1981). Analysis of voice quality or timbre may lead to more precision in the measurement of acoustic cues to emotion (Scherer, 1986). Never- theless, the problem of measuring emotion pro- sody and relating it to the motor sequences that cause it will remain enormous: vocalizations are produced by the joint action of deeply concealed muscles involved in respiration, phonation and ar- ticulation. The mapping between phonatory- articulatory actions and characteristic changes in the speech signal is not one-to-one: similar acoustic results can be produced by a variety of mechanisms (see Scherer, 1986). In sum, we know that emo- tions are reliably conveyed by speech prosody, and that they convey information about discrete emo- tions and not just about emotion dimensions such as arousal or pleasantness as was once thought, though much remains to be discovered.

Prosodic cues are analysed not just for affective information but for person-specific information (the identity, sex and age of the speaker) and linguistic information as well. Prosody has been partially taken over for linguistic purposes: Bol- inger (1964, 1972) describes intonation as a 'half- tamed servant of language'. Prosody operates at many linguistic levels, conveying lexical, syntactic, semantic and discourse information. For example, pitch cues are used to minimally distinguish words in tone languages such as Thai or Chinese. Stress can distinguish nouns and noun phrases in English (*dark room* versus *darkroom*) and the different readings of ambiguous sentences such as *He read the speech naturally*. Prosody also conveys dis- course information, for example whether a sen- tence is a question or statement. Finally, the fact that language uses the speech signal for non- prosodic information constrains prosody: the basic units of language (phonemes, morphemes) must be recognizable, and this defines the limits of prosodic variation (Scherer, 1981).

Prosody is a particularly interesting domain of study for neuropsychologists because it provides an opportunity to look at the ways in which the functional significance of perceptual cues influences their neural organization.

Lateralization

Research conducted thus far has consistently demonstrated a right hemisphere superiority for the recognition of emotion prosody. In dichotic listening studies with normal adults, a left ear (right hemisphere) advantage has been found for recognition of emotional prosody (Haggard and Parkinson, 1971; Ley and Bryden, 1982). This finding extends even to children as young as five (Saxby and Bryden, 1984). RH damaged patients have shown a far greater impairment than LH damaged patients in recognizing emotion conveyed through prosody (Bowers et al., 1987; Benowitz et al., 1983; Heilman et al., 1975; Heilman et al., 1984; Tucker et al., 1977; but see also Schlanger et al., 1976). These results have appeared consistently despite differences in the way the sentences are presented: some have used sentences with neutral or emotional content; others have altered the sentences acoustically so that frequency bands conveying lexical content are filtered out, or so that cues to rhythm and tempo are destroyed by randomly cutting very brief segments out of speech tapes.

It is not yet clear how best to describe the skill for which lateralization is shown. The majority of the studies have used experimental techniques that require relating a stimulus to a person's stored knowledge about the signal, such as pointing to a face with the same emotion as a sentence and/or ascribing a verbal label to the emotional pattern. However, Tucker et al. (1977) found that RH damaged patients were impaired even in a simple discrimination task – they were far poorer than controls at saying whether two sentences conveyed the same or different emotion when they varied in prosody. Although these patients were given a prosody *recognition* task as well (pointing to a face,

providing a name corresponding to the sentence's prosody), their performances on the two tasks were not submitted to a correlational analysis to see if recognition deficit was found over and above a simple perceptual deficit (which of course would lead to a recognition deficit as a consequence). In examining their data, however, there is some suggestion that a recognition deficit may exist even if discrimination is preserved: at least one patient showed relatively preserved discrimination, yet this patient was as severely impaired as the others in recognizing the emotion.

Finally, Benowitz et al. (1983, 1984) report an unusual pattern of preservation and loss of ability to recognize emotional prosody in a 20-year-old patient who had undergone a radical right hemispherectomy at age 8. They used two separate procedures, one in which sentences were acoustically manipulated by random splicing, which mainly masks or distorts rhythm and tempo, and another in which sentences were content filtered, which largely affects voice quality, leaving intonation and timing relatively intact. (One must keep in mind, however, that these are relatively crude techniques: prosodic cues cannot be removed in the same way that one can remove a single instrument from an orchestra.) Benowitz et al. found a dramatic difference in the ability of this patient's isolated left hemisphere to decode emotion from random spliced speech (virtually nil) and from content-filtered speech (well preserved). Such a pattern was not found with unilaterally brain damaged patients: RH damaged patients were worse than LH patients on both tasks. Studies with intact adults suggest that accuracy declines only slightly and by about the same amount when the signal is altered by these techniques (Johnson et al., 1986). The finding from the hemispherectomy patient suggests that the left hemisphere maturing in isolation may be heavily reliant on emotion cues provided by rhythm and tempo (at least in combination with other cues) and less able to use voice quality cues (at least when they are isolated from rhythm and tempo cues). Such an interpretation is in line with findings of a left hemisphere superiority for the processing of hythmic components of music in dichotic listening tudies of normal adults (e.g. Gordon, 1978) and of ·ilateral involvement in the perception of musical hythm (in contrast to the demonstrated RH control of musical pitch perception) in brain-damaged patients (Shapiro et al., 1981).

Before leaving these studies, two general points eed to be made. First, the range of emotions ested in these studies has usually been limited — 1ost have looked only at recognition of happiness, nger and sadness, or only at emotions described 1ore generally as positive or negative. Whether the esults will hold when a full range of emotions is ested is unknown. However, if there exist parallels etween the lateralization of the recognition of acial expression and of the recognition of emotion ·rosody, the most likely emotions to show large ight hemisphere advantages would be fear and lisgust, neither of which has been specifically ested. Second, there is no standard set of stimuli vailable because we do not yet know how to capture ·recisely the psychophysical differences among the motions. Thus, it is possible that there are wide ·ariations in the samples used and the means by vhich the emotions are being conveyed in these tudies. Of course, this strengthens rather than veakens the impact of these studies: differences are ikely to add noise, and consistent results would be ess expected.

Relation to the recognition of other information ontained in the speech signal

Relation to recognition of semantic content. Several studies have found a clear dissociation between the processing of neutral (unemotional) iemantic content and the processing of the emotional tone in which it is said. For example, in lichotic listening studies with normal adults and :hildren, Bryden and his collaborators (Ley and Bryden, 1982; Saxby and Bryden, 1984) have found a left ear (right hemisphere) advantage for :he perception of emotional tone of voice, and a ·ight ear (left hemisphere) advantage for the ·ecognition of the actual content or words spoken

in these sentences. Papanicolaou et al. (1983) provided electrophysiological evidence for a similar dissociation: they found greater attenuation of evoked potential amplitudes to a probe click over the right hemisphere when intact adults were reporting the emotion conveyed by speakers, and greater attenuation over the left hemisphere when the same subjects were detecting target syllables. The authors assume that greater hemispheric attenuation to a probe click indicates greater hemispheric involvement in the task it is performing when the click is presented. Finally, Heilman et al. (1975) found that RH patients displayed an impairment in recognizing emotion from tone of voice, but no impairment in recognizing the content of the sentences presented to them.

Studies which have used emotional rather than neutral semantic content also suggest that the right hemisphere does not play an essential role in recognizing literal semantic content even when that content is emotional. Safer and Leventhal (1977) found that when intact adults listened to passages that were positive, negative or neutral in content and/or in voice tone, the right hemisphere (left ear) tended to rely on information from voice tone in making affect judgements while the left hemisphere relied more on the sentence's literal content. Bowers et al. (1987) found that RH damaged patients, already poor at perceiving emotion prosody, showed a further severe decline in performance when conflicting as opposed to redundant information was provided by semantic content (e.g. when the sentence *all the puppies are dead* was said in a happy or sad voice). Presumably this is because the output of their intact LH predominates in their responses. Several other studies have found that RH patients are able to attach emotional meaning to verbal descriptions of emotion-eliciting situations (e.g. Cicone et al., 1978; Etcoff, 1984b; Kolb and Taylor, 1981).

Relation to recognition of prosody conveying lexical and phonological information. The studies just reviewed suggest that the decoding of the meaning of words and the emotion tone in which they are uttered involve separate processors with different neural substrates. Other research suggests that this is true even when the same acoustic features (prosody) provide information for each type of judgement.

The first source of evidence comes from tone languages such as Thai or Chinese, where pitch variations serve a linguistic function by distinguishing between words that are otherwise identical. In a series of dichotic listening studies, Van Lancker and Fromkin (1973, 1978) have shown that native Thai speakers recognize pitch contrasts which have linguistic significance better in the right ear (left hemisphere) but show no ear advantage when discriminating the same pitch in hummed tones. Native English speakers show no ear advantage for the perception of either contrast. Similarly, Gandour and Dardarananda (1983) found the perception of phonemic pitch contrast impaired in left but not right hemisphere damaged Thai speakers. The complementary syndrome was documented by Hughes et al. (1983), who found that the perception of emotion prosody was impaired for RH damaged speakers of Mandarin Chinese. Interestingly, the patients did not differ from normal controls in their ability to perceive phonemic pitch contrasts.

In English, stress patterns are phonological templates that are assigned to individual word roots and then modified by the structure of the whole word, phrase or sentence in which the root is found. Hence stress can distinguish otherwise homophonous lexical items. For example, it distinguishes between certain noun compounds and noun phrases (*darkroom* and *dark room*) and between some nouns and verbs such as *CONvict* and *conVICT*. The earliest studies in this area (Blumstein and Goodglass, 1972; Weintraub et al., 1981) were often interpreted as evidence for a *right* hemisphere dominance for this skill, and as evidence that a global deficit in recognizing prosody was associated with RH damage. A close look at their findings, however, suggests that this was premature, and recent evidence strongly suggests that the *left* hemisphere is more proficient at this

task. There were several limitations in the early studies: neither included a control group of patients with brain damage (in one study, LH damaged patients were compared only to intact adults, in the other RH damaged patients were compared to intact adults) or tasks other than those involving linguistic prosody. The interpretive problems associated with such designs have already been discussed. Second, Blumstein and Goodglass (1972) did find significant differences between the LH group and the intact controls: they made significantly more errors overall, and more errors involving random responses and involving responses specifically attributed to decoding stress. However, the differences between the two groups in stress errors did not reach statistical significance. The authors and many others have interpreted the findings as evidence for preservation of the ability to distinguish stress contrast in LH damaged patients. However, given the high percentage of errors in this study, many of which involved random choices, it is likely that problems in comprehension may have masked the more subtle problem in recognizing stress contrast. Weintraub et al. (1981) found that RH patients were impaired in discriminating stress in single words: this conclusion, however, rests on a comparison of RH patients with intact adults who performed at virtually 100% accuracy on the task.

More recent evidence unambiguously suggests that the left, not the right, hemisphere is crucial for distinguishing words minimally differing in stress. Emmorey (1987) presented LH patients, RH patients and matched controls with a task virtually identical to that used by Blumstein and Goodglass (1972). She eliminated some items that were particularly difficult in order to maximize the likelihood of errors due to discrimination of stress rather than to more global comprehension problems (the results indicate she was successful). LH damaged patients performed significantly worse than did RH patients and controls, with RH patients not differing from their matched controls. Other research indicates that intact adults show a right ear (left hemisphere) advantage for identify ng stress placement in word pairs minimally contrasting in stress (Behrens, 1985). Interestingly, when phonetic and semantic information was eliminated by filtering and only the stress pattern remained, a left ear (RH) advantage emerged. Finally, nonsense word pairs that were similar to stress-contrasted minimal word pairs but lacked semantic content did not show an ear asymmetry. It seems that when stress has more of a linguistic function to perform, the left hemisphere gains an advantage.

Research on the perception of pitch contrasts in speakers of tone languages and of stress contrast in English thus provides consistent evidence that hemispheric specialization depends on the particular computation performed (linguistic versus nonlinguistic) and not on the presence of certain prosodic features themselves. Word recognition and discrimination appear to be subserved by the left hemisphere, regardless of which acoustic cues distinguish them. Prosody conveying emotion is subserved by the right. This research also suggests that, more generally, prosody stripped of linguistic meaning (hummed tones, filtered or nonsense stress contrasts) shows either no hemispheric advantage or a right hemisphere advantage.

Relation to recognition of prosody conveying sentence-level information. Prosodic cues can indicate whether a sentence is meant as a statement, as a question or as a command. Emmorey (1987) has described this level of linguistic prosody as 'sentential', by which she means that it is separated from the grammatically conveyed content (one can understand the literal content of the sentence without understanding its intent as a statement or question), and that it operates on the sentence as a whole rather than on isolated words or phrases. In addition, uttering a statement in a commanding or questioning tone can convey pragmatic information that is not entirely unrelated to emotional information. The distinction between questions, statements and commands inherently pertains to the speaker's intentions, and this 'illocutionary force' can easily be combined with more obviously

emotional aspects of the speaker's state to convey impatience, surprise, sarcasm, contradiction, and so on. Several authors have suggested that the RH plays a dominant role in understanding pragmatic aspects of communication (see Foldi et al., 1983, for a review). All of this suggests that sentence-level prosody may stand somewhere between the emotional prosody and word-level prosody: it gives information that can be woven together with both. It would not be surprising, then, if it showed neither strong left nor right specialization.

There has been very little research on this issue, and the research that has been done has used filtered speech or meaningless sentences (repeated syllables) so that information about content is unavailable. For example, Blumstein and Cooper (1974), using a dichotic listening format, presented examples of different sentence types (statements, questions, commands and conditionals) to intact subjects. They found a right hemisphere superiority when the task was 'nonlinguistic', requiring the subject to match two sentences or to match a sentence to a visually presented contour. No hemispheric advantage emerged in a 'linguistic' condition, where subjects had to identify the sentence's type (question, statement, etc.). Similar findings were reported by Heilman et al. (1984), who presented RH patients and LH patients with filtered sentences. Subjects were asked to judge either the emotion conveyed, or the sentence type, which they had to identify by selecting one of a set of printed punctuation marks: '!', '.' '?'. Although only the RH patients had difficulty with the emotion prosody task, both RH and LH patients were worse than controls in recognizing sentence type. The two studies together suggest that, at least for meaningless sentences, both hemispheres are involved in the recognition of sentence type from prosody. Finally, Weintraub et al. (1981) presented real sentences that either differed in which word was stressed, differed in whether they were statements or questions, or were identical. RH patients were more impaired than control subjects in this task. Since the comparison was only between RH patients and intact controls this evidence can be seen as suggestive.

The evidence to date suggests that both hemispheres participate in recognizing sentence-level prosody conveying discourse or illocutionary information. More conclusive evidence must await studies that examine such recognition in linguistically meaningful sentences, in particular sentences where such prosodic information might enhance the left hemisphere's ability to carry out linguistic decisions (see Zurif, 1974; Zurif and Mendelsohn, 1972) or where it might be crucially woven in with emotional information (e.g. a question conveyed sarcastically or literally).

To summarize, it appears that both hemispheres can decode prosodic cues. When these cues are crucially involved in linguistic decisions, a left hemisphere advantage emerges; when the task calls for recognizing emotion, a right hemisphere advantage emerges. We will next examine whether there is any evidence that the RH superiority in recognizing emotion prosody is not part of a more global skill in recognizing all forms of non-linguistic prosody.

Relation to the recognition of non-linguistic prosody. Research suggests that the RH is superior to the LH in recognizing nonlinguistic auditory information such as environmental sounds and melodies (e.g. Kimura, 1967). It also appears better than the left in recognizing speaker identity (e.g. Assal et al., 1981; Riley and Sackheim, 1982). It would be of great interest to see whether one could find evidence for a dissociation between the perception of these nonlinguistic sorts of information (e.g. the identity, age or sex of the speaker) and the perception of emotional state from tone of voice. Unfortunately, currently no relevant evidence exists.

Relation to other aspects of emotion
As in the literature on the perception of facial expressions of emotion, several authors have informally noted that difficulties in perceiving emotion from speech prosody are associated with the presence of disturbances in emotional behavior,

such as denial or indifference (e.g. Heilman et al., 1975, Tucker et al., 1977; Ross, 1981). However, no studies have been conducted that look for causal relations or even correlations within individual patients between anomalies of emotional behavior and disturbances of emotional prosody. Similarly, several studies have found disturbances in both perception and in production of emotion prosody in their RH patients (Tucker et al., 1977; Weintraub et al., 1981). Here again, the extent to which the two deficits are found *within the same individuals* has not been systematically explored. Finally, there has been no evidence for differential hemispheric specialization for emotions of different valences in the limited set of emotions tested (as mentioned, these have been mainly happiness, sadness, and anger). Interestingly, recognition studies suggest that the relative difficulty of perceiving the various emotions differs for prosody and facial expression. Whereas happiness is the easiest facial expression to recognize, sadness appears to be the easiest vocal prosodic expression to recognize (Apple and Hecht, 1982; Johnson et al., 1986).

Localization
Studies of patients with unilateral cortical lesions suggest that the circuits underlying the ability to recognize emotion prosody may be in the right temporoparietal or right parietal region (e.g. Heilman et al., 1975, 1984; Ross, 1981; Tucker et al., 1977). There is evidence suggesting that parietal structures are more crucially involved than temporal structures; Benowitz et al.'s (1984) patient who was selectively impaired at recognizing emotion through prosody but not through facial expressions had right parietal damage, as did Etcoff's (in preparation) patient with the same pattern of deficits. Such findings may explain the one reported failure to find differences between RH and LH patients on a test of emotion prosody recognition (Schlanger et al., 1976): the authors included only three temporoparietal and no purely parietal patients in their sample of 20 RH damaged patients. However, whether only right parietal or

right temporoparietal patients will show selective impairments in the recognition of emotion prosody awaits verification through testing of patients with widely differing lesion sites. Thus far, the majority of studies have confined their patient groups to those with lesions in the temporoparietal regions.

Conclusion

Many have conceptualized 'emotion' as a single faculty that resides in the right hemisphere of the brain. When one examines the neuropsychological literature with an eye toward verifying this claim, however, one finds complex patterns of data that at first glance do not support this simple view. Such discrepancies could lead to a pessimistic viewpoint that the literature on the lateralization of emotion using neuropsychological data is contradictory or messy, or that the whole topic is somehow misguided. I hope to have shown in this chapter that any such pessimism would be unfounded. True, emotion is not subserved by a global faculty loosely situated in an entire hemisphere, but we should not have expected it to be. Each emotion has a particular function and evolutionary history, and each perceptual channel expressing emotions defines a particular kind of mapping between emotions and physical signals that derive from the physiological constraints on the organs producing those signals. Furthermore, channels are not uniquely dedicated to communicating emotion but contain several kinds of information superimposing their effects. Once these external constraints are recognized, it is not surprising that there is no evidence for a global analyser for emotion situated in the right hemisphere, or for other global faculties such as a general analyser for prosody, for all complex visuospatial information, or for decoding the meaning of facial muscle movements. Rather, there seem to be distinct circuits in the brain with particular purposes, each one defined in terms of the channel of communication involved and by the kind of information that is extracted from it. Most of the circuits for emotion recognition, though not

all of them, are indeed found in the right hemisphere, and most of them seem to make contributions to our emotional life that can be teased apart both in normal and in impaired functioning. When the distinctions between emotional subfaculties are recognized and properly formulated, the neuropsychological literature appears much more orderly, with widely divergent populations and techniques giving rise to converging conclusions.

Acknowledgements

Steve Pinker provided many helpful comments on this chapter, for which I thank him. Preparation of this paper was supported by NIH Grant 1R NS26926, and by the MIT Center for Cognitive Science under a grant from the Alfred P. Sloan Foundation.

References

Andrew RJ: The origin and evolution of the calls and facial expressions of the primates. *Behaviour: 20*, 1 – 109, 1963.

Apple W, Hecht K: Speaking emotionally: the relation between verbal and vocal communication of affect. *J. Pers. Soc. Psychol.: 42*, 864 – 875, 1982.

Assal G, Aubert C, Buttet J: Asymmetrie cerebrale et reconnaissance de la voix. *Rev. Neurol.: 137*, 255 – 268, 1981.

Baker-Shenk C: A microanalysis of the nonmanual components of questions in American Sign Language. Unpublished Ph.D. Dissertation. University of California, Berkeley, 1983.

Bear DM: Hemispheric specialization and the neurology of emotion. *Arch. Neurol.: 40*, 195 – 202, 1983.

Behrens SJ: The perception of stress and lateralization of prosody. *Brain Lang.: 26*, 332 – 348, 1985.

Benowitz LI, Bear DM, Mesulam, M-M, Rosenthal R, Zaidel E, Sperry RW: Nonverbal sensitivity following lateralized cerebral injury. *Cortex: 19*, 5 – 12, 1983.

Benowitz LI, Bear DM, Mesulam M-M, Rosenthal R, Zaidel E, Sperry RW: Contributions of the right cerebral hemisphere in perceiving paralinguistic cues of emotion. In Vaina L, Hintikka J (Editors), *Cognitive Constraints on Communication*. New York: Reidel, 1984.

Bisiach E, Vallar G, Perani D, Papagno C, Berti A: Unawareness of disease following lesions of the right hemisphere: anosognosia for hemiplegia and anosognosia for hemianopia. *Neuropsychologia: 24*, 471 – 482, 1986.

Blumstein S, Cooper WE: Hemispheric processing of intonation contours. *Cortex: 10*, 146 – 158, 1974.

Blumstein S, Goodglass H: The perception of stress as a semantic cue in aphasia. *J. Speech Hear. Res.: 15*, 800 – 806, 1972.

Bolinger D: *Intonation as universal.* In Proceedings of the Ninth International Congress of Linguistics. The Hague,

Netherlands: Mouton, 1964.

Bolinger D: *Intonation: Selected Readings.* Harmondsworth, England: Penguin, 1972.

Borod JC, Caron H: Facedness and emotion related to lateral dominance, sex, and expression type. *Neuropsychologia: 18,* 237 – 241, 1980.

Borod JC, Koff E, Lorch MP, Nicholas M: Channels of emotional expression in patients with unilateral brain damage. *Arch. Neurol.: 42,* 345 – 348, 1985.

Borod JC, Koff E, Lorch MP, Nicholas M: The expression and perception of facial emotion in brain-damaged patients. *Neuropsychologia: 24,* 169 – 180, 1986.

Bowers D, Bauer RM, Coslett HB, Heilman KM: Processing of faces by patients with unilateral hemispheric lesions. I. Dissociation between judgments of facial affect and facial identity. *Brain Cognition: 4,* 258 – 272, 1985.

Bowers D, Coslett HB, Bauer KM, Speedie LJ, Heilman KM: Comprehension of emotional prosody following unilateral hemispheric lesions: processing defect versus distraction defect. *Neuropsychologia: 25,* 317 – 328, 1987.

Bruyer R, Laterre C, Seron X, Feyereisen P, Strypstein E, Pierrard E, Rectem D: A case of prosopagnosia with some preserved covert remembrance of familiar faces. *Brain Cognition: 2,* 257 – 284, 1983.

Buck R, Duffy R: Nonverbal communication of affect in brain damaged patients. *Cortex: 16,* 351 – 362, 1980.

Campbell R: Asymmetries in interpreting and expressing a posed facial expression. *Cortex: 14,* 327 – 342, 1978.

Campbell R: The lateralisation of lipread sounds: a first look. *Brain Cognition: 5,* 1 – 21, 1986.

Campbell R, Landis T, Regard M: Face recognition and lipreading: a neurological dissociation. *Brain: 109,* 509 – 521, 1986.

Chevalier-Skolnikoff S: Facial expression of emotion in nonhuman primates. In Ekman P (Editor), *Darwin and Facial Expression.* New York: Academic Press, 1973.

Cicone M, Wapner W, Gardner H: Sensitivity to emotional expressions and situations in organic patients. *Cortex: 16,* 145 – 158, 1980.

Corina DD: Recognition of affective and noncanonical linguistic facial expressions in hearing and deaf subjects. Unpublished manuscript: The Salk Institute for Biological Studies, 1987.

Cosmides L: Invariances in the acoustic expression of emotion during speech. *J. Exp. Psychol.: 9,* 864 – 881, 1983.

Darwin C: *The expression of the emotions in man and animals.* London: John Murray, 1872. (Current edition, Chicago: University of Chicago Press, 1965).

Davidson RJ, Fox NA: Cerebral asymmetry and emotion: Developmental and individual differences. In Segalowitz S, Molfese D (Editors), *Developmental Implications of Brain Lateralization.* New York: Guilford, in press.

Davidson RJ, Schaffer CE, Saron C: Effects of lateralized presentations of faces on self-reports of emotion and EEG asymmetry in depressed and non-depressed subjects. *Psychophysiology: 22,* 353 – 364, 1985.

DeKosky ST, Heilman KM, Bowers D, Valenstein E: Recognition and discrimination of emotional faces and pictures. *Brain Lang.: 9,* 206 – 214, 1980.

De Renzi E, Spinnler H: Facial recognition in brain-damaged

patients: an experimental approach. *Neurology: 16,* 145 – 152, 1966.

Dimond S, Farrington L, Johnson P: Differing emotional responses from right and left hemispheres. *Nature: 261,* 690 – 692, 1976.

Ekman P: Facial signs: facts, fantasies, and possibilities. In Sebeok T (Editor), *Sight, Sound, and Sense.* Bloomington, IN: Indiana University Press, 1978.

Ekman P: Expression and the nature of emotion. In Scherer K, Ekman P (Editors), *Approaches to Emotion.* Hillsdale, NJ: Lawrence Erlbaum, 1984.

Ekman P, Friesen WV: Felt, false, and miserable smiles. *J. Nonverbal Behav.: 6,* 238 – 252, 1982.

Ekman P, Friesen WV: A new pan-cultural facial expression of emotion. *Motiv. Emotion: 10,* 159 – 168, 1986.

Ekman P, Friesen WV, Ellsworth P: What emotion categories or dimensions can observers judge from facial behavior? In Ekman P (Editor), *Emotion in the Human Face* (Second edition). Cambridge: Cambridge University Press, 1982.

Emmorey KD: The neurological substrates for prosodic aspects of speech. *Brain Lang.: 30,* 305 – 320, 1987.

Etcoff NL: Hemispheric differences in the perception of emotion in faces. Unpublished doctoral dissertation, Boston University, 1983.

Etcoff NL: Selective attention to facial identity and facial emotion. *Neuropsychologia: 22,* 281 – 295, 1984a.

Etcoff NL: Perceptual and conceptual organization of facial emotions: hemispheric differences. *Brain Cognition: 3,* 385 – 412, 1984b.

Etcoff NL: The neuropsychology of emotional expression. In Goldstein G, Tarter RE (Editors), *Advances in Clinical Neuropsychology. Vol. 3.* New York: Plenum, 1986.

Etcoff NL: Recognition and expression of emotion. *Exp. Brain Res.:* in press.

Etcoff NL: Deficits in the recognition of vocal but not facial affect: a case study. Manuscript in preparation.

Freud S: Fragment of an analysis of a case of hysteria (1905). *Collected Papers, Vol. 3.* New York: Basic Books, 1959.

Foldi NS, Cicone M, Gardner H: Pragmatic aspects of communication in brain-damaged patients. In Segalowitz SJ (Editor), *Language Functions and Brain Organization.* New York: Academic Press, 1983.

Fried I, Mateer C, Ojemann G, Wohns R, Fedio P: Organization of visuospatial functions in human cortex. *Brain: 105,* 349 – 371, 1982.

Gainotti G: Emotional behavior and hemispheric side of lesion. *Cortex: 8,* 41 – 55, 1972.

Gandour J, Dardarananda: Identification of tonal contrasts in Thai aphasic patients. *Brain Lang.: 180,* 98 – 114, 1983.

Gazzaniga MS, Risse GL, Springer SP, Clark E, Wilson DH: Psychologic and neurologic consequences of partial and complete cerebral commisurotomy. *Neurology: 25,* 10 – 15, 1975.

Gordon HW: Left hemisphere dominance for rhythmic elements in dichotically-presented melodies. *Cortex: 14,* 58 – 70, 1978.

Hager JC, Ekman P: Long distance transmission of facial affect signals. *Ethol. Sociobiol.: 1,* 77 – 82, 1979.

Hager JC, Ekman P: The asymmetry of facial actions is inconsistent with models of hemispheric specialization. *Psycho-*

physiology: 22, 307 – 318, 1985.

Haggard MP, Parkinson AM: Stimulus and task factors as determinants of ear advantages. *Q. J. Exp. Psychol.: 23,* 168 – 177, 1971.

Heilman KM, Scholes HD, Watson RT: Auditory affective agnosia. *J. Neurol. Neurosurg. Psychiatry: 38,* 69 – 72, 1975.

Heilman KM, Schwartz HD, Watson RT: Hypoarousal in patients with neglect and emotional indifference. *Neurology: 28,* 229 – 232, 1978.

Heilman KM, Bowers D, Speedie L, Coslett HB: Comprehension of affective and nonaffective prosody. *Neurology: 34,* 917 – 921, 1984.

Heller W, Levy J: Perception and expression of emotion in right handers and left handers. *Neuropsychologia: 19,* 263 – 272, 1981.

Hirschman RS, Safer MA: Hemispheric differences in perceiving positive and negative emotions. *Cortex: 18,* 569 – 580, 1982.

Hughes CP, Chan JL, Su MS: Aprosodia in Chinese patients with right cerebral hemisphere lesions. *Arch. Neurol.: 50,* 732 – 736, 1983.

Johnson WF, Emde RN, Scherer KR, Klinnert MD: Recognition of emotion from vocal cues. *Arch. Gen. Psychiatry: 43,* 280 – 283, 1986.

Kimura D: Functional asymmetries of the brain in dichotic listening. *Cortex: 3,* 163 – 178, 1967.

Kinsbourne M, Bemporad B: Lateralization of emotion: a model and the evidence. In Fox NA, Davidson RJ (Editors), *The Psychobiology of Affective Development.* Hillsdale, NJ: Lawrence Erlbaum, 1984.

Kolb B, Milner B: Observations of spontaneous facial expression after focal cerebral excisions and after intracarotid injection of sodium amytal. *Neuropsychologia: 19,* 505 – 514, 1981.

Kolb B, Taylor L: Affective behavior in patients with localized cortical excisions: role of lesion site and side. *Science: 214,* 89 – 90, 1981.

Ladavas E, Umiltà C, Ricci-Bitti PE: Evidence for sex differences in right-hemisphere dominance for emotions. *Neuropsychologia: 18,* 361 – 366, 1980.

Landis E, Assal G, Perret E: Opposite cerebral hemispheric superiorities for visual associative processing of emotional facial expressions and objects. *Nature: 278,* 739 – 740, 1979.

Lanzetta JT, Kleck RE: Encoding and decoding of nonverbal affect in humans. *J. Pers. Soc. Psychol.: 16,* 12 – 19, 1970.

Lehiste I: *Suprasegmentals.* Cambridge, MA: MIT Press, 1970.

Ley RG, Bryden MP: Hemispheric difference in processing emotions and faces. *Brain Lang.: 7,* 127 – 138, 1979.

Ley RG, Bryden MP: A dissociation of right and left hemispheric effects for recognizing emotional tone and verbal content. *Brain Cognition: 1,* 3 – 9, 1982.

Ley RG, Strauss E: Hemispheric asymmetries in the perception of facial expressions by normals. In Bruyer R (Editor), *The Neuropsychology of Face Perception and Facial Expression.* Hillsdale, NJ: Lawrence Erlbaum, 1986.

Liddell SK: *American Sign Language Syntax.* The Hague: Mouton, 1980.

McGurk H, MacDonald J: Hearing lips and seeing voices. *Nature: 264,* 746 – 748, 1976.

Milner B: Hemispheric specialization: Scope and limits. In Schmidt FO, Worden FG (Editors), *The Neurosciences Third Study Program.* Cambridge, MA: MIT Press, 1974.

Morrow L, Vrtunski PB, Kim Y, Boller F: Arousal responses to emotional stimuli and laterality of lesion. *Neuropsychologia: 19,* 65 – 71, 1981.

Natale M, Gur RE, Gur RC: Hemispheric asymmetries in processing emotional expressions. *Neuropsychologia: 21,* 555-565, 1983.

O'Sullivan M, Ekman P, Friesen WV: Emotion recognition: measuring affect specific abilities. Manuscript in preparation.

Papanicolaou AC, Levin HS, Eisenberg HM, Moore BT: Evoked potential indices of selective hemispheric engagement in affective and phonetic tasks. *Neuropsychologia: 21,* 401 – 405, 1983.

Perrett DI, Smith PAJ, Potter DD, Mistlin AJ, Head AS, Milner AD, Jeeves: Neurones responsive to faces in the temporal cortex: studies of functional organization, sensitivity to identity and relation to perception. *Hum. Neurobiol.: 3,* 197 – 208, 1984.

Pizzamiglio L: Disturbi del riconoscimento e della espressione di emozioni nei soggetti cerebrolesi. Paper presented at the International Conference on Emotions and Hemispheric Specialization, Rome, Italy, November, 1986.

Pizzamiglio L, Zoccolotti P, Mammucari A, Cesaroni R: The independence of face identity and facial expression recognition mechanisms: relation to sex and cognitive style. *Brain Cognition: 2,* 176 – 188, 1983.

Reuter-Lorenz P, Davidson RJ: Differential contribution of the two cerebral hemispheres to the perception of happy and sad faces. *Neuropsychologia: 19,* 609 – 613, 1981.

Riley EN, Sackheim HA: Ear asymmetry in recognition of unfamiliar voices. *Brain Cognition: 1,* 245 – 258, 1982.

Rizzolatti G, Umilta C, Berlucchi G: Opposite superiorities of the right and left cerebral hemispheres in discriminating reaction time to physiognomical and alphabetical material. *Brain: 94,* 431 – 442, 1971.

Rolls ET: Neurons in the cortex of the temporal lobe and in the amygdala of the monkey with responses selective for faces. *Hum. Neurobiol.: 3,* 209 – 222, 1984.

Ross ED: The aprosodias: functional-anatomical organization of the affective components of language in the right hemisphere. *Arch. Neurol.: 38,* 561 – 569, 1981.

Ross, ED: Modulation of affect and nonverbal communication by the right hemisphere. In Mesualm M-M (Editor), *Principles of Behavioral Neurology.* Philadelphia: F.A. Davis, 1985.

Ross ED, Mesulam M-M: Dominant language functions in the right hemisphere? *Arch. Neurol.: 36,* 144 – 148, 1979.

Safer MA: Sex and hemisphere differences in access to codes for processing emotional expressions and faces. *J. Exp. Psychol. Gen.: 1,* 86 – 100, 1981.

Safer MA: Individual differences in the metacontrol of lateralization for recognizing facial expressions of emotion. *Cortex: 20,* 19 – 25, 1984.

Safer MA, Leventhal H: Ear differences in evaluating emotional tones of voice and verbal content. *J. Exp. Psychol. Hum. Percep. Perform.: 3,* 75 – 82, 1977.

Saxby L, Bryden MP: Left-ear superiority in children for processing auditory emotional material. *Dev. Psychol.: 20,*

72 – 80, 1984.

Scherer KR: Speech and emotional states. In Darby J (Editor), *Speech Evaluation in Psychiatry*. New York: Grune and Stratton, 1981.

Scherer KR: Vocal affect expression: a review and a model for future research. *Psychol. Bull.: 99,* 143 – 165, 1986.

Schlanger BB, Schlanger P, Gerstman LJ: The perception of emotionally toned sentences by right hemisphere-damaged and aphasic subjects. *Brain Lang.: 3,* 396 – 403, 1976.

Shapiro BE, Grossman M, Gardner H: Selective musical processing deficits in brain damaged populations. *Neuropsychologia: 19,* 161 – 169, 1981.

Shuttleworth EL, Syring V, Allen N: Further observations on the nature of prosopagnosia. *Brain Cognition: 1,* 307 – 332, 1982.

Silberman EK, Weingartner H: Hemispheric lateralization of functions related to emotion. *Brain Cognition: 5,* 322 – 353, 1986.

Spencer H: *Essays, Scientific, Political, and Speculative,* 1863.

Strauss S, Moscovitch M: Perception of facial expressions. *Brain Lang.: 13,* 308 – 332, 1981.

Tranel D, Damasio AR: Recognition of gender, age, and meaning of facial expression can be dissociated from recognition of facial identity. Paper presented at the 39th Annual Meeting of the American Academy of Neurology, New York, April, 1987.

Tucker DM, Watson RT, Heilman KM: Discrimination and evocation of affectively toned speech in patients with right parietal disease. *Neurology: 27,* 947 – 950, 1977.

Van Lancker D, Fromkin V: Hemispheric specialization for pitch and tone: Evidence from Thai. *J. Phonetics: 1,* 101 – 109, 1973.

Van Lancker D, Fromkin VA: Cerebral dominance for pitch contrasts in tone language speakers and in musically untrained and trained English speakers. *J. Phonetics: 6,* 19 – 23, 1978.

Weintraub S, Mesulam M, Kramer L: Disturbances in prosody: a right hemisphere contribution of language. *Arch. Neurol.: 38,* 742 – 744, 1981.

Williams CE, Stevens KM: Emotions and speech: some acoustic correlates. *J. Acoust. Soc. Am.: 52,* 1238 – 1250, 1972.

Young AW, McWeeny KH, Hay DC, Ellis AW: Matching familiar and unfamiliar faces on identity and expression. *Psychol. Res.: 48,* 63 – 68, 1986.

Zoccolotti P, Scabini D, Violani C: Electrodermal responses in patients with unilateral brain damage. *J. Clin. Neuropsychol.: 4,* 143 – 150, 1982.

Zurif EB: Auditory lateralization: prosodic and syntactic factors. *Brain Lang.: 1,* 391 – 404, 1974.

Zurif EB, Mendelsohn M: Hemispheric specialization for the perception of speech sounds: The influence of intonation and structure. *Percept. Psychophys.: 11,* 329 – 332, 1972.

CHAPTER 18

Facial expression of emotion

L. Pizzamiglio[1], C. Caltagirone[2] and P. Zoccolotti[1]

[1] Dipartimento di Psicologia, Universita' di Roma 'La Sapienza', and [2] Clinica Neurologica, II Universita' di Roma
'Tor Vergata', Rome, Italy

Introduction

Several convergent developments have contributed in the past decade to a renaissance of interest in research on facial expression of emotion.

Although the hypothesis of a direct and close relationship between facial expression and emotional experience has been anchored in neurobiological thinking since the seminal studies of C. Darwin (1872, 1965), only in comparatively recent times have empirical, theoretical and cross-cultural studies definitively demonstrated that this issue can be investigated in a rigorous and creative way (see Lanzetta and McHugo, 1989, for a review).

From a neuropsychological point of view the basic question underlying different neuropsychological models of emotion is related to evidence of a special mechanism for processing of emotional experience. The way we respond to internal or external situations inducing an emotion may require processing which is separate from all other kinds of experience. A related question is whether or not this processing is supported by a specialized neural system.

Interest in this issue was sparked following the publication of research results which indicated either a differential impairment produced by the two cerebral hemispheres in different emotional experiences or, alternatively, the responsibility of the right hemisphere for several aspects of emotion (see Kinsbourne and Bemporad, 1985; Gainotti, 1989, for a review).

Data relevant to these issues have been collected in recent years both for normal subjects and for brain-damaged patients suffering from focal unilateral lesions. In the fifties through the use of the amytal technique different affective changes were observed following a unilateral injection either to the left or to the right hemisphere. Later, Gainotti (1969, 1972) described different mood changes in patients with focal lesions to the left or right hemisphere.

It was speculated that each hemisphere is involved with either positive or negative emotions. Alternatively, the right hemisphere was considered the activation site for the experience of emotion (see Gainotti, 1989).

Within this general interest a number of systematic investigations were undertaken to look for the differential role of the two hemispheres in processing information with emotional value, in organizing emotional expression and in producing autonomic responses.

The present chapter will review the evidence gathered on asymmetry in emotional expression and more specifically the evidence for possible asymmetrical control of emotional facial expressions.

Facial communication has been widely studied because it is apparently easy to observe. Nevertheless, the very brief duration and the dynamic changes which occur during a natural interactive communication pose a number of methodological problems which are still a matter of debate. Furthermore, facial expression subserves emotional as well as non-emotional communication. Therefore the question is whether the two kinds of communicative system are served by a unitary neural control or by separate units or modules for each of the two processes.

Evidence for the possible asymmetry of the two expressive channels will be reviewed and data collected on normal subjects and on focal brain-damaged patients will be reported. The picture of our recent knowledge of this issue will be completed by the scanty neuroanatomical bases for such asymmetry.

The study of facial expression of emotions

The measurement of facial expression
For a critical comprehension of the current literature on facial expression, methodological issues will be discussed and some important distinctions will be made between different forms of expressive behavior.

The first problem is related to measurement of facial expression. We commonly make inferences about the feelings of others with whom we interact from the gestaltic perception of their facial expression. This gestaltic capacity develops very early in life (Spitz, 1965). There is also some evidence that the ability of the child to deal with physiognomic and emotional information through the face follows a developmental route different from that of the perception of different classes of stimuli (Carey and Diamond, 1977). This powerful and generalized ability suggested the idea of measuring facial expressions produced in experimental situations in which either naive or experienced judges were asked to evaluate the facial emotional responses by means of subjective techniques.

The economy and simplicity of this approach justify its wide use, but at the same time reduce the chances of capturing the quickly developing sequence of events occurring in an emotional expression, often of very short duration, as well as subtle asymmetries in the facial movements of possible theoretical interest.

As for the problem of evaluating facial asymmetries in the expression of emotions, an ingenious technique consists of using composite or 'chimeric' pictures of face. They are obtained by combining one hemiface with its own specular image, thereby producing a complete face composed of the same part of the face. Using this procedure, Wolff (1933) found that naive observers judged differently chimeric pictures made out of left or right hemifaces: the left chimeric faces were described as 'smiling, frank, active, social' while the right chimeric faces were considered as 'concentrated, reticent, passive and solitary'. Wolff's stimuli were based on neutral expressions. More recent studies used posed emotional expressions (Sackeim and Gur, 1983) or pictures in which, for example, a right half of a relaxed face is put together with the opposite half of the same face performing a certain emotional expression (e.g. smiling; Campbell, 1978).

In studies based on this methodology independent judges are generally required to evaluate the composite picture in terms of relative expressiveness or intensity of expression.

The above technique, even if very useful in studies on normal subjects, needs some clarification and has some limitations. With regard to the former, the mechanism through which a given facial expression is elicited (i.e. spontaneous or posed) has to be specified (Ekman, 1980). The limitations derive from the difficulty of capturing the apex of a facial expression; in any case information about the dynamic progression of the entire expression is lost. Furthermore, the data collected in this way depend on the perceptual ability of the perceiver.

More 'objective' techniques to describe facial emotional expressions have been developed in recent years. Izard and Dougherty (1982) developed a technique which allows the description of the sequence of different emotional expressions produced by the subjects as a function of time. Ekman and Friesen (1978) developed the Facial Action Coding System (FACS), the hitherto most elaborate and detailed behavioral technique for describing all the facial movements produced by the subject during an emotional or non-emotional communication through the face. This coding system allows any Action Unit (AU), i.e. any perceivable movement of the face, to be classified and related to the underlying group of muscles producing the movement. In order to do so repeated viewing of frame by frame videotape recordings is required, not live action. Consequently, it is possible to describe with high reliability the presence, intensity and duration of movements (i.e., the increase, apex and decrease in activity over time) as well as possible asymmetries between the two hemifaces separately for each AU. However, it should be observed that in most studies, particularly with normal subjects, the analysis has been limited to the evaluation of these parameters at the apex of the expressions. These two techniques, although having the advantage of giving more accurate information, demand considerable skill on the part of the scorer and take a long time to administer.

Finally, the electromyographic recording of single muscles provides a reliable measure of facial activity. This technique proves to be particularly useful when no movements are visually detectable (Schwartz, 1982; Lanzetta and McHugo, 1989). EMG recordings have been found to provide accurate information about the valence of experienced emotion (Cacioppo et al., 1986; Englis et al., 1982) and to differentiate between several negative emotions (Fridlund et al., 1984; Smith et al., 1986).

One limitation is that the presence of electrodes may inhibit, to some extent, the spontaneous reactivity of the subject, over and above the typical artificial conditions of laboratory testing. The number of constraints that each of these techniques imply and the very infrequent direct comparison between results obtained with more than one scoring system on the same subjects call for caution in comparing data obtained with different methodologies.

For instance, in a study on spontaneous expression recorded in neurological patients a difference was present between controls and brain-damaged patients when the FACS was used, while it disappeared when two different kinds of subjective evaluations were used (Mammucari et al., 1988).

Voluntary versus spontaneous expression of emotion

A second important distinction should be discussed between different forms of facial emotional expressions.

If a friend tells me a joke or some bad news about someone I know, I smile or display my sadness without any effort. But if I am asked to put on a 'happy' or a 'sad' face, I certainly experience, especially in the latter case, considerable difficulty in carrying out the task. With the exception of smiling, normal people at any age may well prove unable to deliberately pose basic emotions such as sadness, fear, disgust, surprise or anger, in a comparatively high percentage of cases (Caltagirone et al., 1989; Smith et al., 1986).

Does this phenomenological difference in producing spontaneous or voluntary emotional expressions correspond to different neurological mechanisms underlying the two ways by which we express emotions through the face?

Clinical neurology has indicated a number of clear dissociations between the impairment in voluntary and involuntary emotional expressions: Rinn (1984) sums up the most important evidence in 4 points.

The first example comes from the frequent dissociation found in patients who have suffered from paralysis after a lesion of the motor cortex or its projections: these patients show a facial paralysis contralateral to the side of the lesion although they can smile spontaneously without any asymmetry. Occasionally, in a spontaneous smile, the contraction of the corner of the mouth in the affected (contralateral) side is observed to be even stronger than on the opposite side. This paradoxical behavior is supposed to result from a lack of inhibition by the damaged cortex (Brodal, 1981).

The second source of evidence comes from patients with basal ganglia disorders, and particularly from patients with Parkinson's disease. Clinically these patients show as a typical symptom an 'amimic or masked face'; however, the same patients can pose a smile or any other emotion like normal subjects.

A third type of evidence comes from patients suffering from peripheral paralysis of the VII nerve who undergo surgical anastomosis linking a branch of another cranial nerve (accessory nerve) and the peripheral fibres of the facial nerve. The recovery of these patients brings them to progressively reacquire voluntary control of the movement of the facial mimic muscles (with or without concomitant movements of the shoulder, in the case of the anastomosis with accessory nerve): nevertheless, no improvement is observed in spontaneous emotional expression (Kahn, 1966).

A fourth type of evidence of dissociation between spontaneous and voluntary emotional expressions comes from cases of gelastic and diacristic epilepsy as well as from pathological laughing and crying (Poeck, 1969, 1985). In both these pathological phenomena, patients produce all the facial movements appropriate to the smile or the crying; moreover, they exhibit the same autonomic concomitants of the normally elicited situation although the expression is performed in a stereotyped way, rapidly reaching the apex. However, the patients do not experience the affect corresponding to the expression and in any case this behavior is not triggered by the appropriate stimulus.

A model for interpreting all these pathological events can be provided by hypothesizing the existence of two distinct neurological systems, one basically responsible for the voluntary production of an appropriate pattern of facial actions, the other responsible for the production of the involuntary ones.

The inability of the patients with pyramidal lesions to intentionally produce emotional expressions, while remaining capable of producing spontaneous ones, indicates that the pyramidal pathway is responsible for the intentional control of the face movements. In contrast, no spontaneous facial expression of emotion can usually be produced in the presence of lesions affecting the extrapyramidal system.

The case of pathological laughing and crying is generally explained as a consequence of the disconnection between the pyramidal system and the subcortical structures, releasing the latter ones from an inhibitory control and therefore allowing a sudden outburst of a motor program which produces facial expressions, disconnected from any corresponding feeling (Rinn, 1984). This last interpretation explicitly suggests the idea that the relationship between the two systems can be conceived in terms of relative functional autonomy, but also of a distinct modulating activity of the pyramidal system on extrapyramidal activity.

The anatomical substrates of facial expression

A neuroanatomical survey is necessary to elucidate the significance of possible differences in various forms of facial expressions and to interpret possible asymmetries in mimic activity.

The facial expressive features are produced by a variety of non skeletal muscles, all innervated by the VII nerve, and by four skeletal muscles (temporalis, masseter, internal and external pterygoid) which are controlled by the trigeminal nerve and partly contribute to mimicry of the face.

The voluntary movements of the face are regulated by a direct corticobulbar tract, which has special characteristics. The representation of the lower part of the face in area 4 in man is larger than that of the upper part (brows and forehead). Furthermore, the pyramidal tract moving the lower face synapses completely with the controlateral nuclei of the VII nerve. The fibres reaching the nuclei for the orbicularis oculi are predominantly controlateral. The cortical connection of the brows and forehead are evenly distributed ipsi- and contralaterally (Kuypers, 1958). Therefore, the fine motor control of the oral region of the face and the possibility of unilateral movements is supported by a large contingent of strictly controlateral corticobulbar fibres. On the other side, the movements of the upper part of the face (more often produced bilaterally) are simultaneously controlled by the two sides of the motor cortex. The trigeminal muscles relevant to the facial expressiveness receive completely bilateral cortical input (Crosby et al., 1962).

A second indirect cortico-bulbar system regulates the facial movements: this cortico-bulbar tract connects the cortex to the efferent motoneurons via interneurons in the reticular formation. These connections are also bilateral (Holstege et al., 1977). Probably, this indirect cortico-bulbar system conveys cortical modulation to the periphery, but, at the same time, receives information from a variety of extrapyramidal structures (Rinn, 1984).

A large number of clinical observations (see discussion above) point to the relevance of the extrapyramidal system, and the fronto-limbic structures, in producing spontaneous emotional behavior, but a specification of the anatomical structures involved and of the role played by each structure is much less easy to obtain.

A great variety of basal ganglia disorders, such as Parkinson's disease (Buck and Duffy, 1980). Huntington's disease, progressive supranuclear palsy, Wilson's disease, Sydenhan's chorea and Meige's disease (Marsden, 1976), often produce reduction of facial expressiveness, involuntary facial movements, pathological laughing and crying (see Mayeux, 1983, for a review). In spite of the frequent occurrence of a disordered facial mobility, there are no descriptions of any impairment in which a particular emotion is selectively impaired. An equally vague picture emerges with regard to a number of limbic structures known to produce perturbation of emotional expressiveness. Bilateral lesions of the cingulate gyrus (Amyes and Nielsen, 1955) or bilateral cingulotomy (Le Beau, 1951) produced akinetic mutism and facial inexpressiveness. Unilateral lesion to the cingulate gyrus yielded the same facial disorders, which subsided in a few days and were slightly more intense on the side controlateral to the lesion. The electrical stimulation of the same structure (Talairach et al., 1973) was followed by difficulty in expressing emotion through the face, and was associated with a variety of emotional feelings.

The pathology of fronto-limbic structures seems to interfere with the production of spontaneous facial expression of emotions, although it is not clear whether these symptoms reveal a specific control of the encoding of facial emotional expressions or whether they are a consequence of the emotional changes that these patients experience (Damasio and Van Hoesen, 1983). In some cases (supplementary motor area), the facial sequelae are observed to an equal extent in left and right lesions and affect both sides of the face: however, they tend to be more intense on the opposite side of the lesion.

Unilateral corticectomy of the supplementary motor area on either side produced an 'emotional facial paralysis' on both sides, although more evident in the controlateral hemiface (Laplane et al., 1977).

Comments

Some important considerations can be inferred from the above discussion for the purpose of making reasonable predictions about possible asymmetries of the facial expression of emotions.

Firstly, the clinical literature indicates that there are two distinct neural subsystems, one of which deals with voluntary expression of emotions and another which is predominantly involved in the encoding of spontaneous facial expression. This distinction can be mitigated by considering that, when we are interacting with other people and communicating our feelings through the face, it is certainly possible that we intentionally modulate our spontaneous mimicry according to some internal 'display rules' (Ekman and Friesen, 1975b). Nevertheless, in any research on facial expression a clear distinction must be maintained between these two domains, and special care should be taken to explicitly determine to what extent any particular kind of observed behavior can be considered 'spontaneous' or under voluntary control.

'Spontaneous' involuntary facial expression of emotion seems to be predominantly under extrapyramidal influence, perhaps with the contribution of limbic structures. The neural pathways encoding facial movements are almost exclusively bilaterally represented. Furthermore, none of the described pathologies has ever been associated with any asymmetrical consequences in terms of facial expressiveness: even in cases where the reduced facial expressions were more intense on the controlateral face, emotional expressive disorders resulting from unilateral lesions of the basal ganglia or of the limbic structures did not differ according to the side of the brain injury. These observations do not immediately lead to a strong expectation of cerebral asymmetry in the spontaneous expression of emotions.

Voluntary expression, on the other hand, is controlled by a direct corticobulbar path, which is strictly controlateral for the lower and more mobile face. Although there are no compelling reasons to expect that any activity under pyramidal control should end up in functional asymmetry, it is conceivable that a higher cortical function modulating and controlling emotional responses might be lateralized to one hemisphere, as occurs for other well-known cognitive abilities.

If this position is to be considered, in order to predict a predominance of the right hemisphere, one of two further hypotheses should be explicitly made. The first is that, just as the left hemisphere is dominant in organizing complex sequences of movements of the limbs, the right hemisphere may show a dominant role in controlling the complex facial activity necessary to convey emotional and non-emotional communication. Alternatively, the stronger hypothesis could be advanced that the right hemisphere has developed a special module or subsystem which is selectively involved in regulating facial emotional communication. In any case it seems plausible to expect that, if any asymmetry for voluntary expressions is found, the lower face would probably show such an effect to a greater extent than the upper face. Linking this observation to the described techniques for studying facial expression, it seems reasonable to point out that all the observations based on 'gestaltic'

evaluation of the subject's face are more likely to lose relevant information in the clarification of this problem.

Cerebral lateralization of facial expression of emotion

Studies on facial expressiveness have been carried out on both normal subjects and brain-damaged patients. While these two paradigms have been used to test similar hypotheses, methodologies as well as underlying assumptions are considerably different. In the case of studies with unilateral brain-damaged populations, emotional facial expressions displayed by right and left brain-damaged patients are usually compared. It is reasoned that, if an emotional expression is mainly subserved by a cerebral hemisphere, then damage to that hemisphere will preferentially impair that emotional expression. Within-subject comparisons of the relative expressivity of the two hemifaces are usually not carried out since they may be confounded by the presence of facial hemiparesis. In the case of studies involving normal subjects, attention is typically focused on differences in the intensity of expression between the two halves of the face. The underlying rationale is that such asymmetries may reflect hemispheric specialization for facial and/or emotional expressions (e.g., Sackeim and Gur, 1983).

For this hypothesis to hold it is important to evaluate whether or not the face is itself an asymmetrical stimulus. Reviewing a large body of literature from orthodontic, anthropological and psychological studies, Sackeim (1985) concludes that while specific morphological asymmetries of the face at rest may be present they are equally likely to occur in either direction. Therefore, morphological asymmetries cannot account for asymmetries in the expression of emotion.

However, it must be added that the presence of a larger right hemiface has been reported in a number of studies (Figalova, 1969; Burke, 1971; Koff et al., 1985, 1981). If this effect were to prove reliable, it could be expected that symmetrical ovements, being distributed on areas of different zes, will erroneously appear to be asymmetrical Nelson and Horowitz, 1980). However, studies irectly testing this hypothesis have generally eported the absence of any predictive value of norphological asymmetry (Koff et al., 1981; ackeim and Gur, 1980; Sackeim et al., 1984).

acial movements without emotional value

n some studies, normal subjects were asked to intentionally produce unilateral facial movements uch as winking, moving the eyes to either side, or ulling the mouth up and down or to one side Chaurasia and Goswami, 1975; Koff et al., 1981; orod et al., 1983; Alford, 1983). Their performance was judged on subjective scales of facial expressiveness by either naive or experienced observrs. In all cases the movements produced by the eft hemiface were more intense or better performd. Campbell (1986) notes that these findings are ndependent of cultural influence, since similar ata were obtained using Indian and White American subjects. More intense left-sided movenents were also found in a study in which the subects were performing bilateral facial actions Campbell, 1982).

Studying patients with localized cortical removals, Kolb and Milner (1981a) found no impairnent in single facial movements in any of the ubgroups studied as compared to the performance f normal controls. Patients with frontal lobe excisions performed more poorly in sequences of facial novements than patients with central, parietal or emporal removals; however, this result seems to ndicate a general deficit in motor programming, not specific to the face, since these patients were imilarly impaired in copying sequences of arm nd hand movements.

All the previously described studies were based n subjective evaluations of facial expressiveness. n three recent investigations a wide and representative repertoire of possible action units (raising yebrows, wrinkling the nose, pulling up the corner of one's lips, stretching eyelids, etc.) were collected in a population of children (Ekman et al.,

1980), normal young adults (Hager and Ekman, 1985) and brain-damaged and normal controls (Pizzamiglio et al., 1987). The imitation of facial movements was analysed using the FACS scoring system (Ekman and Friesen, 1978). In neither study, looking at different ages and independent of sex, did normal subjects show any systematic bias toward one side of the face or the other. Occasionally, when imitating some individual movement, there were unilateral biases (Hager and Ekman, 1985). An important finding was that these lateral differences were stronger for deliberate requested actions than for spontaneous ones. However, biases were peculiar to specific actions, with some showing a prevalence on the left side (brow lowered, smiling) and some on the right side (nose wrinkled, lip corners down, brow raised), and were present for actions involving both the upper and the lower parts of the face. In commenting on their results, Hager and Ekman (1985) pointed out that the relatively few observed asymmetries do not fit any model of cerebral asymmetry for emotional information processing.

Pizzamiglio et al. (1987) found that, using different scoring criteria, both left and right braindamaged groups did not differ or were only slightly worse than the normal controls in this task. Right brain-damaged patients differed from the left-brain-damaged patients only in that they performed the movements after greater delay and made less use of facilitating movements. Oral apraxia and facial movement imitation were found to be largely independent and no patients were found to show severe impairment in imitating facial movements, unlike what was observed in other forms of apraxia. Furthermore, no intrahemispheric locus of the lesions was found to produce greater impairment in this task. Therefore there seems to be no evidence of cerebral asymmetry in the control of facial movement. The difficulty in producing apraxia for facial movements and in localizing a neural structure controlling this task would suggest that the facial movements have a multiple representation in both hemispheres. This conclusion is similar to Geschwind's (1975) statement about the representation of central axial and extrinsic eye movements.

Voluntary expression of emotions through the face

A number of studies have been addressed more directly to the question of how normal and brain-damaged subjects intentionally produce facial emotional expressions.

Chimeric stimuli. An initial attempt consisted of using pictures of actors trained to move a complex pattern of mimic muscles in order to produce an emotional expression. With the photographic material previously published by Ekman and Friesen (1975a), Sackeim et al. (1978) made composite pictures of the two left or the two right hemifaces and asked naive subjects to judge which of the two composites expressed the emotion more intensely. The majority of the so called 'negative' emotions (sadness, fear, disgust and anger) were judged to be more intense for the left composite pictures. No left or right bias was present for the smile: in commenting on these results, Ekman (1980) pointed out that the pictures of smiles were taken from spontaneous smiling, while the pictures of other emotions were produced by asking experienced posers to deliberately move the various AUs involved in a given facial expression. A consistent left face bias for smiling was obtained by Campbell (1978) using similar chimeric pictures. In the same study, Campbell (1978) found that, when judging chimeric faces made out of two relaxed hemifaces, the left chimeric was judged to be sadder than the right. With a similar technique a left bias was also found by Heller and Levy (1981).

Using chimeric stimuli, Rubin and Rubin (1980) demonstrated asymmetries toward the left face for posed smiles in children.

Somewhat less clear results have been recently reported by Braun et al. (1988). Across all stimuli and expressions they observed a small left face superiority; however, this effect varied in unpredicted ways with the posed emotion (e.g., sadness was significantly right-side dominant).

A different picture arises when a chimeric face is judged in terms of its similarity to the original face. In this case, it was observed that the subject evaluated the right chimeric face as more similar to the original (Gilbert and Bakan, 1973). This effect has been confirmed by a number of studies (Bennet et al., 1987; Kolb et al., 1983; Lawson, 1978). Gilbert and Bakan (1973) interpreted this effect as due to a functional asymmetry of the cerebral hemispheres. During the free vision of a face the two hemifaces would stimulate different hemispheres; the right hemiface would mainly stimulate the left hemifield and would be processed by the right hemisphere, which is believed to be superior in face recognition (cf. Benton, 1980). Therefore, this asymmetry was interpreted as due to a perceptual asymmetry of the observer (Gilbert and Bakan, 1973). Consistent with a hemispheric asymmetry interpretation is the finding that the right hemiface preference is present in right-handed but not left-handed observers (Lawson, 1978). Furthermore, this effect disappears when the chimeric faces are evaluated by patients with a lesion in right temporal or parieto-occipital lobes (Kolb et al., 1983).

Recently, Grega et al. (1988) proposed an interpretation of the phenomenon based on a hemispatial rather than a hemifield bias in central processing. They found that the preference for the right chimeric face is maintained when stimuli are presented centrally moving through a small vertical slit. It may be observed that this interpretation maintains that the effect is due to a hemispheric asymmetry of the perceiver.

While these findings are not directly relevant to the problem of asymmetry of facial expression, they nevertheless indicate that in observing a face in free viewing condition a non-experienced judge shows an asymmetrical bias, a finding potentially important in interpreting results on facial asymmetry obtained using different scoring techniques. As for facial expressions, using chimeric faces (half-smile – half-neutral), Levy et al. (1983) found that smiles appearing in the left hemifield of the observer were more expressive than those appearing in the right. In contrast, this effect was independent of poser biases; that is, this preference was present whether the left or right face of the poser appeared in the left hemifield of the observer.

A more direct attempt to evaluate the role of the perceptual bias has been put forward by Sackeim and Grega (1987), who requested their posers to produce deliberately asymmetrical facial expressions (happiness and sadness). Right-side-accentuated expressions appeared more intense when the accentuated side was on the left (normal presentation) than on the right (mirror image presentation) of the judge's view. The effect was not significant for left-side-accentuated expressions. These findings give some support to the idea that, in producing an overall subjective evaluation of expressiveness, judges give greater weight to the portion of the face stimulus appearing on the left hemispace.

Asymmetry in full face viewing. In a different line of research, using subjective estimates of asymmetry of expression with full face viewing, further evidence accumulated to indicate a left-facedness in voluntary expressions (Borod and Caron, 1980; Borod et al., 1981, 1983).

The research of Borod and coworkers indicated some interactions of these findings with the 'valence' of emotions and with the sex: chiefly left-facedness was more evident for negative emotions in females, while men were left-biased for both positive and negative emotions (Borod et al., 1983).

Ekman et al. (1981) found that posed smiles in children were more intense on the left side of the face as assessed by the FACS.

The fact that positive emotions have not been found to be consistently asymmetrical can be explained (Etcoff, 1986) in two ways: one is that usually positive emotion is basically represented by the smile, while negative emotions may be expressed in a variety of ways, and, most importantly, the smile is an expression which does not exclusively depict happiness, but is also used as an emblem for general social communication, and is therefore an overlearned and conventional expression. These

two arguments may very well account for the symmetrical facial performance and bilateral control of positive emotions.

Asymmetry in brain-damaged patients. In research on brain-damaged patients voluntary emotional expressions are rarely described in single case studies and only few group studies are available.

Bruyer (1981) used chimeric stimuli made out of faces of patients with a unilateral brain lesion. Left faces of left brain-damaged patients were more expressive than right faces and the opposite was found for right brain-damaged patients; this effect was greater for patients with clinical signs of facial paralysis but it was still present for patients without them. These results can be interpreted most parsimoniously by suggesting that even subclinical signs of facial paralysis may orient the gestaltic preference of the judges toward the uninjured hemiface; overall, they indicate the difficulty in applying the chimeric face technique to unilaterally brain-damaged patients.

Using a full-face-viewing technique, Borod et al. (1986) did not observe a differential impairment of right versus left brain-damaged patients in posing a group of so-called negative emotions. The absence of a hemispheric dissociation for these expressions was confirmed by Caltagirone et al. (1989) on a larger group of left and right brain-damaged patients. Their results did not change whether the analyses were based on the FACS technique or on subjective evaluations of blind judges.

For positive expressions, Borod et al. (1986) reported that right brain-damaged patients appeared less expressive than left brain-damaged patients. However, no difference was observed in the study by Caltagirone et al. (1989); they also noted that it proved difficult to establish whether the smiles of their patients were posed or spontaneous and suggested that results on positive expressions be viewed with caution.

In both studies, it was observed that facial performance was unrelated to the presence and degree of facial paralysis and oral apraxia (Caltagirone et al., 1989; Borod et al., 1988).

Summarizing the literature on voluntary emotional expressions, there is no convincing evidence for a lateralization of the control of facial movements to either hemisphere; on the contrary, a suggestion seems to emerge for a multiple cortical representation of this activity.

As for the voluntary production of emotional expression there is some support for the idea of a left-facedness based on normal subjects. However, since left-facedness is not coherent with the results of the pathological literature it seems premature to conclude that the observed facial asymmetry is a direct consequence of right hemispheric control of emotional expressions (see conclusive remarks).

Spontaneous facial expression of emotion
As for other aspects of emotional expression, also in studies on spontaneous expression, data are generally collected by means of a variety of experimental procedures: videotaping everyday actions, inducing emotion by showing slides or movies and recording facial movements at the same time. In all cases, what seems really important in order to obtain a meaningful sample of spontaneous behavior is that the subject must be unaware of being observed.

Studies on normal subjects. Studies on normal subjects pointed to a predominantly symmetrical response of the two hemifaces, or, when asymmetries were found, the biases to the left or to the right were evenly distributed (Lynn and Lynn, 1938, 1943; Ekman et al., 1981). However only smiles were considered in these studies.

In another more ecological kind of research, by observing unaware people in restaurants or during conversation in the laboratory, Moscovitch and Olds (1982) found that most facial actions were bilateral; however, when the face moved in a non-symmetrical way (about 20% of cases), the left side moved more vivaciously than the right. Dopson et al. (1984) trained the subjects to generate a particular mood and then to verbally describe it: under these conditions they observed a bias for the left side of the face. That is, the left chimeric faces of their subjects appeared more expressive than the

right ones to naive judges. In both these studies facial expressions were measured while subject were speaking. The possibility has been raised that in this case, facial expressions may serve as conversational signals rather than true expressions of emotion (Ekman et al., 1981).

Inducing emotional expressions by showing pleasant and unpleasant slides, Borod et al. (1983) found a left-facedness effect, although their evidence was particularly clear for negative expressions and it was found for pleasant stimuli only in men, but not in women.

Recording EMG responses from different facial muscles, Schwartz et al. (1979) stressed left hemiface mobility in expressing negative emotions while the opposite was found for movement related to smiles.

The studies on positive emotions do not always point to an asymmetric expression. This finding is not perhaps surprising in the light of the above considerations concerning the use of the smile for both social and emotional communication. On the other hand, most of the evidence points to a left facedness for a variety of 'negative' emotions such as disgust, fear, anger, etc. Although it is not always convincing how some inducing situations can really elicit spontaneous behaviors (Dopson et al., 1984) or how the recording through electrodes can maintain the experimental setting as a spontaneous one (Schwartz et al., 1979), the variety of conditions in which these phenomena were observed requires an appropriate explanation (see conclusive remarks).

Studies on brain-damaged patients. The information collected on brain-damaged patients does not show a very coherent picture.

Ross and Mesulam (1979) described two right brain-damaged patients as being inexpressive in their faces; interestingly, they were showing a dissociation between their intact emotional feeling and the severely impaired ability to produce a corresponding facial expression. This inability to use facial expressiveness has not been reported in the case of aphasic patients (Buck and Duffy, 1980; Katz et al., 1978). More systematic research on

brain-damaged responses to emotion-inducing stimuli was performed by Buck and Duffy (1980) and
Borod et al. (1985). In both cases the patients were
presented with slides of pleasant, unpleasant and
neutral situations and their facial behaviors were
recorded and evaluated according to the intensity
of their expressions. Right brain-damaged patients
were judged to be less expressive. Buck and Duffy
(1980) also included a group of Parkinsonians,
who were the least expressive of all four groups of
patients.

In addition Borod et al. (1985) partialled out a
subsample of patients with frontal lobe lesions,
and found a particularly low expressiveness in patients with right frontal lobe involvement.

In contrast with these findings, Kolb and Milner
(1981b) evaluated the facial responses given by
their patients during the neuropsychological testing: no hemispheric group was found to be less expressive, while frontal lobe patients of both sides
showed less mobility and expressiveness in their
faces. Unfortunately, in combining expressions
such as smiles, different brow movements, and
others (e.g., yawns) Kolb and Milner (1981b) failed
to distinguish between facial movements with an
emotional meaning and facial movements presumably serving as conversational signals (cf. Ekman,
1979). This distinction is important both
qualitatively and quantitatively. In fact, these two
types of facial action may be controlled by different mechanisms (Ekman, 1979); moreover, conversational signals are the most frequent expressions in interpersonal interaction. In this respect, it
might be important to note that in the same study
the patients with left frontal lobe removals were
less talkative (Kolb and Taylor, 1981).

On a different line of thinking, Sackeim et al.
(1982) reviewed a large body of literature suggesting that predominantly right brain damage and
left epileptic focuses were more likely to produce
pathological laughing; pathological crying was
more often produced by specular lesions and epileptic focuses.

These pathological symptoms are certainly informative about the mechanisms of carrying out

patterns of facial movements, but not about emotions, since they do not necessarily correspond
with the emotional feelings (Poeck, 1985). In spite
of these disssociations Sackeim et al. (1982) suggested that these findings supported the hypothesis
of two different roles played by the two hemispheres in controlling emotional experience for
negative and positive emotions. Also it should be
observed that Strauss, Wada and Losaka (1983)
made direct observations of pathological outbursts
of laughing and crying during epiletic crisis but did
not confirm the findings of Sackeim et al. (1982).

In the study by Mammucari et al. (1988) a large
population of brain-damaged patients with focal
lesions in either hemisphere was examined with a
control group. The induction of emotions consisted of the projection of positive and negative
movies; the patients' performances were scored
with the Ekman and Friesen's (1978) Facial Action
Coding System, as well as with the subjective scale
of intensity of expression previously used by Buck
and Duffy (1980) and by Borod et al. (1985). In
spite of the variety of indexes used to score facial
responses, no difference emerged between the left
and right hemispheric groups, or between different
locations of the lesions on either side of the brain,
either for positive or for negative emotional situations.

However, in spite of the quantitative and qualitative similarities of the two hemispheric groups in
producing facial emotional expressions and with a
good verbal description of the emotional meaning
of the presented scenes, control and left brain-
damaged patients showed, in association with, or
independently from, facial expressions, some aversive movements of the eyes or the head when
presented with a very distressing stimulus. This
behavior was extremely infrequent in right brain-
damaged patients.

In a different study, in which the same sample of
subjects was examined, it was found that autonomic responses (heart rate and skin conductance
responses) elicited by means of inducing movies
were clearly reduced in right brain-damaged patients for the emotional stimuli (Zoccolotti et al.,

1986; Caltagirone et al., 1989). In contrast, left brain-damaged patients exhibited autonomic responses very similar to the control group. This evidence confirmed previous studies pointing to a reduction of autonomic concomitants in the right brain-damaged group (Heilman et al., 1978; Morrow et al., 1981; Zoccolotti et al., 1982).

Moreover, in the above-mentioned study (Caltagirone et al., 1989) it emerged that, in accordance with the facial feed-back hypothesis, the occurrence of facial emotional expression was coupled in left brain-damaged and control patients with a more intense reactivity as measured by heart rate modifications. Furthermore the occurrence of aversive reactions was inversely correlated with the cardiac parameter and that again only in the left brain-damaged and control groups. This latter finding is in agreement with earlier systematic studies on the role of avoidance reactions in modulating the autonomic response to negative stimuli (Malcuit, 1973; Sandman, 1975). In other terms, right brain-damaged patients showed an impairment in the relationship between autonomic reactivity and facial expressions of emotions.

Pizzamiglio and Mammucari (1989), considering this pattern of data, speculated that, while the control of facial emotional expressiveness is not lateralized, the right hemisphere might be responsible for a differential involvement of the patients with the 'emotional' meaning of the stimuli, as documented by the absence of averting movements and the modifications of autonomic responses.

Concluding remarks

Neural substrates of spontaneous facial expression of emotion
The distinction made in the introduction between voluntary and involuntary facial movements conveying emotional facial information is clearly supported by the neurological literature (Rinn, 1984). However, this review indicates that it is still difficult to provide a precise definition of the neural systems involved in these two processes.

By focusing attention on spontaneous emotional expression some indications can be derived from the contribution of brain pathology. Lesions restricted to the fronto-limbic system (Damasio and Van Hoesen, 1983) or to the basal ganglia (Mayeux, 1983) produce disorders of spontaneous facial expression. These deficits are largely independent of the side of the lesion. Involuntary release of laughing or crying represents another kind of pathology related to spontaneous facial activity. The disorder may derive from lesions very different in their aetiology and level of nervous system involvement. In fact, these patterns of facial movements can be produced as a consequence of vascular lesions affecting various cortical or subcortical areas disconnecting those regions from the motor nuclei of the pons, as is the case of pseudo-bulbar palsy (Poeck, 1985); alternatively, they can be associated with several cortical or subcortical epileptic foci activating or not many deep structures, as in the case of gelastic epilepsy (Myslobodsky, 1983). The possible role of lateralization in the case of this disorder is controversial. Sackeim et al. (1982) claimed a differential association of emotional outbursts of laughing and crying, with right and left hemispheric lesions, respectively. However, several considerations limit the generality of this conclusion. An analysis of Sackeim et al.'s data reveals that the association with the side of the lesion strongly depended on the sex variable. Moreover, it has been observed that the more frequent left localization of the epileptic foci causing irrepressible laughing (Moslobodsky, 1983; Sackeim et al., 1982) cannot be easily compared with the very infrequent epileptic outbursts of crying (Feyereisen, 1986). Finally, recent systematic observations failed to confirm different emotional reactions according to the lateralization of the epileptic focus (Strauss et al., 1983). Similar inconsistent results have been observed in studies examining the role of unilateral cortical lesions. Some studies found that the spontaneous expression of emotion was reduced after right hemispheric lesion (Ross and Mesulam, 1979; Buck and Duffy, 1980; Borod et al., 1985). However, these conclusions were based on very limited samples of patients; furthermore they were not replicated by other studies (Kolb and Milner, 1981b; Mammucari et al., 1988). Similar inconsistent patterns of asymmetry have been found in studies on normal subjects (Lynn and Lynn, 1938, 1943; Ekman et al., 1981; Moscovitch and Olds, 1982; Borod et al., 1983; Dopson et al., 1984).

Overall these findings provide a very incomplete description of the neural pathways responsible for the control of spontaneous facial expression. As for the role of the two cerebral hemispheres, it seems important to restate the question specifically addressed in this paper. While the literature on emotions was first moved by clinical observations of differential mood changes induced either by pharmacological inactivations or by unilateral lesions (see Gainotti for a review, 1989), the question we are dealing with does not concern the relative involvement of one or the other hemisphere with the emotional experience in a general sense. Rather, one is forced to conclude that there is a lack of convincing evidence concerning hemispheric superiority in controlling the 'machinery' for expressing an emotional experience through the face. This operational definition obviously goes beyond any theoretical postulate for interpreting the emotional experience as being causally dependent upon feedback from the face (see Feyereisen, 1986).

Neural substrates of voluntary facial expression of emotion

As for the control of intentional emotional movements of the face the first problem is whether they are regulated in the same way as other classes of non-emotional facial movements. It has been established that the execution, on verbal command or on imitation, of 'oral movements', such as those clinically used to test oral apraxia ('put out your tongue', 'bite your teeth', 'cough', 'whistle', etc.) is impaired in patients with left frontal lesions. This finding is similar to what is observed for intentional movements of the upper limbs (e.g., De Renzi et al., 1968). While the cortico-bulbar pathway represents the neural efferent system con-

trolling all voluntary facial movements, there is evidence indicating that the mimic movements of the face represent a particular class of actions which do not share the same neural control as the above-described oral movements. Thus, oral apraxia has been found to be unrelated to the ability to pose emotional expressions (Borod et al., 1988; Damasio and Van Hoesen, 1983; Caltagirone et al., 1989) or to imitate isolated mimic movements (Pizzamiglio et al., 1987). In summarizing these results, Pizzamiglio et al. (1987) have suggested that the control unit for mimic facial movements may have a multiple representation across the cortex, similar to what has been suggested for central axial and extrinsic eye movements by Geschwind (1975).

Much of the research on the voluntary control of facial expression has focused on evaluating the possible role of the two hemispheres in modulating this behavior. However, the available data appear contradictory and do not easily fit a unitary interpretation. In trying to understand these findings, it is important that differences in the observed asymmetry patterns seem to depend on the type of scoring technique used (subjective vs. objective) and the type of population studied (normal subjects vs. brain-damaged patients). Thus, when intentional facial movements without emotional value were studied in normal subjects by means of subjective estimates of expressiveness (Campbell, 1982; Chaurasia and Goswami, 1975; Koff et al., 1981; Borod et al., 1983; Alford, 1983) movements produced by the left hemiface were judged as more intense or better performed. However, in studies in which an objective scoring technique (FACS) was used, the imitation of facial movements performed by young adults did not reveal any systematic asymmetry toward either side of the face (Hager and Ekman, 1985). Furthermore, studies comparing patients with left or right lesions failed to observe deficits in the production of single non-emotional facial movements (Kolb and Milner, 1981a; Pizzamiglio et al., 1987).

A similar contradictory picture arises in the case of posed expressions of emotions. In some studies, in which normal subjects were examined under different experimental paradigms based on subjective judgements, the left hemiface was judged as more expressive particularly in the case of negative emotions (Sackeim et al., 1978; Borod and Caron, 1980; Campbell, 1978; Borod et al., 1981, 1983). For positive expressions, results vary widely, with some studies finding left-facedness (e.g., Campbell, 1978), and some no laterality (e.g., Sackeim et al., 1978). Another unexplained feature of these results is their frequent variation with the sex of the poser (Borod et al., 1983). As for the case of non-emotional facial movements, asymmetries are not found when an objective scoring technique of facial asymmetry is used in either controls or unilateral brain-damaged patients (Caltagirone et al., 1989).

In summary, asymmetries have been most often reported in the studies based on subjective estimates of differences in the intensity of movements between the two halves of the face in normal subjects. It has been proposed that these effects indicate a specific role of the right cerebral hemisphere in controlling this behavior (e.g., Borod et al., 1983; Sackeim and Gur, 1983). However, inconsistent with this interpretation is the much less clear-cut evidence of lateral asymmetry of the studies using objective scoring techniques or comparing populations of patients with left or right unilateral brain damage. Additional difficulty for a cerebral hemispheric interpretation arises from the characteristics of the neural pathways involved. Neuroanatomical evidence indicates that the cortico-bulbar pathway which controls voluntary facial movements is strictly contralateral only for the lower and more mobile face (Rinn, 1984). Therefore, earlier in this paper we have suggested that expectations about possible asymmetries of voluntary expressions should be biased particularly toward this region of the face. However, when present, left facedness effects have been observed both for movements involving the upper face and for movements of the lower face (e.g., Ladavas, 1982). In general, these effects seem to be largely non-specific: they appear both

in the case of active facial movements and in the case of a relaxed face (e.g., Campbell, 1978); they are typically present for both right-handers and left-handers (e.g., Campbell, 1986), for both emotional and non-emotional expressions (e.g., Borod and Caron, 1980; Borod and Koff, 1983), and for both posed and spontaneous facial expressions (Borod et al., 1983; Dopson et al., 1984). Finally, it may be observed that facedness seems to follow an ontogenic development, the effect emerging only around 11 years of age (Ladavas, 1982). This finding is in clear contrast with the fact that virtually all other laterality effects are present in all testable age groups and do not show any development trend (for a review, see Young, 1982). All these features are inconsistent with the hypothesis of a specific involvement of the right hemisphere in the production of facial expressions of emotion.

Alternatively, it has been proposed that all facial asymmetries are related to hemispheric specialization of emotion (Sackeim and Gur, 1983); for example, according to this hypothesis, the left face would be more mobile because of the greater use due to the right hemispheric control of (mainly) negative emotions. A similar interpretation is offered for the expressive asymmetries of the face at rest (e.g., Wolff, 1933). Such a broad hypothesis may prove difficult to test. Furthermore, it should be stressed once again that a major assumption of Sackeim and Gur (1983) is the presence of an asymmetrical neural control of spontaneous facial expression. As we have seen, the present neuroanatomical knowledge is inconsistent with this view.

Issues still deserving clarification

In spite of these considerations, one might still observe that the data gathered with subjective scoring techniques (particularly that of chimeric faces) on normal subjects repeatedly point to asymmetries of facial expressions which demand some explanation. Stated in this way, the literature presents some support for the idea that the left hemiface is more expressive than the right. Overall, this 'facedness' effect is present for both emotional and non-emotional facial movements and is somewhat stronger for posed than spontaneous emotional expressions (see Campbell, 1986). As we have seen, the lack of confirmatory data from the studies with pathological populations does not provide solid ground for interpreting observed facial asymmetries as related to the activity of a central, specialized subsystem in either hemisphere.

Several alternative hypotheses have been proposed, none of which at the present time seems able to explain all the published findings. The fact that such a hypothesis should be able to explain why facedness effects vary with the nature (subjective-objective) of the scoring technique seems particularly critical.

An initial hypothesis is that *facedness is a perceptual phenomenon of the observer* rather than an expressor asymmetry. In particular, it has been proposed that the left hemiface may erroneously appear more expressive because of a smaller size than the right hemiface (Nelson and Horowitz, 1980). This interpretation would comply with the above-described requirement; in fact, it seems reasonable that a subjective evaluation is much more prone to such a bias than a scoring in which each facial action unit is compared with itself across time regardless of the relative size of the left or the right muscles. Also, this interpretation would be consistent with the absence of an emotional – non-emotional differentiation in the observed asymmetries. However, apart from the reliability of the morphological asymmetries in size (see Sackeim, 1985), most studies have failed to observe a direct correlation between these asymmetries and facedness effects (Koff et al., 1981; Sackeim and Gur, 1980; Sackeim et al., 1984).

This possibility has been recently re-examined by Vannucci et al. (1989), who suggested that morphological influence on the left facedness effects in chimeric stimuli can only be evaluated in faces for which no clear asymmetry of movement is present. When the totality of their chimeric stimuli was considered, a left face superiority in expressiveness was present, independent of differences in size between the two hemifaces. Scoring facial asym-

metries according to the FACS, about 25% of faces showed clear asymmetries of movement. When only the stimuli considered symmetrical according to FACS were taken into account, the overall effect of left facedness was still present. However, the pattern of results varied for the different expressions: angry and disgusted expressions were no longer asymmetrical; also, surprised and sad expressions were judged more expressive the smaller the left hemiface of the poser, a finding consistent with the hypothesis that symmetrical movements distributed on a smaller area would appear more intense (Nelson and Horowitz, 1980). An opposite tendency was present in the case of happy expressions, indicating that a smile is perceived as more expressive if it appears over a larger facial area. Overall, these findings suggest that some portion of the facedness effects in chimeric stimuli may be due to static, not dynamic, asymmetries in the face. Also, they raise the possibility that at least some of the differences observed between positive and negative expressions may be related to morphological not hemispheric asymmetries. More research is needed in this area to evaluate the possibility that morphological factors other than hemifacial size may contribute to the determination of left facedness effects.

Sackeim and Gur (1983) have suggested that a different interpreter bias might be at work in the case of studies evaluating asymmetries on full faces. Since, as we have seen, subjects seem to rely particularly on facial features appearing on the left hemifield (Gilbert and Bakan, 1973), they suggested that the greater expressivity of the left face may be underestimated by the judges since the left hemiface of the poser stimulates mainly the right hemifield of the observer. The bias may be present in the case of studies in which an overall subjective comparison of the two hemifaces is requested (e.g., Borod et al., 1983; Moscovitch and Olds, 1982). On the other hand, it seems unlikely that an interpreter bias can affect objective scoring such as FACS since this requires repetitive analytical viewing of facial actions, separately for each side of the face (e.g., Hager and Ekman, 1985; Ekman et al., 1981). However, opposite to Sackeim and Gur's (1983) suggestion, an overall effect of left facedness is observed in the former but not in the latter studies.

Another possibility to be considered is that *facedness effects in normals are due to asymmetries in the poser but are not,* or are only indirectly, *related to hemispheric lateralization.* Campbell (1982, 1986) has speculated that the two hemifaces may be different in muscle tone, thereby producing asymmetrical baselines for the movements to be judged. Indeed, indirect support for this hypothesis comes from the presence of facial asymmetries in the resting face; for example, left composites of the face appear sadder than right composites (Campbell, 1978). Campbell (1982, 1986) interprets this asymmetry by suggesting that the left hemiface might be more relaxed than the right. It would be interesting to evaluate whether or not these asymmetries at rest are related to the frequently observed asymmetries in size between the two hemifaces.

An additional explanation hypothesizes that *the cognitive processes, preliminary to the encoding of facial expression, may be lateralized to the right hemisphere and influence the neural system dealing with the contralateral facial movements.* The nature of such preliminary processes might differ. Campbell (1986) suggests that, in order to produce a facial expression, one might centrally activate a mental image, which guides the encoding of facial movements. It has been proposed that the right hemisphere is better equipped for such a process (see Erhlichman and Bonet, 1983, for a thorough discussion of this hypothesis). Alternatively, it can be speculated that an emotionally inducing stimulus, although cognitively understood by both hemispheres, does not equally produce an appropriate emotional activation in one or the other side of the brain. The absence of averting responses and of the expected autonomic changes in the right brain-damaged patients would support this interpretation (Caltagirone et al., 1989; Mammucari et al., 1988).

Following Kinsbourne's (1970) model of hemispheric lateralization one may speculate that the activation of these unilateral processors will spread more strongly to the neural systems controlling face movements in the same (right) hemisphere. According to this reasoning, asymmetrical expression would not be the result of asymmetrical neural control of the face; rather, symmetrical systems controlling facial movements would be differentially influenced by other cortical areas active in the cognitive processes preliminary to the production of facial expression. This interpretation is consistent with the findings of clearer facial asymmetries in normals than in unilateral brain-damaged patients; in fact, according to Kinsbourne's hypothesis, unilateral cortical lesions, while affecting other affective behaviours, should leave facial behavior unimpaired.

Certainly none of these speculations can account for all the data observed both in normal and in brain-damaged subjects. A better understanding of this issue requires further research. In particular, in the case of normal subjects it might prove particularly useful to evaluate facial asymmetries by applying different scoring techniques on the same stimuli. Information on different expressive modalities collected on the same patients in the case of brain pathology would also be informative. As a final methodological point, we think that intensive studies of single cases, rather than group studies, may be particularly sensitive for dissociating different mechanisms underlying emotional expressions.

References

Alford RD: Sex differences in lateral facial facility; the effects of habitual functional concealment. *Neuropsychologia: 21,* 567 – 570, 1983.

Amyes EW, Nielsen JM: Clinicopathologic study of vascular lesion of the anterior cingulate region. *Bull. Los Ang. Neurol. Soc.: 20,* 112 – 130, 1955.

Bennet HL, Delmonico RL, Bond CF: Expressive and perceptual asymmetries of the resting face. *Neuropsychologia: 25,* 681 – 687, 1987.

Benton AL: The neuropsychology of facial recognition. *Am. Psychol.: 35,* 176 – 186, 1980.

Borod J, Caron HS: Facedness and emotion in relation to

lateral dominance, sex, and expression type. *Neuropsychologia: 18,* 237–241, 1980.

Borod J, Caron HS, Koff E: Asymmetry in positive and negative facial expressions: sex differences. *Neuropsychologia: 19,* 819–824, 1981.

Borod J, Koff E: Hemiface mobility and facial expression asymmetry. *Cortex: 19,* 327–332, 1983.

Borod J, Koff E, White B: Facial asymmetry in posed and spontaneous expressions of emotion. *Brain Cognition: 2,* 165–175, 1983.

Borod JC, Koff E, Perlman Lorch M, Nicholas M: Channels of emotional expression in patients with unilateral brain damage. *Arch. Neurol.: 42,* 345–348, 1985.

Borod JC, Koff E, Perlman Lorch M, Nicholas M: The expression and perception of facial emotion in brain-damaged patients. *Neuropsychologia: 24,* 169–180, 1986.

Borod JC, Koff E, Perlman Lorch M, Nicholas M: Emotional and non-emotional facial behavior in patients with unilateral brain damage. *J. Neurol. Neurosurg. Psychiatry: 51,* 826–832, 1988.

Braun MJ, Baribeau JMC, Ethier M, Guerette R, Proulx R: Emotional facial expressive and discriminative performance and lateralization in normal young adults. *Cortex: 24,* 77–90, 1988.

Brodal A: *Neurological Anatomy.* New York: Oxford Press, 1981.

Bruyer R: Asymmetry of facial expression in brain damaged subjects. *Neuropsychologia: 19,* 615–624, 1981.

Buck R, Duffy R: Nonverbal communication of affect in brain damaged patients. *Cortex: 16,* 351–362, 1980.

Burke PH: Stereophotogrammatic measurement of normal facial asymmetry in children. *Hum. Biol.: 43,* 536–548, 1971.

Cacioppo, JT, Petty RE, Losch ME, Kim H: Electromyografic activity over facial muscle regions can differentiate the valence and intensity of affective reactions. *J. Pers. Soc. Psychol.: 50,* 260–268, 1986.

Caltagirone C, Ekman P, Friesen W, Gainotti G, Mammucari A, Pizzamiglio L, Zoccolotti P: Posed emotional expression in brain damaged patients. *Cortex:* in press, 1989.

Caltagirone C, Zoccolotti P, Originale G, Daniele A, Mammucari A: Autonomic reactivity and facial expression of emotion in brain damaged patients. In Gainotti G, Caltagirone C (Editors), *Emotion and the Dual Brain.* New York: Springer Verlag, 1989.

Campbell R: Asymmetries in interpreting and expressing a posed facial expression. *Cortex: 14,* 327–342, 1978.

Campbell R: Asymmetries in moving faces. *Br. J. Psychol.: 73,* 95–103, 1982.

Campbell R: Asymmetries of facial action: some facts and fancies of normal face movements. In Bruyer R (Editor), *The Neuropsychology of Face Perception and Facial Expression.* Hillsdale: Erlbaum L., Ch. II, pp. 247–267, 1986.

Carey S, Diamond R: From piecemeal to configurational representation of faces. *Science: 195,* 312–314, 1977.

Chaurasia BD, Goswami HK: Functional asymmetry in the face. *Acta Anatom.: 91,* 154–160, 1975.

Crosby EC, Humphrey T, Lauer EW: *Correlative Anatomy of the Nervous System.* New York: Macmillan, 1962.

Damasio AR, Van Hoesen GW: Emotion disturbances associated with focal lesions of the limbic frontal lobe. In Heilman K, Satz P (Editors), *Neuropsychology of Human Emotion.* New York: The Guilford Press, Ch. 4, pp. 85–110, 1983.

Darwin C: *The Expression of the Emotions in Man and Animals.* Chicago & London: The University of Chicago Press, 1965.

De Renzi E, Pieczuro A, Vignolo LA: Ideational apraxia: a quantitative study. *Neuropsychologia: 6,* 41–52, 1968.

Dopson WG, Beckwith BE, Tucker DM, Bullard-Bates, PC: Asymmetry of facial expression in spontaneous emotion. *Cortex: 20,* 243–251, 1984.

Ehrlichman H, Bonet J: Right hemisphere specialization for mental imagery: a review of the evidence. *Brain Cognition: 2,* 55–76, 1983.

Ekman P: Universal and cultural differences in the facial expressions of emotion. In Cole JK (Editor), *Nebraska Symposium on Motivation.* Lincoln: University of Nebraska Press, Ch. 19, pp. 207–283, 1971.

Ekman P: Asymmetry in facial expression. *Science: 209,* 833–834, 1980.

Ekman P, Friesen WV: *Pictures of Facial Affect.* Palo Alto, CA: Consulting Psychologist Press, 1975a.

Ekman P, Friesen WV: *Unmasking the Face.* Englewood Cliffs, NJ: Prentice-Hall, 1975b.

Ekman P, Friesen WV: *Facial Action Coding System.* Palo Alto, CA: Consulting Psychologists Press, 1978.

Ekman P, Roper G, Hager JC: Deliberate facial movement. *Child Dev.: 51,* 886–891, 1980.

Ekman P, Hager JC, Friesen WV: The symmetry of emotional and deliberate facial actions. *Psychophysiology: 18,* 101–106, 1981.

Englis B, Vaughan K, Lanzetta JT: Conditioning of counter-empathetic emotional responses. *J. Exp. Soc. Psychol.: 18,* 375–391, 1982.

Etcoff NL: The neuropsychology of emotional expression. In Goldstein G, Tarter E (Editors), *Advances in Clinical Neuropsychology.* New York: Plenum, 1986.

Feyereisen P: Production and comprehension of emotional facial expression in brain-damaged subjects. In Bruyer R (Editor), *The Neuropsychology of Face Perception and Facial Expression.* Hillsdale, NJ: Erlbaum L., Ch. 10, pp. 221–245, 1986.

Figalova P: Asymmetry of the face. *Anthropologie: 7,* 31–34, 1969.

Fridlund A, Schwartz G, Fowler S: Pattern recognition of self-reported emotional state from multiple-site facial EMG activity during affective imagery. *Psychophysiology: 21,* 622–636, 1984.

Gainotti G: Reactions 'catastrophiques' et manifestations d'indifférence au cours des atteintes cerebrales. *Neuropsychologia: 7,* 195–204, 1969.

Gainotti G: Emotional behavior and hemispheric side of the lesion. *Cortex: 8,* 41–55, 1972.

Gainotti G: Disorders of emotions and affect in patients with unilateral brain damage. In Boller F, Grafman J (Editors), *Handbook of Neuropsychology, Vol. 3.* Amsterdam: Elsevier, Ch. 16 of this volume, 1989.

Geschwind N: The apraxias: neural mechanisms of disorders of learned movements. *Am. Sci.: 63,* 188–195, 1975.

Gilbert C, and Bakan P: Visual asymmetry in perception of faces. *Neuropsychologia: 11*, 355 – 362, 1973.

Grega DM, Sackeim HA, Sanchez E, Cohen BH, Hough S: Perceiver bias in the processing of human faces: neuropsychological mechanisms. *Cortex: 24*, 91 – 117, 1988.

Hager JC, Ekman P: The asymmetry of facial actions is inconsistent with models of hemispheric specialization. *Psychophysiology: 23*, 307 – 318, 1985.

Heilman KM, Schwartz HD, Watson RT: Hypoarousal in patients with neglect and emotional indifference. *Neurology: 28*, 229 – 232, 1978.

Heller W, Levy J: Perception and expression of emotion in right handers and left handers. *Neuropsychologia: 19*, 263 – 272, 1981.

Holstege G, Kuypers GHJM, Dekker JJ: The organization of bulbar fibre connections to the trigeminal facial and hypoglossal motor nuclei. *Brain: 100*, 265 – 286, 1977.

Kahn FA: On facial expression. In: *Clinical Neurosurgery, Proceedings of the Congress of Neurological Surgeons.* Florida, 1964. Baltimore, MD: Williams and Wilkins, 1966.

Katz RC, LaPointe LL, Markel NN: Coverbal behavior and aphasic speakers. In Brookshire RH (Editor), *Clinical Aphasiology. Proceedings of the conference.* Minneapolis: BRK Publishers, pp. 164 – 173, 1978.

Kinsbourne MA: A model for the mechanism of unilateral neglect of space. *Trans. Am. Neurol. Assoc.: 95*, 143 – 146, 1970.

Kinsbourne MA, Bemporad B: Lateralization of emotion: a model and the evidence. In Fox and Davidson (Editor), *Psychobiology of Affect.* Erlbaum Press: Hillsdale, 1985.

Koff E, Borod J, White B: Asymmetries for hemiface size and mobility. *Neuropsychologia: 19*, 825 – 830, 1981.

Koff E, Borod J, Strauss E: Development of hemiface size asymmetry. *Cortex: 21*, 153 – 156, 1985.

Kolb B, Milner B: Performance of complex arm and facial movements after focal brain lesions. *Neuropsychologia: 19*, 491 – 503, 1981a.

Kolb B, Milner B: Observations of spontaneous facial expression after cerebral excisions and after intracarotid injection of sodium amytal. *Neuropsychologia: 19*, 505 – 514, 1981b.

Kolb B, Taylor L: Affective behavior in patients with localized cortical excisions: role of lesion site and side. *Science: 214*, 89 – 91, 1981.

Kolb B, Milner B, Taylor L: Perception of faces by patients with localized cortical excisions. *Can. J. Psychol.: 37*, 8 – 18, 1983.

Kuypers MGJM: Corticobulbar connexions to the pons and lower brain-stem in man. *Brain: 81*, 364 – 388, 1958.

Izard CE, Dougherty LM: Two complementary systems for measuring facial expressions in infants and children. In Izard CE (Editor), *Measuring Emotions in Infants and Children.* Cambridge, England: Cambridge University Press, 1982.

Ladavas E: The development of facedness. *Cortex: 18*, 535 – 545, 1982.

Landis T, Graves R: Mouth asymmetry variation with task in aphasia. Lisbon: Communication at the INS Meeting, 1983.

Lanzetta JT, McHugo GJ: Facial expressive and psychophysiological correlates of emotion. In Gainotti G, Caltagirone C (Editors), *Emotion and the Dual Brain.* New York: Springer Verlag, 1989.

Laplane D, Talairach J, Meininger V, Bancaud J, Orgogozo JM: Clinical consequences of corticectomies involving the supplementary motor area in man. *J. Neurol. Sci.: 34*, 301 – 314, 1977.

Lawson NC: Inverted writing in right and left-handers in relation to lateralization of face recognition. *Cortex: 14*, 207 – 211, 1978.

Le Beau J: The cingular and precingular areas in psychosurgery (agitated behavior, obsessive compulsive states, epilepsy). *Acta Psychiatr. Neurol. Scand.: 27*, 305 – 316, 1952.

Levy J, Heller W, Banich MT, Burton LA: Asymmetry of perception in free viewing of chimeric faces. *Brain Cognition: 2*, 404 – 419, 1983.

Lynn JG, Lynn DR: Face-hand laterality in relation to personality. *J. Abnorm. Soc. Psychol.: 33*, 291 – 322, 1938.

Lynn JG, Lynn DR: Smile and hand dominance in relation to basic modes adaptation. *J. Abnorm. Soc. Psychol.: 38*, 250 – 276, 1943.

Malcuit G: Cardiac responses in aversive situation with and without avoidance possibility. *Psychophysiology: 10*, 295 – 306, 1973.

Mammucari A, Caltagirone C, Ekman P, Friesen W, Gainotti G, Pizzamiglio L, Zoccolotti P: Spontaneous facial expression of emotion in brain damaged patients. *Cortex: 24*, 521 – 533, 1988.

Mardsen CD: Blepharospasm-oromandibular dystonia syndrome (Brueghel's syndrome). A variant of adult-onset torsion dystonia? *J. Neurol. Neurosurg. Psychiatry: 39*, 1204 – 1209, 1976.

Mayeux R: Emotional changes associated with basal ganglia disorders. In Heilman K, Satz P (Editors), *Neuropsychology of Human Emotion.* New York: The Guilford Press, Ch. 6, pp. 141 – 164, 1983.

Mislobodsky MS (Editor): Epileptic laughter. In *Hemisyndromes: Psychobiology, Neurology, Psychiatry.* New York: Academic Press, pp. 239 – 263, 1983.

Morrow L, Vrtunski B, Kim Y, Boller F: Arousal responses to emotional stimuli and laterality of lesion. *Neuropsychologia: 19*, 65 – 71, 1981.

Moscovitch M, Olds J: Asymmetries in spontaneous facial expressions and their possible relation to hemispheric specialization. *Neuropsychologia: 20*, 71 – 81, 1982.

Nelson CA, Horowitz FD: Asymmetry in facial expression. (Letter) *Science: 209*, 834, 1980.

Pizzamiglio L, Mammucari A: Disorders of emotional facial expressions in brain damaged patients. In Gainotti G, Caltagirone C (Editors), *Emotion and the Dual Brain.* New York: Springer Verlag, 1989.

Pizzamiglio L, Caltagirone C, Mammucari A, Ekman P, Friesen WV: Imitation of facial movements in brain damaged patients. *Cortex: 23*, 207 – 221, 1987.

Poeck K: Pathophysiology of emotional disorders associated with brain damage. In Vinken PJ, Bruyn GW (Editors), *Handbook of Clinical Neurology, Vol. 3.* New York: Elsevier, Ch. 20, pp. 343 – 367, 1969.

Poeck K: Pathological laughter and crying. In Fredericks JAM (Editor), *Handbook of Clinical Neurology, Vol. 1, 45.* New York: Elsevier, Ch. 16, pp. 219 – 225, 1985.

Rinn WE: The neuropsychology of facial expression: a review of the neurological and psychological mechanisms for producing facial expressions. *Psychol. Bull.: 95,* 52 – 77, 1984.

Ross ED, Mesulam M-M: Dominant language functions of the right hemisphere? Prosody and emotional gesturing. *Arch. Neurol.: 36,* 144 – 148, 1979.

Rubin DA, Rubin RT: Differences in facial asymmetry between left and right-handed children. *Neuropsychologia: 16,* 473 – 481, 1980.

Sackeim HA: Morphological asymmetry of the face: a review. *Brain Cognition: 4,* 296 – 312, 1985.

Sackeim HA, Gur R: Lateral asymmetry in intensity of emotional expression. *Neuropsychologia: 16,* 473 – 481, 1978.

Sackeim HA, Gur R: Asymmetry in facial expression. (Letter) *Science: 209,* 834 – 835, 1980.

Sackeim HA, Gur R: Facial asymmetry and the communication of emotion. In Cacioppo JT, Petty RE, Shapiro D (Editors), *Social Psychophysiology. A Sourcebook.* New York: The Guilford Press, 1983.

Sackeim HA, Gur R, Saucy MC: Emotions are expressed more intensely on the left side of the face. *Science: 202,* 434 – 436, 1978.

Sackeim HA, Greenberg MS, Weiman AL, Gur RC, Hungerbuhler JP, Geschwind N: Hemispheric asymmetry in the expression of positive and negative emotions: neurologic evidence. *Arch. Neurol.: 39,* 210 – 218, 1982.

Sackeim HA, Weiman AL, Forman BD: Asymmetry of the face at rest: size, area and emotional expression. *Cortex: 20,* 165 – 178, 1984.

Sandman C: Physiological responses during escape and non escape from stress in field independent and field dependent subjects. *Biol. Psychol.: 2,* 205 – 216, 1975.

Schwartz GE: Psychophysiological patterning and emotion revisited: a systems prospective. In Izard C (Editor), *Measuring Emotion in Infants and Children.* Cambridge, England: Cambridge University Press, 1982.

Schwartz GE, Ahern GL, Brown SL: Lateralized facial muscle response to positive and negative emotional stimuli. *Psychophysiology: 16,* 561 – 571, 1979.

Smith C, McHugo G, Lanzetta J: The facial muscle patterning of posed and imagery-induced expressions of emotion by expressive and non-expressive posers. *Motiv. Emotion: 10,* 133 – 157, 1986.

Spitz RA: *The First Year of Life. A Psychoanalytic Study of Normal and Deviant Development of Direct Relation.* New York: International Universities Press, 1965.

Strauss E, Wada J, Losaka B: Spontaneous facial expressions occurring at the onset of focal seizure activity. *Arch. Neurol.: 40,* 545 – 547, 1983.

Talairach J, Bancaud J, Geier S, Bordas-Ferrer M, Bonis A, Szikla G, Rusu M: The cingulate gyrus and human behaviour. *Electroencephalogr. Clin. Neurophysiol.: 34,* 45 – 52, 1973.

Vannucci S, Zoccolotti P, Mammucari A: Asymmetries in expressivity and similarity judgements of emotional facial expressions: the effect of writing posture and hemiface size of the poser. Technical Report, Dept. of Psychology, University of Rome, 1989.

Wolff W: The experimental study of forms of expression. *Charact. Pers.: 2,* 168 – 176, 1933.

Young AW: Asymmetry of cerebral hemispheric function development. In Dickerson JWT, McGurk H (Editors), *Brain and Behavioural Development,* Glasgow: Blackie, pp. 168 – 202, 1982.

Zoccolotti P, Scabini D, Violani C: Electrodermal responses in patients with unilateral brain damage. *J. Clin. Neuropsychol.: 4,* 143 – 150, 1982.

Zoccolotti P, Caltagirone C, Benedetti N, Gainotti G: Perturbation des responses vegetatives aux stimuli emotionnels au cours des lesions hemispheriques unilaterales. *L'Encephale: 12,* 263 – 268, 1986.

© 1989 Elsevier Science Publishers B.V. (Biomedical Division)
Handbook of Neuropsychology, Vol. 3
F. Boller and J. Grafman (Eds)

CHAPTER 19

Arousal and emotions

Kenneth M. Heilman and Robert T. Watson

Department of Neurology, J. Hills Miller Health Center, University of Florida, College of Medicine, Gainesville, FL 32610, U.S.A

Introduction

Emotion is primarily a behavioral control system that motivates behavior. There appear to be three major systems that motivate behavior. One system (primary drive system) is dependent on changes in the internal mileau of the organism. The best examples of primary drives are thirst and hunger. The second behavioral control system directly involves emotions. This behavioral control system, like the primary control system, depends upon internal sensations which act to drive behavior. However, these sensations may be induced by exteroceptive stimuli either directly (e.g. nociceptive stimuli) or indirectly after perceptual-cognitive interpretation. Just as sensations induced directly by stimuli may be pleasant, unpleasant or even painful, internal sensations induced by stimulus interpretation can also be pleasant, unpleasant or painful. Internal sensations induced by stimulus interpretation or memory are called emotional feelings. Although both the primary drive system and the emotional drive system rely on internal sensations or feelings to motivate behavior, they differ in that the primary drive system is activated by internal stimuli whereas the emotional system (under normal circumstances) is activated by external stimuli (or memories of these stimuli). Emotional feelings motivate behavior because the organism, under normal circumstances, wishes to avoid unpleasant or painful sensations (direct or indirect) and experience pleasure. In higher organisms, there is a third behavioral control system which is related to emotions and primary drive systems but motivates behavior even in the absence of internal sensations induced either by changes of the internal milieu or by external stimuli. Some organisms such as humans have well-developed cognitive systems that allow them to determine the set of environmental circumstances which will be likely to lead either to changes of the internal milieu or to emotion-inducing stimuli. This knowledge drives behavior in such a way that the organism attempts to avoid circumstances that lead to unpleasant feelings and to promote circumstances that lead to pleasant sensations. The systems that mediate this behavior are mainly neocortical and probably include the frontal lobes as well as the temporoparietal regions. In this chapter, our discussion will be limited to the emotional system that involves feelings.

In addition to functioning as a motivating system emotions also have at least two important adaptive features. First, emotions have a communicative property. Secondly, emotions help prepare an organism to deal with the environment. That is, emotions are associated with changes in both the central nervous system and the body which help the organism prepare to analyse the situation and develop a plan of action.

Almost all theories of emotion imply that arousal is a critical element. The purpose of this chapter is to discuss the neuropsychology of emotion as it pertains to arousal. As we will discuss, arousal may play a critical role in developing feelings. During emotions, arousal may also be critical for activating the central nervous system, which enhances stimulus analysis, cognitive activity and motor preparation for action. Central nervous system arousal may also lead to changes in the autonomic nervous system (peripheral arousal) and in the endocrine system that help prepare the body for action. Although there has been abundant neurophysiological and neuroanatomic research pertaining to arousal, and it has been clearly established that there is a strong relationship between arousal and emotions, there has been a paucity of research that deals with hemispheric specialization and other neuropsychological factors of arousal as they pertain to emotion.

In this chapter we will first discuss the neurophysiology, neurochemistry and neuroanatomy of arousal. In this discussion we will mainly address arousal as it pertains to the central nervous system. In the next section we will discuss the relationship between arousal and emotion and the role arousal plays in subjective emotional feelings. Lastly, we will discuss the adaptive value of emotional arousal.

Arousal

Arousal has both behavioral and electrophysiological definitions. Behaviorally, arousal varies from low arousal where the organism is in a pathological state of coma to various degrees of alertness and/or waking. Physiologically, arousal describes the excitability of the nervous system or portions of the nervous system.

A change in neuronal excitation can affect the manner in which stimuli are detected and processed. Arousal may also affect cognitive activity and influence the premotor and motor systems. The arousal processes that influence the premotor and motor systems may be dissociable from those that affect the sensory-perceptual and cognitive systems. As suggested by Pribram and McGuinness (1975) we will call the former process activation or intention, the latter arousal.

Arousal

Behavioral

When we are presented with a new or meaningful stimulus, we orient our sensory organs (e.g., eyes and ears) to the source of the stimulus. Pavlov initially called this orienting response the 'investigating' or 'what is it?' reaction. If an organism is at rest, muscle tone is increased and autonomic changes occur, including pupil dilation, increased sweating, peripheral vasoconstriction or dilation, and alterations in heart rate and respiration. Sensory thresholds are also lowered (Lynn, 1966).

Physiology

Beck (1890) and Berger (1930) showed in human subjects that the EEG voltage decreased and frequency increased with sensory stimulation. However, it was Adrian and Matthews (1934) who first suggested that these changes in the EEG depend on attention to the stimulus.

Moruzzi and Magoun (1949) demonstrated that electrical stimulation of the reticular formation of the mesencephalon in animals would evoke EEG desynchronization similar to that occurring during natural arousal. Bilateral lesions of the mesencephalic reticular formation induced coma, the opposite of arousal. These studies demonstrated that perturbations of a nonspecific brain area could affect the way the brain interacted with its environment. During the last 25 years, the arousal-activation theory has received criticism. One of the major problems is the dissociation of behavior and EEG activity. For example, while low-voltage fast EEG rhythms should be associated with alert wakefulness, they can also be associated with coma (Loeb et al., 1959). Although slowing of EEG rhythms usually indicates decreased arousal, atropine induces EEG slowing without particularly affecting behavior (Vanderwolf and Robinson, 1981). It also appears that many areas of the reticular formation have a motor function (Siegal and Tomaszewski, 1983).

In spite of the criticism of arousal theory, the mesencephalic reticular formation can effect sensory function so as to augment the excitability of neurons to stimuli, as Moruzzi and Magoun (1949) predicted. For example, visual potentials in the lateral geniculate body of the monkey are increased by electrical stimulation of the mesencephalic reticular formation (Doty et al., 1973). Facilitation of single neurons can also be seen in the monkey striate cortex. Singer (1973, 1977) recorded from cells in the lateral geniculate of the cat and noted that bursts of inhibitory postsynaptic potentials (IPSPs) were synchronous with the slow waves in the EEG. Mesencephalic stimulation not only desynchronized the slow waves but also obliterated the IPSPs, allowing for more effective transmission of visual information through the lateral geniculate nucleus.

Wurtz and Mohler (1976) showed that neurons in the monkey striate cortex have, in an attentional task, enhanced responses before saccades. This enhancement was not spatially selective and therefore related to arousal rather than to selective attention. Robinson and Fuchs (1969) showed a similar enhancement for neurons in the prestriate cortex. Motter and Mountcastle (1981) compared the response of light-sensitive neurons in the posterior parietal cortex to visual stimuli when the animal was actively looking at a fixation point with the response of these neurons to the same stimuli flashed when the animal was not actively fixating. Active fixation was associated with significant increase in the excitability of the parietal neurons. This was not induced only by a visual interaction with the target, because the increased excitability persisted even when the central fixation target disappeared.

Anatomy

Although no direct connections have been satisfactorily demonstrated from the mesencephalic reticular formation to the cerebral cortex (Nauta and Kuypers, 1958; Ropert and Steriade, 1981), there are two pathways by which mesencephalic reticular activity can influence cortical processing.

The mesencephalic reticular formation activity may be relayed through the medial thalamus. Steriade and Glenn (1982) showed that neurons in the centralis lateralis – paracentralis complex of the cat thalamus project to the cerebral cortex and that some of these cells could be excited monosynaptically from the ipsilateral mesencephalic reticular formation. The thalamic projections to the cortex appear to be specific. For example, cells that could be excited from the pericruciate cortex could not be excited from the middle suprasylvian gyrus. While the pericruciate region is a specific somatosensory cortical association area (Mountcastle, 1957), the middle suprasylvian cortex is a visual association area (Palmar et al., 1978). These results suggest that different sensory systems can be facilitated independently by reticular activation.

The mesencephalic reticular formation may also affect cortical activity by influencing the reticular nucleus of the thalamus. Direct projections from the mesencephalic reticular formation to the reticular nucleus of the thalamus have been demonstrated (Ben-Ari et al., 1976). Based on the structure of the reticular nucleus, Scheibel and Scheibel (1967) postulated that the reticular nucleus of the thalamus could inhibit modality-specific thalamic nuclei. Subsequently, Waszak and Schlag (1971) noted that when the reticular nucleus discharged, it inhibited relay in other thalamic nuclei. Stimulation of the mesencephalic reticular formation inhibits the reticular nucleus of the thalamus, and this disinhibition facilitates the relay through thalamic nuclei.

Neurochemistry

Because the locus coeruleus – norepinephrine system projects diffusely to cortical structures it would appear to be an ideal mediator of arousal. Although the locus coeruleus is in the pons, the area of the mesencephalon stimulated by Moruzzi and Magoun (1949) contains the ascending norepinephrine systems. While the norepinephrine system would be an ideal candidate to mediate cortical arousal (Jouvet, 1977), locus coeruleus ablation does not affect behavioral or physiological evidence of arousal (Jacobs and Jones, 1978). The dopaminergic system appears to be critical in the activation-intentional systems, but because blockade of both synthesis and receptors does not appear to affect EEG desynchronization (Whishaw et al., 1978) it appears not to be the neurochemical systems mediating arousal.

Mesencephalic reticular activating system stimulation not only induces arousal but also increases the rate of acetylcholine released from the neocortex (Kanai and Szerb, 1965). Shute and Lewis (1967) described an ascending cholinergic reticular formation, but its role in behavioral arousal is not clear. Cholinergic agonists induce neocortical desynchronization, and antagonists abolish desynchronization (Bradley, 1968). However, the drugs do not appear to influence behavioral arousal. Although Vanderwolf and Robinson (1981) suggest that there may be two types of cholinergic input to the neocortex, only one of which is affected by drugs such as atropine, the role of the cholinergic system in arousal remains to be determined.

Control of arousal systems

Cortical-reticular relationships

Sokolov (1963) proposed a model whereby afferent stimuli are transmitted to the cortex by the classic sensory pathways and to the reticular system via afferent collaterals. The cortex makes a model of stimulus characteristics, and if the stimulus is new or has biological significance the cortex induces excitation of the reticular system and the reticular system mediates an arousal response. If the stimulus is unimportant (not new or significant) an arousal response does not occur.

Heilman (1977) and Watson et al. (1981) have proposed a detailed neurological model based on the seminal work of Sokolov (1963). According to this model, primary sensory areas project to their association areas and unimodal association areas converge upon polymodal association areas. In the monkey these polymodal areas are the prefrontal cortex (periarcuate, prearcuate, orbitofrontal) and both banks of the superior temporal sulcus (STS) (Pandya and Kuypers, 1969). The caudal inferior parietal lobe (IPL) also receives projections from unimodal association cortex as well as receiving projections from polymodal convergence areas such as the prefrontal cortex and both banks of the STS (Mesulam et al., 1977). Polymodal convergence areas may not only be critical for cross-modal associations and polymodal sensory synthesis but also may be important in detecting biological significance (e.g., 'Is the stimulus new or important?') while the unimodal association cortex may project to specific parts of the NR and gate modality-specific input, multimodal convergence areas may have a more general inhibitory action on NR and thereby provide further arousal after cortical analysis. These convergence areas also may project to the MRF, which may induce a generalized arousal. General arousal may be mediated by the two systems discussed earlier. Evidence that cortical polymodal areas mediate arousal comes from neurophysiological studies showing that stimulation of the prearcuate region and both banks of STS induces an evoked response in the MRF (French et al., 1955) and a generalized arousal response (Segundo et al., 1955). When these cortical sites are ablated there is both behavioral and EEG evidence of ipsilateral hypoarousal (Watson et al., 1978). Although determining whether a stimulus is new may be mediated by sensory association cortex, the behavioral significance of a stimulus is determined by knowledge and by the needs of the organism (motivational state). Limbic system input into brain regions important for determining stimulus significance might provide information about motivational states and supramodal areas may contain knowledge about the meaning of the stimulus. The dorsolateral frontal lobes might provide input about goals that are neither directly stimulus-dependent nor motivated by a change in the internal milieu.

It has been demonstrated that polymodal (e.g., STS) and supramodal (IPL) areas have prominent

imbic and frontal connections. The prefrontal
cortex and STS project to the cingulate gyrus, and
the cingulate gyrus projects to the IPL (Baleydier
and Mauguiere, 1980). In addition, the prefrontal
cortex, STS and IPL have strong reciprocal connections (Pandya and Kuypers, 1969). The connections of STS and IPL with limbic and frontal
systems may provide an anatomic substrate by
which motivational states (e.g., biological needs,
sets and long-term goals) may influence stimulus
processing and arousal.

Each hemisphere may in part have its own
arousal system. Stimulation of the mesencephalic
reticular area induces greater desynchronization of
the ipsilateral hemisphere than of the contralateral
hemisphere (Moruzzi and Magoun, 1949).
Unilateral lesions of the mesencephalic reticular
area induce both a behavioral and an EEG defect
of the orienting reflex to contralateral stimuli but
with preserved orienting to ipsilateral stimuli
(Reeves and Hagamen, 1971; Watson et al,. 1974).
Discrete unilateral cortical lesions in animals
(Heilman et al., 1970; Welch and Stuteville, 1958)
and humans (Critchley, 1953; Heilman and
Valenstein, 1972) induce a similar defect in the
orienting response.

In summary, the anatomic, physiological and
behavioral studies just reviewed provide evidence
that reciprocal relationships exist between the
reticular system and certain neocortical areas.
While the reticular formation influences the activity of the cortex, the activity of the reticular system
may be controlled by certain cortical areas.

Hemispheric asymmetries

As mentioned above, cortical and subcortical lesions in man may induce a defect in the orienting
reflex. This orienting defect is a part of the neglect
syndrome and is thought to be at least in part induced by defective arousal (see Heilman et al.,
1985). Gainotti et al. (1972) and Costa et al. (1969)
demonstrated that neglect was more frequent after
right than left hemisphere lesions. Although the
galvanic skin response (GSR) is a peripheral
measure of arousal, it correlates with central

measures of arousal. Heilman et al. (1978) studied
patients with right or left temporoparietal lesions
as well as controls without brain lesions by
stimulating the hands ipsilateral to the lesioned
hemisphere and recording galvanic skin responses.
When compared to left hemisphere brain-damaged
controls and to controls who are without brain
damage, patients with right hemisphere lesions had
a reduced response, suggesting decreased arousal.
Trexler and Schmidt (1981) replicated these results
and Morrow et al. (1981) described similar results.
Another peripheral measure of arousal is heart rate
change. Using this measure Yokoyama et al. (in
press) found again that patients with right
hemisphere lesions were less responsive.

Heilman, Gilmore, Van Den Abell and Watson
(unpublished observations) using an EEG recorded
from the undamaged hemisphere of awake right
and left hemisphere damaged patients. Patients
with right-side lesions showed more theta and delta
activity over the undamaged left hemisphere than
those with left-side lesions showed over their right
hemisphere. These studies of both peripheral and
central arousal suggest that the right hemisphere
may have a special role in mediating the arousal
response.

When studying the galvanic skin response of
brain-damaged subjects we noted that not only did
the right hemisphere damaged patients have a
reduced level of arousal but that the left
hemisphere damaged group, when compared to
non-brain-damaged controls, had an increased
arousal response. Trexler and Schmidt (1981)
found similar results. Yokoyama (in press), using
heart rate measures, also found left hemisphere
damaged patients to be more responsive. Unfortunately, no studies have been performed using
central measures such as EEG to compare left
hemisphere damaged to non-brain-damaged controls. However, studies of peripheral arousal suggest that the left hemisphere exerts inhibitory control on the arousal mechanisms mediated by the
right hemisphere. The manner in which this control is exerted is not known.

Activation (intention)

Activation refers to the brain's preparation to initiate a movement. Since relatively little is known about the relationship between central nervous system activation and emotion we will not discuss this in as much detail as we discussed arousal. For a more detailed discussion of activation one may refer to our recent review (Heilman et al., 1987).

One way to study the brain's role in activation is to study behavioral states where there is a loss of activation. These include akinesia, hypokinesia, bradykinesia and hypometria. Akinesia is the failure to respond to a meaningful (or novel) stimulus that calls for action if the failure to respond cannot be attributed to weakness, sensory loss or inattention. Hypokinesia is a milder form of akinesia where there is a delay in responses. Bradykinesia refers to a decreased rate and hypometria a decreased amplitude of movement. Ablative studies in both animals and man have revealed that behavioral activation defects may be associated with lesions of the dorsolateral (Watson et al., 1973; Ch. 5 of this volume) and mesial frontal lobe (Watson et al., 1973; Meador, 1986). The frontal lobe is connected with both the neocortical monomodal sensory association areas and temporo-parietal poly- and supramodal areas (Pandya and Kuypers, 1969). These connections may provide the frontal lobe with information about the stimulus and the meaning of the stimulus. The frontal lobe has reciprocal connections with the cingulate gyrus, a part of the Papez limbic circuit from which the frontal lobes may derive motivational information. The frontal lobes also have connections with the mesencephalic reticular system, which may be important in arousal. Psychological studies provide evidence for the important role of the frontal lobe in activation. The pre-movement slow potential which may reflect motor preparatory processes is best recorded from the frontal vertex (Walter, 1973). Single cell recordings prior to either limb (Suzuki and Azuma, 1977) or eye movement (Bruce and Goldberg, 1985) also demonstrate that the frontal

lobes have a role in movement preparation.

As discussed, the dorsolateral frontal lobes have strong connections with the polymodal area of the temporoparietal lobes and lesions in these areas may also induce akinesia (Valenstein et al., 1982; Critchley, 1953).

Akinesia can also be seen with a variety of brain lesions including the basal ganglia (Valenstein and Heilman, 1981), the ventrolateral thalamus (Velasco and Velasco, 1979) and the medial thalamus (centromedian-parafascicularis) (Watson et al., 1981). Watson et al. (1981) have proposed a complex frontal lobe basal ganglia thalamic network that mediates activation.

It has also been well demonstrated that lesions of the dopaminergic system or dopaminergic blockade may induce akinesia, hypokinesia, hypometria and bradykinesia. Dopaminergic pathways originate in the pars compacta of the substantia nigra and from the ventral tegmental area just medial to the substantia nigra. These neurons project to the neostriatum (the nigrostriatal pathway), to limbic areas of the basal forebrain (nucleus accumbens septi and olfactory tubercle – the mesolimbic pathway) and to the cerebral cortex (frontal lobes and cingulate gyrus – the mesocortical pathway (Lindvall et al., 1974; Ljundberg and Ungerstedt, 1978). The exact role of each of these systems in activation has not been determined.

With regard to hemispheric asymmetries, warning stimuli prepare an organism for action and thereby reduce reaction times (Lansing et al., 1959). De Renzi and Faglioni (1965) measured reaction times of the hand ipsilateral to a lesion in patients with unilateral cerebral lesions. While lesions of either hemisphere slowed the reaction times, right hemisphere lesions were associated with greater slowing than left hemisphere lesions. While De Renzi and Faglioni attributed these differences to lesion size, Howes and Boller (1975) studied patients whose lesions of the right hemisphere were not larger than those of the left and found similar results. Because patients with right hemisphere lesions have been shown to have

reduced behavioral evidence of activation, we proposed that the right hemisphere may dominate the
mediation of the activation process. If the right
hemisphere dominates activation or intention, activation asymmetries in normal subjects should be
discernible. Heilman and Van Den Abell (1979)
presented normal subjects with warning stimuli in
the right and left visual half-field. These warning
stimuli were followed by central imperative stimuli
and reaction times were measured. We found that
warning stimuli projected to the right hemisphere
reduced right-hand reaction times more than warning stimuli projected to the left hemisphere reduced left-hand reaction times. In addition, the warning stimuli projected to the right hemisphere reduced reaction times of the right (ipsilateral) hand
even more than warning stimuli projected directly
to the left hemisphere. These results in normals,
together with observations in brain-damaged subjects, support the postulate that the right
hemisphere plays a critical role in activation.

Emotion and arousal

Since Lindsley's (1970) work, most investigators
have noted a close relationship between emotions
and arousal whether it be measured centrally or
peripherally. However, arousal and emotion are
not synonymous. For example, there are circumstances where arousal is increased (e.g., exercise) but there is no emotion. In our definition of
emotion we stated that emotion under normal circumstances is generated by a stimulus (or memory
of a stimulus). Based on our definition, since the
stimulus must be interpreted, emotions must contain a perceptual or cognitive element. When we
state that emotion has a cognitive element we do
not mean that cognition has to be mediated by
language or that the knowledge has to be learned.
There is nonverbal knowledge and it may be
transmitted genetically and be 'hardwired'. All we
mean by cognitive is that the organism contains
representations that allow it to determine at some
level the meaning of the stimulus.

Emotional changes after hemispheric damage

Studies of brain-damaged patients suggest that
hemispheric lesions may differentially affect emotional feeling. Babinski (1914), Hecaen et al.
(1951) and Denny-Brown et al., (1952) noted that
right hemisphere lesioned patients were often indifferent or emotionally flat. Goldstein (1948)
noted that patients with left hemisphere lesions
were often depressed, agitated and anxious – the
catastrophic reaction. Gainotti (1972) studied 160
subjects with right or left hemisphere damage and
was able to replicate the previous reports of emotional changes associated with hemispheric disease.

It has now been well established (see Chapter 16)
that right hemisphere damaged patients have a
variety of emotional communicative disorders.
These patients are not only unable to recognize the
emotional prosody of speech (Heilman et al., 1975,
1984; Ross, 1981) but may have difficulty expressing emotional prosody in speech (Tucker et al.,
1977; Ross, 1979). Similarly, patients with right
hemisphere dysfunction may not only have difficulty recognizing emotional faces and scenes
(DeKosky et al., 1980; Cicone et al., 1980) but also
may have difficulty making facial emotional expressions (Buck and Duffy, 1980). Patients with
left hemisphere lesions who are aphasic can often
emotionally intone speech and make emotional
faces. The studies reviewed thus far suggest that
patients with right hemisphere dysfunction may
have more difficulty than patients with left
hemisphere disease in comprehending and expressing affectively intoned speech as well as comprehending and expressing emotional facial expressions. Patients with right hemisphere disease may
also have more difficulty remembering emotionally charged speech or faces. These perceptual,
cognitive and expressive deficits might underlie
and account for the change seen with right or left
hemisphere disease. Alternatively, these perceptual, cognitive, expressive deficits may not reflect
the patient's underlying mood.

To learn more about mood, Gasparrini et al.

(1978) administered the Minnesota Multiphasic Personality Inventory (MMPI) to patients with unilateral hemisphere lesions. The patients were matched for severity of cognitive (e.g., IQ) and motor defects (e.g., motor tapping). The MMPI is widely used as an index of underlying affective experience, and the completion of this inventory does not require the perception or expression of affectively intoned speech or of facial expressions. Patients with left hemisphere disease showed an elevation on the depression scale but patients with right hemisphere disease did not. These findings suggest that the differences in emotional reactions of patients after right versus left hemisphere disease cannot be attributed entirely to difficulties in perceiving or expressing affective stimuli or to differences in the severity of cognitive or motor defects.

Many patients with right hemisphere disease who have emotional indifference may not appear depressed because they have anosognosia, do not recognize that they are disabled, and therefore have no reason to be depressed. However, we also see patients who do not explicitly deny illness, in that they recognize that they have had a stroke, are in the hospital, and have a left hemiparesis, but nevertheless appear unconcerned (anosodiaphoria) (Critchley, 1953). Although a portion of this flattening and unconcern may be induced by a loss of ability to express affective intonations in speech or to use affective facial expressions, even when one uses propositional speech to assess affect these patients still convey emotional indifference.

As previously mentioned in our discussion of arousal, patients who had right hemisphere lesions and were indifferent had evidence of reduced arousal as determined by skin conductance (Heilman et al., 1978; Morrow et al., 1981; Trexler and Schmidt, 1981) and by heart rate (Yokoyama et al., in press). Patients with left hemisphere lesions were found in several studies to have increased evidence of arousal (Heilman et al., 1978; Trexler and Schmidt 1981; Yokoyama et al., in press). Perhaps the difference in emotional feelings between the right and left hemisphere subjects is at least partially related to differences in arousal.

Models of emotional feeling

Although it is clear that arousal is associated with emotions and that emotions are induced by stimuli which must be interpreted, it is not clear how these lead to the internal or subjective sensation we call emotional feelings. There have been three significant models proposed to explain the basis for emotional feelings: (1) the James-Lange feedback or the body reaction theory; (2) the Maranon-Schacter or cognitive arousal theory; and (3) the Cannon or central theory. We will briefly describe each of these theories, discuss how they relate to neuropsychological observations, discuss their limitations and finally propose a revised theory.

Feedback hypothesis
There are two feedback hypotheses, the visceral and the motor.
Visceral feedback. According to James's (1890) theory, emotion-provoking stimuli induce bodily changes, and our feelings of these changes as they occur is the emotion. James, however, noted that there were also 'cerebral' forms of pleasure and displeasure that did not require bodily changes or perception of these changes. James felt it was the visceral response rather than muscle or facial response that was critical for feeling an emotion. Although one of Cannon's (1927) five criticisms of James's theory was that the same visceral responses occur for different feelings, there is evidence that refutes Cannon's critique and supports James's theory. Some research demonstrates that different bodily reactions can be associated with different emotions (Ax, 1953; Ekman et al., 1983).

Unfortunately James's theory does not tell us how different stimuli induce different bodily responses and what portion or portions of the brain perceive these bodily responses. More importantly, as pointed out by Dana (1929), spinal cord injuries in humans that separate the viscera from the brain do not prevent the animal or person from experiencing emotion. More recently, however, Hohmann (1966) studied emotions in patients with spinal damage and found that although patients whose viscera were disconnected from their brain experienced emotion, patients with higher cord lesions experienced less emotion than those with lower cord disease, thereby also providing partial support for James's theory. There is also some evidence that adrenergic beta blockers which do not cross into the brain may reduce anxiety in some subjects, and experiments in animals demonstrate that sympathectomy affects adversive conditioning (Di Giusto and King, 1972), most likely because it reduces fear.

While these latter observations suggest that feedback may embellish an emotion, feedback is not critical. In addition, even if feedback were critical to feeling an emotion in order to support James's theory, one would have to demonstrate that feedback even in the absence of a stimulus or cognitive state could induce emotion. Maranon (1924) in his classic study induced peripheral sympathetic arousal by giving normal subjects epinephrine. Although some subjects felt physical effects and others had 'as if' feelings, emotions were not experienced with the medication alone.

Motor feedback. Ekman and Friesen (1971) and Izard (1971) have clearly demonstrated that facial expressions associated with emotions are the same and independent of race and culture. In addition, they demonstrated seven basic or primary facial expressions (happiness, sadness, fear, anger, surprise, interest, disgust). Tomkins (1963) posited that the feed-back from facial muscles was important for the subjective feeling of emotion.

Although Tomkins's theory would explain how patients with spinal cord injury may experience emotional feelings, one can see patients in the clinic who despite facial akinesia experience emotion. Even more important is the observation of patients with pseudobulbar affect who despite having a facial expression of grief with crying do not feel sad (Wilson, 1924).

The self attribution theory – cognitive arousal interaction

As mentioned above, the relationship between arousal and emotion was studied in 1924 by Maranon, who induced physiological arousal by administering sympathomimetic drugs to normal subjects. He reported that most of his subjects reported feeling 'no emotions', although many reported that they experienced 'as if' feelings. When Maranon induced an affective memory that was not strong enough to produce an emotion in the normal state, emotional reactions occurred if there was a concomitant pharmacological arousal. The notion that a cognitive state must interact with arousal is the basis of Schacter's (1970) self attribution theory of emotion. Schacter (1970) pharmacologically aroused normal subjects, placed them in stressful situations, and found both subjective and objective evidence of emotional states. Pharmacological arousal alone did not produce emotional states. The stressful situation produced less emotion when the subjects were not pharmacologically aroused than when they were.

The self attribution theory appears to explain not only why patients with right hemisphere disease may have flattened affects but also why patients with left hemisphere disease are depressed and have the catastrophic reaction.

Patients with right hemisphere disease have difficulty comprehending affectively intoned speech and recognizing affective facial expressions and scenes. These deficits may interfere with the development of an appropriate cognitive state. In addition, patients with right hemisphere disease and the indifference reaction are also inadequately aroused (Heilman et al., 1978). Patients with left hemisphere damage may be able to develop an appropriate cognitive state and have, when compared to controls, increased arousal (Heilman et al., 1978).

Although the self attribution theory may help explain why patients with right and left hemisphere dysfunction have different emotional feelings there are several important observations it cannot explain.

First of all, epinephrine induces peripheral (sympathetic) arousal. While central arousal may occur it is not clear whether arousal that leads to emotions occurs through feedback or entirely depends on central mechanisms. Perhaps even more important is the observation that even in the absence of the appropriate cognitive state animals and man can experience emotion. Emotions may be seen either with stimulation of the limbic system in animals (see Valenstein, 1973, for a review) or man (e.g., Heath, 1964) or during seizures that emanate from the limbic system of man (partial seizures with complex symptomatology).

Central theories

Cannon (1927) proposed that feelings or subjective emotions depended on central nervous system activity, and that the thalamus was the critical structure. He felt that signals emanating from the thalamus were not only important for the expression of emotion but when they reached the cortex they were also important in subjective emotional experience or feelings. Cannon also thought that the systems important for expressing emotion and feeling emotion may be at least in part independent and that the sympathetic activity associated with certain emotions served adaptive purposes rather than as a source of emotional feelings.

The observation that peripheral arousal (changes in the peripheral autonomic nervous system) can influence emotion, although not being capable of inducing an emotion, might appear to refute Cannon's theory. Visceral afferent nerves may, however, provide the brain with information about autonomic activity that helps, along with information about external stimuli, to develop emotional feelings.

Although Cannon suggested that the thalamus was the major effector organ of emotion, subsequent studies by Bard (1934) demonstrated that it was actually the hypothalamus. The hypothalamus appears to control both the autonomic nervous system and the endocrine system through the pituitary.

Central-peripheral theory

Although Bard demonstrated that the major effector was the hypothalamus rather than the thalamus, Cannon's concept that emotional feelings depend on diencephalic cortical interaction has not been refuted and was the basis of the classic theory of Papez (1937). Papez (1937) agreed with Cannon that although the hypothalamus was critical for emotional expression it was the cortex that was critical for subjective feelings. He also proposed that afferent stimuli, after passing through the thalamus, go either to the hypothalamus or to the cortex. Information passes from the hypothalamus through the mammillothalamic tract to the anterior nucleus of the thalamus and then to the cingulate gyrus. The cingulate gyrus has extensive connections with the cortex and it is, according to Papez, this interconnection that is critical for subjective emotional feelings. Papez also recognized that the hippocampus was one of the main efferent outputs from the cortex to the hypothalamus (hippocampus-fornix-mammillary bodies).

Unfortunately, although animal research can examine emotional behavior, it cannot examine human subjective emotional feeling. Only research with humans can do that. The research that is performed in humans has been limited for the most part to examining patients with lesions, or epilepsy, or both. With regard to lesions, most patients with extensive bilateral medial frontal (cingulate) lesions have akinetic mutism and their subjective emotional experiences cannot be obtained. Although cingulotomy has been used to treat depression, obsessive compulsive neurosis, pain and addiction, according to Teuber et al. (1977) these patients continue to have subjective emotional feelings. However, it should be recalled that while the cingulum bundle is interrupted in these cases, the cingulate gyrus, for the most part, remains intact. Although certain portions of the hippocampus can be damaged with anoxia, this damage is partial and it is unusual to find bilateral damage whether from stroke, tumor, infection, trauma or surgical ablation that is restricted to the hippocampus. Most of these lesions involve structures such as the amygdalae which are not considered parts of Papez's circuit. As regards seizures and brain stimulation, although fear may be associated with seizures emanating from the cingulate gyrus and medial temporal lobes in the latter case it is more likely to be the amygdala that is involved than the hippocampus. In general, therefore, while some portions of Papez's circuit may be involved in the mediation of emotion this circuit seems to be more important in mediating memory than emotions.

The amygdala, which is part of Yakolov's (1948) lateral limbic circuit (orbitofrontal cortex, uncinate fasciculus, anterior temporal lobe, amygdala, medial dorsal thalamus, orbitofrontal lobe). also has extensive connections with the hypothalamus. Ablation of the amygdala induces placidity (Kluver and Bucy, 1937; Woods, 1956), and stimulation or seizures induce fear and perhaps rage (Mark and Ervin, 1970). Ablation of the septal region may be associated with rage (Brady and Nauta, 1955) and stimulation may be associated with pleasure and sexual feelings (Olds, 1958; Hearth, 1964).

The purpose of this discussion is not to review the entire anatomy of the limbic system or fully discuss its role in emotion (see Chapter 13), but to demonstrate that the limbic system may play a critical role in the experiencing of emotions and that different portions of the limbic system are associated with different emotions.

Although during a seizure or electrical stimulation an emotion can be felt without the appropriate cognitive stimulus, it does not mean that under normal circumstances the cognitive state induced by a stimulus does not influence the limbic system, for it is well known that the cortex has sensory input into both the Papez circuit and Yakolov's circuit (as well as other areas of the limbic system). In addition, peripheral autonomic feedback through visceral afferents may also affect the limbic system. For example, vagal afferents from the heart project to the nucleus of the tractus solitarius, and this nucleus in turn projects to the amygdala. The limbic system (especially the cingulate gyrus and amygdala) not only receives projections from the cortex but also projects back to the cortex. We suspect that emotional feelings depend on two feedback systems: the autonomic nervous system that feeds back to the limbic system, and the limbic system that feeds back to the cortex. Davidson et al. (1981) noted that in the absence of psychophysiological feedback, normal subjects tap their left hand in concordance with their heart beat more often than they do with their right hand, suggesting that the right hemisphere may be the chief recipient of autonomic nervous system feedback. The cortex is important for perception and cognition. It also controls the arousal system and has input to the limbic systems. The limbic system (together with cortical systems) influences arousal, which is mediated by the reticular activating system, and the limbic system also has important input into the hypothalamus, which both controls the autonomic nervous system and influences the endocrine systems. As mentioned, visceral afferents feed back to the limbic system and the limbic system feeds back to the cortex. Because the cortex receives all the critical elements (e.g., feedback from limbic, arousal and cognitive systems) and is critical for conscious experience (awareness), we suspect it is the cortex that interprets emotional feelings. Because the right hemisphere plays a critical role in the cognitive arousal and feedback elements of emotion, we believe the right cortex is also dominant for the interpretation of emotion and feeling, but further research is needed.

Emotions: adaptive aspects

In the introduction, we proposed that there were at least three functions that emotion may serve. These included communicative, motivational and preparatory. The communicative aspects of emotion are discussed in Chapter 12. We have linked emotional feelings to motivation and have already discussed the realtionship of arousal to emotional feelings. Although all emotions are associated with feelings and have motivational significance, not all emotions appear to have a strong preparatory function. Some emotions such as fear and anger may be associated with more preparatory functions than others such as happiness. In this last section we will briefly discuss the preparatory function of emotion and how these preparatory functions relate to central and peripheral arousal as well as to activation.

Arousal as mediated by the cortical-limbic-thalamic-reticular network alters the stimulus-processing capabilities of the organism. For example, an aroused organism has lower sensory thresholds and can more rapidly process sensory stimuli (see Lynn, 1966, for a review). Arousal is critical to cognitive functioning and plays a crucial role in the attentional systems. For example, increased levels of arousal are associated with increased vigilance and decreased distractibility.

Emotion is also associated with changes in the autonomic nervous system (ANS). The ANS controls some viscera functions, including the cardiovascular, the pulmonary, the gastrointestinal, the genitourinary, the integumentary (e.g., sweat glands) and ocular (e.g., part of the pupils) systems. In addition to maintaining the baseline activity needed for sustaining life, phasic changes in these organs are often necessary to adapt to different needs placed on the organism. Changes in the activity of the organs (e.g., heart, sweat glands, pupils) are often, but not exclusively, associated with emotion and this peripheral arousal is mediated by the ANS.

There are two subdivisions of the ANS: the sympathetic (SNS) and parasympathetic (PNS). These two systems often act reciprocally (e.g., sympathetic activity dilates the pupil and parasympathetic constricts the pupil), but not always (e.g., sweating). The SNS and the PNS differ in anatomy (e.g., sympathetic preganglionic nerves are derived from thoracic and lumbar cord and PNS are derived from the brainstem and sacral cord). The PNS and SNS may also have different neurotransmitters at a specific site (for a review of the anatomy and neurochemistry, see Le Doux, 1986). The adrenal medulla, also under control of the SNS, releases norepinephrine and epinephrine (sympathetic neurotransmitters), which may reach target organs through the blood stream.

It was initially proposed by Cannon that there may be only one pattern of autonomic peripheral (arousal) activity. According to Cannon's theory, autonomic arousal prepared the organism for fight or flight and mainly involved an increase in sympathetic activity. For example, during sympathetic activity, glycogen is released from the liver and turns into glucose needed for energy. Blood is redistributed from the skin into muscles. The heart increases its output, which in turn delivers more blood to critical organ systems. More recent studies, however, have suggested that different emotions may be associated with different changes in the autonomic nervous system. Eckman et al. (1983) asked subjects to relive past emotional experiences. The author found that negative emotions increased heart rate and changed finger temperature more than pleasant emotions (happiness); however, there were even differences in the autonomic nervous system between negative emotions (e.g., heart rate was low in surprise and high in anger and fear; skin temperature was high in anger and low in fear).

These results suggest that the hypothalamus may differentially activate portions of the ANS, and the pattern of activation may be related to the specific instruction it receives from the cortex or limbic system.

Although many of the changes in the body induced by the ANS are adaptive (prepare the body for action) it is not clear why there are differences in ANS activity with different emotions. Different emotions may have to differentially prepare the organism. However, it remains possible that not all the changes are adaptive.

With regard to activation or motor preparation, Lansing et al. (1959), using a reduction of reaction time paradigm, showed that motor preparation is closely linked to arousal. Verfaellie et al. (in press), however, noted that motor set may be altered independently of arousal. Unfortunately, little is known about the relationship of motor set and emotion. We would not be surprised, however, if the emotions that are often associated with action (e.g., fear or anger) induce more of the motor preparatory set than do emotions that are not closely associated with action (e.g., happiness).

We have already discussed research which provides evidence that the right hemisphere plays a critical role in arousal and appears to be dominant in the mediation of ANS activation. In addition, the right hemisphere also appears to be dominant for activation or motor preparation. Since the right hemisphere appears to be dominant for mediating central nervous system arousal, autonomic nervous system activity and activation (motor preparation) it would appear that the right hemisphere plays a special role in the adaptive-preparatory aspect of emotions.

References

Adrian ED, Matthews BC: The interpretation of potential waves in the cortex. *J. Physiol. Lond.: 81,* 440 – 471, 1934.

Ax: The physiological differentiation between fear and anger in humans. *Psychosom. Med.: 15,* 433 – 442, 1953.

Babinski J: Contribution a l'etude des troubles mentaux dans l'hemisplegie organique cerebrale (anosognosie). *Rev. Neurol.: 27,* 845 – 848, 1914.

Baleydier C, Mauguiere F: The duality of the cingulate gyrus in monkey – neuroanatomical study in functional hypothesis. *Brain: 103,* 525 – 554, 1980.

Bard P: Emotion. I: The neuro-humoral basis of emotional reactions. In Murchison C (Editor), *Handbook of General Experimental Psychology.* Worcester, MA: Clark University Press, 1934.

Beck A: Die Bestimmung der Localisation der Gehirn- und Ruckenmarkfunctionen vermittelst der electrischen Erscheinungen (the determination of localization of brain and spinal cord function by means of electrical phenomena). *Zentralbl. Physiol.: 4,* 473 – 476, 1890: (Cited by M.A.B. Brazier. Trails leading to the concept of the ascending reticular system. In Hobson JA, Brazier MAB (Editors), *The Reticular Formation Revisited.* New York: Raven, pp. 31 – 52, 1980.

Ben-Ari Y, Dingledine R, Kanazawa I, Kelly JS: Inhibitory effects of acetylcholine on neurons in the feline nucleus reticularis thalami. *J. Physiol. Lond.: 261,* 647 – 671, 1976.

Berger H: Uber das Elektrenkephalogramm des Menschen. *J. Psychol. Neurol.: 40,* 160 – 179, 1930.

Bradley PB: The effect of atropine and related drugs on the EEG and behavior. *Prog. Brain Res.: 28,* 3 – 13, 1968.

Bruce CJ, Goldberg ME: Primate frontal eye fields. I. Single neurons discharging before saccades. *J. Neurophysiol.: 53,* 603 – 635, 1985.

Buck P, Duffy R: Nonverbal communication of affect in brain-damaged patients. *Cortex: 16,* 351 – 362, 1980.

Cannon WB: The James-Lange theory of emotion: A critical examination and an alternative theory. *Am. J. Psychol.: 39,* 106 – 124, 1927.

Cicone M, Waper W, Gardner H: Sensitivity to emotional expressions and situation in organic patients. *Cortex: 16,* 145 – 158, 1980.

Costa LP, Vaughn HG, Horwitz M, Ritter W: Patterns of behavioral deficits associated with visual spatial neglect. *Cortex: 5,* 242 – 263, 1969.

Critchley M: *The Parietal Lobes.* New York: Hafner, 1953.

Davidson RJ, Horowitz ME, Schwartz GE, Goodman DY: Lateral differences in the latency between finger tapping and heart beat. *Psychophysiology: 18,* 36 – 41, 1981.

DeKosky S, Heilman KM, Bowers D, Valenstein E: Recognition and discrimination of emotional faces and pictures. *Brain Lang.: 9,* 206 – 214, 1980.

Denny-Brown D, Meyer JS, Horenstein D: The significance of perceptual rivalry resulting from parietal lesions. *Brain: 75,* 434 – 471, 1952.

De Renzi E, Faglioni P: The comparative efficiency of intelligence and vigilance tests detecting hemispheric change. *Cortex: 1,* 410 – 433, 1965.

Di Guisto EL, King MG: Chemical sympathectomy and aniodane learning. *Natl. J. Comp. Psysiol-Psychol.: 81,* 491 – 500, 1972.

Doty W, Wilson PD, Bartlett JR, Pecci-Saavedra J: Mesencephalic control of lateral geniculate nucleus in primates. I. Electrophysiology. *Exp. Brain Res.: 18,* 189 – 203, 1973.

Ekman P, Friesen WV: Constants across culture in the face and emotion. *J. Pers. Soc. Psychol.: 17,* 124 – 129, 1971.

Ekman P, Levenson RW, Friesen WV: Autonomic nervous system activity distinguishes emotions. *Science: 221,* 1208 – 1210, 1983.

French JD, Hernandez-Peon R, Livingston RB: Projections from cortex to cephalic brain stem (reticular formation) in monkey. *J. Neurophysiol.: 18,* 74 – 95, 1955.

Gainotti G: Emotional behavior and hemispheric side of lesion. *Cortex: 8,* 41 – 55, 1972.

Gainotti G, Messerli P, Tissot R: Quantitative analysis of unilateral spatial neglect in relation to laterality of cerebral lesions. *J. Neurol. Neurosurg. Psychiatry: 35,* 545 – 550, 1972.

Gasparrini WG, Satz P, Heilman KM, Coolidge FL: Hemispheric asymmetries of affective processing as determined by the Minnesota multiphasic personality inventory. *J. Neurol. Neurosurg. Psychiatry: 41,* 470 – 473, 1978.

Goldstein K: *Language and Language Disturbances.* New York: Grune and Stratton, 1948.

Heath RG: Pleasure response of human subjects to direct stimulation of the brain: physiologic and psychodynamic considerations. In Heath RG (Editor), *The Role of Pleasure in Behavior.* New York: Harper and Row, 1964.

Hecaen H, Ajuriaguerra J de, Massonet J: Les troubles visuoconstructifs par lesion parieto-occipitale droit. *Encephale: 40,* 122 – 179, 1951.

Heilman KM: Neglect and related disorders. In Heilman KM, Valenstein E (Editors), *Clinical Neuropsychology.* New York: Oxford University Press, pp. 268 – 307. 1979.

Heilman KM, Van Den Abell T: Right hemisphere dominance for mediating cerebral activation. *Neuropsychologia: 17,* 315 – 321, 1979.

Heilman KM, Pandya DN, Geschwind N: Trimodal inattention following parietal lobe ablations. *Trans. Am. Neurol. Assoc.: 95,* 259 – 261, 1970.

Heilman KM, Scholes R, Watson RT: Auditory affective agnosia: disturbed comprehension of affective speech. *J. Neurol. Neurosurg. Psychiatry: 38,* 69 – 72, 1975.

Heilman KM, Schwartz HD, Watson RT: Hypoarousal in patients with the neglect syndrome and emotional indifference. *Neurology: 28,* 229 – 232, 1978.

Heilman KM, Bowers D, Speedie LJ, Coslett HB: The comprehension of affective and nonaffective prosody. *Neurology: 34,* 917 – 221, 1984.

Hohmann G: Some effects of spinal cord lesions on experimental emotional feelings. *Psychophysiology: 3,* 143 – 156, 1966.

Izard CE: *The Face of Emotion.* New York: Appleton, 1971.

James W: *The Principles of Psychology.* New York: Holt, 1890.

Kanai T, Szerb JC: Mesencephalic reticular activating system and cortical acetylcholine output. *Nature (Lond).: 205,* 80 – 82, 1965.

Kluver H, Bucy PC: 'Psychic blindness' and other symptoms following bilateral temporal lobectomy in rhesus monkeys. *Am. J. Physiol.: 119,* 352 – 353, 1937.

Lansing RW, Schwartz E, Lindsley DB: Reaction time and EEG activation under alerted and nonalerted conditions. *J. Exp. Psychol.: 58,* 1 – 7, 1959.

le Doux JE: The neurobiology of emotion. In LeDoux JE, Hirst W (Editors), *Mind and Brain.* New York: Cambridge University Press. 1986.

Le Doux, JE: Emotion. *Handbook of Physiology – The Nervous System Vol. 5, Part II.* Bethesda, MD: The American Physiological Society, 1987.

Lindsley D: The role of nonspecific reticulo-thalamo-cortical systems in emotion. In Black P (Editor), *Physiological Correlates of Emotion* New York: Academic Press, 1970.

Lindvall O, Bjorklund A, Moore RY, Stenevi U: Mesencephalic dopamine neurons projecting to neocortex. *Brain Res.: 81,* 325 – 331, 1974.

Ljungberg T, Understedt U: Sensory inattention produced by 6-hydroxydopamine-induced degeneration of ascending dopamine neurons in the brain. *Exp. Neurol.: 53,* 585 – 600, 1976.

Loeb C, Rosadini G, Poggio GF: Electroencephalograms during coma: normal and borderline records in 5 patients. *Neurology: 9,* 610 – 618, 1959.

Lynn R: *Attention, Arousal and the Orientation Reaction.* Oxford: Pergamon, 1966.

Maranon G: Contribution a l'etude de l'action emotive de l'adrenaline. *Rev. Franc. endocrinol.: 2,* 301 – 325, 1934.

Mark VH, Ervin FR: *Violence and the Brain.* New York: Harper and Row, 1970.

Meador K, Watson RT, Bowers D, Heilman KM: Hypometria in the hemispatial and limb motor neglect. *Brain: 109,* 293 – 305, 1986.

Mesulam M, Van Hoesen GW, Pandya DN, Geschwind N: Limbic and sensory connections of the inferior parietal lobule (area PG) in the rhesus monkey: a study with a new method for horseradish peroxidase histochemistry. *Brain Res.: 136,* 393 – 414, 1977.

Morrow L, Urtunski PB, Kim Y, Boller F: Arousal responses to emotional stimuli and laterality of lesion. *Neuro-psychologia: 19,* 65 – 71, 1981.

Moruzzi G, Magoun HW: Brainstem reticular formation and activation of the EEG. *Electroencephalogr. Clin. Neurophysiol.: 1,* 455 – 473, 1949.

Motter BC, Mountcastle VB: The functional properties of the light sensitive neurons of the posterior parietal cortex studied in waking monkeys: foveal sparing and opponent vector organization. *J. Neurosci.: 1,* 3 – 26, 1981.

Nauta WJH, Kuypers HGJM: Some ascending pathways in the brainstem reticular formation. In Jasper HH, Proctor LD, Knighton RS, Noshay WC, Costello RT (Editors), *Reticular Formation of the Brain.* Boston, MA: Little, Brown, pp. 3 – 30, 1958.

Olds J: Self-stimulation of the brain. *Science: 127,* 315 – 324, 1958.

Palmer LA, Rosenquist AL, Tusa R: The retinotopic organization of lateral suprasylvian visual area in the cat. *J. Comp. Neurol.: 177,* 237 – 256, 1978.

Pandya DM, Kuypers HGJM: Cortico-cortical connections in the rhesus monkey. *Brain Res.: 13,* 13 – 26, 1969.

Papez JW: A proposed mechanism of emotion. *Arch. Neurol. Psychiatry: 38,* 725 – 743, 1937.

Pribram KH, McGuiness D: Arousal, activation and effort in the control of attention. *Psychol. Rev.: 182,* 116 – 149, 1975.

Reeves AG, Hagemen WD: Behavioral and EEG asymmetry following lesions of the forebrain and midbrain of cats. *Electroencephalogr. Clin. Neurophysiol.: 30,* 83 – 86, 1971.

Robinson DA, Fuchs AF: Eye movements evoked by stimulation of frontal eye fields. *J. Neurophysiol.: 32,* 637 – 648, 1969.

Ropert N, Steriade M: Input-output organization of midbrain reticular core. *J. Neurophysiol.: 46,* 17 – 31, 1981.

Ross ED: The aprosodias: functional-anatomic organization of the affective components of language in the right hemisphere. *Ann. Neurol.: 38,* 561 – 589, 1981.

Ross ED, Mesulam MM: Dominant language functions of the right hemisphere? Prosody and emotional gesturing. *Arch. Neurol.: 36,* 144 – 148, 1979.

Schachter S: The interaction of cognitive and physiological determinants of emotional state. In Berkowitz (Editor), *Advances in Experimental Social Psychology, Vol. 1.* New York: Academic Press, 1970.

Scheibel ME, Scheibel AM: Structural organization of nonspecific thalamic nuclei and their projection toward cortex. *Brain Res.: 6,* 90 – 94, 1967.

Segundo JP, Naquet R, Buser, P: Effects of cortical stimulation on electrocortical activity in monkeys. *J. Neurophysiol.: 18,* 236 – 245, 1955.

Shute CCD, Lewis PR: The ascending cholinergic reticular system, neocortical, olfactory and subcortical projections. *Brain: 90,* 496 – 520, 1967.

Siegel JM: Behavioral functions of the reticular formation. *Brain Res. Rev.: 1,* 69 – 105, 1979.

Siegel JM, Tomaszewski KS: Behavioral organization of reticular formation: studies in the unrestrained cat. I. Cells related to axial, limb, eye, and other movements. *J. Neurophysiol.: 50,* 696 – 716, 1983.

Singer W: The effect of mesencephalic reticular stimulation on intracellular potential of cat lateral geniculate. *Brain Res.: 61,* 55 – 68, 1973.

Singer W: Control of thalamic transmission by corticofugal and ascending reticular pathways in the visual system. *Physiol. Rev.: 57,* 386 – 420, 1977.

Sokoloy YN: *Perception and the Conditioned Reflex.* Oxford: Pergamon, 1963.

Steriade M, Glenn LL: Neocortical and caudate projections of intralaminar thalamic neurons and their synaptic excitation from midbrain reticular core. *J. Neurophysiol.: 48,* 352 – 371.

Suzuki H, Azuma M: Prefrontal neuronal activity during gazing at a light spot in the monkey. *Brain. Res.: 126,* 497 – 508, 1977.

Teuber HL, Corkin S, Twitchell TE: A study of cingulotomy in man. In Psychosurgery. PHEW Publication No. (DS) 77-0002. Washington DC: US Government Printing Office, 1977.

Tomkins SS, McCarter R: What and where are the primary affects? Some evidence for a theory. *Percept. Motor Skills: 18,* 119 – 158, 1964.

Trexler LE, Schmidt ND: Autonomic arousal associated with complex affective stimuli in lateralized brain injury. Paper presented before International Neuropsychological Society, Bergen, Norway.

Valenstein ES: *Brain Control: A Critical Examination of Brain Stimulation and Psychosurgery.* New York: Wiley-Interscience, 1973.

Valenstein E, Heilman KM: Unilateral hypokinesia and motor extinction. *Neurology: 31,* 445 – 448, 1981.

Valenstein E, Van Den Abell T, Watson RT, Heilman KM: Non-sensory neglect from parietotemporal lesions in monkeys. *Neurology: 32,* 1198 – 1201, 1982.

Vanderwolf CH, Robinson TE: Reticulo-cortical activity and behavior: a critique of arousal theory and a new synthesis. *Behav. Brain Sci.: 4,* 459 – 514, 1981.

Velasco F, Velasco M: A reticulothalamic system mediating proprioceptive attention and tremor in man. *Neurosurgery: 4,* 30 – 36, 1979.

Walter WG: Human frontal lobe function in sensory-motor association. In Pribram KH, Luria AR (Editors), *Psychophysiology of the Frontal Lobes.* New York: Academic Press, pp. 109 – 122, 1973.

Watson RT, Heilman KM, Cauthen JC, King FA: Neglect after cingulectomy. *Neurology: 24,* 1003 – 1007, 1973.

Watson RT, Heilman KM, Miller BD, King FA: Neglect after mesencephalic reticular formation lesions. *Neurology: 24,* 294 – 298, 1974.

Watson RT, Andriola M, Heilman KM: The EEG in neglect. *J. Neurol. Sci.: 34,* 343 – 348, 1977.

Watson RT, Miller BD, Heilman KM: Nonsensory neglect. *Ann. Neurol.: 3,* 505 – 508, 1978.

Watson RT, Valenstein E, Heilman KM: Thalamic neglect: the possible role of the medial thalamus and nucleus reticularis thalami in behavior. *Arch. Neurol.: 38,* 501 – 507, 1981.

Welch K, Stuteville P: Experimental production of unilateral neglect in monkeys. *Brain: 81,* 341 – 347, 1958.

Whishaw IQ, Robinson TE, Schallert T, De Ryck M, Ramirez VD: Electrical activity of the hippocampus and neocortex in rats depleted of brain dopamine and norepinephrine: relations to behavior and effects of atropine. *Exp. Neurol.: 62:* 748 – 767, 1978.

Wilson SAK: Some problems in neurology. II: Pathological laughing and crying. *J. Neurol. Psychopathol.: 16,* 299 – 333, 1924.

Woods JW: Taming of the wild Norway rat by rhinocephalic lesions. *Nature: 170,* 869, 1956.

Wurtz RH, Mohler CW: Organization of monkey superior colliculus: enhance visual response of superficial layer cells. *J. Neurophysiol.: 39,* 745 – 765, 1976.

Yakolev PI: Motility, behavior, and the brain: stereodynamic organization and neural coordinates of behavior. *J. Nerv. Ment. Dis.: 127,* 490 – 502, 1948.

Yokoyama K, Jennings R, Ackles P, Hood P, Boller F: Lack of heart rate changes during an attention demanding task after right hemisphere lesions. *Neurology:* in press.

CHAPTER 20

Laterality and emotion: an electrophysiological approach

Richard J. Davidson and Andrew J. Tomarken

Department of Psychology, University of Wisconsin-Madison, WI, U.S.A.

Introduction

Although functional differences between the two cerebral hemispheres in the control of emotional behavior have been noted for over fifty years (e.g., Alford, 1933; Goldstein, 1939), relatively little systematic study of this problem occurred prior to the last decade. During this latter period there has been a dramatic increase in research on this topic. Furthermore, this accumulating body of work encompasses a wide variety of methodological approaches. For example, neurological, psychiatric and normal populations have all been studied extensively, and a range of assessment techniques have been used. These latter include self-report and behavioral indices of emotion, and behavioral, electrophysiological and other indices of regional brain activity (for reviews, see Davidson, 1984; Leventhal and Tomarken, 1986; Silberman and Weingartner, 1986; Tucker, 1981; Tucker and Frederick, in press). In addition to this large corpus of new data in humans, animal findings consistent with the human data have been obtained, and promising animal models of the lateralization of emotion have been developed (for reviews, see Denenberg and Yutzey, 1985; Glick and Shapiro, 1985).

In this chapter, we will first present a brief review of representative findings in the area of lateralization and emotion. In the process, we will highlight several key conclusions from these data and discuss some significant gaps in our current understanding of the hemispheric substrates of emotion. After presenting this brief overview, we will consider some specific methodological requirements for research on the psychobiology of emotion. We will then present recent electrophysiological research from our laboratory on both task-dependent emotion-related EEG asymmetries and on individual differences in resting patterns of asymmetry which predict emotional reactivity.

Asymmetry and emotion: previous empirical observations

Although there has been a notable convergence of findings and conclusions across studies using different methodological approaches, there have also been inconsistent findings and differing interpretations of those results that have proven replicable (e.g., Davidson, 1984; Levy, 1983; Tucker and Williamson, 1984). Previously, we (Davidson, 1984; Leventhal and Tomarken, 1986) have argued that one major reason for disagreements and inconsistencies in this area is the failure to distinguish between the *perception* or *decoding* of emotional information, and the *experience* or *expression* of emotion. Additionally, investigators have often failed to distinguish regional variations in specialization or activation within a hemisphere, along the rostral-caudal axis. Taking these two sets of factors into account, a number of converging lines of evidence indicate that the posterior regions of the right hemisphere are relatively more specialized for the perception, or decoding, of affective information.

Posterior right hemisphere superiority for the perception of emotional information is supported by evidence from both brain-damaged and normal populations. Concerning the former, several studies have shown that posterior right hemisphere lesions impair the ability to detect the emotional tone of speech. No such impairments were found in patients with left hemisphere lesions (e.g., Heilman et al., 1975; Tucker et al., 1976). Right hemisphere parietal lesions have been found to impair the ability to recognize emotional faces, while comparable lesions in the homologous left hemisphere region have little effect (Etcoff, 1986). Consistent with these clinical findings, a plethora of studies in normal adults and children have shown right hemisphere superiority for the perception of emotional information. In the auditory modality, investigators have examined hemispheric differences in the ability to judge the emotional tone of speech or to identify non-verbal emotional sounds. For example, Carmon and Nachson (1973), in one of the first studies to evaluate hemispheric differences in the perception of emotional information, found that accuracy of emotional sound identification (e.g., baby crying) was better in the left ear (whose fibers project predominantly, although not exclusively, to the right hemisphere) than the right ear. In the visual modality, many similar studies have been performed. The essential method used in these studies has been to compare either reaction time or accuracy of recognition in response to hemi-retinal presentations of visual stimuli. When such stimuli are exposed to the left visual field, they project directly to the right hemisphere and vice versa. These studies have repeatedly found enhanced performance when emotional stimuli are presented directly to the left versus right visual field (e.g., Ley and Bryden, 1979; Saxby and Bryden, 1985; Suberi and McKeever, 1979).

Most of the studies which were designed to examine hemispheric differences in the processing of emotional versus non-emotional information have not explicitly considered the valence of the emotional stimuli. For example, some studies have not used an equal number of positive and negative emotional stimuli (e.g., Carmon and Nachson, 1973; Schwartz et al., 1975). Most studies which have carefully compared differences in performance as a function of the valence of the emotional cues have not found systematic differences in the processing of positive and negative stimuli. Right hemisphere superiority is typically found for both types of cue (e.g., Ley and Bryden, 1979; for review, see Etcoff, 1986; Silberman and Weingartner, 1986). Some studies, however, have reported hemispheric differences in the perception of positive and negative emotional information, with left hemisphere superiority in the perception of positive cues and right hemisphere superiority in the perception of negative cues (e.g., Reuter-Lorenz and Davidson, 1981; Reuter-Lorenz et al., 1983; Natale et al., 1983). We have suggested that the differences between studies may in part reflect the degree to which affect is actually recruited by experimental stimuli (Davidson, 1984).

In contrast to the preponderance of evidence relating to hemispheric substrates of emotional perception, evidence concerning the experience or spontaneous expression of emotion underscores the importance of valence. Specifically, certain left hemisphere regions are activated during the experience or spontaneous expression of particular positive emotions, while corresponding regions of the right hemisphere are relatively more activited during the experience or expression of particular negative emotions. Furthermore, this pattern of asymmetry is most strongly linked to activity in the *anterior* regions of the cerebral hemispheres.

Evidence from several sources supports this conclusion. Studies on the affective correlates of unilateral brain damage indicate that lesions in the left anterior region are more likely to result in depressive symptomatology compared with comparable right hemisphere lesions. In one of the first systematic studies to compare the emotional consequences of left versus right-sided brain damage, Gainotti (1972) reported that left-lesioned patients had significantly more negative affect and depressive symptomatology compared with right-lesioned patients. Sackeim et al. (1982), in a review of the literature on pathological laughter and crying subsequent to unilateral brain damage, found a similar pattern indicating relative left hemisphere specialization for laughter and relative right hemisphere specialization for crying. More recently, using rigorous quantitative assessment of lesion location inferred from CT-scan evidence, Robinson and his colleagues (Robinson et al., 1984) reported a very strong correlation between the proximity of a lesion to the frontal pole within the left hemisphere and severity of depressive symptomatology based on a composite index (see also Kolb and Milner, 1981; Robinson and Benson, 1981; Robinson and Szetela, 1981).

Electrophysiological studies on non-lesioned populations point toward a similar conclusion. Such studies have typically used spectral analysis of the EEG to make inferences about patterns of regional activation (see Davidson, 1988, for an overview of these methods). In the next part of this chapter we will review an extensive series of studies from our laboratory which use such methods. A number of other workers, using similar measures, have reported effects similar to ours. This evidence indicates that the anterior region of the right hemisphere is relatively more activated during negative compared with positive emotion (e.g., Ahern and Schwartz, 1985; Tucker et al., 1981). In addition, depressives have been reported to show more relative right-sided activation in anterior electrode sites compared with non-depressed subjects (see Henriques and Davidson, 1989, for review).

A strong linkage between anterior regions of the cerebral hemispheres and affective experience is additionally consistent with evidence of the extensive neuroanatomical reciprocity between prefrontal and anterior temporal regions of the cerebral cortex and limbic circuits known to be directly involved in the control of motivation and emotion (e.g., Kelly and Stinus, 1984; Nauta, 1971). As a caveat, we should note, however, that recent evidence from our laboratory (to be reviewed below) also indicates an association between at least one affective state (clinical depression) and asymmetries in posterior regions. That the pattern of posterior asymmetry in this case is opposite to that found in anterior regions once again underscores the importance of regional specificity. It should be noted that this posterior asymmetry is most related to cognitive dysfunction which accompanies depression and may not be specifically associated with the primary affective disturbance.

Prior to reviewing our own recent studies in this area, we should note several significant unexplored or unresolved issues pertaining to evidence for hemispheric differences in emotion. One of the most significant among the unexplored issues concerns the temporal coordination among different response systems which specify emotion. For example, do the changes in asymmetrical anterior activation precede, accompany or follow changes in the subjective experience or facial expression of emotion? Another significant unexplored issue is the relationship between electrophysiological measures of emotion-related asymmetries and other biological indices (e.g., regional cerebral metabolism as assessed by emission-computed tomography). A final unexplored issue is the relationship between patterns of cortical and sub-cortical activation in specific brain circuits implicated in emotion and motivation. We know from extensive animal evidence that emotion and motivation are represented at various levels of the neuraxis from the brainstem to the cortex (e.g., Gallistel, 1980a). Some have suggested that heightened activation in a particular cortical region is associated with decreased activation in underlying subcortical tissue (e.g., Tucker and Frederick, in press). According to one variant of this view, relative *left-sided* anterior activation in *cortical* regions is associated with relative *right-sided* activation in *subcortical* regions (e.g., Levy, 1983). One source of evidence which we believe militates against such an interpretation is data from patients with subcortical lesions who have been found to show emotional symptoms which are highly similar to those found in patients with cortical damage to the same hemisphere. Specifically, Starkstein et al., (1987) have found that left anterior lesions, *both* cortical *and* subcortical, are associated with the presence of depressive symptomatology. Other investigators have observed similar effects (e.g., Cummings and Mendez, 1984).

In this chapter, we will review recent findings from our laboratory that indicate differential contributions of the cerebral hemispheres to the experience or spontaneous expression of emotion. We will concentrate on the results of our most recent studies using electrophysiological methods, specifically spectral-analysed EEG. Two general types of studies will be reviewed. The first type focuses on changes in EEG measures of activation asymmetry brought about by the experimental induction of emotional *states* in normal subjects. In such studies, emotional states have typically been induced by visual stimuli (e.g., affective film clips or slides) or by the self-generation of positive and negative emotional imagery. The second type of study focuses on *individual differences* in patterns of resting activation, assessed while subjects are sitting quietly, in the absence of exposure to an emotion elicitor. Studies in this latter category assess whether patterns of resting asymmetry can discriminate between diagnostic groups (depressives and normals), or whether such patterns can predict the affective responses of normals when subjects are exposed to emotion elicitors at a later point in time. We will first review our recent work on EEG asymmetries associated with the elicitation of emotional states. Before doing so, however, it is useful to note a number of unique methodological requirements for research on the psychophysiological manifestations of emotional states (from Davidson et al., in press).

Methodological desiderata in psychophysiological research on emotional states

Research on the psychophysiology of emotion has traditionally been hindered by the failure to adhere to a number of important methodological desider-

ata particular to studies in this area. Fulfillment of these requirements helps ensure that valid exemplars of the intended emotions are compared or measures which are appropriately chosen to reflect changes brought about by the induction of emotion. Below, we note eight such desiderata for research on the biological substrates of human emotion. These apply to studies of both autonomic and central nervous system components of emotion. In this section, and in the subsequent section reviewing our own research on EEG correlates of emotional states, we note the degree to which these desiderata are satisfied in our own studies.

1. Emotion must actually be elicited. While this requirement may seem trivial, many experiments which purport to study emotion may not actually elicit significant emotion in subjects. Some studies focus more on the perception of affective cues. Other studies, particularly those that focus on subject's perceptions of how they *would* think and feel in hypothetical situations, may focus more on the structure of subjects' beliefs about emotions, or the language that they use to describe emotion. If the goal of the research is to characterize the psychophysiology of emotion, then there must be evidence that emotion was actually produced.

We acknowledge that researchers studying the psychophysiological correlates of negative emotions may face valid ethical constraints that may limit their ability to fulfill this requirement. For example, the elicitation of intense, phobic-like fear in the absence of any benefit to subjects is not acceptable. There are, however, options which permit the transcendence of such constraints. For example, in some of our current research, we are inducing emotion in therapeutic contexts, for example during the course of exposure treatment for phobias.

2. Adequate procedures must be used to verify the presence of the intended emotion. One of the noteworthy characteristics of emotion is the lack of an isomorphic relationship between an elicitor and a particular emotion (see Ekman, 1984). In other words, the same elicitor will often produce an array of different emotions across subjects.

even in response to elicitors that are specifically chosen to target a particular discrete emotion, subjects typically will report a range of different emotions if given the opportunity (cf. Ekman et al., 1980). In our recent work, we have attempted to produce emotion using film stimuli that induce relatively 'pure emotion' (e.g., high levels of sadness, low levels of other emotions). Our experiences selecting film clips for use in these experiments have underscored for us the relatively non-specific effects of the great majority of affective stimuli. It is particularly difficult to dissociate specific combinations of emotions. For example, we have found that the overwhelming majority of film clips that elicit significant disgust in subjects also elicit significant fear. Clearly, self-report instruments used to assess affective responses must assess both the targeted emotion and other emotions that may also be elicited. The failure to assess multiple emotions is particularly grievous in work designed to assess emotion-specific psychophysiological profiles.

3. Epochs of different discrete emotions must be separable. Not only is it likely that any given elicitor will produce more than one emotion, the relative intensities of different emotions may also change sequentially over time. Unfortunately, studies on the psychophysiology of emotion typically ignore this possibility by aggregating data over the entire duration of the eliciting stimulus. Simply put, it is imperative to identify separate periods of time during which different discrete emotions are present. Only in this way can the physiology that accompanies different emotions be directly compared.

Note that this requirement necessitates a method which provides a continuous or near-continuous measure of emotional state. One possibility here would be to have subjects continuously rate their emotional experiences using a joy-stick or similar device (e.g., Davidson et al., 1979a). However, one obvious limitation of this method is that the requirement of continuous rating may distract subjects from the experimental stimulus and weaken its emotional impact. As a better alternative, in our recent studies, we have surreptitiously videotaped subjects' affective facial expressions during exposure to stimuli. Using this unobtrusive method, we have been able to extract those periods in time during which particular discrete emotions were present.

4. The physiological measures chosen for study must have a sufficiently fast time constant to reflect brief periods of emotion. Quite often, emotional states are relatively fleeting, lasting perhaps less than four seconds (Ekman, 1984). High levels of emotional intensity are especially likely to be brief. It is clear that only those physiological events which have a relatively fast time constant are capable of being the core substrate for such affective phenomena. Correspondingly, only those measures that have sensitive temporal resolution are capable of tracking the physiological correlates of emotion in these circumstances. In our work, a major reason that we have relied on EEG measures of emotion is the excellent time resolution of EEG relative to competing techniques (e.g., cerebral blood flow, PET) for assessing the neural correlates of emotional states (see Davidson, 1988, for a review of the relative strengths and weaknesses of EEG). Certainly, when affective phenomena are more long-lasting (e.g., clinical depression), other physiological systems and measures whose response properties are slower may also be appropriate foci of study.

5. At least two emotions must be compared. An experimental design which allows for assessment of the effects of only one emotion makes it impossible to conclude whether any physiological changes observed are unique to that specific emotion or are non-specific changes associated with *any* emotion. Thus, at least two emotion conditions are required. In addition, it is preferable to have a baseline condition against which to compare the emotion-arousing conditions. It is possible that two emotion conditions will differ from one another, but only one condition will differ significantly from baseline. Such a finding could have an important bearing on the interpretation of a particular result.

6. Each emotion under consideration should be induced by at least two distinct stimuli or methods. This requirement is an extension of the preceding one. Simply put, in the absence of multiple stimuli or methods for inducing each emotion, it is unclear whether experimental effects are produced by emotion per se, or by the unique, potentially non-emotion-related, features of the stimulus. In our recent work, where feasible, we have endeavored to use at least two exemplars of each emotion category (e.g., two distinct film clips designed to elicit happiness) and to replicate results across multiple methods.

7. The intensity of the elicited emotion must be matched between conditions. When two or more emotions are compared, it is imperative to match the intensity of emotions so that differences in intensity do not confound the emotion-specific comparisons. Unfortunately, many investigators who have compared two or more emotions have not utilized any procedure to match the intensity of the elicited emotions (e.g., Schwartz et al., 1981). If two emotions that differ in intensity also differ in some physiological parameter, it is impossible to say whether emotion-specific factors or intensity account for the physiological differences.

It is important to note that stimuli matched under certain contextual conditions may not remain matched under others. For example, in our experience, ratings of the happiness elicited by film clips tend to be higher when subjects view films, and make ratings, in a group setting, rather than alone. Conversely, fear and disgust ratings tend to be higher when subjects are run individually rather than in a group. Thus, two sets of emotional stimuli matched on intensity in a group context may not be matched in an individualized setting. This point highlights the need to make the stimulus selection context as similar as possible to the actual experimental context.

8. For each emotion under study, a sufficient duration of data must be obtained from each subject. In order to obtain stable estimates of physiological activity, a certain minimum amount of artifact-free data is required. Precisely what con-

stitutes a sufficient duration will vary as a function of the physiological measures of interest. If the dependent measure is EEG, a minimum of approximately 10 seconds would be required in order to obtain a stable estimate of spectral power (Davidson, 1988). In order to have sufficient durations of data, we have frequently used a within-subject aggregation strategy. For example, if physiological activity during smiling was of interest, all instances of the artifact-free physiology during target smiles would be extracted, analysed and then aggregated for each subject.

Patterns of brain electrical asymmetry during emotional states

Before reviewing our recent studies on patterns of EEG asymmetry during facial signs of emotion in adults and infants, we will briefly describe the EEG recording and analysis methodology which is common to all of the studies from our laboratory reviewed in this chapter. For additional details, the reader is referred to Davidson (1988).

In certain respects, brain electrical activity measures are ideally suited for the study of neural activity underlying emotional behavior. For example, such measures can be recorded non-invasively from the scalp surface. In addition, as noted above, brain electrical activity measures have a very fast time resolution. Indeed, events in the millisecond range can be resolved with certain measures. This makes them ideally suited for the study of emotion, where the critical periods for analysis are often very brief due to the fleeting nature of affect. In studies of emotional state, we often examine brain electrical activity which is coincident with brief facial expressions of emotion. We use the face as a flag to provide us with information on periods during which peak emotional activity is present. The brain activity is then extracted for these periods and subjected to quantitative analysis.

There are two salient disadvantages of brain electrical activity measures in the study of emotion which should also be noted. The first is a problem endemic to all applications of these measures. Topographic differences in scalp-recorded brain electrical activity do not necessarily reflect activity from underlying neural tissue. The source generators of scalp-recorded brain electrical activity are difficult to unambiguously describe, particularly for neural activity which may be generated by large, multiple regions of the brain. Thus, the spatial resolution of this method is less than ideal. The second problem is that most features of brain electrical activity which are recorded from the scalp surface and analysed using the methods described below are generated in the cortex. Since we know that significant contributions to emotional behavior are made by structures which are subcortical, the analysis of cortical activity may seem tangential to the study of the neural substrates of emotion.

As we will illustrate below, certain cortical regions do participate in emotional behavior. It is those cortical areas which have extensive anatomical connections with limbic structures implicated in the control of emotion. The crude spatial resolution of EEG remains a significant methodological obstacle. However, confidence in the localization findings is increased as convergence across methods is obtained. As we note below, there are now striking parallels in the findings on regional electrophysiological asymmetries in 'non-neurological' depressed subjects and the effects of localized unilateral lesions on depressive symptomatology.

The principal method of quantitative analysis that will be presented in this chapter is the Fast Fourier Transform (FFT). This procedure decomposes the complex waveforms of the EEG into their underlying sine-wave constituents. From this analysis, estimates of power in different frequency bands can be obtained. To obtain stable estimates of spectral power for brain activity accompanying a particular emotional expression, we require a minimum of about 10 seconds of artifact-free EEG. Once power values are obtained, they are log-transformed to normalize their distribution. Before analysis, all data are artifact-scored by hand to eliminate data confounded by eye movements,

muscle activity and other sources of artifact. The FFT is then performed on artifact-free epochs of EEG. When analysing EEG contemporaneous with facial expressions, these epochs are approximately 1 second in duration. They are extracted via a Hamming window, which minimizes spurious frequency components (see Davidson, 1988, for a detailed discussion of these technical issues), and are overlapped by 75%. The output of the FFT is then averaged over all epochs extracted from the same condition so that a minimum of 10 seconds is obtained.

In the studies presented in the second part of this chapter on individual differences in asymmetry and their relation to affective reactivity, brain electrical activity is measured during a short resting period when subjects are sitting quietly. Due to the greater proportion of artifact-free data during resting baselines, the epoch length for the baseline-period FFTs is approximately two seconds in duration. The output of the FFT is aggregated over all epochs within the baseline period.

Although we typically extract, and perform statistical analyses upon, measures of power density in several frequency bands, in studies using adult subjects our experimental hypotheses and major analyses concern the alpha frequency band (8 – 13 Hz). This is because there is a wealth of evidence indicating that increased alpha activity is associated with decreased cerebral activation (e.g., Shagass, 1972) and because asymmetrical activation in this frequency band has been most consistently linked both to emotional states and to individual differences (for reviews, see Davidson, 1988; Davidson et al., 1989). The specific measure of asymmetry derived is the difference between the log of alpha power in the right hemisphere and the log of alpha power in the homologous left hemisphere region (i.e., log right alpha – log left alpha). Since increased alpha indicates decreased cortical activity, higher scores on this index indicate greater relative left hemisphere activation. In our studies with infants in the first year of life, we began by examining whole band power (1 – 12 Hz), since the specific frequency equivalent of alpha activity in the infants is not definitively known. In adults, measures of whole band power (1 – 30 Hz) have been found to change in a fashion quite similar to alpha activity (see Davidson, 1988). In more recent studies with infants, we have found that most of the variance in both task-dependent changes in EEG asymmetry as well as individual differences in resting activation are in the 6 – 8 Hz frequency band (see review in Davidson and Fox, 1988).

Below we will briefly review two recent studies performed in our laboratory which examine EEG asymmetry during facial signs of emotion. The first experiment was a collaborative study with Ekman and Friesen (Davidson et al., in press) in which right-handed adult subjects were presented with brief film clips designed to elicit happiness and disgust. We chose happiness and disgust since these were emotions that we expected to be associated with approach and withdrawal respectively. As will be discussed more extensively below, we have hypothesized that approach vs. withdrawal may be the underlying dimension indexed by asymmetries in anterior regions. Subjects were presented with two positive and two negative film clips in a darkened room while we unobtrusively videotaped them and recorded brain electrical activity from the left and right mid-frontal, central, anterior temporal and parietal regions. All EEG leads were referenced to vertex.

In accord with the methodological desiderata described above, the films were carefully selected to elicit positive and negative affect at comparable intensities. The predominant emotion elicited by the positive clips was amusement and by the negative films the predominant emotion was disgust. The mean intensity of amusement reported in response to the two positive film clips (on a 0 – 8 point scale) was 5.88. The mean intensity of disgust reported in response to the two negative film clips was 5.44. These self-report data suggest that the two classes of films were well matched on the intensity of the predominant emotion elicited by each.

The video record of each subject was coded with

Ekman and Friesen's (1978) Facial Action Coding System FACS). FACS distinguishes 44 action units. These are the minimal units that are anatomically separate and visually distinctive. Any facial movement can be described in terms of the particular action unit, or units, that produced it. The scorer identifies the action units, such as the one which pulls the lip corners up, or which lowers the brow, rather than making inferences about underlying emotional states such as happiness or anger. FACS scoring of the facial data from this experiment revealed that the two types of expression which occurred with the most frequency were happy expressions in response to the positive film clips and disgust expressions in response to the negative film clips. For each subject, the onset and offset of each happy and disgust expression was identified with FACS. These times were then entered into the computer so that the EEG coincident with these expressions could be extracted.

Artifact-free EEG during facial expressions of happiness and disgust was Fourier transformed to yield measures of power density. As noted above, power density in the alpha frequency band was of prime interest, and it is these data that will be reported below. Based on previous findings from our laboratory and other laboratories reviewed above, we hypothesized greater relative right hemisphere activation in anterior regions during

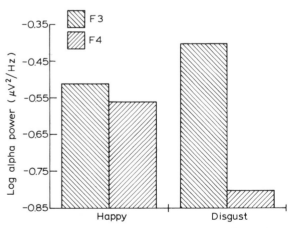

Fig. 1. Mean log-transformed alpha-power (in $\mu V^2/Hz$) from the left and right mid-frontal regions (F3 and F4) during facial signs of happiness and disgust. From Davidson et al. (in press).

facial expressions of disgust compared to facial expressions of happiness. As shown in Fig. 1, the data supported our hypothesis. In the mid-frontal region, assessed by the F3 and F4 electrode sites in the international 10 – 20 system, disgust periods were associated with greater right-sided activation (i.e., less alpha power) than happy periods. The pattern of greater right-sided activation during disgust compared with happiness was also found in the anterior temporal region. That no significant between-condition differences were found for the central and parietal regions underscores the regional specificity of the effects observed.

Fig. 2 displays frontal asymmetry scores (log right minus log left alpha power) from the happy and disgust periods for individual subjects. Two aspects of this figure are noteworthy. First, every subject shows a lower score during disgust expressions than happy expressions. Thus, *100%* of the subjects showed more relative right-sided frontal activation during disgust compared with happy periods. The second important feature of these data is the pronounced individual variability in the absolute magnitude of the asymmetry scores. Some subjects show highly positive asymmetry scores overall, denoting tonic left-sided frontal activation, while other subjects show highly negative asymmetry scores denoting overall right-sided

frontal activation. In other words, the between-condition differences in asymmetry (i.e., between happy and disgust) are superimposed upon widely varying individual differences in the overall magnitude and direction of asymmetry. As will be considered in the next section of this paper, these individual differences in tonic asymmetry may be related to important dimensions of affective style.

In order to examine whether the procedures we used to verify the presence of an emotion (i.e., facial expression) actually made an important difference in uncovering patterns of asymmetry, we performed the type of analysis which is more typical in research on the psychophysiology of emotion. We simply compared all artifact-free EEG epochs extracted from the positive film clips with the comparable epochs extracted from the negative film clips. The epochs used for this analysis were selected irrespective of the subject's facial behavior. While the means were in the expected direction for the frontal leads, with the negative film clips producing more right-sided activation compared with the positive clips, we found no significant differences between these conditions on any of the measures of asymmetry. The lack of significant effects when the analyses were performed independent of facial behavior suggests that our method of using the facial expressivity to flag epochs of peak emotional state was effective. In this study, significant between-condition differences in asymmetry were obtained only when facial expression was used to verify the presence of emotional states. We should note, however, that previous studies in our laboratory and other laboratories (e.g., Ahern and Schwartz, 1985; Tucker et al., 1981) have found EEG differences between positive and negative emotional states without using facial expressive measures as an index of peak emotional intensity. Thus, the presence of discrete facial expressions of emotion does not appear to be a *necessary* condition for the emergence of hemispheric asymmetries relevant to emotion.

One line of research from our laboratory that has used both a facial-expressive strategy and the more traditional whole-epoch strategy is a series of

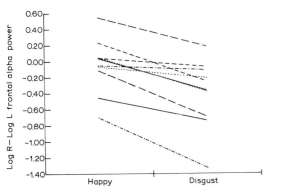

Fig. 2. Frontal asymmetry laterality scores (log right – log left alpha power) for individual subjects during facial signs of happiness and disgust. Higher numbers on this index denote greater relative left-sided activation. Note that every subject shows a higher score during happiness compared with disgust. Based upon data from Davidson et al. (in press).

collaborative studies with Nathan Fox. Focusing on EEG asymmetries in infants, this research effort has been designed to document the early manifestations of cerebral asymmetries which underlie emotion. In our first study with this age group (Davidson and Fox, 1982), we presented 10-month-old infants with a videotape of an actress displaying laughter and distress while EEG was recorded from the left and right frontal and parietal regions. We found that the positive condition elicited more left-sided frontal activation than the negative condition. This finding was obtained in two separate samples of infants. In a more recent study, we (Fox and Davidson, 1986) tested newborn infants to determine whether this asymmetry was present at birth. Neonates were presented with tastes which differed in hedonic valence while brain electrical activity was recorded. We found that tastes which produced facial signs of disgust were associated with more right-sided activation compared with tastes which produced a more positive facial expression (sucrose). In this study, we found that the asymmetry difference between conditions was present in both the frontal and parietal regions. Whether this reflects the lack of functional differentiation in these cortical regions at this age is a question that must await additional research.

In more recent work with Fox (Fox and Davidson, 1988), we have studied brain electrical activity during the expression of different facial signs of emotion in 10-month-old infants. Emotion was elicited via the approach of a mother and a stranger. Of prime interest to us was a comparison between two types of smile. One of these involves activity in both the zygomatic muscle (cheek) *and* orbicularis oculi (around the eye) while the other involves activity only in the zygomatic region. The difference between these two smile types was first described by the French anatomist Duchenne (1862). Duchenne's work figured heavily in Darwin's 1872 book *The Expression of the Emotions in Man and Animals*. According to Darwin's discussion, Duchenne suggested that the emotion of 'frank joy' is accompanied by activity in both the

zygomatic and orbicularis oculi muscles, while smiles not associated with felt happiness are accompanied only by activity in the zygomatic region. Ekman and Friesen (1982) provided the first modern empirical support for this proposal by showing that smiles involving activity in both of these facial regions were much more highly correlated with self-reports of happiness than smiles produced by activity in only the zygomatic region. In the light of this evidence, we were intrigued by the possibility that these two types of smile could be discriminated electrophysiologically.

Artifact-free EEG data were obtained on 19 infants, all born to two right-handed parents. EEG was recorded from the left and right frontal and parietal regions and quantified in the same manner as described above for the study with adults. Infants were exposed to episodes of both mother approach and stranger approach. Facial behavior and EEG were recorded in response to each episode. Facial behavior was coded with Ekman and Friesen's (1984) EM-FACS system.

We first computed the incidence of each of the two smile types in response to both stranger and mother approach. Seventy-five percent of the infants displayed smiles without orbicularis oculi activity to the stranger, while in response to mother approach 78% of the infants displayed smiles with orbicularis oculi activity. The difference in the frequency of occurrence of these two smile types is highly significant ($p < 0.005$). In other words, smiles indicative of felt happiness were more likely to occur in the situation in which genuine positive affect would be expected (mother approach), while a potentially threatening situation (stranger approach) was more likely to elicit 'unfelt happiness'. We also coded the duration of the two smile types, since Darwin (1872) suggested that the more 'genuine' smiles (i.e., those with orbicularis activity) were longer in duration compared with the other type of smile. Our results confirmed Darwin's (1872) suggestion: the mean duration of smiles with orbicularis activity was 2.39 seconds, while the mean duration of smiles without orbicularis activity was 1.49 seconds ($p < 0.01$). The central question which we posed in this study was whether the two smile types could be discriminated on the basis of frontal brain electrical asymmetry. We specifically predicted that smiles with orbicularis activity would be accompanied by more relative left-sided frontal activation compared with the other smiles. As shown in Fig. 3, the data strongly supported this hypothesis. Consistent with the majority of our previous findings, regional specificity was once again indicated by the absence of significant differences in the parietal region (see Fig. 3).

We have recently examined EEG asymmetry during these two types of smile in adults (Ekman et al., in press). In this study, we were also able to examine the relationship between the duration of these smile types and self-reports of emotion. We found that higher intensities of self-reported amusement were associated with increased duration of smiles with orbicularis oculi ($r = 0.70$), while the duration of smiles without orbicularis activity were not associated with self-reports of amusement ($r = 0.14$). Most importantly, smiles with orbicularis activity were associated with significantly more left anterior activation than smiles lacking orbicularis activity. This pattern of anterior asymmetry is precisely the same found to discriminate between these two smile types in infants.

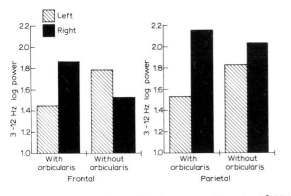

Fig. 3. Mean log-transformed band power ($3 - 12$ Hz in $\mu V^2/Hz$) for the left and right frontal and parietal regions during two types of smile in 10-month-old infants. One smile type includes activity in orbicularis oculi and the other does not. Adapted from Fox and Davidson (1988).

Anterior asymmetry, affective style and psychopathology

In recent years, we have begun exploring individual differences in resting anterior EEG asymmetry and its relation to emotional reactivity and psychopathology. We have adopted two converging strategies in our studies in this area. The first strategy involves comparing groups of subjects who differ on a known psychological or behavioral variable which theoretically should be related to anterior asymmetry. One of the most important variables we have examined is depression. The second strategy is to examine the relationship between individual differences in resting anterior activation asymmetry and affective reactivity at a later point in time in an unselected, normal cohort. Studies which represent each of these two approaches will be presented below.

Our first study in this area (Schaffer et al., 1983) was designed to determine whether patterns of resting frontal asymmetry would discriminate between depressed subjects and non-depressed subjects. Subjects for this study were selected on the basis of extreme scores on the Beck Depression Inventory. They were required to score at the extremes on two separate occasions separately by approximately 6 weeks. We then examined resting frontal and parietal EEG asymmetry using methods described above. As hypothesized, we found that the depressed subjects showed more relative right-sided frontal activation at rest compared with the non-depressed subjects. The difference between groups was primarily in the left frontal region, with the depressed subjects showing less activation.

We have recently replicated this study on a much larger sample size ($n = 23$ per group) and found the same pattern of results (Davidson et al., 1987). Depressed subjects were found to exhibit less relative left-sided frontal activation compared with non-depressed subjects. We also found that the depressed subjects showed less relative right-sided parietal activation at the same points in time. This pattern of parietal asymmetry was the same as we found in the original study (Schaffer et al., 1983), but, given the small sample size in that first study, it was not significant. In the replication study, both the frontal and parietal asymmetry differences between groups were significant.

These findings indicate the pronounced specificity which typifies regional brain asymmetry. Simultaneously, the frontal and parietal regions showed opposite patterns of asymmetry. Clearly, hemispheres as a whole are not activated in a uniform fashion. Rather, different regions within a hemisphere may become very selectively activated. Our findings indicating EEG differences between depressives and non-depressives are also noteworthy because of their convergence with recent neurological data on the emotional sequelae of unilateral brain damage. Our finding of decreased left anterior EEG activation in depressives is paralleled by a recent finding by Robinson and his colleagues (Robinson et al., 1984) which indicates a very high correlation ($r = 0.92$) between the proximity of a lesion to the frontal pole within the left hemisphere (based upon CT scan evidence) and the severity of depressive symptomatology. Consistent with our data, in Robinson et al.'s study the closer the left hemisphere lesion to the frontal pole, the more severe was the depressive symptomatology. Our finding that depressives show less relative right-sided activation in posterior regions is also consistent with Robinson et al.'s data. In addition to reporting an association between left anterior lesions and depression, these authors observed that right posterior lesions were associated with depression.

Both our findings and those of Robinson et al. (1984) suggest that there may be two neuropsychological paths to depression: (1) deficits in left anterior activation, and (2) deficits in right posterior activation. The latter type of deficit would be expected to result in impairments in certain forms of visuo-spatial processing. We (Davidson et al., 1987) recently compared subclinically depressed subjects and non-depressed controls on psychometrically matched verbal and spatial tasks. The verbal task consisted of word-finding pro-

blems and the spatial task consisted of dot-localization problems. The tasks were matched on overall difficulty, the standard deviation of item difficulty, and internal consistency reliability. As predicted, the depressed subjects showed a selective deficit on the spatial task. No differences between groups were found for the verbal task. These findings confirm the suggestion in the literature that depression is associated with a selective impairment on right hemisphere cognitive tasks (for a review, see Silberman and Weingartner, 1986). Some investigators (e.g., Willner, 1985) have speculated that the right hemisphere cognitive performance deficit in depressives may underlie certain symptoms of depression, such as deficits in interpersonal skills and in the perception of nonverbal emotional information. For example, individuals with such a deficit may show impairments in the recognition of facial expressions and intonation patterns which specify emotion.

One important question to which we have recently turned is the degree to which the differences between depressed and non-depressed subjects in resting asymmetry are state-independent. That is, does the pattern of asymmetry characteristic of depression vary as a function of the clinical status of the individual, or is it a trait marker that pre-dates the onset of depression and/or remains stable despite changes in clinical status? In a recent study, we (Henriques and Davidson, in press) have addressed this question by comparing two groups of subjects who were currently non-depressed. One group ($n = 9$) had a past history of major or minor depression according to Research Diagnostic Criteria (Spitzer et al., 1978), as assessed by the Schedule for Affective Disorders and Schizophrenia (SADS). All subjects in this group had been free from depressive symptoms for at least one year and free of all psychoactive medication for at least one month. We compared this group to a group of non-depressed subjects who had never been depressed ($n = 11$). Subjects in this latter group were additionally required to have an absence of psychiatric illness in their first-degree relatives. The groups did not differ in age, sex distribution or socioeconomic status. Most importantly, the groups did not differ in the current depression, as assessed both by the Beck Depression Inventory (M for past depressed group = 1.67 (SD = 2.25); for never depressed group = 1.43 (SD = 2.15)) and the Hamilton Depression Rating Scale (M for past depressed group = 1.16 (SD = 1.60); for never depressed group = 1.75 (SD = 1.49)).

EEG was recorded during an eyes-open and an eyes-closed baseline period from 14 scalp locations. In this study, we derived the EEG with three different reference montages. Since the major effects were significant with each reference montage, only the data from the averaged ears reference will be presented here*. No differences in asymmetry were found between the two baseline types and the data were combined across them. As we predicted, the differences in asymmetry that we found in previous studies to differentiate between acutely depressed and non-depressed subjects were present in this sample when we compared previously depressed and never depressed subjects. Specifically, there was a significant ($p < 0.05$) Group × Hemisphere interaction for the mid-frontal region (F3/F4 electrode sites)**. The previously depress-

ed group showed less activation in the left frontal region compared with the never depressed group. The trend in the parietal region was opposite to that observed in the frontal region, although this difference did not reach significance. This pattern of decreased left frontal and decreased right parietal activation can be easily observed in a topographic difference map. Fig. 4 presents the difference between the mean alpha power data for the never depressed subjects and the previously depressed subjects (i.e., never depressed − previously depressed). In this figure, lighter shading indicates greater activation (i.e., less alpha power). As can be seen from this topographic map, the never depressed subjects show more activation in both the left frontal and right posterior regions compared with the previously depressed subjects.

These results indicate that patterns of asymmetry characteristic of depression (decreased relative left frontal activation and decreased relative right parietal activation) remain even when depres-

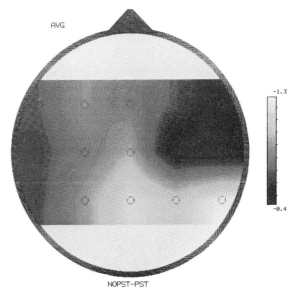

Fig. 4. Topographic map displaying the difference in mean log-transformed alpha power between never depressed and past depressed subjects. Lighter shading denotes areas where the never depressed subjects have more activation (i.e., less alpha power) than the past depressed subjects. Actual electrode locations used in producing the map are denoted by the circles. From Henriques and Davidson (in press).

* We developed the averaged ears reference to eliminate a potential problem with the more traditional linked ears reference. A number of electrophysiologists (e.g., Nunez, 1981) have suggested that physically linking the ears provides a low-resistive shunt across the head which attenuates the magnitude of observed asymmetry since it forces the two sides of the head to be isoelectric. Some researchers have empirically found that the magnitude of observed asymmetry is attenuated with a linked ears reference compared with other reference montages (e.g., Van Petten and Kutas, 1988). We developed a procedure which eliminates this possibility yet also permits us to reference to the two ears. We record each electrode referred to vertex (Cz). In addition, we record two channels of Cz, one referred to A1 (left ear) and the other referred to the right ear (A2). We then average these two channels and use this average of the two ears to re-compute each channel with respect to this new reference.
** The mid-frontal region is measured by activity in the F3 and F4 electrode sites. These are sites which we have previously found to differentiate between acutely depressed and non-depressed subjects. In addition, they were the sites used in the studies described in the first part of this chapter on state-dependent changes in frontal asymmetry in response to affect elicitors.

sion is remitted. In turn, these findings suggest that 'depressogenic' asymmetry patterns may be a *state-independent* marker that indexes risk for depression. Clearly, to more comprehensively test this hypothesis, a prospective design is required in which subjects are classified on the basis of asymmetry patterns and followed-up over time. We would predict that, relative to comparison groups, a higher proportion of subjects who demonstrate decreased left anterior activation and right posterior activation would develop subsequent psychopathology. We will be conducting such a study in the future.

Although we have not yet conducted a prospective, longitudinal study on the development of psychopathology, we have recently conducted several studies which indicate that patterns of resting asymmetry can indeed *predict* affective reactions at a later point in time. These studies have been conducted with both infant and adult samples. We have completed two studies to date in adults (Tomarken et al., 1989). These examined the relationship between resting baseline asymmetry measures obtained at the beginning of an experimental session and subjects' subsequent reactivity to short emotional film clips.

The design of each of the two studies was similar, although the subject samples were entirely independent and the film clips used in each study were different. In the first study, 24 right-handed females were assessed. Resting measures of EEG asymmetry from a 30-second eyes-open period were recorded at the beginning of the session. Subjects were then presented with two positive film clips, followed by two negative film clips. The positive clips were designed to elicit happiness and amusement and the negative film clips were designed to elicit fear and disgust. The duration of each film clip was approximately 2 minutes. Following each baseline and film trial, subjects were asked to rate their emotional experience during the clip on a series of 0−8 rating scales.

The major issue addressed in this study was the relationship between the resting measures of asymmetry (log right minus log left alpha power) taken at the start of the session and subjects' subsequent reports of their emotional responses to the film clips. We found that relative right frontal activation at rest significantly predicted fear responses to each of the two film clips ($r = -0.45$ and -0.43, $p < 0.05$) and composite (i.e., mean) fear responses across the two clips ($r = -0.48$, $p < 0.025$). Correlations between frontal asymmetry and disgust responses were not significant, although trends in the predicted direction were evident. The results of several additional sets of analyses were also revealing. First, the correlations between resting anterior asymmetry and fear responses were not simply due to the confounding effects of pre-existing mood at the time of the baselines. Resting EEG was uncorrelated with all individual mood scales assessed at the time of the baseline. In addition, it was uncorrelated with composite mood indices (e.g., composite negative affect). Moreover, when baseline mood was partialed out, correlations between frontal asymmetry and fear responses remained significant and almost identical in magnitude to their zero-order values (e.g., partial r between frontal asymmetry and composite fear $= -0.47$, $p < 0.05$). Thus, consistent with the notion that anterior asymmetry is a state-independent marker indexing affective predispositions, it predicted fear responses in this sample independent of concurrent mood state.

A second, revealing set of analyses focused on the relationship between anterior asymmetry and both positive and negative affective responses. In this sample, although the correlation was in the predicted direction, frontal asymmetry did not significantly predict happiness responses to positive films ($r = 0.18$). However, for both fear and disgust, frontal asymmetry was significantly correlated with the *difference* between negative affective responses to negative films and positive affective responses to positive films. The correlation between resting asymmetry and the disgust − happiness difference score was -0.41 ($p < 0.05$) and the correlation between resting asymmetry and the fear − happiness difference score was -0.59 ($p < 0.01$). This important finding suggests that resting anterior asymmetry may primarily index the individual's *relative balance* of positive and negative affective response tendencies.

That anterior asymmetry significantly predicted the *difference* between positive and negative affective responsivity also suggests that it does *not* index generalized emotional reactivity. This is an important observation given recent findings by Diener and his colleagues. This research group has identified stable individual differences in affective reactivity that are independent of the valence of emotion (e.g., Diener et al., 1985; Larsen et al., 1986). To conduct a more direct test of a generalized affective reactivity interpretation of frontal asymmetry, we computed what might be considered a 'generalized reactivity' index consisting of the *sum* of subjects' negative affective responses to negative films and positive affective responses to positive films. For both fear and disgust, frontal asymmetry was uncorrelated with this index (fear + happiness $r = 0.10$; disgust + happiness $r = 0.09$). These data indicate that it is not affective reactivity per se that is indexed by anterior asymmetry but a valence-specific bias in reactivity.

One additional set of results in this study is also noteworthy. Specifically, for all analyses conducted, resting asymmetry in parietal sites was unrelated to any measure of affective reactivity (e.g., zero-order r between parietal asymmetry and composite fear = 0.13). This observation once again underscores the regional specificity of the relationship between resting asymmetry and emotional responsivity.

In the second study in this series (Tomarken et al., 1989; Study II), subjects were 15 right-handed females. As in the first experiment, EEG was recorded during a 30-second eyes-open resting baseline, after which subjects completed a set of $0-8$ scales assessing current mood. Subjects then watched two positive and six negative film clips selected from contemporary movies (e.g., The Godfather) and rated their emotional responses immediately after each clip. Film clips were different from those used in Experiment 1. EEG was recorded from three sets of anterior sites: mid-

frontal (F3/F4), lateral frontal (F7/F8) and anterior temporal (T3/T4). In addition, EEG was recorded from two posterior sites: posterior temporal (T5/T6) and parietal (P3/P4).

We computed correlations between resting EEG asymmetry and composite fear and disgust responses across the four films which elicited at least moderate fear and disgust and we computed correlations between resting asymmetry and happiness ratings across the two films which elicited at least moderate happiness. As in the first experiment, greater relative right hemisphere activation in the mid-frontal site was associated with greater fear ($r = -0.35$), although this correlation was not significant due to the small sample size ($n = 14$). Furthermore, resting asymmetry in both the mid-frontal and lateral frontal sites was highly correlated with disgust responses to negative films ($r = -0.62$ and -0.68, respectively; $p < 0.025$). In addition, although resting frontal asymmetry did not predict happiness responses, anterior temporal asymmetry was significantly correlated with composite happiness ratings ($r = 0.52$), in the direction hypothesized (greater relative left anterior temporal activation associated with increased happiness).

As in Experiment 1, resting anterior asymmetry predicted affective responses independent of concurrent mood at the time of the baselines. Resting asymmetry was either uncorrelated with baseline mood, or correlated in a direction opposite to that which would be expected. Furthermore, when baseline mood was partialed out, correlations remained significant, and either identical or actually somewhat greater in magnitude (e.g., $r = 0.71$ between anterior temporal asymmetry and happiness). Finally, as in the previous experiment, EEG asymmetry in posterior sites failed to significantly predict any affective responses to films.

Although there were some inconsistencies across the two studies (e.g., the significant prediction of fear but not disgust in Experiment 1, and the reversal of this pattern in Experiment 2), the findings from these two studies indicate that in normal, unselected cohorts of adults, resting frontal asymmetry can predict positive and negative responses to affect elicitors. We have recently extended these findings and conclusions in a study examining the relationship between individual differences in resting asymmetry and affective reactivity in infants (Davidson and Fox, 1989). In this study, resting EEG asymmetry was measured from 14 female 10-month-old infants prior to their exposure to a brief episode of maternal separation. The episode was 60 seconds in duration unless the infant was judged by the experimenter to be extremely upset, at which point the episode was terminated. We focused on individual differences in response to this stressor, since several researchers have noted the pronounced differences among infants of this age in response to maternal separation (e.g., Shiller et al., 1986; Weinraub and Lewis, 1977). Moreover, infants' response to maternal separation at this age period is one component of a constellation of behaviors that are associated with individual differences in vulnerability to distress. This is a dimension of temperament for which impressive longitudinal stability has been demonstrated (for a review, see Kagan, 1984).

From the videotaped record of the session, we coded infants' responses to the maternal separation challenge. Examination of these responses revealed that 7 infants cried and 7 did not cry. An infant was classified as a non-crier only if she showed no evidence of crying for the entire duration of the maternal separation episode. The classification of an infant as a crier or non-crier was done prior to any EEG analysis and was therefore completely blind.

In accord with our previous findings, we predicted that infants who responded with distress to maternal separation would show more relative right frontal activation during a baseline assessment of EEG than infants who were not distressed by the situation. As indicated by Fig. 5, infants who cried in response to maternal separation did in fact show greater right-frontal and less left-frontal activation at rest than the non-criers. Consistent with our previous findings in adult subjects, parietal asymmetry recorded at the same time as

the frontal asymmetry measures failed to discriminate between groups.

In order to examine the consistency of the group difference in frontal asymmetry on an individual subject basis, we computed a laterality difference score for each subject (log right minus log left power). As before, higher numbers on this metric indicate more relative left-sided activation. As shown in Fig. 6, every one of the criers fell below the mean score for the non-criers and every one of the non-criers fell above the mean score for the criers. Moreover, all but one of the criers had absolute right-sided frontal activation.

One concern which might be raised about these findings is that the difference in asymmetry between the two groups might simply reflect differences in pre-existent mood, with the criers perhaps in a more irritable mood at the time of the resting baselines. In order to obtain data relevant to this issue, we coded infants' facial behavior during the resting baseline according to Izard's MAX

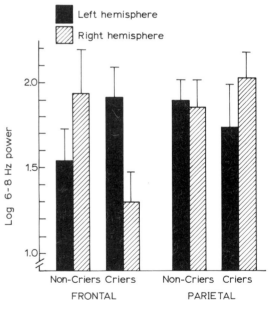

Fig. 5. Mean log-transformed band power (6–8 Hz) for the resting baseline period in the left and right frontal and parietal regions for criers and non-criers. Decreases in 6–8 Hz power are indicative of increases in activation. From Davidson and Fox (1989).

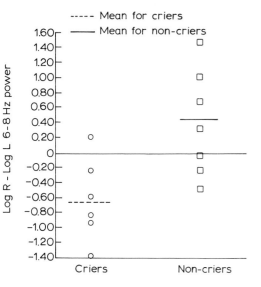

Fig. 6. Frontal asymmetry laterality scores (log right – log left power) for individual infants, split by which infants subsequently cried or did not cry in response to a brief episode of maternal separation. The means for each group are denoted by the lines. Note that all the criers fell below the mean of non-criers and all the non-criers fell above the mean of the criers. Based upon data from Davidson and Fox (1989).

TABLE 1

Facial signs of emotion during the baseline period

		Criers	Non-criers
Interest	M	9.5	11.3
	SD	8.6	7.8
No expression	M	17.0	15.1
	SD	8.2	8.9
Joy/surprise	M	2.4	3.2
	SD	2.9	3.2
Negative affect	M	0.5	1.4
	SD	0.9	1.3

Mean duration in seconds of facial affect for criers ($n = 6$) and non-criers ($n = 7$) during the baseline period. The 'no expression' category represents the mean number of seconds during which no facial signs of emotion were present. The 'negative affect' category represents the mean number of seconds during which facial signs of any of the negative emotions (anger, fear, distress, sadness and disgust) were expressed. From Davidson and Fox (1989).

system. Table 1 presents the duration in seconds of different facial signs of emotion during the baseline period. As indicated by this table, on all facial signs of emotion, those infants who subsequently cried in response to maternal separation failed to differ from those who did not cry. While certainly not definitive, these findings do suggest that the two groups of infants were not in a different emotional state at the time that the EEG measures were recorded.

In sum, we have conducted two adult studies and one infant study, each of which assessed the relationship between resting EEG asymmetry and subsequent affective responses to an emotion elicitor. In each study, we found evidence that resting asymmetry recorded from anterior sites can predict affective responses to emotion elicitors. Furthermore, in each study, anterior asymmetry predicted affective responses independent of subjects' emotional state at the time of the baselines. Taken together, these two sets of findings suggest the following conclusions: (1) anterior asymmetry is a state-independent marker indexing the individual's readiness or predisposition for affective responsivity, and (2) this readiness is only released when the individual is exposed to a sufficiently potent affect elicitor. Finally, in each of these three studies, resting EEG asymmetry in posterior sites did not significantly predict subsequent affective responses. Thus, regional specificity is indicated.

We should note that our findings on the relationship between resting *anterior* asymmetry and affective responsivity parallel our previous results (Davidson et al., 1979), and those of other investigators (e.g., Furst, 1976; Glass and Butler, 1977), which indicate a relationship between resting asymmetry in *posterior* sites and performance on cognitive tasks. This evidence indicates that resting asymmetries recorded from parietal or posterior temporal sites predict performance on verbal and spatial cognitive tasks in a manner consistent with neuro-anatomical specialization for these functions (e.g., greater relative left hemisphere activation associated with better performance on verbal tasks). Similar findings have been obtained in studies assessing the functional significance of individual differences in cerebral blood flow (e.g., Dabbs and Chou, 1980; Gur and Reivich, 1980). In addition, Levy and her colleagues have found strong relationships between behavioral indicators of hemispheric arousal and performance on verbal and non-verbal cognitive tasks (Levy et al., 1983). As Levy (1983) has argued, these findings support a distinction between hemispheric *specialization* for particular cognitive functions and hemispheric *activation*. In this view, diversity among individuals in activation may be '. . . superimposed on a relatively invariant pattern (Levy, 1983, p. 476) . . .,' in specialization, and account for individual differences in cognitive performance.

By the same token, variation among subjects in resting *anterior* asymmetry may be superimposed on invariant patterns of hemispheric specialization for emotion. One pattern of specialization has been revealed by the studies that we reviewed in the earlier section on EEG responses during experimentally induced affective states. These studies revealed that negative affective states were associated with relative right anterior activation and that positive affective states are associated with relative left anterior activation. Our findings on individual differences in resting anterior asymmetry suggest that diversity among individuals in resting activation may account for differences in affective reactivity that occur despite invariant patterns of affective specialization.

One possible conceptualization of the effects of such individual differences is that they represent differences in *thresholds* for affective responsivity. According to such a view, individuals with relative right anterior activation have a relatively low threshold for negative affective responses to affect elicitors, while individuals with relative left anterior activation have a relatively high threshold. Thus, a more potent affective stimulus may be required to trigger negative affect in the latter group, relative to the former. The converse would be expected in the case of reactivity to positive affective elicitors.

This conceptualization is consistent with recent evidence that individual differences in emotion or temperament are linked to altered thresholds for perception of, or responses to, affective stimuli (for a review, see Derrybery and Rothbart, 1984). Our interpretation is also consistent with infrahuman research indicating that activation of neural structures known to regulate important aspects of emotion does in fact produce altered thresholds for significant stimuli. An example of such threshold adjustment is the finding that an increase in electrical current administered to the lateral hypothalamus of a rat produces a *downward* shift in the concentration gradient of sugar water that rats are willing to consume (Stellar et al., 1979). Gallistel (1980a, 1980b) has reviewed infrahuman evidence of this sort, and has eloquently described the process of threshold adjustment as one of *selective potentiation and depotentiation* of lower-order effectors by higher-order centers (e.g., the hypothalamus) that regulate behavior in motivational contexts.

In future studies, we hope to test the threshold adjustment notion more directly by assessing the relationship between resting anterior asymmetry and responses to affective stimuli that vary parametrically in intensity. In addition, consistent with the argument that a process of threshold adjustment may underlie mood-congruent biases and other effects of emotions on cognitive processes (e.g., Derrybery and Rothbart, 1984; Esposito, 1984), we plan to assess whether resting anterior asymmetry predicts selective processing of positive and negative affective stimuli in cognitive tasks.

An additional important question addressed by current, on-going research is the stability of anterior asymmetry over time. Simply put, if resting anterior asymmetry does in fact index individual differences in affective predispositions and/or risk for psychopathology, it should be a stable attribute of the individual. Previous evidence has indicated that individual differences in resting EEG asymmetry recorded from posterior sites are highly stable over a 1 – 3 week period (Ehrlichman and Wiener, 1979; see also Amochaev nd Salamy, 1979). The stability of posterior EEG symmetry is probably a specific feature of the more general stability of the spectral composition of the resting EEG (e.g., Gasser et al., 1985; Mocks and Gasser, 1984). Unfortunately, to our knowledge, no studies have as yet assessed the stability of EEG asymmetry recorded from anterior sites. As a result, we are currently conducting a study designed to assess the test-retest stability of resting EEG asymmetry in adults over the course of a 3–4-week period. In addition, we will assess whether it is specifically those subjects with both *stable* and *extreme* patterns of asymmetry who are most likely to demonstrate notable affective responses to stimuli. For instance, are those subjects with stable, extreme right anterior activation most likely to respond with negative affect to emotion elicitors?

Future research directions

An additional goal of our current and anticipated future work is relevant to research both on EEG patterns during experimentally elicited affective states and on the affective correlates of individual differences in resting asymmetry. This goal is to clarify the underlying dimensional basis of affective asymmetry. Previously, Davidson (1984) and Kinsbourne (1978) have speculated that anterior asymmetries reflect a fundamental neuro-anatomical asymmetry in the control of approach and withdrawal behaviors. This speculation is consistent with the evidence that approach and withdrawal are fundamental components of motivation (e.g., Schneirla, 1959), and that this dichotomy is a useful framework for a functional analysis of neural structures implicated in important aspects of motivation and emotion (e.g., Depue and Iacono, 1989; Glickman and Schiff, 1967; Stellar et al., 1979; Stellar and Stellar, 1985; Wise and Bozarth, 1987).

Our findings to date are at least broadly consistent with the notion that anterior asymmetries for emotion assess the relative balance of approach and withdrawal tendencies. For example, studies reviewed above have shown that experimentally induced disgust (Davidson et al., in press; Fox and Davidson, 1986) is associated with relative right frontal activation and that resting right anterior activation predicts subsequent fear and disgust responses to affect elicitors (Tomarken et al., 1989). These results are notable given that both fear and disgust are commonly associated with *withdrawal* from eliciting stimuli (cf. Davidson et al., in press; Marks, 1987). Indeed this may be the major commonality between the two emotions.

Our findings indicating a linkage between frontal asymmetry and depression (e.g., Schaffer et al., 1983; Henriques and Davidson, in press) may also be consistent with the notion that anterior asymmetry indexes the relative balance of approach and withdrawal motivation. From this perspective, in accord with several recent conceptualizations of affective disorders (e.g., Depue and Iacono, 1989; Higgins, 1987; Tellegen, 1985), depression may primarily index a deficit in approach motivation. In this regard, it is notable that difficulty initiating voluntary actions, psychomotor retardation, lowered energy and an apparent absence of reward-oriented motivation are all cardinal features of depression. It may well be that this set of symptoms co-occur because they all reflect disrupted functioning in neural structures that regulate approach-oriented motivation toward positive hedonic stimuli (cf. Depue and Iacono, 1989). Notably, in our data, the greatest differences between depressives and non-depressives have consistently been observed in the left frontal region, with depressives showing left frontal *hypo-activation*. It is also significant that lesions in the left frontal region most consistently result in depression in patients with unilateral cortical lesions (Robinson et al., 1984). Perhaps, then, the specific activation levels of the left anterior region reflect the strength of the individual's approach motivation.

In future research, we hope to test these speculations by assessing whether a more fine-grained classification of patterns of anterior asymmetry can yield better prediction of discrete affective responses. For example, is a pattern of left frontal hypo-activation selectively associated with sadness or depression, while right frontal hyper-activation is selectively associated with fear and disgust? This possibility would be consistent with the model of the dimensional structure of emotion recently advanced by Tellegen and his associates (e.g., Tellegen, 1985; Watson and Tellegen, 1985). They have characterized fear and disgust as heightened negative affect and sadness and depression as lowered positive affect.

We also intend to test the approach-withdrawal model through experiments designed to forge a linkage between our research focusing on cortical asymmetries and that of other investigators studying the neurochemistry of approach and withdrawal systems. Dopamine is a neurotransmitter which has been directly implicated in reward motivation. Dopamine agonists have been found to increase self-stimulation behavior elicited from dopamine-rich sites in mesolimbic and mesocortical regions (see review by Kelly and Stinus, 1984). A variety of recent evidence has uncovered asymmetries in dopamine concentration and receptor density in both human and non-human species (see Tucker and Williamson, 1984, for review). For example, Glick and his associates (e.g., Glick and Shapiro, 1984) have reported higher concentrations of dopamine on the side contralateral to the direction in which rats habitually turn. Even more relevant to the research described in this chapter, Schneider et al. (1982) have found that the density of D2 dopamine receptors is 23% higher in the left compared with the right nigrostriatal region in rats. Alterations in the normal pattern of dopamine asymmetry may also be found in certain forms of psychopathology. For example, Reynolds (1983; Reynolds and Czudek, 1987) has reported significant differences in the concentration of dopamine in the left and right amygdala of schizophrenic patients based upon post-mortem examination of brains. In the light of the documented importance of dopamine to positive affect, reward and approach motivation and animal findings suggestive of a left-sided lateralization of dopamine in

at least some brain regions, we believe that the examination of the relationships between dopamine levels, emotion and electrophysiological measures of asymmetry is warranted. We are currently addressing this issue by studying Parkinson's patients who exhibit cyclic changes in motor function and mood over the course of a medication cycle. Such patients have been labeled as exhibiting 'on-off' phenomena (e.g., Cantello et al., 1986; Girotti et al., 1986). We are measuring changes in EEG asymmetry in patients of this type over the course of several medication cycles. In addition to the electrophysiological measures, we are also carefully assessing changes in affect using both self-report and behavioral measures. Finally, both the electrophysiological and the behavioral changes will be related to cyclic changes in levels of dopamine and its metabolites that we assay from repeated plasma samples.

Because they are completely non-invasive, relatively inexpensive and possess excellent time resolution, quantitative electrophysiological methods are ideally suited to the study of emotion. We have illustrated how such methods can be used to make inferences about regional patterns of brain asymmetry which are associated with different emotional states and, when they occur in the resting state, predict trait-like characteristics of emotional reactivity. In the future, the combined use of brain electrical activity measures and behavioral measures of emotional expression in patients with well-defined neurological disorders offers great promise in furthering our understanding of the brain systems which underlie human emotional behavior.

Acknowledgements

The research reported in this chapter was supported in part by NIMH grants MH40747 and MH43454 and by grants from the John D. and Catherine T. MacArthur Foundation to R.J.D. and by an NIMH post-doctoral fellowship to A.J.T.

References

Ahern GL, Schwartz GE: Differential lateralization for positive and negative emotion in the human brain: EEG spectral analysis. *Neuropsychologia: 23,* 745 – 756, 1985.

Alford LB: Localization of consciousness and emotion. *Am. J. Psychiatry: 12,* 789 – 799, 1933.

Amochaev A, Salamy A: Stability of EEG laterality effects. *Psychophysiology: 16,* 242 – 246, 1979.

Carmon A, Nachson I: Ear asymmetry in the perception of emotional non-verbal stimuli. *Acta Psychol.: 37,* 351 – 357, 1973.

Cantello R, Gilli M, Ricco A, Bergamasco B: Mood changes associated with 'end-of-dose deterioration' in Parkinson's disease: a controlled study. *J. Neurol. Neurosurg. Psychiatry: 49,* 1182 – 1190, 1986.

Cummings JL, Mendez MF: Secondary mania with focal cerebrovascular lesions. *Am. J. Psychiatry: 141,* 1084 – 1087, 1984.

Dabbs JM, Chou G: Left-right carotid blood flow predicts specialized mental ability. *Neuropsychologia: 18,* 711 – 713, 1980.

Darwin C: *The Expression of the Emotions in Man and Animals.* Chicago: University of Chicago Press, 1872/1965.

Davidson RJ: Affect, cognition and hemispheric specialization. In Izard CE, Kagan J, Zajonc R (Editors), *Emotion, Cognition and Behavior.* New York: Cambridge University Press, 1984.

Davidson RJ: EEG measures of cerebral asymmetry: Conceptual and methodological issues. *Int. J. Neurosci.: 39,* 71 – 89, 1988.

Davidson RJ, Fox NA: Asymmetrical brain activity discriminates between positive versus negative affective stimuli in human infants. *Science: 218,* 1235 – 1237, 1982.

Davidson RJ, Fox NA: Cerebral asymmetry and emotion: developmental and individual differences. In Molfese DL, Segalowitz SJ (Editors), *Brain Lateralization in Children: Developmental Implications.* New York: Guilford Press, pp. 191 – 206, 1988.

Davidson RJ, Fox NA: Frontal brain asymmetry predicts infants' response to maternal separation. *J. Abnorm. Psychol.: 98,* 127 – 131, 1989.

Davidson RJ, Schwartz GE, Saron C, Bennett J, Goleman DJ: Frontal versus parietal EEG asymmetry during positive and negative affect. *Psychophysiology: 16,* 202 – 203, 1979a.

Davidson RJ, Taylor N, Saron C: Hemisphericity and styles of information processing: individual differences in EEG asymmetry and their relationship to cognitive performance. *Psychophysiology: 16,* 197, 1979b.

Davidson RJ, Schaffer CE, Saron C: Effects of lateralized stimulus presentations on the self-report of emotion and EEG asymmetry in depressed and non-depressed subjects. *Psychophysiology: 22,* 353 – 364, 1985.

Davidson RJ, Chapman JP, Chapman LJ: Task-dependent EEG asymmetry discriminates between depressed and non-depressed subjects. *Psychophysiology: 24,* 585, 1987.

Davidson RJ, Ekman P, Saron C, Senulis J, Friesen W: Approach/withdrawal and cerebral asymmetry. Emotional expression and brain physiology, I. *J. Pers. Soc. Psychol.:* in press.

Davidson RJ, Chapman JP, Chapman LP, Henriques JB: Asymmetrical brain electrical activity discriminates between psychometrically-matched verbal and spatial cognitive tasks. Submitted for publication, 1989.

Denenberg VH, Yutzey DA: Hemispheric laterality, behavioral asymmetry and the effects of early experience in rats. In Glick SD (Editor), *Cerebral Lateralization in Nonhuman Species.* New York: Academic Press, pp. 109 – 133, 1985.

Derryberry D, Rothbart MK: Emotion, attention and temperament. In Izard CE, Kagan J, Zajonc RB (Editors), *Emotion, Cognition and Behavior.* New York: Cambridge University Press, pp. 132 – 166, 1984.

Depue RA, Iacono WG: Neurobehavioral aspects of affective disorders. In Rosenzweig MR, Porter LY (Editors), *Annual Review of Psychology.* Palo Alto: Annual Reviews, Inc., pp. 457 – 492, 1989.

Diener E, Larsen RJ, Levine S, Emmons RA: Intensity and frequency: dimensions underlying positive and negative affect. *J. Pers. Soc. Psychol.: 48,* 1253 – 1265, 1985.

Duchenne B: *Mechanisme de la physionomie humaine ou analyse electrophysiologique de l'expression des passions.* Paris: Bailliere, 1862.

Ehrlichman H, Wiener MS: Consistency of task-related EEG asymmetries. *Psychophysiology: 16,* 247 – 252, 1979.

Ekman P: Expression and nature of emotion. In Scherer KR, Ekman P (Editors), *Approaches to Emotion.* Hillsdale, NJ: Lawrence Erlbaum Associates, pp. 319 – 343, 1984.

Ekman P, Friesen WV: Felt, false and miserable smiles. *J. Nonverbal Behav.: 6,* 238 – 252, 1982.

Ekman P, Friesen WV: *Emotion Facial Action Coding System (EM-FACS).* San Fransisco: University of California, San Fransisco, 1984.

Ekman P, Friesen WV, Ancoli S: Facial signs of emotional experience. *J. Pers. Soc. Psychol.: 39,* 1125 – 1134, 1980.

Ekman P, Davidson RJ, Friesen WV: The Duchenne smile. Emotional expression and brain physiology, II. *J. Pers. Soc. Psychol.:* in press.

Esposito RU: Cognitive-affective integration: some recent trends from a neurobiological perspective. In Weingartner H, Parker ES (Editors), *Memory Consolidation: Psychobiology of Cognition.* Hillsdale, NJ: Lawrence Erlbaum Associates, 1984.

Etcoff NL: The neuropsychology of emotional expression. In Goldstein G, Tarter RE (Editors), *Advances in Clinical Neuropsychology, Vol. 3.* New York: Plenum Press, pp. 127 – 179, 1986.

Fox NA, Davidson RJ: Taste-elicited changes in facial signs of emotion and the asymmetry of brain electrical activity in human newborns. *Neuropsychologia: 24,* 417 – 422, 1986.

Fox NA, Davidson RJ: Patterns of brain electrical activity during facial signs of emotion in ten month old infants. *Dev. Psychol.: 24,* 230 – 236, 1988.

Furst CJ: EEG asymmetry and visuospatial performance. *Nature: 260,* 254 – 255, 1976.

Gainotti G: Emotional behavior and hemispheric side of lesion. *Cortex: 8,* 41 – 55, 1972.

Gallistel CR: *The Organization of Action: A New Synthesis.* Hillsdale, NJ: Lawrence Erlbaum Associates, 1980a.

Gallistel CR: From muscles to motivation. *Am. Sci.: 68,*

398 – 409, 1980b.

Gasser T, Bacher P, Steinberg H: Test-retest reliability of spectral parameters of the EEG. *Electroencephalogr. Clin. Neurophysiol.: 60,* 312 – 319, 1985.

Girotti F, Carella F, Grassi MP, Soliveri P, Marano R, Caraceni T: Motor and cognitive performances of Parkinsonian patients in the on and off phases of the disease. *J. Neurol. Neurosurg. Psychiatry: 49,* 657 – 660, 1986.

Glass A, Butler SR: Alpha EEG asymmetry and speed of left hemisphere thinking. *Neurosci. Lett.: 4,* 231 – 235, 1977.

Glick SD, Shapiro RM: Functional and neurochemical asymmetries. In Geschwind N, Galaburda AM (Editors), *Cerebral Dominance: The Biological Foundations.* Cambridge, MA: Harvard University Press, pp. 147 – 166, 1984.

Glick SD, Shapiro RM: Functional and neurochemical mechanisms of cerebral lateralization in rats. In Glick SD (Editor), *Cerebral Lateralization in Nonhuman Species.* New York: Academic Press, pp. 157 – 183, 1985.

Glickman SE, Schiff BB: A biological theory of reinforcement. *Psychol. Rev.: 74,* 81 – 109, 1967.

Goldstein K: *The organism.* New York: Academic Press, 1939.

Gur RC, Reivich M: Cognitive task effects on hemispheric blood flow in humans: evidence for individual differences in hemispheric activation. *Brain Lang.: 9,* 78 – 92, 1980.

Heilman KW, Scholes R, Watson TR: Auditory affective agnosia: disturbed comprehension of affective speech. *J. Neurol. Neurosurg. Psychiatry: 38,* 69 – 72, 1975.

Henriques JB, Davidson RJ: Asymmetrical brain electrical activity discriminates between previously depressed subjects and healthy controls. *J. Abnorm. Psychol.:* in press.

Higgins ET: Self-discrepancy: a theory relating self and affect. *Psychol. Rev.: 94,* 319 – 340, 1987.

Kagan J: *The Nature of the Child.* New York: Basic Books, 1984.

Kelly A, Stinus L: Neuroanatomical and neurochemical substrates of affective behavior. In Fox NA, Davidson RJ (Editors), *The Psychobiology of Affective Development.* Hillsdale, NJ: Lawrence Erlbaum Associates, 1984.

Kinsbourne M: The biological determinants of functional bisymmetry and asymmetry. In Kinsbourne M (Editor), *Asymmetrical Functions of the Brain.* New York: Cambridge University Press, 1978.

Kolb B, Milner B: Observations on spontaneous facial expression after focal cerebral excisions and after intracarotid injection of sodium amytal. *Neuropsychologia: 19,* 505 – 514, 1981.

Larsen RJ, Diener E, Emmons RA: Affect intensity and reactions to daily life events. *J. Pers. Soc. Psychol.: 51,* 803 – 814, 1986.

Leventhal H, Tomarken AJ: Emotion: today's problems. In Rosenzweig MR and Porter LY (Editors), *Annual Review of Psychology,* Vol. 37. Palo Alto: Annual Reviews, Inc., pp. 565 – 610, 1986.

Levy J: Individual differences in cerebral hemisphere asymmetry: Theoretical issues and experimental considerations. In Hellige JB (Editor), *Cerebral Hemisphere Asymmetry: Method, Theory and Application.* New York: Praeger, 1983.

Levy J, Heller W, Banich MT, Burton LA: Are variations among right-handed individuals in perceptual asymmetries caused by characteristic arousal differences between the hemispheres? *J. Exp. Psychol. Hum. Percept. Performance: 9,* 329 – 359, 1983.

Ley R, Bryden M: Hemispheric differences in processing emotions and faces. *Brain Lang.: 7,* 127 – 138, 1979.

Marks IM: *Fears, Phobias and Rituals.* New York: Oxford University Press, 1987.

Mocks J, Gasser T: How to select epochs of the EEG at rest for quantitative analysis. *Electroencephalogr. Clin. Neurophysiol.: 58,* 89 – 92, 1984.

Natale M, Gur RE, Gur RC: Hemispheric asymmetries in processing emotional expressions. *Neuropsychologia: 21,* 555 – 565, 1983.

Nauta WJH: The problem of the frontal lobe: a reinterpretation. *J. Psychiatric Res.: 8,* 167 – 187, 1971.

Nunez PL: *Electric Fields of the Brain: The Neurophysics of EEG.* New York: Oxford University Press, 1981.

Perris C, Monakhov K: Depressive symptomatology and systemic structural analysis of the EEG. In Gruzelier J, Flor-Henry P. (Editors), *Hemisphere Asymmetries of Function in Psychopathology.* New York: Elsevier/North Holland, 1979.

Reuter-Lorenz P, Davidson RJ: Differential contributions of the two cerebral hemispheres to the perception of happy and sad faces. *Neuropsychologia: 19,* 609 – 613, 1981.

Reuter-Lorenz P, Givis RP, Moscovitch M: Hemispheric specialization and the perception of emotion: evidence from right-handers and from inverted and non-inverted left-handers. *Neuropsychologia: 21,* 687 – 692, 1983.

Reynolds GP: Increased concentrations and lateral asymmetry of amygdala dopamine in schizophrenia. *Nature: 305,* 527 – 529, 1983.

Reynolds GP, Czudek C: Neurochemical laterality of the limbic system in schizophrenia. In Takahashi R, Flor-Henry P, Gruzelier J, Niwa S (Editors), *Cerebral Dynamics, Laterality and Psychopathology.* Amsterdam: Elsevier, pp. 451 – 456, 1987.

Robinson RG, Benson DF: Depression in aphasic patients: frequency, severity and clinical-pathological correlations. *Brain Lang.: 14,* 282 – 291, 1981.

Robinson RG, Kubos KL, Starr LB, Rao K, Price TR: Mood disorders in stroke patients: importance of location of lesion. *Brain: 107,* 81 – 93, 1984.

Robinson RG, Szetela B: Mood change following left hemispheric brain injury. *Ann. Neurol.: 9,* 447 – 453, 1981.

Saxby L, Bryden MP: Left visual field advantage in children for processing visual emotional stimuli. *Dev. Psychol.: 21,* 253 – 261, 1985.

Sackeim HA, Weinman AL, Gur RC, Greenberg M, Hungerbuhler JP, Geschwind N: Pathological laughter and crying: functional brain asymmetry in the expression of positive and negative emotions. *Arch. Neurol.: 39,* 210 – 218, 1982.

Schaffer CE, Davidson RJ, Saron C: Frontal and parietal EEG asymmetries in depressed and non-depressed subjects. *Biol. Psychiatry: 18,* 753 – 762, 1983.

Schneider LH, Murphy RB, Coons EE: Lateralization of striatal dopamine (D2) receptors in normal rats. *Neurosci Lett.: 33,* 281 – 284, 1982.

Schneirla TC: An evolutionary and developmental theory of biphasic processes underlying approach and withdrawal. In Jones MR (Editor), *Nebraska Symposium on Motivation.* Lincoln: University of Nebraska Press, pp. 1 – 42, 1959.

Schwartz GE, Davidson RJ, Maer F: Right hemisphere lateralization for emotion in the human brain: interaction with cognition. *Science: 190,* 286 – 288, 1975.

Schwartz GE, Weinberger DA, Singer JA: Cardiovascular differentiation of happiness, sadness, anger and fear following imagery and exercise. *Psychosom. Med.: 43,* 343 – 364, 1981.

Shagass C: Electrical activity of the brain. In N.S. Greenfield NS, Sternbach RA (Editors), *Handbook of Psychophysiology.* New York: Holt, Rinehart and Winston, pp. 263 – 328, 1972.

Shiller VM, Izard CE, Hembree EA: Patterns of emotion expression during separation in the strange situation. *Dev. Psychol.: 22,* 378 – 383, 1986.

Silberman EK, Weingartner H: Hemispheric lateralization of functions related to emotion. *Brain Cognition: 5,* 322 – 353, 1986.

Spitzer RL, Endicott J, Robins E: Research diagnostic criteria: rationale and reliability. *Arch. Gen. Psychiatry: 35,* 773 – 782, 1978.

Starkstein SE, Robinson RG, Price TR: Comparison of cortical and subcortical lesions in the production of poststroke mood disorders. *Brain: 110,* 1045 – 1059, 1987.

Stellar JR, Stellar E: *The Neurobiology of Motivation and Reward.* New York: Springer-Verlag, 1985.

Stellar JR, Brooks FH, Mills LE: Approach and withdrawal analysis of the effects of hypothalamic stimulation and lesions in rats. *J. Comp. Physiol. Psychol.: 93* 446 – 466, 1979.

Suberi M, McKeever WF: Differential right hemispheric memory storage of emotional and non-emotional faces. *Neuropsychologia: 15,* 757 – 768, 1977.

Tellegen A: Structures of mood and personality and their relevance to assessing anxiety, with an emphasis on self-report. In Tuma AH, Maser J (Editors), *Anxiety and the Anxiety Disorders.* Hillsdale, NJ: Erlbaum, pp. 681 – 706, 1985.

Tomarken AJ, Davidson RJ, Henriques JB, Saron CD, Straus A, Senulis J: Anterior activation asymmetries predict emotional reactivity to film clips. In preparation, 1989.

Tucker DM: Lateral brain function, emotion and conceptualization. *Psychol. Bull.: 89,* 19 – 46, 1981.

Tucker DM, Frederick SL: Emotion and brain lateralization. In Wagner H, Manstead T (Editors), *Handbook of Psychophysiology: Emotion and Social Behaviour.* London: Wiley, in press.

Tucker DM, Williamson PA: Asymmetric neural control systems in human self-regulation. *Psychol. Rev.: 91,* 185 – 215, 1984.

Tucker DM, Watson RT, Heilman KM: Discrimination and evocation of affectively intoned speech in patients with right parietal disease. *Neurology: 27,* 947 – 950, 1977.

Tucker DM, Stenslie CE, Roth RS, Shearer SL: Right frontal lobe activation and right hemisphere performance decrement during a depressed mood. *Arch. Gen. Psychiatry: 38,* 169 – 174, 1981.

Van Petten C, Kutas M: The use of event-related potentials in the study of brain asymmetries. *Int. J. Neurosci.: 39,* 91 – 99, 1988.

Watson D, Tellegen A: Toward a consenual structure of mood. *Psychol. Bull.: 98,* 219 – 235, 1985.

Weinraub M, Lewis M: The determinants of children's responses to separation. *Monogr. Soc. Res. Child Dev.: 42,* (Serial No. 172).

Willner P: *Depression: A Psychobiological Synthesis.* New York: Wiley, 1985.

Wise RA, Bozarth MA: A psychomotor stimulant theory of addiction. *Psychol. Rev.: 94,* 469 – 492, 1987.

© 1989 Elsevier Science Publishers B.V. (Biomedical Division)
Handbook of Neuropsychology, Vol. 3
F. Boller and J. Grafman (Eds)

CHAPTER 21

Neuropsychological mechanisms of anxiety and depression

Don M. Tucker and Mario Liotti

University of Oregon, Psychology Clinic, Eugene, OR 97403, U.S.A

Introduction

In current research on emotional disorders, crossing levels can be difficult. Most psychologists seem to view biological approaches to psychopathology as alternatives to psychological ones, rather than as possible ways of illuminating psychological processes. Biological psychiatrists often seem to reason from receptor mechanisms to diagnostic classifications with little consideration of intervening psychological mechanisms. What this shows is the difficulty of reasoning across the mind – body chasm. Our concepts seem to cling to one side or the other. Yet spanning the chasm is exactly the challenge for neuropsychology.

In this chapter we review key findings in both psychological and biological domains, and we consider the mechanisms of anxiety and depression that might be reflected in both domains. Anxiety and depression are probably the most important emotional states in psychopathology, and they are also integral to normal emotional experience. We begin by considering psychological findings that show unique influences of anxiety and depression on attention and memory. These findings raise several questions for neuropsychological theory. We then consider models of neurochemical and neurophysiological dysfunction in clinical anxiety and depression. Although so far these explanations at a neurophysiological level have not shed much light on the psychology of anxiety and depression, they provide an important perspective on brain mechanisms for neuropsychologists to consider. We then review evidence that would generally be considered neuropsychological, evidence dealing with brain structures and their emotional functions: frontal – limbic interactions and left versus right hemisphere involvement in anxiety and depression. Because other chapters in this volume more thoroughly review the neuropsychological evidence relevant to epilepsy (Strauss), lesion effects (Gainotti), and psychopathology (Flor-Henry), our emphasis is on the key neuropsychological findings that suggest mechanisms that might proceed from a biochemical substrate to regulate psychological phenomena.

Psychological phenomena

Given the difficulty of specifying what emotions are exactly, it is perhaps not surprising that research on anxiety and depression has often searched for somatic symptoms that might be more definite markers for these disorders. Clinical depression may be accompanied by disorders of eating or sleeping, and anxiety may be accompanied by exaggerated autonomic responses. Yet, with the possible exception of panic disorders, in which the visceral responses themselves are frightening, the somatic components of anxiety and depression are not the critical factors. It is the disturbance of thoughts and feelings that brings most patients to clinical attention.

Psychological approaches to anxiety and depression have emphasized the role of negative thinking in producing the emotional disturbance. In addition, there is evidence that the emotional states of anxiety and depression can themselves influence cognition. We will focus on the bottom-up influence – the influence of emotional states on cognition – because it is this direction of causality that raises the most interesting questions of what the neuropsychological mechanisms might be. Over the years, many research studies have shown that anxious or depressed persons perform worse than normals on certain tests of attention and memory (Silberman and Weingartner, 1986). Although many of these effects could be attributed to decreased motivation or general malaise, there are certain qualitative effects of anxiety and depression that provide clues to the roles of these states in directing attention and memory.

Although depression and anxiety often occur together, and separating their effects is a difficult task in clinical research, there are indications that they have different influences on attention and memory. We will organize our review of psychological findings around two themes. Anxiety and depression seem to produce appraisal biases, systematic changes in evaluating self and the world. They also seem to produce structural biases, changes in the structure or organization of perception and cognition. These are the phenomena to be explained by neuropsychological mechanisms.

Depression and negative thinking
In clinical work with depressed persons, it becomes apparent that many patients are predisposed to construe negative views of themselves and their lives. A beginning clinician's tendency is to emphasize a more optimistic way of seeing things, and the result is instructive: in almost every case this approach is met by the depressive's insistence on maintaining a pessimistic outlook. Based on his experience with depressive negativism, Beck (1967) proposed that the depressed person is predisposed to view the world in negative terms, and that this is what leads to the dysphoric affect. Cognitive therapy is then required to restructure the person's way of thinking. Similarly, Abramson et al. (1978) drew from social psychological models of cognition to suggest that the depressed person has a style of making attributions about life events that

highlights his or her role in causing failures.

Experimental studies of cognition in depressed persons have supported the clinical observations of negative thinking. Lloyd and Lishman (1975), for example, found that greater depression in psychiatric patients was correlated with faster reports of negative memories, but slower reports of positive ones. The use of cognitive psychology methods has been accompanied by explanations of the effects of depressive mood in terms of current models of cognitive associations. Bower (1981) reported that memory for items encoded in an emotional state could be facilitated if the subject were in the same state during the recall test. He suggested that an emotional state could serve as an association cue in the cognitive network, much like a perceptual or semantic cue, such that the presence of the mood state would facilitate recall of information that was encoded in a similar state.

Although the ability to draw on cognitive research methods is proving to be an important advantage in researching the cognitive biases of clinical disorders, there are several suggestions that emotion may not be accurately characterized as just another cue in the semantic network (Isen, 1984). Bower and his associates have reported difficulty in replicating the mood-state congruent effects (Bower and Mayer, 1984). Not all methods of assessing cognitive bias in depressives show significant differences from normals (MacLeod et al. 1987). Furthermore, some effects of emotion on cognition have seemed to operate in parallel to, rather than within, the cognitive associational network. Johnson and Tversky (1983) had normal subjects read a story about a threatening event, such as a homicide, and then in an ostensibly different context had them rate their estimate of the likelihood of several negative life events. The expectation was that, due to spreading activation through the network of cognitive associations, other risks similar to that in the story, such as violent crimes, would have greater subjective probability. They found that the affect induction did increase the perception of risk, but the effect was a global one, increasing the perceived likelihood of all negative events. The implication seems to be that the emotional state influenced cognitive appraisal in parallel with the cognitive semantic network, rather than spreading through the associations between the ideas in the network.

Another finding that challenges cognitive explanations of negative thinking in depression has been that the negative thinking may not appear until the depressed mood state is observed, and it may disappear when the depression clears. Lewinsohn et al. (1981) observed a high rate of negative appraisals in a community sample of depressed persons. But the negative cognition was not present in an assessment conducted some time before the depressive episode, nor in a later assessment for those persons who were no longer depressed.

Further evidence in support of a dynamic influence of current emotional state on cognitive appraisal has been provided by experimental induction of negative or positive mood states in normals. Teasdale and Fogarty (1979) induced a depressed mood in normals and found it to slow the recall of positive memories (although unlike the Lloyd and Lishman findings, the depressed mood did not speed the recall of negative memories). In a series of experiments, Isen (1984) has shown that inducing a state of positive affect in normals, with manipulations as innocuous as giving subjects refreshments or a small gift, can facilitate access to emotionally positive information. From these effects with normals, together with those observed in depressed persons by Lewinsohn et al. (1981), it seems as if the negative thinking of depressed persons may be as much an effect of the depressed emotion itself as it is a reflection of the depressive's characteristic ways of thinking.

Anxiety and the perception of threat

Patients suffering from anxiety often seem to be preoccupied with the possibility of some impending physical harm or social insult. Recent research with laboratory cognitive methods has confirmed that anxious as well as depressed patients show a negative bias in cognition, and this research has

suggested some interesting differences between anxiety and depression in the nature of the biases these emotions introduce (Mathews and Eysenck, in press). For example, Watts et al. (1986) found that when asked to name the color of the ink of words in a Stroop task, subjects with a spider phobia showed a specific interference in color-naming when the words were related to their phobic object (e.g., web). Using a similar method, Mathews and MacLeod (1986) tested the color-naming speed of patients whose anxiety centered around either physical harm or social embarrassment. Controls showed no slowing of color-naming when the words denoted threats. Both of the anxiety groups were slowed for social threats, and those patients fearing physical harm showed a slowing of color-naming for words related to this fear. This suggests that the person's specific concerns may influence access to the semantic content. Based on an analysis of results in which content-specific versus general threat priming occurred, Mathews and Eysenck (in press) hypothesize that anxious persons have a preattentive mechanism that is sensitive to threatening material generally, and that with more extensive cognitive processing, specific anxieties may come to influence the perceptual process.

To relate these laboratory findings to the clinically significant disorders of anxious persons, we would need to assume that a high level of anxiety enhances the person's sensitivity to threatening information in a variety of contexts. Although research linking the laboratory findings to clinical observations is at an early stage, Butler and Mathews (1983) have reported that anxious persons show a negative bias in the perception of risk of life events, and that this bias is particularly strong for personally relevant events.

As with the research on depression, an important question is the extent to which the cognitive bias is a trait of the person or is specific to the anxious state. Two kinds of results have suggested that at least some effects are specific to the emotional state of anxiety. Mathews and MacLeod (1986) found that the interference of color-naming by threat words was correlated with the subject's state anxiety. Watts et al. (1986) found that the interference of color-naming by phobia-related words was eliminated after successful treatment for the phobia.

Differential effects of anxiety and depression
Both of these emotional conditions thus seem to be associated with a negative cognitive bias, but are they equivalently negative? Although the evidence is tentative, there have been suggestions that anxiety and depression have specific influences, both on the locus of the cognitive effect – memory versus attention – and on the content of the events that are primed – pleasures versus threats.

In reviewing the laboratory findings with anxious and depressed patients, Mathews and Eysenck (in press) conclude that, although a negative bias in memory has been shown in some studies of anxiety, this has not been as robust as the bias in attention. On the other hand, research with depressives has shown a fairly consistent negative bias in memory, but not in attention (MacLeod et al., 1986). Mathews and Eysenck suggest that if these emotional states do act on different cognitive mechanisms, this might explain why depressed patients often seem preoccupied with past losses or failures, whereas anxious patients are vigilant toward threats from events in the future. In addition to fitting the descriptive evidence, this model could be relevant to the etiology of these disorders, since it would suggest that depression might result from a history of negative life events whose psychological impact was strongest after they had occurred, whereas anxiety might result from negative events that remained impending for some time.

Another model of specific cognitive influences of anxiety and depression has been derived from research on the dimensionality of normal emotion. Psychometric studies of emotion have suggested that two underlying dimensions account for most of the variance in how people use words to describe emotional states. Traditional interpretations of the two major factors have proposed that one dimension describes whether the emotion is positive or negative, and the other dimension describes the degree of arousal or intensity. Tellegen (1985) has recently argued that another, and equally statistically valid, rotation of these factors would describe one dimension as Negative Affect, which varies from calm to tense and hostile, and another dimension as Positive Affect, which varies from lethargic to cheerful and excited. This rotation thus describes two dimensions of intensity or arousal, one pleasant and the other aversive. This view of mood state dimensionality agrees well with psychometric studies of subjects' reports of their current state of physiological arousal (Thayer, 1978). Tucker et al. (in press) proposed that the dimensions identified by Tellegen may be informative for neuropsychological models of emotion, including disordered as well as normal states. They suggest that these two dimensions reflect a specific priming of cognitive contents by two neural systems, a tonic motor activation system that, when strongly engaged, is associated with anxiety and hostility, and a phasic perceptual arousal system that produces the experience of elation. Both of these affective mechanisms are hypothesized to prime adaptively-specific cognitive representations: anxiety primes the representations of threats, and elation primes representations of pleasures. Applied to the cognitive biases of anxiety and depression, this model would suggest differential priming effects, whereby depression would be characterized more by a decreased priming of pleasurable cognition than by an active priming of aversive cognition, and, conversely, anxiety would be characterized by priming of threats rather than a decreased priming of pleasures.

Several findings are consistent with this proposal. Watson and Tellegen (1985) report that clinical depression is better characterized by low scores on the Positive Affect dimension than by high scores on Negative Affect. Nasby and Yando (1982) reported that when a sad mood was induced in children it did not facilitate recall of negative information, but rather impaired recall of positive information. The research inducing a depressed mood in normals by Teasdale and Fogarty (1979) showed a slower recall of positive events, but did not find a faster recall of negative events. However, other findings have not shown a differential affective priming. Johnson and Tversky (1983), for example, found that inducing a positive mood could decrease the risk appraisal for negative events.

What is required to test the notion of differential priming of threats and pleasures is research that controls the psychometric sensitivity of the measures of priming of both these kinds of information, such that differences in results for one content versus the other reflect substantive rather than measurement effects. In a first effort in this direction, Vannatta (unpublished) assessed normal subjects' levels on Tellegen's Positive and Negative Affect dimensions, and had the subjects rate the likelihood and subjective impact of positive and negative life events. Although the relation between emotional state and risk appraisals was not strong, a regression analysis did show a differential effect, whereby the subject's Negative Affect (anxiety/hostility versus relaxation) was related to appraisal of threats but not pleasure, whereas the subject's Positive Affect (elation versus depression) was related to greater or lesser appraisal of pleasures but not threats.

Emotional state and the structure of attention and memory

Since the pioneering observations of Yerkes and Dodson (1908), psychologists have been interested in how performance changes with motivation or arousal level. Yerkes and Dodson observed an inverted U-function: improvements in performance with higher drive level up to a certain point, after which higher drive produces poorer performance. In research with humans, a popular way to manipulate drive level became selecting subjects of high or low anxiety. Spence (1958) and his associates initiated a series of experiments examining predictions from Hullian learning theory on the effects of high drive or anxiety. In addition to

facilitating the rate of conditioning of simple responses, such as eyeblink to a puff of air, high anxiety was found to have cognitive effects on verbal learning tasks in the early trials before strong associations were formed. High anxious subjects were found not to differ from low anxious ones in learning nonsense associations, but were superior to low anxious subjects in learning word pairs that are closely related to each other. This effect is consistent with the notion that high anxiety facilitates responses that are dominant in the organism's habit repertoire.

Other classic effects of anxiety are those observed in perception. Reviewing a number of studies on stress and anxiety, Easterbrook (1958) proposed that high anxiety serves to enhance attention to central cues, and decrease attention to peripheral cues. Although this hypothesis has received support in many experiments, it has become clear that the effect is an attentional one, rather than a perceptual one (e.g., Longenecker, 1962). Thus, anxious subjects may be quite able to see stimuli presented in the periphery, indeed they may look for them (Solso et al., 1968), but when focused on a task they seem to give greater priority to central cues.

If we search for a common thread to unite the effects of anxiety on word association with those on perception, it would seem to involve a restriction or focusing of attention. This is not a general decrease in attentional capacity, although it could appear as such when the task demands attention to low-probability or novel cues (Patton and Kotrick, 1972), but rather seems to represent a qualitative shift of attention toward information that is more salient or familiar. This effect is all the more interesting when it is contrasted with what appears to be an opposite shift in attention that occurs with a different state of emotional arousal, elation.

Clinical descriptions of manic elation often emphasize grandiosity and expansive thinking. Research on categorization in psychiatric patients and creative artists (Andreasen and Powers, 1975) showed that whereas schizophrenics were underinclusive thinkers, manics were like the artists in being overinclusive. Further indication of a link between mania and expansive thinking was suggested by the unexpectedly high proportion of affective disorders in a sample of creative writers and their families (Andreasen and Canter, 1974).

Some manic patients complain that lithium treatment impairs their creativity (Schou, 1979). Shaw et al. (1986) administered a test of creative thinking, an associational fluency task, to bipolar patients on and off lithium in a double-blind design. They found that being taken off lithium enhanced the remoteness of the patients' word associations, and when lithium was reinstated the patients' associations were again restricted.

Although in mania expansive thinking is an indication of psychopathology, we must assume that it is an adaptive mode of attention for creative writers. Research with normals has suggested that a state of elation can enhance novelty in problem-solving and can increase the ability to access remote associations in memory. A traditional method of assessing creativity has been to require a novel approach on a problem-solving task. Subjects in whom a mild state of elation has been induced show enhanced performance of the Duncker candle-tack-box task (Isen and Hastorf, 1982). That this effect reflects a qualitative change in cognitive strategy rather than just enhanced effort is suggested by the finding that induction of positive affect causes subjects to adopt an impressionistic and impulsive problem-solving strategy, rather than one that is methodical and effortful (Isen and Hastorf, 1982).

More direct evidence that mild elation expands attentional scope was provided when Isen et al. (1985) administered a first asssociates task in which the subjects' responses were compared to the Palermo and Jenkins (1964) norms. Positive affect was induced in one experiment by serving refreshments during the experimental session and in another by having the subjects generate word associations to ten positive affect words. Following both of these manipulations, subjects showed significantly more remote associations to neutral words. Isen proposes that positive affect can have an integrative effect on memory, facilitating access to a broad range of experience.

Particularly for the studies of word associations, in which quite similar methods have been used to study anxiety, mania, and normal elation, the evidence suggests that differing emotional states can have opposite influences on the structure of attention. Anxiety seems to constrict the scope of attention, focusing it on central cues and high-probable associations. Elation seems to expand attentional scope, facilitating access to remote or unusual associations. Most likely in normal functioning these two influences balance each other, but when they are unbalanced, as in a state of anxious depression, the person's cognition can become highly constrained by emotional influences.

We suggest that these attentional effects represent a second set of psychological phenomena to be explained by neuropsychological mechanisms. Not only can anxiety and depression bias the contents of attention and memory, influencing the accessibility of representations of pleasures and threats; these states also seem to dynamically regulate cognitive structure as well.

In this section we have attempted to characterize the most elementary influences of anxiety and depression at the psychological level. In the next section we approach anxiety and depression from the elementary neurophysiological level, considering the biochemical mechanisms that drug studies have implicated in these clinical disorders of emotion.

Biological psychiatry of anxiety and depression

Neurophysiological mechanisms of depression

In the last three decades much effort has been devoted to discovering the etiology of depression by researching the mechanism of action of antidepressant drugs. Although several important models of neurotransmitter system function in depression have been developed, we still have only a limited understanding of the effects of antidepressants on brain neurotransmitter systems.

The classical hypothesis is that noradrenergic transmission is altered in depression. Yet there may be syndromes in which serotoninergic, cholinergic and GABAergic systems are affected as well (Post and Bellanger, 1984). Based on the several biochemical mechanisms that have been implicated, researchers have questioned whether there may be several different syndromes of depression, each with a different symptomatology, clinical progression, and response to therapy.

Noradrenergic transmission

In 1965 Schildkraut presented the catecholamine hypothesis of mood disorders. This hypothesis proposed that depression is produced by decreased levels of brain norepinephrine (NE), and possibly dopamine (DA), while manic states are associated with excessive functioning of these catecholamine neurotransmitter systems. The primary support for the hypothesis came from effects of drugs, both illicit and therapeutic drugs. Amphetamine-abusers were found to show an increase in norepinephrine metabolites in their urine during the euphoric or high phase after drug ingestion, and a decrease in these metabolites during the depressive phase (Schildkraut, 1965). The implication seemed to be that high levels of NE produced the elation, and when NE was depleted, depression set in.

Antidepressant drugs also act on NE, at least in their acute effects. Both drugs that decrease the breakdown of catecholamines in the presynaptic terminal and synapse (monoamine oxidase inhibitors) and those that block the pre-synaptic reuptake of amines into the nerve terminal, prolonging their effects in the synapse, can result in an increase of NE availability at the post-synaptic terminals, and, inferentially, can relieve depression (Prange, 1964; Schildkraut, 1965; Sulser, 1983). Although questions of therapeutic drug action and the mechanisms of depression have become substantially more complex than this, an understanding of the function of NE pathways remains essential for a biological model of depression.

Most of brain NE fibers originate in cell bodies of the mesencephalic nucleus locus coeruleus. In spite of the small number of cells (about 1400 in the rat), efferent connections are widespread. The major NE pathway is a dorsal one that bilaterally innervates all of the cerebral cortex, the hippocampal formation, and the amygdala. A ventral pathway innervates the hypothalamus, the cerebellum and the lower brainstem, including the reticular formation (Brodal, 1981; Ungerstedt, 1971). Neurons in the locus coeruleus show both short- and long-term patterns of activity. A long-term cycle of activity occurs during the day, reflecting changes in the behavioral state of the organism, with a low NE activity during slow wave sleep, absence of activity during REM sleep, and increased NE activity when the animal is awake (Aston-Jones and Bloom, 1981a; Hobson et al., 1975). When the animal is exposed to sensorial inputs leading to behavioral arousal, locus coeruleus neurons respond quickly and vigorously to any sensory inputs that are accompanied by orienting responses (Aston-Jones and Bloom, 1981b). A facilitation of emotional response by NE function has been suggested by the observation that stimulation of the locus coeruleus may increase the excitatory response in the hippocampus to a significant stimulus (Segal and Bloom, 1976). Furthermore, locus coeruleus neurons habituate rapidly to non-significant stimuli (Jones et al., 1979).

In the animal work, the enhanced activity of regions modulated by NE pathways when significant stimuli are perceived, and the reduction of activity in response to stimuli that lack significance, suggest a role for NE in selective attention (Mason and Iversen, 1979). Several pharmacological effects support the role of NE pathways in human attention and cognition. Antidepressants or amphetamine, thought to potentiate NE transmission, can increase alertness and enhance at least certain cognitive functions (Olpe et al., 1983). Several drugs used in the treatment of cognitive deficits in older patients (vincamine, hydergine, piracetam) share the property of activating neurons in the locus coeruleus (Olpe and Steinmann, 1982).

When applied extracellularly, NE produces a suppression of spontaneous firing of cortical and cerebellar neurons (Aston-Jones and Bloom, 1981b). This inhibition begins slowly and has a duration of several seconds (Segal and Bloom, 1976). The effect appears to be mediated by an activation of post-synaptic β-adrenergic receptors, since it is blocked by β-receptor antagonists, whereas it is potentiated by NE re-uptake blockers (tricyclics) (Segal and Bloom, 1976). Other effects of NE terminals are excitatory. These are mediated by α-1 post-synaptic receptors. A second type of α-receptor, α-2, is pre-synaptic. It provides a negative feedback regulation of the synthesis and release of NE at the pre-synaptic level (Waterhouse et al., 1981).

Although the initial catecholamine hypothesis was framed in terms of the acute effects of drugs on NE pathways (Schildkraut, 1965), it soon became clear that longer-term, neurophysiological rather than biochemical, mechanisms must be considered for the therapeutic actions of antidepressants. Although the acute biochemical effects on NE and other neurotransmitters occur quickly, the therapeutic effects of antidepressants may not appear for two weeks or more. Thus, the chronic effects of antidepressants seem crucial for an understanding of neurophysiological mechanisms (Charney and Heninger, 1983). Much of the interest in these longer-term effects has been focused on changes in post-synaptic receptors.

β-Adrenergic receptors

A variety of antidepressant treatments, including tricyclic antidepressants, atypical antidepressants such as mianserin, monoamine oxidase inhibitors and electroconvulsive therapy (ECT), when chronically administered, reduce the production of NE-stimulated cAMP in vivo and in vitro studies on animal brain. The converse happens with reserpine or propanolol, two agents which may precipitate depressive reactions in humans. The site of action for this effect has been shown to be the β-adrenergic receptor (Frazer and Mendels, 1983; Vetulani and Sulser, 1975; Sulser, 1983). Binding studies using radioactive agonists or antagonists have also shown that the number of β-

adrenergic receptors in brain membranes is lowered by antidepressants or ECT.

The treatments that cause a decreased sensitivity to NE stimulation of cAMP also cause a decrease in the density of β receptors, with the important exception of mianserin. REM sleep deprivation, which may have antidepressant effects, also decreases the density of these receptors (Charney et al., 1981; Maggi et al., 1980; Rosenblatt et al., 1979). Since both the cAMP and β-adrenergic receptor effects occur after a time lag similar to that observed for the therapeutic action of antidepressants, Vetulani and Sulser (1975) suggested that the biochemical events and the therapeutic efficacy might be related. The down-regulation of β-adrenergic receptors by blockers of NE uptake is thought to occur because a higher amount of NE remains in the synaptic cleft when its uptake is blocked by the drugs. As a result, high levels of transmitter accumulate extracellularly and the β-adrenergic recognition site is persistently occupied by the agonist; therefore, the site is down-regulated (Costa et al., 1986). This mechanism does not apply to atypical antidepressants, like mianserin, which fail to inhibit the re-uptake of NE but do reduce the activation of NE-stimulated cAMP (Gandolfi et al., 1984).

Physiological studies recording the activity of single neurons are consistent with the binding data showing a decrease in the sensitivity of β receptors. In the cingulate cortex and cerebellum of the rat brain, long-term treatment with tricyclic antidepressants produces a decrease in responsiveness of neurons to NE. Both β-receptor sensitivity and density return to normal levels when drug treatment is discontinued (Charney et al., 1981).

α-Adrenergic receptors

As mentioned above, two α-adrenergic NE receptors have been identified. Alpha-1 receptor blocking from antidepressants appears to be similar in the acute and chronic phases of treatment. Alpha-1 receptor blocking is accompanied by an increase in receptor density, paralleling an increased responsivity to NE in single cell studies. Most antidepressants show little ability to directly block the α-2 receptor, with the exception of mianserin, and at a lesser extent, amytriptiline. In chronic treatment with amytriptiline there is a decreased α-2 receptor density (Hall and Ogren, 1981; Tsukamoto et al., 1982). This reduction corresponds to a decrease of the functional response of neurons in the locus coeruleus (which contains many α-2 receptors) after chronic tricyclic antidepressant treatment in single cell studies (McMillen et al., 1980). The feedback mechanism mediated by the receptor is thought to become less sensitive due to antidepressant therapy (Garcia-Sevilla et al., 1981). More NE is then released from the nerve terminal.

Alpha-2 binding sites have been identified on blood platelets, allowing receptor studies with an easily obtained sample in humans. Chronic antidepressant treatment reduces the number of α-2 binding sites on platelet membranes, whereas pretreatment numbers of receptors were the same as controls. Interest in platelet effects as a model for brain effects has been stimulated by this finding, because, as described above, the decrease in α-2 receptors in brain neurons has been postulated to be the mechanism by which long-term tricyclic therapy increases the release of NE (Garcia et al., 1981; Wood and Coppen, 1981). Furthermore, the specific binding of clonidine (an α-2 agonist) in human platelet membranes is greater in depressed than in normal subjects. Conversely, the binding for clonidine decreases after treatment of depressed patients with tricyclics or ECT (Smith et al., 1981).

An important animal model of depression which supports the noradrenergic hypothesis has been developed with the 'learned helplessness' paradigm. Behavioral depression is produced in rats by repeated exposure to strong uncontrollable shock. This treatment gives rise to a substantial depletion of NE in the region of the locus coeruleus (Weiss et al., 1986). The infusion of α-2 antagonists in the locus coeruleus produces behavioral depression in the rat, whereas behavioral activation can be produced by infusion of NE or α-2 agonists such as clonidine. If α-2 agonists or monoamine oxidase inhibitors are infused in the locus coeruleus after uncontrollable shock, they prevent the behavioral depression (Simson et al., 1986). These results support the idea that the stimulation of α-2 autoreceptors by clonidine in the locus coeruleus essentially replaces the NE-depleted by the learned helplessness paradigm. These findings also support the notion that a change in sensitivity of α-2 receptors plays an important role in the mechanism of antidepressant therapies (Costa et al., 1986).

Dopaminergic transmission

The cortical DA terminals are restricted to the deep layers of prefrontal and cingulate cortex (Berger et al., 1974). Monoamine oxidase inhibitors and tricyclic antidepressants increase brain DA as well as NE in their acute effects. Furthermore, a decreased sensitivity in presynaptic autoreceptors has been observed after long-term treatment with tricyclics. This has been interpreted as a potentiation of DA transmission at the mesolimbic level (McNeal and Cimbolic, 1986). In a subclass of patients (about 25%) with psychomotor retardation and with slow DA turnover, the use of DA agonists (L-Dopa) may be indicated (Van Praag and Korf, 1975). However, it is not clear whether low DA function causes psychomotor retardation or is a result of it. L-Dopa administered to normals has an activating psychomotor effect, but has minimal effects on mood (Amsel et al., 1980). It is the case that Parkinsonian patients are found to be more depressed on the Hamilton rating scale than correspondingly severe non-neurological patients (Robins, 1976).

Serotoninergic system

The pontine dorsal raphe nuclei are the primary origins of serotoninergic fibers. The ascending efferents are widespread in the rat and in the cat. They supply the mesencephalon, the hypothalamus, intralaminar thalamus, cerebellum, amygdala, the hippocampal formation, the septum, the caudate and putamen and the cerebral cortex, with especially dense innervation of the frontal cortex

(Brodal, 1981).

In 1969 Glassmann proposed that a deficiency in serotonergic function may contribute to depressive symptoms in at least some patients. Tertiary amines like amytriptiline have greater effects on 5-HT than NE pre-synaptic uptake and are thought to be more effective than secondary amines (e.g., imipramine) in those patients with a disorder in 5-HT neurotransmission (Maas, 1975). Chronic administration of tricyclic antidepressants produces a decrease in the binding (BMax) of imipramine-recognition sites and increases the BMax of 5-HT uptake (Barbaccia et al., 1983). Rats chronically receiving tricyclics show a down-regulation of 5-HT-2 receptors (Petroutka and Snyder, 1980).

According to some authors, the 5-HT involvement in depression may not explain the pathogenesis of the primary mood disorder, but may reflect a trait or vulnerability factor (Costa et al., 1986). This vulnerability may be particularly relevant to impulsiveness, as seen in suicidal behavior or aggressiveness (Van Praag, 1984). Serotonergic transmission also seems to be implicated in neuroendocrine dysfunction in depression. An impaired response on the dexamethasone suppression test, i.e., an increase in cortisol levels, can be induced by stimulation of the 5-HT-system by giving 5-HTp. In one experiment, 5-HTp was given to depressives, manics, and normals. All showed increase in cortisol but this increase was significantly greater in mania and depression, suggesting a supersensitivity of the 5-HT receptor in pituitary or hypothalamus (Meltzer et al., 1984).

Cholinergic system
Cholinergic (ACh) projections to cortex and hippocampus coming from the forebrain (area Ch4 including substantia innominata in animals and the nucleus basalis of Meinhart in humans) have a wide distribution in the deep layers of cortex (Fibiger, 1982). Recent neuropathological evidence shows that the cholinergic system is depleted in Alzheimer's dementia. Furthermore, cholinergic blockade in healthy subjects causes a substantial

learning deficit in episodic memory (Kopelman, 1986).

Janowsky et al. (1972) proposed that depression and mania are hyper- and hypocholinergic states, respectively. In normals, physostigmine produces a syndrome marked by an expressionless face, slowed thought and speech, and psychomotor retardation. The strength of these effects was found to be greater in depressed patients, suggesting a supersensitivity of the cholinergic system to physostigmine challenge (Janowsky et al., 1973, 1978). In addition, physostigmine significantly decreases the intensity of manic behavior in bipolar patients in the manic phase (Janowsky et al., 1980). Most antidepressants block muscarinic receptors, producing an immediate anticholinergic effect (Chuang and Costa, 1984). Muscarinic ACh receptors show increased density after long-term amytriptiline treatment (McNeal and Cimbolic, 1986). However, the notion that a cholinergic deficit is primary in the etiology of depression has been questioned because the anticholinergic effects of antidepressants do not correlate with their clinical potency, and may simply reflect side-effects (Beckmann and Schmauss, 1983; Sulser, 1983).

In a second version of the cholinergic hypothesis, Janowsky and associates proposed that depression and mania involve an imbalance of the noradrenergic and cholinergic systems (Janowsky et al., 1980; see also Disalver and Greden, 1984; Disalver, 1986). This proposal seems consistent with recent neuroendocrine and polysomnographic data. Corticotropin releasing factor (CRF) and adrenocorticotropic hormone (ACTH) secretions in vivo and in vitro are stimulated by muscarinic agonists and inhibited by catecholamines. ACh activates the hypothalamic-pituitary-adrenal axis (e.g., cortisol secretion) and β-endorphin secretion under several conditions (baseline, stress, etc.) (Janowsky et al., 1983; Kaplanski and Smelik., 1983). This activation is greater in depressed patients, confirming the supersensitivity of the cholinergic system (Risch,

982; Risch et al., 1980). Physostigmine injection causes an impairment of dexamethasone suppression in normals (Doerr and Berger, 1983). This impairment is accompanied by the mood and behavioral changes described for physostigmine administration above.

In clinical depression there may be a reduction in low-wave sleep, shortened REM latency, and increased REM activity and density (Feinberg et al., 982; Kupfer and Foster, 1972; Kupfer et al., 976). REM sleep deprivation has been shown to improve the mood of many patients, at least temporarily (Van Den Hoofdakker and Beersma, 986). These sleep abnormalities can be mimicked by cholinergic overdrive (Hobson et al., 1975; Hobson, 1981) and abolished by cholinoceptor blockade (Sagels et al., 1969). It has been proposed that the regulation of the phasic aspects of sleep involves interaction between cholinergic neurons of the pontine-gigantocellular-tegmental field and noradrenergic neurons of the locus coeruleus Hobson, 1981). Anticholinergic drugs and monoamine inhibitors both suppress REM sleep Karczmar et al., 1976). The suppression of REM sleep that, induced by imipramine, is antagonized by cholinergic activation (George et al., 1964). Further, concurrent induction of cholinergic overdrive and monoamine depletion causes marked increases in the duration and density of REM sleep Karczmar et al., 1976). These several findings suggest that a better understanding of cholinergic and noradrenergic mechanisms and their interaction could provide important new perspectives on arousal and mood.

GABAergic transmission

Depressed patients have been observed to have low cerebrospinal fluid GABA (Berrettini and Post, 1984), suggesting that a low GABAergic tone might be a trait associated with mood disorders Costa et al., 1986). In rats, repeated ECTs produce a decrease in GABA turnover, possibly due to increased efficiency of the GABA receptor (Green et al., 1978). Several features of depression, including learned helplessness in animals, sleep disorders, cortisol hypersecretion and anorexia, could be relevant to a deficiency in GABAergic tone.

Interaction of amine systems

A recent hypothesis suggests that it may be an interaction between NE and 5-HT systems that causes depression (Costa et al., 1986). According to this line of reasoning, at least some depressions may result from a complex transsynaptic interaction between neurotransmitter systems. Adrenergic and 5-HT neurons must be intact to produce the down-regulation of β-adrenoreceptors after chronic imipramine treatment (Dumbrill-Ross and Tang, 1983). Some antidepressants may exert effects on 5-HT pathways through intimate connections with NE pathways (Charney et al., 1984). It has been suggested that imipramine acts on 5-HT synapses and modifies the β-receptor transynaptically. However, compounds that act on postsynaptic receptors at 5-HT junctions do not require the integrity of 5-HT terminals to down-regulate β-adrenergic receptors (atypical antidepressants and monoamine inhibitors). Costa et al. speculate that in affective disorders an interneuronal system that links 5-HT to NE neurons fails to function. Through this system, long-lasting changes in 5-HT tone can modulate the sensitivity of beta-adrenergic receptors to NE. GABA and glutamate, the two most general neurotransmitter signals involved in synaptic communication, are likely candidates for the neuronal loop coordinating between 5-HT and NE systems (Costa et al., 1986).

From this brief review of neurotransmitter models of depression, we can see the complexity of the neurophysiological mechanisms that must be considered to understand the biology of this emotional disorder. Although the evidence for some kind of deficit in the NE system is strong, it is clear that NE transmission works in concert with 5-HT and ACh systems, and that a better understanding of the functions of each of these major control systems will be required before we can understand which aspects of clinical depression can be related to which neurophysiological deficits.

Neurophysiological mechanisms of anxiety

Although anxiety is a major part of several forms of psychopathology, it may take different forms in different disorders. As with subtypes of depression, the manifestions of anxiety in panic disorder, phobic disorder, generalized anxiety disorder and obsessive-compulsive disorder are associated with differing symptomatologies, clinical histories and responses to treatment, suggesting to some workers that these conditions may be associated with distinct neural substrates (Kuhar, 1986). As with depression, models of the neurophysiology of anxiety have been developed largely from research on the mode of action of therapeutic drugs.

GABAergic transmission

The molecular mechanism of action of benzodiazepines (BZs), the class of drugs most widely used in the treatment of anxiety, has recently been clarified. BZs produce their pharmacological effects by regulating a GABA/BZ receptor complex. Recognition sites for BZs on GABAergic synapses allosterically modulate the receptor for the primary transmitter, GABA, facilitating the receptor's binding of GABA. The GABA-transmission facilitation operates through enhancing the opening of chloride ion channels, resulting in hyperpolarization of the cell. This hyperpolarization appears directly relevant to the decreased neural excitability that marks the anxiolytic and anticonvulsant effects of BZ drugs (Costa and Guidotti, 1979). A similar mechanism seems to hold for Barbiturates. They have an independent binding site at the level of the chloride channel, facilitating its opening and favoring hyperpolarization (Costa and Guidotti, 1979).

In an animal model of anxiety, the proconflict paradigm, rats are deprived of water and are given electric foot-shock when they try to drink. After a number of trials, they stop trying to drink and become fearful and inhibited. The number of GABA receptors has been shown to be reduced by 50% in these rats for 30 min after the foot-shock. Diazepam infused in the rats after the foot-shock reverses the decrement in GABA-receptor density induced by the stress (Biggio et al., 1981). The same anticonflict effect is shared by GABA-receptor agonists, whereas GABA-receptor antagonists block the anticonflict effect of BZs (Corda and Biggio, 1986).

A category of BZ inverse agonists with anxiogenic properties, the β-carbolines, has been recently identified (Braestrup et al., 1980). These agents produce proconflict effects in rats and panic attacks in humans and animals (Dorow et al., 1983). They bind the GABA–BZ receptor complex in vitro and in vivo, and they produce a reduction in the density of GABA receptors in the cortex, hippocampus and cerebellum that is indistinguishable from that produced by foot-shock stress. When chronically administered, β-carbolines induce a persistent down-regulation of the synthesis of GABA receptors. Rats receiving this treatment show signs of panic attacks, and they easily develop convulsions (Biggio et al., 1984). These findings suggest that the GABAergic system plays an important role in the anticonflict effect of BZs as well as in the proconflict effect of β-carbolines, and they suggest that some anxiety states in humans may result from diminished GABAergic transmission at the level of the GABA–BZ receptor complex.

Recently, an endogenous modulator of GABA transmission has been identified, the diazepam binding inhibitor (DBI). DBI coexists in vesicles with GABA, and once co-released, it acts as a negative modulator of GABA-activated chloride-channel opening. When infused intraventricularly in rodents, DBI elicits proconflict or aggressive responses. It has been suggested that DBI may play an important role in determining the clinical signs of human and animal anxiety (Guidotti, 1986).

DBI is highly localized in the brain, with a regional distribution similar to that of the GABA–BZ receptors. Studies of immunoreactivity to DBI in human brains at autopsy have shown its concentrations to be highest in the hippocam-

ous, amygdala, hypothalamus and cerebellum, and
o be lowest in the pituitary, basal ganglia and in
white matter (Ferrero et al., 1986).

Dopaminergic transmission

Cortical dopaminergic terminals are restricted to
the prefrontal, anterior cingulate and enthorinal
regions. They are concentrated in the deep layers
(laminae V – VI). The prefrontal dopaminergic
fibers have their origin in the mesencephalic
ventro-tegmental A10 cell group, as well as in the
medial part of the substantia nigra pars compacta
(Lindvall et al., 1974). This pathway appears
necessary to support self-stimulation of the medial
pre-frontal cortex in rats and monkeys. Attenuation of self-stimulation is produced by drugs that
interfere with DA metabolism or DA receptors.
DA depletion in the prefrontal cortex by about
90% produces a long-lasting decrease in self-
stimulation behavior (Mora and Ferrer, 1986).

DA agonists stimulate adenylate cyclase activity
in the dorsal hippocampus, and this effect is blocked by haloperidol, a DA-receptor antagonist. In
normal rats, chronic treatment with haloperidol
produces up-regulation of DA receptors in the
striatum, accumbens and substantia nigra. However, DA receptors present in the prefrontal cortex, unlike those in the nigro-striatal system, do
not seem to be affected by chronic treatment with
haloperidol and do not develop tolerance (Memo
et al., 1986).

The mesolimbic – prefrontal dopaminergic pathway has been implicated in anxiety by the finding
that in rats that are stressed by electric foot-shock,
DA metabolism is activated in the medial prefrontal cortex. This is shown by an increase in the content of DOPAC, a DA metabolite. An increase of
in the activity of the mesolimbic DA neurons is
found when stress is pharmacologically induced by
the anxiogenic beta-carbolines. Conversely,
diazepam or BZ-receptor agonists decrease the activity of the mesolimbic DA system, and these
drugs reduce DA metabolism in the prefrontal cortex (Giorgi et al., 1986). GABA agonists, including
BZs, decrease striatal DA release (Wilson et al.,

1983). Chronic activation of the GABA system in
rats consequent to injection of a GABA-trans-
aminase inhibitor leads to DA supersensitivity, an
increase in DA-receptor binding, and a decrease in
GABA-receptor binding in the striatum (Sivam et
al., 1987).

Serotoninergic transmission

A role for 5-HT pathways in modulating anxiety
has been suggested by the observation that administration of BZs into the region of dorsal raphe
nuclei resulted in behavioral effects that were interpreted an anxiolitic. Furthermore, destruction of
serotonergic neurons with a specific neurotoxin
prevented the BZ anxiolitic action (Kuhar, 1986).

Noradrenergic transmission

Electrical stimulation of the locus coeruleus in
monkeys has been found to produce a pattern of
behavior that may be associated with fear and anxiety. The behavior includes teeth grinding, hair
pulling, struggling, and jerking of the body; these
responses are similar to those occurring during
threatening confrontations by humans. These
responses are reduced after destruction of the locus
coeruleus. Similar responses can be reproduced
pharmacologically by injecting α-2 antagonists
that increase the firing rate of locus coeruleus
neurons, whereas effects similar to locus coeruleus
lesions are produced by injecting α-2 agonists,
such as clonidine, that decrease the activity of
locus coeruleus cells. Clonidine has anxiolitic and
sedative effects in humans, whereas α-2 blockers
provoke a fear – anxiety syndrome (for a review of
the findings see Robbins et al., 1985; Kuhar, 1986).
It has been proposed that noradrenergic pathways
might be involved with alerting and selective attention in normal individuals, whereas clinical anxiety
might reflect an imbalance or dysfunction of this
system (Gray, 1982).

Research on the neurophysiological substrates
of anxiety, guided by the actions of anxiolitic
drugs, has thus shown some remarkable
mechanisms. The receptors for GABA and their
modulating factors appear and disappear in

dynamic fashion, and seem highly sensitive to recent experience. Although the interactions of neuromodulators and receptors are exceedingly complex, the final effect seems to be to regulate membrane polarization, and thus the excitability of the neuron. It is tempting to reason directly from this neuronal excitability to the aversive psychological excitability of the anxious patient.

A primary opponent process of GABAergic modulation of neural function seems to be dopaminergic excitation, as suggested by the increase of DA metabolism in prefrontal cortex in animal models of anxiety produced by foot-shock or by injection of anxiogenic drugs. A similar increase of DA metabolism seems likely also in humans, given the similarity of the anxiogenic response to these agents. Although exaggerated dopaminergic transmission seems a reasonable hypothesis for human anxiety, the electrophysiological and pharmacological evidence in animals shows that serotonergic, and possibly, noradrenergic, transmission are also relevant to fearful and anxious behavior.

Neuropsychological models

Because we are only beginning to understand the psychological significance of neurotransmitter pathways and various forms of receptor modulation, it is difficult to consider which aspects of anxiety or depression are influenced by a hypothesized transmitter or receptor pathology. Is there a defect of arousal? Hedonic tone? In this section we review research that relates anxiety and depression to certain brain structures, such as regions of the frontal lobes or one of the cerebral hemispheres. This research allows us to begin to formulate neural mechanisms of anxiety and depression by considering the psychological functions of the brain structures that seem to be most involved in these emotional states.

Frontal – limbic circuits
Before the discovery of drug treatments for psychiatric disorders, over 20 000 patients had

received various forms of frontal lobotomy by 1951 (Flor-Henry, 1977). Most of these were chronic schizophrenics. Given the seriousness of this intervention, it is remarkable that lesioning the frontal lobes became a widespread practice without controlled outcome studies. From Moniz's initial case reports in 1936, which brought him the Nobel prize, the descriptions of outcome in the published literature report fairly consistently that, although largely ineffective in treating the essential mental defects of schizophrenia, surgical lesions of the frontal lobe may substantially reduce symptoms of anxiety and depression (Flor-Henry, 1977). Most effective in reducing these emotional symptoms were lesions of the orbital region of the frontal lobe. Because it seemed to be the lesions of the dorsolateral regions that produced both the cognitive impairments and the personality disinhibition of the post-leucotomy syndrome, restricting psychosurgery to orbital targets became a standard procedure.

Findings from accidental frontal-lobe lesions have been consistent in several respects with the observations in the psychosurgery literature. Frontal damage may lead to a disinhibition syndrome, including loss of social and sexual impulse control (Hecaen, 1964). The particular involvement of the ventral or orbital surface of the frontal lobes in anxiety is suggested by the pseudopsychopathic syndrome which may occur with orbital frontal lesions (Blumer and Benson, 1975). Considering the findings from psychosurgery together with those from accidental lesions thus suggests that excessive anxiety and depression may be alleviated by planned orbital lesions, and when a normal brain is lesioned in this area the result may be a lack of normal anxiety and concern.

Particularly relevant to anxiety seem to be the interconnections of orbital cortex with ventral limbic structures, including the amygdala (Damasio and VanHoesen, 1983). Cytoarchitectonic similarities suggest that orbital cortex has evolved from the paleocortex of the ventral limbic system (Sanides, 1970). Both animal and human lesion studies have shown decreased aggressiveness after amygdala lesions (Aggleton and Mishkin, 1983; Flor-Henry, 1977). Aggleton and Mishkin suggest that, with its input from various sensory modalities, the amygdala is well-suited to providing the affective elaboration of perceptual experience. Judging from the lesion evidence on anxiety and depression in humans, orbital frontal cortex may be involved in integrating the limbic processing of affect with the executive functions of the frontal lobe.

It is probably not accidental that the dopaminergic pathway thought to be most important to anxiety and schizophrenia, the mesolimbic pathway, projects to ventral limbic structures and prefrontal cortex. As noted above, foot-shock stress in animals augments frontal lobe DA metabolism, as do anxiogenic drugs, whereas benzodiazepines decrease it (Giorgi et al., 1986). In humans given doses of a benzodiazepine described as producing a mild euphoria (Mathew et al., 1985), a decrease in regional cerebral blood flow was observed specifically in frontal regions. As with several frontal lobe findings to be reviewed below, the effect was asymmetric, with a greater reduction of flow on the right side.

Reasoning from the localization of neurotransmitter mechanisms implicated in anxiety and depression, it may thus be possible to integrate the biochemical models with the evidence on frontal and limbic lesions. Liotti et al. (in preparation) suggest that it may be possible to explain many of the neuropsychological effects of anxiety by considering the predilection of anxiolytic drugs for limbic and frontal structures. Kuhar (1986) emphasizes that in addition to their anxiolytic effects, benzodiazepines have anticonvulsant properties, and this may be important to their actions on ventral limbic structures such as the amygdala, which show a particular susceptibility to seizure phenomena.

From animal evidence it is clear that elementary emotional mechanisms involve limbic – hypothalamic circuits (Panksepp, 1982). Yet there has been remarkably little progress in relating this animal evidence to human psychopathology. Based on

parallels between the behavior of rats given benzodiazepines and the behavior of rats with lesions of the septo-hippocampal region, Gray (1979, 1982) has proposed that this septo-hippocampal system may serve as a model for human anxiety. In rats, the lesion findings suggest that this system regulates behavioral inhibition in response to novelty, punishment, and frustrative non-reward. In Gray's model, anxiolytic drugs decrease the transmission of ascending monoaminergic projections (particularly NE), thus reducing the excitatory input to the septo-hippocampal system, thereby decreasing anxiety.

Whereas too much septal-hippocampal inhibition could lead to the behavioral incapacity sometimes observed in anxiety states, too little inhibition might figure in the impulsivity of psychopathy. This notion was originally advanced by Gorenstein and Newman (1980), who proposed from the rat lesion literature that some dysfunction of the septo-hippocampal system may underlie a variety of human disinhibition syndromes. The model has led Newman and his associates to test predictions from the animal learning studies, both with psychopaths (Newman and Kosson, 1986) and with normal extroverts (Newman et al., 1985) with their varying degrees of behavioral disinhibition. Like the septo-hippocampal lesioned rats, both human groups have been found to have difficulty in using punishment to inhibit approach behavior, particularly in the presence of opportunities for reward. Thus with models of septal-hippocampal function, as with the findings with human orbital-frontal cortex lesions (Flor-Henry, 1977; Benson and Geschwind, 1974), we find anxiety and psychopathy on opposite ends of a self-regulatory continuum.

Another frontal region with close connections to limbic structures is the supplementary motor area, represented on the dorsal and medial surface (Goldberg, 1985). The cytoarchitectonics of this region suggests it has evolved from the archiocortex of the dorsal limbic system (Sanides, 1970), and it remains highly interconnected with the cingulate cortex in humans (Damasio and

VanHoesen, 1983). Lesions of the dorsomedial frontal cortex may produce loss of initiative and, in the extreme case, akinetic mutism, suggesting to Goldberg (1985) that this region is important to limbic contributions to emotionally significant actions. It may be relevant that the cingulate cortex receives a particularly rich innervation from NE pathways (Descarries and Lapierre, 1973), and that single unit studies in monkeys suggest that cingulate neurons respond preferentially to stimuli with adaptive significance (Mesulam, 1981). Electrical stimulation of cingulate cortex in epileptic patients produces a general alerting function, often accompanied by an elated affective response (Damasio and VanHoesen, 1983).

An important addition to the traditional findings on frontal lobe function from psychosurgery and accidental lesions has been evidence provided by recent advances in neural imaging methods. Although dorsomedial regions of frontal-limbic cortex have been implicated in a variety of tasks that place demands on attention (Goldberg, 1985; Roland, 1984), it has been the orbital surface that has been most strongly implicated in emotion, particularly in anxiety. In positron emission tomographic (PET) studies with normal subjects, Gur (1983) observed that the procedure, which requires arterial injection with a radioactive tracer fresh from a cyclotron, induces anxiety in some subjects. Gur found that, up to a certain point, higher reported state anxiety in his subjects was correlated with higher metabolism of the right orbital-frontal region; beyond this point, further increases in anxiety were associated with decreases in activity of this region.

Other imaging studies have found increased orbital-frontal activity related to anxiety, and have found this to be asymmetric, but with greater activity in the left hemisphere. Baxter et al. (1987) found the PET scans of obsessive-compulsive patients to show high metabolism in the left orbital-frontal cortex compared both to normal controls and to depressed patients. Johanson et al. (1986) had anxiety-disorder patients free-associate to threatening stimuli. During this procedure the pa-

tients showed increased cerebral blood flow of the orbital-frontal region of the left hemisphere. These findings emphasize the importance of relating frontal-limbic mechanisms in anxiety and depression to the differential emotional functions of the left and right hemispheres.

Hemispheric specialization

Because it has been possible to study hemispheric specialization in normal as well as brain-injured persons, research on this topic has yielded a large body of knowledge on the cognitive and perceptual features that differ between the left and right hemispheres. In the last decade, the methods of lateralization research have been applied to questions of emotional specialization, and have documented the right hemisphere's importance to many kinds of receptive and expressive skills dealing with emotional information (see Chapters 17 and 18 of this volume). Given that a major role for the right hemisphere in emotion has been demonstrated, it has become possible to develop theoretical models of how the right hemisphere's cognitive and perceptual skills support its unique contributions to emotional experience and behavior (Buck, 1985; Tucker, 1986).

From this line of reasoning, we might expect that the clinically significant emotions of anxiety and depression would find their primary elaboration in the right hemisphere. However, from the observation that the right hemisphere plays the major role in emotional communication, we cannot conclude that all aspects of motivation and emotion are right-lateralized. Evidence from studies of brain lesions, psychiatric patients and normal emotion shows that the left hemisphere's functioning is of major importance to emotion generally, and to anxiety and depression in particular. In the studies of lesions and sedation, depression is the emotional disorder most often examined, although several observations may suggest that a hemispheric lesion can influence anxiety as well. Similarly, in studies of psychiatric patients, most of the evidence comes from studies of depression, but there are also indications of brain lateralization related to anxiety. Although there are only a few findings with normals relating brain lateralization to anxiety and depression, these have been important in suggesting that the hemispheres' differing contributions to these emotional states are relevant not just to brain pathology, but to normal neuropsychological mechanisms as well.

Because the evidence on lateralization for emotion is reviewed extensively in this volume, we emphasize only the findings that are essential to understanding hemispheric contributions to anxiety and depression, particularly those that may illuminate the neurophysiological mechanisms underlying the psychological phenomena.

Emotion and hemispheric lesions

It had been remarked upon for some time in the neurological literature that a depressive-catastrophic response to brain injury was more common after left than right hemisphere lesions (Goldstein, 1952; Hecaen, 1962). In the first controlled assessment of this issue, Gainotti (1972) confirmed that, when emotional responses occur following a unilateral lesion, depressive-catastrophic responses are more common after left hemisphere injury, whereas denial of problems or even inappropriate cheerfulness are more frequent after right hemisphere injury. Further indication of some sort of differential hemispheric role in emotion was provided by the evidence that sedation of the left hemisphere was often accompanied by a catastrophic emotional reaction, whereas after right hemisphere sedation an elated state often seemed to occur (Rossi and Rosadini, 1967). Although these findings have been most often referred to in the literature as indicating different hemispheric roles in depression, Gainotti (1972) pointed out that the emotional orientations following lesions were unlike a typical psychiatric depression. The catastrophic quality of the emotional responses described both after lesions and after sedation suggests that anxiety may have been as important as depression in the patient's emotional state.

The question raised by these observations was which hemisphere is contributing to the changed emotional outlook. The most reasonable interpretation would be that the patient's emotion reflected the normal emotion of the undamaged hemisphere. Reasoning in this fashion, Kinsbourne (1978) proposed that the left hemisphere may have become specialized for approach behaviors, leading to a more positive emotional tone, while the right hemisphere has become specialized for withdrawal, involving a more negative affective tone. More recently, Davidson (1984; Ch. 20 of this volume) has elaborated on this notion, emphasizing that its sequential mode of motor control may facilitate the left hemisphere's organization of approach behavior, whereas the right hemisphere's more holistic contribution to motor organization may be called upon for rapid withdrawal.

Sackeim et al. (1982) reviewed the unilateral lesion effects and case reports in the literature on emotional behavior following unilateral seizures or hemispherectomy, in an attempt to determine whether the emotional changes observed after unilateral lesion reflected a decrease or an increase in the hemisphere's normal emotional functioning. Because laughter during epileptic seizures was more frequent with left hemisphere foci, they concluded that the left hemisphere must have an inherently positive emotional orientation, and thus the depressive-catastrophic response following left hemisphere lesions must represent the right hemisphere's normal orientation. Strauss (Ch. 15 of this volume) points out, however, that because the emotional expressions during ictal states are typically not accompanied by mood changes, the ictal laughter observations may not be a strong basis for inferences on hemispheric roles. Another interpretation of the unilateral lesion and sedation evidence was suggested by one of us (Tucker, 1981), who argued that a classical neurological principle is that a cortical lesion can disinhibit more primitive functioning (Hall et al., 1968), and thus that the depressive-catastrophic response could reflect a pathological exaggeration of the left hemisphere's normal emotional bias. Furthermore, following unilateral sedation, the emotional responses were only observed after the sedated hemisphere's EEG had returned to an activated state (Rossi and Rosadini, 1967). Because release of the contralateral hemisphere would be expected to be most strong during actual sedation, this finding incidates that the observed emotional responses after sedation may reflect an exaggeration of the normal orientation of the hemisphere recovering from the drug rather than the opposite hemisphere (Tucker, 1981).

Additional complexity in the interpretation of which hemisphere contributes to which emotional orientation has been introduced by the finding that the characteristic emotional effects of unilateral lesions occur primarily with frontal lesions (Robinson et al., 1984). Robinson and his associates have studied depression that results from stroke, and have found that measures of depression show opposite correlations with the location of lesions in the two hemispheres: greater depression occurs with more anterior lesions in the left hemisphere, but less depression occurs with more anterior lesions in the right hemisphere. Thus, the depressive-catastrophic and indifference responses observed by Gainotti (1972) are replicated by Robinson et al. for the left and right hemispheres, respectively, but only for lesions that involve the frontal lobe.

What are the implications of the frontal lobe specificity for understanding normal hemispheric roles in emotion? Given the importance of inhibitory control from frontal structures (Goldman-Rakic, 1984; Guitton et al., 1985; Hecaen, 1964), this evidence could be seen as consistent with the notion that the typical effect of a unilateral lesion is to disinhibit the hemisphere's normal emotional orientation. However, as we have seen above, there appear to be major differences between the functions of orbital and of dorsolateral frontal cortex. Is it dorsolateral frontal lesions that disinhibit the hemisphere's functioning? Is there some reciprocal inhibition between orbital and dorsolateral frontal regions, such that a more dorsal lesion could lead to exaggerated orbital functioning? Is there some inherent lateral asymmetry in the functions mediated by these frontal regions in the normal brain?

Hemispheric asymmetry in depression
Neuropsychological studies of depressed patients often find a pattern of performance suggesting right hemisphere dysfunction (see Flor-Henry, 1979). In a pre-test assessment prior to an electroconvulsive therapy ECT study, for example, Goldstein et al. (1977) found depressives to show poor right hemisphere performance. Adopting the usual interpretation of neuropsychological tests, which indicates that poor performance reflects brain dysfunction, these findings are not easily related to the reports on emotional effects of unilateral lesions; in those reports it was left hemisphere damage that was associated with depression. However, it seems clear that in psychiatric depressives the right hemisphere performance impairment does not reflect brain damage, because this impairment is alleviated with clinical improvement of the depressed mood. Kronfol et al. (1978) found that for those patients whose mood improved with ECT, right hemisphere performance also improved. A specific improvement in right hemisphere function with treatment of depression has been reported in children treated with tricyclics (Brumback et al., 1980; Wilson and Staton, 1984), in a woman who presented with severe left-sided neurological signs which recovered following right-sided ECT (Freeman et al., 1985), and in a patient with a known posterior right hemisphere lesion whose visuospatial impairment was no longer present after successful drug therapy for depression (Fogel and Sparadeo, 1985).

What mechanism is suggested by this dynamic variation of right hemisphere function with mood level? Tucker (1981) proposed that the right hemisphere arousal and function may be particularly dependent on the brain's mood systems. Several EEG studies have shown unusual EEG or ERP findings from depressives' right hemispheres (D'Elia and Perris, 1973; Perris 1975; Flor-Henry, 1979). An indication of the functional significance of these findings was suggested by Von Knorring's (1983) finding that depressives did not show the normal pattern of increased right hemisphere EEG activation while listening to music, as if the right hemisphere were somehow unresponsive or under-aroused.

Two findings have suggested shifts in neuropsychological performance between depression and mania that may indicate changes in right hemisphere functioning. Kushnir et al. (1980) describe a patient whose holistic perceptual skills were impaired while she was depressed; these skills improved during her manic phase. Sackeim et al. (1983) describe a patient who showed a bias to localize sounds toward the left while manic, suggesting relatively greater right hemisphere activation, and a bias to localize them toward the right while depressed, suggesting relatively greater left hemispheric activation. This man's change in auditory attentional bias was similar to that observed by Tucker et al. (1981), who induced a depressed mood in normal subjects. When depressed, the subjects showed a bias to report tones to the left ear as less loud than those to the right ear.

An important clue to the importance of the right hemisphere to emotional disorders is its role in understanding and expressing emotion, through such channels as facial expression or tone of voice (Borod et al., 1986; see Chapters 17 and 18 of this volume). Does the variation in right hemisphere function in depression reflect some mechanism for regulating emotionality as a function of current adaptive success?

Another perspective on lateralization in depression is provided by evidence of right hemisphere specialization for controlling certain aspects of attention and arousal (see Ch. 19 of this volume; Heilman and Van Den Abel, 1979; Posner et al., 1983). In reviewing neuropsychological systems of attentional control, Mesulam (1981) emphasizes the importance of the right parietal region, and points out the interconnection of parietal regions with arousal mechanisms of the thalamus and midbrain, including the control nuclei for both noradrenergic and serotonergic pathways.

The suggestion that serotonergic mechanisms may be important to the right hemisphere abnormalities in depression was provided when Gottfries et al. (1974) related CSF levels of a serotonin metabolite to brain event-related potential measures of psychiatric patients and observed significant correlations only for right hemisphere locations. Asymmetries in left and right hemisphere serotonin function in mouse brains were observed by Mandell and Knapp (1979) to be enhanced by cocaine and decreased by lithium.

An indication that dyscontrol of thalamic activation mechanisms of the right hemisphere may induce a mood disorder is the finding that in cases of clinical mania secondary to unilateral diencephalic lesions, 10 of 12 cases had lesions on the right side (Cummings and Mendez, 1984). Oke et al. (1978) assayed NE in the thalamus of human brains at autopsy and found greater amounts on the right side for most regions examined. Remarkably, animal studies have also suggested that NE may be particularly important to right hemisphere function. Pearlson and Robinson (1981) found that lesions of the right but not left frontal lobe decreased NE levels in the cortex and the locus coeruleus bilaterally. In addition to these neurotransmitter findings, rat studies have shown several effects that suggest the potential to illuminate human studies of emotional lateralization. Denenberg (1981) and his associates have found that right hemisphere lesions have a preferential effect for several measures of emotionality, but only for animals that are handled during early development. Dewberry et al. (1986) showed that the hyperactivity observed after right hemisphere lesions (Robinson, 1979) is not due to release of transcallosal inhibition, since it still obtains for rats commisurotomized in infancy (see also Crowne et al., 1987).

In research with brain-lesioned patients, the right parietal lobe has been found to be particularly important in regulating arousal and attention (Heilman and Van Den Abel, 1979). Posner and his associates (Posner et al., 1983) have developed sensitive attentional tasks using reaction time measures that discern the parietal contribution to orienting attention in space. When they induced a depressed mood in normal subjects, Ladavas et al. (1984) found reaction times slowed to the left visual half field (right hemisphere) specifically. Liotti et al. (in preparation) used these methods with clinically depressed patients and confirmed the right hemisphere attentional impairment.

The importance of right frontal control of arousal suggested by the animal evidence on NE (Pearlson and Robinson, 1981) has been paralleled by findings that right frontal lobe EEG activity in humans may be associated with a depressed mood state. Perris et al. (1978) statistically analysed the symptoms of psychiatric patients in relation to EEG from various brain regions. Whereas left frontal EEG activity was correlated with symptoms of anxiety, right frontal activity correlated with ratings of the degree of the patient's depressed mood. When Tucker et al. (1981) induced a depressed mood in normal subjects, they found alpha-desynchronization, indicating increased activation, of the right frontal lobe. Given that in the same paradigm they had previously observed a relative decrease in left ear loudness judgments, they proposed that the right frontal activity in depression may represent an inhibitory influence, operating to suppress posterior right hemisphere functioning.

In a series of studies with normal adults and children, Davidson and his associates have found frontal lobe asymmetries in emotional states, with greater left frontal activation usually observed in more positive emotional states, and relatively greater right frontal activation in negative emotion (see Davidson, 1984, and Ch. 20 of this volume). In what may be an intermediate paradigm between the studies of normal and psychiatric depression, Schaffer et al. (1983) selected university students who obtained Beck Depression Inventory scores in the depressed range on two separate occasions. In a resting EEG, these students differed from the non-depressed subjects in showing a significant alpha-desynchrony (activation) over the right frontal region.

Thus, whereas lesions of the left hemisphere have been found to lead to a depressive, or perhaps anxious, response, the evidence from both psychiatric and normal samples suggests that in a depressed mood state the activity of the right hemisphere seems most strongly implicated. The functions of the right hemisphere that seem most relevant to explaining its association with depression seem to be its roles in emotional communication and in the regulation of arousal and attention. The dependence of arousal and attention on elementary mechanisms mediated by specific neurotransmitters provides an important possibility for researching the links between higher neuropsychological function – which seems to be inherently asymmetric – and the molecular neurophysiology of depression.

Hemispheric asymmetry in anxiety
The evidence relating anxiety to hemispheric function has raised several interesting questions for a neuropsychological model of emotion. Given the indications of right hemisphere specialization for emotional communication, we might expect it to be involved in anxiety. Although there are several findings suggesting that it is, other evidence seems to implicate left hemisphere processes in both clinical and normal anxiety. If both lines of evidence are correct, then by differentiating the two hemispheres' roles it may become possible to clarify specific underlying processes that make up what we term as anxiety.

An initial suggestion that situational anxiety could engage right hemisphere cognitive processing in normals was provided when Tucker et al. (1977) found that subjects in a stressful situation produced a greater number of leftward lateral eye movements as they considered their response to questions asked by the experimenter. Given the finding that questions with emotional content elicit more leftward reflective eye movements (Schwartz et al., 1975), the stress effects seemed to suggest that anxiety is another emotion that could be related to the right hemisphere. As noted above Gur (1983) observed that higher state anxiety was related to greater metabolism of the right orbital frontal region.

Heightened activation of the parahippocampal gyrus of the right hemisphere was found in patients with panic disorder by Reiman et al. (1984). Using PET methods for a three-dimensional assessment of regional cerebral blood flow, they found greater right than left parahippocampal flow in seven of ten panic disorder patients. Because the patients were not experiencing a panic attack at the time of the scan, Reiman et al. suggest this finding represents a trait or dispositional factor.

Evidence that left hemisphere function is important to anxiety has also come from studies with both normals and psychiatric patients. After observing the increase in left lateral eye movements in state anxiety, Tucker and his associates went on to select normal subjects who were high or low in trait anxiety (Tucker et al., 1978). Unexpectedly, higher trait anxiety was associated with fewer left eye movements, and with a bias to judge tones presented to both ears as louder in the right ear. These results suggested relatively greater left hemisphere activation in the more anxious subjects. Yet on a tachistoscopic task, the subjects highest in trait anxiety showed markedly poor performance for stimuli, both verbal and spatial, presented to the right visual field. Tucker et al. (1978) concluded that the highly anxious subjects seemed to rely heavily on left hemisphere processing, to the point that it seemed overactivated on certain tasks.

This pattern of preferential left hemisphere activation, and yet in some cases left hemisphere dysfunction, was also observed by Gur (1978) for schizophrenic subjects. In Gur's research, greater left hemisphere activation was suggested by a high proportion of rightward reflective eye movements, and left hemisphere dysfunction was suggested by poor right visual field performance on a tachistoscopic task. In addition to pointing to emotional aspects of left hemisphere function, these results suggested the possibility that a better understanding of left hemisphere activity in normal anxiety might help explain the findings of left hemisphere overactivation and dysfunction in schizophrenia (Walker and McGuire, 1982; Flor-Henry, Ch. 22 of this volume). Posner et al. (1988) have recently examined schizophrenics' performance in a visual attention paradigm and have confirmed a right visual field impairment.

Tyler and Tucker (1982) continued work with normal subjects, examining how high and low trait anxious students performed under conditions of high and low situational stress (loud white noise). They found that for nonverbal tasks, presumably drawing on right hemisphere skills, the low trait anxious subjects performed better under stress, whereas the high trait anxious subjects did worse. On a perceptual task that assesses the degree to which subjects adopt a global versus an analytic strategy in perception, they found high trait anxious subjects to be significantly more analytic, consistent with the prediction that they would adopt a more left hemisphere dominated perceptual strategy.

Recently, Gruzelier and Bennett (Gruzelier, 1986) extended the findings on left hemisphere activation and dysfunction to patients diagnosed with anxiety disorder. Using a tachistoscopic task that reliably produces a right field (left hemisphere) advantage with normals, they observed an absence of the right field advantage in anxious patients. Yet on a cognitive style questionnaire, the anxious patients endorsed characteristics of a left hemisphere cognitive style. In their examination of anxiety-disorder patients with Posner's attentional tasks, Liotti et al. (in preparation) found them to show a trend toward impaired right visual field performance.

Perris et al. (1978) found that for the psychiatric symptoms of rumination and anxiety, it was the EEG from the anterior left hemisphere that was most predictive. Considered together with the metabolism and blood findings implicating the left orbital frontal region in anxiety disorder (Johanson et al., 1986) and in obsessive-compulsive disorder (Baxter et al., 1987), this finding suggests that frontal regulation of left hemisphere functioning may be a central issue in anxiety. Flor-Henry et al. (1979) also found anterior left hemisphere EEG abnormalities in obsessive-compulsives, as well as a pattern of neuropsychological test performance that suggested dysfunction of the anterior left hemisphere. They proposed that the ideative ruminations shown by obsessive patients may result from a disinhibition of the posterior left hemisphere's cognitive processing, due to frontal lobe dysfunction. Judging from the findings of increased metabolism and blood flow in left orbital frontal cortex, the dysfunction inferred by Flor-Henry et al. must be accompanied by some sort of a high degree of activation of at least some regions at the left frontal lobe.

An interesting perspective on the interaction between anterior and posterior systems in the left hemisphere is provided by the evidence on anterior versus posterior lesions in aphasia. Consistent with the findings of Robinson et al. (1984), more anterior (Broca's) aphasias are associated with more negative affect, while posterior (Wernicke's) aphasias may be associated with indifference or even inappropriately positive affect (Benson and Geschwind, 1975). The differing speech characteristics of these patients suggest differing kinds of control offered by anterior and posterior regions of the left hemisphere. The aphasics with anterior left hemisphere lesions show expressive deficits, with difficulty finding words. Yet the few words that are expressed are highly meaningful (Benson and Geschwind, 1975). In contrast, a posterior lesion may produce jargon aphasia, in which there is fluent, but meaningless, verbalization. The implication is that the posterior left hemisphere performs a self-monitoring function which applies semantic and syntactic constraints on speech production. Is there an exaggeration of critical self-monitoring from the posterior left hemisphere in anxiety?

In the left hemisphere's self-monitoring is important to self-control in a general sense, it might be expected that inadequate left hemisphere function would be found in certain disorders, such as psychopathy (Flor-Henry, 1976; Tucker, 1981). Studies using neuropsychological tests (Fedora and Fedora, 1983) and research with dichotic listening and tachistoscopic methods of assessing laterality (Hare and McPherson, 1984) have supported this reasoning.

Finding that left hemisphere activity seems to be important to anxiety, we can then question how its cognitive processes figure in anxiety's clinical manifestations. The more elementary aspects of exaggerated arousal in anxiety would seem more difficult to relate to left hemisphere function, since evidence reviewed above points to right hemisphere function in regulating arousal. However, Tucker and Williamson (1984) have proposed that certain brain systems regulating motor readiness – what Pribram and McGuinness (1975) have described as a tonic activation system – may be especially important to the attentional control of the left hemisphere. Several findings have suggested that, although they are certainly bilateral, dopaminergic pathways may be asymmetric and more important to left hemisphere function. In animals, pharmacological and behavioral evidence suggests there may be a left-lateralization of DA systems (Glick and Ross, 1981). In humans, Gottfries et al. (1974) found that CSF levels of a DA metabolite, homovanilic acid, were related to event-related potential amplitudes over the left but not the right hemisphere. In unmedicated schizophrenics, exaggerated left hemisphere EEG activation is observed, which becomes symmetric after neuroleptic therapy (Serafetinides, 1973). Higher-amplitude event-related potentials have been observed in the left than in the right hemisphere in unmedicated schizophrenics (Tomer et al., 1982). Post-mortem analysis of DA in the amygdala of schizophrenics' brains shows it to be higher in the left hemisphere (Reynolds, 1983). In normals given neuroleptics, the EEG slowing is most evident over the left hemisphere (Laurian et al., 1983).

Because GABAergic modulation is so important to the models of DA function in anxiety, hypotheses of asymmetric action of GABAergic agents (Frumkin and Grimm, 1981) are certainly relevant to questions of lateralization and anxiety. Although some autopsy data have suggested an asymmetric distribution of GABA in substantia nigra (Rossor et al., 1980), it remains to be determined how important brain lateralization will be for understanding the action of anxiolytics.

Questions of mechanisms

Reading the psychological literature on emotion and cognition, then reading the receptor physiology models of psychiatric disorders, one wonders if brain and mind could be woven of the same cloth. The neuropsychological literature does attempt to deal both with brain structures and their functions, yet the danger is that it will operate in still another unrelated domain, of hemispheres and lobes, and it will incorporate neither the ephemeral workings of mental processes nor the wet stuff of neural networks.

The emerging evidence on neurotransmitters, receptors and modulators is providing a picture of elementary processes in the physiology of neural systems that have major effects in controlling the brain activity. At least from gross observations on clinical effects of drugs, it is clear that these effects must be integral both to the brain's control of its arousal and to the disordered emotional states observed in psychiatric patients. Yet in psychological theories of emotion, the concepts available to describe such phenomena as 'arousal' are limited at best (Mandler, 1985; Schacter and Singer, 1962), and these provide no help in understanding the adaptive functions of neurophysiological control mechanisms.

Self-regulation through activation and arousal

In reviewing the evidence on neural systems regulating arousal and attention, Pribram and McGuinness (1975) emphasized that a major distinction can be drawn between mechanisms that augment arousal in a phasic fashion and those that produce a tonic increment in function. They suggested that perceptual systems seem to have their arousal regulated in a more phasic fashion, with rapid habituation, whereas motor systems appear to be held in readiness through a tonic activation system. Tucker and Williamson (1984) proposed that these concepts could be helpful in differentiating the qualitative controls applied to neural function by activating neurotransmitter pathways, specifically DA and NE. In contrast to traditional

psychological theories of arousal, which consider only a quantitative increase or decrease in activity, the evidence on neurochemically specific pathways suggests that these mechanisms modulate the brain's activity in qualitatively unique ways.

In the animal literature, DA lesions impair motor behavior, consistent with the role of this pathway in motor readiness. Yet DA agonists do not simply augment motor function quantitatively. With increasing dopaminergic modulation, rats show a restriction of novel behavior, and they engage in a limited range of species-specific behavior (Iversen, 1977). With still larger doses of DA agonists, the rats' behavior degrades into motor stereotypes. Drawing again from Pribram's (1981) notions of frontal cortical control, Tucker and Williamson (1984) concluded that the motor readiness system seems to apply a redundancy bias to behavior. This is a qualitative form of neural cybernetics, a control system that is essential for sequential motor organization, and that may be integral to higher levels of cognitive control which require focusing of attention. Given the left hemisphere's importance to fine motor control (Kimura, 1977), its sequential mode of organizing events across time (Cohen, 1973), and its focal attentional qualities (Kinsbourne, 1970) underlying its analytic cognitive skills, Tucker and Williamson (1984) theorized that the primitive redundancy bias may be integral to the left hemisphere's cognitive function.

The evidence on neuromodulators shows that not only do they have attentional effects, they seem to have unique affective features as well. Emphasizing the vigilance and paranoia observed with exaggerated DA function with chronic amphetamine abuse (Kokkinidis and Anisman, 1980), Tucker and Williamson suggested that anxiety may be inherent to the operation of the motor readiness system. This suggestion would be consistent with the evidence of stress, benzodiazepine modulation and the mesolimbic – frontocortical DA pathways described above. It would also offer opportunities for integrating this evidence with the implications of left-hemisphere activity in anxiety.

The primary NE pathway, the dorsal noradrenergic bundle, was proposed by Tucker and Williamson to be a candidate for supporting the phasic arousal system. At least some of the attentional effects of the NE pathway appear to be exerted by a habituation mechanism, whereby the selection of adaptively relevant stimuli is aided by a rapid decrement in the brain's response to repetitive stimuli that are not selected as relevant (see Mason, 1981). Like the tonic motor readiness system, the phasic arousal system acts directly to control neural activity, but in a qualitatively specific way. The habituation bias selects for novelty. Over a period of time, selection for novelty acts to fill short-term representation capacity with unique information. This produces an expansive mode of attentional control that Tucker and Williamson proposed is integral to the right hemisphere's holistic cognitive and perceptual skills.

Drawing both from the catecholamine hypothesis, that NE modulation is low in depression and high in mania, and from the indication that the euphoriant effects of street drugs like cocaine are mediated at least in part by NE effects (Cooper et al., 1974), Tucker and Williamson proposed that elation is the emotional state asssociated with the phasic arousal system, and that the qualitative attentional effects of this system may explain such clinical observations as stimulus-seeking and expansive thinking in an elated state.

Tucker and Williamson attempted to formulate primitive control mechanisms, such as would be provided by neurotransmitter pathways, that might begin to account for more complex psychological phenomena. Their model predicts that anxiety restricts attention whereas elation expands it. These predictions are consistent with several findings described in the psychological literature on anxiety and mania described above. The advantage of this kind of theorizing is that it suggests how elementary neurophysiological mechanisms may at the same time produce distinct emotional states and qualitative controls on attention. However, the broad scope of the tonic activation and phasic arousal constructs in the Tucker and Williamson model caused several important issues to be glossed over. It is clear that many complexities of the neurophysiological literature were ignored by the selection of DA and NE systems as representative mechanisms for tonic and phasic controls. Furthermore, the psychological controls theorized by Tucker and Williamson are clearly controls on working memory, and yet their model attempts to reason from brainstem control mechanisms to cortical function without considering the limbic structures that are essential to both memory and to elementary emotional states.

The emphasis in Tucker and Williamson's version of the activation and arousal model was on the bottom-up direction of control, theorizing how primitive neural controls could influence more complex dimensions of brain function. Yet perhaps the key question for integrating neuropsychology with biological psychiatry is how the regulatory influences from neuromodulator systems are in turn directed by the cognitive functioning of higher brain systems. It is this top-down control that could help explain how the cognitive appraisal of lack of control could lead to the neurophysiological changes involved in a depressed mood, including the hedonic and attentional changes that may further impair coping efforts.

Lateralization and the anterior – posterior dimension

An important challenge for any model that relates brain lateralization to emotion and psychopathology will be to proceed beyond global concepts of the hemisphere's psychological roles to formulate how frontal-limbic mechanisms differentially regulate hemispheric function. The need to consider frontal – posterior interactions within each hemisphere has become apparent in current models of emotional lateralization (Davidson, 1984; Kinsbourne, in press; Tucker and Frederick, 1989). An integral aspect of the Tucker and Williamson (1984) framework was the speculation that laterality is not orthogonal to caudality; left hemisphere specialization seems to have evolved to draw on the cybernetics of the motor readiness system of the system of the anterior brain, whereas at least many of the right hemisphere's cognitive skills seem to have emerged as dependent on the control properties of more phasic perceptual orienting systems.

The need to interpret the evidence on lateralization within the traditional emphasis on anterior – posterior differentiation (Pribram, 1981) has also been considered by Kinsbourne (in press) in his recent account of emotional lateralization. Kinsbourne proposes that the right hemisphere's emotional functions involve a sensitivity to the external context, and an interruption of internal processes in response to external events. In contrast, the left hemisphere seems to maintain continuity to behavior, especially to internally directed, motivated actions. Kinsbourne argues that these more general aspects of lateralization are consistent with the Tucker and Williamson formulation that the right hemisphere's emotional functions vary on a depression – elation dimension, whereas those of the left hemisphere vary on the relaxation – anxiety dimension.

Although these models thus attempt to integrate the lateralization evidence within the context of more general anterior – posterior differentiation, they provide little in the way of explanations for how frontal-limbic regulatory mechanisms operate differentially on the two hemispheres. Yet this is what is indicated, by the asymmetries of emotional effects of frontal lesions (Robinson et al., 1984), the asymmetries of frontal EEG effects in normal emotion (Davidson, 1984; Tucker et al., 1981) and psychiatric disorders (Perris et al., 1978) and the asymmetries of orbital frontal metabolism and blood flow observed in psychiatric anxiety (Johanson et al., 1986; Baxter et al., 1987). Furthermore, it is becoming clear that the functional differentiation of regions within the frontal lobe must be understood to explain the evidence on frontal control of emotion. For example, it is lesions of the left frontal lobe that appear most likely to produce a depressive-catastrophic emotional response (Robinson et al., 1984). Yet depression and anxiety are decreased by orbital lesions (Flor-Henry, 1977), and anxiety is accompanied by increased left

orbital activity specifically (Johanson et al., 1986; Baxter et al., 1987). Does this mean that there is a reciprocity between orbital and dorsolateral regions of the frontal lobe?

The anatomical connections of the frontal lobes are well-suited to interaction with widespread cortical regions (Goldman-Rakic, 1984). Roland's (1984) blood flow findings suggest that the frontal lobes 'tune' the activity in other cortical regions to orchestrate attention. The main clue to the adaptive functions of frontal regions would seem to be their developmental roots in limbic structures (Goldberg, 1985; Sanides, 1970). Thus at many turns in the neuropsychological literature, the most interesting questions lead to the limbic system. And the limbic mechanisms would seem essential to not only the notions of control of working memory, but to the priming of cognitive representations as a function of threats and pleasures.

Concepts of limbic function

Gray's (1979, 1982) model draws from evidence on limbic system function derived from the animal literature to explain aspects of human anxiety. This model suggests ways of relating effects of drugs such as the benzodiazepines to control mechanisms with specific influences on learning and behavior. The deductions from the septo-hippocampal model by Newman and his associates (Newman and Kosson, 1986; Newman et al., 1985) have led to successful predictions in the opposite direction, explaining the behavior control deficits of humans with limited inhibitions. However, there are only certain aspects of anxiety that can be explained by a behavioral inhibition model. Furthermore, the reasoning on which Gray's model of anxiety rests is indirect. Because anxiolitics produce disinhibition, it is not a necessary conclusion that another cause of disinhibition, septo-hippocampal lesions, can be equated with anxiety. In fact, the evidence Gray (1982) reviews on effects of atropine on hippocampal theta would seem to suggest that cholinergic pathways are better candidates for septal influences on hippocampal function than benzodiazepines. The close relation of

BZ actions to the mesolimbic DA pathways reviewed above would be more consistent with the notion that modulation of motor readiness is integral to anxiety. If so, then the action of BZs as muscle relaxants would not be irrelevant to their anxiolytic effects, as Gray suggests, but rather quite relevant.

A third clinical use of benzodiazepines is as anticonvulsants. While this neurophysiological action may seem far removed from anxiolytic effects, it may provide clues to mechanism as well. When Papez (1937) first proposed a limbic system, its anatomical circuitry was defined by the tendency of seizure activity to propagate rapidly through this circuit. Recent studies of the neurophysiological mechanisms of seizures have shown that limbic structures, including the mammillary bodies, mammillothalamic tract and anterior nuclei of the thalamus, may be involved in the development and propogation of certain kinds of epileptic activity (Dichter and Ayala, 1987). The fact that these structures of the Papez circuit also appear to be essential to human memory (Squire, 1986) raises interesting questions about whether the unique electrophysiological sensitivity of limbic structures may be integral to their role in providing the cortex with the capacity for memory.

The relevance of seizure sensitivity to anxiety is suggested by the observation that GABAergic modulation of the mammillothalamic circuit can gate its seizure propagation (Dichter and Ayala, 1987). GABAergic inhibition of seizures also seems to involve specific actions on dopamine pathways, such that various forms of seizure activity are blocked by infusion of GABAergic agents into the substantia nigra, or by destruction of the substantia nigra (Dichter and Ayala, 1987). It is the GABAergic modulation of mesolimbic DA projections that seems to be the best clue to the role of benzodiazepines in attenuating the brain's response to stress and anxiety (Giorgi et al., 1986). A better understanding of these neurophysiological regulatory mechanisms would lead to important insights into the nature of both subjectively felt emotional states and the tuning of neural networks in learning and memory.

Although attempts to relate the neuropharmacology and receptor physiology literature to psychological phenomena will by necessity have a theoretical reach that will generate controversy, it seems clear that this is what is required to understand the cognitive effects of anxiety and depression. Whatever the limbic system does to allow the cortex to form memories (Squire, 1986), it seems likely this will be done in close association with the organism's hedonic interests and adaptive needs.

One insight into limbic-cortical interactions has been anatomical. Based on an analysis of architectonic features, Sanides (1970) has proposed that dorsal regions of the primate cortex, with their large pyramidal layer, have evolved from the archiocortex of the dorsal limbic system, whereas the ventral cortical regions, with their more granular appearance, seem to have emerged from the paleocortex of the ventral limbic system. This dorsal–ventral distinction has proven to be a critical one in understanding the neuropsychology of memory. In work on visual memory in primates, Mishkin and his associates (Mishkin, 1972; Malamut et al., 1984) find that the route for higher-order processing of spatial information leads through a dorsal, parietal pathway to hippocampus, whereas processing of object qualities of visual stimuli leads through the ventral pathway to temporal lobe and the amygdala. Studies of motor organization suggest that there is a differential limbic control of action, with a dorsal pathway from cingulate cortex to dorsomedial frontal cortex, and a more ventral route to orbital and lateral frontal surfaces (Goldberg, 1985).

Thus, the functional organization of the neocortex may be understood by appreciating its developmental origins within dorsal and ventral limbic structures. Are there qualities of adaptive, emotional function that differentiate between the dorsal archiocortex and the ventral paleocortex? Bear (1983) has proposed that there are, and that these may relate to hemispheric specialization. He reviews evidence on functions of the dorsal pathway coursing through the parietal lobe and suggests that its functions in spatial localization and its interconnections with cingulate cortex cause the dorsal system to be particularly important to emotional surveillance. In contrast, the ventral pathway seems to be closely connected with learned emotional responses that are integrated with motor functions through interconnections of the ventral pathway to orbital frontal cortex.

Bear theorizes that the left and right hemispheres have different degrees of interconnection of their cortical functions with limbic controls. Geschwind (1965) emphasized the importance of non-limbic, transcortical connections in the evolution of language. Bear suggests that left hemisphere specialization has involved greater separation of its cognitive functions from limbic controls. In contrast, the right hemisphere's emotional functions may be seen as retaining a high degree of limbic elaboration.

An important set of observations made on temporal lobe epileptics by Bear and Fedio (1977; see also Fedio and Martin, 1983) can be seen as consistent with this reasoning. Psychometric data showed patients with left temporal lobe foci to have 'ideative' concerns, involving ruminations about ideas with philosophical or religious significance. Patients with right temporal foci showed more 'emotional' characteristics. Bear and Fedio concluded that these personality patterns reflected a 'functional hyperconnection' of cortical with limbic processes in each hemisphere. Thus when overly infused with limbic involvement, left hemisphere functioning seemed to reflect an intellectualized quality, whereas exaggerated limbic involvement in right hemisphere functioning seemed to enhance its emotional qualities.

Another aspect of the psychometric data on Bear and Fedio's temporal lobe epileptics may provide another clue to asymmetries of limbic-cortical interaction. The two groups showed opposite biases in their self-report styles. Compared with ratings by observers, the right temporal patients denied problems and emphasized their positive traits, whereas the left temporal patients were overly self-critical. These asymmetries in emotional orientation are quite relevant to the emotional asymmetries observed in research on brain lesions, psychiatric disorders and normal emotion, and may suggest that there are inherent lateral asymmetries in the organization and function of the limbic system. It may be necessary to understand these limbic asymmetries in order to explain differential hemispheric function in emotion. These limbic mechanisms may provide important insights into how primitive representations of pleasures and anxieties act upon attention and memory.

Conclusion

We began this chapter by attempting to frame a context for considering mechanisms of anxiety and depression, a context formed at one level by patterns of thoughts and feelings and at another level by the dynamics of receptor physiology. Until the neuropsychological evidence is considered, these two levels seem very difficult to put together. Within the neuropsychological evidence itself, however, we have found suggestions of brain mechanisms that are relevant to both these levels, and the problem is not so much figuring how to integrate various mechanisms, but how to separate them. We find asymmetries of neurotransmitter function that seem interpretable only if we understand the hemispheres' different roles in emotion; we find a controversy over hemispheric contributions that seems resolvable only through clarification of frontal lobe controls; from the frontal lobes we find not only asymmetries but what seem to be opposite influences from the dorsal and orbital regions of frontal-limbic cortex.

Thus, if we are to be localizationists in studying anxiety and depression, we must be interdependent localizationists, recognizing the functional integrity that cuts across multiple levels of neural organization. Anxiety and depression clearly touch on the most elementary mechanisms of neural networks, yet they seem to be integral to the most complex of the brain's executive functions as well. Perhaps what the interdependence of these various brain systems suggests most clearly is that anxiety and depression are not isolated disease processes, but mechanisms that are integral to the brain's, and the person's, self-regulation.

References

Abramson LY, Seligman MEP, Teasdale JD: Learned helplessness in humans: critique and reformulation. *J. Abnorm. Psychol.: 87,* 49 – 74, 1978.

Aggleton JP, Mishkin M: The amygdala: sensory gateway to the emotions. In Plutchik R, Kellerman H (Editors), *Emotion: Theory, Research and Experience.* Vol. 3. New York: Academic Press, 1983.

Amsel A, Stanton M: Ontogeny and phylogeny of paradoxical reward effects. *Adv. Stud. Behav.: 11,* 227 – 274, 1980.

Andreasen NJC, Canter A: The creative writer: psychiatric symptoms and family history. *Compr. Psychiatry: 15,* 123 – 131, 1974.

Andreasen NJC, Powers PS: Creativity and psychosis: an examination of conceptual styles. *Arch. Gen. Psychiatry: 32,* 70 – 73, 1975.

Aston-Jones G, Bloom FE: Activity of norepinephrine-containing locus coeruleus neurons in behaving rats anticipates fluctuations in the sleep – waking cycle. *J. Neurosci.: 1,* 876 – 886, 1981a.

Aston-Jones G, Bloom FE: Norepinephrine-containing locus coeruleus neurons in behaving rats exhibit pronounced responses to non-noxious environmental stimuli. *J. Neurosci.: 1,* 887 – 900, 1981b.

Barbaccia ML, Gandolfi O, Chuang DM, Costa E: *Proc. Natl. Acad. Sci. USA: 80,* 5134 – 5138, 1983.

Baxter LR, Phelps ME, Mazziotta JC, Guze, BH: Local cerebral glucose metabolic rates in obsessive-compulsive disorder: a comparison with rates in unipolar depression and in normal controls. *Arch. Gen. Psychiatry,* 1987.

Bear DM: Hemispheric specialization and the neurology of emotion. *Arch. Neurol.: 40,* 195 – 202, 1983.

Bear DM, Fedio PD: Quantitative analysis of interictal behavior in temporal lobe epilepsy. *Arch. Neurol.: 34,* 454 – 467, 1977.

Beck AT: *Depression: Clinical, Experimental, and Theoretical Aspects.* New York: Harper and Row, 1967.

Beckmann H, Schmauss M: Clinical investigations into antidepressant mechanisms. I. Antihistaminic and cholinolytic effects: amitriptyline versus promethazine. *Arch. Psychiatrie Nervenkrankh.: 233,* 59 – 70, 1983.

Benson DF, Geschwind N: The aphasias and related disturbances. In Baker AB, Balar LD (Editors), *Clinical Neurology.* New York: Harper & Row, 1975.

Berger B, Tassin JP, Blanc G, Moyne V, Tierry AM: Histochemical confirmation for dopaminergic innervation of the rat cerebral cortex after destruction of the noradrenergic ascending pathways. *Brain Res.: 81,* 332 – 337, 1974.

Berrettini WH, Post RM: In Post RM, Ballanger JC (Editors), *Frontiers in Clinical Neuroscience.* Vol. 1. Baltimore/London: Williams & Wilkins, pp. 673 – 685, 1984.

Biggio G, Corda MG, Concas A, De Montis G, Rossetti Z,

Gessa GL: Rapid changes in GABA binding induced by stress in different areas of the rat brain. *Brain Res.: 229,* 363 – 369, 1981.

Biggio G, Concas M, Serra M, Salis M, Corda MG, Nurchi V, Crisponi C, Gessa GL: Stress and Beta-carbolines decrease the density of low affinity GABA binding sites, an effect reversed by diazepam. *Brain Res.: 305,* 13 – 18, 1984.

Blumer D, Benson DF: Personality changes with frontal and temporal lobe lesions. In Benson DF, Blumer D (Editors), *Psychiatric Aspects of Neurologic Disease.* New York: Grune and Stratton, 151 – 170, 1975.

Borod JC, Koff E, Buck R: The neuropsychology of facial expression: data from normal and brain-damaged adults. In Blanc P, Buck R, Rosenthal R (Editors), *Nonverbal Communication in the Clinical Context.* University Park, PA: Penn State Press., 1986.

Bower GH: Mood and Memory. *Am. Psychol.: 36,* 129 – 148, 1981.

Bower H, Mayer JD: Failure to replicate mood-dependent retrieval. *Bull. Psychomic Soc.,* 1984, (in press).

Braestrup C, Nielsen M, Olsen CE: Urinary and brain Beta-carboline-3-carboxylates as point inhibitors of brain benzodiazepine receptors. *Proc. Natl. Acad. Sci.: 77,* 2288 – 2292, 1980.

Brodal A: *Neurological Anatomy.* New York: Oxford University Press, 1981.

Brumback RA, Staton RD, Wilson H: Neuropsychological study of children during and after remission of endogenous depressive episodes. *Percept. Mot. Skills: 50,* 1163 – 1167, 1980.

Buck R: Prime theory: an integrated view of motivation and emotion. *Psychol. Rev.: 92,* 389 – 413, 1985.

Butler G, Mathews A: Cognitive processes in anxiety. *Adv. Behav. Res. Ther.: 5,* 51 – 62, 1983.

Charney DS, Menkes DB, Heninger GB: Receptor sensitivity and the mechanism of action of antidepressant treatment. *Arch. Gen. Psychiatry: 38,* 1160 – 1180, 1981.

Charney DS, Heninger GR, Sternberg DE: Serotonin function and mechanism of action of antidepressant treatment. *Arch. Gen. Psychiatry: 41,* 359 – 365, 1984.

Chuang DM, Costa E: In Lajtha A (Editor), *Handbook of Neurochemistry. 6,* 307 – 330. New York: Plenum Press, 1984.

Cohen G: Hemispheric differences in serial versus parallel processing. *J. Exp. Psychol.: 97,* 349 – 356, 1973.

Cooper JR, Bloom FE, Roth RH: *The Biochemical Basis of Neuropharmacology.* New York: Oxford University Press, 1974.

Corda MG, Biggio G: Proconflict effect of GABA receptor complex antagonists. Reversal by diazepam. *Neuropharmacology: 5,* 541 – 544, 1986.

Costa E, Guidotti A: Molecular mechanism in the receptor action of benzodiazepine. *Ann. Rev. Pharmacol. Toxicol.: 19,* 531 – 545, 1979.

Costa E, Ravizza L, Barbaccia ML. Evaluation of current theories on the mode of action of antidepressants. In G. Bartholini et al., *L.E.R.S.* 4. New York: Raven Press, 1986.

Crowne DP, Richardson CM, Dawson KA: Lateralization of emotionality in right parietal cortex of the rat. *Behav. Neurosci.: 101,* 134 – 138, 1987.

Cummings JL, Mendez MF: Secondary mania with focal cerebrovascular lesions. *Am. J. Psychiatry,* 1984.

D'Elia G, Parris G: Cerebral functional dominance and depression: an analysis of EEG amplitude in depressed patients. *Acta Psychiatr. Scand.: 49,* 191–197, 1973.

Damasio AR, Van Hoesen GW: Emotional disturbances associated with disturbances of the limbic frontal lobe. In Heilman KM and Satz P (Editors), *The Neuropsychology of Human Emotion: Recent Advances.* New York: Guilford Press, 1983.

Davidson RJ: Affect, cognition and hemispheric specialization. In Izard CE, Kagan J, Zajonc R (Editors), *Emotion, Cognition and Behavior.* New York: Cambridge University Press, (in press), 1984.

Denenberg VH: Hemispheric laterality in animals and the effects of early experience. *Behav. Brain Sci.: 4,* 1–49, 1981.

Descarries L, Lapierre Y: Norepinephrine and axon terminals in the cerebral cortex of the rat. *Brain Res.: 51,* 141–160, 1973.

Dewberry RG, Lipsey JR, Saad K, Moran TH, Robinson RG: Lateralized response to cortical injury in the rat: interhemispheric interaction. *Behav. Neurosci.: 100,* 556–562, 1986.

Dichter MA, Ayala GF: Cellular mechanisms of epilepsy: a status report. *Science: 237,* 157–164, 1987.

Disalver SC: Cholinergic mechanisms in depression. *Brain Res. Rev.: 11,* 285–316, 1986.

Disalver SC, Greden JF: Antidepressants withdrawal-induced activation (hypomania and mania): mechanisms and theoretical significance. *Brain Res. Rev.: 7,* 29–48, 1984.

Doerr P, Berger M: Physostigmine-induced escape from dexamethasone in normal subjects. *Biol. Psychiatry: 18,* 261–268, 1983.

Dorow R, Horowski R, Paschelke G, Amin M, Braestrup C: Severe anxiety induced by FG7142, a Beta-carboline ligand for benzodiazepine receptors. *Lancet: July 9,* 98–99, 1983.

Dumbrill-Ross A, Tang SW: Noradrenergic and serotoninergic input necessary to imipramine-induced changes in beta but not S2 receptor densities. *Psychiatr. Res.: 9,* 207–215, 1983.

Easterbrook JA: The effect of emotion on cue utilization and the organization of behavior. *Psychol. Rev.: 66,* 183–201, 1959.

Fedio P, Martin A: Ideative–emotive behavioral characteristics of patients following left or right temporal lobectomy. *Epilepsia: 24,* 117–130, 1983.

Fedora O, Fedora S: Some neuropsychological and psychophysiological aspects of psychopathic and nonpsychopathic criminals. In Flor-Henry P, Gruzelier J (Editors), *Laterality and Psychopathology.* Vol 2. Amsterdam: Elsevier, 1983.

Feinberg M, Gillin JC, Carroll BJ et al.: EEG studies of sleep in the diagnosis of depression. *Biol. Psychiatry: 17,* 305–316, 1982.

Ferrero P, Tarenzi L, Bergamasco B: Diazepam binding inhibitor in human cerebrospinal fluid. Studies in neuropsychiatric disorders. Paper presented at the II Conference of the Italian Society of Neuroscience, Pisa, December 1986.

Fibiger HC: The organization and some projections of cholinergic neurons of the mammalian forebrain. *Brain Res. Rev.: 4,* 327–388, 1982.

Flor-Henry P: Lateralized temporal-limbic dysfunction and psychopathology. *Ann. New York Acad. Sci.: 280,* 777–797, 1976.

Flor-Henry P: Progress and problems in psychosurgery. In Maserman JH (Editor), *Current Psychiatric Therapies.* New York: Grune & Stratton, 1977.

Flor-Henry P: On certain aspects of the localization of cerebral systems regulating and determining emotion. *Biol. Psychiatry: 14,* 677–698, 1979.

Flor-Henry P, Yeudall LT, Koles Z, Howarth B: Neuropsychological and power spectral EEG investigations of the obsessive-compulsive syndrome. *Biol. Psychiatry: 14,* 119–130, 1979.

Fogel BS, Sparadeo FR: Focal cognitive deficits accentuated by depression. *J. Nerv. Ment. Dis.: 73,* 120–124, 1985.

Frazer A, Mendels J: Effects of antidepressant drugs on adrenergic responsiveness and receptors. In Mendels J, Amsterdam JD (Editors), *The Psychobiology of Affective Disorders.* New York: Karger, 1983.

Freeman RL, Galaburda AM, Cabal RD, Geschwind N: The neurology of depression. *Arch. Neurol.: 42,* 289–291, 1985.

Frumkin LR, Grimm P: Is there pharmacological asymmetry in the human brain? An hypothesis for the differential hemispheric action of barbiturates. *Int. J. Neurosci.: 13,* 187–197, 1981.

Gainotti G: Emotional behavior and hemispheric side of the lesion. *Cortex: 8,* 41–55, 1972.

Gandolfi O, Barbaccia ML, Costa E: *J. Psychopharmacol. Exp. Ther.: 229,* 782–786, 1984.

Garcia-Sevilla JA, Zis AP, Zelnick TC, Smith GB: Tricyclic antidepressant drug treatment decreases alpha-2-adrenoreceptors on human platelet membranes. *Eur. J. Pharmacol.: 69,* 121–123, 1981.

George R, Haslett WL, Jenden DJ: A cholinergic mechanism in the brainstem reticular formation: induction of paradoxical sleep. *Int. J. Neuropharmacol.: 3,* 541–552, 1964.

Geschwind N: Disconnection syndromes in animals and man. *Brain: 88,* 237–294, 1965.

Glassmann A: Indolamines and affective disorder. *Psychosom. Med.: 31,* 107–114, 1969.

Giorgi O, Corda MG, Culurgioni F, Marras M, Biggio G: Dopamine metabolism in the rat prefrontal cortex: opposite effects of anxiolytic and anxiogenic Beta-Carbolines. Paper presented at the Second Conference of the Italian Neuroscience Society, Pisa, December, 1986.

Glick SD, Ross DA: Lateralization of function in the rat brain: basic mechanism may be operative in humans. *Trends Neurosci.: 4,* 196–199, 1981.

Goldberg G: Supplementary motor area structure and function: review and hypotheses. *Behav. Brain Sci.: 8,* 567–616, 1985.

Goldman-Rakic PS: The frontal lobes: uncharted provinces of the brain. *Trends Neurosci.: 7,* 428–429, 1984.

Goldstein K: The effect of brain damage on the personality. *Psychiatry: 15,* 245–260, 1952.

Goldstein SG, Filskov SB, Weaver LA, Ives J: Neuropsychological effects of electroconvulsive therapy. *J. Clin. Psychol.: 33,* 798–806, 1977.

Gorenstein EE, Newman JP: Disinhibitory psychopathology: a new perspective and a model for research. *Psychol. Rev.: 87,* 301–315, 1980.

Gottfries CG, Perris C, Roos BE: Visual averaged evoked responses (AER) and monoamine metabolics in cerebrospinal fluid (CSF). *Acta Psychiatr. Scand.: 255,* 135 – 142, 1974.

Gray JA: A neuropsychological theory of anxiety. In Izard CE (Editor), *Emotions in Personality and Psychopathology.* New York: Plenum Press, 1979.

Gray JA: Precis of the neuropsychology of anxiety: an inquiry into the functions of the septo-hippocampal system. *Behav. Brain Sci.: 5,* 469 – 534, 1982.

Green AR, Peralta E, Hong JS, Mao CC, Aterwill CK, Costa E: *J. Neurochem.: 31,* 607 – 611, 1978.

Gruzelier JH: Individual differences in dynamic process asymmetries in the normal and pathological brain. In Glass A (Editor), *Individual Differences in Hemispheric Specialization.* New York: Plenum Press, 1986. In press.

Guidotti A: Endogenous ligands for benzodiazepine binding sites. Paper presented at the II Conference of the Italian Neuroscience Society, Pisa, December 1986.

Guitton D, Buchtel HA, Douglas RM: Frontal lobe lesions in man cause difficulties in suppressing reflexive glances and in generating goal-directed saccades. *Exp. Brain Res.: 58,* 455 – 472, 1985.

Gur RC: Measurement and imaging of regional brain function: implications for neuropsychiatry. In Flor-Henry P, Gruzelier J (Editors), *Laterality in Psychopathology.* Amsterdam: Elsevier, 1983.

Gur RE: Left hemisphere dysfunction and left hemisphere overactivation in schizophrenia. *J. Abnorm. Psychol.: 87,* 226 – 238, 1978.

Hall H, Ogren SO: Effects of antidepressant drugs on different receptors in the brain. *Eur. J. Pharmacol.: 70,* 393 – 407, 1981.

Hall MM, Hall GC, Lavoie P: Ideation in patients with unilateral or bilateral midline brain lesions. *J. Abnorm. Psychol.: 73,* 526 – 531, 1968.

Hare RD, McPherson LM: Psychopathy and perceptual asymmetry during verbal dichotic listening. *J. Abnorm. Psychol.: 93,* 141 – 149, 1984.

Hecaen H. Clinical symptomatology in right and left hemisphere lesions. In Mountcastle VB (Editor), *Interhemispheric Relations and Cerebral Dominance,* Baltimore: Johns Hopkins Press, 1962.

Hecaen H: Mental symptoms associated with tumors of the frontal lobe. In Warren JM, Akert K (Editors), *The Frontal Granular Cortex and Behavior.* New York: McGraw-Hill, 1964.

Heilman KM, Van Den Abel T: Right hemisphere dominance for mediating cerebral activation. *Neuropsychologia: 17,* 1979.

Hobson JA: The reciprocal interaction model of sleep cycle control: discussion in the light of Giuseppe Moruzzi's concepts. In Pompeiano O, Ajmone N (Editors), *Brain Mechanisms and Perceptual Awareness.* New York: Raven, pp. 379 – 404, 1981.

Hobson JA, McCarley RW, Wyzinski PW: Sleep cycle oscillation: reciprocal discharge by two brainstem neural groups. *Science: 198,* 55 – 58, 1975.

Isen AM: Toward understanding the role of affect in cognition. In Wyer RS Jr., Srull TK (Editors), *Handbook of Social Cognition.* Vol. 3. Hillsdale, NJ: Lawrence Erlbaum, 1984.

Isen AM, Daubman KA: The influence of affect on categoriza-

tion. *J. Pers. Soc. Psychol.: 47,* 1206 – 1217, 1984.

Isen AM, Hastorf AH: Some perspectives on cognitive social psychology. In Hastorf AH, Isen AM (Editors), *Cognitive Social Psychology.* New York: Elsevier, 1982.

Isen AM, Daubman KA, Gorgoglione, JM: In Snow R, Farr M (Editors), *Aptitude, Learning and Instruction: Affective and Conative Processes,* Hillsdale, NJ: Lawrence Erlbaum, 1985.

Iversen SD: Brain dopamine systems and behavior. In Iversen LL, Iversen SD, Snyder SH (Editors), *Handbook of Psychopharmacology.* Vol. 8: *Drugs, Neurotransmitters and Behavior.* New York: Plenum Press, 333 – 384, 1977.

Janowsky DS, El-Yousef MK, Davis JM et al.: A cholinergic adrenergic hypothesis of mania and depression. *Lancet: 2,* 632 – 635, 1972.

Janowsky DS, Davis JM, El-Yousef MK et al.: Acetylcholine and depression. *Psychosom. Med.: 35,* 568, 1973.

Janowsky DS, Abrams, Groom G, Judd L: Antagonism of cholinergic inhibition by lithium. Presented at the 131st Annual Meeting of the American Psychiatric Association in Atlanta GA, 1978. New Research Abstract NRIS.

Janowsky DS, Risch SC, Parker D et al.: Increased vulnerability to cholinergic stimulation in affect disorder patients. *Psychopharmacol. Bull.: 16,* 29 – 31, 1980.

Janowsky DS, Risch SC, Huey LY, Judd L, Rausch JL: Hypothalamic-pituitary-adrenal regulation: neurotransmitters and affective disorders. *Peptides: 4,* 775 – 784, 1983.

Johanson AM, Risberg J, Silfverskiold P, Smith G: Regional changes of cerebral blood flow during increased anxiety in patients with anxiety neurosis. In Hentsche U, Smith G, Draguns JG (Editors), *The Roots of Perception.* Amsterdam: Elsevier, 1986.

Johnson EJ, Tversky AT: Affect, generalization and the perception of risk. *J. Pers. Soc. Psychol.: 45,* 20 – 31, 1983.

Jones G, Segal M, Foote S, Bloom FE: Locus coeruleus neurons in freely moving rats exhibit pronounced alterations of discharge rates during sensory stimulation. In Usdin E, Copin E, Barchas J (Editors), *Catecholamines, Basic and Clinical Frontiers.* New York: Pergamon Press, 1979.

Kaplanski J, Smelik PG: Analysis of the inhibition of ACTH release by hypothalamic implants of atropine. *Acta Endocrinol.: 73,* 651 – 659, 1983.

Karczmar AG, Longo VG, Scotti De Carolis A: A pharmacological model of paradoxical sleep: the role of cholinergic and monoamine systems. *Physiol. Behav.: 5,* 175 – 182, 1976.

Kimura D: Acquisition of a motor skill after left-hemisphere damage. *Brain: 100,* 527 – 542, 1977.

Kinsbourne M: The cerebral basis of lateral asymmetries in attention. *Acta Psychol.: 33,* 193 – 201, 1970.

Kinsbourne M: The biological determinants of functional bisymmetry and asymmetry. In Kinsbourne M (Editor), *Asymmetrical Functions of the Brain.* pp. 3 – 13, New York: Cambridge University Press, 1978.

Kinsbourne M: Hemisphere interactions in depression. Unpublished manuscript, 1987.

Kokkinidis L, Anisman H: Amphetamine models of paranoid schizophrenia: an overview and elaboration of animal experimentation. *Psychol. Bull.: 88,* 551 – 578, 1980.

Kopelman MD: The cholinergic neurotransmitter system in

human memory and dementia: a review. *Q. J. Exp. Psychol.: 38A,* 535–573, 1986.

Kronfol Z, Hamsher K, Digre K, Waziri R: Depression and hemisphere functions: changes associated with unilateral ECT. *Br. J. Psychiatry: 132,* 560–567, 1978.

Kuhar MJ: Neuroanatomical substrates of anxiety: a brief survey. *Trends Neurosci.: 7,* 307–311, 1986.

Kupfer DJ, Foster FG: Interval between onset of sleep and rapid eye movement sleep as an indicator of depression. *Lancet: 2,* 684–686, 1972.

Kupfer DG, Foster FG, Reich L et al.: EEG sleep changes as predictors in depression. *Am. J. Psychiatry: 133,* 622–626, 1976.

Kushnir M, Gordon H, Heifetz A: Cognitive asymmetries in bipolar and unipolar depressed patients. Paper presented to the International Neuropsychological Society, San Francisco, February, 1980.

Ladavas E, Nicoletti R, Rizzolatti G, Umilta' C: Right hemisphere interference during negative affect: a reaction time study. *Neuropsychologia: 22,* 479–485, 1984.

Laurian S, Gaillard JM, Le PK, Schopf J: Topographic aspects of EEG profile of some psychotropic drugs. In Kemali D, Perris C (Editors), *Advances in Biological Psychiatry.* 1983.

Lewinsohn PM, Steinmetz JL, Larson DW, Franklin J. Depression-related cognitions: antecedent or consequence? *J. Abnorm. Psychol.: 90,* 213–219, 1981.

Lindvall O, Bjorklund A, Moore RY, Steveni U: Mesencephalic dopamine neurons projecting to the neocortex. *Brain Res.: 81,* 325–331, 1974.

Liotti M, Sava D, Caffarra P, Rizzolatti G: Hemispheric differences in patients affected by depression and anxiety. Manuscript in preparation, University of Parma, 1987.

Lloyd GG, Lishman WA: Effect of depression on the speed of recall of pleasant and unpleasant experience. *Psychol. Med.: 5,* 173–180, 1975.

Longenecker ED: Perceptual recognition as a function of anxiety, motivation, and the testing situation. *J. Abnorm. Soc. Psychol.: 64,* 215–221, 1962.

Maas JW: Biogenic amines and depression: biochemical and pharmacological separation of two subtypes of depression. *Arch. Gen. Psychiatry: 32,* 1357–1361, 1975.

MacLeod C, Mathews A, Tata P: Attentional bias in emotional disorders. *J. Abnorm. Psychol.: 95,* 15–20, 1986.

Maggi A, U'Prichard DC, Enna SJ: Differential effects of antidepressant treatment on brain monoaminergic receptors. *Eur. J. Pharmacol.: 61,* 91–98, 1980.

Malamut BL, Saunders RC, Mishkin M: Monkeys with combined amygdalo-hippocampal lesions succeed in object discrimination learning despite 24-hour intertrial intervals. *behav. Neurosci.: 98,* 759–769, 1984.

Mandell AJ, Knapp S: Asymmetry and mood, emergent properties of serotonin regulation. *Arch. Gen. Psychiatry: 36,* 909–916, 1979.

Mandler G: *Mind and Body: Psychology of Emotion and Stress.* New York: W.W. Norton and Company, 1985.

Mason ST: Noradrenaline in the brain: progress in theories of behavioral function. *Prog. Neurobiol.: 16,* 262–303, 1981.

Mason ST, Iversen SD: Theories of dorsal bundle extinction effect. *Brain Res. Rev.: 1,* 107–137, 1979.

Mathew RJ, Wilson WH, Daniel DG: The effect of nonsedating doses of diazepam on regional cerebral blood flow. *Biol. Psychiatry: 20,* 1109–1116, 1985.

Mathews A, Eysenck M: Clinical anxiety and cognition. In Eysenck M, Martin (Editors), *Theoretical Foundations of Behavior Therapy.* Plenum Press (in press).

Mathews A, MacLeod C: Discrimination of threat cues without awareness in anxiety states. *J. Abnorm. Psychol.: 93,* 131–138, 1986.

MacLeod C, Tata P, Mathews A: Perception of emotionally valenced information in depression. *Br. J. Clin. Psychol.: 26,* in press, 1987.

McMillen BA, Warnack W, German DC, Shore PA: Effects of chronic desipramine treatment on rat brain noradrenergic response to alpha-adrenergic drugs. *Eur. J. Pharmacol.: 61,* 239–246, 1980.

McNeal ET, Cimbolic P: Antidepressants and biochemical theories of depression. *Psychol. Bull.: 3,* 361–374, 1986.

Meltzer HY, Umber-Koman-Witta, Robertson A, Tricou BJ, Lowy M, Perline R: Effects of 5-hydroxytryptophan on serum cortisol levels in major affective disorders. I. Enhanced response in depression and mania. *Arch. Gen. Psychiatry: 41,* 366–374, 1984.

Memo M, Nisoli E, Pizzi M, Missale C, Carruba MO, Spano PF: Pharmacological characterization and plasticity of dopamine receptors in mesolimbic-cortical and nigro-striatal systems after chronic treatment with different neuroleptics. Paper presented at the II Conference of the Italian Neuroscience Society, Pisa, December 1986.

Mesulam, MM: A cortical network for directed attention and unilateral neglect. *Ann. Neurol.: 10,* 309–325, 1981.

Mishkin, M: Cortical visual areas and their interaction. In Karczman AG, Eccles JC (Editors), *The Brain and Human Behavior.* Berlin: Springer-Verlag, 1972.

Mora F, Ferrer JMR: Neurotransmitters, pathways and circuits as the neural substrates of self-stimulation of the pre-frontal cortex: facts and speculations. *Behav. Brain. Res.: 22,* 127–140, 1986.

Nasby W, Yando R: Selective encoding and retrieval of affectively valent information. *J. Pers. Soc. Psychol.: 43,* 1244–1255, 1982.

Newman JP, Kosson DS: Passive avoidance learning in psychopathic and non-psychopathic offenders. *J. Abnorm. Psychol.: 95,* 257–263, 1986.

Newman JP, Widom CS, Nathan S: Passive-avoidance in syndromes of disinhibition: psychopathy and extraversion. *J. Pers. Soc. Psychol.: 48,* 1316–1327, 1985.

Oke A, Keller R, Meffort I, Adams RV: Lateralization of norepinephrine in human thalamus. *Science: 200,* 1141–1143, 1978.

Olpe HR, Jones RSG, Steinmann MW: The locus coeruleus: actions of psychoactive drugs. *Experientia: 39,* 242–249, 1983.

Olpe HR, Steinmann MW: The effect of vincamine, hydergine and piracetam on the firing rate of the locus coeruleus neurons. *J. Neural Transm.: 55,* 101–109, 1982.

Palermo DS, Jenkins JJ: Word association norms. Minneapolis: University of Minnesota Press, 1964.

Panksepp J: Toward a general psychobiological theory of emotions. *Behav. Brain Sci.: 5,* 407–467, 1982.

Papez JW: A proposed mechanism of emotion. *Arch. Neurol. Psychiatry: 38,* 725–744, 1937.

Patton WRG, Kotrick CA: Visual exploratory behavior as a function of manifest anxiety. *J. Psychol.: 82,* 349–353, 1972.

Pearlson GD, Robinson RG: Suction lesions of the frontal cerebral cortex in the rat induce asymmetrical behavioral and catecholaminergic responses. *Brain Res.: 218,* 233–242, 1981.

Perris C: EEG techniques in the measurement of the severity of depressive syndromes. *Neuropsychobiology: 1,* 16–25, 1975.

Perris C, Monakhov K, VonKnorring L, Botskarev V and Nikiforov A: Systemic structural analysis of the EEG of depressed patients. *Neuropsychobiology: 4,* 207–228, 1978.

Posner MI, Friedrich FJ, Walker J, Rafal R: Neural control of the direction of covert visual orienting. Paper presented at the meetings of the Psychonomic Society, November 1983.

Posner MI, Early TS, Reiman EM, Pardo PJ, Dhawan M: Asymmetries in hemispheric control of attention in schizophrenia. *Arch. Gen. Psychiatry: 45,* 814–821, 1988.

Post RM, Bellanger JC: Frontiers of Clinical Neuroscience. Vol. I. Baltimore/London: William and Wilkins, 1984.

Prange AJ: The pharmacology and biochemistry of depression. *Dis. Nerv. Syst.: 25,* 217–221, 1964.

Pribraum KH: Emotions. In Filskov SK, Boll TJ (Editors), *Handbook of Clinical Neuropsychology.* New York: Wiley-Interscience, 1981.

Pribraum KH, McGuinness D: Arousal, activation, and effort in the control of attention. *Psychol. Rev.: 82,* 116–149, 1975.

Reiman EMM, Raichle ME, Butler FK, Herscovitch P, Robins E: A focal brain abnormality in panic disorder, a severe form of anxiety. *Nature: 310,* 683–685, 1984.

Reynolds GP: Increased concentrations and lateral asymmetry of amygdala dopamine in schizophrenia. *Nature: 305,* 527–528, 1983.

Risch SC: Beta-endorphin hypersecretion in depression: possible cholinergic mechanisms. *Biol. Psychiatry: 17,* 1071–1079, 1982.

Risch SC, Cohen PM, Janowsky DS, Kalin NH, Murphy DL: Mood and behavioural effects of physostigmine on humans are accompanied by elevations in plasma beta-endorphin and cortisol. *Science: 209,* 1545–1546, 1980.

Robbins TW, Everitt BJ, Cole BJ, Archer T, Mohammed A: Functional hypotheses of the coeruleocortical noradrenergic projection: a review of recent experimentation and theory. *Physiol. Psychol.: 13,* 127–150, 1985.

Robins AH: Depression in patients with Parkinsonism. *Br. J. Psychiatry: 128,* 141–145, 1976.

Robinson RG: Differential behavioral and biochemical effects of right and left hemispheric cerebral infarction in the rat. *Science: 205,* 707–710, 1979.

Robinson RG, Kubos KL, Rao K, Price TR: Mood disorders in stroke patients: importance of location of lesion. *Brain: 107,* 81–93, 1984.

Roland PE: Metabolic measures of the working frontal cortex in man. *TINS:* 430–435, 1984.

Rosenblatt JE, Tellman JF, Pert CB, Pert A, Bunney WE: The effect of imipramine and lithium on alpha- and beta-receptor binding in rat brain. *Brain Res.: 160,* 186–191, 1979.

Rossi GF, Rosadini G: Experimental analysis of cerebral dominance in man. In Millikan CH, Darley FL (Editors), *Brain Mechanisms Underlying Speech and Language.* New York: Grune and Stratton, 1967.

Rossor M, Garret N, Iversen L: No evidence for lateral asymmetry of neurotransmitters in postmortem human brain. *J. Neurochem.: 35,* 743–745, 1980.

Sackeim HA, Greenberg MS, Weiman AL, Gur RC, Hungerbuhler JP, Geschwind M: Hemispheric asymmetry in the expression of positive and negative emotions: neurologic evidence. *Arch. Neurol.: 39,* 210–218, 1982.

Sackeim HA, Decina P, Epstein D, Bruder GE, Malitz S: Possible reversed affective lateralization in a case of bipolar disorder. *Am. J. Psychiatry: 140,* 1191–1193, 1983.

Sagels T, Erill S, Domino EF: Differential effects of scopolamine and chlorpromazine in REM and NREM sleep in normal male subjects. *Clin. Pharmacol. Ther.: 10,* 522–529, 1969.

Sanides F: Functional architecture of motor and sensory cortices in primates in the light of a new concept of neocortex evolution. In Noback CR, Montagna W (Editors), *The Primate Brain: Advances in Primatology.* Vol. 1. New York: Appleton-Century-Crofts, 1970.

Schacter F, Singer JE: Cognitive social and physiological determinants of emotional states. *Psychol. Rev.: 69,* 379–399, 1962.

Schaffer CE, Davidson RJ, Saron C: Frontal and parietal electroencephalogram asymmetry in depressed and nondepressed subjects. *Biol. Psychiatry: 18,* 753–762, 1983.

Schildkraut, J: The catecholamine hypothesis of affective disorders: a review of supporting evidence. *Am. J. Psychiatry: 122,* 509–522, 1965.

Schou M: Artistic productivity and lithium prophylaxis in manic-depressive illness. *Br. J. Psychiatry: 135,* 97–103, 1979.

Schwartz GE, Davidson RJ, Maer F: Right hemisphere lateralization for emotion in the human brain: interactions with cognition. *Science: 190,* 286–288, 1975.

Serafetinides EA: Voltage laterality in the EEG of psychiatric patients. *Dis. Nerv. Syst.: 34,* 190–191, 1973.

Segal M, Bloom TE: The action of norepinephrine in rat hippocampus: the effects of locus coeruleus stimulation on evoked hippocampal unit activity. *Brain Res.: 107,* 513–525, 1976.

Shaw ED, Mann JJ, Stokes PE, Manevitz Z: AZA effects of lithium carbonate on associative productivity and idiosyncracy in bipolar outpatients. *Am. J. Psychiatry: 143,* 1166–1169, 1986.

Silberman EK, Weingartner H: Hemispheric lateralization of functions related to emotion. *Brain Cogn.: 5,* 322–353, 1986.

Simson PC, Weiss JM, Hoffmann LJ, Ambrose MJ: Reversal of behavioural depression by infusion of an alpha-2 adrenergic agonist into the locus coeruleus. *Neuropharmacology: 4,* 385–389, 1986.

Sivam SP, Hudson PM, Tilson HA, Hong GS: GABA and dopamine interaction in the basal ganglia: dopaminergic supersensitivity following chronic elevation of brain gamma-aminobutyric acid levels. *Brain Res.: 412,* 29–35, 1987.

Smith CB, Garcia-Sevilla JA, Hollingsworth PJ: Alpha-2-adrenoreceptors in rat brain and decreased after long-term tricyclic antidepressant drug treatment. *Brain Res.: 210,* 413 – 418, 1981.

Solso RL, Johnson E, Schatz GC: Perceptual perimeters and generalized drive. *Psychon. Sci: 13,* 71 – 72, 1968.

Spence KW: A theory of emotionally based drive (D) and its relation to performance in simple learning situations. *Am. Psychol.: 13,* 131 – 141, 1958.

Squire LR: Mechanisms of memory. *Science: 232,* 1612 – 1619, 1986.

Sulser F: Mode of actions of antidepressant drugs. *J. Clin. Psychiatry: 44,* 14 – 20, 1983.

Teasdale JD, Fogarty SJ: Differential effects of induced mood on retrieval of pleasant and unpleasant events from episodic memory. *J. Abnorm. Psychol.: 88,* 248 – 257, 1979.

Tellegen A: Structures of mood and personality and their relevance to assessing anxiety, with an emphasis on self-report. In Tuma AH, Maser JD (Editors), *Anxiety and the Anxiety Disorders.* Hillsdale, NJ: Lawrence Erlbaum Associates, 1985.

Thayer RE: Toward a psychological theory of multidimensional activation (arousal). *Motiv. Emot.: 2,* 1 – 34, 1978.

Tomer R, Mintz M, Myslobodsky MS: Left hemisphere hyperactivity in schizophrenia: abnormality inherent to psychosis or neuroleptic side effect? *Psychopharmacology: 77,* 168 – 170, 1982.

Tsukamoto T, Asakura M, Hasegawa K: Long-term antidepressant treatment increases alpha-2-adrenergic receptor binding in rat cerebral cortex and hippocampus. In Langer SZ, Takahashi R, Segawa T, Briley M (Editors), *New Vistas in Depression.* New York: Pergamon Press, 1982.

Tucker DM: Lateral brain function, emotion, and conceptualization. *Psychol. Bull.: 89,* 19 – 46, 1981.

Tucker DM: Neural control of emotional communication. In Blanck P, Buck R, Rosenthal R (Editors), *Nonverbal Communication in the Clinical Context.* Cambridge: Cambridge University Press, 1986.

Tucker DM, Frederick SL: Emotion and brain lateralization. In Wagner H, Manstead T (Editors), *Handbook of Psychophysiology: Emotion and Social Behaviour.* New York: John Wiley, 1989.

Tucker DM, Williamson PA: Asymmetric neural control systems in human self-regulation. *Psychol. Rev.: 91,* 185 – 215, 1984.

Tucker DM, Roth RS, Arneson BA, Buckingham V: Right hemispheric activation during stress. *Neuropsychologia: 15,* 697 – 700, 1977.

Tucker DM, Antes JR, Stenslie CE, Barnhardt TN: Anxiety and lateral cerebral function. *J. Abnorm. Psychol.: 87,* 380 – 383, 1978.

Tucker DM, Stenslie CE, Roth RS, Shearer S: Right frontal lobe activation and right hemisphere performance decrement during a depressed mood. *Arch. Gen. Psychiatry: 38,* 169 – 174, 1981.

Tucker DM, Vannatta K, Rothlind J: Activation and arousal systems and the adaptive control of cognitive priming. Paper presented in the symposium, Psychological and Biological Processes in the Development of Emotion. University of Chicago, September, 1986.

Tyler SK, Tucker DM: Anxiety and perceptual structure: individual differences in neuropsychological function. *J. Abnorm. Psychol.: 91,* 210 – 220, 1982.

Ungerstedt U: Stereotaxic mapping of the monoamine pathways in the rat. *Acta Physiol. Scand. Suppl.: 367,* 1971.

Van den Hoofdakker RH, Beersma DGM: The course of depression and the timing of sleep. Proceedings of the 8th European Compr. Sleep Research. Szeged, Hungary, 1986.

Vannatta K: Specific affective priming. Manuscript in preparation, University of Oregon, 1987.

Van Praag HM: In Post RM, Ballanger JC (Editors), *Frontiers in Clinical Neuroscience.* Vol. 1. Baltimore/London: Williams and Wilkins, 1984.

Van Praag HM, Korf J: Central monoamine deficiency in depression: causative or secondary phenomenon? *Pharmacopsychiatry: 8,* 321 – 326, 1975.

Vetulani J, Sulser F: *Nature: 257,* 495 – 496, 1975.

Von Knorring L: Interhemispheric EEG differences in affective disorders. In Flor-Henry P, Gruzelier J (Editors), *Laterality and Psychopathology.* Amsterdam: Elsevier, 1983.

Walker E, McGuire M: Intra- and inter-hemispheric information processing in schizophrenia. *Psychol. Bull.: 29,* 701 – 725, 1982.

Waterhouse BD, Moises HC, Woodward DJ: Alpha-receptor mediated facilitation of somatosensory cortical neuronal responses to excitatory synaptic inputs and iontophoretically applied acetylcholine. *Neuropharmacology: 20,* 907 – 920, 1981.

Watson D, Tellegen A: Toward a consensual structure of mood. *Psychol. Bull.: 98,* 219 – 235, 1985.

Watts FN, McKenna FT, Sharrock R, Trezise L: Colour-naming of phobic-related words. *Br. J. Psychol.: 77,* 97 – 108, 1986.

Weiss JM, Simpson PC, Hoffmann LJ, Ambrose MJ, Cooper S, Webster A: Infusion of adrenergic receptor agonists and antagonists into the locus coeruleus and ventricular system of the brain. *Neuropharmacology: 25,* 367 – 384, 1986.

Wilson H, Staton RD: Neuropsychological changes in children associated with tricyclic antidepressant therapy. *Int. J. Neurosci.: 24,* 307 – 312, 1984.

Wilson WE, Mietling SW, Hong JS: Automated HPLC analysis of tissue levels of dopamine, serotonin and several prominent amine metabolites in extracts from various brain regions. *J. Liq. Chromatogr.: 12,* 871 – 886, 1983.

Wood K, Coppen A: Platelet alpha-adrenoreceptor sensitivity in depressive illness. In Mendlewicz J, Van Praag HM (Editors), *The Psychobiology of Affective Disorders.* New York: Krager, 1981.

Yerkes RM, Dodson JD: The relation of strength stimulus to rapidity of habit formation. *J. Comp. Neurol. Psychol.: 18,* 459 – 482, 1908.

CHAPTER 22

Psychopathology and hemispheric specialization: left hemisphere dysfunction in schizophrenia, psychopathy, hysteria and the obsessional syndrome

Pierre Flor-Henry

Alberta Hospital Edmonton, Box 307, Edmonton, Alberta, Canada T5J 2J7

Schizophrenia

The catatonic syndrome first described by Kahl-baum (1874) was characterized by apathy, excite-ment, mental confusion, verbal incoherence, ver-bigerations, motility abnormalities progressing to a terminal state of defect and dementia. Remark-ably in his clinico-pathological studies Kahlbaum wrote: "The predilection of exudate formation in the vicinity of the left Sylvian fissure and of the se-cond and third left frontal gyri, i.e. in the very areas which, on the basis of aphasia, are regarded as the sites of mental speech formation. It is note-worthy that clinical symptoms related to speech, mutism and verbigeration are very prominent in catatonia. Thus on the basis of the frequency of symptoms related to speech and the predilection of sites for the position of certain exudates it is feasi-ble to assume a relationship between clinical symp-toms and disturbances in the pertinent parts of the brain, which are the left temporal and left frontal regions." Southard (1915), who was director of the Boston Psychopathic Hospital and professor of neuropathology at Harvard Medical School, found in post-mortem investigations a striking lateraliza-tion to the left in 25 cases of dementia praecox. In 25% the lesions were unilateral on the left side, in the other cases the lesions were diffuse and in only one patient the lesions were unilateral in the right

hemisphere. Modern quantitative neuropathologi-cal studies implicate the left hemisphere in schizo-phrenia. Bogerts et al. (1985) in the morphometric study of brain volume and shrinkage of 13 schizo-phrenic brains, compared to normal brains, re-ported that the medial limbic structures of the tem-poral lobe (amygdala, hippocampal formation, parahippocampal gyrus) were significantly smaller in the schizophrenic group. (The brain specimens were collected between 1928 and 1953, i.e. before the introduction of neuroleptics: right hemisphere specimens were not available.) Of importance was the observation that the changes were atrophic in nature, without evidence of gliosis, hence not the result of infective processes. Jacob and Beckmann (1986) examined 64 brains from schizophrenic pa-tients which were compared to ten control brains. Two-thirds of the schizophrenic brains were ab-normal with deviant sulcogyral patterns in the tem-poral lobes and in one-third abnormal cytoarchi-tectonic patterns in the limbic allocortex were found. The anatomical abnormalities were asym-metric with poorly developed and heterotopic dis-placement of cells in the upper cortical layers of the parahippocampal and insular regions, sug-gesting a prenatal developmental disturbance of the limbic allocortex. All hebephrenic forms with chronic deficit symptomatology fell in the neuro-pathologically abnormal group, while paranoid forms usually did not show anatomical abnormalities. Brown et al. (1986) carried out systematic measurements of several brain regions (anterior coronal slice at the level of the interventricular foramina) in the post-mortem analysis of 41 schizophrenics and 29 patients with affective psychoses. There was significant thinning of the left parahippocampal cortex in the schizophrenics and relative thinning of the right parahippocampal gyrus in the affective patients, who, in addition, had a significantly smaller caudate nucleus on the right side than on the left. The thickness of the corpus callosum was similar in both psychoses. Neuroradiological investigations of schizophrenic patients (CT scans) confirm the presence of structural changes in the left hemisphere. Takahashi et al. (1981) found in 257 schizophrenics that atrophy of the dominant hemisphere was associated with defect symptomatology and blunted affect and that, overall, cortical atrophy and/or ventricular dilatation was significantly more pronounced in male than in female schizophrenics. In both sexes auditory hallucinations were associated with left temporal cortical atrophy. Similar findings were reported by Uchino et al. (1984), who were able to correctly classify 92.5% of schizophrenics and 100% of normals with CT area measurements and who found that enlargement of the left sylvian fissure and dilatation of the left anterior horn of the lateral ventricle were both associated with auditory hallucinations.

Golden et al. (1980) studied the actual CT scan density numbers in 21 chronic schizophrenics compared to 22 age-matched normal controls whose neurological examinations were all negative. It was found that the density of the left hemisphere was greater than that of the right in both groups. In addition, the schizophrenics (compared to the normals) had reduced density in both hemispheres, this bilateral reduction of brain density being more pronounced for the left hemisphere, since one of the right hemisphere comparisons did not significantly differ between schizophrenics and controls, whereas all the left hemisphere measures were significant. In a later, slightly expanded report

Berg et al. (1981) and Golden et al. (1981) conclude that abnormal density distribution is particularly evident in the dominant frontal region. Coffman et al. (1984) also observed reduced density of the left hemisphere in schizophrenia and, reviewing CT density studies published to date, conclude that, overall, they indicate reduced left hemisphere density. Reveley et al. (1987) have shown the presence of relative hypodensity of the left hemisphere in 11 monozygotic twins, discordant for schizophrenia when compared with their healthy co-twin or with control twins. In normals the tendency is for the left hemisphere to have a higher density than the right.

Thus, for over a hundred years, neuroanatomical evidence has shown that, when lateralized abnormalities are found in schizophrenia, they implicate the dominant hemisphere.

Hillbom and Kaila (1949) extracted 81 cases of psychosis from 1821 brain-injured soldiers. Of these, 20 were schizophrenic-paranoid psychoses, 17 of whom had temporal lesions, with a significant excess on the left side. Subsequently, Hillbom (1960), having expanded his series to 3552 cases, took a random sample ($n = 415$), and established a temporal localization and a left-sided association with psychosis. In cases without psychiatric disabilities the incidence of right and left wounds was comparable, but as psychiatric disability increased, there was a regular trend by which left-sided wounds outnumbered right-sided injuries; this became significant when left temporal lesions alone were considered. Remarkably similar were the findings of Lishman (1968), who studied 670 patients with penetrating head injuries, extracted from an initial cohort of 1024 on the basis of documentation for adequate analysis. Psychiatric disability and intellectual disorders correlated with brain damage and involvement of the left hemisphere but were independent of generalized intellectual impairment, physical disability, post-traumatic amnesia, and post-traumatic epilepsy. Left temporal lesions showed a strong association with psychiatric disability. Affective disorders were associated with right hemisphere damage and there was a trend for right frontal lesions to lead to the 'post-traumatic syndrome' and left frontal lesions to sexual and psychopathic changes. Davison and Bagley (1969) selected 40 cases of schizophrenic psychoses associated with closed head injuries and with skull fracture from the international literature, on the basis of adequacy of information provided. They found significant associations between temporal lesions, left hemisphere injuries, closed head injuries and unconsciousness of more than 24 hours.

Bingley (1958), studying mental symptoms in temporal lobe gliomas, reported that in 198 dextral patients there was a moderate association between mental symptoms and papilloedema. If the lobes were considered separately, however, there was no association with the dominant lobe but a marked association between papilloedema, mental symptoms and the nondominant lobe. Furthermore, with dominant lesions mental symptoms occurred before the appearance of papilloedema, and in cases without papilloedema dominant gliomas had more psychic symptoms. Also, blunting of affect was strongly associated with dominant gliomas. These remarkable relationships again emphasize the importance of dominant temporal pathology in the genesis of psychiatric symptomatology. Davison and Bagley (1969) culled 77 cases of schizophrenic psychoses associated with cerebral tumors and found that, compared to unselected series of cerebral tumours, the tumour site in the psychotic group had a temporal localization ($p < 0.001$). In a correlation analysis made between individual symptoms and lesion site in 80 cases with circumscribed lesions, the most significant statistical relationships that emerged related primary delusions and catatonic symptomatology to left hemisphere, particularly left temporal localization ($p < 0.001$).

The study of psychopathological manifestations encountered in temporal lobe epilepsy, as this writer has already extensively discussed (Flor-Henry, 1969, 1972a,b, 1976), demonstrates very significant laterality effects with respect to psychosis, psychopathic personality deviation, and affective disturbances. There is a very strong association linking dominant temporal epilepsy with schizophrenic and paranoid psychoses and with psychopathy. There is a weaker, but nevertheless quite definite, relationship between nondominant temporal epilepsy and manic-depressive psychoses, and, more generally, with dysphoric states of neurotic type (Falconer and Taylor, 1970). Interestingly, Mnoukhine and Dinabourg (1965), investigating 139 children with cerebral palsy, hemiparesis and epilepsy, observed that cerebral insult lateralized to the dominant hemisphere produced profound intellectual retardation and blunting of affectivity, whereas lateralization to the nondominant hemisphere led to "distinct intensification of emotional manifestations, abrupt excitability, melancholic depression." Abrams and Taylor (1980), while they found a left temporal lateralization in the clinical EEG of 27 schizophrenics and a right parietal lateralization in 132 manic depressives, reported that, irrespective of diagnosis, left-sided EEG abnormalities were associated with blunted affect. Kurachi et al. (1987) noted that regional cerebral blood flow in the left frontal region was bimodal in chronic schizophrenics: in the group with reduced left frontal flow there was a significant association with blunted affect and emotional withdrawal. The crucial role of left frontal disorganization in schizophrenia is further emphasised by Golden et al. (1985), who found that reduction of left anterior gray flow is particularly predictive of Luria-Nebraska neuropsychological impairment. Trimble (1984) reviewed the published evidence to that date on focus lateralization in the schizophrenic psychoses of epilepsy: ten investigations between 1963 and 1982 yielded a total of 180 cases. Unilateral epilepsy of the left hemisphere was found in 112 patients (62%); of the right hemisphere in 27 patients (15%) and bilateral foci in 41 cases (or 22%). The excess of left-sided foci is significant at the 95% confidence intervals for population (binomial). Interestingly when, a few years later, I reviewed the international literature relating to depression and laterality of focus in epilepsy, cumulating a total of 185 cases (published between 1969 and 1984), the distribution of foci was as follows: unilateral right 141, unilateral left 33, and bilateral 11, again a significant segregation of right hemisphere epilepsies correlated with neurotic or psychotic forms of depression, or with dysphoric affective auras or dacrystic epilepsy. Considering the 15% of cases with right temporal lobe epilepsy and schizophrenia it is noteworthy that there is a striking increase in sinistrality in temporal lobe epilepsy with psychosis, compared to temporal lobe epilepsy without psychosis. Reviewing five studies giving information on hand preference in temporal lobe epilepsy with and without psychosis (between 1975 and 1982), the overall frequency of sinistrality is 22% in the schizophrenics and 9% in those without psychosis (Flor-Henry, 1986). In the series of Sherwin et al. (1982) the incidence of sinistrality was an astonishing 71% in the temporal lobe epileptics with schizophrenia. Since 87% of patients with prenatal or early post-natal left hemisphere lesions (3 months to 5 years) are sinistral − while 100% of patients with right hemisphere lesions sustained during the same developmental period are dextral (Vargha-Khadem et al., 1985) − it is clear that in a proportion of subjects with right temporal lobe epilepsy and schizophrenia, the right hemisphere will in fact be the dominant hemisphere. Overall, an increased incidence of sinistrality is also found in the endogenous schizophrenias. In general, sinistrality in schizophrenia is associated with chronic forms evolving towards deficit symptomatology in males, while more florid psychoses with good prognosis may have an excess of dextrality (see Yan et al., 1985, for discussion.)

Profound affinities link the autistic and schizophrenic syndromes: in both there is a striking excess of males, in both there is an over-representation of first and last-born in the sibship, in both vestibular abnormalities are found, in both there is an excess of sinistrality and in both there are genetic-constitutional ('idiopathic') and acquired forms. Satz et al. (1985), who discuss handedness subtypes in autism, review 12 studies published after 1975 which indicated that the prevalence of manifest sinistrality across the 12 studies was 34%. In their own investigations they observe 20% sinistrality and 40% non-dextrality (mixed handedness).

Rutter and Lockyer (1967) and Rutter et al. (1967) have shown that a central aspect of the syndrome is the absence, or impairment, of language functions and in keeping with this DeMyer et al. (1974) found that the mean verbal IQ of a group of 115 autistic children was 35, while the performance IQ was 50. Of great interest was the observation that there was a positive relationship between the ability to relate emotionally and verbal IQ. Bartak et al. (1975), to further test the hypothesis that a specific cognitive defect involving language impairment underlies the syndrome of autism, studied autistic children of normal nonverbal intelligence whom he compared to children with sensory aphasia of developmental origin but without autism. Nineteen autistic males with a mean nonverbal IQ of 70 or over and 23 males with sensory aphasia were investigated with the WISC, the Merrill-Palmer Scale of Mental Tests, Colored Progressive Matrices, Peabody Picture Vocabulary Test, Free Speech, Gestural Comprehension and Expression. In addition, their reading and social behaviour were rated. The dysphasic children had more defects of articulation than the autistic, in whom gestural language was more impaired, who showed less 'chatter', were more echolalic, and who showed more stereotyped utterances, and metaphorical and pronominal language misuse. The mean verbal/performance IQ discrepancy was significantly greater in the autistic group: verbal = 66, performance = 96 (difference = 30), as opposed to verbal = 76, performance = 90, in the sensory aphasias (difference = 14). Also, the comprehension, similarities and vocabulary subtests were significantly lower in the autistic subjects ($p < 0.005$). Interestingly, block design and object assembly, the two subtests most sensitive to nondominant hemisphere dysfunction were quite normal in the autistic group. A neuropsychological study by Hoffmann and Prior (1982) of ten high-functioning autistic children (average IQ = 87) (in order to eliminate the non-specific impact of intellectual retardation) who were compared to mental-age-matched and chronologically age-matched children showed that the autistic group was significantly impaired on left-hemisphere tests. In particular they had significant deficits on WISC vocabulary, comprehension and similarities subtests, while they had normal scores on WISC Block Design and Object Assembly and a Target Test. The similarity with WAIS Subtest patterns seen in adult schizophrenia or even in children at risk for schizophrenia (reviewed in Flor-Henry, 1983b) is striking.

This evidence thus implies that the autistic syndrome is organic and critically dependent on disturbances of function of those brain regions that determine language mechanisms, including nonverbal language, i.e. gestural communication. A notable confirmation was provided by Hauser et al. (1975), who showed by air-encephalographic investigation that a group of autistic patients were characterized by central atrophy of the dominant temporal lobe. Abnormalities of vestibular functions have been established in both schizophrenia (Fitzgerald and Stengel, 1945; Levy et al., 1978) and autism (Ornitz, 1970). From this are probably derived the perceptual and motility abnormalities characteristic of autism, since the central connections of the vestibular system appear to be essential in maintaining sensory-motor integration. The autistic syndrome may be acquired; this is shown by the very high incidence of epilepsy, its association with maternal rubella (where the incidence increases by a factor of 100) and retrolental fibroplasia as well as with postmaturity (Lobascher et al., 1970). In the majority of instances the etiology appears to be genetically determined. Folstein and Rutter (1977) reported in a genetic study of 21 same-sex twin pairs a 36% pair-wise concordance for autism in monozygotic and 0% concordance in dizygotic pairs. In 12 of the 17 pairs discordant for autism, the autistic had a history of a perinatal brain damage event.

Rutter and Bartak (1971) have further shown

that language delay occurred in one-fourth of the parents and siblings of children with autism, is gender-related, and in this way linked to the more vulnerable dominant hemisphere of the males. Males are particularly susceptible to this syndrome (sex ratio male/female in autism = 400:100) as they are, for the same reason, to developmental dyslexia (same male excess as in autism), developmental aphasia (sex ratio male/female = 500:100), or even mesial temporal sclerosis of the left hemisphere following febrile convulsive hypoxia (Taylor and Ounsted, 1971).

The implications of Taylor's analysis of the probability of occurrence of left and right mesial temporal sclerotic lesions in boys and girls after convulsive hypoxia – an apparently generalized cerebral insult – are far-reaching. He showed that the left hemisphere of the male was more often affected than that of females, in whom the probability of a right or left brain lesion was about equal, because in the male the left hemisphere was at risk for a longer period (first 4 years of life) than in the female (first 2 years of life). The early-onset, poor-prognosis schizophrenias as well as the autistic syndrome, for both of which males are especially at risk, become immediately understandable in this maturational perspective. Of particular importance was the finding of DeMyer et al. (1974) that in autism the ability to establish normal rapport was correlated with verbal IQ and hence related to the integrity of the dominant hemisphere. Bingley (1958) had found that blunting of affect was associated with temporal lobe gliomas of the dominant hemisphere but unrelated to the presence or absence of aphasia. Thus the ability to establish normal emotional rapport and appropriate mood responses (as distinct from dysphoric mood states) seems to relate to dominant hemispheric mechanisms. A link is thereby suggested between the blunted and incongruous affectivity of schizophrenia, the total absence of emotional rapport of autism, and the peculiar affective coldness of schizoid and aggressive psychopathy, all overwhelmingly male character deviations.

The study of vestibular functions in man after

hemispherectomy and in patients with lateralized cerebral tumors had demonstrated that the caloric nystagmus reactions with tumors not involving the temporal lobes are normal. With tumors of the temporal lobe there is a central facilitation of induced labyrinthine nystagmus, with a directional preponderance toward the side of the lesion. The determination of directional preponderance hinges on the fact that in normals the duration of the nystagmic reaction to cold (water at 30°C) is longer − by 5 to 15 seconds − than is the reaction to hot (water at 44°C). With directional preponderance to the right, the left ear has a longer nystagmic response to cold, and the right ear a more prolonged reaction to hot stimulation; the converse relationship occurs in directional preponderance to the left, with the left ear having a shorter reaction to cold and a longer reaction to hot stimulation. Thus directional preponderance depends on the 'independent but complementary clues each provided by the reactions of one ear' (Fitzgerald and Hallpike, 1942). It was therefore of particular interest that Fitzgerald and Stengel (1945) in investigations of caloric stimulation of the vestibular system of 50 chronic schizophrenics in Edinburgh should find absolutely normal responses in ten, a generally normal pattern in 27, diminished or absent responses in six patients, and directional preponderance in 18. In 16 of these 18, the directional preponderance of the slow component of the nystagmic response was to the left. In the intact central nervous system there are tonic impulses from the labyrinth through the ipsilateral vestibular nuclei, which then cross over to the contralateral oculomotor nuclei, on the one hand, and tonic impulses originating in the temporal lobe, modulating the contralateral vestibular nuclei, on the other. These maintain the normal symmetry of the nystagmic reaction to caloric labyrinthine stimulation. It is clear that in such a system the reduction or absence of the tonic impulses of temporal lobe origin will shift the equilibrium of the system toward a directional preponderance on the same side.

Levy et al. (1978), studying the vestibular responses in 25 chronic schizophrenics and 29 acute schizophrenics compared to other psychotic groups and controls, did not replicate the earlier findings in schizophrenia as only one significant difference was found: the schizophrenics had more dysrhythmic responses. Their data indicate that, in schizophrenics (although not in non-schizophrenics) neuroleptics are partly responsible for dysrhythmic responses. The authors consider that technical differences in testing method may be responsible for their divergent findings. It is probable that the patient-populations are not the same, since in the study of Levy et al. (1978) the diagnostic criteria seem to have been based on DSM-II and on elements such as "autistic logic, contamination on the Rorschach test, peculiar verbalizations, preoccupation with deterioration and fragmentation." Thus Levy's schizophrenics in 1978 Chicago are not likely to be as homogeneous as those of Fitzgerald and Stengel in 1945 Edinburgh, who were essentially suffering from dementia praecox and who, of course, in 1945, had never received neuroleptic medication.

Eye tracking functions also depend on the integrity of the vestibular system and its central projections. They consist of two different but interlocked components: smooth pursuit eye movements and saccadic eye movements that are determined by independent but overlapping neural pathways. The saccadic system centers a moving object on the fovea. A response to target displacement, it is under voluntary control. The smooth pursuit system adjusts the eyeball velocity to the target velocity, making a stable retinal image possible. It is not under voluntary control. Holzman and collaborators (1974) showed that schizophrenics, and a high proportion of their healthy first-degree relatives, had abnormal smooth pursuit tracking, both qualitatively and quantitatively. The estimation of the qualitative aspect depends on the fact that within critical frequencies of target oscillations (i.e. a pendulum), the corresponding eye movements are regular and sinusoidal. A quantitative estimation is made by calculating the number of times the eyes stopped following the target during tracking, the 'velocity arrest.' Holzman established a significant and high correlation between the qualitative and quantitative scores. It was found that 86% of chronic schizophrenics, 52% of acute schizophrenics, 22% of manic-depressives and 8.3% of normal controls had deviant eye tracking. Forty-four percent of the healthy first-degree relatives of schizophrenics had abnormal patterns. Holzman and Levy (1977) observed that as early as 1908 Diefendorf and Dodge, photographing the corneal light reflection to measure eye pursuit of a pendulum, had already found deviant tracking to be characteristic of schizophrenia, but not of manic-depressive illness, epilepsy or intellectual retardation. In this review Holzman and Levy report their investigation of eye tracking in a series of twins discordant for schizophrenia: with strict criteria 75% of the monozygotic and 97% of the dizygotic twins were discordant for schizophrenia. Regardless of the presence or absence of schizophrenia there was a significant congruence for good or bad eye tracking in monozygotic but not in dizygotic twins. Of the schizophrenic sample 68% had deviant eye tracking, an incidence similar to that found in singleton schizophrenics. The authors conclude that smooth pursuit eye movement disorder is not a reflection of psychosis nor a predictor of later psychosis but is associated with a predisposition to psychosis, a neurophysiological disturbance of 'cognitive centering' which under certain circumstances increases the statistical occurrence of schizophrenia.

A related finding by Iacono and Lykken (1979) shows that in normal monozygotic twins, high scorers on psychoticism scales had more abnormal eye tracking performance than low scorers. Iacono et al. (1981) next considered remitted schizophrenics during smooth pursuit (a luminous spot driven by a waveform generator) and during saccadic eye tracking (a spot driven by a rectangular wave generator which switched abruptly from side to side at unpredictable intervals). A psychomotor tracking task was also included, the subjects controlling the position of the dot within a moving circle with their preferred hand. An important dissociation was found: the schizophrenics were impaired on the smooth pursuit psychomotor tracking tasks but were identical to normal controls for the saccadic eye tracking tasks. Thus motivational factors, attentional deficits, or a disturbance in the subcortical neural systems common to slow and saccadic tracking cannot be responsible for the slow tracking deficit. The cortical centre controlling smooth pursuit, and not the distinct centre that mediates saccadic eye movements, must be implicated.

A confirmation is provided by Latham et al. (1981) in the study of optokinetic nystagmus in schizophrenia. The basic finding is that partial-field optokinetic nystagmus (OKN) is impaired but not full-field optokinetic responses in schizophrenia. Full-field OKN stabilizes the visual field on the retina when the subject is in motion; it depends on full-field stimulation, is inhibited by stationary contours in the visual field, and is accompanied by a subjective feeling of rotation. On sudden interruption of visual stimulation an optokinetic after-nystagmus persists for about 10 seconds. Partial-field OKN stabilizes moving objects and not the whole visual field, is not associated with subjective rotation, is not followed by after-nystagmus, and is abolished, or impaired, after cortical lesions ipsilaterally – in contrast to full-field OKN, which is unaffected by cortical lesions or even by decortication. It has been considered that partial-field OKN corresponds to smooth pursuit eye movement tracking with refixation saccades. The neural system which subtends the full-field response is essentially a subcortical retinal-optic tract, lateral geniculate, cerebellar, vestibular circuit integrated in the paramedian pontine reticular region. The partial-field optokinetic reflex depends on a much more complex cortical-subcortical network involving cortical projections from the fronto-parietal cortex to the pontine reticular formation, there fusing with the full-field system through efferent relays to the oculomotor nuclei. Thus, this second dissociation in schizophrenia between the impaired partial-field and the normal full-field optokinetic systems again suggests the presence of cortical dysfunction in the syndrome with intact brain-stem reticular functions. Lateral eye movements denote the shifts in gaze to the right or to the left which take place when subjects engage in reflective thinking. It is generally found, in dextrals, that verbal cognitive processes lead to an excess of lateral saccades to the right, and spatial processing to an excess of saccades to the left. Ehrlichman and Weinberger (1978) conclude in a critical review of the methodology and assumptions of lateral eye movement research: "Enough positive results have certainly been provided to conclude that there is some correlation between types of questions and eye movements." Inferentially the direction of lateral saccades is postulated to be an index of relative hemispheric activation, since other parameters, i.e. lateralized alpha power desynchrony, response accuracy, or reaction time measurements during tachistoscopic presentation of verbal and/or spatial stimuli, imply a corresponding lateralized hemispheric activation. However, as Ehrlichman and Weinberger emphasized there was, at the time of their review, no direct empirical evidence formally proving the 'hemisphericity' assumption of lateral eye movement deviations. Shevrin et al. (1980) provided this first empirical demonstration; they found a significant lateralized asymmetry in the amplitude of positive visual evoked response at P 90, which was larger on the right side in left-looking, and larger on the left side in right-looking subjects. This shows that a certain asymmetry of brain response is correlated with preferred direction of lateral gaze.

Tomer et al. (1981) studied smooth pursuit eye movement patterns in 20 schizophrenic patients, incorporating in design their interaction with verbal and spatial cognitive activation, compared with two control groups: normals with a preponderance of right lateral eye movements and normals with a preponderance of left lateral eye movements (LEM).

Tomer and her collaborators in Tel Aviv found that the schizophrenics had impaired smooth pur-

suit tracking, but were similar to the right-mover (LEM) normals. Only the left-mover normals were significantly superior. Cognitive activation similarly led to a considerable deterioration in eye tracking in both schizophrenics and right-movers, but not in left movers. Furthermore, schizophrenics and right movers had significantly more saccadic interruptions and velocity arrests when following a light from extreme right to extreme left (i.e., when activating their left hemisphere), than when the light moved in the opposite direction. Taken together with the reports that have shown a statistical preponderance of lateral eye movements to the right in schizophrenia, independent of cognitive activation (Gur, 1978; Schweitzer et al., 1978; Schweitzer, 1979), these various observations support a hypothesis of abnormal left hemisphere activation, or hyperreactivity, in schizophrenia.

Matsue and Okuma (1984) investigated the time relationship between horizontal smooth pursuit eye movement (SPEM) and tracking target in the leftward or rightward directions in 21 normal and 32 schizophrenic patients. Normals showed a relative advance of SPEM in relation to the target greater in leftward (contralateral to the right visuospatial hemisphere) than in rightward pursuit. In the schizophrenics the relative advance was greatest with rightward pursuit. Thus left hemisphere dysfunctional overactivation is suggested by both lateral saccadic and smooth pursuit eye movement characteristics in schizophrenia. Matsue et al. (1985), in a second study of 12 schizophrenics and 14 normal subjects, measured SPEM during eye fixation and eye tracking with mental tasks of a verbal nature taking place at the same time. There was a marked increase in tracking saccades and a significant advance of SPEM to the target in rightward pursuit. The findings here suggest that the left hemisphere of schizophrenics is more easily activated during verbal tasks than in normals. In a third study Ueno et al. (1986) found that manic or depressed patients with delusions or hallucinations also had a relative advance of SPEM to the target in rightward pursuit, while manics or depressed patients in remission were similar to normals. This would suggest that, irrespective of diagnosis, delusional-hallucinatory states implicate left hemispheric systems. This is consistent with the now extensive body of evidence which indicates that auditory hallucinations are the result of altered left temporal structures (see Flor-Henry, 1987a, for review).

Power spectral EEG investigations and auditory evoked potential studies in general reveal left hemispheric abnormalities in schizophrenia (see Flor-Henry, 1987a,b, for review). Similarly neuropsychological approaches demonstrate the presence of bilateral fronto-temporal dysfunction, left > right, in strictly defined schizophrenia (i.e. Taylor et al., 1979; Flor-Henry and Yeudall, 1979; Flor-Henry, 1983a). Overall neurometabolic (PET) studies indicate that acute schizophrenias show a hypermetabolic pattern in the fronto-temporal regions, left > right, while chronic deficit symptomatology schizophrenias are asymmetrically hypometabolic, an effect most pronounced in the left frontal region (see Flor-Henry, 1987b, for review). More esoteric research approaches continue to demonstrate the ubiquitous left hemisphere abnormality in schizophrenia. For example Crayton et al. (1977) showed that alpha-motor neurone excitability was abnormal in psychotic patients, with reduction of the peak of secondary facilitation in chronic schizophrenics, while the following trough in the recovery cycle was reduced in acute schizophrenia. The Hoffman reflex is the electrically evoked spinal monosynaptic reflex elicited by a stimulating electrode in the popliteal fossa by square wave pulses of 1 ms duration, the muscle potentials being recorded from the soleus muscle. Excitability cycles were established by finding the stimulus intensity for the maximum H-response then by giving pairs of identical stimuli at varying delays from 50 ms to 5 s between stimuli and plotting the height of the second stimulus divided by the first, expressed as a percentage against the inter-stimulus delays, thus generating a recovery curve. In the study of 36 schizophrenic and schizo-affective patients Goode et al. (1981)

observed that the recovery curve height of the right leg was associated with negative, deficit symptomatology, while relative elevation of the left leg was significantly correlated with depressive symptoms. Recovery curve height was positively correlated with the number of RDC symptoms for schizophrenia and is elevated in Parkinson's disease and substantially reduced in humans by intravenous amphetamines. Generally it is elevated in chronic and reduced in acute schizophrenia. Consequently the lateral asymmetries in alpha motor neurone excitability, which are the opposite directionality for schizophrenic and depressive symptom clusters, reflect either lateral changes in cortico-spinal descending neural inhibitory modulation, or bilaterally asymmetrical cortical/subcortical amine activity, biased towards the left for schizophrenic and towards the right for depressive symptoms. Bracha (1987) studied asymmetric rotational behaviour (circling) in ten schizophrenic patients who had either never been medicated or who had been off neuroleptics for at least 6 months. This was done with a rotometer, a device on a belt with a position sensor monitoring changes in orientation in the dorsal–ventral axis, the subjects being monitored for 8 hours. Eighty-five normal controls showed equal left and right turning. All ten schizophrenics showed left-sided turning behaviour; i.e. exhibited right-sided neglect. As Bracha states: "circling behaviour is . . . dopaminergically mediated and related to asymmetry in dopaminergic activity between the left and right basal ganglia or left and right frontal cortex" with rotation towards the side with lower dopamine activity. Reynolds (1983) reported in several neurochemical investigations of schizophrenic brains, compared to controls, the presence of a significant increase of dopamine concentrations in the left amygdaloid of the schizophrenics, a striking lateralization that he confirmed in two subsequent post-mortem series. Presumably these would be hyperdopaminergic, acute, positive symptomatology schizophrenias that should preferentially turn to the right. Neurological examination in schizophrenia, when soft neurological signs, both motor and sensory, are considered, again implicates the left hemisphere (Manschreck and Ames, 1984).

Psychopathy and hysteria

Serafetinides (1965) showed that aggressive psychopathy in epilepsy was related to early-onset epilepsy of the dominant hemisphere in males. The relationship of aggressive, paranoid, psychopathic personality to temporal lobe epilepsy of the left or dominant hemisphere has been confirmed by Taylor (1969), Sherwin (1977) and Lindsay et al. (1979). In the prospective Oxford series of Lindsay et al. (1979), following from birth 100 subjects with pure limbic epilepsy, 12 of the 87 patients surviving at the age of 15 years had exhibited severe antisocial/aggressive behaviour: in all 12 the focus was contralateral to the preferred hand! A very significant lateralization. Ten of the 12 were males. Catastrophic rage reactions were significantly associated with onset of epilepsy before the age of 1 year and with a significant decrement of verbal IQ for both sexes, again demonstrating disorganization of dominant hemisphere systems. Investigations of large samples of aggressive psychopaths (homicide, rape, physical assault) by Yeudall (1977) and Yeudall and Fromm-Auch (1979) with an extensive neuropsychological battery consisting of 32 tests revealed that in this group, which satisfied Cleckley's criteria for primary psychopathy, the neuropsychological profile was abnormal in 90% of the cases. In 72% the pattern of cerebral dysfunction was bilateral frontal, left > right and left temporal. A reduced verbal compared to performance IQ was found, with a particular vulnerability of the Comprehension subtest on the Wechsler Scales (WAIS) (Yeudall et al., 1981). Wardell and Yeudall (1980) found that psychopaths with the largest verbal/performance discrepancy in a large sample were characterized by psychopathy and schizophrenia elevations in the MMPI and by an excess of sinistrality in 14%. Fedora and Fedora (1983), using a very extensive neuropsychological battery, compared psycho-

pathic criminals, non-psychopathic criminals and carefully matched controls. The psychopathic and non-psychopathic criminals differed from the controls only on neuropsychological variables considered left hemisphere and frontal impulsivity markers. Thus psychopathy arises because of disruptions of left temporal neural systems brought about by epilepsy early in life, or through genetic-constitutional factors impinging on these critical cerebral regions in the male. It is worth noting that the psychopaths with the largest verbal decrement compared to performance IQ and with excess sinistrality, both indices of left hemisphere dysfunction, show elevations of both the psychopathic deviate and schizophrenia scales of the Minnesota Multiphasic Personality Inventory (MMPI). A commonality between psychopathy, certain forms of schizophrenia and dominant dysfunction is thereby implied. The underlying affinity between the two syndromes is also suggested by a number of the clinical characteristics common to the two syndromes: the asocial aggressive premorbid personality of early-onset, poor-prognosis schizophrenias in males; the pseudo-psychopathic schizophrenias described in earlier classifications; the 'schizophrenia spectrum' disorders found principally in the male first-degree relatives of schizophrenics; the personality characteristics in monozygotic twins discordant for schizophrenia where the non-schizophrenic twin, if male, is psychopathic, if female, neurotic (Cadoret, 1973). Again both syndromes sometimes share a startling and shocking absence of human empathy.

Wechsler (1958) had noted that adolescent male psychopaths have a relative deficit of verbal compared to performance IQ. Nachshon (1983) reviewed the numerous studies confirming this effect in delinquents, sociopaths, acting-out juveniles, criminal offenders and female delinquents (one study, Bernstein and Corsini, 1953). Prentice and Kelly (1963), considering 24 studies, concluded that delinquents were similar to normals for performance IQ but were significantly lower for verbal IQ. Yeudall et al. (1981) found a significant reduction of verbal/performance IQ of 9 IQ points in psychopaths, of 7 points in rapists and of 6 points in assaultive criminals. Homicidal prisoners, however, did not exhibit the verbal < performance pattern. For purposes of comparison, the verbal IQ of 128 patients with unilateral left hemisphere lesions was 87 and the performance IQ 91, while in 204 patients with unilateral right hemisphere lesions the average verbal IQ was 97 and performance IQ 85 (Woods, 1980). Yeudall et al. (1987) observed a significant increase in left parietal alpha power in the eyes-closed condition in ten murderers and four individuals with a history of repetitive physical violence − a finding which might perhaps suggest a defect of left hemisphere inhibitory regulation. Seventy-five percent of 15 outpatient violent aggressive subjects showed left-sided asymmetry of brain-stem auditory evoked responses. Hare and Frazelle (1981) found that in the tachistoscopic presentation of stimuli requiring complex semantic processing, psychopaths, unlike normals, failed to show a right visual field superiority: this would be predicted on a left hemisphere dysfunction hypothesis (cited by Nachshon, 1983). Hare and McPherson (1984), in a verbal dichotic listening task under divided attention, or directed attention, showed that psychopaths had a smaller right ear advantage than non-psychopaths, a result which once again is consistent with left hemisphere deficit in psychopathy. The third lateralizing observation published by Hare relates to the slower electrodermal recovery time for the left hand to tone signals of high intensity found in psychopaths. Nachshon (1987) studied 127 criminals with two dichotic tasks: verbal stimuli (digits) and analytically processed non-verbal stimuli (tonal). The prisoners consisted of three groups: murderers, violent offenders and non-violent criminals. There were no significant differences between the groups on the digit test; however, for the tone test (identification in one ear of one of four tones as identical to target tone, previously delivered to one of the ears) the murderers and non-violent offenders showed a right ear advantage − similar to normals − while the violent offenders had a left

ear advantage. In addition the violent offenders had a significant decrease in right ear scores compared to the other offenders with no decrease in the left ear scores. These results indicate clearly the presence of unilateral deficit in the left hemisphere of violent offenders. Nachshon explains the paradox of the murderers being similar to the non-violent criminals by the fact that, in this study, they were usually non-violent individuals guilty of a single criminal act, in contrast to the violent offenders, most of whom were recidivists. Gabrielli and Mednick (1980) related lateral preference (measured in 1972) to subsequent criminal behaviour (1978). Sixty-five percent of the sinistrals were arrested once, but only 30% of the dextrals; 33% of criminals with multiple arrests were sinistral, of those with a single crime 11% and in non-offenders 7%. Nachshon and Denno (1987) investigated the correlation of lateral preference and criminality, starting with a cohort of 2958 black children studied in Philadelphia in a perinatal project between 1959 and 1962. Selecting only males, with complete laterality data taken at age 7 and who were resident in Philadelphia up to the age of 18, a final sample of 1066 black males was obtained. Police records showed that 313 (or 29%) had been criminally charged and 10% were violent. Unexpectedly, left-handedness was significantly more frequent in non-offenders than in offenders; there were no differences in foot or eye preference. Violent and non-violent offenders were similar for hand and foot preference but there was a significant difference for eye preference: 60% of the non-offenders and 64% of the non-violent offenders showed right eye preference whereas only 40% of the very violent offenders ($n = 57$, murder, rape, aggravated assault) were right eye preferent ($p < 0.008$). Sixty-three percent of the very violent and 60% of the violent offenders had cross-preferences as opposed to 47% in all other groups. Citing evidence indicating that in males birth stress is associated with left eye (but not left hand) preference, and that visual evoked potentials are of higher amplitude from the dominant than the non-dominant eye, and thus that there may be a hemisphere-eye association, Nachshon and Denno conclude that their results suggest the presence of left hemisphere dysfunction in violent criminals, possibly the result of birth trauma. In the female, hysteria and anti-social criminality are associated. Familial investigations have shown that psychopathy in the male and hysteria in the female are linked through familial transmission: hence psychopathy and hysteria would appear to be fundamentally the same syndrome, modified in its expression by the male or female pattern of cerebral organization. The investigations of Cloninger and Guze (1975) show that this was true for the clinical syndrome. Spalt (1980) showed that the same associations are found in a non-patient university sample and Kriechman (1987) showed that these gender-related associations were also found in families in which two sibs shared a somatoform disorder. In psychopaths the cerebral dysfunction is left > right; in hysteria right > left. However, in a neuropsychological analysis of hysteria, schizophrenia, normals and psychotic depressives three clusters emerge: normals, depression, and hysteria and schizophrenia falling together in a single cluster (Flor-Henry et al., 1981). This suggests that in hysteria, although the severity of dysfunction is greater on the right, the fundamental locus is in the dominant hemisphere and responsible for the essential features of hysteria: the imprecise verbalizations, the affective incongruity ('la belle indifférence') and the chronic pain and conversion symptomatology as a result of defective analysis of endogenous somatic signals and of impaired somatosensory integration. Through disruption of left brain inhibitory regulation of specific right brain modalities (affective lability and depression, the left-sided preponderance of unilateral conversion symptomatology (true only in women)), the sexual dysfunctions emerge: the more flamboyant (but secondary) facade of feminine hysteria.

Obsessive-compulsive syndrome

Following extensive intracerebral electrical stim-

ulation studies, and considering the effects of small multiple thermocoagulations in the orbital – frontal, anterior – temporal and cingulate regions (anterior), Grey-Walter (1966) concluded that altered activity in the fronto – temporal system was related to affective disturbances, while disruption of the cingulate system led to "compulsive-obsessional and ritualistic behaviour." Talairach et al. (1973) observed that electrical stimulation of the anterior cingulate gyrus evoked in the conscious subject continuous movements, contralateral to the stimulated gyrus "that were involuntary, sometimes the subject was able to resist performing them, at other times not. The subject either experienced the behaviour as something wholly foreign to himself or else attempted to explain it away as a reaction to something felt." Stereotactic lesions in the orbital frontal regions are effective for the relief of treatment-refractory chronic depressive states, while lesions in the anterior cingulate are almost specific in the relief-intractable obsessional illnesses (Lewin, 1973). Given the importance of the crossed cingulate – orbital mesial frontal pathways (Yakovlev and Locke, 1961) these various observations strongly suggest that dysregulation of critical frontal systems underlies obsessive-compulsive disorders. Because in the neuropsychological and quantitative EEG study of a small group of 11 unmedicated obsessionals, 27% of whom were sinistral, we found evidence of bilateral frontal, left > right and left temporal EEG hypovariability, we proposed (Flor-Henry et al., 1979) that the syndrome was a reflection of dominant frontal dysfunction, with loss of normal inhibitory processes in that zone, which accounted for the fundamental aspect of obsessions: the inability to inhibit verbal-ideational mental representations and their motor consequences. A subsequent neuropsychological study of 15 obsessionals showed that when compared to normals, neurotic depression and hysteria, although the pattern of deficit was remarkably similar in obsessions and neurotic depressions, the obsessive-compulsive group had maximal deficits on the following tests: Halstead Category, Wisconsin Card Sorting, written word fluency and oral word fluency. This is clearly a pattern indicative of bilateral frontal dysfunction, left > right (Flor-Henry, 1983a). Shagass et al. (1984), in their somatosensory EP investigations of obsessive compulsive disorders, compared to other neurotics, non-patients, schizoprenics and major depressives, found a unique pattern which distinguished the obsessionals from all the other groups: right somatosensory contralateral scores higher than left for SEP 90 and anterior peak for N130 higher than posterior. This pattern of increased EP amplitude in the left anterior quadrant, as Shagass points out, is that which would be predicted by a local defect of neural inhibition in that zone. Ciesielski et al. (1981) report the presence of a significantly shorter latency of the response of the N220 component of the visual evoked response with increasing complexity of cognitive task in obsessionals. As Ciesielski notes, this reduced latency is in keeping with the reports of a significant decrease in serotonin (an inhibitory neurotransmitter) in obsessionals first reported by Yaryura-Tobias et al. (1977). That serotonin mediation is central in the syndrome is shown by the fact, that while the serotonin potentiator clomipramine (a powerful inhibitor of serotonin uptake) is effective in 50% of cases, nortryptyline (a relatively pure noradrenaline uptake blocker) is no better than placebo (Thorén et al., 1980), and by the fact that the efficacy of clomipramine is quite independent of its antidepressant action (Flament et al., 1985). In the first PET study of obsessions, Baxter et al. (1987) examined 14 obsessional patients compared to normals and unipolar depressives. The obsessives had significantly increased neuro-metabolic activity in the left orbital frontal gyrus and bilaterally in the caudate nuclei, when compared to either the normals or the depressives. The levels of anxiety, tension and depression were similar in the obsessives and in the depressed patients. Solyom (1985, personal communications) described a single case, that of a 19-year-old man who had suffered from crippling obsessive-compulsive symptoms from the age of 10 and who attempted to kill himself, the bullet penetrating the base of the left frontal lobe. Three weeks after the cerebral injury there was a striking improvement in the obsessional symptomatology, which persisted in a 2-year follow up. Before the injury the WAIS-R scores were verbal = 115, performance = 117 and full scale = 116. Two years later they had risen to verbal = 121, performance = 140 with a full scale of 133, the left hemispheric insult leading to a global increase in intellectual efficiency. There are a number of features to the obsessional syndrome which are remarkably similar to those seen in schizophrenia. Birth trauma or perinatal injuries are associated with later schizophrenic breakdown; Capstick and Seldrup (1977) found a history of abnormal birth events in one-third of unselected obsessionals. In schizophrenia there is a statistically significant excess of first- or last-born in males. Snowdon (1979), analysing birth order in obsessional neurosis (*n* = 156, of whom 70 were males matched against 500 male and 500 female controls matched for sex, year of birth and social class) found a significant excess of first-born males in the obsessionals. In schizophrenia the earlier the age of onset, the greater the male incidence and the more likely is a chronic evolution. Rasmussen and Tsuang (1986), although they have more women (two-third) than men in their clinical-demographic survey of 44 obsessionals, reported that a deteriorating course was more likely in men with early onset of illness. Men had a significantly earlier age of onset (15.5 years) than women (23 years) − again strikingly similar to the age of onset and sex characteristics of schizophrenia − both shifted of course to an earlier onset in the obsessions. Hollingsworth et al. (1980), reviewing 8367 child and adolescent in- and out-patients in Los Angeles between the years 1959 and 1975, found 17 cases meeting strict criteria for the obsessional syndrome: 13 were male and only four were female. In a study of childhood obsessive-compulsive disorders Rapoport et al. (1981) have an initial series of 11 patients, average age of 14, nine of whom are boys. Expanding the series to 17 adolescents there are 14 boys and three girls (Behar et al., 1984).

Sinistrality is associated with schizophrenia, and, in some investigations, such as the very large scale survey of Dvirsky (1983) in the USSR, significantly more in males than in female schizophrenics. In a personal series of 29 obsessionals (unpublished) we find 70% non-dextrality in those whose neuro-psychological state is normal, or dysfunctional, left > right, who are predominantly male, but on-ly 40% non-dextrality in patients with dysfunc-tional right > left, who are predominantly female. In the general population non-dextrality as defined by Annett (1970) is of the order of 35%. There was a history of birth-trauma or twin births in 20%. Behar et al. (1984) had found that their adolescent obsessionals, although of good in-telligence, were impaired on the Money Road Map Test and on Stylus Maze Learning, while they per-formed normally on the Rey-Osterrieth Complex Figure test. Frontal dysfunction with sparing of right hemispheric functions is implied. All three tests have visuo-spatial components, but the Rey-Osterrieth is especially sensitive for pure visuo-spatial processing. Since the obsessive subjects are normal on this test but abnormal on the Road Map Test and on the Maze test, this suggests that it is an impairment of strategy, but not of visual perception, which accounts for the defective per-formance, hence principally because of left frontal deficit. (This is not the authors' interpretation!) Insel et al. (1983) administered the Halstead – Reitan Battery to 18 adult obsessionals and report that as a group they are essentially in the normal range, but have a significant decrement of performance as compared to verbal IQ and that they were significantly impaired on Tactual Per-formance, non-preferred hand, both hands, time and location. Here the dysfunction is thus bilateral frontal, right > left, and right temporo-parietal. In our own as yet unpublished series of 29 adult obsessive-compulsive patients, the severity dimen-sion of the illness was significantly correlated with poor performance on the (sex-corrected) scores on Dynamometric Hand Strength, Finger Tapping bilaterally and on the Tactual Performance Test, all indicators of frontal lobe functions. Thus, the neuropsychological evidence to date indicates bilateral frontal lobe dysfunction in obsessions, while the EEG, evoked potential and positron emission tomography data reveal left frontal ab-normalities consistent with defective serotonin-mediated neural inhibition in that zone and conse-quent abnormal local activation.

Conclusion

Evidence derived from neuropathology, from the localization of lesions in symptomatic schizo-phrenias, from the nature of the central dysfunc-tion responsible for the anomalies of vestibular, smooth-pursuit and lateral saccadic eye move-ments, partial field optokinetic nystagmus, from EEG, evoked potential, positron emission tomo-graphy, from the asymmetric recovery curves of alpha-motor neuron spinal excitability recovery curves, circling behaviours and neurochemical asymmetries all indicate, in a surprising con-vergence, that a dysfunctional dominant hemi-sphere is the basis of the schizophrenic syndrome.

The interaction between early age of onset, the male sex and perturbed left hemisphere organiza-tion is common to autism, the poor-prognosis chronic schizophrenias, psychopathy and the ob-sessional syndrome. Pathology of affect, its absence in autism, its incongruous or blunted character in schizophrenia and the total absence of human empathy in psychopathy, a form of affec-tive 'agnosia', can all be related, empirically, to abnormal left hemispheric organization. Again, a similar implication follows from the increased sinistrality seen in autism, psychopathy, poor-prognosis schizophrenias and early-onset obses-sive-compulsive states, all male syndromes. Psy-chopathy and hysteria can be viewed as equivalent syndromes, the expression of which is modified by gender: in the male strong, in the female weak right hemispheric systems.

The fundamental nature of the psychopatholo-gical syndromes of the dominant hemisphere can be formulated in the following manner:
1. in schizophrenia, alteration of the cerebral

systems responsible for the verbal-linguistic infrastructure of thought;

2. in autism, developmentally based absence of language, and its implications;

3. in psychopathy, disruption of the left hemispheric systems regulating behaviour, social awareness, empathy and anticipatory planning;

4. in hysteria, subtle abnormality in verbal efficiency associated with correspondingly discordant affect, with a defect in somatosensory integration and impaired cerebral processing of endogenous somatic signals, seen as deriving from perturbed left hemispheric functions;

5. in obsessive-compulsive states, a defective inhibition of unwanted, or random, verbal-linguistic and/or affective intrusions on account of impaired dominant frontal neural inhibitory regulation.

References

Abrams R, Taylor MA: *Psychopathology and the electro-encephalogram. Biol. Psychiatry: 15*, 871–878, 1980.

Annett M: A classification of hand preferences by association analysis. *Br. J. Psychol.: 61*, 303–321, 1970.

Bartak L, Rutter M, Cox A: A comparative study of infantile autism and specific developmental receptive language disorder: I. Children. *Br. J. Psychiatry: 126*, 127–145, 1975.

Baxter LR, Phelps ME, Mazziotta JC, Guze BH, Schwartz JM, Selin CE: Local cerebral glucose metabolic rates in obsessive-compulsive disorder. *Arch. Gen. Psychiatry: 44*, 211–218, 1987.

Behar D, Rapoport JL, Berg CJ, Denckla MB, Mann L, Cox C, Fedio P, Zahn T, Wolfman MG: Computerized tomography and neuropsychological test measures in adolescents with obsessive-compulsive disorder. *Am. J. Psychiatry: 141*, 363–368, 1984.

Berg R, Golden C, Graber B et al: *Localized Brain Deficits in Schizophrenia as Measured by CT Scan Density.* Presented at the Ninth Annual International Neuropsychological Society Meeting, Atlanta, GA, 1981.

Bernstein R, Corsini RJ: Wechsler–Bellevue patterns of female delinquents. *J. Clin. Psychol.: 9*, 176–179, 1953.

Bingley T: Mental symptoms in temporal lobe epilepsy and temporal lobe gliomas. *Acta Psychiatr. Neurol. Scand.: 33*, 136–151, 1958.

Bogerts B, Meertz E, Schonfeldt-Bausch R: Basal ganglia and limbic system pathology in schizophrenia. *Arch. Gen. Psychiatry: 42*, 784–791, 1985.

Bracha HS: Asymmetric rotational (circling) behaviour, a dopamine-related asymmetry: preliminary findings in un-medicated and never-medicated schizophrenic patients. *Biol. Psychiatry: 22*, 995–1003, 1987.

Brown R, Colter N, Corsellis JAN, Crow TJ, Frith CD, Jagoe R, Johnstone EC, Marsh L: Postmortem evidence of structural brain changes in schizophrenia. *Arch. Gen. Psychiatry: 43*, 36–42, 1986.

Cadoret RI: Toward a definition of the schizoid state. Evidence from studies of twins and their families. *Br. J. Psychiatry: 122*, 679–685, 1973.

Capstick N, Seldrup J: A study in the relationship between abnormalities occurring at the time of birth and the subsequent development of obsessional symptoms. *Acta Psychiatr. Scand.: 56*, 427–431, 1977.

Ciesielski KT, Beech HR, Gordon PK: Some electrophysiological observations in obsessional states. *Br. J. Psychiatry: 138*, 479–484, 1981.

Cloninger CR, Guze S: Hysteria and parental psychiatric illness. *Psychol. Med.: 5*, 27–31, 1975.

Coffman JA, Andreasen NC, Nasrallah HA: Left hemispheric density deficits in chronic schizophrenia. *Biol. Psychiatr: 19*, 1237–1247, 1984.

Crayton JW, Meltzer HY, Goode DJ: Motoneuron excitability in psychatric patients. *Biol. Psychiatry: 12*, 545–561, 1977.

Davison K, Bagley CR: Schizophrenia-like psychoses associated with organic disorders of the central nervous system: a review of the literature. In Herrington RN (Editor), *Current Problems in Neuropsychiatry.* Ashford, Kent, England: Royal Medico-Psychological Association, Headley Brothers, Ltd., pp. 113–184, 1969.

DeMyer MK, Barton S, Alpern GD, Kimberlin C, Allen J, Yang E, Steele R: The measured intelligence of autistic children. *J. Autism Child. Schizophrenia: 1*, 42–60, 1974.

Dvirsky AE: Clinical manifestations of schizophrenia in right-handed and left-handed patients. *J. Neuropathol. Psychiatry (Korsakov): 83*, 724–727 (in Russian), 1983.

Ehrlichman H, Weinberger A: Lateral eye movements and hemispheric asymmetry: a critical review. *Psychol. Bull.: 85*, 1080–1101, 1978.

Falconer MA, Taylor DC: Temporal lobe epilepsy: clinical features, pathology, diagnosis and treatment. In Price JH (Editor), *Modern Trends in Psychological Medicine.* London: Butterworths, 1970.

Fedora O, Fedora S: Some neuropsychological and psychophysiological aspects of psychopathic and non-psychopathic criminals. In Flor-Henry P, Gruzelier JH (Editors), *Laterality and Psychopathology.* Amsterdam: Elsevier, pp. 41–58, 1983.

Fitzgerald G, Hallpike CS: Studies in human vestibular function: 1: Observations on the directional preponderance ('nystagmusbereitschaft') of caloric nystagmus resulting from cerebral lesions. *Brain: 65*, 115–137, 1942.

Fitzgerald G, Stengel E: Vestibular reactivity to caloric stimulation in schizophrenics. *J. Ment. Sci.: 91*, 93–101, 1945.

Flament MF, Rapoport JL, Berg CJ, Sceery W, Kilts C, Mellström B, Linnoila M: Clomipramine treatment of childhood obsessive-compulsive disorder. A double-blind controlled study. *Arch. Gen. Psychiatry: 42*, 977–983, 1985.

Flor-Henry P: Psychosis and temporal lobe epilepsy. A controlled investigation. *Epilepsia: 10*, 363–395, 1969.

Flor-Henry P: Ictal and interictal psychiatric manifestations in epilepsy: specific or non-specific? *Epilepsia: 13*, 773 – 783, 1972a.

Flor-Henry P: Schizophrenia-like reactions and affective psychoses associated with temporal lobe epilepsy: etiological factors. *Am. J. Psychiatry: 126*, 400 – 404, 1972b.

Flor-Henry P: Epilepsy and psychopathology. In Granville-Grossman K (Editor), *Recent Advances in Clinical Psychiatry.* 2nd edn., Edinburgh: Churchill Livingstone, 1976.

Flor-Henry P: The Obsessive-compulsive syndrome. *Cerebral Basis of Psychopathology*, Ch. 11. Littleton: MA. PSG-Wright Inc., pp. 301 – 311, 1983a.

Flor-Henry P: Neuropsychological studies in patients with psychiatric disorders. In Heilman KM, Satz P (Editors), *Neuropsychology of Human Emotion.* New York: The Guilford Press, pp. 193 – 220, 1983b.

Flor-Henry P: Epilepsy and schizophrenia. In Burrows GD, Norman TR, Rubinstein G (Editors), *Handbook of Studies of Schizophrenia, Part 1.* Amsterdam: Elsevier, pp. 201 – 214, 1986.

Flor-Henry P: Schizophrenic hallucinations in the context of psychophysiological studies of schizophrenia. In Kunzendorf RG, Sheikh AA (Editors), *Psychophysiology of Mental Imagery: Theory, Research and Application.* Farmingdale: NY: Baywood, 1987a.

Flor-Henry P: Cerebral dynamics, laterality and psychopathology: a commentary. In Takahashi R, Flor-Henry P, Gruzelier J, Niwa S-I (Editors), *Cerebral Dynamics, Laterality and Psychopathology.* Amsterdam: Elsevier, 1987b.

Flor-Henry P, Yeudall LT: Neuropsychological investigation of schizophrenia and manic-depressive psychoses. In Gruzelier J, Flor-Henry P (Editors), *Hemispheric Asymmetries of Function in Psychopathology.* Amsterdam: Elsevier, pp. 341 – 362, 1979.

Flor-Henry P, Yeudall LT, Koles ZJ, Howarth BG: Neuropsychological and power spectral EEG investigations of the obsessive-compulsive syndrome. *Biol. Psychiatry: 14*, 119 – 130, 1979.

Flor-Henry P, Fromm-Auch D, Tapper M, Schopflocher D: A neuropsychological study of the stable syndrome of hysteria. *Biol. Psychiatry: 16*, 601 – 626, 1981.

Folstein S, Rutter M: Infantile autism: a genetic study of 21 twin pairs. *J. Child Psychol. Psychiatry: 18*, 297 – 391, 1977.

Gabrielli WF, Mednick SA: Sinistrality and delinquency. *J. Abnorm. Psychol.: 89*, 654 – 661, 1980.

Golden CJ, Graber B, Coffman J, Berg R, Block S, Brogan D: Brain density deficits in chronic schizophrenia. *Psychiatry Res. 3*, 179 – 184, 1980.

Golden CJ, Graber B, Coffman J, Berg RA, Newlin DB, Block S: Structural brain deficits in schizophrenia. Identification by computed tomographic scan density measurements. *Arch. Gen. Psychiatry: 38*, 1014 – 1017, 1981.

Golden CJ, Scott M, Strider MA, Chou-Chu C, Ruedrich S, Graber B: Neuropsychological deficit and regional cerebral blood flow in schizophrenic patients. *Hillside J. Clin. Psychiatry: 7*, 3 – 15, 1985.

Goode DJ, Manning AA, Middleton JF: Cortical laterality and asymmetry of the Hoffman reflex in psychiatric patients. *Biol. Psychiatry: 16*, 1137 – 1152, 1981.

Grey-Walter W: Appendix A. In Smythies JR (Editor), *The Neurological Foundation of Psychiatry.* Oxford: Blackwell, 1966.

Gur RE: Left hemisphere dysfunction and left hemisphere overactivation in schizophrenia. *J. Abnorm. Psychol.: 87*, 226 – 238, 1978.

Hare RD, Frazelle J: Psychobiological correlates of criminal psychopathy. Paper presented at a symposium of biosocial correlates of crime and delinquency, Annual meeting of the American Society of Criminology, Washington DC: November 1981.

Hare RD, McPherson LM: Psychopathy and perceptual asymmetry during verbal dichotic listening. *J. Abnorm. Psychol.: 23*, 141 – 149, 1984.

Hauser SL, DeLong GR, Rosman NP: Pneumographic findings in the infantile autism syndrome. A correlation with temporal lobe disease. *Brain: 98*, 667 – 688, 1975.

Hillbom E: After-effects of brain-injuries. Research on the symptoms causing invalidism of persons in Finland having sustained brain-injuries during the wars of 1939 – 1940 and 1941 – 1944. *Acta Psychiatr. Neurol. Scand.: 35*, 112 – 125, 1960.

Hillbom E, Kaila M: Psychoses after brain-trauma. *Nord. Psykiatr. Medlemsbl.: 3*, 102 – 117, 1949.

Hoffman WL, Prior MR: Neuropsychological dimensions of autism in children: a test of the hemispheric dysfunction hypothesis. *J. Clin. Neuropsychol.: 4*, 27 – 41, 1982.

Hollingsworth CE, Tanquay PE, Grossman L, Pabst P: Long-term outcome of obsessive-compulsive disorder in childhood. *J. Am. Acad. Child Psychiatry: 19*, 134 – 144, 1980.

Holzman PS, Levy DL: Smooth pursuit eye movements and functional psychoses: a review. *Schizophrenia Bull.: 3*, 15 – 27, 1977.

Holzman PS, Proctor LR, Levy DL, Yasillo NJ, Meltzer HY, Hurt SW: Eye-tracking dysfunction in schizophrenic patients and their relatives. *Arch. Gen. Psychiatry: 31*, 143 – 151, 1974.

Iacono WG, Lykken DT: Eye tracking and psychopathology. *Arch. Gen. Psychiatry: 36*, 1361 – 1396, 1979.

Iacono WG, Tuason VB, Johnson RA: Dissociation of smooth pursuit and saccadic eye tracking in remitted schizophrenics. *Arch. Gen. Psychiatry: 38*, 991 – 996, 1981.

Insel TR, Donnelly EF, Lalakea ML, Alterman IS, Murphy DL: Neurological and neuropsychological studies of patients with obsessive-compulsive disorder. *Biol. Psychiatry: 18*, 741 – 751, 1983.

Jakob H, Beckmann H: Prenatal developmental disturbances in the limbic allocortex in schizophrenics. *J. Neural Transm.: 65*, 303 – 326, 1986.

Kahlbaum KL: *Catatonia.* 1874. Levij Y, Pridan T (Translaters). Baltimore, MD: The Johns Hopkins University Press, 1973.

Kriechman AM: Siblings with somatoform disorders in childhood and adolescence. *J. Am. Acad. Child Adolesc. Psychiatry: 26*, 226 – 231, 1987.

Kurachi M, Suzuki M, Kawasaki Y, Kobayashi K, Shimizu A, Yamaguchi N: Regional cerebral blood flow in patients with schizophrenic disorder. In Takahashi R, Flor-Henry P, Gruzelier J, Niwa S-I (Editors), *Cerebral Dynamics, Laterality and Psychopathology.* Amsterdam: Elsevier, 1987.

Latham C, Holzman PS, Manschreck TC, Tole J: Optokinetic nystagmus and pursuit eye movements in schizophrenia.

Arch. Gen. Psychiatry: 38, 997 – 1003, 1981.

Levy DL, Holzman PS, Proctor LR: Vestibular responses in schizophrenia. *Arch. Gen. Psychiatry: 35*, 972 – 981, 1978.

Lewin W: Selective leukotomy: a review. In Laitinen LV, Livingston KE (Editors), *Surgical Approaches in Psychiatry.* England: Medical and Technical Publishing Co. Ltd., 1973.

Lindsay J, Ounsted C, Richards P: Long-term outcome in children with temporal lobe seizures. III. Psychiatric aspects in childhood and adult life. *Dev. Med. Child Neurol.: 21*, 630 – 636, 1979.

Lishman WA: Brain damage in relation to psychiatric disability after head injury. *Br. J. Psychiatry: 114*, 373 – 410, 1968.

Lobascher ME, Kingerlee PE, Gubbay SS: Childhood autism: an investigation of etiological factors in 25 cases. *Br. J. Psychiatry: 117*, 525 – 529, 1970.

Manschreck TC, Ames D: Neurologic features and psychopathology in schizophrenic disorders. *Biol. Psychiatry: 19*, 703 – 719, 1984.

Matsue Y, Okuma T: Relative advance of eye movement to the target in the rightward tracking in schizophrenics. *Tohoku J. Exp. Med.: 143*, 345 – 349, 1984.

Matsue Y, Saito H, Tomiyama T, Onizawa T, Aneha S, Ueno T, Matsuoka H, Okuma T: Disorder of smooth pursuit eye movements and left hemispheric overactivation in schizophrenia. *Folia Psychiatr. Neurol. Jpn.: 39*, 101, 1985.

Mnoukhine SS, Dinabourg EY: Epileptiform manifestations in early right sided and left sided lesions of the brain in children. *Zh. Nevropatol. Psikhiatr. SS Korsakova: 65*, 1073 – 1077, 1965.

Nachshon I: Hemisphere dysfunction in psychopathy and behaviour disorders. In Myslobodsky M (Editor), *Hemisyndromes: Psychobiology, Neurology, Psychiatry.* New York: Academic Press, Ch. 15, pp. 389 – 414, 1983.

Nachshon I: Hemisphere function in violent offenders. In Mednick SA, Moffitt TE (Editors), *Biological Bases of Antisocial Behaviour.* Boston: Nijhoff, 1987.

Nachshon I, Denno D: Violent behaviour and hemisphere function. In Mednick SA, Moffitt TE (Editors), *Biology and Antisocial Behaviour.* Cambridge: Cambridge University Press, 1987.

Ornitz EM: Vestibular dysfunction in schizophrenia and childhood autism. *Compr. Psychiatry: 11*, 159 – 173, 1970.

Prentice W, Kelly FJ: Intelligence and delinquency: a reconsideration. *J. Soc. Psychol.: 60*, 327 – 337, 1963.

Rapoport JL, Elkins R, Langer DH, Sceery W, Buchsbaum MS, Gillin JC, Murphy DL, Zahn TP, Lake R, Ludlow C, Mendelson W: Childhood obsessive-compulsive disorder. *Am. J. Psychiatry: 138*, 1545 – 1554, 1981.

Rasmussen SA, Tsuang MT: Clinical characteristics and family history in DSM-III obsessive-compulsive disorder. *Am. J. Psychiatry: 143*, 317 – 322, 1986.

Reveley MA, Reveley AM, Baldy R: Left cerebral hemisphere hypodensity in discordant schizophrenic twins. A controlled study. *Arch. Gen. Psychiatry: 44*, 625 – 632, 1987.

Reynolds GP: Increased concentrations and lateral asymmetry of amygdala dopamine in schizophrenia. *Nature: 305*, 527 – 529, 1983.

Rutter M, Bartak L: Causes of infantile autism: some considerations from recent research. *J. Aut. Child Schizophrenia: 1*, 20 – 32, 1971.

Rutter M, Greenfeld D, Lockyer L: A five to fifteen year follow-up study of infantile psychosis. II. Social and behavioural outcome. *Br. J. Psychiatry: 113*, 1183 – 1199, 1967.

Rutter M, Lockyer L: A five to fifteen year follow-up study of infantile psychosis. I. Description of sample. *Br. J. Psychiatry: 113*, 1169 – 1182, 1967.

Satz P, Soper HV, Orsini DL, Henry RR, Zvi JC: Handedness subtypes in autism. *Psychiatr. Ann.: 15*, 447 – 450, 1985.

Schweitzer L: Differences of cerebral lateralization among schizophrenics and depressed patients. *Biol. Psychiatry: 14*, 721 – 733, 1979.

Schweitzer L, Becker E, Welsh H: Abnormalities of cerebral lateralization in schizophrenic patients. *Arch. Gen. Psychiatry: 35*, 982 – 985, 1978.

Serafetinides EA: Aggressiveness in temporal lobe epileptics and its relation to cerebral dysfunction and environmental factors. *Epilepsia: 6*, 33 – 42, 1965.

Shagass C, Roemer RA, Straumanis JJ, Josiassen RC: Distinctive somatosensory evoked potential features in obsessive-compulsive disorder. *Biol. Psychiatry: 19*, 1507 – 1524, 1984.

Sherwin I: Clinical and EEG aspects of temporal lobe epilepsy with behaviour disorder. The role of cerebral dominance. *McLean Hosp. J. June*, 40 – 50, 1977.

Sherwin I, Peron-Magnan P, Bancaud J, Bonis A, Talairach J: Prevalence of psychosis in epilepsy as a function of the laterality of the epileptogenic lesion. *Arch. Neurol.: 39*, 621 – 625, 1982.

Shevrin H, Smokler I, Kooi KA: An empirical link between lateral eye movements and lateralized event-related brain potentials. *Biol. Psychiatry: 5*, 691 – 697, 1980.

Snowdon J: Family-size and birth-order in obsessional neurosis. *Acta Psychiatr. Scand.: 60*, 121 – 128, 1979.

Southard EE: On topographical distribution of cortex lesions and anomalies in dementia praecox, with some account of their functional significance. *Am. J. Insanity: 71*, 603 – 671, 1915.

Spalt L: Hysteria and antisocial personality. *J. Nerv. Ment. Dis.: 168*, 456 – 464, 1980.

Takahashi R, Inaba Y, Inanaga K, Kato N, Kunashiro H, Nishimura T, Okuma T, Otsuki S, Sakai T, Sato T, Shimazono Y: *CT Scanning and the Investigation of Schizophrenia.* Proceedings of the Third World Congress of Biological Psychiatry, Stockholm, (S371) 1981.

Talairach J, Bancaud J, Geier S, Bordes-Ferrer M, Bonis A, Szikla G, Rusu M: The cingulate gyrus and human behaviour. *Electroencephalogr. Clin. Neurophysiol.: 34*, 45 – 52, 1973.

Taylor DC: Aggression and epilepsy. *J. Psychosom. Res.: 13*, 229 – 236, 1969.

Taylor DC, Ounsted C: Biological mechanisms influencing the outcome of seizures in response to fever. *Epilepsia: 12*, 33 – 45, 1971.

Taylor MA, Greenspan B, Abrams R: Lateralized neuropsychological dysfunction in affective disorder and schizophrenia. *Am. J. Psychiatry: 136*, 1031 – 1034, 1979.

Thorén P, Åsberg M, Cronholm B, Jörnestedt L, Träskman L: Clomipramine treatment of obsessive-compulsive disorder. I. A controlled clinical trial. *Arch. Gen. Psychiatry: 37*, 1281 – 1285, 1980.

Tomer R, Mintz M, Levy A, Myslobodsky M: Smooth pursuit pattern in schizophrenic patients during cognitive task. *Biol. Psychiatry: 16*, 131 – 144, 1981.

Trimble MR: Interictal psychoses of epilepsy. *Acta Psychiatr. Scand.: 69*, 9 – 20, 1984.

Uchino J, Araki K, Tominaga Y, Niwa H, Nakama I, Michitsu-ji S, Ishizawa M, Ohta Y, Nakane Y, Takahashi R: Correlation between CT findings of schizophrenics and their clinical symptoms (2): using discriminatory analysis and chi-square test. *Folia Psychiatr. Neurol. Jpn.: 38*, 179, 1984.

Ueno T, Tomiyama S, Goto Y, Saitoh H, Aneha S, Matsue Y, Okuma T: Smooth pursuit eye movements in manic-depressive patients and cerebral lateralization. *Jpn. J. Psychiatry Neurol.: 40*, 130 – 131, 1986.

Vargha-Khadem F, O'Gorman AM, Watters GV: Aphasia and handedness in relation to hemispheric side, age at injury and severity of cerebral lesion during childhood. *Brain: 108*: 677 – 696, 1985.

Wardell D, Yeudall LT: A multidimensional approach to criminal disorders. The assessment of impulsivity and its relation to crime. *Adv. Behav. Res. Ther.: 2*, 159 – 177, 1980.

Wechsler D: Sex differences in intelligence. In *The Measurement and Appraisal of Adult Intelligence*. Edn. 4, Baltimore Williams & Wilkins, pp. 144 – 151, 1958.

Woods BT: The restricted effects of right-hemisphere lesions after age one: Wechsler test data. *Neuropsychologia: 18*, 65 – 70, 1980.

Yakovlev PI, Locke S: Limbic nuclei of thalamus and connection of limbic cortex. III Corticocortical connections of the anterior cingulate gyrus, the cingulum, and the subcallosal bundle in monkey. *Arch. Neurol.: 5*, 364 – 400, 1961.

Yan S-M, Flor-Henry P, Chen D, Li T, Qi S, Ma Z: Imbalance of hemispheric functions in the major psychoses: a study of handedness in the People's Republic of China. *Biol. Psychiatry: 20*, 906 – 917, 1985.

Yaryura-Tobias JA, Bebirian RR, Nziroglu FA, Bhagavan HN: Obsessive-compulsive disorders as a serotoninergic defect. *Res. Comm. Psychol. Psychiatry Behav.: 2*, 279, 1977.

Yeudall LT: Neuropsychological assessment of forensic disorders. *Can. Ment. Health: 7* – 15, 1977.

Yeudall LT, Fromm-Auch D: Neuropsychological impairments in various psychopathological populations. In Gruzelier JH, Flor-Henry P (Editors), *Hemisphere Asymmetries of Function in Psychopathology*. Amsterdam: Elsevier, pp. 401 – 428, 1979.

Yeudall LT, Fedora O, Fedora S, Wardell D: Neurosocial perspective on the assessment and etiology of persistent criminality. *Austr. J. Forensic Sci.: 13*, 131 – 159: 14: 159 – 177, 1981.

Yeudall LT, Fedora O, Fromm D: A neuropsychosocial theory of persistent criminality: implications for assessment and treatment. In Rieber RW (Editor), *Advances in Forensic Psychology and Applied Disciplines: An Interdisciplinary Review. Vol. 2*. Norward, NY: ABLAX Publication, pp. 119 – 191, 1987.

Index